Cooking Light®

ANNUAL
RECIPES 2005

Oxmoor
House®

Our Favorite Recipes

Not all recipes are created equal. At *Cooking Light*®, only those that have passed muster with our Test Kitchens staff and food editors—not an easy crowd to please—make it onto the pages of our magazine. We rigorously test each recipe, often two or three times, to ensure not only that they're healthy and reliable, but also that they taste as good as they possibly can. So which of our recipes are our favorites? They're the ones readers keep calling and writing about, the ones our staff whip up for their own families and friends. They're not always the ones that rated the highest, but they're the dishes that are definitely the most memorable.

◀ **Pressed Cubano with Bacon** *(page 185)*:

Pressing typical sandwich ingredients with a cast-iron skillet takes them to the next level by creating crunchy bread, hot filling, and gooey cheese.

◀ **Cornflake-Crusted Halibut with Chile-Cilantro Aïoli** *(page 72)*:

Your family will never believe that this fish isn't fried. Try the crumb coating on other mild white fish, such as catfish, cod, haddock, or snapper.

◀ **Pumpkin-Orange Cake** *(page 348)*:

Enjoy the tastes of the fall season with this moist cake. It's crowned with cream cheese frosting and set with jewel-like mandarin oranges and pomegranate seeds.

◀ **Chocolate Soufflés with Pistachios** *(page 48)*:

The delicate crunch of pistachios makes every bite of these rich chocolate soufflés even better.

◀ **Smoky Bacon and Blue Cheese Chicken Salad Pitas** *(page 151)*:

With a combination of pungent blue cheese, crisp lettuce, savory chicken, smoky bacon, and juicy tomatoes—what's not to love?

◀ **Garlicky Pasta with Fresh Tomatoes and Basil** *(page 104)*:

Eight everyday ingredients combine perfectly in this fresh take on a comforting weeknight dinner.

◀ **Shrimp in Green Sauce** *(page 26)*:

This quick-to-prepare entrée, reminiscent of shrimp scampi, gets a flavor boost from parsley and green onions. Preparation is a breeze, thanks to help from a food processor.

▲Italian Sausage Soup *(page 232)*:

The deep, rich flavor of this Parmesan-dusted soup belies the fact that it's ready in less than 20 minutes.

◄Corn Fritter Casserole *(page 296)*:

This homey, side-dish casserole tastes like a sweet corn fritter. Packaged corn muffin mix makes it a cinch to make.

◄Summer Pappardelle with Tomatoes, Arugula, and Parmesan *(page 278)*:

Sweet tomatoes; peppery arugula; and sharp, nutty cheese are rounded by a fresh dressing of lemon juice, garlic slivers, and olive oil.

◄Tofu Fried Rice *(page 322)*:

You can have your favorite Chinese restaurant standby in less time than it would take for it to be delivered to your home—and with tastier results.

◄Pepperoni, Provolone, and Pesto Stromboli *(page 328)*:

No one will ever know that you've snuck soy pepperoni into this saucy filled bread with old-fashioned pizza-parlor taste.

◄Louisiana Crab Cakes with Creole Tartar Sauce *(page 248)*:

A double dose of spicy, vinegary hot pepper sauce in the tartar sauce and the crab cakes puts a Creole twist on a Maryland classic.

◄Beef Daube Provençal *(page 373)*:

Slow cooking renders the beef in this comforting French stew meltingly tender. It's quick and easy to put together, and hands-off cooking leaves you free to attend to other things.

◄Smoked Salmon *(page 175)*:

Not like the cold smoked salmon you get on a bagel, this grilled fish gains a buttery texture and delicious flavor from a quick soak in a dill-flavored brine.

◄Key Lime Pie Parfaits *(page 268)*:

Creamy layers of Key lime custard and whipped cream are sandwiched between layers of graham cracker crumbs. Enjoy the texture and flavor of a pie with a fraction of the effort.

Our Favorite Recipes   3

▲ Orange Crisp and Coconut Topping
(page 411):

Enhanced with orange liqueur and topped with a crunchy butter-coconut streusel, juicy oranges star in an unusual dessert that will have your friends asking for the recipe.

▲ Whole Wheat Pasta with Sausages, Leeks, and Fontina
(page 417):

Whole wheat pasta stands up to the assertive flavors of cabbage, leeks, and sausage. Fontina cheese adds creamy richness.

▲ Red Raspberry Velvet Cake
(page 447):

A fruity raspberry filling adds a new twist to this traditional cake. With its delightful color and velvety cream cheese frosting, it's well suited for the holidays or for birthday parties.

▲ Cardamom-Date Snack Cake
(page 394):

Dates give this sweet treat a moist texture; cardamom makes it a unique spice cake.

Our Year at *Cooking Light*®

Since the last volume of *Cooking Light Annual Recipes*, I think it's fair to say that a lot has happened within the pages of the magazine. We've run more than 1,000 recipes, incorporated hundreds of photos, and edited scores of stories. Knowing the magazine from the inside out, I'd like to tell you about some of the highlights that have made 2004 special, both for *Cooking Light* and for this cookbook:

- Our January/February feature, "Power Up Your Plate," started the year right by suggesting eight surprisingly nutritious foods, from berries to beans, and offered terrific recipes that highlighted each one (page 16).
- Starting in March, we've included a recipe with each Enlightened Traveler column. We began with a recipe from San Juan's Parrot Club for Mango Mahi Seviche (page 51).
- The magazine's popular "Cooking Class" series focused this year on chefs who share their mastery of techniques and cuisines with our readers. Among the leading chefs we've featured: Mark Bittman (page 25), Martin Yan (page 219), and Bruce Aidells (page 173).
- July featured quick, high-energy dishes that could be toted along to the office in "What to Eat After a Workout" (page 252). Recipes for super smoothies and slushes ("Refresher Course," page 245) and terrific meals for competitors ("The Gourmet Athlete," page 244) rounded out the package.
- The magazine's Web site, **CookingLight.com**, has always generated extraordinary reader interaction. This year was no exception. Reader exchanges on the bulletin boards resulted in more than 400 *Cooking Light* supper clubs around the country. We celebrated in a special entertaining series in September, complete with menus, recipes, party themes, and how-to's (starting on page 295).
- We wrapped up the year in December with our traditional gift to our readers—*Cooking Light* magazine's complete holiday cookbook (beginning on page 433).

I'm delighted to add this volume of *Cooking Light Annual Recipes* to my cookbook library. I hope you, too, find it appetizing, intriguing, inspiring—and key to your pursuit of living well.

Very truly yours,

Mary Kay Culpepper

Editor in Chief

contents

Our Favorite Recipes   2

Our Year at *Cooking Light*®   4

January-February   7

March   41

April   81

May   125

June   173

July   219

August   255

September   295

October   331

November   373

December featuring   417
The *Cooking Light*® Holiday Cookbook   433

Menu Index   456
Recipe Title Index   461
Month-by-Month Index   469
General Recipe Index   478
Nutritional Analysis/Credits   496

©2004 by Oxmoor House, Inc.
Book Division of Southern Progress Corporation
P.O. Box 2463, Birmingham, Alabama 35201

ISBN: 0-8487-2797-5
ISSN: 1091-3645

Printed in the United States of America
First printing 2004

Be sure to check with your health-care provider before making any changes in your diet.

Oxmoor House, Inc.

Editor in Chief: Nancy Fitzpatrick Wyatt
Executive Editor: Katherine M. Eakin
Art Director: Cynthia R. Cooper
Copy Chief: Allison Long Lowery

Cooking Light Annual Recipes 2005
Editor: Heather Averett
Copy Editor: Jacqueline B. Giovanelli
Editorial Assistants: Jessica Lynn Dorsey, Shannon Friedmann, Terri Laschober, Dawn Russell
Publishing Systems Administrator: Rick Tucker
Director of Production: Phillip Lee
Production Manager: Greg A. Amason
Production Assistant: Faye Porter Bonner

Contributors:
Designer: Carol Damsky
Indexer: Mary Ann Laurens

To order additional publications, call 1-800-765-6400, or visit **oxmoorhouse.com**

Cover: *Blueberry-Blackberry Shortcakes* (page 237)
Page 1: *Asian Chicken Noodle Soup* (page 294)

Cooking Light®

Editor in Chief: Mary Kay Culpepper
Executive Editor: Billy R. Sims
Art Director: Susan Waldrip Dendy
Managing Editor: Maelynn Cheung
Senior Food Editor: Alison Mann Ashton
Senior Editor: Anamary Pelayo
Projects Editor: Mary Simpson Creel, M.S., R.D.
Editorial Coordinator: Carol C. Noe
Food Editor: Krista Ackerbloom Montgomery, M.S., R.D.
Associate Food Editor: Ann Taylor Pittman
Assistant Food Editor: Susan Stone, R.D.
Assistant Editors: Cindy Hatcher, Rachel Seligman
Contributing Beauty Editor: Lauren McCann
Test Kitchens Director: Vanessa Taylor Johnson
Food Stylist: Kellie Gerber Kelley
Assistant Food Stylist: M. Kathleen Kanen
Test Kitchens Staff: Sam Brannock, Kathryn Conrad, Jan Jacks Moon, Tiffany Vickers, Mike Wilson
Assistant Art Director: Maya Metz Logue
Senior Designer: Fernande Bondarenko
Designer: J. Shay McNamee
Assistant Designer: Brigette Mayer
Senior Photographer: Becky Luigart-Stayner
Photographer: Randy Mayor
Senior Photo Stylist: Cindy Barr
Photo Stylists: Melanie J. Clarke, Jan Gautro
Digital Photo Stylist: Jan A. Smith
Studio Assistant: Celine Chenoweth
Copy Chief: Maria Parker Hopkins
Senior Copy Editor: Susan Roberts
Copy Editor: Tara Trenary
Production Manager: Liz Rhoades
Production Editors: Joanne McCrary Brasseal, Hazel R. Eddins
Office Manager: Rita K. Jackson
Editorial Assistants: Melissa Hoover, Brandy Rushing
Correspondence Editor: Michelle Gibson Daniels
Intern: Alicia Reece

CookingLight.com
Editor: Jennifer Middleton
Online Producer: Abigail Masters

Congratulations! As a buyer of *Cooking Light Annual Recipes* 2005, you have exclusive access to the *Cooking Light* Web site on America Online. Simply go to www.cookinglight.com. When prompted, log on with this Web site access code: **CLAR2797**

Effective until December 31, 2005

A Perfect Winter's Day

The ingredients are simple—snow, skates, and stew.

Warming Winter Menu
serves 6

Crisp and Spicy Snack Mix

Broccoli, Orange, and Watercress Salad

Beef Stew

Creamy Mashed Potatoes

Sloppy Joes

Hearty Wheat Bread

Mulled Cranberry-Apple Cider

Oatmeal-Walnut Cookies

Cranberry and Apple Crumble

QUICK & EASY • MAKE AHEAD
Crisp and Spicy Snack Mix

Snack on this party mix before dinner. And if there's any left, toss it on a salad.

- 2 cups crisscross of corn and rice cereal (such as Crispix)
- 1 cup tiny pretzel twists
- ½ cup reduced-fat wheat crackers (such as Wheat Thins)
- ½ cup reduced-fat Cheddar crackers (such as Cheez-It)
- 1½ tablespoons butter, melted
- 1 tablespoon ginger stir-fry sauce (such as Lawry's)
- 1 teaspoon chili powder
- 1 teaspoon ground cumin
- ¼ teaspoon salt
- Cooking spray

1. Preheat oven to 250°.
2. Combine first 4 ingredients in a bowl. Combine butter, stir-fry sauce, powder, cumin, and salt; drizzle over cereal mixture, tossing to coat. Spread mixture into jelly-roll pan coated with cooking spray.

Bake at 250° for 30 minutes or until crisp, stirring twice. Yield: 4 cups (serving size: ½ cup).

CALORIES 117 (30% from fat); FAT 3.9g (sat 1.7g, mono 0.7g, poly 0.5g); PROTEIN 2.2g; CARB 18.5g; FIBER 0.8g; CHOL 6mg; IRON 2.6mg; SODIUM 368mg; CALC 17mg

QUICK & EASY
Broccoli, Orange, and Watercress Salad

To save time, steam the broccoli ahead; cover and chill. Section the oranges ahead, too.

DRESSING:
- ¼ cup cider vinegar
- 2 tablespoons rice vinegar
- 1 tablespoon olive oil
- 2 teaspoons sugar
- 1 teaspoon honey mustard
- ¼ teaspoon salt
- ⅛ teaspoon coarsely ground black pepper

SALAD:
- 4 cups thinly sliced iceberg lettuce
- 3 cups small broccoli florets, steamed
- 3 cups trimmed watercress
- 2 cups orange sections (about 4 oranges)

1. To prepare dressing, combine first 7 ingredients in a jar. Cover tightly; shake vigorously.
2. To prepare salad, combine lettuce and remaining ingredients in a large bowl. Add dressing; toss well to coat. Yield: 6 servings (serving size: 1½ cups).

CALORIES 88 (28% from fat); FAT 2.8g (sat 0.4g, mono 1.8g, poly 0.5g); PROTEIN 3.7g; CARB 15g; FIBER 4.3g; CHOL 0mg; IRON 1.1mg; SODIUM 130mg; CALC 88mg

Beef Stew
(pictured on page 21)

Serve this Mediterranean-inspired stew over Creamy Mashed Potatoes (recipe on page 8). Make and keep warm in a Dutch oven or slow cooker.

- 1½ teaspoons olive oil
- 1½ pounds beef stew meat, cut into 1-inch pieces
- 3½ cups halved mushrooms (about 8 ounces)
- 2 cups diagonally cut carrot
- 1½ cups coarsely chopped onion
- 1½ cups sliced celery
- 2 garlic cloves, minced
- 1½ cups water
- 1 cup Cabernet Sauvignon or other dry red wine
- ½ teaspoon dried thyme
- 1¼ teaspoons kosher salt
- ¼ teaspoon coarsely ground black pepper
- 2 (14.5-ounce) cans no-salt-added stewed tomatoes, undrained
- 2 bay leaves
- 1 (2¼-ounce) can sliced ripe olives, drained
- 2 tablespoons red wine vinegar
- ¼ cup chopped fresh flat-leaf parsley

1. Heat oil in a large Dutch oven over medium-high heat. Add beef; cook 5 minutes, browning on all sides. Remove from pan. Add mushrooms and next 4 ingredients to pan; cook 5 minutes, stirring occasionally. Return beef to pan. Stir in water and next 6 ingredients; bring to a boil. Cover, reduce heat, and simmer 1 hour. Stir in olives, and cook 30 minutes or until beef is tender. Discard bay leaves. Stir in vinegar. Sprinkle with parsley. Yield: 6 servings (serving size: 1⅓ cups).

CALORIES 288 (32% from fat); FAT 10.3g (sat 3.3g, mono 5g, poly 0.6g); PROTEIN 25.2g; CARB 20.1g; FIBER 5.7g; CHOL 71mg; IRON 5.5mg; SODIUM 584mg; CALC 100mg

Creamy Mashed Potatoes

Horseradish adds a peppery kick, but the potatoes are also good without it.

2¼ pounds cubed peeled Yukon gold potato
⅔ cup 2% reduced-fat milk, warmed
2 tablespoons butter, softened
2 teaspoons prepared horseradish
1 teaspoon kosher salt
¼ teaspoon coarsely ground black pepper

1. Place potatoes in a saucepan; cover with water. Bring to a boil. Reduce heat, and simmer 15 minutes or until tender. Drain. Return potatoes to pan. Add milk and remaining ingredients; mash to desired consistency. Cook over low heat until warm. Yield: 8 servings (serving size: ⅔ cup).

CALORIES 174 (28% from fat); FAT 5.5g (sat 3.4g, mono 1.4g, poly 0.2g); PROTEIN 3.2g; CARB 28.6g; FIBER 1.9g; CHOL 15mg; IRON 0.5mg; SODIUM 315mg; CALC 29mg

Sloppy Joes

Kids and adults alike love this sweet-savory sandwich. Keep the meat mixture warm in a slow cooker set on low. Carrots and vegetable chips make great sides.

¾ cup chopped onion
½ cup chopped green bell pepper
¾ pound ground round
2 cups no-salt-added tomato sauce
2 tablespoons tomato paste
1 tablespoon prepared mustard
1 teaspoon chili powder
2 teaspoons Worcestershire sauce
½ teaspoon salt
½ teaspoon sugar
½ teaspoon dried oregano
⅛ teaspoon black pepper
12 (1½-ounce) rolls, split

1. Heat a large nonstick skillet over medium heat. Add onion, bell pepper, and beef; cook until beef is browned, stirring to crumble. Stir in tomato sauce and next 8 ingredients; reduce heat to medium-low. Cover and cook 15 minutes, stirring occasionally. Spoon ¼ cup beef mixture over bottom half of each bun. Cover with top halves. Yield: 12 servings (serving size: 1 sandwich).

CALORIES 202 (27% from fat); FAT 6.2g (sat 2g, mono 2.9g, poly 0.7g); PROTEIN 10.2g; CARB 27g; FIBER 2.5g; CHOL 19mg; IRON 2.6mg; SODIUM 392mg; CALC 68mg

Hearty Wheat Bread

Strong coffee and stout give this wheat bread a hearty flavor and alluring aroma.

½ cup warm strong brewed coffee (100° to 110°)
½ cup warm Guinness Stout (100° to 110°)
1 package dry yeast (about 2¼ teaspoons)
1 cup whole wheat flour
¼ cup toasted wheat germ
1½ cups bread flour, divided
1⅛ teaspoons salt
Cooking spray
1 tablespoon cornmeal

1. Combine coffee and stout in a large bowl. Dissolve yeast in coffee mixture; let stand 5 minutes. Lightly spoon whole wheat flour into a dry measuring cup; level with a knife. Add whole wheat flour and wheat germ to yeast mixture; stir well to combine. Cover and let stand at room temperature 30 minutes to create a sponge (mixture will rise slightly and bubbles will form across surface).

2. Lightly spoon bread flour into dry measuring cups; level with a knife. Stir 1¼ cups bread flour and salt into sponge; stir until a soft dough forms. Turn dough out onto a floured surface. Knead until smooth and elastic (about 8 minutes); add enough of remaining bread flour, 1 tablespoon at a time, to prevent dough from sticking to hands (dough will feel tacky).

3. Place dough in a large bowl coated with cooking spray, turning to coat top. Cover and let rise a second time in a warm place (85°), free from drafts, 1 hour or until doubled in size. (Gently press two fingers into dough. If indentation remains, dough has risen enough.) Punch dough down. Cover and let rise in a warm place (85°), free from drafts, 1 hour or until doubled in size. Punch dough down; cover and let rest 5 minutes. Shape dough into an 8-inch oval; place on a baking sheet sprinkled with 1 tablespoon cornmeal. Lightly coat surface of dough with cooking spray. Cover and let rise in a warm place (85°), free from drafts, 30 minutes or until doubled in size.

4. Preheat oven to 400°.

5. Cut a shallow ¼-inch slash down center of loaf. Bake at 400° for 20 minutes or until loaf is browned on bottom and sounds hollow when tapped. Cool on a wire rack. Yield: 14 servings (serving size: 1 slice).

CALORIES 114 (6% from fat); FAT 0.8g (sat 0.1g, mono 0.1g, poly 0.4g); PROTEIN 4.5g; CARB 22g; FIBER 2.1g; CHOL 0mg; IRON 1.5mg; SODIUM 222mg; CALC 8mg

Mulled Cranberry-Apple Cider

A swivel-bladed vegetable peeler works well for removing the orange peel. Be sure to remove only the colored part of the peel—which contains the flavorful oils—and no more; the white pith is bitter.

4 cups cranberry juice cocktail
4 cups apple cider or apple juice
3 tablespoons brown sugar
5 (3 x 1-inch) strips orange rind
8 whole cloves
4 whole allspice
2 (3-inch) cinnamon sticks, halved
1 whole nutmeg

1. Combine all ingredients in a large saucepan. Bring to a boil; cover, reduce heat, and simmer 30 minutes. Strain mixture through a fine sieve, and discard solids. Serve cider warm. Yield: 8 servings (serving size: about 1 cup).

CALORIES 151 (0% from fat); FAT 0.1g (sat 0g, mono 0g, poly 0.1g); PROTEIN 0g; CARB 38.2g; FIBER 0.1g; CHOL 0mg; IRON 0.3mg; SODIUM 17mg; CALC 8mg

Oatmeal-Walnut Cookies

You can make these cookies ahead of time and store them in an airtight container, but they're best served warm.

½ cup granulated sugar
⅓ cup packed dark brown sugar
¼ cup butter, softened
1 teaspoon vanilla extract
1 large egg
¾ cup all-purpose flour
1 cup regular oats
¼ teaspoon salt
⅔ cup golden raisins
¼ cup chopped toasted walnuts
Cooking spray

1. Preheat oven to 350°.
2. Place first 5 ingredients in a large bowl. Beat with a mixer at medium speed until well blended. Lightly spoon flour into a dry measuring cup; level with a knife. Add flour, oats, and salt to egg mixture; beat well. Stir in raisins and walnuts.
3. Drop by level tablespoons, 1½ inches apart, onto a baking sheet coated with cooking spray. Bake at 350° for 12 minutes or until lightly browned. Remove from oven, and let stand 2 minutes. Remove cookies from baking sheet; cool on wire racks. Yield: 2 dozen (serving size: 1 cookie).

CALORIES 109 (28% from fat); FAT 3.4g (sat 1.4g, mono 0.9g, poly 0.9g); PROTEIN 2.1g; CARB 18.3g; FIBER 1.1g; CHOL 14mg; IRON 0.7mg; SODIUM 24mg; CALC 12mg

Cranberry and Apple Crumble

Serve this simple, satisfying dessert with vanilla ice cream. We used Braeburn apples, but any other tart variety will do.

½ cup all-purpose flour
¼ cup granulated sugar
¼ cup packed brown sugar
¼ cup chilled butter, cut into small pieces
6 cups sliced peeled Braeburn apple
1 cup fresh cranberries
⅓ cup fresh orange juice
2 tablespoons granulated sugar
1 tablespoon cornstarch

1. Preheat oven to 375°.
2. Lightly spoon flour into a dry measuring cup; level with a knife. Combine flour, ¼ cup granulated sugar, brown sugar, and butter in a food processor; pulse 10 times or until mixture resembles coarse meal.
3. Combine apple and cranberries in a large bowl. Combine juice, 2 tablespoons sugar, and cornstarch; pour over apple mixture. Toss well. Spoon apple mixture into a 2-quart baking dish. Sprinkle with flour mixture. Bake at 375° for 40 minutes or until bubbly and golden brown. Serve warm. Yield: 8 servings (serving size: ⅔ cup).

CALORIES 211 (26% from fat); FAT 6.1g (sat 3.6g, mono 1.7g, poly 0.4g); PROTEIN 1.2g; CARB 40.1g; FIBER 3.4g; CHOL 15mg; IRON 0.7mg; SODIUM 61mg; CALC 17mg

enlightened cook

On the Greens Path

Chef Annie Somerville finds her place at a notable San Francisco restaurant.

Annie Somerville never expected to find her life's work when she arrived at Greens Restaurant in 1981. She was—and remains—a member of the San Francisco Zen Center, which opened the restaurant in the historic Fort Mason, overlooking San Francisco Bay, in 1979. "I thought I was coming for a short stay, and 22 years later, I'm still here," Somerville says.

Not only did Somerville take over as executive chef in 1985, but along the way, she wrote the two best-selling cookbooks *Fields of Greens: New Vegetarian Recipes from the Celebrated Greens Restaurant* and, most recently, *Everyday Greens.*

Although the recipes in her cookbooks are from Greens, Somerville tested them in a home-style test kitchen in a nearby apartment—to ensure they'd work for her readers. Since home cooks don't have the benefit of a prep crew and exotic ingredients available at all times, she adapted recipes by simplifying steps or suggesting substitutions for certain ingredients.

Pizza with Escarole, Roasted Peppers, and Olives

1 Pizza Dough (recipe on page 10)
Cooking spray
1 tablespoon cornmeal
1 large yellow bell pepper
1 cup vertically sliced red onion
½ teaspoon salt
¼ teaspoon black pepper
1 tablespoon minced garlic (about 3 cloves)
4 cups chopped escarole
1 tablespoon sherry vinegar
½ cup (2 ounces) shredded fontina cheese
6 chopped pitted kalamata olives
3 tablespoons (about 1 ounce) grated fresh Parmesan cheese
1 teaspoon finely chopped fresh oregano

1. Roll prepared pizza dough into a 12-inch circle on a floured surface. Place dough on a 12-inch pizza pan or baking sheet coated with cooking spray and sprinkled with 1 tablespoon cornmeal. Crimp edges of dough with fingers to form a rim.
2. Preheat broiler. Cut bell pepper in half lengthwise; discard seeds and membranes. Place halves, skin sides up, on a foil-lined baking sheet; flatten with hand. Broil 15 minutes or until blackened. Place in a zip-top plastic bag; seal. Let stand 15 minutes. Peel and cut into strips.
3. Preheat oven to 500°.
4. Heat a large skillet lightly coated with cooking spray over medium-high heat. Add onion, salt, and black pepper; sauté 3 minutes or until tender. Stir in garlic; cook 1 minute. Add escarole; sauté 2 minutes or until escarole wilts. Remove from heat, and stir in vinegar.
5. Spread escarole mixture evenly over pizza crust; top with fontina cheese, roasted pepper, and olives. Bake at 500° for 14 minutes or until crust is golden. Remove pizza from oven, and sprinkle with Parmesan and oregano. Bake 2 minutes or until Parmesan melts. Yield: 6 servings (serving size: 1 slice).

CALORIES 239 (30% from fat); FAT 8.3g (sat 3.1g, mono 4g, poly 0.7g); PROTEIN 10g; CARB 33.3g; FIBER 2.6g; CHOL 14mg; IRON 2.3mg; SODIUM 533mg; CALC 135mg

Mexican Pizza

Pepitas—hulled pumpkinseeds—top this pizza. They're a popular ingredient in many Mexican kitchens.

    1 Pizza Dough (recipe at right)
  Cooking spray
    1 tablespoon cornmeal
    1 large red onion, cut into
       ¼-inch-thick slices and separated
       into rings
    ½ teaspoon salt, divided
    ¼ teaspoon freshly ground black
       pepper, divided
    1 poblano chile
    1 (7-ounce) can chipotle chiles in
       adobo sauce
    ¼ pound tomatillos, husked and
       coarsely chopped
    ½ cup (2 ounces) grated sharp white
       Cheddar cheese
    ½ cup (2 ounces) crumbled queso
       fresco
    2 tablespoons coarsely chopped
       fresh cilantro
    1 tablespoon unsalted pumpkinseed
       kernels, toasted

1. Preheat oven to 450°.
2. Roll prepared pizza dough into a 12-inch circle on a floured surface. Place dough on a 12-inch pizza pan or baking sheet coated with cooking spray and sprinkled with 1 tablespoon cornmeal. Crimp edges of dough with fingers to form a rim.
3. Place onion rings in a large bowl. Lightly spray with cooking spray, and sprinkle with ¼ teaspoon salt and ⅛ teaspoon black pepper; toss well to coat. Arrange onion on a jelly-roll pan coated with cooking spray. Bake at 450° for 15 minutes, stirring halfway through; cool.
4. Preheat broiler.
5. Place poblano chile on a foil-lined baking sheet, and broil 3 inches from heat 8 minutes or until blackened and charred, turning after 6 minutes. Place in a zip-top heavy-duty plastic bag, and seal. Let stand 15 minutes. Peel and discard skins. Cut a lengthwise slit in poblano chile; discard seeds and stem. Cut roasted poblano chile into thin strips. Sprinkle strips with remaining ¼ teaspoon salt and ⅛ teaspoon

black pepper, and set aside. Reduce oven temperature to 500°.
6. Place chipotles in a food processor or blender, and process until smooth. Spread ½ tablespoon chipotle purée over pizza crust using back of spoon. Reserve remaining chipotle purée for another use. Arrange chile strips in an even layer over pizza crust; top with onions, tomatillos, Cheddar, and queso fresco. Bake at 500° for 17 minutes or until crust is golden. Remove pizza from oven, and sprinkle with cilantro and pumpkinseeds. Yield: 6 servings (serving size: 1 slice).

CALORIES 225 (30% from fat); FAT 7.8g (sat 3.4g, mono 2.4g, poly 0.8g); PROTEIN 8.9g; CARB 31.2g; FIBER 2.5g; CHOL 13mg; IRON 2.4mg; SODIUM 374mg; CALC 100mg

Pizza Dough

Double this recipe and freeze half after you knead it; you'll have fresh pizza for another night. Place frozen dough in refrigerator overnight or until completely thawed.

    ½ teaspoon sugar
    1 package dry yeast (about 2¼
       teaspoons)
    ⅔ cup warm water (100° to 110°)
  1½ cups bread flour
  1½ tablespoons cornmeal
    2 teaspoons extravirgin olive oil
    ½ teaspoon salt
    2 tablespoons bread flour
  Cooking spray

1. Dissolve sugar and yeast in warm water in a large bowl; let stand 5 minutes. Lightly spoon flour into dry measuring cups; level with a knife. Add flour, cornmeal, oil, and salt to yeast mixture; stir until a soft dough forms. Turn dough out onto a floured surface. Knead 5 minutes. Add 2 tablespoons bread flour, as needed, to prevent dough from sticking to hands (dough will feel tacky).
2. Place dough in a large bowl coated with cooking spray, turning to coat top. Cover and let rise in a warm place (85°), free from drafts, 45 minutes or until doubled in size. (Gently press two fingers into dough. If indentation remains, dough has risen enough.) Punch dough

down; shape into a ball. Lightly respray bowl; place dough in bowl, turning to coat top. Cover; let rise in a warm place (85°), free from drafts, 30 minutes.
3. Place dough on a lightly floured surface. Shape and top according to specific pizza instructions. Yield: 6 servings (serving size: 1 slice).

CALORIES 138 (12% from fat); FAT 1.9g (sat 0.2g, mono 1.3g, poly 0.3g); PROTEIN 4.9g; CARB 27g; FIBER 1.3g; CHOL 0mg; IRON 1.7mg; SODIUM 198mg; CALC 1mg

Mixed Pepper Pizza with Basil and Pine Nuts

To save time, substitute bottled roasted red peppers for the bell peppers here.

    1 Pizza Dough (recipe at left)
  Cooking spray
    1 tablespoon cornmeal
    2 teaspoons olive oil
    2 cups vertically sliced Vidalia or
       other sweet onion
    ½ teaspoon salt
    ¼ teaspoon black pepper
    1 tablespoon minced garlic (about
       3 cloves)
    1 yellow bell pepper, cut into
       ¼-inch strips
    1 red bell pepper, cut into ¼-inch strips
    ¼ cup water
    1 tablespoon capers, drained
    ¾ cup (3 ounces) crumbled
       reduced-fat feta cheese
    ½ cup chopped fresh basil
    2 tablespoons pine nuts, toasted
    ¼ cup (1 ounce) grated fresh
       Parmesan cheese

1. Preheat oven to 500°.
2. Roll prepared pizza dough into a 12-inch circle on a floured surface. Place dough on a 12-inch pizza pan or baking sheet coated with cooking spray and sprinkled with 1 tablespoon cornmeal. Crimp edges of dough with fingers to form a rim.
3. Heat olive oil in a large skillet over medium-high heat. Add onion, salt, and black pepper; sauté 3 minutes or until tender. Add garlic; cook 1 minute. Reduce heat to low. Add bell peppers; cook

10 minutes, stirring occasionally. Stir in water; cook 10 minutes or until peppers are soft and water has almost evaporated. Remove from heat; stir in capers.

4. Spread pepper mixture evenly over pizza crust; sprinkle with feta. Bake at 500° for 15 minutes or until crust is golden. Remove from oven. Sprinkle with basil and pine nuts; top with Parmesan. Bake an additional 3 minutes or until Parmesan melts. Yield: 6 servings (serving size: 1 slice).

CALORIES 236 (30% from fat); FAT 9.3g (sat 3.1g, mono 3.6g, poly 1.2g); PROTEIN 12.7g; CARB 36g; FIBER 3.1g; CHOL 11.4mg; IRON 2.5mg; SODIUM 643mg; CALC 116mg

dinner tonight

Breakfast Tonight

Sometimes, the best breakfasts are those you eat for dinner.

Bell Pepper Frittata Menu
serves 4

Red Bell Pepper Frittata

Toasted English muffins with jam

Roasted vanilla-scented apples*

*Combine 2 cups sliced Granny Smith apples, 1½ tablespoons vanilla syrup, and 1 teaspoon walnut oil or melted butter in an 8-inch square baking dish coated with cooking spray. Bake at 400° for 15 minutes or until tender.

Game Plan

1. While oven heats for apples and water for couscous comes to a boil:
  - Slice onion and bell pepper
  - Mince garlic
  - Combine egg mixture

2. While apples roast and couscous stands:
  - Toast English muffins
  - Cook frittata

Red Bell Pepper Frittata

Cooked couscous makes this meatless entrée more filling. Substitute 1 cup left-over cooked orzo, spaghetti, or vermicelli, if you prefer.

TOTAL TIME: 30 MINUTES

  ½ cup water
  ⅓ cup uncooked couscous
  1 tablespoon water
  ¾ teaspoon salt
  ¼ teaspoon black pepper
  4 large egg whites
  3 large eggs
  Cooking spray
  2 cups red bell pepper strips
  1 cup thinly vertically sliced onion
  2 garlic cloves, minced
  ⅓ cup (1½ ounces) shredded Manchego or Monterey Jack cheese

1. Preheat oven to 350°.
2. Bring ½ cup water to a boil in a small saucepan; gradually stir in couscous. Remove from heat; cover and let stand 5 minutes. Fluff with a fork.
3. Combine 1 tablespoon water, salt, black pepper, egg whites, and eggs in a medium bowl, stirring with a whisk.
4. Heat a 10-inch ovenproof nonstick skillet coated with cooking spray over medium-high heat. Add bell pepper, onion, and garlic; sauté 5 minutes. Stir in couscous and egg mixture; cook over medium heat 5 minutes or until almost set. Sprinkle with cheese. Bake at 350° for 10 minutes or until set. Let stand 5 minutes before serving. Yield: 4 servings (serving size: 1 wedge).

CALORIES 204 (30% from fat); FAT 6.8g (sat 3g, mono 2.3g, poly 0.7g); PROTEIN 15g; CARB 20.6g; FIBER 2.9g; CHOL 167mg; IRON 1.3mg; SODIUM 716mg; CALC 169mg

Huevos Rancheros Menu
serves 4

Huevos Rancheros with Queso Fresco

Orange, pineapple, and coconut ambrosia*

Margaritas

*Drain 1 (15¼-ounce) can pineapple chunks in juice and 1 (14-ounce) jar fresh orange sections. Combine pineapple, orange, and 2 tablespoons powdered sugar, tossing to coat. Sprinkle with ⅓ cup flaked sweetened coconut.

Game Plan

1. Prepare ambrosia; cover and chill until serving time.
2. While tomato mixture cooks:
  - Chop cilantro
  - Squeeze lime juice
  - Heat beans
3. While eggs cook:
  - Heat tortillas
  - Prepare margaritas

Huevos Rancheros with Queso Fresco

Queso fresco is a soft, crumbly, salty Mexican cheese. Look for it in the dairy section of large grocery stores and Hispanic markets. Substitute crumbled feta or goat cheese, if you prefer.

TOTAL TIME: 25 MINUTES

QUICK TIP: Corn tortillas may be substituted for the flour tortillas.

  1 (10-ounce) can diced tomatoes and green chiles, undrained
  1 (10-ounce) can red enchilada sauce
  ⅓ cup chopped fresh cilantro
  1 tablespoon fresh lime juice
  2 tablespoons water
  1 (16-ounce) can pinto beans, rinsed and drained
  Cooking spray
  4 large eggs
  4 (8-inch) fat-free flour tortillas
  1 cup (4 ounces) crumbled queso fresco cheese

Continued

1. Combine tomatoes and enchilada sauce in a medium saucepan; bring to a boil. Reduce heat; simmer 5 minutes or until slightly thick. Remove from heat; stir in cilantro and juice. Set aside.

2. Place water and beans in a microwave-safe bowl, and partially mash with a fork. Cover and microwave at HIGH 2 minutes or until hot.

3. Heat a large nonstick skillet coated with cooking spray over medium-high heat. Add eggs; cook 1 minute on each side or until desired degree of doneness.

4. Warm tortillas according to package directions. Spread about ⅓ cup beans over each tortilla; top each tortilla with 1 egg. Spoon ½ cup sauce around each egg; sprinkle each serving with ¼ cup cheese. Yield: 4 servings (serving size: 1 topped tortilla).

CALORIES 340 (26% from fat); FAT 9.8g (sat 3.2g, mono 2.7g, poly 1g); PROTEIN 15.7g; CARB 37.8g; FIBER 6.1g; CHOL 222mg; IRON 2.1mg; SODIUM 970mg; CALC 153mg

---

Shrimp and Grits Menu
serves 6

Southern Shrimp and Grits

Green salad with avocado and tomatoes*

Orange sorbet

*Combine 4 cups chopped romaine lettuce, 1 cup halved cherry tomatoes, ½ cup thinly vertically sliced red onion, and 1 sliced ripe avocado. Combine 2 tablespoons fresh lime juice, 2 teaspoons extravirgin olive oil, 1 teaspoon bottled minced garlic, ¼ teaspoon salt, and ¼ teaspoon black pepper, stirring with a whisk. Drizzle dressing over salad; toss gently to coat.

Game Plan

1. Prepare salad; cover and chill until serving time.

2. While water for grits comes to a boil:
- Combine shrimp, lemon juice, and hot sauce
- Chop bacon and green onions
- Shred cheese

3. While shrimp mixture cooks:
- Cook grits

Southern Shrimp and Grits

This shellfish specialty of the Carolina low country, sometimes called "breakfast shrimp," tastes great anytime. To minimize prep time, start with frozen bell pepper and onion, as well as prepeeled and deveined shrimp.

TOTAL TIME: 33 MINUTES

QUICK TIP: Quick-cooking grits are a welcome weeknight alternative to stone-ground versions, which can take 45 minutes to cook.

    3 tablespoons fresh lemon juice
    ½ teaspoon hot sauce (such as
       Tabasco)
    1½ pounds peeled and deveined large
       shrimp
    2 bacon slices, chopped
    1 cup frozen chopped onion
    ¼ cup frozen chopped green bell
       pepper
    1½ teaspoons bottled minced garlic
    1 cup fat-free, less-sodium chicken
       broth
    ½ cup chopped green onions,
       divided
    5 cups water
    1½ cups uncooked quick-cooking
       grits
    1 tablespoon butter
    1 teaspoon salt
    ¾ cup (3 ounces) shredded sharp
       Cheddar cheese

1. Combine first 3 ingredients; set aside.

2. Cook bacon in a large nonstick skillet over medium heat until crisp. Add onion, bell pepper, and garlic to drippings in pan; cook 5 minutes or until tender, stirring occasionally. Stir in shrimp mixture, broth, and ¼ cup green onions; cook 5 minutes or until shrimp are done, stirring frequently.

3. Bring water to a boil in a medium saucepan; gradually add grits, stirring constantly. Reduce heat to low; simmer, covered, 5 minutes or until thick, stirring occasionally. Stir in butter and salt. Serve shrimp mixture over grits; sprinkle with cheese and remaining green onions. Yield: 6 servings (serving size: ⅔ cup shrimp mixture, ⅔ cup grits, 2 tablespoons cheese, and 2 teaspoons green onions).

CALORIES 408 (28% from fat); FAT 12.5g (sat 5.6g, mono 4.1g, poly 1.3g); PROTEIN 32.8g; CARB 39.9g; FIBER 2g; CHOL 246mg; IRON 5.1mg; SODIUM 890mg; CALC 154mg

---

Joe's Special Menu
serves 4

Joe's Special

Crisp oven potatoes*

Beer

*Combine 2¼ cups frozen hash brown potatoes with onions and peppers (such as Ore-Ida Potatoes O'Brien), 1 tablespoon vegetable oil, 1 teaspoon bottled minced garlic, ½ teaspoon salt, ¼ teaspoon hot paprika, and ¼ teaspoon black pepper on a jelly-roll pan coated with cooking spray. Bake at 450° for 20 minutes or until browned, stirring once.

Game Plan

1. While oven heats for potatoes:
- Combine potato mixture
- Chop chard
- Toast bread

2. While potatoes cook:
- Prepare scramble

Joe's Special

This San Francisco specialty turns straightforward scrambled eggs into a distinctive dish. To stay true to the recipe's roots, serve with toasted sourdough bread.

TOTAL TIME: 30 MINUTES

QUICK TIP: Replace the chard with packaged, washed spinach. Use baby spinach to avoid chopping altogether.

    ½ teaspoon dried basil
    ¼ teaspoon salt
    4 large egg whites
    3 large eggs
    4 ounces hot turkey Italian sausage
    2 cups chopped onion
    6 cups chopped Swiss chard (about
       ½ pound)
    4 (1½-ounce) slices sourdough
       bread, toasted

1. Combine first 4 ingredients in a medium bowl, stirring with a whisk.

2. Remove casings from sausage. Cook sausage in a large nonstick skillet over medium-high heat until lightly browned; stir to crumble. Add onion; cook 3 minutes or until onion is tender. Stir in chopped chard; cover and cook 3 minutes or until chard wilts, stirring occasionally. Uncover and cook 1 minute or until liquid evaporates. Stir in egg mixture; cook 3 minutes or until eggs are set, stirring frequently. Serve with toast. Yield: 4 servings (serving size: 1 cup egg mixture and 1 toast slice).

CALORIES 335 (23% from fat); FAT 8.6g (sat 2.4g, mono 3.3g, poly 1.8g); PROTEIN 20.9g; CARB 43.2g; FIBER 4.3g; CHOL 183mg; IRON 3.7mg; SODIUM 931mg; CALC 116mg

reader recipes

Feeding the Mind

A grad student takes a break from the books and hits the kitchen.

Marisa Szelag was glad to leave undergraduate life—cramped dorms and mundane dining-hall meals—behind. Currently living on her own and pursuing a law degree at the University of Notre Dame in South Bend, Indiana, she says cooking helps her to unwind.

"Now that I'm in a condo and actually have enough room to cook, I thoroughly enjoy it," she says.

She finds the creative process and the light physical activity of cooking soothing and refreshing. Cooking for others also brings rewards. "My friends appreciate the food and enjoy the time we spend together," she adds.

Marisa used the flavor profile of a Greek avgolemono soup from a restaurant to create this satisfying main dish, which she calls Lemon Chicken and Rice with Artichokes. She recommends it for weeknights because it's simple, and for casual entertaining because she has found that its flavors please almost everyone.

QUICK & EASY

Lemon Chicken and Rice with Artichokes

(pictured on page 23)

Cooking spray
- 1 pound skinless, boneless chicken breast, cut into ½-inch strips
- 2¼ cups chopped onion
- 1 cup chopped red bell pepper
- 2 cups instant rice
- ¼ cup fresh lemon juice
- ¼ teaspoon salt
- ¼ teaspoon black pepper
- 1 (14-ounce) can fat-free, less-sodium chicken broth
- 1 (14-ounce) can quartered artichoke hearts, drained
- 2 tablespoons grated Romano cheese

1. Heat a Dutch oven coated with cooking spray over medium-high heat. Add chicken, chopped onion, and red bell pepper; sauté 5 minutes. Stir in rice, lemon juice, ¼ teaspoon salt, black pepper, and broth; bring to a boil. Cover, reduce heat, and simmer 15 minutes or until rice is tender. Stir in artichokes, and cook 1 minute or until thoroughly heated. Sprinkle with cheese. Yield: 4 servings (serving size: 2 cups).

CALORIES 324 (8% from fat); FAT 2.8g (sat 1g, mono 0.7g, poly 0.5g); PROTEIN 35g; CARB 40.7g; FIBER 8.3g; CHOL 69mg; IRON 3.1mg; SODIUM 773mg; CALC 120mg

MAKE AHEAD

Wholesome Morning Granola

"This cereal is wonderful with warm milk."
—Meg Wilson, Anderson, South Carolina

- 4 cups regular oats
- 2 cups puffed rice cereal (such as Arrowhead Mills)
- ½ cup flaked sweetened coconut
- ½ cup oat bran
- ¼ cup sliced almonds, toasted
- 3 tablespoons turbinado sugar
- ¾ cup pineapple juice
- ½ cup apple juice
- ¼ cup honey
- Cooking spray
- ¼ cup dried blueberries

1. Preheat oven to 325°.

2. Combine first 6 ingredients in a large bowl. Combine juices in a small saucepan. Bring to a boil; cook until reduced to ⅔ cup. Remove from heat; stir in honey. Slowly pour juice mixture over oat mixture, tossing to coat. Spread oat mixture evenly onto a jelly-roll pan coated with cooking spray. Bake at 325° for 40 minutes or until golden, stirring occasionally. Cool slightly; stir in blueberries. Cool completely, and store in an airtight container. Yield: 7½ cups (serving size: ½ cup).

CALORIES 252 (19% from fat); FAT 5.2g (sat 1.6g, mono 1.6g, poly 1.4g); PROTEIN 8.4g; CARB 46.2g; FIBER 5.6g; CHOL 0mg; IRON 2.6mg; SODIUM 10mg; CALC 36mg

QUICK & EASY • MAKE AHEAD

Garlic and Sun-Dried Tomato Hummus

"I came up with this recipe while exploring ways to get more fiber in my diet. The tomatoes give it a warm, coral-like color."
—Teresa Leerssen, Charleston, South Carolina

- Cooking spray
- 2 (6-inch) pitas, each cut into 10 wedges
- ¼ cup water
- 2 tablespoons chopped oil-packed sun-dried tomato halves
- ½ teaspoon salt
- ¼ teaspoon freshly ground black pepper
- 2 garlic cloves
- 1 (15-ounce) can chickpeas (garbanzo beans), drained

1. Preheat oven to 425°.

2. Coat a baking sheet with cooking spray. Place pita wedges on pan, and coat with cooking spray. Bake at 425° for 6 minutes or until golden.

3. Combine water, tomato, salt, pepper, garlic, and beans in a food processor, and process until smooth. Serve with pita wedges. Yield: 5 servings (serving size: ¼ cup hummus and 4 pita wedges).

CALORIES 175 (9% from fat); FAT 1.7g (sat 0.2g, mono 0.5g, poly 0.6g); PROTEIN 6.6g; CARB 33.7g; FIBER 4.5g; CHOL 0mg; IRON 1.9mg; SODIUM 623mg; CALC 52mg

Golden Gazpacho

"My mother and I re-created this refreshing soup after enjoying a similar one at a café."
—Sarah Petersen, Scottsdale, Arizona

    3   cups orange juice
    2½ cups chopped peeled mango
    2   cups finely diced peeled
        cantaloupe
    1   cup finely diced peeled jícama
    1   cup tomato juice
    ¾   cup finely diced yellow bell pepper
    ⅓   cup thinly sliced green onions
    ¼   cup finely chopped fresh cilantro
    2   tablespoons rice vinegar
    ½   teaspoon salt
    ¼   teaspoon black pepper

1. Combine all ingredients in a large bowl; stir well. Cover and chill. Yield: 9 servings (serving size: 1 cup).

CALORIES 94 (4% from fat); FAT 0.5g (sat 0.1g, mono 0.1g, poly 0.1g); PROTEIN 1.6g; CARB 22.9g; FIBER 2.5g; CHOL 0mg; IRON 0.6mg; SODIUM 234mg; CALC 24mg

inspired vegetarian

Appalachian Menu

Here's a classic mountain wintertime meal that's perfectly hearty and vegetarian.

Appalachian Menu
serves 8
Simple Slaw
Quick Buttermilk Corn Bread
Winter Greens and Potato Casserole
Corn Chow-Chow
Savory Soup Beans
Unfried Apple Pies

Simple Slaw

Prepare and refrigerate this crunchy side several hours before serving if you like. For more color in the dish, toss in red bell pepper strips.

    ½   cup fat-free buttermilk
    ⅓   cup low-fat mayonnaise
    ½   teaspoon celery salt
    ½   teaspoon freshly ground black
        pepper
    12 cups thinly sliced green
        cabbage
    ½   cup finely chopped green onions

1. Combine first 4 ingredients, stirring with a whisk. Place cabbage and onions in a large bowl. Spoon buttermilk mixture over cabbage; toss to coat. Yield: 8 servings (serving size: about 1 cup).

CALORIES 52 (17% from fat); FAT 1g (sat 0.1g, mono 0.2g, poly 0.5g); PROTEIN 2.1g; CARB 9.8g; FIBER 2.7g; CHOL 0mg; IRON 0.7mg; SODIUM 221mg; CALC 70mg

Quick Buttermilk Corn Bread

Moist, tender corn bread is traditionally crumbled into a bowl of soup beans. If you have trouble turning out the baked bread, just serve it from the pan.

    2   tablespoons canola oil
    2   cups yellow cornmeal
    1   teaspoon salt
    ½   teaspoon baking powder
    ½   teaspoon baking soda
    1¾ cups fat-free buttermilk
    ⅛   teaspoon black pepper
    1   large egg, lightly beaten

1. Preheat oven to 450°.
2. Pour oil into a 9-inch cast-iron skillet. Place skillet in oven 10 minutes.
3. Combine cornmeal, salt, baking powder, and baking soda in a large bowl. Combine buttermilk, pepper, and egg, stirring with a whisk. Add egg mixture to cornmeal mixture, stirring just until moist. Remove pan from oven. Tip pan to coat bottom and sides with oil;

carefully pour excess oil into batter, stirring to combine. Pour batter into pan, spreading evenly. Bake at 450° for 15 minutes or until a wooden pick inserted into center comes out clean. Let stand 5 minutes before serving. Yield: 8 servings (serving size: 1 wedge).

CALORIES 170 (27% from fat); FAT 5.1g (sat 0.8g, mono 1.3g, poly 2.6g); PROTEIN 5.2g; CARB 26.5g; FIBER 2.2g; CHOL 28mg; IRON 1.2mg; SODIUM 473mg; CALC 88mg

Winter Greens and Potato Casserole

Earthy kale, mustard greens, and potatoes make this hearty dish a comfort on a cold winter night. Provolone cheese is not typically used in an Appalachian dish, but we enjoyed its pronounced flavor. Use any kind of cheese you like.

    8   cups water
    12 cups chopped kale, stems
        removed (about ½ pound)
    12 cups chopped mustard greens,
        stems removed (about ½ pound)
    6   cups (⅛-inch-thick) slices red
        potatoes (about 2 pounds),
        divided
        Cooking spray
    2   cups vertically sliced onion,
        divided
    ¾   teaspoon salt, divided
    1   cup (4 ounces) shredded sharp
        provolone cheese, divided
    ½   cup canned vegetable broth

1. Preheat oven to 350°.
2. Bring water to a boil in a Dutch oven. Add kale and mustard greens, and cook 5 minutes or until tender, stirring occasionally. Drain; set aside.
3. Arrange 2 cups potato slices in a single layer in a 13 x 9-inch baking dish coated with cooking spray; top with 1 cup onion. Sprinkle with ¼ teaspoon salt; top with half of kale mixture. Sprinkle kale mixture with ½ cup cheese. Repeat layers once, ending with kale mixture. Top kale mixture with remaining 2 cups potatoes, and sprinkle with remaining ½ cup cheese. Pour broth evenly over potato mixture, and

sprinkle with remaining ¼ teaspoon salt. Cover with foil. Bake at 350° for 45 minutes. Uncover and bake 30 minutes or until lightly browned and potatoes are tender. Yield: 8 servings.

CALORIES 170 (27% from fat); FAT 5.1g (sat 2.6, mono 1.5g, poly 0.4g); PROTEIN 7.9g; CARB 25.2g; FIBER 4g; CHOL 14mg; IRON 1.9mg; SODIUM 472mg; CALC 191mg

QUICK & EASY • MAKE AHEAD
Corn Chow-Chow

This mustard-laced relish gets better the longer it sits. It pairs well with beans, such as our Savory Soup Beans (recipe at right), or peas, such as black-eyed peas or crowder peas. Cane syrup is golden, thick, and very sweet; use dark corn syrup in its place if you can't find it.

  1 cup water
  2 cups frozen whole-kernel corn
  1 tablespoon whole-grain Dijon mustard
  1 tablespoon cane syrup
  2 teaspoons cider vinegar
  ½ teaspoon celery salt
  ⅓ cup finely chopped onion
  ¼ cup finely chopped red bell pepper

1. Bring water to a boil in a small saucepan. Add corn; cover, reduce heat, and simmer 5 minutes. Drain.
2. Combine mustard, syrup, vinegar, and celery salt in a medium bowl, stirring with a whisk. Add onion and bell pepper, stirring to coat. Stir in corn. Let stand at least 30 minutes before serving. Yield: 8 servings (serving size: ¼ cup).

CALORIES 46 (8% from fat); FAT 0.4g (sat 0.1g, mono 0.1g, poly 0.1g); PROTEIN 1.4g; CARB 11g; FIBER 1.2g; CHOL 0mg; IRON 0.3mg; SODIUM 145mg; CALC 7mg

MAKE AHEAD
Savory Soup Beans

This dish is traditionally made with bacon; the smoked paprika gives this vegetarian version a similar smoky, savory flavor. You can order the paprika online at www.ethnicgrocer.com, www.thespicehouse.com, or www.tienda.com.

  3 cups dried pinto beans
  2 tablespoons olive oil
  3 cups finely chopped onion
  2 teaspoons Spanish smoked paprika
  6 garlic cloves, minced
  7 cups water
  2 bay leaves
  2½ teaspoons salt

1. Sort and wash beans; place in a large saucepan. Cover with water to 2 inches above beans; bring to a boil. Cook 2 minutes; remove from heat. Cover and let stand 1 hour. Drain.
2. Wipe pan dry with a paper towel. Heat oil in pan over medium-high heat. Add onion, paprika, and garlic, and sauté 4 minutes or until tender. Stir in beans, 7 cups water, and bay leaves, and bring to a boil. Cover, reduce heat, and simmer 1½ hours or until beans are tender. Stir in salt. Discard bay leaves. Remove from heat, and partially mash beans. Yield: 8 servings (serving size: about 1½ cups).

CALORIES 289 (14% from fat); FAT 4.4g (sat 0.7g, mono 2.7g, poly 0.7g); PROTEIN 14.8g; CARB 49.6g; FIBER 15.8g; CHOL 0mg; IRON 4.6mg; SODIUM 739mg; CALC 98mg

STAFF FAVORITE • MAKE AHEAD
Unfried Apple Pies

Hot milk dissolves the shortening in the pastry, resulting in a soft, easy-to-work dough.

CRUST:
  1 cup all-purpose flour
  ½ teaspoon salt
  ¼ teaspoon baking powder
  ⅓ cup hot fat-free milk
  ¼ cup vegetable shortening

FILLING:
  1 cup dried apples, chopped
  ½ cup dried cranberries
  ½ cup water
  ½ cup apple cider
  ¼ cup packed brown sugar

REMAINING INGREDIENTS:
  Cooking spray
  1 large egg white
  1 tablespoon water
  1½ teaspoons turbinado sugar or granulated sugar

1. To prepare crust, lightly spoon flour into a dry measuring cup; level with a knife. Combine flour, salt, and baking powder, stirring with a whisk. Combine milk and shortening in a large bowl, stirring until shortening dissolves. Gradually add flour mixture to milk mixture, tossing with a fork just until blended. Turn dough out onto a piece of plastic wrap. Knead into a ball (dough will feel sticky). Cover and chill at least 2 hours.
2. To prepare filling, combine dried apples, dried cranberries, ½ cup water, and apple cider in a small saucepan. Bring to a boil over medium-high heat. Cover; reduce heat, and simmer 10 minutes or until fruit is tender, stirring occasionally. Stir in brown sugar, and cool to room temperature.
3. Preheat oven to 450°.
4. Divide dough into 8 equal portions. Working with 1 dough portion at a time (cover remaining portions to prevent drying), roll each portion into a 6-inch circle on a lightly floured surface. Spoon about 2 tablespoons filling onto half of each circle; moisten edges of dough with water. Fold dough over filling; press edges together with a fork to seal. Place pies on a baking sheet coated with cooking spray. Combine egg white and 1 tablespoon water, stirring with a whisk; brush over pies. Sprinkle with turbinado sugar. Bake at 450° for 12 minutes or until golden. Place on a wire rack. Serve warm or at room temperature. Yield: 8 servings (serving size: 1 pie).

CALORIES 203 (27% from fat); FAT 6.2g (sat 1.5g, mono 2g, poly 1.6g); PROTEIN 2.5g; CARB 34.2g; FIBER 1.9g; CHOL 0mg; IRON 1mg; SODIUM 188mg; CALC 32mg

Power Up Your Plate

Eight surprisingly nutritious foods and easy ways to eat more of them.

We asked registered dietitians, medical doctors, and researchers why you should include the power foods featured here in your diet. See "Power Foods for Your Diet" on page 17 for their answers and our recipes for incorporating them into your meal plans.

Chicken Braised in Walnut Sauce

This traditional Persian dish is made with ingredients you may likely have on hand.

2 teaspoons olive oil
4 (8-ounce) chicken breast halves, skinned
⅓ cup finely chopped onion
1 garlic clove, minced
½ cup finely chopped walnuts
2 tablespoons all-purpose flour
½ teaspoon ground cinnamon
¼ teaspoon ground red pepper
1 (14-ounce) can fat-free, less-sodium chicken broth
¼ cup finely chopped fresh parsley
1 tablespoon white wine vinegar
¼ teaspoon salt
¼ teaspoon freshly ground black pepper
2 cups hot cooked long-grain white and wild rice

1. Heat oil in a large nonstick skillet over medium heat. Add chicken; cook 3 minutes on each side or until browned. Remove from pan. Add onion and garlic to pan; sauté 2 minutes or until tender. Add walnuts, and sauté 1 minute or until toasted and fragrant. Combine flour, cinnamon, and red pepper, and sprinkle over walnuts, stirring to coat. Add broth; stir with a whisk. Return chicken to pan, breast side up. Cover and simmer 15 minutes or until chicken is done and sauce is slightly thick. Stir in parsley, vinegar, salt, and black pepper. Serve over rice. Yield: 4 servings (serving size: 1 chicken breast half, ½ cup sauce, and ½ cup rice).

CALORIES 452 (29% from fat); FAT 14.5g (sat 1.8g, mono 3.5g, poly 7.8g); PROTEIN 46.5g; CARB 32.7g; FIBER 2.2g; CHOL 99mg; IRON 3.1mg; SODIUM 918mg; CALC 57mg

MAKE AHEAD
Irish Oatmeal Bread

2¼ cups boiling water
1¾ cups steel-cut oats
1 tablespoon salt
3 tablespoons butter
3 tablespoons light brown sugar
Dash of granulated sugar
2 packages dry yeast (about 2¼ teaspoons)
½ cup warm water (100° to 110°)
3¼ cups all-purpose flour, divided
3 cups whole wheat flour
Cooking spray
1 large egg, lightly beaten

1. Combine first 5 ingredients in bowl of a stand-up mixer, and let stand 25 minutes.
2. Dissolve granulated sugar and yeast in warm water; let stand 5 minutes or until foamy. Add to oat mixture. Lightly spoon flours into dry measuring cups; level with a knife. Gradually add 2¾ cups all-purpose flour and 3 cups whole wheat flour to oat mixture. Beat at medium speed until well blended. Turn dough out onto a floured surface. Knead until smooth and elastic (about 8 minutes); add enough of remaining all-purpose flour, 1 tablespoon at a time, to prevent dough from sticking to hands (dough will feel sticky).
3. Place dough in a large bowl coated with cooking spray, turning to coat top. Cover and let rise in a warm place (85°), free from drafts, 1 hour or until doubled in size. (Gently press two fingers into dough. If indentation remains, dough has risen enough.) Punch dough down; cover and let rest 5 minutes. Divide in half. Working with one portion at a time (cover remaining dough to prevent drying), roll each portion into a 14 x 8-inch rectangle on a floured surface. Roll up each rectangle tightly, starting with a short edge, pressing firmly to eliminate air pockets; pinch seam and ends to seal. Place each loaf, seam sides down, in a 9-inch loaf pan coated with cooking spray. Cover and let rise 30 minutes or until doubled in size.
4. Preheat oven to 350°.
5. Uncover dough, and brush egg evenly over loaves. Bake at 350° for 45 minutes or until loaves are browned on bottom and sound hollow when tapped. Remove from pans, and cool on wire racks. Yield: 2 loaves, 14 servings per loaf (serving size: 1 slice).

CALORIES 154 (15% from fat); FAT 2.5g (sat 1g, mono 0.7g, poly 0.4g); PROTEIN 5.1g; CARB 28.9g; FIBER 3g; CHOL 11mg; IRON 1.8mg; SODIUM 267mg; CALC 15mg

MAKE AHEAD
Cran-Grape Syrup

Stir into iced tea or lemonade, or use as a glaze for chicken and pork. It's delicious served over pancakes, waffles, or ice cream, too.

4 cups cranberry-grape juice drink
2 tablespoons honey

1. Bring juice to a boil in a medium saucepan. Reduce heat; simmer until thick and reduced to ¾ cup (about 45 minutes to an hour). Remove from heat; stir in honey. Cover and chill 8 hours (syrup will thicken as it cools). Yield: 12 servings (serving size: 1 tablespoon).
NOTE: Store in refrigerator up to 1 week.

CALORIES 56 (2% from fat); FAT 0.1g (sat 0g, mono 0g, poly 0g); PROTEIN 0.2g; CARB 14.3g; FIBER 0.1g; CHOL 0mg; IRON 0mg; SODIUM 3mg; CALC 7mg

Power Foods for Your Diet

Soybean Superlatives

"The FDA recommends 25 grams of soy protein daily to support cardiovascular health. Soy fiber may also prevent the gyrations of blood sugar in those with type II diabetes. It also helps conserve calcium for stronger bones, lessen hot flashes and other menopausal symptoms, and can lower blood cholesterol."
–Stephen Holt, M.D., author of *The Soy Revolution* and adjunct professor at New Jersey Institute of Technology

Keep an Eye on Kale

"Kale is a great source of beta-carotene. It is also a rich source of antioxidants, which are associated with eye health. Kale is also packed with: potassium to prevent hypertension; vitamin C; fiber; and calcium for bone health."
–Wahida Karmally, R.D., Dr.P.H., director of nutrition, Irving Center for Clinical Research, Columbia University

Dried Plum Particulars

"Prunes, or dried plums as we call them, are a rich source of fiber and iron. This is good news for women on vegetarian or reduced-calorie diets, who often don't get enough iron. And don't forget about antioxidants. Dried plums have carotenoids and other antioxidant compounds that may help reduce the risk of heart disease and cancer."
–Jo Ann Hattner, R.D., spokesperson for the American Dietetic Association

Jazzy Combo in Cran-Grape Juice

"Grape juice is rich in flavonoids that help the heart by preventing LDL ('bad') cholesterol from oxidizing and perhaps by reducing inflammation in the arteries. Cranberry juice also contains flavonoids as well as tannins, which dramatically lower the risk of the development of urinary tract infections."
–Amy Howell, Ph.D., research scientist, Rutgers University

Yogurt and the Calcium Connection

"High levels of calcium in yogurt seem to trigger the body to burn more fat and reduce the amount of new fat. The body does this by suppressing the release of the hormone calcitriol, which signals the cells to make more fat and burn less."
–Michael Zemel, Ph.D., professor of nutrition, University of Tennessee

Take Walnuts to Heart

"The FDA suggests that eating 1.5 ounces of walnuts a day as part of a diet low in saturated fat and cholesterol may reduce the risk of heart disease. The ability of the omega-3 fatty acids in walnuts to reduce inflammation and clumping of platelets may have broad health implications for many chronic diseases facing us."
–Beverly Utt, health consultant, R.D., M.S., M.P.H.

Oatmeal Beyond Breakfast

"Oatmeal is rich in soluble fiber which can improve heart health. The FDA recommends 1½ cups of oatmeal a day to help reduce LDL cholesterol levels. The fiber can also lower your risk for type II diabetes. Oatmeal is a good source of iron, as well."
–Julie Walsh, R.D., spokesperson for the American Dietetic Association

Benefits from Berries

"Berries are little storehouses of fiber; antioxidants; the vitamins A, C, E, and folic acid; and the minerals potassium and calcium. They also contain ellagic acid and lignans, plant compounds that may reduce the risk of some cancers. Studies show that the phytochemicals in berries may also help promote heart health in humans and reduce the risk of age-related conditions, such as Alzheimer's disease.
–Gary Stoner, Ph.D., chair of environmental health, Ohio State University

Pork Loin with Dried-Plum Stuffing

Stuff pork up to a day ahead. Two tablespoons of dried plums in each serving provide 1.5 grams of fiber.

STUFFING:
Cooking spray
1⅓ cups finely chopped red onion
½ cup finely chopped celery
2 garlic cloves, minced
1 cup finely chopped dried plums
⅓ cup finely chopped pecans
1 tablespoon grated orange rind
¼ cup fresh orange juice (about 1 orange)
2 tablespoons minced fresh parsley
1 tablespoon chopped fresh thyme
1 tablespoon chopped fresh rosemary
½ teaspoon salt
¼ teaspoon freshly ground black pepper
1 (2-pound) pork loin, trimmed
¼ teaspoon salt
¼ teaspoon freshly ground black pepper

SAUCE:
1 tablespoon all-purpose flour
1½ cups fat-free, less-sodium chicken broth, divided
¼ cup port
1 tablespoon Dijon mustard
¼ teaspoon salt
⅛ teaspoon freshly ground black pepper
Flat-leaf parsley (optional)

1. Preheat oven to 425°.
2. To prepare stuffing, heat a large skillet coated with cooking spray over medium heat. Add onion, celery, and garlic; cook 7 minutes or until tender, stirring frequently. Remove from heat. Stir in dried plums and next 8 ingredients; set aside.
3. Slice pork lengthwise, cutting to, but not through, other side. Open halves, laying pork flat. Place plastic wrap over pork; pound to ½-inch thickness using a meat mallet or rolling pin.
4. Spread stuffing over pork, leaving a 1-inch border. Roll up tightly; secure at 1½-inch intervals with twine. Rub pork
Continued

with ¼ teaspoon salt and ¼ teaspoon pepper. Place pork on a rack in a broiler pan coated with cooking spray. Bake at 425° for 40 minutes or until a meat thermometer inserted in center of pork registers 155°, turning pork after 20 minutes. Place pork on a cutting board; let stand 10 minutes. Cut into thin slices.

5. To prepare sauce, whisk together flour and ¼ cup broth. Place roasting pan over medium heat. Add port, stirring to loosen browned bits. Whisk in flour mixture, mustard, and 1¼ cups broth. Cook 2 minutes or until slightly thick, stirring frequently with a whisk. Stir in ¼ teaspoon salt and ⅛ teaspoon pepper. Serve with pork. Garnish with parsley, if desired. Yield: 8 servings (serving size: 3 ounces pork and 3 tablespoons sauce).

CALORIES 260 (27% from fat); FAT 7.8g (sat 1.7g, mono 3.9g, poly 1.6g); PROTEIN 26.2g; CARB 20.1g; FIBER 2.9g; CHOL 74mg; IRON 2.5mg; SODIUM 489mg; CALC 39mg

Savory Yogurt Cheesecake with Caramelized Onions

Serve with crackers or toasted baguette slices. The yogurt for the filling drains overnight. Spread any leftover drained yogurt on whole wheat toast for breakfast. Prepare the onions while the crust bakes.

FILLING:
- 1 (32-ounce) carton plain low-fat yogurt
- ½ cup (4 ounces) block-style fat-free cream cheese, softened
- 1 cup part-skim ricotta cheese
- ½ teaspoon salt
- ¼ teaspoon freshly ground black pepper
- 1 large egg yolk

CRUST:
- ½ cup all-purpose flour
- ½ cup yellow cornmeal
- 1 teaspoon sugar
- ½ teaspoon salt
- Dash of freshly ground black pepper
- 2½ tablespoons butter, chilled and cut into small pieces
- ¼ cup ice water
- Cooking spray

ONIONS:
- 1 teaspoon butter
- 8 cups sliced onion (about 1½ pounds)
- 1 tablespoon sugar
- ½ teaspoon salt
- ¼ teaspoon freshly ground black pepper
- 1 teaspoon dried thyme

1. To prepare filling, place colander in a 2-quart glass measure or medium bowl. Line colander with 4 layers of cheesecloth, allowing cheesecloth to extend over outside edges. Spoon yogurt into colander. Cover loosely with plastic wrap; refrigerate 12 hours. Spoon 1¾ cups yogurt cheese into a bowl; discard liquid. Place cream cheese in a bowl; beat with a mixer at medium speed until smooth. Add yogurt cheese, ricotta cheese, ½ teaspoon salt, ¼ teaspoon pepper, and egg yolk. Beat at low speed just until blended.

2. Preheat oven to 350°.

3. To prepare crust, lightly spoon flour into a dry measuring cup; level with a knife. Place flour, cornmeal, 1 teaspoon sugar, ½ teaspoon salt, and dash of pepper in a food processor; pulse 3 times or until combined. Add 2½ tablespoons butter; pulse 4 times or until mixture resembles coarse meal. With processor on, add ice water through food chute, processing just until moist (do not form a ball). Press cornmeal mixture into bottom of an 8-inch springform pan coated with cooking spray. Bake at 350° for 15 minutes or until lightly browned. Cool on a wire rack.

4. To prepare onions, while crust bakes, melt 1 teaspoon butter in a large nonstick skillet over medium heat. Add onion; cook 15 minutes, stirring occasionally. Stir in 1 tablespoon sugar, ½ teaspoon salt, and ¼ teaspoon pepper. Cover and cook 25 minutes or until browned and tender, stirring occasionally. Stir in thyme.

5. Spread yogurt mixture into prepared crust. Bake at 350° for 35 minutes or until almost set. Cool on a wire rack. (Cheesecake will continue to set as it cools.) Serve at room temperature. Cut cheesecake into wedges, and serve with

onions. Yield: 10 servings (serving size: 1 cheesecake wedge and about 2 tablespoons onions).

CALORIES 198 (30% from fat); FAT 6.5g (sat 3.7g, mono 1.9g, poly 0.4g); PROTEIN 10.2g; CARB 25.6g; FIBER 2.5g; CHOL 37mg; IRON 1.1mg; SODIUM 454mg; CALC 240mg

STAFF FAVORITE
Spicy Yellow Soybean, Lentil, and Carrot Curry

Look for canned soybeans next to the garbanzo beans in the supermarket.

- 1 tablespoon olive oil
- 2⅓ cups finely chopped onion
- 1 tablespoon red curry paste
- 4 cups vegetable broth, divided
- 2 cups finely chopped carrot
- 2 tablespoons minced peeled fresh ginger
- ⅛ teaspoon ground red pepper
- 3 garlic cloves, minced
- 1 cup dried small red lentils
- 1 (15-ounce) can yellow soybeans, rinsed and drained
- ⅓ cup minced fresh cilantro
- ¼ teaspoon salt
- ¼ teaspoon freshly ground black pepper
- 6 tablespoons plain fat-free yogurt
- Cilantro sprigs (optional)

1. Heat oil in a large saucepan over medium-high heat. Add onion; sauté 3 minutes or until tender. Stir in curry paste; cook 1 minute. Add ½ cup broth, carrot, ginger, red pepper, and garlic; cook 6 minutes or until carrot is tender, stirring occasionally. Add 3½ cups broth, lentils, and soybeans; bring to a boil. Reduce heat; simmer 10 minutes or until lentils are tender. Stir in cilantro, salt, and black pepper. Place 1 cup curry in each of 6 bowls; dollop with yogurt. Garnish with cilantro sprigs, if desired. Yield: 6 servings (serving size: 1 cup curry and 1 tablespoon yogurt).

CALORIES 314 (28% from fat); FAT 9.7g (sat 1.3g, mono 3.2g, poly 3.9g); PROTEIN 22.8g; CARB 39.5g; FIBER 11.8g; CHOL 0mg; IRON 6.2mg; SODIUM 937mg; CALC 163mg

Breakfast Polenta with Warm Berry Compote

COMPOTE:

    1   tablespoon butter
    3   tablespoons honey
    1   tablespoon fresh lemon juice
    Dash of ground cinnamon
    1   (12-ounce) bag assorted frozen
        berries

POLENTA:

    3   cups 1% low-fat milk
    ½   cup dry instant polenta
    2   tablespoons sugar
    ½   teaspoon salt

1. To prepare compote, melt butter in a medium saucepan over medium heat. Add honey, juice, cinnamon, and berries; bring to a boil. Reduce heat; simmer 5 minutes or until thoroughly heated. Keep warm.
2. To prepare polenta, bring milk to a boil in a medium saucepan. Slowly add polenta, stirring constantly with a whisk. Stir in sugar and salt, and cook 5 minutes or until thick, stirring constantly. Serve with compote. Yield: 4 servings (serving size: ⅔ cup polenta and ⅓ cup compote).

CALORIES 285 (15% from fat); FAT 4.9g (sat 3g, mono 1.4g, poly 0.2g); PROTEIN 8.5g; CARB 54.2g; FIBER 3.9g; CHOL 15mg; IRON 1.2mg; SODIUM 386mg; CALC 541mg

Braised Kale with Bacon and Cider

(pictured on page 23)

    2   bacon slices
    1¼ cups thinly sliced onion
    1   (1-pound) bag chopped kale
    ⅓   cup apple cider
    1   tablespoon apple cider vinegar
    1½ cups diced Granny Smith apple
        (about 10 ounces)
    ½   teaspoon salt
    ¼   teaspoon freshly ground black
        pepper

1. Place a Dutch oven over medium heat. Add bacon; cook 5 minutes or until crisp, stirring occasionally. Remove bacon from pan, reserving 1 teaspoon drippings in pan. Crumble bacon; set aside.

2. Increase heat to medium-high. Add onion to pan; cook 5 minutes or until tender, stirring occasionally. Add kale, and cook 5 minutes or until wilted, stirring frequently. Add cider and vinegar; cover and cook 10 minutes, stirring occasionally. Add apple, salt, and pepper; cook 5 minutes or until apple is tender, stirring occasionally. Sprinkle with bacon. Yield: 6 servings (serving size: ⅔ cup).

CALORIES 75 (28% from fat); FAT 2.3g (sat 0.8g, mono 0.9g, poly 0.4g); PROTEIN 2.5g; CARB 12.7g; FIBER 2.1g; CHOL 3mg; IRON 1mg; SODIUM 255mg; CALC 71mg

happy endings

While the Iron Is Hot

A cast-iron skillet can work wonders for classic desserts, to give crispy edges, golden fruit, and tasty results.

QUICK & EASY
Chocolate Chip Dutch Baby

A Dutch baby is a puffy, baked pancake. A preheated cast-iron skillet enables the batter to cook immediately and causes it to puff.

    ¾   cup 2% reduced-fat milk
    ½   cup all-purpose flour
    2   tablespoons sugar
    ¼   teaspoon salt
    2   large eggs
    2   tablespoons butter, divided
    ⅓   cup semisweet chocolate chips
    3   large firm bananas, halved
        lengthwise
    ½   cup coffee-flavored liqueur (Kahlúa)
    ½   cup frozen reduced-calorie
        whipped topping, thawed

1. Preheat oven to 450°.
2. Place a 9-inch cast-iron skillet in a 450° oven 15 minutes. Combine first 5 ingredients; stir with a whisk until smooth. Melt 1 tablespoon butter in preheated pan until browned, swirling to evenly coat pan. Add batter; sprinkle

evenly with chocolate chips. Bake at 450° for 10 minutes or until puffed and browned.
3. Meanwhile, cut banana halves in half crosswise. Melt 1 tablespoon butter in a large skillet over medium-high heat. Add bananas; cook 2 minutes on each side or until browned. Add liqueur; simmer 1 minute. Serve with Dutch baby; top with whipped topping. Yield: 6 servings (serving size: 1 Dutch baby wedge, 2 banana pieces, and about 1½ tablespoons whipped topping).

CALORIES 326 (28% from fat); FAT 10g (sat 5.7g, mono 2.9g, poly 0.6g); PROTEIN 5.3g; CARB 47.8g; FIBER 2.5g; CHOL 83mg; IRON 1.3mg; SODIUM 175mg; CALC 55mg

Chocolate Pudding Cake

(pictured on page 24)

Serve this gooey dessert with a spoon.

    1   cup all-purpose flour
    2¼ cups sugar, divided
    ½   cup unsweetened cocoa
    2   teaspoons baking powder
    ¼   teaspoon salt
    ¾   cup 2% reduced-fat milk
    ¼   cup melted butter, divided
    1   teaspoon vanilla extract
    1½ cups water

1. Preheat oven to 375°.
2. Lightly spoon flour into a dry measuring cup; level with a knife. Sift together flour, ¾ cup sugar, cocoa, baking powder, and salt over a large bowl. Add milk, 3 tablespoons butter, and vanilla, stirring until smooth. Set aside.
3. Combine 1½ cups sugar and water in a small saucepan. Bring to a boil, stirring to dissolve sugar. Remove from heat.
4. Place a 10-inch cast-iron skillet in a 375° oven 15 minutes. Place 1 tablespoon melted butter in preheated pan, swirling to evenly coat pan. Add batter; spreading evenly over pan. Pour water mixture slowly over batter; do not stir (mixture will bubble). Bake at 375° for 28 minutes or until cake is set. Let stand 10 minutes before serving. Yield: 8 servings.

CALORIES 351 (18% from fat); FAT 7g (sat 4.3g, mono 2g, poly 0.3g); PROTEIN 3.5g; CARB 72.6g; FIBER 2.2g; CHOL 17mg; IRON 1.7mg; SODIUM 267mg; CALC 108mg

Tarte Tatin

The delicious syrup becomes the topping when the tart is inverted. Tangy crème fraîche offsets the tart's sweetness.

1½ cups all-purpose flour
6 tablespoons butter, softened
6 tablespoons water, divided
1 large egg
1 cup sugar
4 Golden Delicious apples, peeled, cored, and quartered (about 2 pounds)
¼ teaspoon ground cinnamon
10 teaspoons crème fraîche

1. Lightly spoon flour into dry measuring cups; level with a knife. Place flour in a medium bowl, and cut in butter with a pastry blender or 2 knives until mixture resembles coarse meal. Combine 2 tablespoons water and egg, stirring with a whisk. Add egg mixture to flour mixture, stirring just until moist. Turn dough out onto a large piece of heavy-duty plastic wrap; knead lightly 5 times (dough will be sticky). Pat dough into a disk. Cover with additional plastic wrap, and chill 30 minutes.

2. Combine 4 tablespoons water and sugar in a 9-inch cast-iron skillet over medium-high heat. Cook 10 minutes or until golden, stirring only until sugar dissolves. Remove from heat; gently stir in small circles to evenly distribute cooked sugar. Let stand 5 minutes.

3. Preheat oven to 400°.

4. Arrange apple quarters tightly in a circular pattern over sugar in pan, beginning at outside edge. Cut 2 apple quarters in half, and arrange, points up, in center of pan. Place pan over medium heat; cook 20 minutes (do not stir), pressing apples slightly to extract juices. Remove from heat; let stand 10 minutes. Sprinkle cinnamon over apples.

5. Remove plastic wrap covering dough. Turn dough out onto a lightly floured surface; roll dough into an 11-inch circle. Place over apple mixture, fitting dough between apples and skillet. Bake at 400° for 20 minutes or until lightly browned. Let cool 10 minutes. Invert tart onto a plate. Serve with crème fraîche.

Yield: 10 servings (serving size: 1 tart slice and 1 teaspoon crème fraîche).

CALORIES 285 (30% from fat); FAT 9.6g (sat 5.6g, mono 2.7g, poly 0.6g); PROTEIN 3g; CARB 48.4g; FIBER 3g; CHOL 44mg; IRON 1.1mg; SODIUM 79mg; CALC 24mg

---

STAFF FAVORITE

Pineapple-Coconut-Banana Upside-Down Cake

A cast-iron skillet gives the cake a crisp edge, cooks it evenly, and keeps it moist.

2 tablespoons butter
¾ cup packed brown sugar
1 (15½-ounce) can pineapple slices in juice, undrained
1 cup flaked sweetened coconut
1 cup all-purpose flour
½ cup granulated sugar
1 teaspoon baking powder
½ teaspoon baking soda
½ teaspoon ground cinnamon
¼ teaspoon salt
½ cup mashed ripe banana (about 1 banana)
2 tablespoons vegetable oil
1 large egg

1. Preheat oven to 375°.

2. Melt butter in a 9-inch cast-iron skillet; sprinkle evenly with brown sugar. Drain pineapple slices over a bowl, reserving ½ cup juice. Place 1 pineapple ring in center of skillet. Cut remaining pineapple rings in half; arrange around center pineapple ring. Sprinkle evenly with coconut. Set aside.

3. Lightly spoon flour into a dry measuring cup, and level with a knife. Combine flour and next 5 ingredients in a large bowl. Combine reserved juice, banana, oil, and egg, stirring with a whisk. Add pineapple juice mixture to flour mixture, stirring until combined. Pour flour mixture over coconut. Bake at 375° for 30 minutes or until a wooden pick inserted in center comes out clean. Invert onto a wire rack. Serve warm or at room temperature. Yield: 10 servings (serving size: 1 slice).

CALORIES 301 (27% from fat); FAT 9g (sat 4.9g, mono 1.6g, poly 1.8g); PROTEIN 2.5g; CARB 54.8g; FIBER 1.4g; CHOL 27mg; IRON 1.4mg; SODIUM 231mg; CALC 55mg

---

Brown-Bag Lunch Menu
serves 1

Pasta salad with chicken*

Carrot and cucumber sticks

Pecan Bar Cookies

*Combine 1 cup cooked small seashell pasta, ½ cup shredded cooked chicken, ½ cup chopped plum tomato, 3 tablespoons crumbled feta cheese, 1 tablespoon chopped fresh basil, 1 teaspoon olive oil, ⅛ teaspoon salt, and ⅛ teaspoon black pepper; toss to combine. Cover and chill.

MAKE AHEAD

Pecan Bar Cookies

Though these delicate cookies have a crisp outside, they're soft inside.

1½ cups all-purpose flour
1 teaspoon baking powder
½ teaspoon baking soda
¼ teaspoon salt
½ cup granulated sugar
½ cup packed dark brown sugar
¼ cup butter, softened
1 teaspoon maple flavoring
1 large egg
½ cup chopped pecans
3 tablespoons semisweet chocolate chips, melted

1. Preheat oven to 350°.

2. Lightly spoon flour into dry measuring cups; level with a knife. Combine flour, baking powder, baking soda, and salt, stirring with a whisk.

3. Place sugars and butter in a large bowl; beat with a mixer at medium speed 3 minutes or until well combined. Add maple flavoring and egg; beat until combined. Add flour mixture; stir until well combined. Stir in pecans. Spread mixture evenly in a 9-inch cast-iron skillet. Bake at 350° for 30 minutes. Cool in pan 10 minutes on a wire rack.

4. Remove from pan, and drizzle with melted chocolate. Cool completely. Yield: 12 servings.

CALORIES 210 (36% from fat); FAT 8.4g (sat 3.3g, mono 3.4g, poly 1.3g); PROTEIN 2.7g; CARB 31.6g; FIBER 0.8g; CHOL 28mg; IRON 1.2mg; SODIUM 190mg; CALC 37mg

Beef Stew, page 7

Hearty Sour Rye Bread, page 36

Lemon Chicken and Rice with
Artichokes, page 13

Braised Kale with Bacon and Cider,
page 19

Shrimp in Green Sauce, page 26

Chocolate Pudding Cake, page 19

The Minimalist Mark Bittman

Meet the master of turning ordinary ingredients into extraordinary, yet simple, dishes.

Mark Bittman, a cookbook author and food columnist for *The New York Times*, is a self-taught cook with a knack for translating the unusual in a simple, accessible way. This cooking style has drawn a legion of loyal Bittman fans. We asked him to kick off our Cooking Class series, in which we will spotlight contemporary cooks who will show you how to adapt their signature styles. While all of the following recipes reflect Bittman's love of international food, they're also great examples of how to prepare good food fast with the fewest ingredients necessary.

Chicken with Green Olives

This North African dish is also served in southern Spain and Italy. It's made as a stew because the region's farm-raised chickens require long cooking for tenderness. This version is quicker because chickens in American supermarkets are more tender. Lightly blanching the olives brings out the true flavor of the fruit.

- 1 tablespoon olive oil
- 8 chicken thighs (about 2 pounds), skinned
- ¾ teaspoon black pepper, divided
- ¼ teaspoon salt
- 2 cups chopped onion
- 1 tablespoon minced fresh garlic
- 2 teaspoons minced peeled fresh ginger
- 1 teaspoon ground cumin
- 1 teaspoon paprika
- ½ teaspoon ground turmeric
- Dash of ground red pepper
- 1 (3-inch) cinnamon stick
- 1 bay leaf
- 2 cups fat-free, less-sodium chicken broth
- ⅔ cup pitted green olives
- 2 tablespoons fresh lemon juice
- ¼ cup chopped fresh cilantro
- 3 cups hot cooked couscous

1. Heat olive oil in a large nonstick skillet over medium-high heat. Sprinkle chicken with ¼ teaspoon black pepper and ¼ teaspoon salt. Add chicken to pan; cook 10 minutes, browning on all sides. Remove chicken from pan; reduce heat to medium.
2. Add ½ teaspoon black pepper, onion, and next 8 ingredients; cook 5 minutes, stirring occasionally. Add broth; bring to a boil. Return chicken to pan, and reduce heat. Simmer, uncovered, 15 minutes or until chicken is done. Discard cinnamon and bay leaf.
3. While chicken cooks, place olives in a small saucepan; cover with water. Bring to a boil; drain. Repeat procedure. Add olives and juice to chicken mixture; sprinkle with cilantro. Serve over couscous. Yield: 4 servings (serving size: 2 chicken thighs, ½ cup sauce, and ¾ cup couscous).

CALORIES 397 (27% from fat); FAT 12.1g (sat 2.2g, mono 6.4g, poly 2g); PROTEIN 33.1g; CARB 37.8g; FIBER 4g; CHOL 107mg; IRON 3mg; SODIUM 933mg; CALC 66mg

Shrimp Lo Mein

Fresh lo mein noodles are available in Asian markets—often in the freezer case. If you can't find them, substitute fettuccine.

- 2½ tablespoons soy sauce
- 8 ounces large shrimp, peeled, deveined, and coarsely chopped
- 8 ounces fresh lo mein noodles
- 1½ tablespoons peanut oil, divided
- 3 cups thinly vertically sliced onion
- 5 cups broccoli florets (about 1 pound)
- 2 cups red bell pepper strips
- 1 tablespoon minced fresh garlic
- 1 tablespoon minced peeled fresh ginger
- ¾ cup fat-free, less-sodium chicken broth
- ¼ teaspoon salt
- ¼ cup unsalted cashews, coarsely chopped

1. Combine soy sauce and shrimp; cover and refrigerate 30 minutes. Drain through a sieve over a bowl, reserving soy sauce.
2. Prepare noodles according to package directions, omitting salt and fat. Drain and rinse; drain well. Toss noodles with 1 teaspoon oil. Set aside.
3. Heat 2 teaspoons peanut oil in a large nonstick skillet over medium-high heat. Add onion; stir-fry 3 minutes. Add broccoli and bell pepper; stir-fry 3 minutes. Add garlic and ginger; stir-fry 1 minute. Remove vegetable mixture from pan.
4. Heat 1½ teaspoons peanut oil in pan. Add shrimp, and stir-fry 1 minute. Add reserved soy sauce, broth, and salt, and bring to a boil. Add noodles, vegetable mixture, and nuts, and toss well to combine. Yield: 4 servings (serving size: 2¼ cups).

CALORIES 408 (26% from fat); FAT 12g (sat 2.1g, mono 5g, poly 3.5g); PROTEIN 26g; CARB 51.8g; FIBER 8.3g; CHOL 128mg; IRON 5.2mg; SODIUM 941mg; CALC 122mg

Mark Bittman's approach to bringing back a recipe from abroad is to re-create it in ways that maintain its integrity and make it accessible.

QUICK & EASY

Asparagus Salad with Mustard-Soy Dressing

Asparagus is tossed with an emulsified vinaigrette that's laced with soy sauce. Soy and ground mustard are a common combination in Japan, resulting in a unique wasabi-like flavor. Since the egg yolk goes into the dressing raw, use a pasteurized egg—most grocery stores stock them.

 1 teaspoon ground mustard
 1 teaspoon extravirgin olive oil
 1 large pasteurized egg yolk
 1 teaspoon fresh lemon juice
 1 teaspoon soy sauce
 1 pound asparagus spears, steamed
    and chilled

1. Combine mustard, olive oil, and egg yolk, stirring with a whisk. Stir in juice and soy sauce. Drizzle dressing over asparagus, and toss gently to coat. Serve immediately. Yield: 4 servings.

WINE NOTE: When it comes to wine pairings, asparagus, egg yolk, and soy sauce are considered problem foods since each can make a wine taste flat. The range of possible wine pairings is admittedly small, but one type really works well: New Zealand Sauvignon Blanc. It is bold, zesty, and herbal. Try Nautilus Sauvignon Blanc 2003 from Marlborough, New Zealand ($12).

CALORIES 61 (40% from fat); FAT 2.7g (sat 0.6g, mono 1.3g, poly 0.3g); PROTEIN 3.5g; CARB 5.2g; FIBER 2.5g; CHOL 53mg; IRON 0.7mg; SODIUM 78mg; CALC 32mg

STAFF FAVORITE • QUICK & EASY

Shrimp in Green Sauce

(pictured on page 24)

This Iberian dish is similar to shrimp scampi. Serve with bread to soak up the rich sauce.

 3½ tablespoons extravirgin olive oil
  6 garlic cloves, peeled
  1 cup coarsely chopped green onions
  1 cup coarsely chopped fresh
     flat-leaf parsley
 ½ teaspoon salt
 ½ teaspoon freshly ground black
     pepper
 ¼ teaspoon crushed red pepper
 2¼ pounds large shrimp, peeled and
     deveined
 ⅓ cup dry white wine
  6 ounces sourdough or French bread,
     torn into 6 (1-ounce) pieces

1. Preheat oven to 500°.
2. Place olive oil and garlic in a food processor; process until garlic is finely chopped, scraping sides of bowl occasionally. Add green onions and parsley in food processor; pulse until minced. Spoon garlic mixture into a large bowl. Add ½ teaspoon salt, black pepper, red pepper, and shrimp to garlic mixture, and toss well to coat.
3. Spoon shrimp mixture into a shallow roasting pan, and add wine. Bake at 500° for 7 minutes or until shrimp are done, stirring once. Serve with bread. Yield: 6 servings (serving size: about 5 ounces shrimp mixture and 1 ounce bread).

CALORIES 352 (30% from fat); FAT 11.8g (sat 1.8g, mono 6.6g, poly 2g); PROTEIN 37.6g; CARB 19.5g; FIBER 2g; CHOL 259mg; IRON 5.6mg; SODIUM 630mg; CALC 131mg

Start the rice first, then tend to the fish. While the fish cooks, begin the snow pea stir-fry. Have everything for the stir-fry prepared and ready to go; once you begin cooking, everything moves quickly.

Sweet Black Pepper Fish

Snow pea and red pepper stir-fry*

Steamed white rice

*Heat 1 teaspoon canola oil and ½ teaspoon dark sesame oil in a large nonstick skillet over medium-high heat. Add ½ teaspoon bottled minced fresh ginger and 2 minced garlic cloves; stir-fry 30 seconds. Add 2 cups trimmed snow peas, 1 cup red bell pepper strips, and ¼ teaspoon salt; stir-fry 3 minutes or until crisp-tender. Drizzle with 2 teaspoons low-sodium soy sauce; stir to coat.

Sweet Black Pepper Fish

For most of its flavor, this Vietnamese classic relies on sugar and pepper, which everyone has on hand. The sugar is used to make a slightly bitter caramel sauce, and the results are spectacular.

- ½ cup water, divided
- 3 tablespoons sugar
- 2½ tablespoons Thai fish sauce
- 3 tablespoons minced peeled fresh lemongrass
- 1 tablespoon minced fresh garlic
- 1 teaspoon freshly ground black pepper
- 1 cup coarsely chopped green onions
- 4 (6-ounce) halibut fillets
- 1 tablespoon chopped fresh cilantro

1. Combine ¼ cup water, sugar, and fish sauce in a large nonstick skillet; bring to a boil, stirring to dissolve sugar. Add lemongrass, garlic, and pepper. Cook 1½ minutes or until slightly reduced. Add ¼ cup water, onions, and fish, and cook over medium-high heat 7 minutes

or until fish flakes easily when tested with a fork, turning once. Sprinkle with cilantro. Yield: 4 servings (serving size: 1 fillet and 2 tablespoons sauce).

CALORIES 247 (14% from fat); FAT 3.9g (sat 0.6g, mono 1.3g, poly 1.3g); PROTEIN 36.3g; CARB 13.9g; FIBER 1.2g; CHOL 54mg; IRON 1.9mg; SODIUM 911mg; CALC 89mg

QUICK & EASY
Pasta with Anchovies and Walnuts

"Pasta with walnuts is seen in countless forms in the Italian region of Liguria—some creamy, some with tomatoes or other vegetables. But my favorite, and by far the simplest, is this version. It's really no more than pasta with garlic and oil, incorporating two of the region's most distinctive ingredients: anchovies and walnuts."

—Mark Bittman

- 4 quarts water
- 1 teaspoon salt
- 1 pound uncooked linguine
- 1½ tablespoons extravirgin olive oil
- 1 tablespoon minced fresh garlic
- 2 (3.5-ounce) cans anchovies, drained and chopped
- ½ cup chopped walnuts, toasted
- 2 tablespoons chopped fresh flat-leaf parsley

1. Bring water and salt to a boil in a stockpot. Add pasta; cook 10 minutes or until al dente. Drain in a colander over a bowl, reserving ½ cup cooking liquid.
2. While pasta cooks, heat oil in a large nonstick skillet over medium heat. Add garlic; cook 3 minutes or until lightly browned, stirring frequently. Add anchovies, and cook 1 minute, stirring frequently. Remove from heat. Combine anchovy mixture, pasta, and reserved liquid; toss well to coat. Stir in walnuts; sprinkle with parsley. Yield: 6 servings (serving size: 1⅓ cups).

CALORIES 413 (28% from fat); FAT 12.8g (sat 1.8g, mono 4.1g, poly 5.5g); PROTEIN 17.4g; CARB 58.2g; FIBER 3.1g; CHOL 16mg; IRON 3.7mg; SODIUM 796mg; CALC 72mg

Jook
Rice Porridge

Jook—also known as *congee*—is eaten in Chinese communities around the world. Despite its odd name, it has wide-ranging appeal and has become one of Mark Bittman's favorites. The dish takes many guises in restaurants but can easily be made at home. Use it as a side dish with chicken, pork, or beef. You can also stir in fish, shrimp, chicken, or cooked egg to make it a main dish. While glutinous sushi rice gives the dish a sticky-creamy texture, Arborio adds extra texture because it retains more of its bite after the long cooking time.

- ½ cup sushi rice
- ½ cup Arborio rice
- 5 cups water
- 2 cups fat-free, less-sodium chicken broth
- ½ teaspoon salt
- 1 (3-inch) piece peeled fresh ginger, thinly sliced
- ⅓ cup chopped dry-roasted peanuts
- ¼ cup minced green onions
- 4 bacon slices, cooked and crumbled

1. Place rices in a sieve, and rinse thoroughly with cold water. Combine rices, 5 cups water, and broth; bring to a boil. Cover, reduce heat, and simmer 1½ hours, stirring occasionally. Add salt and ginger. Cover and cook 1 hour or until mixture has a porridgelike consistency, stirring occasionally. Place rice mixture on each of 6 plates. Top each serving with peanuts, onions, and bacon. Yield: 6 servings (serving size: 1⅓ cups rice mixture, 2½ teaspoons peanuts, 2 teaspoons onions, and 2 teaspoons bacon).

CALORIES 173 (30% from fat); FAT 5.8g (sat 1.3g, mono 2.8g, poly 1.4g); PROTEIN 5.9g; CARB 23.8g; FIBER 1.7g; CHOL 4mg; IRON 0.8mg; SODIUM 474mg; CALC 6mg

Tuna with Miso-Chile Sauce

Here, a standard red wine sauce is enhanced by miso, an ingredient similar to Parmesan cheese in its complexity, usefulness, and incredible flavor. The sauce is equally good with beef or pork.

  1 teaspoon butter
  1 teaspoon minced shallots
 ½ teaspoon minced peeled fresh ginger
 ⅛ teaspoon chile paste with garlic
  1 garlic clove, minced
 ½ cup dry red wine
1½ tablespoons mirin (sweet rice wine)
  1 tablespoon red miso (soybean paste)
  1 tablespoon vegetable oil
  4 (6-ounce) tuna steaks
 ¼ teaspoon salt
 ¼ teaspoon black pepper

1. Melt butter in a small saucepan over medium heat. Add shallots, ginger, chile paste, and garlic; cook 3 minutes, stirring frequently. Add wine and mirin; bring to a boil. Cook until reduced to 3 tablespoons (about 8 minutes); remove from heat. Stir in miso.
2. Heat vegetable oil in a large nonstick skillet over medium-high heat. Sprinkle tuna steaks with salt and pepper. Add tuna to pan; cook 3 minutes on each side until fish is medium-rare or desired degree of doneness. Serve tuna steaks with sauce. Yield: 4 servings (serving size: 1 steak and 1 tablespoon sauce).

CALORIES 245 (23% from fat); FAT 6.2g (sat 1.5g, mono 1.4g, poly 2.6g); PROTEIN 40.4g; CARB 3.5g; FIBER 0.2g; CHOL 79mg; IRON 1.5mg; SODIUM 409mg; CALC 33mg

Pork Tenderloin with Xec

Xec, a sweet-tart Mayan citrus salsa, is simple to prepare and uses everyday ingredients—yet it's truly remarkable with broiled meat. When the weather turns warmer, grill the tenderloin.

PORK:

  1 (1-pound) pork tenderloin, trimmed
 ¼ teaspoon salt
 ¼ teaspoon black pepper
Cooking spray

XEC:

  1 cup coarsely chopped orange sections
  1 cup coarsely chopped grapefruit sections
 ¼ cup coarsely chopped lemon sections
  2 tablespoons chopped fresh cilantro
1½ teaspoons minced seeded habanero pepper
 ⅛ teaspoon salt

1. Preheat broiler.
2. To prepare pork, sprinkle pork with ¼ teaspoon salt and black pepper. Place pork on a broiler pan coated with cooking spray. Broil 15 minutes or until a thermometer registers 160° (slightly pink). Let stand 5 minutes, and cut into ¼-inch-thick slices.
3. To prepare xec, combine orange and remaining ingredients, and serve with pork. Yield: 4 servings (serving size: 3 ounces pork and ½ cup salsa).

CALORIES 160 (27% from fat); FAT 4.8g (sat 1.6g, mono 2.1g, poly 0.5g); PROTEIN 18.4g; CARB 11.3g; FIBER 2.2g; CHOL 56mg; IRON 1.3mg; SODIUM 262mg; CALC 34mg

superfast

...And Ready in Just About 20 Minutes

Here we offer several dishes with international flair.

For example, try pork chops with a French influence, featuring olives, tomatoes, and garlic. Fajita seasoning and cilantro give chicken sandwiches a Mexican theme. A fresh lemon rind, garlic, and parsley garnish turns simple scallops into an Italian-inspired meal. And for those nights when you want something homey and familiar, try Pork Chops with Country Gravy and Mashed Potatoes; Chicken and Barley Stew; or baked fish with a Parmesan cheese-breadcrumb topping.

QUICK & EASY
Spiced Turkey Cutlets

The raisins and sweet spices give the sauce and the vegetables a Middle Eastern flavor. Serve over couscous.

  1 tablespoon vegetable oil
  8 (2-ounce) turkey cutlets
 ½ teaspoon salt
 ¼ teaspoon black pepper
 ½ cup sliced green onions
  1 medium red bell pepper, cut into (¼-inch-thick) slices
  1 cup fat-free, less-sodium chicken broth
 ¼ cup raisins
  1 tablespoon brown sugar
  1 teaspoon ground allspice
 ½ teaspoon ground cinnamon
 ½ teaspoon ground cumin

1. Heat vegetable oil in a large nonstick skillet over medium-high heat. Sprinkle turkey cutlets with salt and black pepper. Add turkey cutlets to pan, and cook 3½ minutes on each side or until done. Remove turkey cutlets from pan, and keep warm.

Using fewer ingredients not only makes for faster, easier cooking—it can also mean food with clearer, more pronounced flavor.

2. Add onions and bell pepper to pan; sauté 2 minutes. Add remaining 6 ingredients. Bring to a boil; cook until reduced to 1 cup (about 3 minutes). Serve with turkey. Yield: 4 servings (serving size: 2 cutlets and ¼ cup bell pepper mixture).

CALORIES 230 (27% from fat); FAT 6.9g (sat 1.6g, mono 1.5g, poly 3g); PROTEIN 26.3g; CARB 15.3g; FIBER 2.2g; CHOL 74mg; IRON 2.5mg; SODIUM 490mg; CALC 43mg

QUICK & EASY
Sautéed Pork Chops Niçoise

In Nice, France, olives, tomatoes, and garlic are the defining ingredients. Serve the pork chops and sauce over rice or packaged cooked potato wedges (such as Simply Potatoes).

    1 teaspoon vegetable oil
       Cooking spray
    4 (4-ounce) boneless center-cut
       loin pork chops (about ½ inch
       thick)
    ½ teaspoon salt
    ¼ teaspoon black pepper
    3 tablespoons all-purpose flour
    2 teaspoons bottled minced garlic
    3 tablespoons dry white wine
    4 teaspoons chopped pitted niçoise
       olives
    1 (14.5-ounce) can diced tomatoes,
       undrained
    2 tablespoons chopped fresh parsley

1. Heat vegetable oil in a large nonstick skillet coated with cooking spray over medium-high heat. Sprinkle pork with salt and pepper. Place flour in a shallow bowl. Dredge pork in flour, turning to coat; shake off excess flour. Add pork to pan; cook 3½ minutes on each side or until browned. Remove pork from pan. Add garlic to pan; sauté 10 seconds. Add wine, olives, and tomatoes; cook 2 minutes. Return pork to pan; cook 1 minute. Sprinkle with parsley. Yield: 4 servings (serving size: 1 pork chop and about ¼ cup sauce).

CALORIES 206 (38% from fat); FAT 8.7g (sat 2.8g, mono 3.8g, poly 1.2g); PROTEIN 22.3g; CARB 7.3g; FIBER 1.9g; CHOL 58mg; IRON 1.3mg; SODIUM 494mg; CALC 48mg

QUICK & EASY
Crab Cakes with Rémoulade

These crab cakes are on the bready side, so if that's not your preference, omit a couple tablespoons of breadcrumbs. Serve with a green salad.

CRAB CAKES:

    2 teaspoons olive oil
    1 cup dry breadcrumbs
    ½ cup thinly sliced green
       onions
    ½ pound lump crabmeat, shell
       pieces removed
    1 (4-ounce) jar diced pimiento,
       drained
    1 tablespoon Dijon mustard
    1 tablespoon fresh lemon
       juice
    ¼ teaspoon salt
    1 large egg

RÉMOULADE:

    ⅓ cup low-fat mayonnaise
    2 teaspoons 2% reduced-fat
       milk
    1 teaspoon capers, chopped
    ⅛ teaspoon ground red
       pepper
    1 small garlic clove, minced

1. To prepare crab cakes, heat oil in a large nonstick skillet over medium-high heat. Combine breadcrumbs, onions, crabmeat, and pimiento in a medium bowl. Combine mustard, juice, salt, and egg, stirring with a whisk. Add egg mixture to crab mixture, tossing gently to combine. Divide crab mixture into 4 equal portions, shaping each into a 1-inch-thick patty.
2. Add crab cakes to skillet; cook 2 minutes. Turn cakes; reduce heat to medium. Cook 3 minutes or until golden brown.
3. To prepare rémoulade, combine mayonnaise and remaining 4 ingredients, stirring with a whisk. Serve with crab cakes. Yield: 4 servings (serving size: 1 crab cake and 2 tablespoons rémoulade).

CALORIES 246 (27% from fat); FAT 7.4g (sat 1.4g, mono 2.2g, poly 2.9g); PROTEIN 16.1g; CARB 28.5g; FIBER 1.6g; CHOL 97mg; IRON 3.1mg; SODIUM 870mg; CALC 136mg

QUICK & EASY
Scallops Gremolata

    1½ tablespoons olive oil
       Cooking spray
    3 tablespoons Italian-seasoned
       breadcrumbs
    1½ pounds sea scallops
    ¼ cup chopped fresh flat-leaf parsley
    1 tablespoon grated lemon rind
    ¾ teaspoon bottled minced garlic
    ¼ teaspoon salt
    ⅛ teaspoon black pepper

1. Heat oil in a large nonstick skillet coated with cooking spray over medium-high heat. Place breadcrumbs in a large zip-top plastic bag; add scallops. Seal bag; shake to coat. Add scallops to pan; cook 4 minutes. Turn scallops; cook 3 minutes or until done. Remove from heat. Add parsley and remaining 4 ingredients; stir gently to coat. Yield: 4 servings (serving size: about 5 ounces scallops).

CALORIES 217 (28% from fat); FAT 6.7g (sat 0.8g, mono 3.8g, poly 0.9g); PROTEIN 29.3g; CARB 8.5g; FIBER 0.6g; CHOL 56mg; IRON 1mg; SODIUM 557mg; CALC 60mg

QUICK & EASY
Garlic-Rosemary Lamb Pita

    2 teaspoons olive oil
    1 tablespoon chopped fresh rosemary
    1 teaspoon bottled minced garlic
    ½ teaspoon salt, divided
    ¼ teaspoon black pepper
    1 pound boneless leg of lamb, cut
       into (¾-inch) cubes
    1½ cups finely chopped seeded
       cucumber
    1 tablespoon fresh lemon juice
    ⅛ teaspoon black pepper
    1 (6-ounce) container plain low-fat
       yogurt
    4 (6-inch) whole wheat pitas

1. Heat oil in a large nonstick skillet over medium-high heat. Combine rosemary, garlic, ¼ teaspoon salt, ¼ teaspoon pepper, and lamb, tossing to coat. Add lamb mixture to pan; sauté 4 minutes or until done.

Continued

2. While lamb cooks, combine ¼ teaspoon salt, cucumber, lemon juice, ⅛ teaspoon pepper, and yogurt. Place lamb mixture on each of 4 pitas, and drizzle with sauce. Yield: 4 servings (serving size: about 3 ounces lamb, 1 pita, and ⅔ cup sauce).

CALORIES 391 (26% from fat); FAT 11.5g (sat 3.5g, mono 4.8g, poly 1.5g); PROTEIN 32.7g; CARB 40.8g; FIBER 5.3g; CHOL 77mg; IRON 4.4mg; SODIUM 742mg; CALC 117mg

---

QUICK & EASY

Spicy Chicken and Arugula Sandwich

We found plain focaccia, perfect for this sandwich, at the deli counter. The arugula adds a peppery bite, but any other salad green will work.

- 2 teaspoons olive oil
- 2 (6-ounce) skinless, boneless chicken breast halves
- 1 tablespoon fajita seasoning
- ¼ cup light mayonnaise
- 3 tablespoons chopped fresh cilantro
- 1 teaspoon grated lime rind
- 1 tablespoon fresh lime juice
- 1 (9-ounce) round loaf focaccia, halved horizontally
- 1 medium ripe tomato, thinly sliced (about 4 ounces)
- 1½ cups trimmed arugula

1. Heat oil in a large nonstick skillet over medium-high heat. Place plastic wrap over chicken; pound each piece to a ¼-inch thickness using a meat mallet or rolling pin. Sprinkle both sides of chicken with fajita seasoning. Add chicken to pan; cook 2 minutes on each side or until done. Cut into 1-inch-thick slices.
2. While chicken cooks, combine mayonnaise, cilantro, rind, and juice; spread evenly over cut sides of bread. Arrange chicken on bottom half of bread; top with tomato and arugula. Cover with top half of bread. Cut into 4 wedges. Yield: 4 servings (serving size: 1 wedge).

CALORIES 341 (26% from fat); FAT 9.9g (sat 2.3g, mono 2.7g, poly 4.4g); PROTEIN 24.9g; CARB 37.6g; FIBER 1.7g; CHOL 53mg; IRON 2.5mg; SODIUM 545mg; CALC 35mg

---

QUICK & EASY

Chicken and Barley Stew

Frozen chopped onion makes this dish even quicker to prepare. If you use them, add with the frozen mixed vegetables.

- 1 cup uncooked quick-cooking barley
- 3 (14-ounce) cans fat-free, less-sodium chicken broth
- 1 tablespoon olive oil
- 1¾ cups chopped onion
- 1 (10-ounce) package frozen mixed vegetables
- 1 cup chopped cooked chicken
- ¼ teaspoon salt
- ¼ teaspoon dried thyme
- ¼ teaspoon black pepper

1. Bring barley and broth to a boil in a large saucepan. Reduce heat, and simmer 5 minutes.
2. While barley cooks, heat oil in a large nonstick skillet over medium-high heat. Add chopped onion, and sauté 3 minutes. Add mixed vegetables, and sauté 2 minutes. Add vegetable mixture, chicken, salt, thyme, and pepper to barley mixture; simmer 4 minutes. Yield: 4 servings (serving size: about 1¾ cups).

CALORIES 356 (19% from fat); FAT 7.5g (sat 1.5g, mono 1.9g, poly 3.3g); PROTEIN 22.7g; CARB 50.7g; FIBER 12.1g; CHOL 31mg; IRON 3.1mg; SODIUM 763mg; CALC 54mg

---

QUICK & EASY

Tamale Pie

Use a fork to crumble the firm polenta.

- 1½ (16-ounce) tubes of polenta, crumbled
- Cooking spray
- 2 (15-ounce) cans low-fat turkey chili
- 1 cup (4 ounces) preshredded sharp Cheddar cheese
- 6 tablespoons bottled salsa
- 6 tablespoons reduced-fat sour cream

1. Preheat oven to 475°.
2. Place crumbled polenta in an 11 x 7-inch baking dish coated with cooking spray.

Top with chili and Cheddar cheese. Bake at 475° for 13 minutes or until bubbly. Top each serving with 1 tablespoon salsa and 1 tablespoon reduced-fat sour cream. Yield: 6 servings.

CALORIES 324 (27% from fat); FAT 9.7g (sat 5.5g, mono 2.5g, poly 1g); PROTEIN 18.8g; CARB 40.6g; FIBER 6.6g; CHOL 46mg; IRON 2.8mg; SODIUM 881mg; CALC 223mg

---

QUICK & EASY

Curried Couscous with Broccoli and Feta

Using bagged broccoli florets and pre-shredded carrots all but eliminates the prep for this vegetarian entrée. If you want to add meat, use chopped chicken or thin strips of flank steak.

- 1¾ cups water
- 1 cup uncooked couscous
- 1½ cups small broccoli florets
- ½ cup finely chopped red onion
- ⅓ cup shredded carrot
- ¼ cup raisins
- ¼ cup dry-roasted cashews, chopped
- 2 tablespoons white wine vinegar
- 1½ tablespoons olive oil
- 1 tablespoon sugar
- 1½ teaspoons curry powder
- 1 teaspoon bottled minced fresh ginger
- ¾ teaspoon salt
- 1 (15-ounce) can chickpeas (garbanzo beans), rinsed and drained
- ¾ cup (3 ounces) crumbled feta cheese

1. Bring 1¾ cups water to a boil in a medium saucepan; gradually stir in couscous. Remove from heat; cover and let stand 5 minutes. Fluff with a fork.
2. While couscous stands, steam broccoli florets, covered, 3 minutes or until tender.
3. Combine couscous, broccoli, onion, and next 10 ingredients, tossing gently. Sprinkle with cheese. Yield: 5 servings (serving size: about 1¼ cups).

CALORIES 402 (27% from fat); FAT 12.2g (sat 3.8g, mono 5.8g, poly 1.6g); PROTEIN 13.4g; CARB 61.4g; FIBER 7.4g; CHOL 15mg; IRON 2.7mg; SODIUM 827mg; CALC 145mg

Mexican Corn and Bean Soup

For a vegetarian supper, you can substitute vegetable broth for the chicken broth.

    2   teaspoons olive oil
    ½   cup frozen chopped onion
    1   teaspoon ground cumin
    1   teaspoon bottled minced garlic
    ½   teaspoon dried oregano
    1   cup frozen whole-kernel corn
    ¼   teaspoon black pepper
    1   (14-ounce) can fat-free, less-sodium chicken broth
    1   (15-ounce) can black beans, rinsed and drained
    1   (14.5-ounce) can diced tomatoes and green chiles, undrained
    3   lime slices

1. Heat oil in a large saucepan over medium-high heat. Add onion, cumin, garlic, and oregano; sauté 1½ minutes. Stir in corn, pepper, broth, beans, and tomatoes; bring to a boil. Reduce heat; simmer 10 minutes. Serve with lime slices. Yield: 3 servings (serving size: 1⅔ cups soup and 1 lime slice).

CALORIES 241 (16% from fat); FAT 4.2g (sat 0.5g, mono 2.4g, poly 0.5g); PROTEIN 12.7g; CARB 44.7g; FIBER 12.4g; CHOL 0mg; IRON 3.2mg; SODIUM 722mg; CALC 87mg

Ginger Beef

    1   (3½-ounce) bag boil-in-bag long-grain rice
    1   teaspoon vegetable oil
        Cooking spray
    ¼   cup low-salt beef broth
    3   tablespoons low-sodium soy sauce
    1   tablespoon cornstarch
    1   tablespoon dry sherry
    2   teaspoons bottled minced fresh ginger
    1   teaspoon bottled minced garlic
        Dash of crushed red pepper
    1½ cups vertically sliced onion
    1   (1-pound) flank steak, trimmed and cut into ¼-inch strips
    4   lime slices

1. Prepare rice according to package directions, omitting salt and fat.
2. While rice cooks, heat oil in a large nonstick skillet coated with cooking spray over medium-high heat.
3. Combine broth and next 6 ingredients. Add onion to pan; sauté 2 minutes. Add steak; sauté 5 minutes or until desired degree of doneness. Stir in broth mixture; cook 10 seconds until slightly thick, stirring constantly. Serve over rice with lime slices. Yield: 4 servings (serving size: ½ cup ginger beef, ½ cup rice, and 1 lime slice).

CALORIES 330 (28% from fat); FAT 10.1g (sat 3.6g, mono 4g, poly 1.1g); PROTEIN 28.4g; CARB 29g; FIBER 1.8g; CHOL 68mg; IRON 3.5mg; SODIUM 468mg; CALC 18mg

Pork Chops with Country Gravy and Mashed Potatoes

Refrigerated mashed potatoes are widely available and are already seasoned, so no additional salt is needed. The five-ingredient gravy would go well over pan-sautéed or oven-fried chicken. It's also great over an open-faced turkey sandwich.

    ¾   teaspoon salt, divided
    4   (4-ounce) boneless center-cut loin pork chops (about 1 inch thick)
    1   teaspoon butter
    1⅓ cups 1% low-fat milk
    3   tablespoons all-purpose flour
    ¼   teaspoon poultry seasoning
    ¼   teaspoon black pepper
    1   (20-ounce) package refrigerated mashed potatoes (such as Simply Potatoes)

1. Heat a large nonstick skillet over medium-high heat. Sprinkle ¼ teaspoon salt evenly over both sides of pork. Add 1 teaspoon butter to pan, stirring until butter is melted. Add pork to pan, and cook pork 3 minutes on each side. Remove pork from pan, and keep warm.
2. Combine low-fat milk and flour, stirring with a whisk. Add milk mixture to pan, stirring with a whisk. Stir in remaining ½ teaspoon salt, poultry seasoning, and black pepper. Return pork to pan. Cover; reduce heat, and simmer 7 minutes or until gravy is thick and pork is done.
3. While pork cooks, prepare potatoes according to package directions. Serve with pork. Yield: 4 servings (serving size: 1 pork chop, ⅔ cup potatoes, and ¼ cup gravy).

CALORIES 322 (29% from fat); FAT 10.5g (sat 3.7g, mono 3.9g, poly 0.5g); PROTEIN 26.7g; CARB 29g; FIBER 2.2g; CHOL 65mg; IRON 1mg; SODIUM 908mg; CALC 125mg

Parmesan-Herb Baked Flounder

Mayonnaise helps the breadcrumbs adhere to the fish. Serve with white and wild rice or on a hoagie roll with lettuce and tomato for a fish sandwich.

    4   (6-ounce) flounder fillets
        Cooking spray
    ⅓   cup (about 1½ ounces) grated Parmesan cheese
    ¼   cup low-fat mayonnaise
    2   tablespoons minced green onions
    ¼   cup dry breadcrumbs
    1   teaspoon dried basil
    1   teaspoon dried oregano
    ¼   teaspoon salt
    ¼   teaspoon black pepper

1. Preheat oven to 400°.
2. Place fish on a foil-lined baking sheet coated with cooking spray. Combine cheese, mayonnaise, and onions; spread evenly over fish. Combine breadcrumbs and remaining 4 ingredients; sprinkle evenly over fish. Lightly coat fish with cooking spray. Bake at 400° for 10 minutes or until fish flakes easily when tested with a fork. Yield: 4 servings (serving size: 1 fillet).

CALORIES 241 (21% from fat); FAT 5.5g (sat 1.9g, mono 1.1g, poly 0.7g); PROTEIN 35.9g; CARB 10g; FIBER 0.7g; CHOL 87mg; IRON 1.6mg; SODIUM 606mg; CALC 157mg

Cajun Sausage and Rice Skillet

- 2 teaspoons vegetable oil
- 1 cup presliced mushrooms
- 1 cup chopped onion
- 1 tablespoon salt-free Cajun seasoning
- 8 ounces andouille sausage, sliced
- 2 (3½-ounce) bags boil-in-bag long-grain rice
- 4 cups fat-free, less-sodium chicken broth
- 1 (15-ounce) can kidney beans, rinsed and drained
- ½ teaspoon salt

1. Heat oil in a large nonstick skillet over medium-high heat. Add mushrooms, onion, Cajun seasoning, and sausage; sauté 5 minutes. Remove rice from bags; add to pan. Stir in broth and beans. Bring mixture to a boil; cover, reduce heat, and simmer 10 minutes or until rice is tender. Stir in salt. Yield: 6 servings (serving size: about 1¼ cups).

CALORIES 383 (21% from fat); FAT 8.9g (sat 3g, mono 1.5g, poly 2g); PROTEIN 16g; CARB 58.1g; FIBER 6.1g; CHOL 27mg; IRON 2.9mg; SODIUM 955mg; CALC 54mg

Hoisin Chicken and Broccoli Stir-Fry

- 1 tablespoon vegetable oil
- Cooking spray
- ⅓ cup fat-free, less-sodium chicken broth
- 3 tablespoons hoisin sauce
- 2 tablespoons dry sherry
- 2 tablespoons orange juice
- 1 teaspoon cornstarch
- 2 teaspoons bottled minced garlic
- 2 teaspoons bottled minced fresh ginger
- ½ teaspoon sesame oil
- 1 pound chicken breast tenders
- 3 cups bagged broccoli florets
- 1 (8-ounce) can whole water chestnuts, drained

1. Heat vegetable oil in a large nonstick skillet coated with cooking spray over medium-high heat. Combine broth and next 7 ingredients. Add chicken to pan, and sauté 2 minutes. Add broccoli, and sauté 5 minutes. Add water chestnuts, and sauté 2 minutes. Add broth mixture; cook 1½ minutes or until sauce is slightly thick, stirring constantly. Yield: 4 servings (serving size: 1 cup).

CALORIES 246 (22% from fat); FAT 6g (sat 1g, mono 1.5g, poly 2.7g); PROTEIN 28.7g; CARB 17.3g; FIBER 4.6g; CHOL 66mg; IRON 1.2mg; SODIUM 324mg; CALC 21mg

Asian Noodles with Asparagus and Shrimp

- 6 ounces uncooked soba (buckwheat noodles)
- ⅔ cup fat-free, less-sodium chicken broth
- 2 tablespoons rice vinegar
- 2 tablespoons low-sodium soy sauce
- 1 tablespoon peanut butter
- 2 teaspoons sugar
- 1 teaspoon bottled minced fresh ginger
- ½ teaspoon dark sesame oil
- 1 tablespoon vegetable oil
- 1 teaspoon bottled minced garlic
- 2 cups (2-inch) diagonally cut asparagus
- 1 pound peeled and deveined large shrimp
- ¼ cup thinly sliced green onions

1. Cook noodles according to package directions, omitting salt and fat.
2. While noodles cook, combine chicken broth and next 6 ingredients, stirring well.
3. Heat vegetable oil in a large nonstick skillet over medium-high heat. Add garlic; sauté 45 seconds. Add asparagus, and sauté 2 minutes. Add shrimp, and sauté 2 minutes or until shrimp are done. Add broth mixture and onions to pan, and cook over medium heat until hot. Add noodles, tossing gently to coat. Yield: 4 servings (serving size: 1½ cups).

CALORIES 357 (21% from fat); FAT 8.4g (sat 1.5g, mono 2.4g, poly 3.7g); PROTEIN 32.7g; CARB 40.3g; FIBER 2g; CHOL 172mg; IRON 4.7mg; SODIUM 868mg; CALC 91mg

season's best

Hoppin' John

In the South, a simple meal of black-eyed peas is a New Year's Day tradition—the legumes are thought to bring a year's worth of luck and prosperity.

Hoppin' John

- 1 tablespoon vegetable oil
- ⅔ cup chopped onion
- ½ cup chopped green bell pepper
- ⅓ cup chopped celery
- 2 garlic cloves, minced
- 1 teaspoon dried thyme
- 1 teaspoon crushed red pepper
- ½ teaspoon salt
- ¼ teaspoon ground black pepper
- 2 bay leaves
- 4 cups water
- 2 smoked ham hocks (about 1½ pounds)
- 1 (16-ounce) bag frozen black-eyed peas
- 1 cup uncooked jasmine or basmati rice
- ¾ cup chopped red bell pepper
- ⅓ cup chopped green onion tops

1. Heat oil in a Dutch oven over medium-high heat. Add onion, green bell pepper, celery, and garlic; sauté 5 minutes. Add thyme, red pepper, salt, black pepper, and bay leaves; cook 1 minute. Add water and ham hocks, and bring to a boil. Cover, reduce heat, and simmer 30 minutes. Add peas; cook an additional 30 minutes.
2. Remove ham hocks from pan; cool. Remove ham from bones; finely chop. Discard bones, skin, and fat. Add rice and red bell pepper to pan; bring to a boil. Cover, reduce heat, and simmer 15 minutes. Remove from heat; stir in ham. Discard bay leaves. Spoon into a serving dish, and sprinkle with green onions. Yield: 8 servings (serving size: about 1 cup).

CALORIES 226 (12% from fat); FAT 2.7g (sat 0.7g, mono 1.2g, poly 0.6g); PROTEIN 13.6g; CARB 37g; FIBER 4.5g; CHOL 17mg; IRON 2.2mg; SODIUM 622mg; CALC 31mg

Prairie Home Baking

Try these old-fashioned breads for a wonderful taste of history.

The everyday breads of the Mennonites reflect their ancestral travels, from their first migration from the Netherlands to Prussia, to the steppes of Russia, and eventually, to a great swath of North America. Each bread reflects a particular taste and culture, from toasted zwieback and celebratory babka, to the hearty Russian bierocks and the contemporary Prairie Fields Wheat and Soy Bread. When you bake any of these breads, you get a flavorful taste of history.

STAFF FAVORITE • FREEZABLE
Bierocks

These savory meat, onion, and cabbage "pies" are also known as *runzas*. Enclosed in sweetened yeast dough, the portable snacks are great for school lunches, picnics, and long car trips. Serve with mustard.

FILLING:

- ¼ cup chopped onion
- ½ pound ground turkey
- Cooking spray
- 2 cups finely shredded cabbage
- ½ teaspoon freshly ground black pepper
- ¼ teaspoon salt

DOUGH:

- ¼ cup sugar
- 1 package dry yeast (about 2¼ teaspoons)
- ½ cup warm water (100° to 110°)
- ½ cup 1% low-fat milk
- ¼ cup vegetable oil
- ¾ teaspoon salt
- 2 large eggs, lightly beaten
- 4 cups bread flour, divided

1. To prepare filling, cook onion and turkey in a large nonstick skillet coated with cooking spray over medium-high heat until turkey is browned, stirring to crumble. Add cabbage; cook until cabbage wilts, stirring constantly. Stir in pepper and ¼ teaspoon salt. Cover and chill.

2. To prepare dough, dissolve sugar and yeast in warm water in a large bowl; let stand 5 minutes. Stir in milk, oil, ¾ teaspoon salt, and eggs. Lightly spoon flour into dry measuring cups; level with a knife. Add 3½ cups flour to yeast mixture; stir to form a soft dough. Turn dough out onto a lightly floured surface. Knead until smooth and elastic (about 8 minutes); add enough of remaining flour, 1 tablespoon at a time, to prevent dough from sticking to hands (dough will feel tacky).

3. Place dough in a large bowl coated with cooking spray, turning to coat top. Cover and let rise in a warm place (85°), free from drafts, 1 hour or until doubled in size. (Gently press two fingers into dough. If indentation remains, dough has risen enough.) Punch dough down; cover and let rest 5 minutes.

4. Divide dough in half. Roll each half into a 10½ x 7-inch rectangle on a lightly floured surface. Cut each rectangle into 6 (3½-inch) squares. Working with 1 portion at a time (cover remaining dough to keep from drying), spoon about ¼ cup filling into center of each portion, and bring 2 opposite corners to center, pinching points to seal. Bring remaining 2 corners to center, pinching points to seal. Pinch 4 edges together to seal. Place bierocks, seam sides down, on a large baking sheet covered with parchment paper. Cover and let rise 20 minutes.

5. Preheat oven to 375°.

6. Uncover bierocks. Bake at 375° for 15 minutes or until bierocks are browned on bottom and sound hollow when tapped.

Remove bierocks from pan, and cool on wire racks. Yield: 12 servings (serving size: 1 bierock).

NOTE: To freeze, cool completely, and wrap individually in foil. Place wrapped bierocks in a heavy-duty zip-top plastic bag; freeze up to 3 months. To reheat, thaw in refrigerator. Place foil-wrapped bierocks in a preheated 350° oven for 15 minutes.

CALORIES 244 (27% from fat); FAT 7.4g (sat 1.6g, mono 2.1g, poly 3.3g); PROTEIN 10.8g; CARB 35.6g; FIBER 1.6g; CHOL 52mg; IRON 2.6mg; SODIUM 237mg; CALC 29mg

MAKE AHEAD
Sour Cream Babka

Russian immigrants gloried in Easter babkas—enriched yeast breads studded with dried fruits and nuts. For a more traditional babka, use dried sour cherries and candied cherries in place of cranberries and raisins.

DOUGH:

- 1 cup dried cranberries
- 1 tablespoon amaretto (almond-flavored liqueur)
- 1 cup evaporated fat-free milk
- 1 (8-ounce) carton low-fat sour cream
- 1 package dry yeast (about 2¼ teaspoons)
- ¼ cup warm water (100° to 110°)
- ½ cup granulated sugar
- 2 large eggs
- 2 large egg yolks
- 1 teaspoon almond extract
- ½ teaspoon salt
- 6 cups all-purpose flour, divided
- Cooking spray
- 1 tablespoon granulated sugar
- 1 cup golden raisins
- ½ cup slivered almonds

ICING:

- 1½ cups powdered sugar
- ¼ cup evaporated fat-free milk
- ¼ teaspoon almond extract

1. To prepare dough, combine cranberries and amaretto in a small bowl; set aside. Heat milk over medium-high heat
Continued

in a small, heavy saucepan to 180° or until tiny bubbles form around edge (do not boil). Remove from heat; stir in sour cream. Cool to room temperature.

2. Dissolve yeast in warm water, and let stand 5 minutes. Place ½ cup granulated sugar, eggs, and egg yolks in a large bowl; beat with a mixer at high speed until thick and pale (about 2 minutes). Add milk mixture, yeast mixture, 1 teaspoon almond extract, and salt; beat until well blended.

3. Lightly spoon flour into dry measuring cups; level with a knife. Add 5½ cups flour to egg mixture; stir until a soft dough forms. Turn dough out onto a floured surface. Knead until smooth and elastic (about 5 minutes); add enough of remaining flour, 1 tablespoon at a time, to prevent dough from sticking to hands (dough will feel tacky).

4. Place dough in a large bowl coated with cooking spray, turning to coat top. Cover and let rise in a warm place (85°), free from drafts, 1 hour or until doubled in size. (Gently press two fingers into dough. If indentation remains, dough has risen enough.) Punch dough down; cover and let rest 10 minutes.

5. Coat a 12-cup Bundt pan with cooking spray; dust with 1 tablespoon granulated sugar. Knead cranberry mixture, raisins, and almonds into dough. With floured hands, pat dough into an 8-inch circle. Form a 2-inch hole in center of dough; place dough in prepared pan, allowing center of Bundt pan to emerge through hole in dough. Gently press dough into pan. Lightly coat top of dough with cooking spray; cover and let rise 45 minutes or until doubled in size.

6. Preheat oven to 350°.

7. Uncover dough. Bake at 350° for 45 minutes or until loaf is browned and sounds hollow when tapped. Cool in pan 5 minutes on a wire rack.

8. To prepare icing, combine powdered sugar, ¼ cup milk, and ¼ teaspoon almond extract, stirring with a whisk. Remove babka from pan, and place on a serving platter. Drizzle with icing; cool completely. Yield: 28 servings.

CALORIES 216 (14% from fat); FAT 3.3g (sat 1g, mono 1.1g, poly 0.5g); PROTEIN 5.4g; CARB 40.7g; FIBER 1.6g; CHOL 35mg; IRON 1.6mg; SODIUM 66mg; CALC 63mg

Is It Tacky?

Various factors can cause dough to become too wet or too dry, but the most common cause by far is over- or under-measuring the flour. Even our method—lightly spooning the flour into a dry measuring cup—isn't foolproof. Professional bakers do away with the guesswork by using a scale to weigh flour (1 cup all-purpose flour weighs 4.5 ounces).

Short of a scale, the best course is to measure the flour lightly and add more flour incrementally until the dough matches the texture described in the recipe. Soft dough, for example, should feel like the fleshy area between your thumb and index finger. Tacky dough should feel like partially dried paint.

Prussian Leaf-Wrapped Breadsticks

Mennonites from west Prussia brought with them the tradition of baking dough on leaves. Serve this novelty bread on a large platter with a bowl of sour cream.

12 young beet leaves (6-8 inches long), stems trimmed
1 package dry yeast (about 2¼ teaspoons)
⅓ cup warm water (100° to 110°)
½ cup low-fat buttermilk
½ teaspoon salt
1¼ cups bread flour, divided
1 cup all-purpose flour
Cooking spray
2 tablespoons butter, melted
½ teaspoon kosher salt
Low-fat sour cream (optional)

1. Wash beet leaves. Pat dry; set aside.

2. Dissolve yeast in warm water in a large bowl; let stand 5 minutes. Stir in buttermilk and ½ teaspoon salt. Lightly spoon flours into dry measuring cups; level with a knife. Add 1 cup bread flour and all-purpose flour to buttermilk mixture; stir to form a soft dough. Turn dough out onto a lightly floured surface. Knead until smooth and elastic (about 8

minutes); add enough of remaining bread flour, 1 tablespoon at a time, to prevent dough from sticking to hands (dough will feel tacky).

3. Place dough in a large bowl coated with cooking spray, turning to coat top. Cover and let rise in a warm place (85°), free from drafts, 1 hour or until doubled in size. (Gently press two fingers into dough. If indentation remains, dough has risen enough.) Punch dough down; cover and let rest 5 minutes.

4. Roll dough into a 12 x 4-inch rectangle on a lightly floured surface. Cut rectangle crosswise into 12 (1-inch) strips. Working with 1 portion at a time (cover remaining dough to prevent drying), wrap a leaf around middle of dough strip, starting with stem end. (Ends of breadsticks should not be covered by leaf.) Place breadsticks, leaf tips down, on a baking sheet covered with parchment paper. Brush breadsticks with melted butter; sprinkle with kosher salt. Cover and let rise 45 minutes or until doubled in size.

5. Preheat oven to 375°.

6. Uncover breadsticks. Bake at 375° for 35 minutes or until browned on bottom and lightly browned on top. Remove from pan; cool on a wire rack. Serve with sour cream, if desired. Yield: 12 servings (serving size: 1 breadstick).

CALORIES 105 (17% from fat); FAT 2g (sat 1.4g, mono 0g, poly 0g); PROTEIN 3.9g; CARB 18.9g; FIBER 1.9g; CHOL 6mg; IRON 2.3mg; SODIUM 265mg; CALC 50mg

How to Wrap Breadsticks

Wrap a leaf around middle of each dough strip, starting with the stem end. (Ends of breadsticks should not be covered by leaf.)

Miller's Cinnamon-Raisin Bread

Contemporary Mennonite farmers take their harvested wheat to the local co-op and grain elevator. The co-op then sells the grain to places like Stafford County Flour Mills in Kansas, which makes this fine-crumbed bread with its all-purpose Hudson Cream Flour. You can purchase the flour at www.staffordcountyflourmills.com, or use bread flour, as we did.

⅔ cup raisins
1 cup plus 2 tablespoons 1% low-fat milk
2½ tablespoons unsalted butter
3 cups bread flour, divided
¼ cup packed brown sugar
1 tablespoon ground cinnamon
¾ teaspoon salt
1 package dry yeast (about 2¼ teaspoons)
2 large eggs, lightly beaten
Cooking spray

1. Place raisins in a small saucepan, and cover with water; bring to a boil. Remove from heat; cover and let stand 15 minutes. Drain well.

2. Heat milk over low heat in a small, heavy saucepan to between 100° and 110°; remove from heat. Add butter to pan; stir until butter melts.

3. Lightly spoon flour into dry measuring cups, and level with a knife. Combine 2¾ cups flour, brown sugar, cinnamon, ¾ teaspoon salt, and yeast in a large bowl, stirring with a whisk. Add warm milk mixture and eggs to flour mixture, and stir until a soft dough forms. Add raisins. Turn dough out onto a lightly floured surface. Knead until smooth and elastic (about 8 minutes); add enough of remaining flour, 1 tablespoon at a time, to prevent dough from sticking to hands (dough will feel tacky).

4. Place dough in a large bowl coated with cooking spray, turning to coat top. Cover and let rise in a warm place (85°), free from drafts, 1 hour or until doubled in size. (Gently press two fingers into dough. If indentation remains, dough has risen enough.) Punch dough down; cover and let rest 5 minutes.

5. Roll dough into a 14 x 7-inch rectangle on a lightly floured surface. Roll up rectangle tightly, starting with a short edge, pressing firmly to eliminate air pockets; pinch seam and ends to seal. Place roll, seam side down, in a 9 x 5-inch loaf pan coated with cooking spray. Cover and let rise 30 minutes or until doubled in size.

6. Preheat oven to 350°.

7. Uncover dough. Bake at 350° for 40 minutes or until loaf is browned on bottom and sounds hollow when tapped. Remove from pan; cool on a wire rack. Yield: 14 servings.

CALORIES 164 (16% from fat); FAT 3g (sat 1.8g, mono 0.3g, poly 0.1g); PROTEIN 5.5g; CARB 30.6g; FIBER 1.4g; CHOL 37mg; IRON 1.9mg; SODIUM 148mg; CALC 37mg

Prairie Fields Wheat and Soy Bread

In the late 19th century, many farmers milled their own grain for household needs. You can do the same with a food processor or a coffee grinder. To freeze baked loaves, wrap each in foil, then place in a zip-top plastic bag. They will keep about 3 months.

5¼ cups bread flour, divided
4 cups whole wheat flour
1 cup soy flour
1 tablespoon salt
2 packages dry yeast (about 2¼ teaspoons each)
3½ cups warm water (100° to 110°)
½ cup honey
⅓ cup olive oil
Cooking spray
1 tablespoon unsalted butter, melted

1. Lightly spoon flours into dry measuring cups, and level with a knife. Combine 3 cups bread flour, 1 tablespoon salt, and yeast in a large bowl, stirring with a whisk. Stir in water, ½ cup honey, and olive oil. Add 2 cups bread flour, whole wheat flour, and soy flour to yeast mixture, and stir until a soft dough forms. Turn dough out onto a lightly floured surface. Knead until smooth and elastic (about 8 minutes), adding enough of remaining bread flour, 1 tablespoon at a time, to prevent dough from sticking to hands (dough will feel tacky).

2. Place dough in a large bowl coated with cooking spray, turning to coat top. Cover and let rise in a warm place (85°), free from drafts, 1 hour or until doubled in size. (Gently press two fingers into dough. If indentation remains, dough has risen enough.) Punch dough down; cover and let rest 10 minutes.

3. Divide dough into thirds. Working with 1 dough portion at a time (cover remaining dough to prevent drying), roll portion into a 14 x 7-inch rectangle on a lightly floured surface. Roll up rectangle tightly, starting with a short edge, pressing firmly to eliminate air pockets; pinch seam and ends to seal. Place rolls, seam sides down, in a 9 x 5-inch loaf pan coated with cooking spray. Cover and let rise 45 minutes or until doubled in size.

4. Preheat oven to 350°.

5. Uncover dough. Bake dough at 350° for 25 minutes or until loaves are browned on bottom and sound hollow when tapped. Remove from pans, and brush tops of loaves with melted butter. Cool on wire racks. Yield: 3 loaves, 12 servings each loaf (serving size: 1 slice).

CALORIES 150 (17% from fat); FAT 2.9g (sat 0.5g, mono 1.5g, poly 0.3g); PROTEIN 5.3g; CARB 27.5g; FIBER 2.7g; CHOL 1mg; IRON 1.7mg; SODIUM 195mg; CALC 9mg

Pair soy bread with soups and stews for a hearty, Mennonite-style meal that reflects the influences of the Mennonites' ancestral travels.

Hearty Sour Rye Bread
(pictured on page 22)

These loaves of sour rye were everyday fare for Mennonites living on the Russian steppes. They were made with a natural sourdough starter and baked in ovens that were fueled by prairie grasses. In this recipe, yogurt replaces the sourdough starter.

    2 tablespoons vegetable oil
    ¾ cup chopped onion
    ¼ teaspoon sugar
    1 package dry yeast (about
         2¼ teaspoons)
    2 tablespoons warm water (100° to
         110°)
    1¼ cups plain low-fat yogurt
    1 tablespoon caraway seeds
    1½ teaspoons salt
    ¾ teaspoon white pepper
    1 large egg, lightly beaten
    2¼ cups bread flour, divided
    1¼ cups stone-ground rye flour
         (such as Bob's Red Mill)
    Cooking spray
    1 tablespoon water
    1 large egg yolk, lightly
         beaten
    ½ teaspoon kosher salt

1. Heat vegetable oil in a large skillet over medium heat. Add onion; cover and cook 10 minutes or until golden brown, stirring frequently. Remove from heat; cool completely.

2. Dissolve sugar and yeast in warm water in a large bowl; let stand 5 minutes. Stir in yogurt, caraway seeds, salt, and pepper. Add egg; stir well with a whisk.

3. Lightly spoon flours into dry measuring cups, and level with a knife. Add 2 cups bread flour and rye flour to yeast mixture, 1 cup at a time, stirring until a soft dough forms. Stir in chopped onion. Turn dough out onto a lightly floured surface. Knead until smooth and elastic (about 8 minutes); add enough of remaining flour, 1 tablespoon at a time, to prevent dough from sticking to hands (dough will feel tacky).

4. Place dough in a large bowl coated with cooking spray, turning to coat top.

Cover and let rise in a warm place (85°), free from drafts, 45 minutes or until doubled in size. (Gently press two fingers into dough. If indentation remains, dough has risen enough.) Punch dough down; cover and let rest 5 minutes.

5. With floured hands, knead dough 5 times. Shape into a round 7-inch loaf. Place loaf on a large baking sheet covered with parchment paper. Cover and let rise 30 minutes or until doubled in size. Make 3 diagonal cuts ¼-inch deep across top of loaf using a sharp knife.

6. Preheat oven to 350°.

7. Combine 1 tablespoon water and egg yolk; gently brush over dough. Sprinkle with ½ teaspoon kosher salt. Bake at 350° for 35 minutes or until loaf sounds hollow when tapped. Cool on a wire rack. Yield: 12 servings.

CALORIES 168 (20% from fat); FAT 3.8g (sat 0.9g, mono 1g, poly 1.6g); PROTEIN 6.5g; CARB 28.1g; FIBER 2.4g; CHOL 37mg; IRON 1.7mg; SODIUM 394mg; CALC 59mg

Zwieback

These rolls, whose name means "twice baked" in German, start off as soft yeast rolls enriched with butter, sugar, and eggs. Though they're traditionally shaped like doughnuts with topknots, we decided to shape them into classic dinner rolls. Russian Mennonites enjoy fresh zwieback with coffee at celebrations and funerals. Sliced and baked a second time, the slightly sweet bread slices have a crisp, nutty flavor and keep for weeks.

    ½ cup 1% low-fat milk
    2 tablespoons unsalted butter, cut
         into small pieces
    1 tablespoon vegetable oil
    2 tablespoons sugar, divided
    ¾ teaspoon salt
    1 package dry yeast (about
         2¼ teaspoons)
    ¼ cup warm water (100° to 110°)
    1 large egg, lightly beaten
    3 cups all-purpose flour
    Cooking spray

1. Heat milk over medium-high heat in a small, heavy saucepan to 180° or until tiny bubbles form around edge (do not boil). Remove from heat. Add butter; stir until melted. Stir in oil, 5 teaspoons sugar, and salt; cool to room temperature.

2. Dissolve 1 teaspoon sugar and yeast in warm water in a large bowl; let stand 5 minutes. Add milk mixture to yeast mixture; stir to combine. Add egg; stir well with a whisk. Lightly spoon flour into dry measuring cups; level with a knife. Add flour to yeast mixture, 1 cup at a time, stirring until a soft dough forms. Turn dough out onto a lightly floured surface; knead 5 minutes (dough will feel slightly tacky).

3. Place dough in large bowl coated with cooking spray, turning to coat top. Cover and let rise in a warm place (85°), free from drafts, 30 minutes or until doubled in size. (Gently press two fingers into dough. If indentation remains, dough has risen enough.) Punch dough down; cover and let rise 30 minutes or until doubled in size. Punch dough down; cover and let rest 5 minutes.

4. Divide dough in half; divide each half into 6 equal portions. Roll each portion into a ball. Working with 1 ball at a time (cover remaining dough to prevent drying), gently press or roll ball into a 2½-inch-long oval on a floured surface. Roll up oval tightly, starting with a long edge, pressing firmly to eliminate air pockets; pinch seam and ends to seal. Place rolls, seam sides down, on a large baking sheet covered with parchment paper. Cover and let rise 45 minutes or until doubled in size.

5. Preheat oven to 375°.

6. Uncover rolls. Bake at 375° for 15 minutes or until rolls are browned on bottom and lightly browned on top. Remove from pan, and cool on wire racks. Yield: 12 servings (serving size: 1 roll).

NOTE: To toast zwieback, preheat oven to 300°. Slice each roll lengthwise into ½-inch-thick slices. Arrange slices in a single layer on a baking sheet. Bake at 300° for 20 minutes or until lightly browned; turn slices over and bake an additional 5 minutes or until crisp. Remove from pan; cool on wire racks.

CALORIES 147 (21% from fat); FAT 3.5g (sat 1.6g, mono 0.9g, poly 0.4g); PROTEIN 4.1g; CARB 25.9g; FIBER 0.9g; CHOL 23mg; IRON 1.6mg; SODIUM 156mg; CALC 14mg

In the Red

An ancient cooking technique based on soy sauce infuses today's cuts of meat with juicy, complex flavor.

The Chinese method of red cooking begins with four elements: soy sauce, an aromatic root or herb (such as ginger), a sweetener (often just a little sugar), and a fortifier (usually some type of wine). Food braises slowly in this sweetened soy sauce broth. Heating mellows the flavor, and the soy sauce imparts a nutty taste and its signature red-umber color.

Traditional red-cooked dishes simmer fatty cuts of meat for hours to render them juicy and fork-tender. However, we find that leaner cuts of chicken, beef, and pork—even tofu—are well-suited for this technique, and they cook in a fraction of the time.

Asian Chicken over Noodles

Stewing a whole chicken in a soy sauce-based broth yields a juicy, flavorful bird. In this recipe, you serve the meat over cellophane noodles with crisp cucumbers. You could instead serve the chicken with its cooking liquid as a dipping sauce.

- ¾ cup low-sodium soy sauce
- ½ cup water
- ¼ cup sake (rice wine)
- 1 tablespoon sugar
- 2 tablespoons (¼-inch) slices peeled fresh ginger
- 1 whole garlic head, cloves separated, crushed, and peeled
- 1 (3½-pound) whole chicken, skinned
- 4 ounces cooked bean threads (cellophane noodles)
- 2 cucumbers, peeled, halved lengthwise, seeded, and thinly sliced (about 2½ cups)
- ⅓ cup thinly sliced green onions
- ¼ cup chopped unsalted, dry-roasted peanuts

1. Combine soy sauce, water, and next 4 ingredients in a large Dutch oven, and bring to a boil. Remove from heat; cover and steep 10 minutes.

2. Add chicken, breast-side down; bring to a boil. Cover, reduce heat, and simmer 45 minutes, turning chicken every 15 minutes.
3. Remove from heat; let chicken stand, breast-side down, 20 minutes. Transfer chicken to a cutting board, reserving cooking liquid; cool completely. Strain liquid through a sieve into a bowl; discard solids. Return liquid to pot; bring to a boil. Cook until reduced to ¾ cup (about 15 minutes).
4. Remove chicken from bones, and cut meat into bite-sized pieces. Discard bones. Place noodles on a platter, and top with chicken, cucumbers, green onions, and peanuts. Drizzle with reserved cooking liquid. Serve immediately. Yield: 8 servings (serving size: about 1⅓ cups).

CALORIES 220 (27% from fat); FAT 6.6g (sat 1.5g, mono 2.7g, poly 1.7g); PROTEIN 19.1g; CARB 18.8g; FIBER 0.8g; CHOL 48mg; IRON 1.1mg; SODIUM 1,005mg; CALC 25mg

Chinese Essentials

In ancient China, soy sauce was one of the seven essential items considered necessary in a home for daily life. The other six items were firewood, rice, vinegar, salt, oil, and tea.

Glossary of Ingredients

All ingredients in these recipes are available in Asian markets, gourmet markets, and health-food stores. If you can't find them, check the Web for online Asian grocers.

Fermented Chinese black beans are soybeans preserved in salt and spices. Buy them in clear pouches, so you can tell that the beans are fresh. Store in the refrigerator. Typical dried black beans are very different from these, and the two are not interchangeable.

Peanut oil should smell fragrant and earthy, like peanuts. Because it has a high smoke point, which keeps it from burning over high heat, it's a good choice for stir-frying or sautéing. You can substitute canola or vegetable oil.

Rice vinegar comes in many colors, but we call for white, unseasoned vinegar. Made from glutinous rice, it has a very mild taste and can be stored indefinitely at room temperature. Substitute cider vinegar in a pinch.

Sambal oelek (chile paste) is an Indonesian condiment often added to stews as a flavoring. It's essentially puréed fresh chiles. Some varieties have bean paste or garlic added; we prefer the basic variety in our red-cooked dishes.

Soy sauce is available in many varieties. These recipes specify low-sodium soy sauce, which provides a subtle flavor without adding copious amounts of sodium to the dishes.

Szechuan peppercorns are not peppercorns at all. The dried berries of a prickly ash tree add a mild, aromatic tang to Szechuan dishes—not the heat, which usually comes from chiles. Pink peppercorns are a good substitute, but don't use black peppercorns.

The sweet and spicy flavors are balanced, forming a harmonious and delicious union in Spicy Orange Beef.

Spicy Orange Beef

To avoid the bitter pith underneath the orange's skin, use a vegetable peeler or zester to remove just the colored peel. This Szechuan dish is spicy, but you can tame the heat by using fewer chiles, or by removing them from the Dutch oven before adding the beef. Substitute orange juice or another orange liqueur for the Grand Marnier if you like.

  2   teaspoons peanut oil
  6   dried hot red chiles
  4   (1 x 4-inch) orange rind strips
  2   garlic cloves, thinly sliced
2½   cups (1-inch-thick) slices carrot
1½   pounds lean beef stew meat
  1   cup water
  ½   cup fat-free low-salt beef broth
  ⅓   cup low-sodium soy sauce
  1   tablespoon Grand Marnier
      (orange-flavored liqueur)
  1   tablespoon honey
  3   tablespoons water
  2   tablespoons cornstarch
  3   cups hot cooked rice

1. Heat oil in a Dutch oven over medium-high heat. Add chiles, rind, and garlic; sauté 4 minutes or until rind is lightly browned. Add carrot and beef; sauté 1 minute. Stir in 1 cup water, broth, soy sauce, Grand Marnier, and honey; bring to a boil. Cover, reduce heat, and simmer 1 hour and 10 minutes or until beef is tender, stirring occasionally.

2. Combine 3 tablespoons water and cornstarch, stirring well with a whisk. Add cornstarch mixture to beef mixture; bring to a boil. Cook 1 minute or until thick, stirring constantly. Serve with rice. Yield: 6 servings (serving size: ⅔ cup beef mixture and ½ cup rice).

CALORIES 357 (25% from fat); FAT 9.8g (sat 3.3g, mono 4.2g, poly 0.9g); PROTEIN 25.9g; CARB 38g; FIBER 2.5g; CHOL 70mg; IRON 4.3mg; SODIUM 604mg; CALC 34mg

Barbecue Beef Sandwiches

The flavors of this dish are actually better the next day, when the spices have had time to infuse the beef. We enjoyed this Asian-inspired barbecue served on sandwich rolls or hamburger buns, and then sprinkled with sesame seeds.

1½   cups low-sodium beef broth
  ½   cup low-sodium soy
      sauce
  ½   cup water
  ¼   cup rice vinegar
  2   tablespoons dark brown
      sugar
  2   tablespoons molasses
  2   teaspoons five-spice powder
  1   teaspoon crushed red pepper
  ½   teaspoon freshly ground black
      pepper
  1   cup chopped onion
  2   pounds flank steak, trimmed
  1   tablespoon hoisin sauce
  ¼   cup chopped fresh cilantro
  8   (2½-ounce) hoagie rolls

1. Combine first 9 ingredients in a large Dutch oven over medium-high heat, and bring to a boil. Add onion and beef; return to a boil. Cover, reduce heat, and simmer 1 hour and 45 minutes or until beef is tender, stirring occasionally. Remove from heat; let stand 10 minutes. Transfer beef to a cutting board, reserving cooking liquid in pan. Shred beef with 2 forks. Return shredded beef to pan; stir in hoisin sauce. Bring mixture to a boil; reduce heat, and simmer 20 minutes or until most of liquid evaporates, stirring occasionally. Remove from heat, and let stand 5 minutes. Stir in cilantro. Serve on rolls. Yield: 8 servings (serving size: ¾ cup beef and 1 roll).

CALORIES 439 (27% from fat); FAT 13.2g (sat 6.2g, mono 4.5g, poly 1.4g); PROTEIN 33.5g; CARB 44.2g; FIBER 2.6g; CHOL 46mg; IRON 4.3mg; SODIUM 1,057mg; CALC 125mg

Black Bean Chicken

Fermented Chinese black beans are sometimes labeled as salty black beans. Soak only the amount you'll need for this recipe in water before they're added to the dish. Keep any extra in the refrigerator up to 6 months.

  ⅓   cup fermented Chinese black
      beans
  2   tablespoons peanut oil
  2   cups chopped onion
  1   garlic clove, minced
  ⅔   cup fat-free, less sodium chicken
      broth
  ⅓   cup low-sodium soy sauce
  1   teaspoon sugar
  4   cups broccoli florets
  1   pound boneless, skinless chicken
      breast, sliced into ¼-inch strips
  1   tablespoon cornstarch
  1   tablespoon dry sherry

1. Place beans in a bowl, and cover with warm water. Cover and let stand 30 minutes. Drain and rinse with cold water; drain well.

2. Heat oil in a large nonstick skillet or wok over medium-high heat. Add onion and garlic; sauté 30 seconds. Add beans; sauté 10 seconds. Stir in broth, soy sauce, and sugar; bring to a boil. Add broccoli and chicken; bring to a boil. Cover, reduce heat, and simmer 5 minutes or until chicken is done, stirring occasionally.

3. Combine cornstarch and sherry, stirring well with a whisk. Add cornstarch mixture to chicken mixture, and bring to a boil. Cook mixture 1 minute, stirring constantly. Yield: 4 servings (serving size: 1½ cups).

CALORIES 294 (29% from fat); FAT 9.5g (sat 1.6g, mono 3.5g, poly 2.7g); PROTEIN 33.9g; CARB 17g; FIBER 3.5g; CHOL 66mg; IRON 2.4mg; SODIUM 970mg; CALC 90mg

QUICK & EASY
Pork and Plantains

Pork and bananas are a traditional Szechuan combination. Chinese bananas, much starchier than their Western counterparts, are rarely available, so we substituted plantains.

1½ pounds pork tenderloin, trimmed
2 tablespoons peanut oil
¾ cup sliced green onions
2 tablespoons minced peeled fresh ginger
1 teaspoon Szechuan or pink peppercorns, crushed
1 serrano chile, thinly sliced
3 plantains, quartered lengthwise and sliced into 1-inch-thick pieces (about 3 cups)
1 cup fat-free, less-sodium chicken broth
½ cup low-sodium soy sauce
¼ cup white rum
1 tablespoon dark brown sugar
2 tablespoons water
1 tablespoon cornstarch

1. Cut pork into 2 x ¼-inch-wide strips. Heat oil in a large nonstick skillet or wok over medium-high heat. Add onions, ginger, peppercorns, and chile; stir-fry 30 seconds. Add pork; stir-fry 1 minute. Add plantains; stir-fry 30 seconds. Stir in broth, soy sauce, rum, and sugar; bring to a boil. Cover, reduce heat, and simmer 15 minutes, or until plantains soften.
2. Combine water and cornstarch, stirring well with a whisk. Add cornstarch mixture to pork mixture, stirring well; bring to a boil. Cook 1 minute or until thick, stirring constantly. Yield: 6 servings (serving size: 1 cup).

WINE NOTE: With spicy, salty, and sweet fruity flavors all rolled together, this pork dish is a delicious challenge for wine. Something bold and full-bodied is in order, all the better if the wine has some spice, too. The ideal answer: Gewürztraminer from Alsace, France. Alsatian Gewürztraminers are dry but powerful and riveting in their spiciness. If you haven't tried one, let this dish be your welcome excuse. Buy a 2002 from Domaine Weinbach, Hugel, or Trimbach (price range $15 to $40). All are top producers.

CALORIES 334 (26% from fat); FAT 9.6g (sat 2.4g, mono 4.3g, poly 2g); PROTEIN 27g; CARB 30.1g; FIBER 2.2g; CHOL 71mg; IRON 1.8mg; SODIUM 946mg; CALC 30mg

> When simmered in a sweetened soy sauce broth, foods such as pork, chicken, and tofu emerge sweet, salty, nutty, and mellow.

Tofu and Mushrooms

Tofu showcases its spongelike ability to pick up flavors in this traditional Chinese dish. Because silken tofu is delicate, it's added at the end; it steeps in the broth just long enough to pick up the flavors without disintegrating.

1½ tablespoons peanut oil
3 cups quartered shiitake mushroom caps (about 8 ounces)
½ cup chopped carrot
½ cup minced green onions
2 tablespoons minced peeled fresh ginger
1 garlic clove, minced
1 cup fat-free, less-sodium chicken broth
5 tablespoons low-sodium soy sauce
2 tablespoons sake (rice wine)
1 teaspoon sugar
1 teaspoon sambal oelek (chile paste)
1 tablespoon cornstarch
2 teaspoons water
1 teaspoon rice vinegar
1 (12.3-ounce) package extrafirm silken tofu, drained and cut into ½-inch cubes
2 cups hot cooked brown rice

1. Heat oil in a large nonstick skillet over medium-high heat. Add mushrooms, carrot, onions, ginger, and garlic; sauté 2 minutes. Stir in broth, soy sauce, sake, sugar, and sambal oelek. Cover, reduce heat, and simmer 10 minutes, stirring occasionally.
2. Combine cornstarch, water, and vinegar, stirring well with a whisk. Add cornstarch mixture to broth mixture, stirring well; bring to a boil. Cook 1 minute or until thick, stirring constantly. Remove from heat; add tofu. Cover and let stand 10 minutes. Serve over rice. Yield: 4 servings (serving size: 1 cup tofu mixture and ½ cup rice).

CALORIES 271 (26% from fat); FAT 7.7g (sat 1.3g, mono 3g, poly 2.9g); PROTEIN 12.7g; CARB 35.1g; FIBER 3.1g; CHOL 0mg; IRON 2.7mg; SODIUM 997mg; CALC 52mg

Pork and Chestnuts

One-fourth cup may seem like a lot of ginger, but its flavor mellows as it cooks. Look for a large piece of fresh ginger that has taut skin—wrinkles are a sign of age.

1½ pounds boneless pork loin, cut
    into 1-inch cubes
1   (10-ounce) can cooked shelled
    chestnuts, halved
1   cup fat-free, less-sodium chicken
    broth
1   cup water
¾   cup sliced green onions
½   cup low-sodium soy sauce
⅓   cup dry sherry
¼   cup chopped peeled fresh ginger
1   tablespoon sugar
4   cinnamon sticks
2   pods star anise
1   tablespoon water
4   teaspoons cornstarch
8   ounces udon noodles (thick
    Japanese noodles)
    Sliced green onions (optional)

1. Combine pork loin, chestnuts, and next 9 ingredients in a large Dutch oven over medium-high heat, and bring to a boil. Cover, reduce heat, and simmer 1 hour and 20 minutes or until meat is tender, stirring occasionally. Discard cinnamon and star anise.
2. Combine water and cornstarch, stirring well with a whisk. Add cornstarch mixture to pork mixture, stirring well, and bring to a boil. Cook 1 minute or until thick, stirring constantly. Remove from heat.
3. Cook noodles according to package directions, omitting salt and fat. Place ½ cup noodles into each of 6 bowls; top with ¾ cup pork mixture. Garnish each serving with sliced green onions, if desired. Yield: 6 servings.

CALORIES 310 (19% from fat); FAT 6.4g (sat 2.1g, mono 2.9g, poly 0.8g); PROTEIN 30.2g; CARB 29.3g; FIBER 0.8g; CHOL 62mg; IRON 1.8mg; SODIUM 960mg; CALC 42mg

---

lighten up

Surfing for Succulence

An Illinois reader submits an Internet recipe for a makeover.

Cindy Geier of Vernon Hills, Illinois, found the recipe for Cajun Shrimp and Catfish on the Internet. It received a five-star rating from one of the Web site's users, and persuaded by their testimonies, Cindy just had to try it.

Cindy agreed with the online comments regarding flavor but instinctively knew the recipe needed to be lightened. So she turned to us for help.

We replaced the mayonnaise with a small amount of low-fat buttermilk and omitted the butter used to cook the catfish, which ultimately eliminated nearly 90 grams of fat. We abandoned the heavy sauce of condensed soup and butter for a more contemporary version. A blend of chicken broth and a prepared Alfredo sauce now coats the fish, and shaves 559 calories from the dish. The savings allowed us to top the recipe with Parmesan cheese, which added to the flavor and gave the dish a great appearance.

Cindy's now convinced that anyone who tries this will give it top ratings.

BEFORE	AFTER
SERVING SIZE	
¾ cup shrimp mixture and ⅔ cup rice	
CALORIES PER SERVING	
532	382
FAT	
27.9g	12g
PERCENT OF TOTAL CALORIES	
47%	28%

Cajun Shrimp and Catfish

2   tablespoons low-fat buttermilk
1   tablespoon low-salt blackening
    seasoning
1½ pounds catfish fillets, cut into
    ½-inch strips
    Cooking spray
1   tablespoon butter
1   cup chopped green onions
1   cup presliced mushrooms
½   cup chopped fresh parsley
1   pound small shrimp, peeled and
    deveined
½   cup light Alfredo sauce (such as
    Contadina)
1   tablespoon fat-free, less-sodium
    chicken broth
2   tablespoons grated fresh Parmesan
    cheese
5½ cups hot cooked long-grain rice
    Parsley sprigs (optional)

1. Preheat oven to 350°.
2. Place buttermilk and blackening seasoning in a large bowl, stirring to blend. Add catfish; toss gently to coat.
3. Heat a large nonstick skillet coated with cooking spray over medium-high heat. Add catfish mixture; cook 3 minutes, stirring frequently. Place catfish mixture in a 2½-quart shallow casserole coated with cooking spray.
4. Melt butter in pan over medium-high heat. Add onions, mushrooms, and chopped parsley; sauté 3 minutes. Add shrimp; sauté 3 minutes. Spoon shrimp mixture over catfish. Combine Alfredo sauce and broth, stirring with a whisk. Drizzle over shrimp mixture; sprinkle with cheese. Bake shrimp mixture at 350° for 20 minutes or until bubbly. Serve shrimp mixture over rice. Garnish with parsley sprigs, if desired. Yield: 8 servings (serving size: about ¾ cup shrimp mixture and about ⅔ cup rice).

CALORIES 382 (28% from fat); FAT 12g (sat 4.4g, mono 3.8g, poly 1.9g); PROTEIN 30.4g; CARB 35.7g; FIBER 1.1g; CHOL 139mg; IRON 3.7mg; SODIUM 511mg; CALC 110mg

Warming Trend

Heat up the last days of winter with a steamy baked pasta casserole.

Even though the components have to be readied, these toss-together casseroles are actually more accommodating to busy schedules than the stovetop pastas, which require last-minute cooking. Simply combine the ingredients, and ease them into a baking dish. Then put them in the refrigerator until you're ready—or you can send them straight to the oven. All you need to round out dinner is a green salad or a simple side vegetable.

MAKE AHEAD
Baked Sesame Chicken Noodles

Asian vegetables, fresh ginger, and soy sauce imitate the taste of lo mein. Break the spaghetti in half before cooking to make it easier to prepare and serve.

- 8 ounces uncooked spaghetti or linguine, broken in half
- 1 tablespoon dark sesame oil
- 1 cup red bell pepper strips
- 8 ounces shiitake mushroom caps, sliced
- 2 (6-ounce) skinless, boneless chicken breast halves, cut into ½-inch pieces
- 1 teaspoon minced fresh ginger
- 3 garlic cloves, minced
- ¼ cup low-sodium soy sauce
- 1 cup fat-free, less-sodium chicken broth
- 1 tablespoon cornstarch
- 2 tablespoons cream sherry
- 1 tablespoon rice vinegar
- ½ teaspoon crushed red pepper
- 2 cups thinly sliced bok choy
- ¾ cup sliced green onions
- 1 tablespoon sesame seeds, divided
- Cooking spray
- 1 cup panko (coarse, dry) breadcrumbs
- 2 tablespoons butter, melted

1. Preheat oven to 400°.

2. Cook pasta according to package directions, omitting salt and fat. Drain well.

3. Heat oil in a Dutch oven over medium-high heat. Add bell pepper and mushrooms; sauté 2 minutes. Add chicken, ginger, and garlic; sauté 3 minutes. Stir in soy sauce; cook 2 minutes, stirring frequently.

4. Combine broth and cornstarch, stirring well with a whisk. Add broth mixture to pan, and cook 2 minutes or until slightly thick, stirring constantly. Remove from heat; stir in sherry, vinegar, and crushed red pepper. Add pasta, bok choy, onions, and 2 teaspoons sesame seeds to pan, tossing well to combine. Spoon pasta mixture into an 8-inch square baking dish lightly coated with cooking spray.

5. Combine breadcrumbs, butter, and 1 teaspoon sesame seeds; sprinkle evenly over pasta mixture. Bake at 400° for 20 minutes or until breadcrumbs begin to brown. Yield: 4 servings.

CALORIES 505 (23% from fat); FAT 12.7g (sat 4.5g, mono 3.4g, poly 2.6g); PROTEIN 32.6g; CARB 60.5g; FIBER 4g; CHOL 65mg; IRON 8.1mg; SODIUM 936mg; CALC 92mg

MAKE AHEAD
Roasted Butternut Squash and Bacon Pasta

(pictured on page 57)

Mini penne pasta works well in this dish. You can also use elbow macaroni, shell pasta, or orecchiette.

- ¾ teaspoon salt, divided
- ½ teaspoon dried rosemary
- ¼ teaspoon freshly ground black pepper
- 3 cups (1-inch) cubed peeled butternut squash
- Cooking spray
- 6 sweet hickory-smoked bacon slices
- 1 cup thinly sliced shallots
- 8 ounces uncooked mini penne (tube-shaped pasta)
- ¼ cup all-purpose flour
- 2 cups 2% reduced-fat milk
- ¾ cup (3 ounces) shredded sharp provolone cheese
- ⅓ cup (1½ ounces) grated fresh Parmesan cheese

1. Preheat oven to 425°.

2. Combine ¼ teaspoon salt, rosemary, and pepper. Place squash on a foil-lined baking sheet coated with cooking spray; sprinkle with salt mixture. Bake at 425° for 45 minutes or until tender and lightly browned. Remove squash from oven. Increase oven temperature to 450°.

3. Cook bacon in a large nonstick skillet over medium heat until crisp. Remove bacon from pan, reserving 1½ teaspoons drippings in pan; crumble bacon. Increase heat to medium-high. Add shallots to pan; sauté 8 minutes or until tender. Combine squash, bacon, and shallots; set aside.

4. Cook pasta according to package directions, omitting salt and fat. Drain well.

5. Combine flour and ½ teaspoon salt in a Dutch oven over medium-high heat. Gradually add milk, stirring constantly with a whisk; bring to a boil. Cook 1 minute or until slightly thick, stirring constantly. Remove from heat. Add provolone; stir until cheese melts. Add pasta to cheese mixture, tossing well to combine. Spoon pasta mixture into an 11 x 7-inch baking dish lightly coated with cooking spray; top with squash mixture. Sprinkle evenly with Parmesan cheese. Bake at 450° for 10 minutes or until cheese melts and begins to brown. Yield: 5 servings.

CALORIES 469 (28% from fat); FAT 14.4g (sat 7.3g, mono 4.4g, poly 0.9g); PROTEIN 22.1g; CARB 66.6g; FIBER 6.8g; CHOL 40mg; IRON 3.5mg; SODIUM 849mg; CALC 443mg

Create a Casserole

To invent your own baked pasta combinations, try a mix-and-match approach. Four components comprise the formula: pasta, sauce, basic ingredients, and toppings.

Pasta

Generally, pasta shapes should be short. Penne, rigatoni, ravioli, and ziti capture sauce and are bite-size, so they're easy to serve and eat. When you choose a long, thin variety, such as spaghetti, break it in half so it's more manageable for cooking and eating. Slightly undercook the pasta because it will finish cooking in the oven. This will also help the pasta soak up the tasty sauce.

Sauce

Simple sauces—embellished with various types of seasonings—provide a backdrop for the pasta and basic ingredients. While it's expedient to use purchased pasta sauce, freshly made sauce can come together in the time it takes to cook the pasta and prepare the other ingredients. Reprise a favorite sauce recipe, or consult the Kitchen Assistant at CookingLight.com for fresh ideas.

Basic Ingredients

Diced meat, poultry, or vegetables round out the one-dish meal. The choices are wide ranging, as our recipes illustrate. For example, they feature meats such as chicken, shrimp, and Italian turkey sausage. Other options include turkey breast, lean pork, and tuna.

Toppings

A crusty topping is an essential contrast to pasta. Breadcrumbs, nuts, flaxseed, or crushed unsweetened whole-grain cereals add both crunch and nutrients. Melted cheese renders a rich, satisfying flavor. Whatever you use, make sure the topping browns before you remove the dish from the oven.

Creamy Gruyère and Shrimp Pasta

Gruyère has a nutty, slightly sweet flavor; Swiss cheese makes a fine substitute. Vary this dish by using chicken in place of the shrimp.

- 8 ounces uncooked cavatelli or orecchiette pasta ("little ears" pasta)
- ¼ cup all-purpose flour
- ½ teaspoon salt
- 2 cups 2% reduced-fat milk
- 1¼ cups (5 ounces) shredded Gruyère cheese, divided
- 1 tablespoon butter
- 1½ pounds large shrimp, peeled and deveined
- 3 garlic cloves, minced
- 2 tablespoons dry white wine
- ¼ teaspoon ground red pepper
- 2 cups frozen green peas, thawed
- Cooking spray
- Parsley sprigs (optional)

1. Preheat oven to 375°.
2. Cook pasta according to package directions, omitting salt and fat. Drain well.
3. Combine flour and salt in a Dutch oven over medium heat. Gradually add milk, stirring constantly with a whisk; bring to a boil. Cook 1 minute or until slightly thick, stirring constantly with a whisk. Remove from heat. Stir in ¾ cup cheese, stirring until melted.
4. Heat butter in a large nonstick skillet over medium-high heat. Add shrimp and garlic; sauté 3 minutes. Stir in wine and pepper, and cook 1 minute or until shrimp is done.
5. Add pasta, shrimp mixture, and peas to cheese mixture, tossing well to combine. Spoon pasta mixture into a 13 x 9-inch baking dish lightly coated with cooking spray; sprinkle evenly with ½ cup cheese. Bake at 375° for 20 minutes or until cheese melts and begins to brown. Garnish with parsley, if desired. Serve immediately. Yield: 6 servings.

CALORIES 459 (27% from fat); FAT 13.8g (sat 7.1g, mono 3.7g, poly 1.6g); PROTEIN 39.6g; CARB 41.2g; FIBER 2.5g; CHOL 210mg; IRON 4.1mg; SODIUM 535mg; CALC 415mg

---

Mushroom Pasta Bake

A full cup of Italian Asiago cheese gives body and flavor to the velvety sauce, which is laced with sherry.

- 8 ounces uncooked gigli or radiatore pasta
- 2 teaspoons butter
- ¼ cup sliced shallots
- 8 ounces sliced shiitake mushroom caps
- 4 ounces sliced cremini mushrooms
- 1 tablespoon chopped fresh thyme
- ½ teaspoon salt
- ¼ teaspoon freshly ground black pepper
- 3 garlic cloves, minced
- 1 tablespoon dry sherry
- ¼ cup all-purpose flour
- 2 cups 2% reduced-fat milk
- 1 cup (4 ounces) grated Asiago cheese, divided
- Cooking spray
- Thyme sprigs (optional)

1. Preheat oven to 375°.
2. Cook pasta according to package directions; omit salt and fat. Drain well; set aside.
3. Melt butter in a large nonstick skillet over medium-high heat. Add shallots; sauté 3 minutes. Add mushrooms, chopped thyme, salt, pepper, and garlic; sauté 8 minutes or until mushrooms are tender. Add sherry; cook 1 minute, stirring frequently. Remove from heat.
4. Place flour in a Dutch oven over medium-high heat; gradually add milk, stirring constantly with a whisk. Bring to a boil; cook 1 minute or until slightly thick, stirring constantly with a whisk. Remove from heat; add ½ cup cheese, stirring until melted. Add pasta and mushroom mixture to cheese mixture, tossing well to combine. Spoon pasta mixture into an 8-inch square baking dish lightly coated with cooking spray; sprinkle evenly with ½ cup cheese. Bake at 375° for 30 minutes or until cheese melts and begins to brown. Garnish with thyme sprigs, if desired. Yield: 4 servings.

CALORIES 474 (30% from fat); FAT 16g (sat 8g, mono 4.6g, poly 2.2g); PROTEIN 21.8g; CARB 61.4g; FIBER 3.3g; CHOL 40mg; IRON 3.9mg; SODIUM 745mg; CALC 386mg

Casserole Get Ahead Guide

If time is an issue, assemble the baked pasta dishes the day before you plan to serve them, and refrigerate them until you're ready to bake. Follow these tips from our Test Kitchens for the best results:

• Assemble the casserole, cover with foil, and refrigerate up to 24 hours before baking.

• Dishes with fresh seafood are best assembled and baked immediately.
• Add cheese, breadcrumbs, or other toppings just before baking.
• If the casserole was refrigerated ahead, bake it an additional 10 to 15 minutes to heat through and brown the top.

MAKE AHEAD
Easy Ravioli Bake

This recipe pairs the convenience of store-bought pasta with a quick, easy homemade sauce. Chop tomatoes right in the can, snipping them with kitchen scissors. We enjoyed chicken ravioli in this dish, though any variety will work.

    2 (9-ounce) packages refrigerated
       chicken ravioli (such as Monterey
       Pasta Company)
  Cooking spray
    1 cup chopped onion
    ½ cup chopped green bell
       pepper
    ½ teaspoon dried oregano
    4 garlic cloves, minced
    6 tablespoons tomato paste
    ¼ cup dry white wine
    ¾ teaspoon salt
    ½ teaspoon dried basil
    ¼ teaspoon crushed red pepper
    ⅛ teaspoon black pepper
    4 (14.5-ounce) cans no-salt-added
       whole tomatoes, undrained and
       chopped
    ½ cup (2 ounces) shredded
       part-skim mozzarella cheese

1. Cook pasta according to package directions, omitting salt and fat. Drain well.
2. Preheat oven to 400°.
3. Heat a Dutch oven coated with cooking spray over medium-high heat. Add onion, bell pepper, oregano, and garlic; sauté 5 minutes or until vegetables are tender. Add tomato paste and next 6 ingredients, stirring well to combine; bring to a boil. Reduce heat, and simmer 20 minutes, stirring frequently. Remove from heat. Add pasta to tomato mixture, tossing well to combine. Spoon pasta mixture into an 8-inch square baking dish lightly coated with cooking spray, and sprinkle evenly with cheese. Bake at 400° for 30 minutes or until cheese melts and begins to brown. Yield: 4 servings.

CALORIES 444 (27% from fat); FAT 13.3g (sat 7.8g, mono 3.3g, poly 1.1g); PROTEIN 21.9g; CARB 60.4g; FIBER 8g; CHOL 76mg; IRON 4.5mg; SODIUM 855mg; CALC 361mg

Baked Ziti with Shrimp and Scallops

This casserole has a silky sauce made from jarred roasted bell peppers and cream cheese puréed in the blender. Let the dish stand a few minutes after it emerges from the oven so the sauce can set.

    8 ounces uncooked ziti (short
       tube-shaped pasta)
    ½ cup hot water
    1 (12-ounce) bottle roasted red bell
       peppers, drained
    1 (8-ounce) block fat-free cream
       cheese, softened
    1 tablespoon olive oil
    ⅛ teaspoon salt
    8 ounces large shrimp, peeled,
       deveined, and chopped
    8 ounces bay scallops
    4 garlic cloves, minced
    1 tablespoon chopped fresh
       parsley
  Cooking spray
    ¾ cup (3 ounces) shredded sharp
       provolone cheese

1. Preheat oven to 400°.
2. Cook pasta according to package directions, omitting salt and fat. Drain well.
3. Combine hot water, roasted peppers, and cream cheese in a food processor; process until smooth, scraping sides.
4. Heat oil in a Dutch oven over medium-high heat. Add salt, shrimp, scallops, and garlic; sauté 2 minutes or until shrimp and scallops are almost done. Add pepper mixture to pan; bring to a simmer. Reduce heat; cook 2 minutes, stirring frequently. Add pasta and parsley to shrimp mixture, tossing well to combine. Spoon pasta mixture into an 8-inch square baking dish lightly coated with cooking spray, and sprinkle evenly with shredded cheese. Bake at 400° for 20 minutes or until cheese melts; remove from oven.
5. Preheat broiler.
6. Return dish to oven; broil 2 minutes or until cheese begins to brown. Remove from oven; let stand 10 minutes. Yield: 4 servings.

CALORIES 508 (21% from fat); FAT 11.7g (sat 4.7g, mono 4.3g, poly 1.3g); PROTEIN 43.3g; CARB 53.4g; FIBER 2.4g; CHOL 130mg; IRON 4mg; SODIUM 977mg; CALC 388mg

MAKE AHEAD
Ziti Baked with Spinach, Tomatoes, and Smoked Gouda

Substitute smoked Cheddar for the Gouda, if you like.

    8 ounces uncooked ziti
    1 tablespoon olive oil
    1 cup chopped onion
    1 cup chopped yellow bell
       pepper
    3 garlic cloves, minced
    1 (14.5-ounce) can diced tomatoes
       with basil, garlic, and oregano,
       undrained
    1 (10-ounce) can Italian seasoned
       diced tomatoes (such as Rotel
       Bold Italian), undrained
    4 cups baby spinach
  1¼ cups (5 ounces) shredded smoked
       Gouda cheese, divided
  Cooking spray

Continued

1. Preheat oven to 375°.
2. Cook pasta according to package directions, omitting salt and fat. Drain well.
3. Heat oil in a Dutch oven over medium-high heat. Add onion and pepper; sauté 5 minutes. Add garlic; sauté 2 minutes or until onion is tender. Stir in tomatoes; bring to a boil. Reduce heat, and simmer 5 minutes, stirring occasionally. Add spinach to pan; cook 30 seconds or until spinach wilts, stirring frequently. Remove from heat. Add pasta and ¾ cup cheese to tomato mixture, tossing well to combine. Spoon pasta mixture into an 11 x 7-inch baking dish lightly coated with cooking spray; sprinkle evenly with ½ cup cheese. Bake at 375° for 15 minutes or until cheese melts and begins to brown. Yield: 5 servings.

CALORIES 382 (30% from fat); FAT 12.7g (sat 5.7g, mono 4.6g, poly 0.9g); PROTEIN 17g; CARB 52.3g; FIBER 4.3g; CHOL 33mg; IRON 4.4mg; SODIUM 977mg; CALC 334mg

Italian Sausage Puttanesca

If you're in the mood for something spicy rather than creamy, this is it. For a little less heat, use mild turkey Italian sausage instead of hot.

    8   ounces uncooked penne pasta
    8   ounces hot turkey Italian sausage
    1   cup chopped onion
    1   cup chopped green bell pepper
    3   garlic cloves, minced
Cooking spray
    2   (14.5-ounce) cans no-salt-added whole tomatoes, undrained and chopped
    ½   cup halved pitted kalamata olives
    2   tablespoons tomato paste
    1   tablespoon capers, drained
    1   teaspoon anchovy paste
    ½   cup (2 ounces) finely shredded Parmesan cheese

1. Preheat oven to 400°.
2. Cook pasta according to package directions, omitting salt and fat. Drain well.
3. Remove casings from sausage. Place sausage, onion, pepper, and garlic in a Dutch oven coated with cooking spray over medium-high heat; sauté 8 minutes, stirring to crumble.
4. Add tomatoes and next 4 ingredients to pan; bring to a boil. Reduce heat, and simmer 5 minutes. Remove from heat. Add pasta, tossing well to combine. Spoon pasta mixture into an 8-inch square baking dish coated with cooking spray; sprinkle evenly with cheese. Bake at 400° for 15 minutes or until cheese melts and begins to brown. Yield: 4 servings.

CALORIES 482 (30% from fat); FAT 16g (sat 4.6g, mono 6.9g, poly 2.6g); PROTEIN 24.7g; CARB 63.3g; FIBER 6.1g; CHOL 42mg; IRON 4.7mg; SODIUM 983mg; CALC 231mg

lighten up

Snack Time

An alternative ingredient helps a new version of a classic cake win this grandmother's praise.

When her grandkids make a surprise visit, Chrystine Morrill of Tomkins Cove, New York, is likely to mix up her Apple Spice Cake. "It's that fast. I just need a moment's notice," she says. With fresh apple and a blend of sweet spices, the moist, tender snack cake might appear a wholesome treat for the boys. But Chrystine was aware of the excessive amount of vegetable oil in the batter, so she knew that the cake wasn't so innocent. Although the vegetable oil made the cake moist, it contributed more than 108 grams of fat to the recipe.

We halved the vegetable oil and made up the difference in volume by using fat-free cream cheese. The combination extended the oil's moisturizing and tenderizing effect yet saved 4.5 grams of fat per serving in the process. Our savings allowed us to add 2 eggs to the batter, which improved the cake's texture, as well. And the egg whites aided in leavening, while the yolks made it creamier.

Chrystine and her grandsons were delighted with the lighter version. "The recipe worked like magic," Chrystine says. "The cake was as moist and dense as the original."

BEFORE	AFTER
SERVING SIZE	
1 piece	
CALORIES PER SERVING	
224	205
FAT	
9.5g	5.8g
PERCENT OF TOTAL CALORIES	
38%	25%

Apple Spice Cake

    1   cup packed dark brown sugar
    ⅓   cup (3 ounces) block-style fat-free cream cheese, softened
    ¼   cup vegetable oil
    1   teaspoon vanilla extract
    2   large eggs
    1½   cups all-purpose flour
    1   teaspoon baking soda
    1   teaspoon cinnamon
    ½   teaspoon salt
    ½   teaspoon ground cloves
    ½   teaspoon ground nutmeg
    1   cup low-fat buttermilk
    1   cup chopped peeled Braeburn apple
    2   tablespoons brandy (optional)
Cooking spray
    2   teaspoons powdered sugar

1. Preheat oven to 350°.
2. Place first 4 ingredients in a large bowl, and beat with a mixer at medium speed until well blended (about 3 minutes). Add eggs, 1 at a time, beating well after each addition.
3. Lightly spoon flour into dry measuring cups; level with a knife. Combine flour and next 5 ingredients, stirring with a whisk. Add flour mixture and buttermilk alternately to sugar mixture, beginning and ending with flour mixture; beat well after each addition. Stir in apple and brandy, if desired. Spoon mixture into an 8-inch square baking pan coated with cooking spray.
4. Bake at 350° for 30 minutes or until a wooden pick inserted in center comes out clean. Cool in pan on a wire rack

10 minutes. Remove from pan; cool completely on wire rack. Sprinkle with powdered sugar. Yield: 12 servings.

CALORIES 205 (25% from fat); FAT 5.8g (sat 1.1g, mono 1.4g, poly 2.8g); PROTEIN 4.4g; CARB 33.1g; FIBER 0.8g; CHOL 38mg; IRON 1.3mg; SODIUM 278mg; CALC 66mg

reader recipes

Muffin Magic

With a few tricks up her sleeve, a Florida reader perfects a lighter recipe.

Lorraine Fina Stevenski of Clearwater, Florida, is adept at lightening recipes—especially muffins.

Lorraine focuses on individual ingredients and determines the best way to reduce fat in each. She reduces butter and oil and sometimes replaces them with applesauce; she uses low-fat sour cream instead of full-fat; and she uses chocolate sparingly. In batters, Lorraine replaces a portion of nuts with raisins, and in toppings, she replaces nuts with oatmeal to keep the crunch.

Muffins fill her freezer, wrapped and ready to give away. Every week, another couple of recipes join her muffin repertoire. Here's an example.

MAKE AHEAD • FREEZABLE
Low-Fat Strawberry-Cinnamon Muffins

1½ cups all-purpose flour
½ cup sugar
2½ teaspoons baking powder
1 teaspoon ground cinnamon
¼ teaspoon salt
⅔ cup vanilla fat-free yogurt
¼ cup butter, melted
3 tablespoons 1% low-fat milk
1 large egg, lightly beaten
Cooking spray
¼ cup strawberry jam
1 tablespoon sugar
½ teaspoon ground cinnamon

1. Preheat oven to 375°.

2. Lightly spoon flour into dry measuring cups; level with a knife. Combine flour and next 4 ingredients in a large bowl, stirring well with a whisk. Make a well in center of mixture. Combine yogurt, butter, milk, and egg in a bowl, stirring well with a whisk. Add yogurt mixture to flour mixture, stirring just until moist.

3. Place 12 foil cup liners in muffin cups; coat liners with cooking spray. Spoon 1 tablespoon batter into each liner. Top each with 1 teaspoon jam. Top evenly with remaining batter. Combine 1 tablespoon sugar and ½ teaspoon cinnamon; sprinkle over batter. Bake at 375° for 15 minutes or until a wooden pick inserted in center comes out clean. Cool in pan on a wire rack 15 minutes. Remove from pan; place on a wire rack. Yield: 1 dozen (serving size: 1 muffin).

CALORIES 165 (24% from fat); FAT 4.4g (sat 2.6g, mono 1.3g, poly 0.3g); PROTEIN 3g; CARB 29g; FIBER 0.6g; CHOL 28mg; IRON 1mg; SODIUM 206mg; CALC 94mg

MAKE AHEAD
Lemony Fruit Dip

"I lightened this fruit dip recipe, and it received rave reviews. It looks lovely and tastes great." Serve with fresh fruit such as strawberries, pineapple, or apple.

—Janice Van Mullem,
Huntington Beach, California

¼ cup sugar, divided
1 large egg
2½ tablespoons fresh lemon juice
¼ cup water
1½ teaspoons cornstarch
½ teaspoon vanilla extract
1½ cups frozen reduced-calorie whipped topping, thawed

1. Combine 2 tablespoons sugar, egg, and lemon juice in a small bowl; stir well with a whisk. Combine 2 tablespoons sugar, water, and cornstarch in a small saucepan; bring to a boil. Cook 30 seconds or until thickened, stirring constantly. Remove from heat. Slowly pour beaten egg mixture into water mixture, stirring constantly. Cook over medium heat 2 minutes or until thick, stirring constantly. Remove from heat; stir in vanilla. Cool completely. Fold in whipped topping. Yield: 14 servings (serving size: about 2 tablespoons).

CALORIES 39 (28% from fat); FAT 1.2g (sat 1g, mono 0.1g, poly 0.1g); PROTEIN 0.5g; CARB 6g; FIBER 0g; CHOL 15mg; IRON 0.1mg; SODIUM 7mg; CALC 2mg

Warm Eggplant and Goat Cheese Sandwiches

"This sandwich was born when I brought home adorable baby eggplants from the local farmers' market. Eggplant and goat cheese go together perfectly."

—Lisa Richardson, Glendale, California

1 teaspoon olive oil
2 (¼-inch) vertical slices small eggplant
Cooking spray
¼ teaspoon salt
¼ teaspoon freshly ground black pepper
¼ cup (2 ounces) goat cheese, softened
2 (1½-ounce) rustic sandwich rolls
2 (¼-inch) slices tomato
1 cup arugula

1. Preheat oven to 275°.

2. Brush oil over eggplant.

3. Heat a large nonstick skillet coated with cooking spray over medium-high heat. Add eggplant; cook 5 minutes on each side or until lightly browned. Sprinkle with salt and pepper.

4. Spread goat cheese evenly over cut sides of roll halves. Place rolls on a baking sheet, cheese sides up; bake at 275° for 8 to 10 minutes or until thoroughly heated.

5. Remove from oven; top bottom half of each roll with 1 eggplant slice, 1 tomato slice, and ½ cup arugula. Top sandwiches with top halves of rolls. Yield: 2 servings.

CALORIES 299 (33% from fat); FAT 11.1g (sat 5.1g, mono 4.3g, poly 1g); PROTEIN 12g; CARB 40g; FIBER 9g; CHOL 13mg; IRON 3mg; SODIUM 647mg; CALC 137mg

Triple Sesame Asparagus

"My husband and I eat a lot of Asian food. This has become our favorite asparagus recipe."

—Jennifer Holcomb, Raleigh, North Carolina

  1 pound asparagus spears, trimmed
  1 teaspoon white sesame seeds, toasted
  1 teaspoon black sesame seeds, toasted
  1 teaspoon dark sesame oil
  ½ teaspoon kosher salt

1. Place asparagus in a large saucepan of boiling water; cook 3 minutes or until crisp-tender. Drain and plunge asparagus into ice water; drain. Combine asparagus, sesame seeds, and remaining ingredients in a large bowl, tossing well to coat. Yield: 4 servings.

CALORIES 51 (35% from fat); FAT 1.8g (sat 0.2g, mono 0.5g, poly 0.5g); PROTEIN 3g; CARB 5g; FIBER 2g; CHOL 0mg; IRON 3mg; SODIUM 235mg; CALC 24mg

Louisiana Goulash

"This recipe name is actually a joke. My dad couldn't think of 'jambalaya,' so he said, 'Pass the Louisiana goulash.'"

—David Dilley, Royal Oak, Michigan

  3¼ cups chopped tomato
  ¾ cup (¼-inch-thick) slices celery
  ½ cup water
  ⅓ cup chopped onion
  ½ teaspoon paprika
  ½ teaspoon dried thyme
  ½ teaspoon dried rubbed sage
  ¼ teaspoon ground red pepper
  ¼ teaspoon Cajun seasoning
  10 ounces andouille sausage, cut into ¼-inch-thick slices
  1 (14-ounce) can fat-free, less-sodium chicken broth
  1 garlic clove, minced
  1¼ cups uncooked long-grain brown rice
  ½ pound medium shrimp, peeled and deveined

1. Combine first 12 ingredients in a Dutch oven; bring to a boil. Stir in rice; cover, reduce heat, and simmer 45 minutes or until rice is tender. Add shrimp; cook 3 minutes or until shrimp are done. Yield: 8 servings (serving size: 1 cup).

CALORIES 245 (29% from fat); FAT 8g (sat 2.8g, mono 3.3g, poly 1.3g); PROTEIN 15.2g; CARB 28.2g; FIBER 2.3g; CHOL 68mg; IRON 2.3mg; SODIUM 451mg; CALC 34mg

White Pizza

"Our favorite local restaurant has wonderful white pizza, but they aren't always open when I have a craving. So I decided to try my hand at my own white pizza; it was simply delicious and maybe even better than theirs."

—Lynn Brandt, Franklin, Pennsylvania

  1 cup part-skim ricotta cheese
  1 cup (4 ounces) preshredded part-skim mozzarella cheese
  ¼ cup (1 ounce) grated Parmigiano-Reggiano cheese
  1 (1-pound) Italian cheese-flavored pizza crust (such as Boboli)
  1 cup thinly sliced fresh basil
  ½ cup thinly sliced shallots
  ½ cup finely chopped spinach
  ½ to 1 teaspoon crushed red pepper
  ½ teaspoon black pepper
  ½ teaspoon dried oregano
  ¼ teaspoon garlic powder
  1 cup thinly sliced plum tomatoes

1. Preheat oven to 425°.
2. Combine first 3 ingredients in a medium bowl. Spread cheese mixture over pizza crust, leaving a ½-inch border. Sprinkle with basil and next 6 ingredients. Arrange tomato slices in a single layer on top. Place pizza on a baking sheet. Bake at 425° for 10 minutes. Remove pizza to cutting board; cut into 6 slices. Yield: 6 servings (serving size: 1 slice).

CALORIES 339 (27% from fat); FAT 10.2g (sat 4.6g, mono 2.1g, poly 0.3g); PROTEIN 18g; CARB 43g; FIBER 2g; CHOL 26mg; IRON 3mg; SODIUM 712mg; CALC 303mg

Southeast Asian Grilled Beef Salad

"I love the strong flavors of Thai food, especially the combination of lime juice and beef. This dish is great for company because you can prep all the ingredients ahead, and then everything comes together quickly."

—Patty Lister, Falls Church, Virginia

BEEF:
  2 tablespoons low-sodium soy sauce
  2 tablespoons minced peeled fresh ginger
  1 tablespoon freshly ground black pepper
  1 tablespoon thinly sliced green onions
  1 teaspoon kosher salt
  6 garlic cloves, minced
  1 (1½-pound) flank steak, trimmed
  Cooking spray

DRESSING:
  ¼ cup fresh lime juice
  2 tablespoons finely chopped fresh basil
  2 tablespoons finely chopped fresh cilantro
  1 tablespoon low-sodium soy sauce
  1 teaspoon sugar
  1 teaspoon dark sesame oil

SALAD:
  8 cups mixed salad greens
  2 cups grape or cherry tomatoes, halved
  1½ cups fresh bean sprouts
  1 cup thinly sliced yellow or red bell pepper
  ½ cup thinly sliced red onion

1. To prepare beef, combine first 6 ingredients. Rub over beef; cover and refrigerate 30 minutes.
2. Prepare grill.
3. Place beef on grill rack coated with cooking spray; grill 8 minutes on each side or until desired degree of doneness. Cut beef diagonally across grain into thin slices.
4. To prepare dressing, combine juice and next 5 ingredients; stir well with a whisk.
5. To prepare salad, combine greens and remaining 4 ingredients in a large bowl.

Drizzle dressing over salad; toss gently to coat. Divide salad evenly among 6 plates; top with beef. Yield: 6 servings (serving size: about 3 cups salad and 3 ounces beef).

CALORIES 236 (36% from fat); FAT 9.5g (sat 3.7g, mono 3.7g, poly 0.9g); PROTEIN 25.6g; CARB 13.3g; FIBER 4g; CHOL 54mg; IRON 4.3mg; SODIUM 676mg; CALC 71mg

MAKE AHEAD • FREEZABLE
Moist 'n' Dark Nut Bread

"This is the only date-nut bread I've come across that tastes good, has a moist and chewy texture, and improves with age. Wrapped in plastic, it lasts a long time in the refrigerator and freezes beautifully."
—Linda M. Roth,
Wilmington, Massachusetts

  2 cups chopped pitted dates
  2 teaspoons baking soda
  2 cups boiling water
  2 cups sugar
  1 tablespoon vegetable shortening
  1 teaspoon salt
  1 teaspoon vanilla extract
  1 large egg
3½ cups all-purpose flour
  1 cup chopped pecans, toasted
Cooking spray

1. Combine dates and baking soda in a medium bowl. Pour water over date mixture; stir and let cool.
2. Preheat oven to 350°.
3. Place sugar and next 4 ingredients in a large bowl; beat with a mixer at medium speed until well blended.
4. Lightly spoon flour into dry measuring cups; level with a knife. Add flour and date mixture alternately to sugar mixture, beginning and ending with flour mixture. Stir in pecans.
5. Pour batter into 3 (8½ x 4½-inch) loaf pans coated with cooking spray. Bake at 350° for 40 to 45 minutes or until a wooden pick inserted in center comes out clean. Cool 10 minutes in pans on wire racks; remove from pans. Cool completely. Yield: 3 loaves, 16 servings per loaf (serving size: 1 slice).

CALORIES 107 (19% from fat); FAT 2.3g (sat 0.3g, mono 1.2g, poly 0.7g); PROTEIN 1.5g; CARB 21g; FIBER 1g; CHOL 4mg; IRON 0.6mg; SODIUM 103mg; CALC 6mg

Meals That Add Up
Real-world strategies for keeping balance in your diet.

At *Cooking Light*, we typically give you recipes that carry moderate amounts of fat. But in this story we show you that there's room to splurge and still stay within the overall guidelines of a healthful diet.

Here's the gist: If you're entertaining friends on Saturday night, eat light and lean at breakfast and lunch. Then indulge in a glass of Merlot, and sizzle a steak and all the fixings to impress company. Go ahead and top it off with rich Chocolate Soufflés with Pistachios (recipe on page 48). The lighter meals from earlier in the day will balance the totals.

Social Saturday Menu

When it's time to entertain, don't skip the spectacular dessert. Just offset an indulgent dinner by eating a breakfast and a lunch that are low in fat. If lunch is on the go, look for sandwiches made with lean meats and lots of vegetables.

	Cal	Fat	% Calories from Fat
Breakfast			
Bran flakes (1½ cups)	150	1.5g	9%
1% milk (1 cup)	102	2.6g	23%
Banana	140	0.7g	1%
Subtotal	392	4.8g	11%
Lunch			
Subway (6-inch) turkey breast (on wheat with American cheese, 1 tablespoon light mayonnaise, and all the vegetables)	365	13.0g	32%
Baked Lays potato chips (1.5 ounces)	165	2.3g	13%
Diet soda	1	0g	0%
Subtotal	531	15.3g	26%
Dinner			
Olive assortment (6 olives)	120	12.0g	90%
Peppercorn-Crusted Filet Mignon with Port Jus (recipe on page 48)	257	12.0g	42%
Creamy Parmesan Orzo (recipe on page 48)	236	6.4g	24%
Chive Green Beans (recipe on page 48)	53	1.9g	32%
Merlot 1 (5-ounce) glass	102	0g	0%
Chocolate Soufflés with Pistachios (recipe on page 48)	221	9.0g	37%
Subtotal	989	41.3g	38%
DAILY TOTAL	1,912	61.4g	29%

Continued

Chocolate Soufflés with Pistachios

Use your favorite chopped nut in place of pistachios, if desired.

  Cooking spray
  7 tablespoons plus 1 teaspoon sugar, divided
1½ tablespoons butter
  1 ounce semisweet chocolate
  2 tablespoons unsweetened cocoa powder
  2 tablespoons all-purpose flour
  ⅛ teaspoon salt
  ½ cup 1% low-fat milk
  3 large egg whites
  4 teaspoons chopped pistachio nuts

1. Preheat oven to 375°.
2. Coat 4 (6-ounce) ramekins or custard cups with cooking spray, and dust each with 1 teaspoon sugar. Place on a baking sheet.
3. Combine 3 tablespoons sugar, butter, and chocolate in a small saucepan. Cook over low heat until melted. Add cocoa, flour, and salt, stirring with a whisk until blended. Gradually stir in milk; cook over medium heat until mixture thickens (about 3 minutes), stirring constantly. Remove from heat. Cool.
4. Beat egg whites with a mixer at high speed until foamy. Add 3 tablespoons sugar, 1 tablespoon at a time, beating until stiff peaks form. Gently fold one-fourth of egg white mixture into chocolate mixture; repeat procedure with remaining egg white mixture, one-fourth at a time. Spoon into prepared ramekins; sprinkle each serving with 1 teaspoon nuts. Bake at 375° for 20 minutes. Serve immediately. Yield: 4 servings.

CALORIES 221 (37% from fat); FAT 9g (sat 4.8g, mono 3.1g, poly 0.6g); PROTEIN 5.7g; CARB 33.1g; FIBER 1.5g; CHOL 13mg; IRON 1.1mg; SODIUM 174mg; CALC 52mg

Chive Green Beans
(pictured on page 60)

Leave green beans whole for a restaurant-caliber look. Or try this recipe with other vegetables, such as steamed carrots or fresh asparagus. This dish is a good example of how you should consider grams of fat as well as the percentage of calories from fat, which here is more than 30%. Yet the 1.9 grams of fat in the recipe is low.

  1 pound fresh green beans, trimmed
  1 tablespoon chopped fresh chives
  1 tablespoon chopped fresh parsley
  2 teaspoons butter
  ½ teaspoon stone-ground mustard
  ¼ teaspoon salt
  ⅛ teaspoon pepper

1. Steam green beans, covered, 5 minutes or until crisp-tender. Remove from steamer; toss with chives and remaining ingredients. Yield: 4 servings (serving size: ¾ cup).

CALORIES 53 (32% from fat); FAT 1.9g (sat 1.2g, mono 0.6g, poly 0.1g); PROTEIN 1.5g; CARB 7.1g; FIBER 4.2g; CHOL 5mg; IRON 0.6mg; SODIUM 175mg; CALC 58mg

Creamy Parmesan Orzo
(pictured on page 60)

Unlike traditional pasta, this orzo isn't cooked in a pot of boiling water. Instead, it's cooked slowly in a flavorful broth that captures its starch.

  1 tablespoon butter
  1 cup orzo
1¼ cups fat-free, less-sodium chicken broth
1¼ cups water
  ¼ cup (1 ounce) grated fresh Parmesan cheese
  2 tablespoons chopped fresh basil
  ¼ teaspoon salt
  ¼ teaspoon freshly ground black pepper
  4 teaspoons pine nuts, toasted

1. Heat butter in a medium saucepan over medium heat. Add orzo, and cook 3 minutes, stirring constantly. Stir in broth and water; bring to a boil. Reduce heat; simmer until liquid is absorbed and orzo is done (about 15 minutes). Remove from heat; stir in cheese, basil, salt, and pepper. Sprinkle with pine nuts. Serve immediately. Yield: 4 servings (serving size: ½ cup).

CALORIES 236 (24% from fat); FAT 6.4g (sat 3.2g, mono 1.8g, poly 0.8g); PROTEIN 9.9g; CARB 34.8g; FIBER 1.7g; CHOL 12mg; IRON 1.8mg; SODIUM 412mg; CALC 82mg

Peppercorn-Crusted Filet Mignon with Port Jus
(pictured on page 60)

Filet mignon is a lean cut of beef, and pairing the filet with fat-free orzo provides the opportunity to whisk in chilled butter to finish the sauce.

  2 teaspoons cracked black pepper
  4 (4-ounce) beef tenderloin steaks, trimmed (1 inch thick)
  ¼ teaspoon salt
  ½ cup port or other sweet red wine
  ½ cup fat-free less-sodium beef broth
  1 tablespoon chilled butter, cut into small pieces

1. Heat a cast-iron skillet over medium-high heat. Rub pepper evenly over steaks. Sprinkle salt over bottom of pan. Add steaks to pan; cook 2 minutes on each side or until browned. Remove steaks from pan; set aside.
2. Stir in port and broth, scraping pan to loosen browned bits. Reduce heat to medium. Return steaks to pan; cook 2 minutes on each side or until desired degree of doneness. Remove steaks from pan. Reduce liquid to ¼ cup. Remove pan from heat. Add butter to pan; stir with a whisk until melted. Drizzle sauce over steaks. Yield: 4 servings (serving size: 1 steak and 1 tablespoon jus).

CALORIES 257 (42% from fat); FAT 12g (sat 5.2g, mono 4.3g, poly 0.5g); PROTEIN 24g; CARB 4.3g; FIBER 0.3g; CHOL 78mg; IRON 3.6mg; SODIUM 313mg; CALC 15mg

Relaxing Sunday Menu

The brunch menu is substantial enough to carry you until dinner, but if you need an afternoon snack opt for a piece of fruit.

	Cal	Fat	% Calories from Fat
Brunch			
Mushroom and Bell Pepper Omelet with Fontina (recipe below)	272	17.7g	59%
Sweet Potato Hash (recipe at right)	200	3.6g	16%
Sesame-seed bagel (3 ounces) (1 bagel with 1 tablespoon preserves and 1 tablespoon butter)	313	12.3g	35%
Cubed melon (1 cup)	62	0.5g	7%
Bloody Mary (8 ounces)	177	0.2g	1%
Subtotal	1,024	34.3g	30%
Dinner			
Moroccan Chicken with Almond Couscous (recipe on page 50)	590	15.9g	24%
Lemony Asparagus-Mushroom Stir-Fry (recipe on page 50)	55	2.7g	44%
Light vanilla ice cream (½ cup)	130	4.5g	31%
Subtotal	775	23.1g	27%
Daily Total	1,799	57.4g	29%

Mushroom and Bell Pepper Omelet with Fontina

You can use 1 cup egg substitute in place of 4 of the eggs, which cuts about 45 calories and 5 grams of fat per serving. If the vegetable mixture leaves some liquid in the pan, wipe it dry with a paper towel before adding the egg mixture.

 1 teaspoon olive oil, divided
Cooking spray
 ¼ cup chopped green onions
 ½ green bell pepper, thinly sliced
 2 cups sliced shiitake mushrooms
     (about 6 ounces)
 ½ cup chopped seeded plum tomato
 ½ teaspoon salt, divided
 ⅛ teaspoon black pepper
 2 teaspoons chopped fresh parsley
 8 large eggs
 2 large egg whites
 ½ teaspoon butter
 ½ cup (2 ounces) shredded fontina
     cheese
 ¼ cup reduced-fat sour cream

1. Heat ½ teaspoon oil in a large non-stick skillet coated with cooking spray over medium-high heat. Add onions; sauté 1 minute. Add bell pepper; sauté 1 minute. Add mushrooms; cook 3 minutes, stirring frequently. Stir in tomato, ¼ teaspoon salt, and black pepper; cook 30 seconds. Remove vegetable mixture from pan; cover and keep warm.
2. Place ¼ teaspoon salt, parsley, eggs, and egg whites in a bowl; stir well with a whisk.
3. Place ½ teaspoon oil and butter in skillet over medium-high heat until butter melts. Add egg mixture to pan; cook until edges begin to set (about 2 minutes). Slide front edge of a spatula between edge of omelet and pan. Gently lift edge of omelet, tilting pan to allow some uncooked egg mixture to come in contact with pan. Repeat procedure on opposite edge of omelet. Continue cooking until center is just set (about 7 minutes).
4. Spoon vegetable mixture evenly over ½ of omelet; top vegetable mixture with cheese. Loosen omelet with a spatula; fold in half. Carefully slide omelet onto a serving platter. Cut omelet into 4 wedges; top with sour cream. Serve immediately. Yield: 4 servings (serving size: 1 wedge and 1 tablespoon sour cream).

CALORIES 272 (59% from fat); FAT 17.7g (sat 7.3g, mono 6.5g, poly 1.8g); PROTEIN 19.4g; CARB 7.1g; FIBER 1.3g; CHOL 448mg; IRON 2.4mg; SODIUM 576mg; CALC 145mg

STAFF FAVORITE • QUICK & EASY
Sweet Potato Hash

High carbohydrate, low-fat sweet potatoes are a nutritious contrast for the Mushroom and Bell Pepper Omelet with Fontina (recipe at left).

 1½ pounds sweet potatoes, peeled
      and diced
 ⅓ cup water
 1½ teaspoons olive oil
 2 (1-ounce) links turkey breakfast
     sausage
 1¼ cups chopped onion
 ¾ teaspoon salt, divided
 1½ tablespoons maple syrup
 1 tablespoon water
 ¼ teaspoon black pepper
 ⅛ teaspoon ground nutmeg

1. Place sweet potatoes and ⅓ cup water in a large microwave-safe bowl. Cover with plastic wrap; microwave at HIGH 15 minutes or until potatoes are tender. Carefully uncover; drain and keep warm.
2. Heat oil in a large nonstick skillet over medium-high heat. Remove casings from sausage. Add onion to pan; sauté 6 minutes or until tender. Add sausage and ¼ teaspoon salt; cook 4 minutes or until sausage is done, stirring to crumble. Stir in sweet potatoes, ½ teaspoon salt, syrup, 1 tablespoon water, pepper, and nutmeg. Cook until liquid is absorbed and sweet potatoes begin to brown (about 5 minutes). Yield: 4 servings (serving size: about 1 cup).

CALORIES 200 (16% from fat); FAT 3.6g (sat 0.8g, mono 1.8g, poly 0.7g); PROTEIN 5.2g; CARB 37.8g; FIBER 4.5g; CHOL 11mg; IRON 1.2mg; SODIUM 571mg; CALC 43mg

Continued

Moroccan Chicken with Almond Couscous

Two of the best features of this recipe are that standard pantry spices coat the chicken, and that the chicken and sauce are made in the same skillet. If you don't have couscous, boil-in-bag rice—either brown or white—makes a quick substitute.

CHICKEN:

- 1 tablespoon all-purpose flour
- 1 teaspoon ground coriander
- 1 teaspoon ground cumin
- 1 teaspoon paprika
- 1 teaspoon brown sugar
- ½ teaspoon cinnamon
- ¼ teaspoon salt
- ¼ teaspoon garlic powder
- ¼ teaspoon freshly ground pepper
- 8 chicken thighs (about 2 pounds), skinned
- 1 tablespoon olive oil
- 1¼ cups shallots, peeled and quartered
- 1¼ cups fat-free, less-sodium chicken broth, divided
- 12 whole pitted dates, chopped
- 1 tablespoon chopped fresh cilantro

COUSCOUS:

- ¾ cup fat-free, less-sodium chicken broth
- ¾ cup water
- ¼ teaspoon salt
- ⅛ teaspoon ground cumin
- ¾ cup uncooked couscous
- ¼ cup slivered almonds, toasted

1. Preheat oven to 375°.
2. To prepare chicken, combine first 9 ingredients in a shallow dish. Dredge chicken in flour mixture. Reserve remaining flour mixture.
3. Heat oil in a large ovenproof nonstick skillet over medium-high heat. Add chicken; cook 3 minutes on one side. Turn chicken; remove skillet from heat. Combine reserved flour mixture and shallots; add to skillet. Stir in ¼ cup broth and dates. Bake at 375° for 25 minutes or until chicken is done.

4. Remove chicken from skillet. Place skillet over medium heat; stir in 1 cup broth. Cook 1 minute; stir in cilantro. Return chicken to pan. Cover; remove pan from heat.
5. To prepare couscous, combine ¾ cup broth, water, ¼ teaspoon salt, and ⅛ teaspoon cumin in a medium saucepan; bring to a boil. Stir in couscous. Remove from heat; cover and let stand 5 minutes. Fluff with a fork. Stir in almonds. Serve with chicken and sauce. Yield: 4 servings (serving size: 2 thighs, ¼ cup sauce, and ¾ cup couscous).

CALORIES 590 (24% from fat); FAT 15.9g (sat 3g, mono 7.2g, poly 3.3g); PROTEIN 53.8g; CARB 57.3g; FIBER 5.4g; CHOL 188mg; IRON 4.4mg; SODIUM 725mg; CALC 87mg

---

QUICK & EASY

Lemony Asparagus-Mushroom Stir-Fry

The parsley and lemon rind topping adds a fresh, bright flavor that complements the Moroccan Chicken with Almond Couscous (recipe at left).

- 2 teaspoons olive oil
- 2 cups (1½-inch) diagonally cut asparagus
- 2 cups sliced mushrooms
- 1 cup snow peas, trimmed and diagonally cut
- 1 garlic clove, minced
- ⅓ cup finely chopped fresh parsley
- 1½ teaspoons grated lemon rind
- ¼ teaspoon kosher salt
- ⅛ teaspoon coarsely ground black pepper

1. Heat oil in a large nonstick skillet over medium-high heat. Add asparagus, mushrooms, and snow peas; sauté 7 minutes or until vegetables are tender. Add garlic; sauté 1 minute.
2. Combine parsley and remaining 3 ingredients. Sprinkle over vegetables. Serve immediately. Yield 4 servings (serving size: ½ cup).

CALORIES 55 (44% from fat); FAT 2.7g (sat 0.4g, mono 1.8g, poly 0.3g); PROTEIN 3.2g; CARB 6.4g; FIBER 2.5g; CHOL 0mg; IRON 1.6mg; SODIUM 124mg; CALC 32mg

---

QUICK & EASY

Sesame Tofu Stir-Fry over Rice

Be careful when stir-frying sesame seeds as they tend to pop and splatter. If you can't find black sesame seeds, use light sesame seeds instead.

- 1 tablespoon sesame seeds
- 1 tablespoon black sesame seeds
- ½ teaspoon salt, divided
- 1 (1-pound) package firm or extrafirm tofu, drained and cut into 1-inch cubes
- 2 teaspoons peanut oil
- 2 teaspoons dark sesame oil
- Cooking spray
- 4 cups thinly sliced shiitake mushroom caps (about ¾ pound)
- 3 cups (2-inch) slices asparagus (about 1 pound)
- ¼ cup thinly sliced green onions
- ½ cup fat-free, less-sodium chicken broth
- 2 tablespoons hoisin sauce
- 1½ tablespoons low-sodium soy sauce
- 1 teaspoon cornstarch
- 1 teaspoon chili garlic sauce (such as Lee Kum Kee)
- 2 cups cooked long-grain brown rice

1. Combine sesame seeds and ¼ teaspoon salt. Add tofu cubes; toss gently to coat. Combine oils in a large nonstick skillet over medium-high heat. Add tofu; stir-fry 5 minutes or until tofu is golden. Remove from pan; keep warm.
2. Return pan to heat; coat with cooking spray. Add mushrooms; stir-fry 3 minutes or until mushrooms begin to brown. Add asparagus; stir-fry 4 minutes or until asparagus is crisp-tender. Reduce heat to medium; stir in green onions.
3. Combine broth and next 4 ingredients. Add broth mixture to pan; remove from heat (sauce will thicken). Add tofu and ¼ teaspoon salt; toss gently to combine. Serve over rice. Yield: 4 servings (serving size: ½ cup rice and 1½ cups mushroom mixture).

CALORIES 423 (38% from fat); FAT 18g (sat 2.7g, mono 5.4g, poly 8.8g); PROTEIN 26.3g; CARB 43.1g; FIBER 8.5g; CHOL 0mg; IRON 15.4mg; SODIUM 737mg; CALC 853mg

Busy Weekday Menu

Since a fast-food breakfast can be high in calories and fat, balance it with a lunch that focuses on lean meats, pasta or bread, and plenty of fruit and veggies.

	Cal	Fat	% Calories from Fat
Breakfast			
Egg McMuffin	290	12.0g	37%
Hash browns	130	8.0g	55%
Orange juice (12 ounces)	150	0.9g	5%
Black coffee (6 ounces)	0	0g	0%
Subtotal	570	20.9g	33%
Snack			
Oats and Honey Granola Bar	97	3.6g	33%
Lunch			
Roasted Chicken and Bow Tie Pasta Salad (recipe below)	363	14.4g	36%
Rye dinner roll (1.5 ounces)	122	1.5g	11%
Apple	82	0.5g	5%
Iced tea (unsweetened)	4	0g	0%
Subtotal	571	16.4g	26%
Dinner			
Sesame Tofu Stir-Fry over Rice (recipe at left)	423	18.0g	38%
Fresh pineapple (1 cup cubed)	76	0.7g	8%
Fortune cookie	28	0.1g	3%
Lite Beer (12 ounces)	92	0g	0%
Subtotal	619	18.8g	27%
Daily Total	1,857	59.7g	29%

QUICK & EASY • MAKE AHEAD

Roasted Chicken and Bow Tie Pasta Salad

To cut preparation time, use rotisserie chicken from the deli.

- 3 cups uncooked farfalle (bow tie pasta) (about 8 ounces)
- 1/3 cup fresh orange juice
- 1/4 cup fresh lemon juice
- 2 tablespoons extravirgin olive oil
- 1 tablespoon stone-ground mustard
- 2 teaspoons sugar
- 1 1/4 teaspoons salt
- 1/2 teaspoon freshly ground black pepper
- 1 1/2 teaspoons rice vinegar
- 2 cups shredded cooked chicken breast (about 2 breasts)
- 1 1/2 cups seedless red grapes, halved
- 1 cup thin diagonally cut celery
- 1/3 cup finely chopped red onion
- 1/3 cup coarsely chopped walnuts, toasted
- 3 tablespoons chopped fresh chives
- 2 tablespoons chopped fresh parsley

1. Cook pasta according to package directions, omitting salt and fat; drain. Cool completely.
2. Combine orange juice and next 7 ingredients in a large bowl, stirring with a whisk. Add pasta, chicken, and remaining ingredients; toss gently to combine. Yield: 6 servings (serving size: about 1 2/3 cups).

CALORIES 363 (36% from fat); FAT 14.4g (sat 2.4g, mono 5.5g, poly 4.8g); PROTEIN 18.5g; CARB 42g; FIBER 3.1g; CHOL 33mg; IRON 2.2mg; SODIUM 553mg; CALC 45mg

enlightened traveler

Puerto Rico

Colorful history, Latin style, and Caribbean flair mingle breezily in this nearby American commonwealth.

Puerto Rico is only a 90-minute flight from Miami, and if you are ever there, you need to be sure to check out the Parrot Club—one of the best places for cocktails. Unlike most trendy spots, food there is treated with respect. After a couple of drinks at the bar, you'll be ready to settle in at a courtyard table for a sampling of Chef Robert Trevino's recipes. But if you can't make it to Puerto Rico, here's one of Trevino's best.

QUICK & EASY • MAKE AHEAD

Mango Mahi Seviche

Chef Robert Trevino serves this refreshing seviche to diners at the hip Parrot Club in Old San Juan, Puerto Rico. Ask your fishmonger for mahimahi that's trimmed of the bloodline (the dark area) for a more visually appealing seviche. Serve with plantain chips.

- 1 cup vertically sliced onion
- 3/4 cup fresh lemon juice
- 1/4 teaspoon salt, divided
- 1 pound mahimahi fillet, cut into thin slices
- 1 cup diced peeled mango
- 1 cup diced red bell pepper
- 1/2 cup chopped fresh cilantro
- 1/4 teaspoon black pepper

1. Combine onion, juice, 1/8 teaspoon salt, and fish in a large bowl. Let stand 10 minutes. Add 1/8 teaspoon salt, mango, bell pepper, cilantro, and black pepper; toss gently to coat. Cover and chill 1 hour. Yield: 5 servings (serving size: 1 cup).

CALORIES 129 (6% from fat); FAT 0.9g (sat 0.2g, mono 0.2g, poly 0.2g); PROTEIN 17.8g; CARB 13.7g; FIBER 2.1g; CHOL 66mg; IRON 1.4mg; SODIUM 202mg; CALC 32mg

New Orleans Brunch

Taste the food that deliciously supports the Crescent City's claim as the birthplace of brunch.

After Sunday morning mends Saturday night's misdeeds, reason to celebrate lies ahead: brunch, New Orleans style. We hope you'll love these lightened New Orleans classics as much as we do.

Grillades and Gravy over Grits

4   teaspoons vegetable oil, divided
2   pounds thin beef or breakfast steaks
½   teaspoon salt
2   teaspoons black pepper, divided
1   cup diced onion
½   cup chopped celery
½   cup chopped green bell pepper
¼   cup minced fresh garlic (about 8 cloves)
2   tablespoons all-purpose flour
1   (14.5-ounce) can diced tomatoes, undrained
1   (8-ounce) can tomato sauce
1   (2¼-ounce) can sliced ripe olives, undrained
1   (14-ounce) can low-sodium beef broth
2   tablespoons minced fresh basil
1   teaspoon chopped fresh thyme
1   teaspoon hot pepper sauce
½   cup sliced green onions
¼   cup minced fresh parsley
4   cups hot cooked grits

1. Heat 2 teaspoons oil in a large cast-iron skillet over medium-high heat. Sprinkle steak with salt and 1 teaspoon black pepper. Add one-third of steak to pan; cook 45 seconds on each side. Remove from pan; keep warm. Repeat procedure with remaining steak.
2. Add 2 teaspoons oil to pan. Add diced onion, celery, bell pepper, and garlic; sauté 3 minutes or until vegetables are tender. Sprinkle flour over vegetables, and stir well. Add tomatoes, tomato sauce, and olives; stir well. Add broth; stir until well blended. Add 1 teaspoon black pepper, basil, thyme, and pepper sauce.

3. Return steak to pan; bring to a boil. Reduce heat, and simmer 1 hour or until steak is tender. Stir in green onions and parsley. Serve over grits. Yield: 8 servings (serving size: about 3 ounces steak, about ⅓ cup gravy, and ½ cup grits).

CALORIES 326 (30% from fat); FAT 10.8g (sat 3.2g, mono 4.1g, poly 1.9g); PROTEIN 29.8g; CARB 27.1g; FIBER 2.2g; CHOL 65mg; IRON 4.3mg; SODIUM 791mg; CALC 62mg

Café Brûlot

Brûlot in French means "spicy" or "burned" with sugar. This beverage, a blend of dark roast coffee with cognac or brandy, spiced with cinnamon and orange peel, is attributed to Dominique Youx, top lieutenant to the 18th-century Louisiana pirate Jean Lafitte. Traditionally, every household in New Orleans had a brûlot bowl—a silver or copper bowl that could be heated. The coffee was then made with much fanfare. We have simplified the method for a similar result.

1   orange
1   lemon
6   whole cloves
1¼ cups Triple Sec (orange-flavored liqueur)
2   tablespoons brandy
2   (3-inch) cinnamon sticks
5   cups hot strong brewed coffee
2   tablespoons fresh orange juice
1   teaspoon fresh lemon juice

1. Carefully remove rind from orange and from lemon in continuous strips using a vegetable peeler, making sure to avoid white pithy part of rind. Stud orange rind piece with 3 cloves. Stud lemon rind piece with 3 cloves.
2. Combine Triple Sec, brandy, and cinnamon sticks in a medium saucepan over medium-low heat. Bring to a simmer. Ignite Triple Sec mixture with a long match. Carefully hold orange and lemon rinds with tongs over flames, turning frequently. Let flames die down; add orange and lemon rinds to Triple Sec mixture.
3. Pour coffee into one side of saucepan. Stir in juices. Discard rinds. Serve in demitasse cups. Yield: 10 servings (serving size: about ½ cup).

CALORIES 98 (1% from fat); FAT 0.1g (sat 0g, mono 0g, poly 0.1g); PROTEIN 0.2g; CARB 12.1g; FIBER 0g; CHOL 0mg; IRON 0.1mg; SODIUM 4mg; CALC 3mg

Pain Perdu
(pictured on page 57)

Pain Perdu—literally "lost bread"—was a simple breakfast of day-old French bread dredged in beaten eggs and pan-fried in butter.

1½ cups fat-free milk
¾   cup egg substitute
¼   cup granulated sugar
½   teaspoon ground cinnamon
½   teaspoon ground nutmeg
¼   teaspoon salt
1½ teaspoons vanilla extract
16 (1-inch-thick) slices diagonally cut French bread baguette
¼   cup butter, divided
2   cups water
½   cup dry white wine
¼   cup granulated sugar
1   tablespoon cornstarch
2   cups fresh raspberries
1   cup fresh blackberries
1   cup fresh blueberries
½   cup fresh strawberry halves
1   tablespoon powdered sugar

1. Combine first 7 ingredients, stirring well with a whisk. Arrange bread slices in a single layer in a large shallow dish. Pour milk mixture over bread, and let stand until milk is absorbed (about 2 minutes).

2. Melt 2 tablespoons butter in a large cast-iron skillet over medium heat. Arrange 8 bread slices in pan; cook 3 minutes on each side or until bread is golden brown. Remove from pan; keep warm. Repeat procedure with 2 tablespoons butter and 8 bread slices.

3. Combine 2 cups water, wine, ¼ cup granulated sugar, and cornstarch in a large saucepan, stirring with a whisk. Bring to a boil; cook until reduced to 1 cup (about 5 minutes). Remove pan from heat. Add fruit to pan, stirring well to coat. Serve sauce with bread slices. Sprinkle each serving with powdered sugar. Yield: 8 servings (serving size: 2 bread slices and about ½ cup sauce).

CALORIES 270 (26% from fat); FAT 7.8g (sat 4g, mono 2.3g, poly 1g); PROTEIN 7.6g; CARB 40.9g; FIBER 4.7g; CHOL 16mg; IRON 1.7mg; SODIUM 373mg; CALC 112mg

Eggs Hussarde

This dish originated with the New Orleans restaurant Brennan's, which is famous for its breakfast. A typical recipe for Hollandaise sauce calls for ½ pound butter and an additional egg yolk, but milk and cornstarch replace most of the butter in this version.

MARCHANDS DE VIN SAUCE:

- ¾ cup Merlot or other dry red wine
- 2 teaspoons cornstarch
- 1 (14-ounce) can low-salt beef broth
- 2 tablespoons butter

HOLLANDAISE SAUCE:

- 1½ tablespoons cornstarch
- ½ teaspoon dry mustard
- ⅔ cup 1% low-fat milk
- 1 large egg yolk
- 2½ tablespoons fresh lemon juice
- 1 tablespoon butter
- ⅛ teaspoon salt

REMAINING INGREDIENTS:

- 12 (¼-inch-thick) slices tomato
- Cooking spray
- 12 slices Canadian bacon
- 12 large eggs
- 6 English muffins, split and toasted

1. To prepare Marchands de vin sauce, combine first 3 ingredients in a saucepan; bring to a boil. Reduce heat, and cook until reduced to 1 cup (about 30 minutes). Remove pan from heat. Add 2 tablespoons butter; stir until butter melts. Set aside; keep warm.

2. To prepare Hollandaise sauce, combine 1½ tablespoons cornstarch and mustard in a 2-cup glass measure. Gradually add milk and egg yolk, stirring with a whisk. Microwave at HIGH 1 minute, and stir well. Microwave at HIGH 30 seconds or until thick. Add lemon juice, 1 tablespoon butter, and salt; stir with a whisk.

3. To prepare remaining ingredients, preheat broiler.

4. Place tomato slices on a broiler pan coated with cooking spray, and broil 5 minutes or until lightly browned. Add water to a large skillet, filling two-thirds full; bring to a boil. Reduce heat; simmer. Add bacon, and cook 1 minute. Remove bacon with a slotted spoon. Drain bacon on paper towels, and keep warm. Break eggs into pan; cook 8 minutes. Remove eggs from water with a slotted spoon.

5. Place 1 slice bacon on each muffin half; top each with an egg. Drizzle each serving with 4 teaspoons Marchands de vin sauce and 4 teaspoons Hollandaise sauce, and top with a tomato slice. Yield: 12 servings.

CALORIES 248 (41% from fat); FAT 11.2g (sat 4.3g, mono 4g, poly 1.4g); PROTEIN 15.9g; CARB 17.7g; FIBER 1g; CHOL 253mg; IRON 1.9mg; SODIUM 667mg; CALC 253mg

QUICK & EASY
Bloody Mary

If you're not starting brunch with Champagne in New Orleans, you're probably having one of these.

- 7 cups low-sodium tomato juice
- ¾ cup vodka
- 3 tablespoons fresh lime juice
- 2 tablespoons prepared horseradish
- 2 tablespoons Worcestershire sauce
- 1½ teaspoons hot sauce
- 1 teaspoon garlic salt
- 1 teaspoon ground celery seed
- 1 teaspoon black pepper

1. Combine all ingredients in a pitcher, stirring well. Chill. Serve over ice. Yield: 8 servings (serving size: 1 cup).

CALORIES 97 (2% from fat); FAT 0.2g (sat 0g, mono 0g, poly 0.1g); PROTEIN 1.8g; CARB 10.5g; FIBER 2g; CHOL 0mg; IRON 1.5mg; SODIUM 231mg; CALC 28mg

inspired vegetarian

The Lenten Tastes of Greece

Peppery olive oil and pungent herbs deliciously figure into the country's vegetarian cuisine.

MAKE AHEAD
Lemony Lentils with Black Olives

Warm lentils flavored with lemon juice, olive oil, oregano, and salty kalamata olives make a nice addition to a *mezzes*, or appetizer, buffet. Though they're served warm here, they're also good cold or at room temperature.

DRESSING:

- 2 teaspoons grated lemon rind
- 3 tablespoons fresh lemon juice
- 1 tablespoon extravirgin olive oil
- 2 teaspoons chopped fresh or
- ¾ teaspoon dried oregano
- ½ teaspoon salt
- ¼ teaspoon freshly ground black pepper
- 1 garlic clove, minced

LENTILS:

- 3 cups water
- 1 cup dried lentils
- ½ cup chopped carrot
- 2 garlic cloves, crushed
- 1 thyme sprig
- 1 rosemary sprig
- ½ cup chopped seeded plum tomato
- ⅓ cup chopped pitted kalamata olives
- ¼ cup chopped fresh parsley
- ¼ cup chopped green onions

Continued

1. To prepare dressing, combine first 7 ingredients, stirring with a whisk.

2. To prepare lentils, combine water and next 5 ingredients in a medium saucepan; bring to a boil. Cover, reduce heat, and simmer 18 minutes or until lentils are tender. Drain; discard thyme and rosemary. Place lentil mixture in a large bowl; stir in tomato, olives, parsley, and onions. Pour dressing over lentil mixture; toss to coat. Yield: 6 servings (serving size: about ½ cup).

CALORIES 179 (30% from fat); FAT 6g (sat 0.8g, mono 4.3g, poly 0.7g); PROTEIN 9.7g; CARB 23.1g; FIBER 10.8g; CHOL 0mg; IRON 3.3mg; SODIUM 410mg; CALC 35mg

---

MAKE AHEAD

Baked Eggplant with Savory Cheese Stuffing

Eggplant makes a satisfying vegetarian dinner when stuffed with tomato and peppers and served with rice. Feta cheese adds tang and body to the stuffing.

> 2 eggplants, each cut in half lengthwise (about 2 pounds)
> Cooking spray
> 1 (1-ounce) slice white bread
> 1 teaspoon extravirgin olive oil
> 1½ cups finely chopped onion
> 1¼ cups finely chopped red bell pepper
> 1 cup finely chopped seeded plum tomato
> 1 teaspoon chopped fresh or ¼ teaspoon dried oregano
> 2 garlic cloves, minced
> ¾ cup (3 ounces) crumbled feta cheese
> ¼ cup chopped fresh flat-leaf parsley
> ¾ teaspoon salt
> ¼ teaspoon freshly ground black pepper

1. Preheat oven to 400°.

2. Score cut side of each eggplant half by making 4 crosswise cuts. Place eggplant halves, cut sides down, on a foil-lined baking sheet coated with cooking spray. Bake at 400° for 25 minutes or until tender. Remove from oven; cool on pan 10 minutes. Carefully remove pulp, leaving a ⅓-inch-thick shell; reserve eggplant shells. Chop pulp.

3. Reduce oven temperature to 350°.

4. Place bread in a food processor; pulse 10 times or until coarse crumbs measure ½ cup. Drizzle breadcrumbs with olive oil, and pulse to combine.

5. Heat a large nonstick skillet coated with cooking spray over medium-high heat. Add onion; sauté 3 minutes. Stir in chopped eggplant, bell pepper, tomato, oregano, and garlic; cover, reduce heat, and simmer 10 minutes, stirring occasionally. Uncover and cook 5 minutes or until liquid evaporates, stirring occasionally. Remove from heat; stir in cheese, parsley, salt, and black pepper. Stuff each eggplant shell with about ½ cup onion mixture; sprinkle with breadcrumb mixture. Place on a baking sheet; bake at 350° for 30 minutes or until thoroughly heated and lightly browned. Yield: 4 servings (serving size: 1 stuffed eggplant half).

CALORIES 178 (28% from fat); FAT 5.5g (sat 2.6g, mono 2g, poly 0.6g); PROTEIN 8.3g; CARB 28.4g; FIBER 8.5g; CHOL 8mg; IRON 1.6mg; SODIUM 749mg; CALC 126mg

---

MAKE AHEAD

Tomato and Lentil Soup

This soup is served during Lent and on other fasting days. Add a slice of crusty bread and a few black olives to finish the meal. Use a food processor to chop the vegetables if you're short on time.

> 2 tablespoons extravirgin olive oil
> 1½ cups finely chopped onion
> ½ cup finely chopped carrot
> ½ cup finely chopped celery
> 2 garlic cloves, minced
> 5½ cups water
> 1½ cups dried lentils
> 2 tablespoons chopped fresh dill, divided
> 2 bay leaves
> 1 dried red chile pepper
> 1 (8-ounce) can tomato sauce
> 1 tablespoon balsamic vinegar
> ¾ teaspoon salt
> ¼ teaspoon freshly ground black pepper
> ¾ cup (3 ounces) crumbled feta cheese

1. Heat oil in a large Dutch oven over medium heat. Add onion, carrot, celery, and garlic; cook 10 minutes or until vegetables are tender, stirring frequently. Add water, dried lentils, 1 tablespoon dill, bay leaves, chile, and tomato sauce. Bring to a boil; reduce heat, and simmer 30 minutes or until lentils are tender. Stir in 1 tablespoon dill, vinegar, salt, and black pepper; discard bay leaves and chile. Sprinkle with cheese. Yield: 6 servings (serving size: about 1 cup soup and 2 tablespoons cheese).

CALORIES 276 (27% from fat); FAT 8.2g (sat 2.8g, mono 4.1g, poly 0.8g); PROTEIN 16.7g; CARB 36.4g; FIBER 16.4g; CHOL 13mg; IRON 5mg; SODIUM 700mg; CALC 118mg

---

MAKE AHEAD

Tzatziki

This simple cucumber-yogurt combination is great with pita bread as a starter or alongside other dishes as a salad or condiment. Paper towels or coffee filters work well in place of cheesecloth when draining the yogurt.

> 1 (32-ounce) carton plain fat-free yogurt
> 1½ cups shredded English cucumber
> ¾ teaspoon salt, divided
> 2 tablespoons chopped fresh mint
> ¼ teaspoon freshly ground black pepper
> 2 garlic cloves, minced
> 1 tablespoon extravirgin olive oil

1. Place a colander in a large bowl. Line colander with 4 layers of cheesecloth, allowing cheesecloth to extend over outside edges. Spoon yogurt into colander. Cover loosely with plastic wrap, and refrigerate 12 hours. Spoon drained yogurt into a bowl, and discard liquid. Cover and refrigerate drained yogurt.

2. Place cucumber in colander; sprinkle with ½ teaspoon salt. Toss well to combine. Drain 15 minutes. Place cucumber on paper towels; squeeze until barely moist. Combine drained yogurt, cucumber, ¼ teaspoon salt, mint, pepper, and garlic. Drizzle with oil. Yield: 12 servings (serving size: ¼ cup).

CALORIES 29 (37% from fat); FAT 1.2g (sat 0.2g, mono 0.8g, poly 0.1g); PROTEIN 1.8g; CARB 3.7g; FIBER 0.1g; CHOL 1mg; IRON 0.1mg; SODIUM 121mg; CALC 53mg

MAKE AHEAD
Baked Gigantes in Tomato Sauce

Look for *gigantes*, beans as big as your thumb, in Greek groceries. We found ours in a market that specializes in Mediterranean foods. Substitute large lima beans if you can't find gigantes.

    1   pound dried gigantes beans or
        large dried lima beans (about
        2½ cups)
    ¼   cup extravirgin olive oil
    3   cups chopped onion
    1   cup chopped celery
    1   cup finely chopped carrot
    3   garlic cloves, minced
    2   teaspoons dried oregano
    1   (28-ounce) can crushed tomatoes,
        undrained
    ¼   cup chopped fresh flat-leaf
        parsley
    2   tablespoons chopped fresh or
        2 teaspoons dried dill
    2   teaspoons honey
    1¼ teaspoons salt
    ½   teaspoon freshly ground black
        pepper
        Cooking spray

1. Sort and wash beans; place in a large Dutch oven. Cover with water to 2 inches above beans; cover and let stand 8 hours or overnight. Drain beans. Cover with water to 2 inches above beans, and bring to a boil. Cover, reduce heat, and simmer 1 hour or until beans are tender. Drain beans.
2. Preheat oven to 325°.
3. While beans cook, heat oil in a large nonstick skillet over medium heat. Add onion, celery, carrot, and garlic; cook 10 minutes, stirring occasionally. Stir in oregano and tomatoes; simmer 10 minutes. Stir in parsley, dill, honey, salt, and pepper. Combine cooked beans and tomato mixture in a 3-quart casserole coated with cooking spray. Bake at 325° for 1 hour. Yield: 8 servings (serving size: about 1 cup).

CALORIES 325 (20% from fat); FAT 7.3g (sat 1g, mono 5g, poly 0.8g); PROTEIN 15g; CARB 52.1g; FIBER 14.5g; CHOL 0mg; IRON 5.5mg; SODIUM 643mg; CALC 112mg

Wilted Greens with Rice

This is a version of *spanakorizo*, a popular Lenten dish of rice and greens flavored with fresh dill. Reserving half of the spinach and mustard greens to add at the end keeps the color fresh and vibrant. Though you start with a lot of greens, they cook down quite a bit.

    3   tablespoons extravirgin olive oil
    1½ cups finely chopped onion
    2   garlic cloves, minced
    1   cup uncooked basmati rice
    1½ cups water
    3   tablespoons chopped fresh dill,
        divided
    3   (6-ounce) packages fresh baby
        spinach, thinly sliced and divided
        (about 24 cups)
    8   ounces mustard greens, stems
        removed, thinly sliced, and
        divided (about 4 cups)
    ¼   cup fresh lemon juice
    ¾   teaspoon salt
    ¼   teaspoon freshly ground black
        pepper
    ⅛   teaspoon crushed red
        pepper

1. Heat oil in a large Dutch oven over medium heat. Add onion; cook 5 minutes or until tender, stirring occasionally. Add garlic; saute 1 minute. Add rice; cook 2 minutes, stirring frequently. Add water, 1½ tablespoons dill, half of spinach, and half of mustard greens. Bring to a boil; cover, reduce heat, and simmer 20 minutes or until liquid is absorbed. Stir in remaining spinach, remaining mustard greens, 1½ tablespoons dill, lemon juice, salt, and peppers; cook 30 seconds, stirring constantly. Yield: 8 servings (serving size: 1 cup).

CALORIES 171 (28% from fat); FAT 5.4g (sat 0.7g, mono 3.8g, poly 0.5g); PROTEIN 4.5g; CARB 26.2g; FIBER 2.6g; CHOL 0mg; IRON 2.5mg; SODIUM 279mg; CALC 111mg

MAKE AHEAD
Feta-Chile Spread

Anaheim chiles are quite mild and add a flavor similar to that of green bell peppers.

    2   Anaheim or poblano chiles
    2   cups (8 ounces) crumbled feta
        cheese
    ½   cup plain fat-free yogurt
    2   tablespoons fresh lemon juice
    4   pitas, each cut into 8 wedges

1. Preheat broiler.
2. Place chiles on a foil-lined baking sheet, and broil 7 minutes or until lightly blackened, turning after 3½ minutes. Peel and cut a lengthwise slit in each chile; discard seeds and stems. Chop chiles.
3. Place cheese, yogurt, and juice in a food processor; process until smooth. Spoon cheese mixture into a medium bowl, and stir in chopped chiles. Chill at least 1 hour before serving with pita wedges. Yield: 8 servings (serving size: 3 tablespoons spread and 4 pita wedges).

CALORIES 158 (28% from fat); FAT 4.9g (sat 3.1g, mono 1.3g, poly 0.3g); PROTEIN 8.6g; CARB 21.3g; FIBER 1.2g; CHOL 10mg; IRON 0.9mg; SODIUM 520mg; CALC 148mg

Greek Black-Eyed Peas and Greens

In Greece in the spring, markets fill with bunches of wild greens labeled *horta*—sweet, sour, bitter, and peppery leaves of plants collected from the rocky hillsides. Swiss chard, spinach, and arugula are the best choices, but you can use any combination of greens you would like in this homey dish.

1¼ cups dried black-eyed peas (about 8 ounces)
2 tablespoons extravirgin olive oil
2 cups finely chopped onion
1 cup finely chopped celery
4 garlic cloves, minced
7 cups torn Swiss chard (about 8 ounces)
6 cups baby spinach (about 6 ounces)
6 cups trimmed arugula (about 6 ounces)
¾ teaspoon salt
¼ teaspoon freshly ground black pepper
1 (14½-ounce) can petite diced tomatoes, undrained
1 cup (4 ounces) crumbled feta cheese

1. Sort and wash peas. Place peas in a large saucepan; cover with water to 2 inches above peas. Bring to a boil; drain. Return peas to pan; cover with water to 2 inches above peas. Bring to a boil. Reduce heat to medium; cook 30 minutes or just until tender. Drain.
2. Heat oil in large Dutch oven over medium heat. Add onion, celery, and garlic; cook 6 minutes or until tender, stirring occasionally. Stir in chard and next 5 ingredients. Cover and cook 20 minutes or until tender, stirring occasionally. Stir in peas; cover and cook 15 minutes. Stir in cheese; cook 5 minutes or until cheese melts, stirring occasionally. Yield: 6 servings (serving size: 1 cup).

CALORIES 262 (30% from fat); FAT 8.6g (sat 2.8g, mono 4.2g, poly 0.9g); PROTEIN 15.1g; CARB 35.3g; FIBER 10.6g; CHOL 7mg; IRON 5mg; SODIUM 748mg; CALC 218mg

Braised Baby Artichokes and New Potatoes

Artichokes appear in the spring in Greece, and the small, tender baby variety works nicely in braised dishes like this one. Because they're so tender, it's not necessary to remove the fuzzy choke from the center of the heart. If fresh baby artichokes are unavailable, substitute frozen artichoke hearts, and skip the step of soaking them in lemon water.

4 cups water, divided
3 tablespoons fresh lemon juice, divided
12 baby artichokes (about 1½ pounds)
3 tablespoons extravirgin olive oil
2 cups thinly vertically sliced onion
1½ cups fresh green peas
1 cup chopped carrot
2½ cups small red potatoes, quartered (about 1 pound)
2 tablespoons chopped fresh dill
2 tablespoons chopped fresh mint
1 teaspoon salt
¼ teaspoon freshly ground black pepper

1. Combine 2 cups water and 1 tablespoon juice in a large bowl. Cut off stem of each artichoke to within 1 inch of base; peel stem. Remove bottom leaves and tough outer leaves, leaving tender heart and bottom. Cut each artichoke in half lengthwise; place in water mixture, tossing to coat.
2. Heat oil in a large nonstick skillet over medium heat. Add onion; cook 5 minutes or until tender, stirring frequently. Add 2 cups water, peas, and carrot; bring to a boil. Drain artichokes; add artichokes and potatoes to pan. Cover, reduce heat, and simmer 45 minutes or until artichokes are tender. Uncover; cook 3 minutes. Stir in dill, mint, salt, and pepper. Remove from heat; stir in 2 tablespoons juice. Yield: 6 servings (serving size: 1⅓ cups).

CALORIES 239 (27% from fat); FAT 7.3g (sat 1g, mono 5g, poly 0.8g); PROTEIN 9g; CARB 39g; FIBER 12.1g; CHOL 0mg; IRON 3.2mg; SODIUM 539mg; CALC 96mg

Smoky Eggplant Purée with Crostini

Place the eggplant halves about 1 inch from the broiler to slightly char the skin, which is discarded. This procedure gives the purée a smoky flavor.

1 eggplant, cut in half lengthwise (about 1 pound)
Cooking spray
1 tablespoon fresh lemon juice
½ teaspoon salt
¼ teaspoon freshly ground black pepper
1 tablespoon extravirgin olive oil
½ cup finely chopped onion
1 garlic clove, minced
½ cup finely chopped seeded plum tomato
1 tablespoon chopped fresh parsley
18 (¼-inch-thick) slices diagonally cut French bread baguette, toasted (about 4 ounces)

1. Preheat broiler.
2. Place eggplant, cut sides down, on a foil-lined baking sheet coated with cooking spray. Lightly coat eggplant with cooking spray; broil 30 minutes or until tender. Cool slightly. Remove pulp; discard skin. Place eggplant, juice, salt, and pepper in a food processor; process until smooth.
3. Heat oil in a nonstick skillet over medium heat. Add onion and garlic; cook 9 minutes or until lightly browned, stirring occasionally. Remove from heat; add eggplant mixture, tomato, and parsley. Spoon mixture into a bowl; cover and chill at least 2 hours before serving with bread. Yield: 6 servings (serving size: about 3 tablespoons purée and 3 bread slices).

CALORIES 101 (27% from fat); FAT 3g (sat 0.5g, mono 1.9g, poly 0.4g); PROTEIN 2.8g; CARB 16.7g; FIBER 2.9g; CHOL 0mg; IRON 0.9mg; SODIUM 315mg; CALC 25mg

Pain Perdu, page 52

Roasted Butternut Squash and Bacon Pasta,
page 41

Thin French Apple Tart, page 65

Seared Scallops, Sweet Potato, and
Pecan Salad, page 77

Chicken Breasts Stuffed with Goat Cheese and
Sun-Dried Tomatoes, page 67

Peppercorn-Crusted Filet Mignon with Port Jus, page 48,
Creamy Parmesan Orzo, page 48, and Chive Green Beans, page 48

Irish Inspired

A hearty menu with stew and quick bread conjures a late winter's day on the Emerald Isle.

Irish-Inspired Menu

Cabbage and Mixed Greens Salad with Tangy Herb Vinaigrette

Vegetable-Beef Stew

Brown Soda Bread

Gingered Pear Crisp

QUICK & EASY

Cabbage and Mixed Greens Salad with Tangy Herb Vinaigrette

Make the dressing ahead and chill it in the refrigerator, but add the herbs just before tossing the salad.

DRESSING:

- 2 tablespoons water
- 2 tablespoons balsamic vinegar
- 1 tablespoon chopped fresh chives
- 1 tablespoon fresh lemon juice
- 1 tablespoon stone-ground mustard
- 2 teaspoons olive oil
- 1 teaspoon chopped fresh dill
- 1 teaspoon honey
- ¼ teaspoon freshly ground black pepper
- ⅛ teaspoon salt

SALAD:

- 4 cups mixed salad greens
- 2 cups thinly sliced Savoy cabbage
- 1 cup grape or cherry tomatoes, halved
- ½ cup diagonally cut green onions

1. To prepare dressing, combine first 10 ingredients, stirring well with a whisk.
2. To prepare salad, combine salad greens, cabbage, tomatoes, and onions in a large bowl. Drizzle dressing mixture over salad

mixture; toss gently to coat. Serve immediately. Yield. 4 servings (serving size: 2 cups).

CALORIES 72 (34% from fat); FAT 2.7g (sat 0.4g, mono 1.7g, poly 0.4g); PROTEIN 2.3g; CARB 10.7g; FIBER 3.6g; CHOL 0mg; IRON 1.3mg; SODIUM 197mg; CALC 53mg

---

MAKE AHEAD • FREEZABLE

Vegetable-Beef Stew

We enjoyed this hearty stew with beef, but cubed leg of lamb would work, as well. For robust Irish flavor, use Guinness Stout or another stout for the beer that's specified in the recipe.

- 2 teaspoons vegetable oil
- 1 pound beef stew meat
- 1 (14-ounce) can low-salt beef broth
- 1 (12-ounce) bottle beer
- 1½ cups cubed peeled baking potato
- 1 cup (½-inch) cubed peeled turnips (about 2 medium)
- 1 cup thinly sliced leek (about 1 large)
- 1 cup (½-inch-thick) slices carrot
- ½ teaspoon salt
- ¼ teaspoon freshly ground black pepper
- 3 thyme sprigs
- 1 bay leaf
- ¼ cup water
- 2 tablespoons all-purpose flour
- 1 tablespoon fresh lemon juice
- 1 teaspoon sugar
- ¼ cup chopped fresh parsley
- Thyme sprigs (optional)

1. Heat oil in a Dutch oven over medium-high heat. Add beef, and cook 5 minutes, browning on all sides. Add broth and next 9 ingredients, stirring to combine; bring to a boil. Cover, reduce heat, and simmer 45 minutes or until vegetables are tender, stirring occasionally. Discard bay leaf and thyme sprigs.
2. Combine ¼ cup water, flour, lemon juice, and sugar, stirring well with a whisk. Add flour mixture to beef mixture, stirring constantly; bring to a boil. Cook 3 minutes or until slightly thick, stirring constantly. Remove from heat, and stir in parsley. Garnish with thyme

sprigs, if desired. Yield: 4 servings (serving size: 1½ cups).

CALORIES 337 (30% from fat); FAT 11.3g (sat 3.5g, mono 3.9g, poly 2.1g); PROTEIN 24.6g; CARB 27.5g; FIBER 3.7g; CHOL 55mg; IRON 4.4mg; SODIUM 434mg; CALC 56mg

---

MAKE AHEAD • FREEZABLE

Brown Soda Bread

Quick breads like this one, leavened with baking powder and baking soda, come together easily, even for weeknights.

- 2 cups whole wheat flour
- 1 cup all-purpose flour
- 2 tablespoons brown sugar
- 2 teaspoons baking powder
- 1 teaspoon baking soda
- 1 teaspoon caraway seeds
- ½ teaspoon salt
- 2 tablespoons chilled butter, cut into small pieces
- 1¼ cups low-fat buttermilk
- Cooking spray

1. Preheat oven to 350°.
2. Lightly spoon flours into a dry measuring cup; level with a knife. Combine whole wheat flour and next 6 ingredients in a large bowl; cut in butter with a pastry blender or 2 knives until mixture resembles coarse meal.
3. Make a well in center of flour mixture; add buttermilk. Stir just until moist.
4. Turn dough out onto a lightly floured surface; knead lightly 5 or 6 times. Pat dough into an 8-inch circle on a baking sheet lightly coated with cooking spray. Using a sharp knife, score dough by making 2 lengthwise cuts ¼ inch deep across top of loaf to form an X. Bake at 350° for 35 minutes or until a wooden pick inserted in center comes out clean. Cool on a wire rack. Cut into 12 wedges. Yield: 12 servings (serving size: 1 wedge).

CALORIES 146 (17% from fat); FAT 2.7g (sat 1.5g, mono 0.7g, poly 0.3g); PROTEIN 5.1g; CARB 26.5g; FIBER 2.7g; CHOL 6mg; IRON 1.3mg; SODIUM 329mg; CALC 94mg

Gingered Pear Crisp

Choose the ripest Bartlett pears you can find. Their soft, juicy texture and sweet flavor make a big difference in this dessert.

- ¼ cup golden raisins
- ¼ cup granulated sugar
- 1 teaspoon grated orange rind
- 1 tablespoon fresh orange juice
- 1 teaspoon chopped peeled fresh ginger
- ½ teaspoon vanilla extract
- 4 cups (½-inch) chopped peeled Bartlett pears (about 4 pears)
- Cooking spray
- ¼ cup all-purpose flour
- ½ cup regular oats
- ¼ cup packed brown sugar
- ¼ teaspoon ground cinnamon
- ⅛ teaspoon salt
- 3 tablespoons chilled butter, cut into small pieces
- 2 tablespoons chopped pecans

1. Preheat oven to 375°.
2. Combine first 6 ingredients in a large bowl, stirring to combine. Add pears; toss gently to coat. Spoon pear mixture into a shallow 2-quart baking dish lightly coated with cooking spray.
3. Lightly spoon flour into a dry measuring cup; level with a knife. Combine flour, oats, brown sugar, cinnamon, and salt in a medium bowl. Cut in butter with a pastry blender or 2 knives until mixture resembles coarse meal, and stir in nuts. Sprinkle flour mixture over pear mixture.
4. Bake at 375° for 35 minutes or until topping is lightly browned. Cool on a wire rack 10 minutes. Yield: 6 servings (serving size: about 1 cup).

CALORIES 272 (31% from fat); FAT 9.5g (sat 3.8g, mono 3.1g, poly 1.2g); PROTEIN 2.8g; CARB 48g; FIBER 4g; CHOL 15mg; IRON 0.9mg; SODIUM 112mg; CALC 32mg

Foolproof Dinners with Pam Anderson

Learn to sauté, sauce, and serve a first-rate entrée in less than 30 minutes.

QUICK & EASY
Sautéed Tilapia with Lemon-Peppercorn Pan Sauce

The sauce is perfect over plain white fish. Use freshly squeezed lemon juice for the brightest flavor. Serve with white rice.

- ¾ cup fat-free, less-sodium chicken broth
- ¼ cup fresh lemon juice
- 1½ teaspoons drained brine-packed green peppercorns, lightly crushed
- 1 teaspoon butter
- 1 teaspoon vegetable oil
- 2 (6-ounce) tilapia or sole fillets
- ¼ teaspoon salt
- ¼ teaspoon freshly ground black pepper
- ¼ cup all-purpose flour
- 2 teaspoons butter
- Lemon wedges (optional)

1. Combine first 3 ingredients.
2. Melt 1 teaspoon butter with oil in a large nonstick skillet over low heat.
3. While butter melts, sprinkle fillets with salt and black pepper. Place flour in a shallow dish. Dredge fillets in flour; shake off excess flour.
4. Increase heat to medium-high; heat 2 minutes or until butter turns golden brown. Add fillets to pan; sauté 3 minutes on each side or until fish flakes easily when tested with a fork. Remove fillets from pan. Add broth mixture to pan, scraping to loosen browned bits. Bring to a boil; cook until reduced to ½ cup (about 3 minutes). Remove from heat. Stir in two teaspoons butter with a whisk. Serve sauce over fillets. Garnish with lemon wedges, if desired. Yield: 2 servings (serving size: 1 fillet and 2 tablespoons sauce).

CALORIES 282 (26% from fat); FAT 8.3g (sat 3.2g, mono 2g, poly 2.1g); PROTEIN 35g; CARB 15.3g; FIBER 0.8g; CHOL 92mg; IRON 1.5mg; SODIUM 739mg; CALC 43mg

QUICK & EASY
Sautéed Chicken Breasts with Balsamic Vinegar Pan Sauce

Use small breasts, about 4 to 5 ounces each. Serve with polenta or orzo.

- ½ cup fat-free, less-sodium chicken broth
- ½ cup balsamic vinegar
- 2 teaspoons honey
- 1 tablespoon butter
- 1 tablespoon vegetable oil
- 4 (5-ounce) skinless, boneless chicken breast halves
- ¼ teaspoon salt
- ¼ teaspoon freshly ground black pepper
- ¼ cup all-purpose flour
- 2 tablespoons finely chopped shallots
- Chopped parsley (optional)

1. Combine broth, vinegar, and honey.
2. Melt butter and oil in a large nonstick skillet over low heat.
3. While butter melts, sprinkle chicken with salt and pepper. Place flour in a shallow dish. Dredge chicken in flour; shake off excess flour.
4. Increase heat to medium-high; heat 2 minutes or until butter turns golden brown. Add chicken to pan; cook 4

minutes on each side or until golden brown. Remove chicken from pan; keep warm. Add shallots, and sauté 30 seconds. Add broth mixture, scraping to loosen browned bits. Bring to a boil, and cook until reduced to ½ cup (about 3 minutes). Serve sauce over chicken. Garnish with chopped parsley, if desired. Yield: 4 servings (serving size: 1 breast and 2 tablespoons sauce).

CALORIES 269 (27% from fat); FAT 8.1g (sat 2.7g, mono 2g, poly 2.5g); PROTEIN 34g; CARB 13.1g; FIBER 0.2g; CHOL 90mg; IRON 1.7mg; SODIUM 331mg; CALC 29mg

How to Sauté Chicken Breasts

1. *A hot skillet is the key to nicely browned cuts. Butter provides flavor, while oil prevents burning.*

2. *Resist the temptation to move the cut once it's in the skillet. A golden-brown crust requires at least 3 uninterrupted minutes of heat.*

Sautéing and Saucing

The Finesse of Sautéing

The key to successful sautéing is to start with a relatively thin cut. Skinless, boneless chicken breasts, boneless pork chops, turkey cutlets, and fish fillets are all good candidates. You can pound the chicken breasts to make them thinner, but it really isn't necessary. Just keep in mind, if the cut is too thick, the outside will be burned by the time the inside is fully cooked.

The skillet's size is also important. Too small, and your food will steam instead of sauté. Too large, and your food may burn. When cooking for four, select a large (12-inch) heavy-bottomed nonstick skillet. Reach for a 10-inch skillet when you're cooking for two. And grab an eight-inch skillet when it's just for one.

The third and possibly most important point in sautéing is properly heating up the skillet. A hot skillet will create a nice crust on the cutlet. Add a combination of oil and butter to the skillet before the pan gets hot. It takes several minutes to bring a cold skillet up to sautéing temperature, so begin slowly heating the pan early. Then you'll be ready to sauté when the cuts are prepared. Use butter for flavor, and oil—vegetable or pure olive—to increase the butter's smoke point and keep it from burning. While the pan slowly and calmly heats, gather the meat and scoop a little flour into a pie plate. Regardless of the cut, the seasoning procedure is the same. Sprinkle both sides with salt and pepper, then dredge it in the flour.

A couple of minutes before sautéing, turn the burner from low heat to medium-high. When the butter stops foaming, the milk solids turn golden brown, and the first wisps of smoke start to rise from the pan, add the prepared cuts of meat—not a moment sooner. If the pan's not hot enough, you'll end up overcooking the cut before browning it.

At this point, it's very important to set a timer and walk away. If you don't, you might be tempted to pick, poke, or prod the cut, which will keep it from forming a gorgeous golden brown crust. Take these few minutes to set the table, clean up your mess, or measure the ingredients for the pan sauce.

And here's a sure method concerning cooking times: Sauté the cut until it's beautifully brown on the first side. Don't worry about how the second side browns after you turn the cut; remember, no one ever sees the bottom. If you're looking for exact times, keep three minutes a side in the back of your head. You'll never go too far wrong with those times. When you remove the cut from the pan, place it in an oven set on low to keep warm.

The Art of the Sauce

Now that you have a crisp, browned cutlet, adorn it with a flavorful sauce. The pan sauces offered in our recipes are ready to pour over the sautéed cutlets in less than five minutes. These pan sauces are made of three components—liquid, flavorings, and enrichment. Simply pour the liquid (chicken broth, orange juice, or wine) into the hot skillet, scrape any browned bits remaining in the pan, bring it to a boil, and reduce for about three to five minutes. Reducing concentrates and thickens the liquid. Next, add flavorings— shallots, mustard, cranberries, capers, and jam work well. To finish, some sauces are enriched with a swirl of butter at the end to give a silky finish and rich taste.

Pam's healthy eating strategy: Moderation and little deprivation.

How to Make a Pan Sauce

For a flavorful sauce, place the liquid in the hot skillet, then scrape up any browned bits.

Sautéed Turkey Cutlets with Orange-Cranberry Pan Sauce

The sauce also goes well with chicken breasts. Serve with a wild rice mix.

- 1 tablespoon butter
- 1 tablespoon vegetable oil
- 8 (2-ounce) turkey cutlets
- ½ teaspoon salt
- ¼ teaspoon freshly ground black pepper
- ¼ cup all-purpose flour
- 1 cup fresh orange juice
- 2 teaspoons Dijon mustard
- ⅓ cup dried cranberries

1. Melt butter and oil in a large nonstick skillet over low heat.
2. While butter melts, sprinkle cutlets with salt and pepper. Place flour in a shallow dish. Dredge cutlets in flour; shake off excess flour.
3. Increase heat to medium-high; heat 2 minutes or until butter turns golden brown. Add cutlets to pan; cook 2 minutes on each side or until golden brown. Remove cutlets from pan; keep warm. Add juice, mustard, and cranberries to pan, scraping to loosen browned bits. Bring to a boil; cook until reduced to ⅔ cup (about 5 minutes). Serve sauce over cutlets. Yield: 4 servings (serving size: 2 cutlets and about 2½ tablespoons sauce).

CALORIES 271 (25% from fat); FAT 7.4g (sat 2.5g, mono 1.9g, poly 2.4g); PROTEIN 29.4g; CARB 19.9g; FIBER 1.2g; CHOL 78mg; IRON 1.9mg; SODIUM 439mg; CALC 24mg

Pork Medallions with Port Wine-Dried Cherry Pan Sauce

Here, a pork tenderloin is cut into 16 medallions, an ideal shape and size for sautéing. Butter is whisked into the red wine mixture at the end, creating a velvety, rich sauce. Serve with plain or garlic-flavored couscous.

- 1 cup ruby port or other sweet red wine
- ⅓ cup dried sweet cherries
- 4 teaspoons seedless raspberry jam
- 1 teaspoon Dijon mustard
- 1 tablespoon vegetable oil
- 1½ pounds pork tenderloin, trimmed
- ½ teaspoon salt
- ¼ teaspoon freshly ground black pepper
- 1 tablespoon butter
- Parsley sprigs (optional)

1. Combine first 4 ingredients.
2. Heat oil in a large nonstick skillet over low heat 2 minutes. Cut pork crosswise into 16 pieces. Sprinkle evenly with salt and pepper.
3. Place pork in pan; cook 4 minutes on each side or until golden brown. Remove pork from pan. Stir in wine mixture, scraping to loosen browned bits. Increase heat to high; bring to a boil. Cook until reduced to ½ cup (about 3 minutes). Remove from heat. Stir in butter with a whisk. Serve sauce over pork. Garnish with parsley, if desired. Yield: 4 servings (serving size: 4 pieces pork and 2 tablespoons sauce).
WINE NOTE: The fruitiness of dried cherries and raspberry jam, the earthiness of pork, plus the port in the sauce all point to wine as a perfect counterpoint. Should that wine be a port? Probably not. Sweet and full-bodied, port is best left to the end of the meal—either on its own as dessert or with a bit of cheese. Instead, serve Pinot Noir. Its flavors will beautifully mirror this dish. A very good one: Robert Mondavi Pinot Noir 2001 (Napa Valley, California), $21. Earthy and supple, its classic aromas and flavors of earth, dried leaves, sandalwood, mushrooms, dried cherries, and raspberries are fascinating.

CALORIES 269 (27% from fat); FAT 8.1g (sat 2.9g, mono 2.9g, poly 1.8g); PROTEIN 24.4g; CARB 12.7g; FIBER 0.7g; CHOL 79mg; IRON 1.6mg; SODIUM 295mg; CALC 16mg

Salmon with Sweet-and-Sour Pan Sauce

Sautéing the salmon creates a beautiful crust. This sauce is thin but flavorful.

- 1 tablespoon vegetable oil
- ¼ cup fat-free, less-sodium chicken broth
- 2 tablespoons brown sugar
- 2 tablespoons fresh lime juice
- 1 tablespoon low-sodium soy sauce
- 1 tablespoon fish sauce
- 2 garlic cloves, minced
- 4 (6-ounce) salmon fillets (about 1 inch thick)
- ¼ teaspoon salt
- ¼ teaspoon freshly ground black pepper

1. Heat oil in a large nonstick skillet over low heat.
2. Combine broth and next 5 ingredients.
3. Increase heat to medium-high, and heat 3 minutes.
4. While pan heats, sprinkle fillets with salt and pepper. Add fillets to pan; cook 4 minutes on each side or until fish flakes easily when tested with a fork. Remove fillets from pan.
5. Drain fat from pan, and discard fat. Add broth mixture to pan, scraping to loosen browned bits. Bring to a boil; cook 30 seconds. Remove from heat. Serve sauce over fish. Yield: 4 servings (serving size: 1 fillet and 1½ tablespoons sauce).

CALORIES 309 (41% from fat); FAT 14.2g (sat 3.3g, mono 5.9g, poly 3.8g); PROTEIN 37g; CARB 6.3g; FIBER 0.1g; CHOL 87mg; IRON 0.9mg; SODIUM 736mg; CALC 31mg

Getting an Edge

With three indispensable knives, you can master any culinary challenge.

With just a chef's knife, a paring knife, and a long serrated knife, you can cover an array of tasks. Learn to use them efficiently and safely to improve your speed and finesse in the kitchen. Tips and instructions begin on page 66.

Tips and instructions begin on page 66.

MAKE AHEAD
Chicken, Date, and Apricot Tagine

Use a chef's knife to cut up the chicken, onion, fruit, and herbs, and use a small paring knife to section the lemon and remove the strips of rind.

  1 (3½-pound) whole chicken
  1 tablespoon olive oil
  1 cup chopped onion
  1 teaspoon ground turmeric
  1 teaspoon ground cumin
  ½ teaspoon ground ginger
  ½ teaspoon ground cinnamon
  ⅛ teaspoon ground red pepper
  5 garlic cloves, minced
1½ cups fat-free, less-sodium chicken broth
  ⅓ cup sliced whole pitted dates
  ⅓ cup sliced dried apricots
  2 teaspoons (1-inch) julienne-cut lemon rind
  ½ teaspoon salt
  ⅓ cup chopped fresh parsley
  ⅓ cup lemon sections, peeled and chopped
  2 tablespoons chopped fresh cilantro
  3 cups hot cooked couscous

1. Skin and cut chicken into 2 drumsticks, 2 thighs, 2 breast halves, and 2 wings. Reserve chicken wings for another use. Discard back and giblets.
2. Heat oil in a Dutch oven over medium-high heat. Add chicken; cook 5 minutes on each side or until browned. Add onion and next 6 ingredients; cook 4 minutes, stirring occasionally. Add broth, dates, apricots, rind, and salt. Bring to a boil; cover, reduce heat, and simmer 30 minutes or until chicken is tender. Remove from heat; stir in parsley, lemon sections, and cilantro. Serve over couscous. Yield: 4 servings (serving size: 1 breast half or 1 thigh and 1 drumstick, ¾ cup fruit mixture, and ¾ cup couscous).

CALORIES 477 (15% from fat); FAT 8.2g (sat 1.6g, mono 3.8g, poly 1.4g); PROTEIN 45g; CARB 54.8g; FIBER 5.5g; CHOL 118mg; IRON 3.8mg; SODIUM 605mg; CALC 77mg

Thin French Apple Tart
(pictured on page 58)

To prepare the apples for this simple dessert, use a paring knife.

  ½ (15-ounce) package refrigerated pie dough (such as Pillsbury)
  ¼ cup sugar
  ½ teaspoon ground cinnamon
  2 pounds Golden Delicious apples, peeled, cored, and thinly sliced
2½ tablespoons honey
  ½ teaspoon vanilla extract

1. Preheat oven to 425°.
2. Place dough on a lightly floured surface; roll into a 12-inch circle. Place on a 12-inch pizza pan. Combine sugar and cinnamon. Sprinkle 1 tablespoon sugar mixture over dough. Arrange apple slices spokelike on dough, working from outside edge to center. Sprinkle apple slices with remaining sugar mixture. Bake at 425° for 30 minutes.
3. Combine honey and vanilla in a microwave-safe bowl. Microwave at HIGH 40 seconds. Brush honey mixture over warm tart. Serve warm. Yield: 8 servings (serving size: 1 wedge).

CALORIES 220 (30% from fat); FAT 7.3g (sat 2.9g, mono 3.2g, poly 0.9g); PROTEIN 0.6g; CARB 39g; FIBER 1.9g; CHOL 5mg; IRON 0.2mg; SODIUM 100mg; CALC 6mg

How to Choose the Right Knife

Is there really a difference between a $100 knife and one that costs $20? Absolutely. Inexpensive knives wear out more quickly and don't hold their edge as well. If you're a casual cook, these knives are probably fine for you. But if you're a more serious cook, opt for a higher-quality knife. How do you find the right one? "First, you want it to be a comfortable weight for your hand," says master chef Ron DeSantis, associate dean at The Culinary Institute of America. And there's no hard and fast measure for that. Look for the following features:

• A grip with smooth—not sharp—edges so nothing scratches or rubs your hand as you hold the knife.
• Rounded edges near the bolster (where the blade meets the handle).
• When gripping the handle of the knife to cut, it should feel balanced without tilting on its own toward or away from the tip.

When shopping for knives, take them for a test drive. For a chef's knife, hold its blade on a flat surface as though you're chopping, and rock it back and forth, keeping the tip on the board. Look for the length that feels most comfortable in that motion. Think of the paring knife as an extension of your hand, and hold it as if to peel an apple. Then imagine you're using the tip to slice a garlic clove or "write" a design on dough. Go for the blade that makes you feel in control with the easiest grip in those positions. Pantomime the way you would use a serrated knife, too, and choose the most comfortable length and style.

The Paring Knife

With its blade of 2½ to 4 inches, this looks like a miniature chef's knife, but its use is very different. The paring knife is great for peeling fruits and vegetables; slicing a single garlic clove or shallot; controlled, detailed cutting, such as cutting shapes or vents into dough; and scoring designs and patterns on surfaces of food. Use it for any job that requires precise and delicate work, like removing the ribs from a jalapeño or coring an apple.

Unlike the chef's knife, which is always used on a cutting board, you can cut with the paring knife while holding it aloft, as though it's an extension of your hand. The small handle gives the cook maximum control over the tip and the edge of the blade.

Three More Tasks for a Paring Knife

Hull strawberries: Use the tip of the knife to remove the stem and carve out the white center core from the stem end of each berry.

Section an orange or lemon: Hold the fruit over a bowl to catch all the juice that drips down. Peel the fruit to the flesh, then cut between the white membranes to extract each section. Because you hold the fruit as you cut it, this job is much safer when performed with a paring knife than with a chef's knife.

Devein shrimp: Cut a shallow slit down the outside curve of the shrimp; remove the dark vein, and rinse the shrimp under cold water.

The Chef's Knife

This is probably the largest knife you'll own. And, according to master chef Ron DeSantis, it's also "the most versatile knife you'll ever have." The chef's knife is the workhorse of the kitchen, used for more tasks than any other. It works for almost all chopping: herbs, onions, garlic, fruits, and vegetables. It's also great for cutting boneless meats (even through small bones, such as those of chicken and fish), slicing and dicing, and general cutting tasks.

Many chefs choose a 12-inch-long chef's knife. "But most home cooks are comfortable with an 8-inch," DeSantis says. "No one size is uniformly best—it's a matter of personal comfort."

From left to right: Pairing knife, chef's knife, serrated knife.

The curved blade and relatively heavy weight of the knife give it an advantage for chopping. Leave the tip of the knife on the chopping board, and rock the rest of the knife back and forth with a subtle movement of the wrist and forearm. The weight of the thickest part of the blade, near the handle, adds force as it slices through food. A heavy handle also does more of the work for you, reducing the amount of force with which your arm has to move the knife.

Three More Tasks for a Chef's Knife

Peel and crush garlic: Place a garlic clove on a cutting board, and place the knife blade flat on top of the garlic. Forcefully hit the blade onto the garlic clove to crush it and separate the peel.

Pit olives: Follow instructions above for crushing and peeling garlic. The olive will pop open, exposing the pit for easy removal.

Cut up a whole chicken: The size and weight of the knife make this job smooth and easy.

The Serrated Knife

Serrated knives, with their scalloped, toothlike edge, are ideal for cutting through foods with a hard exterior and softer interior, such as a loaf of crusty bread. The principle behind a serrated knife is similar to that of a saw: The teeth of the blade catch and then rip as the knife smoothly slides through the food. Crusty bread is easier and neater to cut using a serrated knife because the crust will splinter less. It also cuts cleanly through the resistant skin and juicy flesh of a ripe tomato without crushing it.

Three More Tasks for a Serrated Knife

Slice whole citrus fruits: Because citrus skin is tough and slick, the serrated blade is best for this task.

Cut baked phyllo dough: The blade gently saws through the delicate pastry so it crumbles less.

Slice a layer cake: A serrated knife is thinner and more delicate than a chef's knife and cuts cleanly through tender, moist cakes.

Sourdough Panzanella with Grilled Flank Steak

The design of a serrated knife makes it ideal to cut through the skin of soft, juicy tomatoes as well as to cube the bread for this salad. Mincing shallots, slicing flank steak and onions, and chiffonading basil are all tasks well suited to a chef's knife.

BEEF:

¼ cup minced shallots
2 tablespoons fresh lemon juice
2 tablespoons low-sodium soy sauce
1 tablespoon red wine vinegar
½ teaspoon dried thyme
½ teaspoon hot sauce
1 pound flank steak, trimmed

SALAD:

½ cup thinly vertically sliced red onion
1 tablespoon red wine vinegar
1 tablespoon balsamic vinegar
2 teaspoons extravirgin olive oil
½ teaspoon salt
¼ teaspoon freshly ground black pepper
2 tomatoes, each cut into 8 wedges (about 1 pound)
1 (10-ounce) cucumber, peeled, halved lengthwise, and thinly sliced (about 1½ cups)
Cooking spray
5 cups (½-inch) cubed sourdough bread, toasted (about 8 ounces)
⅓ cup thinly sliced fresh basil leaves

1. To prepare beef, combine first 7 ingredients in a zip-top plastic bag. Seal bag. Marinate in refrigerator 2 hours.
2. To prepare salad, combine onion and next 7 ingredients in a large bowl. Cover and let stand at room temperature 2 hours, stirring occasionally.
3. Prepare grill.
4. Remove steak from bag, discarding marinade. Place steak on grill rack coated with cooking spray; grill 5 minutes on each side or until desired degree of doneness. Let stand 5 minutes. Cut steak diagonally across grain into thin slices. Add bread and basil to cucumber mixture; toss well. Serve salad immediately

with steak. Yield: 4 servings (serving size: 1½ cups salad and 3 ounces steak).

CALORIES 402 (29% from fat); FAT 12.8g (sat 4.3g, mono 5.8g, poly 1.2g); PROTEIN 29.2g; CARB 42g; FIBER 4g; CHOL 54mg; IRON 4.7mg; SODIUM 884mg; CALC 78mg

Chicken Breasts Stuffed with Goat Cheese and Sun-Dried Tomatoes
(pictured on page 59)

Use a paring knife to cut the small pocket in the chicken breasts. Serve with orzo or rice.

1 cup boiling water
⅓ cup sun-dried tomatoes, packed without oil
2 teaspoons olive oil, divided
½ cup chopped shallots, divided
1½ teaspoons sugar
3 garlic cloves, minced
2½ tablespoons balsamic vinegar, divided
½ cup (2 ounces) crumbled goat cheese
2 tablespoons chopped fresh basil
¾ teaspoon salt, divided
4 (6-ounce) skinless, boneless chicken breast halves
⅛ teaspoon freshly ground black pepper
¾ cup fat-free, less-sodium chicken broth
¼ teaspoon dried thyme
2 teaspoons cornstarch
2 teaspoons water

1. Combine boiling water and tomatoes in a bowl; cover and let stand 30 minutes or until soft. Drain and finely chop.
2. Heat 1 teaspoon oil in a large nonstick skillet over medium heat. Add ⅓ cup shallots, sugar, and garlic; cook 4 minutes or until lightly browned, stirring frequently. Spoon into a bowl; stir in 1½ teaspoons vinegar.

3. Combine chopped tomatoes, shallot mixture, cheese, basil, and ¼ teaspoon salt, stirring well.
4. Cut a horizontal slit through thickest portion of each chicken breast half to form a pocket. Stuff about 2 tablespoons cheese mixture into each pocket. Sprinkle chicken evenly with ½ teaspoon salt and pepper.
5. Heat 1 teaspoon oil in pan over medium-high heat. Add chicken; cook 6 minutes on each side or until done. Remove chicken from pan; cover and keep warm. Add broth, remaining shallots, 2 tablespoons vinegar, and thyme; bring to a boil. Combine cornstarch and 2 teaspoons water, stirring with a whisk. Add cornstarch mixture to pan; bring to a boil. Cook 1 minute or until sauce is slightly thick, stirring constantly. Serve sauce over chicken. Yield: 4 servings (serving size: 1 chicken breast half and 2 tablespoons sauce).

CALORIES 296 (23% from fat); FAT 7.6g (sat 3g, mono 2.9g, poly 0.8g); PROTEIN 43.8g; CARB 11.3g; FIBER 0.9g; CHOL 105mg; IRON 2.4mg; SODIUM 787mg; CALC 62mg

Bread, beef, and tomatoes make the panzanella salad like a chopped roast beef sandwich.

How to Cut a Small Pocket in a Chicken Breast

Cut a horizontal slit through thickest portion of each chicken breast half to form a pocket.

Built Right: The Best Blades and Handles

Most professional cooks use a high-carbon steel, forged knife with a full tang, meaning the blade metal runs from the tip of the knife through the handle to the opposite end.

The Blade: In a forged knife, the blade is formed from heated metal and is individually hammered. The best blades are made from a mixture of alloys that help a knife take and hold a sharp cutting edge and resist corrosion. Look for a high-carbon stainless-steel blade with a Rockwell rating of at least 55, which indicates the knife sharpens easily and holds its edge. The Rockwell Scale is a measure of steel hardness, and it should be listed on the knife's product description.

Handle: Look for a handle with a precise fitting and no gaps or burrs. It should feel comfortable and secure. Materials range from wood to Bakelite to stainless steel and should have enough weight to balance the blade.

Thai Shrimp Rolls with Julienne of Vegetables

The chef's knife is used to create uniform vegetable strips for the summer rolls. Use a paring knife to remove the lettuce leaf ribs. Using lettuce leaves to line the rice paper helps prevent the paper from tearing as you form the rolls.

SAUCE:

- 3 tablespoons rice vinegar
- 1 tablespoon honey
- 1 teaspoon fish sauce
- ⅛ teaspoon Thai red curry paste

ROLLS:

- 1 ounce uncooked rice sticks
- 4 romaine lettuce leaves
- 4 (8-inch) round sheets rice paper
- 8 large fresh basil leaves
- 8 medium shrimp, peeled, steamed, and halved lengthwise (about 4 ounces)
- 20 (2-inch) julienne-cut seeded peeled cucumber strips
- 20 (2-inch) julienne-cut carrot strips
- 20 (2-inch) julienne-cut green onion tops
- 12 fresh mint leaves

1. To prepare sauce, combine first 4 ingredients, stirring with a whisk. Set aside.

2. To prepare rolls, cook rice sticks according to package directions; drain and rinse with cold water. Drain.

3. Trim fibrous ribs from lettuce leaves to flatten leaves.

4. Add hot water to a large, shallow dish to a depth of 1 inch. Place 1 rice paper sheet in dish; let stand 30 seconds or until soft. Place sheet on a flat surface. Arrange 1 lettuce leaf over sheet. Top lettuce with 2 basil leaves, 4 shrimp halves, 2 tablespoons rice sticks, 5 cucumber strips, 5 carrot strips, 5 onion strips, and 3 mint leaves. Fold sides of sheet over filling, and roll up jelly-roll fashion. Gently press seam to seal. Place roll, seam side down, on a serving platter (cover to prevent drying). Repeat procedure with remaining rice sheets, lettuce, basil, shrimp, rice sticks, cucumber, carrot, onion, and mint. Serve with sauce. Yield: 4 servings (serving size: 1 roll and about 1 tablespoon sauce).

CALORIES 127 (5% from fat); FAT 0.7g (sat 0.1g, mono 0.1g, poly 0.3g); PROTEIN 7.8g; CARB 22.5g; FIBER 2.2g; CHOL 43mg; IRON 1.4mg; SODIUM 171mg; CALC 42mg

Butterflied Shrimp and Vegetable Stir-Fry

A paring knife easily deveins and butterflies the shrimp, while a chef's knife can cut the vegetables, garlic, and ginger.

- 1¼ cups fat-free, less-sodium chicken broth
- 2 tablespoons cornstarch, divided
- 3 tablespoons low-sodium soy sauce, divided
- 3 tablespoons sake (rice wine), divided
- 4 teaspoons honey, divided
- 2 teaspoons chile paste with garlic
- 1 teaspoon dark sesame oil
- 1 pound large shrimp
- 2½ tablespoons peanut oil, divided
- 1 cup (1-inch) slices green onions
- 2 tablespoons minced peeled fresh ginger
- 4 garlic cloves, thinly sliced
- 1 cup (¼-inch-thick) red bell pepper strips
- ¾ cup (¼-inch-thick) diagonally cut carrot
- 1½ cups snow peas, trimmed (about 4 ounces)
- 4 cups hot cooked wide lo mein or udon noodles (about 8 ounces uncooked pasta)

1. Combine broth, 1½ tablespoons cornstarch, 2 tablespoons soy sauce, 2 tablespoons sake, 2 teaspoons honey, chile paste, and sesame oil, stirring with a whisk; set aside.

2. Peel shrimp, leaving tails intact. Starting at tail end, butterfly each shrimp, cutting to, but not through, underside of shrimp; remove and discard vein. Combine 1½ teaspoons cornstarch, 1 tablespoon soy sauce, 1 tablespoon sake, and 2 teaspoons honey in a large bowl, stirring with a whisk. Add shrimp; toss gently to coat.

3. Heat 1½ tablespoons peanut oil in a large nonstick skillet or a wok over medium-high heat. Add shrimp mixture; sauté 4 minutes or until shrimp are done. Remove shrimp from pan. Wipe pan clean with paper towels. Add 1 tablespoon peanut oil to pan. Stir in onions, ginger, and garlic, and sauté 30 seconds.

Add bell pepper and carrot; sauté 2 minutes. Add snow peas; sauté 1 minute. Stir in shrimp and broth mixture. Bring to a boil; cook 1 minute or until slightly thick, stirring constantly. Add noodles; cook 1 minute or until thoroughly heated. Yield: 6 servings (serving size: 1¼ cups).

CALORIES 344 (20% from fat); FAT 7.8g (sat 1.3g, mono 3.1g, poly 2.7g); PROTEIN 20.8g; CARB 45.2g; FIBER 2.8g; CHOL 115mg; IRON 4.4mg; SODIUM 507mg; CALC 59mg

---

QUICK & EASY
Tricolor Bitter Greens Salad

Any combination of sweet lettuces, such as romaine, Bibb, and Boston, can substitute for the bitter greens. Julienne the greens with a chef's knife. This salad pairs well with ham and sweet potatoes.

DRESSING:
- 1 tablespoon minced shallots
- 1 tablespoon fresh lemon juice
- 1 teaspoon Dijon mustard
- ½ teaspoon salt
- ⅛ teaspoon freshly ground black pepper
- 1½ teaspoons walnut oil or extravirgin olive oil

SALAD:
- 2 cups trimmed arugula
- 2 cups thinly sliced Belgian endive (about 2 small heads)
- 2 cups thinly sliced radicchio
- 2 tablespoons shaved Parmigiano-Reggiano cheese

1. To prepare dressing, combine first 5 ingredients. Gradually add oil, stirring with a whisk.
2. To prepare salad, combine arugula and 1 tablespoon dressing; toss to coat. Arrange ½ cup arugula mixture on each of 4 salad plates. Combine Belgian endive, radicchio, and remaining dressing; toss to coat. Arrange about 1 cup endive mixture over each serving. Top each serving with 1½ teaspoons cheese. Serve immediately. Yield: 4 servings.

CALORIES 45 (58% from fat); FAT 2.9g (sat 0.8g, mono 0.7g, poly 1.2g); PROTEIN 2.3g; CARB 3.2g; FIBER 1.2g; CHOL 2mg; IRON 0.6mg; SODIUM 395mg; CALC 78mg

---

Savory Dill-Salmon Strudel

Use a serrated knife to slice this strudel and help keep the flaky phyllo dough intact. Score the dough before it's baked to keep it from crumbling as you cut into it. Using canned salmon is convenient because you can skip the step of cooking fresh fish.

- 1½ cups cooked long-grain white rice
- ½ cup plain fat-free yogurt
- ⅓ cup (3 ounces) ⅓-less-fat cream cheese, softened
- ¼ cup chopped fresh parsley
- ¼ cup chopped green onions
- 2 tablespoons chopped fresh dill
- 2 tablespoons fresh lemon juice
- 1 tablespoon Dijon mustard
- ¼ teaspoon salt
- ¼ teaspoon freshly ground black pepper
- 2 (6-ounce) cans skinless, boneless pink salmon in water, drained (such as Black Top)
- 8 (18 x 14-inch) sheets frozen phyllo dough, thawed
  Cooking spray
- ¼ cup dry breadcrumbs
- 1 tablespoon butter, melted

1. Preheat oven to 400°.
2. Combine first 10 ingredients in a large bowl; gently fold in salmon.
3. Place 1 phyllo sheet on a large cutting board or work surface (cover remaining phyllo dough with a damp towel to prevent drying); lightly coat with cooking spray. Sprinkle about 1½ teaspoons breadcrumbs evenly over phyllo. Repeat layers with remaining phyllo, cooking spray, and breadcrumbs, ending with phyllo.
4. Spoon salmon mixture along 1 long edge of phyllo, leaving a 2-inch border. Fold over short edges of phyllo to cover 2 inches of salmon mixture on each end. Starting at long edge, roll up jelly-roll fashion.
5. Place strudel, seam side down, on a baking sheet coated with cooking spray. Brush butter over top of strudel. Cut 4 diagonal slits into top of strudel using a serrated knife. Bake at 400° for 25 minutes or until golden. Let stand 5 minutes.

Cut strudel into 4 portions using a serrated knife. Yield: 4 servings.

CALORIES 394 (30% from fat); FAT 13.1g (sat 5.5g, mono 4.3g, poly 1.9g); PROTEIN 26.8g; CARB 46.6g; FIBER 1.6g; CHOL 74mg; IRON 3.2mg; SODIUM 863mg; CALC 91mg

---

Owner's Manual

Sharpening: It can be tedious, but regular sharpening is the most important aspect of maintaining your knives. For most people, a sharpening steel is the most practical tool for regular sharpening. To keep your knife sharp, hone it on a steel before each use. Purchase the steel made by your knife's manufacturer to be sure that the metal used in the steel is harder than that of your knives. To hone your knife, hold the steel at arm's length in front of you. Draw the blade across the steel several times at the angle recommended by the manufacturer, and repeat the same number of times on each side of the blade.

If your knife seems too dull no matter how often you steel it, have it professionally sharpened. Check with specialty knife stores, butcher shops, or fabric stores (which often sharpen scissors and knives).

Cleaning: While many manufacturers claim their knives can go in the dishwasher, you should always wash knives by hand. Washing in the dishwasher can dull the blade. Use a soft sponge and warm, soapy water to maximize the life and performance of your knife. And avoid soaking knives in water; prolonged immersion can loosen the handles.

Storing: Keep your knives in a knife block, on a magnetic strip designed to hold knives that's mounted somewhere safe, or in a special drawer insert that has slots for the blades. Never store them loose in a drawer—the free movement could result in nicked or dulled blades, as well as nicked hands when you reach in to pull them out.

Chicken with Rice Is Nice

The two combine in delightful ways in recipes from around the world.

These recipes are simple versions of classics, or dishes that use just a few ingredients to create an easy one-skillet dinner. Although all start with chicken and rice, the flavors and textures vary according to the seasonings and the type of rice used—from aromatic, tender long-grain basmati to creamy, al dente medium-grain Arborio. We hope some of these meals find their way onto your weeknight table.

Shireen Palow
Afghan Orange Rice with Chicken

Shireen palow soaks up sweet flavors from orange rind, caramelized onions, and sugar. Use a heavy chef's knife or cleaver to cut the chicken breasts in half.

    2   chicken breast halves, skinned and
        cut in half (about 1 pound)
    4   chicken thighs, skinned (about
        1 pound)
    ¾   teaspoon salt, divided
    ¼   teaspoon freshly ground black
        pepper
    2   tablespoons butter, divided
    2   cups vertically sliced onion
    ¼   teaspoon saffron threads, crushed
    1   garlic clove, minced
    1   tablespoon sugar
    2   teaspoons grated orange rind
    2¼ cups fat-free, less-sodium chicken
        broth
    1½ cups uncooked basmati rice
    2   tablespoons raisins
    6   tablespoons chopped pistachios

1. Sprinkle chicken with ½ teaspoon salt and pepper. Melt 1 tablespoon butter in a Dutch oven over medium-high heat. Add chicken, and cook 5 minutes,

browning on all sides. Remove chicken from pan; cover and keep warm.
2. Melt 1 tablespoon butter in Dutch oven over medium heat. Add onion; cook 10 minutes or until golden brown, stirring occasionally. Add saffron and garlic, and cook 1 minute, stirring constantly. Stir in sugar and rind; cook 1 minute, stirring constantly. Add ¼ teaspoon salt, broth, rice, and raisins; bring to a boil. Add chicken, nestling into rice mixture. Cover, reduce heat, and simmer 25 minutes or until rice is tender. Let stand 5 minutes. Sprinkle with pistachios. Yield: 6 servings (serving size: 2 thighs or 1 breast piece, ¾ cup rice mixture, and 1 tablespoon pistachios).

CALORIES 408 (23% from fat); FAT 10.5g (sat 3.6g, mono 3.9g, poly 2.1g); PROTEIN 27.2g; CARB 51.5g; FIBER 2.1g; CHOL 74mg; IRON 1.6mg; SODIUM 604mg; CALC 35mg

STAFF FAVORITE • QUICK & EASY
Pilaf with Chicken, Spinach, and Walnuts

Pilaf has many variations. This Turkish version gains flavor from popcorn-scented basmati rice and fresh dill. Don't stir the rice as it simmers; doing so makes it gummy. Use leftover meat from a roasted chicken, or pick up a rotisserie chicken from your supermarket.

    1½ tablespoons olive oil,
        divided
    1   cup chopped onion
    1½ cups uncooked basmati rice
    1   cup diced plum tomato
    ½   teaspoon salt
    1   (14-ounce) can fat-free,
        less-sodium chicken broth
    1   (3-inch) cinnamon stick
    1   (6-ounce) package fresh baby
        spinach
    2   cups chopped roasted skinless,
        boneless chicken breasts (about
        2 breasts)
    ½   cup coarsely chopped walnuts,
        toasted
    1   tablespoon finely chopped fresh
        dill

1. Heat 1 tablespoon oil in a large non-stick skillet over medium-high heat. Add

onion; sauté 10 minutes or until lightly browned. Stir in rice, and cook 1 minute, stirring constantly. Stir in 1½ teaspoons oil, tomato, salt, broth, and cinnamon stick; bring to a boil. Cover, reduce heat, and simmer 15 minutes or until liquid is absorbed.
2. Stir in spinach; cook 2 minutes or until spinach wilts. Stir in chicken. Sprinkle evenly with walnuts and dill. Discard cinnamon stick. Yield: 6 servings (serving size: 1⅓ cups).

CALORIES 368 (29% from fat); FAT 11.9g (sat 1.8g, mono 4g, poly 5.6g); PROTEIN 19.8g; CARB 47.5g; FIBER 2.1g; CHOL 33mg; IRON 1.5mg; SODIUM 616mg; CALC 58mg

Arroz con Pollo

Cuban chicken and rice comes in many variations; however, it always starts with *sofrito*, a sautéed mixture of onion, bell pepper, and garlic. We use turmeric to color the rice yellow; other versions use annatto seeds or saffron.

    6   chicken drumsticks (about
        1½ pounds), skinned
    6   chicken thighs (about
        1½ pounds), skinned
    1½ teaspoons dried oregano,
        divided
    ½   teaspoon salt
    ¼   teaspoon freshly ground black
        pepper
    1   tablespoon vegetable oil
    2   tablespoons fresh lime
        juice
    1   cup chopped onion
    ½   cup chopped green bell
        pepper
    2   garlic cloves, minced
    1   teaspoon ground turmeric
    ¾   teaspoon ground cumin
    1½ cups uncooked Arborio rice
    ½   cup diced ham
    2¼ cups fat-free, less-sodium chicken
        broth
    1   (14.5-ounce) can diced tomatoes,
        undrained
    ½   cup frozen petite green peas,
        thawed
    ½   cup chopped pimiento-stuffed
        green olives

1. Sprinkle chicken with 1 teaspoon oregano, salt, and black pepper. Heat oil in a Dutch oven over medium-high heat. Add chicken; cook 8 minutes, browning on all sides. Remove chicken from pan; drizzle with lime juice. Cover; keep warm.
2. Add onion, bell pepper, and garlic to pan. Cover, reduce heat to low, and cook 10 minutes or until tender. Stir in ½ teaspoon oregano, turmeric, and cumin, and sauté 1 minute. Stir in rice and ham; cook 1 minute. Increase heat to medium. Add broth and tomatoes; bring to a boil. Add chicken, nestling into rice mixture. Cover, reduce heat, and simmer 18 minutes or until liquid is almost absorbed. Stir in peas; cover and cook 3 minutes. Remove from heat; let stand, uncovered, 5 minutes. Sprinkle with olives. Yield: 6 servings (serving size: 1 drumstick, 1 thigh, and 1 cup rice mixture).

CALORIES 469 (20% from fat); FAT 10.2g (sat 2.3g, mono 3.7g, poly 2.8g); PROTEIN 34.6g; CARB 55.5g; FIBER 4.1g; CHOL 108mg; IRON 3.1mg; SODIUM 797mg; CALC 75mg

Chicken and Shrimp Paella

Typically, paella is made with medium-grain rice like Arborio or Valencia, which can absorb the flavors in the broth without overcooking. Saffron, the exotic spice with a distinct, earthy flavor, gives this Spanish dish its characteristic yellow hue. It's a bit soupy when first prepared but quickly absorbs the liquid.

6   chicken thighs (about 1½ pounds), skinned
1   teaspoon chopped fresh or ¼ teaspoon dried rosemary
¾   teaspoon salt, divided
¼   teaspoon freshly ground black pepper
2   teaspoons vegetable oil
1   (4-ounce) link hot turkey Italian sausage
1   cup chopped onion
½   cup chopped red bell pepper
1½ cups uncooked Arborio or Valencia rice
½   cup diced plum tomato

1   teaspoon Hungarian sweet paprika
¼   teaspoon saffron threads, crushed
1   garlic clove, minced
3   cups fat-free, less-sodium chicken broth
¾   pound large shrimp, peeled and deveined
1   cup (1-inch) diagonally cut asparagus
½   cup frozen green peas, thawed

1. Preheat oven to 400°.
2. Sprinkle chicken with rosemary, ½ teaspoon salt, and black pepper. Heat oil in a large nonstick skillet over medium-high heat. Add chicken; cook 3 minutes on each side or until lightly browned. Remove chicken from pan; cover and keep warm.
3. Remove casings from sausage. Add sausage to pan; cook 1 minute, stirring to crumble. Add onion and bell pepper; cook 7 minutes, stirring constantly. Add rice and next 4 ingredients; cook 1 minute, stirring constantly. Return chicken to pan. Add broth and ¼ teaspoon salt; bring to a boil. Wrap handle of pan with foil; cover pan. Bake at 400° for 10 minutes. Stir in shrimp, asparagus, and peas. Cover and bake an additional 5 minutes or until shrimp are done. Yield: 6 servings (serving size: 1 chicken thigh and about 1 cup rice mixture).

CALORIES 433 (15% from fat); FAT 7g (sat 1.6g, mono 2g, poly 2.5g); PROTEIN 34.8g; CARB 52.8g; FIBER 3g; CHOL 156mg; IRON 3.2mg; SODIUM 787mg; CALC 73mg

Two simple ingredients, chicken and rice, create seven distinctly different one-dish meals.

Chicken Fried Rice with Bok Choy

Use cold rice because it retains its shape and stays separate, so each grain will be evenly coated with the seasonings. You can also use long-grain brown rice, or a combination of white and brown. If you can't find baby bok choy, substitute 6 cups coarsely chopped regular bok choy.

1   pound skinless, boneless chicken thighs, cut into bite-size pieces
3   tablespoons low-sodium soy sauce, divided
1   tablespoon canola oil
½   cup chopped shallots
2   teaspoons minced peeled fresh ginger
2   garlic cloves, minced
4   cups thinly sliced shiitake mushroom caps (about 6 ounces mushrooms)
3   cups cold cooked sushi rice or other short-grain rice
1   teaspoon dark sesame oil
¼   teaspoon crushed red pepper
1   pound baby bok choy, quartered lengthwise
1   large egg, lightly beaten
2   teaspoons sesame seeds, toasted

1. Combine chicken and 1 tablespoon soy sauce, tossing to coat.
2. Heat canola oil in a Dutch oven over medium-high heat. Add shallots, ginger, and garlic; sauté 10 seconds. Add chicken mixture and mushrooms; sauté 4 minutes. Add 2 tablespoons soy sauce, rice, sesame oil, and red pepper; sauté 1 minute. Add bok choy; sauté 2 minutes.
3. Push rice mixture to one side of pan. Add egg to empty side of pan; cook 1 minute or until almost set, stirring constantly. Stir egg into rice mixture. Sprinkle with sesame seeds. Yield: 6 servings (serving size: 1½ cups).

CALORIES 293 (24% from fat); FAT 7.7g (sat 1.6g, mono 2.3g, poly 2.8g); PROTEIN 20.9g; CARB 33.7g; FIBER 2.4g; CHOL 98mg; IRON 3.8mg; SODIUM 400mg; CALC 110mg

Asopao

This stewlike dish is popular in Puerto Rico and Cuba. Manchego is a firm Mexican cheese that's making its way into many markets, but you can use other sharp cheeses that can be grated, such as pecorino Romano or Parmesan, if you wish.

- ¾ pound skinless, boneless chicken breasts, cut into bite-size pieces
- ½ pound skinless, boneless chicken thighs, cut into bite-size pieces
- 1 teaspoon dried oregano
- ¼ teaspoon freshly ground black pepper
- ⅛ teaspoon salt
- 2 teaspoons vegetable oil
- 1 cup chopped onion
- ½ cup chopped green bell pepper
- 1 garlic clove, minced
- 4 cups fat-free, less-sodium chicken broth
- 1 teaspoon paprika
- 1 (14.5-ounce) can diced tomatoes, undrained
- 1 cup uncooked long-grain rice
- ½ cup chopped bottled roasted red bell peppers
- 1 tablespoon capers
- ¾ cup (3 ounces) grated Manchego cheese

1. Sprinkle chicken with oregano, black pepper, and salt. Heat oil in a large nonstick skillet over medium-high heat. Add chicken; sauté 4 minutes or until lightly browned. Remove chicken from pan; cover and keep warm.
2. Add onion, green bell pepper, and garlic to pan. Cover, reduce heat to low, and cook 10 minutes or until tender. Add broth, paprika, and tomatoes; bring to a boil. Stir in rice. Cover, reduce heat, and simmer 18 minutes or until rice is almost tender. Stir in chicken; cover and cook 4 minutes or until chicken is done. Stir in red bell peppers and capers. Sprinkle each serving with cheese. Yield: 6 servings (serving size: 1⅓ cups rice mixture and 2 tablespoons cheese).

CALORIES 335 (21% from fat); FAT 8g (sat 3.4g, mono 2.1g, poly 1.7g); PROTEIN 30.1g; CARB 33.1g; FIBER 2g; CHOL 77mg; IRON 3mg; SODIUM 677mg; CALC 180mg

Chicken Biriyani

Biriyani is a baked Indian dish of spiced rice combined with chicken, seafood, or other meats. This version omits the baking step while maintaining the authentic flavors. Whole-milk yogurt keeps its creamy texture when cooked; don't substitute low-fat yogurt, which will curdle.

- 3 cups water
- 2 teaspoons salt, divided
- ¼ teaspoon saffron threads, crushed
- 1½ cups uncooked basmati rice
- 1 (3-inch) cinnamon stick
- 1 pound skinless, boneless chicken thighs, cut into bite-size pieces
- 1 tablespoon vegetable oil
- 1 cup chopped onion
- 2 teaspoons curry powder
- 1 teaspoon minced peeled fresh ginger
- ½ teaspoon ground cardamom
- ⅛ teaspoon ground red pepper
- 2 garlic cloves, minced
- 2 serrano chiles, seeded and minced
- 1 cup plain whole-milk yogurt
- ½ cup golden raisins
- ½ cup chopped dry-roasted cashews
- ¼ cup fresh cilantro

1. Bring water, 1 teaspoon salt, and saffron to a boil in a medium saucepan. Add rice and cinnamon stick to pan. Cover, reduce heat, and simmer 20 minutes or until liquid is absorbed. Discard cinnamon stick.
2. Sprinkle chicken with ½ teaspoon salt. Heat oil in a large nonstick skillet over medium-high heat. Add chicken; sauté 5 minutes or until lightly browned. Remove chicken from pan; cover and keep warm. Add onion and ½ teaspoon salt to pan.
3. Cover, reduce heat to low, and cook 10 minutes or until lightly browned, stirring occasionally. Add curry and next 5 ingredients; cook 3 minutes, stirring frequently. Add yogurt, stirring with a whisk; cook 3 minutes or until slightly thick, stirring constantly. Add chicken and raisins; cook 4 minutes or until thoroughly heated. Add rice; stir well to combine. Sprinkle evenly with cashews and cilantro. Yield: 6 servings (serving size: 1⅓ cups).

CALORIES 435 (26% from fat); FAT 12.7g (sat 3.2g, mono 5.1g, poly 3.2g); PROTEIN 22.8g; CARB 59.2g; FIBER 1.9g; CHOL 68mg; IRON 2.3mg; SODIUM 942mg; CALC 84mg

Fish Fillets

These fish fillets require only simple preparation and deliver great flavor.

Halibut Menu
serves 4

Cornflake-Crusted Halibut with Chile-Cilantro Aïoli

Oven fries*

Cabbage salad

*Cut 2 large Yukon gold potatoes into ½ x 1-inch sticks; toss with 2 teaspoons olive oil, and spread in a single layer on a baking sheet lightly coated with cooking spray. Bake at 450° for 30 minutes or until golden, turning after 15 minutes. Toss with ½ teaspoon salt; serve immediately.

Game Plan

1. While oven heats:
- Prepare Chile-Cilantro Aïoli
- Cut potatoes
- Combine milk and egg white
- Prepare cornflake mixture

2. While potatoes cook:
- Prepare fish
- Toss salad

STAFF FAVORITE • QUICK & EASY

Cornflake-Crusted Halibut with Chile-Cilantro Aïoli

We gave this recipe our highest rating. Make the mayonnaise-based aïoli ahead, if you like. To crush the cornflakes, place them in a zip-top plastic bag, seal, and press with a rolling pin.

TOTAL TIME: 25 MINUTES

AÏOLI:

- 3 tablespoons fat-free mayonnaise
- 2 tablespoons minced fresh cilantro
- 1 serrano chile, seeded and minced
- 1 garlic clove, minced

FISH:

1 cup fat-free milk
1 large egg white, lightly beaten
2 cups cornflakes, finely crushed
¼ cup all-purpose flour
½ teaspoon salt
¼ teaspoon black pepper
2 tablespoons olive oil
4 (6-ounce) halibut fillets
4 lemon wedges

1. To prepare aïoli, combine first 4 ingredients, stirring well.
2. To prepare fish, combine milk and egg white in a shallow dish, stirring well with a whisk. Combine cornflakes, flour, salt, and black pepper in a shallow dish.
3. Heat oil in a large nonstick skillet over medium-high heat. Dip fish in milk mixture; dredge in cornflake mixture. Add fish to pan; cook 4 minutes on each side or until fish flakes easily when tested with a fork. Serve with mayonnaise mixture and lemon wedges. Yield: 4 servings (serving size: 1 fish fillet, about 1 tablespoon mayonnaise mixture, and 1 lemon wedge).

CALORIES 367 (27% from fat); FAT 11.2g (sat 1.6g, mono 6.3g, poly 1.9g); PROTEIN 40.8g; CARB 25.1g; FIBER 2.2g; CHOL 56mg; IRON 2.4mg; SODIUM 645mg; CALC 166mg

---

Pan-Seared Cod Menu

serves 4

Pan-Seared Cod with Basil Sauce

Garlic smashed potatoes*

Sautéed spinach

*Place 4 cups cubed peeled Yukon gold potatoes in a saucepan; cover with water. Bring to a boil; cook 6 minutes or until tender. Drain. Return potatoes to pan. Add ¼ cup fat-free, less-sodium chicken broth, ¼ cup reduced-fat sour cream, 2 tablespoons butter, ½ teaspoon salt, and 3 minced garlic cloves; mash with a potato masher to desired consistency.

Game Plan

1. While potatoes cook, prepare basil sauce.
2. While fish cooks:
  • Finish potatoes
  • Prepare spinach

QUICK & EASY

Pan-Seared Cod with Basil Sauce

If you have a minichopper, use it to make the basil sauce. Otherwise, take the time to chop the herb finely before stirring in the remaining ingredients.

TOTAL TIME: 22 MINUTES

¼ cup fresh basil, minced
¼ cup fat-free, less-sodium chicken broth
2 tablespoons grated fresh Parmesan cheese
4 teaspoons extravirgin olive oil
1 teaspoon salt, divided
2 garlic cloves, minced
4 (6-ounce) cod fillets
¼ teaspoon freshly ground black pepper
Cooking spray

1. Combine basil, broth, cheese, oil, ½ teaspoon salt, and garlic in a small bowl.
2. Sprinkle fish with ½ teaspoon salt and pepper. Heat a large nonstick skillet coated with cooking spray over medium-high heat. Add fish; sauté 5 minutes on each side or until fish flakes easily when tested with a fork. Serve fish with basil mixture. Yield: 4 servings (serving size: 1 fillet and about 1½ tablespoons basil sauce).

CALORIES 199 (30% from fat); FAT 6.6g (sat 1.3g, mono 3.5g, poly 0.8g); PROTEIN 32g; CARB 1.3g; FIBER 0.6g; CHOL 76mg; IRON 0.7mg; SODIUM 765mg; CALC 85mg

---

QUICK & EASY

Asian Marinated Striped Bass

Although it contains only 4 ingredients, this marinade packs a lot of flavor.

TOTAL TIME: 33 MINUTES

3 tablespoons fish sauce
2 tablespoons minced fresh cilantro
1 tablespoon sugar
2 garlic cloves, minced
4 (6-ounce) striped bass fillets
Cooking spray

1. Combine first 4 ingredients in a large zip-top plastic bag; add fish to bag. Seal. Marinate in refrigerator 20 minutes; turn once. Remove fish from bag; reserve marinade.
2. Heat a large nonstick skillet coated with cooking spray over medium-high heat. Add fish to pan; cook 4 minutes on each side or until fish flakes easily when tested with a fork. Remove fish from pan. Add marinade to pan; bring to a boil. Cook 30 seconds; serve with fish. Yield: 4 servings (serving size: 1 fillet and about 2 teaspoons sauce).

CALORIES 185 (19% from fat); FAT 4g (sat 0.9g, mono 1.1g, poly 1.3g); PROTEIN 31g; CARB 4.2g; FIBER 0.1g; CHOL 136mg; IRON 1.6mg; SODIUM 1,146mg; CALC 10mg

---

Striped Bass Menu

serves 4

Asian Marinated Striped Bass

Rice noodles*

Steamed baby bok choy

*Soak 4 ounces rice noodles in warm water 20 minutes. Drain; toss with 2 teaspoons peanut oil. Heat 2 teaspoons peanut oil in a large nonstick skillet over medium-high heat; sauté ½ cup thinly sliced shallots 1 minute. Add noodles to pan; cook 3 minutes or until thoroughly heated, tossing well. Stir in ¼ cup chopped green onions, ¼ cup chopped fresh cilantro, 1 tablespoon fish sauce, and 2 teaspoons sugar. Top each serving with 1 teaspoon chopped peanuts.

Game Plan

1. While fish marinates:
  • Soak noodles
  • Slice shallots
  • Chop green onions, cilantro, and peanuts
  • Steam bok choy, and keep warm
2. While fish cooks, prepare rice noodles.

Trout with Lentils

Mixed greens salad with goat
cheese croutons*

Angel food cake with lemon curd

*Spread 2 teaspoons goat cheese onto each of 8 (1-ounce) French bread baguette slices; broil 1 minute. Combine 2 teaspoons extravirgin olive oil, 2 teaspoons sherry vinegar, 1 teaspoon honey, ¼ teaspoon salt, and ⅛ teaspoon freshly ground black pepper, stirring with a whisk. Toss 4 cups mixed salad greens with vinegar mixture; serve with cheese croutons.

Game Plan

1. While lentils cook:
- Chop celery and parsley
- Preheat broiler
2. Broil trout
3. While cheese croutons broil:
- Stir trout into lentil mixture
- Toss salad

QUICK & EASY
Trout with Lentils

Serve this dish warm or as a chilled salad over a bed of greens. If you purchase smoked trout, the recipe will come together even faster.

TOTAL TIME: 42 MINUTES

    1 teaspoon olive oil
    ¼ cup chopped leek
    ¼ cup finely chopped carrot
    2 garlic cloves, minced
    1 cup dried lentils
    ½ cup water
    1 (14-ounce) can fat-free,
       less-sodium chicken broth
    ¼ cup chopped celery
    1 tablespoon finely chopped fresh
       parsley
    1 tablespoon sherry vinegar
    ¾ teaspoon salt, divided
    ½ teaspoon freshly ground black
       pepper, divided
    2 (6-ounce) trout fillets
Cooking spray

1. Heat oil in a medium saucepan over medium-high heat. Add leek, carrot, and garlic; sauté 2 minutes. Stir in lentils, water, and broth; bring to a boil. Cover, reduce heat. Simmer 25 minutes or until lentils are tender and liquid is nearly absorbed. Remove from heat. Add celery, parsley, vinegar, ½ teaspoon salt, and ¼ teaspoon pepper to lentil mixture; stir to combine.
2. Preheat broiler.
3. Sprinkle fillets with ¼ teaspoon salt and ¼ teaspoon pepper. Place fish on a baking sheet coated with cooking spray; broil 5 minutes or until fish flakes easily when tested with a fork. Break fish into chunks; add to lentil mixture, tossing gently to combine. Yield: 4 servings (serving size: 1 cup).

CALORIES 311 (18% from fat); FAT 6.2g (sat 1.6g, mono 2.2g, poly 1.9g); PROTEIN 32.8g; CARB 31.3g; FIBER 15.2g; CHOL 50mg; IRON 5mg; SODIUM 668mg; CALC 96mg

passport

The Basque Way

In the heart of Spain's Basque region, a hotbed of young culinary talent brings new vibrancy to European cuisine.

Chicken with Morels
Pollo con Jugo de Morillas

This recipe is based loosely on a dish served by Chef Aitor Elizegi at Restaurante Gaminiz outside Bilbao.

    1¼ cups dried morels (about 1 ounce)
     1 cup boiling water
Cooking spray
     8 chicken thighs (about 2 pounds),
        skinned
     1 teaspoon salt
     ½ teaspoon black pepper
     1 cup fat-free, less-sodium chicken
        broth
     2 bay leaves
     3 cups hot cooked rice

1. Combine mushrooms and water in a bowl; cover and let stand 15 minutes. Drain.
2. Heat a large nonstick skillet coated with cooking spray over medium-high heat. Sprinkle chicken with salt and pepper. Add chicken to pan, and sauté 4 minutes on each side or until browned. Add mushrooms, broth, and bay leaves. Cover, reduce heat, and simmer 20 minutes or until chicken is done. Discard bay leaves. Serve with rice. Yield: 4 servings (serving size: 2 chicken thighs, about ⅓ cup broth, and ¾ cup rice).

CALORIES 375 (14% from fat); FAT 6g (sat 1.5g, mono 2g, poly 1.4g); PROTEIN 33g; CARB 43.6g; FIBER 1.3g; CHOL 115mg; IRON 4.9mg; SODIUM 823mg; CALC 23mg

Deconstructed Flan

While keeping the traditional flavor profile of flan with all of its ingredients intact, this recipe rearranges them.

YOGURT CHEESE:
    1 (32-ounce) carton vanilla low-fat
       yogurt

ICE CREAM:
    ¼ cup sugar
    3 large eggs
    1 cup whole milk
    1 cup half-and-half
    1 vanilla bean, split lengthwise

SAUCE:
    ⅓ cup sugar
    ½ cup boiling water
    1 vanilla bean, split lengthwise

1. To prepare yogurt cheese, place a colander in a 2-quart glass measure or medium bowl. Line colander with 4 layers of cheesecloth, allowing cheesecloth to extend over outside edges. Spoon yogurt into colander. Cover loosely with plastic wrap, and refrigerate 12 hours. Spoon yogurt cheese into a bowl; discard liquid. Cover and refrigerate.
2. To prepare ice cream, combine ¼ cup sugar and eggs in a medium bowl, stirring well with a whisk. Combine milk and half-and-half in a heavy saucepan

over medium-high heat. Scrape seeds from 1 vanilla bean, and add seeds and bean to milk mixture. Heat to 180° or until tiny bubbles form around edge of pan, stirring frequently (do not boil). Gradually add milk mixture to egg mixture, stirring constantly with a whisk. Return milk mixture to pan; cook over medium heat until thick (about 5 minutes), stirring constantly. Remove from heat. Place pan in a large ice-filled bowl until mixture cools to room temperature (about 25 minutes), stirring occasionally. Remove vanilla bean. Pour mixture into freezer can of an ice-cream freezer, and freeze according to manufacturer's instructions. Spoon ice cream into a freezer-safe container; cover and freeze 1 hour or until firm.

3. To prepare sauce, place ⅓ cup sugar in a small, heavy saucepan over medium-high heat; cook until sugar dissolves, stirring as needed to dissolve sugar evenly (about 6 minutes). Continue cooking about 1 minute or until golden. Remove from heat, and carefully stir in water (caramelized sugar will seize slightly and stick to spoon). Place pan over medium-high heat until caramelized sugar melts. Scrape seeds from 1 vanilla bean, and add seeds and bean to pan. Cook 2 minutes or until reduced to 6 tablespoons, stirring occasionally. Remove from heat, and let stand 10 minutes. Discard vanilla bean.

4. Place ¼ cup yogurt cheese in each of 6 bowls; top with 1 tablespoon sauce and ½ cup ice cream. Serve immediately. Yield: 6 servings.

CALORIES 319 (27% from fat); FAT 9.7g (sat 5.5g, mono 3.2g, poly 0.5g); PROTEIN 13.2g; CARB 43.8g; FIBER 0g; CHOL 140mg; IRON 0.5mg; SODIUM 172mg; CALC 366mg

Clams with Cherry Tomatoes
Almejas con Tomates

Appearing in a variety of guises and dishes, clams are popular in the Basque region. The locals enjoy them simply steamed, in fish stew, and prepared in many other ways, as well.

2 tablespoons olive oil
1 pint cherry tomatoes
¼ cup dry white wine
2 pounds littleneck clams, scrubbed
2 garlic cloves, minced
1 large lemon, cut into 12 wedges
½ cup chopped fresh parsley
8 (1-ounce) slices diagonally cut French bread (about 1 inch thick)

1. Heat oil in a large nonstick skillet over medium-high heat. Add tomatoes; sauté 6 minutes or until lightly browned. Add wine, clams, garlic, and lemon, stirring to coat; cover, reduce heat, and cook 8 minutes or until shells open. Discard any unopened shells. Sprinkle with parsley. Serve clam mixture with French bread. Yield: 4 servings (serving size: about 7 clams, 5 tomatoes, 3 lemon wedges, 2½ tablespoons broth, and 2 bread slices).

CALORIES 303 (28% from fat); FAT 9.5g (sat 1.4g, mono 5.8g, poly 1.3g); PROTEIN 15g; CARB 39g; FIBER 4.1g; CHOL 23mg; IRON 11.9mg; SODIUM 395mg; CALC 104mg

Winter Fruit Compote
Compota de Frutas

A typical Basque dessert uses both fresh and dried fruit. Serve it with fresh cheese or spooned over pound cake.

6 dried figs
6 prunes
6 dried apricots
½ cup golden raisins
½ cup Calvados (apple brandy)
1 cup dry white wine
1 cup water
¼ cup sugar
2 teaspoons grated orange rind
1 teaspoon grated lemon rind
1 apple, peeled and cut into 12 wedges
1 pear, peeled and cut into 12 wedges

1. Combine first 5 ingredients in a microwave-safe bowl. Microwave at HIGH 1 minute.
2. Combine white wine and next 4 ingredients in a medium saucepan, stirring well;

bring to a boil. Add fig mixture; cover, reduce heat, and simmer 10 minutes, stirring occasionally. Add apple; cover and cook 5 minutes, stirring occasionally. Add pear; cover and cook 5 minutes, stirring occasionally. Remove from heat. Cover and let stand at room temperature 2 hours. Yield: 8 servings (serving size: ⅔ cup).

CALORIES 199 (2% from fat); FAT 0.4g (sat 0.1g, mono 0.1g, poly 0.1g); PROTEIN 1.2g; CARB 36.7g; FIBER 3.7g; CHOL 0mg; IRON 1.1mg; SODIUM 5mg; CALC 38mg

Lamb Stew
Txilindron de Cordero

The peppers traditionally used, *pimiento choricero*, are longish red peppers, which are roasted for a smoky taste. *Piquillo* peppers are a good substitute and are available canned or in jars in most supermarkets. In a pinch, roasted red bell peppers and a dash of red pepper flakes will give the appropriate flavor.

3 pounds lamb shoulder, trimmed and cut into 1-inch pieces
1 teaspoon salt
Cooking spray
4 cups vertically sliced onion
1 tablespoon all-purpose flour
1 cup dry white wine
6 garlic cloves, thinly sliced
1 cup sliced bottled piquillo or sliced bottled roasted red bell peppers

1. Sprinkle lamb with salt. Heat a large Dutch oven coated with cooking spray over medium-high heat. Add half of lamb, browning on all sides; remove lamb from pan. Repeat procedure with remaining lamb.
2. Add onion to pan; sauté 4 minutes or until lightly browned. Stir in flour. Add lamb, wine, and garlic, stirring to combine. Cover, reduce heat, and cook 1 hour, stirring occasionally. Stir in peppers; cover and cook 15 minutes or until lamb is tender, stirring occasionally. Yield: 5 servings (serving size: 1 cup).

CALORIES 486 (42% from fat); FAT 22.8g (sat 8.7g, mono 9.2g, poly 2.1g); PROTEIN 45.5g; CARB 15.5g; FIBER 1.8g; CHOL 159mg; IRON 4mg; SODIUM 673mg; CALC 68mg

Farm Hand Potatoes
Papas de Caserio

A traditional recipe, this rural dish is cooked gently in a pot over an open fire. This version is more accessible.

- 2 tablespoons olive oil
- 4 garlic cloves, thinly sliced
- 1 cup chopped onion
- 1 tablespoon all-purpose flour
- 4 cups peeled baking potatoes, cut into ½-inch pieces
- 2 cups water
- ¾ teaspoon salt
- ½ teaspoon black pepper
- ½ cup minced fresh parsley

1. Heat oil in a large Dutch oven over medium-high heat. Add garlic, and sauté 1 minute or until lightly browned. Remove garlic from pan. Add onion to pan; sauté 3 minutes or until tender. Stir in flour; cook 1 minute. Stir in garlic, potatoes, water, salt, and pepper; bring to a boil. Cover, reduce heat, and simmer 20 minutes or until potatoes are tender. Remove from heat. Stir in parsley. Yield: 5 servings (serving size: 1 cup).

CALORIES 176 (29% from fat); FAT 5.7g (sat 0.8g, mono 4g, poly 0.6g); PROTEIN 3.6g; CARB 29g; FIBER 2.8g; CHOL 0mg; IRON 1.6mg; SODIUM 367mg; CALC 28mg

Potato and Cabbage Mash
Patatas y Berzas

Truffle oil makes the difference here. Try pairing this dish with Chicken with Morels (recipe on page 74).

- 4 cups cubed peeled Yukon gold potatoes (about 1½ pounds)
- 4 cups water
- 4 cups Savoy cabbage
- 1 teaspoon salt
- 1 teaspoon truffle oil

1. Place potatoes in a large saucepan; cover with water. Bring to a boil. Reduce heat; simmer 20 minutes or until tender. Drain and return to pan. Mash potatoes with a potato masher.

2. While potatoes cook, bring 4 cups water to a boil in a large Dutch oven. Add cabbage; cook 5 minutes or until tender. Drain in a colander over a bowl, reserving ½ cup cooking liquid. Combine cabbage and reserved cooking liquid in a food processor; process until smooth. Add cabbage to potatoes; cook over medium-high heat 3 minutes or until thoroughly heated, stirring constantly. Stir in salt and oil. Yield: 6 servings (serving size: ⅔ cup).

CALORIES 113 (6% from fat); FAT 0.8g (sat 0.1g, mono 0.6g, poly 0.1g); PROTEIN 3.6g; CARB 22.9g; FIBER 2.8g; CHOL 0mg; IRON 1.2mg; SODIUM 413mg; CALC 16mg

Fresh Tuna Stew
Marmitako

This dish derives its name from the *marmita*, a type of pot used for stews.

- 1 tablespoon olive oil
- ½ cup finely chopped carrot
- 1½ cups finely chopped onion
- ½ cup finely chopped red bell pepper
- 2 tablespoons finely chopped seeded Anaheim chile
- 3 cups (½-inch) cubed peeled Yukon gold potato (about 1 pound)
- 2 garlic cloves, minced
- 1 bay leaf
- 1½ cups canned vegetable broth
- ½ cup dry white wine
- ¾ teaspoon kosher salt
- ¼ teaspoon crushed red pepper flakes
- 2 tablespoons chopped fresh parsley
- ¾ pound Yellowfin tuna, cut into ½-inch cubes

1. Heat oil in a large Dutch oven over medium heat. Add carrot; cook 5 minutes, stirring occasionally. Add onion, bell pepper, and chile; cook 15 minutes or until vegetables are tender, stirring occasionally. Add potato, garlic, and bay leaf; cook 3 minutes, stirring frequently. Add broth, wine, salt, and red pepper flakes, stirring to combine; bring to a boil. Cover, reduce heat, and simmer 10 minutes or until potatoes are tender, stirring occasionally. Remove from heat. Discard bay leaf. Stir in parsley. Place

½ cup tuna into each of 4 bowls. Ladle 1¼ cups potato mixture into each bowl. Yield: 4 servings.

CALORIES 273 (16% from fat); FAT 5g (sat 0.7g, mono 2.7g, poly 0.7g); PROTEIN 24.2g; CARB 28.9g; FIBER 4.2g; CHOL 38mg; IRON 2.1mg; SODIUM 777mg; CALC 53mg

season's best

Posole

March's mercurial nature makes meal-planning a challenge.

This recipe will satisfy no matter what the weather. *Posole*, a warm Mexican stew, is characterized by its spicy aroma, long-simmered flavors, and hearty ingredients, which make it ideal for cooler days. Yet, its finishing touches—crisp radishes, tender lettuce, and cilantro—are gentle reminders of spring. It's the best of both seasons.

Posole

- 1½ teaspoons salt, divided
- 2 teaspoons paprika
- 1 teaspoon black pepper
- 2 pounds boneless Boston butt pork roast
- 2 cups chopped onion
- 3 garlic cloves, minced
- 1½ cups water
- ¼ cup raisins
- 1 teaspoon ground coriander
- 1 teaspoon ground cumin
- 1 teaspoon dried oregano
- 1 (14.5-ounce) can no-salt-added stewed tomatoes, undrained
- 1 (14-ounce) can low-salt beef broth
- 1 (14-ounce) can fat-free, less-sodium chicken broth
- 1 (7-ounce) can chipotle chiles in adobo sauce
- 2 (15.5-ounce) cans golden hominy, drained
- 1¼ cups shredded Boston lettuce
- ⅔ cup unsalted baked tortilla chips
- ⅔ cup minced fresh cilantro
- ⅔ cup thinly sliced radishes

1. Combine 1 teaspoon salt, paprika, and pepper. Trim fat from pork. Cut pork into 2-inch pieces; trim any additional fat. Combine pork and paprika mixture, tossing well to coat.

2. Heat a large Dutch oven over medium-high heat. Add pork; cook 5 minutes, browning on all sides. Remove pork from pan. Add onion and garlic to pan; sauté 3 minutes. Return pork to pan; stir in water and next 7 ingredients.

3. Remove 1 large chile and 2 tablespoons adobo sauce from can; reserve remaining chiles and sauce for another use. Remove seeds from chile; finely chop. Stir chile and adobo sauce into pork mixture. Bring to a boil; cover, reduce heat, and simmer 2 hours or until pork is tender. Remove pork from pan using a slotted spoon, and place pork in a large bowl. Shred pork using 2 forks. Add tomato mixture to pork in bowl. Let cool to room temperature; cover and chill overnight.

4. Skim solidified fat from surface of stew. Combine stew, ½ teaspoon salt, and hominy in a large Dutch oven, and bring to a boil over medium-high heat. Reduce heat; simmer 5 minutes. Ladle 1 cup stew into each of 10 bowls; top each with about 2 tablespoons lettuce, about 1 tablespoon chips, about 1 tablespoon cilantro, and about 1 tablespoon radishes. Yield: 10 servings.

CALORIES 321 (27% from fat); FAT 9.6g (sat 2.7g, mono 3.7g, poly 1.6g); PROTEIN 22.5g; CARB 36.1g; FIBER 5.1g; CHOL 62mg; IRON 2.8mg; SODIUM 952mg; CALC 88mg

enlightened cook

Gimme the Skinny

Maggie Melanson went from corporate worker bee to queen bee of Boston catering.

As president of Gimme the Skinny Catering, located in Boston's South Shore, Melanson serves good health and good times. Low-fat dishes such as those listed here are icons for her approach to healthful food, which allows natural beauty and fresh flavors to shine.

Easy Entertaining Menu
serves 4

Serve this dip with pita wedges or toasted baguette slices for a tasty starter to the meal. You can make and refrigerate the dip up to one day ahead.

Caramelized Onion Dip

Pork chops with tomato chutney*

Mashed potatoes

Collard greens

*Heat 2 teaspoons vegetable oil in a large nonstick skillet over medium-high heat. Sprinkle 4 (6-ounce) bone-in pork chops evenly with ¼ teaspoon salt and ¼ teaspoon black pepper. Add pork to pan; cook 4 minutes on each side or until desired degree of doneness. Microwave ¼ cup bottled tomato chutney at HIGH 30 seconds or until warm. Serve chutney with chops.

MAKE AHEAD
Caramelized Onion Dip

Make this recipe ahead so the flavors can blend and mellow. Serve with pita chips.

Cooking spray
3 cups chopped onion (about 2 medium)
3 tablespoons low-fat sour cream, divided
2 tablespoons (1 ounce) block-style ⅓-less-fat cream cheese, softened
3 tablespoons light mayonnaise
¼ teaspoon Worcestershire sauce
⅛ teaspoon salt
Dash of ground red pepper

1. Heat a large nonstick skillet coated with cooking spray over medium-high heat. Add onion; sauté 2 minutes. Reduce heat to low; cover and cook 20 minutes or until golden brown, stirring frequently. Remove from heat; cool.

2. Combine 1 tablespoon sour cream and cream cheese, stirring well. Add 2 tablespoons sour cream, mayonnaise, and remaining 3 ingredients, and stir well to combine. Stir in onion. Cover

---

and refrigerate overnight. Yield: 16 servings (serving size: 1 tablespoon).

CALORIES 30 (54% from fat); FAT 1.8g (sat 0.5g, mono 0.1g, poly 0.1g); PROTEIN 0.7g; CARB 3.3g; FIBER 0.5g; CHOL 3mg; IRON 0.1mg; SODIUM 53mg; CALC 11mg

Seared Scallops, Sweet Potato, and Pecan Salad
(pictured on page 59)

This recipe can also serve 8 appetizer portions. Maple syrup balances the tangy mustard in the vinaigrette.

VINAIGRETTE:
1 tablespoon white wine vinegar
1 tablespoon olive oil
1 teaspoon Dijon mustard
1 teaspoon maple syrup
Dash of salt
Dash of freshly ground black pepper

SALAD:
3 cups (½-inch) cubed peeled sweet potato
Cooking spray
¾ teaspoon salt, divided
¼ teaspoon freshly ground black pepper
1 pound sea scallops
6 cups gourmet salad greens
1 cup seedless red grapes, halved
1 large red bell pepper, cut into thin strips
¼ cup pecans, toasted

1. To prepare vinaigrette, combine first 6 ingredients, stirring with a whisk.

2. Preheat oven to 400°.

3. To prepare salad, arrange sweet potato in a single layer on a baking sheet lightly coated with cooking spray. Lightly coat potato with cooking spray; sprinkle with ½ teaspoon salt and ¼ teaspoon black pepper. Bake at 400° for 25 minutes or until potato is tender, turning once after 15 minutes. Cool completely.

4. Sprinkle scallops with ¼ teaspoon salt. Heat a large nonstick skillet coated with cooking spray over medium-high heat. Add scallops, and cook 2 minutes on each side or until done. Combine
Continued

sweet potato, greens, grapes, and bell pepper in a large bowl. Drizzle vinaigrette over potato mixture; toss gently to coat. Place 1⅓ cups salad mixture on each of 6 plates; divide scallops evenly among salads. Sprinkle each serving with 2 teaspoons pecans. Yield: 6 servings.

CALORIES 230 (27% from fat); FAT 7g (sat 0.8g, mono 3.8g, poly 1.7g); PROTEIN 15.6g; CARB 27.7g; FIBER 4.5g; CHOL 25mg; IRON 1.8mg; SODIUM 483mg; CALC 74mg

---

MAKE AHEAD
Skinny Turkey-Spinach Meat Loaf

Ground beef and ground turkey breast combine to yield a moist, tasty meat loaf.

    Cooking spray
    1   cup finely chopped onion
    3   garlic cloves, minced
    1   cup dry breadcrumbs
    ½   cup fat-free milk
    1   tablespoon Worcestershire
        sauce
    1   teaspoon salt
    ½   teaspoon freshly ground black
        pepper
    4   large egg whites
    1½ pounds ground turkey breast
    ½   pound extralean ground beef
    2   (10-ounce) packages frozen leaf
        spinach, thawed, drained, and
        squeezed dry
    ½   cup ketchup

1. Preheat oven to 350°.
2. Heat a large nonstick skillet coated with cooking spray over medium-high heat. Add onion, and sauté 4 minutes. Add garlic, and sauté 30 seconds. Remove from heat. Combine onion mixture, breadcrumbs, and next 8 ingredients, stirring well.
3. Shape meat mixture into a 12 x 5-inch loaf on a broiler pan coated with cooking spray. Brush ketchup over top of loaf. Bake at 350° for 45 minutes or until a meat thermometer registers 160°; let stand 10 minutes before slicing. Yield: 8 servings (serving size: 1 slice).

CALORIES 292 (30% from fat); FAT 9.6g (sat 2.9g, mono 3.7g, poly 1.8g); PROTEIN 31g; CARB 20.2g; FIBER 3.1g; CHOL 66mg; IRON 4.2mg; SODIUM 765mg; CALC 154mg

---

...And Ready in Just About 20 Minutes

Rely on soups and stews when you're in the mood for comforting foods.

Twenty-Minute Chili and Mediterranean Vegetable Stew over Soft Polenta are sure to please. If you're ready for spring dishes, try the Shrimp Salad with White Beans, Broccoli, and Toasted Garlic; or Marinated Salmon with Mango-Kiwi Relish. Meatless black bean quesadillas, Asian-flavored tuna, or chicken sandwiches seasoned with sun-dried tomatoes round out your selections.

QUICK & EASY
Sesame-Crusted Tuna with Ginger-Peanut Rice

If you like your tuna cooked rare, buy sushi-grade tuna.

RICE:
    1   (3½-ounce) bag boil-in-bag
        long-grain rice
    ¼   cup sliced green onions
    1   tablespoon Thai peanut sauce
    2   teaspoons bottled minced fresh
        ginger
    ¼   teaspoon salt

TUNA:
    1   tablespoon sesame oil
    4   (6-ounce) Yellowfin tuna steaks
        (about ¾ inch thick)
    3   tablespoons low-sodium soy
        sauce, divided
    ¼   teaspoon salt
    ⅓   cup sesame seeds, toasted
    2   tablespoons sliced green onions

1. To prepare rice, cook rice according to package directions, omitting salt and fat. Stir in ¼ cup onions, peanut sauce, ginger, and ¼ teaspoon salt; keep warm.
2. To prepare tuna, heat oil in a large nonstick skillet over medium-high heat.

Combine tuna and 2 tablespoons soy sauce in a bowl, tossing gently to coat. Sprinkle tuna with ¼ teaspoon salt. Dredge edges of tuna in sesame seeds. Add tuna to pan, and cook 3 minutes on each side or until desired degree of doneness. Serve tuna over rice. Drizzle with 1 tablespoon soy sauce; sprinkle with 2 tablespoons onions. Yield: 4 servings (serving size: 1 tuna steak, about ½ cup rice, and about 1 teaspoon sauce).

CALORIES 491 (21% from fat); FAT 11.3g (sat 1.8g, mono 3.9g, poly 4.5g); PROTEIN 45.2g; CARB 50g; FIBER 1.9g; CHOL 77mg; IRON 4.6mg; SODIUM 690mg; CALC 30mg

---

QUICK & EASY
Black Bean Quesadillas with Corn Salsa

Heating all of the quesadillas at the same time in the oven is faster than cooking them one at a time in a skillet.

QUESADILLAS:
    1   tablespoon olive oil
    1½ teaspoons bottled minced garlic
    2   cups chopped plum tomatoes
    ½   cup chopped fresh cilantro
    1   (15-ounce) can black beans,
        drained and rinsed
    4   (8-inch) flour tortillas
        Cooking spray
    ¾   cup (3 ounces) preshredded
        Mexican blend cheese

SALSA:
    1   cup frozen whole-kernel corn
    ½   cup chopped fresh cilantro
    2   tablespoons fresh lime juice
    ½   teaspoon bottled minced garlic
    1   red bell pepper, chopped

1. To prepare quesadillas, preheat broiler.
2. Heat oil in a large skillet over medium-high heat. Add 1½ teaspoons garlic; sauté 30 seconds. Add tomatoes, ½ cup cilantro, and beans; cook 5 minutes or until liquid evaporates, stirring occasionally. Place tortillas on a baking sheet coated with cooking spray. Top each tortilla with ½ cup bean mixture and 3 tablespoons cheese; fold in half. Lightly coat tops with cooking spray. Broil 3 minutes or until cheese melts and

tortillas begin to brown. Cut each tortilla into 3 wedges.

3. To prepare salsa, combine corn and remaining 4 ingredients in a small saucepan. Bring to a boil over high heat, and cook 2 minutes, stirring frequently. Serve with quesadillas. Yield: 4 servings (serving size: 3 quesadilla wedges and about ⅓ cup salsa).

CALORIES 420 (31% from fat); FAT 14.4g (sat 5.5g, mono 6.4g, poly 1.3g); PROTEIN 17.8g; CARB 60g; FIBER 10.3g; CHOL 19mg; IRON 4.2mg; SODIUM 590mg; CALC 272mg

---

Sandwich Night Menu
serves 4

Sweet potatoes provide a pleasant contrast to the salty bacon and tangy sour cream in the salad, but you can substitute red-skinned potatoes, if you prefer.

Chicken Sandwich with Arugula and Sun-Dried Tomato Vinaigrette

Sour cream and bacon potato salad*

Bread-and-butter pickles

*Cook 1 pound halved fingerling potatoes and 1 pound (1-inch) cubed peeled sweet potatoes in boiling water until tender. Drain; place in a large bowl. Add ½ cup reduced-fat sour cream, ¼ cup chopped green onions, ½ teaspoon salt, ¼ teaspoon ground red pepper, and 3 cooked and crumbled bacon slices; stir gently to combine.

QUICK & EASY

Chicken Sandwich with Arugula and Sun-Dried Tomato Vinaigrette

Cooking spray
- 4 (6-ounce) skinless, boneless chicken breast halves
- ¼ teaspoon salt, divided
- ¼ teaspoon black pepper
- ¼ cup chopped drained oil-packed sun-dried tomato halves
- ¼ cup balsamic vinegar
- 1 garlic clove, minced
- 4 (2-ounce) onion sandwich buns
- 2 cups trimmed arugula

1. Preheat broiler.

2. Heat a grill pan coated with cooking spray over medium-high heat. Place each chicken breast half between 2 sheets of heavy-duty plastic wrap, and pound each piece to ¼-inch thickness using a meat mallet or rolling pin. Sprinkle both sides evenly with ⅛ teaspoon salt and black pepper. Add chicken to pan, and cook 4 minutes on each side or until done.

3. While chicken cooks, combine ⅛ teaspoon salt, tomatoes, vinegar, and garlic, stirring with a whisk.

4. Place buns, cut sides up, on a baking sheet. Broil 1 minute or until lightly toasted. Place 1 chicken breast half on bottom half of each bun. Add arugula to tomato mixture, and toss gently to coat. Arrange about ½ cup arugula mixture over each chicken breast half. Cover with tops of buns. Yield: 4 servings.

CALORIES 376 (15% from fat); FAT 6.4g (sat 2.3g, mono 1.7g, poly 1.7g); PROTEIN 45.4g; CARB 32.4g; FIBER 1.7g; CHOL 99mg; IRON 3.3mg; SODIUM 570mg; CALC 109mg

---

QUICK & EASY

Mediterranean Vegetable Stew over Soft Polenta

Serve this simple meatless stew with a green salad.

- 2 teaspoons olive oil
- 2 cups (¼-inch) slices zucchini
- 1½ teaspoons bottled minced garlic
- ¼ teaspoon black pepper
- 2 (14.5-ounce) cans diced tomatoes, undrained
- 1 (14½-ounce) can Italian-style stewed tomatoes, undrained
- 1 (15-ounce) can chickpeas (garbanzo beans), drained and rinsed
- 3 cups water
- 1 cup dry polenta
- 1½ cups (6 ounces) preshredded fresh Parmesan

1. Heat oil in a large Dutch oven over medium-high heat. Add zucchini and garlic; sauté 30 seconds. Stir in pepper, tomatoes, and chickpeas. Reduce heat; simmer 10 minutes, stirring occasionally.

2. While stew cooks, bring 3 cups water to a boil in a medium saucepan. Add polenta, stirring with a whisk. Reduce heat; simmer 3 minutes or until done, stirring occasionally. Stir in cheese. Serve stew over polenta. Yield: 6 servings (serving size: about ⅔ cup polenta and about 1 cup stew).

CALORIES 351 (22% from fat); FAT 8.7g (sat 4.2g, mono 3.1g, poly 0.8g); PROTEIN 17g; CARB 53.6g; FIBER 8.6g; CHOL 16mg; IRON 3.1mg; SODIUM 943mg; CALC 375mg

---

QUICK & EASY

Marinated Salmon with Mango-Kiwi Relish

Serve over mixed greens, steamed couscous, or on toasted sourdough bread for a fish sandwich.

SALMON:
- 1 tablespoon honey
- 2 teaspoons low-sodium soy sauce
- 1 teaspoon olive oil
- ¼ teaspoon black pepper
- 4 (6-ounce) salmon fillets (about 1 inch thick)
- Cooking spray

RELISH:
- ½ cup diced peeled mango
- ½ cup cubed peeled kiwifruit
- ¼ cup chopped fresh cilantro
- ¼ cup fresh orange juice

1. To prepare salmon, combine first 4 ingredients in a large zip-top plastic bag. Add fish to bag; seal. Marinate 10 minutes, turning occasionally.

2. While fish marinates, heat grill pan or large nonstick skillet over medium-high heat. Remove fish from bag, discarding marinade. Coat pan with cooking spray. Add fish, and cook 5 minutes on each side or until fish flakes easily when tested with a fork.

3. While fish cooks, prepare relish. Combine mango and remaining 3 ingredients. Serve over fish. Yield: 4 servings (serving size: 1 salmon fillet and ¼ cup relish).

CALORIES 321 (39% from fat); FAT 13.8g (sat 3.2g, mono 6.1g, poly 3.3g); PROTEIN 36.8g; CARB 10.9g; FIBER 1.3g; CHOL 87mg; IRON 0.8mg; SODIUM 128mg; CALC 33mg

Shrimp Salad with White Beans, Broccoli, and Toasted Garlic

Crisp Italian bread rounds out the menu. Using bagged broccoli florets cuts several minutes of preparation time.

    4   cups bagged broccoli florets
    2   tablespoons olive oil
    4   garlic cloves, thinly sliced
    ¼   cup fresh lemon juice
    2   tablespoons chopped fresh dill
    ¼   teaspoon salt
    ¼   teaspoon black pepper
    1   pound peeled and deveined large
        shrimp
    2   cups canned small white beans,
        rinsed and drained
    ½   cup (2 ounces) grated fresh
        Parmigiano-Reggiano cheese
    Dill sprigs (optional)

1. Cook broccoli in boiling water 3 minutes or until crisp-tender. Drain and rinse with cold water.

2. While broccoli cooks, heat oil in a large nonstick skillet over medium heat. Add garlic, and cook 5 minutes or until golden, stirring frequently. Remove garlic with a slotted spoon; drain on paper towels. Pour excess oil from pan into a small bowl. Add juice, chopped dill, salt, and pepper; stir with a whisk.

3. Heat pan over medium-high heat. Add shrimp, and cook 3 minutes or until done, stirring frequently.

4. Combine broccoli, lemon mixture, shrimp, beans, and cheese, tossing gently to coat. Sprinkle with garlic. Garnish with dill sprigs, if desired. Yield: 4 servings (serving size: 1½ cups).

CALORIES 403 (27% from fat); FAT 12.1g (sat 3.2g, mono 6.2g, poly 1.7g); PROTEIN 38.7g; CARB 36.3g; FIBER 8.5g; CHOL 180mg; IRON 7.5mg; SODIUM 509mg; CALC 322mg

Chicken Tenders with Apricots and Sautéed Spinach

Serve over couscous or rice.

    5   teaspoons olive oil, divided
    1½ pounds chicken breast tenders
    ¼   teaspoon freshly ground black
        pepper
    ⅛   teaspoon salt
    1   cup Italian-seasoned breadcrumbs
    1   (16-ounce) can apricot halves in
        light syrup, undrained
    1   tablespoon lemon juice
    ¼   teaspoon salt
    1   (10-ounce) package fresh spinach

1. Heat 1 tablespoon oil in a large non-stick skillet over medium-high heat. Sprinkle chicken evenly with pepper and ⅛ teaspoon salt. Place chicken and breadcrumbs in a large zip-top plastic bag; seal bag, and shake to coat. Add chicken to pan; cook 2½ minutes on each side or until browned.

2. Drain apricots in a colander over a bowl; reserve ½ cup liquid. Add apricot halves and ½ cup reserved liquid to pan; cover and cook 3 minutes or until chicken is done. Remove chicken mixture from pan; keep warm.

3. Wipe pan with a paper towel. Heat 2 teaspoons oil in pan over medium-high heat. Add lemon juice, ¼ teaspoon salt, and spinach; cook 3 minutes or until spinach is slightly wilted. Serve spinach with chicken and apricots. Yield: 4 servings (serving size: about 4 ounces chicken, 3 apricot halves, and about ⅓ cup spinach).

CALORIES 432 (18% from fat); FAT 8.8g (sat 1.6g, mono 5g, poly 1.3g); PROTEIN 46.2g; CARB 41.8g; FIBER 5g; CHOL 99mg; IRON 4.6mg; SODIUM 819mg; CALC 131mg

Twenty-Minute Chili

Serving chili over rice is popular in Texas. We also recommend serving it with corn bread sticks.

    1   (3½-ounce) bag boil-in-bag
        long-grain rice
    1   tablespoon vegetable oil
    1   cup chopped onion
    ¾   cup chopped green bell pepper
    ½   pound ground turkey breast
    1   tablespoon chili powder
    1   teaspoon Worcestershire sauce
    ½   teaspoon ground cumin
    ½   teaspoon dried oregano
    ¼   teaspoon salt
    ¼   teaspoon black pepper
    1   (15-ounce) can kidney beans,
        rinsed and drained
    1   (14.5-ounce) can Mexican-style
        stewed tomatoes with jalapeño
        peppers and spices, undrained
    1   (5.5-ounce) can tomato juice
    ¼   cup (1 ounce) preshredded
        reduced-fat Cheddar cheese

1. Cook rice according to package directions, omitting salt and fat.

2. While rice cooks, heat oil in a large nonstick skillet over medium-high heat. Add onion, bell pepper, and turkey, and cook 3 minutes or until done, stirring to crumble. Stir in chili powder and next 8 ingredients; bring to a boil. Cover, reduce heat, and simmer 10 minutes. Serve over rice, and sprinkle with cheese. Yield: 4 servings (serving size: 1¼ cups chili, ½ cup rice, and 1 tablespoon cheese).

CALORIES 380 (26% from fat); FAT 10.5g (sat 2.8g, mono 2.6g, poly 3.3g); PROTEIN 21.4g; CARB 51g; FIBER 11.2g; CHOL 50mg; IRON 4mg; SODIUM 739mg; CALC 125mg

Delightful Dumplings

Almost every country has its own version, whether stuffed or dropped. You'll love them all.

Steamed Pork Buns

The Chinese make these steamed dumplings from yeast dough as part of a collection of steamed and fried delicacies known as *dim sum*. Here, the dough surrounds the filling, then gets pinched and twisted to form a pouch. Make the filling while the dough rises, and make the dipping sauce while the filling marinates. To keep the dough from sticking to the steamer, line the basket with lettuce leaves.

DOUGH:

- ¾ cup warm fat-free milk (100° to 110°)
- ¼ cup warm water (100° to 110°)
- 1 teaspoon sugar
- 1 package dry yeast (about 2¼ teaspoons)
- 3 cups all-purpose flour, divided
- ½ teaspoon salt
- Cooking spray

FILLING:

- ⅓ cup rice vinegar
- ⅓ cup low-sodium soy sauce
- 3 tablespoons sugar
- 1 teaspoon grated peeled fresh ginger
- ¼ teaspoon salt
- ¼ teaspoon crushed red pepper
- 4 garlic cloves, minced
- 1½ pounds boneless Boston butt pork roast, trimmed and cut into 2-inch pieces
- 12 romaine lettuce leaves

SAUCE:

- ⅓ cup low-sodium soy sauce
- 3 tablespoons rice vinegar
- 1 teaspoon sesame seeds, toasted

1. Combine milk and water in a large bowl. Dissolve 1 teaspoon sugar and yeast in milk mixture, and let stand 5 minutes. Lightly spoon flour into dry measuring cups, and level with a knife. Add 2¾ cups flour and ½ teaspoon salt to yeast mixture, and stir until dough forms. Turn out onto a floured surface. Knead until smooth and elastic (about 10 minutes); add enough of remaining flour, 1 tablespoon at a time, to prevent dough from sticking to hands (dough will feel tacky).

2. Place dough in a large bowl coated with cooking spray; turn to coat top. Cover and let rise in a warm place (85°), free from drafts, 1 hour or until doubled in size. (Press two fingers into dough; if indentation remains, dough has risen enough.) Punch dough down; cover and let rise in a warm place (85°) 30 minutes or until doubled in size.

3. Preheat oven to 475°.

4. To prepare filling, combine ⅓ cup vinegar and next 6 ingredients in a zip-top plastic bag. Add pork; seal and marinate in refrigerator 30 minutes, turning bag to coat. Strain mixture through a sieve over a bowl; reserve marinade. Place pork in a shallow roasting pan coated with cooking spray. Bake at 475° for 25 minutes or until done. Let stand 5 minutes; finely chop. Pour marinade into a saucepan; bring to a boil. Cook until reduced to ¼ cup (about 8 minutes). Combine pork and reduced marinade.

5. Divide dough into 24 portions. Working with 1 portion at a time (cover remaining dough to prevent drying), roll each portion into a 3½-inch circle on a floured surface. Spoon about 1 tablespoon filling onto center of circle. Moisten edges of dough with water; gather edges together to encase filling, pinching edges to seal. Gently twist sealed edges to form a pouch shape.

6. Line each tier of a 2-tiered (10-inch) bamboo steamer with 3 lettuce leaves. Arrange 6 dumplings, 1 inch apart, in each steamer basket. Stack tiers; cover with steamer lid. Add water to a large skillet to a depth of 1 inch; bring to a boil. Place steamer in pan, and steam dumplings 10 minutes or until dough is translucent (dumplings will be puffy and spongy). Remove dumplings from steamer. Repeat procedure with remaining lettuce leaves and dumplings.

7. To prepare sauce, combine ⅓ cup soy sauce, 3 tablespoons vinegar, and seeds. Serve dumplings immediately with sauce. Yield: 24 servings (serving size: 1 dumpling and about 1 teaspoon sauce).

NOTE: To reheat dumplings, place cooked dumplings on a plate or platter lined with wax paper; cover with a damp paper towel. Microwave on HIGH 30 seconds to 1 minute to reheat.

CALORIES 110 (20% from fat); FAT 2.5g (sat 0.8g, mono 1.1g, poly 0.3g); PROTEIN 7.9g; CARB 13.4g; FIBER 0.6g; CHOL 19mg; IRON 1.3mg; SODIUM 334mg; CALC 21mg

How to Make Pork Buns

Twist top of dough 90° to tightly seal.

Steamy Situation

As a general rule, prepared dumpling dough shouldn't stand too long. Cook dumplings soon after they're formed, and eat soon after they're cooked. Little pockets of steam trapped inside make them tender. Once the steam dissipates, the dumplings toughen and become dense.

Buttered Spaetzle

These tiny, irregularly shaped egg dumplings are a favorite side dish in southern Germany and Alsatian France.

1⅔ cups all-purpose flour
¾ teaspoon salt
¼ teaspoon baking powder
¾ cup 1% low-fat milk
2 large eggs, lightly beaten
2 quarts water
2 tablespoons butter, divided

1. Lightly spoon flour into dry measuring cups; level with a knife. Sift together flour, salt, and baking powder. Combine milk and eggs; stir with a whisk. Add milk mixture to flour mixture; stir with a whisk until combined. Let stand 10 minutes.
2. Bring 2 quarts water to a boil in a large saucepan. Hold a colander with large holes (about ¼-inch in diameter) over boiling water; spoon about ½ cup dough into colander. Press dough through holes with a rubber spatula (droplets will form spaetzle); set colander aside. Cook 3 minutes or until done (spaetzle will rise to surface). Remove with a slotted spoon; drain in a strainer (spaetzle will stick to a paper towel). Repeat procedure with remaining dough.
3. Melt 1 tablespoon butter in a large nonstick skillet over medium-high heat. Add 2 cups cooked spaetzle; cook 2 minutes or until lightly browned, stirring frequently. Repeat with 1 tablespoon butter and remaining spaetzle. Yield: 6 servings (serving size: ⅔ cup).

CALORIES 198 (28% from fat); FAT 6.1g (sat 3.1g, mono 1.9g, poly 0.5g); PROTEIN 6.7g; CARB 28.2g; FIBER 0.9g; CHOL 82mg; IRON 1.9mg; SODIUM 387mg; CALC 63mg

---

How to Make Spaetzle

Make the dough thin enough to press through the holes of a colander. If the dough is too thin, add flour, 1 tablespoon at a time. Press the dough through the colander directly into boiling water. Place the cooked spaetzle in a strainer; allow excess water to drain. Don't use paper towels to blot the water; the spaetzle will stick to them.

Spaetzle Baked with Ham and Gruyère

Spaetzle help to make a satisfying main-dish casserole.

1⅔ cups all-purpose flour
1 teaspoon salt, divided
¼ teaspoon baking powder
2¼ cups 1% low-fat milk, divided
2 large eggs, lightly beaten
2 quarts water
Cooking spray
1 cup finely chopped onion
¾ cup finely diced ham (about 4 ounces)
2 tablespoons all-purpose flour
¼ teaspoon black pepper
2 large eggs, lightly beaten
¾ cup (3 ounces) shredded Gruyère cheese

1. Preheat oven to 375°.
2. Lightly spoon flour into dry measuring cups, and level with a knife. Sift together 1⅔ cups flour, ½ teaspoon salt, and baking powder. Combine ¾ cup milk and 2 eggs, stirring with a whisk. Add milk mixture to flour mixture, stirring with a whisk until combined. Let stand 10 minutes.
3. Bring 2 quarts water to a boil in a large saucepan. Hold a colander with large holes (about ¼-inch in diameter) over boiling water; spoon about ½ cup dough into colander. Press dough through holes with a rubber spatula (droplets will form spaetzle); set colander aside. Cook 3 minutes or until done (spaetzle will rise to surface). Remove with a slotted spoon; drain in a strainer (spaetzle will stick to a paper towel). Repeat procedure with remaining dough.
4. Heat a medium nonstick skillet coated with cooking spray over medium heat. Add onion, and cook 5 minutes or until lightly browned, stirring frequently. Remove from heat; stir in ham. Combine spaetzle and onion mixture in a 2-quart baking dish coated with cooking spray, tossing gently.
5. Combine ½ teaspoon salt, 1½ cups milk, 2 tablespoons flour, pepper, and 2 eggs, stirring with a whisk. Pour milk mixture over spaetzle mixture. Sprinkle evenly with cheese. Bake at 375° for 35 minutes or until cheese is lightly browned. Yield: 6 servings (serving size: about 1 cup).

CALORIES 310 (28% from fat); FAT 9.6g (sat 4.4g, mono 2.9g, poly 0.9g); PROTEIN 18.8g; CARB 35.7g; FIBER 1.5g; CHOL 165mg; IRON 2.4mg; SODIUM 786mg; CALC 288mg

---

How to Make Rosemary Dumplings

Use two spoons to drop the sticky dumplings into the soup.

Chicken and Rosemary Dumplings

Spoonfuls of seasoned buttermilk biscuit dough form light, fluffy dumplings in this classic American dish.

SOUP:

4 cups fat-free, less-sodium chicken broth
3 cups water
1 pound chicken drumsticks, skinned
1 pound skinless, boneless chicken breast halves
2 thyme sprigs
2 teaspoons olive oil
1½ cups diced carrots
1½ cups chopped celery
1 cup diced onion
2 garlic cloves, minced
½ teaspoon salt

DUMPLINGS:

1¼ cups all-purpose flour
1 tablespoon chopped fresh or
 ½ teaspoon dried rosemary
2 teaspoons baking powder
¼ teaspoon salt
2 tablespoons butter, softened
½ cup low-fat buttermilk
1 large egg, lightly beaten
¼ cup all-purpose flour
¼ cup water

REMAINING INGREDIENT:

Freshly ground black pepper

1. Combine first 5 ingredients in a large Dutch oven over medium-high heat; bring to a boil. Reduce heat, and simmer, uncovered, 15 minutes or until chicken is done. Remove pan from heat. Remove chicken pieces from broth; cool slightly. Strain broth through a sieve into a large bowl; discard solids. Remove chicken from bones. Discard bones; chop chicken into bite-size pieces. Set chicken aside.

2. Heat oil in pan over medium-high heat. Add carrots, celery, onion, and garlic; sauté 6 minutes or until onion is tender. Add reserved broth mixture and ½ teaspoon salt; simmer 10 minutes. Keep warm.

3. To prepare dumplings, lightly spoon 1¼ cups flour into dry measuring cups; level with a knife. Combine 1¼ cups flour, rosemary, baking powder, and ¼ teaspoon salt in a large bowl. Cut in butter with a pastry blender or 2 knives until mixture resembles coarse meal. Combine buttermilk and egg, stirring with a whisk. Add buttermilk mixture to flour mixture, stirring just until combined.

4. Add chopped chicken to broth mixture; bring to a simmer over medium-high heat. Combine ¼ cup flour and ¼ cup water, stirring with a whisk until well blended to form a slurry. Add slurry to pan; simmer 3 minutes. Drop dumpling dough, 1 tablespoon per dumpling, onto chicken mixture to form 12 dumplings. Cover and cook 7 minutes (do not let broth boil). Sprinkle with black pepper. Yield: 6 servings (serving size: 2 dumplings and 1⅓ cups soup).

CALORIES 366 (24% from fat); FAT 9.7g (sat 3.8g, mono 3.5g, poly 1.3g); PROTEIN 32.5g; CARB 35.1g; FIBER 2.9g; CHOL 115mg; IRON 3.3mg; SODIUM 936mg; CALC 169mg

Pierogi Dough

Pierogi [peer-OH-gee] is one of Poland's most popular foods. These "little pies" are delicious stuffed with almost anything and can be served as a side dish, a main dish, or even as dessert. Here's a basic pierogi dough that we use in Potato Pierogi (recipe at right) and Sweet Vanilla Cheese Pierogi (recipe on page 84).

2 cups all-purpose flour
¼ teaspoon salt
¼ cup reduced-fat sour cream
¼ cup water
1 tablespoon vegetable oil
1 large egg, lightly beaten
Cooking spray

1. Lightly spoon flour into dry measuring cups, and level with a knife. Combine flour and salt in a large bowl. Combine sour cream, water, oil, and egg, stirring with a whisk. Add sour cream mixture to flour mixture; stir until combined. Turn dough out onto a floured surface. Knead until smooth and elastic (about 7 minutes). Place dough in a bowl coated with cooking spray, turning to coat top. Cover and let rest 15 minutes. Yield: dough for 16 pierogi.

CALORIES 1,199 (21% from fat); FAT 28.5g (sat 8.6g, mono 5.3g, poly 9.6g); PROTEIN 34.9g; CARB 195.4g; FIBER 6.9g; CHOL 244mg; IRON 12.3mg; SODIUM 688mg; CALC 163mg

How to Make Potato Pierogi

Gently fold dough over filling and seal by pinching edges.

Potato Pierogi

Pierogi puff when they boil but begin to deflate almost immediately. They're almost flat when you cook them. Serve these potato pierogi as a side dish.

1 pound peeled baking potatoes, cut into 1-inch pieces
2 tablespoons egg substitute
2 tablespoons reduced-fat sour cream
1 tablespoon butter
1 tablespoon minced fresh chives or green onions
1 teaspoon white wine vinegar
¾ teaspoon salt
Pierogi Dough (recipe at left)
2 quarts water
1 tablespoon butter, divided
⅛ teaspoon salt
⅓ cup reduced-fat sour cream

1. Place potatoes in a saucepan; cover with water. Bring to a boil. Reduce heat, and simmer 10 minutes or until tender; drain. Place potatoes in a large bowl; mash with a potato masher or fork until smooth. Add egg substitute and next 5 ingredients; blend well with potato masher.

2. Divide Pierogi Dough into 16 equal portions, shaping each into a ball. Working with one portion at a time (cover remaining dough to prevent drying), roll each ball into a 3½-inch circle on a lightly floured surface.

3. Spoon 1 rounded tablespoon of potato mixture onto half of each dough circle. Bring opposite sides of dough circle together; pinch to seal, beginning with center and pinching down both sides to form a half-moon shape.

4. Bring 2 quarts water to a boil in a large saucepan. Add half of pierogi; cook 7 minutes or until done (pierogi will rise to surface). Remove pierogi with a slotted spoon; drain in a colander (pierogi will stick to a paper towel). Place pierogi in a single layer on a baking sheet or platter. Repeat procedure with remaining pierogi.

5. Heat 1½ teaspoons butter in a large nonstick skillet over medium-high heat. Add 8 pierogi; cook 2 minutes on each side or until golden brown. Remove

Continued

pierogi; keep warm. Repeat procedure with 1½ teaspoons butter and 8 pierogi. Sprinkle cooked pierogi with ⅛ teaspoon salt. Serve with ⅓ cup sour cream. Yield: 8 servings (serving size: 2 pierogi and about 2 teaspoons sour cream).

(Totals include Pierogi Dough) CALORIES 248 (30% from fat); FAT 8.2g (sat 3.8g, mono 2.2g, poly 1.4g); PROTEIN 6.2g; CARB 37.2g; FIBER 1.8g; CHOL 42mg; IRON 1.8mg; SODIUM 384mg; CALC 36mg

Sweet Vanilla Cheese Pierogi

The filling in these dessert pierogi is very soft. Freezing firms it, making pierogi easier to prepare.

½ cup 2% low-fat cottage cheese
⅔ cup sugar
1 tablespoon all-purpose flour
1 vanilla bean
6 ounces ⅓-less-fat cream cheese, softened
Pierogi Dough (recipe on page 83)
2 quarts water
1 tablespoon butter, divided
1 cup applesauce

1. Spoon cottage cheese into a cheesecloth-lined sieve over a medium bowl; let stand 1 hour. Scrape drained cottage cheese into a food processor or blender. Combine sugar and flour. Add sugar mixture to cottage cheese; process until well blended. Scrape seeds from vanilla bean; add seeds to cheese mixture, reserving bean for another use. Add cream cheese to cheese mixture; pulse until smooth. Place cheese mixture in a bowl; chill in freezer 30 minutes.

2. Divide Pierogi Dough into 16 equal portions, shaping each into a ball. Working with one portion at a time (cover remaining dough to prevent drying), roll each ball into a 3½-inch circle on a lightly floured surface.

3. Spoon 1 rounded teaspoon cheese mixture onto half of each circle. Bring 2 opposite sides of circle to center. Pinch to seal, beginning with center and pinching down both sides to form a half-moon shape.

4. Bring 2 quarts water to a boil in a large saucepan. Add half of pierogi; cook 7 minutes or until done (pierogi will rise to surface). Remove pierogi with a slotted spoon, and drain in a colander (pierogi will stick to a paper towel). Place pierogi in a single layer on a baking sheet or platter. Repeat procedure with remaining pierogi.

5. Heat 1½ teaspoons butter in a large nonstick skillet over medium-high heat. Add 8 pierogi; cook 2 minutes on each side or until golden brown. Remove pierogi; keep warm. Repeat procedure with 1½ teaspoons butter and 8 pierogi. Serve with applesauce. Yield: 16 servings (serving size: 1 pierogi and 1 tablespoon applesauce).

(Totals include Pierogi Dough) CALORIES 155 (30% from fat); FAT 5.1g (sat 2.6g, mono 1.4g, poly 0.7g); PROTEIN 4.2g; CARB 23.1g; FIBER 0.6g; CHOL 25mg; IRON 0.9mg; SODIUM 121mg; CALC 21mg

Potato Gnocchi with Bolognese

Gnocchi [NYOH-kee], feather-light Italian dumplings, can be made from spinach, ricotta, polenta, or semolina flour, but are most commonly made from potatoes. Their thin grooves catch the Bolognese sauce.

SAUCE:
1 teaspoon vegetable oil
½ pound beef stew meat, trimmed and cut into 2-inch pieces
½ pound pork stew meat, trimmed and cut into 2-inch pieces
1½ cups chopped onion
½ cup chopped celery
½ cup chopped carrot
⅓ cup dried chopped porcini mushrooms (about ⅜ ounce)
2 garlic cloves, minced
1½ cups 2% reduced-fat milk
¾ teaspoon salt
1 (28-ounce) can diced tomatoes, undrained
1 bay leaf
½ cup finely chopped fresh flat-leaf parsley
1 tablespoon chopped fresh or 1 teaspoon dried thyme

GNOCCHI:
2½ pounds large baking potatoes
1¼ cups all-purpose flour, divided
¼ teaspoon salt
2 large egg yolks, lightly beaten
1 gallon water

REMAINING INGREDIENT:
6 tablespoons (1½ ounces) grated fresh Parmesan cheese

1. To prepare sauce, heat oil in a large Dutch oven over medium-high heat. Add beef and pork; cook 3 minutes, browning on all sides. Remove meat from pan, and cool slightly. Finely chop meat.

2. Heat pan over medium heat. Add onion, celery, carrot, porcini, and garlic; cook 10 minutes, stirring occasionally. Add chopped meat, milk, ¾ teaspoon salt, tomatoes, and bay leaf; bring to a boil. Cover, reduce heat, and simmer 1 hour. Uncover and cook 45 minutes, stirring occasionally. Stir in parsley and thyme; cook 15 minutes or until slightly thick, stirring occasionally. Discard bay leaf.

3. To prepare gnocchi, preheat oven to 400°.

4. Bake potatoes at 400° for 1½ hours or until done; cool slightly. Cut each potato in half lengthwise; scoop out pulp. Discard skins. Mash pulp. Place 4 cups mashed potatoes in a large bowl, reserving remaining mashed potatoes for another use. Lightly spoon flour into dry measuring cups; level with a knife. Add 1 cup flour, ¼ teaspoon salt, and egg yolks to 4 cups mashed potatoes, and stir to combine. Knead until smooth (about 2 minutes); add enough of remaining flour, 1 tablespoon at a time, to prevent dough from sticking to hands (dough will feel tacky).

5. Divide dough into 6 portions. Shape each portion into a 10-inch-long rope. Cut each rope into 10 (1-inch) pieces; roll each piece into a ball. Working with one dough piece at a time (cover remaining dough to prevent drying), using your thumb or index finger, roll dough piece down tines of a lightly floured fork (gnocchi will have ridges on one side and an indention on the other). Place gnocchi on a lightly floured baking sheet.

6. Bring 1 gallon water to a boil in a large stockpot. Add half of gnocchi; cook 3 minutes or until done (gnocchi will rise to surface). Remove cooked gnocchi with a slotted spoon; place in a colander. Repeat procedure with remaining gnocchi. Serve immediately with sauce. Sprinkle with cheese. Yield: 6 servings (serving size: 10 gnocchi, ¾ cup sauce, and 1 tablespoon cheese).

CALORIES 475 (22% from fat); FAT 11.6g (sat 4.5g, mono 4.3g, poly 1.5g); PROTEIN 31.4g; CARB 67.7g; FIBER 8.4g; CHOL 129mg; IRON 6.9mg; SODIUM 788mg; CALC 271mg

How to Make Potato Gnocchi

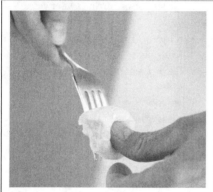

To create grooves in the gnocchi and an indention to hold sauce, use your thumb to indent and roll dough down tines of fork.

Chochoyones in Black Bean Soup

Chochoyones are popular throughout the Oaxaca region of Mexico.

SOUP:
- 2   teaspoons olive oil
- 2   cups chopped onion
- 2   teaspoons aniseed
- 1   teaspoon cumin seeds
- 3   garlic cloves, minced
- 4   cups fat-free, less-sodium chicken broth
- 3   cups water
- ¼   teaspoon salt
- 2   (15-ounce) cans black beans, rinsed and drained

DUMPLINGS:
- 1   cup masa harina
- 1   teaspoon baking powder
- ¼   teaspoon salt
- 2   tablespoons butter, softened
- ¾   cup boiling water
- ¼   cup minced fresh cilantro

REMAINING INGREDIENT:
- 1   tablespoon white wine vinegar

1. To prepare soup, heat oil in a Dutch oven over medium heat. Add onion; cook 5 minutes, stirring frequently. Add aniseed, cumin, and garlic; cook 2 minutes, stirring constantly. Stir in broth and next 3 ingredients; bring to a boil. Reduce heat to low; simmer 45 minutes. Place half of bean mixture in blender; process until smooth. Pour puréed mixture into a large bowl. Repeat procedure with remaining bean mixture. Return puréed mixture to pan.

2. To prepare dumplings, lightly spoon masa into a dry measuring cup, and level with a knife. Combine masa, baking powder, and ¼ teaspoon salt. Cut in butter with a pastry blender until mixture resembles coarse meal. Stir in boiling water and cilantro. Divide dough into 10 portions, shaping each into a ball (dust hands with masa to prevent sticking). Make a small indention in each dumpling. Bring bean mixture to a boil. Add dumplings. Reduce heat, and simmer 10 minutes, stirring frequently. Stir in vinegar. Yield: 5 servings (serving size: 1 cup soup and 2 chochoyones).

CALORIES 412 (19% from fat); FAT 8.5g (sat 3.5g, mono 3.1g, poly 1.2g); PROTEIN 20.8g; CARB 65.6g; FIBER 18.4g; CHOL 12mg; IRON 6.2mg; SODIUM 1,018mg; CALC 164mg

Matzo Ball Soup

These much-loved dumplings are made from ground unleavened matzo cracker. They're a favorite during Passover. Chicken thighs and drumsticks flavor the broth, but aren't included in the soup. Make chicken salad with the cooked chicken.

- 7   cups fat-free, less-sodium chicken broth, divided
- 1½ cups unsalted matzo meal
- 2   tablespoons minced fresh onion
- 3   tablespoons vegetable oil
- ½   teaspoon salt, divided
- 2   large egg yolks, lightly beaten
- 1   garlic clove, minced
- 4   cups chopped onion
- 4   cups water
- 1½ cups chopped carrot
- 1½ cups chopped celery
- 10 garlic cloves, crushed
- 8   thyme sprigs
- 8   parsley sprigs
- 4   chicken thighs, skinned (about 1⅓ pounds)
- 4   chicken drumsticks, skinned (about 1⅓ pounds)
- Cooking spray
- 2   tablespoons chopped fresh dill

1. Combine 1¾ cups chicken broth, matzo meal, minced onion, oil, ¼ teaspoon salt, yolks, and minced garlic, stirring well. Cover and chill 1 hour.

2. While matzo mixture chills, combine 5¼ cups broth, ¼ teaspoon salt, chopped onion, and next 8 ingredients; bring to a boil. Reduce heat, and simmer 1 hour, skimming surface as needed. Remove chicken; reserve for another use. Strain broth mixture through a colander into a large bowl; discard solids. Return broth to pan; bring to a boil. Reduce heat, and simmer.

3. Lightly coat hands with cooking spray. Divide matzo mixture evenly into 24 (1½-inch) balls. Gently drop balls into simmering broth. Cover, reduce heat to medium-low, and cook 5 minutes or until done (matzo balls will rise to surface). Remove from heat; stir in dill. Yield: 6 servings (serving size: 1 cup soup and 4 matzo balls).

CALORIES 198 (41% from fat); FAT 9.1g (sat 1.6g, mono 2.4g, poly 4.3g); PROTEIN 9.1g; CARB 19.9g; FIBER 1.2g; CHOL 78mg; IRON 1.4mg; SODIUM 741mg; CALC 23mg

Caldo de Bolas

Caldo de Bolas is a dumpling soup found throughout Ecuador. The dumplings don't traditionally contain flour, but we found them lighter and easier to handle with some added. Use plantains that are heavily mottled and will turn black within a day or two.

FILLING:

¼ cup finely chopped onion
¼ cup finely chopped green bell pepper
½ pound ground sirloin
1 garlic clove, minced
¼ cup low-sodium beef broth
1 tablespoon raisins
1 tablespoon peanut butter

SOUP:

2 teaspoons vegetable oil
1 cup finely chopped onion
⅔ cup finely chopped green bell pepper
3¼ cups low-sodium beef broth
2 cups water
1 teaspoon cumin seed
¼ teaspoon salt
1 (14.5-ounce) can diced tomatoes
1 minced jalapeño pepper, undrained
2 ripe plantains, each cut crosswise into 3 pieces
½ cup all-purpose flour
1 large egg, lightly beaten
½ cup chopped fresh cilantro

1. To prepare filling, cook first 3 ingredients in a large nonstick skillet over medium-high heat until browned, stirring to crumble. Add garlic; cook 5 minutes, stirring frequently. Stir in ¼ cup broth, raisins, and peanut butter. Bring to a boil; cook 2 minutes or until thick. Set aside.
2. To prepare soup, heat oil in a Dutch oven over medium-high heat. Add 1 cup onion and ⅔ cup bell pepper; sauté 5 minutes or until browned. Add 3¼ cups broth and next 5 ingredients; bring to a boil. Reduce heat. Add plantains; simmer 15 minutes or until plantains are tender. Remove plantains from soup; let cool slightly.
3. Place plantains in a large bowl; mash with a potato masher until smooth. Lightly spoon flour into a dry measuring cup; level with a knife. Add flour to plantains; stir until combined. Stir in egg.

Turn dough out onto a floured surface; knead 3 times. Divide dough into 12 equal portions, shaping each portion into a ball. Working with 1 portion at a time (cover remaining dough to prevent drying), place dough on a floured surface. Flatten; make an indention in center using thumb. Spoon about 1 tablespoon beef mixture into indention. Gather edges to encase filling, pinching to seal. Gently roll, using both hands, to form a ball. Return broth to a simmer. Gently drop balls into broth; cover and cook 10 minutes. Sprinkle with cilantro. Yield: 6 servings (serving size: ⅔ cup soup and 2 bolas).

CALORIES 296 (33% from fat); FAT 10.8g (sat 3.4g, mono 4.3g, poly 1.8g); PROTEIN 14.7g; CARB 37.4g; FIBER 4g; CHOL 61mg; IRON 2.8mg; SODIUM 283mg; CALC 48mg

Asian Flavors Menu
serves 4

The gyoza recipe serves 12, so freeze the remaining uncooked dumplings; steam them, unthawed, an extra minute before sautéing.

Vegetarian Gyoza with Spicy Dipping Sauce

Tofu stir-fry*

Hot cooked short-grain rice

*Drain 1 (15-ounce) package extrafirm water-packed tofu; cut tofu into 1-inch pieces. Heat 2 teaspoons vegetable oil in a large nonstick skillet over medium-high heat. Add tofu; sauté 8 minutes or until browned on all sides. Remove tofu from pan; add 1 teaspoon vegetable oil to pan. Add 3 cups coarsely chopped bok choy, 1 cup red bell pepper strips, 1 cup trimmed snow peas, and 3 minced garlic cloves; sauté 3 minutes. Stir in ¼ cup hoisin sauce and tofu.

Vegetarian Gyoza with Spicy Dipping Sauce

Originating in China, where they're known as *jai-ozi*, or pot stickers, these ravioli-like dumplings are now equally popular in Japan. The traditional filling is pork and cabbage, but they're often stuffed with chicken, seafood, or vegetables. This recipe includes directions to make the wrappers, but in a pinch, you can substitute refrigerated wonton wrappers.

SAUCE:

⅓ cup rice vinegar
¼ cup chopped green onions
¼ cup low-sodium soy sauce
½ teaspoon crushed red pepper

WRAPPERS:

2 cups all-purpose flour
⅔ cup water

FILLING:

Cooking spray
4 cups diced shiitake mushroom caps (about ¾ pound)
4 cups finely chopped green cabbage
2 tablespoons chopped green onions
2 tablespoons mirin (sweet rice wine)
2 tablespoons low-sodium soy sauce
2 teaspoons grated peeled fresh ginger
½ teaspoon salt
¼ teaspoon dark sesame oil
3 garlic cloves, minced

REMAINING INGREDIENTS:

24 lettuce leaves
2 tablespoons peanut oil, divided

1. To prepare sauce, combine first 4 ingredients; set aside.
2. To prepare wrappers, lightly spoon flour into dry measuring cups; level with a knife. Combine flour and water in a bowl. Turn dough out onto a floured surface; knead 5 minutes. Cover dough; let rest 30 minutes.
3. To prepare filling, heat a large nonstick skillet coated with cooking spray over medium-high heat. Add mushrooms; cook 3 minutes or until moisture evaporates, stirring frequently. Add cabbage; cook 3 minutes or until softened, stirring frequently. Stir in 2 tablespoons green onions and next 6 ingredients; simmer 2 minutes. Remove from heat; set aside.
4. Divide dough into 4 equal portions. Roll each portion into a 1-inch-thick rope. Cut each rope into 12 equal pieces. Shape each dough piece into a ball. Roll each ball into a 4-inch circle on a floured

surface (cover circles with a damp towel to prevent drying).

5. Working with 1 wrapper at a time, spoon 2 teaspoons mushroom mixture into center of wrapper. Fold in half. Fold top edge of wrapper at ½-inch intervals to form pleats, pressing against bottom edge to seal. Place dumplings, pleated sides down, on a large baking sheet dusted with flour; cover loosely with towel to prevent drying.

6. Line each tier of a 2-tiered (10-inch) bamboo steamer with 3 lettuce leaves. Arrange 6 dumplings, 1-inch apart, in each steamer basket. Stack tiers; cover with steamer lid. Add water to a large skillet to a depth of 1 inch; bring to a boil. Place steamer in pan, and steam dumplings 5 minutes. Remove dumplings from steamer. Repeat procedure with remaining lettuce and dumplings.

7. Heat 1½ teaspoons oil in a large non-stick skillet over medium-high heat. Add 12 dumplings; cook 1½ minutes on each side or until browned. Repeat procedure 3 times with remaining oil and dumplings. Serve with sauce. Yield: 12 servings (serving size: 4 gyoza and 1 tablespoon sauce).

CALORIES 128 (19% from fat); FAT 2.7g (sat 0.4g, mono 1.1g, poly 0.9g); PROTEIN 3.7g; CARB 21.1g; FIBER 1.8g; CHOL 0mg; IRON 1.8mg; SODIUM 377mg; CALC 20mg

How to Make Vegetarian Gyoza

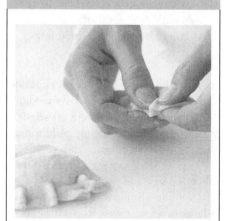

Start at one end of folded wrapper and form pleats at ½-inch intervals.

Putting a Wrap on Spring

A California reader creates Asian appetizers packed with crisp vegetables and shrimp.

Fifteen years ago, Jane Shapton, a freelance writer and classical pianist from Tustin, California, enjoyed eating spring rolls at a small Thai restaurant in San Francisco. She liked them so much that she decided to make some of her own. She remembered their fresh vegetable filling and the spicy dipping sauce served alongside. Developing the recipe was a matter of "pulling things together," Shapton says. "In the back of my mind, I knew I would find something to match them."

Fresh Spring Rolls with Dipping Sauce

DIPPING SAUCE:

2 tablespoons fresh lime juice
1 tablespoon fish sauce
1 tablespoon water
1 tablespoon chile paste with garlic
2 teaspoons grated peeled fresh ginger
1 teaspoon sugar
2 garlic cloves, minced

SPRING ROLLS:

12 (8-inch) round sheets rice paper
3 green leaf lettuce leaves, quartered
3 cups fresh broccoli sprouts or alfalfa sprouts
36 (2-inch) julienne-cut carrot strips
36 (2-inch) julienne-cut cucumber strips
36 (2-inch) julienne-cut yellow bell pepper strips
24 medium shrimp, cooked, peeled, and halved lengthwise
36 fresh mint leaves

1. To prepare sauce, combine first 7 ingredients, stirring with a whisk until sugar dissolves; set aside.

2. To prepare spring rolls, add hot water to a large, shallow dish to a depth of 1 inch. Place 1 rice paper sheet in dish; let stand 30 seconds or just until soft. Place rice paper sheet on a flat surface. Arrange 1 lettuce piece in center of sheet. Top lettuce with ¼ cup sprouts, 3 carrot strips, 3 cucumber strips, 3 bell pepper strips, 4 shrimp halves, and 3 mint leaves. Fold sides of sheet over filling; roll up jelly-roll fashion. Gently press seam to seal. Place spring roll, seam side down, on a serving platter (cover to prevent drying).

3. Repeat procedure with remaining rice paper, lettuce, sprouts, carrot, cucumber, bell pepper, shrimp, and mint. Serve with dipping sauce. Yield: 6 appetizer servings (serving size: 2 rolls and 2 teaspoons sauce).

CALORIES 101 (7% from fat); FAT 0.8g (sat 0.2g, mono 0.1g, poly 0.3g); PROTEIN 7.8g; CARB 16.8g; FIBER 2.1g; CHOL 44mg; IRON 1.7mg; SODIUM 418mg; CALC 40mg

QUICK & EASY
Apricot-Glazed Roasted Asparagus

"When asparagus is in season, it's gorgeous, fresh, and cheap. I came up with this recipe in a moment of creativity; I had a lot of asparagus on hand and wanted to give it a different twist."

—Trisha Kruse, Boise, Idaho

1 pound asparagus spears, trimmed
Cooking spray
2 tablespoons apricot preserves
1 tablespoon low-sodium soy sauce
¼ teaspoon minced garlic
⅛ teaspoon salt

1. Preheat oven to 400°.

2. Place asparagus on a foil-lined jelly-roll pan coated with cooking spray. Combine apricot preserves, soy sauce, garlic, and salt; pour over asparagus. Toss well to coat. Bake at 400° for 10 minutes or until asparagus is crisp-tender. Serve immediately. Yield: 4 servings.

CALORIES 58 (0% from fat); FAT 0g; PROTEIN 3g; CARB 11.6g; FIBER 2.6g; CHOL 0mg; IRON 0.6mg; SODIUM 210mg; CALC 28mg

Slow Cooker Beef Stew

"It's been a long time since I got the original version of this recipe from a high school friend, and I've been tweaking it over the years. Sometimes I'll bake the stew in the oven, but it works just as well in a slow cooker."

—Connie Mudore, Black Earth, Wisconsin

2 tablespoons uncooked granulated tapioca
1 tablespoon sugar
1 tablespoon garlic powder
1 teaspoon salt
3 (5.5-ounce) cans tomato juice
4 cups chopped onion
3 cups chopped celery
2½ cups (¼-inch-thick) slices carrots
2 (8-ounce) packages presliced mushrooms
2 pounds beef stew meat

1. Place first 5 ingredients in a blender, and process until smooth.
2. Combine onion, celery, carrots, mushrooms, and beef in an electric slow cooker, and add juice mixture. Cover and cook on HIGH 5 hours or until beef is tender. Yield: 6 servings (serving size: about 1¾ cups).

CALORIES 345 (29% from fat); FAT 11.1g (sat 4g, mono 4.7g, poly 0.7g); PROTEIN 34.1g; CARB 28.8g; FIBER 5.9g; CHOL 95mg; IRON 5.3mg; SODIUM 811mg; CALC 81mg

Salmon with Roasted Cherry Tomatoes

"It isn't necessary to season the salmon; the tomatoes, thyme, and garlic create such a flavorful sauce. Serve with rice or couscous."

—Teri Goldberg, Los Angeles, California

2 cups cherry tomatoes
1½ teaspoons chopped fresh thyme
1 teaspoon olive oil
¼ teaspoon salt
¼ teaspoon black pepper
2 garlic cloves, minced
Cooking spray
2 (6-ounce) salmon fillets (about 1 inch thick)
2 tablespoons fresh lemon juice

1. Preheat oven to 400°.
2. Combine first 6 ingredients in a jelly-roll pan coated with cooking spray; toss to coat tomatoes. Bake at 400° for 15 minutes. Add fish to pan. Bake 10 minutes or until fish flakes easily when tested with a fork. Serve tomato mixture over fish. Drizzle with lemon juice. Yield: 2 servings (serving size: 1 fillet and ½ cup tomato mixture).

CALORIES 265 (43% from fat); FAT 12.6g (sat 2.7g, mono 6g, poly 2.8g); PROTEIN 28.7g; CARB 9.6g; FIBER 1.8g; CHOL 65mg; IRON 1.2mg; SODIUM 368mg; CALC 37mg

Chocolate and Peanut Butter Cookies

"My husband and I love to create new variations of this recipe, and this is our favorite. We keep the dough in the freezer and make just a few cookies at a time. That way, there's always dough ready for those times when unexpected guests come by for a visit."

—Katie Pewthers, Yorba Linda, California

1 cup all-purpose flour
½ teaspoon baking powder
½ cup granulated sugar
½ cup packed brown sugar
¼ cup butter, softened
2 tablespoons creamy peanut butter
1½ teaspoons vanilla extract
1 large egg white
¾ cup regular oats
½ cup raisins
½ cup semisweet chocolate chips
Cooking spray

1. Preheat oven to 350°.
2. Lightly spoon flour into a dry measuring cup, and level with a knife. Combine flour and baking powder in a small bowl, stirring well with a whisk. Place granulated sugar and next 5 ingredients in a large bowl; beat with a mixer at medium speed until well blended (about 2 minutes). Add flour mixture, oats, raisins, and chocolate chips, stirring until well combined. Cover and freeze 10 minutes.
3. Divide dough into 30 equal portions, shaping each into a ball. Place 2 inches apart on baking sheets coated with cooking spray, and flatten with bottom of a glass. Bake at 350° for 15 minutes. Remove cookies from pans, and cool completely on wire racks. Yield: 30 cookies (serving size: 1 cookie).

CALORIES 91 (31% from fat); FAT 3.1g (sat 1.6g, mono 1g, poly 0.3g); PROTEIN 1.3g; CARB 15.4g; FIBER 0.6g; CHOL 4mg; IRON 0.5mg; SODIUM 33mg; CALC 12mg

Mediterranean Shrimp and Pasta

"I was looking for a recipe to use some of the abundant fresh basil I grow in pots on my back deck, so I modeled this recipe after dishes I've had in local restaurants. It's easy, fresh, and colorful—and a very quick dinner."

—Kelly Lacy, Orlando, Florida

2 teaspoons olive oil
Cooking spray
2 garlic cloves, minced
1 pound medium shrimp, peeled and deveined
2 cups chopped plum tomato
¼ cup thinly sliced fresh basil
⅓ cup chopped pitted kalamata olives
2 tablespoons capers, drained
¼ teaspoon freshly ground black pepper
4 cups hot cooked angel hair pasta (about 8 ounces uncooked pasta)
¼ cup (2 ounces) crumbled feta cheese

1. Heat oil in a large nonstick skillet coated with cooking spray over medium-high heat. Add garlic; sauté 30 seconds. Add shrimp; sauté 1 minute. Add tomato and basil; reduce heat, and simmer 3 minutes or until tomato is tender. Stir in olives, capers, and pepper.
2. Combine shrimp mixture and pasta in a large bowl; toss well. Top with cheese. Yield: 4 servings (serving size: 1½ cups pasta mixture and 1 tablespoon cheese).

CALORIES 424 (21% from fat); FAT 9.7g (sat 3.1g, mono 3.6g, poly 1.7g); PROTEIN 33.4g; CARB 49.7g; FIBER 3g; CHOL 185mg; IRON 6mg; SODIUM 564mg; CALC 163mg

Passover Suite

This collection of savory side dishes and desserts rounds out a Passover table—or any meal—in fine style.

These recipes for both sweets and savories will appeal to everyone at any time—with the added benefit that they work for a Passover menu.

Matzo, Mushroom, and Onion Kugel

The secret to success here is to first brown the matzo in the oven. This savory dish can replace any stuffing served with turkey.

10 (6-inch) matzo crackers
2½ cups fat-free, less-sodium chicken broth
1 cup hot water
¼ cup vegetable oil
3 cups diced onion
⅔ cup grated carrot
1 teaspoon salt
1 teaspoon paprika
½ teaspoon garlic powder
¼ teaspoon freshly ground black pepper
3 garlic cloves, minced
2 (8-ounce) packages presliced mushrooms
2 tablespoons chopped fresh parsley
4 large egg whites
2 large eggs
Cooking spray
Parsley sprigs (optional)

1. Preheat oven to 375°.
2. Place crackers in a single layer on a baking sheet; bake at 375° for 5 minutes or until lightly browned. Break crackers into small pieces, and place in a large bowl. Pour broth and water over matzo, and let stand 10 minutes, stirring occasionally.
3. Heat oil in a large nonstick skillet over medium heat. Add onion; cover and cook 5 minutes, stirring occasionally.

Add carrot and next 6 ingredients; cover and cook 5 minutes or until onion is tender. Add mushroom mixture and chopped parsley to matzo mixture, stirring well. Combine egg whites and eggs in a bowl; stir with a whisk. Add egg mixture to matzo mixture; stir well.
4. Press matzo mixture into a 10-inch deep-dish pie plate coated with cooking spray. Bake, covered, at 375° for 20 minutes. Uncover and bake an additional 18 minutes or until lightly browned. Let kugel stand 5 minutes, and cut into wedges. Garnish with parsley sprigs, if desired. Yield: 12 servings (serving size: 1 wedge).

CALORIES 216 (29% from fat); FAT 7g (sat 1.1g, mono 1.8g, poly 3.6g); PROTEIN 7.6g; CARB 30.6g; FIBER 2.1g; CHOL 43mg; IRON 1.4mg; SODIUM 390mg; CALC 28mg

STAFF FAVORITE • MAKE AHEAD
Matzo Buttercrunch

Toasting the matzo enhances the flavor and helps it stay crisp. Keep a close eye on the buttercrunch as they bake. Spread the sugar mixture evenly over the matzo crackers, and remove them from the oven as soon as they begin to bubble. This recipe is sticky, so cover your baking sheet with aluminum foil and parchment paper for easy cleanup.

6 (6-inch) unsalted matzo crackers
½ cup unsalted butter
1 cup packed brown sugar
½ cup semisweet chocolate minichips, finely chopped

1. Preheat oven to 375°.
2. Line a jelly-roll pan with aluminum foil; cover foil with parchment paper. Arrange crackers in a single layer on pan, cutting as necessary to fit; bake at 375° for 5 minutes or until lightly browned. Reduce oven temperature to 350°.
3. Combine butter and sugar in a small heavy saucepan; bring to a boil, stirring frequently. Cook 3 minutes, stirring constantly; pour mixture over matzo. Bake at 350° for 10 minutes or until mixture bubbles. Sprinkle evenly with chocolate. Cool slightly; refrigerate 30 minutes or until chocolate is set. Break into 36 pieces. Yield: 36 servings (serving size: 1 piece).

CALORIES 72 (40% from fat); FAT 3.2g (sat 2g, mono 1g, poly 0.1g); PROTEIN 0.5g; CARB 10.8g; FIBER 0.1g; CHOL 7mg; IRON 0.4mg; SODIUM 28mg; CALC 12mg

MAKE AHEAD
Homemade Beet Horseradish

This is the quintessential Passover side—it's great served with beef. Allow at least a day for the flavors to mellow and mature. Refrigerate up to 2 weeks. Use the grating disk of a food processor to shred the beets and horseradish finely before pulsing with the steel blade.

2 (10-ounce) beets, peeled and finely shredded
1 fresh horseradish root (about 2½ ounces), trimmed, peeled, and finely shredded
½ cup red wine vinegar
½ cup sugar
2 teaspoons salt

1. Combine beets and horseradish in a food processor, and pulse 20 times. Add vinegar, sugar, and salt; process 2 minutes or until pasty. Spoon into a bowl; cover and chill overnight. Yield: 2 cups (serving size: 2 tablespoons).

CALORIES 39 (2% from fat); FAT 0.1g (sat 0g, mono 0g, poly 0.1g); PROTEIN 0.5g; CARB 9.8g; FIBER 0.8g; CHOL 0mg; IRON 0.2mg; SODIUM 295mg; CALC 9mg

Passover Chopped Layered Salad

Use jarred beets and jarred bell peppers. Assemble up to three days ahead, but add beets and eggs just before serving.

DRESSING:

⅓ cup vegetable broth
¼ cup red wine vinegar
2 tablespoons olive oil
1 teaspoon sugar
½ teaspoon salt
½ teaspoon dried Italian seasoning
¼ teaspoon freshly ground black pepper
3 garlic cloves, minced

SALAD:

4 cups finely chopped romaine lettuce
2 cups finely chopped iceberg lettuce
½ cup finely chopped radicchio
½ cup thinly sliced Belgian endive (about 1 small head)
1½ cups finely chopped English cucumber
½ cup finely chopped celery
1 cup finely shredded carrot
1¾ cups finely chopped red bell pepper
1 cup diced seeded plum tomato (about 4 tomatoes)
1 cup finely chopped red onion
½ cup thinly sliced green onions
2 cups diced cooked beets
3 hard-cooked large eggs, finely chopped
1 tablespoon chopped fresh flat-leaf parsley (optional)

1. To prepare dressing, combine first 8 ingredients, stirring with a whisk. Set aside.
2. To prepare salad, arrange romaine in bottom of a 2-quart glass bowl or trifle dish; top with iceberg. Layer radicchio and next 8 ingredients evenly over lettuces. Drizzle with dressing. Cover and chill 4 hours or overnight.
3. Arrange beets over green onions; top with eggs. Garnish with parsley, if desired. Yield: 10 servings (serving size: about 1 cup).

CALORIES 82 (33% from fat); FAT 3.3g (sat 0.7g, mono 1.7g, poly 0.5g); PROTEIN 3.8g; CARB 10.7g; FIBER 3.6g; CHOL 53mg; IRON 1.5mg; SODIUM 244mg; CALC 53mg

Sweet Potato and Carrot Tzimmes

A glaze of ginger ale and cranberry and orange juices gives this casserole a sweet flavor. Traditionally, this dish consists of dried plums instead of the dried apricots and raisins used in this recipe.

1 cup (¼-inch-thick) slices carrot
2 pounds sweet potato, peeled and cut into 2-inch wedges
3 tablespoons vegetable oil
½ cup dried apricots, cut into ¼-inch strips
½ cup packed brown sugar
¼ cup golden raisins
¼ teaspoon salt
¼ teaspoon freshly ground black pepper
½ cup ginger ale
¼ cup cranberry juice cocktail
2 tablespoons fresh orange juice

1. Preheat oven to 350°.
2. Place carrot and potato in a 13 x 9-inch baking dish. Drizzle with oil, and toss well. Sprinkle apricots and next 4 ingredients over potato mixture; toss to combine. Combine ginger ale and juices; drizzle over potato mixture. Bake, covered, at 350° for 1 hour and 15 minutes or until potato is tender, stirring once after 45 minutes. Uncover; bake an additional 15 minutes or until liquid is slightly thick. Yield: 10 servings (serving size: about ¾ cup).

CALORIES 270 (18% from fat); FAT 5.3g (sat 0.8g, mono 1.2g, poly 3g); PROTEIN 2.6g; CARB 54.2g; FIBER 4.4g; CHOL 0mg; IRON 1.3mg; SODIUM 33mg; CALC 55mg

---

How to Make Your Own Matzo Cake Meal

Matzo cake meal is nothing more than very finely processed matzo meal. If you're unable to find it, you can easily make your own. Measure the amount of matzo meal that the recipe specifies, and pulse it about 10 times in a food processor.

Passover Baklava Cake

This rich, nutty confection is soaked in a honey-citrus syrup, giving it a flavor much like baklava. For the best flavor, soak overnight, and serve chilled.

CAKE:

Cooking spray
¾ cup granulated sugar
¼ cup packed brown sugar
2 tablespoons vegetable oil
3 large egg whites
2 large eggs
½ cup matzo cake meal
½ cup finely chopped walnuts
¼ cup finely chopped hazelnuts
3 tablespoons fresh orange juice
¼ teaspoon salt
¼ teaspoon ground cinnamon

SYRUP:

⅔ cup granulated sugar
¼ cup honey
⅓ cup fresh orange juice
3 tablespoons water
1 tablespoon fresh lemon juice
¼ teaspoon ground cinnamon

1. Preheat oven to 350°.
2. To prepare cake, coat a 9-inch round cake pan with cooking spray. Place ¾ cup granulated sugar and next 4 ingredients in a large bowl; beat with a mixer at medium speed 2 minutes. Lightly spoon matzo cake meal into a dry measuring cup, and level with a knife. Stir in matzo cake meal and next 5 ingredients, beating until well blended. Pour into prepared pan; bake at 350° for 35 minutes or until cake springs back when lightly touched. Cool completely.
3. To prepare syrup, combine ⅔ cup granulated sugar and remaining 5 ingredients in a heavy saucepan; bring to a boil. Reduce heat; simmer 25 minutes or until slightly thick, stirring occasionally. Cool completely. Pierce top of cake several times with a fork; pour syrup over cake. Cover and chill. Yield: 12 servings.

CALORIES 233 (30% from fat); FAT 7.8g (sat 0.9g, mono 2.9g, poly 3.7g); PROTEIN 3.6g; CARB 39.3g; FIBER 0.8g; CHOL 35mg; IRON 0.7mg; SODIUM 76mg; CALC 20mg

Apple, Rhubarb, and Sour Cherry Passover Cobbler

Potato starch is sometimes called potato flour. This sweet-tart cobbler is a refreshing change from traditional Passover desserts.

TOPPING:
- 1 cup unsalted matzo meal
- ½ cup potato starch
- ½ cup packed brown sugar
- ¼ teaspoon salt
- Dash of ground cinnamon
- ½ cup chilled butter, cut into small pieces
- 2 tablespoons fresh orange juice

FILLING:
- 5 cups sliced peeled McIntosh apples (about 1¾ pounds)
- 1 cup chopped frozen rhubarb, thawed
- ⅔ cup granulated sugar
- ½ cup canned pitted sour cherries, drained
- ¼ cup fresh orange juice
- 2 tablespoons potato starch
- ½ teaspoon ground cinnamon

REMAINING INGREDIENT:
- Cooking spray

1. Preheat oven to 350°.
2. To prepare topping, spoon matzo meal into a dry measuring cup; level with a knife. Combine matzo meal and next 4 ingredients, stirring with a whisk. Cut in butter with a pastry blender or 2 knives until mixture resembles coarse meal. Add 2 tablespoons orange juice; stir just until moist.
3. To prepare filling, combine apples and next 6 ingredients; toss gently.
4. Press 1½ cups matzo mixture in bottom of an 11 x 7-inch baking dish coated with cooking spray. Spoon filling over crust; top evenly with remaining matzo mixture. Bake at 350° for 45 minutes or until filling is bubbly and crust is lightly browned. Let stand 10 minutes before serving. Yield: 10 servings.

CALORIES 291 (30% from fat); FAT 9.8g (sat 5.7g, mono 2.8g, poly 0.5g); PROTEIN 1.3g; CARB 52.3g; FIBER 3.3g; CHOL 25mg; IRON 1.2mg; SODIUM 157mg; CALC 27mg

Passover Pecan Bars

This dessert is reminiscent of pecan pie—with the extra sweetness of maple syrup and flaked coconut baked right in.

CRUST:
- 1 cup matzo cake meal
- ½ cup matzo meal
- 1 cup packed brown sugar
- ¼ cup ground toasted pecans
- ½ teaspoon ground cinnamon
- ¼ teaspoon salt
- 6 tablespoons unsalted butter
- 1 large egg white, lightly beaten
- Cooking spray

FILLING:
- 1⅓ cups packed brown sugar
- ½ cup maple syrup
- 2 tablespoons unsalted butter, melted
- 1 tablespoon vanilla extract
- 1 teaspoon fresh lemon juice
- ⅛ teaspoon salt
- 5 large egg whites, lightly beaten
- 1 large egg, lightly beaten
- ⅓ cup flaked sweetened coconut
- 2 tablespoons finely chopped pecans

1. Preheat oven to 350°.
2. To prepare crust, lightly spoon matzo cake meal and matzo meal into dry measuring cups, and level with a knife. Combine matzo cake meal, matzo meal, and next 4 ingredients, stirring with a whisk; cut in 6 tablespoons unsalted butter with a pastry blender or 2 knives until mixture resembles coarse meal. Add 1 egg white, stirring just until moist; press into bottom of a 13 x 9-inch baking pan coated with cooking spray. Bake at 350° for 20 minutes or until edges begin to brown; cool 15 minutes.
3. To prepare filling, combine 1⅓ cups brown sugar and next 7 ingredients, stirring well with a whisk. Stir in coconut and chopped pecans. Pour over prepared crust. Bake at 350° for 30 minutes or until set. Cool to room temperature. Cover and chill at least 1 hour. Cut into bars. Yield: 48 servings (serving size: 1 bar).

CALORIES 89 (29% from fat); FAT 2.9g (sat 1.5g, mono 1g, poly 0.3g); PROTEIN 1g; CARB 15.3g; FIBER 0.2g; CHOL 10mg; IRON 0.4mg; SODIUM 51mg; CALC 14mg

season's best
Pasta Primavera

Tender asparagus and tiny fresh green peas are the quintessential ingredients in this Italian classic.

Pasta Primavera

- ½ pound uncooked fusilli (short twisted spaghetti)
- 2 cups (1-inch) diagonally cut thin asparagus (about ¾ pound)
- ½ cup shelled green peas (about ¾ pound unshelled green peas)
- 1 teaspoon olive oil
- Cooking spray
- 1 small yellow bell pepper, cut into julienne strips
- 1 small red onion, thinly sliced
- 2 garlic cloves, minced
- 1 cup halved cherry tomatoes
- ⅔ cup fat-free, less-sodium chicken broth
- ⅓ cup whipping cream
- ½ teaspoon salt
- ½ teaspoon crushed red pepper
- ¼ cup (1 ounce) grated fresh Parmesan cheese
- ¼ cup thinly sliced fresh basil

1. Cook pasta according to package directions, omitting salt and fat. Add asparagus and peas during last minute of cooking. Drain; place in a large bowl.
2. Heat oil in a large nonstick skillet coated with cooking spray over medium-high heat. Add bell pepper, onion, and garlic; sauté 5 minutes. Add tomatoes; sauté 1 minute. Stir in broth, whipping cream, salt, and red pepper; cook 2 minutes or until thoroughly heated.
3. Add tomato mixture to pasta mixture; toss to coat. Sprinkle with cheese and basil. Serve immediately. Yield: 4 servings (serving size: 1½ cups).

CALORIES 364 (28% from fat); FAT 11.2g (sat 6g, mono 3.4g, poly 0.6g); PROTEIN 14.1g; CARB 54g; FIBER 5.4g; CHOL 31mg; IRON 3.2mg; SODIUM 476mg; CALC 125mg

Popovers Anytime

Now a California reader can enjoy a family favorite every day.

As a youngster, Andrea Lawson of San Clemente, California, really enjoyed popovers. Her grandmother lovingly prepared them on special occasions and holidays. But with 50 percent of the calories from fat, this recipe pushed the seemingly wholesome bread over the limits.

The first small adjustment was to switch from whole milk to 1% low-fat milk, which saved almost 50 calories and 5.5 grams of fat. Cutting the number of eggs in half decreased the fat by another 5.5 grams. But the most significant cut in fat—22.5 grams—resulted when we slashed two-thirds of the original amount of butter. These changes more than halved the fat without changing the popovers' voluptuous shape, golden crust, and, most important, flavor.

Popovers

(pictured on page 110)

Use a pastry brush to oil the popover cups. A muffin tin works, also, but the cups are smaller, so you'll get popovers that need 5 minutes less time in the oven. The popovers puff more when you take some of the chill out of the eggs and milk. Although it's tempting, don't open the oven door to peek at the popovers—use the oven light and view through the glass to see if they're golden brown.

  1 cup all-purpose flour
  ½ teaspoon salt
  1 cup 1% low-fat milk
  2 large eggs, lightly beaten
  1 tablespoon butter, melted
Cooking spray
  1 teaspoon vegetable oil

1. Preheat oven to 375°.

2. Lightly spoon flour into a dry measuring cup; level with a knife. Combine flour and salt, stirring with a whisk. Combine milk and eggs in a medium bowl, stirring with a whisk until blended; let stand 30 minutes. Gradually add flour mixture, stirring well with a whisk. Stir in butter.

3. Coat 9 popover cups with cooking spray; brush oil evenly in cups to coat. Place popover cups in a 375° oven for 5 minutes. Divide batter evenly among prepared popover cups. Bake at 375° for 40 minutes or until golden. Serve immediately. Yield: 9 servings (serving size: 1 popover).

CALORIES 141 (32% from fat); FAT 5g (sat 2.1g, mono 1.5g, poly 0.8g); PROTEIN 5.6g; CARB 18.1g; FIBER 0.6g; CHOL 78mg; IRON 1.2mg; SODIUM 257mg; CALC 62mg

BEFORE	AFTER
SERVING SIZE	
1 popover	
CALORIES PER SERVING	
198	141
FAT	
10.9g	5g
PERCENT OF TOTAL CALORIES	
50%	32%

Something for Everyone

These hearty party dishes bring vegetarians and carnivores together happily.

Preparing entrées that appeal to both meat eaters and vegetarians takes a lot of the stress out of entertaining. You don't have to worry about serving something that one or more of your guests won't eat. A strict vegetarian will not eat meat or fish, but a dedicated carnivore will rarely refuse a luscious plate of pasta. With these satisfying dishes, all you need to round out the meal is a salad and good bread.

Polenta with Smoky Mushroom Ragoût

Baking polenta in the oven, as opposed to using the traditional method of stovetop cooking, frees you so you can prepare the mushroom topping. Oyster mushrooms are fan-shaped and have a peppery bite that softens during cooking. The smokiness of chipotle chiles unexpectedly complements the mushrooms.

POLENTA:

  6 cups water
1½ cups dry polenta
  1 tablespoon butter, cut into small
     pieces
1½ teaspoons salt

RAGOÛT:

  1 tablespoon olive oil
  2 cups chopped onion
  8 cups sliced oyster mushroom caps
     (about 1½ pounds)
  ½ teaspoon salt
  ¼ cup Côtes du Rhône or other
     fruity red wine
  1 tablespoon chopped drained canned
     chipotle chiles in adobo sauce
  1 teaspoon dried oregano
  3 garlic cloves, minced
  1 (28-ounce) can whole tomatoes,
     drained and chopped

REMAINING INGREDIENTS:

  2 cups (8 ounces) crumbled queso
     fresco cheese
  2 tablespoons chopped fresh cilantro

1. Preheat oven to 350°.

2. To prepare polenta, combine first 4 ingredients in a 13 x 9-inch baking dish, stirring well. Bake at 350° for 1 hour or until liquid is absorbed. Cover polenta, and keep warm.

3. To prepare ragoût, while polenta bakes, heat oil in a large Dutch oven over medium-high heat. Add onion, and sauté 5 minutes or until tender. Add mushrooms and ½ teaspoon salt; cook 10 minutes or until mushrooms release moisture and begin to brown, stirring occasionally. Add wine, chiles, oregano, and garlic. Reduce heat to medium, and cook 1 minute or until liquid evaporates, stirring constantly. Stir in chopped tomatoes, and cook over low heat 15 minutes or until mixture thickens slightly, stirring occasionally.

4. Spoon ragoût over polenta; sprinkle evenly with cheese. Bake at 350° for 15 minutes or until cheese begins to melt. Sprinkle with cilantro. Yield: 8 servings.

CALORIES 250 (20% from fat); FAT 5.6g (sat 2.0g, mono 2.4g, poly 0.3g); PROTEIN 11.3g; CARB 38.9g; FIBER 5.8g; CHOL 13mg; IRON 2.5mg; SODIUM 769mg; CALC 108mg

---

STAFF FAVORITE

Mushroom Lasagna with Creamy Béchamel

Lots of porcini, shiitake, and cremini mushrooms are smothered in a creamy sauce for this tasty entrée. The white sauce, or béchamel, for the lasagna is thinner than traditional ones. It will just coat the back of a wooden spoon, but it thickens and soaks into the noodles as the lasagna bakes.

MUSHROOM FILLING:

- 2 cups boiling water
- 1 cup dried porcini mushrooms (about 1 ounce)
- 1 tablespoon olive oil
- 2 cups chopped onion
- 4 garlic cloves, minced
- 8 cups sliced shiitake mushroom caps (about 1½ pounds)
- 3 cups sliced cremini mushrooms (about ½ pound)
- ½ teaspoon salt
- ½ cup Côtes du Rhône or other fruity red wine
- 1 tablespoon low-sodium soy sauce
- ¼ cup chopped fresh parsley
- 2 teaspoons chopped fresh or ¾ teaspoon dried rosemary
- ¼ teaspoon freshly ground black pepper

BÉCHAMEL:

- 3 cups 1% low-fat milk
- 2 tablespoons butter
- 3 tablespoons sifted all-purpose flour
- ½ teaspoon salt
- ¼ teaspoon freshly ground black pepper
- ⅛ teaspoon ground nutmeg

REMAINING INGREDIENTS:

- Cooking spray
- 1 (8-ounce) package precooked lasagna noodles
- 1 cup (4 ounces) grated fresh Parmesan cheese

1. To prepare filling, combine water and porcini in a small bowl; let stand 30 minutes. Drain porcini through a sieve over a bowl, squeezing porcini to extract liquid. Reserve 1½ cups liquid; discard remaining liquid. Rinse porcini, and drain. Chop coarsely; set aside.

2. Heat oil in a large Dutch oven over medium-high heat. Add onion; sauté 5 minutes or until tender. Add garlic; sauté 30 seconds. Add shiitake mushrooms, cremini mushrooms, and ½ teaspoon salt. Sauté 5 minutes or until mushrooms release moisture and begin to brown. Stir in porcini, wine, and soy sauce. Cook 4 minutes or until liquid almost evaporates, stirring frequently. Stir in parsley and rosemary. Add reserved porcini liquid; bring to a simmer. Cook until liquid is reduced to ¾ cup (about 10 minutes). Remove from heat; stir in ¼ teaspoon pepper.

3. To prepare béchamel, place milk in a 4-cup glass measure. Microwave at HIGH 3 minutes or until hot; stir after 2 minutes. Melt butter in a large, heavy saucepan over medium heat. Add flour; stir with a whisk. Cook 1 minute or until bubbly; stir constantly. Gradually add milk; stir constantly with a whisk. Bring to a simmer; cook over low heat 8 minutes or until slightly thick, stirring frequently. Remove from heat, and stir in ½ teaspoon salt, ¼ teaspoon pepper, and nutmeg.

4. Preheat oven to 350°.

5. Spread ½ cup béchamel in bottom of an 11 x 7-inch baking dish coated with cooking spray. Arrange 3 noodles over béchamel; top with ½ cup béchamel. Top with 1 cup mushroom mixture. Sprinkle with ¼ cup cheese. Repeat layers three times (dish will be very full). Cover with foil; place baking dish on a baking sheet. Bake at 350° for 30 minutes. Uncover lasagna; bake an additional 15 minutes or until cheese melts. Yield: 8 servings.

CALORIES 304 (30% from fat); FAT 10.3g (sat 5g, mono 3.5g, poly 0.9g); PROTEIN 17.5g; CARB 37.4g; FIBER 3.7g; CHOL 21mg; IRON 3.5mg; SODIUM 671mg; CALC 304mg

---

Southwestern Veggie Plate Menu

serves 9

Bagged slaw and purchased ice cream round out an easy, homey casserole.

Southwestern Succotash Pot Pie

Creamy coleslaw*

Vanilla ice cream with fat-free caramel sauce

*Combine 7 cups cabbage-and-carrot coleslaw, 1 cup yellow bell pepper strips, and 1 cup (1-inch) slices green onions in a large bowl. Combine ⅓ cup light mayonnaise, ¼ cup low-fat buttermilk, 1 tablespoon sugar, 2½ tablespoons cider vinegar, 2 teaspoons Dijon mustard, ½ teaspoon salt, and ½ teaspoon black pepper, stirring with a whisk. Drizzle dressing over slaw; toss to coat.

MAKE AHEAD

Southwestern Succotash Pot Pie

Ancho chile powder gives this casserole a mild, slightly fruity chile flavor. Most supermarkets now carry ancho chile powder, but if you can't find it, substitute regular chili powder. Make and refrigerate the filling up to a day ahead. Serve a colorful coleslaw on the side.

SUCCOTASH:

- Cooking spray
- 3 cups chopped onion
- 4 garlic cloves, minced
- 2 jalapeño peppers, seeded and finely chopped
- 7 cups chopped zucchini (about 2 pounds)
- 3 cups fresh corn kernels (about 5 ears)
- 1 tablespoon ancho chile powder (such as McCormick's)
- 1 teaspoon salt
- ½ teaspoon freshly ground black pepper
- 1 cup (4 ounces) crumbled feta cheese
- 2 (15-ounce) cans black beans, rinsed and drained

Continued

TOPPING:

- 1 cup whole wheat flour
- 1 cup all-purpose flour
- 2 teaspoons baking powder
- 1 teaspoon dried oregano
- ½ teaspoon baking soda
- ¼ teaspoon salt
- ¼ cup chilled butter, cut into small pieces
- ½ cup 1% low-fat milk
- ½ cup plain fat-free yogurt
- 1 large egg, lightly beaten

1. To prepare succotash, heat a large nonstick skillet coated with cooking spray over medium-high heat. Add onion; sauté 5 minutes or until tender. Add garlic and jalapeño; sauté 30 seconds. Add zucchini; sauté 5 minutes or until zucchini is crisp-tender. Stir in corn; sauté 5 minutes or until corn is crisp-tender. Remove from heat; stir in chile powder, 1 teaspoon salt, and black pepper. Combine zucchini mixture, cheese, and beans in a 13 x 9-inch baking dish coated with cooking spray.

2. Preheat oven to 375°.

3. To prepare topping, lightly spoon flours into dry measuring cups, and level with a knife. Combine flours, baking powder, oregano, baking soda, and ¼ teaspoon salt in a medium bowl, stirring with a whisk. Cut in butter with a pastry blender or 2 knives until mixture resembles coarse meal. Combine milk and yogurt, and add milk mixture to flour mixture, stirring just until moist. Drop dough by tablespoonfuls onto zucchini mixture. Brush beaten egg over topping. Bake at 375° for 30 minutes or until topping is golden. Yield: 9 servings.

CALORIES 322 (28% from fat); FAT 10.1g (sat 5.6g, mono 2.6g, poly 1.1g); PROTEIN 14.6g; CARB 50.4g; FIBER 8.9g; CHOL 49mg; IRON 3.8mg; SODIUM 913mg; CALC 227mg

Winter Vegetable Stew over Couscous

This dish serves a crowd. Prepare the couscous as the vegetable mixture simmers. Try serving with *harissa*, a Tunisian hot sauce found in Middle Eastern markets and large grocery stores.

- 11½ cups water, divided
- 4 cups vertically sliced onion
- 3 cups (1-inch) cubed peeled turnips (about 1 pound)
- 2 cups thinly sliced leek
- 1½ cups (½-inch-thick) slices carrot
- 1 bay leaf
- 4 cups (1-inch) cubed peeled butternut squash (about 1½ pounds)
- 1 teaspoon ground cumin
- ¾ teaspoon ground red pepper
- ½ teaspoon ground cinnamon
- Dash of saffron
- 4 garlic cloves, minced
- 1 (15½-ounce) can chickpeas (garbanzo beans), rinsed and drained
- 6 cups chopped Swiss chard (about 12 ounces)
- ½ cup chopped cilantro
- 2½ teaspoons salt, divided
- ½ teaspoon freshly ground black pepper
- 2 tablespoons fresh lemon juice
- 3 cups uncooked couscous
- 2 tablespoons extravirgin olive oil
- 1½ cups (6 ounces) crumbled goat or feta cheese

1. Combine 10 cups water, onion, and next 4 ingredients in a large Dutch oven; bring to a boil. Cover, reduce heat, and simmer 30 minutes. Remove 2 cups cooking liquid; set aside. Add squash and next 6 ingredients to onion mixture. Simmer

25 minutes or until squash is tender. Stir in chard, cilantro, 2 teaspoons salt, and black pepper; cook 5 minutes or until chard wilts. Stir in juice. Discard bay leaf.

2. Place couscous in a large bowl. Combine reserved cooking liquid and 1½ cups water in a small saucepan; bring to a boil. Stir in ½ teaspoon salt and oil. Pour oil mixture over couscous; stir well to combine. Cover and let stand 20 minutes or until liquid is absorbed. Fluff with a fork. Serve vegetable mixture over couscous. Top with crumbled cheese. Yield: 10 servings (serving size: ¾ cup couscous, about 1 cup vegetable mixture, and about 2½ tablespoons cheese).

CALORIES 381 (18% from fat); FAT 7.6g (sat 3g, mono 3.1g, poly 0.9g); PROTEIN 13.7g; CARB 66.1g; FIBER 9.3g; CHOL 8mg; IRON 3.3mg; SODIUM 833mg; CALC 141mg

Sweet Pepper and Green Bean Risotto

Having all the necessary ingredients prepared before beginning a risotto is best—the dish needs constant attention once it's started.

- 2 quarts water
- 3½ cups (2-inch) cut green beans (about ¾ pound)
- 3 (14½-ounce) cans vegetable broth
- 2 cups water
- 2 tablespoons olive oil
- 1 cup finely chopped onion
- 4 cups red bell pepper strips (about 3 peppers)
- 2 teaspoons chopped fresh or ¾ teaspoon dried thyme
- 3 garlic cloves, minced
- 2½ cups uncooked Arborio rice
- ¾ cup dry white wine
- ¼ teaspoon saffron threads, crushed
- ½ cup (2 ounces) grated fresh Parmesan cheese
- 2 tablespoons fresh lemon juice
- ½ teaspoon salt
- ½ teaspoon freshly ground black pepper

1. Bring 2 quarts water to a boil in a large Dutch oven. Cook beans 4 minutes

The key to vegetarian entertaining
is to choose **dramatic**,
yet familiar, dishes.

or until crisp-tender; drain Rinse with cold water until cool; drain.

2. Combine broth and 2 cups water in a medium saucepan; bring to a simmer (do not boil). Keep warm over low heat.

3. Heat oil in a large Dutch oven over medium-high heat. Add onion; sauté 3 minutes. Add bell pepper, thyme, and garlic; sauté 5 minutes. Add rice; cook 2 minutes, stirring constantly. Reduce heat to medium. Add wine and saffron; cook 2 minutes or until wine is nearly absorbed, stirring constantly. Add 1 cup broth mixture; cook 4 minutes or until liquid is nearly absorbed, stirring constantly. Add remaining broth mixture, ½ cup at a time, stirring constantly until each portion is absorbed before adding next (about 25 minutes total). Stir in beans, and cook 1 minute or until thoroughly heated. Remove from heat, and stir in cheese, juice, salt, and black pepper. Serve immediately. Yield: 8 servings (serving size: about 1⅓ cups).

CALORIES 371 (15% from fat); FAT 6g (sat 1.7g, mono 3g, poly 0.4g); PROTEIN 10.4g; CARB 67.3g; FIBER 4.1g; CHOL 5mg; IRON 1.4mg; SODIUM 900mg; CALC 140mg

MAKE AHEAD
Yellow Squash Gratin

The essence of comfort food, this dish will please kids as well as adults.

Cooking spray
  2 cups chopped onion
  3 garlic cloves, minced
 12 cups yellow squash, halved length-
     wise and cut into ¼-inch-thick
     slices (about 3 pounds)
 ½ cup chopped fresh flat-leaf parsley
1½ teaspoons salt
  1 teaspoon chopped fresh or
     ½ teaspoon dried thyme
 ½ teaspoon freshly ground black
     pepper
  3 cups cooked long-grain rice
 ¾ cup (3 ounces) grated Gruyère or
     Swiss cheese
  3 large eggs, lightly beaten
  1 (1-ounce) slice white bread
 ¼ cup (1 ounce) grated fresh
     Parmesan cheese
  1 tablespoon butter, melted

1. Preheat oven to 375°.
2. Heat a Dutch oven coated with cooking spray over medium-high heat. Add onion, and sauté 5 minutes or until tender. Add garlic; sauté 30 seconds. Add squash; sauté 7 minutes or just until tender. Remove from heat; stir in parsley, salt, thyme, and pepper. Add rice, Gruyère, and eggs, stirring until well combined. Spoon squash mixture into a 13 x 9-inch baking dish coated with cooking spray.
3. Place bread in a food processor; pulse 10 times or until fine crumbs measure ½ cup. Combine breadcrumbs, Parmesan, and butter, tossing to combine. Sprinkle breadcrumb mixture over squash mixture. Bake at 375° for 30 minutes or until topping is lightly browned and filling is set. Let stand 5 minutes before serving. Yield: 8 servings.

CALORIES 247 (29% from fat); FAT 8g (sat 4.1g, mono 2.5g, poly 0.6g); PROTEIN 11.2g; CARB 32.4g; FIBER 4.9g; CHOL 98mg; IRON 2.4mg; SODIUM 599mg; CALC 220mg

Greek Greens and Sweet Onion Pie

Fresh dill and feta cheese flavor this double phyllo-crusted pie. Serve with vegetable soup and crusty bread. Cutting slits into the top phyllo layer allows steam to escape so the crust will be crisp. To serve a larger crowd, double the recipe, and bake the pies side by side in the oven.

  2 quarts water
 12 cups torn Swiss chard (about
     ¾ pound)
  8 cups torn spinach (about ½ pound)
Cooking spray
  2 cups chopped Vidalia or other
     sweet onion
  2 garlic cloves, minced
 ¼ cup chopped fresh dill
 ¼ cup chopped fresh flat-leaf parsley
 ¾ cup (3 ounces) crumbled feta cheese
  2 large eggs, lightly beaten
  2 large egg whites, lightly beaten
 ½ teaspoon freshly ground black
     pepper
 ¼ teaspoon salt
 10 sheets frozen phyllo dough, thawed

1. Bring 2 quarts water to a boil in a large Dutch oven. Add chard and spinach; cook 2 minutes or until tender. Drain well. Place chard mixture on several layers of paper towels; squeeze until barely moist.
2. Preheat oven to 375°.
3. Heat a large nonstick skillet coated with cooking spray over medium-high heat. Add onion; sauté 5 minutes or until tender. Add garlic; sauté 1 minute. Add chard mixture, dill, and parsley, stirring well to combine. Cook 1 minute or until thoroughly heated. Remove from heat. Combine chard mixture, cheese, eggs, and egg whites, tossing well to combine. Stir in pepper and salt.
4. Place 1 phyllo sheet on a large cutting board or work surface (cover remaining dough to prevent drying); lightly coat phyllo sheet with cooking spray. Place phyllo sheet in a 9-inch pie plate coated with cooking spray, allowing edges to overlap plate rim. Repeat procedure with 6 additional phyllo sheets, placing sheets in a crisscross design. Spoon chard mixture into prepared pie plate. Lightly coat 3 phyllo sheets with cooking spray, and place sheets over chard mixture in a crisscross design. Roll excess phyllo into dish to create a decorative edge; press lightly to hold. Cut 4 (2-inch) slits in top of pie; cover with foil. Bake at 375° for 10 minutes. Uncover and bake an additional 30 minutes or until crust is crisp and golden. Cut pie into 8 wedges. Yield: 4 servings (serving size: 2 wedges).

CALORIES 312 (30% from fat); FAT 10.5g (sat 4.8g, mono 3.5g, poly 1.1g); PROTEIN 16.1g; CARB 40.3g; FIBER 5.9g; CHOL 125mg; IRON 6.1mg; SODIUM 955mg; CALC 264mg

Spring Showers

With these make-ahead recipes and scene-setting tips, hosting a party for a bride- or mom-to-be will be a piece of cake.

Spring is a great time to host a shower. The recipes feature crisp, clean flavors and components to make ahead. See our "Tips for Hosting a Shower," on page 98.

Mix-and-Match Shower Menu
serves 12

Grilled Chicken Salad with Feta and Cucumbers

Shrimp and White Bean Salad over Watercress

Spanish Tortilla with Almond Romesco

Salad of Papaya, Mango, and Grapefruit

Fennel, Orange, and Parmigiano Salad

Millet Muffins with Honey-Pecan Butter

Raspberry-Almond Muffins

Strawberries and Oranges with Vanilla-Scented Wine

MAKE AHEAD
Grilled Chicken Salad with Feta and Cucumbers

Stir together all ingredients except herbs; stir in herbs just before serving. You may easily broil the chicken instead of grilling it.

8   (6-ounce) skinless, boneless chicken breast halves
1   tablespoon olive oil
¾   teaspoon salt, divided
¼   teaspoon freshly ground black pepper
Cooking spray
4   cups (½-inch) cubed peeled English cucumber (about 2 large)
2   cups chopped red onion
2   cups (8 ounces) crumbled feta cheese
6   tablespoons chopped fresh mint
6   tablespoons chopped fresh dill
1   tablespoon grated lemon rind
¼   cup fresh lemon juice
Mint sprigs (optional)

1. Prepare grill.
2. Brush chicken with oil; sprinkle with ½ teaspoon salt and pepper. Place chicken on grill rack coated with cooking spray; grill 5 minutes on each side or until done. Place chicken on platter; let cool 5 minutes. Cut each chicken breast half in half lengthwise, and cut chicken pieces crosswise into thin slices.
3. Combine chicken, cucumber, and next 6 ingredients. Sprinkle with ¼ teaspoon salt; toss to combine. Garnish with mint sprigs, if desired. Yield: 12 servings (serving size: 1⅓ cups).

CALORIES 202 (30% from fat); FAT 6.7g (sat 3.4g, mono 2.1g, poly 0.6g); PROTEIN 29.5g; CARB 4.9g; FIBER 1g; CHOL 83mg; IRON 1.2mg; SODIUM 433mg; CALC 121mg

---

MAKE AHEAD
Shrimp and White Bean Salad over Watercress

Combine and chill the shrimp and white bean mixture a day before the party. Be sure to stir the mixture before spooning it over the watercress. You can purchase precooked, peeled shrimp to save time.

2½   pounds large shrimp, peeled and deveined
¾   teaspoon salt, divided
½   teaspoon freshly ground black pepper, divided
Cooking spray
2   (15-ounce) cans cannellini beans, rinsed and drained
¼   cup avocado oil (such as Elysian Isle)
2   tablespoons fresh lemon juice
6   cups trimmed watercress (about 3 bunches)
3   tablespoons chopped fresh chives
Lemon wedges (optional)

1. Prepare grill.
2. Thread shrimp onto 12-inch skewers; sprinkle with ¼ teaspoon salt and ¼ teaspoon pepper. Place skewers on a grill rack coated with cooking spray; grill 3 minutes on each side or until done. Cool completely; remove shrimp from skewers. Place shrimp and beans in a large bowl; toss gently to combine.
3. Combine oil and lemon juice, stirring with a whisk; stir in ½ teaspoon salt and ¼ teaspoon pepper. Drizzle dressing over shrimp mixture; toss gently to combine.
4. Arrange watercress on a large platter, and top with shrimp mixture. Sprinkle evenly with chives. Serve with lemon wedges, if desired. Yield: 12 servings (serving size: about ¾ cup).

CALORIES 190 (30% from fat); FAT 6.4g (sat 0.9g, mono 3.6g, poly 1.3g); PROTEIN 22g; CARB 9.9g; FIBER 2.5g; CHOL 144mg; IRON 3.2mg; SODIUM 421mg; CALC 90mg

---

Whether you're a novice or an entertaining pro, giving a shower can be easy if you plan ahead.

Spanish Tortilla with Almond Romesco

(pictured on page 109)

In Spain, a tortilla is a thin omelet served at room temperature. Roasted potato slices fill this version, while a sharp, tangy red bell pepper sauce tops it. The sauce can be prepared up to 3 days ahead; serve warm, at room temperature, or chilled. Continue your head start by roasting the potato slices early on the day of the party.

ROMESCO:

1 red bell pepper
½ cup chopped seeded plum tomato
2 tablespoons slivered almonds, toasted
2 tablespoons water
2 tablespoons sherry or cider vinegar
1 teaspoon paprika
1 teaspoon extravirgin olive oil
¼ teaspoon salt
¼ teaspoon freshly ground black pepper
⅛ teaspoon crushed red pepper
1 garlic clove, minced
½ (1-ounce) slice white bread, toasted

TORTILLA:

1½ pounds baking potatoes, peeled and cut into ⅛-inch-thick slices
2 teaspoons extravirgin olive oil
Cooking spray
½ teaspoon salt, divided
½ teaspoon freshly ground black pepper, divided
1 cup egg substitute
3 large eggs

1. Preheat broiler.
2. To prepare romesco, cut bell pepper in half lengthwise; discard seeds and membranes. Place bell pepper halves, skin sides up, on a foil-lined baking sheet; flatten with hand. Broil 6 minutes or until blackened. Place in a zip-top plastic bag; seal. Let stand 20 minutes. Peel and chop bell pepper. Place chopped bell pepper in a food processor. Add tomato and next 10 ingredients; process mixture until smooth.
3. Preheat oven to 350°.

4. To prepare tortilla, combine potato and 2 teaspoons oil on a jelly-roll pan coated with cooking spray. Arrange potato slices in a single layer; sprinkle with ¼ teaspoon salt and ¼ teaspoon black pepper. Bake at 350° for 40 minutes or until tender, turning after 20 minutes. Remove from oven.
5. Preheat broiler.
6. Combine egg substitute and eggs in a large bowl; stir with a whisk until foamy (about 2 minutes). Stir in potato slices, ¼ teaspoon salt, and ¼ teaspoon black pepper.
7. Heat a large nonstick ovenproof skillet coated with cooking spray over medium-high heat. Pour egg mixture into pan, spreading potatoes in an even layer with a spatula. Reduce heat to medium; cook 4 minutes or until edges are set and bottom is lightly browned. Wrap handle of skillet with foil; broil 4 minutes or until set. Remove from oven; invert onto a serving platter. Cool at least 5 minutes or to room temperature before serving with romesco sauce. Yield: 12 servings (serving size: 1 tortilla wedge and about 1 tablespoon sauce).

CALORIES 99 (28% from fat); FAT 3.1g (sat 0.6g, mono 1.7g, poly 0.5g); PROTEIN 5.1g; CARB 13.2g; FIBER 1.3g; CHOL 53mg; IRON 1mg; SODIUM 213mg; CALC 22mg

Salad of Papaya, Mango, and Grapefruit

To save time, use bottled grapefruit sections and mango slices from the produce section. Combine ingredients a few hours ahead, but stir in mint just before serving.

2 cups grapefruit sections (about 2 large grapefruit)
2 peeled ripe mangoes, each cut into 12 wedges
1 peeled ripe papaya, cut into thin slices
2 tablespoons fresh lime juice
2 tablespoons extravirgin olive oil
¼ teaspoon salt
⅛ teaspoon black pepper
3 tablespoons chopped fresh mint
12 lime slices

1. Combine first 3 ingredients in a large bowl. Combine juice, oil, salt, and pepper, stirring with a whisk. Drizzle dressing over fruit; sprinkle with mint. Toss gently to combine. Serve with lime slices. Yield: 12 servings (serving size: about ¾ cup).

CALORIES 77 (28% from fat); FAT 2.4g (sat 0.3g, mono 1.7g, poly 0.2g); PROTEIN 0.7g; CARB 15.2g; FIBER 3.5g; CHOL 0mg; IRON 0.1mg; SODIUM 50mg; CALC 18mg

Fennel, Orange, and Parmigiano Salad

(pictured on page 109)

If possible, use a mandoline to cut the fennel into uniform, paper-thin slices. Make the vinaigrette up to 3 days in advance, and shave the cheese up to a day ahead; store separately in the refrigerator.

VINAIGRETTE:

2 teaspoons grated orange rind
6 tablespoons fresh orange juice
2 tablespoons white wine vinegar
2 tablespoons honey
1 tablespoon extravirgin olive oil
½ teaspoon salt
¼ teaspoon freshly ground black pepper
2 garlic cloves, minced

SALAD:

6 cups very thinly sliced fennel bulb (about 3 small bulbs)
6 cups torn Bibb lettuce
2½ cups orange sections
1 cup loosely packed fresh flat-leaf parsley leaves
¾ cup (3 ounces) shaved Parmigiano-Reggiano cheese

1. To prepare vinaigrette, combine first 8 ingredients, stirring with a whisk.
2. To prepare salad, combine fennel, lettuce, orange sections, parsley, and cheese in a large bowl; toss well. Drizzle with vinaigrette; toss gently to combine. Yield: 12 servings (serving size: 1 cup).

CALORIES 95 (30% from fat); FAT 3.2g (sat 1.3g, mono 1.4g, poly 0.2g); PROTEIN 4.3g; CARB 13.9g; FIBER 3.4g; CHOL 5mg; IRON 1.2mg; SODIUM 247mg; CALC 147mg

Getting Started

• Schedule a bridal or baby shower about two months before the big day. The bride will be busy with last-minute details closer to the wedding date, so this timing works best. It also gives the mom-to-be time to set up the nursery with the gifts she receives. Don't plan the event too close to the due date in case the baby arrives early.

• When compiling the guest list, first determine how many people will comfortably fit in your space. Then consult with the guest of honor to obtain names and addresses of invitees. Guests could include family, friends, and coworkers, but in the case of a bridal shower, you'll need to make sure the guests are also invited to the wedding.

• Mail invitations three to four weeks before the party to allow guests time to purchase a gift and to RSVP. Enclose a map with directions.

Get the Look

The ambience you create for your party literally sets the scene.

• Invitations are the first indication of the tone and look of the party. Heavy card stock with calligraphy signifies a formal affair, while a handwritten invitation on homemade paper indicates a more casual gathering.

• Choose accessories that celebrate the guest of honor. If she's an avid cook, make the centerpiece a bouquet of ribbon-wrapped wooden spoons that you'll send home as party favors. If she likes France, decorate with toile prints. Or if she's a spa queen, play soft music, light lavender-scented candles, and use subtle white flower arrangements.

• Achieve a classic look with new table linens or flea market cloths paired with mismatched china.

• If you're hosting a large crowd, look to rental centers for dishes, silverware, stemware, and tablecloths.

• Pretty stemware looks elegant. If you're hosting a crowd, though, consider serving wine Italian-style in sturdy tumblers (or your favorite juice glasses) to reduce breakage.

• Arrange produce rather than flowers for table decor. Immerse radishes in shallow glass vases or jam jars, and rhubarb in a taller vase. Stack oranges and lemons in a bowl with flowers tucked into the crevices (florist tubes keep flowers fresh).

• Use colorful dish towels as napkins. Guests will have a generous swath of fabric to protect their laps, and you'll have a stash of towels after the party.

Gifts

• Ask the guest of honor if she's having any other showers where guests are asked to bring a specific type of gift (for the kitchen or garden, for example). Choose a different theme for the gifts for your shower to avoid overlap, and specify this on the invitations.

• Find out where the couple is registered, and print this information on the invitations. Or ask the selected stores to provide you with drop-in cards that you'll include with the invitations.

• Set up a table for gifts near where your guest of honor will open her presents, whether in the living room, dining room, or on the patio.

• After eating, gather your guests together to view the gift opening. To keep things moving in an orderly fashion, ask four guests to assist: one to record each gift and giver, one to pass around gifts for people to view, one to repackage each gift in the appropriate box with the gift card, and one to dispose of gift wrap.

Organization Makes It Easy

• Optimize flow by setting up a drink station away from the food. A drink table near the entry welcomes arriving guests with a beverage.

• Start your party with an empty dishwasher and empty trash can.

• Enlist help, even if you can't afford a caterer. Ask your aspiring pastry-chef neighbor to make dessert in exchange for your carpool services the next week. The high schooler next door might be available (for a small fee) to send out for ice or run last-minute errands.

• Set the table the day before, and decide what recipes to serve in which dish. If you're short, you'll have time to borrow a platter.

• Put cutlery and napkins at the end of the buffet table so guests don't have to juggle while serving themselves.

Serving Shortcuts

If time is an issue, make one "wow" recipe, then round out the menu with items you've bought at the market and dressed up a little.

• Bagged salads are a great shortcut to embellish in lots of ways. Serve the greens on a shallow platter rather than a deep salad bowl so everyone can enjoy the toppings you sprinkle on top.

• Make a salad more memorable with flavorful oils, like the avocado oil we use in Shrimp and White Bean Salad over Watercress (recipe on page 96). Since the flavors really pop, you can use less oil.

• Stir vinaigrette into drained canned white beans for a simple, filling dish. Spoon them onto a bed of greens, and splurge on a special farmstead cheese to crumble on top.

• Composed butters, like the honey-pecan butter that goes with our Millet Muffins (recipe on page 99), add variety. Make a savory version by mixing minced herbs into softened butter.

• Use frozen bread dough to make free-form flatbreads. Thaw the dough overnight in the fridge, spread on a baking sheet, drizzle with oil, and top with caramelized onions and blue cheese, or a jarred spread like pesto or caponata and shredded mozzarella. Bake at 425° for about 20 minutes or until golden.

• Assemble an antipasto platter composed from your grocer's fancy-food shelf. Use your creativity to arrange green and black olives, sun-dried tomatoes in oil, dried figs and apricots, chickpeas, marinated artichoke hearts, and roasted red bell peppers.

Millet Muffins with Honey-Pecan Butter

Look for millet, a round, pale yellow grain, in health-food stores or in the organic sections of large supermarkets. If you don't have a spice grinder, pulse the millet in a mini food processor or blender, or lightly crush with a mortar and pestle. If using paper muffin cup liners, coat with cooking spray before filling. Make the muffins up to 2 days ahead, and the butter up to 5 days in advance.

MUFFINS:

⅔ cup uncooked millet
¾ cup packed brown sugar
1 large egg
1 cup fat-free buttermilk
¼ cup butter, melted
1½ cups all-purpose flour
1 teaspoon baking powder
¼ teaspoon baking soda
¼ teaspoon salt
Cooking spray

BUTTER:

2 tablespoons butter, softened
2 tablespoons finely chopped pecans, toasted
1 tablespoon honey

1. Preheat oven to 375°.
2. To prepare muffins, place millet in a spice or coffee grinder; pulse 6 times or until lightly crushed. Set aside.
3. Place sugar and egg in a large bowl; beat with a mixer at medium speed until well combined. Stir in millet, buttermilk, and ¼ cup butter.
4. Lightly spoon flour into dry measuring cups; level with a knife. Combine flour, baking powder, baking soda, and salt, stirring with a whisk. Make a well in center of mixture. Add buttermilk mixture; stir just until moist. Let batter stand 5 minutes. Spoon batter into 12 muffin cups coated with cooking spray. Bake at 375° for 18 minutes or until muffins spring back when touched lightly in center. Cool in pan 5 minutes on a wire rack. Remove muffins from pan; place on wire rack.
5. To prepare butter, combine 2 tablespoons butter, pecans, and honey, stirring well to combine. Serve with muffins. Yield: 12 servings (serving size: 1 muffin and 1 teaspoon butter).

CALORIES 229 (30% from fat); FAT 7.6g (sat 3.8g, mono 2.4g, poly 0.8g); PROTEIN 4.3g; CARB 36.3g; FIBER 1.5g; CHOL 33mg; IRON 1.5mg; SODIUM 284mg; CALC 67mg

Raspberry-Almond Muffins

Almond paste is coarser in texture and less sweet than marzipan, but either will work for this recipe. Both can be found on the baking aisle of the supermarket. To make mini muffins, spoon 1 heaping teaspoon of batter into each of 48 miniature muffin cups; bake at 375° for 10 to 12 minutes. To get ahead, bake 2 days before the party.

½ cup granulated sugar
½ cup packed brown sugar
2½ tablespoons almond paste
¼ cup butter, softened
2 large eggs
½ cup fat-free buttermilk
1 teaspoon vanilla extract
1 teaspoon fresh lemon juice
2 cups all-purpose flour
½ teaspoon baking powder
½ teaspoon baking soda
¼ teaspoon salt
1½ cups fresh raspberries
Cooking spray
2 tablespoons turbinado sugar or granulated sugar

1. Preheat oven to 375°.
2. Place first 3 ingredients in a food processor, and process until well blended. Add butter, and pulse 4 or 5 times or just until combined. Add eggs, 1 at a time, pulsing 1 or 2 times after each addition. Add buttermilk, vanilla, and lemon juice; pulse until blended.
3. Lightly spoon flour into dry measuring cups; level with a knife. Combine flour, baking powder, baking soda, and salt in a large bowl, stirring with a whisk. Make a well in center of mixture. Add buttermilk mixture; stir just until moist. Gently fold in raspberries. Let batter stand 5 minutes. Spoon batter into 12 muffin cups coated with cooking spray. Sprinkle with turbinado sugar. Bake at 375° for 22 minutes or until muffins spring back when touched lightly in center. Remove muffins from pans immediately; place on a wire rack. Yield: 12 servings (serving size: 1 muffin).

CALORIES 222 (23% from fat); FAT 5.7g (sat 2.7g, mono 2g, poly 0.6g); PROTEIN 4g; CARB 39.1g; FIBER 1.8g; CHOL 46mg; IRON 1.5mg; SODIUM 186mg; CALC 50mg

Strawberries and Oranges with Vanilla-Scented Wine

Late-harvest Riesling is sweeter than other Rieslings. If you can't find it, try an equally sweet dessert wine such as Sauternes, Muscat, or late-harvest Gewürztraminer. Prepare and chill this refreshingly light dessert earlier in the day. If hosting a baby shower, honor the mom-to-be with a nonalcoholic version using white grape juice in place of the wine.

2 cups late-harvest Riesling or other dessert wine
6 (4-inch) strips orange rind
1 cup fresh orange juice
2 tablespoons sugar
1 (6-inch) piece vanilla bean, split lengthwise
6 cups halved strawberries
2½ cups orange sections
Mint sprigs (optional)

1. Combine first 4 ingredients in a medium saucepan. Scrape seeds from vanilla bean; add seeds and bean to wine mixture. Bring to a boil; reduce heat, and simmer 5 minutes. Strain mixture through a sieve over a large bowl; discard solids. Let cool 30 minutes. Stir in strawberries and orange sections. Cover and chill. Garnish with mint sprigs, if desired. Yield: 12 servings (serving size: ⅔ cup).

CALORIES 60 (6% from fat); FAT 0.4g (sat 0g, mono 0.1g, poly 0.2g); PROTEIN 1g; CARB 14.5g; FIBER 2.7g; CHOL 0mg; IRON 0.5mg; SODIUM 4mg; CALC 31mg

The Chef Shapes Up

Late hours and easy access to high-fat foods took their toll on Chef James Boyce until he turned his life around.

James Boyce's résumé touts a degree from the Culinary Institute of America and tours of duty at New York's famed Le Cirque, Las Vegas's Caesars Palace, and San Diego's Loews Coronado Bay Resort. He garnered more accolades when he ran food operations at The Phoenician resort in Scottsdale, Arizona, from 1999 to 2002. At its headlining restaurant, Mary Elaine's, he earned top rankings from Mobil and AAA, and was nominated best Southwest chef by the James Beard Foundation in 2002.

But Boyce's weight soared along with his career. By 1998, he weighed nearly 300 pounds and decided to make a change. And he did. Here are some of his recipes.

Seared Scallops with Port-Poached Figs and Apple Salad

This salad contrasts temperatures and flavors—the warm scallops rest atop cool greens, and the combination of tart apples and vinegar is tamed with the sweetness of figs and port.

 1 cup dried figs
 1 cup port or other sweet red wine
 2 tablespoons sugar
 2 tablespoons balsamic vinegar
 2 tablespoons orange juice
 2 Granny Smith apples, peeled and
    sliced (about 1 pound)
 1 tablespoon extravirgin olive oil,
    divided
 ½ teaspoon salt
 ¼ teaspoon freshly ground black
    pepper
 1 pound sea scallops
 4 cups gourmet salad greens
 1 tablespoon minced fresh chives

1. Trim stems from figs. Combine figs and next 4 ingredients in a small saucepan; bring to a boil. Cover, reduce heat, and simmer 45 minutes or until tender. Remove from heat. Remove figs with a slotted spoon, reserving cooking liquid. Cool figs slightly, and cut in half lengthwise. Combine figs and apple in a bowl. Combine cooking liquid and 1 teaspoon oil, stirring well with a whisk. Pour over apple mixture; toss gently to coat.

2. Sprinkle salt and pepper over scallops. Heat 2 teaspoons oil in a large nonstick skillet over medium-high heat. Add scallops; cook 2 minutes on each side or until scallops are done.

3. Place 1 cup greens on each of 4 plates. Divide apple mixture and scallops evenly among salads; sprinkle evenly with chives. Yield: 4 servings.

CALORIES 424 (11% from fat); FAT 5.2g (sat 0.7g, mono 2.7g, poly 1g); PROTEIN 21.6g; CARB 61.3g; FIBER 7.9g; CHOL 37mg; IRON 1.9mg; SODIUM 493mg; CALC 128mg

Oven-Braised Cornish Hens with Cider Vinegar and Warm Vegetable Sauce

Warm crusty bread is all you need to round out this meal. Use it to soak up the last drops of the tart broth.

 2 (1¼-pound) Cornish hens
 3 tablespoons all-purpose flour
 ½ teaspoon salt
 ¼ teaspoon freshly ground black
    pepper
 1½ teaspoons butter
 1 teaspoon olive oil
 2 cups (1-inch) slices leek (about
    2 large)
 ½ pound cremini mushrooms,
    halved
 2 garlic cloves, minced
 3 cups fat-free, less-sodium chicken
    broth
 1 cup cider vinegar
 3 plum tomatoes, quartered
 1 Granny Smith apple, peeled and
    cut into ½-inch slices
 ½ pound small red potatoes,
    quartered
 2 tablespoons chopped fresh parsley

1. Preheat oven to 350°.

2. Rinse hens with cold water; pat dry. Remove skin; trim excess fat. Split hens in half lengthwise. Combine flour, salt, and pepper in a shallow dish; dredge hens in flour mixture. Melt butter in a large Dutch oven over medium-high heat. Add oil and hens, and cook 4 minutes on each side or until browned. Remove from pan.

3. Add leek, mushrooms, and garlic to pan; sauté 5 minutes. Add broth and vinegar, stirring to loosen browned bits. Return hens to pan; add tomatoes, apple, and potatoes. Bring mixture to a simmer. Cover and bake at 350° for 30 minutes or until hens are done. Place hens on a serving platter, and keep warm. Remove vegetable mixture from pan with a slotted spoon; place in a serving bowl. Reserve 2 cups cooking liquid in pan; discard remaining liquid. Bring reserved cooking liquid to a boil; cook 8 minutes or until reduced to 1 cup, stirring occasionally. Pour over vegetable mixture. Sprinkle with parsley. Serve with hens. Yield: 4 servings (serving size: 1 hen half and 1 cup vegetable mixture).

CALORIES 487 (27% from fat); FAT 14.4g (sat 5g, mono 4.7g, poly 2.6g); PROTEIN 56.5g; CARB 31.5g; FIBER 3.9g; CHOL 237mg; IRON 4.7mg; SODIUM 842mg; CALC 78mg

Roasted Loin of Pork with Apricot-Rum Glaze

This easy apricot glaze will keep up to 1 week if refrigerated. Try pairing it with chicken, as well.

 1 cup dried apricots
 ¾ cup water
 ½ cup dark rum
 1 teaspoon olive oil
 ½ cup chopped onion
 4 garlic cloves, minced
 ¼ cup honey
 2 teaspoons chopped fresh thyme
 1 (4-pound) boneless pork loin
    roast, trimmed
Cooking spray
 1¼ teaspoons salt
 ½ teaspoon freshly ground black
    pepper

1. Preheat oven to 400°.
2. Combine first 3 ingredients in a small microwave-safe bowl. Microwave at HIGH 4 minutes.
3. Heat oil in a medium saucepan over medium heat. Add onion and garlic; cook 5 minutes or until tender, stirring frequently. Add apricot mixture, and cook 10 minutes or until apricots are soft. Stir in honey and thyme. Place apricot mixture in a food processor, and process until smooth, scraping sides. Reserve ½ cup apricot mixture to serve with pork.
4. Place pork on rack of a broiler pan coated with cooking spray. Sprinkle pork with salt and pepper. Brush ½ cup apricot mixture over pork. Bake at 400° for 10 minutes. Reduce oven temperature to 350° (do not remove pork from oven). Bake 1 hour or until thermometer registers 155°, brushing with ½ cup apricot mixture after 30 minutes. Let stand 10 minutes before slicing. Serve with reserved ½ cup apricot mixture. Yield: 12 servings (serving size: 3 ounces pork and about 2 teaspoons sauce).

CALORIES 235 (37% from fat); FAT 9.7g (sat 3.3g, mono 4.5g, poly 1g); PROTEIN 22.2g; CARB 10.1g; FIBER 0.2g; CHOL 73mg; IRON 1.5mg; SODIUM 261mg; CALC 32mg

sound bites

The Essential Egg

Eggs play a crucial role in many recipes.

We're glad to see the nutrition guidelines for eggs relaxed, as they're crucial to so many dishes—dishes that simply wouldn't be the same without them.

For example, soufflés wouldn't be soufflés without the airy lift of beaten egg whites. Sauces such as citrus curd require the use of egg yolks to emulsify and thicken. And while you can certainly make a frittata or a quiche with egg substitute, it will lack the moist, light texture whole eggs give. When hard-cooked, eggs add richness and textural contrast to salads.

Key Lime Cheesecake

You won't use all of the sweet-tart lime curd for the cheesecake; serve leftovers over angel food cake or fresh fruit. Lightly blotting the lime rind on a paper towel makes it easier to sprinkle over the cheesecake batter.

CRUST:
- 8 sheets honey-flavored graham crackers
- 2 tablespoons apple juice
- 1 tablespoon butter, melted
- Cooking spray

FILLING:
- ¾ cup Key Lime Curd
- ⅓ cup sugar
- 1 tablespoon cornstarch
- 2 large eggs
- 1 large egg white
- 1 (12.3-ounce) package soft silken tofu, drained
- 1 (8-ounce) block fat-free cream cheese
- 1 tablespoon grated lime rind

1. Preheat oven to 350°.
2. To prepare crust, place crackers in a food processor; process until crumbly. Add apple juice and butter; pulse 4 or 5 times or until moist. Press mixture into bottom and ½ inch up sides of a 9-inch springform pan coated with cooking spray. Bake at 350° for 8 minutes. Cool.
3. To prepare filling, combine Key Lime Curd and next 6 ingredients in food processor; process until smooth. Pour into prepared pan. Sprinkle evenly with rind.
4. Bake at 350° for 15 minutes. Reduce oven temperature to 325° (do not remove cheesecake from oven); bake an additional 20 minutes or until almost set. Turn oven off, and partially open oven door. Cool cheesecake in oven 20 minutes. Remove from oven; run a knife around outside edge. Cool to room temperature. Cover and chill 8 hours or overnight. Yield: 8 servings (serving size: 1 wedge).

(Totals include Key Lime Curd) CALORIES 239 (30% from fat); FAT 7.9g (sat 2.8g, mono 2.6g, poly 1.7g); PROTEIN 10g; CARB 30.9g; FIBER 0.5g; CHOL 131mg; IRON 1.3mg; SODIUM 277mg; CALC 112mg

KEY LIME CURD:
- ½ cup sugar
- ½ cup bottled key lime juice (such as Nellie and Joe's)
- 5 large egg yolks, lightly beaten
- 1½ tablespoons butter, cut into small pieces

1. Combine first 3 ingredients in a medium, heavy saucepan. Cook over medium heat 7 minutes or until thick; stir constantly with a whisk. Remove from heat. Add butter; stir with a whisk until butter melts. Place pan in a large ice-filled bowl 20 minutes or until lime curd comes to room temperature; stir occasionally. Cover and chill. Yield: about 1½ cups (serving size: 1½ tablespoons).

CALORIES 54 (45% from fat); FAT 2.7g (sat 1.2g, mono 0.9g, poly 0.3g); PROTEIN 0.9g; CARB 7g; FIBER 0g; CHOL 69mg; IRON 0.2mg; SODIUM 13mg; CALC 8mg

Ham and Potato Omelet

Serve with fruit salad and toast for breakfast, or sautéed Swiss chard and garlic bread for later in the day. Use chicken in place of ham, if you prefer.

- ¼ cup 1% low-fat milk
- ½ teaspoon salt
- ¼ teaspoon black pepper
- 4 large egg whites, lightly beaten
- 3 large eggs, lightly beaten
- 1 tablespoon vegetable oil
- 4 cups packaged frozen hash brown potatoes with onions and peppers (such as Ore-Ida Potatoes O'Brien)
- 1 cup chopped 33%-less-sodium ham

1. Preheat oven to 450°.
2. Combine first 5 ingredients, stirring with a whisk.
3. Heat oil in a large cast-iron skillet over medium-high heat. Add potatoes; sauté 5 minutes. Stir in ham; sauté 1 minute. Stir in egg mixture. Bake at 450° for 12 minutes or until set. Cover and let stand 10 minutes. Cut into 8 wedges. Yield: 4 servings (serving size: 2 wedges).

CALORIES 287 (27% from fat); FAT 8.5g (sat 2.2g, mono 2.8g, poly 2.7g); PROTEIN 17g; CARB 36.4g; FIBER 3.7g; CHOL 172mg; IRON 3mg; SODIUM 703mg; CALC 67mg

How to Cook Perfect Hard-Cooked Eggs

Carefully place large eggs in a saucepan. Add just enough cold water to cover eggs 1 inch. Bring the water to a boil over medium-high heat. Just as the water comes to a full rolling boil, cover the saucepan, and remove it from the heat. Let eggs stand in the hot water 15 minutes. Drain water from pan and cover eggs immediately with cold tap water. When cool to the touch, tap eggs gently on all sides to crack shells. Remove shells under running water.

Particular about how they look? After about 5 minutes of standing in hot water, uncover, gently stir the eggs, and re-cover. Before the eggs are stirred, the yolks are surrounded by partially cooked whites and aren't in the center of the egg. The gentle stirring helps reposition the yolks.

Berry French Toast

This dish is great for lazy mornings when you don't feel like standing at the stove. Egg-rich French toast bakes atop a mixture of sweetened berries.

    2   cups frozen blueberries
 1½   cups frozen blackberries
 1½   cups frozen raspberries
    ¾   cup granulated sugar
    1   tablespoon cornstarch
    1   teaspoon ground cinnamon
Cooking spray
    1   cup fat-free milk
    1   teaspoon vanilla extract
    4   large egg whites, lightly beaten
    1   large egg, lightly beaten
    1   (8-ounce) loaf French bread,
        cut into 1-inch slices
    1   tablespoon granulated sugar
    1   tablespoon powdered sugar

1. Preheat oven to 350°.
2. Combine first 6 ingredients in a 13 x 9-inch baking dish coated with cooking spray.

3. Combine milk, vanilla, egg whites, and egg in a large, shallow baking dish, stirring well with a whisk. Add bread slices, turning to coat. Let stand 5 minutes, turning bread occasionally. Arrange bread in a single layer over berries. Sprinkle evenly with 1 tablespoon granulated sugar. Bake at 350° for 30 minutes or until golden brown and bubbly. Sprinkle evenly with powdered sugar. Yield: 6 servings.

CALORIES 374 (6% from fat); FAT 2.7g (sat 0.6g, mono 0.9g, poly 0.7g); PROTEIN 9.2g; CARB 80.4g; FIBER 7.4g; CHOL 36mg; IRON 2.1mg; SODIUM 300mg; CALC 114mg

Field Greens with Eggs and Enoki Mushrooms

Hard-cooked eggs are a welcome addition to this refreshing Asian-inspired salad. If your grocer doesn't have enoki mushrooms, substitute sliced button mushrooms.

    2   tablespoons minced fresh
        cilantro
    4   teaspoons rice vinegar
    1   tablespoon low-sodium soy
        sauce
    1   teaspoon sugar
    ½   teaspoon vegetable oil
    ¼   teaspoon salt
    ⅛   teaspoon ground red
        pepper
    6   cups gourmet salad greens
    2   cups enoki mushrooms, roots
        trimmed (about 3 ounces)
    2   tablespoons thinly sliced green
        onions
    1   tomato, cut into 8 wedges (about
        ½ pound)
    2   hard-cooked large eggs, thinly
        sliced

1. Combine first 7 ingredients, stirring with a whisk.
2. Combine salad greens, mushrooms, onions, and tomato. Pour vinegar mixture over salad, tossing gently to coat. Top with egg slices. Yield: 4 servings (serving size: about 1¼ cups).

CALORIES 79 (41% from fat); FAT 3.6g (sat 1g, mono 1.2g, poly 0.9g); PROTEIN 5.5g; CARB 7.3g; FIBER 2.9g; CHOL 106mg; IRON 1.8mg; SODIUM 336mg; CALC 61mg

Roasted Garlic and Corn Soufflé

Beaten egg whites give this savory side dish its characteristic airy texture, while whole eggs add richness to the soufflé base. Don't coat the sides of the soufflé dish with cooking spray; the egg mixture needs the extra traction so it can rise up the sides of the dish. Serve with ham, turkey, chicken, or pork.

    2   whole garlic heads
    2   cups fresh corn kernels (about
        4 ears), divided
Cooking spray
    3   tablespoons all-purpose flour
 1½   cups 2% reduced-fat milk
    4   large eggs, lightly beaten
    2   teaspoons chopped fresh chives
    1   teaspoon chopped fresh thyme
    ½   teaspoon salt
    ¼   teaspoon ground nutmeg
    ¼   teaspoon black pepper
    ⅛   teaspoon ground red pepper
    4   large egg whites
    ½   teaspoon cream of tartar

1. Preheat oven to 350°.
2. Remove white papery skin from garlic heads (do not peel or separate cloves). Wrap each head separately in foil. Bake at 350° for 1 hour; cool 10 minutes. Separate cloves, and squeeze to extract garlic pulp. Discard skins. Place garlic pulp and 1 cup corn in a blender or food processor; process until smooth. Set aside.
3. Cut a piece of foil long enough to fit around a 2-quart soufflé dish, allowing a 1-inch overlap; fold foil lengthwise into thirds. Lightly coat one side of foil and bottom of dish with cooking spray. Wrap foil around outside of dish, coated side against dish, allowing it to extend 4 inches above rim to form a collar; secure with string or masking tape.
4. Place flour in a medium saucepan. Gradually add milk, stirring with a whisk until well blended. Stir in garlic mixture; bring to a boil over medium heat. Cook 1 minute or until thick, stirring constantly.
5. Preheat oven to 400°.
6. Place 4 eggs in a large bowl. Gradually add hot milk mixture to eggs, stirring

constantly with a whisk. Stir in 1 cup corn, chives, and next 5 ingredients. Place egg whites and cream of tartar in a large bowl; beat with a mixer at high speed until stiff peaks form. Gently stir one-fourth of egg white mixture into corn mixture. Gently fold in remaining egg white mixture. Pour mixture into prepared dish. Bake at 400° for 10 minutes. Reduce oven temperature to 350° (do not remove soufflé from oven); bake an additional 45 minutes or until puffed and golden. Carefully remove foil collar. Serve immediately. Yield: 6 servings.

CALORIES 162 (29% from fat); FAT 5.2g (sat 1.8g, mono 1.6g, poly 0.5g); PROTEIN 11.1g; CARB 19.1g; FIBER 0.7g; CHOL 146mg; IRON 1.1mg; SODIUM 314mg; CALC 110mg

Mediterranean-Style Poached Eggs

Eggs gently cook atop a savory mixture of onion, bell pepper, tomatoes, and artichoke hearts in this version of *pipérade*. Served over toasted bread, it makes a filling one-dish meal.

    2 teaspoons olive oil
 1½ cups chopped onion
    1 cup green bell pepper strips
    1 garlic clove, minced
  ½ teaspoon ground cumin
  ½ teaspoon paprika
 2½ cups canned crushed tomatoes
  ¼ teaspoon black pepper
    1 (14-ounce) can artichoke hearts, drained and cut in half
    4 large eggs
  ¼ cup chopped fresh parsley
  ¼ cup chopped pitted kalamata olives
  ¼ cup (1 ounce) grated fresh Parmesan cheese
    4 (1½-ounce) slices French bread, toasted

1. Heat oil in a large nonstick skillet over medium-high heat. Add onion, bell pepper, and garlic; sauté 5 minutes. Add cumin and paprika; sauté 1 minute. Reduce heat to medium; stir in tomatoes, black pepper, and artichokes. Cook 5 minutes, stirring occasionally. Form 4

(3-inch) indentations in vegetable mixture using back of a spoon or bottom of a large custard cup. Break 1 egg into each indentation. Cover and cook 8 minutes or until eggs are done. Sprinkle with parsley, olives, and cheese. Serve over bread. Yield: 4 servings (serving size: 1 bread slice, ¾ cup vegetable mixture, and 1 egg).

CALORIES 355 (30% from fat); FAT 11.9g (sat 3.5g, mono 5.4g, poly 1.5g); PROTEIN 17.8g; CARB 46.2g; FIBER 7.5g; CHOL 217mg; IRON 3.8mg; SODIUM 1,050mg; CALC 197mg

dinner tonight

Pasta Tonight

Four inspired, quick dinners made with pasta, our favorite pantry staple.

Fettuccine with Shrimp and Portobellos

Serve this entrée in a bowl with toasted bread to soak up the flavorful broth.

TOTAL TIME: 30 MINUTES

    8 ounces uncooked fettuccine
    1 (4-inch) portobello mushroom cap (about 5 ounces)
    1 tablespoon olive oil
    1 cup finely chopped onion
  ¼ cup chopped fresh flat-leaf parsley
  ¼ teaspoon salt
    1 garlic clove, minced
    1 cup fat-free, less-sodium chicken broth
  ¼ cup dry white wine
  ¾ pound large shrimp, peeled and deveined
  ½ cup (2 ounces) shredded Asiago cheese
    1 tablespoon chopped fresh chives

1. Cook pasta according to package directions, omitting salt and fat. Drain and rinse with cold water. Drain.
2. Remove brown gills from underside of mushroom cap using a spoon; discard gills. Cut cap into thin slices. Cut slices in half crosswise.
3. Heat oil in a large saucepan over medium-high heat. Add mushroom, onion, parsley, salt, and garlic; sauté 4 minutes or until mushroom releases moisture, stirring frequently. Stir in broth, wine, and shrimp; bring to a boil. Add pasta, and cook 3 minutes or until shrimp are done, tossing to combine. Sprinkle with cheese and chives. Yield: 4 servings (serving size: 1¾ cups shrimp mixture, 2 tablespoons cheese, and about 1 teaspoon chives).

CALORIES 384 (21% from fat); FAT 9.1g (sat 3.3g, mono 2.7g, poly 0.9g); PROTEIN 23.8g; CARB 48.9g; FIBER 2.8g; CHOL 114mg; IRON 4.5mg; SODIUM 540mg; CALC 156mg

Garlicky Pasta Menu

serves 6

Garlicky Pasta with Fresh Tomatoes and Basil

Sautéed broccoli rabe*

Fresh berries

*Heat a large nonstick skillet over medium-high heat. Add ¼ cup chopped shallots, 1 tablespoon butter, and 2 minced garlic cloves; sauté 4 minutes. Add 1 teaspoon salt, ½ teaspoon crushed red pepper, and 1½ pounds broccoli rabe; sauté 1 minute. Add ¾ cup fat-free, less-sodium chicken broth; cover and cook 2 minutes or until crisp-tender.

Game Plan

1. While pasta cooks:
- Chop tomatoes, shallots, and mince garlic
- Clean berries
- Grate cheese

2. While broccoli rabe cooks:
- Chop basil
- Toss pasta

STAFF FAVORITE • QUICK & EASY

Garlicky Pasta with Fresh Tomatoes and Basil

Simplicity is a virtue—particularly if you have good tomatoes. The garlic flavor is pronounced; reduce the amount to 2 cloves, if you prefer. If you can't find campanella, try orecchiette, fusilli, or shells.

TOTAL TIME: 24 MINUTES

QUICK TIP: To remove garlic peels, place the garlic clove on a flat surface, and crush with the blunt side of a chef's knife.

- 3 tablespoons extravirgin olive oil
- 3 garlic cloves, minced
- 5 cups chopped plum tomatoes (about 2 pounds)
- 6 cups hot cooked campanella (about 12 ounces uncooked pasta)
- ⅓ cup chopped fresh basil
- ¼ cup (1 ounce) grated fresh Parmesan cheese
- 1½ teaspoons salt
- ¼ teaspoon freshly ground black pepper

1. Heat oil in a large Dutch oven over medium-high heat. Add garlic; sauté 30 seconds. Add tomatoes; cook 2 minutes or until thoroughly heated, stirring occasionally. Add pasta and remaining ingredients, tossing gently to combine. Yield: 6 servings (serving size: 1⅓ cups).

CALORIES 310 (27% from fat); FAT 9.4g (sat 1.9g, mono 5.5g, poly 1.2g); PROTEIN 9.8g; CARB 47.4g; FIBER 3.6g; CHOL 3mg; IRON 2.8mg; SODIUM 677mg; CALC 81mg

---

QUICK & EASY

Lasagna Rolls with Roasted Red Pepper Sauce

These rolls require some assembly time but are a nice change of pace from layered pasta.

TOTAL TIME: 40 MINUTES

QUICK TIP: Use baby spinach to eliminate the task of trimming stems.

LASAGNA:

- 8 uncooked lasagna noodles
- 4 teaspoons olive oil
- ½ cup finely chopped onion
- 1 (8-ounce) package presliced mushrooms
- 1 (6-ounce) package fresh baby spinach
- 3 garlic cloves, minced
- ½ cup (2 ounces) shredded mozzarella cheese
- ½ cup part-skim ricotta cheese
- 2 tablespoons minced fresh basil
- ½ teaspoon salt
- ¼ teaspoon crushed red pepper

SAUCE:

- 1 tablespoon red wine vinegar
- ¼ teaspoon salt
- ¼ teaspoon freshly ground black pepper
- 2 garlic cloves, minced
- 1 (14.5-ounce) can diced tomatoes, undrained
- 1 (7-ounce) bottle roasted red bell peppers, undrained
- ⅛ teaspoon crushed red pepper

REMAINING INGREDIENT:

- 2 tablespoons minced fresh basil

1. To prepare lasagna, cook noodles according to package directions, omitting salt and fat. Drain and rinse with cold water. Drain.

2. Heat oil in a large nonstick skillet over medium-high heat. Add onion, mushrooms, spinach, and 3 garlic cloves; sauté 5 minutes or until onion and mushrooms are tender. Remove from heat, and stir in cheeses and next 3 ingredients.

3. To prepare sauce, place vinegar and next 6 ingredients in a blender; process until smooth.

4. Place cooked noodles on flat surface; spread ¼ cup cheese mixture over each noodle. Roll up noodles, jelly-roll fashion, starting with short side. Place rolls, seam sides down, in a shallow 2-quart microwave-safe dish. Pour ¼ cup sauce over each roll, and cover with heavy-duty plastic wrap. Microwave at HIGH 5 minutes or until thoroughly heated. Sprinkle with 2 tablespoons basil. Yield: 4 servings (serving size: 2 rolls).

CALORIES 393 (27% from fat); FAT 11.7g (sat 4.3g, mono 3.6g, poly 1.5g); PROTEIN 19.3g; CARB 58.3g; FIBER 5.9g; CHOL 20mg; IRON 3.8mg; SODIUM 924mg; CALC 253mg

---

Lasagna Rolls Menu

serves 4

Lasagna Rolls with Roasted Red Pepper Sauce

Sugar snap peas

Amaretto pears*

*Cut 2 pears into thin slices. Combine pear slices, 2 tablespoons toasted sliced almonds, 1 tablespoon brown sugar, and 1 tablespoon amaretto.

Game Plan

1. While water boils:
- Chop onion and mince garlic
- Mince basil
- Shred cheese

2. While noodles cook:
- Prepare sauce
- Prepare pears
- Blanch snap peas

Greek Pasta Salad Menu

serves 4

Greek Pasta Salad

Pita crisps*

Orange sorbet

*Preheat broiler. Cut each of 4 pitas into 8 wedges. Arrange wedges in a single layer on a baking sheet coated with cooking spray. Lightly brush with 2 teaspoons olive oil; sprinkle with ½ teaspoon dried basil and 2 tablespoons freshly grated Parmesan cheese. Broil 2 minutes or until cheese is melted and pita is lightly browned.

Game Plan

1. While pasta cooks:
- Heat broiler
- Heat grill pan
- Chop onion, slice cucumber and olives, and halve tomatoes

2. While tuna cooks:
- Prepare dressing
- Prepare pita crisps

QUICK & EASY
Greek Pasta Salad

TOTAL TIME: 30 MINUTES

QUICK TIP: To save time, buy sliced olives and crumbled cheese.

SALAD:
- 3 cups uncooked farfalle (bow tie pasta)
- Cooking spray
- 1 (8-ounce) tuna steak (about ¾ inch thick)
- ⅛ teaspoon salt
- 1½ cups sliced peeled cucumber
- ¾ cup (3 ounces) crumbled feta cheese with peppercorns
- ¼ cup coarsely chopped red onion
- ¼ cup sliced kalamata olives
- ¼ teaspoon freshly ground black pepper
- 12 cherry tomatoes, halved

DRESSING:
- ¼ cup fresh lemon juice
- 2 teaspoons extravirgin olive oil
- 1 teaspoon dried oregano
- ¼ teaspoon freshly ground black pepper
- ⅛ teaspoon salt

1. To prepare salad, cook pasta according to package directions, omitting salt and fat. Drain and rinse with cold water. Drain; place in a large bowl.

2. Heat a large grill pan coated with cooking spray over high heat. Sprinkle tuna with ⅛ teaspoon salt. Add tuna to pan; cook 5 minutes on each side or until desired degree of doneness. Remove from pan; cool slightly. Cut tuna into 1-inch pieces. Add tuna, cucumber, and next 5 ingredients to pasta.

3. To prepare dressing, combine lemon juice and remaining 4 ingredients, stirring with a whisk. Drizzle over salad, and toss gently to coat. Yield: 4 servings (serving size: 2 cups).

CALORIES 352 (30% from fat); FAT 11.8g (sat 4.1g, mono 5g, poly 1.2g); PROTEIN 23.2g; CARB 39.6g; FIBER 2.8g; CHOL 44mg; IRON 2.5mg; SODIUM 567mg; CALC 144mg

enlightened traveler

Gourmet Getaways

Take a culinary retreat to learn a new cuisine or hone your skills in the kitchen.

A culinary experience is a food lover's dream vacation—and a great way to learn about a place and its culture. Culinary vacations allow you to immerse yourself in the sights, smells, and gastronomic traditions through hands-on cooking classes, visits to working farms, and meetings with local food artisans. Other gourmet getaways might include a day at a famous culinary school or an afternoon farm tour to learn more about a region's produce. No matter your interests, there is a culinary vacation for you. Here is an example of a type of recipe you might learn to make on a culinary vacation.

Fresh Tomato Lasagna

We loved this simple, light, fresh lasagna from The Culinary Institute of America.

- 1 tablespoon olive oil
- 1 cup finely chopped onion
- 4 garlic cloves, minced
- 7 cups chopped peeled tomato (about 4 pounds)
- ⅔ cup thinly sliced fresh basil
- 1 teaspoon salt, divided
- ¼ teaspoon black pepper, divided
- 2 cups part-skim ricotta cheese
- 1 cup (4 ounces) shredded part-skim mozzarella cheese
- Cooking spray
- 8 cooked lasagna noodles
- ½ cup (2 ounces) finely shredded fresh Parmesan cheese
- 1 tablespoon thinly sliced fresh basil

1. Heat oil in a small Dutch oven over medium heat; add onion and garlic. Cook 10 minutes or until tender, stirring occasionally. Add tomato; bring to a boil. Reduce heat, and simmer 1 hour and 20 minutes or until slightly thickened. Remove from heat; stir in ⅔ cup basil, ¾ teaspoon salt, and ⅛ teaspoon pepper. Set aside.

2. Preheat oven to 375°.

3. Heat ricotta in a medium saucepan over medium heat until hot; stir in mozzarella, stirring until melted. Remove from heat; stir in ¼ teaspoon salt and ⅛ teaspoon pepper.

4. Spread 2 cups tomato mixture in bottom of a 13 x 9-inch baking dish coated with cooking spray. Arrange 4 noodles over tomato mixture; top with ricotta mixture. Arrange 4 noodles over ricotta mixture; top with remaining tomato mixture. Sprinkle evenly with Parmesan. Bake at 375° for 15 minutes or until cheese melts and filling is bubbly. Remove from oven; sprinkle with 1 tablespoon basil. Let stand 5 minutes. Yield: 8 servings.

CALORIES 290 (37% from fat); FAT 11.8g (sat 6.1g, mono 4g, poly 0.8g); PROTEIN 17.9g; CARB 29.2g; FIBER 3g; CHOL 32mg; IRON 2.1mg; SODIUM 575mg; CALC 381mg

Easter Dinner Alfresco

Usher in the first sensational flavors of spring with this easy menu.

Easter Dinner Alfresco Menu

serves 4

Mushroom and Parmigiano Bruschetta

Rosemary and Pepper-Crusted Pork Tenderloin

Three-Grain Risotto with Asparagus Spears

Green salad

Strawberry Granita

Mushroom and Parmigiano Bruschetta

Use any combination of fresh mushrooms in this appetizer. The mushroom topping would also be good over pasta. Shaved Parmigiano-Reggiano cheese looks handsome, but you can also grate the cheese and stir it into the topping.

½ cup chopped seeded plum tomato
2 tablespoons sherry vinegar or red wine vinegar
1 teaspoon capers
½ teaspoon sugar
¼ teaspoon crushed red pepper
⅛ teaspoon salt
10 thinly sliced basil leaves
2 teaspoons butter
⅓ cup sliced cremini mushrooms
⅓ cup sliced shiitake mushroom caps
⅓ cup sliced baby portobello mushroom caps
¼ cup chopped green onions
1 garlic clove, minced
8 (½-inch-thick) slices diagonally cut French bread baguette, toasted
¼ cup (1 ounce) shaved Parmigiano-Reggiano cheese

1. Combine first 7 ingredients in a medium bowl; set aside.
2. Melt butter in a medium nonstick skillet over medium heat. Add mushrooms, onions, and garlic; cook 5 minutes or until tender, stirring frequently. Add mushroom mixture to tomato mixture; toss well to combine.
3. Spoon about 1 tablespoon mushroom mixture onto each bread slice. Sprinkle evenly with cheese. Serve immediately. Yield: 4 servings (serving size: 2 topped bruschetta).

CALORIES 145 (30% from fat); FAT 4.8g (sat 2.6g, mono 1.5g, poly 0.4g); PROTEIN 6.1g; CARB 19.5g; FIBER 1.8g; CHOL 10mg; IRON 1.3mg; SODIUM 420mg; CALC 114mg

---

QUICK & EASY

Rosemary and Pepper-Crusted Pork Tenderloin

(pictured on page 111)

Use a mortar and pestle to crush the fennel and celery seeds; or place them in a zip-top plastic bag and crush with a rolling pin.

2 teaspoons cracked black pepper
1 teaspoon dried rosemary, crushed
½ teaspoon kosher salt
½ teaspoon fennel seeds, crushed
½ teaspoon celery seeds, crushed
½ teaspoon dry mustard
1 (1-pound) pork tenderloin, trimmed
Cooking spray
2 tablespoons chopped fresh flat-leaf parsley

1. Preheat oven to 425°.
2. Combine first 6 ingredients; rub over pork. Place pork in a shallow roasting pan coated with cooking spray. Bake at 425° for 30 minutes or until a thermometer registers 160° (slightly pink). Let stand 5 minutes; cut into thin slices. Sprinkle with parsley. Yield: 4 servings (serving size: 3 ounces).

CALORIES 158 (31% from fat); FAT 5.4g (sat 1.8g, mono 2.2g, poly 0.5g); PROTEIN 24.7g; CARB 1.3g; FIBER 0.6g; CHOL 75mg; IRON 1.8mg; SODIUM 289mg; CALC 23mg

---

Three-Grain Risotto with Asparagus Spears

(pictured on page 111)

Rice, barley, and quinoa give this risotto contrasting textures—creaminess from the rice, chewiness from the barley, and crunch from the quinoa. Flowering herbs make a pretty garnish.

⅛ teaspoon saffron threads, crushed
1 (14-ounce) can fat-free, less-sodium chicken broth
1 tablespoon olive oil
¼ cup finely chopped shallots (about 2 medium)
½ cup uncooked Arborio or other short-grain rice
½ cup uncooked quick-cooking barley
¼ cup uncooked quinoa
½ cup dry white wine
1 cup water
1 cup (4 ounces) shredded part-skim mozzarella cheese
⅔ cup 1% low-fat milk
2 teaspoons fresh lemon juice
½ teaspoon salt
½ teaspoon freshly ground black pepper
12 asparagus spears, steamed
1 tablespoon pine nuts, toasted

1. Bring saffron and broth to a simmer in a small saucepan (do not boil). Keep warm over low heat.
2. Heat oil in a large saucepan over medium-high heat. Add shallots; sauté 3 minutes. Add rice, barley, and quinoa; sauté 2 minutes. Add wine; cook 2 minutes or until liquid is nearly absorbed. Stir in 1 cup water; cook 5 minutes or until liquid is nearly absorbed, stirring constantly. Add broth mixture, ½ cup at a time, stirring constantly until each portion is absorbed before adding next (about 25 minutes total).
3. Remove from heat; stir in cheese and next 4 ingredients. Top with asparagus; sprinkle with pine nuts. Yield: 4 servings (serving size: about 1 cup risotto, 3 asparagus spears, and about 1 teaspoon nuts).

CALORIES 393 (24% from fat); FAT 10.5g (sat 3.9g, mono 4.5g, poly 1.4g); PROTEIN 17.3g; CARB 57.3g; FIBER 6.3g; CHOL 18mg; IRON 2.9mg; SODIUM 638mg; CALC 275mg

Strawberry Granita

(pictured on page 111)

This frozen dessert requires no ice-cream maker—just freeze the mixture in a pan, and scrape with a fork. If you'd like to spruce up the granita, top with chopped or halved fresh strawberries and grated lemon zest.

½ cup sugar
½ cup warm water
3 cups sliced strawberries
2 tablespoons fresh lemon juice

1. Combine sugar and water in a blender; process until sugar dissolves. Add strawberries and juice; process until smooth. Pour mixture into an 8-inch square baking dish. Cover and freeze 3 hours; stir well. Cover and freeze 5 hours or overnight.
2. Remove mixture from freezer; let stand at room temperature 10 minutes. Scrape entire mixture with a fork until fluffy. Yield: 4 servings (serving size: 1 cup).

CALORIES 136 (3% from fat); FAT 0.5g (sat 0g, mono 0.1g, poly 0.2g); PROTEIN 0.8g; CARB 34.4g; FIBER 2.9g; CHOL 0mg; IRON 0.5mg; SODIUM 2mg; CALC 18mg

in season

Little Red Radishes

Why it's high time to rethink these crisp, colorful roots.

Spring is a good time to rediscover radishes. A cousin of mustard, they're ruby-red, zingy, and quite mild. (Radishes harvested in the summer heat have a much sharper, almost biting taste.)

When purchasing radishes, always look for bunches with the leaves still attached. The greens are a guarantee of the roots' freshness. Wilted, desiccated leaves above are a sure sign of mealy radishes below. Look beyond the relish tray and welcome these versatile, colorful roots into slaws, soups, salads, and sauces.

Radish Slaw with New York Deli Dressing

In this colorful slaw, peppery radishes stand in for cabbage. Use a shredding blade in a food processor for easier preparation. The vinegar-based dressing gets a big flavor boost from mustard oil; its pungent bite enhances the radish flavor. It's worth seeking out—look for it with other specialty oils. Or try the mayonnaise-based dressing given as a variation below.

4 cups shredded radishes (about 40 radishes)
2 cups finely chopped yellow bell pepper
1½ cups shredded carrot
½ cup white wine vinegar
4 teaspoons sugar
1 tablespoon chopped fresh dill
1 tablespoon mustard oil or olive oil
½ teaspoon salt
½ teaspoon black pepper

1. Combine first 3 ingredients in a large bowl. Combine vinegar and remaining 5 ingredients, stirring with a whisk. Drizzle dressing over slaw; toss well to combine. Serve immediately. Yield: 10 servings (serving size: ¾ cup).

CALORIES 46 (35% from fat); FAT 1.8g (sat 0.2g, mono 0.9g, poly 0.4g); PROTEIN 0.9g; CARB 7.4g; FIBER 1.6g; CHOL 0mg; IRON 0.5mg; SODIUM 136mg; CALC 20mg

CREAMY DILL VARIATION:
4 cups shredded radishes (about 40 radishes)
2 cups finely chopped yellow bell pepper
1½ cups shredded carrot
½ cup low-fat mayonnaise
2 tablespoons white wine vinegar
1 tablespoon chopped fresh dill
2 teaspoons sugar
1 teaspoon dry mustard
½ teaspoon salt
½ teaspoon black pepper

1. Combine first 3 ingredients in a large bowl. Combine mayonnaise and remaining 6 ingredients, stirring with a whisk. Drizzle dressing over slaw; toss well to combine. Serve immediately. Yield: 10 servings (serving size: ¾ cup).

CALORIES 52 (23% from fat); FAT 1.3g (sat 0.1g, mono 0.2g, poly 0.5g); PROTEIN 0.9g; CARB 9.9g; FIBER 1.6g; CHOL 0mg; IRON 0.5mg; SODIUM 247mg; CALC 20mg

Radish Raita

Inspired by the cooling yogurt condiment served with spicy meats in India, this sweet, zesty sauce complements spice-rubbed grilled salmon, chile-spiced pork tenderloin, or barbecued chicken. Use the large holes of a box grater to grate the cucumber.

1 cucumber, peeled, halved lengthwise, and seeded
1 cup diced radishes (about 6 radishes)
¾ cup plain low-fat yogurt
2 tablespoons chopped golden raisins
1 tablespoon fresh lime juice
¼ teaspoon salt
¼ teaspoon ground cumin
⅛ teaspoon hot pepper sauce

1. Grate cucumber into a medium bowl. Add radishes and remaining ingredients, and stir gently to combine. Cover and chill 2 hours or overnight. Yield: 8 servings (serving size: ¼ cup).

CALORIES 31 (15% from fat); FAT 0.5g (sat 0.3g, mono 0.1g, poly 0g); PROTEIN 1.8g; CARB 5.3g; FIBER 0.7g; CHOL 1mg; IRON 0.3mg; SODIUM 94mg; CALC 55mg

---

Storing Radishes

Once you get radishes home, chop off the greens, wash them well, and store them between paper towels in a zip-top plastic bag. Store the radish roots in breathable plastic bags in your hydrator. The greens have a mild, aromatic flavor, and can go raw into salads or cooked into soups. Should the radishes become spongy after a few days, crisp them by placing them in a bowl of ice water for up to one hour.

Chardonnay-Braised Radishes

Cooked radishes turn delicately mild and sweet. Braise them just until tender but not soft. Insert a sharp knife into the radish to check doneness. A properly cooked (but not overdone) radish will easily yield to the knife, but it should stay on the blade without falling off.

Cooking spray
¼ cup minced red onion
1 teaspoon minced fresh thyme
3 cups small radishes (about 1 pound)
1 cup Chardonnay or other dry white wine
1 tablespoon butter
½ teaspoon salt
1 tablespoon chopped fresh parsley

1. Heat a medium saucepan coated with cooking spray over medium-low heat. Add onion and thyme; cook 3 minutes, stirring frequently. Stir in radishes; cook 1 minute, stirring constantly. Add wine; bring to a boil. Cover, reduce heat, and simmer 5 minutes or just until radishes are tender.
2. Remove radishes from pan with a slotted spoon. Cook wine mixture 2 minutes or until slightly thick, stirring occasionally. Remove from heat; stir in butter and salt. Pour wine mixture over radishes, and sprinkle with parsley. Serve immediately. Yield: 6 servings (serving size: ½ cup).

CALORIES 36 (58% from fat); FAT 2.3g (sat 1.2g, mono 0.6g, poly 0.1g); PROTEIN 0.6g; CARB 3.6g; FIBER 1.2g; CHOL 5mg; IRON 0.4mg; SODIUM 235mg; CALC 22mg

MAKE AHEAD
Radish Vichyssoise

Chilled overnight, this soup is a refreshing crowd-pleaser on a warm spring day. Radishes add an earthy, turniplike flavor. Use white pepper to keep the soup creamy white.

1 tablespoon butter
1½ cups thinly sliced onion
20 radishes, halved (about 1 pound)
1½ pounds baking potatoes, peeled and cut into 1-inch pieces
3 cups fat-free, less-sodium chicken broth
2 cups 2% reduced-fat milk
¾ cup reduced-fat sour cream
1 teaspoon salt
¼ teaspoon black pepper
⅛ teaspoon ground nutmeg
¼ cup chopped fresh chives
2 radishes, thinly sliced (optional)

1. Melt butter in a large saucepan over medium heat. Add onion; cook 5 minutes or until tender, stirring frequently. Add halved radishes and potatoes, tossing to coat with butter. Stir in broth and milk; bring to a boil. Cover, reduce heat, and simmer 15 minutes or until potatoes are tender. Cool 10 minutes.
2. Place half of radish mixture in a blender; process until smooth. Pour puréed soup into a large bowl. Repeat procedure with remaining radish mixture. Cover and chill at least 2 hours.
3. Add sour cream, salt, pepper, and nutmeg to soup, stirring with a whisk. Cover and chill at least 4 hours or overnight. Sprinkle with chives; garnish with radish slices, if desired. Yield: 12 servings (serving size: ¾ cup).

CALORIES 119 (29% from fat); FAT 3.9g (sat 2.3g, mono 1.1g, poly 0.2g); PROTEIN 4.2g; CARB 17.2g; FIBER 1.9g; CHOL 13mg; IRON 0.4mg; SODIUM 359mg; CALC 91mg

Thai Beef and Radish Salad

Southeast Asian salads are traditionally eaten out of hand, with lettuce leaves for wrappers. To make the prep easier, chill the steak in the freezer for 10 minutes before slicing.

1 tablespoon chile paste with garlic
2 teaspoons minced peeled fresh ginger
1 garlic clove, minced
1 pound (½-inch-thick) boneless sirloin steak, cut diagonally across grain into thin slices
1½ tablespoons fresh lime juice
1 tablespoon fish sauce
2 teaspoons sugar
Cooking spray
2 cups sliced radishes
¼ cup chopped fresh cilantro
2 tablespoons chopped fresh mint
1 serrano chile, seeded and finely chopped
8 Bibb lettuce leaves

1. Combine chile paste, ginger, and garlic in a large zip-top plastic bag; add steak, tossing to coat. Marinate in refrigerator 30 minutes, turning once.
2. Combine lime juice, fish sauce, and sugar, stirring with a whisk; set dressing aside.
3. Heat a large nonstick skillet coated with cooking spray over medium-high heat. Remove steak from bag; discard marinade. Add steak to pan; cook 2 minutes or until desired degree of doneness, turning once. Cut steak into 1-inch pieces; place in a medium bowl. Add radishes, cilantro, mint, and serrano. Pour lime juice mixture over beef mixture, tossing to coat. Spoon about ⅓ cup salad into each lettuce leaf, and serve immediately. Yield: 4 servings (serving size: 2 filled lettuce leaves).

CALORIES 223 (41% from fat); FAT 10.2g (sat 3.9g, mono 4.2g, poly 0.4g); PROTEIN 25.7g; CARB 6.8g; FIBER 1.4g; CHOL 76mg; IRON 3.1mg; SODIUM 471mg; CALC 35mg

Fennel, Orange, and Parmigiano Salad, page 97 and
Spanish Tortilla with Almond Romesco, page 97

Popovers, page 92

Strawberry Granita,
page 107

Rosemary and Pepper-Crusted Pork Tenderloin, page 106
and Three-Grain Risotto with Asparagus Spears, page 106

Chicken with Citrus, page 113

Susan Loomis: An American Near Paris

From her cooking school in Louviers, this émigré teaches French farmhouse cuisine.

Susan Loomis is the proprietor of On Rue Tatin, a cooking school in Louviers, France. She is also a popular cookbook author who gets involved with her subjects. When she researched *The Great American Seafood Cookbook*, she joined the crews of fishing trawlers. For her *Farmhouse Cookbook*, she traveled across the United States collecting recipes from farm cooks. She moved to France in pursuit of information for her *French Farmhouse Cookbook*. Susan's food style is homey, casual, and down-to-earth.

Susan Loomis's Philosophy

"The first—and key—component in my cooking philosophy is to use the freshest ingredients possible, preferably organic. The majority of ingredients I use grow in fields within a 12-mile radius of town. I buy from growers at our farmers' market, and I purchase seafood directly from the fishermen. If you don't have access to such resources, you can still make wise choices about ingredients by sticking to the ideas of seasonal freshness and quality, and by buying as directly as possible.

The second component in my philosophy stresses the importance of method: You must complete steps one and two before going to step three. Even though French cooking isn't hopelessly labor-intensive or complicated, I write my recipes very deliberately. That is because I think it's vital to follow all the steps to achieve a great dish.

Technique also plays a critical role. Always read a recipe carefully and understand that each term is specific. If a recipe calls for a minced ingredient, the pieces should be tiny, not just small. Likewise, the term "julienne" refers to strips that look almost like thick hair, not matchsticks. Good knife skills are the key to slicing and dicing.

Cooking techniques have specific intended results, as well, and there are methods you should become familiar with. For example, browning is best achieved over medium-high heat. To deglaze, add liquid to the pan, scraping all those succulent caramelized bits from the bottom so the flavor will not be lost. A reduction thickens and concentrates the flavor of liquids as moisture evaporates.

The final part of my philosophy is to layer flavors to create a harmonious whole. A French braise tastes rich because after browning, deglazing, and reducing, it cooks long and slow, as in Beef Cooked with Carrots, Onions, and Dried Plums (recipe on page 115). A French roast is succulent and tender because it's slathered with mustard, which protects it in the hot oven as it cooks. French desserts are light and lively because they begin with fresh ingredients—gorgeous strawberries and other seasonal fruits. Unorthodox, yet complementary, combinations add the final touch—berries with vinegar, sugar, and black pepper, for example. It's all easy, but it isn't always obvious."

Chicken with Citrus
(pictured on page 112)

Enjoy this simple dish in winter or early spring when citrus is still at its peak. Free-range chickens are worth the extra expense for their fresh, pure flavor, but this recipe will work with a commercial chicken, too.

- 1 (3¼-pound) whole free-range chicken
- 2 teaspoons dried oregano, divided
- 1 teaspoon sea salt, divided
- ½ teaspoon freshly ground black pepper
- 1 lemon, cut in half
- 1 orange, cut in half
- 1 tablespoon unsalted butter, softened
- Cooking spray
- 2 cups water, divided

1. Preheat oven to 450°.
2. Remove and discard giblets and neck. Rinse chicken with cold water; pat dry. Sprinkle 1 teaspoon oregano, ½ teaspoon salt, and pepper in body cavity. Place lemon halves and orange halves in cavity (this will be a tight fit).
3. Combine 1 teaspoon oregano and butter. Starting at neck cavity, loosen skin from breast and drumsticks by inserting fingers, gently pushing between skin and meat. Rub butter mixture under loosened skin. Lift wing tips up and over back; tuck under chicken. Tie legs together with cord. Place chicken, breast side up, on a rack coated with cooking spray. Place rack in a broiler pan; add 1½ cups water to pan. Bake at 450° for 50 minutes or until a thermometer inserted in meaty part of thigh registers 170°. Let stand 20 minutes. Remove fruit from cavity; set aside. Remove skin; discard. Sprinkle chicken evenly with ½ teaspoon salt.
4. Place a zip-top plastic bag inside a 2-cup glass measure. Pour drippings from pan into bag; add ½ cup water. Let stand 2 minutes (fat will rise to the top). Seal bag; carefully snip off 1 bottom corner of bag. Drain drippings into measuring cup, stopping before fat layer reaches opening; discard fat. Return drippings to broiler pan, and place over medium heat,

Continued

scraping pan to loosen browned bits. Simmer 8 minutes or until reduced to ¼ cup. Cut chicken into serving pieces; squeeze juice from reserved fruit over chicken. Serve with sauce. Yield: 4 servings (serving size: about 3 ounces meat and 1 tablespoon sauce).

CALORIES 287 (39% from fat); FAT 12.4g (sat 4.4g, mono 4.4g, poly 2.3g); PROTEIN 36g; CARB 6.4g; FIBER 1.7g; CHOL 114mg; IRON 2.3mg; SODIUM 711mg; CALC 51mg

Spring Vegetables

Late spring is a perfect moment in the life of a vegetable: It's tender, sweet, flavorful, and juicy. Prepare this dish with the freshest vegetables, particularly spring onions, which look like large green onions. The fresh lettuce "melts" gently into the peas and carrots, a true celebration of the season.

 2   tablespoons unsalted butter, divided
2½   cups (¼-inch) slices carrot
 ½   cup sliced spring onion, trimmed and peeled
 ½   cup sliced shallots
 ½   teaspoon sea salt
 ¼   teaspoon freshly ground black pepper
 ½   cup water
 2   cups shelled green peas (about 2 pounds unshelled)
 8   Bibb lettuce leaves (about ¼ pound)

1. Melt 1 tablespoon butter in a large saucepan over medium heat. Add carrot and next 4 ingredients, stirring to combine. Cover and cook 7 minutes, stirring occasionally.
2. Add water and peas; place lettuce leaves on top of mixture. Cover and cook 5 minutes or until peas are tender. Remove from heat; gently stir in 1 tablespoon butter. Yield: 10 servings (serving size: about ½ cup).
WINE NOTE: Don't miss the Henri Bourgeois Sancerre Grande Reserve 2000 ($16), a zesty white that has a dagger of refreshing acidity.

CALORIES 115 (20% from fat); FAT 2.6g (sat 1.5g, mono 0.7g, poly 0.2g); PROTEIN 4g; CARB 21.2g; FIBER 5.8g; CHOL 6mg; IRON 1.5mg; SODIUM 180mg; CALC 47mg

Normandy Seafood Stew

The parsley, thyme, and bay leaf bundle is classically referred to as a *bouquet garni.* When the stew is done, it's removed from the broth.

 3   cups chopped onion, divided
 1   cup dry white wine
30   medium mussels (about 1½ pounds), scrubbed and debearded
 6   flat-leaf parsley sprigs, divided
 2   tablespoons butter
2½   cups finely chopped fennel bulb
 2   cups finely chopped leeks (about 1 pound)
 4   cups boiling water
 2   extralarge fish-flavored bouillon cubes (such as Knorr)
 3   thyme sprigs
 1   bay leaf
 ½   cup half-and-half
 ¼   cup crème fraîche
 2   large egg yolks, lightly beaten
1¾   pounds cod or other firm white fish fillets, cut into 1-inch pieces
12   ounces sea scallops
 ¼   cup chopped fresh flat-leaf parsley
 1   tablespoon (1-inch) julienne-cut lemon rind
 ½   teaspoon sea salt
 ¼   teaspoon black pepper

1. Combine 1½ cups onion, wine, mussels, and 3 parsley sprigs in a Dutch oven; bring to a boil over medium-high heat. Cover and cook 2 minutes or until mussels open; discard any unopened shells. Remove mussels with a slotted spoon; set aside. Strain cooking liquid through a sieve into a bowl, reserving liquid, and discard solids. Remove meat from mussels. Discard shells.
2. Place Dutch oven over medium heat; melt butter. Add 1½ cups onion, fennel, and leeks; cook 10 minutes or until tender, stirring occasionally. Combine water and bouillon, stirring until bouillon cubes dissolve. Add bouillon mixture and reserved cooking liquid to onion mixture, stirring to combine.
3. Place 3 parsley sprigs, thyme, and bay leaf on a double layer of cheesecloth. Gather edges of cheesecloth together, and tie securely. Add cheesecloth bag to

broth mixture; bring to a boil. Reduce heat, and simmer 10 minutes. Remove bag, and discard.
4. Combine half-and-half, crème fraîche, and egg yolks in a medium bowl, stirring well with a whisk. Gradually add 1½ cups hot broth mixture to egg mixture, stirring constantly with a whisk. Add egg mixture to pan. Cook 5 minutes or until soup thickens slightly (do not boil), stirring constantly. Add fish and scallops; cook 5 minutes or until fish is done, stirring frequently. Stir in mussels, ¼ cup chopped parsley, and lemon rind; cook 1 minute or until thoroughly heated. Stir in salt and pepper. Yield: 8 servings (serving size: 1½ cups).

CALORIES 329 (31% from fat); FAT 11.2g (sat 5.2g, mono 3g, poly 1.3g); PROTEIN 37.4g; CARB 12.9g; FIBER 1.9g; CHOL 153mg; IRON 5mg; SODIUM 1,062mg; CALC 122mg

Fire-Grilled Pork Chops

These pork chops crisp slowly on the outside, yet stay moist and juicy inside. If you don't have a grill, simply broil them. Marinating them overnight will allow the flavor to more fully penetrate the meat, but you can cook them as soon as an hour after seasoning.

 4   (6-ounce) bone-in center-cut pork chops (about ¾ inch thick)
 2   teaspoons extravirgin olive oil
1½   tablespoons herbes de Provence
 ½   teaspoon freshly ground black pepper
Cooking spray
 1   teaspoon coarse sea salt

1. Brush both sides of pork evenly with oil; sprinkle with herbes de Provence and pepper. Cover and marinate in refrigerator 12 hours or overnight.
2. Prepare grill.
3. Place pork on grill rack coated with cooking spray. Grill 5 minutes on each side or until desired degree of doneness. Sprinkle evenly with salt. Yield: 4 servings (serving size: 1 pork chop).

CALORIES 263 (39% from fat); FAT 11.3g (sat 3.3g, mono 6g, poly 1.9g); PROTEIN 37.7g; CARB 0.5g; FIBER 0.3g; CHOL 105mg; IRON 0.3mg; SODIUM 689mg; CALC 8mg

A *bouquet garni* can include any combination of **herbs**. Typically they're tied together or placed in a **cheesecloth** bag. This allows for **easy** removal.

Beef Cooked with Carrots, Onions, and Dried Plums

This dish is so well loved, it vies with dishes like bouillabaisse, tarte Tatin, roast chicken, and veal stew as a favorite in the annals of French cooking. It's a homey dish, the kind served to family or on the menu in a café or bistro. For a wonderful Sunday night supper, serve with freshly cooked pasta. Note that this dish cooks for about three hours, beginning on the stovetop and finishing in the oven.

    1   (2½-pound) boneless chuck roast, trimmed
    2   teaspoons sea salt
    1   teaspoon freshly ground black pepper
    2   teaspoons extravirgin olive oil or grapeseed oil
    3   cups thinly sliced onion
    4   cups warm water
    2   rosemary sprigs
    20   thyme sprigs
    1   sage sprig
    3   bay leaves
    1   pound baby carrots
    2   cups pitted dried plums
Sage leaves (optional)

1. Preheat oven to 350°.
2. Tie roast at 2-inch intervals with twine; rub with salt and pepper. Heat oil in a Dutch oven over medium-high heat. Add roast; cook 12 minutes, browning on all sides. Remove roast from pan. Add onion and water to pan, scraping pan to loosen browned bits. Return meat to pan.
3. Place rosemary, thyme, sage sprig, and bay leaves on a double layer of cheesecloth. Gather edges of cheesecloth together; tie securely. Add cheesecloth bag to pan; bring to a simmer. Cover and bake at 350° for 1½ hours. Turn roast, and bake, covered, an additional 45 minutes. Add carrots and plums; bake, covered, an additional 45 minutes or until carrots are tender.
4. Place roast, carrots, and plums on a platter; keep warm. Reserve cooking liquid. Discard bag.
5. Place a zip-top plastic bag inside a 2-cup glass measure. Pour cooking liquid into bag; let stand 2 minutes (fat will rise to the top). Seal bag; carefully snip off 1 bottom corner of bag. Drain drippings into measuring cup, stopping before fat layer reaches opening; discard fat. Slice roast; garnish with sage leaves, if desired. Serve with carrot mixture and sauce. Yield: 8 servings (serving size: about 3 ounces beef, ½ cup carrot mixture, and about 1½ tablespoons sauce).
WINE NOTE: Try the Château de Fieuzal Grand Cru Classé de Graves Bordeaux 2000 ($35). Its espresso and dark chocolate flavors act as bookends to a core of blackberry.

CALORIES 316 (27% from fat); FAT 9.4g (sat 3.2g, mono 4.4g, poly 0.5g); PROTEIN 30.5g; CARB 28g; FIBER 4.6g; CHOL 76mg; IRON 3.7mg; SODIUM 716mg; CALC 59mg

Leg of Lamb with Herbs and Mustard

Leg of lamb is delicious any time of year, but particularly in the spring. Lamb roasted with herbs and mustard is a dish fit for the finest occasion. Press the herb mixture into the slits in the meat, brush the leg with mustard, and chill in the refrigerator; it will macerate, allowing the flavor to permeate the lamb.

    2   tablespoons minced fresh thyme
    ¼   teaspoon ground bay leaves
    1   garlic clove, minced
    1   (4-pound) rolled boneless leg of lamb
    1¼   teaspoons sea salt, divided
    1   teaspoon freshly ground black pepper
    ⅓   cup Dijon mustard
    6   rosemary sprigs
    ½   cup water
    ½   cup low-salt beef broth

1. Combine first 3 ingredients, stirring well. Unroll roast; trim fat. Reroll roast; secure at 1-inch intervals with twine. Cut 10 (½-inch-deep) slits in surface of roast; stuff thyme mixture into slits. Sprinkle with ¾ teaspoon salt and pepper. Brush mustard over roast. Cover and chill 12 hours.
2. Preheat oven to 425°.
3. Arrange 3 rosemary sprigs crosswise on rack of a broiler pan, and top with roast. Arrange 3 rosemary sprigs on top of roast. Bake at 425° for 50 minutes or until a thermometer in thickest portion of roast registers 145° (medium-rare) or desired degree of doneness. Discard rosemary. Let roast stand 20 minutes before slicing.
4. Combine water and broth; add to broiler pan. Place over medium heat; bring to a boil, scraping pan to loosen browned bits. Cook 4 minutes or until reduced to ½ cup; stir in ½ teaspoon salt. Slice roast; serve with sauce. Yield: 8 servings (serving size: 3 ounces lamb and 1 tablespoon sauce).
WINE NOTE: A nice match is Château La Nerthe Châteauneuf-du-Pape 1999 ($40), which is replete with chocolate, black licorice, espresso, and grenadine flavors.

CALORIES 119 (33% from fat); FAT 4.3g (sat 1.5g, mono 1.9g, poly 0.3g); PROTEIN 15.9g; CARB 0.6g; FIBER 0.2g; CHOL 49mg; IRON 1.3mg; SODIUM 855mg; CALC 9mg

Strawberry Parfait with Fresh Normandy Cream

Try to purchase locally grown strawberries that have ripened on the plant.

STRAWBERRIES:
- ½ cup packed light brown sugar
- 3 tablespoons raspberry or balsamic vinegar
- 2 cups sliced strawberries

CREAM:
- ¼ cup crème fraîche
- 1½ teaspoons granulated sugar

SORBET:
- 2 cups sliced strawberries
- ¼ cup granulated sugar
- 2½ teaspoons fresh lemon juice
- ⅛ teaspoon freshly ground black pepper
- Mint sprigs (optional)

1. To prepare strawberries, combine brown sugar and vinegar in a medium bowl, stirring with a whisk; add 2 cups strawberries, stirring gently to coat. Cover and chill 4 hours, stirring occasionally.

2. To prepare cream, combine crème fraîche and 1½ teaspoons sugar, stirring until sugar dissolves. Cover and chill.

3. To prepare sorbet, combine 2 cups strawberries, ¼ cup granulated sugar, juice, and pepper in a blender or food processor; process until smooth. Strain strawberry mixture through a sieve over a large bowl, and discard solids. Pour mixture into freezer can of an ice-cream freezer; freeze according to manufacturer's instructions. Spoon sorbet into a freezer-safe container; cover and freeze 1 hour or until firm.

4. To assemble parfaits, spoon 3 tablespoons sorbet into each of 8 champagne flutes, and top each with 3 tablespoons strawberries. Spoon 1½ teaspoons cream over each serving. Drizzle remaining juices from strawberries over each serving. Garnish with mint sprigs, if desired. Yield: 8 servings.

CALORIES 135 (17% from fat); FAT 2.6g (sat 1.7g, mono 0.8g, poly 0.1g); PROTEIN 0.9g; CARB 28.6g; FIBER 2.3g; CHOL 6mg; IRON 0.7mg; SODIUM 12mg; CALC 39mg

In a Pinch

Deftly dispensed, salt can enhance the flavor of many foods.

Coarse salt sprinkled on pretzels is there for one reason—to deliver a burst of flavor. But most of the time, used correctly, salt isn't so obvious.

"Salt both gives flavor and brings out [a food's] intrinsic flavors," says Steven Raichlen, a Miami-based cookbook author whose most recent book is *Big Flavor Cooking.* "It's pretty hard to imagine any food that wouldn't benefit from a sprinkle of salt."

Cooking teachers and food scientists say that when you salt may be as important as how much you salt. And, they say, salt's influence encourages other flavors to come to the fore.

Eggplant, Tomato, and Smoked Mozzarella Tart

Salting the eggplant draws out some of the bitter flavor and moisture. Less moisture in turn minimizes the amount of oil the eggplant will absorb.

CRUST:
- 1 cup all-purpose flour
- 1 tablespoon toasted wheat germ
- 1 teaspoon baking powder
- ½ teaspoon freshly ground black pepper
- ¼ teaspoon salt
- ¼ cup water
- 1 tablespoon olive oil
- Cooking spray

FILLING:
- 1 (1-pound) eggplant, cut crosswise into ¼-inch-thick slices
- ¾ teaspoon salt, divided
- ½ teaspoon olive oil
- 4 garlic cloves, thinly sliced
- 1 tablespoon chopped fresh basil
- 1½ teaspoons chopped fresh oregano
- 1½ teaspoons chopped fresh mint
- 2 plum tomatoes, thinly sliced (about 6 ounces)
- ½ cup (2 ounces) shredded smoked mozzarella cheese, divided
- 2 tablespoons grated fresh Parmesan cheese

1. Preheat oven to 400°.

2. To prepare crust, lightly spoon flour into a dry measuring cup; level with a knife. Combine flour and next 4 ingredients in a large bowl, stirring with a whisk; make a well in center of mixture. Add water and 1 tablespoon oil, stirring to form a soft dough. Turn dough out onto a lightly floured surface; knead lightly 4 times. Gently press dough into a 4-inch circle on plastic wrap; cover and chill 15 minutes.

3. Slightly overlap 2 sheets of plastic wrap on a slightly damp surface. Unwrap dough, and place chilled dough on plastic wrap. Cover with 2 additional sheets of overlapping plastic wrap. Roll dough, still covered, into an 11-inch circle. Remove top sheets of plastic wrap. Fit dough, plastic-wrap side up, into a 10-inch round removable-bottom tart pan coated with cooking spray. Remove remaining plastic wrap. Press dough against bottom and sides of pan. Pierce bottom and sides of dough with a fork; bake at 400° for 10 minutes. Cool completely on a wire rack.

4. To prepare filling, arrange eggplant on several layers of heavy-duty paper towels. Sprinkle eggplant with ½ teaspoon salt; let stand 15 minutes. Pat dry with paper towels; brush eggplant with ½ teaspoon oil. Arrange eggplant in a single layer on a baking sheet coated with cooking spray. Bake at 400° for 20 minutes. Stack eggplant slices on a plate; cover with plastic wrap. Let eggplant stand 7 minutes to steam.

5. Heat a large nonstick skillet coated with cooking spray over medium heat. Add garlic; sauté 1 minute. Remove from heat; stir in ¼ teaspoon salt, basil, oregano, mint, and tomatoes.

6. Sprinkle 2 tablespoons mozzarella on bottom of baked crust. Layer eggplant and tomato mixture in crust; sprinkle with 6 tablespoons mozzarella and Parmesan. Bake at 400° for 10 minutes or until cheese melts. Cut into 8 wedges. Yield: 4 servings (serving size: 2 wedges).

CALORIES 260 (30% from fat); FAT 8.8g (sat 3.1g, mono 4.2g, poly 0.9g); PROTEIN 9.8g; CARB 37g; FIBER 4.6g; CHOL 13mg; IRON 2.6mg; SODIUM 681mg; CALC 210mg

MAKE AHEAD
Vanilla-Nut Pudding

Use any nuts for pistachios and almonds.

    6   tablespoons sugar
    2   tablespoons cornstarch
    2   cups 1% low-fat milk, divided
    ⅛   teaspoon salt
    1   large egg, lightly beaten
    1   teaspoon vanilla extract
    2   tablespoons finely chopped
        pistachios, toasted
    1   tablespoon finely chopped
        blanched almonds, toasted
    Grated whole nutmeg (optional)

1. Combine sugar and cornstarch in a medium heavy saucepan. Add ½ cup milk; stir with a whisk until well blended. Add 1½ cups milk and salt; bring to a simmer over medium heat, stirring frequently. Reduce heat to medium-low; cook 9 minutes, stirring frequently.

2. Place egg in a medium bowl. Gradually add hot milk mixture, stirring constantly with a whisk. Place egg mixture in pan; cook over medium-low heat 3 minutes or until thick, stirring constantly. Remove from heat; stir in vanilla. Pour into a bowl; cover surface with plastic wrap. Cool completely. Uncover and sprinkle with nuts. Garnish with nutmeg, if desired. Yield: 4 servings (serving size: ½ cup).

CALORIES 197 (25% from fat); FAT 5.4g (sat 1.5g, mono 2.4g, poly 1g); PROTEIN 6.9g; CARB 30.1g; FIBER 0.7g; CHOL 58mg; IRON 0.5mg; SODIUM 151mg; CALC 166mg

Salt Facts

Which Salt, What Result?

The difference in flavor between plain and specialty salts is subtle because all salt shares the same chemical profile: 40 percent sodium and 60 percent chloride.

Sea salt is harvested without purification or additives (table salt is processed with a small amount of an anticaking agent to make it pourable). It does have tiny amounts of other minerals, which lend nuances of flavor.

But once it dissolves, the role of any salt—whether table, sea, or kosher—is the same. For that reason, you needn't add expensive sea salt to a soup that will simmer for hours. Use it instead as a finishing flavor note for a dish.

So what salt do chefs use most often? "I'm a big fan of coarse salts, either kosher or sea salt," says cookbook author Steven Raichlen. "They don't completely dissolve when sprinkled on meat or fish." And that offers the occasional hit of salt flavor, or what Raichlen refers to as "a pointillistic burst" of salt flavor.

Food scientist Shirley Corriher is fond of the flavor of "the dirty gray one," or what the French call *sel gris,* Celtic gray sea salt.

The consensus among food professionals is that coarse salts, particularly kosher salt, beat table salt for routine kitchen duties for two simple reasons. First, coarse salts have larger, flakier crystals that dissolve more slowly on the tongue, and are therefore easier to taste. Second, coarse salts are easy to measure out and control. Rather than measuring salt, most chefs simply "pinch" out the amount they need.

Most of these recipes call for table salt, which is common in most kitchens. However, if you use kosher salt, allow for its larger crystals by substituting double the amount of table salt called for. For instance, if a recipe calls for ¼ teaspoon salt, use ½ teaspoon kosher salt. Kosher salts do vary by brand, so if you're concerned about oversalting, start with 50 percent more, and add to taste.

Sodium Concerns

The Food and Drug Administration (FDA) recommends limiting your daily sodium intake to 2,400mg or less. While *Cooking Light* has no specific rules for the amount allowed per recipe, we strive to be mindful of the recommendation—taking into consideration the role the dish plays in a day. For example, we allow higher amounts of sodium for a one-dish meal than for an appetizer or smaller dish.

Salt to the Rescue

In addition to being nature's most adept flavor enhancer, salt plays a few other key roles in cooking.

Salt in bread and pizza dough helps control the action of the yeast and improves the dough's ability to rise. If salt is left out, the finished product will be coarser and taste bland.

Salting slices of eggplant removes bitterness and excess moisture, so it absorbs less fat.

Salt also performs these other kitchen tasks:

• Add a little salt to gelatin; it will set more quickly.

• Throw in a pinch of salt to whipping cream or egg whites before beating to increase volume.

• Wash kale, spinach, and other greens in salt water for easy removal of dirt.

• Combine salt and lemon juice to remove fishy odors from hands and utensils.

• Sprinkle a hefty amount of salt on pie juices that bubble over in the oven to make them easier to clean. The mess will bake to a dry crust that's a cinch to wipe away once it's cool.

Bell Pepper and Tomato Penne with Meatballs

This recipe illustrates how layering salt throughout cooking brings all the flavors of a dish together. The pasta cooks in salted water. The sauce gets seasoned at a couple of steps along the way—first to enhance the flavor of the onion and bell peppers, and later to tame the sharpness of the tomatoes and vinegar.

MEATBALLS:

- 1 (¾-ounce) slice firm white bread (such as Pepperidge Farm)
- ⅓ cup minced fresh onion
- ¼ cup finely chopped cremini mushrooms
- 2 tablespoons finely chopped fresh parsley
- 2 tablespoons grated fresh Parmesan cheese
- ¼ teaspoon salt
- ¼ teaspoon dried oregano
- ¼ teaspoon crushed red pepper
- 1 large egg yolk
- ½ pound lean ground turkey
- Cooking spray

SAUCE:

- 2 teaspoons olive oil
- ¾ cup chopped onion
- 4 garlic cloves, thinly sliced
- ½ cup julienne-cut yellow bell pepper
- ½ cup julienne-cut orange bell pepper
- ½ teaspoon salt, divided
- 3 cups chopped seeded plum tomato (about 2 pounds)
- ½ cup tomato juice
- ¼ cup quartered pitted kalamata olives
- 2 tablespoons balsamic vinegar
- 1 teaspoon sugar
- ½ teaspoon dried oregano
- ¼ teaspoon freshly ground black pepper
- ¼ cup thinly sliced fresh basil

PASTA:

- ⅛ teaspoon salt
- 8 ounces uncooked penne (about 2 cups tube-shaped pasta)

1. Preheat oven to 400°.

2. To prepare meatballs, place bread in a food processor; pulse 10 times or until fine crumbs measure ½ cup. Combine breadcrumbs, ⅓ cup onion, and next 8 ingredients; stir well to combine. Lightly coat hands with cooking spray. Shape turkey mixture into 20 (1-inch) meatballs. Place on a baking sheet coated with cooking spray. Bake at 400° for 12 minutes or until done; cover and keep warm.

3. To prepare sauce, heat oil in a large nonstick skillet over medium-high heat. Add ¾ cup onion; sauté 3 minutes. Add garlic; sauté 1 minute. Add bell peppers and ¼ teaspoon salt; sauté 2 minutes. Add tomato and next 6 ingredients; bring to a boil. Reduce heat; simmer, uncovered, 13 minutes or until sauce thickens. Stir in basil and ¼ teaspoon salt. Add meatballs; stir to coat.

4. To prepare pasta, while sauce cooks, bring 3 quarts water to a boil in a large saucepan; add ⅛ teaspoon salt and pasta. Cook 10 minutes or until al dente; drain. Serve meatball mixture over pasta. Yield: 4 servings (serving size: 1 cup pasta and 1½ cups meatball mixture).

CALORIES 473 (26% from fat); FAT 13.8g (sat 3.2g, mono 6.5g, poly 2.1g); PROTEIN 23.3g; CARB 65.7g; FIBER 6g; CHOL 100mg; IRON 4.6mg; SODIUM 911mg; CALC 116mg

---

Steak and Potatoes Menu
serves 6

This easy lineup works well for either a weeknight meal or casual entertaining. If you don't have time to marinate the meat, brush the marinade on the meat as it grills.

Asiago, Potato, and Bacon Gratin

Grilled marinated flank steak*

Steamed green beans

*Combine 3 tablespoons Worcestershire sauce, 1 tablespoon low-sodium soy sauce, 1 tablespoon fresh lemon juice, 2 teaspoons honey, and 2 minced garlic cloves in a large zip-top plastic bag; add a 1½-pound flank steak to bag. Seal and marinate in refrigerator 1 hour, turning bag occasionally. Preheat grill; grill steak 6 minutes on each side or until desired degree of doneness.

Asiago, Potato, and Bacon Gratin

- 1½ pounds peeled Yukon gold potatoes, cut into ¼-inch-thick slices
- 1 teaspoon salt, divided
- Cooking spray
- 2 tablespoons minced shallots
- ¼ cup all-purpose flour
- 2 cups 1% low-fat milk, divided
- ¾ cup (3 ounces) grated Asiago cheese
- ¼ cup chopped fresh chives
- ¼ teaspoon freshly ground black pepper
- 4 bacon slices, cooked and crumbled
- ¼ cup (1 ounce) grated fresh Parmesan cheese

1. Preheat oven to 350°.

2. Place potatoes in a large saucepan; cover with water. Bring to a boil. Reduce heat; simmer 5 minutes or until potatoes are almost tender. Drain. Sprinkle potatoes evenly with ¼ teaspoon salt; set aside, and keep warm.

3. Heat a medium saucepan coated with cooking spray over medium heat. Add shallots; cook 2 minutes or until tender, stirring frequently. Lightly spoon flour into a dry measuring cup; level with a knife. Sprinkle flour over shallots. Gradually add ½ cup milk, stirring with a whisk until well blended. Gradually add 1½ cups milk, stirring with a whisk. Cook over medium heat 9 minutes or until thick, stirring frequently. Remove from heat; stir in ¾ teaspoon salt, Asiago, chives, pepper, and bacon.

4. Arrange half of potato slices in an 8-inch square baking dish coated with cooking spray. Pour half of cheese sauce over potato slices. Top with remaining potato slices and cheese sauce; sprinkle with Parmesan. Bake at 350° for 35 minutes or until cheese is bubbly and lightly browned. Yield: 6 servings.

CALORIES 250 (30% from fat); FAT 8.2g (sat 4.6g, mono 2.7g, poly 0.5g); PROTEIN 12.3g; CARB 31.9g; FIBER 2.3g; CHOL 23mg; IRON 0.9mg; SODIUM 618mg; CALC 306mg

Pan-Seared Pork Chops with Molasses-Plum Sauce

Aside from seasoning the meat, salt also brings the sweet-savory flavors of the sauce into balance. If you prefer, you can easily substitute chopped dried cherries or cranberries for the blueberries and still get a great-tasting dish. Serve these saucy pork chops alongside rice or couscous.

2 teaspoons olive oil
½ cup chopped onion
¾ cup fat-free, less-sodium chicken broth
¼ cup dried blueberries
3 tablespoons cider vinegar
2 tablespoons molasses
¼ teaspoon salt
¼ teaspoon freshly ground black pepper
⅛ teaspoon ground coriander
3 plums, pitted, peeled, and coarsely chopped (about 1¾ cups)
Cooking spray
¼ teaspoon salt
¼ teaspoon freshly ground black pepper
4 (6-ounce) bone-in center-cut pork chops (about 1 inch thick)
Parsley sprigs (optional)

1. Heat oil in a medium saucepan over medium heat. Add onion; cook 3 minutes or until tender, stirring frequently. Stir in broth and next 7 ingredients; bring to a boil. Reduce heat, and simmer 20 minutes or until plums are tender and mixture is thick.
2. Heat a large nonstick skillet coated with cooking spray over medium-high heat. Sprinkle ¼ teaspoon salt and ¼ teaspoon pepper over pork chops. Add pork chops to skillet; cook 2 minutes on each side or until browned. Reduce heat to medium; cook 4 minutes or until done. Remove pork chops from pan; cover and keep warm. Add plum mixture to pan; bring to a simmer. Cook 2 minutes, scraping pan to loosen browned bits. Spoon plum mixture over pork. Garnish with parsley, if desired. Yield: 4

servings (serving size: 1 pork chop and ¼ cup plum mixture).

CALORIES 299 (29% from fat); FAT 9.6g (sat 2.9g, mono 5g, poly 0.8g); PROTEIN 27.1g; CARB 26.6g; FIBER 1.9g; CHOL 69mg; IRON 1.7mg; SODIUM 434mg; CALC 61mg

---

MAKE AHEAD • FREEZABLE
Orange-Pecan Tea Bread

A small amount of salt in a quick bread or cake batter balances its sweetness.

1¾ cups all-purpose flour
1 teaspoon baking powder
½ teaspoon baking soda
¼ teaspoon salt
¼ teaspoon ground nutmeg
¼ teaspoon ground allspice
½ cup granulated sugar
½ cup low-fat buttermilk
¼ cup chopped pecans, toasted
3 tablespoons 1% low-fat milk
3 tablespoons vegetable oil
3 tablespoons orange marmalade
2 teaspoons grated orange rind
2 large eggs, lightly beaten
Cooking spray
½ cup powdered sugar
2 teaspoons fresh orange juice
1½ teaspoons chopped pecans, toasted

1. Preheat oven to 350°.
2. Lightly spoon flour into dry measuring cups; level with a knife. Combine flour and next 5 ingredients in a large bowl; stir with a whisk. Make a well in center of mixture. Combine granulated sugar and next 7 ingredients; stir with a whisk. Add to flour mixture; stir just until moist.
3. Spoon into an 8 x 4-inch loaf pan coated with cooking spray. Bake at 350° for 45 minutes or until a wooden pick inserted in center comes out clean. Cool 10 minutes in pan on a wire rack; remove from pan. Cool completely on a wire rack.

4. Combine powdered sugar and juice, stirring until smooth. Drizzle glaze over bread, and sprinkle with 1½ teaspoons pecans. Yield: 14 servings (serving size: 1 slice).

CALORIES 171 (29% from fat); FAT 5.6g (sat 0.9g, mono 2g, poly 2.4g); PROTEIN 3.2g; CARB 27.4g; FIBER 0.7g; CHOL 31mg; IRON 1mg; SODIUM 144mg; CALC 44mg

---

Tuscan Bean and Wilted Arugula Salad

Beans become tough if cooked in salted water, so salt them after they're cooked and tender. Salt the arugula before combining with the other ingredients.

¾ cup dried white kidney beans
1 bay leaf
¾ teaspoon salt, divided
⅛ teaspoon freshly ground black pepper
5 teaspoons extravirgin olive oil, divided
4 garlic cloves, thinly sliced
1 tablespoon fresh lemon juice
6 cups trimmed baby arugula (about 8 ounces)
¾ cup thinly vertically sliced red onion

1. Sort and wash beans; place in a large bowl. Cover with water to 2 inches above beans; cover and let stand 8 hours or overnight. Drain beans. Place beans in a large saucepan. Cover with water to 3 inches above beans; add bay leaf. Bring to a boil. Reduce heat; simmer, uncovered, 1 hour and 15 minutes or until tender. Drain beans; discard bay leaf. Place beans in a large bowl; sprinkle with ¼ teaspoon salt and pepper. Let stand 5 minutes. Drizzle with 1 teaspoon oil; toss gently to coat.

Continued

The point is not to use as much salt as possible, but to use it sparingly when and where it will have the most impact.

2. Heat 4 teaspoons oil in a small nonstick skillet over medium heat. Add garlic; sauté 45 seconds or just until garlic begins to brown. Remove from heat; stir in juice. Place arugula in a large bowl; sprinkle with ½ teaspoon salt. Add warm bean mixture, garlic mixture, and onion; toss gently to combine. Yield: 6 servings (serving size: 1 cup).

CALORIES 128 (30% from fat); FAT 4.3g (sat 0.5g, mono 2.8g, poly 0.5g); PROTEIN 5.6g; CARB 18g; FIBER 0.9g; CHOL 0mg; IRON 1.9mg; SODIUM 305mg; CALC 92mg

Chicken and Soba Noodle Soup

In this Asian soup, salt flavors the stock as it cooks and softens the bitter bok choy.

    2 teaspoons dark sesame oil
    1 cup chopped carrot
    1 cup thinly sliced celery
    ¾ cup chopped onion
    1 tablespoon minced peeled fresh ginger
    ¾ teaspoon salt, divided
    3 garlic cloves, minced
    5 cups water
    2 tablespoons low-sodium soy sauce
    ½ teaspoon hot chile sauce with garlic (such as KA-ME)
    2 (14-ounce) cans fat-free, less-sodium chicken broth
    2 (8-ounce) chicken breast halves, skinned
    2 ounces uncooked soba noodles
    4 cups shredded bok choy
    1 cup (½-inch) slices green onions
    3 tablespoons thinly sliced fresh basil
    ¼ teaspoon freshly ground black pepper
    1 tablespoon fresh lime juice

1. Heat oil in a Dutch oven over medium heat. Add carrot, celery, and chopped onion; cook 5 minutes or until tender, stirring frequently. Add ginger, ¼ teaspoon salt, and garlic; cook 1 minute, stirring constantly. Add ¼ teaspoon salt, water, soy sauce, chile sauce, broth, and chicken. Bring to a boil; reduce heat, and simmer 1 hour. Remove chicken from pan; cool slightly. Remove chicken from bones; discard bones. Shred meat with 2 forks. Add chicken to pan; bring to a boil. Add soba; cook 5 minutes. Stir in bok choy; reduce heat, and simmer 3 minutes. Stir in ¼ teaspoon salt, green onions, basil, and pepper; cook 2 minutes. Remove from heat; stir in lime juice. Yield: 6 servings (serving size: about 1½ cups).

CALORIES 149 (16% from fat); FAT 2.6g (sat 0.4g, mono 0.8g, poly 0.9g); PROTEIN 15.5g; CARB 15.4g; FIBER 3g; CHOL 29mg; IRON 1.6mg; SODIUM 731mg; CALC 82mg

Fig and Mascarpone Focaccia

Coarse kosher salt sprinkled on focaccia both tastes and looks great. Mascarpone melts into the dough to create a rich, buttery crust that won our Test Kitchen's highest rating.

    1   teaspoon honey
    1   package dry yeast (about 2¼ teaspoons)
    1¼ cups warm water (100° to 110°), divided
    2   tablespoons olive oil
    3¼ cups all-purpose flour, divided
    1   teaspoon kosher salt, divided
    Cooking spray
    ¼   cup (2 ounces) mascarpone cheese
    3   dried figs, quartered
    ½   teaspoon olive oil

1. Dissolve honey and yeast in ½ cup warm water in a large bowl; let stand 10 minutes. Add ¾ cup warm water and 2 tablespoons oil; stir until blended. Lightly spoon flour into dry measuring cups; level with a knife. Add 2¾ cups flour and ½ teaspoon salt to yeast mixture; stir until blended. Turn dough out onto a floured surface. Knead until smooth and elastic (about 10 minutes); add enough of remaining ½ cup flour, 1 tablespoon at a time, to prevent dough from sticking to hands (dough will feel sticky).
2. Place dough in a large bowl coated with cooking spray, turning to coat top. Cover and let rise in a warm place (85°), free from drafts, 1 hour or until doubled in size. (Gently press two fingers into dough. If indentation remains, dough has risen enough.)

3. Punch dough down. Place dough in a 13 x 9-inch baking pan coated with cooking spray. Pat dough to fit pan. Cover and let rise 30 minutes. Uncover dough. Make indentations in top of dough using handle of a wooden spoon or fingertips. Cover and let rise 45 minutes or until doubled in size.
4. Preheat oven to 400°.
5. Uncover dough. Spoon small dollops of cheese over dough. Gently spread cheese over dough. Sprinkle figs evenly over cheese. Drizzle ½ teaspoon oil over dough. Sprinkle with ¼ teaspoon salt. Bake at 400° for 23 minutes or until browned on bottom and loaf sounds hollow when tapped. Sprinkle with ¼ teaspoon salt. Serve warm or at room temperature. Yield: 14 servings (serving size: 1 piece).

CALORIES 155 (25% from fat); FAT 4.3g (sat 1.4g, mono 2.2g, poly 0.3g); PROTEIN 3.6g; CARB 25.5g; FIBER 1.4g; CHOL 5mg; IRON 1.5mg; SODIUM 138mg; CALC 15mg

---

Supporting Role

It might help to think of salt as a supporting player, one that lets the tastes of other ingredients shine and creates harmony among all the components in a dish, explains Shirley Corriher, an Atlanta-based food scientist. She says salt is especially adept at suppressing bitter flavors in greens, sweets, and just about any food. Skeptical? Try this experiment: Take a sip of plain tonic water, and focus on the bitter quinine flavor. Next, add a little salt to the tonic water, and taste it again. "It's amazing; it tastes almost like sugar water after the salt has been added," says Corriher, who first tried this test at a recent meeting of the International Association of Culinary Professional Board Members.

"Salt is powerful when it comes to eliminating bitterness," she says. "That's why pastry chefs always tell you to add a pinch of salt to desserts. It suppresses bitter notes and brings out sweetness."

. . . And Ready in Just About 20 Minutes

Sometimes the best bet for dinner is breakfast.

Sausage and Egg Burrito offers familiar, comforting foods in an easy-to-eat package. Ham and Asparagus Frittata and Ham and Cheese Hash Browns offer A.M. simplicity for the P.M. meal. Not hungry for breakfast? Cashew Chicken Salad Sandwiches and Roast Chicken Chimichangas become complete meals with fresh fruit and a beverage. Pasta is always good, too. Try angel hair pasta with chicken and spinach, or fettuccine with asparagus and prosciutto. For a meatless option, try Macadamia Nut-Pesto Fettuccine.

QUICK & EASY
Shrimp Creole

To quickly thaw frozen vegetables, place them in a colander, and rinse them with hot tap water. Serve this dish with bottled hot sauce.

1 (3½-ounce) bag boil-in-bag long-grain rice
1 tablespoon vegetable oil
1 teaspoon Old Bay seasoning
¼ teaspoon ground red pepper
1½ pounds medium shrimp, peeled and deveined
1 cup frozen chopped onion, thawed
1 cup frozen diced green pepper, thawed
1 cup chopped celery
1 teaspoon bottled minced garlic
½ teaspoon dried oregano
½ teaspoon dried thyme
1 (14.5-ounce) can diced tomatoes with onion and garlic, undrained
1 (14.5-ounce) can no salt-added diced tomatoes, undrained

1. Cook rice according to package directions, omitting salt and fat.
2. While rice cooks, heat oil in a large nonstick skillet over medium-high heat. Add Old Bay, red pepper, and shrimp; sauté 1 minute. Remove from pan.
3. Add onion, green pepper, celery, and garlic to pan; sauté 4 minutes or until tender. Add oregano, thyme, and tomatoes; bring to a boil. Reduce heat to medium-low; cook 5 minutes. Return shrimp to pan, and cook 2 minutes or until shrimp are done. Serve over rice. Yield: 4 servings (serving size: 1½ cups shrimp mixture and ½ cup rice).

CALORIES 391 (17% from fat); FAT 7.4g (sat 1.1g, mono 3g, poly 1.5g); PROTEIN 40.2g; CARB 41.6g; FIBER 4.7g; CHOL 259mg; IRON 8mg; SODIUM 988mg; CALC 152mg

QUICK & EASY
Spicy Chicken Pasta

You'll need only about 8 minutes of hands-on prep for this recipe. Gather the remaining ingredients as the pasta cooks. If you have leftover chicken, use 1½ cups in place of the honey-roasted chicken.

1 (9-ounce) package fresh angel hair pasta
Cooking spray
1 cup vertically sliced onion
1 tablespoon dried basil
1½ teaspoons bottled minced garlic
½ teaspoon crushed red pepper
1 cup half-and-half
¼ cup reduced-fat sour cream
1 teaspoon all-purpose flour
¼ teaspoon salt
⅛ teaspoon black pepper
1 (6-ounce) package honey-roasted chicken breast cuts (such as Louis Rich)
1 (10-ounce) package frozen chopped spinach, thawed, drained, and squeezed dry
1 tablespoon grated fresh Parmesan cheese

1. Cook pasta according to package directions, omitting salt and fat. Drain in a colander over a bowl, reserving ¼ cup cooking liquid.
2. While pasta cooks, heat a large non-stick skillet coated with cooking spray over medium-high heat. Add onion; sauté 2 minutes. Add basil, garlic, and red pepper; sauté 1 minute. Combine half-and-half, sour cream, and flour, stirring with a whisk. Add reserved pasta cooking liquid and half-and-half mixture to pan; bring to a boil. Stir in salt, black pepper, chicken, and spinach; bring to a boil. Stir in pasta, and cook 1 minute or until thoroughly heated. Sprinkle with cheese. Yield: 4 servings (serving size: about 1¾ cups).

CALORIES 383 (29% from fat); FAT 12.4g (sat 6.2g, mono 3.8g, poly 1.2g); PROTEIN 20.5g; CARB 46.1g; FIBER 6g; CHOL 108mg; IRON 5.3mg; SODIUM 784mg; CALC 253mg

QUICK & EASY
Crab Quesadillas

These quesadillas finish in the oven under the broiler. If you prefer, brown them in a nonstick skillet coated with cooking spray. Serve sour cream and salsa on the side.

¼ cup chopped green onions
2 tablespoons fat-free sour cream
1 tablespoon minced fresh cilantro
¾ teaspoon bottled minced garlic
1 jalapeño pepper, seeded and finely chopped
½ pound lump crabmeat, shell pieces removed
½ cup (2 ounces) shredded Monterey Jack cheese
4 (8-inch) fat-free flour tortillas

1. Preheat broiler.
2. Combine first 6 ingredients, stirring well. Sprinkle 2 tablespoons cheese over each tortilla. Divide crab mixture evenly among tortillas. Fold in half, pressing gently to seal.
3. Place filled tortillas on a baking sheet. Broil 1 minute or until tortillas are lightly browned. Yield: 4 servings (serving size: 1 quesadilla).

CALORIES 275 (28% from fat); FAT 8.6g (sat 3.7g, mono 3.2g, poly 0.9g); PROTEIN 18.5g; CARB 30g; FIBER 2g; CHOL 58mg; IRON 2.2mg; SODIUM 484mg; CALC 187mg

QUICK & EASY

Roast Chicken Chimichangas

These chimichangas are oven-browned
instead of deep-fried. The filling uses *queso
fresco*. If it's not available, try shredded
Monterey Jack.

2½ cups shredded roasted skinless,
   boneless chicken breasts
  1 cup (4 ounces) crumbled queso
   fresco cheese
 ¼ cup chopped green onions
  1 teaspoon dried oregano
 ¼ teaspoon ground cumin
  1 garlic clove, minced
  1 (4.5-ounce) can chopped green
   chiles, drained
  1 (16-ounce) can fat-free refried
   beans
  6 (8-inch) flour tortillas
Cooking spray
 ½ cup bottled green salsa

1. Preheat oven to 500°.
2. Combine first 7 ingredients in a large
bowl; toss well.
3. Spread ¼ cup beans down center of
each tortilla. Top each tortilla with ⅔
cup chicken mixture; roll up. Place
rolls, seam sides down, on a large
baking sheet coated with cooking
spray. Coat tops of chimichangas with
cooking spray. Bake at 500° for 7 minutes. Serve with salsa. Yield: 6 servings
(serving size: 1 chimichanga and about
4 teaspoons salsa).

CALORIES 380 (23% from fat); FAT 9.7g (sat 3.1g, mono 4.1g,
poly 1.6g); PROTEIN 28.8g; CARB 42.5g; FIBER 6.5g; CHOL 55mg;
IRON 3.8mg; SODIUM 728mg; CALC 157mg

QUICK & EASY

Cashew Chicken Salad Sandwiches

This sandwich goes together as fast as an
ordinary turkey sandwich but is much more
interesting. Add lettuce and tomato, if
you'd like.

 ¼ cup fat-free sour cream
  1 tablespoon light mayonnaise
 ¼ teaspoon curry powder
  2 cups chopped roasted skinless,
   boneless chicken breasts (about
   2 breasts)
 ⅓ cup chopped celery
  2 tablespoons chopped dry-roasted
   cashews
  1 tablespoon finely chopped green
   onions
  2 (2-ounce) whole wheat
   hamburger buns

1. Combine first 3 ingredients in a large
bowl, stirring until well blended. Add
chicken, celery, cashews, and green
onions; stir well. Serve chicken salad on
buns. Yield: 2 servings (serving size: ⅔
cup chicken salad and 1 bun).

CALORIES 353 (26% from fat); FAT 10.3g (sat 2.6g, mono 1.5g,
poly 1.8g); PROTEIN 31.6g; CARB 35.8g; FIBER 4.8g; CHOL 69mg;
IRON 1.8mg; SODIUM 925mg; CALC 115mg

QUICK & EASY

Pasta with Asparagus, Lemon, and Prosciutto

Cook prosciutto, the Italian salt-cured ham,
quickly; it becomes tough if overcooked.

  1 (9-ounce) package fresh
   fettuccine
  2 teaspoons olive oil
  5 cups (1-inch) slices asparagus
   (about 1½ pounds)
  2 teaspoons grated lemon rind
  2 tablespoons fresh lemon
   juice
 ½ teaspoon dried oregano
 ¼ teaspoon salt
  4 ounces very thin slices prosciutto,
   coarsely chopped
 ¾ cup (3 ounces) grated fresh
   Parmesan cheese

1. Cook pasta according to package
directions, omitting salt and fat.
2. While pasta cooks, heat oil in a large
nonstick skillet over medium heat. Add
asparagus and next 4 ingredients. Cover
and cook 5 minutes or until tender, stirring occasionally. Stir in prosciutto;
cook, uncovered, 1 minute. Combine
asparagus mixture, pasta, and cheese in a
large bowl, tossing to coat. Yield: 4 servings (serving size: 1¼ cups).

CALORIES 374 (29% from fat); FAT 12.1g (sat 4.7g, mono 3.2g,
poly 1g); PROTEIN 24.9g; CARB 44g; FIBER 6.2g; CHOL 84mg;
IRON 4.2mg; SODIUM 990mg; CALC 256mg

QUICK & EASY

Ham and Cheese Hash Browns

This recipe, a great use for leftover Easter
ham, resembles a hearty potato hash.

  3 cups frozen hash brown
   potatoes with onions and
   peppers (such as Ore-Ida
   Potatoes O'Brien)
 ⅓ cup fat-free, less-sodium chicken
   broth
 ½ cup drained canned quartered
   artichoke hearts, chopped
 ¼ cup chopped green onions
 ⅛ teaspoon black pepper
  3 ounces smoked ham, cut into
   bite-size pieces
 ½ cup (about 2 ounces) shredded
   Monterey Jack cheese

1. Combine potatoes and broth in a
1-quart microwave-safe casserole. Cover
with lid, and microwave at HIGH 12
minutes, stirring after 6 minutes.
2. Uncover dish. Stir in artichoke hearts,
green onions, black pepper, and ham.
Sprinkle with cheese. Microwave, uncovered, at HIGH 1 minute. Yield: 2 servings
(serving size: 1¾ cups).

CALORIES 378 (30% from fat); FAT 12.5g (sat 6.2g, mono 2.7g,
poly 1.4g); PROTEIN 20g; CARB 41.8g; FIBER 6.1g; CHOL 55mg;
IRON 1.3mg; SODIUM 817mg; CALC 204mg

Macadamia Nut-Pesto Fettuccine

This pesto gets its richness from half-and-half. The result is a creamy mixture similar to an Alfredo sauce but with pestolike flavor. Serve it with a tossed garden salad and a French bread baguette.

- 1 (9-ounce) package fresh fettuccine
- 3 cups fresh basil leaves
- ¼ cup half-and-half
- 3 tablespoons roasted macadamia nuts
- 3 tablespoons grated fresh Parmesan cheese
- 2 tablespoons fresh lemon juice
- ¾ teaspoon salt
- ½ teaspoon freshly ground black pepper

1. Cook pasta according to package directions, omitting salt and fat.
2. While pasta cooks, place basil and remaining 6 ingredients in a food processor; process until smooth. Combine basil mixture and pasta in a large bowl, tossing to coat. Yield: 3 servings (serving size: about 1⅓ cups).

CALORIES 374 (30% from fat); FAT 12.4g (sat 3.8g, mono 6.4g, poly 1.1g); PROTEIN 14.6g; CARB 51.5g; FIBER 5.8g; CHOL 77mg; IRON 4.6mg; SODIUM 756mg; CALC 197mg

Salsa Chicken

Personalize this recipe by using your favorite tomato-based salsa. Or try a fruit salsa such as peach, cranberry, or pineapple. Serve over white rice.

- 1 pound skinless, boneless chicken breasts, cut into bite-size pieces
- 2 teaspoons taco seasoning
- Cooking spray
- ⅔ cup bottled salsa
- ⅔ cup (about 2½ ounces) shredded reduced-fat Cheddar cheese
- 1 (4-ounce) can whole green chiles, drained and thinly sliced
- ¼ cup fat-free sour cream
- 2 tablespoons sliced ripe olives

1. Preheat oven to 475°.
2. Combine chicken and seasoning in a medium bowl, tossing to coat. Heat a large nonstick skillet coated with cooking spray over medium-high heat. Add chicken; cook 4 minutes or until browned, stirring occasionally. Arrange chicken in an 8-inch square baking dish coated with cooking spray; top with salsa, cheese, and chiles. Bake at 475° for 8 minutes or until chicken is done and cheese is melted. Top each serving with 1 tablespoon sour cream and 1½ teaspoons olives. Yield: 4 servings.

CALORIES 207 (15% from fat); FAT 3.5g (sat 1.4g, mono 1.1g, poly 0.5g); PROTEIN 33.4g; CARB 9.5g; FIBER 2.1g; CHOL 71mg; IRON 1.5mg; SODIUM 587mg; CALC 130mg

Sausage and Egg Burrito

Use two beaten large eggs in place of the egg substitute, if desired.

- Cooking spray
- ½ cup chopped red bell pepper
- ¼ cup chopped onion
- 3 ounces turkey breakfast sausage
- ½ cup egg substitute
- ¼ cup (1 ounce) shredded reduced-fat Cheddar cheese
- 6 tablespoons bottled salsa, divided
- 2 (8-inch) fat-free flour tortillas
- ¼ cup reduced-fat sour cream

1. Heat a nonstick skillet coated with cooking spray over medium-high heat. Add bell pepper, onion, and sausage; cook 4 minutes or until browned, stirring to crumble sausage. Add egg substitute; cook 2 minutes, stirring frequently. Remove from heat; stir in cheese and 2 tablespoons salsa. Cover and let stand 2 minutes.
2. Heat tortillas according to package directions. Spoon half of egg mixture down center of each tortilla; roll up. Serve with 4 tablespoons salsa and sour cream. Yield: 2 servings (serving size: 1 burrito, 2 tablespoons salsa, and 2 tablespoons sour cream).

CALORIES 314 (28% from fat); FAT 9.6g (sat 4.4g, mono 3.1g, poly 1.8g); PROTEIN 20.7g; CARB 26.9g; FIBER 3.9g; CHOL 50mg; IRON 2.6mg; SODIUM 915mg; CALC 148mg

Mediterranean Vegetable Soup

- Cooking spray
- ½ cup chopped onion
- 1 cup chopped zucchini
- 1 cup chopped yellow squash
- 1 cup water
- ½ teaspoon dried oregano
- ¼ teaspoon crushed red pepper
- 1 (15½-ounce) can chickpeas (garbanzo beans), drained and rinsed
- 1 (14.5-ounce) can diced tomatoes, undrained
- 1 (14½-ounce) can vegetable broth
- ¼ cup plain low-fat yogurt

1. Heat a large saucepan coated with cooking spray over medium-high heat. Add onion; sauté 3 minutes. Add zucchini and yellow squash; sauté 3 minutes. Add water and next 5 ingredients; bring to a boil. Reduce heat, and simmer 5 minutes. Serve with yogurt. Yield: 4 servings (serving size: 1½ cups soup and 1 tablespoon yogurt).

CALORIES 185 (10% from fat); FAT 2.1g (sat 0.3g, mono 0.4g, poly 0.6g); PROTEIN 9g; CARB 35.5g; FIBER 6.2g; CHOL 1mg; IRON 1.9mg; SODIUM 951mg; CALC 132mg

Guacamole and Turkey Sandwiches

If you like hot foods, add minced jalapeño peppers to the avocado mixture.

- ½ cup coarsely mashed avocado
- 1 tablespoon fresh lime juice
- 8 (1-ounce) slices whole grain bread
- 4 plum tomatoes, each cut into 4 slices
- ¼ teaspoon salt
- ⅛ teaspoon ground red pepper
- ⅔ cup alfalfa sprouts
- ½ cup thinly sliced red onion
- ¼ cup chopped fresh cilantro
- 8 ounces thinly sliced deli turkey

1. Combine avocado and lime juice. Spread 2 tablespoons avocado mixture

Continued

on each of 4 bread slices. Arrange tomato slices over avocado mixture; sprinkle evenly with salt and pepper. Divide sprouts, onion, cilantro, and turkey evenly over tomato slices. Top with remaining bread slices. Yield: 4 servings (serving size: 1 sandwich).

CALORIES 205 (22% from fat); FAT 5g (sat 1g, mono 2.2g, poly 0.7g); PROTEIN 14g; CARB 31.4g; FIBER 10.4g; CHOL 23mg; IRON 3.1mg; SODIUM 954mg; CALC 188mg

Balsamic Rosemary Pork

2 teaspoons olive oil
1 pound pork tenderloin, cut crosswise into ½-inch-thick slices
1 tablespoon chopped fresh rosemary
½ teaspoon salt
⅛ teaspoon black pepper
½ cup fat-free, less-sodium chicken broth
¼ cup balsamic vinegar
2 tablespoons honey

1. Heat oil in a large nonstick skillet over medium-high heat. Sprinkle pork with rosemary, salt, and pepper. Add pork to pan; cook 3 minutes on each side or until done. Remove pork from pan; keep warm.
2. Combine broth, vinegar, and honey, stirring with a whisk; add to pan, scraping to loosen browned bits. Bring to a boil; reduce heat, and simmer 6 minutes or until reduced to ⅓ cup. Return pork to pan; cook until thoroughly heated. Yield: 4 servings (serving size: 3 ounces pork and about 1 tablespoon sauce).

CALORIES 201 (28% from fat); FAT 6.2g (sat 1.7g, mono 3.4g, poly 0.6g); PROTEIN 24.3g; CARB 11.3g; FIBER 0.1g; CHOL 74mg; IRON 1.6mg; SODIUM 408mg; CALC 13mg

Scallops with Cucumber-Horseradish Sauce

Serve with a salad and bread or over cooked angel hair pasta tossed with a little olive oil and salt. Add extra horseradish if you want more heat in the sauce.

1 tablespoon olive oil
Cooking spray
1 cup chopped seeded peeled cucumber
1 cup plain fat-free yogurt
2 tablespoons finely chopped fresh parsley
1½ tablespoons prepared horseradish
⅛ teaspoon kosher salt
⅛ teaspoon coarsely ground black pepper
2 tablespoons Italian-seasoned breadcrumbs
12 large sea scallops (about 1½ pounds)

1. Heat oil in a large nonstick skillet coated with cooking spray over medium-high heat.
2. Combine cucumber and next 5 ingredients; set aside. Place breadcrumbs in a shallow dish; dredge scallops in breadcrumbs.
3. Add scallops to pan; cook 4 minutes on each side or until done. Serve immediately with sauce. Yield: 4 servings (serving size: 3 scallops and about ⅓ cup sauce).

CALORIES 220 (25% from fat); FAT 6g (sat 1.4g, mono 3.1g, poly 0.8g); PROTEIN 28.2g; CARB 11.7g; FIBER 0.4g; CHOL 50mg; IRON 0.8mg; SODIUM 393mg; CALC 174mg

Ham and Asparagus Frittata

Extend whole eggs with egg whites for a generous serving size. Serve the frittata with fruit and toasted English muffins and jam for an Easter brunch for two.

⅔ cup chopped 33%-less-sodium ham (about 3 ounces)
½ cup (2 ounces) shredded low-fat Jarlsberg cheese
¼ teaspoon black pepper
⅛ teaspoon salt
3 large egg whites, lightly beaten
2 large eggs, lightly beaten
Cooking spray
½ cup finely chopped onion
½ cup finely chopped bell pepper
½ cup (1-inch) slices asparagus
¼ teaspoon dried Italian seasoning

1. Preheat broiler.
2. Combine first 6 ingredients, stirring well with a whisk.
3. Heat a 9-inch nonstick skillet coated with cooking spray over medium-high heat. Add onion, bell pepper, and asparagus; sauté 3 minutes. Add egg mixture; reduce heat to medium. Cook, covered, 3 minutes or until almost set. Sprinkle with Italian seasoning. Wrap handle of pan with foil; broil 3 minutes or until egg is set. Cut into 4 wedges. Yield: 2 servings (serving size: 2 wedges).

CALORIES 251 (33% from fat); FAT 9.2g (sat 3.4g, mono 3.5g, poly 1.1g); PROTEIN 31.3g; CARB 9.6g; FIBER 2g; CHOL 247mg; IRON 2.1mg; SODIUM 791mg; CALC 373mg

A Legacy of Soulful Food

Charla Draper learned much more than cooking from her mother and grandmothers. As a Mother's Day tribute, she lightens her family's favorite recipes.

Jerk-Style Chicken

A family friend from Haiti inspired this version of Caribbean jerk-style chicken. The chicken marinates quickly and is loaded with flavor.

    1   teaspoon grated lime rind
    ¼   cup fresh lime juice
    2   tablespoons olive oil
    1   to 2 tablespoons finely chopped
        jalapeño pepper
    1   tablespoon ground allspice
    1   tablespoon brown sugar
    1   teaspoon salt
    1   teaspoon coarsely ground black
        pepper
    1   teaspoon dried thyme
    1   teaspoon ground cinnamon
    ½   teaspoon ground nutmeg
    3   garlic cloves, chopped
    ½   cup chopped onion
    6   skinless, boneless chicken thighs
        (about 1 pound)
    3   (6-ounce) skinless, boneless
        chicken breast halves
    Cooking spray
    Parsley sprigs (optional)
    Lime slices (optional)

1. Combine first 12 ingredients in a blender; process until well blended. Pour mixture into a large heavy-duty zip-top plastic bag; add onion and chicken. Seal bag; marinate in refrigerator 1 to 2 hours, turning bag occasionally.
2. Prepare grill.
3. Remove chicken from bag; discard marinade. Place chicken on grill rack coated with cooking spray. Grill chicken, covered, 5 minutes on each side or until done. Garnish with parsley and lime slices, if desired. Yield: 6 servings (serving size: 2 thighs or 1 breast half).

CALORIES 169 (29% from fat); FAT 5.4g (sat 1.1g, mono 2.5g, poly 0.9g); PROTEIN 26.1g; CARB 2.6g; FIBER 0.8g; CHOL 84mg; IRON 1.3mg; SODIUM 287mg; CALC 25mg

QUICK & EASY
Island Rice

This slightly sweet, risotto-like dish is a soothing side for the spicy Jerk-Style Chicken (recipe at left). It also goes well with other highly seasoned dishes, such as barbecued pork or blackened fish.

    2½ cups water
    1   cup uncooked long-grain rice
    ½   cup chopped dried pineapple
    2   teaspoons butter
    ½   teaspoon grated lime rind
    ¼   teaspoon salt
    ¼   cup chopped fresh cilantro
    1   tablespoon chopped green onions
    2½ tablespoons fresh lime juice

1. Bring 2½ cups water to a boil in a medium saucepan; add rice and next 4 ingredients. Cover, reduce heat, and simmer 20 minutes or until liquid is absorbed. Remove from heat; stir in cilantro, onions, and juice. Yield: 6 servings (serving size: ½ cup).

CALORIES 171 (9% from fat); FAT 1.8g (sat 0.8g, mono 0.4g, poly 0.1g); PROTEIN 2.7g; CARB 35.4g; FIBER 0.5g; CHOL 3mg; IRON 1.6mg; SODIUM 117mg; CALC 26mg

MAKE AHEAD
Lemon Pound Cake with Mixed Berries

Draper says she will *never* reveal the original recipe for her grandmother Alice Walker's lemon pound cake, but her lighter variation pays tribute to it. Use any combination of berries you like for the topping.

CAKE:
    Cooking spray
    2   teaspoons all-purpose
        flour
    1   cup all-purpose flour
    ¼   teaspoon baking powder
    ⅔   cup sugar
    ⅓   cup butter, softened
    2   large egg whites
    1   large egg
    1   teaspoon grated lemon rind
    1   teaspoon lemon extract
    ¼   cup vanilla low-fat
        yogurt

TOPPING:
    1   cup sliced strawberries
    ½   cup fresh blueberries or
        blackberries
    1   (10-ounce) package frozen
        raspberries in light syrup, thawed
        and undrained
    1   cup vanilla low-fat
        yogurt

1. Preheat oven to 350°.
2. Coat an 8 x 4-inch loaf pan with cooking spray; dust with 2 teaspoons flour.
3. To prepare cake, lightly spoon 1 cup flour into a dry measuring cup; level with a knife. Combine 1 cup flour and baking powder, stirring with a whisk; set aside.
4. Place sugar and butter in a large bowl; beat with a mixer at high speed until fluffy (about 2 minutes). Add egg whites and egg, one at a time, beating well after each addition. Beat in rind and extract. Add flour mixture and ¼ cup yogurt alternately to sugar mixture, beginning and ending with flour mixture; mix well after each addition. Spoon batter into prepared pan. Bake at 350° for 45 minutes
Continued

or until a wooden pick inserted in center comes out clean. Cool in pan 10 minutes on a wire rack; remove from pan. Cool completely on wire rack.

5. To prepare topping, combine berries, tossing well. Cut cake into 8 slices. Top each slice with ¼ cup berry mixture and 2 tablespoons yogurt. Yield: 8 servings.

CALORIES 286 (28% from fat); FAT 9g (sat 5.3g, mono 2.6g, poly 0.5g); PROTEIN 5.8g; CARB 46.7g; FIBER 2.8g; CHOL 49mg; IRON 1.2mg; SODIUM 141mg; CALC 92mg

---

QUICK & EASY
Bayou Catfish Fillets

(pictured on page 145)

The spicy cornmeal breading stays crispy when the fish is baked on a ventilated broiler pan. You can also use yellow cornmeal. Try this breading on other white fish fillets.

  2 tablespoons white cornmeal
1½ teaspoons seasoned salt
1½ teaspoons dried oregano
  1 teaspoon garlic powder
  1 teaspoon onion powder
  ¾ teaspoon ground red pepper
  ½ teaspoon chili powder
  ¼ teaspoon ground cumin
  ¼ teaspoon black pepper
  6 (6-ounce) catfish fillets
Cooking spray
  6 lemon wedges (optional)

1. Preheat broiler.
2. Combine first 9 ingredients in a zip-top plastic bag. Add 1 catfish fillet. Seal bag; shake well. Remove fillet from bag; place on a broiler pan coated with cooking spray. Repeat procedure with remaining fillets and cornmeal mixture. Broil 6 inches from heat 6 minutes. Carefully turn fillets over, and broil 6 minutes or until fish flakes easily when tested with a fork. Serve with lemon wedges, if desired. Yield: 6 servings (serving size: 1 fillet and 1 lemon wedge).

CALORIES 247 (48% from fat); FAT 13.2g (sat 3.1g, mono 6.1g, poly 2.8g); PROTEIN 27g; CARB 3.8g; FIBER 0.8g; CHOL 80mg; IRON 1.3mg; SODIUM 474mg; CALC 27mg

---

Dry-Rub Chicken with Honey Barbecue Sauce

Celebrate Mother's Day—and the return of warm weather—with a backyard cookout. The star of the meal is this succulent, spicy chicken with an irresistible sweet-and-sour barbecue sauce.

CHICKEN:

  1 (3-pound) whole chicken
  1 tablespoon paprika
  2 teaspoons lemon pepper
  ½ teaspoon garlic powder
  ¼ teaspoon black pepper
  ⅛ teaspoon seasoned salt
Cooking spray

SAUCE:

  ½ cup ketchup
  ¼ cup fresh lemon juice
  2 tablespoons cider vinegar
  2 tablespoons honey
  ½ teaspoon garlic powder
  ¼ teaspoon black pepper

1. To prepare chicken, remove and discard giblets and neck from chicken. Rinse chicken with cold water; pat dry. Trim excess fat. Place chicken, breast side down, on a cutting surface. Cut chicken in half lengthwise along backbone (do not cut through breastbone). Turn chicken over. Starting at neck cavity, loosen skin from breast and drumsticks by inserting fingers, gently pushing between skin and meat.
2. Combine paprika and next 4 ingredients. Rub paprika mixture under loosened skin, and rub over breast and drumsticks. Gently press skin to secure. Cut a 1-inch slit in skin at bottom of each breast half; insert tips of drumsticks into slits.
3. To prepare grill for indirect grilling, place a disposable aluminum foil pan in grill; pour water in pan. Arrange charcoal around pan; heat to medium. Coat grill rack with cooking spray; place rack on grill. Place chicken, breast side down, on grill rack over foil pan. Cover and grill 1½ hours or until a thermometer registers 180°. Remove chicken from grill; place on a clean cutting surface. Cover with foil, and let stand 5 minutes.

4. To prepare sauce, combine ketchup and remaining 5 ingredients in a small saucepan. Bring sauce to a simmer over medium-low heat; cook 15 minutes, stirring frequently. Remove skin from chicken, and brush chicken with ⅓ cup sauce. Serve remaining sauce with chicken. Yield: 4 servings (serving size: about 4 ounces chicken and 4 teaspoons sauce).

CALORIES 265 (26% from fat); FAT 7.8g (sat 2.1g, mono 2.9g, poly 1.9g); PROTEIN 29.3g; CARB 20.3g; FIBER 1g; CHOL 85mg; IRON 2.2mg; SODIUM 650mg; CALC 27mg

---

How to Butterfly a Chicken

1. *Kitchen shears are better at cutting down the backbone than a knife.*

2. *Once the chicken is cut, it will open up and lie flat on the grill for even cooking.*

Cajun Garlic Pork Roast

This much-loved recipe was created for the National Pork Board.

1½ tablespoons minced fresh garlic
  1 tablespoon dried oregano
  2 teaspoons black pepper
  1 teaspoon seasoned salt
  1 teaspoon chili powder
  1 teaspoon ground cumin
  ½ teaspoon crushed red pepper
  1 (2-pound) boneless pork loin
    roast, trimmed
  Cooking spray

1. Preheat oven to 350°.
2. Combine first 7 ingredients, and rub over roast; place on a broiler pan coated with cooking spray. Bake at 350° for 1½ hours or until a thermometer registers 155°. Let stand 10 minutes. Yield: 8 servings (serving size: 3 ounces).

CALORIES 168 (33% from fat); FAT 6.2g (sat 2.1g, mono 2.8g, poly 0.7g); PROTEIN 25.1g; CARB 1.7g; FIBER 0.7g; CHOL 62mg; IRON 1.5mg; SODIUM 246mg; CALC 42mg

Field Greens with Mississippi Caviar

Nutritious, inexpensive black-eyed peas have been a Southern kitchen staple for three centuries. This salad is typical of Draper's recipe makeover approach: She heightens the seasoning profile and uses little added fat.

¾ cup water
  1 garlic clove, minced
  Dash of black pepper
  4 cups fresh or frozen black-eyed
    peas
  1 cup (1-inch) julienne-cut yellow
    bell pepper
  1 cup chopped tomato
  ½ cup bottled reduced-calorie Italian
    dressing
  ⅓ cup chopped fresh parsley
  ¼ cup chopped red onion
  ¼ teaspoon salt
  6 cups mixed salad greens

1. Combine first 3 ingredients in a large saucepan; bring to a boil. Add peas;

cover and cook over medium-low heat 30 minutes or until tender. Drain.
2. Combine peas, bell pepper, and next 5 ingredients in a large bowl; toss gently. Cover and chill 3 hours or overnight. Serve over salad greens. Yield: 6 servings (serving size: 1 cup pea mixture and 1 cup greens).

CALORIES 197 (14% from fat); FAT 3g (sat 0.5g, mono 0.5g, poly 1.7g); PROTEIN 11.2g; CARB 33.5g; FIBER 9.3g; CHOL 1mg; IRON 3.7mg; SODIUM 281mg; CALC 68mg

lighten up

She Takes the Cake

A Californian receives a healthful update of a simple-to-prepare recipe.

By her own confession, Susan Mann of La Jolla, California, says she's a lousy cook. About 25 years ago, however, she made a fabulous cake. "Chalk it up to having foolproof directions," Susan says with a laugh. Since then, she's prepared it for all types of special occasions. Yet, she noted, "The cake is obscenely decadent and past due for an update."

Reducing the amount of eggs to one egg and four whites saved more than 25 grams of fat in the recipe. But eggs are essential for volume in this cake, so we doubled the amount of baking soda to give the cake the same stately appearance as the original. We saved another 46 calories and 5 grams of fat per serving by cutting the butter to an ample one-half cup.

	BEFORE	AFTER
SERVING SIZE		
	1 slice	
CALORIES PER SERVING		
	349	253
FAT		
	19.1g	8g
PERCENT OF TOTAL CALORIES		
	49%	28%

Sour Cream Coffee Cake

This cake keeps well in an airtight container for several days. If you don't have a Bundt pan, use a 10-inch tube pan.

  Cooking spray
  2 tablespoons dry breadcrumbs
  3 cups all-purpose flour
  1 teaspoon baking soda
  ¾ teaspoon salt
  2 cups sugar
  ½ cup butter, softened
  1 teaspoon grated lemon rind
  2 teaspoons fresh lemon juice
  ½ teaspoon almond extract
  4 large egg whites
  1 large egg
1½ cups low-fat sour cream
  ¼ cup finely chopped walnuts,
    toasted
  2 teaspoons powdered sugar

1. Preheat oven to 350°.
2. Coat a 12-cup Bundt pan with cooking spray; dust with breadcrumbs.
3. Lightly spoon flour into dry measuring cups; level with a knife. Combine flour, baking soda, and salt, stirring well with a whisk. Place sugar and butter in a large bowl; beat with a mixer at medium speed until light and fluffy (about 3 minutes). Add rind, juice, and extract, beating until well blended. Add egg whites and egg, 1 at a time, beating well after each addition. Add flour mixture and sour cream alternately to sugar mixture, beginning and ending with flour mixture. Stir in walnuts.
4. Spoon batter into prepared pan. Bake at 350° for 50 minutes or until a wooden pick inserted in center comes out clean. Cool in pan 15 minutes on a wire rack; remove from pan. Cool completely on wire rack. Sprinkle with powdered sugar. Yield: 18 servings.

CALORIES 253 (28% from fat); FAT 8g (sat 4.4g, mono 1.8g, poly 1.1g); PROTEIN 4.4g; CARB 42g; FIBER 0.7g; CHOL 32mg; IRON 1.1mg; SODIUM 261mg; CALC 37mg

London's Calling

If London makes you think of tea and crumpets, you should think again.

London is a city steeped in tradition, but it's also a thriving 21st-century metropolis. That makes for an exciting food scene. Here's one example of the current recipe trends.

Smoked Paprika-Spiced Chicken over Lentils with Yogurt-Cumin Sauce

This recipe from Brian Glover echoes the current trend of using modern Spanish and North African ingredients and spices found at London's Borough Market.

2   tablespoons olive oil, divided
½   teaspoon grated lemon rind
2   tablespoons fresh lemon juice, divided
1   teaspoon salt, divided
½   teaspoon Spanish smoked paprika
½   teaspoon freshly ground black pepper, divided
4   (6-ounce) skinless, boneless chicken breast halves
1   cup plain whole-milk yogurt
3   tablespoons chopped fresh parsley, divided
1   tablespoon chopped fresh mint
½   teaspoon ground cumin
2   garlic cloves, minced
½   cup finely chopped seeded cucumber
1   cup dried lentils
2   parsley sprigs
1   (½-inch-thick) slice onion
1   thyme sprig
1   bay leaf
4   very thin slices Serrano ham or prosciutto (about 1 ounce)
¾   cup minced fresh onion
3   cups thinly sliced zucchini
1   (6-ounce) bag prewashed baby spinach

1. Combine 1 tablespoon oil, rind, 1 tablespoon lemon juice, ¼ teaspoon salt, paprika, and ¼ teaspoon pepper in a medium bowl. Add chicken; turn to coat. Marinate in refrigerator 2 hours.
2. Combine ¼ teaspoon salt, yogurt, 1 tablespoon chopped parsley, mint, cumin, and garlic in a food processor; process until smooth. Place yogurt mixture in a medium bowl; stir in cucumber. Cover and chill.
3. Preheat oven to 375°.
4. Place lentils, parsley sprigs, onion slice, thyme sprig, and bay leaf in a large saucepan; cover with water to 2 inches above lentils. Bring to a boil; cover, reduce heat, and simmer 20 minutes or until tender. Drain. Discard parsley sprigs, onion slice, thyme sprig, and bay leaf.
5. While lentils cook, wrap 1 ham slice around each chicken breast. Place chicken in an 11 x 7-inch baking dish. Bake at 375° for 25 minutes or until done.
6. While chicken cooks, heat 1 tablespoon oil in a large Dutch oven over medium heat. Add minced onion; cook 3 minutes, stirring occasionally. Add zucchini; cook 15 minutes or until zucchini is very tender, stirring occasionally. Stir in lentils, spinach, ½ teaspoon salt, and ¼ teaspoon pepper; cook 5 minutes or until spinach wilts, stirring occasionally. Stir in 1 tablespoon lemon juice and 2 tablespoons chopped parsley. Serve chicken over lentil mixture; drizzle with yogurt sauce. Yield: 4 servings (serving size: 1 breast half, 1 cup lentil mixture, and ⅓ cup sauce).

CALORIES 513 (22% from fat); FAT 12.7g (sat 3.2g, mono 6.2g, poly 1.5g); PROTEIN 60.1g; CARB 41.1g; FIBER 17.6g; CHOL 113mg; IRON 7.9mg; SODIUM 908mg; CALC 200mg

---

London's Best Market

Food lovers will appreciate the old-fashioned charm of Borough Market (8 Southwark St.; 011-44-20-7407-1002, www.boroughmarket.org.uk), located on the south side of London Bridge. A wholesale fruit and vegetable market for London's restaurants during the week, it comes into its own on Fridays and Saturdays, when produce stalls are joined by others selling a selection of the world's best gourmet foods.

Scoop of the Day

Limeade and tofu are transformed into a tongue-tingling dessert.

Tofu is not the kind of food that sets off a feeding frenzy in the typical American kitchen. But for Rachel Bush, 25, a piano teacher in Lebo, a small town in eastern Kansas, tofu is a superstar. "It's a silken wonder," she says.

"Tofu is much misunderstood," says Bush, who admits that it wasn't an instant hit at her family table. "It was bland and mild, and calling it bean curd made it sound bad," she says. But she realized tofu's potential.

Experimentation drove Bush to incorporate surplus frozen limeade, left over from her grandparents' 50th-anniversary party, and tofu into a sweet-tart dessert. In fact, her Arctic Lime Freeze calls for only a can of limeade, some water, and a package of tofu. The final result, Bush says, is a "tongue-tingling dessert that's a cross between Italian ice and tart sherbet."

MAKE AHEAD • FREEZABLE
Arctic Lime Freeze

1   (12-ounce) can thawed limeade concentrate, undiluted
1   (12.3-ounce) package reduced-fat silken firm tofu, drained
1½   cups water
     Mint sprigs (optional)
     Grated lime rind (optional)

1. Combine limeade and tofu in a blender, and process until smooth. Add water, and pulse to combine. Pour mixture into freezer can of an ice-cream freezer; freeze according to manufacturer's instructions. Spoon mixture into a freezer-safe container; cover and freeze 2 hours or until firm. Garnish with mint sprigs and rind, if desired. Yield: 5 servings (serving size: 1 cup).

CALORIES 196 (14% from fat); FAT 3.1g (sat 0g, mono 0.7g, poly 1.7g); PROTEIN 7.8g; CARB 36.8g; FIBER 1.8g; CHOL 0mg; IRON 1.2mg; SODIUM 6mg; CALC 36mg

Tex-Mex Beef Tacos

"This recipe satisfies my craving for Mexican food. You can also serve it with fresh cilantro, sliced green onions, salsa, and fat-free sour cream."

—Lorraine Nielsen, Billings, Montana

Cooking spray
1 cup chopped onion
2 garlic cloves, minced
1 pound ground sirloin
1 cup frozen whole-kernel corn
½ cup water
¼ teaspoon salt
⅛ teaspoon black pepper
1 (15-ounce) can black beans, rinsed and drained
1 (8-ounce) can tomato sauce
1 to 3 drained canned chipotle chiles in adobo sauce, chopped
10 (8-inch) fat-free flour tortillas

1. Heat a large nonstick skillet over medium-high heat. Coat pan with cooking spray. Add onion, garlic, and beef; cook 6 minutes or until browned, stirring to crumble beef. Stir in corn and next 6 ingredients. Bring to a boil; reduce heat, and simmer 10 minutes. Warm tortillas according to package directions. Spoon ½ cup beef mixture into each tortilla. Yield: 10 servings (serving size: 1 taco).

CALORIES 266 (25% from fat); FAT 7.3g (sat 2.7g, mono 3g, poly 0.5g); PROTEIN 13g; CARB 27.6g; FIBER 4.6g; CHOL 31mg; IRON 1.9mg; SODIUM 547mg; CALC 25mg

Springtime Pea Soup

"This has become a spring and summer staple paired with tuna- or egg-salad sandwiches. The color of the soup is especially inviting when it's served up in white bowls."

—Ellen Landers, St. Louis, Missouri

1 (10-ounce) package frozen petite green peas, thawed and divided
1½ cups fat-free, less-sodium chicken broth
½ cup reduced-fat sour cream
¼ teaspoon salt
¼ teaspoon black pepper

1. Place 2 tablespoons peas in a small bowl, and set aside. Combine remaining peas, broth, and sour cream in a blender; process until smooth. Strain mixture through a fine sieve into a bowl; discard solids. Stir in salt and pepper. Cover and chill thoroughly. Ladle ½ cup soup into each of 5 bowls; top each serving with about 1 teaspoon peas. Yield: 5 servings.

CALORIES 88 (33% from fat); FAT 3.2g (sat 1.9g, mono 0.9g, poly 0.2g); PROTEIN 5g; CARB 9.8g; FIBER 2.7g; CHOL 12mg; IRON 0.9mg; SODIUM 330mg; CALC 53mg

Cactus Salad

"When I lived in California, cacti always grew wild around us. Because we also had a large Hispanic population and influence, I came up with this Latin-inspired recipe."

—Pam Norby, Amery, Wisconsin

2 medium cactus pads (nopales)
1 teaspoon olive oil
2 garlic cloves, minced
½ cup canned black beans, rinsed and drained
3 tablespoons chopped green onions
3 tablespoons chopped fresh cilantro
1 tablespoon fresh lime juice
1 teaspoon sugar
½ teaspoon ground cumin
¼ teaspoon chipotle chile powder
2 tomatoes, diced
6 cups shredded leaf lettuce
6 tablespoons crumbled queso fresco cheese
2½ tablespoons fat-free sour cream

1. Shave thorns from cactus pads with a vegetable peeler, leaving green skin; cut cactus pads into thin strips.
2. Heat oil in a large nonstick skillet over medium-high heat. Add cactus and garlic; sauté 7 minutes or until cactus is tender. Combine cactus mixture, beans, and next 7 ingredients. Arrange 1½ cups lettuce on each of 4 plates; top each serving with ½ cup cactus mixture, 1½ tablespoons cheese, and about 2 teaspoons sour cream. Yield: 4 servings.

CALORIES 122 (29% from fat); FAT 3.9g (sat 1.4g, mono 1.4g, poly 0.7g); PROTEIN 6.9g; CARB 15.9g; FIBER 4.8g; CHOL 9mg; IRON 2.5mg; SODIUM 163mg; CALC 184mg

Italian Garbanzo Salad

"This can be served as a first course or antipasti with Italian food, or as a side to grilled chicken. It's even better the next day over salad greens."

—Lori Cohen-Sanford, Austin, Texas

3 cups finely chopped fennel bulb
2 cups chopped tomato
1¾ cups finely chopped red onion
1 cup chopped fresh basil
⅓ cup balsamic vinegar
1 tablespoon olive oil
1 teaspoon freshly ground black pepper
¼ teaspoon salt
4 garlic cloves, minced
2 (15½-ounce) cans chickpeas (garbanzo beans), rinsed and drained
½ cup (2 ounces) crumbled feta cheese

1. Combine all ingredients except cheese in a bowl; toss well. Let stand 30 minutes; sprinkle with cheese. Yield: 8 servings (serving size: about 1 cup).

CALORIES 159 (29% from fat); FAT 5.2g (sat 1.3g, mono 2.3g, poly 1.3g); PROTEIN 5.9g; CARB 23.9g; FIBER 5.9g; CHOL 6mg; IRON 2.2mg; SODIUM 368mg; CALC 103mg

Rachel's Tropical Fruit Salsa

"Serve this salsa with baked tortilla chips, or grilled chicken or fish."

—Rachel Lamb, Brookfield, Wisconsin

1 cup diced peeled ripe mango
1 cup diced pineapple
¼ cup finely chopped red onion
¼ cup minced fresh cilantro
¼ cup fresh lime juice
2 teaspoons ground cumin
⅛ teaspoon salt
⅛ teaspoon black pepper
1 jalapeño pepper, seeded and minced

1. Combine all ingredients. Yield: 4 servings (serving size: ½ cup).

CALORIES 60 (9% from fat); FAT 0.6g (sat 0.1g, mono 0.1g, poly 0.1g); PROTEIN 0.8g; CARB 14.8g; FIBER 2g; CHOL 0mg; IRON 0.6mg; SODIUM 77mg; CALC 20mg

Chickpeas with Spinach

"This vegetarian dish is easy and requires very little oil. Add ground red pepper if you'd like it spicier. I like to serve this dish with Indian flatbread and yogurt."

—Rajita Elhence,
Middleburg Heights, Ohio

     1   teaspoon olive oil
  1½   cups chopped onion
     1   teaspoon bottled ground
         fresh ginger (such as Spice
         World)
     2   garlic cloves, minced
     ¼   cup water
     2   tablespoons tomato paste
     2   cups chopped spinach
     1   teaspoon chili powder
     ⅛   teaspoon salt
     1   (15½-ounce) can chickpeas,
         (garbanzo beans), rinsed and
         drained
     1   teaspoon fresh lemon
         juice
     1   cup hot cooked basmati
         rice
  Lemon wedges (optional)
  Grated lemon rind (optional)

1. Heat oil in a large nonstick skillet over medium-high heat. Add onion, ginger, and garlic; sauté 4 minutes or until mixture begins to brown. Add water and tomato paste; cook 2 minutes or until liquid evaporates, stirring constantly. Stir in spinach, chili powder, salt, and chickpeas; cover. Reduce heat; cook 5 minutes or until spinach wilts and mixture is heated. Stir in juice. Serve over rice. Garnish with lemon wedges and rind, if desired. Yield: 2 servings (serving size: about 1 cup chickpea mixture and ½ cup rice).

CALORIES 403 (11% from fat); FAT 5g (sat 0.7g, mono 2.3g, poly 1.3g); PROTEIN 14.2g; CARB 77.4g; FIBER 11.8g; CHOL 0mg; IRON 4.9mg; SODIUM 707mg; CALC 126mg

Beyond Olive Oil

A world of flavor awaits.

If you're well-acquainted with the bottle of extravirgin olive oil in your pantry, then it's time to get to know specialty oils, such as avocado, walnut, and hazelnut. They're often packaged in elegant bottles that speak enticingly from the shelves. But these oils also work wonders in typical as well as unexpected applications—from salads to oatmeal to desserts.

Wild Mushroom Pizza with Truffle Oil

Truffle oil takes this pizza from fine to sublime. In a pinch, extravirgin olive oil will work, too.

     1   teaspoon sugar
     1   package quick-rise yeast (about
         2¼ teaspoons)
     ½   cup warm water (100° to 110°)
  1½   cups all-purpose flour,
         divided
     ½   teaspoon salt, divided
  Cooking spray
     2   teaspoons cornmeal
     2   teaspoons olive oil
     2   cups thinly sliced shiitake
         mushroom caps (about 4
         ounces)
     2   cups sliced cremini mushrooms
         (about 4 ounces)
  1½   cups (¼-inch-thick) slices
         portobello mushrooms (about
         4 ounces)
     ⅔   cup (about 2½ ounces) grated
         fontina cheese, divided
     2   teaspoons chopped fresh
         thyme
     ½   teaspoon truffle oil
     ¼   cup (1 ounce) grated fresh
         Parmesan cheese
     ¼   teaspoon sea salt

1. Dissolve sugar and yeast in warm water in a large bowl; let stand 5 minutes. Lightly spoon flour into dry measuring cups; level with a knife. Add 1¼ cups flour and ¼ teaspoon salt to yeast mixture, and stir until a soft dough forms. Turn dough out onto a lightly floured surface. Knead until smooth and elastic (about 10 minutes); add enough of remaining flour, 1 tablespoon at a time, to prevent dough from sticking to hands (dough will feel tacky).

2. Place dough in a large bowl coated with cooking spray, turning to coat top. Cover and let rise in a warm place (85°), free from drafts, 30 minutes or until doubled in size. (Gently press two fingers into dough. If indentation remains, dough has risen enough.) Punch dough down; cover and let stand 5 minutes. Line a baking sheet with parchment paper; sprinkle with cornmeal. Roll dough into a 12-inch circle on a floured surface. Place dough on prepared baking sheet. Crimp edges of dough with fingers to form a rim; let rise 10 minutes.

3. Preheat oven to 475°.

4. While dough rises, heat 2 teaspoons olive oil in a large nonstick skillet over medium heat. Add ¼ teaspoon salt and mushrooms, and cook 7 minutes or until mushrooms soften and moisture almost evaporates, stirring frequently.

5. Sprinkle ¼ cup fontina evenly over dough, and arrange mushroom mixture evenly over fontina. Sprinkle with thyme; drizzle evenly with truffle oil. Sprinkle remaining fontina and Parmesan cheese evenly over top. Bake at 475° for 15 minutes or until crust is lightly browned. Remove to cutting board, and sprinkle with sea salt. Cut into 8 slices. Serve immediately. Yield: 4 servings (serving size: 2 slices).

CALORIES 331 (29% from fat); FAT 10.6g (sat 4.9g, mono 4.2g, poly 0.8g); PROTEIN 14.8g; CARB 42.8g; FIBER 3.1g; CHOL 25mg; IRON 3.5mg; SODIUM 693mg; CALC 180mg

Handle with Care

These oils are sensitive to heat and light. Try to buy small quantities and use within six months of opening. Store in an enclosed cabinet away from the stove or in the refrigerator (unless otherwise specified by the manufacturer).

Take a Dip

To familiarize yourself with the oil's flavor, pour a little into a bowl, and dip a baguette slice into it. This will give you a clue as to how strong it is and how its flavor will accentuate your dish.

Good News

You have choices when it comes to keeping your heart healthy.

Researchers are finding that peanut products, including peanut oil, are just as effective as olive oil in protecting against heart disease. Olive oil has other competitors, too: Almond, avocado, and hazelnut oils are all high in monounsaturated fat, which can lower your total cholesterol level.

Walnut oil embodies the same heart-healthy fat, known as omega-3 fatty acid, contained in many types of fish. Omega-3s have been shown to lower triglyceride and blood pressure levels, thereby reducing the overall risk of heart disease and stroke.

Walnut Oil

What to look for: A light golden color, darker than vegetable oil
Our favorite brand: Loriva (www.faraway-foods.com)
Flavor profile: Full-bodied, pleasing tasteful aroma
Uses: Blend with cream cheese and a bit of honey to make a delicious spread for a slice of quick bread (especially banana bread). Like hazelnut oil, it's a great addition to most vinaigrettes.

Hazelnut Oil

What to look for: A light golden color, slightly darker than vegetable oil
Our favorite brands: From France—Jean-Marc Montegottero Virgin Hazelnut Oil (www.dibruno.com) and Les Moulins Dorés (www.splendidpalate.com)
Flavor profile: Toasty, smooth, delicate, buttery flavor
Uses: Great on sliced pears and Brie cheese, or drizzled over butternut squash with brown sugar. Can be used in place of vegetable oils in most vinaigrettes.

Roasted Peanut Oil

What to look for: Label should read "roasted" or "toasted" peanut oil. It will be darker and more flavorful than plain peanut oil, which is made from "steamed" peanuts, resulting in a mild flavor.
Our favorite brand: Loriva (www.faraway-foods.com)
Flavor profile: Surprisingly strong peanut flavor, like fresh-packed peanuts
Uses: Drizzle over grilled shrimp or fish; toss with roasted asparagus; brush over grilled pineapple, and serve with vanilla ice cream.

Pistachio Oil

What to look for: The darker green, the more flavor; slightly thicker than other nut oils
Our favorite brands: Castelmuro (www.chefbernard.com) and Les Moulins Dorés (www.splendidpalate.com)
Flavor profile: Strong but pleasant flavor, faintly sweet with a lingering finish
Uses: Sprinkle over fresh mozzarella with balsamic vinegar and cracked black pepper; brush over eggplant slices before grilling; toss with roasted beets and beet greens; use in homemade pesto.

Avocado Oil

How it's made: Oil is extracted from the flesh (not the seed) of ripe fruits. The riper the avocado, the darker and more flavorful the oil.
What to look for: Dark green color
Our favorite brand: Elysian Isle (www.nzimportsinc.com)
Flavor profile: Slightly nutty, full-bodied
Uses: Drizzle over gazpacho; add to salsas; drizzle over toasted bread slices, and top with chopped fresh tomatoes; whisk with soy sauce and wasabi powder for a flavorful sushi or sliced cucumber dipping sauce. This oil has a higher smoking point than nut oils, so it can be used to grill, sauté, or stir-fry.

Truffle Oil

How it's made: A truffle is a highly prized mushroom that grows underground. Truffle oil isn't pressed directly from the truffle; rather the truffle infuses the oil, most commonly olive oil or grapeseed oil.
What to look for: Unfortunately, there are no good visual cues to help select fine quality truffle oil. Price seems to be the better guide, and it's pricey. If stored for long periods, even high-quality truffle oil will lose its aroma and flavor, so buy in small quantities. Black and white truffle oils are the most common. White truffle oil is slightly milder than black truffle oil.
Our favorite brand: Sabatino Tartufi (www.sabatinostore.com)
Flavor profile: Intense earthy flavor, pungent aroma
Uses: Use sparingly—a little bit goes a long way. Drizzle over pasta dishes; stir into homemade mushroom soup; use as a dipping oil for bread.

QUICK & EASY
Pistachio Rice

With a quality pistachio oil, this rice will have an intense flavor even without the chopped nuts. It's excellent with lamb or chicken.

- 2 cups water
- 1 cup basmati rice
- ¾ teaspoon salt, divided
- 2 tablespoons dried currants or golden raisins
- 1½ tablespoons chopped pistachios
- 1 tablespoon chopped fresh parsley
- 2 tablespoons pistachio oil
- ¼ teaspoon freshly ground black pepper
- Parsley sprigs (optional)

1. Bring water to a boil in a medium saucepan; add rice and ¼ teaspoon salt. Cover, reduce heat, and simmer 18 minutes or until liquid is absorbed and rice is done. Remove from heat; fluff with a fork. Stir in ½ teaspoon salt, currants, and next 4 ingredients. Cover; let stand 5 minutes. Garnish with parsley sprigs, if desired. Yield: 6 servings (serving size: about ½ cup).

CALORIES 186 (29% from fat); FAT 5.9g (sat 0.8g, mono 3.8g, poly 1.3g); PROTEIN 2.4g; CARB 33.1g; FIBER 1.3g; CHOL 0mg; IRON 1.2mg; SODIUM 294mg; CALC 8mg

QUICK & EASY
Cranberry Walnut Tabbouleh

This version takes liberties with the classic Mediterranean salad. Olive oil, tomatoes, and cucumber have been replaced with walnut oil, cranberries, and walnuts.

- 1 cup bulgur wheat
- ½ cup chopped dried cranberries
- 1 cup boiling water
- ½ cup chopped fresh parsley
- ¼ cup minced red onion
- ¼ cup fresh lemon juice
- 2 tablespoons chopped walnuts, toasted
- 2 tablespoons chopped fresh mint
- 1½ tablespoons walnut oil
- ¾ teaspoon salt
- ¼ teaspoon freshly ground black pepper

1. Combine bulgur and cranberries in a medium bowl. Add boiling water, and let stand 30 minutes or until water is absorbed. Fluff with a fork. Stir in parsley and remaining ingredients, and toss gently to combine. Yield: 6 servings (serving size: ⅔ cup).

CALORIES 164 (30% from fat); FAT 5.4g (sat 0.5g, mono 1.1g, poly 3.5g); PROTEIN 3.5g; CARB 27g; FIBER 5.6g; CHOL 0mg; IRON 1mg; SODIUM 299mg; CALC 22mg

Peanut Chicken Soba Salad

You'll only need about 15 minutes to cook the chicken and noodles for this Asian salad. If short on time, substitute rotisserie chicken or leftover cooked chicken, and purchase preshredded carrots from your supermarket's produce section.

- 2 cups water
- 2 (6-ounce) skinless, boneless chicken breast halves
- 4 black peppercorns
- 1 bay leaf
- 2 tablespoons roasted peanut oil
- 1 tablespoon rice vinegar
- 2 teaspoons low-sodium soy sauce
- 1 teaspoon honey
- 1 teaspoon chili garlic sauce (such as Lee Kum Kee)
- ½ teaspoon salt
- 2 cups cooked soba noodles (about 4 ounces uncooked)
- 1 cup grated carrot
- ½ cup thinly sliced green onions
- ¼ cup minced red onion
- ¼ cup chopped fresh basil
- 4 teaspoons chopped unsalted, dry-roasted peanuts
- Lime wedges (optional)

1. Combine first 4 ingredients in a medium saucepan; bring to a boil. Cover, remove from heat, and let stand 15 minutes or until chicken is done. Remove chicken from pan, and discard peppercorns, bay leaf, and cooking liquid. Shred chicken; place in a large bowl.
2. Combine oil and next 5 ingredients, stirring with a whisk. Pour over chicken; let stand 5 minutes. Add soba noodles and next 4 ingredients to chicken mixture, and toss well. Sprinkle with peanuts. Garnish with lime wedges, if desired. Yield: 4 servings (serving size: 1 cup salad and 1 teaspoon peanuts).

CALORIES 256 (33% from fat); FAT 9.5g (sat 1.7g, mono 4.2g, poly 2.9g); PROTEIN 23.9g; CARB 19.5g; FIBER 2.5g; CHOL 49mg; IRON 1.3mg; SODIUM 538mg; CALC 30mg

STAFF FAVORITE
Cherry-Hazelnut Oatmeal

We enjoyed the hearty texture of steel-cut oats, which are often called Irish oats. To make this recipe with regular rolled oats, reduce the water to 4 cups, and simmer 4 minutes or until desired consistency.

- 6 cups water
- 2 cups steel-cut oats (such as McCann's)
- ⅔ cup dried Bing or other sweet cherries, coarsely chopped
- ¼ teaspoon salt
- 5 tablespoons brown sugar, divided
- ¼ cup chopped hazelnuts, toasted and divided
- ¼ teaspoon ground cinnamon
- 2 tablespoons toasted hazelnut oil

1. Combine first 4 ingredients in a medium saucepan; bring to a boil. Reduce heat, and simmer 20 minutes or until desired consistency, stirring occasionally. Remove from heat. Stir in 3 tablespoons sugar, 1 tablespoon nuts, and cinnamon. Place 1 cup oatmeal in each of 6 bowls; sprinkle each serving with 1 teaspoon sugar. Top each with 1½ teaspoons nuts; drizzle with 1 teaspoon oil. Yield: 6 servings.

CALORIES 350 (29% from fat); FAT 11.1g (sat 1.1g, mono 6.8g, poly 2g); PROTEIN 8.9g; CARB 56.1g; FIBER 6.8g; CHOL 0mg; IRON 3mg; SODIUM 112mg; CALC 52mg

Gourmet oils give everyday fare new complexity and verve.

Baby Spinach Salad with Candied Hazelnuts

Nut oils add a distinct flavor to vinaigrettes. Try this salad with other oil and nut varieties, such as walnuts or almonds.

    ¼   cup chopped hazelnuts
    1½ tablespoons light brown
        sugar
    1½ teaspoons egg white
    ⅛   teaspoon salt
        Cooking spray
    2   teaspoons fresh orange
        juice
    1½ teaspoons toasted hazelnut
        oil
    ½   teaspoon Dijon mustard
    ¼   teaspoon salt
    ¼   teaspoon freshly ground black
        pepper
    1   (7-ounce) package fresh baby
        spinach (about 8 cups)
    1   cup orange sections (about
        4 oranges)

1. Preheat oven to 350°.
2. Combine first 4 ingredients, tossing well to coat. Place hazelnut mixture on a nonstick baking sheet coated with cooking spray; bake at 350° for 6 minutes or until lightly browned. Remove from oven; cool.
3. Combine juice and next 4 ingredients, stirring well with a whisk. Place spinach in a large bowl; drizzle with juice mixture. Toss gently to coat. Place about 1¾ cups salad mixture on each of 4 plates; top with ¼ cup orange sections and 1 tablespoon hazelnut mixture. Yield: 4 servings.

CALORIES 117 (49% from fat); FAT 6.4g (sat 0.5g, mono 4.7g, poly 0.9g); PROTEIN 3.5g; CARB 14.1g; FIBER 3.4g; CHOL 0mg; IRON 2.2mg; SODIUM 286mg; CALC 92mg

MAKE AHEAD
Banana-Walnut Napoleons

Some of the components for this impressive dessert can be made ahead. The pastry cream filling can be stored up to 1 week in the refrigerator. The phyllo dough can be baked 1 to 2 days in advance and stored in an airtight container to keep crisp.

FILLING:

    3   tablespoons granulated sugar
    ⅛   teaspoon salt
    ⅛   teaspoon ground cinnamon
    ⅛   teaspoon ground nutmeg
    1   large egg yolk
    1   cup 1% low-fat milk
    2   tablespoons cornstarch
    1½ teaspoons walnut oil

NAPOLEONS:

    4   (18 x 14-inch) sheets frozen
        phyllo dough, thawed
        Cooking spray

CARAMEL-WALNUT SAUCE:

    ¼   cup packed brown sugar
    2   tablespoons water
    1   tablespoon walnut oil
    1   ripe banana, peeled and cut into
        16 slices
    4   teaspoons finely chopped walnuts,
        toasted

1. To prepare filling, combine first 4 ingredients in a small saucepan, stirring well with a whisk. Add egg yolk, stirring well. Combine milk and cornstarch, stirring with a whisk until well blended. Slowly whisk cornstarch mixture into egg mixture. Bring to a boil over medium heat, stirring constantly with a whisk. Remove from heat. Stir in 1½ teaspoons walnut oil. Pour filling into a bowl. Place plastic wrap on surface; cool to room temperature.
2. Preheat oven to 350°.
3. To prepare Napoleons, place 1 phyllo sheet on a large cutting board or work surface (cover remaining dough to prevent drying); lightly coat with cooking spray. Place another phyllo sheet on top; lightly coat with cooking spray. Repeat layers with remaining phyllo sheets and cooking spray. Gently press phyllo layers together. Cut phyllo stack in half lengthwise. Cut each half crosswise into 4 rectangles. Carefully place rectangles onto a nonstick baking sheet coated with cooking spray. Bake at 350° for 10 minutes or until crisp and lightly browned. Remove phyllo stacks from pan; cool completely on a wire rack.
4. To prepare sauce, combine brown sugar and water in a small saucepan; place over medium-high heat. Bring to a boil;

reduce heat, and simmer 3 minutes. Remove mixture from heat; stir in 1 tablespoon walnut oil. Add banana; stir gently to combine.
5. To assemble, place 1 phyllo stack on each of 4 plates; top each with about ¼ cup filling. Place 4 banana slices on each serving; cover with 1 phyllo stack. Drizzle brown sugar mixture evenly over Napoleons. Sprinkle each serving with 1 teaspoon walnuts. Yield: 4 servings (serving size: 1 Napoleon).

CALORIES 294 (31% from fat); FAT 10g (sat 1.8g, mono 2.7g, poly 4.8g); PROTEIN 4.8g; CARB 47.8g; FIBER 1.4g; CHOL 56mg; IRON 1.3mg; SODIUM 204mg; CALC 100mg

Walnut-Chicken Linguine

Ground walnuts, boosted by walnut oil, render this pasta dish richly flavorful. Crumbled Gorgonzola or other blue cheese would be a great addition.

    ¼   cup ground walnuts, divided
    1   tablespoon all-purpose flour
    8   ounces uncooked linguine
    2½ tablespoons walnut oil, divided
    1   teaspoon salt, divided
    ½   teaspoon freshly ground pepper,
        divided
    2   garlic cloves, minced
    ¼   cup chopped fresh parsley
    1   pound chicken breast tenders

1. Place nuts in a food processor, and process until ground. Combine 2 tablespoons ground nuts and flour in a large zip-top plastic bag; set aside.
2. Cook pasta according to package directions, omitting salt and fat. Drain and place in a large bowl. Add 2 tablespoons ground nuts, 5 teaspoons oil, ¾ teaspoon salt, and ¼ teaspoon pepper, tossing to coat. Heat a large nonstick skillet over medium heat. Add ½ teaspoon oil and garlic; cook 1 minute, stirring constantly. Add garlic mixture and parsley to pasta; toss to combine. Cover and keep warm.
3. Sprinkle chicken evenly with ¼ teaspoon salt and ¼ teaspoon pepper. Add

Continued

chicken to flour mixture in zip-top plastic bag; shake to coat. Heat 2 teaspoons oil in pan over medium-high heat. Add chicken; cook 3 minutes on each side or until done. Serve chicken over pasta. Yield: 4 servings (serving size: 1 cup pasta and about 3 ounces chicken).

CALORIES 467 (30% from fat); FAT 15.7g (sat 1.9g, mono 3g, poly 9.3g); PROTEIN 35.5g; CARB 45.7g; FIBER 2.6g; CHOL 66mg; IRON 3.3mg; SODIUM 660mg; CALC 40mg

Backyard Entertaining Menu
serves 8

When your thoughts turn to grilling, try this casual menu. You'll need to double the salad recipe to serve 8.

Romaine Salad with Avocado-Lime Vinaigrette

Mahimahi fish tacos*

Chips and salsa

Margaritas

*Prepare grill to medium-high heat. Sprinkle 8 (6-ounce) mahimahi fillets with ½ teaspoon salt and ¼ teaspoon ground red pepper. Place fillets on grill rack coated with cooking spray; grill 4 minutes or until fish flakes easily when tested with a fork. Serve each fillet with 2 corn tortillas, 2 tablespoons canned salsa verde, 2 tablespoons chopped tomato, 1 tablespoon chopped green onions, 1 teaspoon chopped fresh cilantro, and 2 lime wedges.

Romaine Salad with Avocado-Lime Vinaigrette

Simple ingredients coax the avocado oil into the limelight.

    1   teaspoon fresh lime juice
    ¼   teaspoon salt
    ¼   teaspoon freshly ground black
        pepper
    1   tablespoon avocado oil
    8   cups shredded romaine lettuce
        (about 15 ounces)
    1   cup cherry tomatoes,
        halved
    ¼   cup vertically sliced red onion

1. Combine first 3 ingredients, stirring with a whisk. Gradually add oil, and stir constantly with a whisk.
2. Combine lettuce, tomatoes, and onion in a large bowl, tossing gently. Drizzle juice mixture over lettuce mixture; toss gently to coat. Serve immediately. Yield: 4 servings (serving size: 2 cups).

CALORIES 61 (58% from fat); FAT 3.9g (sat 0.5g, mono 2.5g, poly 0.7g); PROTEIN 2.3g; CARB 5.8g; FIBER 2.6g; CHOL 0mg; IRON 1.5mg; SODIUM 160mg; CALC 45mg

Toasted Hazelnut Focaccia

Chopped hazelnuts toast nicely on top of the bread as it bakes. Hazelnut oil drizzled over the cooked focaccia boosts the flavor.

    1¼   cups warm water (100° to 110°),
         divided
    1   teaspoon sugar
    1   package dry yeast (about
         2¼ teaspoons)
    1   tablespoon toasted hazelnut oil
    3¾   cups all-purpose flour, divided
    1½   teaspoons kosher salt, divided
    ⅛   teaspoon ground nutmeg
    ½   cup golden raisins
         Cooking spray
    1   teaspoon water
    1   large egg white
    ¼   cup chopped hazelnuts
    1   tablespoon toasted hazelnut oil,
         divided

1. Combine ½ cup water, sugar, and yeast in a large bowl, stirring with a whisk; let stand 10 minutes. Add ¾ cup water and 1 tablespoon oil, stirring with a whisk. Lightly spoon flour into dry measuring cups; level with a knife. Add 1 cup flour, 1 teaspoon salt, and nutmeg to yeast mixture, stirring to combine. Stir in 2½ cups flour. Turn dough out onto a lightly floured surface. Knead until smooth and elastic (about 8 minutes); add enough of remaining flour, 1 tablespoon at a time, to prevent dough from sticking to hands (dough will feel tacky). Arrange raisins over dough, and gently knead 4 or 5 times or just until raisins are incorporated into dough.

2. Place dough in a large bowl coated with cooking spray, turning to coat top. Cover and let rise in a warm place (85°), free from drafts, 45 minutes or until doubled in size. (Gently press two fingers into dough. If indentation remains, dough has risen enough.) Turn dough out into a 13 x 9-inch baking dish coated with cooking spray; gently stretch dough to edges of dish. Cover and let rise in a warm place (85°), free from drafts, 30 minutes or until doubled in size.
3. Uncover dough. Make indentations in top of dough using handle of a wooden spoon or your fingertips. Combine 1 teaspoon water and egg white; brush lightly over dough. Sprinkle with nuts. Cover and let rise in a warm place (85°), free from drafts, 45 minutes or until doubled in size.
4. Preheat oven to 400°.
5. Uncover dough, and drizzle with 2 teaspoons oil. Sprinkle dough with ½ teaspoon salt. Bake at 400° for 24 minutes or until golden. Drizzle bread with 1 teaspoon oil; let cool slightly. Yield: 12 servings.

CALORIES 194 (19% from fat); FAT 4.2g (sat 0.4g, mono 2.9g, poly 0.6g); PROTEIN 4.7g; CARB 34.6g; FIBER 1.6g; CHOL 0mg; IRON 2.1mg; SODIUM 238mg; CALC 13mg

Sandwich Night Menu
serves 8

The nutty focaccia is great for sandwiches, which offer a good way to use leftovers of the bread.

Ham and brie sandwich*

Sweet potato chips

Honeydew melon wedge

*Cut Toasted Hazelnut Focaccia (recipe at left) into 8 equal pieces; cut each piece in half horizontally. Spread 1 teaspoon whole-grain mustard on bottom half of each bread piece. Place 1 ounce thinly sliced smoked ham, 3 thin apple slices, and 1 ounce sliced brie cheese over bottom half of each bread piece. Place bottom halves of bread pieces on a baking sheet; broil 1 minute or until cheese melts. Top with top halves of bread.

Truffled Shrimp and Crab Risotto

The earthiness of truffle oil is an unexpected complement to fresh shellfish.

12 ounces medium shrimp
 6 cups water
 1 tablespoon butter
 2 teaspoons white truffle oil
 ¼ cup minced shallots
 1 cup Arborio rice or other
      short-grain rice
 ½ cup dry white wine
 ¾ teaspoon salt
 2 tablespoons chopped fresh
      parsley
 2 tablespoons chopped fresh
      chives
 2 teaspoons fresh lemon juice
 8 ounces lump crabmeat, shell
      pieces removed
    Chives (optional)

1. Peel and devein shrimp; reserve shells. Coarsely chop shrimp.
2. Combine shells and water in a medium saucepan; bring to a boil. Reduce heat, and simmer 15 minutes. Strain through a sieve into a bowl. Discard solids. Keep shrimp broth warm over low heat (do not boil).
3. Melt butter in a medium saucepan over medium heat. Add oil and shallots; cook 2 minutes, stirring constantly. Add rice; cook 1 minute, stirring constantly. Add wine and salt; cook 2 minutes or until almost absorbed, stirring constantly. Add shrimp broth, ½ cup at a time, stirring frequently until each portion is absorbed before adding next (about 30 minutes total). Add shrimp; cook 2 minutes or until shrimp are done, stirring frequently. Stir in parsley, chopped chives, juice, and crab. Garnish with chives, if desired. Serve immediately. Yield: 4 servings (serving size: 1 cup).

CALORIES 417 (18% from fat); FAT 8.4g (sat 3g, mono 2.2g, poly 2.3g); PROTEIN 33.6g; CARB 46.5g; FIBER 0.9g; CHOL 181mg; IRON 3.1mg; SODIUM 775mg; CALC 117mg

Spiced Shrimp with Avocado Oil

(pictured on page 146)

These shrimp are great on their own, with pasta, or as part of a tapas tray.

1½ pounds medium shrimp, peeled
       and deveined
  1 teaspoon sugar
  ¼ teaspoon kosher salt
  1 tablespoon chili powder
  ½ teaspoon ground cumin
  ½ teaspoon ground coriander
  ½ teaspoon dried oregano
1½ tablespoons avocado oil, divided
     Lime wedges

1. Sprinkle shrimp with sugar and salt. Combine chili powder, cumin, coriander, and oregano. Lightly coat shrimp with spice mixture.
2. Heat a large nonstick skillet over medium-high heat. Add 1 teaspoon oil and half of shrimp; sauté 4 minutes or until done. Remove from pan. Repeat procedure with 1 teaspoon oil and remaining shrimp. Place shrimp on a platter; drizzle 2½ teaspoons oil over shrimp. Serve with lime wedges. Yield: 5 servings (serving size: about 4 ounces shrimp).

CALORIES 193 (32% from fat); FAT 6.9g (sat 1g, mono 3.4g, poly 1.6g); PROTEIN 27.9g; CARB 3.7g; FIBER 0.8g; CHOL 207mg; IRON 3.7mg; SODIUM 335mg; CALC 81mg

inspired vegetarian

Out in the Open

This delicious Italian fare is perfect for casual outdoor dining.

Alfresco fare is simple, and usually emphasizes the foods that have formed the basis of the Italian diet for thousands of years.

With Alfresco entertaining, most dishes are brought out together—save the fruit or dessert, which is placed on the table when the savory dishes have been cleared. The following menus, one from Sicily and one from Tuscany, are ideal for alfresco dining.

Sicilian Menu
serves 6

Shaved Fennel Salad with Almonds and Mint

Baked Frittata Ribbons in Tomato Sauce

Bucatini with Eggplant and Roasted Peppers

Ricotta-Honey Mousse with Summer Berries

WINE NOTE: When many vegetables and several green herbs are used throughout a menu, choose a wine that's fresh, light, thirst quenching, and flexible. A good choice: Pinot Gris (a.k.a. Pinot Grigio). Italy produces dozens of them, but California versions are every bit as easygoing and tasty. A favorite: J Pinot Gris. The 2003 is $18.

QUICK & EASY • MAKE AHEAD
Shaved Fennel Salad with Almonds and Mint

Though you can serve it immediately, this salad is best if it stands 1 hour before being served. To get the thinnest slices from your fennel bulb, quarter it before slicing to create more manageable sections that lie flat on the cutting board.

3½ cups thinly sliced fennel bulb
       (about 1 medium bulb)
  1 cup thinly vertically sliced red
       onion
  2 tablespoons thinly sliced fresh mint
  2 tablespoons fresh lemon juice
  2 teaspoons extravirgin olive oil
  ½ teaspoon salt
  ¼ teaspoon freshly ground black
       pepper
  2 tablespoons sliced almonds,
       toasted

1. Combine first 7 ingredients in a large bowl; toss well to combine. Let stand at room temperature 1 hour. Sprinkle with nuts. Yield: 6 servings (serving size: about ⅓ cup).

CALORIES 46 (51% from fat); FAT 2.6g (sat 0.3g, mono 1.7g, poly 0.4g); PROTEIN 1.2g; CARB 5.4g; FIBER 1.8g; CHOL 0mg; IRON 0.4mg; SODIUM 217mg; CALC 31mg

MAKE AHEAD
Baked Frittata Ribbons in Tomato Sauce

The addition of pecorino, a peppery sheep's milk cheese, gives this country dish a decidedly Sicilian flair. You can prepare it 1 day ahead and reheat under the broiler before serving.

SAUCE:

Cooking spray
2 cups finely chopped onion
2 tablespoons finely chopped fresh flat-leaf parsley
2 tablespoons finely chopped fresh basil
2 garlic cloves, minced
4 cups chopped seeded peeled plum tomatoes (about 2½ pounds)
½ teaspoon salt

FRITTATA:

¼ cup finely chopped fresh flat-leaf parsley
½ teaspoon salt
¼ teaspoon freshly ground black pepper
4 large eggs, lightly beaten
4 large egg whites, lightly beaten
¼ cup (1 ounce) grated fresh pecorino Romano cheese

1. To prepare sauce, heat a large nonstick skillet over medium heat. Coat pan with cooking spray. Add onion and next 3 ingredients; cook 7 minutes or until onion is tender, stirring frequently. Stir in tomatoes and ½ teaspoon salt. Cover, reduce heat to medium-low, and cook 15 minutes, stirring occasionally.

2. Preheat broiler.

3. To prepare frittata, combine ¼ cup parsley and next 4 ingredients, stirring with a whisk until well blended. Heat a large nonstick skillet over medium-high heat; coat pan with cooking spray. Add half of egg mixture, and cook 2 minutes or until bottom is set. Carefully turn frittata over. Cook 1 minute. Place cooked frittata on a cutting board. Repeat procedure with remaining egg mixture.

4. Roll up cooked frittatas, jelly-roll fashion, and cut into ¼-inch-thick slices. Combine sauce, frittata ribbons, and cheese in a medium bowl, tossing to coat. Divide frittata mixture evenly among 6 (6-ounce) ramekins or custard cups. Broil 2 minutes or until cheese melts and mixture is thoroughly heated. Yield: 6 servings.

CALORIES 126 (36% from fat); FAT 5g (sat 1.8g, mono 1.7g, poly 0.7g); PROTEIN 9.7g; CARB 11.6g; FIBER 2.5g; CHOL 146mg; IRON 1.5mg; SODIUM 534mg; CALC 88mg

MAKE AHEAD
Bucatini with Eggplant and Roasted Peppers

Eggplant and capers, which are among Sicily's staple ingredients, add a delectable flavor to this summery pasta sauce. If you can't find bucatini (long, hollow pasta), you can use linguine or spaghetti. Prepare the sauce up to 2 days in advance, and then reheat gently over medium-low heat while you cook the pasta.

2 large yellow bell peppers
1 small eggplant, peeled and cut into ½-inch cubes (about ¾ pound)
1 cup water
2 tablespoons extravirgin olive oil, divided
2 tablespoons minced fresh oregano
2 tablespoons capers
2 garlic cloves, minced
½ teaspoon salt
¼ teaspoon freshly ground black pepper
6 plum tomatoes, seeded and chopped
12 ounces bucatini or linguine
¾ cup (3 ounces) grated ricotta salata or Romano cheese

1. Preheat broiler.

2. Cut bell peppers in half lengthwise, and discard seeds and membranes. Place pepper halves, skin sides up, on a foil-lined baking sheet; flatten with hand. Broil 10 minutes or until peppers are blackened. Place in a zip-top plastic bag, and seal. Let stand 15 minutes. Peel and cut into strips. Reduce oven temperature to 425°.

3. Arrange eggplant cubes in a single layer in a 2-quart baking dish. Pour 1 cup water over eggplant. Bake at 425° for 35 minutes or until eggplant is tender, adding more water as needed.

4. Heat 1 tablespoon oil in a large nonstick skillet over medium-high heat. Add oregano, capers, and garlic; sauté 1 minute. Stir in eggplant, bell pepper strips, salt, black pepper, and tomatoes. Cover, reduce heat, and simmer 15 minutes, stirring occasionally.

5. Cook pasta according to package directions, omitting salt and fat. Drain in a colander over a bowl, reserving ½ cup cooking liquid.

6. Combine pasta, eggplant mixture, and 1 tablespoon oil in a large bowl, tossing to coat. Add reserved cooking liquid, if necessary, to coat pasta. Sprinkle with cheese. Yield: 6 servings (serving size: 1⅔ cups pasta mixture and 2 tablespoons cheese).

CALORIES 336 (26% from fat); FAT 9.7g (sat 3.2g, mono 4.6g, poly 1g); PROTEIN 12.9g; CARB 50.3g; FIBER 5.7g; CHOL 15mg; IRON 2.8mg; SODIUM 461mg; CALC 182mg

MAKE AHEAD
Ricotta-Honey Mousse with Summer Berries

The ricotta mixture and berry mixture may both be prepared hours in advance and layered just before serving. Use a mild-flavored honey, such as orange blossom, for the best flavor. Don't be tempted to use a blender or food processor for the ricotta cheese mixture; doing so will liquefy the ricotta.

⅓ cup honey
1½ teaspoons grated orange rind
12 ounces whole-milk ricotta cheese
1½ cups halved small strawberries
1½ cups raspberries
1½ cups blackberries
¼ cup fresh orange juice
3 tablespoons sugar
1½ tablespoons thinly sliced fresh
    mint
Mint sprigs (optional)

1. Place first 3 ingredients in a medium bowl, and stir well with a whisk. Cover and chill.
2. Combine berries, juice, sugar, and sliced mint, tossing gently to coat. Let stand at room temperature 5 minutes; cover and chill. Spoon ⅓ cup berry mixture into each of 6 parfait glasses or small bowls; top each serving with about ¼ cup ricotta mixture. Divide remaining fruit mixture evenly among servings. Garnish with mint sprigs, if desired. Yield: 6 servings.

CALORIES 231 (30% from fat); FAT 7.8g (sat 4.7g, mono 2.1g, poly 0.5g); PROTEIN 7.3g; CARB 35.6g; FIBER 5.1g; CHOL 29mg; IRON 0.9mg; SODIUM 49mg; CALC 146mg

---

Tuscan Menu
serves 6

Wild Mushroom Bruschetta

Stuffed Onions with Chianti Sauce

Penne in Creamy Basil-Walnut Sauce

Sweet Chocolate Log

WINE NOTE: This Tuscan menu would traditionally be accompanied by Chianti, the famous local wine of Tuscany. Chianti is made primarily from the red Sangiovese grape. Because they're relatively high in acidity, Sangiovese wines cut through the richness of dishes made with olive oil or cream. While you can opt for a straightforward Chianti at about $15, a Chianti Classico (from the traditional "classico" area of Tuscany) will deliver more aroma, more flavor, and more finesse. A favorite: Fonterutoli Chianti Classico 2001, about $26.

MAKE AHEAD
Wild Mushroom Bruschetta

Any combination of mushrooms will work—but the more varieties you use, the more memorable this appetizer will be. Try mixing exotic varieties with common ones for layered flavors. Prepare the topping up to a day in advance; reheat or serve at room temperature over toasted bread.

3 garlic cloves, divided
6½ cups coarsely chopped cremini
    mushrooms (about ½ pound)
3 cups coarsely chopped oyster
    mushroom caps (about 4 ounces)
2½ cups coarsely chopped chanterelle
    mushrooms (about 4 ounces)
2 tablespoons finely chopped
    flat-leaf parsley
1 teaspoon extravirgin olive oil
½ teaspoon salt
⅛ teaspoon freshly ground black
    pepper
12 (½-ounce) slices country bread
Cooking spray
½ cup (2 ounces) shaved
    Parmigiano-Reggiano cheese

1. Mince 2 garlic cloves. Cut remaining clove in half; set aside.
2. Place mushrooms in a food processor; pulse 10 times or until finely chopped. Place minced garlic, parsley, and oil in a large nonstick skillet; cook 30 seconds over medium-high heat. Add mushrooms; cook 6 minutes or until liquid evaporates and mushrooms are tender, stirring constantly. Remove from heat; stir in salt and pepper. Cool slightly.
3. Lightly coat both sides of bread with cooking spray. Heat a grill pan over medium-high heat; add half of bread. Cook 1 minute on each side or until toasted. Rub 1 side of each bread slice with cut sides of garlic clove halves. Repeat procedure with remaining bread and garlic. Spoon about 2 tablespoons mushroom mixture over each bread slice, and top with about 2 teaspoons cheese. Yield: 6 servings (serving size: 2 topped bruschetta).

CALORIES 133 (28% from fat); FAT 4.2g (sat 1.7g, mono 1.3g, poly 0.2g); PROTEIN 8g; CARB 18.2g; FIBER 2.5g; CHOL 6mg; IRON 1.5mg; SODIUM 493mg; CALC 136mg

---

Stuffed Onions with Chianti Sauce

This is one of Tuscany's great dishes—onions baked in Chianti and stuffed with a mixture of cheese, breadcrumbs, and garlic and herbs. Bagged Spanish onions work well because they're usually a uniform shape and weigh about 8 ounces each.

6 (8-ounce) yellow onions
Cooking spray
2 cups Chianti, divided
½ cup dry breadcrumbs
⅓ cup finely chopped fresh flat-leaf
    parsley
¼ cup (1 ounce) grated fresh
    pecorino Romano cheese
¼ teaspoon freshly ground black
    pepper
2 garlic cloves, minced
¾ teaspoon salt, divided
1 tablespoon sugar
1 teaspoon finely chopped fresh
    rosemary

1. Preheat oven to 400°.
2. Peel onions. Cut ½ inch off top of onions; discard tops. Place onions, cut sides down, in an 11 x 7-inch baking dish coated with cooking spray. Pour ½ cup wine over onions. Cover and bake at 400° for 30 minutes. Uncover; turn onions, and bake 20 minutes. Turn onions again, and bake an additional 30 minutes or until tender. Cool onions slightly. Carefully remove pulp from onions, leaving ½-inch-thick shells. Chop pulp to measure ¾ cup. Combine pulp, breadcrumbs, and next 4 ingredients in a medium bowl. Add ½ teaspoon salt, tossing to combine. Sprinkle ⅛ teaspoon salt over onion shells; stuff shells with breadcrumb mixture. Bake at 400° for 15 minutes or until tops are golden.
3. Combine 1½ cups wine, ⅛ teaspoon salt, sugar, and rosemary in a small saucepan; bring to a boil. Cook 15 minutes or until reduced to ½ cup. Serve sauce over onions. Yield: 6 servings (serving size: 1 stuffed onion and about 1 tablespoon sauce).

CALORIES 168 (12% from fat); FAT 2.2g (sat 1g, mono 0.7g, poly 0.3g); PROTEIN 6g; CARB 33.3g; FIBER 3.6g; CHOL 5mg; IRON 1.7mg; SODIUM 441mg; CALC 133mg

Penne in Creamy Basil-Walnut Sauce

Thickening the sauce with milk-soaked bread cuts down on both olive oil and cheese. The sauce will darken quickly, so process the pesto just before serving.

2 (½-ounce) slices white bread
½ cup fat-free milk
2 cups loosely packed fresh basil leaves
½ cup coarsely chopped walnuts
2 tablespoons grated fresh pecorino Romano cheese
1 tablespoon extravirgin olive oil
¾ teaspoon salt
¼ teaspoon freshly ground black pepper
1 garlic clove, peeled
1 pound uncooked penne rigate pasta
Chopped fresh parsley (optional)

1. Trim crusts from bread. Place bread in a shallow dish; pour milk over bread. Let stand 5 minutes. Place bread mixture in a food processor; add basil and next 6 ingredients. Set aside without processing.
2. Cook pasta according to package directions, omitting salt and fat. Drain in a colander over a bowl, reserving 3 tablespoons cooking liquid. Place pasta in a large bowl. Add reserved cooking liquid to basil mixture in food processor, and process until smooth. Add pesto to pasta; toss well to coat. Sprinkle with parsley, if desired. Serve immediately. Yield: 6 servings (serving size: 1⅓ cups).

CALORIES 378 (23% from fat); FAT 9.6g (sat 1.5g, mono 2.6g, poly 4.3g); PROTEIN 13.6g; CARB 61.1g; FIBER 3.7g; CHOL 3mg; IRON 3.3mg; SODIUM 365mg; CALC 95mg

Sweet Chocolate Log

Known as *salame dolce* (sweet salami), thin slices of this rich treat are great with an after-dinner espresso. Crushed vanilla wafers give it the mottled look of salami. Because the wafers are coarsely crushed, the pieces will vary greatly in size. Since the mixture is uncooked, use a pasteurized egg yolk (look for cartons of pasteurized egg yolks or pasteurized in-shell eggs).

⅓ cup sugar
1 large pasteurized egg yolk
2 tablespoons honey
1 tablespoon butter, melted
1 cup unsweetened cocoa
1 tablespoon Marsala wine
1 tablespoon hot water
2 teaspoons grated orange rind (optional)
20 reduced-calorie vanilla wafers, coarsely crushed

1. Place sugar and egg yolk in a medium bowl; beat with a mixer at high speed 3 minutes or until thick and pale. Beat in honey and butter. Add cocoa, ½ cup at a time, beating well after each addition. Stir in wine, water, orange rind, if desired, and wafers.
2. Spoon mixture onto a sheet of wax paper using a rubber spatula (mixture will be stiff). Using moist hands, shape mixture into a 6-inch log. Wrap log tightly with plastic wrap; chill at least 1 hour. Cut log into ½-inch-thick slices. Yield: 6 servings (serving size: 2 slices).

CALORIES 178 (28% from fat); FAT 5.5g (sat 2.6g, mono 1.7g, poly 0.3g); PROTEIN 3.7g; CARB 35g; FIBER 4.8g; CHOL 41mg; IRON 2.4mg; SODIUM 68mg; CALC 32mg

technique
Wrap and Roll

Sheets of phyllo dough create crisp, delicate crusts for all kinds of sweet and savory dishes.

Phyllo is probably the most misunderstood of pastries and its reputation often scares many cooks. But, with the following recipes, you'll be on your way to creating impressive pastries, both sweet and savory, with minimal effort. If it's your first time working with phyllo, try Roasted Salmon and Leeks in Phyllo Packets, Pork Tenderloin in Phyllo, or Apple-Cream Cheese Strudel. None of these recipes require cutting or trimming the dough—instead, you just coat it with cooking spray and roll it up or fold it over a few times to enclose the filling. Phyllo 101 couldn't be simpler.

Strudels are a classic use of phyllo.

Apple-Cream Cheese Strudel

Part apple pie, part cheesecake, this dessert is completely delicious. We used a combination of Rome and Granny Smith apples for a sweet-tart flavor, but you can use any apple you like.

1 teaspoon butter
1¼ cups thinly sliced peeled Rome apple (about 8 ounces)
1¼ cups thinly sliced peeled Granny Smith apple (about 8 ounces)
3 tablespoons thawed apple juice concentrate
2 tablespoons brown sugar
⅛ teaspoon ground cinnamon
⅛ teaspoon ground nutmeg
1½ tablespoons finely chopped walnuts
½ cup (4 ounces) ⅓-less-fat cream cheese, softened
2 tablespoons granulated sugar
2 tablespoons fat-free sour cream
1 teaspoon all-purpose flour
1 teaspoon vanilla extract
Dash of salt
1 large egg white
6 (18 x 14-inch) sheets frozen phyllo dough, thawed
Cooking spray
Dash of nutmeg
1 tablespoon powdered sugar (optional)

1. Preheat oven to 375°.
2. Melt butter in a large nonstick skillet over medium-high heat. Add apples; sauté 3 minutes or until lightly browned. Reduce heat to medium; cook 5 minutes or until tender, stirring frequently. Stir in apple juice concentrate, brown sugar, cinnamon, and ⅛ teaspoon nutmeg. Cook 3 minutes or until sugar melts and mixture is slightly syrupy. Remove from heat; stir in walnuts. Cool.

3. Place cream cheese, granulated sugar, sour cream, and flour in a bowl; beat with a mixer at medium speed until smooth. Beat in vanilla, salt, and egg white.

4. Place 1 phyllo sheet on a large cutting board or work surface (cover remaining dough to prevent drying); lightly coat with cooking spray. Repeat layers with remaining phyllo and cooking spray, ending with phyllo. Gently press phyllo layers together. Lightly coat top phyllo sheet with cooking spray. Spoon apple mixture along 1 short edge of phyllo, leaving a 2-inch border. Drizzle cream cheese mixture over apple mixture. Fold long edges of phyllo over filling (phyllo will not completely cover filling). Starting at short edge with 2-inch border, roll up jelly-roll fashion. (Do not roll too tightly or strudel may split.) Place strudel, seam side down, on a baking sheet coated with cooking spray. Sprinkle with dash of nutmeg.

5. Bake at 375° for 15 minutes or until golden brown. Remove from oven; cool 10 minutes on baking sheet on a wire rack. Sprinkle with powdered sugar, if desired. Cut into 6 equal portions using a serrated knife. Yield: 6 servings.

CALORIES 217 (29% from fat); FAT 7.1g (sat 3.5g, mono 2.2g, poly 1.2g); PROTEIN 4.6g; CARB 34.6g; FIBER 3g; CHOL 16mg; IRON 1mg; SODIUM 219mg; CALC 32mg

How to Make Apple-Cream Cheese Strudel

Shaping the strudel is easy—just fold the phyllo edges over the filling and roll up.

Pork Tenderloin in Phyllo

This recipe is simplicity itself—place the meat on the phyllo, and roll up. You don't even have to tuck in the ends of the dough. To ensure that the meat cooks completely, it's partially cooked before it's wrapped.

  1 (1-pound) pork tenderloin, trimmed
  ½ teaspoon salt
  ¼ teaspoon freshly ground black
      pepper
Cooking spray
  1 tablespoon stone-ground mustard
1½ tablespoons chopped fresh thyme
  8 (18 x 14-inch) sheets frozen
      phyllo dough, thawed
  ½ cup hot mango chutney

1. Preheat oven to 400°.

2. Sprinkle pork with salt and pepper; place on a jelly-roll pan coated with cooking spray. Bake at 400° for 15 minutes, turning once. Remove from oven; let stand 5 minutes or until slightly cool. Coat pork with mustard; sprinkle evenly with thyme, pressing thyme into mustard to adhere.

3. Place 1 phyllo sheet on a large cutting board or work surface (cover remaining dough to prevent drying); lightly coat with cooking spray. Repeat layers with remaining phyllo and cooking spray, ending with phyllo. Gently press phyllo layers together. Lightly coat top phyllo sheet with cooking spray.

4. Arrange pork along 1 short edge of phyllo, leaving a 2-inch border. Starting at short edge with 2-inch border, roll up jelly-roll fashion. (Do not roll tightly). Place roll, seam side down, on jelly-roll pan coated with cooking spray. Bake at 400° for 20 minutes or until roll is golden brown and a thermometer registers 155°. Let stand 10 minutes.

5. Place chutney in a microwave-safe bowl; microwave at HIGH 30 seconds or until warm, stirring once. Cut pork crosswise into 8 slices using a serrated knife; serve with chutney. Yield: 4 servings (serving size: 2 pork slices and 2 tablespoons chutney).

CALORIES 329 (24% from fat); FAT 8.7g (sat 2.7g, mono 4g, poly 1.1g); PROTEIN 26.7g; CARB 34.6g; FIBER 2g; CHOL 75mg; IRON 3.1mg; SODIUM 599mg; CALC 36mg

Phyllo 101

Despite all those delicate, paper-thin layers of golden brown pastry, phyllo is actually pretty easy to handle. The keys to its simplicity are thawing it properly and keeping it from drying out. Follow these helpful tips to make sure your phyllo dishes will be a success:

• Most phyllo comes frozen in a box. It's essential to thaw the dough in the refrigerator for at least 24 hours. Thawing in a microwave or at room temperature can produce uneven results and cause some of the dough sheets to stick together.

• After it's thawed, let the dough stand at room temperature a couple of hours before unwrapping. Remove from the package only the sheets of dough you need. Wrap the rest of the dough tightly in plastic wrap, and store it in the refrigerator up to 1 week.

• Keep the sheets you're not working with covered with a slightly damp towel or paper towel and a layer of plastic wrap to prevent drying. Make sure the towel isn't too wet; if it is, it can make the dough soggy and cause it to stick together.

• Always spray on cooking spray, or lightly brush butter or oil between sheets of phyllo dough. A little fat between the layers makes the pastry crisp and flaky.

• You need a large work surface, and because ample amounts of cooking spray are used to coat the sheets, make sure to remove anything nearby that you don't want sprayed.

• Don't worry if a phyllo sheet buckles or folds—gently pat it down as smoothly as you can. If it tears, patch it with cooking spray or butter.

Roasted Salmon and Leeks in Phyllo Packets

As leeks, carrots, and tarragon steam-roast with the fish, the phyllo locks in the flavors and crisps on the outside to form a delicate, crunchy coating.

½ cup (2-inch) julienne-cut leek
½ cup (2-inch) julienne-cut carrot
2 teaspoons minced fresh tarragon
½ teaspoon salt, divided
4 (6-ounce) salmon fillets (about 1 inch thick)
⅛ teaspoon freshly ground black pepper
12 (18 x 14-inch) sheets frozen phyllo dough, thawed
Cooking spray
2 teaspoons fresh lemon juice
4 lemon wedges

1. Preheat oven to 400°.
2. Cook leek and carrot in boiling water 1 minute; drain. Combine leek mixture, tarragon, and ¼ teaspoon salt in a small bowl, tossing gently. Sprinkle salmon with ¼ teaspoon salt and pepper.
3. Place 1 phyllo sheet on a large cutting board or work surface (cover remaining dough to prevent drying); lightly coat with cooking spray. Repeat layers twice, ending with phyllo. Gently press phyllo layers together. Lightly coat top phyllo sheet with cooking spray. Arrange ¼ cup leek mixture along center of 1 short edge of phyllo, leaving a 4-inch border; top with 1 fillet. Drizzle with ½ teaspoon juice. Fold long edges of phyllo over fish.
4. Starting at short edge with 4-inch border, roll up jelly-roll fashion. Place wrapped fish, seam side down, on a baking sheet coated with cooking spray. Lightly coat wrapped fish with cooking spray. Repeat procedure with remaining phyllo, cooking spray, leek mixture, salmon, and juice. Bake at 400° for 15 minutes or until lightly browned, and let stand 5 minutes before serving. Serve with lemon wedges. Yield: 4 servings (serving size: 1 packet).

CALORIES 457 (32% from fat); FAT 16.5g (sat 3.9g, mono 7.5g, poly 3.7g); PROTEIN 40.6g; CARB 33.4g; FIBER 1.8g; CHOL 87mg; IRON 2.4mg; SODIUM 656mg; CALC 40mg

How to Make Asparagus-Fontina Tart

So nothing is wasted, sprinkle chopped excess phyllo dough into the tart crust.

Asparagus-Fontina Tart

In this recipe, a stack of phyllo is cut into a circle and fitted, like a piecrust, into a tart pan. None of the dough goes to waste; the scraps are chopped and placed on top of the crust. A standard dinner plate is 10 inches in diameter; use it to estimate the 11-inch circle you'll cut from the dough.

16 thin asparagus spears, trimmed (about 8 ounces)
3 large egg whites
1 large egg
3 tablespoons 2% reduced-fat milk
¼ teaspoon salt
⅛ teaspoon ground nutmeg
⅛ teaspoon freshly ground black pepper
8 (18 x 14-inch) sheets frozen phyllo dough, thawed
Cooking spray
½ cup (2 ounces) shredded fontina cheese, divided
½ cup shredded peeled Yukon gold potato (about 4 ounces)

1. Preheat oven to 400°.
2. Cut asparagus spears 4 inches from tips; reserve tips. Coarsely chop remaining asparagus; set aside.
3. Combine egg whites and egg in a medium bowl, stirring with a whisk. Add milk, salt, nutmeg, and pepper. Stir in chopped asparagus.
4. Place 1 phyllo sheet on a large cutting board or work surface (cover remaining dough to prevent drying); lightly coat with cooking spray. Repeat layers with remaining phyllo and cooking spray, ending with phyllo. Gently press phyllo layers together. Lightly coat top phyllo sheet with cooking spray.
5. Cut phyllo stack into an 11-inch circle using a sharp knife; coarsely chop excess dough. Carefully place phyllo circle into a 9-inch tart pan coated with cooking spray; gently press phyllo into pan. Fold edges over. Sprinkle chopped dough over phyllo circle; top with ¼ cup cheese and potato. Place tart pan on a foil-lined baking sheet. Pour egg mixture into tart shell. Arrange asparagus tips spokelike on top of egg mixture with tips toward outside of pan, and sprinkle evenly with ¼ cup cheese. Bake at 400° for 20 minutes. Loosely cover tart with foil. Bake an additional 5 minutes or until tart is set. Yield: 4 servings (serving size: 1 wedge).

CALORIES 240 (30% from fat); FAT 8g (sat 3.2g, mono 2.9g, poly 0.8g); PROTEIN 12.2g; CARB 30.1g; FIBER 2.4g; CHOL 67mg; IRON 2.2mg; SODIUM 482mg; CALC 133mg

How to Make Phyllo Shells for Phyllo Éclairs

To prepare shells, cut 6 (12 x 6-inch) pieces of aluminum foil. Using index fingers as a guide, and starting at a narrow edge, loosely roll up each foil piece jelly-roll fashion to form a cylinder with a 1-inch opening. Lightly coat outside of each cylinder with cooking spray.

How to Fill Phyllo Shells for Phyllo Éclairs

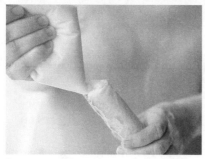

Spoon vanilla cream into a zip-top plastic bag. Seal bag; snip off ½ inch of 1 bottom corner of bag. Pipe vanilla cream evenly into cooled phyllo shells.

MAKE AHEAD
Phyllo Éclairs

You can prepare the phyllo shells and vanilla cream up to 1 day ahead. Store shells in an airtight container at room temperature, and the vanilla cream in a zip-top plastic bag in the refrigerator.

VANILLA CREAM:

    6 tablespoons granulated
       sugar
 ¼ cup cornstarch
Dash of salt
    3 large egg yolks
    1 cup 1% low-fat milk
 ½ cup half-and-half
 ½ teaspoon vanilla extract

SHELLS:

Cooking spray
    4 (18 x 14-inch) sheets frozen
       phyllo dough, thawed
 ¼ cup granulated sugar, divided

REMAINING INGREDIENTS:

 ¼ cup semisweet chocolate
       chips
1½ teaspoons 1% low-fat milk
    1 tablespoon powdered sugar

1. To prepare vanilla cream, combine first 4 ingredients in a small saucepan, stirring with a whisk until well blended. Gradually add 1 cup milk and half-and-half, stirring with a whisk. Cook over medium heat until mixture comes to a boil, stirring constantly. Reduce heat to low; cook 1 minute, stirring constantly. Remove from heat; stir in vanilla. Pour into a bowl. Press plastic wrap onto surface of vanilla cream; chill.

2. Preheat oven to 375°.

3. To prepare shells, cut 6 (12 x 6-inch) pieces of aluminum foil. Using index fingers as a guide, and starting at a narrow edge, loosely roll up each foil piece jelly-roll fashion to form a cylinder with a 1-inch opening. Lightly coat outside of each cylinder with cooking spray.

4. Place 1 phyllo sheet on a large cutting board or work surface (cover remaining dough to prevent drying); lightly coat with cooking spray. Sprinkle evenly with 1 tablespoon granulated sugar. Repeat layers once. Cut phyllo stack lengthwise into 3 equal strips. Repeat procedure with remaining phyllo, cooking spray, and granulated sugar. Place a foil cylinder at bottom of 1 phyllo strip, and roll up phyllo jelly-roll fashion around cylinder. Lightly coat with cooking spray. Place on a parchment-lined baking sheet. Repeat procedure with remaining foil cylinders, phyllo strips, and cooking spray. Bake at 375° for 10 minutes or until lightly browned. Cool completely on a wire rack. Carefully remove foil cylinders from phyllo shells by twisting ends of foil in opposite directions and gently pulling foil from shells.

5. Spoon vanilla cream into a zip-top plastic bag. Seal bag; snip off ½ inch of 1 bottom corner of bag. Pipe vanilla cream evenly into cooled phyllo shells.

6. Place chocolate chips and 1½ teaspoons milk in another zip-top plastic bag. (Do not seal bag.) Microwave at HIGH 45 seconds or until chocolate melts; lightly knead bag until mixture is smooth. Snip off ¼ inch of 1 bottom corner of bag. Drizzle chocolate mixture evenly over stuffed shells. Sprinkle with powdered sugar. Serve immediately. Yield: 6 servings (serving size: 1 éclair).

CALORIES 252 (28% from fat); FAT 7.9g (sat 3.8g, mono 2.9g, poly 0.6g); PROTEIN 4.6g; CARB 40.9g; FIBER 0.7g; CHOL 118mg; IRON 1mg; SODIUM 122mg; CALC 94mg

Feta-Spinach Tarts

These appetizers require the dough to be stacked, cut into squares, and fit into muffin tins. The cups are then filled with a seasoned mixture of spinach and feta cheese, much like the filling in the Greek phyllo triangles called *spanakopita*.

Cooking spray
 ½ cup chopped red onion
    1 garlic clove, minced
 ½ teaspoon freshly ground black
       pepper
 ¼ teaspoon salt
    1 (10-ounce) package frozen
       chopped spinach, thawed,
       drained, and squeezed dry
    3 large egg whites
    1 large egg
    2 tablespoons chopped fresh
       parsley
1½ tablespoons chopped fresh
       oregano
    2 tablespoons 1% low-fat milk
    6 (18 x 14-inch) sheets frozen
       phyllo dough, thawed
 ½ cup (2 ounces) crumbled feta
       cheese

1. Preheat oven to 375°.

2. Heat a nonstick skillet over medium heat. Coat pan with cooking spray. Add onion, and cook 5 minutes, stirring frequently. Add garlic; cook 1 minute, stirring constantly. Stir in pepper and salt. Add spinach; cook 2 minutes, stirring frequently. Remove from heat, and cool slightly. Combine egg whites and egg in a medium bowl, stirring with a whisk. Add spinach mixture, parsley, oregano, and milk, stirring to combine.

3. Place 1 phyllo sheet on a large cutting board or work surface (cover remaining dough to prevent drying); lightly coat with cooking spray. Repeat layers with remaining phyllo and cooking spray, ending with phyllo. Gently press phyllo layers together. Lightly coat top phyllo sheet with cooking spray. Cut stack lengthwise into 3 equal strips (approximately 4½ inches wide), and cut each strip crosswise to form 4 (4½-inch) squares. Carefully place 1 layered square
Continued

into each of 12 muffin cups coated with cooking spray; gently press squares into pan to form cups. Fan corners of phyllo cups. Lightly coat corners of phyllo with cooking spray.

4. Divide spinach mixture evenly among phyllo cups. Bake at 375° for 15 minutes. Remove from oven; sprinkle evenly with cheese. Loosely cover, and bake an additional 3 minutes. Yield: 12 servings (serving size: 1 tart).

CALORIES 62 (30% from fat); FAT 2.1g (sat 1g, mono 0.7g, poly 0.2g); PROTEIN 3.7g; CARB 7.3g; FIBER 1.1g; CHOL 22mg; IRON 1mg; SODIUM 186mg; CALC 64mg

MAKE AHEAD

Cherry-Apricot Turnovers

(pictured on page 148)

Layers of phyllo are brushed with a mixture of melted butter and oil, and then they're sprinkled with graham cracker crumbs and brown sugar. The crumbs help keep the phyllo, which envelopes the moist filling, dry and crisp.

  1 cup apricot nectar
  ½ cup chopped dried apricots
  ⅓ cup packed brown sugar
  ¼ teaspoon grated lemon rind
  2 tablespoons fresh lemon juice
  3 (3-ounce) bags dried sweet cherries
  2 tablespoons chopped almonds
  ½ teaspoon vanilla extract
  2 tablespoons butter, melted
  2 tablespoons canola oil
  6 (18 x 14-inch) sheets frozen phyllo dough, thawed
  ¼ cup graham cracker crumbs, divided
  2 tablespoons brown sugar, divided
Cooking spray

1. Combine first 6 ingredients in a saucepan; bring to a boil. Reduce heat; simmer 20 minutes or until liquid is absorbed, stirring occasionally. Stir in almonds and vanilla. Cool completely.
2. Preheat oven to 375°.
3. Combine butter and oil. Place 1 phyllo sheet on a large cutting board or work surface (cover remaining dough to prevent drying). Lightly brush phyllo sheet with 1 tablespoon butter mixture. Sprinkle with 1 tablespoon crumbs and 1½ teaspoons brown sugar. Repeat layers once. Top with 1 phyllo sheet. Gently press layers together. Lightly coat top phyllo sheet with cooking spray. Cut stack lengthwise into 4 (3½-inch-wide) strips. Cut each strip in half crosswise forming 8 (9 x 3½-inch) rectangles. Spoon 2 tablespoons cherry mixture onto 1 short end of each rectangle, leaving 1-inch borders. Fold 1 corner of each rectangle over mixture, forming a triangle; continue folding back and forth into a triangle to end of each rectangle. Tuck edges under triangles. Place triangles, seam sides down, on a large baking sheet coated with cooking spray; lightly coat triangles with cooking spray. Repeat procedure with remaining phyllo, butter mixture, crumbs, brown sugar, cherry mixture, and cooking spray.
4. Bake at 375° for 15 minutes or until golden brown. Remove from baking sheet, and cool on a wire rack. Yield: 16 turnovers (serving size: 1 turnover).

CALORIES 155 (25% from fat); FAT 4.3g (sat 1.2g, mono 2.1g, poly 0.8g); PROTEIN 1.9g; CARB 27g; FIBER 1.9g; CHOL 4mg; IRON 0.8mg; SODIUM 62mg; CALC 21mg

How to Make Cherry-Apricot Turnovers

To seal the filling in a triangle shape, fold the phyllo like you would a flag.

sidetracked

Chopped Salads

The secret to a great salad: Let the vegetables star.

With minimum help from the cook, these salads go from fridge to table in a few easy steps.

QUICK & EASY • MAKE AHEAD
Versatile Vinaigrette

Cornstarch, commonly used as a thickening agent, gives this red wine vinaigrette body so it can better coat a salad.

  1 cup vegetable broth
  2 teaspoons cornstarch
  2 tablespoons red wine vinegar
  1 tablespoon extravirgin olive oil
  1 teaspoon sugar
  ¼ teaspoon salt
  ⅛ teaspoon freshly ground black pepper

1. Combine broth and cornstarch in a small saucepan, stirring with a whisk. Bring to a boil over medium heat; cook 1 minute, stirring constantly. Remove from heat, and stir in vinegar and remaining ingredients. Cover and chill. Stir before using. Yield: 1 cup (serving size: 2 tablespoons).
NOTE: Store vinaigrette in refrigerator up to 1 week.

CALORIES 21 (77% from fat); FAT 1.8g (sat 0.2g, mono 1.2g, poly 0.1g); PROTEIN 0.3g; CARB 1.3g; FIBER 0g; CHOL 0mg; IRON 0.1mg; SODIUM 199mg; CALC 0mg

DIJON VINAIGRETTE:

Add 2 teaspoons Dijon mustard to broth mixture with red wine vinegar and remaining ingredients.

CALORIES 23 (74% from fat); FAT 1.9g (sat 0.2g, mono 1.3g, poly 0.2g); PROTEIN 0.3g; CARB 1.4g; FIBER 0g; CHOL 0mg; IRON 0.1mg; SODIUM 230mg; CALC 2mg

ROASTED GARLIC VINAIGRETTE:

Add 2 teaspoons bottled minced roasted garlic to broth mixture with red wine vinegar and remaining ingredients.

CALORIES 23 (70% from fat); FAT 1.8g (sat 0.2g, mono 1.2g, poly 0.2g); PROTEIN 0.4g; CARB 1.8g; FIBER 0.1g; CHOL 0mg; IRON 0.1mg; SODIUM 199mg; CALC 3mg

CUMIN-LIME VINAIGRETTE:

Omit vinegar. Add 3 tablespoons fresh lime juice and ¼ teaspoon ground cumin to broth mixture with oil and remaining ingredients.

CALORIES 23 (70% from fat); FAT 1.8g (sat 0.2g; mono 1.2g; poly 0.1g); PROTEIN 0.3g; CARB 1.8g; FIBER 0.1g; CHOL 0mg; IRON 0mg; SODIUM 199mg; CALC 1mg

Napa Cabbage and Snow Pea Slaw

(pictured on page 147)

This salad tastes best after chilling in the refrigerator for about 30 minutes.

DRESSING:
- 2 tablespoons sugar
- 2 tablespoons fresh lime juice
- 1 tablespoon fish sauce
- 1 teaspoon dark sesame oil
- ½ teaspoon grated peeled fresh ginger

Dash of ground red pepper

SLAW:
- 4 cups (¼-inch) slices napa (Chinese) cabbage
- ½ cup snow peas, trimmed and cut lengthwise into (⅛-inch) thin strips
- ½ cup fresh bean sprouts
- ½ cup (⅛-inch) julienne-cut peeled jícama
- ¼ cup (⅛-inch) julienne-cut red bell pepper
- 2 tablespoons thinly sliced green onions
- 2 tablespoons finely chopped fresh cilantro

1. To prepare dressing, combine first 6 ingredients, stirring with a whisk.
2. To prepare slaw, combine cabbage and remaining 6 ingredients in a large bowl. Add dressing, and toss well to coat. Chill 30 minutes. Yield: 4 servings (serving size: 1 cup).

CALORIES 65 (19% from fat); FAT 1.4g (sat 0.2g; mono 0.5g; poly 0.6g); PROTEIN 2.2g; CARB 12.3g; FIBER 2.3g; CHOL 0mg; IRON 1.1mg; SODIUM 396mg; CALC 86mg

Tomato and Cucumber Salad with Feta

The Dijon Vinaigrette variation (recipe on page 142) is also good in this salad.

- 2 cups (½-inch) diced tomato (about 1 pound)
- 1 cup (¼ inch) diced English cucumber
- ¼ cup (1 ounce) crumbled feta cheese
- 1 tablespoon finely chopped fresh mint
- ¼ cup Versatile Vinaigrette (recipe on page 142)

1. Combine first 4 ingredients in a large bowl. Add vinaigrette, and toss gently to coat. Yield: 4 servings (serving size: ¾ cup).

CALORIES 54 (47% from fat); FAT 2.8g (sat 1.2g; mono 1g; poly 0.3g); PROTEIN 2.1g; CARB 6.4g; FIBER 1.3g; CHOL 6mg; IRON 0.6mg; SODIUM 188mg; CALC 46mg

Green and White Salad with Blue Cheese Dressing

To keep the salad fresh and crisp, serve this dish right after you toss it with the dressing.

DRESSING:
- ⅓ cup fat-free cottage cheese
- ⅓ cup fat-free sour cream
- ¼ cup (1-ounce) crumbled blue cheese
- 2 tablespoons 1% low-fat milk
- ¼ teaspoon salt
- ⅛ teaspoon freshly ground black pepper
- 1 garlic clove, minced

SALAD:
- 2½ cups (1-inch) chopped iceberg lettuce
- 2 cups (1-inch) chopped curly leaf lettuce
- ¾ cup (¼-inch) diced cucumber
- ⅓ cup (¼-inch) diced celery
- ¼ cup thinly sliced green onions

1. To prepare dressing, combine first 7 ingredients in a food processor or blender, and process until smooth, scraping sides of bowl once.
2. To prepare salad, combine lettuces, cucumber, celery, and onions in a large bowl. Add dressing; toss well. Serve immediately. Yield: 5 servings (serving size: 1 cup).

CALORIES 59 (27% from fat); FAT 1.8g (sat 1.1g; mono 0.5g; poly 0.1g); PROTEIN 5g; CARB 6.1g; FIBER 1.3g; CHOL 5mg; IRON 0.3mg; SODIUM 301mg; CALC 105mg

Gazpacho Salad with Tomato Vinaigrette

You can serve this refreshing salad like a salsa with chips.

VINAIGRETTE:
- 3 tablespoons tomato juice
- 2 tablespoons red wine vinegar
- 1 tablespoon extravirgin olive oil
- 1 teaspoon Worcestershire sauce
- ¼ teaspoon salt
- ¼ to ½ teaspoon hot sauce
- ⅛ teaspoon freshly ground black pepper

SALAD:
- 2 cups (½-inch) diced tomato (about 1 pound)
- 1½ cups (½-inch) diced cucumber
- ½ cup (¼-inch) diced green bell pepper
- 2 tablespoons minced shallots
- 2 tablespoons coarsely chopped fresh basil

1. To prepare vinaigrette, combine first 7 ingredients, stirring with a whisk.
2. To prepare salad, combine tomato, cucumber, bell pepper, shallots, and basil in a large bowl. Add vinaigrette; toss gently to coat. Yield: 5 servings (serving size: ¾ cup).

CALORIES 57 (49% from fat); FAT 3.1g (sat 0.4g; mono 2g; poly 0.4g); PROTEIN 1.3g; CARB 7.7g; FIBER 2g; CHOL 0mg; IRON 0.7mg; SODIUM 171mg; CALC 20mg

Garden Salad with Citrus Vinaigrette

VINAIGRETTE:

3 tablespoons fresh orange juice
1½ tablespoons fresh lime juice
2½ teaspoons extravirgin olive oil
2 teaspoons honey
1 teaspoon red wine vinegar
¼ teaspoon salt
⅛ teaspoon freshly ground black pepper

SALAD:

1½ cups (1 x ¼-inch) julienne-cut zucchini
1½ cups (1 x ¼-inch) julienne-cut yellow squash
1 cup fresh corn kernels (about 2 ears)
2 tablespoons finely chopped red onion
1 tablespoon finely chopped fresh flat-leaf parsley
1 tablespoon finely chopped fresh basil

1. To prepare vinaigrette, combine first 7 ingredients, stirring with a whisk.
2. To prepare salad, combine zucchini and remaining 5 ingredients in a large bowl. Add vinaigrette; toss well. Cover and chill. Yield: 4 servings (serving size: 1 cup).

CALORIES 101 (30% from fat); FAT 3.4g (sat 0.5g; mono 2.2g; poly 0.5g); PROTEIN 2.6g; CARB 17.4g; FIBER 3.6g; CHOL 0mg; IRON 0.8mg; SODIUM 154mg; CALC 30mg

Roasted Beet Salad with Raspberry Vinaigrette

Serve over curly leaf lettuce or with chicken or pork.

8 beets (about 2½ pounds)
½ cup coarsely chopped red onion
½ cup coarsely chopped celery
2 tablespoons raspberry vinegar
1 tablespoon honey
2½ teaspoons extravirgin olive oil
¼ teaspoon salt
⅛ teaspoon freshly ground black pepper

1. Preheat oven to 425°.
2. Leave root and 1 inch of stem on beets; scrub with a brush. Place beets on a foil-lined baking sheet. Bake at 425° for 45 minutes or until tender; cool. Trim off beet roots and stem; rub off skins. Coarsely chop beets. Combine beets, onion, and celery in a large bowl.
3. Combine vinegar and remaining 4 ingredients. Pour over beet mixture; toss gently to coat. Serve at room temperature or chilled. Yield: 6 servings (serving size: ⅔ cup).

CALORIES 82 (23% from fat); FAT 2.1g (sat 0.3g; mono 1.4g; poly 0.2g); PROTEIN 2g; CARB 15.1g; FIBER 3.5g; CHOL 0mg; IRON 1mg; SODIUM 194mg; CALC 25mg

Green Bean, Corn, and Roasted Poblano Chile Salad

1 poblano chile
2 cups (1-inch) diagonally sliced green beans (about ½ pound)
2 cups fresh corn kernels (about 2 ears)
2 cups chopped spinach
1 cup cherry tomatoes, halved
⅓ cup Cumin-Lime Vinaigrette (recipe on page 143)
3 tablespoons thinly sliced green onions
2 tablespoons finely chopped fresh cilantro
Freshly ground black pepper (optional)

1. Preheat broiler.
2. Place chile on a foil-lined baking sheet; broil 10 minutes or until blackened, turning occasionally. Place in a zip-top plastic bag; seal. Let stand 15 minutes. Peel and cut in half lengthwise. Discard seeds and membranes; chop.
3. Steam green beans, covered, 5 minutes or until crisp-tender; drain. Rinse with cold water; drain well.
4. Combine chopped chile, beans, corn, and next 5 ingredients, tossing gently to coat. Sprinkle with black pepper, if desired. Yield: 6 servings (serving size: 1 cup).

CALORIES 78 (18% from fat); FAT 1.6g (sat 0.2g; mono 0.7g; poly 0.4g); PROTEIN 3.1g; CARB 15.8g; FIBER 3.4g; CHOL 0mg; IRON 1.1mg; SODIUM 106mg; CALC 26mg

Vegetable Salad with Roasted Garlic Vinaigrette

Try this salad with grilled chicken or pork.

1½ cups (¼-inch) diced zucchini
1½ cups (¼-inch) diced plum tomato
1 cup fresh corn kernels (about 2 ears)
⅓ cup Roasted Garlic Vinaigrette (recipe on page 142)
2 tablespoons minced seeded Anaheim chile
¼ teaspoon salt
⅛ teaspoon black pepper
Boston lettuce leaves (optional)

1. Combine all ingredients except lettuce in a large bowl, tossing gently to coat. Spoon onto lettuce leaves, if desired. Yield: 4 servings (serving size: about 1 cup).

CALORIES 80 (24% from fat); FAT 2.1g (sat 0.3g; mono 1g; poly 0.5g); PROTEIN 2.9g; CARB 14.9g; FIBER 3.1g; CHOL 0mg; IRON 0.9mg; SODIUM 243mg; CALC 21mg

Romaine Lettuce with Red Pepper and Olives

The Mediterranean flavors in this salad pair well with pasta and marinara sauce.

4 cups (1-inch) chopped romaine lettuce
⅓ cup (¼-inch) diced red bell pepper
¼ cup (¼-inch) diced red onion
¼ cup (1 ounce) crumbled feta cheese
2 tablespoons coarsely chopped pitted kalamata olives
¼ teaspoon dried oregano
¼ cup fat-free Italian dressing

1. Combine first 6 ingredients in a large bowl. Add dressing; toss well. Yield: 4 servings (serving size: 1 cup).

CALORIES 55 (46% from fat); FAT 2.8g (sat 1.3g; mono 1.1g; poly 0.2g); PROTEIN 2.4g; CARB 5.4g; FIBER 1.6g; CHOL 7mg; IRON 0.9mg; SODIUM 360mg; CALC 68mg

Bayou Catfish Fillets, page 126

Spiced Shrimp with Avocado Oil,
page 135

Napa Cabbage and Snow Pea Slaw, page 143

Filet Mignon with Red Currant-Green
Peppercorn Sauce, page 160

Cherry-Apricot Turnovers, page 142

Soba Noodles with Broccoli and Chicken, page 150

Farmer Bob's Veggie Vision

Chef's Garden founder Bob Jones is on a mission: To raise a crop of kids across America who love to eat vegetables.

Farmer Bob Jones is the founder, patriarch, and visionary behind The Chef's Garden, a thriving, 200-acre family-run farm in Huron, Ohio, that supplies hundreds of restaurants across America with microgreens, heirloom tomatoes, and other specialty crops. But after 20 years of building his enterprise, Jones has turned his sights to kids and nutrition.

Currently, a team of veteran teachers from Erie and Huron counties in Ohio are working with The Culinary Vegetable Institute and Farmer Bob on a pilot program for local schools. These will teach children how important vegetables are to health, as well as what good ones taste like. The centerpiece of the program is a kit that contains soil, seeds, vegetable samples for tastings, recipes, and videos—all designed to make it easy for the teacher to teach and exciting for the children to learn. The eventual goal of the program is to reach every fourth grader in the nation—an effort that may take years to fulfill. But Jones and his cohorts feel their energy, enthusiasm, and farm-tuned patience equip them well for the task.

Grilled-Steak Soft Tacos

Omit the pepper slices for delicate palates.

- 1 cup fresh lime juice (about 8 limes)
- 1 (2-pound) flank steak, trimmed
- 2 tablespoons ground cumin
- 2 tablespoons ground coriander
- ½ teaspoon kosher salt
- ½ teaspoon cracked black pepper
- 6 garlic cloves, minced
- Cooking spray
- 4 ears shucked corn
- 8 (8-inch) fat-free flour tortillas
- 2 cups trimmed arugula
- 2 cups thinly sliced red onion
- 1 cup cilantro sprigs
- 1 cup chopped tomato
- 1 cup diced peeled avocado
- ½ cup sliced seeded jalapeño pepper (about 4 peppers)
- 8 lime wedges

1. Combine lime juice and steak in a large zip-top plastic bag; seal bag. Marinate in refrigerator 1 hour; turn bag occasionally.

2. Prepare grill.

3. Remove steak from bag; discard marinade. Combine cumin and next 4 ingredients; rub over both sides of steak.

4. Place steak on a grill rack coated with cooking spray; grill 8 minutes on each side or until desired degree of doneness. Place on a cutting board; cover loosely with foil. Let stand 5 minutes. Cut steak diagonally across grain into thin slices.

5. Place corn on grill rack coated with cooking spray; grill 8 minutes or until tender, turning occasionally. Cut kernels from ears of corn; discard cobs.

6. Heat tortillas according to package directions. Divide steak evenly among tortillas; top each serving with about ¼ cup corn, ¼ cup arugula, ¼ cup onion, 2 tablespoons cilantro, 2 tablespoons tomato, 2 tablespoons avocado, and 1 tablespoon jalapeño. Fold tortillas in half. Serve with lime wedges. Yield: 8 servings (serving size: 1 taco).

CALORIES 397 (29% from fat); FAT 12.8g (sat 4.3g, mono 5.4g, poly 1g); PROTEIN 28.1g; CARB 34.3g; FIBER 6.7g; CHOL 57mg; IRON 3.6mg; SODIUM 425mg; CALC 56mg

Bell Pepper Chicken with Feta Orzo

Most kids love bell peppers and pasta. Both are featured in this simple, fresh dish. Use red bell peppers, or try any combination of red, yellow, orange, and green.

- 4 ounces uncooked orzo (rice-shaped pasta; about ½ cup)
- 4 teaspoons olive oil, divided
- 4 (6-ounce) skinless, boneless chicken breast halves
- ½ teaspoon salt
- ¼ teaspoon black pepper
- ⅛ teaspoon ground red pepper
- 1 cup red bell pepper strips
- 1 cup green bell pepper strips
- 1 teaspoon dried oregano
- 2 garlic cloves, minced
- 1½ tablespoons fresh lemon juice
- ¾ cup (3 ounces) crumbled feta cheese

1. Cook orzo according to package directions, omitting salt and fat.

2. While orzo cooks, heat 2 teaspoons olive oil in a large nonstick skillet over medium-high heat. Sprinkle chicken with salt, black pepper, and red pepper. Add chicken to pan, and cook 4 minutes on each side or until done. Remove chicken from pan, and keep warm. Add 2 teaspoons olive oil and bell peppers to pan; sauté 2 minutes. Add oregano and garlic, and sauté 1 minute. Remove from heat; stir in lemon juice.

3. Combine orzo and feta, and serve with chicken and bell pepper mixture. Yield: 4 servings (serving size: 1 chicken breast half, ½ cup orzo mixture, and ⅓ cup bell pepper mixture).

CALORIES 404 (26% from fat); FAT 11.7g (sat 4.5g, mono 4.8g, poly 1g); PROTEIN 46.8g; CARB 26.3g; FIBER 2g; CHOL 118mg; IRON 2.8mg; SODIUM 644mg; CALC 143mg

Soba Noodles with Broccoli and Chicken
(pictured on page 148)

Use chicken broth in place of the sake for a nonalcoholic version.

    6 ounces uncooked soba
       (buckwheat noodles)
    ¼ cup sake (rice wine) or dry sherry
    3 tablespoons low-sodium soy sauce
    2 tablespoons rice vinegar
    1 teaspoon honey
    ½ teaspoon crushed red pepper
    1 tablespoon vegetable oil, divided
    ¾ pound chicken breast tenders, cut
       into bite-size pieces
 1½ teaspoons dark sesame oil
    3 cups quartered mushrooms
    3 cups broccoli florets
    1 cup (1-inch) red bell pepper strips
    1 tablespoon bottled ground fresh
       ginger (such as Spice World)
    2 garlic cloves, minced

1. Cook noodles according to package directions; drain.
2. Combine sake and next 4 ingredients.
3. Heat 2 teaspoons vegetable oil in a large nonstick skillet over medium-high heat. Add chicken, and stir-fry 4 minutes or until done. Remove chicken from pan; keep warm. Heat 1 teaspoon vegetable oil and sesame oil in pan over

medium-high heat. Add mushrooms and remaining 4 ingredients; stir-fry 4 minutes or until broccoli is crisp-tender. Return chicken to pan; stir in sake mixture. Cook 1 minute or until thoroughly heated. Serve over noodles. Yield: 4 servings (serving size: 1¼ cups chicken mixture and ½ cup noodles).

CALORIES 357 (18% from fat); FAT 7g (sat 1.2g, mono 1.9g, poly 3.2g); PROTEIN 30.1g; CARB 43.2g; FIBER 3.3g; CHOL 49mg; IRON 3.3mg; SODIUM 810mg; CALC 61mg

Individual Pizzas with Broccoli, Cheese, and Meat Sauce

    1 cup finely chopped onion
    2 garlic cloves, minced
    ½ pound ground round
    3 tablespoons tomato paste
    ½ teaspoon salt, divided
    ¼ teaspoon black pepper
 1½ cups diced fresh tomatoes
    3 cups broccoli florets
 1¼ cups part-skim ricotta cheese
    ½ cup loosely packed basil leaves
    ¼ cup (1 ounce) grated fresh
       Parmesan cheese
    1 teaspoon fresh lemon juice
    6 (4-ounce) Italian cheese-flavored
       pizza crusts (such as Boboli)

1. Preheat oven to 400°.
2. Cook onion, garlic, and beef in a large nonstick skillet over medium-high heat until beef is browned, stirring to crumble. Add tomato paste, ¼ teaspoon salt, pepper, and tomatoes; bring to a boil. Reduce heat, and simmer 5 minutes.
3. Steam broccoli, covered, 4 minutes or until tender. Drain. Place broccoli, ¼ teaspoon salt, ricotta, basil, Parmesan, and juice in a blender or food processor; process until broccoli is finely chopped. Spread about ⅓ cup broccoli mixture over each pizza crust, leaving ½-inch borders; top with ⅓ cup beef mixture.
4. Place pizzas on a baking sheet. Bake at 400° for 18 minutes or until heated. Yield: 6 servings (serving size: 1 pizza).

CALORIES 509 (30% from fat); FAT 17.1g (sat 7.7g, mono 6.7g, poly 1.4g); PROTEIN 29g; CARB 59.1g; FIBER 2.7g; CHOL 45mg; IRON 4.8mg; SODIUM 1,033mg; CALC 538mg

Hummus-Stuffed Pitas with Vegetables

    ¼ cup plain fat-free yogurt
    ¼ cup water
    2 tablespoons fresh lemon juice
    2 tablespoons tahini (sesame-seed
       paste)
    ½ teaspoon salt
    ⅛ teaspoon ground red pepper
    1 (15-ounce) can chickpeas
       (garbanzo beans), rinsed and
       drained
 1½ tablespoons minced fresh cilantro
    6 (6-inch) whole wheat pitas, cut in
       half
    3 cups trimmed arugula
    6 plum tomatoes, thinly sliced
    1 English cucumber, thinly sliced
    1 red onion, thinly sliced

1. Combine first 7 ingredients in a food processor; process until smooth. Stir in cilantro. Spread 2 tablespoons hummus in each pita half; divide arugula, tomatoes, cucumber, and onion evenly among pita halves. Yield: 6 servings (serving size: 2 stuffed pita halves).

CALORIES 275 (19% from fat); FAT 5.9g (sat 0.7g, mono 1.8g, poly 2.7g); PROTEIN 10.8g; CARB 49.7g; FIBER 8.3g; CHOL 0mg; IRON 3.3mg; SODIUM 656mg; CALC 76mg

Pizza Frittata

    ¼ cup water
    ¼ teaspoon salt
    ¼ teaspoon black pepper
    2 (8-ounce) cartons egg substitute
    2 (4-ounce) links sweet turkey
       Italian sausage
    ½ cup finely chopped onion
    1 cup halved cherry or grape
       tomatoes
    1 cup canned cannellini or other
       white beans, rinsed and drained
    ¼ cup (1 ounce) grated fresh
       Parmesan cheese

1. Preheat broiler.
2. Combine first 4 ingredients; set aside.
3. Heat a large nonstick skillet over medium-high heat. Remove casings from

sausage. Add sausage and onion to pan; cook 4 minutes, stirring to crumble sausage. Add tomatoes; cook 2 minutes, stirring frequently. Stir in beans. Pour egg mixture over bean mixture; cover and cook 3 minutes. Uncover; sprinkle with cheese. Wrap handle of skillet with foil. Broil 5 minutes or until set. Yield: 4 servings (serving size: 1 wedge).

CALORIES 239 (28% from fat); FAT 7.5g (sat 2.8g, mono 2.6g, poly 1.9g); PROTEIN 26.8g; CARB 14.6g; FIBER 3.3g; CHOL 53mg; IRON 3.9mg; SODIUM 952mg; CALC 148mg

dinner tonight

New Classic Salads

Pair chicken with fruit, vegetables, or grains for fresh new versions of the classic main-dish salad.

QUICK & EASY
Chicken and Couscous Salad

If you can't find the specified box size of couscous, you can use 1 cup uncooked couscous. If you have any salad left, take it to work for a light lunch.

TOTAL TIME: 25 MINUTES

QUICK TIP: You can toast nuts quickly in a dry skillet over medium-high heat. Stir frequently, and as soon as the nuts become fragrant, remove them from the pan.

SALAD:

- 1¼ cups fat-free, less-sodium chicken broth
- 1 (5.7-ounce) box uncooked couscous
- 1½ cups cubed cooked chicken (about 6 ounces)
- ½ cup thinly sliced green onions
- ½ cup diced radishes (about 3 large)
- ½ cup chopped seeded peeled cucumber
- ¼ cup chopped fresh flat-leaf parsley
- 2 tablespoons pine nuts, toasted

DRESSING:

- ¼ cup white wine vinegar
- 1½ tablespoons extravirgin olive oil
- 1 teaspoon ground cumin
- ½ teaspoon salt
- ⅛ teaspoon freshly ground black pepper
- 1 garlic clove, minced

1. To prepare salad, bring broth to a boil in a medium saucepan; gradually stir in couscous. Remove from heat; cover and let stand 5 minutes. Fluff with a fork. Spoon couscous into a large bowl; cool slightly. Add chicken and next 5 ingredients; toss gently.

2. To prepare dressing, combine vinegar and remaining 5 ingredients, stirring with a whisk. Drizzle dressing over salad; toss to combine. Yield: 4 servings (serving size: 1½ cups).

CALORIES 334 (29% from fat); FAT 10.9g (sat 2g, mono 5.9g, poly 2.1g); PROTEIN 20.9g; CARB 35.8g; FIBER 2.9g; CHOL 39mg; IRON 1.8mg; SODIUM 484mg; CALC 23mg

Chicken and Couscous Salad Menu
serves 4

Chicken and Couscous Salad

Pita crisps*

Lemon sorbet

*Preheat oven to 350°. Split 1 pita in half horizontally; cut each half into 6 wedges. Place wedges in a single layer on a baking sheet. Lightly coat with cooking spray; sprinkle with ⅛ teaspoon salt and ⅛ teaspoon freshly ground black pepper. Bake at 350° for 15 minutes or until pita wedges are crisp and golden brown.

Game Plan

1. While oven heats:
- Prepare couscous
- Prepare dressing
- Season pita wedges

2. While pita wedges cook:
- Prepare salad

Chicken Salad Pita Menu
serves 4

Smoky Bacon and Blue Cheese Chicken Salad Pitas

Herbed carrots*

Fresh berries

*Cook 3 cups (1½-inch) pieces peeled carrots in boiling water 5 minutes or until crisp-tender. Drain well. Rinse with cold water; drain. Combine 3 tablespoons white wine vinegar, 1 tablespoon extravirgin olive oil, 1 teaspoon dried oregano, 1 teaspoon salt, ½ teaspoon freshly ground black pepper, and 1 minced garlic clove; drizzle over carrots. Cover and chill until ready to serve.

Game Plan

1. Prepare carrots; cover and chill
2. While carrots chill:
- Prepare salad
- Place salad in pita halves

QUICK & EASY
Smoky Bacon and Blue Cheese Chicken Salad Pitas

TOTAL TIME: 20 MINUTES

- ¾ cup plain fat-free yogurt
- ¼ cup (1 ounce) crumbled blue cheese
- 2 tablespoons light mayonnaise
- ½ teaspoon freshly ground black pepper
- 3 cups shredded romaine lettuce
- 1½ cups shredded cooked chicken (about 6 ounces)
- 4 bacon slices, cooked and crumbled
- 2 tomatoes, seeded and chopped
- 4 (6-inch) whole wheat pitas, cut in half

1. Combine first 4 ingredients, stirring well. Combine lettuce, chicken, bacon, and tomatoes in a medium bowl, stirring well. Drizzle yogurt mixture over chicken mixture; toss gently to coat. Spoon ½ cup chicken salad into each pita half. Serve immediately. Yield: 4 servings (serving size: 2 stuffed pita halves).

CALORIES 375 (29% from fat); FAT 12.1g (sat 3.7g, mono 3.6g, poly 3.1g); PROTEIN 26.1g; CARB 43.8g; FIBER 6.3g; CHOL 55mg; IRON 3.5mg; SODIUM 696mg; CALC 130mg

Chicken, Red Potato, and Green Bean Salad

Red potatoes work well and add a nice color to this salad, but you can use any waxy potato, such as fingerling or white. If your potatoes aren't small, cut each into 8 wedges.

TOTAL TIME: 35 MINUTES

QUICK TIP: Use a roasted whole chicken purchased at your supermarket's deli, and you'll have leftovers for another meal.

DRESSING:

- ⅓ cup coarsely chopped fresh parsley
- 3 tablespoons red wine vinegar
- 1 tablespoon fresh lemon juice
- 1 tablespoon whole-grain Dijon mustard
- 1 tablespoon extravirgin olive oil
- ½ teaspoon salt
- ¼ teaspoon freshly ground black pepper
- 1 garlic clove, minced

SALAD:

- 1 pound small red potatoes
- 1 teaspoon salt
- ½ pound diagonally cut green beans
- 2 cups cubed cooked chicken (about 8 ounces)
- 2 tablespoons chopped red onion
- 1 (10-ounce) package gourmet salad greens (about 6 cups)

1. To prepare dressing, combine first 8 ingredients, stirring well with a whisk.
2. To prepare salad, place potatoes in a saucepan; cover with water. Add 1 teaspoon salt to pan; bring to a boil. Reduce heat, and simmer 10 minutes or until almost tender. Add beans, and cook 4 minutes or until beans are crisp-tender. Drain. Rinse with cold water; drain well.
3. Quarter potatoes. Place potatoes, beans, chicken, onion, and greens in a large bowl. Drizzle with dressing; toss gently to coat. Serve immediately. Yield: 4 servings (serving size: about 1¾ cups).

CALORIES 269 (29% from fat); FAT 8.8g (sat 1.8g, mono 4.4g, poly 1.6g); PROTEIN 22.4g; CARB 26.1g; FIBER 5.8g; CHOL 53mg; IRON 3.8mg; SODIUM 761mg; CALC 96mg

---

Chicken, Potato, and Green Bean Salad Menu

serves 4

Chicken, Red Potato, and Green Bean Salad

Garlic-Parmesan toasts*

Sliced fresh plum tomatoes with salt and pepper

*Preheat oven to 425°. Combine 2 tablespoons grated fresh Parmesan cheese, 2 tablespoons softened butter, ¼ teaspoon salt, ⅛ teaspoon freshly ground black pepper, and 1 minced garlic clove, stirring well. Spread butter mixture evenly over 8 (1-ounce) baguette slices. Bake at 425° for 6 minutes or until golden brown.

Game Plan

1. While potatoes and green beans cook:
- Preheat oven
- Prepare dressing
- Chop chicken and onion
- Prepare Parmesan toasts
2. While toasts cook:
- Slice tomatoes
- Combine salad

Chicken Salad with Nectarines in Mint Vinaigrette

The mint adds a refreshing note to the dressing, which will also work well in a fresh fruit salad. Use any curly lettuce leaves in place of red leaf.

TOTAL TIME: 22 MINUTES

QUICK TIP: In a pinch, substitute fresh melon for the nectarines. Look for chopped peeled melon in the produce section at the grocery.

DRESSING:

- 1 cup loosely packed fresh mint leaves
- ⅓ cup sugar
- ¼ cup white wine vinegar
- 1 tablespoon fresh lemon juice
- ¼ teaspoon salt
- ¼ teaspoon freshly ground black pepper

SALAD:

- 2 cups chopped cooked chicken breast
- 1 cup chopped seeded cucumber
- ⅓ cup chopped pecans, toasted
- 2 tablespoons minced red onion
- 3 nectarines, peeled, pitted, and chopped
- 5 red leaf lettuce leaves

1. To prepare dressing, place mint and sugar in a food processor; process until finely chopped, scraping sides of bowl. Add vinegar, juice, salt, and pepper, and process 30 seconds.
2. To prepare salad, combine chicken and next 4 ingredients in a medium bowl. Drizzle dressing over salad; toss well to coat. Place 1 lettuce leaf on each of 5 plates; top each serving with ¾ cup salad. Yield: 5 servings.

CALORIES 241 (28% from fat); FAT 7.4g (sat 1g, mono 3.6g, poly 2.1g); PROTEIN 16.7g; CARB 29g; FIBER 3.6g; CHOL 39mg; IRON 3.4mg; SODIUM 163mg; CALC 71mg

---

Chicken Salad with Nectarines Menu

serves 5

Chicken Salad with Nectarines in Mint Vinaigrette

Peppery cheese breadsticks*

Lemonade

*Preheat oven to 375°. Combine ½ cup grated Romano cheese and 1 tablespoon freshly ground black pepper in a shallow dish. Unroll 1 (11-ounce) can refrigerated soft breadsticks; separate into 12 portions. Roll each dough portion in cheese mixture, turning and pressing gently to coat. Twist each dough portion gently; place on a baking sheet coated with cooking spray. Bake at 375° for 13 minutes or until golden brown.

Game Plan

1. While oven heats:
- Prepare dressing
- Prepare breadsticks
2. While breadsticks bake:
- Prepare and toss salad

A Tart Tale of Rhubarb

Try this unique "fruit" in sweet and savory dishes while you can—its season is fleeting.

All About Rhubarb

Rhubarb looks like oversized, crimson-hued celery. While it's actually a vegetable, it's most often used as a fruit, earning the nickname "pie plant" in the United States for its most classic use.

When rhubarb is raw, its texture is similar to celery's—crisp, with fibrous strings. But celery retains its shape and texture in cooking, while cooked rhubarb nearly falls apart, like apples into applesauce. And rhubarb needs to be cooked—to mellow its sharp bite, to soften its texture, and to round out its flavors.

Rhubarb's most defining characteristic is its tart flavor, which is why it's often paired with sweet strawberries (also at their peak in the spring) and lots of sugar.

Because rhubarb requires extra sugar, it's well-suited to desserts like our pudding cake, crumble, sorbet, and classic pie. Yet its tartness also renders it ideal for chutneys, sauces, and compotes that would be excellent with savory chicken or pork entrées.

Whatever you make from it, spring is the time because rhubarb is one of the first crops of the season. Look for stalks of this "fruit" at produce stands and farmers' markets from April to June.

MAKE AHEAD

Lattice-Topped Rhubarb Pie

If you don't feel like weaving the dough strips through one another for the lattice topping, just arrange 6 dough strips over the pie; lay the other 6 strips perpendicular to the first strips without weaving.

CRUST:

1¾ cups all-purpose flour
 3 tablespoons sugar
 ⅛ teaspoon salt
 ¼ cup cold unsalted butter, cut into small pieces
 3 tablespoons vegetable shortening
 5 tablespoons ice water
Cooking spray

FILLING:

 6 cups (1-inch-thick) slices rhubarb (about 1½ pounds)
 1 cup sugar
 3 tablespoons cornstarch
1½ teaspoons grated orange rind
 ¼ teaspoon ground nutmeg

REMAINING INGREDIENTS:

1½ teaspoons 1% low-fat milk
 1 tablespoon sugar

1. To prepare crust, lightly spoon flour into dry measuring cups; level with a knife. Combine flour, 3 tablespoons sugar, and salt in a large bowl; cut in butter and shortening with a pastry blender or 2 knives until mixture resembles coarse meal. Sprinkle surface with ice water, 1 tablespoon at a time; toss with a fork until moist and crumbly (do not form a ball).
2. Gently press two-thirds of dough into a 4-inch circle on heavy-duty plastic wrap; cover with additional plastic wrap. Roll dough into a 12-inch circle. Press remaining dough into a 4-inch circle on heavy-duty plastic wrap, and cover with additional plastic wrap. Roll dough into a 9-inch circle. Freeze dough portions 10 minutes or until plastic wrap can be easily removed.
3. Preheat oven to 425°.
4. Remove 1 sheet of plastic wrap from 12-inch dough circle; fit dough, plastic-wrap side up, into a 9-inch pie plate coated with cooking spray, allowing dough to extend over edge of plate. Remove top sheet of plastic wrap; fold dough edges under, and flute.
5. To prepare filling, combine rhubarb and next 4 ingredients, tossing well to combine. Spoon filling into crust.
6. Remove top sheet of plastic wrap from 9-inch dough circle. Cut dough into 12 (¾-inch) strips. Gently remove dough strips from bottom sheet of plastic wrap, and weave in a lattice design over rhubarb mixture. Seal dough strips to edge of crust. Brush top and edges of dough with milk; sprinkle with 1 tablespoon sugar. Place pie on a baking sheet covered with foil. Bake at 425° for 15 minutes. Reduce oven temperature to 375° (do not remove pie from oven). Bake an additional 30 minutes or until golden (shield crust with foil if it gets too brown). Cool on a wire rack. Yield: 10 servings (serving size: 1 wedge).

CALORIES 276 (29% from fat); FAT 8.8g (sat 3.9g, mono 3.1g, poly 1.3g); PROTEIN 3g; CARB 47.3g; FIBER 2g; CHOL 12mg; IRON 1.2mg; SODIUM 34mg; CALC 69mg

Selecting, Storing, and Preparing Rhubarb

Selecting: Look for firm, red, even-colored, straight stalks (if one has any green or yellow, avoid it). A pound of trimmed rhubarb yields about 4 cups of cut-up fruit.

Storing: Refrigerate unwashed rhubarb in a plastic bag. It keeps up to 2 weeks, depending on freshness. Or to extend the short season, wash, dry, and chop rhubarb; freeze in a heavy-duty zip-top plastic bag up to 9 months.

Preparing: The leaves contain toxic oxalic acid and should be discarded. Rinse rhubarb stalks under cool water just before using. If they seem especially fibrous, peel the outside using a vegetable peeler to remove the strings.

Rhubarb Pudding Cake

Tender, lightly spiced vanilla cake covers a layer of juicy rhubarb. The batter may not cover all the fruit, but it spreads as the pudding cake bakes.

  1   cup all-purpose flour
1¼ teaspoons baking powder
 ⅛ teaspoon salt
  5   tablespoons unsalted butter, softened
1⅓ cups granulated sugar, divided
  1   teaspoon vanilla extract
 ¼ teaspoon ground cinnamon
  1   large egg
 ½ cup 1% low-fat milk
  4   cups (1-inch-thick) slices rhubarb (about 1 pound)
Cooking spray
  1   teaspoon powdered sugar

1. Preheat oven to 350°.
2. Lightly spoon flour into a dry measuring cup; level with a knife. Combine flour, baking powder, and salt, stirring well with a whisk. Place butter in a large bowl, and beat with a mixer at medium speed until smooth. Add ⅔ cup granulated sugar; beat until well blended. Add vanilla, cinnamon, and egg, beating well. Beating at low speed, add flour mixture and milk alternately to sugar mixture, beginning and ending with flour mixture; beat just until smooth.
3. Combine rhubarb slices and ⅔ cup granulated sugar in an 8-inch square baking dish coated with cooking spray. Spoon batter over rhubarb mixture. Bake at 350° for 45 minutes or until a wooden pick inserted in center comes out clean. Sprinkle with powdered sugar. Yield: 9 servings.

CALORIES 249 (26% from fat); FAT 7.3g (sat 4.2g, mono 2.1g, poly 0.4g); PROTEIN 3.1g; CARB 44g; FIBER 1.4g; CHOL 41mg; IRON 1mg; SODIUM 118mg; CALC 109mg

Rhubarb Sorbet

If you've frozen the sorbet overnight or longer, let it stand at room temperature for 10 to 15 minutes to soften before scooping.

  5   cups sliced rhubarb (about 1¼ pounds)
  1   quart water
 ½ cup granulated sugar
 ½ cup packed brown sugar
  1   tablespoon fresh lemon juice

1. Combine rhubarb and water in a large saucepan. Bring to a boil; cook 10 minutes. Remove from heat; strain mixture through a sieve into a bowl, pressing rhubarb with back of a spoon to extract as much liquid as possible. Discard solids. Add granulated sugar, brown sugar, and juice to rhubarb liquid; stir until sugars dissolve. Cover and chill.
2. Pour mixture into freezer can of an ice-cream freezer; freeze according to manufacturer's instructions. Spoon sorbet into a freezer-safe container; cover and freeze 1 hour or until firm. Remove sorbet from freezer 10 minutes before serving. Yield: 8 servings (serving size: ½ cup).

CALORIES 107 (1% from fat); FAT 0.1g (sat 0g, mono 0g, poly 0.1g); PROTEIN 0.3g; CARB 27.4g; FIBER 0.1g; CHOL 0mg; IRON 0.3mg; SODIUM 7mg; CALC 38mg

Rhubarb, Pear, and Apple Compote

Though rhubarb is the star of this sauce, sweet apples and pears help to cut its characteristically sour flavor. Use this compote as an accompaniment to savory entrées, such as pork or poultry. Or serve it as a dessert dolloped with whipped topping.

  2   cups (1-inch-thick) slices rhubarb (about ½ pound)
 ½ cup sugar
  1   teaspoon grated orange rind
 ¼ cup fresh orange juice
  1   (3-inch) cinnamon stick
  1   cup cubed peeled Gala apple
  1   cup cubed peeled Bartlett pear

1. Combine first 5 ingredients in a medium saucepan; bring to a boil over medium-high heat. Reduce heat; simmer 3 minutes. Add apple; cook 2 minutes. Add pear; cook 1 minute or until fruit is tender, stirring gently. Remove from heat; cool. Discard cinnamon stick. Serve chilled or at room temperature. Yield: 3 cups (serving size: ½ cup).

CALORIES 105 (3% from fat); FAT 0.3g (sat 0g, mono 0.1g, poly 0.1g); PROTEIN 0.6g; CARB 26.5g; FIBER 1.8g; CHOL 0mg; IRON 0.2mg; SODIUM 2mg; CALC 41mg

Grilled Pork Chops with Rhubarb Chutney

Serve with rice or couscous to soak up the sauce.

CHUTNEY:

 ½ cup sugar
 ¼ cup balsamic vinegar
 ¼ teaspoon ground coriander
  1   (3-inch) cinnamon stick
  2   cups coarsely chopped rhubarb (about ½ pound)
 ⅓ cup dried cranberries
 ¼ cup chopped green onions
 ¼ teaspoon salt
 ¼ teaspoon ground red pepper

PORK:

 ⅓ cup red currant jelly
  1   tablespoon whole-grain Dijon mustard
 ½ teaspoon salt
 ½ teaspoon black pepper
 ¼ teaspoon ground cumin
  4   (6-ounce) bone-in center-cut pork chops (about ¼ inch thick)
Cooking spray
Thinly sliced green onions (optional)

1. To prepare chutney, combine first 4 ingredients in a small saucepan. Bring to a boil over medium-high heat. Add rhubarb and next 4 ingredients; reduce heat. Simmer 5 minutes or until rhubarb is tender. Spoon into a bowl; cover. Chill at least 2 hours. Discard cinnamon stick.
2. Prepare grill.
3. To prepare pork, combine jelly and mustard in a small bowl; set aside.

4. Combine ½ teaspoon salt, black pepper, and cumin; rub evenly over pork. Place pork on a grill rack coated with cooking spray; grill 4 minutes on each side or until desired degree of doneness, basting occasionally with jelly mixture. Serve pork with chutney; sprinkle with sliced green onions, if desired. Yield: 4 servings (serving size: 1 pork chop and ½ cup chutney).

CALORIES 400 (16% from fat); FAT 7g (sat 2.5g, mono 3.1g, poly 0.6g); PROTEIN 26.2g; CARB 55.9g; FIBER 2.6g; CHOL 69mg; IRON 1.2mg; SODIUM 596mg; CALC 89mg

Rhubarb-Strawberry Crumble

½ cup all-purpose flour
½ cup quick-cooking oats
⅓ cup flaked sweetened coconut
¼ cup granulated sugar
¼ cup packed brown sugar
¼ cup chilled unsalted butter, cut into small pieces
6 cups (½-inch-thick) slices rhubarb (about 1½ pounds)
⅔ cup granulated sugar
2 tablespoons cornstarch
Cooking spray
¼ cup strawberry spread (such as Polaner All Fruit)

1. Preheat oven to 375°.
2. Lightly spoon flour into a dry measuring cup; level with a knife. Combine flour and next 4 ingredients in a medium bowl; cut in butter with a pastry blender or 2 knives until mixture resembles coarse meal.
3. Combine rhubarb, ⅔ cup granulated sugar, and cornstarch in a large bowl, tossing to coat. Spoon rhubarb mixture into an 11 x 7-inch baking dish coated with cooking spray. Drop strawberry spread by spoonfuls over rhubarb mixture; sprinkle with oats mixture. Bake at 375° for 40 minutes or until browned and bubbly. Yield: 9 servings.

CALORIES 244 (24% from fat); FAT 6.4g (sat 4g, mono 1.6g, poly 0.4g); PROTEIN 2.4g; CARB 45.8g; FIBER 2.3g; CHOL 14mg; IRON 0.9mg; SODIUM 16mg; CALC 81mg

Terry Conlan: Redefining Spa Cuisine

This Texan's cooking style is big, bright, and world savvy. Try his strategies to broaden your palate.

By simply tweaking a few techniques and making judicious ingredient choices, any cooking style could be translated beautifully into spa cuisine, according to Terry Conlan, the chef at Lake Austin Spa Resort. Many of the ideas and techniques he's developed will lend themselves readily to your cooking. And armed with a few of his tricks of the trade, you can create lighter, healthier, and more flavorful dishes—without visiting a spa.

Corn Tortillas

Tortilla presses are available at kitchen stores and cooking Web sites for about $20. In a pinch, use a rolling pin as a substitute. Masa harina is sold in many supermarkets; you'll find it by the flour or in the Latin food aisle.

1½ cups masa harina
1 cup plus 1 tablespoon water
½ teaspoon salt

1. Lightly spoon masa harina into dry measuring cups; level with a knife. Combine masa harina, water, and salt in a large bowl, stirring with a whisk. Knead 30 seconds on a lightly floured surface. Cover and let stand 15 minutes.
2. Divide dough into 8 equal portions; shape each portion into a ball. Place 1 dough ball between 2 sheets of heavy-duty plastic wrap (cover remaining balls to prevent drying). Place ball, still covered, on a tortilla press. Close press to flatten dough, moving handle from side to side. Open press; turn dough one-half turn. Close press to flatten. Remove dough. Carefully remove plastic wrap from flattened dough. Repeat procedure with remaining dough balls; stack flattened dough between sheets of wax paper.

3. Heat a large nonstick skillet over medium-high heat. Place 1 tortilla in pan; cook 1 minute or until it begins to brown. Carefully turn tortilla over; cook 1 minute. Turn tortilla once more, and cook 15 seconds. Repeat procedure with remaining tortillas. Yield: 8 servings (serving size: 1 tortilla).

CALORIES 83 (11% from fat); FAT 1g (sat 0.2g, mono 0.2g, poly 0.6g); PROTEIN 2.1g; CARB 17.8g; FIBER 1.9g; CHOL 0mg; IRON 0.7mg; SODIUM 148mg; CALC 43mg

Tortilla Press

A tortilla press is the perfect kitchen tool for making Corn Tortillas.

Chilled Corn Bisque with Basil, Avocado, and Crab

Allow soup to stand 30 minutes at room temperature before serving. The flavor will come through better if you take the chill off. Slice the basil and chop the avocado just before serving so they don't begin to brown.

- 3 cups fat-free, less-sodium chicken broth
- 3 tablespoons cornstarch
- 1 tablespoon butter
- 1 cup finely chopped onion
- 1 garlic clove, minced
- 4 cups fresh corn kernels (about 8 ears)
- ¾ teaspoon salt
- ¼ teaspoon ground red pepper
- ½ cup 2% reduced-fat milk
- ½ cup half-and-half
- 8 ounces lump crabmeat, shell pieces removed (about 1 ½ cups)
- ⅓ cup chopped peeled avocado
- 3 tablespoons chopped fresh basil

1. Combine broth and cornstarch, stirring with a whisk.
2. Melt butter in a large saucepan over medium-high heat. Add onion; sauté 3 minutes. Add garlic; sauté 30 seconds. Stir in broth mixture, corn, salt, and pepper; bring to a simmer. Cook 10 minutes, stirring frequently (do not boil). Place half of corn mixture in a blender, and process until smooth. Pour puréed corn mixture into a large bowl. Repeat procedure with remaining corn mixture. Strain puréed corn mixture through a sieve into a large bowl; discard solids. Stir in milk and half-and-half; chill thoroughly. Let stand 30 minutes at room temperature; stir well.
3. Ladle ⅔ cup soup into each of 8 bowls; top each serving with 3 tablespoons crab, about 2 teaspoons avocado, and about 1 teaspoon basil. Yield: 8 servings.

CALORIES 159 (30% from fat); FAT 5.3g (sat 2.4g, mono 1.9g, poly 0.7g); PROTEIN 10.8g; CARB 18g; FIBER 2.3g; CHOL 34mg; IRON 0.6mg; SODIUM 536mg; CALC 64mg

Camarones Fritoes with Mexican Cocktail Sauce

Use this coating and crisping technique for different fillets of fish, such as halibut or catfish. It will also work in making chicken fingers. Garnish with lime wedges, if desired.

SHRIMP:
- ½ cup all-purpose flour
- ¾ cup low-fat buttermilk
- 1 large egg white, lightly beaten
- 1 (5.5-ounce) bag baked potato chips (such as Lay's)
- 1½ pounds medium shrimp, peeled and deveined
- ¼ teaspoon salt
- ¼ teaspoon freshly ground black pepper
- Cooking spray

SAUCE:
- 6 tablespoons ketchup
- 1 tablespoon fresh lime juice
- 1 tablespoon hot sauce
- 1 teaspoon prepared horseradish
- ½ teaspoon grated orange rind

1. Preheat oven to 400°.
2. To prepare shrimp, lightly spoon flour into a dry measuring cup; level with a knife. Place flour in a shallow dish. Combine buttermilk and egg white in a medium bowl, stirring with a whisk. Place potato chips in a food processor; process until finely ground. Place chip crumbs in a shallow dish.
3. Sprinkle shrimp evenly with salt and pepper. Working with 1 shrimp at a time, dredge shrimp in flour; dip into buttermilk mixture. Dredge shrimp in crumbs, shaking off excess. Place shrimp on a baking sheet coated with cooking spray. Lightly spray top of shrimp with cooking spray. Bake at 400° for 10 minutes or until done.
4. To prepare sauce, combine ketchup and remaining 4 ingredients, stirring well. Serve sauce with shrimp. Yield: 6 servings (serving size: about 7 shrimp and about 4 teaspoons sauce).

CALORIES 301 (16% from fat); FAT 5.3g (sat 0.6g, mono 0.9g, poly 1.4g); PROTEIN 27g; CARB 36.1g; FIBER 2.4g; CHOL 173mg; IRON 3.7mg; SODIUM 641mg; CALC 138mg

Green Chile Sopes with Chipotle Mayonnaise, Shrimp, and Pineapple Slaw

Don't be intimidated by the long ingredient list. You can make the mayonnaise, slaw, and *sopes* ahead. Reheat the sopes in a preheated 400° oven for a few minutes to recrisp them.

MAYONNAISE:
- 1 (7-ounce) can chipotle chiles in adobo sauce
- 2 tablespoons low-fat mayonnaise
- 2 teaspoons fresh lime juice
- 1/8 teaspoon salt
- 1 garlic clove, minced

SLAW:
- 2½ cups very thinly sliced green cabbage
- ¾ cup (½-inch) cubed fresh pineapple
- ½ cup vertically sliced onion
- ½ cup thinly sliced green onions
- ⅓ cup julienne-cut radishes (about 2 large)
- ¼ cup shredded carrot
- ¼ cup finely chopped fresh cilantro
- 2 teaspoons white vinegar
- 1/8 teaspoon salt

CHILE:
- 1 poblano chile

SHRIMP:
- 1/8 teaspoon salt
- 1/8 teaspoon freshly ground black pepper
- 16 medium shrimp, peeled and deveined (about ½ pound)
- Cooking spray

BEANS:
- 1 (15-ounce) can pinto beans, undrained

SOPES:
- 2 cups masa harina
- 1¼ cups water
- ½ teaspoon salt
- 2 tablespoons peanut oil, divided

To add interest, food should have contrast in terms of color, texture, flavor, and temperature.

1. To prepare mayonnaise, remove 1 teaspoon adobo sauce from can; reserve remaining sauce and chiles for another use. Combine 1 teaspoon adobo sauce, mayonnaise, lime juice, 1/8 teaspoon salt, and garlic, stirring well. Cover and chill.

2. To prepare slaw, combine cabbage and next 8 ingredients in a medium bowl, tossing to combine. Cover and chill.

3. Preheat broiler.

4. To prepare chile, place poblano on a foil-lined baking sheet; broil 10 minutes or until blackened, turning occasionally. Place in a zip-top plastic bag; seal. Let stand 15 minutes. Peel chile; cut in half lengthwise. Discard seeds and membranes. Thinly slice chile; set aside.

5. To prepare shrimp, heat a large nonstick skillet over medium-high heat. Sprinkle 1/8 teaspoon salt and black pepper over shrimp. Coat pan with cooking spray. Add shrimp to pan; cook 3 minutes on each side or until done. Remove from pan; keep warm.

6. To prepare pinto beans, place beans in a small saucepan over medium-high heat; bring to a boil. Reduce heat; cover and keep warm.

7. To prepare sopes, combine masa harina, water, and ½ teaspoon salt; stir until a dense dough forms. Divide masa mixture into 8 equal portions. Roll each portion into a ball using moist hands. Pat each ball into a ¼-inch-thick patty.

8. Wipe skillet with a paper towel. Heat pan over medium-high heat. Add 1 tablespoon oil. Place 4 sopes in pan; cook 5 minutes or until browned. Lightly coat tops of sopes with cooking spray. Turn over; cook 5 minutes or until browned. Repeat procedure with 1 tablespoon oil and 4 sopes.

9. Place about 1 cup slaw on each of 4 plates. Arrange 2 sopes on each plate. Using a slotted spoon, spoon 2 tablespoons pinto beans on each sope; top each serving with 2 shrimp. Spoon 1 teaspoon mayonnaise over each sope. Divide poblano strips evenly among servings. Yield: 4 servings.

CALORIES 450 (23% from fat); FAT 14.8g (sat 2.4g, mono 4.6g, poly 4.7g); PROTEIN 14.9g; CARB 70.5g; FIBER 7.9g; CHOL 39mg; IRON 4mg; SODIUM 572mg; CALC 182mg

Green Enchiladas with Crab

In the Southwest, enchiladas are usually covered with chili gravy. Mexican cooks are more likely to take a healthful approach, using a fresh salsa and vegetable topping.

SAUCE:
- 8 medium tomatillos
- 2 quarts water
- ¼ cup chopped peeled avocado
- 2 tablespoons minced fresh cilantro
- 1 tablespoon fresh lime juice
- ¼ teaspoon salt
- 1 serrano chile, seeded
- 1 garlic clove, minced

ENCHILADAS:
- ½ cup (2 ounces) shredded queso chihuahua cheese
- ¼ teaspoon salt
- 1 pound lump crabmeat, drained and shell pieces removed
- 8 (6-inch) corn tortillas
- Cooking spray

TOPPING:
- 2 cups thinly sliced iceberg lettuce
- ½ cup thinly vertically sliced onion
- ¼ cup thinly sliced radishes
- 2 tablespoons minced fresh cilantro
- 2 teaspoons white vinegar
- ¼ teaspoon salt
- ¼ teaspoon dried oregano

Continued

1. Preheat oven to 375°.

2. To prepare sauce, discard husks and stems from tomatillos. Bring 2 quarts water to a boil in a large Dutch oven. Add tomatillos; cook 2 minutes. Drain. Place tomatillos, avocado, and next 5 ingredients in a blender; process until smooth. Strain mixture through a sieve into a medium bowl; discard solids.

3. To prepare enchiladas, combine cheese, ¼ teaspoon salt, and crab. Warm tortillas according to package directions. Spoon about ½ cup crab mixture down center of each tortilla; roll up. Place, seam sides down, in an 11 x 7-inch baking dish coated with cooking spray. Cover and bake at 375° for 12 minutes or until thoroughly heated.

4. To prepare topping, combine lettuce and remaining 6 ingredients. Serve enchiladas with sauce and topping. Yield: 4 servings (serving size: 2 enchiladas, ¾ cup topping, and about ⅓ cup sauce).

CALORIES 304 (29% from fat); FAT 9.7g (sat 3.4g, mono 3.1g, poly 1.8g); PROTEIN 20.6g; CARB 36.6g; FIBER 5.8g; CHOL 58mg; IRON 1.8mg; SODIUM 843mg; CALC 241mg

STAFF FAVORITE • MAKE AHEAD
Café con Leche Cream Pie

¾ cup chocolate wafer crumbs (about 15 cookies, such as Nabisco's Famous Chocolate Wafers)
4 teaspoons butter, melted
Cooking spray
¾ cup extrastrong brewed coffee
1¼ teaspoons unflavored gelatin
1 (8-ounce) block ⅓-less-fat cream cheese
1 (8-ounce) block fat-free cream cheese
1 (14-ounce) can fat-free sweetened condensed milk
3 cups frozen fat-free whipped topping, thawed
½ teaspoon unsweetened cocoa

1. Preheat oven to 350°.

2. Combine chocolate wafer crumbs and butter, tossing with a fork until well combined. Firmly press mixture into bottom of a 9-inch springform pan coated with cooking spray. Bake at 350° for 10 minutes; cool completely.

3. Pour brewed coffee into a medium microwave-safe bowl. Sprinkle gelatin over coffee; let stand 10 minutes. Combine cheeses and milk in a food processor; process until smooth. Microwave coffee mixture at HIGH 20 seconds. Add coffee mixture to cheese mixture, and process until well combined. Pour cheese mixture into prepared crust. Cover and refrigerate overnight. Spread whipped topping evenly over filling; sprinkle cocoa over pie. Chill 1 hour before serving. Yield: 10 servings (serving size: 1 wedge).

CALORIES 284 (27% from fat); FAT 8.4g (sat 5g, mono 2.5g, poly 0.4g); PROTEIN 9.9g; CARB 40.5g; FIBER 0.3g; CHOL 26mg; IRON 0.5mg; SODIUM 353mg; CALC 171mg

Coconut Curry Shrimp Cakes with Papaya-Lime Sauce

Use a ripe papaya for this sauce. It should have a vivid golden-yellow color and give slightly when pressed with the palm. It will blend better and yield a more flavorful and smooth sauce than an unripe one. Garnish with diced papaya, if desired.

SHRIMP CAKES:
¾ teaspoon curry powder
1 cup panko (Japanese breadcrumbs)
3 tablespoons light coconut milk
2 tablespoons flaked sweetened coconut
2 tablespoons finely chopped fresh cilantro
2 tablespoons minced red bell pepper
2 tablespoons minced green onions
1 tablespoon minced peeled fresh ginger
2 teaspoons minced seeded serrano chile
1 teaspoon low-sodium soy sauce
¼ teaspoon salt
12 ounces medium shrimp, peeled, deveined, and chopped
1 large egg, lightly beaten
1 garlic clove, minced
Cooking spray

SAUCE:
1 cup diced peeled papaya
¼ cup water
¼ cup fresh lime juice
2 teaspoons sugar

REMAINING INGREDIENTS:
4 cups gourmet salad greens
2 teaspoons sesame seeds, toasted

1. To prepare shrimp cakes, heat a large nonstick skillet over medium heat. Add curry powder; cook 30 seconds or until lightly toasted and fragrant, stirring constantly. Combine curry powder and next 13 ingredients, stirring well. Cover and chill 1 hour. Divide shrimp mixture into 8 equal portions, and shape each portion into a ½-inch-thick patty. Heat pan over medium-high heat. Coat pan with cooking spray. Add shrimp cakes to pan, and cook 4 minutes on each side or until browned. Remove pan from heat; cover and let stand 5 minutes.

2. To prepare sauce, combine papaya and next 3 ingredients in a food processor; process until smooth.

3. Place 1 cup greens on each of 4 plates. Top each serving with 2 shrimp cakes; spoon about ¼ cup sauce over each serving, and sprinkle with ½ teaspoon sesame seeds. Serve immediately. Yield: 4 servings.

CALORIES 256 (20% from fat); FAT 5.7g (sat 1.9g, mono 1.1g, poly 1.2g); PROTEIN 22.9g; CARB 28.5g; FIBER 3g; CHOL 182mg; IRON 3.4mg; SODIUM 402mg; CALC 101mg

season's best

Muffuletta

In a tiny Italian market and deli in New Orleans, the first muffuletta (pronounced either "muff-uh-LOT-uh" or "moo-foo-LET-ta") was created.

The muffuletta is stuffed with thinly sliced salami, provolone cheese, and the essential "olive salad"—a relishlike mixture of olives and a tangy seasoning. Our version includes marinated grilled vegetables that bring a smoky, hearty flavor. It's perfect for a picnic on a sunny day.

Muffuletta

GRILLED VEGETABLES:

- ¼ cup reduced-fat Italian dressing
- 8 (½-inch-thick) slices eggplant (about 1 pound)
- 2 (½-inch-thick) slices Vidalia or other sweet onion
- 1 yellow squash, thinly sliced
- 1 red bell pepper, cut into 4 wedges

Cooking spray

OLIVE SALAD:

- 1 cup chopped tomato or quartered cherry tomatoes
- ⅓ cup chopped pepperoncini peppers
- ¼ cup sliced pimiento-stuffed olives
- 2 tablespoons pepperoncini juice
- ½ teaspoon dried thyme
- ½ teaspoon cracked black pepper

REMAINING INGREDIENTS:

- 1 (16-ounce) loaf French bread, cut in half horizontally
- 2 ounces thinly sliced provolone cheese
- 2 ounces thinly sliced reduced-fat hard salami (such as Franklin)

1. To prepare grilled vegetables, combine first 5 ingredients in a zip-top plastic bag; seal and marinate in refrigerator 2 hours, turning bag occasionally.
2. Prepare grill.
3. Remove vegetables from plastic bag; place vegetables on grill rack coated with cooking spray. Grill 5 minutes on each side or until vegetables are tender.
4. To prepare olive salad, combine tomato and next 5 ingredients.
5. Hollow out bottom half of bread, leaving a 1-inch-thick shell; reserve torn bread for another use. Arrange cheese in bottom half of bread. Top with salami, grilled vegetables, olive salad, and top half of bread. Wrap loaf with plastic wrap; refrigerate up to 24 hours. Cut into 4 pieces just before serving. Yield: 4 servings (serving size: 1 piece).

CALORIES 384 (28% from fat); FAT 11.9g (sat 4.3g, mono 3.4g, poly 1.9g); PROTEIN 16.3g; CARB 55.1g; FIBER 7.9g; CHOL 23mg; IRON 3.4mg; SODIUM 1,313mg; CALC 204mg

Jam-Packed with Flavor

Turn preserves, jams, and jellies into tasty sauces and glazes that will jazz up your weeknight meals.

We all have jars of sweet jams, preserves, and jellies tucked away in the fridge, waiting for breakfast toast. But there's another use for them: Turn basic and specialty jams and jellies into sauces and glazes for quick entrées.

Apple and Horseradish-Glazed Salmon

Mild apple jelly and hot horseradish pair well with rich salmon. Serve with a neutral-flavored side of couscous or rice.

- ⅓ cup apple jelly
- 2 tablespoons prepared horseradish
- 1 tablespoon finely chopped fresh chives
- 1 tablespoon Champagne vinegar
- ½ teaspoon kosher salt, divided
- 4 (6-ounce) salmon fillets (about 1 inch thick), skinned
- ¼ teaspoon freshly ground black pepper
- 2 teaspoons olive oil

1. Preheat oven to 350°.
2. Combine first 4 ingredients and ¼ teaspoon salt, stirring well with a whisk.
3. Sprinkle salmon with ¼ teaspoon salt and pepper. Heat oil in a large nonstick skillet over medium heat. Add salmon, and cook 3 minutes. Turn salmon over; brush with half of apple mixture. Wrap handle of skillet with foil; bake at 350° for 5 minutes or until fish flakes easily when tested with a fork. Brush with remaining apple mixture. Yield: 4 servings (serving size: 1 fillet).

CALORIES 375 (40% from fat); FAT 16.8g (sat 4.3g, mono 7.7g, poly 3.4g); PROTEIN 36.4g; CARB 18.1g; FIBER 0.1g; CHOL 90mg; IRON 0.7mg; SODIUM 376mg; CALC 30mg

Fig and Chile-Glazed Pork Tenderloin

Basmati rice and black beans go well with the spicy pork. The glaze also enhances chicken thighs.

- ½ cup fig preserves
- ¼ cup rice vinegar
- 1 tablespoon chile paste with garlic
- 1 tablespoon low-sodium soy sauce
- ½ teaspoon kosher salt, divided
- 2 (1-pound) pork tenderloins, trimmed
- ½ teaspoon freshly ground black pepper

Cooking spray
Fresh chives, cut into 1-inch pieces (optional)

1. Prepare grill to medium-high heat.
2. Combine first 4 ingredients and ¼ teaspoon salt, stirring with a whisk.
3. Sprinkle pork with ¼ teaspoon salt and pepper. Place pork on a grill rack coated with cooking spray; grill 18 minutes or until thermometer registers 160° (slightly pink), turning occasionally and basting frequently with fig mixture. Garnish with chives, if desired. Yield: 8 servings (serving size: about 3 ounces).

CALORIES 193 (18% from fat); FAT 3.9g (sat 1.3g, mono 1.8g, poly 0.4g); PROTEIN 24g; CARB 14g; FIBER 0.3g; CHOL 74mg; IRON 1.6mg; SODIUM 274mg; CALC 11mg

Grilled Cornish Hens with Apricot-Mustard Glaze

Serve with grilled fennel bulb quarters and couscous. Preserves are chunkier than jelly and thus adhere better to the Cornish hens. Peach preserves are also a tasty option.

- ½ cup apricot preserves
- ¼ cup stone-ground mustard
- 2 tablespoons chopped fresh flat-leaf parsley
- 2 tablespoons chopped fresh mint
- 2 teaspoons Champagne or white wine vinegar
- 2 (18-ounce) Cornish hens, skinned and quartered
- ¼ teaspoon kosher salt
- ½ teaspoon freshly ground black pepper
- Cooking spray

1. Combine first 5 ingredients, stirring with a whisk.
2. Sprinkle hens with salt and pepper. Place ¼ cup apricot mixture in a large zip-top plastic bag. Add hens; seal and marinate in refrigerator 1 hour, turning bag occasionally.
3. Prepare grill to medium-high heat. Remove hens from bag; discard marinade. Place hens on grill rack coated with cooking spray; grill 12 minutes or until thermometer registers 180°, turning hens occasionally and basting frequently with apricot mixture. Yield: 2 servings (serving size: 1 hen).

CALORIES 417 (15% from fat); FAT 7g (sat 1.7g, mono 2.2g, poly 1.6g); PROTEIN 41.7g; CARB 44.6g; FIBER 3.7g; CHOL 180mg; IRON 2.3mg; SODIUM 608mg; CALC 70mg

---

Elegant Weeknight Dinner Menu
serves 4

This menu is easy enough for an after-work meal yet special enough to serve to company. Be sure to make the polenta at the last minute; it's creamiest when served immediately.

Seared Duck Breast with Ginger-Rhubarb Sauce

Garlic-fontina polenta*

Steamed baby bok choy

*Combine 2 cups 2% reduced-fat milk, ½ cup water, ½ teaspoon salt, ¼ teaspoon freshly ground black pepper, and 1 pressed garlic clove in a medium saucepan. Bring to a boil; gradually add ⅔ cup instant dry polenta, stirring constantly with a whisk. Cook 2 minutes or until thick, stirring constantly. Remove from heat; stir in ½ cup shredded fontina cheese.

QUICK & EASY
Seared Duck Breast with Ginger-Rhubarb Sauce

Serve this dish over creamy polenta with steamed baby bok choy. Use frozen rhubarb if you can't find fresh, and boneless chicken breast halves for the duck, if desired.

- 2 cups dry red wine
- 1 cup finely chopped rhubarb
- 2 tablespoons finely chopped shallots
- 1 bay leaf
- 1 star anise
- ½ cup ginger preserves
- ½ teaspoon kosher salt, divided
- 2 (12-ounce) packages boneless whole duck breast, thawed, skinned, and cut in half
- ½ teaspoon freshly ground black pepper
- 2 teaspoons olive oil

1. Combine first 5 ingredients in a large saucepan. Bring to a boil; cook until reduced to 1 cup (about 18 minutes). Stir in preserves and ¼ teaspoon salt; cook 1 minute. Strain wine mixture through a sieve into a bowl. Discard solids.
2. Sprinkle duck with ¼ teaspoon salt and pepper. Heat oil in a large nonstick skillet over medium heat. Add duck; cook 5 minutes on each side or until desired degree of doneness. Cut duck diagonally across grain into thin slices; serve with sauce. Yield: 4 servings (serving size: 1 duck breast half and about 2 tablespoons sauce).

CALORIES 380 (23% from fat); FAT 9.5g (sat 2.6g, mono 3.7g, poly 1.2g); PROTEIN 34.2g; CARB 23.1g; FIBER 0.6g; CHOL 131mg; IRON 8.3mg; SODIUM 347mg; CALC 29mg

---

QUICK & EASY
Filet Mignon with Red Currant-Green Peppercorn Sauce
(pictured on page 147)

Green peppercorns are soft and a little bit milder than black peppercorns. We prefer jelly for this recipe because it makes a clear, shiny sauce.

- 1½ cups Merlot
- ¼ cup finely chopped shallots
- ¼ cup red currant jelly
- 1 tablespoon drained brine-packed green peppercorns, finely chopped
- 2 teaspoons butter
- 4 (4-ounce) beef tenderloin steaks, trimmed (1 inch thick)
- ¼ teaspoon kosher salt
- ¼ teaspoon freshly ground black pepper

1. Prepare grill to medium-high heat.
2. Combine wine and shallots in a small saucepan. Bring to a boil; cook until reduced to ¼ cup (about 10 minutes). Strain through a sieve into a bowl; discard solids. Return wine to pan, and add jelly and peppercorns. Cook over medium heat until jelly melts (about 2 minutes), stirring occasionally. Remove from heat. Stir in butter; keep warm.
3. Sprinkle steak with salt and black pepper. Place beef on grill rack; cook 4 minutes on each side or until desired degree of doneness. Serve sauce with beef. Yield: 4 servings (serving size: 1 filet and 1 tablespoon sauce).

CALORIES 302 (39% from fat); FAT 13g (sat 5.5g, mono 4.9g, poly 0.5g); PROTEIN 23.3g; CARB 14.9g; FIBER 0.2g; CHOL 77mg; IRON 3.2mg; SODIUM 294mg; CALC 23mg

Blackberry-Zinfandel Quail

Juniper berries are too bitter to eat, so they're crushed to release their flavor and discarded prior to serving. Use this sauce with duck or other game birds.

 1 cup zinfandel or other fruity dry red wine
 ¼ cup finely chopped shallots
 1 teaspoon juniper berries, crushed (optional)
 ½ teaspoon cracked black pepper
 ⅓ cup seedless blackberry jam
 2 teaspoons butter
 4 (4-ounce) semiboneless quail
 ¼ teaspoon kosher salt
 ¼ teaspoon freshly ground black pepper
 Cooking spray

1. Prepare grill to medium-high heat.
2. Combine first 4 ingredients in a small saucepan. Bring to a boil, and cook until reduced to ¼ cup (about 8 minutes). Strain mixture through a sieve into a bowl. Discard solids. Add wine mixture and jam to pan; cook over medium heat 2 minutes, stirring occasionally. Remove from heat; stir in butter. Keep warm.
3. Sprinkle quail with salt and ground black pepper. Place quail on a grill rack coated with cooking spray; grill 2 minutes on each side or until desired degree of doneness. Serve with wine sauce. Yield: 4 servings (serving size: 1 quail and about 1 tablespoon sauce).

CALORIES 325 (43% from fat); FAT 15.6g (sat 5g, mono 5.3g, poly 3.5g); PROTEIN 22.4g; CARB 18.3g; FIBER 0.1g; CHOL 91mg; IRON 4.7mg; SODIUM 227mg; CALC 19mg

Strawberry-Basil Sorbet

This dessert shows just how versatile preserves can be. It's cool and refreshing. You can also use pineapple preserves in place of the strawberry.

 5½ cups water
 2 cups strawberry preserves
 ¼ cup chopped fresh basil
 2 tablespoons fresh lemon juice

1. Combine water and preserves in a large saucepan. Bring to a boil over medium-high heat; cook 2 minutes or until preserves melt. Remove from heat; cool completely. Stir in basil and juice.
2. Pour mixture into freezer can of an ice-cream freezer, and freeze according to manufacturer's instructions. Spoon sorbet into a freezer-safe container; cover and freeze 1 hour or until firm. Yield: 9 servings (serving size: ⅔ cup).

CALORIES 179 (0% from fat); FAT 0g; PROTEIN 0g; CARB 46.6g; FIBER 0.1g; CHOL 0mg; IRON 0.1mg; SODIUM 4mg; CALC 5mg

enlightened cook

The Raw Edge

Chef Jenny Cornbleet says raw food preparation techniques can fit into any cook's repertoire.

 As a Chicago-based chef, Jenny Cornbleet, 31, teaches raw foods "cooking" through her business Enchanted Kitchens (www.enchantedkitchens.com). That the dishes are also healthful, vegetarian, and fairly simple to prepare is important to her, too. But above all, Cornbleet wants people to enjoy her food. "Lots of people want more fruits and veggies in their diet," she says. "This is one way to get there."

Berries and Almond Milk

The almond milk can be made ahead and kept refrigerated up to 1 week. Medjool dates are soft and blend well; their intense natural sweetness flavors the milk.

 ¼ cup whole, raw almonds
 1 cup water, divided
 1 medjool date, pitted
 2 cups mixed berries (such as raspberries, blueberries, and strawberries)
 2 tablespoons maple syrup

1. Combine almonds and ½ cup water in a small bowl; cover and let stand 8 hours or overnight. Drain almonds; rinse. Combine almonds, ½ cup water, and date in a blender or food processor; process until smooth. Spoon mixture into a cheesecloth-lined sieve over a medium bowl. Gather edges of cheesecloth together, and squeeze over sieve. Discard solids.
2. Place 1 cup berries into each of 2 bowls. Drizzle each serving with 1 tablespoon maple syrup, and top each serving with 2 tablespoons almond milk. Serve immediately. Yield: 2 servings.

CALORIES 200 (30% from fat); FAT 6.6g (sat 0.5g, mono 3.9g, poly 1.8g); PROTEIN 3.5g; CARB 34.8g; FIBER 5.4g; CHOL 0mg; IRON 0.8mg; SODIUM 11mg; CALC 65mg

Old-Fashioned Oatmeal

Groats are whole grains with only the hull removed. Oat groats are chewy and firm, and less processed than rolled oats, therefore retaining more nutrients. They need to soak overnight two times to soften enough to be puréed. Look for oat groats in health-food stores. You can make your own almond milk (see Berries and Almond Milk, recipe at left), or you can purchase packaged almond milk on the organic and health-food aisle in the grocery store. We suggest blueberries, but any fruit makes a great accompaniment. For thinner oatmeal, add more water.

 2 cups oat groats
 ¼ cup water
 ¼ cup almond milk
 ¼ cup maple syrup
 ½ teaspoon ground cinnamon
 ¼ teaspoon salt
 1 large apple, peeled and chopped
 1½ cups blueberries

1. Place groats in a large bowl. Cover with water to 2 inches above groats; cover and let stand overnight. Drain and rinse groats; repeat soaking and draining procedure.
2. Combine groats, ¼ cup water, and next 4 ingredients in a food processor;
Continued

process until smooth. Add apple; process until smooth. Place ½ cup oatmeal mixture into each of 6 bowls, and top with ¼ cup berries. Yield: 6 servings.

CALORIES 285 (14% from fat); FAT 4.3g (sat 0.7g, mono 1.3g, poly 1.5g); PROTEIN 8.3g; CARB 56.9g; FIBER 7.3g; CHOL 0mg; IRON 2.8mg; SODIUM 108mg; CALC 49mg

QUICK & EASY • MAKE AHEAD
Ensalada de Repollo
Cabbage Salad

Let the salad stand at least 30 minutes after it's dressed so the flavors can marry.

 7 cups shredded cabbage
 1 cup chopped red bell pepper
 ¼ cup chopped onion
 ¼ cup chopped fresh cilantro
 3 celery stalks, chopped
 3 plum tomatoes, chopped
 1 cucumber, chopped
 ¼ cup fresh lime juice
 2 teaspoons olive oil
 ¾ teaspoon salt
 ¼ teaspoon freshly ground black pepper

1. Combine first 7 ingredients in a large bowl. Combine lime juice, oil, salt, and black pepper, stirring with a whisk. Drizzle lime mixture over cabbage mixture; toss gently to coat. Let salad stand 30 minutes before serving. Yield: 8 servings (serving size: 1½ cups).

CALORIES 45 (30% from fat); FAT 1.5g (sat 0.2g, mono 0.9g, poly 0.3g); PROTEIN 1.6g; CARB 8g; FIBER 2.3g; CHOL 0mg; IRON 0.7mg; SODIUM 250mg; CALC 45mg

QUICK & EASY
Papaya Lime Soup

For a tropical presentation, serve this soup in hollowed-out papaya shell halves, and sprinkle with mint and diced mango. If you prefer thinner soup, add more water or orange juice.

 2 cups diced peeled papaya (about 2 medium papayas)
 1 cubed peeled ripe mango
 1 cup fresh orange juice
 ½ cup water
 2 tablespoons fresh lime juice
 2 tablespoons honey
 Diced mango (optional)
 Chopped fresh mint (optional)

1. Place first 6 ingredients in a blender or food processor; process until smooth.
2. Ladle 1 cup soup into each of 4 bowls; top with diced mango and mint, if desired. Yield: 4 servings.

CALORIES 150 (3% from fat); FAT 0.5g (sat 0.1g, mono 0.1g, poly 0.1g); PROTEIN 1.7g; CARB 38.1g; FIBER 3.6g; CHOL 0mg; IRON 0.4mg; SODIUM 7mg; CALC 50mg

QUICK & EASY
Swiss Chard with Pine Nuts and Raisins

 1 pound trimmed Swiss chard (about 1¼ pounds untrimmed)
 2 tablespoons fresh lemon juice
 1½ teaspoons extravirgin olive oil
 ½ teaspoon salt
 ⅛ teaspoon freshly ground black pepper
 ½ cup golden raisins
 2 tablespoons pine nuts

1. Slice chard leaves crossways into thin strips; place in a large bowl. Combine juice, oil, salt, and pepper, stirring with a whisk. Drizzle juice mixture over chard; toss to coat. Add raisins and pine nuts, and toss to combine. Let stand 15 minutes before serving. Yield: 4 servings (serving size: 1 cup).

CALORIES 111 (29% from fat); FAT 3.6g (sat 0.5g, mono 1.9g, poly 0.9g); PROTEIN 3.5g; CARB 19.8g; FIBER 2.7g; CHOL 0mg; IRON 2.7mg; SODIUM 391mg; CALC 69mg

superfast

. . . And Ready in Just About 20 Minutes

QUICK & EASY
Skillet Stuffed Peppers

This recipe can also be made with red, yellow, or orange bell peppers.

 2 large green bell peppers, halved lengthwise and seeded
 Cooking spray
 ¾ pound ground round
 ½ cup water
 1 (1.25-ounce) package taco seasoning
 1 (20-ounce) package refrigerated mashed potatoes (such as Simply Potatoes)
 ¼ cup (1 ounce) reduced-fat shredded Cheddar cheese
 Cracked black pepper (optional)

1. Place bell pepper halves, cut sides down, on a microwave-safe dish; cover with plastic wrap. Microwave at HIGH 3 minutes and 30 seconds or until pepper halves are crisp-tender. Let stand, covered, 3 minutes (peppers will soften).
2. While peppers cook, heat a large nonstick skillet over medium-high heat. Coat pan with cooking spray. Add beef to pan; cook 3 minutes, stirring to crumble. Stir in water and seasoning. Cover, reduce heat, and cook 5 minutes or until done.
3. While beef cooks and peppers stand, cook potatoes in microwave according to package directions, omitting salt and fat.
4. Spoon ½ cup beef mixture into each pepper half; top each with ⅔ cup potatoes. Sprinkle each pepper half with 1 tablespoon cheese. Garnish with black pepper, if desired. Yield: 4 servings (serving size: 1 stuffed pepper half).

CALORIES 338 (36% from fat); FAT 13.4g (sat 5.3g, mono 5.7g, poly 0.4g); PROTEIN 20.1g; CARB 29.3g; FIBER 5.1g; CHOL 59mg; IRON 2.4mg; SODIUM 663mg; CALC 48mg

Chicken with Cherry Tomato and Olive Topping

Serve with angel hair pasta.

- 4 (6-ounce) skinless, boneless chicken breast halves
- ¼ teaspoon black pepper
- ⅛ teaspoon salt
- 2 teaspoons olive oil
- 1 cup quartered cherry tomatoes
- 2 tablespoons chopped fresh basil
- ¼ teaspoon salt
- ¼ teaspoon crushed red pepper
- 12 kalamata olives, chopped and pitted

1. Heat a large nonstick skillet over medium heat. Sprinkle chicken with black pepper and ⅛ teaspoon salt. Add oil to pan. Add chicken; cook 5 minutes on each side or until done.
2. While chicken cooks, combine tomatoes and remaining 4 ingredients. Serve over chicken. Yield: 4 servings (serving size: 1 chicken breast half and ¼ cup tomato topping).

CALORIES 247 (27% from fat); FAT 7.5g (sat 1.3g, mono 4.6g, poly 1.1g); PROTEIN 39.8g; CARB 2.6g; FIBER 0.5g; CHOL 99mg; IRON 1.5mg; SODIUM 515mg; CALC 27mg

Chicken with Chunky Pepper Sauce

- 1 (16-ounce) package frozen pepper stir-fry, thawed
- 2 teaspoons chopped drained canned chipotle chiles in adobo sauce
- 4 (6-ounce) skinless, boneless chicken breast halves
- Cooking spray
- 1 tablespoon fresh lime juice
- 1 tablespoon olive oil
- ½ teaspoon salt
- ¼ cup chopped fresh cilantro
- ¼ cup reduced-fat sour cream
- 1 lime, quartered

1. Place pepper stir-fry and chiles in a blender or food processor, and pulse 10 times or until coarsely chopped.

2. Heat a large nonstick skillet over medium-high heat. Place chicken breast halves between 2 sheets of heavy-duty plastic wrap; pound to ¼-inch thickness using a meat mallet or rolling pin. Coat pan with cooking spray. Add chicken to pan; cook 5 minutes or until browned. Turn chicken; add pepper mixture. Reduce heat, and simmer 5 minutes or until chicken is done. Remove chicken from pan; keep warm. Add lime juice, oil, and salt to pan; cook 5 minutes, stirring constantly.
3. Spoon ¼ cup pepper sauce onto each of 4 plates; top each serving with one chicken breast half. Sprinkle each with 1 tablespoon cilantro, and top with 1 tablespoon sour cream. Serve with lime quarters. Yield: 4 servings.

CALORIES 286 (25% from fat); FAT 8g (sat 2.2g, mono 3g, poly 0.8g); PROTEIN 41.2g; CARB 11.6g; FIBER 2.7g; CHOL 106mg; IRON 1.6mg; SODIUM 495mg; CALC 58mg

Insalata Pizzas

- 4 (7-inch) pitas
- 2 teaspoons bottled minced garlic
- 1 cup (4 ounces) preshredded part-skim mozzarella cheese
- ½ cup thinly sliced Vidalia or other sweet onion
- 1 tablespoon cider vinegar
- 2 teaspoons extravirgin olive oil
- ¼ teaspoon crushed red pepper
- 1 cup quartered grape tomatoes
- ¼ cup pitted kalamata olives, coarsely chopped
- 2 tablespoons chopped basil leaves
- 4 cups packaged gourmet salad greens

1. Preheat oven to 475°.
2. Place pitas on a baking sheet. Spread ½ teaspoon garlic on each pita. Sprinkle each pita with ¼ cup cheese, and divide onion evenly among pitas. Bake at 475° for 8 minutes or until edges are lightly browned and cheese is bubbly.
3. While pitas bake, combine vinegar, oil, and pepper in a large bowl, stirring with a whisk. Stir in tomatoes, olives, and basil. Add salad greens, and toss gently to coat.

4. Place 1 pita on each of 4 plates; top each with about 1 cup salad. Serve immediately. Yield: 4 servings (serving size: 1 topped pita).

CALORIES 319 (31% from fat); FAT 10.9g (sat 3.7g, mono 5.4g, poly 1.2g); PROTEIN 14.1g; CARB 41.5g; FIBER 3.6g; CHOL 16mg; IRON 2.8mg; SODIUM 656mg; CALC 279mg

Creamy Shrimp and Corn Bowl

Serve with sliced baguette for dipping.

- Cooking spray
- 1½ pounds large shrimp, peeled and deveined
- ¾ cup chopped green onions, divided
- ¼ cup water
- ¾ teaspoon Old Bay seasoning
- 1 (11-ounce) can extrasweet whole-kernel corn, drained
- ¾ cup half-and-half
- ¼ teaspoon salt

1. Heat a large saucepan over medium-high heat. Coat pan with cooking spray. Add shrimp to pan; sauté 3 minutes. Add ½ cup onions, water, seasoning, and corn; bring to a boil. Cover, reduce heat, and simmer 5 minutes.
2. Remove from heat, and stir in half-and-half and salt. Cover; let stand 3 minutes. Sprinkle with ¼ cup onions. Yield: 4 servings (serving size: 1 cup shrimp mixture and 1 tablespoon onions).

CALORIES 279 (26% from fat); FAT 8.1g (sat 3.6g, mono 1.9g, poly 1.1g); PROTEIN 37.3g; CARB 12g; FIBER 2g; CHOL 281mg; IRON 4.3mg; SODIUM 741mg; CALC 149mg

Shrimp-Poblano Rice

Savor the mild taste of poblano chiles, now available in most grocery stores. They're best in the summer and early fall.

- 1 (3½-ounce) bag boil-in-bag long-grain rice
- 3 tablespoons sliced almonds, toasted
- ½ teaspoon salt, divided
- 1½ pounds large shrimp, peeled and deveined
- ½ teaspoon black pepper
- Cooking spray
- 2 tablespoons olive oil, divided
- 1 poblano chile, seeded and chopped
- ¼ cup chopped fresh cilantro
- ¼ cup fresh lemon juice (about 2 lemons)
- 4 lemon wedges

1. Cook rice according to package directions, omitting salt and fat. Stir in almonds and ¼ teaspoon salt. Keep rice mixture warm.

2. While rice cooks, heat a large non-stick skillet over medium-high heat. Sprinkle shrimp with ¼ teaspoon salt and pepper. Coat pan with cooking spray. Add 1½ teaspoons oil to pan. Add poblano; cook 3 minutes or until lightly browned, stirring frequently. Reduce heat to medium. Add shrimp; cook 4 minutes or until shrimp are done. Remove from heat.

3. Combine 1½ tablespoons oil, cilantro, and lemon juice, stirring with a whisk. Add cilantro mixture to shrimp mixture; toss to coat. Place rice on each of 4 plates; top with shrimp mixture. Serve with lemon wedges. Yield: 4 servings (serving size: ½ cup rice mixture, about 1 cup shrimp mixture, and 1 lemon wedge).

CALORIES 385 (31% from fat); FAT 13.2g (sat 1.7g, mono 7.6g, poly 2.6g); PROTEIN 38.4g; CARB 27g; FIBER 1.3g; CHOL 259mg; IRON 5.4mg; SODIUM 572mg; CALC 114mg

Applying Pressure

The pressure cooker makes quick work of fresh ingredients.

It's hard to believe that something that gets so hot can keep your kitchen from overheating. But a pressure cooker does just that—hot steam stays in the pot. Although we tend to think of using a pressure cooker during winter—it's also a cool tool for hot weather. Pressure cooking also intensifies the flavors of food.

Pressure Cooking Know-How

- We tested all the recipes in a 6-quart pressure cooker, using a variety of brands—from expensive models to less costly ones. We found no significant difference in performance among brands.
- We prefer the cold-water method for releasing pressure: Run cold water over the lid of the pot until all pressure has been released. This method discharges less steam into your kitchen.
- Food cooked under pressure has a tendency to increase in volume, so don't fill your pressure cooker more than half full with food or two-thirds full with liquid (as when making soup). Most pressure cookers have a two-thirds indicator inside the pot.
- Dried beans always benefit from a presoak to jump-start the cooking process. With traditional stovetop cooking, beans are soaked in cool water overnight or cooked in boiling water for a couple of minutes before standing for an hour. With the pressure cooker, the presoak time is reduced to a mere minute.
- As with conventional cooking methods, it's important not to salt beans before cooking—doing so will keep the beans tough.
- Herbs don't hold up well under pressure cooking. Add them just before serving.

Lemon-Basil Risotto with Tomato Topping

Citrus-scented risotto cooks in about 10 minutes in the pressure cooker. Once the components are combined, there's no stirring required.

TOPPING:

- 1½ cups chopped seeded tomato
- 2 tablespoons chopped green onions
- 1½ teaspoons extravirgin olive oil
- 1 teaspoon balsamic vinegar
- ¼ teaspoon crushed red pepper
- Dash of sugar
- Dash of salt
- Dash of freshly ground black pepper

RISOTTO:

- 2 tablespoons butter
- 1 cup chopped onion
- 1½ cups Arborio rice
- 2 garlic cloves, minced
- ½ cup dry white wine
- 4 cups fat-free, less-sodium chicken broth
- ½ teaspoon salt
- ¼ teaspoon freshly ground black pepper
- ⅛ teaspoon ground nutmeg
- 1 cup (4 ounces) grated fresh Parmesan cheese
- 1 teaspoon grated lemon rind
- 3 tablespoons fresh lemon juice
- ⅓ cup finely chopped fresh basil

1. To prepare topping, combine first 8 ingredients. Cover and let stand at room temperature.

2. To prepare risotto, melt butter in a 6-quart pressure cooker over medium heat. Add 1 cup onion; cook 2 minutes, stirring frequently. Add rice and garlic; cook 2 minutes, stirring constantly. Add wine; cook 1 minute or until liquid is absorbed, stirring frequently. Stir in broth and next 3 ingredients. Close lid securely, and bring to high pressure over high heat. Adjust heat to medium or level needed to maintain high pressure; cook 6 minutes. Remove from heat; place cooker under cold running water. Remove lid. Stir in cheese, rind, juice, and basil. Top with tomato topping.

Yield: 6 servings (serving size: 1 cup risotto and ¼ cup topping).

CALORIES 368 (24% from fat); FAT 10g (sat 5.7g, mono 3.4g, poly 0.4g); PROTEIN 13.7g; CARB 52.6g; FIBER 2.3g; CHOL 23mg; IRON 1mg; SODIUM 869mg; CALC 262mg

Tortilla Soup

In the pressure cooker, it takes only 20 minutes to make homemade chicken stock. Ground red chiles found in Mexican markets are quite different from regular chili powder or ground red pepper. You can substitute ground New Mexico chile powder.

    8 (6-inch) corn tortillas
    2 cups thinly sliced onion
    ¾ teaspoon salt
    ½ teaspoon coarsely ground black pepper
    Dash of ground allspice
    3 pounds chicken pieces, skinned
    3 (14-ounce) cans fat-free, less-sodium chicken broth
    2 garlic cloves, crushed
    1 carrot, cut into 3 pieces
    1 celery stalk, cut in half crosswise
    1 bay leaf
    ¼ cup ground red chiles
    1 tablespoon dried oregano
    1 tablespoon ground cumin
    1 cup diced peeled avocado
    ½ cup fat-free sour cream
    2 tablespoons chopped fresh cilantro

1. Preheat oven to 350°.
2. Cut each tortilla in half. Cut tortilla halves into ¼-inch strips. Arrange tortilla strips in a single layer on a baking sheet. Bake at 350° for 6 minutes or until lightly browned, stirring after 3 minutes. Cool completely.
3. Combine onion and next 9 ingredients in a 6-quart pressure cooker. Close lid securely; bring to high pressure over high heat. Adjust heat to medium or level needed to maintain high pressure; cook 20 minutes. Remove from heat; place cooker under cold running water. Remove lid. Remove chicken from broth; cool slightly. Remove chicken from bones; cut meat into bite-size pieces. Discard bones.

4. Strain stock through a sieve into a bowl, and discard solids. Return stock to cooker; stir in ground chiles, oregano, cumin, and chicken; let stand 5 minutes.
5. Divide tortilla strips evenly among 8 bowls; top each serving with about 1⅓ cups soup, 2 tablespoons avocado, 1 tablespoon sour cream, and ¾ teaspoon cilantro. Yield: 8 servings.

CALORIES 226 (27% from fat); FAT 6.7g (sat 1.3g, mono 2.7g, poly 1.3g); PROTEIN 22.5g; CARB 20.1g; FIBER 3.6g; CHOL 59mg; IRON 2.9mg; SODIUM 630mg; CALC 105mg

MAKE AHEAD
White Beans with Roasted Red Pepper and Pesto

Add a green salad and crusty bread to this simple rustic dish for a satisfying supper. As with the Barbecue Beans (recipe on page 166), simmer the beans on the stovetop if they're still not tender after cooking under pressure for 12 minutes.

PESTO:

    2 cups loosely packed basil leaves
    ½ cup (2 ounces) grated fresh Parmesan cheese
    2 tablespoons pine nuts, toasted
    2 tablespoons water
    2 tablespoons extravirgin olive oil
    ¼ teaspoon salt
    ⅛ teaspoon freshly ground black pepper
    1 garlic clove, crushed

BEANS:

    1 pound dried Great Northern beans
    10 cups water, divided
    1½ cups coarsely chopped onion
    1 tablespoon chopped fresh sage
    1 tablespoon olive oil
    2 garlic cloves, crushed
    1 teaspoon salt
    ¼ teaspoon freshly ground black pepper
    1 cup chopped bottled roasted red bell peppers
    1 tablespoon balsamic vinegar

1. To prepare pesto, combine first 8 ingredients in a food processor; process until smooth.

2. To prepare beans, sort and wash beans. Combine beans and 4 cups water in a 6-quart pressure cooker. Close lid securely; bring to high pressure over high heat. Adjust heat to medium or level needed to maintain high pressure, and cook 3 minutes. Remove from heat; place cooker under cold running water. Remove lid; drain beans.
3. Combine beans, 6 cups water, onion, sage, 1 tablespoon olive oil, and 2 garlic cloves in cooker. Close lid securely; bring to high pressure over high heat. Adjust heat to medium or level needed to maintain high pressure; cook 12 minutes. Remove from heat; place cooker under cold running water. Remove lid; let bean mixture stand 10 minutes. Drain bean mixture in a colander over a bowl, reserving 1 cup liquid. Return bean mixture and reserved 1 cup liquid to cooker. Add 1 teaspoon salt, ¼ teaspoon black pepper, bell peppers, and vinegar. Stir well to combine. Top bean mixture with pesto. Yield: 8 servings (serving size: about ¾ cup bean mixture and 2 tablespoons pesto).

CALORIES 292 (25% from fat); FAT 8g (sat 2.1g, mono 4.1g, poly 1.2g); PROTEIN 16.3g; CARB 40.5g; FIBER 12.7g; CHOL 5mg; IRON 3.9mg; SODIUM 542mg; CALC 212mg

MAKE AHEAD
Vichyssoise

Though it's also good hot, having this creamy soup chilled is a lifesaver on hot summer evenings. We liked leaving the skins on the potatoes, but you can remove them if you prefer.

    1 tablespoon butter
    8 cups thinly sliced Vidalia or other sweet onion (about 3 medium)
    9 cups (¼-inch-thick) slices baking potato (about 1½ pounds)
    5 cups fat-free, less-sodium chicken broth
    1 teaspoon salt
    ¼ teaspoon white pepper
    ¼ teaspoon ground nutmeg
    1 cup 2% reduced-fat milk
    1 cup reduced-fat sour cream
    ½ cup minced fresh chives

Continued

1. Melt butter in a 6-quart pressure cooker over medium heat. Add onion, and cook 5 minutes or until tender, stirring occasionally. Add potato and broth. Close lid securely; bring to high pressure over high heat. Adjust heat to medium or level needed to maintain high pressure; cook 5 minutes. Remove from heat; place cooker under cold running water. Remove lid; let soup cool 10 minutes.

2. Place half of soup in a blender or food processor; process until smooth. Pour puréed soup into a large bowl. Repeat procedure with remaining soup. Stir in salt, pepper, and nutmeg. Add milk and sour cream, stirring until well blended. Cover and chill. Top with chives just before serving. Yield: 8 servings (serving size: about 1½ cups).

CALORIES 200 (27% from fat); FAT 6g (sat 3.7g, mono 1.7g, poly 0.3g); PROTEIN 7.6g; CARB 29.6g; FIBER 3.3g; CHOL 22mg; IRON 1.1mg; SODIUM 630mg; CALC 125mg

---

QUICK & EASY • MAKE AHEAD
Barbecue Beans

These saucy beans are ready in less than 40 minutes. If you'd like more of a smoky taste, use a mesquite-flavored barbecue sauce; if you prefer a milder flavor, use a regular tomato-based barbecue sauce. Check the beans for doneness after they've cooked for 6 minutes; if they're still a bit firm, simmer them (not under pressure) until tender.

       3 bacon slices
    1½ cups chopped onion
       1 cup finely chopped red bell pepper
       1 cup finely chopped green bell pepper
       4 garlic cloves, minced
       1 pound dried Great Northern beans
     10 cups water, divided
       1 tablespoon vegetable oil
      ¾ cup barbecue sauce
      ½ cup packed dark brown sugar
      ⅓ cup beer
       3 tablespoons maple syrup
       2 tablespoons stone-ground mustard
       1 teaspoon salt

1. Cook bacon slices in a 6-quart pressure cooker over medium-high heat until crisp. Remove bacon from cooker; crumble and set aside. Add onion, bell peppers, and garlic to drippings in cooker; sauté 2 minutes. Remove onion mixture from cooker; set aside.

2. Sort and wash beans. Combine beans and 4 cups water in cooker. Close lid securely; bring to high pressure over high heat. Adjust heat to medium or level needed to maintain high pressure; cook 1 minute. Remove from heat, and place cooker under cold running water. Remove lid; drain beans.

3. Combine beans, 6 cups water, and oil in cooker. Close lid securely; bring to high pressure over high heat. Adjust heat to medium or level needed to maintain high pressure; cook 6 minutes. Remove from heat, and place cooker under cold running water. Remove lid; drain beans. Return beans to cooker; add bacon, onion mixture, barbecue sauce, and remaining ingredients. Bring to a boil; reduce heat, and simmer 12 minutes or until slightly thick. Yield: 16 servings (serving size: ½ cup).

CALORIES 189 (19% from fat); FAT 3.9g (sat 1.2g, mono 1.4g, poly 1g); PROTEIN 7.3g; CARB 31.8g; FIBER 6.8g; CHOL 3mg; IRON 2mg; SODIUM 311mg; CALC 69mg

---

MAKE AHEAD
All-Purpose Southwestern Corn and Black Bean Salad

This recipe makes 12 servings and keeps in the refrigerator up to 5 days. It's quite versatile—add shredded chicken and serve tortillas on the side to make it a main-dish salad. Or serve it as a dip with baked tortilla chips, a side for burgers or grilled chicken, or a salad on a bed of lettuce.

SALAD:

       1 pound dried black beans
   11½ cups water, divided
       1 teaspoon olive oil
       2 teaspoons cumin seeds
       2 garlic cloves, minced
       2 cups fresh corn kernels
       2 cups chopped seeded tomato
       1 cup finely chopped Vidalia or other sweet onion
       1 cup chopped red bell pepper
       1 cup chopped green bell pepper

DRESSING:

      ½ cup fresh lime juice (about 3 limes)
       3 tablespoons olive oil
       1 tablespoon chili powder
       2 teaspoons salt
       2 teaspoons honey
    1½ teaspoons ground cumin
       3 garlic cloves, minced
       2 jalapeño peppers, seeded and minced
      ⅓ cup chopped fresh cilantro

1. To prepare salad, sort and wash beans. Combine beans and 5½ cups water in a 6-quart pressure cooker. Close lid securely; bring to high pressure over high heat. Adjust heat to medium or level needed to maintain high pressure, and cook 1 minute. Remove from heat; place cooker under cold running water. Remove lid. Drain beans; rinse with cold water. Drain and cool.

2. Heat 1 teaspoon oil in cooker over medium heat. Add cumin seeds and 2 garlic cloves; cook 1 minute, stirring frequently. Add beans and 6 cups water. Close lid securely; bring to high pressure over high heat. Adjust heat to medium or level needed to maintain high pressure, and cook 12 minutes. Remove from heat; place cooker under cold running water. Remove lid. Drain bean mixture; rinse with cold water. Drain and cool. Combine bean mixture, corn, tomato, onion, and bell peppers in a large bowl.

3. To prepare dressing, combine juice and next 7 ingredients, stirring with a whisk. Stir in cilantro. Pour dressing over bean mixture; stir gently to combine. Cover and refrigerate at least 30 minutes. Yield: 12 servings (serving size: 1 cup).

CALORIES 216 (21% from fat); FAT 5g (sat 0.7g, mono 3g, poly 0.8g); PROTEIN 10g; CARB 35.7g; FIBER 8g; CHOL 0mg; IRON 2.8mg; SODIUM 408mg; CALC 65mg

Moroccan Summer Vegetable and Sausage Stew

Eggplant, onion, and summer squash join sausage, raisins, and feta cheese for a hearty dish that tastes as though it simmered for hours. Use kitchen scissors to split the sausage casings.

 2 teaspoons olive oil
 2 cups chopped onion
 1 pound hot turkey Italian sausage
 5 cups (¾-inch) cubed eggplant (about 1½ pounds)
 4 cups coarsely chopped yellow squash (about 1 pound)
 1 cup fat-free, less-sodium chicken broth
 1 tablespoon ground cumin
 1 tablespoon ground coriander
 ½ teaspoon salt
 ¼ teaspoon crushed red pepper
 3 garlic cloves, minced
 1 (15½-ounce) can chickpeas (garbanzo beans), rinsed and drained
 1 (14.5-ounce) can diced tomatoes, undrained
 ⅓ cup golden raisins
 3 tablespoons chopped fresh thyme
 6 cups hot cooked couscous
 1 cup (4 ounces) crumbled feta cheese

1. Heat oil in a 6-quart pressure cooker over medium-high heat. Add onion, and sauté 2 minutes. Remove casings from sausage. Add sausage to cooker; cook 2 minutes, stirring to crumble. Add eggplant and next 9 ingredients. Close lid securely; bring to high pressure over high heat. Adjust heat to medium or level needed to maintain high pressure; cook 4 minutes. Remove from heat; place cooker under cold running water. Remove lid, and stir in raisins and thyme. Serve over couscous; sprinkle with cheese. Yield: 8 servings (serving size: about 1⅓ cups stew, ¾ cup couscous, and 2 tablespoons cheese).

CALORIES 401 (24% from fat); FAT 10.8g (sat 4g, mono 3.7g, poly 2.2g); PROTEIN 21.7g; CARB 55.8g; FIBER 8.9g; CHOL 60mg; IRON 2.8mg; SODIUM 885mg; CALC 151mg

Fast From the Sea

Enjoy seafood from around the world with these speedy entrées.

Nearly every culture has a seafood staple. From Provence, France, to Portland, Oregon, we have a variety of cuisines to draw from for a nourishing seafood supper.

The French favor mussels for a quick bistro-style meal, and more American cooks are discovering their convenience, as well. Steamed in tomatoes, wine, and garlic, mussels beg for something else French—a generous chunk of baguette to sop up the flavorful broth.

In the Pacific Northwest, salmon reigns supreme, and our version is matched with a tangy, teriyaki-style marinade. Trout, also an American favorite, has a succulent texture that provides a fine foil for the cool zing of cucumber salsa.

Trout Topped with Cucumber Salsa

Serve with couscous tossed with feta and chopped tomato.

SALSA:

 2 cups finely chopped seeded peeled cucumber
 ⅓ cup rice wine vinegar
 2 tablespoons finely chopped shallots
 1½ tablespoons sugar
 1 tablespoon minced seeded jalapeño pepper
 1½ teaspoons minced fresh cilantro

FISH:

 2 teaspoons butter
 1 tablespoon minced fresh cilantro
 1 teaspoon bottled minced garlic
 ¼ teaspoon salt
 ⅛ teaspoon freshly ground black pepper
 4 (6-ounce) trout fillets

1. To prepare salsa, combine first 6 ingredients. Cover and chill 2 hours.
2. To prepare fish, melt butter in a large nonstick skillet over medium-high heat. Sprinkle 1 tablespoon cilantro, garlic, salt, and black pepper evenly over 1 side of fillets. Add fillets, cilantro side down, to pan; cook 3 minutes. Turn and cook 3 minutes or until fish flakes easily when tested with a fork. Serve with salsa. Yield: 4 servings (serving size: 1 fillet and ½ cup salsa).

CALORIES 284 (35% from fat); FAT 11.2g (sat 3.9g, mono 3.2g, poly 3.2g); PROTEIN 36.2g; CARB 7.8g; FIBER 0.6g; CHOL 106mg; IRON 0.7mg; SODIUM 376mg; CALC 130mg

Citrus Salmon with Garlicky Greens

Serve with mashed red-skin potatoes or orzo tossed with olive oil.

 2 teaspoons grated orange rind
 ½ cup fresh orange juice (about 1 orange)
 ¼ cup low-sodium soy sauce
 4 (6-ounce) salmon fillets (about 1 inch thick)
   Cooking spray
 2 teaspoons vegetable oil
 1 teaspoon bottled minced garlic
 ½ teaspoon salt
 2 (10-ounce) packages fresh spinach (about 20 cups)
 1 tablespoon seasoned rice vinegar
 2 tablespoons green onions, thinly sliced (optional)

1. Combine first 3 ingredients in a zip-top plastic bag; add salmon. Seal bag; marinate in refrigerator 30 minutes.
2. Preheat oven to 500°.
3. Remove fillets from bag, and discard marinade. Place fillets, skin sides down, in a shallow roasting pan coated with cooking spray; bake at 500° for 13 minutes or until fish flakes easily when tested with a fork.
4. Heat oil in a Dutch oven over medium-high heat. Add garlic, salt, and one package of spinach; sauté 1 minute or *Continued*

until spinach wilts. Add remaining spinach; cook 2 minutes or until spinach wilts, stirring frequently. Remove from heat; toss with vinegar. Arrange ⅔ cup spinach mixture on each of 4 plates; top each with a fillet. Garnish with onions, if desired. Yield: 4 servings.

CALORIES 272 (42% from fat); FAT 12.6g (sat 2.7g, mono 4.8g, poly 3.9g); PROTEIN 31.8g; CARB 8.6g; FIBER 4.1g; CHOL 65mg; IRON 4.5mg; SODIUM 807mg; CALC 161mg

---

QUICK & EASY
Mussels with Tomato-Wine Broth

Figure about a pound of mussels per person.

1 tablespoon olive oil
1½ teaspoons bottled minced garlic
¼ teaspoon crushed red pepper
1 cup Pinot Noir or other spicy dry red wine
3 cups chopped seeded peeled tomato
½ teaspoon salt
¼ teaspoon black pepper
2 pounds small mussels, scrubbed and debearded
2 cups trimmed arugula

1. Heat oil in a large skillet over medium heat. Add garlic and red pepper, and cook 1 minute, stirring constantly. Add wine; simmer 3 minutes. Add tomato, salt, and black pepper; cook 1 minute.
2. Add mussels; cover and cook 4 minutes or until shells open. Remove from heat; discard any unopened shells. Stir in arugula; serve immediately. Yield: 2 servings (serving size: about 20 mussels and about 1½ cups sauce).

CALORIES 379 (29% from fat); FAT 12.1g (sat 1.9g, mono 6.1g, poly 2.2g); PROTEIN 26g; CARB 24.1g; FIBER 2g; CHOL 53mg; IRON 9.7mg; SODIUM 873mg; CALC 114mg

---

passport
In Chile

If you like South American food, you'll love the blend of Old and New World cuisines in Chilean cooking.

The topography of this long, thin country contributes to an abundance of excellent vegetables and fruits. While most ingredients used in Chilean cooking are indigenous, the techniques reflect a strong Spanish influence; European immigration has also left its mark.

Pastel de Choclo

There are several interpretations of this Chilean chicken and corn casserole. Here, fresh corn cooks with milk until slightly thick, then whirls in the food processor until smooth. You can achieve similar results with frozen corn if fresh isn't available. Serve this dish with *Pebre*, a pungent fresh herb sauce (recipe on page 169).

4½ cups fresh corn or 2 (16-ounce) packages frozen corn, thawed
½ cup whole milk
2 tablespoons thinly sliced fresh basil
4 teaspoons sugar, divided
1 teaspoon salt, divided
1 cup fat-free, less-sodium chicken broth or water
1 cup thinly sliced onion
½ cup thinly sliced red bell pepper
½ cup thinly sliced carrot
¼ teaspoon freshly ground black pepper
2 garlic cloves, thinly sliced
2 bay leaves
½ pound skinless, boneless chicken breast, cut into bite-size pieces
2 tablespoons minced fresh parsley
Cooking spray

1. Preheat oven to 400°.
2. Combine corn and milk in a large saucepan; bring to a boil. Cover, reduce heat, and simmer 15 minutes. Remove from heat; let stand, covered, 5 minutes. Place corn mixture in a food processor; process until smooth. Stir in basil, 1 teaspoon sugar, and ½ teaspoon salt.
3. Combine broth and next 6 ingredients in a Dutch oven; bring to a boil. Cover, reduce heat, and simmer 15 minutes. Add ½ teaspoon salt, chicken, and parsley. Cover and cook 10 minutes or until chicken is done. Drain; discard bay leaves.
4. Place chicken mixture in bottom of an 8-inch square baking dish coated with cooking spray. Top with corn mixture; sprinkle evenly with 1 tablespoon sugar. Bake at 400° for 25 minutes.
5. Preheat broiler.
6. Broil 3 minutes or until lightly browned. Yield: 4 servings (serving size: about 1½ cups).

CALORIES 328 (10% from fat); FAT 3.6g (sat 1.1g, mono 1g, poly 1.1g); PROTEIN 22.6g; CARB 59.1g; FIBER 7g; CHOL 37mg; IRON 1.8mg; SODIUM 766mg; CALC 67mg

---

MAKE AHEAD • FREEZABLE
Spicy Lentils with Chorizo

You can reduce the amount or omit the pepper sauce if you don't like hot foods. Leftovers freeze well.

1 tablespoon olive oil
1 cup finely chopped onion
¾ cup crumbled Spanish chorizo sausage (about 3 ounces)
½ cup finely chopped carrot
⅓ cup finely chopped red bell pepper
2 garlic cloves, minced
3 cups fat-free, less-sodium chicken broth
3 cups water
2 cups dried lentils
1¾ cups (½-inch) cubed Yukon gold potato
1½ cups chopped tomato
2 teaspoons hot pepper sauce
½ teaspoon salt
½ cup (2 ounces) grated fresh Parmesan cheese

1. Heat oil in a Dutch oven over low heat. Add onion and next 4 ingredients; cook 10 minutes or until tender, stirring frequently. Add broth and next 5 ingredients; bring to a boil. Reduce heat, and simmer 30 minutes or until lentils are tender. Stir in salt. Sprinkle with Parmesan cheese. Yield: 8 servings (serving size: 1 cup of lentil mixture and 1 tablespoon cheese).

CALORIES 306 (24% from fat); FAT 8.3g (sat 2.9g, mono 3.3g, poly 0.8g); PROTEIN 20.1g; CARB 39.6g; FIBER 12.8g; CHOL 15mg; IRON 5.4mg; SODIUM 542mg; CALC 127mg

MAKE AHEAD

Dulce de Leche-Filled Cookies

Alfajores are crisp wafer cookies filled with caramelized sweetened condensed milk. Although you often can find a full-fat version of this product at Hispanic markets, we've made our own fat-free version.

- 1½ cups all-purpose flour
- ¾ cup powdered sugar
- ½ cup butter, softened
- 1 large egg yolk
- 5 tablespoons Caramelized Condensed Milk
- 3 tablespoons powdered sugar

1. Sift flour and ¾ cup sugar together twice. Place flour mixture, butter, and egg yolk in a large bowl; beat with a mixer at low speed 3 minutes (dough will be crumbly). Turn dough out, and knead until combined. Divide dough in half; gently press each portion into a 4-inch circle on plastic wrap. Cover and chill 30 minutes or until firm.
2. Preheat oven to 350°.
3. Working with 1 dough portion at a time, unwrap dough and place on 2 sheets of overlapping plastic wrap. Cover dough with 2 additional sheets of overlapping plastic wrap. Roll dough, still covered, into a 10-inch circle. Freeze dough 5 minutes or until plastic wrap can be easily removed. Remove plastic wrap; cut dough into 15 circles with a 2-inch biscuit cutter. Place dough circles 1 inch apart on baking sheets lined with parchment paper. Bake at

350° for 7 minutes (should not brown). Cool on a wire rack.
4. Gently spread 1 teaspoon of Caramelized Condensed Milk onto each of 15 cookies. Gently top with remaining cookies. Sprinkle cookies with 3 tablespoons powdered sugar. Yield: 15 servings (serving size: 1 cookie sandwich).

(Totals include Caramelized Condensed Milk) CALORIES 150 (39% from fat); FAT 6.5g (sat 3.9g, mono 1.9g, poly 0.3g); PROTEIN 2g; CARB 21g; FIBER 0.3g; CHOL 31mg; IRON 0.6mg; SODIUM 69mg; CALC 23mg

CARAMELIZED CONDENSED MILK:

- 1 (14-ounce) can fat-free sweetened condensed milk

1. Preheat oven to 400°.
2. Pour milk into a 9-inch pie plate, and cover with foil. Place pie plate in a shallow roasting pan. Add enough hot water to pan to come halfway up sides of pie plate (about 4 cups). Bake at 400° for 1½ hours, adding water to pan as needed (about 2 cups).
3. Carefully remove pie plate from water. Uncover and stir milk with a whisk until smooth. Milk should be golden brown. Yield: about 1 cup (serving size: 1 tablespoon).

CALORIES 112 (0% from fat); FAT 0g; PROTEIN 3.1g; CARB 24.4g; FIBER 0g; CHOL 5mg; IRON 0mg; SODIUM 41mg; CALC 102mg

MAKE AHEAD

Pebre

This fresh herb sauce is a staple on Chilean tables. It pairs well with *Pastel de Choclo* (recipe on page 168), grilled meats, and is good stirred into pasta or rice.

- 2 cups fresh parsley leaves (about 1 bunch)
- 2 cups fresh cilantro leaves (about 1 bunch)
- ¾ cup chopped onion
- ¼ cup water
- 1 tablespoon fresh lemon juice
- 1 teaspoon hot pepper sauce or crushed red pepper
- ¾ teaspoon salt
- ¼ teaspoon black pepper
- 2 garlic cloves, minced
- 1½ tablespoons extravirgin olive oil

1. Combine first 9 ingredients in a food processor; pulse until minced, scraping sides occasionally. Place herb mixture in a bowl; cover and refrigerate 1 hour. Stir in oil before serving. Yield: 8 servings (serving size: 2 tablespoons).

CALORIES 37 (66% from fat); FAT 2.7g (sat 0.4g, mono 1.9g, poly 0.2g); PROTEIN 0.8g; CARB 3g; FIBER 0.9g; CHOL 0mg; IRON 1.1mg; SODIUM 240mg; CALC 28mg

Potatoes with Spicy Cheese Sauce

- 4 cups thinly sliced onion, separated into rings
- ⅓ cup fresh lemon juice
- 2 pounds small Yukon gold potatoes
- 3 ounces feta cheese
- 3 ounces 2% reduced-fat cottage cheese
- 1 tablespoon hot pepper sauce
- ¼ cup whole milk
- 12 curly leaf lettuce leaves
- 2 hard-cooked large eggs, each cut into 6 wedges

1. Combine onion and juice in a large zip-top plastic bag; seal and marinate in refrigerator 2 hours, turning bag occasionally. Remove onion from bag, reserving marinade.
2. Place potatoes in a saucepan, and cover with water; bring to a boil. Reduce heat, and simmer 25 minutes or until tender; drain. Cool. Peel and cut potatoes in half.
3. Place reserved marinade, cheeses, hot sauce, and milk in a blender; process until smooth.
4. Arrange 2 lettuce leaves on each of 6 salad plates. Top each serving with ⅔ cup onion, ¾ cup potatoes, 2 tablespoons cheese sauce, and 2 egg wedges. Yield: 6 servings.

CALORIES 230 (22% from fat); FAT 5.6g (sat 3.1g, mono 1.5g, poly 0.5g); PROTEIN 10g; CARB 36.3g; FIBER 4.2g; CHOL 86mg; IRON 1.2mg; SODIUM 266mg; CALC 137mg

Grilled Lamb Chops

This may seem like a lot of dried oregano, but Chileans love it. Use dry white wine instead of sherry, if you like.

      3   tablespoons dried oregano
      1   teaspoon salt
      ½   teaspoon freshly ground black
          pepper
      8   (4-ounce) lamb loin chops,
          trimmed
      4   garlic cloves, thinly sliced
      3   tablespoons dry sherry
    Cooking spray
    Lime wedges (optional)

1. Combine first 3 ingredients; sprinkle evenly over lamb. Place lamb in a heavy-duty zip-top plastic bag. Add garlic and sherry; seal bag, turning to coat. Marinate in refrigerator 3 hours, turning occasionally.
2. Prepare grill or broiler.
3. Place lamb on grill rack or broiler pan coated with cooking spray; cook 5 minutes on each side or until desired degree of doneness. Serve with lime wedges, if desired. Yield: 4 servings (serving size: 2 chops).

CALORIES 187 (33% from fat); FAT 6.9g (sat 2.4g, mono 2.7g, poly 0.6g); PROTEIN 24.4g; CARB 3.5g; FIBER 1.5g; CHOL 75mg; IRON 4.1mg; SODIUM 667mg; CALC 73mg

Mussel Salad

For centuries, Chileans have smoked seafood to preserve it. Adding wood chips to the grill gives fresh mussels smoked flavor. Use a mesh rack, such as a vegetable grilling basket, to keep mussels from falling through the grates as they cook. This zesty dish is ideal on an antipasti platter or as a side to roast chicken, pork, or vegetables.

      ½   cup hickory wood chips
      2   pounds mussels, scrubbed and
          debearded
    1½   tablespoons red wine vinegar
      1   teaspoon olive oil
      1   teaspoon Dijon mustard
      3   cups gourmet salad greens
    1⅓   cups chopped peeled tomato
      1   cup marinated artichoke hearts,
          drained and chopped
      2   tablespoons chopped peeled
          avocado
      1   tablespoon chopped fresh cilantro

1. Soak wood chips in water 30 minutes. Drain well.
2. Prepare grill.
3. Place wood chips on hot coals. Place a mesh rack on a grill rack over hot coals. Place mussels on mesh rack; cover and cook 3 minutes or until shells open. Remove from heat, and discard any unopened shells. Cool mussels. Remove meat from shells; discard shells.
4. Combine vinegar, oil, and mustard in a large bowl, stirring with a whisk. Add mussels, greens, and remaining ingredients; toss gently to coat. Yield: 6 servings (serving size: about 1 cup).

CALORIES 163 (29% from fat); FAT 5.3g (sat 0.9g, mono 1.7g, poly 1.2g); PROTEIN 19.1g; CARB 9.7g; FIBER 1.5g; CHOL 42mg; IRON 6.6mg; SODIUM 491mg; CALC 58mg

happy endings

Meringue Cookies

Egg whites and sugar make these cookies light and airy. The extras—nuts, chocolate, dried fruit, and spices—make them stand out.

MAKE AHEAD
Chocolate-Cherry Chunk Meringues

The edges of the meringues are crisp, but the center pieces are slightly soft. Don't chop the chocolate too finely or it will completely melt in the meringue.

      4   large egg whites
      ¼   teaspoon cream of tartar
      ½   cup granulated sugar
      ¾   cup powdered sugar
      1   teaspoon almond extract
      ½   cup dried tart cherries, chopped
      3   ounces unsweetened chocolate,
          chopped

1. Preheat oven to 200°.
2. Cover a large baking sheet with parchment paper. Draw a 14 x 10-inch rectangle on paper. Turn paper over; secure with masking tape.
3. Place egg whites and cream of tartar in a large bowl, and beat with a mixer at medium speed until soft peaks form. Increase speed to high, and gradually add granulated sugar and then powdered sugar, 1 tablespoon at a time, beating until stiff peaks form. Add extract; beat just until blended. Fold in cherries and chocolate. Spread batter onto drawn rectangle using back of a spoon. Score rectangle into 2-inch squares using tip of a sharp knife.
4. Bake at 200° for 2 hours. Turn oven off, and cool meringue in closed oven 1½ hours or until dry. Carefully remove meringue from paper. Break into 2-inch squares. Yield: 35 cookies (serving size: 1 cookie).

CALORIES 42 (30% from fat); FAT 1.4g (sat 0.8g, mono 0.5g, poly 0g); PROTEIN 0.7g; CARB 7.6g; FIBER 0.4g; CHOL 0mg; IRON 0.2mg; SODIUM 7mg; CALC 3mg

Tweed Meringues

Chocolate and pecans give these cookies the nubby appearance of tweed. Before grinding the toasted nuts, make sure they have cooled completely to keep the chocolate from melting.

  2   large egg whites
 ⅛   teaspoon cream of tartar
 ¼   cup granulated sugar
 ¼   cup powdered sugar
 ¼   teaspoon vanilla extract
 ¼   cup pecans, toasted
  2   tablespoons granulated sugar
 ½   ounce unsweetened chocolate, coarsely chopped

1. Preheat oven to 225°.
2. Line a large baking sheet with parchment paper; secure with masking tape.
3. Place egg whites and cream of tartar in a medium bowl; beat with a mixer at medium speed until soft peaks form. Increase speed to high, and gradually add ¼ cup granulated sugar and then powdered sugar, 1 tablespoon at a time, beating until stiff peaks form. Add vanilla; beat just until combined.
4. Place pecans, 2 tablespoons granulated sugar, and chocolate in a food processor; pulse 6 times or until finely ground. Fold chocolate mixture into egg white mixture.
5. Spoon batter into a large zip-top plastic bag. Seal bag; carefully snip off 1 bottom corner of bag. Pipe 30 S shapes on prepared baking sheet.
6. Bake at 225° for 1½ hours. Turn oven off; cool meringues in closed oven 2 hours or until dry. Carefully remove meringues from paper. Yield: 2½ dozen (serving size: 1 cookie).

CALORIES 24 (38% from fat); FAT 1g (sat 0.2g, mono 0.5g, poly 0.2g); PROTEIN 0.4g; CARB 3.8g; FIBER 0.2g; CHOL 0mg; IRON 0.1mg; SODIUM 4mg; CALC 1mg

Coconut Meringues

Unsweetened, shredded coconut usually can be found in the produce section of your grocery store.

  4   large egg whites
 ¼   teaspoon cream of tartar
 ½   cup granulated sugar
 ¾   cup powdered sugar
  1   cup unsweetened shredded coconut, divided

1. Preheat oven to 225°.
2. Cover 2 large baking sheets with parchment paper; secure paper with masking tape.
3. Place egg whites and cream of tartar in a large bowl; beat with a mixer at medium speed until soft peaks form. Increase speed to high, and gradually add granulated sugar and then powdered sugar, 1 tablespoon at a time, beating until stiff peaks form. Gently fold in ¾ cup coconut.
4. Drop 36 mounds onto prepared baking sheets. Sprinkle ¼ cup coconut evenly over meringues.
5. Bake at 225° for 1½ hours. Turn oven off, and cool meringues in closed oven 2 hours or until dry. Carefully remove meringues from paper. Yield: 3 dozen (serving size: 1 cookie).

CALORIES 30 (18% from fat); FAT 0.6g (sat 0.6g, mono 0g, poly 0g); PROTEIN 0.4g; CARB 6g; FIBER 0.1g; CHOL 0mg; IRON 0mg; SODIUM 11mg; CALC 1mg

---

How to Make Perfect Meringues

- Start with chilled eggs since they're easier to separate without breaking the yolk.
- Use the 4-bowl method for the most foolproof way to separate eggs: Crack the egg on a flat surface, and break it in half. Hold your hand over bowl 1 (practice bowl). Pour the egg into your hand, and let the white run through your fingers. Place the egg yolk in bowl 2 (egg yolk bowl). If it was a clean break, transfer the white to bowl 3 (egg white bowl). If a small amount of yolk got into the white, use a cotton-tipped swab to absorb it before placing the white in bowl 3. If the yolk is broken and can't be cleaned up, transfer the broken yolk and white to bowl 4 (mistake bowl). Cover and refrigerate up to 2 days, and use for another purpose that calls for whole eggs. Before you separate another egg over bowl 1, thoroughly clean the bowl, and wipe with a paper towel moistened with vinegar to remove any trace of fat.
- Large eggs are the best for meringues, but refrigerated whites (such as Eggology or Egg Beaters Egg Whites) are also fine.
- Fat, which is found in yolks, is the enemy of light, airy, stiffly beaten whites. Make sure your bowl and beaters are clean, with no traces of fat.
- The egg whites and cream of tartar (to stabilize eggs) are beaten until soft peaks form before adding sugar. To determine peaks, turn off the mixer, and lift the beaters. The egg whites will fall to one side for soft peaks and stand upright for stiff peaks.
- Sugar is added 1 tablespoon at a time to make sure it dissolves completely for a smooth meringue.
- Batter can be piped out of a pastry bag or a zip-top plastic bag with a corner cut out. Or use a spoon to scoop batter, and use your finger to scrape even-sized mounds onto prepared baking sheets.
- Meringues are baked at low temperatures for at least 1 hour to make them crisp. Turn the heat off, and leave the meringues in the closed oven to dry them out. They're done when their surface is dry and they can be removed from the paper without sticking to fingers.
- Store cooled meringues in an airtight container up to 2 weeks.

Double Vanilla Meringues

The expense of the vanilla bean is worth it—the delicate flavor shines through in these cookies, which taste like toasted marshmallows.

 1 vanilla bean, split lengthwise
 4 large egg whites
 1/4 teaspoon cream of tartar
 1/2 cup granulated sugar
 2/3 cup powdered sugar
 1 tablespoon vanilla extract

1. Preheat oven to 225°.
2. Cover 2 large baking sheets with parchment paper, and secure paper with masking tape.
3. Scrape seeds from vanilla bean. Reserve vanilla bean for another use.
4. Place egg whites and cream of tartar in a large bowl; beat with a mixer at medium speed until soft peaks form. Increase speed to high, and gradually add granulated sugar and then powdered sugar, 1 tablespoon at a time, beating until stiff peaks form. Add vanilla seeds and extract; beat just until blended.
5. Spoon batter into a pastry bag fitted with a large star tip. Pipe 60 mounds onto prepared baking sheets.
6. Bake at 225° for 1½ hours. Turn oven off; cool meringues in closed oven 1½ hours or until dry. Carefully remove meringues from paper. Yield: 5 dozen (serving size: 1 cookie).

CALORIES 13 (0% from fat); FAT 0g; PROTEIN 0.2g; CARB 3.1g; FIBER 0g; CHOL 0mg; IRON 0mg; SODIUM 4mg; CALC 0mg

Thumbprint Meringues

Add the jam mixture just before serving to keep the meringues light and crisp.

 2 large egg whites
 1/8 teaspoon cream of tartar
 1/2 cup granulated sugar
 1/4 cup powdered sugar
 1/2 teaspoon vanilla extract
 1/4 cup seedless raspberry jam
 2 teaspoons raspberry liqueur

1. Preheat oven to 225°.
2. Cover 2 large baking sheets with parchment paper, and secure paper with masking tape.
3. Place egg whites and cream of tartar in a medium bowl; beat with a mixer at medium speed until soft peaks form. Increase speed to high, and gradually add granulated sugar and then powdered sugar, 1 tablespoon at a time, beating until stiff peaks form. Add vanilla; beat just until combined.
4. Spoon batter into a large zip-top plastic bag. Seal bag; carefully snip off 1 bottom corner of bag. Pipe 24 mounds onto prepared baking sheets. Moisten thumb or a spoon with water; press thumb or spoon into center of each mound to form an indentation.
5. Bake at 225° for 1½ hours. Turn oven off; cool meringues in closed oven 2 hours or until dry. Carefully remove meringues from paper.
6. Combine jam and liqueur, stirring with a whisk. Place mixture in a small zip-top plastic bag. Seal bag; carefully snip off 1 bottom corner of bag. Pipe about ½ teaspoon jam mixture into indention in each cookie. Serve immediately. Yield: 2 dozen (serving size: 1 cookie).

CALORIES 37 (0% from fat); FAT 0g; PROTEIN 0.3g; CARB 8.4g; FIBER 0g; CHOL 0mg; IRON 0mg; SODIUM 5mg; CALC 0mg

Peanut Butter-Chocolate Meringue Sandwiches

Peanut butter filling is sandwiched between chocolate meringues, creating a flavor reminiscent of chocolate-peanut butter cups.

 1 ounce unsweetened chocolate, coarsely chopped
 1/3 cup powdered sugar
 1/4 cup unsweetened cocoa
 2 large egg whites
 1/8 teaspoon cream of tartar
 1/3 cup granulated sugar
 1/4 cup reduced-fat peanut butter
 2½ tablespoons powdered sugar
 1½ tablespoons fat-free milk

1. Preheat oven to 225°.
2. Place chocolate in a medium microwave-safe bowl; microwave at HIGH 45 seconds or until almost melted, stirring until smooth. Cool completely.
3. Cover a large baking sheet with parchment paper; secure with masking tape. Sift together ⅓ cup powdered sugar and cocoa.
4. Place egg whites and cream of tartar in a medium bowl; beat with a mixer at medium speed until soft peaks form. Increase speed to high, and gradually add granulated sugar and then cocoa mixture, 1 tablespoon at a time, beating until stiff peaks form. Add ½ cup egg white mixture to melted chocolate; beat just until blended. Add chocolate mixture to remaining egg white mixture, and beat just until blended.
5. Drop 30 mounds onto prepared baking sheet.
6. Bake at 225° for 1 hour and 15 minutes. Turn oven off; cool meringues in closed oven 1½ hours or until dry. Carefully remove meringues from paper.
7. Combine peanut butter, 2½ tablespoons powdered sugar, and milk, stirring with a whisk until smooth. Spread about 1 teaspoon of peanut butter mixture onto flat sides of 15 meringues, and top with remaining meringues. Yield: 15 servings (serving size: 1 cookie sandwich).

CALORIES 70 (35% from fat); FAT 2.7g (sat 1g, mono 1.2g, poly 0.5g); PROTEIN 2.2g; CARB 11.2g; FIBER 1g; CHOL 0mg; IRON 0.4mg; SODIUM 32mg; CALC 7mg

Brining with Bruce Aidells

This scientist-turned-chef shows us how to make lean meats tender and juicy with the help of salt.

Here's a promise: The first time you try brining, you'll master the technique, and it will change the whole way you work with lean pork, poultry, and seafood. Brining is simply a matter of soaking meat in a saltwater solution, but it will ensure that you'll never cook another dried-out pork chop or chicken breast again.

Lemon Tarragon-Brined Whole Chicken

This chicken is best when cooked indirectly on a grill, but you can also roast it in an oven. Fresh tarragon has a brighter flavor than dried, but you can use a third the amount of dried if fresh is unavailable. Toss any leftover chicken with tarragon-flavored mayonnaise for a salad.

    7   cups water, divided
    2   tablespoons grated lemon
        rind
    8   tarragon sprigs
    1   cup kosher salt (such as Diamond
        Crystal)
    ½   cup sugar
    2   cups ice cubes
    1   (4½-pound) roasting chicken
    1   tablespoon chopped fresh
        tarragon, divided
    2   teaspoons freshly ground black
        pepper, divided
    Cooking spray
    ¼   cup fresh lemon juice,
        divided

1. Combine 1 cup water, rind, and tarragon sprigs in a small saucepan. Bring to a boil; remove from heat. Pour in a large bowl; cool to room temperature. Add 6 cups water, salt, and sugar, stirring until salt and sugar dissolve. Place salt mixture in a 2-gallon zip-top plastic bag. Add ice and chicken; seal. Refrigerate 3 hours, turning bag occasionally. Remove chicken from bag; discard brine. Pat chicken dry with paper towels.
2. Prepare grill for indirect grilling, heating one side to medium and leaving one side with no heat.
3. Sprinkle cavity of chicken with 1½ teaspoons chopped tarragon and 1 teaspoon pepper. Lightly coat outside of chicken with cooking spray. Rub 1½ teaspoons chopped tarragon and 1 teaspoon pepper evenly over outside of chicken. Place chicken on grill rack coated with cooking spray over unheated side. Close lid; grill 15 minutes. Brush chicken with 2 tablespoons lemon juice. Close lid; grill an additional 30 minutes. Brush with 2 tablespoons lemon juice. Close lid; grill 15 minutes or until thermometer inserted into meaty part of thigh registers 180°.
4. Place chicken on a platter; cover with foil. Let stand 15 minutes. Discard skin. Yield: 5 servings (serving size: about 4 ounces).

CALORIES 246 (31% from fat); FAT 8.4g (sat 2.3g, mono 3.1g, poly 1.9g); PROTEIN 37g; CARB 3.3g; FIBER 0.1g; CHOL 109mg; IRON 1.8mg; SODIUM 1,505mg; CALC 29mg

Honey and Thyme-Brined Turkey Breast

Briefly boiling the thyme and black pepper extracts the flavor and helps infuse the brine. If the turkey starts to brown too fast, shield it with aluminum foil. Serve with mashed red potatoes and roasted baby carrots.

    7   cups water, divided
    3   tablespoons freshly ground black
        pepper, divided
    6   thyme sprigs
    ½   cup kosher salt (such as Diamond
        Crystal)
    ½   cup honey
    ¼   cup packed brown sugar
    2   cups ice cubes
    1   (6-pound) whole bone-in turkey
        breast, skinned
    2   tablespoons olive oil
    1   tablespoon chopped fresh thyme
    Cooking spray
    Thyme sprigs (optional)

1. Combine 1 cup water, 2 tablespoons pepper, and 6 thyme sprigs in a small saucepan. Bring to a boil, and remove from heat. Pour into a large bowl; cool to room temperature. Add 6 cups water, salt, honey, and sugar, stirring until salt and sugar dissolve. Pour salt mixture into a 2-gallon zip-top plastic bag. Add ice and turkey; seal. Refrigerate 24 hours, turning bag occasionally. Remove turkey from bag; discard brine. Pat turkey dry with paper towels.
2. Rub turkey with oil. Combine 1 tablespoon pepper and chopped thyme; rub over turkey.
3. Preheat oven to 400°.
4. Place turkey on a roasting pan coated with cooking spray. Bake at 400° for 1 hour or until thermometer inserted into thickest portion of breast registers 180°. Place turkey on a platter. Cover with foil, and let stand 15 minutes. Garnish with thyme sprigs, if desired. Yield: 12 servings (serving size: about 4 ounces).

CALORIES 207 (26% from fat); FAT 5.9g (sat 1.5g, mono 2.3g, poly 1.2g); PROTEIN 34g; CARB 2.5g; FIBER 0.2g; CHOL 78mg; IRON 1.8mg; SODIUM 359mg; CALC 29mg

New England-Style Pickled Beef

Soaking meat in a salt solution is exactly how old-fashioned corned beef is made. The three-day brining period is a great technique for keeping the brisket moist. Beef brisket or boneless pork shoulder are excellent in this boiled dinner. Garnish with chopped parsley.

    7   cups water, divided
    2   tablespoons black peppercorns
    2   tablespoons pickling spice
    1   tablespoon juniper berries, crushed
    1   tablespoon coriander seeds
    8   bay leaves
    6   thyme sprigs
    4   garlic cloves, crushed
    ¾   cup kosher salt (such as Diamond Crystal)
    ½   cup sugar
    2   cups ice cubes
    1   (4½-pound) beef brisket, trimmed
    1½   cups (2-inch-thick) slices carrot
    1   (2-pound) head green cabbage, cored and quartered
    9   small red potatoes, quartered
    6   small onions, peeled and halved

1. Combine 1 cup water, peppercorns, and next 6 ingredients in a small saucepan; bring to a boil. Reduce heat, and simmer 5 minutes. Remove from heat. Pour into a large bowl; cool to room temperature. Add 6 cups water, salt, and sugar, stirring until salt and sugar dissolve. Pour salt mixture into a 2-gallon zip-top plastic bag. Add ice and brisket; seal. Refrigerate brisket 3 days, turning bag occasionally. Remove brisket from bag, and discard brine. Pat brisket dry with paper towels.

2. Place brisket in a large stockpot; cover with water. Bring to a boil; skim foam from surface. Cover, reduce heat, and simmer 2½ to 3 hours or until brisket is tender. Remove brisket from pan; keep warm. Reserve cooking liquid. Add carrot, cabbage, potatoes, and onions to reserved cooking liquid; bring to a boil. Reduce heat, and simmer 30 minutes or until tender. Yield: 12 servings (serving size: about 3 ounces beef, 3 potato wedges, 1 onion half, and about ½ cup carrot and cabbage).

CALORIES 256 (34% from fat); FAT 9.8g (sat 3.5g, mono 4.4g, poly 0.4g); PROTEIN 29.9g; CARB 11.2g; FIBER 2.6g; CHOL 88mg; IRON 3.2mg; SODIUM 508mg; CALC 42mg

Fennel-Brined Pork Chops

These chops are best made with both fennel seeds and fresh fennel fronds (the flowery tips of fennel). If you can't find fresh fennel, substitute two additional tablespoons of fennel seeds for the fronds. Serve with a mixed green salad.

    3½   cups water, divided
    ½   cup chopped fennel fronds
    1   tablespoon fennel seeds
    ¼   cup kosher salt (such as Diamond Crystal)
    ¼   cup sugar
    2   tablespoons sambuca or other anise-flavored liqueur
    1   cup ice cubes
    4   (4-ounce) boneless center-cut loin pork chops (about ¾ inch thick)
    Cooking spray
    2   teaspoons chopped fresh rosemary
    1   teaspoon freshly ground black pepper
    2   garlic cloves, minced

1. Combine 1 cup water, fennel fronds, and seeds in a small saucepan. Bring to a boil; remove from heat. Pour into a large bowl; cool to room temperature. Add 2½ cups water, salt, sugar, and liqueur, stirring until salt and sugar dissolve. Pour salt mixture into a large zip-top plastic bag. Add ice and pork; seal. Refrigerate 4 hours, turning bag occasionally.

2. Prepare grill to high heat.

3. Remove pork from bag; discard brine. Pat pork dry with paper towels. Coat pork with cooking spray. Combine rosemary, pepper, and garlic; rub evenly over both sides of pork. Place pork on grill rack coated with cooking spray; grill 3 minutes on each side or until done. Let stand 5 minutes before serving. Yield: 4 servings (serving size: 1 chop).

CALORIES 174 (34% from fat); FAT 6.5g (sat 2.4g, mono 2.9g, poly 0.5g); PROTEIN 24.1g; CARB 3g; FIBER 0.3g; CHOL 65mg; IRON 0.9mg; SODIUM 469mg; CALC 34mg

Orange-Brined Pork Loin

Apples aren't the only fruit that taste great with pork. This orange-flavored brine gives a subtle citrus flavor and makes the meat juicy and tender.

3 cups water, divided
1½ tablespoons grated orange rind
4 cups fresh orange juice (about 12 oranges)
½ cup kosher salt (such as Diamond Crystal)
¼ cup packed brown sugar
¼ cup low-sodium soy sauce
2 cups ice cubes
1 (3-pound) boneless pork loin, trimmed
¼ cup orange marmalade
2 tablespoons fresh orange juice
1 tablespoon low-sodium soy sauce
Cooking spray
Orange slices (optional)
Parsley sprigs (optional)

1. Combine 1 cup water and rind in a small saucepan. Bring to a boil; remove from heat. Pour into a large bowl; cool to room temperature. Add 2 cups water, 4 cups juice, salt, sugar, and ¼ cup soy sauce, stirring until salt and sugar dissolve. Pour salt mixture into a 2-gallon zip-top plastic bag. Add ice and pork; seal. Refrigerate 24 hours, turning bag occasionally.
2. Preheat oven to 450°.
3. Combine marmalade, 2 tablespoons juice, and 1 tablespoon soy sauce in a small saucepan. Bring to a boil; cook 10 seconds or until marmalade melts. Remove from heat.
4. Remove pork from bag, and discard brine. Pat pork dry with paper towels. Place pork on a roasting pan coated with cooking spray. Bake at 450° for 15 minutes. Reduce oven temperature to 325° (do not remove pork from oven); bake an additional 45 minutes. Brush marmalade mixture evenly over pork; bake an additional 5 minutes or until thermometer inserted into thickest portion of pork registers 155° (slightly pink). Place pork on a platter. Cover with foil; let stand 15 minutes. Garnish with orange slices and parsley sprigs, if desired. Yield: 10 servings (serving size: about 3 ounces).

CALORIES 191 (28% from fat); FAT 6g (sat 2.1g, mono 2.7g, poly 0.7g); PROTEIN 25g; CARB 7.8g; FIBER 0.1g; CHOL 62mg; IRON 1mg; SODIUM 472mg; CALC 30mg

STAFF FAVORITE
Smoked Salmon
(pictured on page 183)

This recipe gives you moist smoked salmon—not the drier, thinly sliced type called lox that you purchase at a deli. Start soaking the wood chips while the salmon brines.

3½ cups water
½ cup kosher salt (such as Diamond Crystal)
¼ cup sugar
2 tablespoons dried dill
2 tablespoons low-sodium soy sauce
1 cup ice cubes
1 (1½-pound) salmon fillet (about 1 inch thick)
4 cups hickory wood chips
Cooking spray
Cracked black pepper (optional)
Dill sprigs (optional)

1. Combine first 5 ingredients in a large bowl; stir until salt and sugar dissolve. Pour salt mixture into a large zip-top plastic bag. Add ice and salmon; seal. Refrigerate 2 hours, turning bag occasionally.
2. Soak wood chips in water 1 hour. Drain well.
3. Prepare grill for indirect grilling, heating one side to medium and leaving one side with no heat.
4. Place half of wood chips on hot coals. Remove salmon from bag; discard brine. Pat salmon dry with paper towels. Place salmon on grill rack coated with cooking spray over unheated side. Close lid; grill 10 minutes. Place remaining wood chips on hot coals; close lid, and grill 15 minutes or until fish flakes easily when tested with a fork. Sprinkle with black pepper and garnish with dill sprigs, if desired. Yield: 4 servings (serving size: about 4 ounces salmon).

CALORIES 279 (42% from fat); FAT 13.1g (sat 3.1g, mono 5.7g, poly 3.2g); PROTEIN 36.3g; CARB 1.7g; FIBER 0g; CHOL 87mg; IRON 0.7mg; SODIUM 958mg; CALC 28mg

Five-Spice Chicken Breasts with Hoisin Glaze

Chicken breasts with the skin on aren't usually boneless, so you may need to special order them from your butcher or debone them at home. They don't dry out as easily as the skinless, boneless variety.

3½ cups water
⅓ cup kosher salt (such as Diamond Crystal)
3 tablespoons dark brown sugar
2 tablespoons low-sodium soy sauce
2 tablespoons five-spice powder
4 (6-ounce) boneless chicken breast halves
1 cup ice
2 tablespoons hoisin sauce
2 teaspoons dark sesame oil
2 teaspoons minced fresh ginger
1½ teaspoons dark brown sugar
1½ teaspoons low-sodium soy sauce
¼ teaspoon five-spice powder
Cooking spray

1. Combine first 4 ingredients in a large bowl, stirring until salt and sugar dissolve. Stir in 2 tablespoons five-spice powder. Pour salt mixture into a large zip-top plastic bag. Rinse chicken with cold water. Add chicken and ice to bag; seal. Refrigerate 2 hours, turning bag occasionally. Remove chicken from bag; discard brine. Pat chicken dry with paper towels.
2. Combine hoisin sauce and next 5 ingredients.
3. Prepare grill for indirect grilling, heating one side to medium and leaving one side with no heat.
4. Place chicken, skin side down, on grill rack coated with cooking spray over medium heat side. Close lid, and grill chicken 8 minutes on each side, brushing occasionally with hoisin sauce mixture. Place chicken, skin side up, on unheated side; brush with hoisin sauce mixture. Grill an additional 5 minutes or until done. Discard skin; serve immediately. Yield: 4 servings (serving size: 1 chicken breast half).

CALORIES 241 (18% from fat); FAT 4.7g (sat 0.9g, mono 1.5g, poly 1.6g); PROTEIN 39.8g; CARB 7.4g; FIBER 0.3g; CHOL 99mg; IRON 1.8mg; SODIUM 909mg; CALC 35mg

Shrimp Sautéed with Fresh Tomatoes, Wine, and Basil

Don't overcook the shrimp, or they'll be tough. Although shrimp live in salt water, brining makes them firmer and juicier.

3½ cups water
½ cup kosher salt (such as Diamond Crystal)
1 cup ice cubes
1¼ pounds large shrimp
1½ tablespoons olive oil
¼ cup thinly sliced green onions
3 garlic cloves, thinly sliced
½ cup dry white wine
1 cup coarsely chopped seeded peeled tomato
¼ teaspoon kosher salt
¼ teaspoon freshly ground black pepper
3 cups hot cooked vermicelli (about 6 ounces uncooked pasta)
¼ cup chopped fresh basil

1. Combine water and ½ cup salt in a large bowl, stirring until salt dissolves. Pour salt mixture into a large zip-top plastic bag. Add ice and shrimp; seal. Refrigerate 30 minutes. Remove shrimp from bag; discard brine. Peel shrimp; pat shrimp dry with paper towels.
2. Heat oil in a large nonstick skillet over medium-high heat. Add onions and garlic; sauté 15 seconds. Add shrimp, and sauté 1 minute. Add wine; cook 1 minute, scraping pan to loosen browned bits. Add tomato, ¼ teaspoon salt, and pepper; cook 3 minutes or until shrimp are done. Remove from heat; serve over pasta. Sprinkle with basil. Yield: 4 servings (serving size: ⅔ cup shrimp mixture and ¾ cup pasta).

CALORIES 380 (20% from fat); FAT 8.4g (sat 1.3g, mono 4.2g, poly 1.7g); PROTEIN 34.5g; CARB 35g; FIBER 2.7g; CHOL 216mg; IRON 5.4mg; SODIUM 1,137mg; CALC 100mg

Coffee and Molasses-Brined Pork Chops

Coffee adds a background flavor that helps bring out the sweet yet bitter undertone of the molasses. This brine is also excellent with chicken thighs and drumsticks, and pork or beef ribs. Use any type of hardwood chips if hickory isn't available.

2 cups water
1½ cups chilled strong brewed coffee
¼ cup kosher salt (such as Diamond Crystal)
3 tablespoons dark brown sugar
2 tablespoons molasses
1 tablespoon Worcestershire sauce
1 cup ice cubes
4 (6-ounce) bone-in center-cut pork chops (about ½ inch thick)
1 cup hickory wood chips
⅛ teaspoon kosher salt
8 teaspoons Pepper-Garlic Spice Rub
Cooking spray

1. Combine first 6 ingredients in a large bowl, stirring until salt and sugar dissolve. Pour salt mixture into a large zip-top plastic bag. Add ice and pork; seal. Refrigerate 3 hours, turning bag occasionally.
2. Soak wood chips in water 1 hour. Drain well.
3. Prepare grill for indirect grilling, heating one side to medium-high and leaving one side with no heat.
4. Place wood chips on hot coals. Remove pork from bag; discard brine. Pat pork dry with paper towels. Sprinkle ⅛ teaspoon salt over pork. Rub Pepper-Garlic Spice Rub evenly over both sides of pork. Place pork on grill rack coated with cooking spray over medium-high heat; grill 2 minutes on each side. Place pork on unheated side of grill; grill 3 minutes on each side or until done. Remove from heat. Let stand 5 minutes before serving. Yield: 4 servings (serving size: 1 chop).

CALORIES 254 (31% from fat); FAT 8.7g (sat 3g, mono 3.9g, poly 0.9g); PROTEIN 37.7g; CARB 3.8g; FIBER 3.1g; CHOL 107mg; IRON 1.8mg; SODIUM 584mg; CALC 50mg

PEPPER-GARLIC SPICE RUB:

Store the remaining spice rub in the refrigerator for up to 1 week, and use it on beef or chicken.

2 tablespoons freshly ground black pepper
1 tablespoon Hungarian sweet paprika
1 tablespoon chili powder
1 tablespoon garlic powder
1 tablespoon dark brown sugar
2 teaspoons ground cumin
2 teaspoons chopped fresh sage
1½ teaspoons dry mustard
1 teaspoon ground coriander
1 teaspoon ground red pepper

1. Combine all ingredients. Yield: about ½ cup (serving size: 1 teaspoon).

CALORIES 8 (23% from fat); FAT 0.2g (sat 0g, mono 0g, poly 0.1g); PROTEIN 0.3g; CARB 1.6g; FIBER 0.5g; CHOL 0mg; IRON 0.3mg; SODIUM 4mg; CALC 7mg

Brining vs. Marinating

Technically, a brine is a type of marinade. But marinades principally impart *flavor* to the surface of the meat, while brines penetrate all the way to the center of the meat to improve *texture*.

When it comes to tenderizing moderately tender cuts of meat and poultry, brines are probably more effective than acidic marinades because the brine penetrates the muscle fibers, causing them to swell and soften.

We could find no conclusive answer for how much sodium is absorbed from the brine. Estimates ranged from 10 to 15 percent, so we split the difference and calculated 12.5 percent sodium absorption.

Spanish-Style Brined Pork Tenderloin

Sherry vinegar and paprika give this pork a traditional Spanish flair. Adding vinegar at the end brightens the flavors of the dish.

    3½ cups water
    ¼   cup kosher salt (such as Diamond
        Crystal)
    ¼   cup sugar
    ¼   cup sherry vinegar
    1   cup ice cubes
    1   (1½-pound) pork tenderloin,
        trimmed
    2   tablespoons paprika
    2   teaspoons sugar
    1   teaspoon freshly ground black
        pepper
    1   teaspoon chopped fresh sage
    1   teaspoon chopped fresh thyme
    2   garlic cloves, minced
    2   teaspoons olive oil
    Cooking spray
    2   teaspoons sherry vinegar

1. Combine first 4 ingredients in a large bowl, stirring until salt and sugar dissolve. Pour salt mixture into a 2-gallon zip-top plastic bag. Add ice and pork; seal. Refrigerate 3 hours, turning bag occasionally.
2. Combine paprika and next 5 ingredients.
3. Prepare grill for indirect grilling, heating one side to medium-high and leaving one side with no heat.
4. Remove pork from bag, and discard brine. Pat pork dry with paper towels. Brush oil evenly over pork; rub with paprika mixture. Place pork on grill rack coated with cooking spray over medium-high heat; grill pork 6 minutes, browning on all sides. Place pork on grill rack over unheated side. Close lid, and grill an additional 20 minutes or until thermometer inserted into thickest portion of pork registers 155° (slightly pink), turning pork occasionally. Place pork on a platter. Cover with foil, and let stand 5 minutes. Uncover and drizzle with 2 teaspoons vinegar. Yield: 6 servings (serving size: about 3 ounces pork).

CALORIES 169 (30% from fat); FAT 5.7g (sat 1.6g, mono 2.9g, poly 0.7g); PROTEIN 24.2g; CARB 4.5g; FIBER 0.6g; CHOL 74mg; IRON 2.1mg; SODIUM 343mg; CALC 18mg

---

lighten up

Strata Makeover

Start the day right with this brunch casserole. It won't weigh you down.

After enjoying Goat Cheese, Artichoke, and Smoked Ham Strata at a first communion brunch hosted by her sister, Carolyn Brown of Golf, Illinois, considered it a must-have recipe. It appeared to be simple enough to assemble and perfect to make ahead. But when she received the recipe, she was outdone. The recipe certainly had nutritional shock value—more than half of the ingredients were high in fat.

When lightening a recipe that has "cheese" in its title, we aim to keep as much of the namesake as possible. So, we first eliminated oil and used egg substitute and 1% low-fat milk to bind the bread instead of whole milk, heavy cream, and whole eggs. Only then did we work with the cheese. We used half the original amount of fontina and a third of the Parmesan. We also reduced the amount of goat cheese by a third and blended it with the milk mixture to spread the flavor throughout. The final fat savings came with the switch from marinated artichoke hearts to water-packed. By omitting the added salt and using reduced-sodium ham, we decreased the sodium per serving by about 1,000 milligrams.

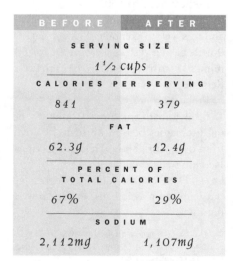

BEFORE	AFTER
SERVING SIZE	
1½ cups	
CALORIES PER SERVING	
841	379
FAT	
62.3g	12.4g
PERCENT OF TOTAL CALORIES	
67%	29%
SODIUM	
2,112mg	1,107mg

Goat Cheese, Artichoke, and Smoked Ham Strata

To make ahead, assemble the strata, cover, and refrigerate overnight. Let stand at room temperature while the oven preheats. Bake, uncovered, as directed. Although sourdough has a nice subtle tanginess, French bread works, too.

    3¼ cups 1% low-fat milk, divided
    1   (8-ounce) carton egg substitute
    1   (4-ounce) package goat cheese
    ¾   teaspoon freshly ground black
        pepper
    ½   teaspoon chopped fresh thyme
    ⅛   teaspoon ground nutmeg
    2   garlic cloves, minced
    10 (1½-ounce) slices sourdough
        bread, cut into ½-inch cubes
    Cooking spray
    ½   cup (2 ounces) grated fresh
        Parmesan cheese
    8   ounces 33%-less-sodium smoked
        ham, coarsely chopped
    2   (14-ounce) cans artichoke hearts,
        drained, rinsed, and coarsely
        chopped
    ½   cup (2 ounces) shredded fontina
        cheese

1. Preheat oven to 350°.
2. Place 1 cup milk, egg substitute, and goat cheese in a blender; process until smooth. Combine goat cheese mixture, 2¼ cups milk, pepper, thyme, nutmeg, and garlic in a large bowl, stirring with a whisk. Add bread cubes; stir gently to combine. Let stand 10 minutes.
3. Place half of bread mixture in a 13 x 9-inch baking dish coated with cooking spray. Arrange Parmesan cheese, ham, and artichoke hearts evenly over bread mixture. Top with remaining bread mixture, and sprinkle evenly with fontina cheese.
4. Bake strata at 350° for 40 minutes or until edges are bubbly. Let stand 15 minutes. Yield: 8 servings (serving size: about 1½ cups).

CALORIES 379 (29% from fat); FAT 12.4g (sat 6.9g, mono 3.8g, poly 0.8g); PROTEIN 25.2g; CARB 40.2g; FIBER 2.7g; CHOL 43mg; IRON 3.8mg; SODIUM 1,107mg; CALC 331mg

Celebration of Heritage

Old World habits foster healthy hearts and wonderful Italian food.

QUICK & EASY
Kale with Garlic and Hot Red Pepper

(pictured on page 181)

Anna Marie Ruggiero, author of the *Roseto Cuisine Cookbook*, prepares robust greens in this simple Italian manner. Washed, chopped, bagged kale makes the side dish as easy as it is tasty. Serve with Roast Pork Porchetta-Style (recipe on page 179).

- 2 cups water
- 1 (1-pound) bag chopped kale
- 2 teaspoons olive oil
- 3 garlic cloves, minced
- ½ teaspoon salt
- ¼ teaspoon freshly ground black pepper
- ¼ teaspoon crushed red pepper

1. Bring 2 cups water to a boil in a large Dutch oven. Add kale; cover and cook 2 minutes or until bright green and wilted. Drain kale in a colander, pressing until barely moist.
2. Place pan over low heat. Add oil and garlic; cook 4 minutes or until garlic is just beginning to brown, stirring occasionally. Stir in kale, salt, black pepper, and red pepper. Increase heat to medium-high, and cook 3 minutes or until tender, stirring constantly. Yield: 6 servings (serving size: ⅔ cup).

CALORIES 54 (35% from fat); FAT 2.1g (sat 0.3g, mono 1.2g, poly 0.4g); PROTEIN 2.6g; CARB 8.2g; FIBER 1.6g; CHOL 0mg; IRON 1.4mg; SODIUM 229mg; CALC 107mg

STAFF FAVORITE
Tomatoes Roasted with Rosemary and Lemon

Proof that simple foods are often best, this colorful multipurpose combination of tomatoes, herbs, and lemon smells almost as good as it tastes. To serve over pasta, cook 12 ounces dried pasta; drain and return pasta to pan. Stir in 3 cups of the roasted tomatoes; cook over low heat until liquid thickens. Serve with grated Parmesan cheese.

- ¼ cup chopped fresh flat-leaf parsley
- 1 tablespoon chopped fresh rosemary
- 1 tablespoon extravirgin olive oil
- 2 teaspoons grated lemon rind
- ½ teaspoon salt
- ½ teaspoon freshly ground black pepper
- 4 pounds plum tomatoes, quartered lengthwise
- 3 garlic cloves, minced

1. Preheat oven to 400°.
2. Place all ingredients in a large bowl, and toss well to combine. Place in a 13 x 9-inch baking dish. Bake at 400° for 30 minutes, stirring every 10 minutes. Remove from oven.
3. Preheat broiler.
4. Broil tomato mixture 10 minutes or until tomatoes begin to brown. Remove from oven; stir gently. Yield: 10 servings (serving size: ½ cup).
NOTE: Place chilled tomatoes in heavy-duty zip-top plastic bags; freeze up to 3 months.

CALORIES 53 (34% from fat); FAT 2g (sat 0.3g, mono 1.1g, poly 0.4g); PROTEIN 1.7g; CARB 9g; FIBER 2.2g; CHOL 0mg; IRON 1mg; SODIUM 134mg; CALC 15mg

Farmers' Market Menu
serves 8

Use any summer squash or pepper for the stuffed vegetables; your favorite field pea variety, such as lady peas, pink-eyed peas, or purple-hull peas; and if you can find wax beans or rattlesnake beans, use them in place of green beans.

Italian Stuffed Summer Vegetables

Field peas with green beans*

Grilled flank steak

*Cook 1 cup chopped onion and 3 chopped bacon slices in a large saucepan over medium heat 4 minutes. Add 4 cups fresh field peas, 2 cups (1-inch) cut green beans, 2 cups water, and 1 (14-ounce) can fat-free, less sodium chicken broth. Bring to a boil; reduce heat, and simmer 30 minutes or until tender.

Italian Stuffed Summer Vegetables

A variety of vegetables makes for a pretty presentation, but this can be made with all bell peppers or squash. If you use only bell peppers, which have no interior flesh, add equal amounts of additional breadcrumbs and tomatoes until you get enough filling. Using soft breadcrumbs adds to the melt-in-your-mouth texture of the tender vegetables. Because the vegetables are covered while baking, moisture stays in, resulting in tender and delicate flesh.

- 1 large red bell pepper, halved lengthwise
- 2 large yellow squash, halved lengthwise (about 1 pound)
- 1 large zucchini, halved lengthwise (about ½ pound)
- Cooking spray
- 3 ounces Italian bread
- 2 garlic cloves, minced
- 1½ cups chopped peeled plum tomato
- ½ cup (2 ounces) finely shredded Parmesan cheese, divided
- ¼ cup chopped fresh parsley
- ½ teaspoon freshly ground black pepper
- ¼ teaspoon salt

1. Preheat oven to 375°.
2. Discard seeds and membranes from bell pepper. Carefully scoop out squash and zucchini pulp, leaving shells intact. Finely chop pulp; set aside. Place bell pepper halves, squash shells, and zucchini shells, cut sides up, in a 13 x 9-inch baking pan coated with cooking spray. Coat shells with cooking spray.
3. Place bread in a food processor; pulse 10 times or until crumbs measure 1½ cups. Heat a large nonstick skillet over medium heat. Coat pan with cooking spray. Add chopped pulp and garlic; cook 4 minutes or until moisture evaporates, stirring frequently. Add tomato; cook 2 minutes or until tomato begins to soften, stirring frequently. Remove from heat. Stir in breadcrumbs, ¼ cup cheese, parsley, black pepper, and salt. Divide mixture evenly among prepared bell pepper halves, squash shells, and zucchini shells; sprinkle evenly with ¼ cup cheese. Cover pan with foil, and bake at 375° for 40 minutes or until shells are tender.
4. Preheat broiler.
5. Remove foil; broil 4 minutes or until cheese is lightly browned. Yield: 8 servings (serving size: 1 stuffed shell).

CALORIES 80 (23% from fat); FAT 2g (sat 1.1g, mono 0.6g, poly 0.3g); PROTEIN 4.5g; CARB 10.9g; FIBER 2.3g; CHOL 4mg; IRON 0.9mg; SODIUM 242mg; CALC 90mg

MAKE AHEAD
Pickled Hot Peppers
(pictured on page 181)

These peppers are full of flavor and fire. The recipe can easily be doubled.

  1 cup sliced seeded Hungarian wax chiles (about 5 ounces)
  ¾ cup white vinegar
  ⅛ teaspoon kosher salt
  ⅛ teaspoon sugar

1. Combine all ingredients in a clean, hot jar. Cover jar with metal lid; screw on band. Refrigerate overnight. Yield: 1 cup (serving size: 1 tablespoon).
NOTE: Store peppers in refrigerator up to 3 weeks.

CALORIES 3 (0% from fat); FAT 0g; PROTEIN 0.1g; CARB 0.6g; FIBER 0g; CHOL 0mg; IRON 0.1mg; SODIUM 16mg; CALC 2mg

MAKE AHEAD
Beet and Red Onion Salad with Ricotta-Provolone Topping

Inspired by a recipe in Anna Marie Ruggiero's *The Roseto Cuisine Cookbook*, this version has less oil. To avoid ruby-red hands, peel beets under running water. Prepare and chill the salad a day or two ahead to allow the flavors to meld. Let stand at room temperature for 15 minutes; prepare cheese mixture and chop basil right before serving.

 2½ pounds small beets
  2 tablespoons red wine vinegar
  2 teaspoons extravirgin olive oil
  ½ teaspoon salt
  ¼ teaspoon freshly ground black pepper
 1½ cups thinly sliced red onion
  ½ serrano chile, seeded and thinly sliced
  ½ cup part-skim ricotta cheese
  ¼ cup (1 ounce) finely shredded sharp provolone cheese
  2 teaspoons hot water
  ⅓ cup thinly sliced fresh basil

1. Leave root and 1 inch of stems on beets, and scrub with a brush. Pierce each beet 2 times with a sharp knife. Place beets in a large heavy-duty zip-top plastic bag, and seal halfway. Microwave at HIGH 20 minutes or until tender, rotating bag every 5 minutes. Remove bag from microwave; cool to room temperature. Remove beets from bag; reserve liquid in bag. Peel beets, and cut into ¼-inch-thick slices.
2. Combine reserved liquid, vinegar, oil, salt, and pepper in a large bowl, stirring with a whisk. Add beets, onion, and serrano; toss gently to coat.
3. Combine ricotta, provolone, and hot water, stirring well. Sprinkle salad with basil; top with cheese mixture. Yield: 6 servings (serving size: 1 cup salad, about 1 tablespoon basil, and about 1 tablespoon cheese mixture).

CALORIES 159 (29% from fat); FAT 5.1g (sat 2.1g, mono 1.7g, poly 0.3g); PROTEIN 7.2g; CARB 23.2g; FIBER 6.2g; CHOL 11mg; IRON 1.9mg; SODIUM 424mg; CALC 135mg

Roast Pork Porchetta-Style
(pictured on page 181)

Porchetta (por-KETT-a), a roast suckling pig seasoned with rosemary and garlic, is served at many Italian gatherings in the Roseto area. It's sliced, heaped on buns, and moistened with tasty pan juices. Home cooks may be challenged to go "whole hog" as the Italian festival chefs do, so this recipe calls for a more manageable pork loin. Use fennel or rosemary in this family-style roast.

  2 tablespoons crushed fennel seeds
  1 teaspoon salt
  ½ teaspoon freshly ground black pepper
  5 garlic cloves, minced
  1 (3½-pound) boneless pork loin roast, trimmed
Cooking spray
  1 cup dry white wine

1. Preheat oven to 350°.
2. Combine first 4 ingredients. Make 12 (1½-inch) slits along 1 side of roast, and stuff slits with some of fennel mixture. Place roast, slit side down, on a shallow roasting pan coated with cooking spray. Rub any remaining fennel mixture over top of roast.
3. Bake at 350° for 1 hour and 10 minutes or until thermometer registers 155° (slightly pink). Transfer roast to a serving platter. Add wine to pan, scraping pan to loosen browned bits. Pour wine mixture into a saucepan. Bring to a boil over medium-high heat. Reduce heat, and simmer until reduced to ⅔ cup (about 8 minutes). Remove from heat. Pour accumulated juices from serving platter into wine mixture. Serve wine mixture with pork. Yield: 10 servings (serving size: about 4 ounces pork and about 1 tablespoon wine mixture).

CALORIES 250 (33% from fat); FAT 9.2g (sat 3.1g, mono 4.2g, poly 1g); PROTEIN 34.4g; CARB 1.5g; FIBER 0.5g; CHOL 94mg; IRON 1.7mg; SODIUM 318mg; CALC 47mg

Oven Fries with Crisp Sage Leaves

As beautiful to look at as they are great to eat, these golden slices of potato are scented and subtly flavored with crisp cooked sage. They're an incredible snack or a perfect savory side to any meal, from chicken to filet mignon. You can double this recipe and use two baking sheets. For even browning, rotate the baking sheets halfway through the first 40 minutes of baking.

  2 small baking potatoes (about
       1 pound)
  1 tablespoon extravirgin olive oil
  ½ teaspoon kosher salt
  12 sage leaves

1. Preheat oven to 400°.
2. Cut each potato lengthwise into 6 equal slices. Place potato slices in a large bowl, and drizzle with oil. Sprinkle with salt; toss well to coat. Remove potato slices from bowl. Reserve remaining oil and salt in bowl, and set aside. Arrange potato slices in a single layer on a baking sheet.
3. Bake at 400° for 40 minutes or until golden brown on bottom. Remove potato slices from oven (leave oven at 400°).
4. Add sage leaves to reserved oil mixture in bowl. Gently rub sage leaves along bottom of bowl, coating both sides. Lift 1 potato slice from baking sheet with a thin spatula. Lay 1 sage leaf on baking sheet, and cover with potato slice, browned side down. Repeat with remaining potato slices and sage leaves.
5. Bake at 400° for 10 minutes. Remove from heat. Using a thin spatula, carefully turn potato slices over with leaves on top. Bake at 400° for an additional 10 minutes or until bottoms begin to brown. Serve immediately. Yield: 3 servings (serving size: 4 potato slices).

CALORIES 205 (21% from fat); FAT 4.7g (sat 0.7g, mono 3.3g, poly 0.4g); PROTEIN 3.5g; CARB 38.2g; FIBER 3.6g; CHOL 0mg; IRON 2.1mg; SODIUM 326mg; CALC 15mg

Peaches Chilled in Red Wine

Use a fruity bottle of Dolcetto or Valpolicella for this dessert. Serve with a dollop of ricotta sweetened with powdered sugar and vanilla extract.

  2 cups thickly sliced peeled ripe
       peaches (about 1¼ pounds)
  ¾ cup fruity Italian red wine
  1½ teaspoons sugar
  Mint sprigs (optional)

1. Combine peaches, wine, and sugar in a bowl, stirring gently. Cover and chill 2 hours, stirring occasionally. Spoon ⅓ cup peach mixture into each of 6 small bowls. Garnish with mint sprigs, if desired. Yield: 6 servings.

CALORIES 49 (2% from fat); FAT 0.1g (sat 0g, mono 0g, poly 0.1g); PROTEIN 0.5g; CARB 7.7g; FIBER 1.1g; CHOL 0mg; IRON 0.2mg; SODIUM 2mg; CALC 5mg

season's best

Fresh Cherry Cobbler

Succulent cherries from the Pacific Northwest are available through the summer.

So get them while the getting is good. Fresh cherries are crisp and explode with rich, sweet flavor, which is the essence of our Fresh Cherry Cobbler. The secret to having a cobbler with a juicy filling and a flaky, crisp crust is an easy, old-fashioned method: Bake the crust separately, and then gently slide it onto the hot, baked cherries. The contrast between the luscious cherries and the sugar-dusted crust is as easy to savor as cherry season itself.

Fresh Cherry Cobbler

  ½ (15-ounce) package refrigerated
       pie dough (such as Pillsbury)
  Cooking spray
  1 large egg white, lightly beaten
  1 tablespoon sugar
  4 cups pitted fresh cherries (about
       1¾ pounds)
  1 cup sugar
  3 tablespoons uncooked
       quick-cooking tapioca
  1 tablespoon fresh lemon juice
  ⅛ teaspoon salt
  2 tablespoons chilled butter, cut
       into small pieces

1. Preheat oven to 375°.
2. Cut dough into 8 (9 x 1-inch) strips. Arrange dough strips in a lattice design on a baking sheet coated with cooking spray. Brush dough with egg white, and sprinkle evenly with 1 tablespoon sugar. Bake at 375° for 15 minutes or until crust is golden brown. Cool on pan, on a wire rack, 10 minutes. Carefully lift crust using 2 spatulas; cool completely on a wire rack.
3. Combine cherries, 1 cup sugar, tapioca, juice, and salt. Let stand 15 minutes. Spoon cherry mixture into an 8-inch baking dish coated with cooking spray. Top with butter. Bake at 375° for 40 minutes or until hot and bubbly. Place crust on top of cherry mixture. Yield: 8 servings.

CALORIES 312 (30% from fat); FAT 10.4g (sat 4.9g, mono 1g, poly 0.3g); PROTEIN 2.3g; CARB 54g; FIBER 1.7g; CHOL 13mg; IRON 0.3mg; SODIUM 171mg; CALC 12mg

Kale with Garlic and Hot Red Pepper,
page 178, Roast Pork Porchetta-Style,
page 179, and Pickled Hot Peppers,
page 179

Carrots with Paprika and Capers,
page 218

Brunch Parfaits, page 190

White Bean and Roasted Chicken Salad,
page 211

Smoked Salmon, page 175

Grilled Chicken and Roasted Red Pepper Sandwiches with
Fontina Cheese, facing page

Great Grilled Sandwiches

Crusty bread on the outside, gooey cheese and delicious fillings on the inside. No wonder the world loves them.

From Italy to Cuba, grilled sandwiches are popular portable lunches and light dinners. But the ingredients needn't be exotic to yield delicious results, as the following recipes prove.

Grilled Chicken and Roasted Red Pepper Sandwiches with Fontina Cheese

(pictured on facing page)

A garlic-herb marinade gives the chicken a flavorful jump start. You can serve an entire quarter or cut each quarter into two wedges. Serve with vegetable chips.

- 1 pound skinless, boneless chicken breast
- 1 tablespoon fresh lemon juice
- 1 tablespoon Dijon mustard
- 2 teaspoons extravirgin olive oil
- ¼ teaspoon dried marjoram
- ¼ teaspoon dried thyme
- 1 garlic clove, minced and divided
- Cooking spray
- 1 cup vertically sliced onion
- 1 teaspoon sugar
- ¾ teaspoon fennel seeds, crushed
- ¼ teaspoon crushed red pepper
- ¼ teaspoon salt
- 4 garlic cloves, minced
- 1 (7-ounce) bottle roasted red bell peppers, drained and sliced
- 1 tablespoon red wine vinegar
- ⅛ teaspoon freshly ground black pepper
- 1 (12-ounce) loaf rosemary focaccia, cut in half horizontally
- 4 teaspoons low-fat mayonnaise
- 3 ounces fontina cheese, thinly sliced

1. Place chicken between 2 sheets of heavy-duty plastic wrap, and pound to ¾-inch thickness using a meat mallet or rolling pin.
2. Combine juice, next 5 ingredients, and chicken in a large zip-top plastic bag; seal. Marinate in refrigerator 2 hours, turning occasionally.
3. Heat a large nonstick skillet over medium-high heat. Coat pan with cooking spray. Add onion and next 5 ingredients, and sauté 1 minute. Add roasted bell peppers; cook 5 minutes or until onions are tender, stirring frequently. Stir in vinegar and black pepper.
4. Prepare grill to medium-high heat.
5. Remove chicken from bag; discard marinade. Place chicken on grill rack coated with cooking spray; grill 5 minutes on each side or until done. Cool slightly; cut chicken into slices.
6. Spread cut sides of bread evenly with mayonnaise. Arrange cheese on bottom half of bread. Arrange chicken and pepper mixture over cheese. Top with top half of bread; press lightly.
7. Place stuffed loaf on grill rack; grill 3 minutes on each side or until cheese melts. Cut into quarters. Yield: 4 servings (serving size: 1 sandwich quarter).

CALORIES 462 (24% from fat); FAT 12.2g (sat 4.7g, mono 3.7g, poly 1.7g); PROTEIN 39.5g; CARB 51.2g; FIBER 5.6g; CHOL 90mg; IRON 3mg; SODIUM 981mg; CALC 199mg

Pressed Cubano with Bacon

Garlic oil gives these sandwiches a crisp, flavorful crust. Hawaiian rolls provide a slightly sweet contrast to the salty ham, pickles, and mustard. To make this easy supper even quicker to prepare, use pre-cooked bacon. Serve with banana peppers.

- 1 teaspoon extravirgin olive oil
- 1 garlic clove, minced
- 4 (3-ounce) Hawaiian rolls, cut in half horizontally
- 2 tablespoons yellow mustard
- 8 (½-ounce) slices reduced-fat Swiss cheese, divided
- 4 bacon slices, cooked and halved
- 12 dill pickle slices
- 2 teaspoons minced fresh cilantro
- 6 ounces thinly sliced 33%-less-sodium ham
- 2 ounces thinly sliced deli roasted turkey breast

1. Combine oil and garlic.
2. Spread cut sides of rolls evenly with mustard. Place 1 cheese slice, 2 bacon halves, 3 pickle slices, and ½ teaspoon cilantro on bottom half of each roll. Divide ham and turkey evenly among bottom halves of rolls; top each serving with 1 cheese slice and top half of roll. Brush garlic oil evenly over outside of rolls.
3. Heat a large nonstick skillet over medium heat. Add 2 sandwiches to pan. Place a cast-iron or heavy skillet on top of sandwiches, and press gently to flatten. Cook 3 minutes on each side or until cheese melts and bread is toasted (leave cast-iron skillet on sandwiches while they cook). Repeat with remaining sandwiches. Yield: 4 servings (serving size: 1 sandwich).

CALORIES 432 (30% from fat); FAT 14.5g (sat 6.3g, mono 4.1g, poly 1.2g); PROTEIN 27.1g; CARB 47.6g; FIBER 2.8g; CHOL 49mg; IRON 3.1mg; SODIUM 1,053mg; CALC 292mg

When you cook a sandwich, the bread becomes wonderfully crunchy, the cheese oozes, and the fillings marry in a way that makes them simply irresistible.

Grilled Goat Cheese Sandwiches with Fig and Honey

These are equally good for breakfast or dinner. Mixing honey with the goat cheese makes the cheese easier to spread over the cinnamon-raisin bread.

  2 teaspoons honey
  ¼ teaspoon grated lemon rind
  1 (4-ounce) package goat cheese
  8 (1-ounce) slices cinnamon-raisin bread
  2 tablespoons fig preserves
  2 teaspoons thinly sliced fresh basil
Cooking spray
  1 teaspoon powdered sugar

1. Combine first 3 ingredients, stirring until well blended. Spread 1 tablespoon goat cheese mixture on each of 4 bread slices; top each slice with 1½ teaspoons preserves and ½ teaspoon basil. Top with remaining bread slices. Lightly coat outside of sandwiches with cooking spray.
2. Heat a large nonstick skillet over medium heat. Add 2 sandwiches to pan. Place a cast-iron or heavy skillet on top of sandwiches; press gently to flatten. Cook 3 minutes on each side or until bread is lightly toasted (leave cast-iron skillet on sandwiches while they cook). Repeat with remaining sandwiches. Sprinkle with sugar. Yield: 4 servings (serving size: 1 sandwich).

CALORIES 243 (31% from fat); FAT 8.5g (sat 4.8g, mono 2.7g, poly 0.5g); PROTEIN 9.8g; CARB 33.1g; FIBER 2.5g; CHOL 13mg; IRON 2.2mg; SODIUM 326mg; CALC 78mg

Pear, Pecorino, and Prosciutto Panini

If you prefer cooked prosciutto, sauté it until it's crisp; you'll add some crunch to this sandwich. Parmigiano-Reggiano is a good substitute for pecorino Romano cheese.

  1 firm, ripe pear, peeled, cored, and cut into 8 wedges
  ½ teaspoon sugar
  1 (12-ounce) loaf focaccia, cut in half horizontally
  4 teaspoons balsamic vinegar
  1 cup trimmed arugula
  ½ cup (2 ounces) fresh pecorino Romano cheese, shaved
 16 very thin slices prosciutto (about 4 ounces)

1. Heat a nonstick skillet over medium-high heat. Add pear to pan, and sprinkle with sugar. Cook 2 minutes on each side or until golden.
2. Brush cut sides of bread with vinegar. Arrange pear slices, arugula, cheese, and prosciutto evenly over bottom half of bread; cover with top half of bread.
3. Heat a large nonstick skillet over medium heat. Add stuffed loaf to pan. Place a cast-iron or heavy skillet on top of stuffed loaf; press gently to flatten. Cook 4 minutes on each side or until bread is toasted (leave cast-iron skillet on stuffed loaf while it cooks). Cut into quarters. Yield: 4 servings (serving size: 1 sandwich quarter).

CALORIES 383 (29% from fat); FAT 12.3g (sat 5.3g, mono 2.7g, poly 1.7g); PROTEIN 18.7g; CARB 50.8g; FIBER 2.7g; CHOL 40mg; IRON 2.8mg; SODIUM 1,019mg; CALC 178mg

Chipotle Pulled-Pork Barbecue Sandwiches

The sweet-sour flavor of bread-and-butter pickles is a tasty foil to the smoky barbecue sauce in this updated Southern-style sandwich. Serve with coleslaw.

  1 (7-ounce) can chipotle chiles in adobo sauce
  ¼ cup barbecue sauce
 1½ teaspoons ground cumin
  1 teaspoon garlic powder
  1 (1-pound) pork tenderloin, trimmed and cut into ½-inch cubes
  1 (14.5-ounce) can diced tomatoes, undrained
  1 tablespoon olive oil
  3 cups thinly sliced onion
  2 teaspoons chopped fresh thyme
  1 teaspoon sugar
  6 (½-ounce) slices provolone cheese
 12 sandwich-cut bread-and-butter pickles
  6 (2½-ounce) Kaiser rolls

1. Remove 1 chile from can; reserve remaining chiles and sauce for another use. Finely chop chile.
2. Place chopped chile, barbecue sauce, and next 4 ingredients in a medium saucepan; bring to a boil over medium-high heat. Cover, reduce heat, and simmer 45 minutes, stirring occasionally. Uncover and cook 10 minutes or until sauce thickens and pork is very tender. Remove from heat. Remove pork from sauce, and shred pork. Return pork to sauce.
3. Heat oil in a large nonstick skillet over medium-high heat. Add onion, thyme, and sugar; cook 10 minutes or until golden, stirring occasionally.
4. Heat a large nonstick skillet over medium heat. Place 1 cheese slice, ½ cup pork mixture, about 2 tablespoons onions, and 2 pickle slices on bottom half of each roll. Cover with top halves of rolls. Add 3 sandwiches to pan. Place a cast-iron or heavy skillet on top of sandwiches, and press gently to flatten. Cook 2 minutes on each side or until

cheese melts and bread is toasted (leave cast-iron skillet on sandwiches while they cook). Repeat procedure with remaining sandwiches. Yield: 6 servings (serving size: 1 sandwich).

CALORIES 431 (26% from fat); FAT 12.4g (sat 3.9g, mono 3.7g, poly 1.8g); PROTEIN 28.3g; CARB 51.4g; FIBER 4.7g; CHOL 59mg; IRON 4.1mg; SODIUM 910mg; CALC 207mg

Grilled Vegetable and Mozzarella Sandwiches

You can use a grilling basket to make it easier to handle the vegetables as they cook. If you can't find a loaf of ciabatta, use focaccia.

    3   cups (⅛-inch-thick) diagonally
        cut zucchini (about 1 pound)
    2   tablespoons balsamic vinegar
    1   teaspoon extravirgin olive oil
    ½   teaspoon salt
    ¼   teaspoon freshly ground black
        pepper
    3   (⅛-inch-thick) slices red onion
    1   red bell pepper, seeded and cut
        into 4 pieces
        Cooking spray
    1   (1-pound) loaf ciabatta, cut in half
        horizontally
    1   cup gourmet salad greens
    5   ounces fresh mozzarella cheese,
        sliced
    8   fresh basil leaves

1. Prepare grill to medium-high heat.
2. Combine first 7 ingredients in a large bowl, tossing to coat. Remove vegetables from bowl, reserving vinegar mixture. Place onion and bell pepper on grill rack coated with cooking spray; grill 7 minutes on each side or until tender. Grill zucchini 3 minutes on each side or until tender.
3. Hollow out bottom half of bread, leaving a ½-inch-thick shell; reserve torn bread for another use. Layer grilled vegetables, greens, cheese, and basil in bottom of loaf; drizzle reserved vinegar mixture on top. Cover with top of bread; press lightly.
4. Place filled loaf on grill rack; grill 4 minutes on each side or until cheese

melts. Cut into quarters. Yield: 4 servings (serving size: 1 sandwich quarter).

CALORIES 338 (30% from fat); FAT 11.1g (sat 5.7g, mono 3.5g, poly 1g); PROTEIN 14.3g; CARB 44.8g; FIBER 4.4g; CHOL 28mg; IRON 2.9mg; SODIUM 785mg; CALC 287mg

QUICK & EASY
Grilled Ham and Cheese with Tomato

Wheat bread is a good stand-in for the white bread in this modified ham-and-cheese sandwich. A creamy spread of sour cream, Dijon mustard, and Parmesan cheese adds lots of flavor.

    2   tablespoons Dijon mustard
    2   tablespoons reduced-fat sour
        cream
    1   tablespoon grated fresh Parmesan
        cheese
    8   (1½-ounce) slices hearty white
        bread
   16   (½-ounce) slices 33%-less-sodium
        ham
    8   (⅛-inch-thick) slices tomato
        (about 1 medium)
    8   (½-ounce) slices reduced-fat
        Swiss cheese
    2   teaspoons chopped fresh chives
        Cooking spray

1. Combine mustard, sour cream, and Parmesan cheese in a small bowl.
2. Spread 2 teaspoons mustard mixture over each bread slice. Top each of 4 bread slices with 4 ham slices, 2 tomato slices, 2 cheese slices, and ½ teaspoon fresh chives. Top with remaining bread slices. Lightly coat outside of sandwiches with cooking spray.
3. Heat a large nonstick skillet over medium heat. Add 2 sandwiches to pan. Place a cast-iron or heavy skillet on top of sandwiches; press gently to flatten. Cook 3 minutes on each side or until cheese melts and bread is toasted (leave cast-iron skillet on sandwiches while they cook). Repeat with remaining sandwiches. Yield: 4 servings (serving size: 1 sandwich).

CALORIES 407 (30% from fat); FAT 13.5g (sat 5.9g, mono 3.7g, poly 0.8g); PROTEIN 28.2g; CARB 47.5g; FIBER 5g; CHOL 54mg; IRON 2.9mg; SODIUM 1,229mg; CALC 337mg

QUICK & EASY
Chicken Philly Sandwiches

Taking a cue from the classic Philly cheese steak, this recipe replaces the traditional beef with chicken but keeps the cheese and onion-bell pepper topping. Pressing the already-warm filling helps the cheese melt and binds the ingredients so they don't fall out as you enjoy the sandwich.

    2   teaspoons olive oil
    ¾   pound skinless, boneless chicken
        breast, cut into (1-inch-thick) strips
    ⅛   teaspoon salt
    ⅛   teaspoon freshly ground black
        pepper
    1   cup red bell pepper strips
    1   cup green bell pepper strips
    1   cup vertically sliced onion
    1½ teaspoons white wine vinegar
    ⅛   teaspoon salt
    2   garlic cloves, minced
    ½   teaspoon hot pepper sauce
    4   (3-ounce) submarine rolls (such as
        Cobblestone Mill brand)
    4   (1-ounce) slices provolone cheese

1. Heat oil in a medium nonstick skillet over medium-high heat. Add chicken to pan; sprinkle with ⅛ teaspoon salt and black pepper. Sauté 5 minutes or until chicken is done. Remove chicken from pan. Add red bell pepper and next 5 ingredients to pan; sauté 6 minutes or until tender. Stir in chicken and pepper sauce; remove from heat.
2. Slice each roll in half horizontally, cutting to, but not through, other side. Place 1 cheese slice and 1 cup chicken mixture on bottom half of each roll, and gently press roll halves together.
3. Heat a large nonstick skillet over medium heat; add 2 sandwiches. Place a cast-iron or heavy skillet on top of sandwiches; press gently to flatten. Cook 4 minutes on each side or until cheese melts and bread is toasted (leave cast-iron skillet on sandwiches while they cook). Repeat with remaining sandwiches. Yield: 4 servings (serving size: 1 sandwich).

CALORIES 490 (28% from fat); FAT 15.4g (sat 6.5g, mono 6.2g, poly 1.5g); PROTEIN 35.2g; CARB 51.3g; FIBER 4.2g; CHOL 69mg; IRON 3.9mg; SODIUM 945mg; CALC 359mg

Currying Flavor

A young cook does her homework to recreate a favorite chicken recipe.

A couple of summers ago, Kelsie Wilson, 19, a junior at Seattle Pacific University majoring in nutrition and dietetics, ate at a waterfront restaurant in British Columbia. There she enjoyed an intriguing sweet and spicy dish of curried chicken with mango chutney and penne. After only two tries, Wilson was able to duplicate the creamy sauce she had eaten at the restaurant.

Curried Chicken Penne with Fresh Mango Chutney

CHUTNEY:

    2 cups diced peeled ripe mango
       (about 2 mangoes)
    1 cup finely chopped onion
    ½ cup water
    2 tablespoons brown sugar
    1 tablespoon curry powder
    1 tablespoon fresh lime juice
    ½ teaspoon black pepper
    ½ teaspoon chopped peeled fresh
       ginger
    ¼ teaspoon salt

CHICKEN:

    1 teaspoon olive oil
    2 garlic cloves, minced
    1 pound skinless, boneless
       chicken breast, cut into 1-inch
       pieces
    1 cup light coconut milk
    2 tablespoons sugar
 1½ teaspoons red curry paste
    1 to 2 teaspoons Thai fish
       sauce
    1 teaspoon salt
    2 cups broccoli florets
    2 cups cauliflower florets
    4 cups hot cooked penne rigate
       (about 2 cups uncooked
       tube-shaped pasta)
    2 tablespoons chopped green
       onions (optional)

1. To prepare chutney, combine first 9 ingredients in a medium saucepan; bring to a boil. Reduce heat, and simmer 15 minutes or until most of liquid evaporates and mixture is thick, stirring occasionally.
2. To prepare chicken, heat oil in a large nonstick skillet over medium-high heat. Add garlic and chicken; sauté 5 minutes. Combine coconut milk and next 4 ingredients, stirring with a whisk. Add coconut mixture to pan; bring to a simmer. Add broccoli and cauliflower; cover and cook 7 minutes or until vegetables are crisp-tender, stirring occasionally. Stir in chutney and pasta; toss well. Sprinkle with green onions, if desired. Yield: 6 servings (serving size: about 1⅓ cups).

CALORIES 216 (18% from fat); FAT 4.3g (sat 1.8g, mono 0.9g, poly 0.4g); PROTEIN 20g; CARB 25.9g; FIBER 3.6g; CHOL 44mg; IRON 1.9mg; SODIUM 724mg; CALC 52mg

QUICK & EASY
Turkey Bolognese

"Two years ago, this was one of the recipes that won over my then fiancé, now husband, Jon, to my cooking. It's still one of our favorites."

—Joann Hoye, Raleigh, North Carolina

    1 tablespoon olive oil
    1 cup chopped onion
    4 garlic cloves, minced
   12 ounces ground turkey breast
    1 tablespoon chopped fresh
       oregano
    1 tablespoon chopped fresh
       basil
    1 tablespoon chopped fresh
       parsley
    1 teaspoon salt
    ½ teaspoon sugar
    ½ teaspoon black pepper
    1 (14.5-ounce) can petite diced
       tomatoes, undrained
    1 (8-ounce) can no-salt-added
       tomato sauce
    4 cups hot cooked penne (about
       ¾ pound uncooked tube-shaped
       pasta)
    ¼ cup (1 ounce) grated fresh Asiago
       cheese

1. Heat oil in a large saucepan over medium heat. Add onion and garlic; cook 5 minutes or until tender, stirring frequently. Increase heat to medium-high. Add turkey, and cook 4 minutes or until turkey is browned, stirring to crumble. Add oregano and next 7 ingredients; bring to a boil. Reduce heat, and simmer 10 minutes. Stir in pasta; cook 2 minutes or until thoroughly heated. Sprinkle with cheese. Yield: 4 servings (serving size: 1½ cups pasta mixture and 1 tablespoon cheese).

CALORIES 447 (25% from fat); FAT 12.5g (sat 3.5g, mono 5.4g, poly 2.3g); PROTEIN 29.7g; CARB 53.9g; FIBER 4.6g; CHOL 61mg; IRON 4.3mg; SODIUM 816mg; CALC 147mg

MAKE AHEAD
Black Bean Soup

"I devised this recipe after a restaurant I loved closed and took with it my favorite soup."

—Carolyn Blanchard, Aberdeen, South Dakota

    1 pound dried black
       beans
    2 bacon slices, chopped
    1 cup chopped onion
    ¾ cup chopped carrot
    ¾ cup chopped celery
    2 garlic cloves, minced
    1 jalapeño pepper, seeded and
       minced
    4 (14-ounce) cans fat-free,
       less-sodium chicken broth
    1 (28-ounce) can crushed tomatoes,
       undrained
    ⅓ cup minced fresh cilantro
    2 tablespoons fresh lime juice
    1 teaspoon salt
    ½ teaspoon freshly ground black
       pepper
    ¾ cup reduced-fat sour cream

1. Sort and wash beans; place in a large bowl. Cover with water to 2 inches above beans; cover and let stand 8 hours or overnight. Drain and rinse beans.
2. Cook bacon in a large Dutch oven over medium-high heat until crisp. Remove bacon from pan, reserving drippings in pan. Add onion, carrot, and

celery to pan; sauté 10 minutes or until tender. Add garlic and jalapeño; sauté 2 minutes. Add beans, bacon, broth, and tomatoes; bring to a boil. Cover, reduce heat, and simmer 1½ hours or until beans are tender. Place 4 cups soup in a blender or food processor; let stand 5 minutes. Process until smooth; return puréed soup to pan. Stir in cilantro, lime juice, salt, and pepper. Serve with sour cream. Yield: 12 servings (serving size: 1 cup soup and 1 tablespoon sour cream).

CALORIES 215 (20% from fat); FAT 4.8g (sat 2.1g, mono 1.6g, poly 0.7g); PROTEIN 12g; CARB 32.5g; FIBER 7.7g; CHOL 8mg; IRON 3mg; SODIUM 570mg; CALC 95mg

Garlic and Bell Pepper Farfalle

"I came up with this dish when I had a half-dozen peppers I wanted to use. You can get a head start by roasting the peppers a couple of days ahead of time."

—Catherine Kohm,
Sherman Oaks, California

　2　red bell peppers
　2　yellow bell peppers
　2　orange bell peppers
　3　bacon slices, chopped
　2　garlic cloves, minced
1½　cups chopped plum tomato
　½　cup kalamata olives, pitted and thinly sliced
　¾　teaspoon salt
　¼　teaspoon freshly ground black pepper
　5　cups hot cooked farfalle (about 4 cups uncooked bow tie pasta)
　6　tablespoons (1½ ounces) grated fresh Parmesan cheese
　¼　cup chopped fresh basil

1. Preheat broiler.
2. Cut bell peppers in half lengthwise, and discard seeds and membranes. Place pepper halves, skin sides up, on a foil-lined baking sheet; flatten with hand. Broil 8 minutes or until blackened. Place in a zip-top plastic bag; seal. Let stand 5 minutes. Peel and chop.
3. Cook bacon in a large nonstick skillet over medium-high heat until crisp.

Remove bacon from pan, reserving 1 teaspoon drippings in pan. Add garlic to pan, and sauté 30 seconds. Add bell peppers, bacon, tomato, olives, salt, and black pepper; cook 3 minutes or until thoroughly heated, stirring occasionally. Combine bell pepper mixture and pasta in a large bowl; sprinkle with cheese and basil. Yield: 6 servings (serving size: 1⅓ cups pasta mixture, 1 tablespoon cheese, and 1 tablespoon basil).

CALORIES 281 (20% from fat); FAT 6.4g (sat 2.5g, mono 2.5g, poly 0.6g); PROTEIN 11.6g; CARB 46.4g; FIBER 4.8g; CHOL 8mg; IRON 2.8mg; SODIUM 568mg; CALC 121mg

Parmesan-Corn Bread Muffins

"These warm, delicious muffins, covered in savory Parmesan cheese, are best right from the oven."

—Jamie Castillo, Pittsburg, California

　1　cup all-purpose flour
　⅔　cup yellow cornmeal
　2　tablespoons sugar
　2　teaspoons baking powder
　¼　teaspoon salt
　⅔　cup fat-free buttermilk
　3　tablespoons vegetable oil
　2　large egg whites, lightly beaten
　　　Cooking spray
　¼　cup (1 ounce) grated fresh Parmesan cheese

1. Preheat oven to 425°.
2. Lightly spoon flour and cornmeal into dry measuring cups; level with a knife. Combine flour, cornmeal, sugar, baking powder, and salt in a medium bowl, stirring with a whisk. Make a well in center of mixture. Combine buttermilk, oil, and egg whites; add to flour mixture, stirring just until moist.
3. Spoon batter into 10 muffin cups coated with cooking spray. Sprinkle evenly with cheese. Bake at 425° for 10 minutes or until muffins spring back when touched lightly in center. Remove muffins from pan immediately; place on

a wire rack. Serve warm. Yield: 10 servings (serving size: 1 muffin).

CALORIES 151 (29% from fat); FAT 4.9g (sat 1.1g, mono 1.2g, poly 2.4g); PROTEIN 4.3g; CARB 21.9g; FIBER 0.6g; CHOL 2mg; IRON 1mg; SODIUM 229mg; CALC 110mg

Southwestern Chicken Roll-Ups

"This recipe is fast and easy, and I can prepare it in advance for guests. Use wooden picks to secure the chicken before dredging."

—Christine Vogel, Sanford, Florida

　6　(6-ounce) skinless, boneless chicken breast halves
　6　tablespoons (about 3 ounces) ⅓-less-fat cream cheese
　6　tablespoons picante sauce
　6　cilantro sprigs
　6　tablespoons Italian-seasoned breadcrumbs
　　　Cooking spray

1. Preheat oven to 350°.
2. Place each chicken breast half between 2 sheets of heavy-duty plastic wrap; pound to ¼-inch thickness using a meat mallet or rolling pin. Top each breast half with 1 tablespoon cheese, 1 tablespoon picante sauce, and 1 cilantro sprig. Roll up jelly-roll fashion, beginning at narrow end.
3. Dredge chicken rolls in breadcrumbs. Place rolls, seam sides down, on a baking sheet coated with cooking spray; lightly coat rolls with cooking spray. Bake at 350° for 20 minutes or until chicken is done. Yield: 6 servings (serving size: 1 chicken roll).

CALORIES 257 (20% from fat); FAT 5.8g (sat 2.7g, mono 1.5g, poly 0.6g); PROTEIN 41.7g; CARB 6.9g; FIBER 0.3g; CHOL 109mg; IRON 1.6mg; SODIUM 385mg; CALC 40mg

Summer Sweethearts

Strawberries may be available year-round, but they have their sweetest, most intense flavor in June—so pick them while you can.

Strawberries are at their peak in June and need very little adornment to become the star of any meal. The best fresh strawberries are typically sweet, with a concentrated aroma. Ingredients like balsamic vinegar, lemon juice, and a light touch of sugar coax out the best of the berries rather than masking or overpowering them.

MAKE AHEAD
Strawberry Pie

Strawberries do double duty in this pie. Some are blended into a purée and combined with gelatin, then more fresh berries are added to the filling.

1¼ cups chocolate wafer crumbs (about 20 cookies, such as Nabisco's Famous Chocolate Wafers)
2½ tablespoons butter, melted
  Cooking spray
1½ cups sliced strawberries
½ cup sugar
⅛ teaspoon salt
3 tablespoons boiling water
1 envelope unflavored gelatin
4 cups sliced strawberries
¼ cup vanilla-flavored baking chips

1. Preheat oven to 400°.
2. Combine wafer crumbs and butter, tossing with a fork until moistened. Press crumb mixture into a 9-inch pie plate coated with cooking spray. Bake at 400° for 9 minutes. Cool on a wire rack.
3. Place 1½ cups strawberries, sugar, and salt in a blender; process until smooth.
4. Combine boiling water and gelatin in a medium bowl; let stand 5 minutes. Stir until gelatin dissolves. Stir in puréed strawberry mixture.

5. Spoon 4 cups strawberries into cooled crust. Pour gelatin mixture evenly over strawberries. Chill, uncovered, 2 hours or until set.
6. Place chips in a small heavy-duty zip-top plastic bag; seal. Submerge bag in very hot water until chips melt. Snip a tiny hole in 1 corner of bag, and drizzle melted chips over pie. Yield: 8 servings (serving size: 1 wedge).

CALORIES 239 (33% from fat); FAT 8.8g (sat 4.7g, mono 2g, poly 0.6g); PROTEIN 3.2g; CARB 38.4g; FIBER 3.1g; CHOL 11mg; IRON 1mg; SODIUM 212mg; CALC 44mg

QUICK & EASY
Frozen Strawberry Daiquiris

3 cups sliced strawberries
1 cup white rum
3 tablespoons fresh lime juice
1 (12-ounce) can limeade concentrate, thawed and undiluted
1 cup crushed ice
6 lime slices (optional)

1. Place first 4 ingredients in a blender; process until smooth. Add ice; process until smooth. Serve immediately; garnish with lime slices, if desired. Yield: 6 servings (serving size: about 1 cup).

CALORIES 219 (2% from fat); FAT 0.4g (sat 0g, mono 0.1g, poly 0.2g); PROTEIN 0.7g; CARB 34.6g; FIBER 2.2g; CHOL 0mg; IRON 0.4mg; SODIUM 1mg; CALC 15mg

MAKE AHEAD
Strawberry-Rhubarb Tart

½ (15-ounce) package refrigerated pie dough (such as Pillsbury)
2 cups sliced rhubarb
½ cup sugar
2 tablespoons cornstarch
2 teaspoons water
¾ teaspoon cinnamon, divided
3 cups sliced strawberries
1 tablespoon sugar

1. Preheat oven to 400°.
2. Press dough into bottom and up sides of a 10-inch removable-bottom tart pan. Line bottom of dough with a piece of foil; arrange pie weights or dried beans on foil.

Bake at 400° for 5 minutes. Remove pie weights and foil. Bake an additional 5 minutes. Cool on a wire rack.
3. Combine rhubarb, ½ cup sugar, cornstarch, water, and ½ teaspoon cinnamon in a medium saucepan. Bring to a boil; reduce heat, and simmer 5 minutes or until rhubarb is tender, stirring frequently. Remove from heat, and stir in strawberries. Spoon strawberry mixture into prepared crust. Combine ¼ teaspoon cinnamon and 1 tablespoon sugar; sprinkle evenly over tart.
4. Place tart on a baking sheet. Bake at 400° for 30 minutes or until filling is set. Cool on a wire rack. Yield: 8 servings (serving size: 1 wedge).

CALORIES 203 (32% from fat); FAT 7.2g (sat 3g, mono 1.7g, poly 1.9g); PROTEIN 1.6g; CARB 34g; FIBER 2.1g; CHOL 5mg; IRON 0.4mg; SODIUM 101mg; CALC 36mg

QUICK & EASY • MAKE AHEAD
Brunch Parfaits
(pictured on page 182)

Assemble everything but the granola and almonds ahead of time, and store in the refrigerator up to 1 hour. Sprinkle with granola and almonds just before serving.

⅓ cup apricot preserves
3 cups sliced strawberries
2 cups low-fat vanilla yogurt
½ cup low-fat granola without raisins (such as Kellogg's)
2 tablespoons slivered almonds, toasted

1. Place apricot preserves in a medium microwave-safe bowl, and microwave at HIGH 10 to 15 seconds or until preserves melt. Add strawberries, and toss gently to coat.
2. Spoon ¼ cup yogurt into each of 4 parfait glasses; top each serving with ⅓ cup strawberry mixture. Repeat layers with remaining yogurt and strawberry mixture. Top each serving with 2 tablespoons granola and 1½ teaspoons almonds. Serve immediately. Yield: 4 servings (serving size: 1 parfait).

CALORIES 279 (14% from fat); FAT 4.2g (sat 1.4g, mono 1.4g, poly 0.6g); PROTEIN 8.7g; CARB 53.5g; FIBER 3.9g; CHOL 6mg; IRON 1mg; SODIUM 94mg; CALC 240mg

Balsamic Strawberry Topping

Stirring the strawberries into the warm syrup at the end helps them keep their shape. Serve over low-fat frozen yogurt or ice cream.

    2   tablespoons light brown sugar
    2   tablespoons balsamic vinegar
    ⅛   teaspoon ground nutmeg
    3   cups sliced strawberries

1. Combine first 3 ingredients in a small saucepan. Bring to a simmer over medium-low heat; cook 2 minutes or until slightly thickened. Stir in strawberries, and remove from heat. Let stand 5 minutes. Yield: 7 servings (serving size: ¼ cup).

CALORIES 34 (8% from fat); FAT 0.3g (sat 0g, mono 0g, poly 0.1g); PROTEIN 0.5g; CARB 8.2g; FIBER 1.6g; CHOL 0mg; IRON 0.4mg; SODIUM 3mg; CALC 14mg

Fresh Strawberry Jam

Store in a plastic container in the refrigerator up to 1 month.

    4   cups halved strawberries
    1   cup sugar
    2   teaspoons fresh lemon juice

1. Combine strawberries and sugar in a medium saucepan, and bring to a simmer over medium-high heat, stirring frequently. Reduce heat to medium, and simmer 1 hour or until thick, stirring occasionally. Remove from heat, and stir in lemon juice. Cool to room temperature. Yield: 2 cups (serving size: 1 tablespoon).

CALORIES 30 (3% from fat); FAT 0.1g (sat 0g, mono 0g, poly 0.1g); PROTEIN 0.1g; CARB 7.6g; FIBER 0.4g; CHOL 0mg; IRON 0.1mg; SODIUM 0mg; CALC 3mg

How to Choose Strawberries

Choose strawberries that are small, shiny, intensely red, and attract you with their sweet fragrance. Eat them within a couple of days—they're fragile and spoil quickly.

Meals to Go

Portable, packable dishes are perfect for brown bag lunches or picnics.

Whether you're attending a holiday cookout or want to take homemade food to work for lunch, try these recipes, many of which can be made ahead. Just be sure to chill your portable foods thoroughly before you leave the house, and refrigerate them in the containers in which they will be traveling.

White Bean, Tomato, and Green Bean Salad

Fresh dill adds zestiness to this salad without overpowering it. You can use cannellini beans or great Northern beans in place of the navy beans.

DRESSING:

    1   tablespoon fresh lemon
        juice
    1   tablespoon balsamic vinegar
    1   tablespoon extravirgin olive oil
    ¼   teaspoon sugar
    ¼   teaspoon salt
    ¼   teaspoon freshly ground black
        pepper
    1   garlic clove, minced

SALAD:

    5   cups (1-inch) cut green beans
        (about 1 pound)
    1   cup finely chopped tomato
    1   tablespoon chopped fresh dill
    1   (15-ounce) can navy beans, rinsed
        and drained
    ½   cup (2 ounces) feta cheese,
        crumbled

1. To prepare dressing, combine first 7 ingredients, stirring with a whisk.
2. To prepare salad, place green beans in a large saucepan of boiling water; cook 5 minutes. Drain and plunge beans into ice water; drain. Place beans in a large bowl. Add tomato, dill, and navy beans; toss to combine. Drizzle with dressing; toss gently to coat. Sprinkle with cheese. Cover and chill at least 1 hour. Yield: 4 servings (serving size: 1½ cups).

CALORIES 214 (30% from fat); FAT 7.1g (sat 2.7g, mono 3.2g, poly 0.7g); PROTEIN 11g; CARB 29.6g; FIBER 8.7g; CHOL 13mg; IRON 3.1mg; SODIUM 698mg; CALC 158mg

Lentil and Fennel Salad

The lentils have an appealing bite because they're cooked just until tender. The crisp fennel adds contrast.

DRESSING:

    2   tablespoons fresh lemon juice
    2   tablespoons extravirgin olive oil
    1   tablespoon balsamic vinegar
    ½   teaspoon salt
    ¼   teaspoon sugar
    ¼   teaspoon freshly ground black
        pepper
    1   garlic clove, minced

SALAD:

    1¼ cups dried lentils
    ¾   cup (¼-inch-thick) red bell
        pepper strips, each cut in half
        crosswise
    ½   cup thinly sliced fennel bulb
    ½   cup thinly vertically sliced red
        onion
    3   tablespoons chopped fresh
        parsley, divided

1. To prepare dressing, combine first 7 ingredients, stirring with a whisk.
2. To prepare salad, place lentils in a large saucepan; cover with water to 2 inches above lentils. Bring to a boil; cover, reduce heat, and simmer 18 minutes or until just tender. Drain. Place lentils in a large bowl; stir in dressing, bell pepper, fennel, onion, and 2 tablespoons parsley. Sprinkle 1 tablespoon parsley over top of salad. Cover and chill at least 1 hour. Yield: 4 servings (serving size: 1 cup).

CALORIES 282 (24% from fat); FAT 7.5g (sat 1g, mono 5.1g, poly 0.9g); PROTEIN 16.3g; CARB 40.1g; FIBER 14.8g; CHOL 0mg; IRON 6.3mg; SODIUM 306mg; CALC 51mg

Orzo-Bell Pepper Salad

Blanching the bell peppers for a few seconds tenderizes them while maintaining their delightful crunch. The marinated cheese provides a shortcut for adding more flavor.

DRESSING:

- 2 tablespoons fresh lemon juice
- 2½ teaspoons extravirgin olive oil
- 2 teaspoons red wine vinegar
- ½ teaspoon salt
- ¼ teaspoon freshly ground black pepper
- 3 garlic cloves, minced

SALAD:

- 1 cup uncooked orzo (rice-shaped pasta)
- ⅓ cup finely chopped red bell pepper
- ⅓ cup finely chopped green bell pepper
- ⅓ cup finely chopped yellow bell pepper
- 1 cup finely chopped tomato
- ½ cup (2 ounces) diced fresh marinated mozzarella cheese (such as Cappiello)
- ¼ cup minced fresh parsley
- ¼ cup finely chopped red onion
- ¼ cup chopped pitted kalamata olives

1. To prepare dressing, combine first 6 ingredients, stirring with a whisk.

2. To prepare salad, cook pasta in boiling water 6 minutes or until al dente. Add bell peppers to pasta in pan; cook 10 seconds. Drain. Combine pasta mixture and half of dressing in a large bowl; cool mixture to room temperature. Add remaining dressing, tomato, and remaining ingredients; toss gently to coat. Cover and chill at least 1 hour. Yield: 4 servings (serving size: 1 cup).

CALORIES 351 (29% from fat); FAT 11.3g (sat 3.4g, mono 5.8g, poly 1g); PROTEIN 11.6g; CARB 48.6g; FIBER 3.4g; CHOL 8mg; IRON 2.7mg; SODIUM 619mg; CALC 134mg

Orecchiette with Tomatoes, Fresh Mozzarella, and Basil

Taking its cue from Italy's *insalata caprese*, this easy dish combines fresh mozzarella cheese with basil and tomatoes. Choose the ripest, most flavorful tomatoes for this sensational pasta salad.

- 2 cups uncooked orecchiette (about 8 ounces uncooked "little ears" pasta)
- 3 cups chopped plum tomato
- 1¼ cups (5 ounces) diced fresh mozzarella cheese
- 1 cup loosely packed chopped fresh basil
- 1 tablespoon extravirgin olive oil
- ¾ teaspoon salt
- ¼ teaspoon crushed red pepper
- 2 garlic cloves, minced

1. Cook pasta according to package directions, omitting salt and fat; drain and rinse with cold water. Drain. Combine pasta, tomato, and remaining ingredients. Cover and chill at least 1 hour. Yield: 4 servings (serving size: 1½ cups).

CALORIES 376 (30% from fat); FAT 12.4g (sat 5.7g, mono 4.2g, poly 1.1g); PROTEIN 15.1g; CARB 50.5g; FIBER 3.4g; CHOL 28mg; IRON 3.4mg; SODIUM 361mg; CALC 239mg

Tomato and Cucumber Salad

Cool, crunchy, refreshing, and simple to make—this side salad would be a welcome addition to a picnic or family reunion.

- 3 cups chopped peeled English cucumber
- 2 cups chopped tomato
- ¾ cup finely chopped red onion
- ¼ cup finely chopped fresh parsley
- 3 tablespoons finely chopped fresh cilantro
- ½ teaspoon salt

1. Combine all ingredients in a large bowl. Cover and chill at least 2 hours.

Serve with a slotted spoon. Yield: 6 servings (serving size: about ¾ cup).

CALORIES 29 (12% from fat); FAT 0.4g (sat 0.1g, mono 0g, poly 0.2g); PROTEIN 1.2g; CARB 6.3g; FIBER 1.6g; CHOL 0mg; IRON 0.6mg; SODIUM 204mg; CALC 20mg

Sesame Farfalle with Roasted Tofu

Baking the tofu in a mixture of soy sauce, ginger, sesame oil, and chile paste accomplishes three goals: It creates a golden crust, gives the tofu a firmer texture, and adds flavor by cooking the seasonings into the tofu.

SALAD:

- 2 cups halved shiitake mushroom caps
- 1 tablespoon low-sodium soy sauce
- 1 teaspoon minced peeled fresh ginger
- 1 teaspoon dark sesame oil
- ½ teaspoon chile paste with garlic
- 1 (14-ounce) package extrafirm water-packed tofu, drained and cut into 1-inch cubes
- 2 cups uncooked farfalle (about 8 ounces uncooked bow tie pasta)
- ¾ cup (1-inch) slices green onions

DRESSING:

- 3 tablespoons fresh lemon juice
- 3 tablespoons low-sodium soy sauce
- 2 tablespoons rice vinegar
- 2 tablespoons chopped fresh cilantro
- 1½ teaspoons dark sesame oil
- 1½ teaspoons vegetable oil
- ¼ teaspoon sugar
- ¼ teaspoon salt
- ¼ teaspoon freshly ground black pepper
- 3 garlic cloves, minced

1. Preheat oven to 425°.

2. To prepare salad, combine first 6 ingredients in a 13 x 9-inch baking dish; toss gently to coat. Bake at 425° for 40 minutes or until mushrooms are tender and tofu is golden brown.

3. Cook pasta according to package directions, omitting salt and fat; drain and rinse with cold water. Drain. Combine pasta, tofu mixture, and onions in a large bowl.

4. To prepare dressing, combine lemon juice and remaining 9 ingredients, stirring well with a whisk. Drizzle dressing over salad; toss well to coat. Cover and chill at least 1 hour. Yield: 6 servings (serving size: 1⅓ cups).

CALORIES 249 (27% from fat); FAT 7.6g (sat 1.4g, mono 2g, poly 3.7g); PROTEIN 14.3g; CARB 33.3g; FIBER 2.9g; CHOL 0mg; IRON 3.1mg; SODIUM 465mg; CALC 92mg

Tofu Teriyaki Noodle Salad

Be sure to pick up the water-packed tofu. It has a spongier texture than silken tofu, which is soft and unsuitable for marinating.

    6 tablespoons fresh lime juice,
       divided
    ¼ cup honey, divided
    3 tablespoons low-sodium soy
       sauce
    1 tablespoon dark sesame oil,
       divided
    2½ teaspoons minced peeled fresh
       ginger, divided
    2 garlic cloves, minced
    1 (12.3-ounce) package reduced-fat
       firm water-packed tofu, drained
       and cut into ½-inch cubes
    4 ounces uncooked bean threads
       (cellophane noodles)
    ½ cup diced red bell pepper
    ¼ cup coarsely chopped dry-roasted
       peanuts
    ¼ cup chopped fresh cilantro

1. Combine 2 tablespoons lime juice, 2 tablespoons honey, soy sauce, 2 teaspoons oil, 2 teaspoons ginger, and garlic in a large zip-top plastic bag; add tofu to bag. Seal and marinate in refrigerator 1 hour. Remove tofu from bag; discard marinade.

2. Prepare noodles according to package directions. Rinse with cold water, and drain. Combine ¼ cup lime juice, 2 tablespoons honey, 1 teaspoon oil, and

½ teaspoon ginger in a large bowl, stirring with a whisk. Add noodles, bell pepper, peanuts, and cilantro; toss gently to coat. Add tofu; stir gently to combine. Yield: 3 servings (serving size: about 1⅔ cups).

CALORIES 399 (24% from fat); FAT 11g (sat 1.5g, mono 4.7g, poly 4.2g); PROTEIN 12.5g; CARB 65.6g; FIBER 1.5g; CHOL 0mg; IRON 1.4mg; SODIUM 723mg; CALC 66mg

Curried Couscous with Pine Nuts and Currants

When added to the cooked couscous, the broth mixture acts as a flavorful dressing and keeps the salad moist.

    ¼ cup vegetable broth
    2 tablespoons fresh lemon juice
    1 tablespoon extravirgin olive oil
    ½ teaspoon salt
    ½ teaspoon grated peeled fresh
       ginger
    ⅛ teaspoon freshly ground black
       pepper
    1½ cups water
    1 cup uncooked couscous
    ¼ cup dried currants
    1½ teaspoons curry powder
    1 cup frozen green peas, thawed
    ½ cup finely chopped red bell
       pepper
    ¼ cup pine nuts, toasted
    ¼ cup thinly sliced green onions

1. Combine first 6 ingredients, stirring well with a whisk.

2. Bring 1½ cups water to a boil in a medium saucepan; gradually stir in couscous, currants, and curry. Remove from heat; cover and let stand 5 minutes. Fluff with a fork.

3. Combine couscous mixture, peas, bell pepper, pine nuts, and onions in a large bowl. Add broth mixture; toss gently to coat. Yield: 4 servings (serving size: 1¼ cups).

CALORIES 315 (24% from fat); FAT 8.5g (sat 1.3g, mono 4.4g, poly 2.4g); PROTEIN 10.3g; CARB 50.8g; FIBER 5.6g; CHOL 0mg; IRON 2.4mg; SODIUM 408mg; CALC 35mg

Roasted Red Pepper Spread Sandwiches

If you like pimiento cheese, you'll enjoy this recipe. Keep the sandwiches well chilled so the cream cheese spread will remain firm. Sturdy, whole-grain bread works best.

    ½ cup finely chopped seeded
       cucumber
    1 (7-ounce) bottle roasted red bell
       peppers, drained and finely
       chopped
    ¾ cup (6 ounces) ⅓-less-fat cream
       cheese, softened
    ⅓ cup (about 3 ounces) block-style
       fat-free cream cheese, softened
    3 tablespoons minced red onion
    ¼ teaspoon salt
    1 garlic clove, minced
    8 (1½-ounce) slices whole-grain
       bread
    8 romaine lettuce leaves

1. Spread cucumber and bell peppers onto several layers of heavy-duty paper towels; let stand 5 minutes to drain excess moisture. Scrape into a medium bowl using a rubber spatula. Add cheeses, onion, salt, and garlic; stir with a fork until well blended. Spread about ½ cup cheese mixture over each of 4 bread slices; top each serving with 2 lettuce leaves and 1 bread slice. Yield: 4 servings (serving size: 1 sandwich).

CALORIES 356 (30% from fat); FAT 11.9g (sat 6.4g, mono 2.9g, poly 0.4g); PROTEIN 14.9g; CARB 43.6g; FIBER 4.1g; CHOL 36mg; IRON 2.9mg; SODIUM 875mg; CALC 173mg

MAKE AHEAD
Couscous-Chickpea Salad with Ginger-Lime Dressing

Couscous is great for make-ahead salads like this one. Turmeric lends a golden hue to the pasta, but it can be omitted.

DRESSING:
- ⅓ cup fresh lime juice
- 1½ tablespoons extravirgin olive oil
- 2 teaspoons grated peeled fresh ginger
- ¾ teaspoon ground cumin
- ½ teaspoon sugar
- ½ teaspoon salt
- ¼ teaspoon freshly ground black pepper
- 1 garlic clove, minced

SALAD:
- 2 cups water
- 1½ cups uncooked couscous
- ½ cup raisins
- ½ teaspoon ground turmeric
- 1 cup chopped tomato
- 1 cup chopped peeled cucumber
- 1 cup (4 ounces) crumbled feta cheese
- ¼ cup thinly sliced green onions
- 2 tablespoons finely chopped fresh mint
- 1 (15½-ounce) can chickpeas (garbanzo beans), rinsed and drained

1. To prepare dressing, combine first 8 ingredients, stirring with a whisk.
2. To prepare salad, bring 2 cups water to a boil in a medium saucepan, and gradually stir in couscous, raisins, and turmeric. Remove from heat; cover and let stand 5 minutes. Fluff with a fork. Place couscous mixture in a large bowl. Add tomato and remaining 5 ingredients. Drizzle with dressing; stir well to coat. Cover and chill at least 1 hour. Yield: 6 servings (serving size: 1⅓ cups).

CALORIES 345 (23% from fat); FAT 9g (sat 3.4g, mono 3.8g, poly 1.2g); PROTEIN 11.2g; CARB 56.2g; FIBER 5.6g; CHOL 17mg; IRON 2mg; SODIUM 529mg; CALC 137mg

Pop Goes the Breakfast

Wake Dad up with one of these imaginative morning meals.

Many of us make a big to-do over Mother's Day, and rightly so. But when Father's Day rolls around, dear old Dad is lucky if someone throws a steak on the grill. This Father's Day, start a new tradition of spoiling your dad with a special breakfast. These recipes from Matt Miller, owner of Orange, a restaurant in Chicago, will provide plenty of inspiration.

QUICK & EASY
Green Eggs and Ham

Tinted green with a zesty dose of basil, this dish makes an intriguing breakfast or brunch item. Add a salad for a light dinner. If you can't find pancetta (unsmoked Italian bacon), substitute prosciutto or bacon.

- 1 (8-ounce) loaf French bread, cut diagonally into 6 slices
- 1 cup egg substitute
- ¼ cup chopped fresh basil
- 2 tablespoons 1% low-fat milk
- ½ teaspoon salt
- ¼ teaspoon freshly ground black pepper
- 1 large egg, lightly beaten
- 2 garlic cloves, minced
- 1 ounce pancetta, diced
- 4 plum tomatoes, thinly sliced lengthwise
- ¼ cup (1 ounce) shredded fontina cheese

1. Preheat broiler.
2. Arrange bread slices in a single layer on a baking sheet. Broil 2 minutes or until tops are toasted. Remove from oven. Turn slices over; set aside on baking sheet.
3. Combine egg substitute and next 5 ingredients, stirring with a whisk.
4. Heat a large nonstick skillet over medium-high heat. Add garlic and pancetta; sauté 3 minutes or until pancetta begins to crisp. Add egg mixture to pan; cook 2 minutes or just until set, stirring gently.
5. Divide egg mixture evenly over bread slices. Top egg mixture with tomatoes, and sprinkle with cheese. Broil 2 minutes or until cheese melts and begins to brown. Serve immediately. Yield: 6 servings (serving size: 1 topped bread slice).

CALORIES 194 (30% from fat); FAT 6.4g (sat 2.5g, mono 2.5g, poly 0.8g); PROTEIN 10.6g; CARB 23.1g; FIBER 1.7g; CHOL 44mg; IRON 2.1mg; SODIUM 592mg; CALC 86mg

MAKE AHEAD
Pan-Seared Oatmeal with Warm Fruit Compote and Cider Syrup

This is oatmeal to get excited about—hearty steel-cut oats are chilled and cut into triangles, then seared in butter and topped with warm fruit. All of the components can be made a day ahead and reheated.

SYRUP:
- 2 cups apple cider

COMPOTE:
- 2 cups water
- ¼ cup packed brown sugar
- ½ teaspoon ground cinnamon
- 1 (7-ounce) package dried mixed fruit bits

OATMEAL:
- 3 cups water
- 1 cup fat-free milk
- ¼ cup packed brown sugar
- ½ teaspoon ground cinnamon
- ¼ teaspoon salt
- 1½ cups steel-cut (Irish) oats
- Cooking spray
- ¼ cup butter, divided

1. To prepare syrup, bring cider to a boil in a small saucepan over medium-high heat. Cook until reduced to ⅓ cup (about 20 minutes); set aside.
2. To prepare compote, combine 2 cups water and next 3 ingredients in a medium saucepan; bring to a boil. Reduce heat, and simmer 20 minutes or until thick.
3. To prepare oatmeal, combine 3 cups water and next 4 ingredients in a large

saucepan. Bring to a boil over medium-high heat; stir in oats. Reduce heat, and simmer 20 minutes or until thick, stirring occasionally. Spoon oatmeal into an 11 x 7-inch baking dish coated with cooking spray; cool to room temperature. Cover and chill at least 1 hour or until set.

4. Using a sharp knife, cut oatmeal into 8 equal rectangles; cut each rectangle in half diagonally to form 16 triangles.

5. Melt 2 tablespoons butter in a large nonstick skillet over medium heat. Add 8 oatmeal triangles; cook 3 minutes on each side or until golden brown. Remove from pan; keep warm. Repeat procedure with 2 tablespoons butter and remaining oatmeal triangles. Place 2 oatmeal triangles on each of 8 plates, and top each serving with 3½ tablespoons fruit compote and about 2 teaspoons syrup. Yield: 8 servings.

CALORIES 314 (23% from fat); FAT 7.9g (sat 3.9g, mono 2.3g, poly 0.9g); PROTEIN 5.8g; CARB 58.7g; FIBER 2.8g; CHOL 16mg; IRON 2.4mg; SODIUM 167mg; CALC 76mg

MAKE AHEAD
Chamomile-Fruit Smoothie

This juice blend is a refreshing, healthful way to greet the morning. Mix a pitcher for your next brunch—and be prepared to pour seconds. Serve well chilled.

 1 cup boiling water
 1 chamomile tea bag
 ½ teaspoon grated peeled fresh
    ginger
 2 peeled ripe mangoes, chopped
 2 carrots, chopped
 1 ripe pear, peeled and cored
 2 cups fresh orange
    juice

1. Pour 1 cup boiling water over tea bag in a small bowl, and steep 10 minutes. Remove and discard tea bag.

2. Combine brewed tea, ginger, mangoes, carrots, and pear in a blender; process until smooth. Stir in orange juice. Cover and chill 8 hours or overnight. Strain mixture through a cheesecloth-lined sieve into a medium bowl, pressing with a wooden spoon or rubber spatula to squeeze out juice;

discard solids. Pour into a pitcher. Yield: 4 servings (serving size: 1 cup).

CALORIES 128 (4% from fat); FAT 0.5g (sat 0.1g, mono 0.1g, poly 0.1g); PROTEIN 1.7g; CARB 31.1g; FIBER 2.9g; CHOL 0mg; IRON 0.4mg; SODIUM 19mg; CALC 32mg

MAKE AHEAD
Coconut Frushi

Frushi, or fruit sushi, is one of Orange's most popular items and makes a beautiful and unusual breakfast addition. Serve it as a side to poached eggs and Canadian bacon or ham. We've used oranges and raspberries for the topping, but any fresh fruit will work. If the fruit won't adhere to the rice, apply it with a dab of honey.

 1¼ cups water
 1 cup uncooked sushi rice or other
    short-grain rice
 ¼ cup sugar
 ¼ cup light coconut milk
 Dash of salt
 Cooking spray
 10 orange sections
 20 fresh raspberries
 1 (6-ounce) carton vanilla fat-free
    yogurt

1. Bring water and rice to a boil in a medium saucepan. Cover, reduce heat, and simmer 15 minutes or until water is almost absorbed. Remove from heat; let stand, covered, 15 minutes.

2. Place rice in a large bowl. Add sugar, coconut milk, and salt; stir gently until well combined. Cover. Let stand 20 minutes.

3. Lightly coat hands with cooking spray. Divide rice mixture into 20 equal portions; shape each into a ball (about 1 rounded tablespoon each). Lightly press each rice ball into an oval between palms; place ovals on a baking sheet lined with wax paper. Top each of 10 ovals with 1 orange section; press gently to adhere. Top each of remaining 10 ovals with 2 raspberries. Cover and chill frushi until ready to serve. Serve with yogurt for dipping. Yield: 5 servings (serving size: 4 frushi pieces and about 2½ tablespoons yogurt).

CALORIES 228 (4% from fat); FAT 1g (sat 0.7g, mono 0.1g, poly 0.1g); PROTEIN 4.2g; CARB 50.2g; FIBER 1.4g; CHOL 1mg; IRON 0.4mg; SODIUM 53mg; CALC 71mg

Coconut French Toast with Grilled Pineapple and Tropical Salsa

This dish is best prepared with day-old bread. You can serve the pineapple slices raw, but the deep, caramelized flavors you get from cooking them in a grill pan are worth the extra effort.

SALSA:
 2 tablespoons flaked sweetened
    coconut
 2 teaspoons fresh lime juice
 2 peeled ripe mangoes, chopped
 1 pint strawberries, chopped

FRENCH TOAST:
 1 cup egg substitute
 1 cup light coconut milk
 1 cup 1% low-fat milk
 ½ cup granulated sugar
 ½ teaspoon vanilla extract
 ¼ teaspoon salt
 2 large eggs, lightly beaten
 1 (16-ounce) loaf French bread,
    cut into 16 slices
 Cooking spray

REMAINING INGREDIENTS:
 1 pineapple, peeled, cored, and cut
    crosswise into 8 slices
 Powdered sugar (optional)

1. To prepare salsa, combine first 4 ingredients; cover and chill.

2. Preheat oven to 400°.

3. To prepare French toast, combine egg substitute and next 6 ingredients in a large bowl, stirring well with a whisk. Place bread in egg mixture; press with spatula to completely submerge bread in egg mixture. Let stand 15 minutes.

4. Arrange soaked bread in a single layer on a jelly-roll pan coated with cooking spray. Bake at 400° for 12 minutes or until set. Remove from oven, and keep warm.

5. While bread bakes, heat a grill pan over medium-high heat. Coat pan with cooking spray. Arrange 4 pineapple slices in pan; cook 4 minutes on each side or until pineapple begins to brown. Remove from pan; keep warm. Repeat procedure with cooking spray and
Continued

remaining pineapple. Arrange 2 toast pieces on each of 8 plates; top each serving with 1 pineapple slice and ½ cup salsa. Sprinkle with powdered sugar, if desired. Yield: 8 servings.

CALORIES 350 (15% from fat); FAT 5.7g (sat 2.3g, mono 1.4g, poly 0.8g); PROTEIN 11.4g; CARB 64.8g; FIBER 4.4g; CHOL 54mg; IRON 2.8mg; SODIUM 523mg; CALC 112mg

MAKE AHEAD
Blueberry Blender

Loaded with antioxidants, this tasty drink can be served chilled, or blended with a few ice cubes just before serving.

3 cups fresh orange juice
¼ cup honey
1 pint fresh or frozen blueberries
1 cucumber, quartered

1. Combine all ingredients in a blender; process until smooth. Cover and chill 8 hours or overnight. Strain mixture through a cheesecloth-lined sieve into a medium bowl, pressing with a wooden spoon or rubber spatula to squeeze out juice; discard solids. Yield: 4 servings (serving size: about 1 cup).

CALORIES 185 (3% from fat); FAT 0.7g (sat 0.1g, mono 0.1g, poly 0.2g); PROTEIN 2g; CARB 45.8g; FIBER 2.3g; CHOL 0mg; IRON 0.6mg; SODIUM 7mg; CALC 32mg

menu of the month

Burger Cookout

Now's the time to fire up the grill and gather outdoors to savor great food and good times.

Summertime Grilling Menu
serves 4

Grilled Vegetable Salad with Creamy Blue Cheese Dressing

Jamaican Jerk Turkey Burgers with Papaya-Mango Salsa

Baked potato chips

Apricot-Cherry Upside-Down Mini Cakes

MAKE AHEAD
Grilled Vegetable Salad with Creamy Blue Cheese Dressing

This is a smart make-ahead dish because the vegetables can be grilled a few hours prior to assembling the salads.

DRESSING:
⅓ cup low-fat mayonnaise
⅓ cup plain low-fat yogurt
¼ cup (1 ounce) crumbled blue cheese
¼ cup 1% low-fat milk
¼ teaspoon freshly ground black pepper
⅛ teaspoon salt

SALAD:
¼ pound green beans, trimmed
¼ pound sugar snap peas, trimmed
¼ pound carrots, peeled and cut diagonally into ½-inch-thick pieces
1 cup (½-inch-thick) slices red onion
Cooking spray
½ teaspoon freshly ground black pepper
¼ teaspoon garlic salt
6 cups torn romaine lettuce
½ cup thinly sliced radishes

1. To prepare dressing, combine first 6 ingredients, stirring with a whisk until well blended. Cover and chill.
2. Prepare grill to medium heat.
3. To prepare salad, cook beans, peas, and carrots in boiling water 3 minutes or until crisp-tender. Drain and plunge into ice water; drain. Place mixture in a large bowl, and add onion. Lightly coat vegetable mixture with cooking spray. Sprinkle with ½ teaspoon pepper and garlic salt; toss gently to coat.
4. Place vegetable mixture in a wire grilling basket coated with cooking spray. Place grilling basket on grill rack, and grill 7 minutes on each side or until lightly browned. Arrange 1½ cups lettuce on each of 4 salad plates. Divide grilled vegetables and radishes evenly among servings. Serve ¼ cup dressing with each salad. Yield: 4 servings.

CALORIES 144 (29% from fat); FAT 4.7g (sat 2g, mono 0.8g, poly 0.3g); PROTEIN 6.8g; CARB 20.4g; FIBER 5.2g; CHOL 8mg; IRON 2.4mg; SODIUM 497mg; CALC 187mg

MAKE AHEAD
Jamaican Jerk Turkey Burgers with Papaya-Mango Salsa

Burgers on the grill are anything but ordinary when they're made with jerk-seasoned ground turkey. Ketchup and mustard step aside for a cool, fruity salsa that offsets the spice of the burgers. Prepare the salsa up to 1 day in advance, and refrigerate.

SALSA:
⅔ cup diced peeled papaya
⅔ cup diced peeled mango
¼ cup finely chopped red bell pepper
¼ cup finely chopped red onion
2 tablespoons chopped fresh cilantro
½ teaspoon grated lime rind
2 tablespoons fresh lime juice

BURGERS:
1 cup finely chopped red onion
½ cup dry breadcrumbs
⅓ cup bottled sweet-and-sour sauce
¼ cup finely chopped red bell pepper
1 tablespoon Jamaican jerk seasoning (such as Spice Islands)
1 large egg white, lightly beaten
1 pound ground turkey
Cooking spray
4 (2-ounce) Kaiser rolls or hamburger buns

1. To prepare salsa, combine first 7 ingredients. Let stand at room temperature at least 30 minutes.
2. Prepare grill to medium heat.
3. To prepare burgers, combine 1 cup onion and next 5 ingredients, stirring well. Add turkey; mix well. Divide turkey mixture into 4 equal portions, shaping each into a 1-inch-thick patty. Cover and refrigerate 20 minutes.
4. Lightly coat patties with cooking spray; place on a grill rack coated with cooking spray. Grill 7 minutes on each side or until done.
5. Cut rolls in half horizontally. Place rolls, cut sides down, on grill rack; grill 1 minute or until lightly toasted. Place 1 patty on bottom half of each roll; top

with ½ cup salsa and top half of roll. Yield: 4 servings (serving size: 1 burger).

CALORIES 424 (22% from fat); FAT 10.4g (sat 2.5g, mono 3.7g, poly 2.9g); PROTEIN 24.1g; CARB 58g; FIBER 3.9g; CHOL 67mg; IRON 4mg; SODIUM 818mg; CALC 121mg

Apricot-Cherry Upside-Down Mini Cakes

This dessert spotlights seasonal apricots and cherries at the peak of perfection.

Cooking spray
1 tablespoon butter, cut into 4 equal pieces
4 teaspoons brown sugar
2 apricots, halved and pitted
16 sweet cherries, pitted and halved
⅔ cup all-purpose flour
½ teaspoon baking soda
¼ teaspoon salt
⅓ cup granulated sugar
2 tablespoons butter, softened
¼ teaspoon vanilla extract
1 large egg, lightly beaten
⅓ cup fat-free milk
6 tablespoons frozen fat-free whipped topping, thawed

1. Preheat oven to 350°.
2. Coat 4 (8-ounce) custard cups or ramekins with cooking spray. Place 1 butter piece in bottom of each cup. Sprinkle 1 teaspoon brown sugar over butter in each cup. Arrange 1 apricot half, cut side up, over brown sugar in each ramekin. Arrange 8 cherry halves, cut sides up, around outside edge of each apricot; set aside.
3. Lightly spoon flour into a dry measuring cup; level with a knife. Combine flour, baking soda, and salt, stirring with a whisk. Place granulated sugar and 2 tablespoons butter in a medium bowl; beat with a mixer at medium speed until well blended. Add vanilla and egg; beat well. Add flour mixture to sugar mixture alternately with milk, beginning and ending with flour mixture; beat well after each addition. Divide batter evenly over fruit in cups. Place cups on a baking sheet.
4. Bake at 350° for 30 minutes or until a wooden pick inserted in center comes out clean. Cool in cups 5 minutes on a wire rack. Loosen edges of cakes with a knife. Place a dessert plate, upside down, on top of each cup; invert onto plates. Drizzle any remaining caramelized syrup evenly over cakes. Serve cake warm with whipped topping. Yield: 4 servings (serving size: 1 cake and 1½ tablespoons whipped topping).

CALORIES 299 (31% from fat); FAT 10.3g (sat 5.8g, mono 3.1g, poly 0.7g); PROTEIN 5.1g; CARB 46.9g; FIBER 1.6g; CHOL 77mg; IRON 1.5mg; SODIUM 423mg; CALC 48mg

dinner tonight

Sauté in No Time

Sauté your way to a delicious meal in minutes.

Pork Tacos Menu
serves 4

Lime-Cilantro Pork Tacos

Black bean salad with bell peppers and onions*

Lemon sorbet

*Combine 1 (15-ounce) can rinsed and drained black beans, 1 cup chopped red bell pepper, ½ cup chopped red onion, ¼ cup chopped fresh parsley, 1½ tablespoons red wine vinegar, 1 tablespoon olive oil, ¼ teaspoon black pepper, ⅛ teaspoon salt, and 1 minced garlic clove. Serve at room temperature.

Game Plan

1. While skillet preheats:
  • Prepare black bean salad
  • Chop jalapeño pepper, tomato, and cilantro
  • Slice onion and squeeze lime juice
2. While tomatoes simmer in sauce, warm tortillas.

Lime-Cilantro Pork Tacos

Browning the pork improves its color, and the browned bits enrich the sauce's flavor. Increase the amount of jalapeño pepper if you enjoy spicy food. Serve with lime wedges.

TOTAL TIME: 30 MINUTES

QUICK TIP: To make the pork tenderloin easier to cut into thin strips, partially freeze it first.

1 pound pork tenderloin, trimmed and cut into thin strips
¼ teaspoon salt
⅛ teaspoon freshly ground black pepper
2 teaspoons olive oil
1½ cups thinly sliced onion
1 small jalapeño pepper, seeded and chopped
½ cup fat-free, less-sodium chicken broth
½ cup chopped plum tomato
3 tablespoons chopped cilantro
2½ tablespoons fresh lime juice
8 (6-inch) flour tortillas

1. Heat a large nonstick skillet over medium-high heat. Sprinkle pork with salt and black pepper. Add oil to pan. Add pork, and sauté 4 minutes or until browned. Remove pork from pan; place in a bowl. Add onion and jalapeño to pan; sauté 5 minutes or until tender. Add broth; reduce heat, and simmer 1 minute, scraping pan to loosen browned bits. Stir in tomato; simmer 2 minutes.
2. Return pork and accumulated juices to pan. Stir in cilantro and lime juice; cook 1 minute or until pork is done.
3. Heat tortillas according to package directions. Spoon ½ cup pork mixture into each tortilla; roll up. Yield: 4 servings (serving size: 2 tacos).

CALORIES 416 (28% from fat); FAT 13.1g (sat 3.6g, mono 6.8g, poly 1.6g); PROTEIN 30.2g; CARB 43.1g; FIBER 3.6g; CHOL 75mg; IRON 3.8mg; SODIUM 569mg; CALC 101mg

QUICK & EASY
Parmesan Chicken and Rice

Rice and broth are added to sautéed chicken, onion, garlic, and mushrooms for a simple entrée that requires only one pan.

TOTAL TIME: 30 MINUTES

1	tablespoon olive oil
½	cup chopped onion
1	teaspoon bottled minced garlic
½	teaspoon dried thyme
1	(8-ounce) package presliced mushrooms
¾	pound skinless, boneless chicken breast, cut into bite-sized pieces
½	cup dry white wine
½	teaspoon salt
¼	teaspoon freshly ground black pepper
1	cup uncooked instant rice
1	cup fat-free, less-sodium chicken broth
½	cup (2 ounces) grated fresh Parmesan cheese
¼	cup chopped fresh parsley

1. Heat oil in a large nonstick skillet over medium-high heat. Add onion, garlic, thyme, and mushrooms; sauté 5 minutes or until onion is tender. Add chicken; sauté 4 minutes or until chicken is lightly browned. Add wine, salt, and pepper; cook 3 minutes or until liquid almost evaporates.

2. Stir in rice and broth. Bring to a boil; cover, reduce heat, and simmer 5 minutes or until liquid is absorbed. Stir in cheese and parsley. Yield: 4 servings (serving size: about 1 cup).

CALORIES 395 (18% from fat); FAT 8g (sat 2.8g, mono 3.7g, poly 0.8g); PROTEIN 29.9g; CARB 44.4g; FIBER 2g; CHOL 57mg; IRON 4.1mg; SODIUM 656mg; CALC 171mg

QUICK & EASY
Rice Noodles with Sesame-Ginger Flank Steak

Have all the vegetables ready to go—once you start, the cooking goes quickly. If you can't find fresh sugar snap peas, use thawed frozen peas, and add them to the dish when you return the steak to the pan. You can also save time by purchasing toasted sesame seeds at Asian markets. Look for bags of shredded carrots in the produce section of your supermarket.

TOTAL TIME: 35 MINUTES

QUICK TIP: To grate ginger easily, place a small piece in a garlic press, and squeeze as you would for garlic.

⅓	cup rice vinegar
3	tablespoons low-sodium soy sauce
1	tablespoon hoisin sauce
2	teaspoons cornstarch
2	teaspoons grated peeled fresh ginger
1½	teaspoons sugar
¼	teaspoon salt
3	garlic cloves, minced
2	teaspoons dark sesame oil, divided
1	(1-pound) flank steak, trimmed and cut into ¼-inch strips
1½	cups shredded carrot
1½	cups sugar snap peas, trimmed
1	cup (¼-inch) red bell pepper strips
½	cup fresh bean sprouts
4	cups hot cooked rice noodles (about 8 ounces uncooked noodles)
½	cup chopped green onions
1	tablespoon sesame seeds, toasted

1. Combine first 8 ingredients, stirring until sugar dissolves.

2. Heat a large nonstick skillet over medium-high heat. Add 1 teaspoon oil. Add half of steak; sauté 4 minutes or until browned. Remove steak from pan. Repeat procedure with 1 teaspoon oil and remaining steak. Add vinegar mixture, carrot, peas, bell pepper, and sprouts to pan; cook 3 minutes, stirring frequently. Return steak to pan. Add noodles; cook 1 minute, stirring constantly. Sprinkle with onions and sesame seeds. Yield: 6 servings (serving size: 1⅓ cups).

CALORIES 369 (25% from fat); FAT 10.4g (sat 3.7g, mono 4g, poly 1.4g); PROTEIN 24.3g; CARB 42.9g; FIBER 4.4g; CHOL 51mg; IRON 3.1mg; SODIUM 542mg; CALC 63mg

Mushroom-Prosciutto Pizza Menu

serves 4

Mushroom-Prosciutto Pizza

Arugula salad with garlic-sherry vinaigrette*

Angel food cake topped with fresh berries

*Combine 1½ teaspoons sherry vinegar, 1 teaspoon extravirgin olive oil, ¼ teaspoon salt, ⅛ teaspoon freshly ground black pepper, and 1 crushed garlic clove in a large bowl, stirring with a whisk. Add 6 cups arugula, ½ cup halved grape tomatoes, and ½ cup chopped yellow bell pepper; toss to coat.

Game Plan

1. While oven preheats:
- Slice mushrooms and prosciutto
- Chop shallots, garlic, and thyme

2. While pizza toppings cook, bake untopped pizza crust.

3. While untopped pizza crust bakes:
- Shred cheese
- Prepare salad

QUICK & EASY

Mushroom-Prosciutto Pizza

For a crisp crust, bake the pizza crust on the lowest rack for a few minutes before adding the toppings. Presliced button mushrooms can substitute for the creminis.

TOTAL TIME: 25 MINUTES

QUICK TIP: Use a fresh thyme sprig that has small leaves so you don't have to chop them; just strip them off the stem.

Cooking spray
8 ounces sliced cremini mushrooms
¼ cup finely chopped shallots
1 garlic clove, minced
1 teaspoon chopped fresh thyme
2 teaspoons sherry vinegar
1 (10-ounce) Italian cheese-flavored thin pizza crust (such as Boboli)
2 ounces prosciutto, cut into thin strips
⅓ cup (about 1½ ounces) shredded fontina cheese

1. Preheat oven to 450°.

2. Heat a 12-inch nonstick skillet over medium-high heat. Coat pan with cooking spray. Add mushrooms and shallots; sauté 7 minutes or until mushrooms are tender. Add garlic and thyme; sauté 1 minute. Stir in vinegar; remove from heat.

3. Place crust on bottom rack of oven. Bake at 450° for 4 minutes.

4. Place crust on a baking sheet. Spread mushroom mixture evenly over crust; sprinkle evenly with prosciutto and fontina cheese. Bake at 450° for 6 minutes or until cheese melts. Yield: 4 servings.

CALORIES 273 (28% from fat); FAT 8.4g (sat 3.7g, mono 2.4g, poly 0.8g); PROTEIN 15.3g; CARB 34.5g; FIBER 0.4g; CHOL 23mg; IRON 2.3mg; SODIUM 723mg; CALC 254mg

---

enlightened cook

Serving Mom's Seviche

Chef Jose Garces shares variations of a childhood favorite with patrons of Philadelphia's Alma de Cuba.

As a youngster growing up on the northwest side of Chicago, Jose Garces always looked forward to Saturday lunch. While other kids knocked back hot dogs, canned spaghetti, or macaroni and cheese, Garces feasted on fresh seviche. The Latin-American dish of fresh fish cured, or "cooked," in citrus juice might have seemed exotic in America at the time—but not in the Garces home. Garces's mother, Magdalena, a talented home cook, was born in Ecuador, where seviche is a national treasure.

"She made clam seviche, oyster seviche, and the classic shrimp or whitefish seviche with a marinade of diced tomatoes, orange juice, cilantro, and red onions," recalls Garces, who is now executive chef at Alma de Cuba in Philadelphia.

Now, seven days a week, Garces treats diners at Alma de Cuba to a variety of exquisite seviches flavored with ingredients from around the globe.

Pineapple Seviche Mixto

Mixto refers to a mix of two or more seafoods—here, shrimp, scallops, and mussels. The sauce designed to go with this dish also pairs well with grilled fish. Coconut water, the natural liquid inside a coconut, is used in the sauce. See "How to Crack a Coconut" on page 200 for more info on how to get coconut water from a fresh coconut.

SAUCE:
Cooking spray
½ cup finely chopped red onion
1 garlic clove, minced
¼ teaspoon saffron threads, crushed
1 cup finely chopped fresh pineapple
¼ cup coconut water
¼ cup water
1 teaspoon cornstarch
2 teaspoons water
½ cup pineapple juice
½ cup fresh lime juice
⅛ teaspoon hot paprika

SEVICHE:
1½ cups water, divided
1 pound medium shrimp, peeled and deveined
1 pound bay scallops
24 mussels (about 1 pound), scrubbed and debearded
1 cup fresh lime juice
¼ cup finely chopped fresh pineapple
2 tablespoons finely chopped red onion
2 tablespoons chopped fresh chives
2 tablespoons minced fresh cilantro
1 jalapeño pepper, seeded and finely chopped

REMAINING INGREDIENT:
¼ cup freshly grated coconut

1. To prepare sauce, heat a nonstick skillet over medium-high heat. Coat pan with cooking spray. Add onion and garlic; sauté 2 minutes. Add saffron; sauté 30 seconds. Stir in 1 cup pineapple, coconut water, and ¼ cup water. Reduce heat to medium; cook 5 minutes or until liquid almost evaporates, stirring occasionally.
Continued

Combine cornstarch and 2 teaspoons water, stirring well with a whisk. Add pineapple juice and ½ cup lime juice, stirring with a whisk. Add cornstarch mixture to pan; bring to a boil. Cook 1 minute, stirring constantly. Remove from heat, and stir in paprika. Cool completely.

2. To prepare seviche, bring ½ cup water to a boil in a large nonstick skillet; add shrimp. Cook, covered, 1 minute or until done. Rinse shrimp with cold water; drain and place in a bowl.

3. Bring ½ cup water to a boil in a large nonstick skillet, and add scallops. Cook, covered, 1 minute or until done. Rinse scallops with cold water; drain and add to shrimp.

4. Bring ½ cup water to a boil in a large nonstick skillet, and add mussels. Cook, covered, 2 minutes or until shells open; discard any unopened shells. Remove meat from mussels, and discard shells. Add meat to shrimp mixture.

5. Combine 1 cup lime juice and next 5 ingredients; stir jalapeño mixture into seafood mixture. Cover and chill 1 hour.

6. Divide seviche evenly among 8 chilled bowls using a slotted spoon; top each serving with 2 tablespoons sauce and 1½ teaspoons grated coconut. Serve immediately. Yield: 8 servings.

CALORIES 213 (18% from fat); FAT 4.3g (sat 1.3g, mono 0.7g, poly 1.1g); PROTEIN 28.5g; CARB 15.5g; FIBER 1.1g; CHOL 121mg; IRON 4.1mg; SODIUM 347mg; CALC 72mg

---

How to Crack a Coconut

Fresh coconut water (the liquid inside a coconut) and coconut meat are essential to this recipe's success. To crack a coconut, drive a long nail through 2 of the 3 eyes with a hammer. Drain the coconut water into a bowl; chill. Place a bed of towels on the floor. Set the coconut on the towels; hit with a hammer until the shell cracks. Cut the white meat from the brown shell using a paring knife. Grate the coconut meat with a box grater or food processor.

Rainbow Seviche

Wrap each type of fish in plastic, and place it in the freezer for about 30 minutes to partially freeze. This makes it easier to dice.

    1   pound sweet potatoes
    ¾   cup lime juice, divided
    ¼   cup chopped red onion
    3   tablespoons chopped fresh
        cilantro, divided
    1   teaspoon freshly ground black
        pepper
    ½   teaspoon sugar
    1   jalapeño pepper, seeded and
        chopped
    8   ounces sushi-grade Yellowfin tuna
        fillets, diced
    ¼   cup low-sodium soy sauce
    8   ounces sushi-grade salmon fillets,
        diced
    8   ounces sushi-grade grouper fillets,
        diced
    1   tablespoon sesame seeds, toasted
    Cilantro sprigs (optional)

1. Preheat oven to 400°.

2. Bake potatoes at 400° for 1 hour or until tender. Cool. Peel potatoes; slice into ¼-inch rounds.

3. Combine ½ cup juice, onion, 2 tablespoons cilantro, black pepper, sugar, and jalapeño, stirring with a whisk. Place 3 tablespoons of jalapeño mixture in a medium bowl; add tuna. Cover and chill 1 hour. Stir soy sauce into remaining jalapeño mixture; add salmon, tossing to coat. Cover and chill. Combine ¼ cup juice and 1 tablespoon cilantro, stirring well; add grouper, tossing well to coat. Cover and chill 1 hour.

4. Divide tuna mixture evenly among 6 (8-ounce) ramekins or custard cups using a slotted spoon; repeat procedure with salmon and grouper. Divide sweet potato slices evenly among servings. Place a small plate upside down on top of each ramekin; invert onto plates. Sprinkle each serving with about ¾ teaspoon sesame seeds, and garnish with cilantro sprigs, if desired. Yield: 6 servings (serving size: 1 ramekin).

CALORIES 251 (20% from fat); FAT 5.7g (sat 1.1g, mono 1.8g, poly 2.1g); PROTEIN 26g; CARB 23.7g; FIBER 2.9g; CHOL 53mg; IRON 1.7mg; SODIUM 423mg; CALC 57mg

---

Ecuadoran Shrimp Seviche

This dish is made with cooked shrimp. Serve with lightly grilled French bread to savor every drop of the sauce, which is made from grilled vegetables. CornNuts are a traditional topping; look for them with other snack foods at the grocery.

SAUCE:

    1   large tomato, cored
    1   small onion, quartered
    1   jalapeño pepper, seeded
    1   small green bell pepper, halved
        and seeded
    Cooking spray
    1   cup fresh orange juice
    ½   cup ketchup
    ¼   cup fresh lime juice

SEVICHE:

    1   cup fresh lime juice
    ½   cup chopped red onion
    ¼   cup chopped green onions
    1½ pounds medium shrimp, cooked
        and peeled

REMAINING INGREDIENTS:

    ½   cup diced peeled avocado
    ¼   cup CornNuts, lightly crushed

1. Prepare grill to medium-high heat.

2. To prepare sauce, lightly coat tomato, quartered onion, and peppers with cooking spray. Place vegetables in a wire grilling basket coated with cooking spray; grill 4 minutes on each side or until vegetables begin to blacken. Remove from heat; cool slightly. Combine orange juice, ketchup, and ¼ cup lime juice in a food processor. Add grilled vegetables; process until smooth, scraping sides of bowl occasionally. Spoon sauce into a large bowl; cover and chill at least 1 hour.

3. To prepare seviche, add 1 cup lime juice, red onion, green onions, and shrimp to sauce; stir well to combine. Cover and chill 1 hour. Divide seviche evenly among 6 chilled dishes; top each with 1½ tablespoons avocado and 2 teaspoons CornNuts. Yield: 6 servings.

CALORIES 230 (19% from fat); FAT 4.8g (sat 0.8g, mono 1.8g, poly 1.3g); PROTEIN 25g; CARB 23.5g; FIBER 2.6g; CHOL 172mg; IRON 3.4mg; SODIUM 432mg; CALC 81mg

Northwest Exposure

Vancouver, British Columbia, serves a full complement of cultures and cuisines. Here's an example of a Korean delicacy.

Korean Beef Strip Steak

This recipe from chef Chris Whittaker of Zin Restaurant showcases the Asian flavors that are so popular in Vancouver. Serve with *kimchi* (spicy fermented vegetables).

STEAK:

- ¼ cup low-sodium soy sauce
- 3 tablespoons chopped green onions
- 1½ tablespoons minced garlic
- 1½ tablespoons sesame seeds, toasted
- 1 tablespoon brown sugar
- 1 teaspoon sesame oil
- ¼ teaspoon freshly ground black pepper
- 4 (4-ounce) New York strip steaks, trimmed
- Cooking spray

BOK CHOY:

- 2 teaspoons vegetable oil
- 1 teaspoon finely chopped shallots
- 1 teaspoon minced garlic
- 10 cups coarsely chopped bok choy (about 1 pound)
- ½ teaspoon salt

REMAINING INGREDIENT:

- 2 cups hot cooked jasmine rice

1. To prepare steak, combine first 7 ingredients in a large zip-top plastic bag. Add steaks; seal and marinate in refrigerator 2 hours, turning bag occasionally.
2. Preheat grill to medium-high heat.
3. Remove steaks from bag, and discard marinade. Place steaks on grill rack coated with cooking spray, and grill 3 minutes on each side or until desired degree of doneness.
4. To prepare bok choy, heat oil in a large skillet over medium-high heat. Add shallots and 1 teaspoon garlic; sauté 30 seconds. Add bok choy, and sauté 1 minute. Sprinkle salt over bok choy. Cover, reduce heat to low, and cook 7 minutes or until bok choy wilts and stems are soft, stirring occasionally. Serve steak with bok choy and rice. Yield: 4 servings (serving size: 1 steak, 1 cup bok choy, and ½ cup rice).

CALORIES 368 (31% from fat); FAT 12.8g (sat 4g, mono 4.7g, poly 2.4g); PROTEIN 28.8g; CARB 33.4g; FIBER 1.8g; CHOL 65mg; IRON 4.7mg; SODIUM 678mg; CALC 153mg

. . . And Ready in Just About 20 Minutes

Here, we've featured 22 superfast recipes ranging from Mexican to Indian fare. Whether you want soup, steak, poultry, or fish, there are enough recipes so you can try a different dish every weeknight.

QUICK & EASY
Pan-Fried Bass

This crisp, crunchy fish has just a fraction of the fat—and none of the mess—of deep-fat frying. Serve with tartar sauce, white-and-wild rice, and steamed broccoli.

- 1 tablespoon all-purpose flour
- ¼ teaspoon salt
- ¼ teaspoon black pepper
- 1 tablespoon water
- 1 large egg white
- ¼ cup seasoned breadcrumbs
- 2 tablespoons cornmeal
- 4 (6-ounce) bass fillets, skinned
- 2 teaspoons vegetable oil
- 1 teaspoon butter
- 4 lemon wedges

1. Heat a large nonstick skillet over medium heat. Combine flour, salt, and pepper in a large zip-top plastic bag. Combine water and egg white in a shallow dish, stirring with a whisk. Combine breadcrumbs and cornmeal in another shallow dish, stirring with a whisk.
2. Place 1 fillet in bag; seal and shake to coat. Dip in egg white mixture, and dredge in breadcrumb mixture. Repeat procedure with remaining fillets, flour mixture, egg white mixture, and breadcrumb mixture.
3. Add oil and butter to pan; cook until butter melts. Add fillets to pan, and cook 5 minutes on each side or until fish flakes easily when tested with a fork. Serve with lemon wedges. Yield: 4 servings (serving size: 1 fillet and 1 lemon wedge).

CALORIES 250 (27% from fat); FAT 7.5g (sat 1.9g, mono 2g, poly 2.8g); PROTEIN 32.8g; CARB 10.9g; FIBER 0.9g; CHOL 139mg; IRON 2mg; SODIUM 485mg; CALC 37mg

QUICK & EASY
Chile-Glazed Shrimp

Serve over rice noodles with steamed sugar snap peas.

- 2 teaspoons dark sesame oil
- 1 teaspoon bottled minced garlic
- 1½ pounds large shrimp, peeled and deveined
- ½ cup thinly sliced green onions
- 1 tablespoon low-sodium soy sauce
- 1 tablespoon honey
- 1 teaspoon sambal oelek (ground fresh chile paste)

1. Heat a large nonstick skillet over medium-high heat. Add oil to pan. Add garlic and shrimp, and stir-fry 2 minutes. Add onions and remaining ingredients; stir-fry 3 minutes or until shrimp are done. Yield: 4 servings (serving size: ¾ cup).

CALORIES 225 (21% from fat); FAT 5.2g (sat 0.9g, mono 1.3g, poly 2.1g); PROTEIN 34.8g; CARB 7.6g; FIBER 0.6g; CHOL 259mg; IRON 4.3mg; SODIUM 441mg; CALC 91mg

Spicy Sausage Pizza

For a more kid-friendly supper, use a milder sausage, such as basil and pine nut.

- 1 (10-ounce) Italian cheese-flavored thin pizza crust (such as Boboli)
- ½ cup pizza sauce or marinara sauce
- 3 (⅛-inch-thick) slices sweet or red onion, separated into rings
- 1 yellow bell pepper, thinly sliced into rings
- 3 ounces chicken sausage with habanero chiles and tequila, chopped (such as Gerhard's)
- 1 cup (4 ounces) preshredded part-skim mozzarella cheese
- 2 tablespoons chopped fresh basil

1. Preheat oven to 425°.
2. Place crust on a baking sheet. Spread sauce evenly over crust, leaving a ½-inch border. Arrange onion and bell pepper evenly over sauce. Top with sausage; sprinkle with cheese. Bake at 425° for 10 minutes or until cheese is melted and bubbly. Remove from heat, and sprinkle with basil. Yield: 4 servings.

CALORIES 314 (30% from fat); FAT 10.4g (sat 4.7g, mono 2.9g, poly 0.8g); PROTEIN 17.5g; CARB 37.4g; FIBER 1.9g; CHOL 32mg; IRON 2.3mg; SODIUM 703mg; CALC 396mg

Southwestern Steak and Pinto Beans

You can round out this dish with your favorite corn bread.

- 1 teaspoon garlic salt
- 1 teaspoon ground cumin
- ¼ teaspoon ground red pepper
- 1 pound boneless sirloin steak, trimmed
- Cooking spray
- 1 teaspoon vegetable oil
- 1 cup diced red bell pepper
- ½ cup bottled chunky salsa, divided
- 1 (15-ounce) can pinto beans, rinsed and drained
- ¼ cup chopped cilantro

1. Heat a grill pan over medium-high heat. Combine first 3 ingredients. Remove 1 teaspoon cumin mixture, and set aside. Sprinkle remaining cumin mixture evenly over steak. Lightly coat steak with cooking spray. Place steak in grill pan; cook 4 minutes on each side or until desired degree of doneness. Remove from pan; let stand 5 minutes. Cut into thin slices.
2. While steak cooks, heat oil in a medium saucepan over medium-high heat. Add bell pepper; sauté 4 minutes or until tender. Add reserved cumin mixture, ¼ cup salsa, and beans; cook 1 minute or until thoroughly heated, stirring mixture constantly.
3. Place ½ cup bean mixture on each of 4 plates; divide beef evenly over bean mixture. Top each serving with 1 tablespoon salsa and 1 tablespoon cilantro. Yield: 4 servings.

CALORIES 267 (27% from fat); FAT 8g (sat 2.6g, mono 2.9g, poly 1.3g); PROTEIN 27.5g; CARB 21g; FIBER 6.4g; CHOL 63mg; IRON 4.6mg; SODIUM 640mg; CALC 73mg

Picadillo Soft Tacos

Chipotle chile powder gives this taco filling a wonderful smoky flavor.

- ½ cup frozen chopped onion
- 2 teaspoons bottled minced garlic
- 12 ounces ground turkey breast
- ¼ cup raisins
- 1 teaspoon chipotle chile powder
- 1 teaspoon ground cumin
- ¾ teaspoon salt
- ¼ teaspoon ground cinnamon
- 1 (14.5-ounce) can diced tomatoes, undrained
- 8 (6-inch) corn tortillas
- ½ cup diced peeled avocado
- 2 tablespoons slivered almonds, toasted
- 2 tablespoons chopped fresh cilantro

1. Heat a large nonstick skillet over medium-high heat. Add onion, garlic, and turkey; cook 4 minutes or until turkey is done, stirring to crumble. Stir in raisins and next 5 ingredients; simmer 6 minutes or until thickened, stirring occasionally.
2. Warm tortillas according to package directions. Spoon about ⅔ cup turkey mixture onto each tortilla; top each tortilla with 1 tablespoon avocado, 1½ teaspoons almonds, and 1½ teaspoons cilantro; fold in half. Yield: 4 servings (serving size: 2 tacos).

CALORIES 341 (22% from fat); FAT 8.2g (sat 1.1g, mono 4.2g, poly 2g); PROTEIN 27.3g; CARB 42.4g; FIBER 6.6g; CHOL 53mg; IRON 3.1mg; SODIUM 727mg; CALC 169mg

Chunky Vegetable Soup with Toasted Cheese Croutons

- 2 teaspoons olive oil
- 1 cup frozen chopped onion
- 1 cup presliced mushrooms
- 1 cup bagged chopped carrot
- 1 cup chopped green bell pepper
- 1 teaspoon dried herbes de Provence
- ¼ teaspoon black pepper
- 1 (14-ounce) can vegetable broth
- 1 (14.5-ounce) can no-salt-added diced tomatoes, undrained
- 1 (15-ounce) can navy beans, rinsed and drained
- 8 (½-inch-thick) slices French bread baguette, toasted
- ¼ cup (1 ounce) grated Asiago cheese

1. Preheat broiler.
2. Heat oil in a Dutch oven over medium-high heat. Add onion, mushrooms, carrot, and bell pepper; cover and cook 3 minutes. Stir in herbes de Provence, black pepper, broth, and tomatoes. Bring to a boil; cover, reduce heat, and simmer 5 minutes. Stir in beans; cover and simmer 5 minutes.
3. While soup cooks, arrange bread slices on a baking sheet. Sprinkle evenly with cheese. Broil 2 minutes or until cheese melts. Spoon 1¾ cups soup into each of 4 bowls, and top each serving with 2 bread slices. Yield: 4 servings.

CALORIES 382 (20% from fat); FAT 8.3g (sat 2.2g, mono 3.1g, poly 2g); PROTEIN 16.8g; CARB 64.1g; FIBER 11.1g; CHOL 6mg; IRON 3.8mg; SODIUM 957mg; CALC 217mg

Linguine Carbonara

1 (9-ounce) package uncooked fresh linguine
3 slices precooked bacon (such as Oscar Mayer Ready-to-Serve bacon)
½ cup fat-free, less-sodium chicken broth
¼ cup dry white wine
1 tablespoon butter
2 garlic cloves, minced
¼ cup egg substitute
¼ teaspoon salt
⅛ teaspoon black pepper
½ cup (2 ounces) grated fresh Parmesan cheese

1. Cook pasta according to package directions, omitting salt and fat.
2. Heat bacon according to package directions. Cool and finely chop; set aside.
3. Combine broth, wine, butter, and garlic in a large nonstick skillet; bring to a boil over medium-high heat. Reduce heat, and simmer 1 minute. Remove from heat; stir in egg substitute, salt, and pepper. Add pasta; toss well. Stir in bacon and cheese; toss well. Yield: 4 servings (serving size: 1 cup).

CALORIES 363 (24% from fat); FAT 9.7g (sat 4.8g, mono 3.1g, poly 1.1g); PROTEIN 16.2g; CARB 48.9g; FIBER 1.6g; CHOL 20mg; IRON 3.1mg; SODIUM 526mg; CALC 163mg

Cider-Glazed Chicken with Dried Cranberries

Spoon the cranberries and the glaze left in the pan over the chicken. Serve with rice.

1½ tablespoons all-purpose flour
¾ teaspoon salt
¼ teaspoon ground allspice
4 (6-ounce) skinless, boneless chicken breast halves
1 tablespoon butter
⅓ cup dried cranberries
½ cup apple cider or apple juice
1 tablespoon cider vinegar or white balsamic vinegar

1. Heat a large nonstick skillet over medium heat. Combine first 3 ingredients in a zip-top plastic bag. Add chicken; seal and shake to coat.
2. Melt butter in pan. Add chicken, and cook 4 minutes. Turn chicken over. Add cranberries, juice, and vinegar; cook 5 minutes or until chicken is done. Yield: 4 servings (serving size: 1 chicken breast half and about 1 teaspoon sauce).

CALORIES 269 (17% from fat); FAT 5g (sat 2.3g, mono 1.3g, poly 0.6g); PROTEIN 39.6g; CARB 13.4g; FIBER 0.9g; CHOL 106mg; IRON 1.4mg; SODIUM 579mg; CALC 21mg

Indian-Spiced Roast Salmon

Serve with sliced cucumbers drizzled with low-fat bottled vinaigrette.

4 (6-ounce) salmon fillets (about 1 inch thick)
Cooking spray
2 tablespoons fresh lime juice
½ teaspoon salt
½ teaspoon ground ginger
½ teaspoon ground coriander
¼ teaspoon ground cumin
⅛ teaspoon ground cinnamon
⅛ teaspoon ground red pepper
⅔ cup plain fat-free yogurt
2 tablespoons chopped fresh cilantro

1. Preheat oven to 425°.
2. Place salmon, skin side down, in a roasting pan or jelly-roll pan coated with cooking spray. Brush evenly with juice. Combine salt and next 5 ingredients, and sprinkle evenly over fish.
3. Bake at 425° for 10 minutes or until fish flakes easily when tested with a fork. Combine yogurt and cilantro, and serve with fish. Yield: 4 servings (serving size: 1 salmon fillet and about 3 tablespoons yogurt mixture).

CALORIES 300 (40% from fat); FAT 13.2g (sat 3.1g, mono 5.7g, poly 3.2g); PROTEIN 38.7g; CARB 4.3g; FIBER 0.3g; CHOL 88mg; IRON 0.8mg; SODIUM 403mg; CALC 107mg

Chicken with Cremini Mushrooms and Asparagus

Serve over angel hair pasta.

1 tablespoon olive oil, divided
4 (6-ounce) skinless, boneless chicken breast halves
½ teaspoon salt
½ teaspoon black pepper
2 cups quartered cremini mushrooms
2 teaspoons bottled minced garlic
¼ teaspoon dried thyme
1 pound asparagus, trimmed and cut into 1-inch pieces
¾ cup fat-free, less-sodium chicken broth
1 teaspoon cornstarch
3 tablespoons balsamic vinegar
1 tablespoon orange juice

1. Heat 2 teaspoons oil in a large nonstick skillet over medium-high heat. Place 1 chicken breast half in a large heavy-duty zip-top plastic bag; pound to a ¼-inch thickness. Repeat procedure with remaining chicken. Sprinkle chicken evenly with salt and pepper. Add chicken to pan; cook 3 minutes on each side or until done. Remove from pan, and keep warm.
2. Heat 1 teaspoon oil in pan over medium-high heat. Add mushrooms, garlic, thyme, and asparagus; cook 3 minutes, stirring frequently. Combine broth and cornstarch, stirring with a whisk. Add broth mixture, vinegar, and juice to pan; bring to a boil. Cook 1 minute or until slightly thick. Serve over chicken. Yield: 4 servings (serving size: 1 chicken breast half and ½ cup asparagus mixture).

CALORIES 275 (19% from fat); FAT 5.7g (sat 1g, mono 3g, poly 0.8g); PROTEIN 43.5g; CARB 9.9g; FIBER 3g; CHOL 99mg; IRON 2.4mg; SODIUM 490mg; CALC 54mg

Olive-Tomato Grilled Cheese Sandwiches

Tomato, basil, and olives are surrounded by melted cheese in this update of a classic lunch or light dinner.

  8 (½-ounce) slices provolone
     cheese
  8 (1½-ounce) slices sourdough
     bread
  2 tablespoons olive spread (such as
     Lindsay Olivada)
 16 large basil leaves
  8 (¼-inch-thick) slices tomato
     Cooking spray

1. Heat a large nonstick skillet over medium heat.
2. To prepare each sandwich, place 1 cheese slice on 1 bread slice. Spread 1½ teaspoons olive spread over cheese. Top with 4 basil leaves, 2 tomato slices, 1 cheese slice, and 1 bread slice.
3. Lightly coat outside of sandwiches with cooking spray. Place 2 sandwiches in pan; cook 3 minutes on each side or until golden brown. Repeat procedure with remaining sandwiches. Yield: 4 servings (serving size: 1 sandwich).

CALORIES 353 (29% from fat); FAT 11.2g (sat 5.4g, mono 3.2g, poly 0.9g); PROTEIN 15.1g; CARB 47.4g; FIBER 3.1g; CHOL 20mg; IRON 2.5mg; SODIUM 827mg; CALC 283mg

Huevos Rancheros Tostados

Serve this meatless main dish with a fruit salad. Most of the seasoning is from the picante sauce, so taste it and make sure you like it before preparing the recipe.

  4 (6-inch) corn tortillas
     Cooking spray
 ½ cup picante sauce
 ¼ cup ketchup
  1 (15-ounce) can pinto beans,
     rinsed and drained
  4 large eggs
 ¼ teaspoon salt
 ¼ cup chopped fresh
     cilantro

1. Preheat oven to 450°.
2. Lightly coat both sides of tortillas with cooking spray, and place on a baking sheet. Bake at 450° for 5 minutes on each side or until crisp.
3. While tortillas bake, combine picante sauce, ketchup, and beans in a large nonstick skillet; bring to a simmer over medium-high heat, stirring frequently. Using a wooden spoon, make 4 small wells in bean mixture, 2 inches apart. Break 1 egg into each well, and sprinkle evenly with salt. Cover and cook 5 minutes or until egg is desired degree of doneness.
4. Place 1 tortilla on each of 4 plates; top each serving with ½ cup bean mixture and 1 egg. Sprinkle each serving with 1 tablespoon cilantro. Yield: 4 servings.

CALORIES 248 (24% from fat); FAT 6.6g (sat 1.6g, mono 2.1g, poly 1.8g); PROTEIN 13.7g; CARB 34.7g; FIBER 7.4g; CHOL 213mg; IRON 2.4mg; SODIUM 854mg; CALC 108mg

Pork Tenderloin with Olive-Mustard Tapenade

A little bit of this tapenade adds a lot of flavor. This quick entrée is great served with couscous and a tossed Greek salad with feta cheese. To quickly flatten pork, press with the heel of your hand.

  1 (1-pound) pork tenderloin,
     trimmed and cut crosswise into
     8 pieces
 ½ teaspoon salt
 ¼ teaspoon black pepper
 ¼ teaspoon ground fennel
     Cooking spray
 ¼ cup chopped pitted kalamata
     olives
 ¼ cup chopped pitted green olives
     or onion-stuffed green olives
  1 tablespoon fresh chopped parsley
  1 tablespoon Dijon mustard
  2 teaspoons balsamic vinegar
 ½ teaspoon bottled minced garlic

1. Heat a large nonstick skillet over medium-high heat. Press pork pieces into ½-inch-thick medallions. Combine salt, pepper, and fennel; rub evenly over pork. Lightly coat pork with cooking spray. Add pork to pan; cook 4 minutes on each side or until done.
2. While pork cooks, combine Kalamata olives and remaining 5 ingredients. Serve olive mixture over pork. Yield: 4 servings (serving size: 2 pork medallions and 2 tablespoons olive mixture).

CALORIES 163 (33% from fat); FAT 6g (sat 1.6g, mono 3.2g, poly 0.7g); PROTEIN 24.3g; CARB 2.2g; FIBER 0.7g; CHOL 74mg; IRON 2.2mg; SODIUM 590mg; CALC 31mg

Sautéed Chicken Breasts with Latin Citrus Sauce

The sauce, also known as *mojo criollo*, requires very little chopping and provides a tangy counterpart to the cumin-rubbed chicken. Serve over white rice.

CHICKEN:
  2 teaspoons brown sugar
  1 teaspoon ground cumin
 ½ teaspoon salt
 ½ teaspoon garlic powder
 ⅛ teaspoon ground red pepper
  4 (6-ounce) skinless, boneless
     chicken breast halves
  1 teaspoon vegetable oil

SAUCE:
 1½ teaspoons bottled minced garlic
 ¼ cup fresh lime juice
 ¼ cup orange juice
  2 tablespoons honey
  2 tablespoons chopped fresh cilantro
  2 tablespoons chopped fresh mint

1. To prepare chicken, combine first 5 ingredients; rub over chicken. Heat oil in a large nonstick skillet over medium-high heat. Add chicken, and cook 5 minutes on each side or until done. Remove from pan; keep warm.
2. To prepare sauce, add garlic to pan; sauté 30 seconds. Add juices and honey; cook 3 minutes or until slightly thickened. Remove from heat; stir in cilantro and mint. Serve with chicken. Yield: 4 servings (serving size: 1 chicken breast half and about 1 tablespoon sauce).

CALORIES 255 (12% from fat); FAT 3.4g (sat 0.7g, mono 0.8g, poly 1.2g); PROTEIN 39.8g; CARB 15g; FIBER 0.5g; CHOL 99mg; IRON 1.6mg; SODIUM 405mg; CALC 34mg

Maple-Orange Chicken

This chicken dish is best served over rice.

Cooking spray
4 (6-ounce) skinless, boneless chicken breast halves
3 tablespoons water
3 tablespoons pure maple syrup
2 tablespoons low-sodium soy sauce
2 tablespoons cider vinegar
1½ teaspoons grated orange rind

1. Heat a large nonstick skillet over medium heat. Coat pan with cooking spray. Add chicken to pan, and cook 6 minutes on each side or until done.
2. Combine water and remaining 4 ingredients. Add to pan; cook 1 minute, turning chicken to coat. Yield: 4 servings (serving size: 1 breast half and about 1 tablespoon sauce).

CALORIES 233 (8% from fat); FAT 2.1g (sat 0.6g, mono 0.5g, poly 0.5g); PROTEIN 39.8g; CARB 11.3g; FIBER 0.1g; CHOL 99mg; IRON 1.5mg; SODIUM 415mg; CALC 31mg

Chicken with Port Wine Sauce

If you aren't a Gorgonzola fan, try crumbled goat cheese instead. Serve with mashed sweet potatoes and steamed sugar snap peas or asparagus.

CHICKEN:
1 teaspoon paprika
1 teaspoon dried thyme
½ teaspoon salt
¼ teaspoon black pepper
4 (6-ounce) skinless, boneless chicken breast halves
Cooking spray

SAUCE:
¼ cup port or other sweet red wine
¼ cup fat-free, less-sodium chicken broth
1 tablespoon butter

REMAINING INGREDIENT:
¼ cup (1 ounce) crumbled Gorgonzola cheese

1. To prepare chicken, heat a large nonstick skillet over medium-high heat. Combine first 4 ingredients; rub evenly over chicken. Lightly coat pan with cooking spray. Add chicken to pan; cook 4 minutes on each side or until done.
2. To prepare sauce, combine port and broth in a small saucepan; bring to a boil. Reduce heat; simmer 3 minutes or until reduced to ¼ cup. Remove from heat; stir in butter until melted. Spoon sauce over chicken, and sprinkle with cheese. Yield: 4 servings (serving size: 1 chicken breast half, 1 tablespoon sauce, and 1 tablespoon cheese).

CALORIES 264 (25% from fat); FAT 7.2g (sat 3.7g, mono 2g, poly 0.8g); PROTEIN 41g; CARB 2.4g; FIBER 0.3g; CHOL 112mg; IRON 1.6mg; SODIUM 460mg; CALC 69mg

Chipotle Pork Tenderloin with Corn Salsa

Serve with flour tortillas or Mexican rice.

1 (1-pound) pork tenderloin, trimmed
1½ teaspoons chipotle chile powder
1 teaspoon ground cumin
½ teaspoon garlic salt
Cooking spray
1 cup frozen whole-kernel corn
½ cup sliced green onions
½ cup picante sauce
2 tablespoons minced fresh cilantro

1. Heat a large nonstick skillet over medium-high heat. Cut pork crosswise into 12 equal pieces; firmly press each piece to ¾-inch thickness. Combine chile powder, cumin, and garlic salt; rub over pork. Coat pan with cooking spray. Add pork to pan; cook 5 minutes on each side or until done. Remove pork from pan. Add corn, onions, and picante sauce to pan; cook 2 minutes or until thoroughly heated, stirring frequently. Spoon salsa over pork, and sprinkle with cilantro. Yield: 4 servings (serving size: 3 pieces pork, ¼ cup salsa, and 1½ teaspoons cilantro).

CALORIES 192 (21% from fat); FAT 4.5g (sat 1.4g, mono 1.9g, poly 0.6g); PROTEIN 25.7g; CARB 12.3g; FIBER 2.2g; CHOL 74mg; IRON 2.2mg; SODIUM 439mg; CALC 24mg

> Vary your weeknight meals with entrées featuring pork, seafood, and lamb—plus a few vegetarian dishes.

Escarole Soup with Ginger and Cilantro

Adjust the curry paste, depending on your heat preference.

2 (14-ounce) cans fat-free, less-sodium chicken broth
½ cup chopped carrot
2 ounces uncooked spaghetti, broken into thirds
2 cups coarsely chopped escarole
1 pound skinless, boneless chicken breast, cut into (½-inch) pieces
2 teaspoons bottled minced fresh ginger
½ teaspoon red curry paste or crushed red pepper flakes
¼ cup chopped fresh cilantro

1. Bring broth to a boil in a 3-quart saucepan. Add carrot and pasta; cover, reduce heat, and simmer 6 minutes, stirring occasionally. Stir in escarole and chicken; cook 3 minutes or until chicken is done.
2. Remove from heat; stir in ginger and curry paste. Ladle soup into 4 bowls; sprinkle with cilantro. Yield: 4 servings (serving size: about 1¼ cups soup and 1 tablespoon cilantro).

CALORIES 207 (8% from fat); FAT 1.8g (sat 0.4g, mono 0.4g, poly 0.5g); PROTEIN 31.1g; CARB 14.2g; FIBER 1.7g; CHOL 66mg; IRON 1.7mg; SODIUM 465mg; CALC 35mg

Turkey Cutlets with Coleslaw

Adding the olive oil to the pan after it's hot keeps the oil from smoking.

COLESLAW:
- 3 tablespoons orange juice
- 2 tablespoons white wine vinegar
- 2 tablespoons light mayonnaise
- ¾ teaspoon sugar
- ½ teaspoon salt
- ⅛ teaspoon freshly ground black pepper
- 1 (16-ounce) package cabbage-and-carrot coleslaw

TURKEY:
- 1 pound turkey cutlets
- ¼ teaspoon salt
- ¼ teaspoon freshly ground black pepper
- 2 teaspoons olive oil
- ⅓ cup water

1. Combine first 6 ingredients in a large bowl. Add coleslaw; toss to coat.
2. Heat a large skillet over high heat. Sprinkle both sides of cutlets evenly with ¼ teaspoon salt and ¼ teaspoon pepper. Add oil to pan. Add turkey, and cook 3 minutes on each side or until done. Remove from pan.
3. Add water to pan; bring to a simmer, scraping pan to loosen browned bits. Pour sauce over cutlets. Serve with coleslaw. Yield: 4 servings (serving size: about 3 ounces turkey, 1 cup coleslaw, and about 1½ teaspoons sauce).

CALORIES 210 (25% from fat); FAT 5.8g (sat 1g, mono 1.8g, poly 0.5g); PROTEIN 30g; CARB 9.4g; FIBER 2.7g; CHOL 73mg; IRON 2.1mg; SODIUM 576mg; CALC 68mg

Pork with Cranberry-Apple Salsa

The salsa can be made ahead and stored in the refrigerator up to 3 days. It's also good with chicken breast halves.

- 1 cup diced Granny Smith apple
- ¾ cup cranberry-orange crushed fruit (such as Ocean Spray)
- 1 teaspoon grated lemon rind
- 1 tablespoon fresh lemon juice
- ¾ teaspoon bottled minced fresh ginger
- 4 (6-ounce) bone-in center-cut pork chops
- ¼ teaspoon salt
- ¼ teaspoon black pepper
- ⅛ teaspoon ground allspice
- Cooking spray

1. Combine first 5 ingredients.
2. Heat a large nonstick skillet over medium-high heat. Sprinkle chops with salt, pepper, and allspice. Coat pan with cooking spray. Add pork to pan; cook 4 minutes on each side or until desired degree of doneness. Serve with salsa. Yield: 4 servings (serving size: 1 chop and ⅓ cup salsa).

CALORIES 223 (19% from fat); FAT 4.7g (sat 1.7g, mono 2.1g, poly 0.4g); PROTEIN 17.2g; CARB 28.6g; FIBER 0.9g; CHOL 46mg; IRON 0.7mg; SODIUM 196mg; CALC 27mg

Curried Lamb Chops with Minted Chutney

- 2 teaspoons curry powder
- ½ teaspoon salt
- ¼ teaspoon crushed red pepper
- 4 (6-ounce) lamb rib chops, trimmed
- ½ cup mango chutney
- 2 tablespoons chopped fresh mint

1. Heat a grill pan over medium-high heat.
2. Combine curry powder, salt, and pepper; rub evenly over lamb. Add lamb to pan; cook 5 minutes on each side or until desired degree of doneness. Combine chutney and mint; serve with lamb. Yield: 4 servings (serving size: 1 chop and 2 tablespoons chutney).

CALORIES 300 (31% from fat); FAT 10.4g (sat 3.7g, mono 4.1g, poly 1g); PROTEIN 36.1g; CARB 14.2g; FIBER 1.2g; CHOL 112mg; IRON 4mg; SODIUM 414mg; CALC 38mg

Creamy Pasta with Chicken and Mushrooms

Ultrafine instant flour dissolves quickly in liquid. All-purpose flour works, too, but it requires more whisking to avoid lumps.

- ½ pound wide egg noodles
- 1 tablespoon olive oil
- ½ cup chopped onion
- 1 (8-ounce) package sliced cremini mushrooms
- ½ pound skinless, boneless chicken breast, cut into bite-sized pieces
- 2 cups prewashed baby spinach
- ½ cup dry white wine
- 1 cup evaporated low-fat milk
- 1 tablespoon instant flour (such as Pillsbury Shake and Blend Flour)
- ¾ teaspoon salt
- ½ teaspoon black pepper

1. Cook noodles according to package directions, omitting salt and fat.
2. While noodles cook, heat oil in a large skillet over medium-high heat. Add onion and mushrooms to pan; sauté 3 minutes or until mushrooms are tender. Add chicken; sauté 4 minutes. Add spinach and wine; cook 2 minutes or until spinach wilts, stirring occasionally.
3. Combine milk and flour, stirring with a whisk. Add milk mixture to pan; cook 2 minutes or until sauce thickens. Stir in salt and pepper. Serve over noodles. Yield: 4 servings (serving size: ¾ cup chicken mixture and 1 cup pasta).

CALORIES 416 (16% from fat); FAT 7.6g (sat 2.2g, mono 3.4g, poly 1.2g); PROTEIN 28.5g; CARB 52.5g; FIBER 3.7g; CHOL 97mg; IRON 4.2mg; SODIUM 592mg; CALC 207mg

Quick One-Dish Wonders

Keep dinner simple with versatile, speedy recipes that are meals unto themselves.

After a long day at work, a satisfying meal in one simple dish is a welcome alternative to a multicourse dinner. These two-serving recipes fill the bill. All combine fresh ingredients with pantry or freezer staples, and most are prepared in just one pan for fast cleanup.

QUICK & EASY
Nutty Pasta Toss with Shrimp

To save time, use bottled minced fresh ginger and bottled minced garlic.

- 3 tablespoons low-sodium soy sauce
- 2 tablespoons crunchy peanut butter
- 1 tablespoon minced fresh cilantro
- 1 tablespoon grated peeled fresh ginger
- 1 teaspoon sugar
- 1 teaspoon rice vinegar
- ¼ teaspoon hot sauce
- 1 garlic clove, minced
- 1 teaspoon dark sesame oil
- 8 ounces medium shrimp, peeled and deveined
- 1 cup vertically sliced onion
- ½ red bell pepper, cut into (¼-inch) strips
- 1 cup bagged prewashed spinach
- 2 cups hot cooked rigatoni (about 1¼ cups uncooked pasta)

1. Combine first 8 ingredients in a medium bowl, stirring well with a whisk.
2. Heat oil in a large nonstick skillet over medium-high heat. Add shrimp, and sauté 3 minutes or until done. Remove shrimp from pan. Add onion and bell pepper to pan; sauté 3 minutes. Add soy sauce mixture, shrimp, and spinach. Reduce heat to medium; cook 2 minutes or until spinach wilts. Serve shrimp mixture over pasta. Yield: 2 servings

(serving size: 1 cup shrimp mixture and 1 cup pasta).

CALORIES 483 (25% from fat); FAT 13.4g (sat 2.4g, mono 5.1g, poly 4.4g); PROTEIN 36.1g; CARB 55.1g; FIBER 4.8g; CHOL 172mg; IRON 6.2mg; SODIUM 1,003mg; CALC 108mg

Bistro Chicken and Peppers

The garlic rub enhances the browning and adds flavor.

- 1 red bell pepper
- 1 yellow bell pepper
- ¼ teaspoon salt
- 1 garlic clove, coarsely chopped
- 2 (6-ounce) skinless, boneless chicken breast halves
- ¾ teaspoon vegetable oil
- 2 tablespoons finely chopped shallots
- ½ cup fat-free, less-sodium chicken broth
- 1 teaspoon curry powder
- ⅛ teaspoon dried thyme
- ⅛ teaspoon fennel seeds
- 2 cups prepared packaged mashed potatoes (such as Simply Potatoes)

1. Preheat broiler.
2. Cut bell peppers in half lengthwise, and discard seeds and membranes. Place pepper halves, skin sides up, on a foil-lined baking sheet; flatten with hand. Broil 15 minutes or until blackened. Place in a zip-top plastic bag; seal. Let stand 20 minutes. Peel and cut into ½-inch strips; set aside.
3. Combine salt and garlic on a cutting board; chop until mixture becomes a coarse paste. Rub garlic mixture over chicken. Heat oil in a large nonstick skillet over medium-high heat. Add chicken; cook 5 minutes or until golden, turning once. Add shallots; cook 1 minute, stirring frequently. Add broth, curry, thyme, and fennel. Cover, reduce heat, and simmer 10 minutes. Add peppers; cook 2 minutes or until chicken is done.
4. Warm mashed potatoes according to package directions. Serve potatoes with chicken and pepper mixture. Yield: 2 servings (serving size: 1 chicken breast

half, ½ cup pepper mixture, and 1 cup potatoes).

CALORIES 411 (14% from fat); FAT 6.5g (sat 0.9g, mono 1g, poly 1.7g); PROTEIN 45g; CARB 42.7g; FIBER 5.5g; CHOL 99mg; IRON 2.5mg; SODIUM 1,074mg; CALC 49mg

QUICK & EASY • MAKE AHEAD
Ginger-Curry Pork and Rice

If you don't have dried apricots on hand, you can substitute golden raisins instead. Fresh ginger livens this dish and gives it a mild, peppery heat.

- 2 (4-ounce) boneless center-cut loin pork chops
- ⅛ teaspoon black pepper
- Dash of salt
- 1 tablespoon vegetable oil, divided
- ½ teaspoon grated lime rind
- 1 tablespoon fresh lime juice
- 1½ teaspoons grated peeled fresh ginger
- ½ cup chopped onion
- ½ teaspoon red curry paste
- 1 cup fat-free, less-sodium chicken broth
- 2 tablespoons chopped dried apricots
- 1 teaspoon honey
- 1 garlic clove, minced
- 1½ cups hot cooked basmati rice
- 2 tablespoons thinly sliced green onions

1. Sprinkle pork with pepper and salt. Heat 2 teaspoons oil in a medium non-stick skillet over medium-high heat. Add pork; cook 2½ minutes on each side or until browned. Remove pork from pan. Combine rind, juice, and ginger in a shallow dish; add pork, turning to coat.
2. Heat 1 teaspoon oil in pan over medium heat. Add onion and curry paste; cook 2 minutes or until onion is tender, stirring frequently. Add pork mixture, broth, apricots, honey, and garlic; bring to a boil. Cover, reduce heat, and simmer 10 minutes or until pork is done. Remove pork from pan. Increase heat to medium-high. Add rice; cook 2 minutes or until thoroughly heated, stirring

Continued

frequently. Serve rice mixture with pork, and top each serving with 1 tablespoon green onions. Yield: 2 servings (serving size: 1 pork chop and 1 cup rice mixture).

CALORIES 486 (26% from fat); FAT 14.3g (sat 3.3g, mono 4.8g, poly 5.1g); PROTEIN 33.5g; CARB 53.7g; FIBER 4.8g; CHOL 62mg; IRON 2mg; SODIUM 965mg; CALC 56mg

QUICK & EASY • MAKE AHEAD
FREEZABLE
Moroccan Chicken and Lentils

This dish freezes well, so you can double the recipe and save half for later.

  2 teaspoons vegetable oil
  8 ounces skinless, boneless chicken thighs, cut into 1-inch pieces
  1 cup chopped onion
  ½ teaspoon salt
  ½ teaspoon ground coriander
  ¼ teaspoon ground cumin
  ¼ teaspoon ground cinnamon
  ⅛ teaspoon ground red pepper
  1 garlic clove, minced
  1 tablespoon tomato paste
  1 cup canned brown lentils, rinsed and drained
  1 cup fat-free, less-sodium chicken broth
  ½ cup water
  2 tablespoons golden raisins
  1 cup hot cooked basmati rice
  2 tablespoons chopped fresh parsley
  1 tablespoon slivered almonds, toasted

1. Heat oil in a large nonstick skillet over medium-high heat. Add chicken; sauté 5 minutes or until browned. Remove chicken from pan. Add onion and next 6 ingredients to pan; sauté 3 minutes. Add tomato paste, and cook 1 minute, stirring constantly. Stir in chicken, lentils, broth, water, and raisins. Reduce heat, and cook 5 minutes or until chicken is done, stirring occasionally. Add rice; cook 1 minute or until thoroughly heated, stirring frequently. Sprinkle with parsley and almonds. Yield: 2 servings (serving size: 1¼ cups).

CALORIES 502 (22% from fat); FAT 12.2g (sat 2.2g, mono 3.8g, poly 4.6g); PROTEIN 37.8g; CARB 61.5g; FIBER 12.8g; CHOL 94mg; IRON 5.9mg; SODIUM 1,061mg; CALC 90mg

---

One-Dish Staples

Keep these items on hand so you can add fresh vegetables and the protein of your choice to pull together a meal:
- Canned fat-free, less-sodium chicken broth
- Pasta
- Rice
- Quick-cooking barley
- Lentils (canned or dried)
- Frozen spinach

QUICK & EASY
Beef and Barley-Stuffed Peppers

The bell peppers are softened in the microwave before they're filled and baked. Quick-cooking barley is a boon for busy weeknights.

  1 cup low-salt beef broth
  ½ cup uncooked quick-cooking barley
  2 large red bell peppers
  6 ounces ground round
  1 cup sliced mushrooms
  1 garlic clove, minced
  ¼ cup tomato purée
  2 tablespoons chopped green onions
  1 tablespoon chopped fresh parsley
  ¼ teaspoon salt
  ¼ teaspoon dried thyme
  ¼ teaspoon dried oregano
  ⅛ teaspoon black pepper
  ½ cup (2 ounces) shredded part-skim mozzarella cheese
  1 tablespoon chopped green onions

1. Preheat oven to 350°.
2. Bring beef broth and barley to a boil in a small saucepan. Cover, reduce heat, and simmer 10 minutes or until liquid is absorbed.
3. Cut each bell pepper in half lengthwise, and discard seeds and membranes. Arrange bell pepper halves in a 9-inch pie plate. Cover with heavy-duty plastic wrap. Microwave at HIGH 5 minutes or until crisp-tender; drain.

---

4. Cook beef, mushrooms, and garlic in a nonstick skillet over medium-high heat 4 minutes or until browned, stirring to crumble. Add barley, tomato purée, and next 6 ingredients, and cook 2 minutes or until thoroughly heated. Divide beef mixture evenly among pepper halves. Top each pepper half with 2 tablespoons cheese and ¾ teaspoon onions. Bake at 350° for 10 minutes or until cheese melts. Yield: 2 servings (serving size: 2 stuffed pepper halves).

CALORIES 510 (35% from fat); FAT 19.6g (sat 8.4g, mono 7.4g, poly 1.4g); PROTEIN 34g; CARB 51.7g; FIBER 12.9g; CHOL 74mg; IRON 5.7mg; SODIUM 655mg; CALC 249mg

QUICK & EASY
Mac and Cheese Florentine

Add spinach and fresh breadcrumbs to macaroni and cheese for a meal that provides half of your daily calcium needs. You can vary this dish by using a different short pasta, such as mini penne or radiatore, and changing the cheese to gouda, Monterey Jack, or provolone.

  ½ (1-ounce) slice white bread
  1 tablespoon butter, melted
Cooking spray
  1 cup thinly sliced onion
  1 cup frozen chopped leaf spinach, thawed, drained, and squeezed dry
  1 teaspoon fresh lemon juice
  ¼ teaspoon ground nutmeg
  2 garlic cloves, minced
  1½ cups fat-free milk
  1½ tablespoons all-purpose flour
  ⅓ cup (about 1½ ounces) shredded Cheddar cheese
  ½ teaspoon salt
  ¼ teaspoon freshly ground black pepper
  2 cups hot cooked elbow macaroni (about 1 cup uncooked)

1. Place bread in a food processor; pulse 10 times or until coarse crumbs measure ¼ cup. Combine breadcrumbs and butter, stirring to coat.
2. Preheat broiler.
3. Heat a large nonstick skillet over medium-high heat. Coat pan with cooking

spray. Add onion; sauté 3 minutes or until tender. Add spinach, juice, nutmeg, and garlic; cook 2 minutes, stirring occasionally. Combine milk and flour, stirring well with a whisk. Gradually add milk mixture to spinach mixture, stirring constantly; bring to a boil. Add cheese, salt, and pepper; cook 30 seconds or until cheese melts, stirring constantly. Remove from heat, and stir in pasta. Spoon mixture into a 1-quart soufflé dish coated with cooking spray. Top evenly with breadcrumb mixture.

4. Broil 3 minutes or until breadcrumbs are lightly browned. Yield: 2 servings (serving size: about 2 cups).

CALORIES 482 (27% from fat); FAT 14.5g (sat 7.8g, mono 3.9g, poly 1.1g); PROTEIN 22.6g; CARB 66.9g; FIBER 5.7g; CHOL 42mg; IRON 4.4mg; SODIUM 975mg; CALC 502mg

simple suppers

Meatless Main

This easy-to-make vegetarian fare will satisfy even the hungriest diners.

QUICK & EASY
Tex-Mex Lasagna

Use a different salsa to vary the flavor of this lasagna. Make it smoky with chipotle salsa, or spice it up with the hot stuff.

- ¾ cup bottled salsa
- 1½ teaspoons ground cumin
- 1 (14.5-ounce) can no-salt-added diced tomatoes, undrained
- 1 (8-ounce) can no-salt-added tomato sauce
- Cooking spray
- 6 precooked lasagna noodles (such as Barilla or Vigo)
- 1 cup frozen whole-kernel corn, thawed
- 1 (15-ounce) can black beans, rinsed and drained
- 2 cups (8 ounces) preshredded reduced-fat 4-cheese Mexican blend cheese
- ¼ cup chopped green onions

1. Preheat oven to 450°.
2. Combine first 4 ingredients; spread ⅔ cup sauce in bottom of an 8-inch square baking dish coated with cooking spray. Arrange 2 noodles over sauce; top with ½ cup corn and half of beans. Sprinkle with ½ cup cheese; top with ⅔ cup sauce. Repeat layers once; top with 2 noodles. Spread remaining sauce over noodles. Sprinkle with 1 cup cheese. Cover and bake at 450° for 30 minutes or until noodles are tender and sauce is bubbly. Let stand 15 minutes. Sprinkle with onions. Yield: 4 servings.

CALORIES 415 (29% from fat); FAT 13.3g (sat 6.1g, mono 3.8g, poly 0.9g); PROTEIN 27.2g; CARB 55.2g; FIBER 10.4g; CHOL 41mg; IRON 3.9mg; SODIUM 970mg; CALC 518mg

QUICK & EASY
Frittata with Mushrooms, Linguine, and Basil

Break the pasta in half before cooking so it's easier to stir into the egg mixture. To save time, use presliced button mushrooms.

- Cooking spray
- 3 cups sliced cremini mushrooms
- 1¼ cups thinly sliced leek (about 2 large)
- ½ cup 1% low-fat milk
- 2 teaspoons butter, melted
- ¾ teaspoon salt
- ⅛ teaspoon freshly ground black pepper
- 4 large egg whites, lightly beaten
- 3 large eggs, lightly beaten
- 2 cups hot cooked linguine (about 4 ounces uncooked pasta)
- ⅓ cup chopped fresh basil
- ½ cup (2 ounces) shredded part-skim mozzarella cheese

1. Preheat oven to 450°.
2. Heat a large nonstick skillet over medium heat. Coat pan with cooking spray. Add mushrooms and leek; cook 6 minutes or until leek is tender, stirring frequently.
3. Combine milk and next 5 ingredients in a large bowl, stirring with a whisk. Add leek mixture, pasta, and basil; toss gently to combine.

4. Heat pan over medium-low heat. Coat pan with cooking spray. Add egg mixture; cook until edges begin to set (about 4 minutes). Gently lift edge of egg mixture, tilting pan to allow some uncooked egg mixture to come in contact with pan. Cook 5 minutes or until almost set. Sprinkle evenly with cheese; wrap handle of pan with foil. Bake 7 minutes or until golden brown. Cut into 8 wedges. Yield: 4 servings (serving size: 2 wedges).

CALORIES 269 (29% from fat); FAT 8.8g (sat 4.1g, mono 2.8g, poly 0.9g); PROTEIN 18.4g; CARB 28g; FIBER 2.8g; CHOL 174mg; IRON 2.6 mg; SODIUM 661mg; CALC 177mg

Dilled Goat Cheese Sandwiches with Roasted Plum Tomatoes

- 8 plum tomatoes, halved lengthwise
- Cooking spray
- ½ teaspoon dried oregano
- ¼ teaspoon salt
- 1 tablespoon chopped fresh dill
- ¼ teaspoon freshly ground black pepper
- 1 (4-ounce) package goat cheese
- 8 (1-ounce) slices multigrain bread, toasted
- 1 cup arugula leaves

1. Preheat oven to 350°.
2. Lightly coat both sides of tomatoes with cooking spray. Arrange tomatoes in a single layer, cut sides up, on a jelly-roll pan coated with cooking spray. Sprinkle evenly with oregano and salt. Bake at 350° for 1 hour.
3. Combine dill, pepper, and cheese; spread 1 tablespoon over each bread slice. Arrange 4 tomato halves and ¼ cup arugula on each of 4 bread slices. Top with remaining bread slices. Serve immediately. Yield: 4 servings (serving size: 1 sandwich).

CALORIES 246 (31% from fat); FAT 8.6g (sat 4.7g, mono 2.3g, poly 0.9g); PROTEIN 12.2g; CARB 32.7g; FIBER 5.2g; CHOL 13mg; IRON 3.3mg; SODIUM 540mg; CALC 109mg

Eggplant Stew over Couscous

Eggplant, peppers, zucchini, and tomatoes make a stew that's light enough to enjoy when the weather is hot.

1½ cups cubed peeled eggplant
  2 tablespoons water
  ½ teaspoon salt
  1 teaspoon olive oil
1½ cups (1-inch) bell pepper strips
  1 cup chopped onion
  2 garlic cloves, minced
  1 zucchini, halved lengthwise and thinly sliced
  ½ teaspoon dried basil
  ½ teaspoon dried oregano
  ¼ teaspoon dried dill
  ⅛ teaspoon black pepper
  1 (14.5-ounce) can no-salt-added diced tomatoes, undrained
  1 (6-ounce) can tomato sauce
  3 cups cooked couscous
  ½ cup (2 ounces) grated fresh Parmesan cheese

1. Combine first 3 ingredients in a large microwave-safe bowl. Cover and microwave at HIGH 8 minutes.
2. Heat oil in a large nonstick skillet over medium-high heat. Add bell pepper, onion, garlic, and zucchini; sauté 8 minutes or until onion is tender. Add eggplant mixture, basil, and next 5 ingredients to pan; cook 8 minutes or until vegetables are tender. Serve over couscous; sprinkle with cheese. Yield: 4 servings (serving size: 1 cup stew, ¾ cup couscous, and 2 tablespoons cheese).

CALORIES 324 (26% from fat); FAT 9.4g (sat 4g, mono 4.1g, poly 0.6g); PROTEIN 15.2g; CARB 46.3g; FIBER 7.2g; CHOL 14mg; IRON 2mg; SODIUM 941mg; CALC 317mg

Pasta with Mushrooms and Radicchio

This pasta dish gets a pleasant bitterness from radicchio and a licorice flavor from fennel. You can use penne, too.

  1 tablespoon butter
  1 teaspoon olive oil
  6 cups chopped mushrooms (about 1½ pounds)
  4 cups chopped fennel bulb (about 2 large bulbs)
  ¾ cup sliced green onions
  ½ cup vegetable broth
  3 tablespoons dry sherry
  ½ cup evaporated fat-free milk
  2 cups chopped radicchio (about 1 head)
  ½ teaspoon salt
  ¼ teaspoon freshly ground black pepper
  8 cups hot cooked fusilli (short twisted spaghetti, about 1 pound uncooked pasta)
  ¾ cup (3 ounces) grated fresh Parmesan cheese
  ½ cup finely chopped fresh parsley

1. Heat a large skillet over medium heat. Add butter and oil to pan; cook until butter melts. Add mushrooms, fennel, and onions; cook 20 minutes or until fennel is tender, stirring frequently. Stir in broth and sherry; cook 3 minutes or until liquid evaporates. Add milk; cook 2 minutes. Add radicchio; cook 2 minutes. Stir in salt and pepper. Combine mushroom mixture and pasta. Sprinkle with cheese and parsley. Yield: 8 servings (serving size: 1½ cups pasta mixture, 1½ tablespoons cheese, and 1 tablespoon parsley).

CALORIES 310 (16% from fat); FAT 5.4g (sat 2.7g, mono 1.5g, poly 0.2g); PROTEIN 14.5g; CARB 51.4g; FIBER 4.4g; CHOL 10mg; IRON 3.1mg; SODIUM 416mg; CALC 192mg

Indian Chickpeas over Garlic Spinach

This recipe relies on several spices, such as fennel seeds, cumin seeds, coriander, and red pepper, for a simple curry powder. Measuring out the separate spices is worth the extra effort; homemade curry powder has a brighter flavor than packaged curry powder. The fennel and cumin seeds add a pleasing crunch and pungency.

  4 teaspoons olive oil, divided
  2 cups sliced onion
1½ cups canned vegetable broth
  1 teaspoon fennel seeds
  1 teaspoon cumin seeds
  1 teaspoon ground coriander
  ¼ teaspoon salt
  ¼ teaspoon ground red pepper
  1 (19-ounce) can chickpeas (garbanzo beans), rinsed, drained, and divided
  2 garlic cloves, chopped
 16 cups chopped spinach (about 12 ounces)
  ½ cup plain fat-free yogurt

1. Heat 2 teaspoons oil in a large nonstick skillet over medium-high heat. Add onion; sauté 5 minutes. Add broth and next 5 ingredients, and bring to a boil. Reduce heat, and simmer 5 minutes.
2. Place ½ cup chickpeas in a food processor; process until minced. Add minced chickpeas and remaining chickpeas to onion mixture. Bring to a boil; reduce heat, and simmer 10 minutes.
3. Heat 2 teaspoons oil in a Dutch oven over medium-high heat. Add garlic, and sauté 30 seconds. Add spinach; sauté 3 minutes or until spinach is just wilted.
4. Spoon ½ cup spinach mixture onto each of 4 plates. Top each serving with ¾ cup chickpea mixture; dollop each serving with 2 tablespoons yogurt. Yield: 4 servings.

CALORIES 247 (26% from fat); FAT 7.4g (sat 0.8g, mono 3.4g, poly 0.6g); PROTEIN 13.8g; CARB 46.1g; FIBER 11.3g; CHOL 1mg; IRON 5.7mg; SODIUM 882mg; CALC 251mg

Rotisserie Chicken

Roasted chicken from the supermarket makes salads, pastas, and pizzas quick and convenient.

Rotisserie chickens keep for three to four days in the refrigerator, so have one tucked away for spur-of-the-moment meals. If you're adding rotisserie chicken to a hot recipe, just stir it in at the end to warm it up (since the chicken is already cooked). Another advantage of using store-cooked chicken: It's easy to slice and remove the meat from the bone. An average 2-pound rotisserie chicken yields 3 to 3½ cups of meat—more than enough for any of these recipes.

STAFF FAVORITE • QUICK & EASY
White Bean and Roasted Chicken Salad

(pictured on page 182)

Great for picnics or lazy-day suppers, this salad stirs together in a flash.

SALAD:

- 2 cups coarsely chopped skinless, boneless rotisserie chicken breast
- 1 cup chopped tomato
- ½ cup thinly sliced red onion
- ⅓ cup sliced fresh basil
- 2 (16-ounce) cans cannellini beans or other white beans, rinsed and drained

DRESSING:

- ¼ cup red wine vinegar
- 2 tablespoons extravirgin olive oil
- 1 tablespoon fresh lemon juice
- 2 teaspoons Dijon mustard
- ½ teaspoon salt
- ¼ teaspoon freshly ground black pepper
- 2 garlic cloves, minced

1. To prepare salad, place first 5 ingredients in a large bowl; stir gently to combine.
2. To prepare dressing, combine vinegar and remaining 6 ingredients, stirring with a whisk. Drizzle over salad, tossing gently to coat. Yield: 5 servings (serving size: about 1¼ cups).

CALORIES 369 (25% from fat); FAT 10.1g (sat 2g, mono 5.7g, poly 1.7g); PROTEIN 29.2g; CARB 41.5g; FIBER 9.6g; CHOL 45mg; IRON 4mg; SODIUM 342mg; CALC 117mg

---

QUICK & EASY
Ratatouille Pizza with Chicken

The addition of chicken to a quick ratatouille makes a great-tasting, satisfying pizza.

- 1 teaspoon olive oil
- 1 Japanese eggplant, halved lengthwise and cut into ¼-inch-thick slices
- 1 red bell pepper, cut into ¼-inch strips
- ½ small red onion, thinly sliced
- 1 cup sliced mushrooms
- ¾ teaspoon dried Italian seasoning
- ¼ teaspoon salt
- 4 garlic cloves, minced
- 1 (10-ounce) Italian cheese-flavored thin pizza crust (such as Boboli)
- 1 cup chopped skinless, boneless rotisserie chicken breast meat
- 1 cup (4 ounces) preshredded reduced-fat pizza-blend cheese
- 3 plum tomatoes, cut into ¼-inch-thick slices
- Cooking spray
- 3 tablespoons finely chopped fresh flat-leaf parsley

1. Preheat oven to 375°.
2. Heat a large nonstick skillet over medium-high heat. Add oil to pan. Add eggplant, bell pepper, and onion; sauté 3 minutes or until eggplant begins to soften. Reduce heat to medium. Add mushrooms, and cook 3 minutes, stirring frequently. Add Italian seasoning, salt, and garlic; cook 1 minute, stirring constantly. Remove from heat.
3. Place crust on a baking sheet. Spread vegetable mixture evenly over crust, leaving a ½-inch border. Arrange chicken over vegetable mixture; sprinkle evenly with cheese. Arrange tomato slices over cheese, and lightly coat with cooking spray. Bake at 375° for 25 minutes or until cheese is bubbly and tomatoes are softened. Sprinkle with parsley. Yield: 6 servings.

CALORIES 249 (30% from fat); FAT 8.3g (sat 3.9g, mono 2g, poly 0.8g); PROTEIN 18.1g; CARB 26.3g; FIBER 1.8g; CHOL 33mg; IRON 2mg; SODIUM 409mg; CALC 273mg

---

STAFF FAVORITE • QUICK & EASY
Gazpacho Panzanella

This colorful salad combines the best of the classic Spanish soup, gazpacho, and the Italian bread salad, panzanella. Chop the vegetables and toast the bread cubes ahead of time, but toss the salad right before serving; the bread will soak up the juices and become soggy if it sits too long. If you prefer a drier panzanella, simply add less dressing. Use olive oil-flavored cooking spray if you have it.

SALAD:

- 4 ounces French bread, cut into ½-inch cubes
- Cooking spray
- 3½ cups chopped seeded tomato (about 2 pounds)
- 2 cups chopped skinless, boneless rotisserie chicken breast meat
- 1¾ cups chopped seeded cucumber (about 1 pound)
- 1 cup chopped green bell pepper
- ½ cup vertically sliced red onion
- ¼ cup chopped fresh flat-leaf parsley

DRESSING:

- ½ cup low-sodium vegetable juice
- ¼ cup red wine vinegar
- 1 tablespoon extravirgin olive oil
- 1 tablespoon water
- 2 garlic cloves, minced
- ½ teaspoon salt
- ⅛ teaspoon freshly ground black pepper

Continued

1. Preheat oven to 350°.

2. To prepare salad, arrange bread cubes in a single layer on a baking sheet. Lightly coat bread cubes with cooking spray. Bake at 350° for 15 minutes or until golden brown, stirring once. Set aside.

3. Place tomato and next 5 ingredients in a large bowl; toss gently to combine.

4. To prepare dressing, combine juice and remaining 6 ingredients, stirring with a whisk. Drizzle over salad, tossing gently to coat. Stir in bread cubes; let stand 5 minutes. Serve immediately. Yield: 4 servings (serving size: 2½ cups).

CALORIES 294 (24% from fat); FAT 7.7g (sat 1.5g, mono 4.1g, poly 1.4g); PROTEIN 26.9g; CARB 29.6g; FIBER 4.4g; CHOL 60mg; IRON 3mg; SODIUM 553mg; CALC 68mg

QUICK & EASY
Chicken and Blue Cheese Slaw

Chopped apple or green grapes would also work well in this fast summer dinner. Ready-to-use slaw and preshredded carrots make short work of this refreshing salad.

SALAD:

2 cups chopped skinless, boneless rotisserie chicken breast meat
2 cups seedless red grapes, halved
1 cup shredded carrot
½ cup thinly sliced red onion
1 (10-ounce) package angel hair slaw

DRESSING:

¼ cup rice vinegar
¼ cup fat-free, less-sodium chicken broth
¼ cup thawed orange juice concentrate
2 teaspoons vegetable oil
¼ teaspoon salt
⅛ teaspoon freshly ground black pepper

REMAINING INGREDIENTS:

3 tablespoons crumbled blue cheese
2 tablespoons coarsely chopped walnuts

1. To prepare salad, place first 5 ingredients in a bowl; toss gently to combine.

2. To prepare dressing, combine vinegar and next 5 ingredients, stirring with a whisk. Drizzle over salad, tossing to coat. Sprinkle with cheese and walnuts, and toss gently to combine. Yield: 4 servings (serving size: 2 cups).

CALORIES 312 (28% from fat); FAT 9.6g (sat 2.6g, mono 2.4g, poly 3.6g); PROTEIN 26.7g; CARB 32g; FIBER 4g; CHOL 64mg; IRON 1.8mg; SODIUM 340mg; CALC 106mg

QUICK & EASY
Asparagus and Chicken Carbonara

This lighter version of pasta carbonara achieves the same texture with egg substitute and fat-free evaporated milk.

8 ounces uncooked spaghetti
2 cups (1-inch) slices asparagus (about ¾ pound)
½ cup egg substitute
½ cup evaporated fat-free milk
2 teaspoons olive oil
½ cup chopped onion
¼ cup dry vermouth
2 cups chopped skinless, boneless rotisserie chicken breast meat
½ cup (2 ounces) grated fresh Parmesan cheese
3 tablespoons finely chopped fresh flat-leaf parsley
¾ teaspoon salt
½ teaspoon freshly ground black pepper
4 bacon slices, cooked and crumbled

1. Cook pasta in boiling water 10 minutes or until al dente; add asparagus during final 2 minutes of cooking. Drain pasta mixture in a colander over a bowl, reserving ⅓ cup cooking liquid. Combine reserved cooking liquid, egg substitute, and milk, stirring with a whisk.

2. Heat a large nonstick skillet over medium-high heat. Add oil and onion to pan; sauté 2 minutes. Add vermouth; cook 1 minute. Stir in pasta mixture. Remove from heat; stir in milk mixture, chicken, and cheese. Place pan over medium heat, and cook 4 minutes or until slightly thick, stirring frequently. Remove from heat; stir in parsley, salt, pepper, and bacon. Serve immediately. Yield: 5 servings (serving size: about 1¼ cups).

CALORIES 416 (23% from fat); FAT 10.8g (sat 3.7g, mono 4.4g, poly 2g); PROTEIN 34.7g; CARB 41.9g; FIBER 3.1g; CHOL 60mg; IRON 3.4mg; SODIUM 700mg; CALC 236mg

QUICK & EASY
Summer Succotash with Chicken

1 tablespoon vegetable oil
3 cups fresh corn kernels (about 6 ears)
1½ cups chopped onion
½ cup chopped red bell pepper
1½ teaspoons Old Bay seasoning
½ teaspoon dried thyme leaves, crushed
¼ teaspoon salt
⅛ teaspoon freshly ground black pepper
4 garlic cloves, minced
1 cup frozen baby lima beans, thawed
1 cup fat-free, less-sodium chicken broth
2 cups chopped skinless, boneless rotisserie chicken
1 cup grape or cherry tomatoes, halved

1. Heat oil in a large nonstick skillet over medium-high heat. Add corn and next 7 ingredients; sauté 4 minutes or until onion is tender. Add beans and broth. Bring to a simmer; cook 2 minutes, stirring frequently. Reduce heat to low. Add chicken and tomatoes; cook 5 minutes or until chicken is thoroughly heated, stirring occasionally. Yield: 4 servings (serving size: 1½ cups).

CALORIES 338 (25% from fat); FAT 9.5g (sat 2g, mono 2.9g, poly 3.8g); PROTEIN 27.5g; CARB 39.3g; FIBER 7.4g; CHOL 56mg; IRON 2.7mg; SODIUM 612mg; CALC 44mg

Chicken Tips

• Pick up a rotisserie chicken at the end of your shopping trip so it stays hot.

• Serve or refrigerate it within two hours (sooner in hot weather).

• Cut, shred, or chop the chicken, and store it, uncovered, in a shallow container in the refrigerator to help it cool quickly. Cover the container when the chicken has cooled.

QUICK & EASY

Couscous Salad with Chicken and Chopped Vegetables

The creamy yogurt dressing has a hint of sweetness from the honey and an extra zing from the vinegar.

SALAD:

- 1½ cups water
- 1 tablespoon olive oil, divided
- ¾ teaspoon salt
- 1 cup uncooked couscous
- 1 cup chopped yellow bell pepper
- ½ cup finely chopped zucchini
- ½ cup chopped mushrooms
- 1½ cups chopped skinless, boneless rotisserie chicken
- ½ cup (⅛-inch-thick) diagonally cut carrot
- ¼ cup thinly sliced green onions
- 3 tablespoons dried currants
- 3 tablespoons finely chopped fresh mint
- ⅛ teaspoon freshly ground black pepper

DRESSING:

- 1 cup plain low-fat yogurt
- 3 tablespoons fresh lemon juice
- 1 tablespoon honey
- 1 tablespoon white wine vinegar

1. To prepare salad, bring water, 1 teaspoon oil, and salt to a boil in a medium saucepan; gradually stir in couscous. Remove from heat; cover and let stand 5 minutes. Fluff with a fork. Place in a large bowl; cool to room temperature.

2. Heat a large nonstick skillet over medium-high heat. Add 2 teaspoons oil to pan. Add bell pepper, zucchini, and mushrooms; sauté 4 minutes or until bell pepper is tender. Add bell pepper mixture, chicken, and next 5 ingredients to couscous; toss gently to combine.

3. To prepare dressing, combine yogurt and remaining 3 ingredients, stirring with a whisk. Drizzle over couscous mixture, tossing gently to combine. Yield: 4 servings (serving size: 1½ cups).

CALORIES 368 (20% from fat); FAT 8g (sat 2.1g, mono 4g, poly 1.2g); PROTEIN 24.1g; CARB 49.4g; FIBER 4.3g; CHOL 46mg; IRON 1.8mg; SODIUM 540mg; CALC 148mg

QUICK & EASY

Southwestern Salad Bar

We had fun putting together our own salads—this lineup has something for everyone.

- 1 tablespoon fajita seasoning
- 2 cups fresh corn kernels (about 4 ears)
- 5 teaspoons fresh lime juice, divided
- 2 teaspoons minced fresh cilantro
- ⅔ cup chopped red onion
- 2 garlic cloves, minced
- 2 (15-ounce) cans black beans, rinsed and drained
- 1 (7-ounce) bottle roasted red bell peppers, drained and chopped
- ½ cup diced peeled avocado
- ¾ cup light ranch dressing
- 1½ teaspoons minced canned chipotle chiles in adobo sauce
- 12 cups packaged chopped romaine lettuce
- 3 cups chopped skinless, boneless rotisserie chicken
- 1½ cups (6 ounces) preshredded reduced-fat Mexican blend or Cheddar cheese
- 1½ cups unsalted baked tortilla chips, crumbled (about 2½ ounces)
- 1 cup bottled sliced peeled mango, chopped
- 1 cup sliced green onions
- ½ cup thinly sliced radishes

1. Cook seasoning in a large saucepan over medium heat 2 minutes or until toasted, stirring frequently. Combine seasoning, corn, 1 tablespoon juice, and cilantro in a medium serving bowl.

2. Combine onion, garlic, beans, and bell pepper in a medium serving bowl. Combine avocado and 2 teaspoons juice in a small serving bowl, tossing gently to coat. Combine dressing and chipotle in a small serving bowl.

3. Place chopped lettuce in a large serving bowl. Place chicken in a medium serving bowl. Place cheese, chips, mango, green onions, and radishes in individual serving bowls. Arrange bowls, buffet-style, beginning with lettuce and ending with dressing. Yield: 8 servings (serving size: 1½ cups lettuce, ¾ cup bean mixture, ¼ cup corn mixture, about ⅓ cup chicken, 3 tablespoons chips, 3 tablespoons cheese, 2 tablespoons mango, 2 tablespoons onions, 1 tablespoon radishes, 1 tablespoon avocado, and 1½ tablespoons dressing).

CALORIES 411 (29% from fat); FAT 12.7g (sat 2.5g, mono 4.6g, poly 4.2g); PROTEIN 32g; CARB 45.9g; FIBER 11.3g; CHOL 55mg; IRON 3.7mg; SODIUM 822mg; CALC 179mg

Use rotisserie chicken to top a pizza, toss with pasta, transform a side dish into an entrée, or anchor a salad.

Basmati Chicken Salad

Oil-packed sun-dried tomatoes and artichokes give this salad richness, as well as a nice tang.

SALAD:

1½ cups water
1 cup uncooked basmati rice
3 garlic cloves, minced
2 cups shredded skinless, boneless rotisserie chicken breast meat
½ cup thinly sliced green onions
¼ cup chopped drained oil-packed sun-dried tomato halves
1 teaspoon grated lemon rind
1 (15½-ounce) can chickpeas (garbanzo beans), rinsed and drained
1 (14-ounce) can artichoke hearts, drained and coarsely chopped

DRESSING:

¼ cup fat-free, less-sodium chicken broth
3 tablespoons fresh lemon juice
3 tablespoons extravirgin olive oil
1 teaspoon Dijon mustard
¾ teaspoon salt
½ teaspoon freshly ground black pepper
¼ teaspoon dried oregano

1. To prepare salad, bring 1½ cups water to a boil in a 3-quart saucepan; add rice and garlic. Cover; reduce heat, and simmer 20 minutes or until liquid is absorbed. Remove from heat, and let stand 5 minutes. Place in a large bowl. Add chicken and next 5 ingredients to rice; stir gently to combine.

2. To prepare dressing, combine broth and remaining 6 ingredients, stirring with a whisk. Drizzle over salad, tossing gently to coat. Yield: 6 servings (serving size: about 1 cup).

CALORIES 397 (23% from fat); FAT 10.1g (sat 1.6g, mono 6.2g, poly 1.5g); PROTEIN 22.8g; CARB 57.4g; FIBER 8.5g; CHOL 40mg; IRON 3.6mg; SODIUM 762mg; CALC 69mg

Peppery Chicken Pasta Salad

Serve this soon after you dress the salad so the pasta stays moist.

SALAD:

8 ounces uncooked farfalle (bow tie pasta)
2 cups (1-inch) cut green beans (about ½ pound)
2 cups chopped skinless, boneless rotisserie chicken breast meat
⅔ cup (⅛-inch-thick) diagonally cut celery
1 red bell pepper, chopped
½ small red onion, thinly sliced

DRESSING:

3 tablespoons light mayonnaise
2 tablespoons water
4 teaspoons fresh lemon juice
4 teaspoons commercial pesto
½ teaspoon freshly ground black pepper
¼ teaspoon salt

1. To prepare salad, cook pasta in boiling water 11 minutes or until al dente. Add green beans during final 5 minutes of cooking. Drain and rinse pasta mixture with cold water. Place pasta mixture, chicken, celery, bell pepper, and onion in a large bowl; toss gently to combine.

2. To prepare dressing, combine mayonnaise and remaining 5 ingredients, stirring with a whisk. Drizzle over pasta mixture, tossing gently to coat. Yield: 6 servings (serving size: 1⅔ cups).

CALORIES 279 (20% from fat); FAT 6.3g (sat 1.4g, mono 2.3g, poly 1.8g); PROTEIN 21.1g; CARB 34g; FIBER 3.5g; CHOL 43mg; IRON 2.2mg; SODIUM 232mg; CALC 66mg

entertaining

Feeding a Crowd

These no-nonsense recipes are great for potluck gatherings, graduation parties, and other casual get-togethers.

Sweet Potato Trifle

The two main ingredients in this dessert, purchased angel food cake and canned sweet potatoes, mean there's no baking required. Prepare and garnish up to 1 day in advance.

1 (16-ounce) angel food cake, cut into (1-inch) cubes
¾ cup sugar, divided
½ cup reduced-fat sour cream
1 (8-ounce) block ⅓-less-fat cream cheese, softened
1 (5-ounce) can evaporated fat-free milk
½ teaspoon vanilla extract
Dash of salt
2 (15-ounce) cans cooked peeled sweet potatoes, drained and mashed
3 tablespoons flaked sweetened coconut, toasted
1 (8-ounce) container frozen fat-free whipped topping, thawed
1 tablespoon chopped pecans, toasted

1. Preheat oven to 350°.

2. Arrange cake cubes in a single layer on a jelly-roll pan. Bake at 350° for 15 minutes or until toasted, turning once.

3. Place ½ cup sugar, sour cream, and cream cheese in a large bowl; beat with a mixer at medium speed until well combined. Gradually add milk, beating until smooth. Add toasted cake cubes; fold gently to combine.

4. Place ¼ cup sugar, vanilla, salt, and sweet potatoes in a large bowl, and beat with a mixer at medium speed until smooth.

5. Spoon half of cake mixture into a trifle dish or 3-quart glass bowl; top with half of sweet potato mixture. Sprinkle 1 tablespoon coconut over sweet potato mixture; top with half of whipped topping. Repeat layers; sprinkle with 1 tablespoon coconut and pecans. Cover and chill at least 1 hour. Yield: 12 servings (serving size: about ⅔ cup).

CALORIES 303 (20% from fat); FAT 6.9g (sat 4g, mono 1.9g, poly 0.5g); PROTEIN 6.2g; CARB 53.5g; FIBER 1.4g; CHOL 19mg; IRON 0.9mg; SODIUM 434mg; CALC 125mg

Taco Rice Salad

Convenience products, such as preseasoned yellow rice and picante sauce, flavor this easy one-dish meal that appeals to kids and adults alike.

SALAD:

Cooking spray
1 pound ground round
1 garlic clove, minced
3 cups cooked yellow rice
1 teaspoon ground cumin
1 teaspoon chili powder
¼ teaspoon salt
¼ teaspoon black pepper
6 cups torn romaine lettuce (about 10 ounces)
3 cups chopped tomato (about 1¼ pounds)
1 cup frozen whole-kernel corn, thawed
½ cup chopped red onion
1 (15-ounce) can black beans, rinsed and drained

DRESSING:

⅔ cup fat-free sour cream
⅔ cup picante sauce
1 teaspoon chili powder
½ teaspoon ground cumin

REMAINING INGREDIENT:

½ cup (2 ounces) shredded reduced-fat sharp Cheddar cheese

1. To prepare salad, heat a large nonstick skillet over medium-high heat. Coat pan with cooking spray. Add beef and garlic, and cook 9 minutes or until browned, stirring to crumble. Drain; return beef mixture to pan. Stir in rice and next 4 ingredients. Cool slightly.
2. Place lettuce and next 4 ingredients in a large bowl; toss to combine.
3. To prepare dressing, combine sour cream and next 3 ingredients, stirring with a whisk. Spoon dressing over lettuce mixture; toss to coat. Place 1⅓ cups lettuce mixture on each of 6 plates. Top each with ¾ cup rice mixture and about 1½ tablespoons cheese. Yield: 6 servings.

CALORIES 360 (30% from fat); FAT 11.9g (sat 5g, mono 4.5g, poly 0.8g); PROTEIN 21.1g; CARB 46.7g; FIBER 6.7g; CHOL 48mg; IRON 4.2mg; SODIUM 994mg; CALC 177mg

Chipotle Shrimp Cups

This quick appetizer gets smoke and savor from commercial salsa. And it's made all the easier by baking purchased wonton wrappers in mini muffin tins instead of preparing a homemade pastry. You can make all the components the night before (store filling in the refrigerator and cups at room temperature), then heat the assembled cups in the oven just before serving.

36 wonton wrappers
Cooking spray
1½ cups (6 ounces) shredded reduced-fat sharp Cheddar cheese
1 cup chopped cooked shrimp
1 cup chopped bottled roasted red bell peppers
1 cup bottled chipotle salsa
½ cup chopped green onions

1. Preheat oven to 350°.
2. Fit 1 wonton wrapper into each of 36 mini muffin cups coated with cooking spray, pressing wrappers into sides of cups. Bake at 350° for 7 minutes or until lightly browned. Keep wontons in muffin cups.
3. Combine cheese and remaining 4 ingredients, and spoon about 1 tablespoon cheese mixture into each wonton cup. Bake at 350° for 6 minutes or until cheese melts. Remove from muffin cups. Serve immediately. Yield: 3 dozen (serving size: 2 filled wonton cups).

CALORIES 98 (24% from fat); FAT 2.6g (sat 1.6g, mono 0.6g, poly 0.4g); PROTEIN 7.6g; CARB 11.8g; FIBER 1.4g; CHOL 28mg; IRON 1mg; SODIUM 202mg; CALC 96mg

Crawfish and Rice Casserole

You can combine the ingredients ahead, refrigerate the dish for a day, then pop it in the oven. If you can't find crawfish in the freezer section of your local market, substitute cooked shrimp.

Cooking spray
1 cup chopped onion
1 cup chopped green bell pepper
2 pounds frozen cooked peeled and deveined crawfish tail meat, rinsed and drained
4 ounces light processed cheese, cubed (such as Velveeta Light)
1 (6.5-ounce) tub light garlic-and-herbs spreadable cheese (such as Alouette Light)
1 (10¾-ounce) can condensed reduced-fat, reduced-sodium cream of mushroom soup, undiluted
3 cups cooked wild rice
2 cups cooked long-grain white rice
1 cup chopped green onions
½ teaspoon salt
¼ teaspoon ground red pepper

1. Preheat oven to 350°.
2. Heat a large nonstick skillet over medium-high heat. Coat pan with cooking spray. Add 1 cup onion and bell pepper; sauté 5 minutes or until tender. Add crawfish, cheeses, and soup. Cook over medium heat until cheese melts, stirring occasionally. Stir in wild rice and remaining ingredients. Spoon into a 13 x 9-inch baking dish coated with cooking spray. Bake at 350° for 30 minutes. Yield: 8 servings (serving size: about 1¼ cups).

CALORIES 323 (21% from fat); FAT 7.7g (sat 4g, mono 1.6g, poly 0.9g); PROTEIN 29.2g; CARB 33.8g; FIBER 2.6g; CHOL 174mg; IRON 2.3mg; SODIUM 719mg; CALC 167mg

Cajun-Spiced Chicken Fettuccine

Instead of plating individual servings of this pasta dish, bake it as a casserole that guests can spoon out for themselves at the table. While the dish bakes, toss together a simple salad to complete the meal. Leftover chicken also works well.

2 pounds skinless, boneless chicken breast
1 teaspoon Cajun seasoning
Cooking spray
2 tablespoons butter
1 cup chopped green bell pepper
1 cup chopped onion
½ teaspoon salt
1 (8-ounce) package presliced cremini mushrooms
1 garlic clove, minced
2 tablespoons all-purpose flour
1 tablespoon Worcestershire sauce
1 tablespoon Creole mustard
3 cups 2% low-fat milk
1 cup thinly sliced green onions, divided
½ cup (2 ounces) grated fresh Parmesan cheese, divided
¼ cup coarsely chopped fresh parsley, divided
8 cups hot cooked fettuccine (about 1 pound uncooked pasta)

1. Preheat oven to 350°.
2. Heat a large nonstick skillet over medium-high heat. Sprinkle chicken with Cajun seasoning. Coat pan with cooking spray. Add chicken to pan; cook 7 minutes on each side or until done. Cut chicken into ¼-inch-thick slices; set aside.
3. Melt butter in a large Dutch oven over medium-high heat. Add bell pepper and next 4 ingredients; sauté 7 minutes or until tender. Sprinkle with flour, and cook 1 minute, stirring constantly. Stir in Worcestershire and mustard; gradually add milk, stirring with a whisk. Bring to a boil; reduce heat, and simmer 3 minutes or until slightly thick. Remove from heat; stir in ¾ cup green onions, 6 tablespoons cheese, and 3 tablespoons parsley. Add chicken and pasta to sauce mixture; toss well to combine.

4. Spoon mixture into a 13 x 9-inch baking dish coated with cooking spray. Sprinkle with ¼ cup green onions, 2 tablespoons cheese, and 1 tablespoon parsley. Cover and bake at 350° for 20 minutes; uncover and bake an additional 5 minutes. Yield: 8 servings (serving size: 1½ cups).

CALORIES 469 (17% from fat); FAT 8.8g (sat 4.7g, mono 2.2g, poly 0.6g); PROTEIN 41.6g; CARB 54.2g; FIBER 4g; CHOL 85mg; IRON 3.5mg; SODIUM 632mg; CALC 233mg

Shrimp, Corn, and Potato Soup

This hearty dish is easy and flavorful. Canned cream-style corn slightly thickens the soup, while frozen corn kernels save preparation time. Canned diced tomatoes with green chiles have a twofold advantage: The tomatoes are already cut, and they add heat to the soup without the cook having to handle a fresh chile.

Cooking spray
1¾ cups chopped red onion
1 cup chopped green bell pepper
½ cup chopped celery
1 garlic clove, minced
2 cups chopped baking potato
2 (14-ounce) cans fat-free, less-sodium chicken broth
1 (16-ounce) package frozen whole-kernel corn, thawed
1 (14¾-ounce) can cream-style corn
1 (10-ounce) can diced tomatoes and green chiles, undrained
1 (6-ounce) can no-salt-added tomato paste
½ teaspoon salt
¼ teaspoon black pepper
1½ pounds medium shrimp, peeled and deveined
¼ cup thinly sliced green onions

1. Heat a large Dutch oven over medium-high heat. Coat pan with cooking spray. Add red onion, bell pepper, celery, and garlic; sauté 5 minutes or until tender. Add potato and next 5 ingredients. Bring to a boil; cook 5 minutes. Stir in salt, black pepper, and shrimp; cook 5 minutes or until shrimp are done. Sprinkle with

green onions. Yield: 8 servings (serving size: 1½ cups).

CALORIES 262 (8% from fat); FAT 2.4g (sat 0.4g, mono 0.4g, poly 1g); PROTEIN 23.4g; CARB 40.1g; FIBER 5g; CHOL 129mg; IRON 3.3mg; SODIUM 769mg; CALC 78mg

Orange-Pecan French Toast Casserole

Making this casserole saves you the trouble of standing over a griddle flipping individual slices of French toast. Assemble the dish the night before your gathering, and pop it in the oven the next morning. Be sure to serve each slice bottom-side up so the pecan mixture is on top.

1 cup packed brown sugar
⅓ cup butter, melted
2 tablespoons light-colored corn syrup
Cooking spray
⅓ cup chopped pecans
1 teaspoon grated orange rind
1 cup fresh orange juice
½ cup fat-free milk
3 tablespoons granulated sugar
1 teaspoon ground cinnamon
1 teaspoon vanilla extract
3 large egg whites, lightly beaten
2 large eggs, lightly beaten
12 (1-inch-thick) slices French bread (about 1 pound)

1. Combine first 3 ingredients; pour into a 13 x 9-inch baking dish coated with cooking spray. Sprinkle pecans evenly over sugar mixture.
2. Combine rind and next 7 ingredients; stir with a whisk. Arrange bread slices over pecans in dish; pour egg mixture over bread. Cover and refrigerate 1 hour or overnight.
3. Preheat oven to 350°.
4. Carefully turn bread slices over to absorb excess egg mixture. Let stand at room temperature 20 minutes. Bake at 350° for 35 minutes or until lightly browned. Yield: 12 servings.

CALORIES 293 (29% from fat); FAT 9.5g (sat 3.9g, mono 3.6g, poly 1.3g); PROTEIN 6.1g; CARB 43.6g; FIBER 1.6g; CHOL 49mg; IRON 1.6mg; SODIUM 323mg; CALC 69mg

Moroccan Barbecue

The vivid flavors of this colorful North African country come alive in this easy alfresco menu.

For a new twist on the traditional American summer barbecue, try a Moroccan barbecue. The barbecue theme combines easy preparation with convenience. Marinate the kebabs of lamb a day ahead to infuse them with the flavor of fresh herbs and spices. On the day of the party grill the kebabs and accompany them with plenty of warm, crusty bread and saucers filled with cooked or raw vegetable salads. For dessert, serve a platter of fresh seasonal fruit, honey-sweet Medjool dates, and Couscous with Apple-Ginger Topping and Orange Sauce—a contemporary adaptation of couscous (a Moroccan staple). Finish off the menu with glasses of syrupy fresh mint tea.

Moroccan Grilling Menu
serves 8

Tomato Salad with Avocado and Preserved Lemons

Brochettes of Lamb

Carrots with Paprika and Capers

Couscous with Apple-Ginger Topping and Orange Sauce

Iced Mint Tea

WINE NOTE: Begin your enjoyment of this Moroccan barbecue with a nicely chilled dry, spicy Gewürztraminer. The bold, piquant flavors and almost thick, smooth texture will act as a thirst-quenching counterbalance to the Tomato Salad. A good one to try: Trimbach Gewürztraminer from Alsace France. The 2002 is $22.

QUICK & EASY
Tomato Salad with Avocado and Preserved Lemons

4 cups diced plum tomato (about 2 pounds)
1 tablespoon minced Quick Preserved Lemons (recipe at right)
2 teaspoons fresh lemon juice
½ teaspoon salt
1 diced peeled avocado
2 tablespoons chopped fresh parsley

1. Combine first 5 ingredients. Sprinkle with parsley. Yield: 8 servings (serving size: ½ cup).

(Totals include Quick Preserved Lemons) CALORIES 60 (63% from fat); FAT 4.2g (sat 0.7g, mono 2.5g, poly 0.6g); PROTEIN 1.3g; CARB 6.3g; FIBER 2.4g; CHOL 0mg; IRON 0.7mg; SODIUM 245mg; CALC 10mg

QUICK & EASY • MAKE AHEAD
Quick Preserved Lemons

Preserving lemons typically takes 4 to 6 weeks to acquire the right consistency and flavor. However, this quick method bypasses the lengthy preservation time and is a great substitute for the real thing. Use the lemon rind to accent a variety of dishes, from seafood to vegetable stir-fries. Mash the pulp in a sauce or a stew, or use it to baste chicken or lamb. The preserved lemons can be made several days ahead and stored in the refrigerator up to 1 week. To distribute the flavor, chop before adding to a dish.

1 cup water
2 tablespoons kosher salt
2 lemons, washed and quartered

1. Combine water and salt in a small saucepan; bring to a boil. Add lemons; cook 30 minutes or until liquid is reduced to ½ cup and lemon rind is tender. Remove from heat; cool to room temperature. Yield: ½ cup (serving size: 1 teaspoon).

CALORIES 2 (0% from fat); FAT 0g; PROTEIN 0.1g; CARB 1g; FIBER 0.4g; CHOL 0mg; IRON 0.1mg; SODIUM 235mg; CALC 6mg

Brochettes of Lamb

Serve with harissa, a hot sauce sold in Middle Eastern markets.

⅓ cup chopped fresh cilantro
2 tablespoons fresh lemon juice
2 teaspoons Hungarian sweet paprika
1 teaspoon ground cumin
¾ teaspoon salt
¼ teaspoon freshly ground black pepper
2 garlic cloves, minced
3 pounds boneless leg of lamb, trimmed and cut into 1-inch cubes
Cooking spray

1. Combine all ingredients except cooking spray in a large bowl. Cover and marinate in refrigerator 2 hours.
2. Prepare grill to medium-high heat.
3. Thread lamb pieces onto 8 (8-inch) skewers. Lightly coat lamb with cooking spray. Place brochettes on grill rack coated with cooking spray; grill 5 minutes on each side or until desired degree of doneness. Yield: 8 servings (serving size: 1 brochette).

WINE NOTE: Spicy or rustic lamb dishes are ideal with wines based on the red grape varieties Syrah, Grenache, and Mourvedre. In particular, Shiraz from Australia (Syrah is called Shiraz there) marries with the succulent meatiness of the lamb. There are loads of moderately priced Shirazes on the market. Try Penfolds Bin 28 "Kalimna" Shiraz. The 2001 is about $22.

CALORIES 149 (31% from fat); FAT 5.2g (sat 1.8g, mono 2.1g, poly 0.5g); PROTEIN 23.5g; CARB 0.8g; FIBER 0.2g; CHOL 73mg; IRON 2.2mg; SODIUM 290mg; CALC 12mg

QUICK & EASY • MAKE AHEAD

Carrots with Paprika and Capers

(pictured on page 181)

Like most Moroccan salads, this can be made up to 1 day ahead and chilled. For the best flavor, bring it back to room temperature before serving.

    4   teaspoons olive oil
    2   teaspoons Hungarian sweet paprika
    1   cup diced sweet onion
    7   cups (⅛-inch) diagonally cut
        carrot (about 2 pounds)
    ½   cup water
    6   garlic cloves, minced
    2   tablespoons capers
    2   tablespoons red wine vinegar
    ½   teaspoon salt
    2   tablespoons chopped fresh parsley

1. Heat oil in a large nonstick skillet over medium-high heat. Add paprika; sauté 30 seconds. Add onion; sauté 5 minutes or until tender. Add carrot, water, and garlic; reduce heat to medium-low. Cover and cook 10 minutes or until carrot is tender. Add capers, vinegar, and salt; uncover and cook 8 minutes or until liquid almost evaporates. Sprinkle with parsley. Yield: 8 servings (serving size: ¾ cup).

CALORIES 89 (26% from fat); FAT 2.6g (sat 0.4g, mono 1.7g, poly 0.3g); PROTEIN 1.9g; CARB 16g; FIBER 4.3g; CHOL 0mg; IRON 0.9mg; SODIUM 315mg; CALC 46mg

Couscous with Apple-Ginger Topping and Orange Sauce

The sauce for this dessert can be made a day ahead and reheated just before serving. Before juicing the oranges, grate 2 teaspoons rind for the couscous.

SAUCE:

    ¾   cup fresh orange juice
    1½ tablespoons Triple Sec
        (orange-flavored liqueur)

COUSCOUS:

    1⅓ cups apple juice
    3   tablespoons butter
    ¼   teaspoon salt
    1   cup uncooked couscous
    2   teaspoons grated orange
        rind

TOPPING:

    2   tablespoons butter
    2   tablespoons dark brown sugar
    2   cups diced peeled Granny Smith
        apple
    2   tablespoons raisins
    2   tablespoons finely chopped
        crystallized ginger
    1½ tablespoons Triple Sec
        (orange-flavored liqueur)
    ½   teaspoon ground cinnamon

REMAINING INGREDIENTS:

    ¼   cup reduced-fat sour cream
        Mint sprigs (optional)

1. To prepare sauce, bring orange juice to a boil in a large saucepan; cook until reduced to ⅓ cup (about 6 minutes). Stir in 1½ tablespoons liqueur. Pour into a small bowl, and set aside.

2. To prepare couscous, bring apple juice, 3 tablespoons butter, and salt to a boil in a saucepan, and gradually stir in couscous and rind. Remove from heat; cover and let stand 5 minutes. Fluff with a fork.

3. To prepare topping, melt 2 tablespoons butter in a medium nonstick skillet over medium-high heat. Add sugar, and cook 1 minute, stirring constantly. Stir in apple and raisins; cook 5 minutes or until apple is tender, stirring frequently. Remove from heat. Stir in ginger, 1½ tablespoons liqueur, and cinnamon.

4. Spoon about ⅓ cup couscous into each of 8 dessert glasses or bowls. Top each serving with about 2 tablespoons topping, 1½ teaspoons sour cream, and about 1 tablespoon sauce. Garnish with mint sprigs, if desired. Yield: 8 servings.

CALORIES 248 (30% from fat); FAT 8.3g (sat 5g, mono 2.3g, poly 0.5g); PROTEIN 3.4g; CARB 38.2g; FIBER 1.9g; CHOL 22mg; IRON 0.7mg; SODIUM 155mg; CALC 32mg

MAKE AHEAD

Iced Mint Tea

Mint tea, made with spearmint, is the traditional drink of Morocco and North Africa. A few leaves of fresh or dried lemon verbena add a lovely citrus flavor. Be sure to use Chinese green tea, such as Gunpowder Green, Young Hyson, or Formosa Oolong. For a lighter minty flavor, remove the mint sprigs before chilling. This tea is traditionally very sweet, but use less sugar, if desired.

    8   cups boiling water
    1   tablespoon loose Chinese green
        tea
    25 fresh mint sprigs (about
        1½ ounces)
    ½   cup sugar

1. Combine water and tea in a medium bowl; cover and steep 2½ minutes. Strain tea mixture through a fine sieve into a bowl, and discard tea leaves. Add mint; steep 5 minutes. Add sugar; stir until sugar dissolves. Cool completely. Serve over ice. Yield: 8 cups (serving size: 1 cup).

CALORIES 52 (2% from fat); FAT 0.1g (sat 0g, mono 0g, poly 0.1g); PROTEIN 0.2g; CARB 13.3g; FIBER 0.4g; CHOL 0mg; IRON 0.3mg; SODIUM 9mg; CALC 18mg

Martin Yan Can Teach

A favorite television chef demystifies traditional, healthful Chinese cooking techniques.

Martin Yan grew up in Guangzhou, China, amid the aromas and tastes of his parents' restaurant and grocery. He went to Hong Kong at age 13 to apprentice in a restaurant and later studied nutrition at the University of California at Davis. While helping a friend in Canada launch a restaurant, Yan was invited to be a guest on a television morning show, which led to an offer to host his own cooking show. He first appeared on PBS in 1978 as the host of *Yan Can Cook*. He was nominated for the 2004 James Beard Award for Best National Television Cooking Show.

For Yan, cooking is a great adventure, a chance to explore and try new things. The following recipes will help you master marinating, steaming, stir-frying, and braising—but most of all, you'll learn that Chinese cooking is fun.

Melon Chicken Salad

Yan's penchant for balancing flavors and textures is evident in this main-dish salad.

¼ cup rice vinegar
2 tablespoons low-sodium soy sauce
2 tablespoons chunky peanut butter
1 tablespoon honey
¾ teaspoon dark sesame oil
3 cups (2 x ¼-inch) strips honeydew melon
3 cups (2 x ¼-inch) strips cantaloupe
2 cups (2 x ¼-inch) strips daikon radish
1 cup (2 x ¼-inch) strips peeled English cucumber
3 tablespoons thinly sliced green onions
2 cups shredded cooked chicken breast
¼ cup chopped fresh cilantro
2 tablespoons chopped walnuts, toasted

1. Combine first 5 ingredients in a large bowl, stirring well with a whisk. Add honeydew and next 4 ingredients; toss well to coat.

2. Place 2 cups melon mixture on each of 4 plates; top each serving with ½ cup chicken. Sprinkle 1 tablespoon cilantro over each serving; top each with 1½ teaspoons walnuts. Serve immediately. Yield: 4 servings.

CALORIES 293 (30% from fat); FAT 9.9g (sat 1.8g, mono 3.3g, poly 3.9g); PROTEIN 22.6g; CARB 32g; FIBER 3.7g; CHOL 48mg; IRON 1.6mg; SODIUM 383mg; CALC 55mg

Staples for Chinese Cooking

Although many Chinese dishes use the same ingredients, they can be combined to create entirely different flavors. Here are staple ingredients to keep on hand so you can cook Chinese food anytime:
• Low-sodium soy sauce
• Ginger
• Garlic
• Green onions
• Dark sesame oil
• Rice vinegar
• Cornstarch
• White pepper
• Chinese rice wine
• Oyster sauce

Three-Pepper Beef
(pictured on page 235)

This stir-fry gets its color and crunch from a variety of bell peppers. Serve with rice.

2½ teaspoons cornstarch, divided
1 teaspoon sugar, divided
½ teaspoon salt
1 pound flank steak, trimmed and thinly sliced across grain
¼ cup less-sodium beef broth
3 tablespoons low-sodium soy sauce
1 teaspoon freshly ground black pepper
1 teaspoon vegetable oil
¼ cup sliced onion
1 teaspoon minced peeled fresh ginger
1 garlic clove, minced
1 cup sugar snap peas, trimmed
1¼ cups cubed red bell pepper
1¼ cups cubed yellow bell pepper
1¼ cups cubed green bell pepper
Parsley sprigs (optional)

1. Combine ½ teaspoon cornstarch, ½ teaspoon sugar, salt, and steak in a medium bowl; toss to coat. Set aside.

2. Combine 2 teaspoons cornstarch, ½ teaspoon sugar, broth, soy sauce, and black pepper, stirring with a whisk until sugar dissolves; set aside.

3. Heat oil in a wok or large nonstick skillet over medium-high heat. Add onions, ginger, and garlic; stir-fry 10 seconds. Add beef mixture, and stir-fry 3 minutes or until done. Remove beef mixture from pan; cover and keep warm. Add peas and bell peppers to pan; stir-fry 4 minutes or until crisp-tender. Add beef and broth mixture to pan; cook 2 minutes or until thickened, stirring constantly. Yield: 4 servings (serving size: about 1¾ cups).

CALORIES 326 (36% from fat); FAT 13g (sat 5.2g, mono 5g, poly 1.3g); PROTEIN 34.1g; CARB 17.6g; FIBER 4.4g; CHOL 76mg; IRON 4.3mg; SODIUM 832mg; CALC 50mg

Martin Yan's Philosophy

Martin Yan's motto has always been, "If Yan can, you can, too!" Classic techniques essential to Chinese cooking, such as steaming, stir-frying, and braising, can indeed be mastered by the home cook. Yan's mission is to teach his television viewers and cookbook readers that cooking can be fun, quick, and easy. "You don't have to be an expert to make delicious food," he says.

One of Yan's favorite things about Chinese cuisine is its versatility. Chinese food uses staple flavor components, but they can be combined in so many ways that "the same ingredients can create a different dish every day for a month," Yan explains. Another advantage of Chinese cooking "is that it's essentially healthy and low-fat." Yan attributes this to the fact that the cuisine relies heavily on vegetables and fish. And techniques such as stir-frying and steaming require little, if any, oil.

Yan's approach to cooking has always emphasized balance. He views it as part of an overall lifestyle. Informed by the Chinese philosophy in which yin and yang represent opposites that reside together in harmony, Yan achieves balance through contrasting flavors and textures—sweet and savory, spicy and mild, creamy and crunchy.

The Essential Tool: The Wok

Most Chinese cooking techniques can be done using a single piece of equipment: a wok. Just about every kind of wok (whether round-bottomed for gas burners or flat-bottomed for electric ranges) is now available with a nonstick coating, so you don't have to use much oil for stir-frying. Yan recommends spending a little extra money on a high-quality nonstick wok because the coating will last longer.

Heat concentrates at the bottom of the wok so that small, uniformly sized pieces of food stir-fry quickly over high heat. The curved shape of the pan makes it easier to move food around so the oil coats it evenly. The centuries-old method of steaming, another of Yan's favorite techniques, also works well in a wok, as most woks come equipped with a steaming rack or insert.

Flavor Builders

Chinese cuisine uses "marinades, such as soy sauce, rice wine or rice vinegar, cornstarch, and white pepper, to add flavor, tenderize, or intensify a food's moisture content," Yan explains. Cornstarch seals in juices, coats meat with a shiny glaze, and thickens sauces and soups. White pepper is milder than black, so its flavor blends seamlessly with other ingredients. In the recipe for Steamed Salmon with Savory Black Bean Sauce (recipe on page 221), for example, the fish is sprinkled with cornstarch, salt, and pepper, then allowed to stand for 10 minutes before cooking. When the cornstarch cooks, it creates a smooth, velvety texture for the fish.

Braising combines the techniques of stir-frying and steaming to deepen flavors. Ingredients are stir-fried in a wok, then allowed to boil in sauce until it thickens and the meat is tender. Yan compares Chinese-style braising to the technique of reducing in Western cooking: The liquid evaporates to concentrate the flavor. It's also a great technique to achieve a tender texture, particularly with inexpensive cuts of meat.

Braised Seafood and Vegetable Noodles

Braising the ingredients together in the sauce for a few extra minutes blends the flavors and makes the seafood very tender. We liked the fresh Chinese noodles found in the produce section the best, but any Asian noodle will do.

 2 teaspoons cornstarch
 2 teaspoons sake or dry sherry
 ½ pound skinless halibut fillets, cut into 1-inch pieces
 ¼ pound medium shrimp, peeled and deveined
 ½ cup fat-free, less-sodium chicken broth
 2 tablespoons sake or dry sherry
 2 tablespoons oyster sauce
 1 teaspoon cornstarch
 ¼ teaspoon white pepper
 2 quarts water
 3 baby bok choy, quartered lengthwise
 8 ounces fresh lo mein noodles or udon noodles (thick, round fresh Japanese wheat noodles)
 1 tablespoon vegetable oil
 ½ cup thinly sliced carrot
 ¼ cup thinly sliced green onions
 ½ cup canned straw mushrooms, drained
 ⅓ cup snow peas, cut in half diagonally
 6 canned whole baby corn, cut in half diagonally

1. Combine first 4 ingredients in a medium bowl, tossing to coat, and let mixture stand 10 minutes.

2. Combine broth and next 4 ingredients, stirring with a whisk; set aside.

3. Bring 2 quarts water to a boil in a large saucepan. Add bok choy; cook 3 minutes or until crisp-tender. Remove bok choy with a slotted spoon; keep warm. Add noodles to boiling water; cook according to package directions, omitting salt and fat. Drain noodles. Arrange noodles and bok choy on a serving platter; cover and keep warm.

4. Heat oil in a wok or large nonstick skillet over medium-high heat. Add fish mixture, carrot, and onions; stir-fry

3 minutes or until shrimp are done and fish flakes easily when tested with a fork. Add broth mixture, mushrooms, snow peas, and corn; bring to a boil, stirring constantly. Cook 2 minutes or until sauce is slightly thick. Spoon over noodles and bok choy. Yield: 4 servings (serving size: 1 cup noodles, 3 bok choy quarters, and about ¾ cup seafood mixture).

CALORIES 348 (17% from fat); FAT 6.4g (sat 0.8g, mono 1.4g, poly 2.8g); PROTEIN 24.6g; CARB 43.9g; FIBER 2.6g; CHOL 61mg; IRON 2.8mg; SODIUM 607mg; CALC 179mg

Grilled Beef Salad with Lemongrass Dressing

DRESSING:
½ cup coarsely chopped fresh mint
¼ cup coarsely chopped fresh cilantro
¼ cup thinly sliced shallots
¼ cup fresh lime juice
2 tablespoons chopped green onions
2 tablespoons chile paste with garlic
1½ tablespoons fish sauce
2 teaspoons sugar
2 teaspoons finely chopped peeled fresh lemongrass

SALAD:
1 (1-pound) flank steak, trimmed
⅛ teaspoon salt
⅛ teaspoon freshly ground black pepper
Cooking spray
2 cups sliced iceberg lettuce
2 cups sliced napa (Chinese) cabbage
½ cup chopped tomato
½ cup thinly vertically sliced red onion

1. Prepare grill.
2. To prepare dressing, combine first 9 ingredients, stirring until sugar dissolves.
3. To prepare salad, sprinkle steak with salt and pepper. Place steak on a grill rack coated with cooking spray; grill 4 minutes on each side or until desired degree of doneness. Remove from grill; place on a cutting board. Let stand 15 minutes. Cut steak diagonally across grain into thin slices. Place steak, lettuce, and remaining 3 ingredients in a large bowl. Pour dressing over salad; toss well

to coat. Serve immediately. Yield: 4 servings (serving size: 1½ cups).

CALORIES 288 (37% from fat); FAT 11.7g (sat 5g, mono 4.6g, poly 0.6g); PROTEIN 33g; CARB 11.2g; FIBER 2.1g; CHOL 76mg; IRON 3.9mg; SODIUM 1,020mg; CALC 57mg

Tips for Steaming

With this method, the food cooks in moist heat, so it doesn't dry out; the cover of the pan keeps both the heat and the moisture in. Follow these general guidelines:

• Marinate the food to be steamed ahead—for a few minutes or even hours, if possible.

• Add seasonings before steaming so their flavors will be infused during the steaming process. Yan likes to use aromatics, such as garlic and ginger; flavorings like sake or citrus juices; and spices, such as five-spice powder or white pepper.

• Woks are great for steaming, but a deep pan or Dutch oven will work, too. You can use a metal steamer rack, cooling rack, or stackable bamboo steamer to hold the food.

• There are two keys to steaming: Cook at a high temperature for a short time, and always keep an eye on the water level. Keep a pot of water simmering nearby so you can add more to keep the water level and temperature constant. Follow these steps for successful steaming:

1. Before cooking, place the rack or basket in the wok or pan, and fill the pan with water 1 to 1½ inches below the rack or basket.
2. Place the food on a heat-resistant dish (such as a glass pie plate) with a diameter smaller than the steamer.
3. Bring the water to a full boil.
4. Set the food dish on the rack or basket, and cover.
5. Begin measuring the cooking time.
6. Always open the lid away from you because the steam is hot and could burn.

Steamed Salmon with Savory Black Bean Sauce

Look for dried wood ear (sometimes called cloud ear, tree ear, or silver ear) mushrooms and jars of black bean sauce in the Asian food aisles of large supermarkets. If you don't have a bamboo steamer, use a round cooling rack to support the pie plate in the wok or skillet.

2 dried wood ear mushrooms
4 (6-ounce) salmon fillets, skinned (about 1 inch thick)
2 teaspoons cornstarch
¼ teaspoon salt
⅛ teaspoon ground white pepper
½ cup thinly sliced green onions
3 tablespoons sake (rice wine)
2 tablespoons black bean sauce
1 tablespoon minced fresh garlic
2 teaspoons dark sesame oil
1 teaspoon sugar
1 to 2 jalapeño peppers, thinly sliced

1. Soak mushrooms in hot water 20 minutes or until soft. Drain; cut into thin strips.
2. Cut 3 (¾-inch) deep lengthwise slits in each fillet. Combine cornstarch, salt, and pepper; sprinkle over fish. Let stand 10 minutes. Stuff mushroom strips and green onions into slits.
3. Place fish in a 9-inch pie plate. Combine sake and remaining 5 ingredients; pour over fish. Place a bamboo steamer basket in a large wok, and add water to wok to a depth of 1½ inches below basket. Bring water to a boil. Place pie plate in bottom of steamer basket; cover and cook 8 minutes or until fish flakes easily when tested with a fork. Yield: 4 servings (serving size: 1 fillet).

WINE NOTE: The sweet earthiness of the mushrooms and black bean sauce as well as the flavor of the salmon form a perfect counterpoint to the earthy flavors and silky texture of a good pinot noir. Try Sebastiani pinot noir 2002 (Russian River Valley, California), $23, with its forestlike aromas of earth, dried leaves, and underbrush, and its seductive flavors of dried cherries, mocha, and vanilla.

CALORIES 335 (42% from fat); FAT 15.8g (sat 3.5g, mono 6.7g, poly 4.3g); PROTEIN 36.7g; CARB 5.8g; FIBER 0.8g; CHOL 87mg; IRON 0.8mg; SODIUM 284mg; CALC 27mg

More of a Good Thing

After our recipe makeover, an Iowa vegetarian finds her corn bread boasts more fresh corn sweetness.

Before they moved to Iowa City, Iowa, Lucy Barker and her husband, Jason, lived in Texas for more than a decade. He loved pork barbecue with spicy red sauce, while Lucy was just as passionate about barbecue's traditional sides. As a vegetarian, Lucy never felt deprived at a Lone Star cookout. "It was easy to make a complete meal with ranch-style beans, salads, and my Corn Bread with Fresh Corn." She describes her corn bread as moist and slightly sweet, but she suspected it had too much butter and shortening. She turned to us for help.

We began by omitting 7 tablespoons of shortening, replacing it with a mere 2 tablespoons of vegetable oil. We replaced the volume and maintained the moisture by tripling the amount of fresh corn. Removing excess butter dropped another 68 grams of fat. Switching from whole milk and half-and-half to 2 percent reduced-fat milk and replacing one egg with an egg white shaved almost 15 more grams of fat.

BEFORE	AFTER
SERVING SIZE	
1 wedge	
CALORIES PER SERVING	
291	181
FAT	
16.7g	5.1g
PERCENT OF TOTAL CALORIES	
52%	25%

Corn Bread with Fresh Corn

Cut kernels from ears of corn in a deep bowl to catch the kernels and juices.

2 ears corn
2 tablespoons vegetable oil, divided
1 tablespoon butter
1¾ cups 2% reduced-fat milk, divided
1 cup all-purpose flour
1½ cups yellow cornmeal
¼ cup sugar
1 tablespoon baking powder
1 teaspoon salt
1 large egg, lightly beaten
1 large egg white, lightly beaten

1. Preheat oven to 400°.
2. Cut kernels from ears of corn into a bowl; scrape "milk" and remaining pulp from cobs using dull side of a knife.
3. Coat a 10-inch cast-iron skillet with 1½ teaspoons oil. Place pan in 400° oven 10 minutes.
4. While pan preheats in oven, melt butter in a medium nonstick skillet over medium-high heat. Add corn mixture; sauté 2 minutes. Remove from heat. Place half of corn and ½ cup milk in a blender or food processor, and process until smooth. Place puréed corn mixture and sautéed corn in a medium bowl.
5. Lightly spoon flour into a dry measuring cup; level with a knife. Combine flour, cornmeal, sugar, baking powder, and salt in a large bowl; make a well in center of mixture. Add 1½ tablespoons oil, 1¼ cups milk, egg, and egg white to corn mixture; stir to combine. Add corn mixture to flour mixture, stirring just until moist. Pour batter into preheated skillet; bake at 400° for 25 minutes or until a wooden pick inserted in center comes out clean. Yield: 12 servings (serving size: 1 wedge).

CALORIES 181 (25% from fat); FAT 5.1g (sat 1.5g, mono 1.2g, poly 1.6g); PROTEIN 5.1g; CARB 30.6g; FIBER 2.2g; CHOL 23mg; IRON 1.3mg; SODIUM 355mg; CALC 115mg

A Plum Recipe for Pork

A New England cook makes a special meal with ripe fruit and pork tenderloin.

In most kitchens, plums are snacks or an ingredient baked into pies. But for Jessica Flaherty, of Canton, Connecticut, plums are transformed into a sauce for a special dinner.

With a paring knife, Flaherty carefully peels the plums and cuts them into small pieces. Then she simmers the fruit in a sweet and tart mixture of balsamic vinegar, white wine, and brown sugar in a skillet. To enhance the flavors, she rubs the pork with a little ginger. "I like to cut the tenderloin into medallions and brown them quickly so they stay moist," she says.

Flaherty serves salad and corn on the cob with her main dish. (Polenta makes a nice accompaniment, too.) For dessert, she serves mocha chip ice cream.

Pork Tenderloin with Plum Sauce

1 teaspoon grated peeled fresh ginger
½ teaspoon kosher salt, divided
¼ teaspoon freshly ground black pepper, divided
1 (1-pound) pork tenderloin, trimmed
1 teaspoon olive oil
2½ tablespoons minced shallots (about 1 medium)
2 cups chopped peeled ripe plums (about 4 medium)
1 tablespoon brown sugar
¼ teaspoon ground ginger
¼ cup dry white wine
1 teaspoon balsamic vinegar
1 teaspoon butter
Cooking spray
1 tablespoon chopped walnuts, toasted

1. Combine fresh ginger, ¼ teaspoon salt, and ⅛ teaspoon pepper. Cut pork crosswise into 8 pieces; rub pork with ginger mixture. Let stand 15 minutes.

2. Heat oil in a large nonstick skillet over medium heat. Add shallots; cook 5 minutes or until tender, stirring frequently. Stir in ¼ teaspoon salt, ⅛ teaspoon pepper, plums, sugar, and ground ginger. Cook 8 minutes or until plums are tender; stir in wine and vinegar. Reduce heat; simmer 10 minutes. Add butter; stir until butter melts.

3. Heat a large nonstick skillet over medium-high heat. Coat pan with cooking spray. Add pork to pan; cook 3 minutes on each side or until desired degree of doneness. Serve sauce over pork. Sprinkle with walnuts. Yield: 4 servings (serving size: 2 pork pieces, ¼ cup sauce, and ¾ teaspoon walnuts).

CALORIES 232 (30% from fat); FAT 7.7g (sat 2.2g, mono 3.4g, poly 1.6g); PROTEIN 25g; CARB 16g; FIBER 1.5g; CHOL 76mg; IRON 1.8mg; SODIUM 305mg; CALC 19mg

---

QUICK & EASY • MAKE AHEAD
White Bean Dip

"I first made this dip years ago when I needed a fast appetizer for an impromptu evening with friends, and I've been making it ever since. I love the lime and cilantro combination; they cut into the flavor so you're not just eating beans. Serve with baked tortilla chips."

—Jo Goren, Moreland Hills, Ohio

½ cup fresh cilantro
2 tablespoons fresh lime juice
1 tablespoon finely chopped canned jalapeño pepper
1½ teaspoons low-sodium soy sauce
1 teaspoon olive oil
¼ teaspoon chili powder
2 (16-ounce) cans cannellini beans or other white beans, rinsed and drained
2 garlic cloves, minced
¼ cup chopped seeded plum tomato
¼ cup minced green onions

1. Place first 8 ingredients in a food processor, and process until smooth. Top with tomato and onions. Yield: 8 servings (serving size: ¼ cup).

CALORIES 93 (10% from fat); FAT 1g (sat 0.1g, mono 0.4g, poly 0.5g); PROTEIN 4.3g; CARB 16g; FIBER 4.4g; CHOL 0mg; IRON 1.6mg; SODIUM 201mg; CALC 36mg

---

MAKE AHEAD
Baked Chiles Rellenos

"Tex-Mex food can be high in fat and calories, but we love it, so I try to re-create the flavors in a lightened version. This is my best dish. It's a great do-ahead meal. I refrigerate the stuffed chiles and sauce separately and bake them together either the same evening or the next day."

—Amy R. Sokol, San Antonio, Texas

5 large poblano chiles
Cooking spray
2½ cups thinly sliced zucchini
1 teaspoon minced garlic
1 teaspoon ground cumin, divided
2 jalapeño peppers
1 (14.5-ounce) can diced tomatoes, drained
1 (8-ounce) can tomato sauce
1½ cups (6 ounces) preshredded part-skim mozzarella cheese
1 cup shredded cooked chicken breast
½ teaspoon salt

1. Preheat broiler.
2. Place poblano chiles on a foil-lined baking sheet; broil 3 inches from heat 8 minutes or until blackened and charred, turning after 6 minutes. Place in a heavy-duty zip-top plastic bag; seal. Let stand 15 minutes. Peel and discard skins. Cut a lengthwise slit in each chile; discard seeds, leaving stems intact.
3. Heat a medium saucepan over medium-high heat. Coat with cooking spray. Add zucchini and garlic; cook 4 minutes or until crisp-tender. Stir in ½ teaspoon cumin, jalapeño peppers, tomatoes, and tomato sauce; bring to a boil. Reduce heat, and simmer 15 minutes. Remove and discard jalapeño peppers.
4. Preheat oven to 350°.
5. Combine ½ teaspoon cumin, cheese, chicken, and salt in a bowl, tossing to combine. Spoon about ½ cup cheese mixture into each chile, and secure with a wooden pick. Place stuffed chiles in an 11 x 7-inch baking dish coated with cooking spray; pour tomato mixture over stuffed chiles. Cover, and bake at 350° for 20 minutes. Uncover; bake an additional

---

10 minutes or until thoroughly heated. Yield: 5 servings (serving size: 1 stuffed chile and about ⅔ cup tomato mixture).

CALORIES 201 (33% from fat); FAT 7.7g (sat 3.8g, mono 2.2g, poly 0.8g); PROTEIN 20g; CARB 15.4g; FIBER 3.9g; CHOL 43mg; IRON 2mg; SODIUM 795mg; CALC 267mg

---

Zucchini-Spinach Bisque

"I find that puréed soups are a filling and easy way to get vegetables into my daily diet—summer or winter. Sometimes, just before serving, I brown and dice low-fat chicken-apple sausage and add it to the soup."

—Sonya Bavvai, Palo Alto, California

4½ cups chopped zucchini (about 1½ pounds)
2 cups fat-free, less-sodium chicken broth
1 cup chopped red onion
¾ cup chopped celery
2 tablespoons Madeira wine
½ teaspoon salt
½ teaspoon chopped fresh dill
⅛ teaspoon black pepper
Dash of ground nutmeg
1 garlic clove, minced
1 (6-ounce) package fresh baby spinach
½ cup fat-free half-and-half
½ cup (2 ounces) grated fresh Asiago cheese

1. Combine first 10 ingredients in a large saucepan; bring to a boil. Reduce heat, and simmer 20 minutes or until zucchini is tender. Stir in spinach; cook 1 minute or until spinach wilts. Let stand 5 minutes. Place half of zucchini mixture in a blender, and pulse until coarsely puréed. Pour puréed mixture into a large bowl. Repeat procedure with remaining zucchini mixture. Stir in half-and-half. Ladle soup into bowls; sprinkle with cheese. Yield: 6 servings (serving size: 1 cup soup and 4 teaspoons cheese).

CALORIES 91 (30% from fat); FAT 3g (sat 1.8g, mono 0.8g, poly 0.2g); PROTEIN 6.1g; CARB 9.7g; FIBER 2.6g; CHOL 8mg; IRON 1.4mg; SODIUM 520mg; CALC 139mg

Zesty Garden Sauce

"I created this scrumptious sauce when my crop of tomatoes overwhelmed my windowsill. It's delicious over pasta and served with French bread to sop up the juices."
—Amanda Nowlin, Worthington, Minnesota

    8   cups chopped peeled tomatoes
        (about 4½ pounds)
    ¾   teaspoon salt
    1   tablespoon butter
    2   cups chopped onion
    1   teaspoon minced garlic
    1   tablespoon chopped fresh basil
    ½   teaspoon chili powder
    ¼   teaspoon freshly ground black
        pepper
    ⅛   teaspoon ground red pepper
    1   cup chopped zucchini
    ¾   cup chopped red bell pepper
    ½   cup chopped green bell pepper

1. Place tomato in a colander; sprinkle with salt. Toss well. Drain in sink 30 minutes.
2. Melt butter in a large saucepan over medium-high heat. Add onion; sauté 4 minutes or until browned. Add garlic; sauté 30 seconds. Add drained tomato, basil, chili powder, black pepper, and ground red pepper; bring to a boil. Reduce heat; simmer 15 minutes. Stir in zucchini and bell peppers; simmer 5 minutes or until peppers are crisp-tender. Yield: 7 cups (serving size: 1 cup).

CALORIES 78 (29% from fat); FAT 2.5g (sat 1.1g, mono 0.6g, poly 0.4g); PROTEIN 2.5g; CARB 14.3g; FIBER 3.6g; CHOL 4mg; IRON 1.3mg; SODIUM 290mg; CALC 23mg

Stuffed Portobellos

"After making a *Cooking Light* recipe for burritos using soy crumbles, my daughter, Jessica, suggested using the crumbles in a low-fat version of Italian sausage-stuffed portobellos. This makes a great meal with wild rice and a mixed green salad."
—Mary Gleason Best, Brighton, Michigan

    6   (4-inch) portobello caps
    1⅓ cups frozen soy crumbles,
        thawed
    ¾   cup canned diced tomatoes,
        drained
    ½   cup minced green onions
    2   tablespoons chopped fresh
        parsley
    2   tablespoons grated fresh Parmesan
        cheese
    2   tablespoons ⅓-less-fat cream
        cheese
    1   teaspoon dried Italian seasoning
    ½   teaspoon salt
    ¼   teaspoon black pepper
    1   garlic clove, minced
    Cooking spray

1. Preheat oven to 350°.
2. Remove and discard stems from mushrooms. Remove brown gills from undersides of mushrooms using a spoon; discard gills.
3. Combine soy crumbles and next 9 ingredients in a medium bowl. Spoon ⅓ cup soy mixture into each mushroom cap. Place caps on a baking sheet coated with cooking spray. Bake at 350° for 30 minutes or until mushrooms are tender and tops are lightly browned. Yield: 6 servings (serving size: 1 stuffed cap).

CALORIES 124 (15% from fat); FAT 2g (sat 0.6g, mono 0.5g, poly 0.2g); PROTEIN 13.4g; CARB 13.4g; FIBER 5g; CHOL 3mg; IRON 0.9mg; SODIUM 541mg; CALC 47mg

Chocolate Chip Zucchini Bread
(pictured on page 235)

"After searching for a chocolate zucchini bread recipe that didn't require a lot of oil, I came up with this winner. My four-year-old son, Andrew, really likes it, and it's great to be able to enjoy something that's healthy and chocolate at the same time."
—Elizabeth Alcorn, Fort Mitchell, Kentucky

    ¾   cup sugar
    3   tablespoons vegetable oil
    2   large eggs
    1   cup applesauce
    2   cups all-purpose flour
    2   tablespoons unsweetened cocoa
    1¼ teaspoons baking soda
    1   teaspoon ground cinnamon
    ¼   teaspoon salt
    1½ cups finely shredded zucchini
        (about 1 medium)
    ½   cup semisweet chocolate chips
    Cooking spray

1. Preheat oven to 350°.
2. Place first 3 ingredients in a large bowl; beat with a mixer at low speed until well blended. Stir in applesauce.
3. Lightly spoon flour into dry measuring cups; level with a knife. Combine flour and next 4 ingredients, stirring well with a whisk. Add flour mixture to sugar mixture, beating just until moist. Stir in zucchini and chocolate chips. Spoon batter into a 9 x 5-inch loaf pan coated with cooking spray. Bake at 350° for 1 hour or until a wooden pick inserted in center comes out almost clean. Cool in pan 10 minutes on a wire rack, and remove from pan. Cool completely on wire rack. Yield: 16 servings (serving size: 1 slice).

CALORIES 161 (29% from fat); FAT 5.1g (sat 1.6g, mono 1.4g, poly 1.7g); PROTEIN 2.9g; CARB 27.3g; FIBER 1.4g; CHOL 27mg; IRON 1.2mg; SODIUM 145mg; CALC 12mg

Inspiration From the Garden

Top chefs tell how their gardens have grown and become key to their cooking.

Most chefs will agree their food is only as good as its ingredients. To ensure they have access to the type and quality of ingredients they want, many chefs cultivate their own gardens. Here, we talk to five whose gardens range from tiny plots to several acres, and learn how what they grow influences their cooking. (See "How Their Gardens Grow" on page 226.)

Maine Lobster and Pepper Salad with Asian Herbs

Flavors reminiscent of spring rolls star in this herb-filled salad from Clark Frasier. Substitute shrimp for lobster, if desired. Look for sweetened chile sauce in Asian markets.

SALAD:
- 2 cups (2-inch) julienne-cut peeled jícama (about ¾ pound)
- 2 cups thinly sliced napa (Chinese) cabbage
- 1 cup (2-inch) red bell pepper strips
- 1 cup (2-inch) yellow bell pepper strips
- ½ cup (2-inch) julienne-cut carrot
- 3 tablespoons thinly sliced fresh cilantro
- 3 tablespoons thinly sliced fresh mint
- 3 tablespoons thinly sliced fresh basil
- 3 tablespoons fresh lime juice
- 1 banana pepper, seeded and thinly sliced

VINAIGRETTE:
- ¼ cup rice wine vinegar
- 2 tablespoons sweetened chile sauce
- 1 tablespoon thinly sliced fresh cilantro
- 1 tablespoon thinly sliced fresh mint
- 1 tablespoon canola oil
- 2 teaspoons fresh lime juice
- 1½ teaspoons minced peeled fresh ginger
- ½ teaspoon chopped seeded serrano chile
- ½ teaspoon fish sauce

REMAINING INGREDIENTS:
- 1 pound cooked lobster meat, cut into bite-sized pieces (about 2 [2-pound] Maine lobsters)
- 4 teaspoons chopped dry-roasted peanuts

1. To prepare salad, combine first 10 ingredients in a large bowl, tossing gently to combine.

2. To prepare vinaigrette, combine vinegar and next 8 ingredients, stirring with a whisk. Pour vinaigrette over salad, and toss gently to coat. Arrange about ¾ cup salad on each of 8 small plates, and top evenly with lobster. Sprinkle each serving with about ½ teaspoon peanuts. Yield: 8 appetizer servings.

WINE NOTE: In choosing a wine for this sensational dish, there are two considerations: the rich, meaty, luxurious flavor of the lobster; and the snappy, fresh, clean, Asian-inspired flavors of the salad and dressing. The best pick is definitely white Bordeaux.

While there are many good white Bordeaux available in the United States, you may want to try one of the truly great examples—especially since this is a "luxury" match for the lobster. Try Château Carbonnieux 2001, from the area in Bordeaux known as Pessac-Léognan, about $30.

CALORIES 130 (30% from fat); FAT 4.4g (sat 1.2g, mono 1.9g, poly 0.9g); PROTEIN 12.8g; CARB 10g; FIBER 3.3g; CHOL 43mg; IRON 0.8mg; SODIUM 381mg; CALC 60mg

Striped Bass with Heirloom Tomatoes and Herbs

Good tomatoes are a must for this dish from Ryan Hardy. He uses heirloom tomatoes from his garden. Try incorporating tomatoes of different colors for the prettiest presentation.

FISH:
- 4 (6-ounce) striped bass fillets
- ¼ teaspoon kosher salt
- ½ teaspoon freshly ground black pepper
- ¼ teaspoon ground red pepper
- 1 teaspoon olive oil

SALAD:
- 3 tomatoes, cut into ½-inch-thick slices (about 1¼ pounds)
- ¾ teaspoon kosher salt, divided
- ⅓ cup fresh mint leaves
- ⅓ cup fresh basil leaves
- ⅓ cup fresh flat-leaf parsley leaves
- ⅓ cup fresh chervil leaves
- ⅓ cup (1-inch) slices fresh chives
- 1 tablespoon extravirgin olive oil
- 1 tablespoon balsamic vinegar
- ¼ teaspoon freshly ground black pepper
- 8 sorrel leaves, coarsely chopped

1. To prepare fish, sprinkle fillets evenly with ¼ teaspoon salt, ½ teaspoon black pepper, and red pepper. Heat 1 teaspoon olive oil in a large nonstick skillet over medium-high heat. Add fillets, skin-side down. Cook 2 minutes or until skin is browned; turn fish over. Reduce heat to medium; cook 10 minutes or until fish flakes easily when tested with a fork.

2. To prepare salad, place tomato slices in a medium bowl; sprinkle evenly with ½ teaspoon salt. Let stand 10 minutes. Combine ¼ teaspoon salt, mint, and remaining 8 ingredients in a small bowl, tossing gently.

3. Divide tomato slices evenly among 4 plates. Top each serving with 1 fillet and ½ cup herb mixture. Yield: 4 servings.

CALORIES 248 (33% from fat); FAT 9.2g (sat 1.6g, mono 4.5g, poly 1.9g); PROTEIN 32.3g; CARB 9.1g; FIBER 2.8g; CHOL 136mg; IRON 3.4mg; SODIUM 609mg; CALC 69mg

Down East Garden

"Our garden came from necessity," says Clark Frasier, who, with partner Mark Gaier, owns and operates Arrows, a critically acclaimed restaurant in Ogunquit, Maine. "When we came [to Maine] in 1988, it was difficult, if not impossible, to get any good ingredients here. Anything more exotic than iceberg lettuce was a problem. We had the land, so we decided to start a kitchen garden."

Today, their garden supplies 80 percent of the produce used at this elegant self-described "farmhouse restaurant," despite Maine's short growing season. From its humble beginnings in 1992, the garden has grown to an intensely cultivated, three-quarter-acre swatch of land behind the restaurant. "Neither of us were really gardeners," Frasier says. "You just kind of throw yourself into it, plant, and see how you do." They no longer grow okra, for example, because it takes up too much space, but love their "beautiful little lettuce cups, sweet and peppery arugula, and really great-tasting green zebra tomatoes."

Returning to His Roots

"As a young kid, I couldn't wait until late summer, when I could have fresh peaches," says Ryan Hardy, chef at The Coach House on Martha's Vineyard, Massachusetts. "The flavor of a [just-picked] peach was what made me want to get in this business."

Hardy grew up eating foods from the garden. "We were forced as kids to go out and kill the weeds," he jokes. "Being able to spend time by myself outside—picking weeds is as much fun for me as tilling. Nothing matches the feeling of seeing something grow that you've planted from seed."

When Hardy first came to the Coach House in 2002, there was no garden. "I lived in cities where I couldn't have a garden, so I really took advantage when I moved someplace where I could grow again. Also, most people don't realize that herbs are more expensive than meats and fish, and you can grow them in a small

amount of space with minimal effort. So obviously, I wanted my own herb garden. Then, well, you can't grow basil without tomatoes, and tomatoes grow so well here."

Small Eden

To Chris Bianco, chef-owner of the acclaimed Pizzeria Bianco in Phoenix, "the word 'garden' is relative. If you're a city kid, you grow onion grass. My grandfather would take me on the side of the New York State Thruway, and we'd pick dandelion greens. It starts with a relationship with the ground. Here, purslane grows through every crack in the sidewalk."

Bianco keeps his kitchen garden at the restaurant small. "My garden is realistic," he says. "You get out of it what you put in, and most of my time goes to my restaurant. I know how hard it is to run a farm. I want to continue to support my local farmers—but I also want to be able to run out my back door and say, 'I want some tarragon!' I want to look at my garden and think, 'Wow, I have to use that'—whatever 'that' is on that day.

"Every day, people come to my back door with produce," he says. "Then there's my little garden. It all finally comes together on the plate."

Bianco believes his small garden doesn't simply inspire but actually dictates what he cooks. It's a combination of fresh ingredients, how they're prepared in the kitchen, and the way in which the food is plated that makes it good.

From Rooftop to Resort

Three years ago, Daniel Orr bought his apartment in New York City specifically because it had outdoor space for a garden. He wanted to bring a little bit of the 1,000-acre farm of his childhood into his city life as a high-profile chef. Until recently, the 25 by 18–foot rooftop garden—tiny by his native Indiana standards but large by city measures—provided bold accent flavors for food Orr served at the 350-seat restaurant Guastivino's,

where he was formerly chef. These days, Orr divides his time between the city and his work as the executive chef at The Cuisinart Resort and Spa in Anguilla, British West Indies, where he's working on a cookbook, developing a series of healthy cooking classes for guests, and "assisting the resort's farmers and gardeners with a hydroponic farm."

Orr's small city garden yields big flavor. "I grow things that are very intense, where the flavors go a long way," he explains. "And I grow things I can't buy." One of Orr's favorites is chiles, and many varieties grow well in his garden, which he says has a microclimate more similar to the Southwest than New York State. "I grow things that love the sun, because there's no shade up here. The sun is intense, and it's warm and dry." In addition to the chiles he grows, Orr's garden yields powerfully flavored herbs and spices, including mountain mint and four kinds of basil.

Ever-Changing Menu

When I travel," explains Johnny Schmitt, owner and chef of the Boonville Hotel in Boonville, California, "I pack some good salt and herbs from my garden. With those things, I know I can make almost anything."

Schmitt has spent his life in restaurants and has never cooked without a kitchen garden. In fact, at one point he decided to leave the industry to pursue another career path: gardener. But, he says, each time he tried to be a gardener, "they'd find out I can cook, and I'd be back behind the stove."

Clearly, Schmitt's inspiration in the kitchen starts with the garden. This Renaissance man—designer, gardener, hotelier, and chef—thinks visually, evidenced by his concentric garden, where he grows herbs, greens, and a variety of fruits and vegetables. His menu changes daily. "I go out into my garden, see what I've got, and write my menu every day based on what's there," Schmitt says. "I wouldn't know how to cook without a garden."

Golden Summer Soup

Daniel Orr's colorful soup has a velvety texture. The garnish of fresh-from-the-garden herbs at the end adds a bright burst of flavor and an appealing textural contrast.

    Cooking spray
 2 garlic cloves, minced
 8 cups chopped yellow tomato
      (about 3½ pounds)
 3 cups chopped Vidalia or other
      sweet onion
 2 cups fresh corn kernels
 1 cup chopped yellow bell
      pepper
 1 teaspoon fine sea salt
 1 teaspoon grated lemon
      rind
 ½ teaspoon freshly ground black
      pepper
 ½ teaspoon hot sauce
 1 tablespoon coarsely chopped
      fresh chervil
 1 tablespoon coarsely chopped
      fresh chives
 1 tablespoon coarsely chopped
      fresh basil
 1 tablespoon coarsely chopped
      fresh flat-leaf parsley
 1 cup halved cherry or grape
      tomatoes

1. Heat a small Dutch oven over medium-high heat. Coat pan with cooking spray. Add garlic; sauté 15 seconds. Add yellow tomato, onion, corn, and bell pepper; bring to a boil. Reduce heat, and simmer 15 minutes or until onion is tender, stirring occasionally. Place half of tomato mixture in a blender; process until smooth. Press puréed tomato mixture through a large sieve into a large bowl, reserving liquid; discard solids. Repeat procedure with remaining tomato mixture. Stir in salt, rind, black pepper, and hot sauce.

2. Combine chervil, chives, basil, and parsley, tossing gently. Ladle 1¼ cups soup into each of 4 bowls; top with ¼ cup cherry tomatoes and 1 tablespoon herb mixture. Yield: 4 servings.

CALORIES 209 (12% from fat); FAT 2.7g (sat 0.4g, mono 0.5g, poly 1.2g); PROTEIN 9.2g; CARB 46.8g; FIBER 11.8g; CHOL 0mg; IRON 3.2mg; SODIUM 636mg; CALC 82mg

Fresh Corn Risotto with Seared Shrimp and Salsa Verde

Any combination of fresh herbs works in this recipe created by Johnny Schmitt.

SALSA:

 ¼ cup water
 3 tablespoons chopped trimmed
      arugula
 3 tablespoons chopped fresh mint
 3 tablespoons chopped fresh
      flat-leaf parsley
 2 tablespoons chopped fresh basil
 1 tablespoon grated lemon rind
 1 tablespoon chopped fresh thyme
 2½ tablespoons extravirgin olive oil
 1½ teaspoons balsamic vinegar
 ¾ teaspoon kosher salt
 ¾ teaspoon anchovy paste
 3 garlic cloves, peeled

RISOTTO:

 24 large shrimp (about 1¼ pounds)
 1 tablespoon extravirgin olive oil,
      divided
 2 teaspoons balsamic vinegar
 ¾ teaspoon salt, divided
 ¼ teaspoon freshly ground black
      pepper, divided
 3 shallots
 3 ears corn
 1 tablespoon butter
 4 cups fat-free, less-sodium chicken
      broth
 2¼ cups water
 3 flat-leaf parsley sprigs
 3 thyme sprigs
 1 bay leaf
 1 rosemary sprig
 1½ cups Arborio rice
 ½ cup (2 ounces) grated
      Parmigiano-Reggiano cheese,
      divided

1. To prepare salsa, combine first 12 ingredients in a food processor; pulse until finely chopped, scraping sides.

2. To prepare risotto, peel shrimp, reserving shells. Combine shrimp, 1 teaspoon oil, 2 teaspoons vinegar, ¼ teaspoon salt, and ⅛ teaspoon pepper, tossing to coat. Cover and marinate in refrigerator 1 hour.

3. Peel and finely chop shallots, reserving skins; set shallots aside. Cut kernels from ears of corn, reserving cobs; set kernels aside. Melt butter in a Dutch oven over medium-high heat; add shrimp shells and shallot skins. Sauté 3 minutes; add corn cobs, broth, and next 5 ingredients. Bring to a boil. Reduce heat, and simmer 15 minutes. Strain through a fine sieve into a large bowl; discard solids. Return stock to pan; keep warm.

4. Combine 2 teaspoons oil and chopped shallots in a large saucepan over medium heat; cook 3 minutes, stirring frequently. Add rice; cook 2 minutes, stirring constantly. Stir in ½ cup reserved stock; cook 2 minutes or until liquid is nearly absorbed, stirring constantly. Add 3 cups stock, ½ cup at a time, stirring constantly until each portion of stock is absorbed before adding next (about 15 minutes total). Stir in reserved corn kernels and ¼ cup cheese; cook 2 minutes, stirring constantly. Stir in remaining stock; cook 5 minutes or until rice is done. Stir in ½ teaspoon salt and ⅛ teaspoon pepper. Keep warm.

5. Heat a large nonstick skillet over medium-high heat; add shrimp. Cook 3 minutes on each side or until done. Spoon 1 cup risotto into each of 6 bowls, and top with 4 shrimp. Drizzle each serving with 1 tablespoon salsa; sprinkle with about 2 teaspoons cheese. Yield: 6 servings.

CALORIES 427 (30% from fat); FAT 14.4g (sat 4.2g, mono 6.7g, poly 1.7g); PROTEIN 18.6g; CARB 58g; FIBER 2.4g; CHOL 55mg; IRON 2mg; SODIUM 1,089mg; CALC 157mg

A good kitchen garden not only inspires but also dictates what to cook.

Pizzeria Bianco Watermelon, Fennel, and Parsley Salad

(pictured on page 233)

Chris Bianco's unlikely combination of fennel, parsley, and watermelon is as refreshing as it is surprising. As with all of Bianco's dishes, he varies the proportions based on the characteristics of the individual ingredients. If his garden yields especially sweet watermelon, for example, he might use a little more lemon juice for balance.

    5   cups cubed seeded watermelon,
        divided
    1   tablespoon fresh lemon juice
    ½   teaspoon sea salt
    ¼   teaspoon freshly ground black
        pepper
    4   cups thinly sliced fennel bulb
        (about 2 medium bulbs)
    1½ cups fresh flat-leaf parsley leaves
        (about 2 ounces)

1. Place 1 cup watermelon in a blender; process until smooth. Strain mixture through a fine sieve into a bowl, reserving ¼ cup watermelon juice; discard solids and remaining watermelon juice. Combine ¼ cup watermelon juice, lemon juice, salt, and pepper in a large bowl, stirring well. Add 4 cups watermelon, fennel, and parsley; toss gently to combine. Yield: 8 servings (serving size: 1 cup).

CALORIES 49 (2% from fat); FAT 0.6g (sat 0.1g, mono 0.1g, poly 0.2g); PROTEIN 1.5g; CARB 10.9g; FIBER 2.2g; CHOL 0mg; IRON 1.2mg; SODIUM 175mg; CALC 45mg

enlightened traveler

Great Places for Active Getaways

Brush up on your favorite sport—or relax in breathtaking scenery—with camps created just for adults.

Recapture youthful glee with a weekend or weeklong stay at a fitness camp. Here's a sample of a recipe that you could enjoy at the Westerbeke Ranch in Sonoma, California.

Grilled Chicken Breasts with Yellow Tomato Curry Sauce and Thai Ratatouille

This recipe, from Chef John Littlewood of Westerbeke Ranch, can also be prepared with tofu. Instead of chicken, cut 1 pound extrafirm tofu into 1-inch cubes, and blot dry with paper towels. Sprinkle evenly with kosher salt; roll in cornstarch, and sauté in 2 teaspoons canola oil over medium-high heat for 6 minutes or until lightly browned.

RATATOUILLE:

    5   cups peeled cubed eggplant
        (about 1¼ pounds)
    ½   teaspoon kosher salt
    1½ tablespoons olive oil, divided
    1   cup diced yellow onion
    ¼   cup dry white wine
    2   tablespoons minced fresh garlic
    2   plum tomatoes, quartered
    ½   teaspoon black pepper
    ¼   cup thinly sliced fresh basil
    ¼   cup thinly sliced fresh mint
    1   teaspoon sugar

SAUCE:

    1   cup coconut milk
    ½   cup diced yellow onion
    ½   cup dry white wine
    1½ tablespoons peeled fresh ginger,
        sliced
    4   garlic cloves, peeled
    1   cup chopped yellow tomato
    1½ teaspoons Thai yellow curry paste
    ½   teaspoon kosher salt

CHICKEN:

    ½   teaspoon ground ginger
    ½   teaspoon black pepper
    ½   teaspoon garlic powder
    ½   teaspoon kosher salt
    4   (6-ounce) skinless, boneless
        chicken breast halves
    Cooking spray

REMAINING INGREDIENT:

    2   cups hot cooked basmati rice

1. To prepare ratatouille, preheat oven to 375°.

2. Place eggplant in a large bowl; sprinkle with ½ teaspoon salt. Toss to coat. Let stand 10 minutes. Heat 1 tablespoon olive oil in a large nonstick skillet over medium-high heat. Add 1 cup onion; sauté 1 minute. Stir in ¼ cup wine and 2 tablespoons garlic. Remove from heat. Add plum tomatoes; cover and set aside.

3. Toss eggplant with 1½ teaspoons oil and ½ teaspoon pepper. Spread eggplant on a baking sheet; bake at 375° for 10 minutes or until lightly browned and tender.

4. Place eggplant, onion mixture, basil, mint, and sugar in a large bowl, and toss gently to combine.

5. To prepare sauce, combine coconut milk and next 4 ingredients in a small saucepan; bring to a boil. Cover, reduce heat to low, and simmer 15 minutes. Place coconut mixture, tomato, curry paste, and ½ teaspoon salt in a blender; process until smooth. Return to pan, and keep warm over low heat.

6. To prepare chicken, combine ground ginger and next 3 ingredients; sprinkle evenly over chicken. Heat a grill pan over medium-high heat. Lightly coat chicken and grill pan with cooking spray. Cook chicken 6 minutes. Turn chicken over; cook chicken 3 minutes or until done.

7. Place ½ cup basmati rice on each of 4 plates. Place 1 cup ratatouille and 1 chicken breast half on each serving of rice. Pour 1 cup sauce over each serving. Yield: 4 servings.

CALORIES 517 (26% from fat); FAT 15.2g (sat 2.4g, mono 9.4g, poly 1.8g); PROTEIN 44.9g; CARB 42.7g; FIBER 5.4g; CHOL 99mg; IRON 3.7mg; SODIUM 948mg; CALC 96mg

Fresh Take On the Fourth

Light up your Independence Day celebration with this no-fuss menu.

Star-Spangled Menu
serves 6

Watermelon Agua Fresca

Summer Baked Beans

Green Bean, Chickpea, and Tomato Salad

Red, White, and Blue Potato Salad

Grilled Summer Squash

Grilled Corn with Creamy Chipotle Sauce

Santa Rosa Plum Crumble

MAKE AHEAD
Watermelon Agua Fresca

Agua fresca is a drink made by combining blended fruit, chopped fruit, water, and sugar, then letting the mixture macerate. This version is popular with both kids and adults. You can make it early in the day and keep it chilled until ready to serve.

    4   cups cubed seeded watermelon,
        divided
    4   cups water
    2   tablespoons sugar
    2   tablespoons fresh lime juice

1. Finely chop 2 cups watermelon, and set aside.
2. Place 2 cups watermelon in a blender; process until smooth. Strain puréed watermelon through a sieve into a pitcher, and discard solids. Add water, sugar, and lime juice; stir until sugar dissolves. Stir in chopped watermelon. Cover and chill at least 1 hour. Yield: 6 servings (serving size: 1¼ cups).

CALORIES 72 (0% from fat); FAT 0g; PROTEIN 0.7g; CARB 22.9g; FIBER 1.4g; CHOL 0mg; IRON 0.5mg; SODIUM 7mg; CALC 14mg

MAKE AHEAD
Summer Baked Beans

Try the quick-soak method: Cover the beans with water, and bring to a boil. Cook 2 minutes, remove from heat, cover, and let stand 1 hour. To make a day or two ahead, prepare the beans up to the point of baking, and refrigerate. The day of the cookout, bring to a simmer on the stovetop, then bake.

    1   pound dried pinto beans
    ¾   teaspoon crushed red pepper
    9   cups water
    2¼   teaspoons salt, divided
    2   tablespoons olive oil
    4   cups chopped onion
    2   cups chopped red bell pepper
    3   garlic cloves, minced
    3   cups chopped tomato
    ¼   cup packed brown sugar
    2   tablespoons chopped fresh mint
    1½   teaspoons paprika
    ¼   teaspoon black pepper
    1   tablespoon balsamic vinegar

1. Sort and wash beans; place in a large Dutch oven. Cover with water to 2 inches above beans; cover and let stand 8 hours or overnight. Drain beans.
2. Combine beans and crushed red pepper in pan; add 9 cups water. Bring to a boil; reduce heat, and simmer 1 hour and 15 minutes or until beans are tender. Drain in a colander over a bowl. Reserve 1 cup cooking liquid; discard remaining cooking liquid. Return beans and reserved cooking liquid to pan. Stir in 1 teaspoon salt. Remove beans from heat, and keep warm.
3. Preheat oven to 325°.
4. Heat oil in a large nonstick skillet over medium-high heat. Add onion and ¾ teaspoon salt; cover and cook 15 minutes or until golden brown, stirring occasionally. Add bell pepper and garlic; cook 1½ minutes or until bell pepper is crisp-tender, stirring frequently. Add tomato; cook 1½ minutes, stirring frequently. Remove from heat. Stir in sugar, mint, paprika, and black pepper. Add onion mixture and ½ teaspoon salt to bean mixture, stirring well to combine. Cover and bake at 325° for 1 hour. Stir in vinegar. Yield: 10 servings (serving size: about ¾ cup).

CALORIES 247 (13% from fat); FAT 3.6g (sat 0.5g, mono 2.1g, poly 0.6g); PROTEIN 11.1g; CARB 45g; FIBER 13.6g; CHOL 0mg; IRON 3.5mg; SODIUM 543mg; CALC 82mg

QUICK & EASY • MAKE AHEAD
Green Bean, Chickpea, and Tomato Salad

The salad holds well and can be tossed a few hours in advance—but leave out the salt until close to serving time, since it will cause the tomatoes to release their juice. Blanch the green beans up to a day ahead, and keep refrigerated.

    2   cups green beans, trimmed
         (8 ounces)
    4   cups coarsely chopped tomato
         (about 2½ pounds)
    1   cup thinly sliced red onion
    ½   cup (2 ounces) crumbled feta
         cheese
    2   tablespoons chopped fresh mint
    2   tablespoons red wine vinegar
    2½   teaspoons extravirgin olive oil
    ½   teaspoon salt
    ¼   teaspoon black pepper
    1   (15½-ounce) can chickpeas
         (garbanzo beans), rinsed and
         drained

1. Place green beans in a large saucepan of boiling water; cook 3 minutes. Drain and plunge beans into ice water. Drain.
2. Combine beans, tomato, and remaining ingredients in a large bowl; toss well to combine. Yield: 6 servings (serving size: 1⅓ cups).

CALORIES 157 (29% from fat); FAT 5.1g (sat 1.8g, mono 2g, poly 0.8g); PROTEIN 6.2g; CARB 24.4g; FIBER 5.9g; CHOL 8mg; IRON 2.1mg; SODIUM 463mg; CALC 91mg

Red, White, and Blue Potato Salad

This recipe uses a trio of potatoes, but use all of one type if you prefer. Blue potatoes are starchier than the others and tend to bleed, so cook them separately. If you need to, prepare this dish a day ahead, but add the blue potatoes just before serving. If your potatoes are larger than the ones we call for, cut them to a uniform size.

2 cups fingerling potatoes, halved lengthwise (about 10 ounces)
2 cups small red potatoes, quartered (about 10 ounces)
2 cups small blue potatoes, halved lengthwise (about 10 ounces)
¼ cup finely chopped red onion
2 tablespoons chopped fresh parsley
1 tablespoon chopped fresh dill
1 tablespoon chopped fresh chives
3 hard-cooked large eggs, finely chopped
¼ cup red wine vinegar
2 tablespoons olive oil
2 teaspoons Dijon mustard
1¼ teaspoons salt
½ teaspoon freshly ground black pepper
1 garlic clove, minced

1. Place fingerling and red potatoes in a saucepan; cover with water. Bring potatoes to a boil. Reduce heat; simmer 15 minutes or until tender. Drain; cool slightly. Place potatoes in a large bowl.
2. Place blue potatoes in a saucepan; cover with water. Bring to a boil. Reduce heat; simmer 10 minutes or until tender. Drain; cool slightly. Add blue potatoes, onion, and next 4 ingredients to bowl; toss gently.
3. Combine vinegar and remaining 5 ingredients. Pour over potato mixture; toss gently to combine. Serve warm, at room temperature, or chilled. Yield: 6 servings (serving size: 1 cup).

CALORIES 250 (27% from fat); FAT 7.5g (sat 1.5g, mono 4.4g, poly 0.9g); PROTEIN 6.9g; CARB 39.6g; FIBER 3.9g; CHOL 106mg; IRON 2.7mg; SODIUM 576mg; CALC 36mg

Grilled Summer Squash

You can use either all yellow squash or zucchini, but the dish is prettiest with a combination of the two.

¼ cup fresh lemon juice
¼ cup plain fat-free yogurt
1 tablespoon olive oil
2 teaspoons chopped fresh rosemary
½ teaspoon freshly ground black pepper
2 garlic cloves, minced
¾ teaspoon salt, divided
3 small yellow squash, halved lengthwise (about 1 pound)
3 small zucchini, halved lengthwise (about 1 pound)
Cooking spray

1. Prepare grill.
2. Combine first 6 ingredients in a 13 x 9-inch baking dish. Add ½ teaspoon salt. Make 3 diagonal cuts ¼-inch-deep across cut side of each squash and zucchini half. Place squash and zucchini halves, cut sides down, in baking dish. Marinate squash and zucchini at room temperature 15 minutes.
3. Remove squash and zucchini from marinade, and discard marinade. Place squash and zucchini on grill rack coated with cooking spray. Grill 5 minutes on each side or until tender. Sprinkle evenly with ¼ teaspoon salt. Yield: 6 servings (serving size: 2 squash halves).

CALORIES 45 (30% from fat); FAT 1.5g (sat 0.2g, mono 0.9g, poly 0.2g); PROTEIN 2.1g; CARB 7.7g; FIBER 2.9g; CHOL 0mg; IRON 0.8mg; SODIUM 202mg; CALC 41mg

Grilled Corn with Creamy Chipotle Sauce

Instead of butter, try this smoky, spicy sauce—it's a savory complement to the sweet corn. To remove the silks from an ear of corn, rub with a damp paper towel or a damp, soft-bristled toothbrush. Though the corn needs to be grilled at the last minute, the sauce can be prepared 1 day ahead.

¼ teaspoon salt
1 drained canned chipotle chile, seeded
1 garlic clove
½ cup 2% reduced-fat cottage cheese
2 tablespoons light mayonnaise
2 tablespoons plain fat-free yogurt
6 ears shucked corn
Cooking spray

1. Prepare grill.
2. Place first 3 ingredients in a food processor; process until minced. Add cottage cheese; process until smooth, scraping sides of bowl occasionally. Add mayonnaise and yogurt; process until blended. Spoon sauce into a bowl; cover and chill.
3. Place corn on grill rack coated with cooking spray. Grill 10 minutes, turning frequently. Serve corn with sauce. Yield: 6 servings (serving size: 1 ear of corn and 2 tablespoons sauce).

CALORIES 116 (25% from fat); FAT 3.2g (sat 0.7g, mono 0.7g, poly 1.5g); PROTEIN 5.7g; CARB 19g; FIBER 2.5g; CHOL 3mg; IRON 0.5mg; SODIUM 245mg; CALC 23mg

Santa Rosa Plum Crumble

Santa Rosa plums are great in this dessert, although any juicy plum will work nicely. Because it's good served either warm or at room temperature, this is a choice make-ahead dessert. After scraping the seeds from the vanilla bean, use it to flavor sugar: Bury the bean in a container of granulated sugar, and store up to 6 months.

14 plums, each cut into 6 wedges
¼ cup granulated sugar
3 tablespoons dry red wine
1 (4-inch) piece vanilla bean, split lengthwise
Cooking spray
¾ cup all-purpose flour
1 cup regular oats
6 tablespoons brown sugar
1½ teaspoons grated orange rind
¼ teaspoon salt
⅛ teaspoon ground nutmeg
5 tablespoons chilled butter, cut into small pieces

1. Preheat oven to 375°.

2. Combine first 3 ingredients. Scrape seeds from vanilla bean; add seeds to plum mixture. Discard bean. Toss gently to combine. Spoon into a 13 x 9-inch baking dish coated with cooking spray.

3. Lightly spoon flour into a dry measuring cup; level with a knife. Combine flour and next 5 ingredients in a medium bowl; cut in butter with a pastry blender or 2 knives until mixture resembles coarse meal. Sprinkle flour mixture evenly over plum mixture. Bake at 375° for 45 minutes or until plum mixture is bubbly and topping is lightly browned. Serve warm or at room temperature. Yield: 9 servings (serving size: about 1 cup).

CALORIES 284 (26% from fat); FAT 8.2g (sat 4.1g, mono 2.8g, poly 0.7g); PROTEIN 3.8g; CARB 52.5g; FIBER 3.9g; CHOL 17mg; IRON 1.3mg; SODIUM 134mg; CALC 24mg

superfast

. . . And Ready in Just About 20 Minutes

These entrées will quickly take your taste buds to exotic locations from Italy to India.

QUICK & EASY
Tomatillo Shrimp Fajitas

The fresh flavors of red onion, bell pepper, and cilantro spark this easy supper.

  Cooking spray
1½ cups red bell pepper strips
  2 teaspoons bottled minced garlic
  1 small red onion, vertically sliced
  ½ cup bottled green salsa
  1 teaspoon ground coriander
  ¼ teaspoon salt
1½ pounds peeled and deveined large shrimp
  8 (6-inch) corn tortillas
  2 tablespoons chopped fresh cilantro

1. Heat a large nonstick skillet over medium-high heat. Coat pan with cooking spray. Add bell pepper, garlic, and onion; sauté 4 minutes. Stir in salsa, coriander, salt, and shrimp; sauté 2 minutes or until shrimp are done. Arrange about ½ cup shrimp mixture down center of each tortilla; sprinkle each tortilla with 1½ teaspoons cilantro. Yield: 4 servings (serving size: 2 fajitas).

CALORIES 333 (12% from fat); FAT 4.5g (sat 0.8g, mono 0.8g, poly 1.8g); PROTEIN 38.4g; CARB 33.8g; FIBER 4.5g; CHOL 259mg; IRON 5.2mg; SODIUM 581mg; CALC 259mg

QUICK & EASY
Grouper with Puttanesca Sauce

Keep your pantry stocked with the sauce ingredients to make this dish anytime. Serve with orzo to soak up the sauce.

  4 (6-ounce) grouper or flounder fillets
  ¼ teaspoon black pepper
  ⅛ teaspoon salt
  Cooking spray
1½ teaspoons olive oil
  1 cup thinly sliced onion
  1 tablespoon bottled minced garlic
  ¼ teaspoon dried oregano
  1 (28-ounce) can whole tomatoes, drained
  ⅓ cup chopped pitted kalamata olives
  2 tablespoons capers
  ¼ cup chopped fresh flat-leaf parsley (optional)

1. Heat a nonstick grill pan over medium-high heat. Sprinkle fish with pepper and salt. Coat pan with cooking spray. Add fish to pan; cook 5 minutes on each side or until fish flakes easily when tested with a fork.

2. While fish cooks, heat oil in a large nonstick skillet over medium heat. Add onion; cook 4 minutes or until tender, stirring frequently. Add garlic, oregano, and tomatoes; bring to a boil. Reduce heat, and simmer 6 minutes, stirring frequently. Stir in olives and capers; cook 1 minute. Spoon tomato mixture over fish. Sprinkle with chopped parsley, if desired. Yield: 4 servings (serving size: 1 fillet, ¾ cup tomato mixture, and 1 tablespoon chopped parsley).

CALORIES 238 (18% from fat); FAT 4.8g (sat 0.8g, mono 2.5g, poly 0.8g); PROTEIN 35.5g; CARB 12g; FIBER 1.5g; CHOL 63mg; IRON 2.4mg; SODIUM 736mg; CALC 142mg

QUICK & EASY
Omelet with Summer Vegetables

This satisfying entrée for one is good for any meal, from breakfast to dinner. Serve with fruit salad.

  Cooking spray
  ⅔ cup frozen whole-kernel corn, thawed
  ½ cup chopped zucchini
  3 tablespoons chopped green onions
  ¼ teaspoon salt, divided
  2 tablespoons water
  ¼ teaspoon black pepper
  3 large egg whites
  1 large egg
  2 tablespoons shredded smoked Gouda cheese

1. Heat a small saucepan over medium-high heat. Coat pan with cooking spray. Add corn, zucchini, onions, and ⅛ teaspoon salt to pan; sauté 4 minutes or until vegetables are crisp-tender. Remove from heat.

2. Heat a 10-inch nonstick skillet over medium-high heat. Combine ⅛ teaspoon salt, water, pepper, egg whites, and egg, stirring well with a whisk. Coat pan with cooking spray. Pour egg mixture into pan; cook until edges begin to set (about 2 minutes). Gently lift edges of omelet with a spatula, tilting pan to allow uncooked egg mixture to come in contact with pan. Spoon corn mixture onto half of omelet; sprinkle corn mixture with cheese. Loosen omelet with a spatula, and fold in half over corn mixture. Cook 2 minutes or until cheese melts. Carefully slide omelet onto a plate. Yield: 1 serving (serving size: 1 omelet).

CALORIES 281 (33% from fat); FAT 10.3g (sat 4.3g, mono 3.4g, poly 1.4g); PROTEIN 24.8g; CARB 25.3g; FIBER 4.2g; CHOL 229mg; IRON 2.1mg; SODIUM 947mg; CALC 162mg

Veal Piccata

Enjoy this lemony Italian favorite with simple steamed green beans and mashed sweet potatoes.

    2   tablespoons all-purpose flour
    ¼   teaspoon black pepper
    Dash of salt
    1   tablespoon water
    1   large egg white
    ⅓   cup Italian-seasoned breadcrumbs
    4   (2-ounce) veal cutlets
    2   teaspoons olive oil
    1   cup fat-free, less-sodium chicken
        broth
    1   teaspoon grated lemon rind
    2   to 3 tablespoons fresh lemon juice
    1   tablespoon capers, drained and
        rinsed
    Lemon wedges (optional)

1. Combine flour, pepper, and salt in a shallow dish. Combine water and egg white in another shallow dish, stirring with a whisk. Place breadcrumbs in a third shallow dish. Working with 1 cutlet at a time, dredge in flour mixture. Dip floured cutlet in egg white mixture; dredge in breadcrumbs.
2. Heat oil in a large nonstick skillet over medium-high heat. Add cutlets to pan; cook 2 minutes on each side or until lightly browned. Remove from pan; keep warm.
3. Add broth, rind, juice, and capers to pan; simmer 2 minutes, stirring constantly. Pour over cutlets; serve immediately. Garnish with lemon wedges, if desired. Yield: 2 servings (serving size: 2 cutlets and 3 tablespoons sauce).

CALORIES 281 (24% from fat); FAT 7.6g (sat 1.2g, mono 4g, poly 0.6g); PROTEIN 30.4g; CARB 21.2g; FIBER 1.3g; CHOL 89mg; IRON 2.2mg; SODIUM 964mg; CALC 89mg

Thai-Style Chicken

This recipe is also good with shrimp in place of the chicken. Serve over rice, and garnish with green onion tops.

    1½ teaspoons vegetable oil
    1   onion, cut into ¼-inch
        wedges
    ¾   cup light coconut milk
    ½   teaspoon red curry paste
    ⅛   teaspoon black pepper
    1   pound chicken breast tenders
    3   tablespoons chopped fresh
        cilantro
    1½ teaspoons fish sauce
    ¼   teaspoon salt
    1   (7-ounce) bottle roasted red bell
        peppers, drained and coarsely
        chopped

1. Heat oil in a large nonstick skillet over medium-high heat. Add onion, and cook 4 minutes or until onion is golden, stirring frequently. Stir in coconut milk, curry paste, and black pepper. Add chicken; bring to a simmer. Cook 8 minutes or until chicken is done, stirring frequently. Stir in cilantro and remaining ingredients, and cook 1 minute. Yield: 4 servings (serving size: 1 cup).

CALORIES 195 (26% from fat); FAT 5.7g (sat 2.2g, mono 0.8g, poly 1.5g); PROTEIN 27.3g; CARB 6.7g; FIBER 0.9g; CHOL 66mg; IRON 1.2mg; SODIUM 601mg; CALC 26mg

Italian Sausage Soup

This soup has that simmered-all-day flavor but takes just minutes to prepare. Serve it with hot crusty bread.

    8   ounces hot or sweet turkey Italian
        sausage
    2   cups fat-free, less-sodium chicken
        broth
    1   (14.5-ounce) can diced tomatoes
        with basil, garlic, and oregano
    ½   cup uncooked small shell pasta
    2   cups bagged baby spinach leaves
    2   tablespoons grated fresh Parmesan
        or Romano cheese
    2   tablespoons chopped fresh basil

1. Heat a large saucepan over medium heat. Remove casings from sausage. Add sausage to pan, and cook 5 minutes or until browned, stirring to crumble. Drain; return to pan.
2. Add broth, tomatoes, and pasta to pan, and bring to a boil over high heat. Cover, reduce heat, and simmer 10 minutes or until pasta is done. Remove from heat; stir in spinach until wilted. Sprinkle each serving with cheese and basil. Yield: 4 servings (serving size: 1⅓ cups soup, 1½ teaspoons cheese, and 1½ teaspoons basil).

CALORIES 216 (30% from fat); FAT 7.1g (sat 2.6g, mono 2.5g, poly 1.8g); PROTEIN 17.4g; CARB 20g; FIBER 1.6g; CHOL 52mg; IRON 3.2mg; SODIUM 1,020mg; CALC 153mg

Grilled Tuna with Avocado Salsa

Serve with tortilla chips and a margarita for a festive summer meal.

    4   (6-ounce) yellowfin tuna steaks
        (about ¾ inch thick)
    ½   teaspoon salt, divided
    1   tablespoon brown sugar
    3   tablespoons lime juice, divided
    Cooking spray
    1   cup chopped tomato
    3   tablespoons chopped fresh cilantro
    1   diced peeled avocado
    1   jalapeño pepper, seeded and
        chopped

1. Heat a large grill pan over medium-high heat.
2. Sprinkle fish with ¼ teaspoon salt. Combine sugar and 1½ tablespoons juice; spread evenly over fish. Coat pan with cooking spray. Add fish to pan, and cook 3 minutes on each side or until desired degree of doneness.
3. While fish cooks, combine ¼ teaspoon salt, 1½ tablespoons juice, tomato, cilantro, avocado, and jalapeño, tossing gently. Serve fish with salsa. Yield: 4 servings (serving size: 1 tuna steak and ¼ cup salsa).

CALORIES 293 (29% from fat); FAT 9.6g (sat 1.7g, mono 5.1g, poly 1.5g); PROTEIN 41.3g; CARB 10.8g; FIBER 3.1g; CHOL 77mg; IRON 2.1mg; SODIUM 366mg; CALC 40mg

Pizzeria Bianco Watermelon, Fennel, and Parsley Salad, page 228

Chipotle Macaroni and Cheese, page 248

Chocolate Chip Zucchini Bread, page 224

Three-Pepper Beef, page 219

Blueberry Cheesecake, page 239

Maine's Got the Blues

During summer, sweet, succulent blueberries dominate—and delight—the state's residents and visitors.

Outsiders may think Maine is all about lobsters, but any summer visitor quickly realizes that the wild blueberry deserves equal billing. Certainly in the estimation of many Mainers, the berry defines the state just as much. That's especially true in Washington County, where most of the crop grows.

Wildflower Inn Blueberry Jam

This all-purpose jam is great on toasted English muffins or biscuits; it's also delicious heated and served as a pancake or waffle topping. The recipe works equally well with fresh or frozen berries. Because it's stored in the refrigerator, there's no need for canning.

 5 cups fresh or frozen, thawed, wild blueberries
5¼ cups sugar
 ⅔ cup fresh orange juice (about 3 oranges)
 1 tablespoon fresh lemon juice
 ¼ teaspoon salt
 1 (6-ounce) package liquid fruit pectin (such as CERTO)

1. Place blueberries in a large saucepan, and crush with a potato masher. Add sugar, juices, and salt; stir well. Let mixture stand 30 minutes.
2. Bring mixture to a boil over medium heat; cook 1 minute, stirring constantly. Remove from heat, and add pectin, stirring until well blended. Pour jam into jars or airtight containers. Cool completely; cover and refrigerate up to 4 weeks. Yield: 7 cups (serving size: 2 tablespoons).

CALORIES 81 (1% from fat); FAT 0.1g (sat 0g, mono 0g, poly 0.1g); PROTEIN 0.1g; CARB 20.8g; FIBER 0.5g; CHOL 0mg; IRON 0mg; SODIUM 11mg; CALC 2mg

Blueberry-Blackberry Shortcakes

(pictured on cover)

The key to tender low-fat shortcakes is to not overwork the dough; so pat it out instead of rolling it. A portion of the blueberries is cooked with sugar and cornstarch to form a blueberry glaze that binds the filling. This dessert is best with fresh berries.

SHORTCAKES:
 2 cups all-purpose flour
 ¼ cup sugar
 1 tablespoon grated lemon rind
 2 teaspoons baking powder
 ½ teaspoon baking soda
 ¼ teaspoon salt
 ¼ cup chilled butter, cut into small pieces
 ½ cup fat-free buttermilk
Cooking spray
 1 teaspoon water
 1 large egg white, lightly beaten
 2 teaspoons sugar

FILLING:
 3 cups fresh wild blueberries, divided
 ½ cup sugar
 2 tablespoons fresh lemon juice
 2 teaspoons cornstarch
 2 cups fresh blackberries
 1 cup frozen reduced-calorie whipped topping, thawed

1. Preheat oven to 400°.

2. To prepare shortcakes, lightly spoon flour into dry measuring cups; level with a knife. Combine flour and next 5 ingredients in a large bowl, stirring with a whisk. Cut in chilled butter with a pastry blender or 2 knives until mixture resembles coarse meal. Add buttermilk; stir just until moist.
3. Turn dough out onto a lightly floured surface; knead lightly 4 times. Pat dough to a ½-inch thickness; cut with a 3-inch biscuit cutter to form 8 dough rounds. Place dough rounds 2 inches apart on a baking sheet coated with cooking spray. Combine water and egg white, stirring with a whisk; brush over dough rounds. Sprinkle evenly with 2 teaspoons sugar. Bake at 400° for 13 minutes or until golden. Remove from oven, and cool on a wire rack.
4. To prepare filling, combine 1 cup blueberries, ½ cup sugar, juice, and cornstarch in a small saucepan. Bring to a boil; reduce heat, and simmer 5 minutes or until slightly thick. Place in a large bowl; add 2 cups blueberries and blackberries, stirring to coat. Cover and chill.
5. Using a serrated knife, cut each shortcake in half horizontally; spoon ½ cup blueberry mixture over bottom half of each shortcake. Top each serving with 2 tablespoons whipped topping and top half of shortcake. Yield: 8 servings (serving size: 1 filled shortcake).

CALORIES 322 (21% from fat); FAT 7.5g (sat 4.7g, mono 1.8g, poly 0.5g); PROTEIN 4.6g; CARB 60.1g; FIBER 4.3g; CHOL 16mg; IRON 1.9mg; SODIUM 354mg; CALC 108mg

---

Two Types of Berries

Cultivated, or high-bush, blueberries are what you see in the produce sections of grocery stores. They're grown on tree-sized shrubs all over the country. Wild, or low-bush, berries grow on sprawling, ankle-high shrubs. These berries are about one-third the size of the cultivated ones. They're firmer, tangier, and more complex in flavor. In a field of wild blueberries, dozens of varieties grow—so you end up with a potpourri of sweet and sour tastes.

MAKE AHEAD • FREEZABLE

Blueberry Gingerbread Cake

Blueberry farmer Robert Ouelette of Old Town, Maine, enjoys this snack cake his wife, Marion, created. Tossing the berries with flour before folding them into the batter prevents them from sinking. Frozen blueberries can be used in place of fresh; however, the batter will be tinted lavender, and the baking time will increase to 40 minutes.

    1   cup fresh or frozen wild blueberries
    2   tablespoons all-purpose flour
    2   cups all-purpose flour
    1   teaspoon baking soda
    1   teaspoon ground cinnamon
    ½   teaspoon salt
    ½   teaspoon ground ginger
    1   cup sugar
    7   tablespoons vegetable shortening, melted
    3   tablespoons molasses
    1   large egg
    1   cup fat-free buttermilk
    Cooking spray

1. Preheat oven to 350°.

2. Combine blueberries and 2 tablespoons flour, tossing gently to coat.

3. Lightly spoon 2 cups flour into dry measuring cups, and level with a knife. Combine 2 cups flour, baking soda, cinnamon, salt, and ginger, stirring with a whisk. Place sugar, shortening, molasses, and egg in a large bowl; beat with a mixer at medium speed until well blended. Add flour mixture and buttermilk alternately to sugar mixture, beginning and ending with flour mixture. Fold in blueberry mixture.

4. Pour batter into a 13 x 9-inch baking pan coated with cooking spray. Bake at 350° for 30 minutes or until a wooden pick inserted in center comes out clean. Yield: 15 servings (serving size: 1 piece).

CALORIES 195 (29% from fat); FAT 6.2g (sat 1.5g, mono 2g, poly 1.5g); PROTEIN 2.9g; CARB 32.1g; FIBER 0.8g; CHOL 15mg; IRON 1.1mg; SODIUM 185mg; CALC 35mg

MAKE AHEAD

Blueberry-Pumpkin Pound Cake

This cake was adapted from a recipe by Debra Ayers of Crawford, Maine. The original recipe earned a blue ribbon at the Machias Blueberry Festival in 1999. Frozen blueberries tint the batter purple.

CAKE:

    Cooking spray
    2   teaspoons all-purpose flour
    3   cups all-purpose flour
    4   teaspoons baking powder
    1½ teaspoons ground cinnamon
    ½   teaspoon ground nutmeg
    ¼   teaspoon salt
    ¼   teaspoon baking soda
    ¼   teaspoon ground cloves
    ¾   cup butter, softened
    1   cup granulated sugar
    ¾   cup packed brown sugar
    1   teaspoon vanilla extract
    3   large eggs
    1⅓ cups canned pumpkin
    ⅓   cup fat-free sour cream
    ½   cup 1% low-fat milk
    2   cups fresh or frozen wild blueberries

GLAZE:

    1   cup sifted powdered sugar
    1   tablespoon canned pumpkin
    2¼ teaspoons 1% low-fat milk
    ¼   teaspoon vanilla extract

1. Preheat oven to 325°.

2. To prepare cake, coat a 10-inch tube pan with cooking spray; dust with 2 teaspoons flour. Set aside.

3. Lightly spoon 3 cups flour into dry measuring cups, and level with a knife. Combine 3 cups flour and next 6 ingredients, stirring with a whisk. Place butter in a large bowl; beat butter with a mixer at medium speed 1 minute or until fluffy. Gradually add granulated and brown sugars and 1 teaspoon vanilla, beating until light and fluffy (about 3 minutes). Add eggs, 1 at a time, beating well after each addition. Add pumpkin and sour cream, and beat well. Beating at low speed, add flour mixture and milk alternately to butter mixture, beginning and ending with flour mixture. Fold in blueberries.

4. Pour batter into prepared pan. Bake at 325° for 1 hour and 15 minutes or until a wooden pick inserted in center comes out clean. Cool in pan 15 minutes on a wire rack. Place a wire rack upside down on top of cake; invert onto rack. Cool completely.

5. To prepare glaze, combine powdered sugar and remaining 3 ingredients, stirring until well blended; drizzle over cooled cake. Yield: 16 servings (serving size: 1 slice).

CALORIES 314 (29% from fat); FAT 10g (sat 5.8g, mono 2.9g, poly 0.6g); PROTEIN 4.6g; CARB 52.8g; FIBER 1.9g; CHOL 64mg; IRON 2mg; SODIUM 342mg; CALC 115mg

Frozen wild blueberries offer a taste of Maine all year long.

Blueberry Cheesecake
(pictured on page 236)

Here's another great recipe we adapted from the award-winning Ayers family of Crawford, Maine. Blueberry purée gives a double shot of delicious berry flavor. Combining the graham cracker and vanilla wafer crumbs makes for a great-tasting crust. The crumb mixture may seem a little dry after it bakes the first time, but it works just fine once it's filled.

CRUST:
- ⅔ cup graham cracker crumbs (about 5 cookie sheets)
- ⅔ cup reduced-fat vanilla wafer crumbs (about 20 cookies)
- 3 tablespoons sugar
- 3 tablespoons butter, melted
- Cooking spray

FILLING:
- 2½ cups fresh or frozen wild blueberries, thawed
- 1 tablespoon cornstarch
- 2 (8-ounce) blocks fat-free cream cheese, softened
- 1 (8-ounce) block ⅓-less-fat cream cheese, softened
- 1 cup sugar
- 2 tablespoons cornstarch
- ¼ teaspoon salt
- 5 large eggs

TOPPING:
- 1½ cups fat-free sour cream
- 2 tablespoons sugar
- ½ teaspoon vanilla extract

SAUCE:
- ¼ cup sugar
- ¼ cup water
- 1 cup fresh or frozen, thawed, wild blueberries

1. Preheat oven to 325°.
2. To prepare crust, combine first 3 ingredients in a medium bowl. Drizzle with butter; toss with a fork until moist. Firmly press mixture into bottom of a 9-inch springform pan coated with cooking spray. Bake at 325° for 10 minutes; cool on a wire rack.

3. To prepare filling, combine 2½ cups blueberries and 1 tablespoon cornstarch in a food processor, and process until smooth. Place purée in a small saucepan; bring to a boil. Cook 6 minutes or until slightly thick, stirring constantly. Cool purée slightly. Reserve ½ cup blueberry purée for sauce; set remaining 1 cup blueberry purée aside.
4. Place cheeses in a large bowl; beat with a mixer at high speed 3 minutes or until smooth. Combine 1 cup sugar, 2 tablespoons cornstarch, and salt. Add sugar mixture to cheese mixture; beat well. Add eggs, 1 at a time, beating well after each addition. Pour batter over prepared crust. Pour 1 cup blueberry purée over batter; gently swirl with a knife. Bake at 325° for 1 hour and 10 minutes or until cheesecake center barely moves when pan is touched. Remove cheesecake from oven (do not turn oven off); place cheesecake on a wire rack.
5. To prepare topping, combine sour cream, 2 tablespoons sugar, and vanilla in a small bowl, stirring well. Spread sour cream mixture evenly over cheesecake. Bake at 325° for 10 minutes. Remove cheesecake from oven; run a knife around outside edge. Cool to room temperature. Cover and chill at least 8 hours. Remove sides of springform pan.
6. To prepare sauce, combine reserved ½ cup blueberry purée, ¼ cup sugar, and water in a small saucepan. Cook over medium heat 8 minutes or until sauce is thick, stirring constantly. Gently fold in 1 cup blueberries. Remove from heat, and cool. Serve sauce with cheesecake. Yield: 16 servings (serving size: 1 cheesecake wedge and 1½ tablespoons sauce).

CALORIES 257 (30% from fat); FAT 8.7g (sat 4.6g, mono 2.6g, poly 0.7g); PROTEIN 9.2g; CARB 36.4g; FIBER 1g; CHOL 89mg; IRON 0.6mg; SODIUM 340mg; CALC 110mg

Blueberry Cinnamon-Burst Muffins

The original version of these muffins won Courtney Ayers of Crawford, Maine, a blue ribbon; this adaptation was lightened a bit. A whole tablespoon of cinnamon in the batter makes these smell heavenly when they bake.

- ¼ cup all-purpose flour
- ¼ cup sugar
- 1 tablespoon ground cinnamon
- 3 tablespoons chilled butter, cut into small pieces
- 1 cup sugar
- ⅓ cup butter, softened
- 2 large eggs
- 2½ cups all-purpose flour
- 5 teaspoons baking powder
- ½ teaspoon salt
- 1 cup 2% reduced-fat milk
- 1½ cups fresh or frozen wild blueberries
- Cooking spray

1. Preheat oven to 400°.
2. Lightly spoon ¼ cup flour into a measuring cup; level with a knife. Combine ¼ cup flour, ¼ cup sugar, and cinnamon in a medium bowl, and cut in 3 tablespoons butter with a pastry blender or 2 knives until mixture resembles coarse meal. Cover and chill 30 minutes.
3. Place 1 cup sugar and ⅓ cup butter in a bowl; beat with a mixer at high speed 1 minute or until combined. Add eggs, 1 at a time, beating well after each addition. Lightly spoon 2½ cups flour into dry measuring cups; level with a knife. Combine 2½ cups flour, baking powder, and salt, stirring with a whisk. Add flour mixture and milk alternately to egg mixture, beginning and ending with flour mixture. Fold in blueberries and cinnamon mixture (batter will be thick).
4. Spoon batter into 18 muffin cups coated with cooking spray. Bake at 400° for 18 minutes or until muffins spring back when touched lightly in center. Cool in pans 5 minutes on a wire rack. Remove muffins from pans; place on wire rack. Yield: 18 servings (serving size: 1 muffin).

CALORIES 193 (29% from fat); FAT 6.3g (sat 3.6g, mono 1.8g, poly 0.4g); PROTEIN 3.3g; CARB 31.5g; FIBER 1.1g; CHOL 39mg; IRON 1.3mg; SODIUM 269mg; CALC 104mg

Spiced Blueberry Muffins

Eat these muffins while they're still warm. This recipe is adapted from the one that won Brittany Ayers, of Crawford, Maine, her first blue ribbon when she was just eight years old. Fresh berries are best for these muffins, but you can also use frozen.

  2 cups all-purpose flour
  ¾ cup sugar
  1 tablespoon baking powder
  ½ teaspoon salt
  ½ teaspoon ground cinnamon
  ⅛ teaspoon ground nutmeg
  ⅛ teaspoon ground cloves
1½ cups fresh or frozen wild blueberries
  1 tablespoon all-purpose flour
  ⅓ cup butter, softened
  1 (8-ounce) block fat-free cream cheese, softened
  ½ cup 2% reduced-fat milk
  2 large eggs
  1 teaspoon vanilla extract
Cooking spray
1½ tablespoons sugar

1. Preheat oven to 425°.
2. Lightly spoon 2 cups flour into dry measuring cups, and level with a knife. Combine 2 cups flour and next 6 ingredients in a large bowl, stirring with a whisk. Make a well in center of mixture.
3. Place blueberries in a small bowl. Sprinkle 1 tablespoon flour over blueberries; toss to coat.
4. Place butter and cream cheese in a medium bowl; beat with a mixer at high speed 1 minute or until blended. Add milk, eggs, and vanilla to butter mixture; beat to combine. Add butter mixture to flour mixture; stir just until moist. Gently fold in blueberry mixture. Spoon batter into 14 muffin cups coated with cooking spray. Sprinkle 1½ tablespoons sugar evenly over batter. Bake at 425° for 15 minutes or until muffins spring back when touched lightly in center. Cool in pans 5 minutes on a wire rack. Remove muffins from pans; place on wire rack. Yield: 14 servings (serving size: 1 muffin).

CALORIES 192 (26% from fat); FAT 5.5g (sat 3.1g, mono 1.6g, poly 0.4g); PROTEIN 5.5g; CARB 29.9g; FIBER 1g; CHOL 46mg; IRON 1.1mg; SODIUM 327mg; CALC 124mg

---

dinner tonight

Tasty Rubs

Instantly supercharge food with flavor with these four tasty rubs.

Rub Menu 1
serves 4

Herbes de Provence-Crusted Lamb Chops

Grilled red potatoes with mint*

Steamed green beans

*Toss 1½ pounds small red potatoes with 1 teaspoon kosher salt and 2 teaspoons olive oil. Place potatoes ¼ inch apart on a grill rack coated with cooking spray. Grill 15 minutes; turn over with tongs. Grill 15 minutes or until done. Cool slightly. Cut potatoes in half; toss with ⅓ cup thinly sliced mint leaves.

Game Plan

1. While grill preheats:
  • Combine potatoes with salt and oil
  • Prepare rub for lamb
  • Wash and trim green beans
2. While potatoes cook on grill:
  • Slice mint for potatoes
  • Steam green beans
  • Place lamb on grill during last 8 minutes of potatoes' cooking time

---

QUICK & EASY
Herbes de Provence-Crusted Lamb Chops

The Dijon mustard and dried herbs rub also tastes great on chicken thighs or beef fillets. Herbes de Provence is a combination of several dried herbs—including lavender, thyme, rosemary, and basil—that evoke flavors from the south of France.

TOTAL TIME: 30 MINUTES

QUICK TIP: Use half the grill to cook the potatoes and the other half for the lamb. Make sure to allow an extra 5 minutes before serving the meal so the potatoes can cool slightly. This also gives the lamb time to stand.

---

  2 tablespoons Dijon mustard
  1 tablespoon dried herbes de Provence
  ½ teaspoon kosher salt
  ¼ teaspoon freshly ground black pepper
  1 garlic clove, minced
  8 (4-ounce) lamb loin chops, trimmed
Cooking spray

1. Prepare grill.
2. Combine first 5 ingredients, and rub evenly over both sides of lamb.
3. Place lamb on a grill rack coated with cooking spray; grill 4 minutes on each side or until desired degree of doneness. Yield: 4 servings (serving size: 2 lamb chops).

CALORIES 220 (41% from fat); FAT 10g (sat 3.4g, mono 4.3g, poly 0.8g); PROTEIN 29.2g; CARB 1.7g; FIBER 0.6g; CHOL 90mg; IRON 2.6mg; SODIUM 505mg; CALC 44mg

Rub Menu 2
serves 4

Lemon and Oregano-Rubbed Chicken Paillards

Greek farmers' salad*

Basmati rice

*Combine 2 tablespoons red wine vinegar, 2 teaspoons Dijon mustard, 1 teaspoon extravirgin olive oil, ½ teaspoon dried oregano, ¼ teaspoon salt, ¼ teaspoon crushed red pepper, and 2 minced garlic cloves, stirring with a whisk. Combine 3 cups coarsely chopped English cucumber, 2 cups halved cherry tomatoes, 1 cup chopped yellow bell pepper, ¼ cup finely chopped red onion, and ¼ cup halved kalamata olives. Drizzle dressing over salad; toss to coat. Chill.

Game Plan

1. While grill preheats:
  • Prepare and chill salad
  • Bring water to a boil for rice
  • Pound chicken breasts
  • Prepare rub for chicken
2. While rice cooks:
  • Grill chicken
  • Chop parsley for chicken

Lemon and Oregano-Rubbed Chicken Paillards

To create paillards, pound the chicken breasts thin with a meat mallet or rolling pin; the increased surface allows you to use even more of the flavorful rub.

TOTAL TIME: 35 MINUTES

QUICK TIP: Using the pounding technique on the chicken not only tenderizes the meat, but also shortens the cooking time and gives the appearance of a heartier portion.

- 4 (6-ounce) skinless, boneless chicken breast halves
- 5 teaspoons grated lemon rind
- 1 tablespoon olive oil
- 1½ teaspoons dried oregano
- ¾ teaspoon kosher salt
- ½ teaspoon freshly ground black pepper
- ¼ teaspoon water
- 2 garlic cloves, minced
- Cooking spray
- 4 lemon wedges
- 2 tablespoons chopped fresh parsley

1. Prepare grill.
2. Place each chicken breast half between 2 sheets of heavy-duty plastic wrap, and pound to ¼-inch thickness using a meat mallet or rolling pin.
3. Combine lemon rind and next 6 ingredients; rub evenly over both sides of chicken. Place chicken on a grill rack coated with cooking spray, and grill 3 minutes on each side or until chicken is done. Remove from heat. Squeeze 1 lemon wedge evenly over each chicken breast half. Sprinkle parsley evenly over chicken. Yield: 4 servings (serving size: 1 chicken breast half).

CALORIES 226 (22% from fat); FAT 5.6g (sat 1g, mono 3g, poly 0.8g); PROTEIN 39.6g; CARB 2.2g; FIBER 0.7g; CHOL 99mg; IRON 1.8mg; SODIUM 465mg; CALC 38mg

Rub Menu 3
serves 4

Classic Steak House Rubbed Filet Mignon

Grilled asparagus with lemon*

Baked potatoes with chives and reduced-fat sour cream

*Combine 1 pound trimmed asparagus spears, 1 teaspoon olive oil, ¼ teaspoon kosher salt, and ¼ teaspoon black pepper in a large zip-top plastic bag. Seal bag; shake well to coat. Place asparagus on a grill rack or in a grilling basket coated with cooking spray; grill 3 minutes or until lightly browned, turning frequently. Garnish with lemon slices, if desired. Serve immediately.

Game Plan

1. While grill preheats:
- Prepare rub for beef
- Combine asparagus with seasonings
- Wash potatoes
- Begin cooking potatoes in microwave
2. While beef cooks on grill:
- Chop chives for potatoes
- Place asparagus on grill during last 3 minutes of beef's cooking time

Classic Steak House Rubbed Filet Mignon

Dry mustard powder has a pleasant bitterness and mild heat that pair well with the tender beef. Peppercorns and rosemary add even more flavor.

TOTAL TIME: 30 MINUTES

- 2 teaspoons black peppercorns
- ¼ teaspoon dried rosemary
- 1 teaspoon dry mustard
- ¾ teaspoon kosher salt
- ½ teaspoon garlic powder
- 4 (4-ounce) beef tenderloin steaks, trimmed (1 inch thick)
- Cooking spray

1. Prepare grill.
2. Place peppercorns and rosemary in a spice or coffee grinder; pulse until pepper is coarsely ground. Combine pepper mixture, dry mustard, salt, and garlic powder; rub evenly over both sides of steaks. Place steaks on a grill rack coated with cooking spray, and grill 3 minutes on each side or until desired degree of doneness. Yield: 4 servings (serving size: 1 steak).

CALORIES 188 (43% from fat); FAT 8.9g (sat 3.2g, mono 3.3g, poly 0.3g); PROTEIN 24.5g; CARB 0.8g; FIBER 0.2g; CHOL 72mg; IRON 3.3mg; SODIUM 407mg; CALC 11mg

Rub Menu 4
serves 4

Grilled Pastrami-Style Salmon (recipe on page 242)

Red cabbage and apple slaw*

Rye bread

*Combine ½ cup fresh orange juice, ¼ cup reduced-fat sour cream, 1 tablespoon malt vinegar, ½ teaspoon caraway seeds, ¼ teaspoon kosher salt, and ¼ teaspoon freshly ground black pepper, stirring well with a whisk. Combine 5 cups thinly sliced red cabbage, 2 shredded Granny Smith apples, and 2 tablespoons chopped toasted walnuts. Drizzle with orange juice mixture, and toss well to combine.

Game Plan

1. While grill preheats:
- Prepare rub for salmon
- Chill salmon with rub
- Prepare dressing for slaw
- Toast nuts for slaw
2. While salmon cooks on grill:
- Slice cabbage for slaw
- Shred apples for slaw
- Toss slaw ingredients together

Continued

Grilled Pastrami-Style Salmon

The classic seasonings associated with beef pastrami taste fantastic on this grilled salmon. Allspice is a fairly strong spice, so if you're sensitive to its "burn," use the lesser amount. Purchase a whole center-cut salmon fillet so that it will cook more evenly than a cut that contains the thinner tail end.

TOTAL TIME: 35 MINUTES

- 1 tablespoon dark brown sugar
- 1 teaspoon kosher salt
- 1 teaspoon garlic powder
- 1 teaspoon ground ginger
- 1 teaspoon ground coriander
- 1 teaspoon coarsely ground black pepper
- ¼ to ½ teaspoon ground allspice
- 1 (1½-pound) center-cut salmon fillet
- ½ teaspoon olive oil
- Cooking spray

1. Prepare grill.
2. Combine first 7 ingredients. Place salmon fillet, skin side down, on a cutting board or work surface; brush evenly with olive oil. Sprinkle spice mixture evenly over salmon, and gently rub mixture into fish. Cover lightly with plastic wrap, and chill 15 minutes.
3. Place fish, skin side down, on a grill rack coated with cooking spray; grill 10 minutes or until fish flakes easily when tested with a fork. Yield: 4 servings (serving size: about 4½ ounces).

CALORIES 230 (41% from fat); FAT 10.5g (sat 2.4g, mono 4.7g, poly 2.4g); PROTEIN 27.4g; CARB 4.9g; FIBER 0.6g; CHOL 65mg; IRON 0.8mg; SODIUM 532mg; CALC 26mg

---

Seaside Supper

Claim your place in the sun, and enjoy the bright citrus flavors of this easy, mostly make-ahead meal.

Seaside Supper Menu
serves 6

Spicy Shrimp and Scallop Seviche

Baked flour tortilla chips

Citrus-Spiked Jícama and Carrot Slaw

Grilled Pork Chops with Tomatillo, Corn, and Avocado Salsa

Basmati rice

Key Lime Pie Ice Cream

Make-Ahead Tips

Here's how to make this summertime menu even simpler.

• Prepare the Citrus-Spiked Jícama and Carrot Slaw (recipe at right) up to 1 day ahead (stir in the cilantro just before serving).

• Mix the salsa (minus the avocado) for the Grilled Pork Chops with Tomatillo, Corn, and Avocado Salsa (recipe on page 243) 1 day in advance.

• The night before, whisk together a batch of the Key Lime Pie Ice Cream (recipe on page 243).

MAKE AHEAD
Spicy Shrimp and Scallop Seviche

To make sturdy baked chips to dip in the seviche, sprinkle flour tortilla wedges with ground red pepper, and bake at 350° until golden brown. Blanching the seafood in boiling water gives it a head start before it finishes "cooking" in the citrus mixture. Marinate the seafood only a couple of hours; if it sits too long, it will become tough.

- 3 cups diced tomato
- 2 cups diced onion
- ½ cup chopped fresh cilantro
- ½ cup fresh lime juice
- 2 tablespoons chopped serrano chile
- ½ teaspoon salt
- ¼ teaspoon freshly ground black pepper
- ½ pound medium shrimp, peeled and deveined
- ½ pound bay scallops
- 1 (16-ounce) bottle no-salt-added tomato juice

1. Combine first 7 ingredients in a large bowl; let stand 30 minutes.
2. Cook shrimp and scallops in boiling water 45 seconds. Drain and plunge shrimp and scallops into ice water; drain. Add shrimp and scallops to tomato mixture. Stir in tomato juice. Cover and chill 2 hours. Yield: 6 servings (serving size: ⅓ cup).

CALORIES 135 (9% from fat); FAT 1.4g (sat 0.2g, mono 0.2g, poly 0.5g); PROTEIN 16.1g; CARB 15.2g; FIBER 2.7g; CHOL 70mg; IRON 2mg; SODIUM 331mg; CALC 54mg

---

MAKE AHEAD
Citrus-Spiked Jícama and Carrot Slaw

A mandoline makes easy work of cutting the jícama and carrot into julienne strips; if you don't have one, coarsely shred them.

- 4 cups (1½-inch) julienne-cut peeled jícama (about 1 pound)
- 2 cups (1½-inch) julienne-cut carrot
- ½ cup thinly vertically sliced red onion
- ¼ cup fresh orange juice
- 1 teaspoon grated lime rind
- 3 tablespoons fresh lime juice
- 1½ teaspoons sugar
- ¼ teaspoon salt
- 1 tablespoon chopped fresh cilantro
- Cilantro sprigs (optional)

1. Combine first 8 ingredients in a large bowl, and toss gently to coat. Let stand 10 minutes. Stir in chopped cilantro just before serving. Garnish with cilantro sprigs, if desired. Yield: 6 servings (serving size: 1 cup).

CALORIES 65 (3% from fat); FAT 0.2g (sat 0g, mono 0g, poly 0.1g); PROTEIN 1.3g; CARB 15.5g; FIBER 5.7g; CHOL 0mg; IRON 0.8mg; SODIUM 116mg; CALC 26mg

---

Grilled Pork Chops with Tomatillo, Corn, and Avocado Salsa

Grilling the tomatillos enhances their natural tartness and softens their tough skin. Serve over basmati rice.

SALSA:
¾ pound tomatillos
1 ear shucked corn
Cooking spray
¼ cup finely chopped red onion
3 tablespoons chopped fresh cilantro
2 tablespoons fresh lime juice
1 tablespoon minced seeded jalapeño pepper
¼ teaspoon salt
⅛ teaspoon freshly ground black pepper
1 garlic clove, minced
½ cup diced peeled avocado

PORK:
6 (6-ounce) bone-in loin pork chops (about 1 inch thick)
1 teaspoon freshly ground black pepper
½ teaspoon salt

1. Prepare grill.
2. To prepare salsa, discard husks and stems from tomatillos. Place tomatillos and corn on a grill rack coated with cooking spray; grill 10 minutes or until browned, turning tomatillos and corn occasionally. Place tomatillos in a food processor; process until smooth. Cut kernels from ear of corn. Combine tomatillo purée, corn, onion, and next 6 ingredients

in a medium bowl; gently stir in avocado just before serving.
3. To prepare pork, sprinkle pork with 1 teaspoon black pepper and ½ teaspoon salt. Place pork on grill rack coated with cooking spray; grill 5 minutes on each side or until done. Serve pork with salsa. Yield: 6 servings (serving size: 1 pork chop and ⅓ cup salsa).

CALORIES 235 (37% from fat); FAT 9.6g (sat 2.9g, mono 4.4g, poly 1.1g); PROTEIN 27.2g; CARB 10.4g; FIBER 2.7g; CHOL 69mg; IRON 1.5mg; SODIUM 350mg; CALC 37mg

---

Key Lime Pie Ice Cream

This ice cream has all the flavors of classic Key lime pie—even the crust. We used bottled Key lime juice for convenience. You can also squeeze the juice from fresh Key limes if your supermarket carries them.

1½ cups 2% reduced-fat milk
½ cup bottled Key lime juice (such as Nellie and Joe's)
½ cup whipping cream
Dash of salt
1 (14-ounce) can fat-free sweetened condensed milk
6 graham crackers (1½ cookie sheets), coarsely crushed, divided
Key lime wedges (optional)

1. Combine first 5 ingredients, stirring with a whisk. Pour mixture into freezer can of an ice-cream freeze; freeze according to manufacturer's instructions. Stir ⅓ cup graham crackers into ice cream. Spoon ice cream into a freezer-safe container; cover and freeze 1 hour or until firm. Sprinkle each serving with 1 teaspoon graham crackers. Garnish with lime wedges, if desired. Yield: 6 servings (serving size: ¾ cup).

CALORIES 317 (27% from fat); FAT 9.5g (sat 5.3g, mono 2.7g, poly 0.3g); PROTEIN 8.8g; CARB 50.3g; FIBER 0.1g; CHOL 36mg; IRON 0.4mg; SODIUM 190mg; CALC 275mg

---

BLT Bread Salad

Most of us are familiar with the acronym BLT. But this recipe is not for a sandwich; it's for a salad.

You'll want to make this refreshing version of panzanella while summertime tomatoes are at their juicy peak. In other words, PDQ—pretty darn quick.

BLT Bread Salad

6 cups (½-inch) cubed French bread or other firm white bread (4 ounces)
Cooking spray
¼ cup white wine vinegar
2 tablespoons water
2 tablespoons fat-free mayonnaise
2½ teaspoons sugar
2 teaspoons extravirgin olive oil
¼ teaspoon salt
¼ teaspoon freshly ground black pepper
⅛ teaspoon ground red pepper
3 cups torn curly leaf lettuce
2 cups chopped seeded tomato
2 tablespoons thinly sliced green onions
4 bacon slices, cooked and crumbled

1. Preheat oven to 400°.
2. Place bread cubes in a single layer on a jelly-roll pan. Lightly coat bread cubes with cooking spray. Bake at 400° for 10 minutes or until golden, stirring once.
3. Combine vinegar and next 7 ingredients in a large bowl, stirring with a whisk. Add toasted bread cubes, lettuce, and tomato; toss gently to coat. Sprinkle with onions and bacon. Serve immediately. Yield: 6 servings (serving size: about 1⅓ cups).

CALORIES 159 (29% from fat); FAT 5.2g (sat 1.2g, mono 2.4g, poly 1.2g); PROTEIN 5g; CARB 23.4g; FIBER 2.1g; CHOL 4mg; IRON 1.7mg; SODIUM 402mg; CALC 48mg

The Gourmet Athlete

Chef Greg Brown cooks for, and coaches, world-class competitors.

High in the mountains of Colorado Springs, Colorado, Carmichael Training Systems coach and chef Greg Brown works with some world-class athletes to provide the proper nutrition required to perform at their best. They need a lot of the appropriate types of calories to fuel their training and competition, Brown notes, but "there's no reason it can't be enjoyable."

Lucky for these athletes, "Coach Greg" is as well versed in the culinary arts as he is in the nutrition needs of competitive cycling. Here are some of his best-loved creations.

QUICK & EASY
Asparagus-Potato Soup

Thickened with potatoes, vanilla soy milk, and yogurt, this slightly sweet soup makes an interesting starter or tasty accompaniment to a grilled cheese sandwich.

2¾ cups vegetable broth
2½ cups cubed peeled red potato
   (about 12 ounces)
¾ cup chopped onion
3 cups (1-inch) slices asparagus
   (about 1 pound)
1 cup vanilla soy milk
½ cup vanilla low-fat yogurt
1 teaspoon fresh lemon
   juice
½ teaspoon salt
¼ teaspoon freshly ground black
   pepper
Asparagus tips (optional)

1. Combine first 3 ingredients in a large saucepan; bring to a boil. Reduce heat, and simmer 12 minutes or until potato is tender. Add 3 cups asparagus; cook 3 minutes or until tender. Let stand 5 minutes. Pour half of vegetable mixture in a blender; process until smooth. Pour puréed vegetable mixture into a large bowl. Repeat procedure with remaining vegetable mixture. Return puréed vegetable mixture to pan; stir in milk and next 4 ingredients. Bring to a simmer over medium heat (do not boil), stirring occasionally. Garnish with asparagus tips, if desired. Yield: 6 servings (serving size: 1 cup).

CALORIES 115 (12% from fat); FAT 1.5g (sat 0.2g, mono 0.2g, poly 0.4g); PROTEIN 5.7g; CARB 22.1g; FIBER 2.8g; CHOL 1mg; IRON 1mg; SODIUM 688mg; CALC 108mg

Easy Gnocchi with Thick Marinara Sauce

Use a food processor to make gnocchi in a flash and help prevent the over-kneading that often leads to too-dense dumplings. Be sure to cook the gnocchi in four batches to avoid overcrowding. Serve as a side anywhere you would normally have rice, pasta, or mashed potatoes.

SAUCE:
1 tablespoon olive oil
2 cups chopped onion (about
   1 medium)
2 garlic cloves, minced
2 cups chopped seeded plum
   tomato
½ cup tomato purée
1 teaspoon sugar
½ teaspoon dried oregano
¼ teaspoon salt
1 (8-ounce) can tomato sauce

GNOCCHI:
1 cup hot water
1 teaspoon salt
1 large egg
1 cup all-purpose flour
2 cups instant potato flakes
1 tablespoon chopped fresh basil
⅛ teaspoon freshly ground black
   pepper
Cooking spray
4 quarts water

1. To prepare sauce, heat oil in a large saucepan over medium-high heat. Add onion and garlic; sauté 4 minutes or until tender. Stir in chopped tomato and next 5 ingredients; bring to a boil. Reduce heat, and simmer 15 minutes or until slightly thickened.

2. To prepare gnocchi, combine 1 cup water, 1 teaspoon salt, and egg in a food processor, and process until blended. Lightly spoon flour into a dry measuring cup; level with a knife. Add flour, potato flakes, basil, and pepper to egg mixture; process just until dough forms a ball.

3. Place dough on a dry, unfloured surface. (If dough sticks to hands, lightly coat hands with cooking spray.) Divide dough into 4 equal pieces. Working with one portion at a time (cover remaining dough to prevent drying), roll each portion into an 18-inch-long rope. Cut each rope into 18 (1-inch) pieces; place dough pieces on a baking sheet coated with cooking spray.

4. Bring 4 quarts water to a boil in a large Dutch oven. Add one-fourth of dough pieces; cook 3 minutes or until gnocchi rise to surface of water. Remove cooked gnocchi with a slotted spoon; place in a colander to drain. Repeat procedure with remaining gnocchi. Serve immediately with sauce. Yield: 6 servings (serving size: 12 gnocchi and ½ cup sauce).

CALORIES 201 (17% from fat); FAT 3.7g (sat 0.7g, mono 2.1g, poly 0.5g); PROTEIN 5.9g; CARB 37.1g; FIBER 3g; CHOL 35mg; IRON 2.1mg; SODIUM 821mg; CALC 32mg

Lentil Couscous with Spinach

Try serving grilled salmon or chicken on a bed of this easy, filling side dish.

Cooking spray
1 cup chopped onion
3 garlic cloves, minced
2 cups water, divided
½ cup dried lentils
½ cup uncooked couscous
1 tablespoon olive oil
10 cups bagged prewashed spinach
   (about 5 ounces)
1¼ teaspoons salt
1 teaspoon ground cumin
¼ teaspoon freshly ground black
   pepper

1. Heat a medium saucepan over medium heat. Coat pan with cooking spray. Add onion to pan; cook 5 minutes or until golden, stirring occasionally. Stir in garlic; cook 30 seconds, stirring constantly. Add 1 cup water and lentils, and bring to a boil. Cover, reduce heat, and simmer 30 minutes or until lentils are tender.

2. While lentils cook, bring 1 cup water to a boil in a large saucepan. Gradually stir in couscous and oil. Remove from heat. Add spinach; cover and let stand 5 minutes. Combine lentil mixture, couscous mixture, salt, cumin, and pepper in a large bowl. Yield: 6 servings (serving size: ⅔ cup).

CALORIES 153 (16% from fat); FAT 2.8g (sat 0.4g, mono 1.7g, poly 0.4g); PROTEIN 8.2g; CARB 25g; FIBER 7.6g; CHOL 0mg; IRON 3.2mg; SODIUM 533mg; CALC 73mg

liquid assets

Refresher Course

Eight sippers that are the perfect cooldown after a long, hot workout.

After working out on a sticky summer day, you could reach for a specially formulated sports drink. But unless you're an endurance athlete exercising for hours at a time, what your body simply needs is something that's fluid, cool, and nutritious.

QUICK & EASY
Frozen Banana Latte

Keep peeled and sliced bananas in your freezer in zip-top bags because you'll want to make this smoothie often.

    1   cup vanilla low-fat frozen yogurt
    1   cup vanilla soy milk
    ½   cup cubed soft silken tofu
    2   to 3 teaspoons instant coffee
        granules
    2   ripe bananas, sliced and frozen
        (about 1½ cups)
    Ground cinnamon (optional)

1. Place first 5 ingredients in a blender; process until smooth and frothy. Sprinkle with cinnamon, if desired. Yield: 3 servings (serving size: about 1 cup).

CALORIES 208 (20% from fat); FAT 4.6g (sat 1.3g, mono 0.4g, poly 1.4g); PROTEIN 6.7g; CARB 37.8g; FIBER 1.9g; CHOL 7mg; IRON 0.9mg; SODIUM 61mg; CALC 184mg

QUICK & EASY
Spicy Mango-Orange Slush

A touch of ground red pepper gives this beverage a vitalizing jolt of heat.

    2   cups cubed peeled ripe mango,
        frozen
    1   cup fresh orange juice
    ½   cup sparkling water, chilled
    1   teaspoon grated lime rind
    2   tablespoons fresh lime juice
    ⅛   teaspoon ground red pepper

1. Place all ingredients in a blender, and process until smooth. Yield: 2 servings (serving size: about 1⅓ cups).

CALORIES 133 (2% from fat); FAT 0.3g (sat 0.1g, mono 0.1g, poly 0.1g); PROTEIN 0.6g; CARB 33g; FIBER 2.3g; CHOL 0mg; IRON 0.2mg; SODIUM 15mg; CALC 16mg

QUICK & EASY
Triple Berry Freeze

Raspberries, blueberries, and blackberries, which are all packed with health-boosting antioxidants, give this drink a rich flavor and a deep, enticing color.

    2   cups sparkling water, chilled
    1   cup lemon sorbet
    ½   cup frozen raspberries
    ½   cup frozen blueberries
    ½   cup frozen blackberries
    1   tablespoon honey

1. Place sparkling water and sorbet in a blender, and process until well blended. Add raspberries, blueberries, blackberries, and honey, and process until smooth. Yield: 4 servings (serving size: 1¼ cups).

CALORIES 106 (3% from fat); FAT 0.3g (sat 0g, mono 0g, poly 0.2g); PROTEIN 0.5g; CARB 27g; FIBER 2.8g; CHOL 0mg; IRON 0.3mg; SODIUM 4mg; CALC 27mg

QUICK & EASY
Ginger-Lemon Tonic

The fresh grated ginger and juice give this beverage a nice kick.

    2   cups chilled apple cider or apple
        juice, divided
    ¼   cup grated peeled fresh ginger,
        divided
    ⅓   cup frozen lemon sorbet
    Lemon slices (optional)

1. Place 1 cup cider in a blender.

2. Place 3 tablespoons grated ginger on several layers of damp cheesecloth. Gather edges of cheesecloth together; squeeze cheesecloth bag over a small bowl. Set 2 tablespoons ginger juice aside, and discard remaining ginger juice and pulp.

3. Add ginger juice and 1 tablespoon grated ginger to blender, and process until smooth. Add 1 cup apple cider and sorbet. Blend until smooth and frothy. Garnish with lemon slices, if desired. Yield: 2 servings (serving size: 1½ cups).

CALORIES 146 (0% from fat); FAT 0g; PROTEIN 0.1g; CARB 35.1g; FIBER 0.5g; CHOL 0mg; IRON 0.4mg; SODIUM 37mg; CALC 16mg

QUICK & EASY • MAKE AHEAD
Tropical Breeze

This juicy, creamy beverage is at its best when served ice cold.

    2   cups chilled mango or papaya
         juice
    1½   cups cubed peeled papaya
    1½   cups cubed fresh pineapple
    ½   cup soft silken tofu
    1   tablespoon minced peeled fresh
         ginger
    1   tablespoon fresh lime
         juice
    1   tablespoon honey

1. Place all ingredients in a blender; process until smooth. Chill thoroughly. Yield: 4 servings (serving size: about 1 cup).

CALORIES 156 (8% from fat); FAT 1.3g (sat 0.2g, mono 0.2g, poly 0.6g); PROTEIN 2.3g; CARB 37.1g; FIBER 2.6g; CHOL 0mg; IRON 0.6mg; SODIUM 7mg; CALC 32mg

Cool Melon Sipper

Mint adds an invigorating zest to this already refreshing beverage.

> 2 cups cubed peeled cantaloupe, divided
> 2 cups cubed peeled honeydew melon, divided
> 1 cup vanilla low-fat frozen yogurt
> ½ cup water
> 6 fresh mint leaves

1. Arrange 1 cup cantaloupe and 1 cup honeydew in a single layer on a baking sheet. Freeze 2 hours.
2. Place frozen cantaloupe, frozen honeydew, 1 cup cantaloupe, 1 cup honeydew, frozen yogurt, water, and mint leaves in a blender, and process until smooth. Yield: 3 servings (serving size: 1 cup).

CALORIES 170 (2% from fat); FAT 0.4g (sat 0.1g, mono 0g, poly 0.2g); PROTEIN 5.5g; CARB 38.7g; FIBER 1.5g; CHOL 2mg; IRON 0.3mg; SODIUM 51mg; CALC 152mg

Blackberry-Peach Smoothie with Walnuts

This smoothie is rich in antioxidants and fiber from berries, potassium from peaches, omega-3 fatty acids from walnuts, vitamin C from orange juice, and soy isoflavones from tofu. Use calcium-fortified orange juice for added nutrition.

> 2 cups frozen sliced peaches
> 1 cup blackberries
> 1 cup orange juice
> ¾ cup chopped soft silken tofu (about 4 ounces)
> ¼ cup honey
> 2 tablespoons fresh lemon juice
> 2 tablespoons chopped walnuts

1. Place first 6 ingredients in a blender, and process until smooth. Top with chopped walnuts. Yield: 3 servings (serving size: 1 cup smoothie and 2 teaspoons walnuts).

CALORIES 237 (18% from fat); FAT 4.7g (sat 0.5g, mono 0.7g, poly 3.1g); PROTEIN 4.4g; CARB 47.1g; FIBER 4.5g; CHOL 0mg; IRON 1mg; SODIUM 7mg; CALC 43mg

Vanilla-Honey-Nut Smoothie

Flaxseed boosts heart health and may enhance vision. You can find it in health-food stores already ground. Or grind whole flaxseed in a spice grinder or with a mortar and pestle. Store it in the refrigerator or freezer to keep it fresh. Enjoying this smoothie also helps you meet your daily calcium needs.

> 2 cups vanilla low-fat frozen yogurt
> ½ cup vanilla soy milk
> ½ cup fat-free milk
> ⅓ cup cubed soft silken tofu
> 1 tablespoon creamy peanut butter
> 1 tablespoon honey
> 1 tablespoon ground flaxseed (optional)

1. Combine first 6 ingredients in a blender; process until smooth. Sprinkle with flaxseed, if desired. Yield: 3 servings (serving size: 1 cup).

CALORIES 270 (30% from fat); FAT 9g (sat 2.8g, mono 2.7g, poly 2g); PROTEIN 9.2g; CARB 41.5g; FIBER 0.6g; CHOL 14mg; IRON 1.8mg; SODIUM 117mg; CALC 250mg

simple suppers

Creative Chicken

Inventive new recipes to prepare the ultimate suppertime standbys—chicken breasts and thighs.

Can you have too many chicken recipes? After all, chicken is affordable, easy to prepare, broadly appealing, and versatile—perfectly suited for new flavors and techniques.

Thread soy-marinated chicken thigh pieces onto skewers, and broil them ever so briefly to create Yakitori, a popular Japanese grilled chicken dish. For skinless, boneless chicken breasts, we offer three tantilizing options. A tangy tarragon-caper sauce makes one entrée worthy of a special evening.

Spiced Chicken with Black-Eyed Peas and Rice

For juicier chicken, sear it on the stovetop and finish in the oven.

> 1 tablespoon olive oil, divided
> 1 teaspoon paprika
> 1 teaspoon Old Bay seasoning
> ½ teaspoon sugar
> ½ teaspoon salt, divided
> 4 (6-ounce) skinless, boneless chicken breast halves
> 1 cup frozen chopped onion, thawed
> 1 teaspoon bottled minced garlic
> 1½ cups cooked long-grain rice
> 1 teaspoon hot pepper sauce (such as Tabasco)
> 1 (15.8-ounce) can black-eyed peas, undrained
> ¼ cup sliced green onions

1. Preheat oven to 350°.
2. Heat 2 teaspoons oil in a large non-stick skillet over medium-high heat. Combine paprika, seasoning, sugar, and ¼ teaspoon salt; sprinkle over chicken. Add chicken to pan; cook 2 minutes on each side. Wrap handle of pan with foil. Place pan in oven. Bake at 350° for 6 minutes or until chicken is done. Cover and keep warm.
3. Heat 1 teaspoon oil in a large saucepan over medium-high heat. Add 1 cup onion and garlic; sauté 3 minutes. Stir in ¼ teaspoon salt, rice, hot pepper sauce, and black-eyed peas; cook 3 minutes or until thoroughly heated, stirring frequently. Spoon about ¾ cup rice mixture into each of 4 bowls; top each serving with 1 chicken breast half. Sprinkle each serving with 1 tablespoon green onions. Yield: 4 servings.

CALORIES 405 (14% from fat); FAT 6.5g (sat 1.3g, mono 3.1g, poly 1.2g); PROTEIN 47g; CARB 37.5g; FIBER 5g; CHOL 99mg; IRON 3.4mg; SODIUM 868mg; CALC 64mg

Chicken, Mushroom, and Cheese Quesadillas

Using preshredded cheese and presliced mushrooms makes these quesadillas a snap to prepare.

    1   teaspoon olive oil
    1   teaspoon ground cumin
    ¼   teaspoon salt, divided
    ¼   teaspoon black pepper, divided
    12 ounces skinless, boneless chicken breast, cut into ¼-inch-thick slices
    ¾   cup chopped onion
    1   (8-ounce) package presliced mushrooms
    1   garlic clove, minced
    1   jalapeño, seeded and chopped
    4   (8-inch) flour tortillas
    1½ cups (6 ounces) preshredded reduced-fat Mexican cheese blend (such as Sargento)

1. Heat oil in a large nonstick skillet over medium-high heat. Combine cumin, ⅛ teaspoon salt, and ⅛ teaspoon pepper; sprinkle over chicken. Add chicken to pan, and sauté 5 minutes or until browned. Remove chicken from pan; set aside. Add onion, mushrooms, garlic, jalapeño, ⅛ teaspoon salt, and ⅛ teaspoon pepper to pan, and sauté 5 minutes. Remove from pan; let stand 5 minutes. Wipe pan with paper towels.
2. Heat pan over medium heat. Sprinkle each tortilla with about ⅓ cup cheese. Arrange ½ cup mushroom mixture over one-half of each tortilla. Arrange chicken evenly over mushroom mixture. Carefully fold each tortilla in half. Add 2 quesadillas to pan; cook 2 minutes on each side or until lightly browned and cheese melts. Repeat procedure with remaining quesadillas. Serve immediately. Yield: 4 servings (serving size: 1 quesadilla).

CALORIES 388 (29% from fat); FAT 12.5g (sat 5.7g, mono 2.5g, poly 0.9g); PROTEIN 38.5g; CARB 31.3g; FIBER 1.7g; CHOL 65mg; IRON 2.8mg; SODIUM 759mg; CALC 429mg

Chicken Breasts with Tarragon-Caper Sauce

It takes careful preparation to keep the skinless, boneless chicken breasts moist. Cook only until the breast feels firm when pressed in the thick center area.

    4   (6-ounce) skinless, boneless chicken breast halves
    2   teaspoons olive oil
    ½   teaspoon salt
    ¼   teaspoon black pepper
    1   tablespoon minced shallots
    1   cup fat-free, less-sodium chicken broth
    1   teaspoon cornstarch
    3   tablespoons fresh lemon juice
    2   tablespoons capers
    2   teaspoons chopped fresh tarragon

1. Place each chicken breast half between 2 sheets of heavy-duty plastic wrap; pound to ½-inch thickness using a meat mallet or rolling pin.
2. Heat oil in a large nonstick skillet over medium-high heat. Sprinkle chicken with salt and pepper. Add chicken to pan; cook 2 minutes on each side or until done. Remove from pan.
3. Add shallots to pan; sauté 1 minute or until tender. Combine broth and cornstarch, stirring with a whisk. Add broth mixture, juice, capers, and tarragon to pan. Bring to a boil; cook until reduced to ½ cup (about 3 minutes), stirring frequently. Serve sauce over chicken. Yield: 4 servings (serving size: 1 chicken breast half and 2 tablespoons sauce).

CALORIES 220 (18% from fat); FAT 4.4g (sat 0.9g, mono 2.2g, poly 0.7g); PROTEIN 40.5g; CARB 2.5g; FIBER 0.1g; CHOL 99mg; IRON 1.4mg; SODIUM 675mg; CALC 26mg

Yakitori

Yakitori (yah-kee-TOH-ree), Japanese for "grilled fowl," most often refers to small pieces of marinated chicken that are placed on skewers, and then grilled. These kebabs are cooked in a grill pan.

    ¼   cup sake (rice wine)
    ¼   cup low-sodium soy sauce
    3   tablespoons sugar
    2   tablespoons grated peeled fresh ginger
    ¼   teaspoon crushed red pepper
    2   garlic cloves, minced
    1   pound skinless, boneless chicken thighs, cut into 24 bite-sized pieces
    5   green onions, each cut into 4 (2-inch) pieces
    Cooking spray

1. Combine first 6 ingredients in a small saucepan. Bring to a boil; cook until reduced to ¼ cup (about 2½ minutes). Remove from heat; cool.
2. Combine soy sauce mixture and chicken. Cover and marinate in refrigerator 1 hour.
3. Heat a large grill pan over medium-high heat.
4. Thread 6 chicken cubes and 5 green onion pieces alternately onto each of 4 (10-inch) skewers. Brush kebabs with soy mixture. Coat pan with cooking spray. Place kebabs in pan, and cook 4 minutes on each side or until chicken is done. Yield: 4 servings (serving size: 1 kebab).

CALORIES 172 (24% from fat); FAT 4.5g (sat 1.1g, mono 1.4g, poly 1.1g); PROTEIN 22.9g; CARB 6.7g; FIBER 0.3g; CHOL 94mg; IRON 1.5mg; SODIUM 366mg; CALC 19mg

Turn Up the Heat

Five fiery condiments—chipotle chiles in adobo sauce, Sriracha, sambal oelek, hot pepper sauce, and wasabi—boost the flavor in everyday dishes.

Louisiana Crab Cakes with Creole Tartar Sauce

The Maryland classic goes Creole with a double dose of spicy, vinegary hot pepper sauce.

TARTAR SAUCE:

- ½ cup low-fat mayonnaise
- 3 tablespoons sweet pickle relish
- 2 tablespoons capers, rinsed and drained
- 1 teaspoon Creole mustard
- ¼ teaspoon salt-free Cajun-Creole seasoning (such as The Spice Hunter)
- ¼ teaspoon hot pepper sauce (such as Tabasco)

CRAB CAKES:

- 4 (1-ounce) slices white bread
- ¼ cup finely chopped onion
- ¼ cup finely chopped red bell pepper
- 1 tablespoon chopped fresh parsley
- 1 tablespoon fresh lemon juice
- 1 tablespoon hot pepper sauce (such as Tabasco)
- ¼ teaspoon freshly ground black pepper
- 1 pound lump crabmeat, shell pieces removed
- 1 large egg, lightly beaten
- 1 large egg white, lightly beaten
- 4 teaspoons vegetable oil, divided
- Parsley sprigs (optional)
- Lemon wedges (optional)

1. To prepare tartar sauce, combine first 6 ingredients, stirring with a whisk. Let stand 10 minutes.
2. To prepare crab cakes, place bread slices in a food processor; pulse 10 times or until coarse crumbs measure 2 cups. Combine 1 cup breadcrumbs, onion, and next 8 ingredients; mix well. Divide crab mixture into 8 equal portions. Form each portion into a ½-inch-thick patty. Place 1 cup breadcrumbs in a shallow dish. Dredge patties, one at a time, in breadcrumbs.
3. Heat 2 teaspoons oil in a large nonstick skillet over medium-high heat. Add 4 patties; cook 3 minutes on each side or until golden brown. Repeat procedure with 2 teaspoons oil and remaining patties. Serve with tartar sauce. Garnish with parsley sprigs and lemon wedges, if desired. Yield: 4 servings (serving size: 2 crab cakes and 2 tablespoons tartar sauce).

CALORIES 331 (30% from fat); FAT 11g (sat 1.8g, mono 2.6g, poly 5.3g); PROTEIN 28.2g; CARB 29.1g; FIBER 1.4g; CHOL 167mg; IRON 2.5mg; SODIUM 992mg; CALC 163mg

Grilled Pork Chops with Fiery Salsa

Sriracha and fish sauce lend the salsa an Asian flavor. Serve it with grilled chicken, shrimp, or even tortilla chips.

- 1½ cups diced tomato
- ⅓ cup diced red onion
- ¼ cup diced avocado
- 1½ tablespoons Sriracha (hot chile sauce, such as Huy Fong)
- 1 tablespoon chopped fresh cilantro
- 2 teaspoons fresh lemon juice
- ½ teaspoon fish sauce
- 1 teaspoon sugar
- ¾ teaspoon garlic powder
- ½ teaspoon ground coriander
- ¼ teaspoon salt
- ⅛ teaspoon freshly ground black pepper
- 4 (4-ounce) boneless center-cut loin pork chops (about ½ inch thick)
- Cooking spray

1. Prepare grill to medium-high heat.
2. Combine first 7 ingredients.
3. Combine sugar and next 4 ingredients; sprinkle evenly over both sides of pork. Place pork on grill rack coated with cooking spray; grill 4 minutes on each side or until done. Serve with salsa. Yield: 4 servings (serving size: 1 chop and about ⅓ cup salsa).

CALORIES 188 (34% from fat); FAT 7g (sat 2.1g, mono 3.2g, poly 0.7g); PROTEIN 22.7g; CARB 8g; FIBER 1.7g; CHOL 65mg; IRON 1.4mg; SODIUM 316mg; CALC 21mg

Chipotle Macaroni and Cheese
(pictured on page 234)

This macaroni and cheese is a favorite of ours because it's incredibly tasty and easy to prepare. You don't even have to make a white sauce for this creamy dish. The acidic tomatoes counter the richness of the cheeses.

- 1 (7-ounce) can chipotle chiles in adobo sauce
- 1 tablespoon butter
- ½ cup finely chopped onion
- ½ cup finely chopped green bell pepper
- 1 garlic clove, minced
- 2 tablespoons all-purpose flour
- 1 (14½-ounce) can diced tomatoes and green chiles, undrained
- 4 cups hot cooked elbow macaroni (about 2 cups uncooked)
- 2 cups (8 ounces) shredded reduced-fat sharp Cheddar cheese
- 1 cup 1% low-fat cottage cheese
- 1 cup 2% reduced-fat milk
- ¼ cup (1 ounce) grated fresh Parmesan cheese
- 1 large egg, lightly beaten
- Cooking spray
- 3 tablespoons dry breadcrumbs

1. Preheat oven to 350°.
2. Remove 1 teaspoon adobo sauce from can; set sauce aside. Remove 2 chipotle chiles from can; finely chop to measure 1 tablespoon. Reserve remaining chiles and adobo sauce for another use.

3. Melt butter in a Dutch oven over medium-high heat. Add chopped chiles, onion, bell pepper, and garlic; cook 4 minutes or until onion is tender, stirring frequently. Sprinkle with flour; cook 30 seconds, stirring constantly. Reduce heat to medium; add tomatoes. Cook 3 minutes or until thickened. Add reserved 1 teaspoon adobo sauce, pasta, and next 5 ingredients; stir to combine. Spoon pasta mixture into a 2-quart baking dish coated with cooking spray; top with breadcrumbs. Bake at 350° for 30 minutes or until bubbly. Yield: 6 servings (serving size: about 1 cup).

CALORIES 324 (24% from fat); FAT 8.5g (sat 4.6g, mono 2.4g, poly 0.6g); PROTEIN 34.2g; CARB 39.6g; FIBER 2g; CHOL 56mg; IRON 2.4mg; SODIUM 756mg; CALC 307mg

---

QUICK & EASY

Thai Roast Duck Salad

Rich, meaty duck breast stands up well to the full-flavored dressing in this Asian-style salad. The sweetness of honey is a nice foil to the spicy sambal oelek.

2 (8-ounce) boneless duck breasts, split into halves
⅛ teaspoon freshly ground black pepper
¼ cup fresh lime juice
2 tablespoons honey
1 tablespoon rice vinegar
1 tablespoon fish sauce
2 to 3 teaspoons sambal oelek (ground fresh chile paste, such as Huy Fong)
1 teaspoon finely chopped shallots
4 cups torn Boston lettuce
2 cups peeled sliced cucumber
¾ cup diagonally sliced carrot
½ cup thinly sliced red onion
½ cup thinly sliced red bell pepper
2 tablespoons chopped fresh cilantro
2 tablespoons chopped fresh mint

1. Preheat oven to 400°.
2. Heat a large ovenproof nonstick skillet over medium-high heat. Sprinkle duck with pepper. Add duck to pan;

cook 2 minutes on each side or until browned. Place pan in oven, and bake at 400° for 15 minutes or until desired degree of doneness. Remove duck from pan; let stand 10 minutes. Remove and discard skin from duck; cut duck crosswise into thin slices.
3. Combine lime juice and next 5 ingredients, stirring with a whisk. Combine Boston lettuce and next 6 ingredients in a large bowl. Drizzle 6 tablespoons juice mixture over lettuce mixture, and toss to coat. Divide salad evenly among 4 plates. Divide duck evenly among salads. Drizzle each serving with 1½ teaspoons juice mixture. Yield: 4 servings (serving size: about 1⅓ cups salad and about 3 ounces duck).

CALORIES 215 (22% from fat); FAT 5.2g (sat 1.6g, mono 1.4g, poly 0.8g); PROTEIN 24.6g; CARB 18.5g; FIBER 2.6g; CHOL 87mg; IRON 5.8mg; SODIUM 462mg; CALC 48mg

---

STAFF FAVORITE • MAKE AHEAD

Seared Chicken with Sriracha Barbecue Dipping Sauce

Use this all-purpose sauce for pork, shrimp, or seared tofu. Make it when you start marinating the chicken. Serve over sticky white rice to counter the heat of the dipping sauce. Toss edamame with soy sauce, garlic, and hoisin to complete the meal.

¼ cup chopped shallots
2 tablespoons sugar
2 tablespoons fresh lime juice
1 tablespoon fish sauce
4 garlic cloves, minced
1½ teaspoons dark sesame oil, divided
8 (2-ounce) skinless, boneless chicken thighs
3 tablespoons ketchup
4 teaspoons rice vinegar
1 tablespoon Sriracha (hot chile sauce, such as Huy Fong)
2 teaspoons honey
1 teaspoon grated peeled fresh ginger

1. Combine first 5 ingredients; stir in ½ teaspoon oil. Place shallot mixture in a large zip-top plastic bag; add chicken to bag.

Seal and marinate in refrigerator 3 hours to overnight, turning bag occasionally.
2. Combine ketchup and next 4 ingredients.
3. Heat 1 teaspoon oil in a large nonstick skillet over medium-high heat. Remove chicken from bag; discard marinade. Add chicken to pan; cook 2 minutes on each side or until browned. Cover, reduce heat to medium-low, and cook 8 minutes or until done, turning twice. Serve with ketchup mixture. Yield: 4 servings (serving size: 2 thighs and 1 tablespoon ketchup mixture).

CALORIES 194 (27% from fat); FAT 5.9g (sat 1.3g, mono 1.9g, poly 1.7g); PROTEIN 22.8g; CARB 11.7g; FIBER 0.3g; CHOL 94mg; IRON 1.4mg; SODIUM 451mg; CALC 20mg

---

QUICK & EASY

Seared Shrimp with Thai Cocktail Sauce

Mint and sambal oelek brighten traditional cocktail sauce. Chili sauce, found near ketchup in the supermarket, is a blend of tomatoes, chili powder, onions, and spices.

½ cup bottled chili sauce (such as Heinz)
4 teaspoons chopped fresh mint
½ teaspoon grated lemon rind
1½ teaspoons fresh lemon juice
1¼ teaspoons sambal oelek (ground fresh chile paste, such as Huy Fong), divided
⅛ teaspoon freshly ground black pepper
21 jumbo shrimp, peeled and deveined (about 1 pound)
2 teaspoons vegetable oil

1. Combine first 4 ingredients; stir in 1 teaspoon sambal oelek. Set aside.
2. Combine ¼ teaspoon sambal oelek, black pepper, and shrimp, tossing gently to coat.
3. Heat oil in a large nonstick skillet over medium-high heat. Add shrimp; cook 2½ minutes on each side or until done. Serve with sauce. Yield: 3 servings (serving size: 7 shrimp and 2½ tablespoons sauce).

CALORIES 191 (27% from fat); FAT 5.7g (sat 0.7g, mono 2.2g, poly 1.9g); PROTEIN 30.8g; CARB 2.3g; FIBER 0.1g; CHOL 230mg; IRON 3.7mg; SODIUM 283mg; CALC 81mg

Bottled Heat

Chipotle Chiles in Adobo Sauce

Country of origin: Mexico; "chipotle" is a combination of the prefix *chi* (for "chile") and *potle* (Aztec word for "smoke")

Main ingredients: chipotle chiles (dried, smoked jalapeños) and adobo sauce (seasoned tomato sauce)

Heat index: medium, with a smoky, slightly sweet, meaty, and savory flavor. Drying and smoking concentrates a jalapeño's heat.

Consistency: rehydrated, soft chiles in tomato sauce

Where to find it: canned, in the Latin foods section of most grocery stores

Best uses: Often used as an ingredient in chili, soups, and sauces. They're usually not added after cooking.

Sriracha

Country of origin: Thailand (named after a seaside town)

Main ingredients: red Thai chiles, sugar, vinegar, salt, and garlic

Heat index: moderately hot and spicy, but rounded with sweetness and deepened with garlic

Consistency: thick, like bottled barbecue sauce

Where to find it: Asian markets, or order from www.ethnicgrocer.com. The most common brand, Huy Fong, comes in a clear plastic squeeze bottle with a rooster on the label and a bright green cap.

Best uses: Enjoyed as a table condiment in Thai and Vietnamese restaurants, it's also great with non-Asian dishes. Try it in place of ketchup on most anything—French fries, omelets or scrambled eggs, pizza, hot dogs, and hamburgers.

Sambal Oelek (ground fresh chile paste)

Country of origin: Indonesia

Main ingredients: chiles with little additional seasoning other than vinegar

Heat index: intense

Consistency: somewhat thin, like tomato purée

Where to find it: Asian markets, or from www.ethnicgrocer.com or www.thegood lifegourmet.com. The brand we use, Huy Fong, comes in a plastic jar with a green lid and gold label depicting a rooster.

Best uses: Stir into sauces, and use in marinades.

Hot Pepper Sauce

Country of origin: United States

Main ingredients: Tabasco sauce, the most recognizable brand, is made with hot peppers grown on Avery Island, Louisiana. The peppers are mashed and fermented in oak barrels up to 3 years, then mixed with vinegar.

Heat index: moderately spicy and vinegary

Consistency: watery

Where to find it: grocery store shelves near the ketchup and barbecue sauce

Best uses: Use on almost anything that needs a little heat.

Wasabi

Country of origin: Japan

Main ingredients: Nicknamed "Japanese horseradish," wasabi is grated from a rare plant that is not actually related to horseradish. The real thing is expensive and hard to find in the United States. (What Americans eat—and our recipes use—is a blend of horseradish and mustard tinted green with food coloring to look like wasabi.)

Heat index: varies; has pungent, intense spiciness that registers first in your sinuses and makes your eyes water

Consistency: thick, toothpastelike texture

Where to find it: Look for tubes of wasabi paste or powder (to reconstitute with water) in the Asian food section of large supermarkets or in Asian markets.

Best uses: Serve with sushi, mix into mashed potatoes, or use in a sauce or marinade for strongly flavored fish.

Spicy Sriracha Bread

This also works in a bread machine.

    ¾ cup warm water (100° to 110°)
    ¼ cup Sriracha (hot chile sauce,
       such as Huy Fong)
    1 package dry yeast (about
       2¼ teaspoons)
    3 cups bread flour, divided
    ¾ teaspoon salt
    1 large egg, lightly beaten
       Cooking spray
    1 teaspoon butter, melted

1. Combine water, Sriracha, and yeast in a large bowl; let stand 5 minutes. Lightly spoon flour into dry measuring cups; level with a knife. Add 2¾ cups flour, salt, and egg to yeast mixture; stir until a soft dough forms. Turn dough out onto a floured surface. Knead until smooth and elastic (about 8 minutes); add enough of remaining flour, 1 tablespoon at a time, to prevent dough from sticking to hands (dough will feel sticky).

2. Place dough in a large bowl coated with cooking spray, turning to coat top. Cover and let rise in a warm place (85°), free from drafts, 1 hour or until doubled in size. (Gently press two fingers into dough. If indentation remains, dough has risen enough.) Punch dough down; cover and let rest 5 minutes. Roll dough into a 14 x 7-inch rectangle on a lightly floured surface. Roll up rectangle tightly, starting with a short edge, pressing firmly to eliminate air pockets; pinch seam and ends to seal. Place roll, seam side down, in an 8½ x 4½-inch loaf pan coated with cooking spray. Lightly coat surface of dough with cooking spray; cover and let rise in a warm place 30 minutes or until doubled in size.

3. Preheat oven to 375°.

4. Bake at 375° for 40 minutes or until lightly browned on bottom and loaf sounds hollow when tapped. Remove from pan, and brush with melted butter. Cool on a wire rack. Yield: 14 servings (serving size: 1 slice).

CALORIES 119 (8% from fat); FAT 1.1g (sat 0.4g, mono 0.3g, poly 0.3g); PROTEIN 4.2g; CARB 22.4g; FIBER 0.8g; CHOL 16mg; IRON 1.4mg; SODIUM 184mg; CALC 7mg

Serve the flavorful kebabs and spicy sauce with warmed small pita bread to make gyro-inspired wraps.

Yogurt-Marinated Beef Kebabs with Wasabi Aïoli

Greek chickpea salad*

Pita bread

*Combine 2 cups chopped English cucumber, 1 cup chopped tomato, ¼ cup chopped red onion, ¼ cup halved kalamata olives, 2 tablespoons chopped fresh parsley, and 1 (15½-ounce) can drained chickpeas in a medium bowl. Combine 3 tablespoons red wine vinegar, 1 tablespoon extravirgin olive oil, ½ teaspoon dried oregano, ¼ teaspoon salt, ¼ teaspoon freshly ground black pepper, and 1 minced garlic clove, stirring with a whisk. Drizzle vinaigrette over salad; toss to coat.

Yogurt-Marinated Beef Kebabs with Wasabi Aïoli

Wasabi is a welcome addition to garlicky aïoli, giving it a green hue and a spicy kick.

- ¼ cup finely chopped onion
- 2 tablespoons fresh lemon juice
- 1 tablespoon grated peeled fresh ginger
- 1 tablespoon low-sodium soy sauce
- ⅛ teaspoon ground red pepper
- 2 garlic cloves, minced
- 1 (6-ounce) carton plain fat-free yogurt
- 1 (1½-pound) boneless sirloin steak, trimmed and cut into 20 (1-inch) cubes
- ⅓ cup fat-free mayonnaise
- 2 teaspoons fresh lemon juice
- 2 teaspoons prepared wasabi paste
- ¼ teaspoon minced fresh garlic
- 16 cherry or grape tomatoes
- 16 (1-inch-long) pieces green onion
- ¼ teaspoon salt
- Cooking spray

1. Combine first 7 ingredients in a large zip-top plastic bag; add beef to bag. Seal and marinate in refrigerator 4 to 6 hours, turning bag occasionally.

2. Combine mayonnaise, 2 teaspoons juice, wasabi, and ¼ teaspoon garlic, stirring with a whisk. Refrigerate at least 1 hour.

3. Prepare grill to medium-high heat.

4. Remove beef from bag; discard marinade. Thread 5 beef cubes alternately with 4 tomatoes and 4 green onion pieces onto each of 4 (12-inch) skewers. Sprinkle salt evenly over kebabs. Place kebabs on grill rack coated with cooking spray; grill 4 minutes on each side or until desired degree of doneness. Serve with mayonnaise mixture. Yield: 4 servings (serving size: 1 kebab and about 2 tablespoons mayonnaise mixture).

CALORIES 198 (30% from fat); FAT 6.7g (sat 2.3g, mono 2.5g, poly 0.3g); PROTEIN 23.4g; CARB 11.2g; FIBER 1.5g; CHOL 66mg; IRON 2.9mg; SODIUM 498mg; CALC 49mg

Chipotle-Bacon Corn Bread

Bacon and chipotle chiles give this corn bread double the smokiness to offset the buttermilk's tang.

- 1 cup all-purpose flour
- ¾ cup yellow cornmeal
- 3 tablespoons sugar
- 1 teaspoon baking powder
- 1 teaspoon salt
- ½ teaspoon ground cumin
- ¼ teaspoon baking soda
- 1⅓ cups fat-free buttermilk
- 2 tablespoons butter, melted
- 1½ tablespoons chopped canned chipotle chiles in adobo sauce
- 1 large egg, lightly beaten
- 3 bacon slices, cooked and crumbled
- Cooking spray

1. Preheat oven to 425°.

2. Combine flour and next 6 ingredients in a large bowl, stirring well. Combine buttermilk, butter, chiles, and egg in a medium bowl, stirring with a whisk. Add buttermilk mixture to flour mixture; stir just until moist. Fold in bacon. Pour batter into an 8-inch square baking pan coated with cooking spray.

3. Bake at 425° for 18 minutes or until a wooden pick inserted in center comes out clean. Cool 10 minutes in pan on a wire rack. Yield: 9 servings.

CALORIES 165 (28% from fat); FAT 5.1g (sat 2.4g, mono 1.6g, poly 0.5g); PROTEIN 4.9g; CARB 25.1g; FIBER 1.2g; CHOL 34mg; IRON 1.3mg; SODIUM 460mg; CALC 82mg

Sesame-Crusted Tuna with Wasabi-Ponzu Sauce

Wasabi comes in different intensities. You may want to experiment with several brands to find the right amount of heat for your taste buds. Some of the sesame seeds might pop out of the pan as the tuna cooks, so use caution and wear an oven mitt as you turn the fish over.

- 2 tablespoons low-sodium soy sauce
- 2 tablespoons fresh orange juice
- 1 tablespoon rice vinegar
- 1 tablespoon chopped green onions
- 1 teaspoon grated lemon rind
- 2 teaspoons fresh lemon juice
- 2 teaspoons honey
- 1¼ teaspoons prepared wasabi paste
- 1 teaspoon grated peeled fresh ginger
- 1 teaspoon brown sugar
- 2 teaspoons vegetable oil
- 4 (6-ounce) tuna steaks (about ¾ inch thick)
- ¼ teaspoon salt
- 3 tablespoons sesame seeds
- 2 tablespoons black sesame seeds
- Sliced green onions (optional)

1. Combine first 10 ingredients, stirring with a whisk.

2. Heat oil in a large nonstick skillet over medium-high heat. Sprinkle tuna with salt. Combine sesame seeds in a shallow dish. Dredge tuna in sesame seeds. Add tuna to pan; cook 3 minutes on each side or until desired degree of doneness. Garnish with green onions, if desired. Serve tuna with sauce. Yield: 4 servings (serving size: 1 tuna steak and 2 tablespoons sauce).

CALORIES 302 (28% from fat); FAT 9.5g (sat 1.4g, mono 3.5g, poly 3.3g); PROTEIN 40g; CARB 9.9g; FIBER 0.2g; CHOL 80mg; IRON 3.2mg; SODIUM 507mg; CALC 54mg

Shrimp Tacos with Spiked Sour Cream

½ cup reduced-fat sour cream
3¼ teaspoons hot pepper sauce (such as Tabasco), divided
1¼ teaspoons chili powder, divided
¾ teaspoon ground cumin
½ teaspoon garlic powder
½ teaspoon hot smoked paprika
¼ teaspoon salt
1½ pounds large shrimp, peeled and deveined
1 tablespoon vegetable oil
3 garlic cloves, minced
1 tablespoon fresh lime juice
8 (6-inch) corn tortillas
2 cups shredded iceberg lettuce
½ cup chopped Vidalia or other sweet onion
¼ cup prepared salsa verde (such as Herdez)

1. Combine sour cream, 1¼ teaspoons hot pepper sauce, and ½ teaspoon chili powder.
2. Combine ¾ teaspoon chili powder, cumin, garlic powder, paprika, and salt in a large bowl. Add shrimp; toss to coat. Let stand 10 minutes.
3. Heat oil in a large nonstick skillet over medium-high heat. Add garlic; sauté 30 seconds. Add shrimp mixture, and sauté 3 minutes or until done. Stir in 2 teaspoons hot pepper sauce and juice. Remove from heat.
4. Heat tortillas according to package directions. Arrange one-fourth of the shrimp, ¼ cup lettuce, and 1 tablespoon onion down center of each tortilla. Serve with sour cream mixture and salsa verde. Yield: 4 servings (serving size: 2 tacos, 1 tablespoon sour cream mixture, and 1 tablespoon salsa).

CALORIES 401 (24% from fat); FAT 10.7g (sat 3g, mono 2.9g, poly 2.9g); PROTEIN 40.7g; CARB 34.9g; FIBER 4.7g; CHOL 269mg; IRON 5.5mg; SODIUM 593mg; CALC 274mg

What to Eat After a Workout

Prepare these quick, high-energy recipes the night before your next lunch-hour workout. They're simple options that will help your body recover.

STAFF FAVORITE • QUICK & EASY
MAKE AHEAD
Roasted Chicken-Artichoke Calzones

Use a microwave or toaster oven to reheat this dish. Let calzones come to room temperature before wrapping to keep the dough from getting soggy. Pack some bottled marinara sauce for dipping.

1 (14-ounce) can artichoke hearts, drained and finely chopped
¼ teaspoon salt
¼ teaspoon freshly ground black pepper
1 garlic clove, minced
2 cups thinly sliced fresh spinach leaves
1¼ cups (5 ounces) shredded sharp provolone cheese
1 cup shredded cooked chicken breast (about 5 ounces)
1 teaspoon olive oil
2 teaspoons cornmeal
1 (13.8-ounce) can refrigerated pizza crust dough

1. Preheat oven to 425°.
2. Pat artichokes dry with paper towels. Combine artichokes, salt, pepper, and garlic in a large bowl. Add spinach, cheese, and chicken; toss gently to combine.
3. Brush oil over a baking sheet; sprinkle with cornmeal. Unroll dough onto prepared baking sheet; cut into 6 equal portions. Cover and let rest 5 minutes. Pat each portion into a 6 x 5-inch rectangle. Spoon ⅔ cup spinach mixture into center of each dough portion. Fold one corner of each dough portion over spinach mixture to form a triangle. Press edges together with fingers to seal. Bake at 425° for 12 minutes or until golden. Yield: 6 servings (serving size: 1 calzone).

CALORIES 347 (30% from fat); FAT 11.6g (sat 4.6g, mono 0.9g, poly 0.3g); PROTEIN 21.6g; CARB 40.1g; FIBER 4.8g; CHOL 44mg; IRON 3.2mg; SODIUM 940mg; CALC 222mg

Quick Dinner for One Menu
serves 1

Fast-cooking couscous pairs with bottled roasted bell peppers, canned artichoke hearts, and a simple vinaigrette for a speedy meal.

Bell Pepper and Fresh Mozzarella Couscous

Green salad

Balsamic-brown sugar strawberries*

*Toss 1 cup halved strawberries with 1 tablespoon brown sugar, 2 teaspoons balsamic vinegar, and 1 teaspoon chopped fresh mint. Let stand at room temperature 20 minutes before serving.

QUICK & EASY • MAKE AHEAD
Bell Pepper and Fresh Mozzarella Couscous

Bottled roasted red peppers and superfast-cooking couscous make this a perfect recipe for your busiest day. It can be doubled to make two meals. Use any leftover artichoke hearts, bell peppers, and mozzarella for a vegetarian pizza.

½ cup water

⅓ cup uncooked couscous

⅛ teaspoon salt

¼ cup chopped bottled roasted red bell peppers

¼ cup canned artichoke hearts, rinsed, drained, and chopped

¼ cup (1 ounce) chopped fresh mozzarella cheese

1 tablespoon chopped fresh basil

1 tablespoon balsamic vinegar

1 teaspoon extravirgin olive oil

⅛ teaspoon freshly ground black pepper

2 kalamata olives, pitted and sliced

1. Bring water to a boil in a small saucepan; gradually stir in couscous and salt. Remove from heat; cover and let stand 5 minutes. Fluff with a fork.

2. Add bell peppers and remaining ingredients; toss gently to combine. Cover and chill. Yield: 1 serving (serving size: 2 cups).

CALORIES 407 (29% from fat); FAT 13.3g (sat 5.1g, mono 4.9g, poly 1g); PROTEIN 14.7g; CARB 54.7g; FIBER 3.5g; CHOL 22mg; IRON 2.2mg; SODIUM 798mg; CALC 197mg

QUICK & EASY • MAKE AHEAD
Curried Chicken Salad

Eat this chicken salad with whole-grain crackers or a toasted baguette to increase your carbohydrates. If you don't have time to cook the chicken, pick up a rotisserie chicken at the supermarket.

1½ cups chopped cooked chicken breast (about 8 ounces)

½ cup halved seedless red grapes

½ cup diced peeled apple

2 tablespoons diced pineapple

1 tablespoon dried currants

3 tablespoons low-fat mayonnaise

1 teaspoon honey

½ teaspoon curry powder

½ teaspoon fresh lemon juice

⅛ teaspoon salt

⅛ teaspoon freshly ground black pepper

1 tablespoon sliced almonds, toasted

1. Combine first 5 ingredients in a large bowl. Combine mayonnaise and next 5 ingredients, stirring with a whisk. Pour

mayonnaise mixture over chicken mixture; toss gently to coat. Sprinkle with almonds. Cover and chill. Yield: 2 servings (serving size: 1¼ cups).

CALORIES 303 (21% from fat); FAT 7.2g (sat 1.3g, mono 2.3g, poly 1.3g); PROTEIN 33.8g; CARB 25.7g; FIBER 1.9g; CHOL 89mg; IRON 1.7mg; SODIUM 435mg; CALC 37mg

Brown-Bag Lunch Menu
serves 2

Double the noodle recipe so you can share, or so you can have both lunch and dinner covered.

Soba Noodles with Shrimp

Sesame green beans*

Orange wedges

*Heat 1½ teaspoons dark sesame oil in a medium nonstick skillet over medium-high heat. Add ½ teaspoon minced peeled fresh ginger and 1 minced garlic clove; sauté 30 seconds. Add 2 cups trimmed green beans, ¼ teaspoon salt, and ⅛ teaspoon freshly ground black pepper; sauté 6 minutes or until crisp-tender. Cover and chill.

QUICK & EASY • MAKE AHEAD
Soba Noodles with Shrimp

Cooking the soba takes about 6 minutes, and you can chop and assemble the remaining ingredients while the noodles cook. Purchase peeled and deveined cooked shrimp, or buy raw shrimp and add them to the boiling water a couple of minutes after adding the noodles. This recipe is easily doubled if you need more than one serving.

2 ounces uncooked soba (buckwheat) noodles

4 cups water

½ cup shredded carrot

1 tablespoon rice vinegar

1 tablespoon dark sesame oil

1 teaspoon low-sodium soy sauce

¼ teaspoon chili garlic sauce (such as Lee Kum Kee)

⅛ teaspoon sugar

½ cup chopped cooked shrimp (about 3 ounces)

¼ cup thinly sliced green onions

1 tablespoon chopped fresh cilantro

1. Break noodles in half. Bring 4 cups water to a boil in a medium saucepan. Add noodles; cook 4 minutes. Add carrot to noodles in pan; cook 2 minutes or until noodles are done. Drain.

2. Combine vinegar, oil, soy sauce, garlic sauce, and sugar in a medium bowl, stirring with a whisk. Add noodle mixture, shrimp, onions, and cilantro; toss to coat. Cover and chill. Yield: 1 serving (serving size: 2 cups).

CALORIES 357 (15% from fat); FAT 6g (sat 1g, mono 2.1g, poly 2.4g); PROTEIN 26.9g; CARB 51.7g; FIBER 3g; CHOL 166mg; IRON 4.7mg; SODIUM 898mg; CALC 72mg

QUICK & EASY • MAKE AHEAD
Lemon Garbanzo Salad with Feta

This makes one serving, but it's easily doubled and is even better the next day.

½ cup boiling water

⅓ cup uncooked bulgur

1½ tablespoons fresh lemon juice, divided

⅓ cup canned chickpeas (garbanzo beans), rinsed and drained

2 tablespoons chopped peeled cucumber

2 tablespoons chopped celery

2 tablespoons diced red onion

1½ tablespoons crumbled feta cheese

1½ teaspoons chopped fresh or ¼ teaspoon dried dill

2 teaspoons extravirgin olive oil

⅛ teaspoon salt

⅛ teaspoon freshly ground black pepper

1. Combine boiling water, bulgur, and 1 tablespoon lemon juice in a medium bowl. Let stand 15 minutes. Add chickpeas and next 5 ingredients; toss gently to combine.

2. Combine 1½ teaspoons lemon juice, oil, salt, and pepper, stirring with a whisk. Drizzle over bulgur mixture, and toss gently to coat. Cover and chill. Yield: 1 serving (serving size: 1½ cups).

CALORIES 390 (31% from fat); FAT 13.6g (sat 3.5g, mono 7.6g, poly 1.5g); PROTEIN 12.3g; CARB 58.9g; FIBER 13g; CHOL 13mg; IRON 2.6mg; SODIUM 713mg; CALC 129mg

In about 15 minutes you can have a make-ahead, portable lunch for one.

QUICK & EASY • MAKE AHEAD

Corn and Sun-Dried Tomato Quesadilla with Smoked Mozzarella

We liked this quesadilla cold, but you can warm it in a toaster oven or microwave. Serve with a tossed salad.

¼ teaspoon olive oil
2 (6-inch) corn tortillas
Cooking spray
⅓ cup fresh or frozen, thawed, corn kernels
1 tablespoon chopped red onion
1½ teaspoons sun-dried tomato sprinkles
⅛ teaspoon salt
⅛ teaspoon freshly ground black pepper
¼ cup (1 ounce) shredded smoked mozzarella cheese

1. Pour oil onto one side of a tortilla. Place second tortilla over oiled side of first tortilla, and rub tortillas together to spread oil evenly over both tortillas.
2. Heat a large nonstick skillet over medium-high heat. Coat pan with cooking spray. Add corn; cook 4 minutes or until lightly browned, stirring occasionally. Place corn in a bowl. Add onion, sun-dried tomato, salt, and pepper to pan; sauté 1 minute. Add to corn mixture. Wipe pan with paper towels; recoat with cooking spray.
3. Heat pan over medium-high heat. Place one tortilla, oiled side down, in pan. Sprinkle 2 tablespoons cheese over tortilla; top with corn mixture. Sprinkle with 2 tablespoons cheese; top with remaining tortilla, oiled side up. Cook 2 minutes on each side or until cheese melts and tortilla is crisp. Cut into 4 wedges. Yield: 1 serving (serving size: 4 wedges).

CALORIES 257 (32% from fat); FAT 9.2g (sat 4.1g, mono 3.2g, poly 1.2g); PROTEIN 10.4g; CARB 36.6g; FIBER 4.6g; CHOL 22mg; IRON 1.3mg; SODIUM 525mg; CALC 242mg

QUICK & EASY • MAKE AHEAD

Edamame and Bean Salad with Shrimp and Fresh Salsa

Edamame can be cooked in the microwave in minutes, and everything else can be purchased already cooked to save time. Triple the recipe if you want to use the whole can of cannellini beans. Have an apple with your lunch, and you'll get close to 45 grams of carbohydrates—and a nice dose of fiber.

¼ cup frozen shelled edamame
½ cup chopped cooked small shrimp (about 3 ounces)
½ cup canned cannellini beans, rinsed and drained
½ cup halved cherry tomatoes
1 to 2 tablespoons chopped red onion
1 teaspoon minced jalapeño pepper
1 tablespoon chopped fresh cilantro
2 teaspoons fresh lime juice
1½ teaspoons extravirgin olive oil
⅛ teaspoon salt

1. Cook edamame according to package directions. Drain and rinse with cold water; drain.
2. Combine edamame, shrimp, and next 4 ingredients. Combine cilantro and next 3 ingredients, stirring with a whisk. Drizzle over edamame mixture, and toss gently to combine. Cover and chill. Yield: 1 serving (serving size: 1⅓ cups).

CALORIES 314 (29% from fat); FAT 10.1g (sat 1g, mono 5g, poly 1.2g); PROTEIN 28.1g; CARB 28g; FIBER 8.2g; CHOL 167mg; IRON 5.8mg; SODIUM 803mg; CALC 94mg

QUICK & EASY • MAKE AHEAD

Kung Pao Tofu Rice Salad

To save on cleanup, microwave the rice in the same container in which you will store your lunch. Carry the dressing in a separate container, and stir it in right before you eat. Packaged grilled tofu can be found in most supermarkets in the refrigerated case along with the other soy and organic products.

SALAD:
1 cup water
½ cup instant brown rice
½ cup shredded carrot
½ cup thinly sliced bok choy
¼ cup chopped green onions
2 tablespoons chopped fresh cilantro
3 ounces packaged grilled tofu, cut into (½-inch) cubes (about ½ cup, such as Marjon)

DRESSING:
1½ tablespoons creamy peanut butter
1 tablespoon rice vinegar
2 teaspoons water
2 teaspoons low-sodium soy sauce
½ teaspoon chili garlic sauce (such as Lee Kum Kee)
⅛ teaspoon salt

1. To prepare salad, combine 1 cup water and rice in a medium microwave-safe bowl; cover. Microwave at HIGH 4 minutes. Microwave at MEDIUM 5 minutes. Fluff with a fork. Let cool to room temperature. Add carrot and next 4 ingredients; toss gently to combine.
2. To prepare dressing, combine peanut butter and next 5 ingredients, stirring with a whisk. Add dressing to salad; toss gently to combine. Yield: 1 serving (serving size: about 2 cups).

CALORIES 434 (37% from fat); FAT 17.9g (sat 3.1g, mono 6.6g, poly 5.6g); PROTEIN 21g; CARB 51.4g; FIBER 6.8g; CHOL 0mg; IRON 2.4mg; SODIUM 941mg; CALC 96mg

cooking class

Keeping It Simple with Sally James

A popular cookbook author encourages you to relax and have fun in the kitchen, and shows how to make the most of in-season, flavorful ingredients.

According to Sally James, enjoying variety doesn't have to be difficult. Sally claims to be a bit of a lazy cook—not one to enjoy long stints in the kitchen. Her cooking style is a clean-as-you-go whirlwind, so she's found shortcuts to create the kind of meals she likes—full of color, flavor, texture, and always a splash of surprise.

Seared Scallops on Braised Wild Mushrooms

The luxury of this dish comes from truffle oil-enhanced mushrooms. A crisp crust on the scallops renders a textural contrast to the tender mushrooms. To get the best crust, be sure your skillet is very hot, and only turn the scallops once during cooking.

    4   teaspoons olive oil, divided
    2   cups sliced cremini mushrooms
        (about 4 ounces)
    1   cup sliced shiitake mushroom caps
        (about 2 ounces)
    1   cup sliced oyster mushroom caps
        (about 2 ounces)
    ½   teaspoon salt, divided
    ½   teaspoon freshly ground black
        pepper, divided
    ¼   cup dry white wine
    1   teaspoon chopped fresh
        thyme
    1   teaspoon fresh lemon
        juice
    1   teaspoon truffle oil or extravirgin
        olive oil
    1½ pounds large sea scallops
    ¼   cup yellow cornmeal
    2   cups trimmed watercress

1. Heat 2 teaspoons olive oil in a large cast-iron skillet over medium-high heat. Add mushrooms, ¼ teaspoon salt, and ¼ teaspoon pepper; sauté 2 minutes or until mushrooms begin to soften. Add wine, thyme, and juice; reduce heat to low, and cook 5 minutes or until mushrooms are tender. Pour mixture into a bowl. Stir in truffle oil; cover and keep warm.
2. Wipe pan dry with paper towels. Pat scallops dry with paper towels; sprinkle with ¼ teaspoon salt and ¼ teaspoon pepper. Place cornmeal in a shallow dish; dredge scallops in cornmeal. Heat 1 teaspoon olive oil in pan over high heat. Add half of scallops; cook 3 minutes on each side or until golden brown. Repeat with remaining oil and scallops. Serve over watercress and mushroom mixture. Yield: 4 servings (serving size: about 4½ ounces scallops, ½ cup watercress, and ½ cup mushroom mixture).

WINE NOTE: While all sorts of white wines work well with scallops, there's a European classic that's not to be missed: albariño. Try Burgans Albariño 2002 (Rías Baixas, Galicia, Spain), $12.

CALORIES 252 (26% from fat); FAT 7.3g (sat 1g, mono 4.3g, poly 1.1g); PROTEIN 31.8g; CARB 14.3g; FIBER 1.7g; CHOL 56mg; IRON 1.8mg; SODIUM 578mg; CALC 69mg

MAKE AHEAD
Zucchini-Buttermilk Soup with Watercress Pesto

Serve this soup either warm or chilled. If reheating leftovers, cook over medium-low heat just until hot; the buttermilk could curdle if allowed to boil.

SOUP:
    Cooking spray
    ½   cup chopped leek
    ½   cup chopped celery
    5   cups chopped zucchini (about
        1¼ pounds)
    1   (14-ounce) can fat-free,
        less-sodium chicken broth
    1   cup fat-free buttermilk
    ½   teaspoon salt
    ¼   teaspoon freshly ground black
        pepper

PESTO:
    ½   cup watercress leaves
    2   tablespoons grated fresh Parmesan
        cheese
    1   tablespoon pine nuts
    1   tablespoon fresh lemon juice
    1   to 2 tablespoons water
    1½ teaspoons extravirgin olive oil

1. To prepare soup, heat a large saucepan over medium-high heat. Coat pan with cooking spray. Add leek and celery; sauté 4 minutes. Add zucchini; sauté 5 minutes. Add broth; bring to a boil. Partially cover, reduce heat, and simmer 20 minutes or until zucchini is very tender. Remove from heat, and cool slightly. Place half of zucchini mixture in a blender; process until smooth. Pour into a medium bowl. Repeat procedure with remaining zucchini mixture. Stir in buttermilk, salt, and pepper.
2. To prepare pesto, place watercress and remaining 5 ingredients in blender; process until smooth (add more water if necessary). Drizzle pesto over soup. Yield: 6 servings (serving size: about ¾ cup soup and 2 teaspoons pesto).

CALORIES 69 (34% from fat); FAT 2.6g (sat 0.7g, mono 1.3g, poly 0.5g); PROTEIN 5g; CARB 7.4g; FIBER 1.7g; CHOL 2mg; IRON 0.8mg; SODIUM 409mg; CALC 106mg

Wild Rice, Asparagus, and Goat Cheese Frittata

Delicately seasoned with basil and lemon rind, this frittata spotlights the contrasting flavors of asparagus, green onions, and grape tomatoes. Wild rice brings an earthy nuttiness and makes this dish a light meal in itself. Cook the rice first so you can prepare the frittata quickly.

  2 tablespoons water
  ½ teaspoon salt
  ¼ teaspoon freshly ground black
      pepper
  5 large eggs, lightly beaten
  4 large egg whites, lightly beaten
Cooking spray
  1 cup (1-inch) slices asparagus
      (about ¼ pound)
  1 garlic clove, minced
  1 cup thinly sliced green onions
  ½ cup halved grape tomatoes
  ½ cup cooked wild rice
  ¼ cup thinly sliced fresh basil
  1 teaspoon grated lemon rind
  ¼ cup (1 ounce) crumbled goat
      cheese

1. Preheat broiler.
2. Combine first 5 ingredients, stirring well with a whisk; set aside.
3. Heat a large nonstick skillet over medium-high heat. Coat pan with cooking spray. Add asparagus and garlic, and sauté 2 minutes. Add onions, and sauté 1 minute or until asparagus is crisp-tender. Add tomatoes, rice, basil, and rind; cook 1 minute or until thoroughly heated. Reduce heat to medium. Pat mixture into an even layer in pan; sprinkle with cheese. Pour egg mixture over rice mixture; cook 4 minutes or until almost set.
4. Wrap handle of pan with foil; broil 4 minutes or until golden brown and set. Yield: 4 servings (serving size: 1 wedge).

CALORIES 172 (42% from fat); FAT 8g (sat 3.1g, mono 2.8g, poly 1g); PROTEIN 14.4g; CARB 10.2g; FIBER 2.4g; CHOL 269mg; IRON 1.6mg; SODIUM 461mg; CALC 57mg

---

MAKE AHEAD

Glazed Peaches in Phyllo Baskets with Ricotta Cream

This delightful dessert is stunning enough to serve at a dinner party but simple enough to prepare as an everyday treat. The pastry baskets can be made a few days ahead and stored in an airtight container at room temperature. Substitute various in-season fruits to make this dish other times of the year. Grind the nuts in a mini food processor or a spice or coffee grinder.

  ½ cup whole-milk ricotta cheese
  3 tablespoons granulated sugar,
      divided
  1 teaspoon vanilla extract
  3 tablespoons chopped hazelnuts,
      toasted and ground
  6 (18 x 14-inch) sheets frozen
      phyllo dough, thawed
1½ tablespoons butter, melted
Cooking spray
  3 cups chopped peeled ripe peaches
  ½ cup apple jelly, melted and
      slightly cooled
  1 tablespoon powdered sugar

1. Preheat oven to 350°.
2. Place ricotta, 1 tablespoon granulated sugar, and vanilla in a medium bowl; beat with a mixer at medium speed until well blended. Cover and chill.
3. Combine 2 tablespoons granulated sugar and hazelnuts. Stack 2 phyllo sheets on a large cutting board or work surface (cover remaining sheets to prevent drying); brush with half of butter. Sprinkle phyllo stack with half of hazelnut mixture. Repeat procedure with 2 phyllo sheets, remaining butter, and remaining hazelnut mixture. Top with remaining 2 phyllo sheets. Gently press phyllo layers together. Lightly coat top phyllo sheet with cooking spray. Cut stack into 6 (7 x 6-inch) rectangles. Carefully place 1 layered rectangle into each of 6 (8-ounce) ramekins coated with cooking spray. Gently press rectangles into ramekins to form baskets (phyllo will extend about 1 inch over tops of ramekins). Place ramekins on a baking sheet. Bake at 350° for 20 minutes or until lightly browned and crisp. Cool in ramekins on a wire rack. Carefully remove phyllo baskets from ramekins.
4. Just before serving, spread about 1 tablespoon cheese mixture into bottom of each phyllo basket. Combine peaches and melted jelly, tossing to coat. Spoon about ½ cup peach mixture into each phyllo cup. Sprinkle evenly with powdered sugar. Serve immediately. Yield: 6 servings (serving size: 1 filled phyllo basket).

CALORIES 264 (29% from fat); FAT 8.5g (sat 3.5g, mono 3.8g, poly 0.7g); PROTEIN 5g; CARB 42.9g; FIBER 2.4g; CHOL 18mg; IRON 0.8mg; SODIUM 201mg; CALC 93mg

---

MAKE AHEAD • FREEZABLE

Macadamia and Ginger Cookies

This recipe is an adaptation of Italian amaretti. It calls for macadamias, but hazelnuts, walnuts, almonds, pistachios, or pine nuts would also be good.

  ½ cup self-rising flour
  ½ cup macadamia nuts
  ¼ to ½ cup crystallized ginger
  2 large egg whites
  ¾ cup sugar
  1 teaspoon honey
  1 teaspoon grated orange rind

1. Preheat oven to 300°.

2. Line 2 baking sheets with parchment paper; secure with masking tape.

3. Lightly spoon flour into a dry measuring cup; level with a knife. Place flour and nuts in a food processor; pulse 10 times or until mixture resembles coarse meal. Reserve 1 tablespoon flour mixture in food processor; set remaining flour mixture aside. Add ginger to food processor; pulse 8 times or until finely minced. Stir into remaining flour mixture; set aside.

4. Place egg whites in a large bowl, and beat with a mixer at high speed 1 minute or until soft peaks form. Beating at high speed, gradually add sugar and honey; beat 4 minutes or until thick and glossy. Gently fold in flour mixture and rind. Drop dough by level tablespoons 2 inches apart onto prepared baking sheets. Bake at 300° for 18 minutes or until set. Remove from baking sheets, and cool on a wire rack. Yield: 30 cookies (serving size: 1 cookie).

CALORIES 51 (30% from fat); FAT 1.7g (sat 0.3g, mono 1.3g, poly 0g); PROTEIN 0.6g; CARB 8.7g; FIBER 0.2g; CHOL 0mg; IRON 0.2mg; SODIUM 37mg; CALC 11mg

Feta and Lemon-Stuffed Lamb with Potato-Parsnip Mash

Goat's milk feta cheese is intensely flavorful. Look for it at Greek or specialty markets; you might also find a goat's and sheep's milk blend, which also has a pleasantly strong taste. For milder flavor, use cow's milk feta.

LAMB:

1 (2¾-pound) rolled boneless leg of lamb, trimmed
⅓ cup (1½ ounces) crumbled goat's milk feta cheese
2 tablespoons chopped fresh or 2 teaspoons dried thyme
2 teaspoons grated lemon rind
¼ cup fresh lemon juice, divided
10 fresh thyme sprigs
¼ cup dry white wine
¼ teaspoon salt
¼ teaspoon freshly ground black pepper

MASH:

5 cups cubed Yukon gold potatoes (about 1¾ pounds)
2 cups chopped peeled parsnip
½ cup plain fat-free yogurt
2 teaspoons olive oil
½ teaspoon salt
¼ teaspoon freshly ground black pepper
Thyme sprigs (optional)

1. Preheat oven to 250°.

2. To prepare lamb, unroll roast. Combine cheese, chopped thyme, and rind; spread over roast. Drizzle with 2 teaspoons juice. Reroll roast; secure at 1-inch intervals with twine. Place 10 thyme sprigs in a shallow 2-quart baking dish; place lamb roast over thyme sprigs in dish. Pour remaining juice and wine over roast. Sprinkle with ¼ teaspoon salt and ¼ teaspoon pepper. Bake at 250° for 1 hour. Turn roast over, and bake an additional 1½ hours or until a thermometer inserted in thickest portion of roast registers 145° (medium rare). Remove from oven. Place roast on a cutting board; let stand 10 minutes.

3. Strain pan juices through a fine sieve into a small saucepan. Discard solids. Cook over medium heat until reduced to 2 tablespoons (about 5 minutes).

4. Remove twine; cut roast into thin slices. Arrange slices on a serving platter; drizzle with reduced pan juices.

5. To prepare mash, cook potatoes and parsnip in boiling water 25 minutes or until very tender. Drain; place in a large bowl. Add yogurt, oil, ½ teaspoon salt, and ¼ teaspoon pepper. Mash with a potato masher to desired consistency. Serve with lamb. Garnish with thyme sprigs, if desired. Yield: 10 servings (servings size: 3 ounces lamb and ½ cup mash).

CALORIES 256 (27% from fat); FAT 7.7g (sat 2.8g, mono 3.4g, poly 0.5g); PROTEIN 23.7g; CARB 22.4g; FIBER 2.8g; CHOL 69mg; IRON 2.1mg; SODIUM 290mg; CALC 74mg

Focus on Quality

Here are easy ways Sally has adapted meals to be more healthful—and more flavorful.

• Use foods with assertive flavors, such as truffle or nut oils, and strong-flavored cheeses like Parmesan, goat, or blue. Just a bit goes a long way and brings food to life.

• Wine not only adds antioxidants to a dish, but it also lends a wonderful depth, body, and flavor that butter or oil normally gives food.

• Substitute nuts for butter or margarine. Their crunch and flavor are wonderful. For example, ground macadamias give the Macadamia and Ginger Cookies (recipe on page 256) a rich flavor and melt-in-your-mouth texture.

• Cook more fish. Opt for fish that's wild, seasonal, and high in omega-3 fatty acids, such as salmon and sardines. Wild, seasonal fish has more flavor and is less likely to have added artificial colors.

• Fresh ricotta cheese is a great alternative to cream and cream cheese. Toss it with pasta, whip it with a little vanilla for desserts, or bake it in tarts.

• Experiment with new ways to enliven your everyday dishes, such as combining cornmeal with flour to add crunch to biscuits, or puréeing parsnips with mashed potatoes for a hint of sweetness.

• Reductions are easy and make flavorful sauces for meat. Just simmer red wine, balsamic vinegar, sugar, and beet juice or orange juice until thick and glossy.

• Season food after you've tasted it; keep the focus on the ingredients rather than masking them with heavy sauces and seasonings.

Tuna Tartare in Endive with Horseradish Sauce

Since it will not be cooked, purchase sushi-grade tuna from your local fish market. It should be firm, shiny, plump, and bright red with no fishy odor. Keep the tuna mixture well chilled, and assemble the appetizers just before serving. The tuna can also be seared, if you prefer: Cook the whole fillet in a pan over high heat for 1 minute on each side; cool and cut into ¼-inch cubes. If you're a fan of wasabi, substitute wasabi paste for the horseradish.

    2   tablespoons finely chopped
        celery
    2   tablespoons capers, drained
    1   tablespoon finely chopped fresh
        chives
    2   teaspoons extravirgin olive oil
    1   teaspoon minced fresh
        thyme
    ½   teaspoon cracked black pepper
    ¼   teaspoon salt
    1   (8-ounce) Yellowfin tuna steak
        (about 1 inch thick), cut into
        ¼-inch cubes
    ¼   cup plain low-fat yogurt
    1   teaspoon fresh lime juice
    1   teaspoon prepared horseradish
    24 Belgian endive leaves (about
        4 heads)
    1   tablespoon finely chopped chives
        (optional)

1. Combine first 8 ingredients, tossing to coat; cover and chill. Combine yogurt, juice, and horseradish, stirring well. Spoon about 1½ tablespoons tuna mixture into each endive leaf. Drizzle each filled leaf with about ½ teaspoon yogurt mixture. Garnish with 1 tablespoon chives, if desired. Yield: 8 servings (serving size: 3 filled leaves).

WINE NOTE: The big-flavored meatiness of the tuna combined with the pizzazz of capers and lime juice requires a wine that's equally dramatic. A good choice: Alsatian Gewürztraminer. Bold, spicy, and aromatic, Gewürztraminer also has a rich, almost lanolin-like texture that's superb with meaty fish. Try Domaine Weinbach Gewürztraminer 2002 (Alsace,

France), $29. Powerful yet elegant litchi, spice, rose petal, and ginger aromas and flavors are followed by a texture that's silky and soft.

CALORIES 91 (21% from fat); FAT 2.1g (sat 0.4g, mono 0.9g, poly 0.4g); PROTEIN 10.3g; CARB 9.6g; FIBER 8.1g; CHOL 13mg; IRON 2.5mg; SODIUM 213mg; CALC 155mg

Grilled Chicken with Pinot-Plum Sauce

Serve this simply seasoned sauce at room temperature or chilled. Taste the plums before using; if they aren't fully ripe, add a little extra sugar. Pour the remaining Pinot Noir with the meal; it makes a graceful, natural pairing.

SAUCE:

    2   cups chopped ripe plums (about
        3 small)
    1   cup Pinot Noir or other dry red
        wine
    2   tablespoons brown sugar
    1   tablespoon red wine vinegar
    ⅛   teaspoon salt

CHICKEN:

    4   (6-ounce) skinless, boneless
        chicken breast halves
    ⅛   teaspoon salt
    ⅛   teaspoon black pepper
        Cooking spray

1. To prepare sauce, combine first 4 ingredients in a small saucepan; bring to a boil. Reduce heat; simmer 25 minutes or until thick, stirring occasionally. Remove from heat; stir in ⅛ teaspoon salt. Pour into a small bowl; cool to room temperature.
2. Prepare grill to medium-high heat.
3. To prepare chicken, sprinkle chicken with ⅛ teaspoon salt and pepper. Place chicken on a grill rack coated with cooking spray. Grill 4 minutes on each side or until done. Serve chicken with plum sauce. Yield: 4 servings (serving size: 1 chicken breast half and about ¼ cup sauce).

CALORIES 215 (9% from fat); FAT 2.1g (sat 0.5g, mono 0.7g, poly 0.5g); PROTEIN 30.2g; CARB 18.3g; FIBER 1.3g; CHOL 74mg; IRON 1.4mg; SODIUM 237mg; CALC 28mg

Cornmeal Shortcakes with Tomato-Ginger Jam

Cornmeal adds a delightful crunch to the shortcakes, which are a twist on everyday biscuits. Tomato jam offers a great way to use up ripe late-summer tomatoes; broiling them first brings out their rich, sweet flavor. Serve the jam chilled or at room temperature. Cover and refrigerate any leftover jam in a nonreactive container, such as a glass bowl, up to 1 week.

JAM:

    1½ pounds cherry tomatoes
    1   tablespoon olive oil
    1½ cups chopped onion
    ½   cup diced peeled Granny Smith
        apple
    2   tablespoons minced peeled fresh
        ginger
    2   tablespoons brown sugar
    ⅔   cup water
    2   tablespoons thinly sliced fresh
        basil
    2   tablespoons cider vinegar
    ¼   teaspoon salt
    ¼   teaspoon freshly ground black
        pepper

SHORTCAKES:

    1½ cups self-rising flour
    1¼ cups yellow cornmeal
    2   teaspoons baking powder
    ¼   teaspoon salt
    ⅔   cup fat-free milk
    2   tablespoons olive oil
    1   tablespoon fresh lemon juice
        Cooking spray

1. Preheat broiler.
2. To prepare jam, arrange tomatoes in a single layer on a jelly-roll pan. Broil 20 minutes or until tomatoes are browned, stirring occasionally.
3. Heat 1 tablespoon oil in a medium saucepan over medium-high heat. Add onion, apple, and ginger; sauté 5 minutes or until tender. Add sugar; cook 1 minute. Add tomatoes, water, and next 4 ingredients, and bring to a boil. Reduce heat, and simmer until reduced to 2 cups (about 45 minutes). Remove tomato mixture from heat; cool.

4. Preheat oven to 400°.

5. To prepare shortcakes, lightly spoon flour and cornmeal into dry measuring cups; level with a knife. Combine flour, cornmeal, baking powder, and ¼ teaspoon salt in a large bowl, stirring with a whisk. Make a well in center of mixture. Combine milk, 2 tablespoons oil, and juice; add to flour mixture. Stir just until moist. Turn dough out onto a lightly floured surface; knead lightly 3 or 4 times. Roll dough into a ½-inch thickness. Cut with a 2½-inch round cutter into 12 rounds; place on a baking sheet coated with cooking spray. Bake at 400° for 15 minutes or until lightly browned. Serve with jam. Yield: 12 servings (serving size: 1 shortcake and about 2½ tablespoons jam).

CALORIES 178 (21% from fat); FAT 4.1g (sat 0.6g, mono 2.6g, poly 0.6g); PROTEIN 4.2g; CARB 31.7g; FIBER 2.6g; CHOL 0mg; IRON 1.4mg; SODIUM 395mg; CALC 134mg

---

Tools for a Healthy Kitchen

Few tools are essential to Sally's style of healthy cooking, aside from a set of sharp knives and imagination. But there are items that make light cooking simpler.

• **Nonstick** and **cast-iron cookware** are her favorites, especially ridged grill pans and nonstick woks. In summer, though, an outdoor grill is her choice.

• **Parchment paper** is wonderful for steaming fish in the oven in a packet (en papillote) with just a splash of flavor.

• A **pepper mill** and **spice grinder** allow you to have fresh, aromatic flavor.

• **Pastry brushes** are ideal for applying minimal amounts of fat to phyllo dough, pans, baking sheets, and vegetables before baking or grilling.

• Ceramic **oil pourers** will keep olive and other oils fresher longer and help control how much you pour.

• A **blender** is essential for making sauces, soups, and smoothies.

• Lemon, lime, or orange zest can really bring a dish to life, so keep a **citrus zester** on hand.

---

lighten up

Charting a Healthy Course

Three Cooking Light *cruisers receive recipe makeovers.*

Each fall, *Cooking Light* sponsors a weeklong cruise to the Caribbean for its readers. The event includes cooking demonstrations, seminars, wine tastings, and fitness classes in addition to land-bound tours and activities. On the last sailing, we decided to build one of the cruise's cooking demonstrations around our popular Lighten Up column, so we asked our cruisers to submit their favorite heavy recipes for lightening. We threw down the anchor for three great candidates, successfully revamped their recipes, and let our attendees taste the results for themselves. Here are the recipes.

STAFF FAVORITE • MAKE AHEAD

Sour Cream Pound Cake with Rum Glaze

Drizzle the brown sugar glaze over the cake while it's still warm so it soaks in nicely.
—Don Milburn, Great Falls, Virginia

CAKE:
Cooking spray
3 tablespoons dry breadcrumbs
3 cups cake flour
1 teaspoon baking powder
¼ teaspoon baking soda
¼ teaspoon salt
¾ cup butter, softened
2 cups granulated sugar
3 large eggs
¼ cup fat-free milk
1 tablespoon dark rum
2 teaspoons vanilla extract
1 cup fat-free sour cream

GLAZE:
½ cup packed brown sugar
2 tablespoons dark rum
2 tablespoons water
1½ tablespoons butter

---

1. Preheat oven to 350°.

2. To prepare cake, coat a 10-inch tube pan with cooking spray; dust with breadcrumbs. Set aside.

3. Lightly spoon flour into dry measuring cups; level with a knife. Combine flour, baking powder, baking soda, and salt, stirring well with a whisk. Place ¾ cup butter and granulated sugar in a large bowl; beat with a mixer at medium speed until light and fluffy. Add eggs, 1 at a time, beating well after each addition. Add milk, 1 tablespoon rum, and vanilla; beat until combined. Beating at low speed, add flour mixture and sour cream alternately to sugar mixture, beginning and ending with flour mixture; beat until just combined.

4. Spoon batter into prepared pan. Bake at 350° for 1 hour or until a wooden pick inserted in center comes out clean. Cool in pan 10 minutes. Loosen cake from sides of pan using a narrow metal spatula. Place a plate upside down on top of cake; invert onto plate. Invert cake again. Pierce cake liberally with a wooden pick.

5. While cake bakes, prepare glaze. Combine brown sugar, 2 tablespoons rum, and water in a small saucepan; bring to a boil, stirring until sugar dissolves. Add 1½ tablespoons butter, stirring until butter melts. Drizzle half of warm glaze evenly over warm cake; allow mixture to absorb into cake. Drizzle remaining glaze over cake. Cool cake completely. Yield: 16 servings (serving size: 1 slice).

CALORIES 325 (30% from fat); FAT 11g (sat 6.3g, mono 3.2g, poly 0.5g); PROTEIN 3.6g; CARB 52.8g; FIBER 0.6g; CHOL 68mg; IRON 1.5mg; SODIUM 232mg; CALC 58mg

BEFORE	AFTER
SERVING SIZE	
1 slice	
CALORIES PER SERVING	
427	325
FAT	
19.4g	*11g*
PERCENT OF TOTAL CALORIES	
41%	*30%*

Fish Chowder

This chunky soup is thickened with a roux of butter and flour.

—Steve Getz, Michigan City, Indiana

2½   cups frozen whole-kernel corn,
       thawed and divided
  8   bacon slices, chopped
  3   cups chopped onion
1½   cups finely chopped celery
1½   cups finely chopped carrot
  1   cup finely chopped shallots
  4   garlic cloves, minced
  ¼   cup chopped fresh flat-leaf parsley
  1   tablespoon chopped fresh thyme
  1   tablespoon paprika
  3   tablespoons butter
  ¼   cup all-purpose flour
  3   cups whole milk
  1   teaspoon salt
  ½   teaspoon freshly ground black
       pepper
  2   (8-ounce) bottles clam juice
  2   bay leaves
1½   pounds Yukon gold potatoes, cut
       into ½-inch cubes (about 4 cups)
  2   pounds halibut or other firm
       white fish fillets, cut into bite-
       sized pieces

1. Place 1 cup corn in a food processor or blender, and process until smooth. Set aside.
2. Cook bacon in a Dutch oven over medium-high heat until crisp. Remove bacon from pan with a slotted spoon, reserving 1 tablespoon drippings in pan; set bacon aside. Add onion and next 4 ingredients to pan; sauté 5 minutes or until tender. Stir in parsley, thyme, and paprika. Remove vegetable mixture from pan; set aside.
3. Melt butter in pan over medium heat. Gradually whisk in flour. Cook over medium heat 2 minutes or until browned. Gradually add milk, stirring with a whisk. Add vegetable mixture, salt, and next 4 ingredients; bring to a boil. Reduce heat, and simmer 10 minutes or until potatoes are almost tender. Stir in puréed corn, 1½ cups corn kernels, and fish; cover and cook 15 minutes or until fish flakes easily when tested with a fork. Discard bay leaves. Top with

bacon. Yield: 10 servings (serving size: 1 cup chowder and 2 teaspoons bacon).

CALORIES 355 (29% from fat); FAT 11.6g (sat 5.5g, mono 3.9g, poly 1.3g); PROTEIN 27.3g; CARB 37.1g; FIBER 4.1g; CHOL 60mg; IRON 2.1mg; SODIUM 572mg; CALC 171mg

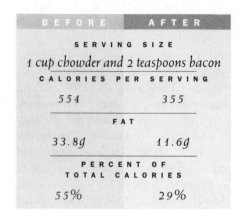

BEFORE	AFTER
SERVING SIZE	
1 cup chowder and 2 teaspoons bacon	
CALORIES PER SERVING	
554	355
FAT	
33.8g	11.6g
PERCENT OF TOTAL CALORIES	
55%	29%

Lobster Newburg

If you don't want to cook live lobsters, use frozen tails. To get 1 cup of chopped meat, use 3 (6-ounce) tails, and steam them for about 8 minutes. You can also use shrimp or crab in place of lobster.

—Carolyn Vessels, Stafford, Arizona

  4   (2.5-ounce) sourdough rolls
  1   tablespoon butter
  ¼   cup finely chopped onion
  1   garlic clove, minced
  3   tablespoons water
1½   tablespoons dry sherry
1½   tablespoons all-purpose flour
1¼   cups 1% low-fat milk
  ¼   cup (2 ounces) ⅓-less-fat cream
       cheese, cut into small pieces
  1   cup chopped cooked lobster meat
  2   teaspoons fresh lemon juice
  ¼   teaspoon salt
  ⅛   teaspoon paprika
  2   teaspoons chopped fresh chives

1. Preheat oven to 375°.
2. Hollow out rolls, leaving about ¼-inch-thick shells; reserve torn bread for another use. Place bread shells on a baking sheet. Bake at 375° for 7 minutes or until lightly toasted. Remove bread shells from oven; set aside.
3. Melt butter in a nonstick skillet over medium heat. Add onion and garlic;

cook 2 minutes or until tender, stirring frequently. Add water and sherry, and cook 1 minute. Sprinkle flour over onion mixture; cook 1 minute, stirring constantly. Gradually add milk, and stir constantly with a whisk; bring to a boil. Reduce heat, and simmer 3 minutes or until thick, stirring constantly. Add cream cheese; stir with a whisk until cheese melts. Stir in lobster, juice, salt, and paprika. Spoon ½ cup lobster mixture into each bread shell; sprinkle each serving with ½ teaspoon chives. Serve immediately. Yield: 4 servings (serving size: 1 stuffed bread shell).

CALORIES 265 (29% from fat); FAT 8.5g (sat 4.7g, mono 2.6g, poly 0.6g); PROTEIN 15.6g; CARB 30.3g; FIBER 1.6g; CHOL 48mg; IRON 1.5mg; SODIUM 668mg; CALC 164mg

BEFORE	AFTER
SERVING SIZE	
1 stuffed bread shell	
CALORIES PER SERVING	
755	265
FAT	
62.8g	8.5g
PERCENT OF TOTAL CALORIES	
75%	29%

reader recipes

Marinara *Magnifica*

CookingLight.com *community members cook up a savory marinara sauce in cyberspace.*

Alysha Russo of Angola, Indiana, and a longtime *Cooking Light* reader, turned to CookingLight.com's online community for help to create the perfect marinara sauce. She described what she wanted, and not very long after submitting her request, people responded with tips for making marinara. Despite its name, which translates to "sailor style," there's nothing fishy about marinara. It's a nuts-and-bolts tomato sauce seasoned with garlic and herbs.

Marinara Magnifica

Dry red wine intensifies the well-blended flavors in this lusciously seasoned tomato sauce—*magnifico!* Serve over your favorite pasta.

1 tablespoon olive oil
6 cups chopped onion (about 3 medium)
1 tablespoon sugar
½ cup dry red wine
1 tablespoon extravirgin olive oil
2 teaspoons dried oregano
1 teaspoon salt
½ teaspoon dried thyme
½ teaspoon dried marjoram
½ teaspoon dried basil
½ teaspoon freshly ground black pepper
¼ teaspoon crushed red pepper
6 garlic cloves, crushed
2 (28-ounce) cans crushed tomatoes, undrained
2 (14.5-ounce) cans diced tomatoes, undrained
2 (6-ounce) cans tomato paste

1. Heat oil in a Dutch oven over medium heat; add onion and sugar. Cook 30 minutes or until golden, stirring occasionally. Stir in wine; cook 1 minute. Add oil and remaining ingredients; bring to a boil. Reduce heat, and simmer 3 hours, stirring occasionally. Yield: 9 cups (serving size: 1 cup).

CALORIES 169 (20% from fat); FAT 3.8g (sat 0.5g, mono 2.3g, poly 0.6g); PROTEIN 5.3g; CARB 30.9g; FIBER 6.5g; CHOL 0mg; IRON 2.9mg; SODIUM 960mg; CALC 131mg

Mango-Cucumber Salad

—Katie Schnorr, Forestville, Wisconsin

4 cups diagonally cut thinly sliced seeded peeled cucumber (about 2 medium)
2 cups thinly sliced peeled mango (about 2 medium)
3 tablespoons fresh lime juice
¼ teaspoon salt
¼ teaspoon ground red pepper

1. Combine all ingredients in a medium bowl; toss gently. Let stand 15 minutes before serving. Yield: 4 servings (serving size: 1 cup).

CALORIES 71 (5% from fat); FAT 0.4g (sat 0.1g, mono 0.1g, poly 0.1g); PROTEIN 1.2g; CARB 18.1g; FIBER 2.4g; CHOL 0mg; IRON 0.3mg; SODIUM 151mg; CALC 26mg

Roast Pork Sandwiches au Jus with Rosemary
(pictured on page 271)

"My husband and I have always liked this roast pork tenderloin, but it seemed a shame to throw out the browned bits and juices. So we made a flavorful *jus* out of them. It's really simple and so good."

—Sherri O'Hare, Ajo, Arizona

2 teaspoons black pepper
1 teaspoon dried rosemary
¾ teaspoon salt
1 garlic clove, minced
1 tablespoon olive oil, divided
1 (1-pound) pork tenderloin, trimmed
1 (14-ounce) can less-sodium beef broth
¼ cup dry sherry
1 tablespoon tomato paste
6 (2-ounce) French bread rolls
Lettuce leaves (optional)

1. Preheat oven to 400°.
2. Combine first 4 ingredients in a small bowl; add 1 teaspoon oil. Rub over pork. Let stand 15 minutes.
3. Heat 2 teaspoons oil in a large ovenproof skillet over medium-high heat. Add pork; cook 4 minutes, browning on all sides. Bake at 400° for 10 minutes or until a thermometer registers 160° (slightly pink). Let stand 5 minutes. Remove pork from pan; cut diagonally across grain into 12 slices.
4. Return pan to medium-high heat, and add broth, scraping pan to loosen browned bits. Add sherry and tomato paste; stir with a whisk. Bring to a boil. Reduce heat; simmer 5 minutes.
5. Cut rolls in half horizontally. Place 2 slices pork on bottom half of each roll; top with lettuce leaf, if desired. Cover with roll tops. Serve with jus. Yield: 6 sandwiches (serving size: 1 sandwich and ¼ cup jus).

CALORIES 270 (23% from fat); FAT 7g (sat 1.9g, mono 3.6g, poly 1.1g); PROTEIN 22g; CARB 28.9g; FIBER 1.5g; CHOL 49mg; IRON 2.7mg; SODIUM 669mg; CALC 83mg

Hearty Fresh Tomato Salsa

"You can adjust the amount of jalapeños and chipotles to your preference of zest and zing; we like it spicy. The recipe makes a lot, but it can be cut in half. We eat it with chips and go through it quickly."

—Doris R. Durkee, St. Charles, Missouri

4 pounds tomatoes, peeled, seeded, and chopped (about 6 cups)
½ teaspoon salt
1 cup fresh corn kernels (about 2 ears)
1 cup minced fresh cilantro
¼ cup finely chopped Vidalia or other sweet onion
¼ cup finely chopped red onion
3 tablespoons fresh lime juice
2 teaspoons sugar
¼ teaspoon freshly ground black pepper
3 jalapeño peppers, seeded and chopped
2 garlic cloves, minced
1 (15-ounce) can black beans, rinsed and drained
1 (7-ounce) can chipotle chiles in adobo sauce

1. Place tomatoes in a colander; sprinkle with salt. Toss gently; drain 30 minutes. Combine tomato mixture, corn, and next 9 ingredients in a large bowl. Remove 1 chipotle chile from can; finely chop. Add chile and 8 teaspoons adobo sauce to corn mixture, stirring to combine. (Reserve remaining chiles and adobo sauce for another use.) Yield: 16 servings (serving size: ½ cup).

CALORIES 86 (12% from fat); FAT 1.1g (sat 0.1g, mono 0.1g, poly 0.3g); PROTEIN 4g; CARB 17.1g; FIBER 4.1g; CHOL 0mg; IRON 1.3mg; SODIUM 253mg; CALC 25mg

Chopstick Noodle Salad

—Ricki McMillian, R.D., Hemphill, Texas

- 2 (8-ounce) packages soba (buckwheat noodles), uncooked
- ⅔ cup sliced green onions
- ¼ cup water
- ¼ cup low-sodium soy sauce
- 2 tablespoons dark sesame oil
- 1 tablespoon fish sauce
- 2 garlic cloves, minced
- 8 cups water
- 1 cup small cauliflower florets
- 1 cup (¼-inch) diagonally cut carrot
- 1 cup small broccoli florets
- 1 cup small yellow squash, halved lengthwise and thinly sliced

1. Cook noodles according to package directions, omitting salt and fat.
2. Combine onions and next 5 ingredients in a small bowl.
3. Bring 8 cups water to a boil in a large saucepan. Add cauliflower, carrot, and broccoli; cook 2 minutes. Add squash, and cook 1 minute. Drain vegetables. Combine noodles, onion mixture, and vegetables in a large bowl; toss to coat. Yield: 6 servings (serving size: about 1½ cups).

CALORIES 353 (13% from fat); FAT 5.1g (sat 0.8g, mono 2g, poly 2.1g); PROTEIN 16.1g; CARB 67g; FIBER 5.5g; CHOL 0mg; IRON 2mg; SODIUM 774mg; CALC 36mg

Steak with Mustard-Caper Sauce

"This steak is great to serve with bulgur and a sauté of zucchini and summer squash."
  —Alicia Brennan, San Francisco, California

- 4 (4-ounce) beef tenderloin steaks, trimmed (1 inch thick)
- ⅛ teaspoon salt
- ⅛ teaspoon freshly ground black pepper
- Cooking spray
- ¼ cup less-sodium beef broth
- ¼ cup dry red wine
- 1 tablespoon Dijon mustard
- 1 teaspoon Worcestershire sauce
- 1½ tablespoons capers
- 2 teaspoons butter

1. Sprinkle steaks with salt and pepper. Heat a large nonstick skillet over medium heat. Coat pan with cooking spray. Add steaks; cook 3 minutes on each side or until browned. Reduce heat to medium-low; cook 1½ minutes on each side or until desired degree of doneness. Place steaks on a platter; keep warm.
2. Add broth, wine, mustard, and Worcestershire sauce to pan; cook 30 seconds, stirring with a whisk to combine. Remove from heat; add capers and butter, stirring until butter melts. Serve over steaks. Yield: 4 servings (serving size: 1 steak and 1 tablespoon sauce).

CALORIES 230 (33% from fat); FAT 8.4g (sat 3.5g, mono 3.3g, poly 0.4g); PROTEIN 33.3g; CARB 1.2g; FIBER 0.2g; CHOL 83mg; IRON 2.6mg; SODIUM 372mg; CALC 16mg

Spicy Corn Relish

"Making special condiments is something of a summer ritual for my mother and me. Corn relish adds spice to otherwise plain chicken tenders or roast pork."
  —Nancy Smith Midgette, Gibsonville, North Carolina

- 2 cups chopped Vidalia or other sweet onion
- 2 cups chopped celery
- 1 cup chopped green bell pepper
- 2 cups cider vinegar
- 1⅓ cups sugar
- 2 teaspoons salt
- 1 teaspoon dry mustard
- 1 teaspoon ground turmeric
- ½ teaspoon crushed red pepper
- 2 (4-ounce) jars diced pimiento, drained
- 4 cups fresh corn kernels (about 8 ears)

1. Place first 3 ingredients in a food processor, and pulse 5 times or until finely chopped.
2. Combine vinegar and next 6 ingredients in a large Dutch oven, stirring to dissolve sugar. Stir in onion mixture and corn; bring to a boil. Reduce heat; simmer 20 minutes, stirring occasionally. Yield: 16 servings (serving size: ½ cup).

CALORIES 127 (5% from fat); FAT 0.7g (sat 0.1g, mono 0.2g, poly 0.3g); PROTEIN 2.1g; CARB 31.2g; FIBER 2.5g; CHOL 0mg; IRON 0.9mg; SODIUM 316mg; CALC 19mg

Feta-Chicken Pasta

"This recipe is born of my husband's love of feta cheese. We use baby red onions, with their green stems, from a local organic farm, but any red onion will do."
  —Katie Marr, Ann Arbor, Michigan

- 3 cups uncooked fusilli (short twisted spaghetti)
- 2 (6-ounce) skinless, boneless chicken breast halves, cut into thin slices
- ⅛ teaspoon salt
- 1 teaspoon olive oil
- ⅔ cup vertically sliced red onion
- ¼ cup sliced ripe olives
- 1 teaspoon chopped fresh oregano
- ¼ teaspoon freshly ground black pepper
- 1 cup (4 ounces) crumbled feta cheese

1. Cook pasta according to package directions, omitting salt and fat.
2. Sprinkle chicken with salt. Heat oil in a large nonstick skillet over medium-high heat. Add chicken; sauté 2 minutes. Add onion; cook 2 minutes, stirring frequently. Stir in cooked pasta, olives, oregano, and pepper; cook 2 minutes or until thoroughly heated. Remove from heat, and stir in cheese. Yield: 6 servings (serving size: 1 cup).

CALORIES 282 (18% from fat); FAT 5.6g (sat 2.5g, mono 1.2g, poly 0.5g); PROTEIN 22g; CARB 33.7g; FIBER 2.8g; CHOL 43mg; IRON 2.5mg; SODIUM 336mg; CALC 97mg

Waterside Menu

Even if you're landlocked, you can savor this meal that's inspired by the sea.

Waterside Menu
serves 4

Herbed Cracker Bread

Roasted Fig and Arugula Salad

Grilled Lemon-Bay Shrimp

Barley Risotto with Fennel and Olives

Cherries in Spiced Wine Syrup with Pound Cake Croutons

Pimm's Cup, Slushy Watermelon Mojitos, or **Sparkling Peach Splash**

MAKE AHEAD
Herbed Cracker Bread

We loved the irregular shape of these savory crackers. Store them in an airtight container up to 3 days. Vary the flavor by using other dried herbs in place of herbes de Provence. Serve with Roasted Fig and Arugula Salad (recipe at right).

  2 cups all-purpose flour
  ⅓ cup (about 1½ ounces) grated fresh Parmesan cheese
  2 teaspoons dried herbes de Provence
1½ teaspoons coarsely ground black pepper
  1 teaspoon baking powder
  1 teaspoon sugar
  ¾ teaspoon salt
  ½ cup fat-free sour cream
  2 tablespoons butter, melted
  1 large egg, lightly beaten
Cooking spray
  3 tablespoons yellow cornmeal

1. Preheat oven to 350°.
2. Lightly spoon flour into dry measuring cups, and level with a knife.

Combine flour and next 6 ingredients in a large bowl, stirring with a whisk.
3. Combine sour cream, butter, and egg, stirring with a whisk. Add egg mixture to flour mixture; stir to form a soft dough. Turn dough out onto a lightly floured surface; knead lightly 7 or 8 times.
4. Divide dough in half. Place 1 dough portion on each of 2 baking sheets coated with cooking spray and sprinkled with 1½ tablespoons cornmeal; turn to coat top of dough. Roll each portion into a 12 x 8-inch rectangle (about ⅛ inch thick). Bake at 350° for 15 minutes or until browned and crisp. Remove from pans, and cool completely on wire racks. Break into 24 crackers. Yield: 12 servings (serving size: 2 crackers).

CALORIES 132 (25% from fat); FAT 3.7g (sat 2g, mono 1g, poly 0.3g); PROTEIN 4.7g; CARB 19.9g; FIBER 0.9g; CHOL 26mg; IRON 1.4mg; SODIUM 278mg; CALC 89mg

Roasted Fig and Arugula Salad

Roasting slightly caramelizes the figs and creates flavorful browned bits that eventually season the vinaigrette. If you don't have molasses on hand, use honey or maple syrup.

  ⅓ cup sherry vinegar or cider vinegar
  1 tablespoon molasses
  2 teaspoons extravirgin olive oil
  ¼ teaspoon salt
  4 large (dark-skinned) fresh figs, halved (such as Black Mission)
Cooking spray
  5 cups trimmed arugula
  ¼ cup (1 ounce) crumbled goat cheese
  ⅛ teaspoon freshly ground black pepper

1. Preheat oven to 425°.
2. Combine first 4 ingredients in a medium bowl, stirring with a whisk. Add figs; toss to coat. Remove figs with a slotted spoon, reserving vinegar mixture.
3. Place figs in a cast-iron or ovenproof skillet coated with cooking spray. Bake at 425° for 8 to 10 minutes. Remove figs from pan; place on a plate. Immediately add reserved vinegar mixture to hot pan, scraping pan to loosen browned bits. Pour into a small bowl; let figs and vinaigrette cool to room temperature.
4. Place arugula on a platter; arrange figs over arugula. Sprinkle with cheese and pepper. Drizzle with cooled vinaigrette. Yield: 4 servings (serving size: 1¼ cups).

CALORIES 109 (34% from fat); FAT 4.1g (sat 1.4g, mono 2.1g, poly 0.4g); PROTEIN 2.4g; CARB 18g; FIBER 2.5g; CHOL 3mg; IRON 1.1mg; SODIUM 182mg; CALC 84mg

QUICK & EASY
Grilled Lemon-Bay Shrimp

The simplicity of this dish belies its incredible taste. Bay leaves and lemon wedges infuse peppered shrimp with woodsy and citrus flavors. If your grocery doesn't carry fresh bay leaves, substitute good-quality dried bay leaves (such as Spice Island) soaked overnight in water. Leave the tails on the shrimp for a prettier presentation.

  2 tablespoons fresh lemon juice
  1 tablespoon olive oil
  ½ teaspoon salt
  ½ teaspoon crushed red pepper
  ½ teaspoon freshly ground black pepper
  2 garlic cloves, minced
 32 large shrimp, peeled and deveined (about 1½ pounds)
 32 fresh bay leaves
  4 large lemons, each cut into 8 wedges
Cooking spray

1. Prepare grill.
2. Combine first 6 ingredients in a large bowl. Add shrimp; toss to coat. Cover and marinate in refrigerator 10 minutes.
3. Place bay leaves and lemon wedges in a large bowl. Coat with cooking spray; toss to coat.

Continued

4. Thread 4 lemon wedges, 4 shrimp, and 4 bay leaves alternately onto each of 8 (10-inch) skewers. Place skewers on grill rack coated with cooking spray, and grill 2 minutes on each side or until shrimp are done. Yield: 4 servings (serving size: 2 skewers).

CALORIES 217 (27% from fat); FAT 6.4g (sat 1g, mono 2.9g, poly 1.4g); PROTEIN 34.8g; CARB 3.1g; FIBER 0.3g; CHOL 259mg; IRON 4.3mg; SODIUM 545mg; CALC 94mg

Barley Risotto with Fennel and Olives

Oil-cured olives have a wrinkled appearance and a pleasant bitter, rich flavor. Substitute any other olive, if desired. You can also make this risotto with Arborio rice instead of barley. Save the feathery, flowery tips of the fennel bulb to chop and use as a garnish.

    1   tablespoon butter
    1½ cups chopped leek, divided
    1   cup finely chopped fennel bulb,
        divided
    ½   cup finely chopped red bell
        pepper
    ¾   cup uncooked pearl
        barley
    1   teaspoon fresh or ¼ teaspoon
        dried thyme
    2   garlic cloves, minced
    3½ cups fat-free, less-sodium chicken
        broth, divided
    ½   cup dry white wine
    ⅓   cup (about 1½ ounces) grated
        fresh Parmesan cheese
    ¼   cup chopped fresh
        parsley
    1   teaspoon freshly ground black
        pepper
    ¼   cup oil-cured olives, pitted and
        chopped
    Chopped fennel fronds (optional)

1. Melt butter in a large saucepan over medium-high heat. Add ¾ cup leek, ½ cup fennel, and bell pepper; sauté 5 minutes or until tender. Add barley, thyme, and garlic; cook 2 minutes, stirring constantly. Stir in 2 cups broth, and cook 10 minutes or until liquid is nearly absorbed,

stirring constantly. Stir in ¾ cup leek, ½ cup fennel, 1½ cups broth, and wine; cook until liquid is nearly absorbed, stirring frequently (about 45 minutes). Stir in cheese, parsley, and black pepper. Sprinkle with olives; garnish with fennel fronds, if desired. Yield: 4 servings (serving size: ¾ cup).

CALORIES 255 (26% from fat); FAT 7.5g (sat 3.8g, mono 2.4g, poly 0.7g); PROTEIN 12.1g; CARB 36.1g; FIBER 8.2g; CHOL 15mg; IRON 3.1mg; SODIUM 693mg; CALC 192mg

Cherries in Spiced Wine Syrup with Pound Cake Croutons

Rosemary, cinnamon, and peppercorns give the red wine sauce a robust flavor.

    ½   teaspoon grated lemon rind
    6   black peppercorns
    1   (3-inch) cinnamon stick
    1   (4-inch) rosemary sprig
    2   cups dry red wine
    ¾   cup brandy
    ½   cup water
    ⅓   cup honey
    2   tablespoons fresh lemon
        juice
    3   cups pitted sweet cherries
    ½   (10.75-ounce) loaf frozen low-fat
        pound cake (such as Sara Lee)
    Cooking spray
    ⅓   cup reduced-fat sour cream
    1   tablespoon honey

1. Place first 4 ingredients on a double layer of cheesecloth. Gather edges of cheesecloth together; tie securely.
2. Combine wine and next 4 ingredients in a medium saucepan; bring to a boil. Add cheesecloth bag, and cook 5 minutes. Reduce heat, and add cherries; simmer 5 minutes, stirring occasionally. Drain cherries in a colander over a bowl, reserving cooking liquid.
3. Place cherries in a medium bowl; discard cheesecloth bag. Return cooking liquid to pan; bring to a boil. Cook 20 minutes or until reduced to 1¼ cups. Pour wine syrup over cherries, and refrigerate 1½ hours or until mixture is completely cool.

4. Preheat oven to 350°.
5. Cut cake into 24 (1-inch) cubes, and arrange cake cubes in a single layer on a nonstick baking sheet coated with cooking spray. Bake at 350° for 12 minutes or until lightly browned, turning cubes every 4 minutes.
6. Combine sour cream and 1 tablespoon honey. Spoon ½ cup cherry mixture into each of 6 bowls or parfait glasses; top each serving with 4 croutons and 1 tablespoon sour cream mixture. Yield: 6 servings.

CALORIES 283 (20% from fat); FAT 6.4g (sat 2.4g, mono 1.9g, poly 0.5g); PROTEIN 3.1g; CARB 48.5g; FIBER 1.7g; CHOL 31mg; IRON 1.3mg; SODIUM 146mg; CALC 48mg

QUICK & EASY
Pimm's Cup
(pictured on page 269)

This refreshing drink gets most of its flavor from Pimm's No. 1, a gin-based aperitif with fruit juices and spices. Cucumber spears make a crunchy garnish.

    ¾   cup Pimm's No. 1
    2   cups ginger ale, chilled
    1⅓ cups sparkling water, chilled
    4   lemon slices
    1   cucumber, halved lengthwise and
        cut into 4 spears

1. Fill 4 tall (12-ounce) glasses with ice cubes.
2. Pour 3 tablespoons Pimm's into each glass. Pour ½ cup ginger ale and ⅓ cup sparkling water into each glass; stir to combine. Garnish each serving with 1 lemon slice and 1 cucumber spear. Serve immediately. Yield: 4 servings.

CALORIES 150 (0% from fat); FAT 0g; PROTEIN 0.8g; CARB 13.3g; FIBER 0.8g; CHOL 0mg; IRON 0.3mg; SODIUM 13mg; CALC 15mg

Slushy Watermelon Mojitos
(pictured on page 269)

The classic Cuban cocktail is the basis for this ruby-hued version. Be sure to keep the limeade frozen so the beverage will be slushy.

5 cups cubed seeded watermelon
1 cup sparkling water, chilled
¾ cup white rum
¼ cup chopped fresh mint
1 (6-ounce) can frozen limeade
   concentrate, undiluted
Mint sprigs (optional)
Lime slices (optional)

1. Arrange watermelon in a single layer on a baking sheet; freeze 2 hours or until completely frozen.

2. Combine watermelon, sparkling water and next 3 ingredients in a blender; process until smooth. Garnish with mint sprigs and lime slices, if desired. Serve immediately. Yield: 8 servings (serving size: about ¾ cup).

CALORIES 119 (3% from fat); FAT 0.4g (sat 0.1g, mono 0.1g, poly 0.2g); PROTEIN 0.7g; CARB 17.5g; FIBER 0.6g; CHOL 0mg; IRON 0.3mg; SODIUM 2mg; CALC 11mg

Sparkling Peach Splash

(pictured on page 269)

Juicy, late-summer peaches create a fruity cocktail based on the popular Bellini. For a nice garnish, place a peach slice onto the rim of each glass before serving.

2 cups chopped peeled peaches
   (about 3 peaches)
½ cup peach schnapps
2 tablespoons fresh lime juice
1 (750-milliliter) bottle Champagne
   or sparkling wine, chilled
8 peach slices (optional)

1. Combine first 3 ingredients in a blender; process until smooth. Freeze 1 hour.

2. Pour Champagne into a pitcher. Spoon peach mixture into pitcher; stir to combine. Garnish with peach slices, if desired. Serve immediately. Yield: 8 servings (serving size: about ¾ cup).

CALORIES 133 (1% from fat); FAT 0.1g (sat 0g, mono 0g, poly 0.1g); PROTEIN 0.4g; CARB 12.1g; FIBER 0.9g; CHOL 0mg; IRON 0.4mg; SODIUM 6mg; CALC 11mg

In Virginia, Romancing French Cuisine

Chef Jacques Haeringer continues a family dynasty, reinterpreting Alsatian classics for American palates.

L'Auberge Chez François's chef, Jacques Haeringer—star of the PBS cooking show *Two for Tonight* and author of a cookbook of the same name, as well as *The Chez François Cookbook*—knows how to romanticize food. Haeringer is the second generation romancing French food in Great Falls, Virginia, at the restaurant started by his father, François.

Haeringer favors free-range meats and poultry, as well as organically grown fruits and vegetables. It's a strategy that he recommends for home cooks—within reason. Get the best ingredients available, he says, but don't avoid a recipe just because you can't obtain organic ingredients. In the end, the goal is to prepare healthful meals that please the senses and, more important, to enjoy the results.

Melon Balls with Port

Sweet cantaloupe, heady port, and fresh mint combine in a light dessert ideal for the end of a hearty meal. Try it after the Spiced Beef with Wine Sauce and Roasted Potatoes (recipe on page 266).

1 cup ruby port or other sweet red
   wine
1 tablespoon sugar
Dash of salt
Dash of cardamom
6 cups cantaloupe balls (about
   2 large cantaloupes)
2 teaspoons chopped fresh mint
Mint sprigs (optional)

1. Combine port and sugar in a small saucepan; bring to a boil. Reduce heat,

and simmer 10 minutes or until reduced to ½ cup. Place port mixture in a large bowl; cool. Stir in salt and cardamom. Add cantaloupe balls and chopped mint; toss gently to coat. Cover and chill 1 hour before serving. Garnish with mint sprigs, if desired. Yield: 6 servings (serving size: 1 cup).

CALORIES 130 (4% from fat); FAT 0.5g (sat 0.1g, mono 0g, poly 0.2g); PROTEIN 1.7g; CARB 21.6g; FIBER 1.4g; CHOL 0mg; IRON 0.5mg; SODIUM 41mg; CALC 23mg

Seafood Salad with Lime Vinaigrette

Although Alsatian cuisine favors rich meat and pork dishes, Haeringer has a deft touch with seafood, too. Citrus juice and cumin in the vinaigrette provide an earthy contrast to the delicate, slightly sweet scallops and shrimp. Serve with herb focaccia for a light summer dinner.

VINAIGRETTE:

1 teaspoon cumin seeds
½ teaspoon salt
1 garlic clove, minced
⅓ cup fresh orange juice (about
   1 medium orange)
3 tablespoons fresh lime juice
1 tablespoon minced shallots
2 teaspoons honey
⅛ teaspoon freshly ground black
   pepper
2 tablespoons extravirgin olive oil

SEAFOOD:

1¼ pounds sea scallops
1¼ pounds large shrimp, peeled and
   deveined
Cooking spray
¼ teaspoon salt
⅛ teaspoon freshly ground black
   pepper

SALAD:

3 cups mixed salad greens
3 cups chopped romaine lettuce
1 cup sliced Belgian endive (about
   2 small heads)
1 cup orange sections
Chopped fresh parsley (optional)

Continued

1. To prepare vinaigrette, toast cumin seeds in a small skillet over medium-high heat 2 minutes or until fragrant, stirring constantly. Combine ½ teaspoon salt and garlic in a small bowl, using a fork to mash into a paste. Add toasted cumin seeds, orange juice, and next 4 ingredients; stir well with a whisk. Add oil, stirring with a whisk until well blended. Set aside.

2. To prepare seafood, lightly coat scallops and shrimp with cooking spray; sprinkle with ¼ teaspoon salt and ⅛ teaspoon pepper. Heat a heavy grill pan over medium-high heat. Lightly coat pan with cooking spray. Add half of seafood; cook 2 minutes on each side or until done. Repeat procedure with remaining seafood. Place seafood in a bowl; drizzle with ⅓ cup vinaigrette, tossing to coat.

3. To prepare salad, combine salad greens, romaine, endive, and orange sections in a large bowl. Drizzle with remaining vinaigrette; toss gently to coat. Divide salad among 6 plates; top with seafood. Garnish with parsley, if desired. Serve immediately. Yield: 6 servings (serving size: about 5 ounces seafood and 1 cup salad).

CALORIES 281 (23% from fat); FAT 7.1g (sat 1g, mono 3.7g, poly 1.3g); PROTEIN 36.6g; CARB 17.2g; FIBER 2.7g; CHOL 175mg; IRON 3.5mg; SODIUM 599mg; CALC 127mg

---

MAKE AHEAD

Vegetables à la Grecque

À la grecque refers to vegetables cooked in olive oil and lemon juice, then chilled and served cold. Use the flat side of a chef's knife to crush the aromatic seeds. Cut any large mushrooms in half so they'll cook evenly. Try preparing this dish with a dry Alsatian Riesling, Gewürztraminer, or Pinot Blanc. Haeringer suggests cooking with purified water, instead of tap water, for a cleaner taste and incorporating the cooking liquid into the recipe to retain the vegetables' nutrients.

 1 tablespoon olive oil
 ½ cup chopped onion
 ½ cup diced carrot
 ¼ cup diced celery
 1 cup dry white wine
 1 cup water
 1 cup diced seeded plum tomato

 ¼ cup fresh lemon juice
 1 teaspoon salt
 ¼ teaspoon freshly ground black pepper
 ¼ teaspoon grated lemon rind
 ¼ teaspoon coriander seeds, crushed
 8 mustard seeds, crushed
 2 garlic cloves, chopped
 1 cup thinly sliced leek
 2 heads cauliflower, cut into large florets
 1 teaspoon chopped fresh thyme
 1 (8-ounce) package small button mushrooms
 8 ounces small cremini mushrooms

1. Heat oil in a Dutch oven over medium heat. Add onion, carrot, and celery; cook 4 minutes or until onion is tender, stirring constantly. Stir in wine and water; bring to a boil.

2. Stir in tomato and next 7 ingredients; reduce heat, and simmer 5 minutes.

3. Stir in leek and cauliflower; cover and simmer 10 minutes. Add thyme and mushrooms, and cook 5 minutes or until vegetables are tender. Remove vegetables from pan with a slotted spoon. Bring cooking liquid to a boil; cook until reduced to ½ cup (about 5 minutes). Drizzle cooking liquid over vegetables. Chill 1 to 4 hours. Let stand at room temperature 15 minutes before serving. Yield: 9 servings (serving size: 1 cup).

CALORIES 100 (18% from fat); FAT 2g (sat 0.3g, mono 1.1g, poly 0.3g); PROTEIN 4.3g; CARB 14.9g; FIBER 4.4g; CHOL 0mg; IRON 1.5mg; SODIUM 315mg; CALC 55mg

---

Spiced Beef with Wine Sauce and Roasted Potatoes

Haeringer gently poaches tenderloin in spiced wine to produce a delicate flavor and tender texture. Use a good-quality red wine for the most robust result.

POTATOES:
1½ pounds fingerling potatoes
 Cooking spray
 ¼ teaspoon salt
 ⅛ teaspoon freshly ground black pepper

BEEF:
 ¼ teaspoon salt
 ⅛ teaspoon freshly ground black pepper
 6 coriander seeds, crushed
 4 juniper berries, crushed
 2 cloves
 1 (1-inch) cinnamon stick
 1 (750-milliliter) bottle Cabernet Sauvignon or other dry red wine
 4 (4-ounce) beef tenderloin steaks, trimmed (1½ inches thick)

SAUCE:
 ½ cup low-salt beef broth, divided
 1 teaspoon sugar
 ¼ teaspoon salt
1½ teaspoons cornstarch
 2 teaspoons butter

1. To prepare potatoes, preheat oven to 400°.

2. Arrange potatoes in a single layer on a jelly-roll pan coated with cooking spray. Lightly coat potatoes with cooking spray; sprinkle with ¼ teaspoon salt and ⅛ teaspoon pepper. Bake at 400° for 40 minutes or until tender, turning after 20 minutes. Remove from oven; keep warm.

3. To prepare beef, combine ¼ teaspoon salt, ⅛ teaspoon pepper, coriander seeds, and next 4 ingredients in a large saucepan; bring to a boil. Reduce heat; simmer 2 minutes. Strain wine mixture through a sieve into a bowl; discard solids. Return wine mixture to pan; bring to a simmer (mixture will just barely bubble). Arrange beef in a single layer in pan; cook 5 minutes or until desired degree of doneness. Remove from pan; keep warm. Reserve ½ cup liquid; discard remaining cooking liquid.

4. To prepare sauce, combine reserved cooking liquid, ¼ cup broth, sugar, and ¼ teaspoon salt in pan; bring to a boil. Reduce heat, and simmer 2 minutes or until reduced to ½ cup. Combine ¼ cup broth and cornstarch, stirring with a whisk. Add cornstarch mixture to pan; bring to a boil. Cook 1 minute, stirring constantly. Remove from heat. Add butter; stir until melted. Yield: 4 servings (serving size: 1 steak, about 2 tablespoons sauce, and about 1 cup potatoes).

CALORIES 438 (22% from fat); FAT 10.9g (sat 4.5g, mono 3.9g, poly 0.5g); PROTEIN 28.8g; CARB 46g; FIBER 4.2g; CHOL 77mg; IRON 5.8mg; SODIUM 541mg; CALC 32mg

Perfectly Parfait

These desserts in a glass are easy as pie—and they're a lot less work.

"Parfait" is the French word for "perfect," and that's the best way to describe this whimsical dessert. Parfaits are simple to make, stunning to look at, and fun to eat. Creamy layers of custard or ice cream and fruit are sandwiched between crumbled cookies. Enjoy the parfait as a shortcut to a fancy dessert.

There's no need to buy a new set of parfait glasses. Any tall, clear glass will do. Parfaits look elegant in small wineglasses or Champagne flutes. For a casual presentation, use jelly jars or pilsner glasses.

MAKE AHEAD
Amaretto-Scented Pear Parfaits with Gingersnaps

Freeze the parfait glasses about 1 hour before assembling to keep the yogurt from melting too quickly.

 3 cups chopped peeled ripe Bosc pears (about 3 large)
 ¼ cup amaretto (almond-flavored liqueur)
 1 tablespoon sugar
 1 cup gingersnap crumbs, (about 4 ounces, crushed)
 3 cups vanilla low-fat frozen yogurt, softened
 ½ cup sliced almonds, toasted

1. Combine first 3 ingredients; cover and chill at least 1 hour.
2. Spoon 1 tablespoon cookie crumbs into each of 8 (8-ounce) glasses; top each with 3 tablespoons pear mixture and 3 tablespoons yogurt. Repeat layers once, ending with yogurt. Top each with 1 tablespoon almonds. Yield: 8 servings (serving size: 1 parfait).

CALORIES 238 (21% from fat); FAT 5.6g (sat 1.2g, mono 3g, poly 1g); PROTEIN 5.6g; CARB 39.9g; FIBER 2.4g; CHOL 4mg; IRON 1.1mg; SODIUM 137mg; CALC 149mg

Funky Monkey Parfaits

This simple chocolate custard, which cooks quickly in the microwave, is layered with the delicious combination of peanut butter and bananas.

 6 tablespoons sugar
 ¼ cup Dutch process cocoa
 2 tablespoons cornstarch
 Dash of salt
 1½ cups 2% reduced-fat milk
 ½ teaspoon vanilla extract
 1 cup peanut butter sandwich cookie crumbs (such as Nutter Butter; about 8 cookies, crumbled)
 3 cups sliced bananas

1. Combine first 4 ingredients in a 2-quart glass measure; stir well. Gradually add milk, stirring with a whisk. Microwave at HIGH 2½ minutes, stirring occasionally. Microwave mixture at MEDIUM-HIGH (70% power) 2½ minutes or until thick, stirring occasionally. Stir in vanilla. Cover surface of mixture with plastic wrap; chill.
2. Spoon 1 tablespoon cookie crumbs into each of 8 (8-ounce) glasses; top each with 3 tablespoons bananas and 1½ tablespoons chocolate mixture. Repeat layers once, ending with chocolate mixture. Serve immediately. Yield: 8 servings (serving size: 1 parfait).

CALORIES 191 (21% from fat); FAT 4.5g (sat 1.4g, mono 1.4g, poly 0.6g); PROTEIN 4g; CARB 37.7g; FIBER 1.9g; CHOL 5mg; IRON 0.9mg; SODIUM 127mg; CALC 53mg

Apple Pie à la Mode Parfaits

 4½ cups chopped peeled cooking apple (such as Braeburn)
 ½ cup sugar
 1 tablespoon fresh lemon juice
 1 teaspoon apple-pie spice
 1 cup oatmeal cookie crumbs, (about 4 ounces, crushed)
 3 cups vanilla low-fat ice cream, softened

1. Combine first 4 ingredients in a medium saucepan, and bring to a boil. Cover, reduce heat, and simmer 5 minutes. Uncover; simmer 5 minutes or until tender, stirring occasionally. Spoon into a bowl; cover and chill.
2. Spoon 1 tablespoon cookie crumbs into each of 8 (8-ounce) glasses; top each with ¼ cup apple mixture and 3 tablespoons ice cream. Repeat layers once, ending with ice cream. Serve immediately. Yield: 8 servings (serving size: 1 parfait).

CALORIES 284 (24% from fat); FAT 7.7g (sat 2.3g, mono 3.7g, poly 0.9g); PROTEIN 4.4g; CARB 51.4g; FIBER 3g; CHOL 9mg; IRON 0.9mg; SODIUM 129mg; CALC 83mg

QUICK & EASY • MAKE AHEAD
Peach and Raspberry Pavlova Parfaits

To make crumbs, place cookies in a plastic bag and gently crush with a rolling pin.

 ½ cup (4 ounces) ⅓-less-fat cream cheese
 ¼ cup sugar, divided
 1 cup vanilla fat-free yogurt
 2 cups sliced peeled peaches (about 6 to 7 peaches)
 1 cup raspberries
 1 cup vanilla meringue cookie crumbs (such as Miss Meringue Minis; about 12 mini cookies, coarsely crushed)
 12 vanilla meringue mini cookies

1. Place cream cheese and 3 tablespoons sugar in a medium bowl; beat with a mixer at high speed 2 minutes or until smooth. Beat in yogurt until blended.
2. Combine 1 tablespoon sugar, peaches, and raspberries in a large bowl, tossing to coat. Let stand 5 minutes.
3. Spoon 2 tablespoons cheese mixture into each of 6 (8-ounce) glasses; top each with ¼ cup peach mixture and 2½ tablespoons cookie crumbs. Repeat layers once with cheese mixture and peach mixture; top each with 2 whole cookies. Cover and chill until ready to serve. Yield: 6 servings (serving size: 1 parfait).

CALORIES 193 (22% from fat); FAT 4.7g (sat 2.9g, mono 1.3g, poly 0.2g); PROTEIN 5.1g; CARB 34.7g; FIBER 2.5g; CHOL 15mg; IRON 0.3mg; SODIUM 111mg; CALC 94mg

Black Forest Cheesecake Parfaits

In the Black Forest region of Germany, the signature dessert is layered with chocolate, cherries, and whipped cream. Here, cream cheese replaces whipped cream.

    4 cups frozen unsweetened
       cherries
    ½ cup black cherry preserves
    ½ cup sugar
    2 tablespoons fresh lemon
       juice
    6 ounces ⅓-less-fat cream
       cheese
    ¾ cup chocolate wafer crumbs
       (about 15 cookies; such as Nabisco's
       Famous Chocolate Wafers)
    Grated lemon rind (optional)

1. Combine cherries and preserves in a medium saucepan, and bring to a boil. Reduce heat to medium-low, and simmer 5 minutes. Remove from heat, and cool completely.
2. Combine sugar, juice, and cheese in a large bowl, and beat with a mixer at medium speed until smooth (about 2 minutes). Cover and chill.
3. Spoon 2 teaspoons crumbs into each of 8 (8-ounce) glasses; top each with 1½ tablespoons cream cheese mixture and 3 tablespoons cherry mixture. Repeat layers once, ending with cherry mixture. Garnish with rind, if desired. Serve immediately. Yield: 8 servings (serving size: 1 parfait).

CALORIES 236 (26% from fat); FAT 6.8g (sat 3.7g, mono 2g, poly 0.7g); PROTEIN 3.5g; CARB 42.6g; FIBER 1.6g; CHOL 16mg; IRON 0.9mg; SODIUM 147mg; CALC 30mg

---

Not Just Stand-Ins

Crumbled oatmeal cookies don't merely stand in as a substitute for a piecrust in the Apple Pie à la Mode Parfaits (recipe on page 267)—they add great flavor, too.

Making a meringue crust for a typical Pavlova is time consuming, but by simply crushing a few meringue cookies you can assemble the Peach and Raspberry Pavlova Parfaits (recipe on page 267) in minutes.

And the Black Forest Cheesecake Parfaits (recipe at left) taste every bit like a traditional cheesecake—without the chore of making a crust and the long baking time.

Key Lime Pie Parfaits

Key limes are smaller, rounder, and have a yellower flesh than traditional limes. If you can find Key limes, use them in this dessert to add a sweet-tartness.

    ½ cup fresh lime juice
    ¼ cup sugar
    ¼ teaspoon grated lime rind
    2 large eggs, lightly beaten
    1 (14-ounce) can fat-free sweetened
       condensed milk
    1½ cups canned whipped light cream
       (such as Reddi-wip)
    1 cup graham cracker crumbs (about
       8 cookie sheets)
    Grated lime rind (optional)

1. Combine first 5 ingredients in a large bowl, stirring with a whisk until smooth; pour into top of a double boiler. Cook over simmering water until mixture thickens (about 6 minutes) or until a thermometer registers 160°, stirring constantly. Remove from heat. Place pan in a large ice-filled bowl 20 minutes or until mixture comes to room temperature, stirring occasionally.
2. Spoon 1 tablespoon whipped cream into each of 8 (8-ounce) glasses; top each serving with 1 tablespoon crumbs and 3 tablespoons lime mixture. Repeat

---

layers once, ending with lime mixture. Top each serving with 1 tablespoon whipped cream; sprinkle with lime rind, if desired. Serve immediately. Yield: 8 servings (serving size: 1 parfait).

CALORIES 258 (17% from fat); FAT 5g (sat 2.1g, mono 1.6g, poly 0.7g); PROTEIN 7.1g; CARB 47g; FIBER 0.4g; CHOL 65mg; IRON 0.6mg; SODIUM 149mg; CALC 161mg

Coconut Cream Pie Parfaits

To toast coconut, spread it on a baking sheet. Bake at 375° for 5 minutes or until lightly brown, stirring occasionally.

    ½   cup all-purpose flour
    ½   cup sugar
    2¼ cups fat-free milk
    2   large eggs, lightly beaten
    ¾   cup flaked sweetened coconut,
        toasted and divided
    2   teaspoons vanilla extract
    1   cup plus 2 tablespoons
        reduced-calorie vanilla wafer
        crumbs (about 26 cookies,
        crushed)
    1½ cups canned whipped light cream
        (such as Reddi-wip)

1. Lightly spoon flour into a dry measuring cup; level with a knife. Place flour and sugar in a medium saucepan; gradually whisk in milk. Cook over medium heat until thick and bubbly, stirring constantly. Place eggs in a bowl; gradually whisk half of milk mixture into eggs. Pour egg mixture into saucepan; stir well. Cook 1 minute or until thick. Remove from heat; stir in ½ cup coconut and vanilla. Cover surface of mixture with plastic wrap; chill.
2. Spoon 1½ tablespoons wafer crumbs into each of 6 (8-ounce) glasses; top each with about 3 tablespoons coconut mixture and 2 tablespoons whipped cream. Repeat layers once, ending with whipped cream. Sprinkle parfaits evenly with ¼ cup coconut. Yield: 6 servings (serving size: 1 parfait).

CALORIES 310 (30% from fat); FAT 10.5g (sat 5.8g, mono 2.5g, poly 0.4g); PROTEIN 7.5g; CARB 46.7g; FIBER 0.9g; CHOL 85mg; IRON 1.4mg; SODIUM 158mg; CALC 149mg

(Left to right): Pimm's Cup, page 264,
Sparkling Peach Splash, page 265, and
Slushy Watermelon Mojitos, page 264

Refrigerator Fig Preserves,
page 290

Lemongrass Shrimp over Rice Vermicelli and Vegetables
Bun Tom Nuong Xa, **page 285**

Roast Pork Sandwiches au Jus with Rosemary,
page 261

Summer Pappardelle with Tomatoes, Arugula, and Parmesan, page 278

Fiery Turkey Fillets with Mango Salsa and Lemon Southwest Rice, page 274

Cooking for the Company

The new recipe for corporate team-building success is in the kitchen.

A dozen professionals—doctors, teachers, entrepreneurs, and managers from the Santa Fe, New Mexico-based International Chamber for Health and Well-Being—gathered in a kitchen at the Santa Fe School of Cooking, negotiating how to share the few cutting boards given to them. Their objective was to strengthen communication and networking skills. Their goal was to get dinner on the table without using flow charts and office politics. With a limited amount of equipment, they were expected to prepare a four-course dinner. Here it is.

Santa Fe Menu
serves 8

Farmers' Market Quesadillas

Red Cabbage and Spinach Salad with Balsamic Vinaigrette

Fiery Turkey Fillets with Mango Salsa

Mexican Chocolate Cake

Lemon Southwest Rice

QUICK & EASY
Farmers' Market Quesadillas

Pair the quesadillas with a salad for a light supper.

- 1 or 2 poblano chiles
- 1 large red bell pepper
- Cooking spray
- 1 onion, thinly sliced
- 1½ cups chopped yellow squash
- 2 garlic cloves, minced
- 1 cup chopped oyster mushrooms
- ½ teaspoon salt
- ¼ teaspoon freshly ground black pepper
- 1 cup (4 ounces) shredded Monterey Jack cheese
- ½ cup (2 ounces) crumbled goat cheese
- 8 (8-inch) fat-free flour tortillas
- 2 tablespoons chopped fresh cilantro

1. Preheat broiler.

2. Place poblano and bell pepper on a foil-lined baking sheet; broil 10 minutes or until blackened, turning occasionally. Place poblano and bell pepper in a zip-top plastic bag; seal. Let stand 15 minutes. Peel poblano and bell pepper; discard seeds and membranes. Cut into thin strips.

3. Heat a large nonstick skillet over medium-high heat. Coat with cooking spray. Add onion; sauté 3 minutes or until lightly browned. Add squash and garlic; sauté 3 minutes. Add poblano and pepper strips and mushrooms; cook 5 minutes or until mushrooms are tender and moisture evaporates, stirring frequently. Sprinkle with salt and black pepper.

4. Sprinkle 2 tablespoons Monterey Jack and 1 tablespoon goat cheese over each of 4 tortillas; top each with ⅔ cup vegetable mixture. Sprinkle 2 tablespoons Monterey Jack, 1 tablespoon goat cheese, and 1½ teaspoons cilantro over each vegetable-topped tortilla; top with remaining tortillas.

5. Heat a large nonstick skillet over medium-high heat. Place 1 quesadilla in pan; cook 5 minutes on each side or until tortillas are crisp. Repeat procedure with remaining quesadillas. Cut each quesadilla into 6 wedges. Yield: 12 servings (serving size: 2 wedges).

CALORIES 140 (34% from fat); FAT 5.3g (sat 2.8g, mono 1.2g, poly 0.2g); PROTEIN 6g; CARB 17.9g; FIBER 1.5g; CHOL 12mg; IRON 1.2mg; SODIUM 360mg; CALC 132mg

QUICK & EASY • MAKE AHEAD
Red Cabbage and Spinach Salad with Balsamic Vinaigrette

This colorful salad can be made ahead; toss the beets in just before serving. The vinaigrette will keep up to 1 week in the refrigerator, so double the vinaigrette ingredients, combine in a jar, and store the extra half for a salad later in the week.

VINAIGRETTE:

- ¼ cup balsamic vinegar
- ¼ cup fat-free, less-sodium chicken broth
- 1 tablespoon frozen orange juice concentrate, thawed
- 2 teaspoons extravirgin olive oil
- 1½ teaspoons sugar
- 1 teaspoon Dijon mustard
- ½ teaspoon salt
- ¼ teaspoon freshly ground black pepper
- 1 garlic clove, minced

SALAD:

- 6 cups coarsely chopped red cabbage (about 1 pound)
- 5 cups thinly sliced spinach leaves (about 8 ounces)
- ¼ cup chopped green onion
- 2 small beets, peeled and shredded

1. To prepare vinaigrette, combine first 9 ingredients, stirring with a whisk.

2. To prepare salad, combine cabbage, spinach, onion, and beets in a large bowl. Drizzle with vinaigrette; toss gently to coat. Serve immediately. Yield: 8 servings (serving size: 1¼ cups).

CALORIES 51 (26% from fat); FAT 1.5g (sat 0.2g, mono 0.9g, poly 0.2g); PROTEIN 2.1g; CARB 8.8g; FIBER 2.6g; CHOL 0mg; IRON 1.3mg; SODIUM 222mg; CALC 63mg

Fiery Turkey Fillets with Mango Salsa

(pictured on page 272)

The marinade gives the turkey fillets interesting color and delicious flavor. The sweet salsa is a good contrast to the spicy turkey. Try serving the salsa as a dip with tortilla chips, as well. Chimayo chile powder, also known as ground New Mexican chili powder, can be found in Latino grocery stores. Garnish with fresh cilantro sprigs.

TURKEY:

½ cup coarsely chopped fresh cilantro

½ cup fresh lime juice (about 2 limes)

¼ cup finely minced onion

3 tablespoons Chimayo or New Mexican chile powder

2 tablespoons chopped fresh oregano

1 tablespoon ancho chile powder

2 tablespoons dry white wine

2 tablespoons extravirgin olive oil

2 tablespoons minced chipotle chiles in adobo sauce

½ teaspoon salt

½ teaspoon ground cumin

3 garlic cloves, minced

1 (3-pound) boneless turkey breast half, skinned and cut into 8 fillets

Cooking spray

SALSA:

2 cups diced peeled ripe mango (about 2 mangoes)

1 cup chopped English cucumber

1 cup chopped red bell pepper

½ cup chopped red onion

1 tablespoon seasoned rice vinegar

1 teaspoon hot sauce

½ teaspoon salt

2 serrano chiles, seeded and minced

1. To prepare turkey, combine first 12 ingredients in a large zip-top plastic bag. Add turkey fillets; seal and marinate in refrigerator 1 hour, turning bag occasionally.

2. Preheat grill to medium-high heat.

3. Remove turkey from bag, reserving marinade. Place marinade in a saucepan. Bring to a boil over medium-high heat; cook 2 minutes. Remove from heat. Set aside ½ cup marinade to serve as a sauce; use remaining marinade for basting.

4. Place fillets on a grill rack coated with cooking spray; grill 5 minutes on each side or until done, basting with marinade.

5. To prepare salsa, combine mango and remaining 7 ingredients. Serve turkey with salsa and ½ cup marinade. Yield: 8 servings (serving size: 1 turkey fillet, ½ cup salsa, and 1 tablespoon marinade).

CALORIES 286 (17% from fat); FAT 5.5g (sat 0.9g, mono 3g, poly 0.9g); PROTEIN 42.7g; CARB 15.8g; FIBER 3.1g; CHOL 112mg; IRON 3.1mg; SODIUM 525mg; CALC 55mg

---

MAKE AHEAD

Mexican Chocolate Cake

This dessert is a great way to finish a Mexican dinner. It's not too sweet, so it provides balance for the hot and spicy flavors of the rest of the meal. Mexican chocolate is sweet, with a hint of cinnamon. Look for it at your local ethnic grocery store, or order a box of Ibarra Mexican Sweet Chocolate disks from www.gourmet-sleuth.com.

Cooking spray

2 teaspoons all-purpose flour

1 cup all-purpose flour

⅓ cup Dutch process cocoa

1 teaspoon ground cinnamon

¾ teaspoon baking powder

½ teaspoon baking soda

¼ teaspoon salt

1 cup packed light brown sugar

¼ cup unsalted butter, softened

3 large egg whites

1 cup plain fat-free yogurt

1 teaspoon vanilla extract

1 large egg

1 tablespoon fat-free milk

1 ounce Mexican chocolate (such as Ibarra), coarsely chopped

2 tablespoons powdered sugar

1. Preheat oven to 350°.

2. Coat an 8-inch round cake pan with cooking spray; line bottom of pan with wax paper. Coat wax paper with cooking spray; dust with 2 teaspoons flour. Set aside.

3. Lightly spoon flour into a dry measuring cup; level with a knife. Sift 1 cup flour and next 5 ingredients into a bowl. Place brown sugar and butter in a large bowl; beat with a mixer at medium speed until well blended (about 5 minutes). Add egg whites, 1 at a time, beating well after each addition. Add yogurt, vanilla, and egg, beating until blended. Gradually add flour mixture, beating until combined. Pour batter into prepared pan; sharply tap pan once on counter to remove air bubbles. Bake at 350° for 35 minutes or until a wooden pick inserted in center comes out clean. Remove from oven; cool 10 minutes in pan. Place a plate upside down on top of cake; invert cake onto plate. Carefully peel off wax paper.

4. Combine milk and chocolate in a small microwave-safe bowl. Microwave at HIGH 30 seconds or until chocolate melts; stir until smooth. Cool slightly; drizzle over cake. Let glaze set; sprinkle with powdered sugar. Yield: 8 servings.

CALORIES 247 (27% from fat); FAT 7.5g (sat 4.4g, mono 2.2g, poly 0.4g); PROTEIN 5.6g; CARB 41.9g; FIBER 1.6g; CHOL 43mg; IRON 2mg; SODIUM 263mg; CALC 127mg

---

QUICK & EASY

Lemon Southwest Rice

(pictured on page 272)

Stir in the cilantro, chiles, and lemon rind at the end for the best flavor.

2 tablespoons butter

1 cup thinly sliced leek

1 tablespoon minced garlic

2 cups uncooked long-grain rice

4 cups fat-free, less-sodium chicken broth

¼ cup fresh lemon juice

¾ teaspoon salt

¼ teaspoon ground coriander

⅛ teaspoon saffron threads, crushed

¼ cup chopped fresh cilantro

¼ cup canned chopped green chiles, undrained

1 teaspoon grated lemon rind

1. Melt butter in a large nonstick skillet over medium heat. Add leek; cook 5 minutes or until tender, stirring frequently. Add garlic; cook 1 minute, stirring constantly. Add rice, and cook 1 minute, stirring constantly. Add broth and next 4 ingredients; bring to a boil. Cover, reduce heat, and simmer 30 minutes or until rice is tender and liquid is absorbed. Stir in cilantro, chiles, and rind. Yield: 6 cups (serving size: ¾ cup).

CALORIES 217 (13% from fat); FAT 3.2g (sat 1.9g, mono 0.9g, poly 0.2g); PROTEIN 5.4g; CARB 40.7g; FIBER 1.2g; CHOL 8mg; IRON 2.3mg; SODIUM 483mg; CALC 25mg

Farmers' Market Treasures

Find ideas for fine fare in the bounty of late-summer produce.

QUICK & EASY
Fresh Corn Frittata with Smoked Mozzarella

Easy to double and simple to prepare, this open-faced omelet is a good light main course. Smoked cheese is a fitting counterpoint to the sweet, fresh corn.

Cooking spray
1½ cups fresh corn kernels (about 3 ears)
¼ cup (1 ounce) shredded smoked mozzarella cheese, divided
1 tablespoon chopped fresh basil
¼ teaspoon sea salt
¼ teaspoon freshly ground black pepper
5 large egg whites, lightly beaten
2 large eggs, lightly beaten

1. Preheat broiler.
2. Heat a medium nonstick skillet over medium-high heat. Coat pan with cooking spray. Add corn, and sauté 5 minutes. Combine corn, 2 tablespoons cheese, basil, and remaining 4 ingredients in a large bowl, stirring with a whisk.
3. Heat skillet over medium heat. Coat pan with cooking spray; add corn mixture. Cover and cook 5 minutes or until almost set. Sprinkle with 2 tablespoons

cheese. Wrap handle of pan with foil. Broil 5 minutes or until set and browned. Yield: 4 servings (serving size: 1 wedge).

CALORIES 129 (33% from fat); FAT 4.7g (sat 1.9g, mono 1.7g, poly 0.7g); PROTEIN 10.7g; CARB 12g; FIBER 1.6g; CHOL 112mg; IRON 0.8mg; SODIUM 263mg; CALC 58mg

Eggplant and Tomato Gratin

Removing strips of eggplant peel makes for a pretty presentation, but you can remove all the peel if you'd rather. Seasonal eggplant from the farmers' market doesn't need to be salted because it's usually so fresh that there's no bitterness. If you're unsure about freshness, place eggplant slices on paper towels, lightly sprinkle with salt, let stand 30 minutes, then blot dry with paper towels.

3 pounds chopped seeded peeled tomato
1 teaspoon olive oil
¼ cup finely chopped celery
3 tablespoons finely chopped onion
3 tablespoons finely chopped carrot
¾ teaspoon sea salt, divided
1 bay leaf
1 thyme sprig
1 basil sprig
2½ pounds eggplant
Cooking spray
¼ teaspoon freshly ground black pepper
3 tablespoons thinly sliced fresh basil
½ cup (2 ounces) grated fresh Parmesan cheese

1. Cook tomato in a medium saucepan over medium heat 20 minutes or until tender, stirring frequently. Place tomato in a food processor, and pulse 5 times or until puréed. Heat oil in pan over medium-high heat. Add celery, onion, and carrot; sauté 2 minutes. Add puréed tomato, ½ teaspoon salt, bay leaf, thyme sprig, and basil sprig. Reduce heat to medium-low; cook 10 minutes or until slightly thick. Discard bay leaf, thyme sprig, and basil sprig. Set sauce aside.
2. Preheat broiler.

3. Cut off both ends of eggplant; peel eggplant, leaving narrow strips of peel attached. Cut eggplant into ½-inch-thick slices. Place on a jelly-roll pan coated with cooking spray. Lightly coat slices with cooking spray; sprinkle with ¼ teaspoon salt and black pepper. Broil 5 minutes on each side or until lightly browned.
4. Reduce oven temperature to 375°.
5. Lightly coat a shallow 2-quart baking dish with cooking spray. Spread ¾ cup tomato sauce in bottom of dish. Arrange ⅓ of eggplant slices in dish, overlapping slices if necessary. Sprinkle with 1 tablespoon sliced basil, and top with ¾ cup tomato sauce. Repeat layers twice with eggplant, sliced basil, and tomato sauce. Sprinkle with cheese. Cover and bake at 375° for 15 minutes. Uncover and bake an additional 15 minutes or until eggplant is tender and cheese is lightly browned. Remove from oven; let stand 10 minutes before serving. Yield: 6 servings.

CALORIES 122 (29% from fat); FAT 3.9g (sat 1.8g, mono 1.4g, poly 0.4g); PROTEIN 6.5g; CARB 18.2g; FIBER 6.3g; CHOL 6mg; IRON 1.2mg; SODIUM 461mg; CALC 138mg

MAKE AHEAD
Apricot-Lavender Sauce

Don't be tempted to make this pretty dessert sauce out of season using canned apricots—wait for fresh ones. Great over ice cream, fresh ricotta cheese, yogurt, or angel food cake, the sauce has a beautiful color and unforgettable flavor. It may be served cold, at room temperature, or slightly warm.

1 cup sugar
½ cup water
3 pounds apricots, halved and pitted (about 8 cups)
1½ teaspoons chopped fresh or ½ teaspoon dried lavender

1. Combine sugar, water, and apricots in a large, heavy saucepan. Cook over high heat 3 minutes or until sugar dissolves, stirring constantly. Reduce heat to medium; cook 30 minutes or until fruit breaks down and mixture is slightly thick, stirring
Continued

frequently. Remove from heat. Stir in lavender; let stand 10 minutes. Strain through a sieve into a large bowl; discard solids. Cool to room temperature. Cover and chill up to 2 weeks. Yield: 3 cups (serving size: 2 tablespoons).

CALORIES 59 (3% from fat); FAT 0.2g (sat 0g, mono 0.1g, poly 0.1g); PROTEIN 0.8g; CARB 14.6g; FIBER 1.4g; CHOL 0mg; IRON 0.3mg; SODIUM 1mg; CALC 8mg

Green Rice with Roasted Chiles and Leeks

A vegetable stock made with herb and vegetable trimmings packs flavor into the rice.

STOCK:

```
 6  cups water
 1  cup thinly sliced celery
 1  cup thinly sliced carrot
 ½  cup thinly sliced leek tops
 ½  cup coarsely chopped flat-leaf
     parsley stems
 ½  cup coarsely chopped cilantro stems
 ½  teaspoon sea salt
 3  black peppercorns
 1  oregano sprig
 1  thyme sprig
```

RICE:

```
 2   poblano chiles
 1   tablespoon vegetable oil
 2   cups thinly sliced leek (about
      3 large)
1½  cups uncooked long-grain rice
 ¾  teaspoon sea salt
 1   bay leaf
 1   cup loosely packed fresh flat-leaf
      parsley leaves
 ½  cup loosely packed fresh cilantro
      leaves
 ½  cup (2 ounces) shredded
      Monterey Jack cheese
```

1. To prepare stock, combine first 10 ingredients in a medium saucepan; bring to a boil. Reduce heat, and simmer 25 minutes. Strain through a cheesecloth-lined colander into a bowl, and discard solids. Set aside 3 cups stock; reserve any remaining stock for another use.
2. Preheat broiler.

3. To prepare rice, place chiles on a foil-lined baking sheet; broil 8 minutes or until blackened and charred, turning after 4 minutes. Place in a zip-top plastic bag; seal. Let stand 15 minutes. Peel and discard skins. Cut a lengthwise slit in each chile; discard seeds and stems. Set chiles aside.
4. Heat oil in saucepan over medium-high heat. Add 2 cups leek and rice; sauté 5 minutes. Add 2¾ cups stock, ¾ teaspoon salt, and bay leaf; bring to a boil. Cover, reduce heat, and simmer 18 minutes or until liquid is absorbed. Remove from heat; discard bay leaf. Fluff rice with a fork.
5. Combine ¼ cup stock, roasted chiles, parsley leaves, and cilantro leaves in a blender or food processor; process until smooth. Gently fold chile mixture into rice. Sprinkle with cheese. Yield: 6 servings (serving size: ⅔ cup rice mixture and 4 teaspoons cheese).

CALORIES 260 (20% from fat); FAT 5.8g (sat 2.1g, mono 1.6g, poly 1.7g); PROTEIN 6.5g; CARB 45.2g; FIBER 2.3g; CHOL 10mg; IRON 3.5mg; SODIUM 551mg; CALC 119mg

QUICK & EASY
Whole Wheat Penne with Broccoli, Green Olives, and Pine Nuts

Fresh broccoli from a farmers' market is sweet and tender. Pungent olives and meaty pine nuts offer nice contrasting flavors. Broccoli stalks add crunch.

```
 9   cups broccoli florets (about 2 pounds)
 1   cup chopped broccoli stalks
 2   tablespoons olive oil
 3   cups chopped yellow onion
 2   garlic cloves, minced
 ¾  cup chopped pitted green olives
 ¼  cup pine nuts, toasted
 2   to 3 tablespoons chopped fresh
      marjoram or oregano
 ½  teaspoon sea salt
 ¼  teaspoon freshly ground black
      pepper
 6   cups hot cooked whole wheat
      penne (about ¾ pound uncooked
      tube-shaped pasta)
 ⅓  cup (1⅓ ounces) grated fresh
      Parmesan cheese
```

1. Cook florets and stalks in boiling water 2 minutes or until crisp-tender, and drain.
2. Heat oil in a Dutch oven over medium-high heat. Add onion; sauté 8 minutes or until golden. Add garlic; sauté 1 minute. Stir in florets, stalks, olives, nuts, marjoram, salt, and pepper; cook 2 minutes or until thoroughly heated. Serve over pasta; sprinkle with cheese. Yield: 6 servings (serving size: 1 cup broccoli mixture, 1 cup pasta, and about 1 tablespoon cheese).

CALORIES 397 (30% from fat); FAT 13.3g (sat 2.8g, mono 7g, poly 2.5g); PROTEIN 18.1g; CARB 59.4g; FIBER 11.3g; CHOL 5mg; IRON 4.6mg; SODIUM 849mg; CALC 218mg

Bruschetta with Warm Tomatoes

Briefly heating the tomatoes intensifies their sweetness while preserving their bright, fresh flavor. Use any variety of small summer tomatoes you find at the market; for a gorgeous look, mix tomato colors and shapes, such as yellow and orange pear tomatoes paired with red grape tomatoes.

```
2½  cups grape, pear, or cherry
      tomatoes
 3   tablespoons thinly sliced fresh
      basil
 2   tablespoons finely chopped
      shallots
 2   teaspoons olive oil
 ¼  teaspoon sea salt
 ¼  teaspoon balsamic vinegar
 ⅛  teaspoon freshly ground black
      pepper
 1   garlic clove, minced
    Cooking spray
 4   (1-ounce) slices ciabatta or
      sourdough bread
 1   garlic clove, halved
```

1. Combine first 8 ingredients, and let stand 1 hour.
2. Heat a medium nonstick skillet over medium heat. Coat pan with cooking spray. Add tomato mixture, and cook 10 minutes or until thoroughly heated, stirring occasionally. Remove from heat.

3. Heat a grill pan over medium-high heat. Coat pan with cooking spray. Add bread; cook 2 minutes on each side or until toasted. Rub 1 side of each toast piece with cut sides of garlic clove halves. Serve tomato mixture over toast. Yield: 4 servings (serving size: 1 toast slice and about ⅓ cup tomato mixture).

CALORIES 122 (27% from fat); FAT 3.6g (sat 0.6g, mono 1.9g, poly 0.7g); PROTEIN 3.5g; CARB 19.8g; FIBER 1.9g; CHOL 0mg; IRON 1.4mg; SODIUM 319mg; CALC 34mg

Potato and Summer Vegetable Stovetop Casserole

This dish affords the chance to improvise with what you find at your local market. Try purple potatoes in place of fingerlings, Maui or Walla Walla onions instead of Vidalias, or sliced beefsteak heirloom tomatoes for the grape or cherry tomatoes.

   1   yellow bell pepper
   1   red bell pepper
   2   tablespoons olive oil, divided
   1   pound fingerling potatoes, peeled and cut into ¼-inch-thick slices
   ¼   cup chopped fresh basil
   1   teaspoon sea salt
   ¼   teaspoon freshly ground black pepper
   3   garlic cloves, thinly sliced
   4   cups thinly vertically sliced Vidalia or other sweet onion
   2   cups (¼-inch-thick) slices zucchini
   1   cup (¼-inch-thick) slices yellow squash
   1   cup grape or cherry tomatoes, halved
   3   tablespoons water
Flat-leaf parsley sprigs (optional)

1. Preheat broiler.
2. Cut bell peppers in half lengthwise, and discard seeds and membranes. Place pepper halves, skin sides up, on a foil-lined baking sheet; flatten with hand. Broil 8 minutes or until blackened. Place in a zip-top plastic bag; seal. Let peppers stand 5 minutes. Peel and cut into strips.

3. Heat 1 tablespoon oil in a deep 10-inch cast-iron skillet over medium heat. Add potatoes, tossing to coat. Spread potatoes in a single layer in pan. Sprinkle with 1 tablespoon basil, ¼ teaspoon salt, ⅛ teaspoon black pepper, and ⅓ of garlic. Arrange onion, zucchini, and squash over seasonings. Sprinkle with 1 tablespoon basil, ¼ teaspoon salt, ⅛ teaspoon black pepper, and ⅓ of garlic. Top with roasted bell peppers, 2 tablespoons basil, ⅓ of garlic, and tomatoes. Drizzle 1 tablespoon oil and water over top; sprinkle with ½ teaspoon salt. Cover, reduce heat to low, and cook 25 minutes or until vegetables are tender. Uncover; increase heat to high, and cook 3 minutes or until liquid almost evaporates. Garnish with parsley, if desired. Yield: 4 servings (serving size: 1 wedge).

CALORIES 225 (30% from fat); FAT 7.6g (sat 1g, mono 5.1g, poly 0.9g); PROTEIN 6.4g; CARB 35.4g; FIBER 7.4g; CHOL 0mg; IRON 2.1mg; SODIUM 592mg; CALC 62mg

on hand

The Long and Short of It

Pasta is at home in a variety of dishes— and cuisines.

Maybe it's because pasta has a long shelf life or it's so versatile, but it seems to partner deliciously with things you already have on hand in the pantry and refrigerator.

Try our Hamburger, Cheddar, and Macaroni Toss or Sesame Pork Lo Mein. Salad and soup lovers can whip up the Tuna and Red Pepper Pasta Salad or the Summer Squash Soup with Pasta and Parmesan. Or if you crave Italian, try Penne Pasta with Roasted Fennel, Cherry Tomatoes, and Olives.

Use the recipes that follow as templates. If one calls for penne, substitute any short pasta, such as rotini or elbow. If it calls for longer pasta like spaghetti, substitute vermicelli or linguine. Just make sure it's about the same size as what's called for in the recipe.

Penne with Mushroom Sauce

Serve this rich dish with a warm baguette and the red wine you opened for the sauce.

   2   tablespoons butter, divided
   ½   cup finely chopped onion
   ¼   cup finely chopped celery
   ¼   cup finely chopped carrot
   1½ tablespoons tomato paste
   1   cup dry red wine
   ⅛   teaspoon dried thyme
   ⅛   teaspoon black pepper
   1   (10½-ounce) can beef consommé
   1   (8-ounce) package presliced mushrooms
   1   tablespoon water
   1   teaspoon cornstarch
   ⅛   teaspoon salt
   4   cups hot cooked penne rigate (8 ounces uncooked pasta)
Flat-leaf parsley sprigs (optional)

1. Melt 1 tablespoon butter in a medium nonstick skillet over medium-high heat. Add onion, celery, and carrot; sauté 5 minutes. Stir in tomato paste; cook 2 minutes, stirring constantly. Add wine; cook 10 minutes or until liquid almost evaporates. Stir in thyme, pepper, and consommé. Bring to a boil; cook until reduced to 1 cup (about 3 minutes). Strain through a sieve into a bowl; discard solids. Keep consommé mixture warm.
2. Melt 1 tablespoon butter in pan over medium-high heat. Add mushrooms, and sauté 5 minutes. Add consommé mixture; bring to a boil. Reduce heat, and simmer 5 minutes. Combine water and cornstarch. Add cornstarch mixture and salt to pan; bring to a boil. Cook 1 minute. Combine sauce and pasta, tossing to coat. Garnish with parsley, if desired. Yield: 4 servings (serving size: 1 cup).

CALORIES 301 (21% from fat); FAT 7.1g (sat 3.9g, mono 1.9g, poly 0.7g); PROTEIN 10.4g; CARB 49.4g; FIBER 3.1g; CHOL 16mg; IRON 3.2mg; SODIUM 441mg; CALC 32mg

Summer Pappardelle with Tomatoes, Arugula, and Parmesan

(pictured on page 272)

If cooked pasta clumps together, just rinse it under hot water, drain thoroughly, and then toss with the tomato mixture and arugula.

9 ounces uncooked pappardelle (wide ribbon pasta)
2 tablespoons extravirgin olive oil
¼ teaspoon crushed red pepper
3 garlic cloves, thinly sliced
1½ cups halved yellow tear-drop cherry tomatoes (pear-shaped)
1½ cups halved grape tomatoes
3 tablespoons fresh lemon juice
1 teaspoon salt
5 cups loosely packed trimmed arugula
⅓ cup (1½ ounces) shaved fresh Parmesan cheese
2 bacon slices, cooked and crumbled

1. Cook pasta according to package directions, omitting salt and fat. Drain; keep warm.
2. Heat oil in a large nonstick skillet over medium heat. Add pepper and garlic to pan; cook 1 minute or until garlic is fragrant. Add tomatoes; cook 45 seconds or just until heated, stirring gently. Remove pan from heat; stir in lemon juice and salt. Combine hot pasta, arugula, and tomato mixture in a large bowl, tossing to coat. Top with cheese and bacon. Yield: 4 servings (serving size: 2 cups).

CALORIES 388 (29% from fat); FAT 12.5g (sat 3.5g, mono 6.6g, poly 1.1g); PROTEIN 15.2g; CARB 55.7g; FIBER 3.8g; CHOL 10mg; IRON 3.1mg; SODIUM 828mg; CALC 189mg

Spicy Noodle Salad with Tofu and Peanut Dressing

To make this dish vegetarian, use vegetable broth instead of chicken broth.

6 cups water
1½ cups (1-inch) diagonally cut asparagus (about ½ pound)
1 cup snow peas, trimmed
6 ounces rice noodles
1 cup red bell pepper strips
1 cup yellow bell pepper strips
1 cup chopped green onions
1 cup fresh bean sprouts
2 teaspoons dark sesame oil
1 (12.3-ounce) package reduced-fat firm tofu, drained and cut into ½-inch cubes
¼ cup fat-free, less-sodium chicken broth
¼ cup water
3 tablespoons peanut butter
2 tablespoons fresh lime juice
1½ tablespoons low-sodium soy sauce
1½ tablespoons dark brown sugar
¼ teaspoon ground red pepper
1 garlic clove

1. Bring 6 cups water to a boil in a large saucepan. Add asparagus, snow peas, and rice noodles; cook 2 minutes. Drain.
2. Combine noodle mixture, bell pepper strips, onions, and bean sprouts.
3. Heat oil in a large nonstick skillet over medium-high heat. Add tofu; sauté 5 minutes or until browned. Add tofu to noodle mixture.
4. Combine broth and remaining 7 ingredients in a blender, and process until smooth. Add to noodle mixture; toss gently to coat. Yield: 4 servings (serving size: 2¼ cups).

CALORIES 410 (28% from fat); FAT 12.6g (sat 1.6g, mono 4.7g, poly 4.9g); PROTEIN 18.3g; CARB 58.4g; FIBER 6.6g; CHOL 0mg; IRON 3.8mg; SODIUM 306mg; CALC 83mg

Sesame Pork Lo Mein

For variety, use shrimp or chicken in place of the pork and chopped red bell pepper instead of mushrooms.

8 ounces uncooked lo mein noodles or vermicelli
6 tablespoons dry sherry
¼ cup low-sodium soy sauce
1 tablespoon bottled minced garlic
1 tablespoon bottled minced fresh ginger
1 tablespoon rice vinegar
2 teaspoons sugar
½ teaspoon crushed red pepper
4 teaspoons dark sesame oil, divided
12 ounces pork tenderloin, trimmed and sliced into thin strips
1 cup fat-free, less-sodium chicken broth
2 teaspoons cornstarch
Cooking spray
¾ cup snow peas, halved crosswise
½ cup thinly sliced carrot
1 (8-ounce) package presliced mushrooms
1 teaspoon sesame seeds, toasted
1 cup diagonally cut green onions

1. Prepare noodles according to package directions; drain.
2. Combine sherry and next 6 ingredients in a medium bowl. Add 1 teaspoon sesame oil and pork; toss to coat.
3. Combine broth and cornstarch, stirring with a whisk.
4. Heat a large nonstick skillet over medium-high heat. Coat pan with cooking spray. Add pork mixture to pan, and cook 3 minutes, stirring frequently. Remove pork using a slotted spoon. Add peas, carrot, and mushrooms to pan; cook 2 minutes. Stir in broth mixture; cook 2 minutes or until thick, stirring constantly.
5. Stir in noodles, 1 tablespoon sesame oil, pork, and sesame seeds. Sprinkle with green onions. Serve immediately. Yield: 6 servings (serving size: about 1⅓ cups).

CALORIES 300 (17% from fat); FAT 5.5g (sat 1.2g, mono 2.2g, poly 1.7g); PROTEIN 18.2g; CARB 39.9g; FIBER 2.6g; CHOL 37mg; IRON 3.5mg; SODIUM 469mg; CALC 18mg

While the vegetables roast, get the rolls ready to go into the oven. Bake them while the pasta cooks.

Penne Pasta with Roasted Fennel, Cherry Tomatoes, and Black Olives

Garlic-Parmesan rolls*

Garden salad

*Preheat oven to 425°. Unroll 1 (13.8-ounce) can refrigerated pizza crust dough on a lightly floured surface; pat into a 15 x 10-inch rectangle. Combine 2 tablespoons melted butter, ¼ teaspoon salt, and 2 minced garlic cloves; brush evenly over dough. Sprinkle evenly with ½ cup thinly sliced fresh basil and ½ cup grated fresh Parmesan cheese. Starting at long edge, roll up jelly-roll fashion. Cut into 12 (1-inch) slices. Place slices, 2 inches apart, on a baking sheet lined with parchment paper. Bake at 425° for 12 minutes or until golden.

STAFF FAVORITE
Penne Pasta with Roasted Fennel, Cherry Tomatoes, and Olives

Roasting the vegetables gives them a slight sweetness that's countered by the briny olives and salty cheese.

½ pound fennel bulb
2 cups cherry tomatoes, halved
½ cup kalamata olives, pitted and halved
2 teaspoons chopped fresh rosemary
1½ teaspoons chopped fresh oregano
⅛ teaspoon freshly ground black pepper
1 tablespoon extravirgin olive oil
8 ounces uncooked penne (tube-shaped pasta)
½ teaspoon salt
¾ cup (3 ounces) freshly grated pecorino Romano cheese

1. Preheat oven to 450°.

2. Cut fennel bulb in half lengthwise; discard core. Chop fennel into bite-sized pieces. Combine fennel, tomatoes, olives, rosemary, and oregano in a 13 x 9-inch baking dish. Sprinkle with pepper; drizzle with oil. Toss well to coat. Bake at 450° for 30 minutes or until fennel is tender, stirring once.

3. Prepare pasta according to package directions, omitting salt and fat. Drain; place in a large bowl. Stir in fennel mixture and salt. Add cheese; toss to combine. Yield: 4 servings (serving size: about 1¾ cups).

CALORIES 370 (29% from fat); FAT 11.8g (sat 4g, mono 5.5g, poly 0.7g); PROTEIN 14.6g; CARB 52g; FIBER 4.2g; CHOL 20mg; IRON 3.3mg; SODIUM 735mg; CALC 250mg

QUICK & EASY
Hamburger, Cheddar, and Macaroni Toss

This is a true one-pot family favorite that's also a good source of fiber and calcium. Prepare the beef mixture in the same pan used to cook the pasta.

1½ cups uncooked medium elbow macaroni
Cooking spray
¾ pound ground round
1 cup chopped yellow onion
2 garlic cloves, minced
2 tablespoons tomato paste
1½ teaspoons chili powder
1 teaspoon paprika
½ teaspoon dried oregano
1 (14½-ounce) can diced tomatoes with green peppers and onions, undrained
1 cup (4 ounces) reduced-fat shredded sharp Cheddar cheese, divided
¼ teaspoon salt
⅛ teaspoon freshly ground black pepper

1. Prepare macaroni in a Dutch oven according to package directions, omitting salt and fat. Drain and set aside.

2. Heat pan over medium-high heat. Coat pan with cooking spray. Add beef; cook 3 minutes or until browned, stirring to crumble. Remove beef with a slotted spoon. Add onion and garlic to pan; sauté 2 minutes. Stir in tomato paste and next 4 ingredients; cook 2 minutes or until mixture thickens, stirring occasionally. Stir in macaroni, beef, and ¾ cup cheese; cook 1 minute or until cheese melts. Stir in salt and pepper. Sprinkle 1 tablespoon cheese over each serving. Yield: 4 servings (serving size: 1½ cups).

CALORIES 446 (31% from fat); FAT 15.4g (sat 7.6g, mono 3.8g, poly 1.7g); PROTEIN 30.9g; CARB 44g; FIBER 4.1g; CHOL 75mg; IRON 4.2mg; SODIUM 912mg; CALC 253mg

QUICK & EASY
Curried Noodles

Serve a simple tofu or chicken stir-fry on a bed of these flavorful noodles.

4 ounces uncooked wide rice stick noodles (*banh pho*)
½ cup water
2 tablespoons low-sodium soy sauce
1 tablespoon honey
¾ teaspoon cornstarch
1 tablespoon vegetable oil
1 cup chopped green onions
1 cup (¼-inch-thick) slices red bell pepper, each cut in half
1 tablespoon grated peeled fresh ginger
1 teaspoon curry powder
1 teaspoon ground cumin
3 garlic cloves, minced

1. Cook noodles according to package directions, omitting salt and fat. Drain.

2. Combine ½ cup water, soy sauce, honey, and cornstarch in a small bowl, stirring with a whisk.

3. Heat oil in a large nonstick skillet over medium-high heat. Add onions and remaining 5 ingredients; sauté 3 minutes. Add noodles and water mixture; cook 1½ minutes or until thoroughly heated and sauce is slightly thick. Yield: 4 servings (serving size: ¾ cup).

CALORIES 183 (18% from fat); FAT 3.7g (sat 0.5g, mono 0.8g, poly 2g); PROTEIN 3.1g; CARB 33.8g; FIBER 2.7g; CHOL 0mg; IRON 1.7mg; SODIUM 274mg; CALC 29mg

Southwestern Pasta with Beans

Children love the shape of wagon wheel pasta in this meatless entrée. Alter this dish for them by leaving out the chipotle chile powder for a milder flavor.

    8 ounces uncooked wagon wheel or
       seashell pasta
    1 tablespoon vegetable oil
    1 cup diced seeded poblano chiles
       (about 2 chiles)
    1 cup chopped onion
    ½ teaspoon chipotle chile powder
    ¼ teaspoon salt
    4 garlic cloves, minced
    1 (14.5-ounce) can stewed
       tomatoes, undrained
    1 (10-ounce) can enchilada sauce
    1 (15-ounce) can pinto beans,
       rinsed and drained
       Cooking spray
    1 cup (4 ounces) shredded
       Monterey Jack cheese
    5 tablespoons chopped fresh
       cilantro
    5 tablespoons reduced-fat sour
       cream

1. Preheat oven to 350°.
2. Cook pasta according to package directions, omitting salt and fat. Drain.
3. Heat oil in a Dutch oven over medium-high heat. Add poblano and onion; sauté 5 minutes or until tender. Add chile powder, salt, and garlic; sauté 2 minutes. Stir in tomatoes and enchilada sauce; bring to a simmer. Cook 5 minutes, stirring occasionally. Stir in beans; remove from heat. Add pasta to tomato mixture, tossing well to combine. Spoon pasta mixture into an 11 x 7-inch baking dish coated with cooking spray; sprinkle evenly with cheese. Bake at 350° for 20 minutes or until cheese melts and begins to brown. Top each serving with 1 tablespoon cilantro and 1 tablespoon sour cream. Yield: 5 servings (serving size: about 1½ cups).

CALORIES 450 (29% from fat); FAT 14.7g (sat 5.8g, mono 3g, poly 2.9g); PROTEIN 19.6g; CARB 63g; FIBER 8.6g; CHOL 32mg; IRON 3.3mg; SODIUM 711mg; CALC 263mg

---

MAKE AHEAD • FREEZABLE
Mushroom and Yellow Pepper Lasagna

Smoky bacon and Marsala wine flavor a rustic lasagna of shiitake, oyster, and button mushrooms layered between pasta and smothered with a creamy béchamel sauce.

MAKE-AHEAD TIP: Assemble the lasagna, cover tightly with foil, and freeze (uncooked) up to 1 month. Let stand at room temperature 30 minutes before baking.

    2 bacon slices
    2 cups sliced shiitake mushroom
       caps (about 4 ounces)
    2 cups sliced oyster mushroom caps
       (about 4 ounces)
    1 (8-ounce) package presliced
       button mushrooms
    1 cup chopped yellow bell pepper
    ¾ cup chopped onion
    2 garlic cloves, minced
 1½   teaspoons salt-free Creole seasoning
    ½ teaspoon dried oregano
    1 teaspoon salt, divided
    ¾ teaspoon black pepper, divided
    1 cup Marsala wine
    2 tablespoons butter
    3 tablespoons all-purpose flour
 2½   cups 1% low-fat milk
    ¾ cup (3 ounces) shredded sharp
       provolone cheese
       Cooking spray
    9 cooked lasagna noodles
    ½ cup (2 ounces) shredded
       part-skim mozzarella cheese

1. Preheat oven to 350°.
2. Cook bacon in a large nonstick skillet over medium-high heat until crisp. Remove bacon from pan, reserving 1 teaspoon drippings in pan. Crumble bacon; set aside. Add mushrooms, bell pepper, onion, and garlic to pan; sauté 10 minutes or until tender. Add Creole seasoning, oregano, ½ teaspoon salt, and ¼ teaspoon black pepper; cook 1 minute, stirring constantly. Add wine; bring to a boil. Cover, reduce heat, and simmer 3 minutes. Uncover and simmer 4 minutes.
3. Melt butter in a medium saucepan over medium heat. Add flour, stirring with a whisk. Gradually add milk, stirring with a whisk until well blended. Cook until slightly thick (about 8 minutes), stirring constantly (do not boil). Remove from heat. Add provolone, ½ teaspoon salt, and ½ teaspoon black pepper, stirring until cheese melts.
4. Spread ½ cup sauce in bottom of a 13 x 9-inch baking dish coated with cooking spray. Arrange 3 noodles over sauce; top with half of mushroom mixture and about ¾ cup sauce. Repeat layers, ending with noodles. Spread remaining sauce over noodles. Cover and bake at 350° for 30 minutes. Uncover; sprinkle evenly with mozzarella and bacon. Bake an additional 10 minutes. Let stand 15 minutes before serving. Yield: 8 servings.

CALORIES 305 (30% from fat); FAT 10.2g (sat 5.5g, mono 3.2g, poly 0.8g); PROTEIN 12.9g; CARB 33g; FIBER 2.1g; CHOL 27mg; IRON 2.3mg; SODIUM 558mg; CALC 239mg

---

Pasta with Roasted Shiitakes and Tomato Purée

Roasting the mushrooms along with the vegetables that form the sauce allows for caramelization, which deepens the flavor of the ingredients. If you have large shiitakes, cut them in half to ensure even roasting. If you can't find orecchiette, substitute any short pasta, such as mini penne, cavatappi, or farfalle.

    1 tablespoon olive oil
    3 garlic cloves, unpeeled
    1 pound shiitake mushrooms, stems
       removed
    1 pound plum tomatoes, cut in half
       lengthwise
    1 small onion, quartered
    1 teaspoon kosher salt
    1 teaspoon dried rosemary
    ½ teaspoon freshly ground black
       pepper
    ½ cup fat-free, less-sodium chicken
       broth
    4 cups hot cooked orecchiette pasta
       (about 8 ounces uncooked "little
       ears" pasta)
    ¼ cup chopped fresh parsley
    1 tablespoon chopped fresh chives
    ½ cup (2 ounces) shaved fresh
       Parmesan cheese

1. Preheat oven to 375°.
2. Combine first 5 ingredients in a shallow roasting pan, and toss well. Sprinkle with salt, rosemary, and pepper. Bake at 375° for 25 minutes or until onion is tender, stirring occasionally. Squeeze garlic cloves to extract pulp; discard skins. Place garlic pulp, onion, tomatoes, and broth in a food processor; process until well blended.
3. Combine mushrooms, tomato mixture, pasta, parsley, and chives in a large bowl, tossing well. Sprinkle with cheese. Yield: 4 servings (serving size: 1¼ cups pasta mixture and 2 tablespoons cheese).

CALORIES 393 (23% from fat); FAT 10g (sat 3.4g, mono 4.3g, poly 1.2g); PROTEIN 17.7g; CARB 57.3g; FIBER 5.2g; CHOL 63mg; IRON 5.5mg; SODIUM 805mg; CALC 216mg

Gemelli Pasta with Clams, Scallops, and Shrimp

Prepare the pasta while the seafood sauce simmers, and you'll have dinner in about 30 minutes.

- 1 tablespoon olive oil
- 1 cup chopped onion
- 1 cup chopped yellow bell pepper
- 3 garlic cloves, minced
- ½ cup dry white wine
- ¼ teaspoon crushed red pepper
- 1 (14.5-ounce) can diced tomatoes, undrained
- ½ cup chopped canned clams, undrained
- ¼ cup chopped fresh flat-leaf parsley
- 2 tablespoons chopped fresh or 1½ teaspoons dried tarragon
- ¼ teaspoon salt
- ¼ teaspoon freshly ground black pepper
- ½ pound medium shrimp, peeled and deveined
- ½ pound bay scallops
- 5 cups hot cooked gemelli (about 6 ounces uncooked short tube-shaped pasta)
- 5 tablespoons grated fresh Parmesan cheese

1. Heat oil in a Dutch oven over medium heat. Add onion and bell pepper; cook 5 minutes, stirring frequently. Add garlic; cook 1 minute, stirring constantly. Stir in wine, crushed red pepper, and tomatoes; bring to a boil. Cover, reduce heat, and simmer 10 minutes. Add clams and next 6 ingredients; cook 3 minutes or until shrimp are done. Serve seafood mixture over pasta, and sprinkle with cheese. Yield: 5 servings (serving size: 1 cup seafood mixture, 1 cup pasta, and 1 tablespoon cheese).

CALORIES 390 (16% from fat); FAT 6.8g (sat 1.9g, mono 2.8g, poly 1.1g); PROTEIN 29.3g; CARB 51.9g; FIBER 4.2g; CHOL 93mg; IRON 4.3mg; SODIUM 582mg; CALC 164mg

Tuna and Red Pepper Pasta Salad

Lemon juice and capers give this simple pasta salad a tangy zip.

- 8 ounces uncooked small seashell pasta
- 1 cup finely chopped red bell pepper
- ½ cup chopped fresh parsley
- ½ cup finely chopped red onion
- ½ cup finely chopped celery
- 1 (6-ounce) can solid white tuna in water, drained
- ⅓ cup fresh lemon juice
- 2 tablespoons extravirgin olive oil
- 2 tablespoons capers
- ½ teaspoon salt
- ¼ teaspoon freshly ground black pepper
- 1 garlic clove, minced

1. Cook pasta according to package directions, omitting salt and fat. Drain and rinse with cold water; drain. Combine pasta, bell pepper, and next 4 ingredients in a large bowl, tossing gently.
2. Combine lemon juice and remaining 5 ingredients in a small bowl, stirring with a whisk. Drizzle over pasta mixture; toss gently to coat. Yield: 4 servings (serving size: 1¼ cups).

CALORIES 324 (24% from fat); FAT 8.7g (sat 1.3g, mono 5.4g, poly 1.3g); PROTEIN 15.6g; CARB 46.3g; FIBER 3.3g; CHOL 13mg; IRON 3.2mg; SODIUM 594mg; CALC 43mg

Soba with Garlic Chives, Mushrooms, and Bok Choy

Garlic chives (also called Chinese chives) have a more pungent scent and flavor than Western chives. If you can't find them, use 3½ cups thinly sliced leeks and 3 tablespoons chopped garlic in their place.

- 3 quarts water
- 1 pound bok choy
- 8 ounces uncooked soba (buckwheat noodles)
- 2½ tablespoons olive oil
- 3 cups (1-inch) slices garlic chives
- 5 cups thinly sliced shiitake mushroom caps (about ½ pound)
- 5 cups thinly sliced cremini mushrooms (about ½ pound)
- ⅓ cup sake (rice wine) or sherry
- ⅓ cup low-sodium soy sauce

1. Bring water to a boil in a large Dutch oven. Cut bok choy diagonally into 1-inch pieces; separate green portions and stalks. Cook stalks in boiling water 2 minutes. Add green portions, and cook 1 minute. Remove bok choy from water with a slotted spoon; place in a colander. Rinse with cold water; drain. Place bok choy in a bowl.
2. Return water to a boil, and add soba. Cook 4 minutes or until al dente. Drain and rinse with warm water; drain.
3. Heat oil in a wok or large nonstick skillet over medium-high heat. Add chives to pan, and stir-fry 10 seconds. Add mushrooms and sake; cover, reduce heat to medium-low, and cook 3 minutes or until mushrooms are tender. Uncover and increase heat to medium-high. Add bok choy and soy sauce; cook 2 minutes, stirring occasionally. Add noodles; cook 2 minutes, tossing to combine. Serve immediately. Yield: 6 servings (serving size: 1⅓ cups).

CALORIES 245 (23% from fat); FAT 6.2g (sat 0.9g, mono 4.3g, poly 0.7g); PROTEIN 10.7g; CARB 36.1g; FIBER 2.7g; CHOL 0mg; IRON 3.2mg; SODIUM 861mg; CALC 118mg

Summer Squash Soup with Pasta and Parmesan

6   cups fat-free, less-sodium chicken broth
3   cups water
6   ounces uncooked farfalle (bow tie pasta)
2   cups finely chopped zucchini
2   cups finely chopped yellow squash
1   tablespoon chopped fresh parsley
1   tablespoon chopped fresh basil
1   tablespoon fresh lemon juice
½   teaspoon chopped fresh thyme
½   teaspoon chopped fresh oregano
½   teaspoon freshly ground black pepper
½   cup (2 ounces) grated Parmigiano-Reggiano cheese
¼   cup thinly sliced fresh basil

1. Bring broth and water to a boil in a Dutch oven. Add pasta; cook 8 minutes or until almost tender. Add zucchini and next 7 ingredients. Reduce heat; simmer 4 minutes or until pasta is done and squash is tender. Sprinkle with cheese and sliced basil. Yield: 4 servings (serving size: about 2 cups).

CALORIES 269 (15% from fat); FAT 4.6g (sat 2.5g, mono 1.2g, poly 0.5g); PROTEIN 16.5g; CARB 39.4g; FIBER 3.4g; CHOL 10mg; IRON 2.6mg; SODIUM 912mg; CALC 210mg

Lemon Noodles with Curry Leaves and Cashews

You'll need to make a trip to your local Indian market for some of these ingredients.

8   ounces skinny rice stick noodles (*py mai fun*)
1   tablespoon vegetable oil
1   teaspoon brown mustard seeds
⅔   cup curry leaves (about 32 leaves, ½ ounce)
⅓   cup cashews (about 2 ounces)
2   teaspoons white gram beans
1   dried seeded hot red chile
¼   cup water
¼   teaspoon ground turmeric
⅔   cup chopped peeled mango
3   tablespoons fresh lemon juice
¾   teaspoon salt

1. Cook noodles according to package directions; drain and rinse with cold water. Drain.
2. Heat oil in a large nonstick skillet over medium-high heat. Add mustard seeds; cover pan, and cook 1 minute or until seeds stop popping. Uncover pan. Stir in curry leaves, nuts, beans, and chile; stir-fry 1 minute or until nuts are golden. Stir in water and turmeric. Add noodles; cook 3 minutes or until thoroughly heated, stirring constantly. Stir in mango, juice, and salt, tossing well. Yield: 4 servings (serving size: 1 cup).

CALORIES 334 (25% from fat); FAT 9.2g (sat 1.6g, mono 3.9g, poly 2.9g); PROTEIN 5.6g; CARB 57.9g; FIBER 1.3g; CHOL 0mg; IRON 2.1mg; SODIUM 524mg; CALC 52mg

Greek Pasta with Seared Tuna

Artichoke hearts, capers, and kalamata olives give this dish a Mediterranean flair.

1   (6-ounce) tuna steak (about ¾ inch thick)
¼   teaspoon freshly ground black pepper
   Cooking spray
2   cups chopped tomato (about 1 large tomato)
½   cup chopped fresh flat-leaf parsley
½   cup drained canned artichoke hearts, coarsely chopped
1   teaspoon grated lemon rind
2   tablespoons fresh lemon juice
2   tablespoons chopped pitted kalamata olives
1   tablespoon capers
1   tablespoon olive oil
3   cups hot cooked linguine (about 6 ounces uncooked pasta)
6   tablespoons grated Parmigiano-Reggiano cheese

1. Heat a small nonstick skillet over medium-high heat. Sprinkle tuna with pepper. Coat pan with cooking spray. Add tuna to pan, and cook 3 minutes on each side or until desired degree of doneness. Keep warm.
2. Combine tomato and next 7 ingredients in a large bowl. Add pasta; toss to combine. Arrange about 1⅓ cups pasta mixture on each of 3 plates. Flake fish with a fork; divide evenly over pasta. Sprinkle each serving with 2 tablespoons cheese. Yield: 3 servings.

CALORIES 447 (29% from fat); FAT 14.2g (sat 3.9g, mono 7.2g, poly 1.7g); PROTEIN 27.5g; CARB 53.1g; FIBER 3.8g; CHOL 29mg; IRON 4.3mg; SODIUM 559mg; CALC 179mg

lunch box chronicles

Air Fare

Travel in comfort with these portable, passenger-friendly dishes.

Prosciutto and Picholine Pasta Salad

Cavatelli are short, tight pasta shells; any small, compact pasta, such as mini penne, will also work.

3   tablespoons red wine vinegar
1   tablespoon extravirgin olive oil
1   tablespoon whole-grain Dijon mustard
1   tablespoon chopped fresh basil
2   teaspoons sugar
¼   teaspoon freshly ground black pepper
⅛   teaspoon salt
8   ounces uncooked cavatelli
¼   cup chopped fresh flat-leaf parsley
¼   cup (1 ounce) grated Parmigiano-Reggiano cheese
¼   cup chopped prosciutto (about 1 ounce)
2   tablespoons chopped pitted picholine or kalamata olives

1. Combine first 7 ingredients in a medium bowl, stirring well with a whisk; set aside.
2. Cook pasta according to package directions, omitting salt and fat. Drain and rinse with cold water. Drain. Add pasta, parsley, and remaining ingredients to vinegar mixture; toss well to coat.

Cover and chill. Yield: 2 servings (serving size: 1½ cups).

CALORIES 430 (29% from fat); FAT 13.8g (sat 4g, mono 7.5g, poly 1.4g); PROTEIN 17.1g; CARB 57g; FIBER 2.9g; CHOL 18mg; IRON 3.6mg; SODIUM 846mg; CALC 202mg

---

MAKE AHEAD
Chicken Saté Wraps

Coconut milk, curry powder, and peanut butter bring Indonesian flair to a quick-fix sandwich.

Cooking spray
½ cup matchstick-cut carrots
⅓ cup chopped green onions
⅔ cup light coconut milk
3 tablespoons creamy peanut butter
1 tablespoon low-sodium soy sauce
1 tablespoon rice vinegar
1 teaspoon curry powder
⅛ teaspoon ground red pepper
2 cups shredded skinless, boneless rotisserie chicken breast
4 (8-inch) fat-free flour tortillas
1⅓ cups packaged angel hair slaw

1. Heat a large nonstick skillet over medium-high heat. Coat pan with cooking spray. Add carrots and onions; sauté 1 minute. Stir in coconut milk and next 5 ingredients; cook 30 seconds, stirring constantly. Add chicken; cook 1 minute, stirring to coat. Remove from heat; cool. Warm tortillas according to package directions. Spoon about ½ cup chicken mixture down center of each tortilla, and top each with ⅓ cup slaw. Roll up. Cover and chill. Yield: 4 servings (serving size: 1 wrap).

CALORIES 321 (28% from fat); FAT 10.1g (sat 3.3g, mono 3.7g, poly 2.1g); PROTEIN 24.1g; CARB 25.5g; FIBER 4.3g; CHOL 49mg; IRON 0.9mg; SODIUM 844mg; CALC 37mg

---

MAKE AHEAD
Moroccan-Spiced Bulgur and Chickpea Salad

Fresh mint gives this dish a pleasant aroma. Dried cranberries offer a hint of sweetness. Use any other dried fruit you like in their place: Try golden raisins, currants, dried cherries, or chopped dried apricots.

3 tablespoons fresh lime juice
1 tablespoon extravirgin olive oil
½ teaspoon salt
¼ teaspoon ground cumin
¼ teaspoon ground coriander
¼ teaspoon freshly ground black pepper
2 cups boiling water
1⅓ cups uncooked bulgur
½ cup matchstick-cut carrots
⅓ cup dried cranberries
3 tablespoons slivered almonds, toasted
2 teaspoons chopped fresh mint
1 (15½-ounce) can chickpeas (garbanzo beans), rinsed and drained

1. Combine first 6 ingredients in a large bowl, stirring with a whisk; set aside.
2. Combine boiling water and bulgur in a large bowl. Cover and let stand 20 minutes or until liquid is absorbed. Add bulgur, carrots, and remaining ingredients to juice mixture, and toss well to coat. Cover and chill. Yield: 3 servings (serving size: 1¼ cups).

CALORIES 451 (22% from fat); FAT 11.2g (sat 1.1g, mono 6.5g, poly 2.9g); PROTEIN 13.8g; CARB 79.3g; FIBER 18.2g; CHOL 0mg; IRON 3.7mg; SODIUM 654mg; CALC 86mg

---

MAKE AHEAD
Barley-Chicken Salad with Fresh Corn and Sweet Onions

Rinsing the onion helps eliminate any strong smell, which your fellow passengers or coworkers will appreciate. Farmer cheese is a good substitute for queso fresco.

1½ tablespoons extravirgin olive oil
1 tablespoon fresh lime juice
½ teaspoon honey
¼ teaspoon salt
¼ teaspoon hot pepper sauce
½ cup uncooked pearl barley
2 cups chopped skinless, boneless rotisserie chicken breast
1½ cups fresh corn kernels (about 2 ears)
¾ cup finely chopped Vidalia or other sweet onion, rinsed and drained
½ cup (2 ounces) crumbled queso fresco
½ cup chopped bottled roasted red bell peppers

1. Combine first 5 ingredients in a large bowl, stirring with a whisk; set aside.
2. Place barley in a medium saucepan; cover with water. Bring to a boil. Reduce heat, and simmer 40 minutes or until tender. Drain and rinse with cold water. Drain. Add barley, chicken, and remaining ingredients to oil mixture; toss well to coat. Cover and chill. Yield: 4 servings (serving size: 1 cup).

CALORIES 345 (27% from fat); FAT 10.2g (sat 2.4g, mono 5.2g, poly 1.7g); PROTEIN 29.1g; CARB 36g; FIBER 6.8g; CHOL 64mg; IRON 2.2mg; SODIUM 310mg; CALC 75mg

---

MAKE AHEAD
Edamame, Quinoa, and Shiitake Mushroom Salad

The combination of lime juice, soy sauce, and honey creates a flavor similar to that of teriyaki; Thai Sriracha sauce adds a hint of heat to balance the sweetness.

¼ cup fresh lime juice
2 tablespoons low-sodium soy sauce
1 tablespoon olive oil
1 tablespoon honey
2 teaspoons Sriracha (hot chile sauce, such as Huy Fong)
½ teaspoon salt
1 cup uncooked quinoa
2 cups frozen shelled edamame (green soybeans)
1 cup chopped shiitake mushroom caps
¼ cup chopped red bell pepper

1. Combine first 6 ingredients in a large bowl, stirring with a whisk; set aside.
2. Place quinoa in a medium saucepan, and cover with water to 2 inches above quinoa. Bring to a boil; cook 3 minutes. Add edamame to pan; return to a boil. Reduce heat, and simmer 5 minutes or until tender. Drain and rinse with cold water. Drain. Add edamame mixture, mushrooms, and bell pepper to juice mixture; toss well to coat. Cover and chill. Yield: 4 servings (serving size: 1¼ cups).

CALORIES 320 (25% from fat); FAT 8.9g (sat 0.7g, mono 3.7g, poly 2.2g); PROTEIN 14.6g; CARB 46.6g; FIBER 7g; CHOL 0mg; IRON 6mg; SODIUM 635mg; CALC 81mg

Cashew Chicken Salad with Mandarin Oranges

3 tablespoons rice vinegar
1 tablespoon minced peeled fresh ginger
1 tablespoon low-sodium soy sauce
2 teaspoons hoisin sauce
1 teaspoon sugar
½ teaspoon salt
4 cups shredded iceberg lettuce
3 cups shredded skinless, boneless rotisserie chicken breast
1½ cups fresh bean sprouts
½ cup chopped green onions
2 tablespoons chopped dry-roasted cashews
1 (11-ounce) can mandarin oranges in light syrup, drained

1. Combine first 6 ingredients, stirring well with a whisk.
2. Combine lettuce and remaining 5 ingredients in a large bowl. Drizzle dressing over salad; toss gently to coat. Yield: 4 servings (serving size: about 2 cups).

CALORIES 300 (30% from fat); FAT 10.1g (sat 2.6g, mono 4g, poly 2.2g); PROTEIN 33.9g; CARB 18g; FIBER 2g; CHOL 94mg; IRON 2.6mg; SODIUM 588mg; CALC 54mg

Toasted Bagels with Avocado-Cilantro Spread

Assemble and wrap up this easy and filling sandwich for a great portable breakfast option. Lime juice keeps the avocado mixture from discoloring.

⅓ cup (3 ounces) fat-free cream cheese
¼ cup minced fresh cilantro
1 small ripe avocado, peeled and seeded
1 tablespoon fresh lime juice
¼ teaspoon salt
⅛ teaspoon hot pepper sauce
4 (2¼-ounce) whole-grain bagels, cut in half and toasted

1. Combine first 3 ingredients in a medium bowl; mash with a fork until smooth. Stir

in juice, salt, and hot sauce. Serve spread with bagels. Yield: 4 servings (serving size: 1 bagel and ¼ cup spread).

CALORIES 235 (20% from fat); FAT 5.3g (sat 0.9g, mono 2.9g, poly 0.9g); PROTEIN 10.8g; CARB 39.7g; FIBER 7.4g; CHOL 2mg; IRON 2.4mg; SODIUM 598mg; CALC 88mg

Lentil Dal Wraps

Pack some carrot and celery sticks to nosh alongside this hearty sandwich.

1 tablespoon vegetable oil
2 cups vertically sliced Vidalia or other sweet onion
1 cup dried small red lentils
1 tablespoon chopped peeled fresh ginger
¼ teaspoon crushed red pepper
1 cinnamon stick
2 cups water, divided
1 cup fat-free, less-sodium chicken broth
1½ tablespoons fresh lemon juice
½ teaspoon salt
4 (1.4-ounce) flatbreads (such as Flatout)
¼ cup plain fat-free yogurt
½ cup julienne-cut cucumber

1. Heat oil in a medium saucepan over medium heat. Add onion; cook 5 minutes or until tender, stirring occasionally. Add lentils, ginger, pepper, and cinnamon; cook 10 minutes, stirring occasionally. Stir in 1 cup water and broth; bring to a boil. Reduce heat, and simmer 10 minutes. Add 1 cup water and juice, and cook 30 minutes or until thick, stirring occasionally. Stir in salt. Remove cinnamon stick; cool lentil mixture completely. Spread about ½ cup mixture over each flatbread. Spread 1 tablespoon yogurt over each serving; divide cucumber evenly among flatbreads. Roll up. Cover and chill. Yield: 4 servings (serving size: 1 wrap).

CALORIES 461 (15% from fat); FAT 7.6g (sat 0.5g, mono 1.2g, poly 3.4g); PROTEIN 23.5g; CARB 73.2g; FIBER 10.3g; CHOL 1mg; IRON 5.7mg; SODIUM 916mg; CALC 103mg

Simple Peach Ice Cream

Summer is time for cannonball contests, grilled burgers, lightweight novels, and our homemade peach ice cream.

With a short list of wholesome ingredients and a no-cook method, this ice cream is ready to freeze quickly. Use an old-fashioned ice-cream freezer, or the newer kind that needs no ice or salt. Either way, you'll wish that summer would never end.

Simple Peach Ice Cream

Let the peaches and sugar stand at room temperature 30 minutes to produce the greatest amount of juice. With perfectly ripe peaches, a potato masher will coarsely chop or mash the fruit just as well as a food processor.

6 cups sliced peeled peaches (about 3 pounds)
¾ cup sugar
2 cups half-and-half
1½ teaspoons vanilla extract
¼ teaspoon salt

1. Combine peaches and sugar in a large bowl. Let stand 30 minutes, stirring occasionally. Place peach mixture in a food processor; pulse 10 times or until coarsely chopped. Return peach mixture to bowl; stir in half-and-half, vanilla, and salt.
2. Pour mixture into freezer can of an ice-cream freezer; freeze according to manufacturer's instructions. Spoon ice cream into a freezer-safe container; cover and freeze 1 hour or until firm. Yield: 12 servings (serving size: ½ cup).

CALORIES 138 (31% from fat); FAT 4.7g (sat 2.9g, mono 1.4g, poly 0.2g); PROTEIN 1.8g; CARB 23.7g; FIBER 1.7g; CHOL 15mg; IRON 0.1mg; SODIUM 65mg; CALC 46mg

Culinary Crossroads

With its Chinese and French influences—plus an emphasis on fresh ingredients and lively flavors—Vietnamese food is ideal for summer.

Lemongrass Shrimp over Rice Vermicelli and Vegetables

Bun Tom Nuong Xa

(pictured on page 271)

You can substitute pork tenderloin, beef sirloin, or chicken for the shrimp. Simply cut the meat into cubes, marinate for 2 hours, then skewer and grill until done. The sauce, called *nuoc cham*, is present at every meal in Vietnam and drizzled over grilled meats, plain rice, or noodles. Homemade herbal oil and fried herbs are widely used in Asia. In Vietnam, shallot oil and fried shallots are the most popular and are used to garnish meat, seafood, rice, and noodle dishes.

SHRIMP:
- ⅓ cup Thai fish sauce (such as Three Crabs)
- ¼ cup sugar
- 2 tablespoons finely chopped peeled fresh lemongrass
- 1 tablespoon vegetable oil
- 2 garlic cloves, minced
- 32 large shrimp, peeled and deveined (about 1½ pounds)

SAUCE:
- 1 cup fresh lime juice (about 9 medium limes)
- ¾ cup shredded carrot
- ½ cup sugar
- ¼ cup Thai fish sauce (such as Three Crabs)
- 2 garlic cloves, minced
- 2 red Thai chiles, seeded and minced

SHALLOT OIL:
- ¼ cup vegetable oil
- ¾ cup thinly sliced shallots

REMAINING INGREDIENTS:
- 8 ounces uncooked rice vermicelli (*banh hoai* or *bun giang tay*)
- 3½ cups shredded Boston lettuce, divided
- 2 cups fresh bean sprouts, divided
- 1¾ cups shredded carrot, divided
- 1 cucumber, halved lengthwise, seeded, and thinly sliced (about 1½ cups), divided
- Cooking spray
- ½ cup chopped fresh mint
- ½ cup unsalted dry-roasted peanuts, finely chopped

1. To prepare shrimp, combine first 6 ingredients in a large zip-top plastic bag; seal. Marinate in refrigerator 1 hour, turning occasionally. Remove shrimp from bag; discard marinade.

2. To prepare sauce, combine lime juice and next 5 ingredients, stirring with a whisk until sugar dissolves. Set aside.

3. To prepare shallot oil, heat ¼ cup oil in a small saucepan over medium heat. Add shallots; cook 5 minutes or until golden brown. Strain shallot mixture through a sieve into a bowl. Reserve oil. Set fried shallots aside.

4. To prepare remaining ingredients, place vermicelli in a large bowl; cover with boiling water. Let stand 20 minutes. Drain. Combine noodles, shallot oil, 1¾ cups lettuce, 1 cup sprouts, 1 cup carrot, and ¾ cup cucumber, tossing well.

5. To cook shrimp, prepare grill to medium-high heat.

6. Place shrimp on grill rack coated with cooking spray; grill 2½ minutes on each side or until done. Place ¾ cup noodle mixture in each of 8 bowls; top each serving with 4 shrimp, about 3 tablespoons sauce, and about 1 tablespoon fried shallots. Serve with remaining lettuce, bean sprouts, carrot, cucumber, mint, and peanuts. Yield: 8 servings.

CALORIES 423 (29% from fat); FAT 13.5g (sat 2.1g, mono 4.1g, poly 6g); PROTEIN 26.6g; CARB 51.9g; FIBER 4.3g; CHOL 129mg; IRON 4.2mg; SODIUM 960mg; CALC 102mg

How to Cut Lemongrass

Remove the tough, fibrous outer layers from lemongrass before chopping. Use only the pale bottom part of the stalk.

Sweet Coconut Tapioca Soup with Bananas

Che Chuoi

- 2 cups water
- 1 (14-ounce) can light coconut milk
- ½ cup sugar
- ¼ cup uncooked pearl tapioca
- ½ teaspoon salt
- 2 large ripe bananas, quartered lengthwise and cut into ½-inch pieces (about 1½ cups)
- 1 teaspoon sesame seeds, toasted (optional)

1. Bring water and coconut milk to a boil in a medium saucepan. Stir in sugar, tapioca, and salt. Reduce heat to medium-low; cook 30 minutes, stirring frequently. Stir in bananas. Remove from heat; cover and let stand 15 minutes. Serve warm or chill 3 hours. Sprinkle with sesame seeds, if desired. Yield: 4 servings (serving size: 1 cup soup and ¼ teaspoon seeds).

CALORIES 245 (22% from fat); FAT 5.9g (sat 3.7g, mono 0.1g, poly 0.2g); PROTEIN 0.8g; CARB 48.8g; FIBER 1.5g; CHOL 0mg; IRON 0.4mg; SODIUM 341mg; CALC 12mg

Vietnamese Pantry

Many of these ingredients are available in the produce and ethnic food aisles at large supermarkets. You can also find them at Asian specialty markets.

Chiles (*ot;* pronounced UT) vary widely in size and color. Very hot Thai or bird's-eye chiles are the most common.

Fish sauce (*nuoc mam;* NYUK MAAM) is an indispensable seasoning made of anchovies. A good quality fish sauce really makes a difference; we like Three Crabs.

Lemongrass (*xa;* SA) adds tangy flavor to stir-fries, stews, and sauces. Remove the outer leaves and dark-green leafy tops to reveal the creamy bulb, which can be chopped, crushed, sliced, or grated.

Mung bean sprouts (*gia;* ZIA) have yellow tips and white stems, and add crunch to salads and soups.

Rice vermicelli (*banh hoai;* BAAN HOY) are thin rice noodles that are used in Vietnamese table salads.

Thai basil (*rau que;* RAO KEH) is among the herbs that traditionally accompany Vietnamese dishes. The stems have a subtle purple hue.

Cilantro (*rau mui;* RAO MOY) leaves are used in finished dishes. Use the stems to flavor stock and rice.

Ginger (*gung;* GUH NG), an important flavoring, is often used in stocks and braised dishes.

Pearl tapioca (*bot bang;* BUT BAANG) is used primarily in sweets with coconut milk.

Rice (*gao te;* GAO TEH) is a staple for nearly half the world's population. Use jasmine rice for tender, separate, and fragrant cooked grains.

Rice sticks (*banh pho;* BAAN PHUH), dried, flat rice noodles, are used in stir-fries and soups.

Hanoi Beef and Rice Noodle Soup
Pho Bo

Traditionally a northern Vietnamese breakfast specialty, *pho bo* is now eaten at any time of day. Partially freeze eye-of-round roast to make it easier to slice. You can also use regular sweet basil in place of Thai basil.

BROTH:

- 3 pounds beef oxtail
- ¾ cup thinly sliced peeled fresh ginger (about 3 ounces)
- ⅔ cup coarsely chopped shallots (about 3 medium shallots)
- 5 quarts water
- 4 cups coarsely chopped daikon radish (about 1 pound)
- 3 tablespoons Thai fish sauce (such as Three Crabs)
- 2 tablespoons sugar
- 1 teaspoon white peppercorns
- 5 whole cloves
- 2 star anise
- 1 large yellow onion, peeled and quartered
- 1 cinnamon stick

REMAINING INGREDIENTS:

- 2 cups vertically sliced onion
- 12 ounces wide rice stick noodles (*banh pho*)
- 2 cups fresh bean sprouts
- 12 ounces eye-of-round roast, trimmed and cut into 1/16-inch slices
- 2 cups cilantro leaves
- 1 cup Thai basil leaves
- 4 red Thai chiles, seeded and thinly sliced
- 8 lime wedges
- 1 tablespoon hoisin sauce (optional)

1. To prepare broth, heat a large stockpot over medium-high heat. Add oxtail, ginger, and shallots; sauté 8 minutes or until ginger and shallots are slightly charred. Add water and next 8 ingredients; bring to a boil. Reduce heat, and simmer 4 hours. Strain broth through a sieve into a large bowl; discard solids. Return broth to pan; bring to a boil. Reduce heat to medium, and cook until reduced to 10 cups (about 30 minutes). Skim fat from surface; discard fat. Keep warm.

2. To prepare remaining ingredients, add sliced onion to broth. Place noodles in a large bowl, and cover with boiling water. Let stand 20 minutes. Drain. Place ⅓ cup bean sprouts in each of 6 soup bowls. Top each serving with 1⅓ cups noodles and 2 ounces eye-of-round. Bring broth to a boil; carefully ladle 1⅔ cups boiling broth over each serving (boiling broth will cook meat). Serve with cilantro, basil, chiles, limes, and hoisin, if desired. Yield: 6 servings.

CALORIES 404 (19% from fat); FAT 8.5g (sat 3.3g, mono 3.7g, poly 0.5g); PROTEIN 23.4g; CARB 58g; FIBER 3.5g; CHOL 57mg; IRON 3.3mg; SODIUM 751mg; CALC 69mg

STAFF FAVORITE • QUICK & EASY
Pan-Fried Tofu with Spicy Lemongrass Sauce
Tofu Nuong Xa

The original version of this dish calls for deep-frying the tofu. Pan-searing renders a healthier version that's just as delicious. This recipe earned our Test Kitchens' highest rating.

- 2 (15-ounce) packages water-packed extrafirm tofu
- Cooking spray
- 2 tablespoons Thai fish sauce (such as Three Crabs)
- 1½ tablespoons sugar
- 2 teaspoons vegetable oil
- ½ cup finely chopped shallots
- 1 garlic clove, minced
- 2 tablespoons chopped peeled fresh lemongrass
- 1 red Thai chile, minced

1. Cut each tofu block crosswise into 8 slices. Arrange tofu in a single layer on several layers of heavy-duty paper towels. Cover with additional paper towels; let stand 15 minutes.

2. Heat a large nonstick skillet over medium-high heat. Coat pan with cooking spray. Add tofu; cook 2 minutes on each side or until browned. Set aside, and keep warm.

3. Combine fish sauce and sugar, stirring with a whisk until blended. Heat oil in a small saucepan over medium-high heat. Add shallots and garlic; sauté 3 minutes or until lightly browned. Add lemongrass and chile; sauté 2 minutes. Stir in sugar mixture, and cook 1 minute. Serve lemongrass sauce with tofu. Yield: 4 servings (serving size: 4 tofu pieces and 1 tablespoon sauce).

CALORIES 180 (32% from fat); FAT 6.4g (sat 1g, mono 1.3g, poly 3.6g); PROTEIN 17g; CARB 14.5g; FIBER 0.5g; CHOL 0mg; IRON 3.2mg; SODIUM 832mg; CALC 82mg

---

Asian Menu
serves 8

Garlic and Ginger Rice

Five-spice shrimp*

Snow peas

*Prepare grill. Combine 1 tablespoon vegetable oil, 2 teaspoons dark sesame oil, 2 teaspoons grated orange rind, 1 teaspoon salt, ¾ teaspoon five-spice powder, and ½ teaspoon crushed red pepper in a large bowl. Add 3 pounds peeled and deveined large shrimp; toss to coat. Thread shrimp onto 10-inch skewers. Place on grill rack coated with cooking spray; grill 2 minutes on each side or until shrimp are done.

Garlic and Ginger Rice
Com Gung Tuong

Asian Chicken Stock (recipe at right) flavors this rice dish. If you're pressed for time, substitute canned chicken broth for the Asian Chicken Stock. Use any leftover rice to make fried rice.

- 2 cups uncooked jasmine rice
- 1 tablespoon vegetable oil
- 1 tablespoon grated peeled fresh ginger
- 2 garlic cloves, minced
- 3 cups Asian Chicken Stock (recipe at right)
- 1 cup chopped fresh cilantro

1. Place rice in a colander in a bowl. Cover rice with water; stir rice until water turns white. Lift colander; drain liquid in bowl. Repeat procedure twice. Drain.

2. Heat oil in a large saucepan over medium heat. Add ginger and garlic; cook 3 minutes, stirring frequently. Add rice; cook 1 minute, stirring constantly. Stir in Asian Chicken Stock; bring to a boil. Cover, reduce heat to medium-low, and cook 15 minutes or until liquid is absorbed. Remove from heat, and stir in cilantro. Cover and let stand 10 minutes. Fluff with a fork. Yield: 8 servings (serving size: ¾ cup).

CALORIES 210 (9% from fat); FAT 2.2g (sat 0.4g, mono 0.6g, poly 1.1g); PROTEIN 4.5g; CARB 46.1g; FIBER 1.5g; CHOL 6mg; IRON 1.6mg; SODIUM 143mg; CALC 9mg

---

Asian Chicken Stock

Use this mild stock for soups or for cooking rice. See Garlic and Ginger Rice (recipe at left).

- 1 gallon water
- 2 cups chopped leek (about 3 leeks)
- 1½ cups thinly sliced peeled fresh ginger (about 4 ounces)
- 1½ cups chopped celery
- 3 tablespoons Thai fish sauce (such as Three Crabs)
- 1 teaspoon black peppercorns
- 10 chicken wings (about 2½ pounds)
- 8 chicken drumsticks (about 2½ pounds)
- 2 bunches cilantro, chopped
- 2 bay leaves
- 1 Vidalia or other sweet onion, peeled and quartered

1. Combine all ingredients in a large Dutch oven; bring to a boil. Reduce heat, and simmer 3 hours. Strain broth through a cheesecloth-lined colander into a bowl; discard solids. Yield: about 2½ quarts (serving size: 1 cup).

CALORIES 36 (35% from fat); FAT 1.4g (sat 0.4g, mono 0.5g, poly 0.3g); PROTEIN 4.7g; CARB 0.8g; FIBER 0.1g; CHOL 15mg; IRON 0.3mg; SODIUM 378mg; CALC 15mg

---

Chicken with Ginger and Green Onion-Salt Dip

Use this pungent dip in small amounts. You can also drizzle some of the dip over the chicken and serve the rest in a small bowl.

- ¼ cup minced green onions
- 2½ tablespoons vegetable oil
- 2 tablespoons grated peeled fresh ginger
- 1½ teaspoons kosher salt
- 3 cups shredded cooked chicken breast
- 2 cups hot cooked rice

1. Combine first 4 ingredients in a medium bowl; stir with a whisk. Arrange chicken over rice; serve with dip. Yield: 4 servings (serving size: ¾ cup chicken, about 2 tablespoons dip, and ½ cup rice).

CALORIES 374 (30% from fat); FAT 12.5g (sat 2.3g, mono 3.3g, poly 5.8g); PROTEIN 34.8g; CARB 27.7g; FIBER 1.3g; CHOL 89mg; IRON 2.5mg; SODIUM 785mg; CALC 17mg

---

Green Papaya Salad
Goi Du Du

Use green mango if green papaya isn't available.

- ½ cup fresh lime juice (about 2 large limes)
- ¼ cup sugar
- 3 tablespoons Thai fish sauce (such as Three Crabs)
- 4 cups (2 x ¼-inch) julienne-cut peeled papaya (about 3 papayas)
- 3 cups matchstick-cut carrots
- 2 red Thai chiles, seeded and thinly sliced
- ⅔ cup chopped fresh cilantro
- ¼ cup finely chopped unsalted, dry-roasted peanuts

1. Combine first 3 ingredients in a medium bowl; stir well with a whisk. Add papaya, carrot, and chiles; toss well. Let stand 20 minutes. Sprinkle with cilantro and peanuts. Yield: 6 servings (serving size: 1 cup).

CALORIES 150 (20% from fat); FAT 3.3g (sat 0.5g, mono 1.6g, poly 1.1g); PROTEIN 3.5g; CARB 30g; FIBER 4.4g; CHOL 0mg; IRON 0.8mg; SODIUM 722mg; CALC 52mg

Wrap It Up

Make a filling, use refrigerated dough, tortillas, or crêpes, and you'll have a sandwich supper all wrapped up.

QUICK & EASY
Thai Beef Salad Wraps

This dish has all the bright, fresh flavors and crunchy textures of a summer roll. The tortilla wrappers make it a satisfying main dish.

TOTAL TIME: 35 MINUTES

QUICK TIP: If the tortillas are dry, revive them by wrapping in damp paper towels and microwaving at HIGH for 10 seconds. This will keep them from cracking when you roll them up.

- 1 (1-pound) flank steak, trimmed
- ¼ teaspoon salt
- ¼ teaspoon black pepper
- Cooking spray
- 1 cup cubed peeled cucumber
- ½ cup grape or cherry tomato halves
- ¼ cup thinly sliced shallots
- 1 tablespoon chopped fresh mint
- 1 tablespoon chopped fresh basil
- 1 tablespoon chopped fresh cilantro
- 3 tablespoons low-sodium soy sauce
- 2 tablespoons fresh lime juice
- 2 tablespoons brown sugar
- ½ teaspoon crushed red pepper
- 6 (10-inch) flour tortillas
- 12 Bibb lettuce leaves

1. Prepare grill to medium-high heat.
2. Sprinkle steak with salt and black pepper. Place steak on a grill rack coated with cooking spray, and grill 4 minutes on each side or until desired degree of doneness. Let rest 5 minutes.
3. Cut steak diagonally across grain into thin slices. Combine sliced steak, cucumber, and next 5 ingredients in a large bowl. Combine soy sauce, juice, sugar, and red pepper. Drizzle over steak mixture; toss well to coat.
4. Warm tortillas according to package directions. Arrange 2 lettuce leaves on each tortilla. Spoon ⅔ cup steak mixture

down center of each tortilla; roll up. Yield: 6 servings (serving size: 1 wrap).

CALORIES 399 (28% from fat); FAT 12.4g (sat 4.3g, mono 5.6g, poly 1.1g); PROTEIN 22.4g; CARB 48.5g; FIBER 3.1g; CHOL 39mg; IRON 4.4mg; SODIUM 760mg; CALC 113mg

Wrap Menu
serves 6

Thai Beef Salad Wraps

Grilled soy-glazed eggplant*

Iced green tea

*Slice 4 Japanese eggplants crosswise into ¼-inch-thick slices. Combine 1½ tablespoons low-sodium soy sauce, 2 teaspoons fresh lime juice, and 1 teaspoon dark sesame oil; brush evenly over both sides of eggplant. Place on a grill rack coated with cooking spray; grill 1 minute on each side or until tender.

Game Plan

1. While grill heats:
- Chop herbs and cucumber for wraps
- Squeeze juice for wraps and eggplant
- Halve tomatoes and slice shallots for wraps
- Prepare soy sauce mixture for wraps
2. While steak grills:
- Slice eggplant
- Brush eggplant slices with soy sauce glaze
3. While steak rests, grill eggplant.

QUICK & EASY
Prosciutto and Gruyère Strombolis

These five ingredients come together quickly to yield tasty Italian sandwiches.

TOTAL TIME: 25 MINUTES

- 1 (11-ounce) can refrigerated French bread dough
- 2 ounces thinly sliced prosciutto
- 1 cup trimmed arugula
- ½ cup (2 ounces) shredded Gruyère cheese
- ¼ cup chopped fresh parsley

1. Preheat oven to 425°.
2. Unroll dough onto a baking sheet; pat into a 14 x 11-inch rectangle. Cut dough into quarters to form 4 (7 x 5½-inch) rectangles. Top each rectangle with ½ ounce prosciutto, ¼ cup arugula, 2 tablespoons cheese, and 1 tablespoon parsley. Beginning at short side of each rectangle, roll up dough, jelly-roll fashion; pinch seam to seal (do not seal ends of rolls). Arrange rolls 4 inches apart on baking sheet. Bake at 425° for 10 minutes or until rolls are lightly browned. Serve warm. Yield: 4 servings (serving size: 1 roll).

CALORIES 275 (28% from fat); FAT 8.5g (sat 4.4g, mono 2.1g, poly 0.5g); PROTEIN 14g; CARB 34.4g; FIBER 1.5g; CHOL 24mg; IRON 2.3mg; SODIUM 754mg; CALC 158mg

Stromboli Menu
serves 4

Prosciutto and Gruyère Strombolis

Tomato-basil soup*

Cantaloupe cubes tossed with mint

*Heat 2 teaspoons olive oil in a medium saucepan. Add ½ cup chopped onion and 3 chopped garlic cloves; sauté 4 minutes or until onion is tender. Add 1 (28-ounce) can whole tomatoes, drained; bring to a boil. Cover, reduce heat, and simmer 10 minutes. Pour tomato mixture into a blender; add ½ cup packed fresh basil leaves, 2 tablespoons whipping cream, and ½ teaspoon salt. Process until smooth.

Game Plan

1. While oven preheats for strombolis:
- Bring tomato mixture to a boil
- Arrange stromboli fillings on dough
- Cut cantaloupe
2. While soup simmers:
- Bake strombolis
- Wash basil for soup
- Chop mint for cantaloupe

Creamy Chicken and Mushroom Crêpes

Buy a rotisserie chicken from the deli counter, and use the breast meat for this recipe. You'll have some leftover chicken for another meal later in the week. If you can't find baby portobello mushrooms, use cremini mushrooms. Look for packaged crêpes in the produce aisle.

TOTAL TIME: 32 MINUTES

1 teaspoon butter
1 cup vertically sliced onion
1 garlic clove, minced
3 cups thinly sliced baby portobello mushroom caps (about 6 ounces)
¾ teaspoon salt
¼ teaspoon freshly ground black pepper
½ cup dry white wine
¾ cup fat-free, less-sodium chicken broth
2 teaspoons chopped fresh thyme
¼ cup crème fraîche
2 cups shredded skinless, boneless rotisserie chicken breast
6 (9-inch) packaged French crêpes (such as Melissa's)
Thyme sprigs (optional)

1. Melt butter in a large nonstick skillet over medium-high heat. Add onion and garlic; sauté 2 minutes or until onion begins to brown. Add mushrooms, salt, and pepper; cook 3 minutes or until liquid evaporates and mushrooms are tender, stirring frequently. Add wine, and cook 3 minutes or until liquid almost evaporates, stirring frequently. Add broth and chopped thyme; cook 2 minutes. Remove from heat; add crème fraîche, stirring until well blended. Add chicken, tossing to coat.
2. Place 1 crêpe on each of 6 plates. Spoon about ⅓ cup mushroom mixture into center of each crêpe; roll up. Garnish with thyme sprigs, if desired. Serve immediately. Yield: 6 servings (serving size: 1 filled crêpe).

CALORIES 272 (30% from fat); FAT 9.1g (sat 5g, mono 2.8g, poly 0.9g); PROTEIN 19.4g; CARB 27.5g; FIBER 0.8g; CHOL 66mg; IRON 2.1mg; SODIUM 643mg; CALC 66mg

Crêpe Menu
serves 6

Creamy Chicken and Mushroom Crêpes

Broccoli with balsamic-butter sauce*

White and wild rice blend

*Place 1 pound broccoli spears in a microwave-safe dish; add 1 tablespoon water. Cover with plastic wrap; vent. Microwave at HIGH 4 minutes or until crisp-tender; drain. Melt 1 tablespoon butter in a large nonstick skillet over medium-high heat. Add 2 tablespoons finely chopped shallots; sauté 2 minutes. Remove from heat. Stir in 2 tablespoons balsamic vinegar, ¼ teaspoon salt, and ¼ teaspoon freshly ground black pepper; drizzle over broccoli.

Game Plan

1. While water for rice comes to a boil:
  • Slice onion and mushrooms, and mince garlic for crêpes
  • Shred chicken
2. While rice cooks:
  • Prepare filling for crêpes
  • Prepare broccoli

Spinach and Feta-Stuffed Focaccia

TOTAL TIME: 40 MINUTES

1 tablespoon olive oil
½ cup chopped onion
3 garlic cloves, minced
2 (6-ounce) packages baby spinach
¾ cup (3 ounces) crumbled feta cheese
⅔ cup golden raisins
3 tablespoons pine nuts, toasted
2 tablespoons fresh lemon juice
1½ teaspoons chopped fresh oregano
¼ teaspoon salt
¼ teaspoon ground red pepper
1 (13.8-ounce) can refrigerated pizza crust dough
Cooking spray
1 tablespoon 2% reduced-fat milk
1 tablespoon water
¼ cup (1 ounce) grated fresh Parmesan cheese

1. Preheat oven to 450°.
2. Heat oil in a large nonstick skillet over medium-high heat. Add onion and garlic; sauté 1 minute. Add half of spinach; cook 1 minute or until spinach wilts. Add remaining spinach; cook 2 minutes or until spinach wilts, stirring constantly. Remove from heat; stir in feta and next 6 ingredients.
3. Place dough on a baking sheet coated with cooking spray; pat dough into a 15 x 12-inch rectangle. Spread spinach mixture lengthwise over half of dough, leaving a 1-inch border. Fold dough over filling; press edges together with a fork. Cut 5 (1-inch) diagonal slits in top of dough.
4. Combine milk and water; brush evenly over dough. Sprinkle with Parmesan. Bake at 450° for 15 minutes or until golden. Yield: 6 servings (serving size: 1 slice).

CALORIES 334 (29% from fat); FAT 10.6g (sat 3.5g, mono 4.6g, poly 1.3g); PROTEIN 12.6g; CARB 48.7g; FIBER 3.5g; CHOL 16mg; IRON 3.9mg; SODIUM 815mg; CALC 201mg

Focaccia Menu
serves 6

Spinach and Feta-Stuffed Focaccia

Romaine, strawberry, and orange salad*

Vanilla low-fat ice cream with caramel sauce

*Combine 6 cups torn romaine lettuce, 1 cup sliced strawberries, 1 cup drained canned mandarin oranges, and ¾ cup thinly vertically sliced red onion in a large bowl. Combine 2 tablespoons fresh lemon juice, 1 tablespoon honey, 2 teaspoons extravirgin olive oil, 1 teaspoon Dijon mustard, ¼ teaspoon salt, and ¼ teaspoon black pepper, stirring with a whisk. Drizzle dressing over salad; toss gently to coat. Sprinkle with ¼ cup shaved Parmesan cheese.

Game Plan

1. While oven preheats for focaccia:
  • Toast nuts for focaccia
  • Prepare filling for focaccia
  • Prepare dressing for salad
2. While focaccia bakes:
  • Prepare remaining salad ingredients

Fresh Figs

Don't miss out on the renaissance of this plump, sweet, and versatile "fruit."

Although we usually think of figs as fruit, they're actually flowers that turn in on themselves. The tiny seeds inside are the real fruit. Fresh figs are best when simply prepared to enhance their natural sweetness, much like you might handle peaches or plums in season.

Fig Varieties

Black Mission is by far the most widely available fig in markets, especially in California (where they're grown) and in the Northeast (where figs must be shipped in). Stunningly beautiful, Black Missions possess deep-purple to black skin and watermelon-colored flesh. *Also known as California Black, Franciscan, Franciscana, and Negra*

Kadota figs have amber-pink flesh with few seeds and luminous caterpillar-green skin that's somewhat thicker than that of other varieties. That's an asset when it comes to shipping, and you're more likely to find these in Eastern markets during the season. *Also known as Dattero, Dottato, and White Kadota*

Adriatic figs have greenish-yellow skin and red flesh. They "eat like raspberry jam," says Bob Steinacher of Maywood Farms in Northern California. *Also known as Grosse Verte, Italian Strawberry, Nebian, Ventura, Verdone, and White Adriatic*

Brown Turkey is a beloved older fig grown in the West and the South and, with winter care, as far Northeast as Connecticut. It has a milder flavor than a Mission, and some say a sweeter taste. Brown Turkey figs have copper-colored skin, often with hints of purple, and white flesh that shades to pink in the center. *Also known as California Brown Turkey, San Pedro, and San Piero*

QUICK & EASY

Fresh Fig Salad with Crème Fraîche, Mint, and Prosciutto

Look for crème fraîche, thickened cream with a nutty flavor, near the gourmet cheeses. If your supermarket doesn't carry it, substitute whole sour cream.

- ⅓ cup crème fraîche
- 1 tablespoon water
- 1 teaspoon grated lemon rind
- 2 teaspoons fresh lemon juice
- ¼ teaspoon salt
- ¼ teaspoon freshly ground black pepper
- 24 small dark-skinned fresh figs, halved (such as Black Mission, Celeste, or Brown Turkey; about 2 pounds)
- ¼ cup chopped fresh mint
- 3 very thin slices prosciutto, cut into ½-inch strips (about ½ cup)
- Mint sprigs (optional)

1. Combine first 6 ingredients, stirring well with a whisk.

2. Arrange figs on a platter. Drizzle with crème fraîche mixture. Sprinkle with chopped mint and prosciutto. Garnish with mint sprigs, if desired. Yield: 6 servings (serving size: about 1 cup).

CALORIES 169 (29% from fat); FAT 5.4g (sat 3.1g, mono 1.7g, poly 0.5g); PROTEIN 3.2g; CARB 29.8g; FIBER 5.1g; CHOL 14mg; IRON 0.7mg; SODIUM 214mg; CALC 81mg

---

MAKE AHEAD

Oven-Dried Figs

These dried figs are much softer and moister than store-bought dried figs. They're great for a snack, in salads, on pizza, or chopped and sprinkled over ice cream. Store them in an airtight container up to 3 days.

- 10 light-skinned fresh figs, halved (such as Kadota, Adriatic, or Panachee; about 1 pound)
- Cooking spray

1. Preheat oven to 250°.

2. Arrange figs in a single layer on a foil-lined baking sheet coated with cooking spray. Bake at 250° for 1½ to 2 hours or until almost dry but still soft. Yield: 1½ cups (serving size: ¼ cup).

CALORIES 56 (3% from fat); FAT 0.2g (sat 0g, mono 0.1g, poly 0.1g); PROTEIN 0.6g; CARB 14.5g; FIBER 2.5g; CHOL 0mg; IRON 0.3mg; SODIUM 1mg; CALC 26mg

---

MAKE AHEAD

Refrigerator Fig Preserves
(pictured on page 270)

Test the thickness of the cooked fruit mixture by spooning a little of it onto a saucer. Place the saucer in the freezer for a few minutes; the mixture should firm to a jam-like consistency. Store in the refrigerator up to 1 month.

- ½ cup sugar
- ¼ cup water
- ¼ cup honey
- ¼ cup light-colored corn syrup
- 2 tablespoons fresh lemon juice
- ⅛ teaspoon salt
- 20 light-skinned fresh figs, quartered (such as Kadota, Adriatic, or Panachee; about 2 pounds)

1. Combine all ingredients in a medium saucepan over medium-high heat; bring to a boil. Reduce heat; simmer 50 minutes or until thick and syrupy, stirring occasionally. Remove from heat; cool. Yield: 2½ cups (serving size: 2 tablespoons).

CALORIES 78 (1% from fat); FAT 0.1g (sat 0g, mono 0g, poly 0.1g); PROTEIN 0.4g; CARB 20.5g; FIBER 1.5g; CHOL 0mg; IRON 0.2mg; SODIUM 20mg; CALC 16mg

Chicken Braised with Leeks and Figs

The sweetness of figs, balsamic vinegar, and honey cuts the richness of chicken thighs and drumsticks. White wine has a delicate flavor, making it a good cooking liquid that won't overpower the figs. Serve this saucy dish over couscous.

    1 tablespoon butter
    3 cups coarsely chopped leek (about
       4 large)
    2 tablespoons all-purpose flour
    ¾ teaspoon salt
    ¼ teaspoon freshly ground black
       pepper
    4 (4-ounce) chicken drumsticks,
       skinned
    4 (4-ounce) chicken thighs,
       skinned
    2 cups dry white wine
    2 tablespoons balsamic
       vinegar
    1 tablespoon honey
    6 parsley sprigs
    1 thyme sprig
   16 light-skinned fresh figs, halved
       (such as Kadota, Adriatic, or
       Panachee; about 1½ pounds)
    1 tablespoon chopped fresh
       parsley
       Thyme sprigs (optional)

1. Melt butter in a large nonstick skillet over medium-high heat. Add leek; sauté 5 minutes or until tender. Remove leek from pan, and set aside.
2. Combine flour, salt, and pepper in a large zip-top plastic bag. Add chicken; seal and shake to coat. Add chicken mixture to pan; cook 10 minutes, browning on all sides. Return leek to pan; add wine and next 4 ingredients. Bring to a boil; cover, reduce heat, and simmer 15 minutes. Add figs; simmer 10 minutes or until chicken is done. Discard parsley sprigs and thyme sprig. Sprinkle with chopped parsley. Garnish with thyme sprigs, if desired. Yield: 4 servings (serving size: 1 drumstick, 1 thigh, 8 fig halves, and about ¼ cup sauce).

CALORIES 387 (19% from fat); FAT 8.3g (sat 3.1g, mono 2.4g, poly 1.6g); PROTEIN 28.8g; CARB 52.4g; FIBER 7g; CHOL 110mg; IRON 4.2mg; SODIUM 607mg; CALC 127mg

MAKE AHEAD

Flatbread with Oven-Dried Figs, Caramelized Onions, and Blue Cheese

Rosemary-scented flatbread is topped with a tasty combination of sweet figs and caramelized onions, meaty walnuts, and pungent blue cheese. It's best served warm and would make a fine accompaniment to a grilled steak and green salad.

    2¾ cups bread flour, divided
     1 package dry yeast (about
        2¼ teaspoons)
     1 cup warm water (100° to 110°),
        divided
     2 tablespoons extravirgin olive oil,
        divided
     1 to 2 teaspoons chopped fresh
        rosemary
    1½ teaspoons salt, divided
        Cooking spray
    2¼ cups vertically sliced red onion
     1 tablespoon sugar
     ½ teaspoon grated orange rind
     ⅛ teaspoon freshly ground black
        pepper
     ¼ cup coarsely chopped walnuts
    20 Oven-Dried Fig halves (recipe on
        page 290)
     ½ cup (2 ounces) crumbled blue cheese

1. Lightly spoon flour into dry measuring cups; level with a knife. Combine ½ cup flour and yeast in a large bowl, stirring with a whisk. Add ½ cup warm water; let stand 30 minutes. Add 2 cups flour, ½ cup water, 1 tablespoon oil, rosemary, and 1¼ teaspoons salt; stir until a soft dough forms. Turn dough out onto a lightly floured surface. Knead until smooth and elastic (about 8 minutes), and add enough of remaining flour, 1 tablespoon at a time, to prevent dough from sticking to hands (dough will feel tacky).
2. Place dough in a large bowl coated with cooking spray, turning to coat top. Cover and let rise in a warm place (85°), free from drafts, 1 hour or until doubled in size. (Press two fingers into dough. If an indentation remains, dough has risen enough.)
3. While dough rises, heat 1 tablespoon oil in a large nonstick skillet over medium heat. Add onion and sugar; cook 15 minutes or until deep golden brown, stirring occasionally. Add ¼ teaspoon salt, orange rind, and pepper. Cool slightly.
4. Preheat oven to 425°.
5. Punch dough down; form into a ball. Place dough on a baking sheet coated with cooking spray; let rest 5 minutes. Roll dough into a 14 x 12-inch rectangle (about ¼ inch thick). Arrange onion mixture, walnuts, and Oven-Dried Fig halves evenly over dough, leaving a ½-inch border on all sides. Sprinkle with cheese, and gently press toppings into dough to adhere. Bake at 425° for 20 minutes or until flatbread is golden brown and cheese melts. Yield: 14 servings (serving size: 1 piece).

CALORIES 160 (26% from fat); FAT 4.7g (sat 1.2g, mono 2g, poly 1.3g); PROTEIN 5g; CARB 26.6g; FIBER 2.3g; CHOL 3mg; IRON 1.5mg; SODIUM 309mg; CALC 40mg

QUICK & EASY

Baked Figs and Nectarines over Ice Cream

This fruit mixture is also great over pound cake or angel food cake. If you have trouble finding late-harvest Riesling, try Gewürztraminer in its place.

   12 light-skinned fresh figs, halved
       (such as Kadota, Adriatic, or
       Panachee; about 1¼ pounds)
    3 nectarines, pitted and quartered
    ¼ cup late-harvest Riesling or other
       sweet white wine
    2 tablespoons honey
    3 tablespoons sugar
    3 cups vanilla reduced-fat ice cream
       (such as Healthy Choice)

1. Preheat oven to 425°.
2. Arrange figs and nectarines in a single layer in a 13 x 9-inch baking dish. Pour wine over fruit, and drizzle with honey. Sprinkle evenly with sugar. Bake at 425° for 25 minutes or until fruit begins to brown. Serve warm with vanilla ice cream. Yield: 6 servings (serving size: about ½ cup fruit mixture and ½ cup ice cream).

CALORIES 271 (9% from fat); FAT 2.6g (sat 1.1g, mono 0.7g, poly 0.2g); PROTEIN 4.3g; CARB 58.3g; FIBER 5.3g; CHOL 5mg; IRON 0.6mg; SODIUM 47mg; CALC 136mg

Fig Tales

Figs have long been prized for their luscious taste and sensuous appeal. Some enthusiasts argue that it was a fig, not an apple, that tempted Eve in the Bible. In Genesis, Adam and Eve "sewed fig leaves together and made themselves aprons."

Other religious traditions are linked to figs. The prophet Muhammad, founder of Islam, is said to have declared, "If I should wish a fruit brought to Paradise, it would, certainly, be the fig." The fig tree also played a part in the birth of Buddhism. Siddhartha Gautama's revelation came to him while he was sitting beneath a Bo tree, a species of fig.

The Romans held figs in high regard and planted them in all the lands they conquered, including what are now France and England. Pliny, a Roman writer in the first century A.D., wrote, "Figs are restorative. They increase the strength of young people, preserve the elderly in better health, and make them look younger with fewer wrinkles." But the seductive taste of the fig was Cleopatra's undoing. Knowing she would reach for a delectable fig, her enemies hid an asp in a basket of them.

The Black Mission fig is closely tied to the history of California. Spanish missionaries planted figs at the San Diego Mission in the mid-18th century and subsequently at every mission north of there.

Fig lore persists today. "It's strange; people come to my booth, taste a fig, and then tell their life story to me," says Bob Steinacher of Maywood Farms in Northern California. "Everybody has a story of a fig that was part of their own family history."

Spiced Fig Upside-Down Cake

Cooking spray
2 tablespoons butter, melted
3 tablespoons brown sugar
10 dark-skinned fresh figs, halved (such as Black Mission, Celeste, or Brown Turkey; about 1 pound)
1½ cups all-purpose flour
2 teaspoons baking powder
1 teaspoon ground ginger
¼ teaspoon ground cinnamon
¼ teaspoon ground cloves
¼ teaspoon ground mace
⅛ teaspoon salt
⅓ cup butter, softened
¾ cup packed brown sugar
½ cup light molasses
2 large egg yolks
½ cup 1% low-fat milk
1 teaspoon vanilla extract
2 large egg whites

1. Preheat oven to 350°.
2. Coat a 9-inch round cake pan with cooking spray. Coat bottom of pan with melted butter, and sprinkle with 3 tablespoons sugar. Arrange fig halves over sugar, cut sides down. Set aside.
3. Lightly spoon flour into dry measuring cups; level with a knife. Combine flour and next 6 ingredients, stirring with a whisk. Place ⅓ cup butter and ¾ cup sugar in a large bowl, and beat with a mixer at medium speed until blended. Add molasses and egg yolks; beat well. Beat in milk and vanilla. Add flour mixture to butter mixture; stir with a whisk just until blended.
4. Place egg whites in a medium bowl; using clean beaters, beat with a mixer at high speed until stiff peaks form. Gently fold egg whites into batter; spoon over figs in prepared pan. Bake at 350° for 55 minutes or until a wooden pick inserted in center comes out clean. Cool 15 minutes in pan on a wire rack. Loosen cake from sides of pan using a narrow metal spatula. Place a plate upside down on top of cake; invert onto plate. Yield: 10 servings (serving size: 1 wedge).

CALORIES 323 (28% from fat); FAT 9.9g (sat 5.7g, mono 2.9g, poly 0.6g); PROTEIN 4.1g; CARB 56.5g; FIBER 2.2g; CHOL 66mg; IRON 2.5mg; SODIUM 246mg; CALC 149mg

Pork Stew with Pearl Onions, Green Olives, and Figs

Green figs, such as Kadota, hold up better when cooked than darker-skinned varieties. You could also make this stew with boneless, skinless chicken thighs in place of the pork.

2 teaspoons olive oil
2 cups finely chopped onion
1 cup chopped carrot
2½ tablespoons all-purpose flour
½ teaspoon salt
¼ teaspoon freshly ground black pepper
2 pounds boneless Boston butt pork roast, trimmed and cut into bite-sized pieces
3 cups fat-free, less-sodium chicken broth
1½ cups frozen pearl onions (about 7 ounces)
1 cup dry white wine
1 tablespoon chopped fresh parsley
1 teaspoon chopped fresh oregano
½ teaspoon chopped fresh thyme
2 bay leaves
½ cup pitted green olives
12 light-skinned fresh figs, halved (such as Kadota, Adriatic, or Panachee; about 1¼ pounds)

1. Heat oil in a Dutch oven over medium-high heat. Add chopped onion and carrot; sauté 5 minutes or until tender. Remove from pan; set aside.
2. Combine flour, salt, and pepper in a large zip-top plastic bag. Add pork; seal and shake to coat. Add pork mixture to pan; cook 10 minutes, browning on all sides. Return carrot mixture to pan. Add broth and next 6 ingredients; bring to a boil. Cover, reduce heat, and simmer

45 minutes. Stir in olives and figs; cook 15 minutes or until pork is tender. Remove and discard bay leaves. Yield: 6 servings (serving size: about 1 cup).

CALORIES 372 (28% from fat); FAT 11.4g (sat 3.3g, mono 5.8g, poly 1.3g); PROTEIN 26.4g; CARB 35.7g; FIBER 5g; CHOL 76mg; IRON 2.6mg; SODIUM 776mg; CALC 88mg

. . . And Ready in Just About 20 Minutes

Warm Salad of Grilled Figs, Grapes, and Bitter Greens

Grilling intensifies the sweetness of figs by caramelizing their natural sugars—a nice contrast to the bitterness of the radicchio and endive.

1½ tablespoons extravirgin olive oil, divided
2 tablespoons sherry vinegar or cider vinegar
½ teaspoon salt
½ teaspoon freshly ground black pepper
2 cups torn radicchio
2 cups thinly sliced fennel bulb
2 cups sliced Belgian endive
2 cups seedless red grapes
12 dark-skinned fresh figs, halved (such as Black Mission, Celeste, or Brown Turkey; about 1¼ pounds)
Cooking spray

1. Prepare grill to high heat.
2. Combine 1 tablespoon oil, vinegar, salt, and pepper in a large bowl. Add radicchio, fennel, endive, and grapes; toss gently to coat. Set aside.
3. Brush 1½ teaspoons oil over cut sides of figs. Place figs on a grill rack coated with cooking spray; grill 1½ minutes on each side or until lightly browned. Place radicchio mixture on a platter; top with grilled figs. Yield: 6 servings (serving size: about 1¼ cups).

CALORIES 154 (24% from fat); FAT 4.1g (sat 0.6g, mono 2.6g, poly 0.5g); PROTEIN 1.8g; CARB 31.3g; FIBER 5.2g; CHOL 0mg; IRON 1mg; SODIUM 219mg; CALC 66mg

Salmon with Wilted Watercress and Balsamic Drizzle

The warm, sweet balsamic dressing tenderizes the peppery watercress to make a bed for the seared salmon.

½ cup balsamic vinegar
½ teaspoon powdered sugar
4 (6-ounce) salmon fillets (about 1 inch thick), skinned
¾ teaspoon kosher salt, divided
Cooking spray
8 cups trimmed watercress (about 8 ounces)
¼ teaspoon freshly ground black pepper

1. Combine vinegar and sugar in a small saucepan over medium-high heat; bring to a boil. Cook until reduced to ¼ cup (about 7 minutes). Place in a large bowl; cool slightly.
2. While vinegar mixture cooks, heat a large nonstick skillet over medium-high heat. Sprinkle fillets with ¼ teaspoon salt. Coat pan with cooking spray. Add fillets; cook 4 minutes on each side or until fish flakes easily when tested with a fork.
3. Add ½ teaspoon salt, watercress, and pepper to vinegar mixture; toss to coat. Place about 1½ cups watercress mixture on each of 4 plates; top each serving with 1 fillet. Yield: 4 servings.

CALORIES 301 (39% from fat); FAT 13.2g (sat 3.1g, mono 5.7g, poly 3.2g); PROTEIN 37.9g; CARB 5.9g; FIBER 0.4g; CHOL 87mg; IRON 1mg; SODIUM 555mg; CALC 112mg

Chicken Scaloppine over Broccoli Rabe

To make cutlets, place chicken breast halves between two sheets of heavy-duty plastic wrap, and pound to ¼-inch thickness using a meat mallet. Serve with baby carrots and roasted new potatoes.

1 tablespoon olive oil
⅓ cup Italian-seasoned breadcrumbs
¼ teaspoon black pepper
4 (6-ounce) skinless, boneless chicken breast halves
½ cup dry white wine
½ cup fat-free, less-sodium chicken broth
3 tablespoons fresh lemon juice
1 teaspoon butter
1 pound broccoli rabe (rapini), cut into 3-inch pieces
2 tablespoons chopped fresh parsley
2 tablespoons capers, rinsed and drained
4 lemon slices (optional)

1. Heat oil in a large nonstick skillet over medium-high heat.
2. Combine breadcrumbs and pepper in a shallow dish; dredge chicken in breadcrumb mixture. Add chicken to pan; cook 3 minutes on each side or until done. Remove from pan; keep warm.
3. Add wine, broth, juice, and butter to pan, scraping pan to loosen browned bits. Stir in broccoli rabe; cover and cook 3 minutes or until broccoli rabe is tender. Stir in parsley and capers. Serve chicken over broccoli rabe mixture. Garnish with lemon slices, if desired. Yield: 4 servings (serving size: 1 chicken cutlet and ½ cup broccoli rabe mixture).

CALORIES 318 (21% from fat); FAT 7.4g (sat 1.7g, mono 3.3g, poly 1g); PROTEIN 44.3g; CARB 14g; FIBER 3.9g; CHOL 101mg; IRON 2.9mg; SODIUM 577mg; CALC 102mg

Asian Chicken Noodle Soup

The pasta will still have a chewy bite when the chicken is ready, but it continues to cook while the soup stands. Serve with rice crackers and lime wedges.

1 tablespoon vegetable oil
1 tablespoon bottled minced garlic
1 tablespoon bottled grated ginger
2 stalks fresh lemongrass, peeled
2 cups water
2 (14-ounce) cans fat-free, less-sodium chicken broth
1 pound chicken breast tenders, cut into bite-sized pieces
4 ounces uncooked angel hair pasta
¼ cup chopped fresh cilantro
1 tablespoon fresh lime juice
½ teaspoon salt
2 green onions, thinly sliced
1 red chile pepper, finely chopped

1. Heat oil in a large nonstick skillet over medium-high heat. Add garlic, ginger, and lemongrass; sauté 3 minutes. Add water and broth, and bring to a boil. Add chicken and pasta; cook 5 minutes or until chicken is done. Remove from heat; stir in cilantro and remaining ingredients. Let stand 5 minutes. Discard lemongrass. Yield: 8 servings (serving size: 1 cup).

CALORIES 289 (17% from fat); FAT 5.3g (sat 0.9g, mono 1.2g, poly 2.5g); PROTEIN 32.6g; CARB 23.9g; FIBER 1g; CHOL 66mg; IRON 2.1mg; SODIUM 738mg; CALC 31mg

Sesame Chicken Salad

Serve this delicious salad soon after mixing, or it will wilt and take on a dull color. For quicker prep, substitute bagged shredded cabbage for the napa.

VINAIGRETTE:
¼ cup rice vinegar
¼ cup low-sodium soy sauce
2 tablespoons creamy peanut butter
1 teaspoon dark sesame oil
1 teaspoon bottled minced fresh ginger
1 teaspoon bottled minced garlic

SALAD:
2½ cups chopped cooked chicken breast
2 cups thinly sliced napa (Chinese) cabbage
1 cup red bell pepper strips
1 cup fresh bean sprouts
1 cup grated carrot
2 tablespoons chopped green onions
1 teaspoon sesame seeds, toasted

1. To prepare vinaigrette, combine first 6 ingredients, stirring with a whisk.
2. To prepare salad, combine chicken and next 5 ingredients in a large bowl. Drizzle with vinaigrette, tossing gently to coat. Sprinkle with sesame seeds. Yield: 4 servings (serving size: 1½ cups).

CALORIES 256 (31% from fat); FAT 8.8g (sat 2g, mono 3.6g, poly 2.5g); PROTEIN 31.9g; CARB 12.1g; FIBER 3g; CHOL 74mg; IRON 2mg; SODIUM 654mg; CALC 54mg

Grilled Portobello-Goat Cheese Pitas

If the tomatoes are ripe, skip grilling them. Serve with a tropical fruit salad of mangoes, cantaloupe, and pineapple sprinkled with toasted coconut.

1½ teaspoons bottled minced garlic
1 teaspoon olive oil
4 (6-inch) pita rounds
½ teaspoon salt, divided
¼ teaspoon black pepper, divided
1 (6-ounce) package portobello mushrooms
2 tomatoes, cut into ¼-inch-thick slices
⅓ cup (3 ounces) goat cheese
½ cup chopped fresh basil

1. Preheat a grill pan over medium heat.
2. Combine garlic and oil; brush evenly over pitas. Sprinkle ¼ teaspoon salt and ⅛ teaspoon pepper evenly over pitas. Place pitas in pan, and cook 2 minutes on each side or until toasted.
3. Sprinkle ¼ teaspoon salt and ⅛ teaspoon pepper evenly over mushrooms and tomatoes. Place mushrooms in pan; cook 6 minutes or until tender, turning once.

Remove mushrooms from pan. Add tomatoes to pan; cook 1 minute.
4. Spread cheese evenly over pitas. Arrange mushrooms and tomatoes evenly over pitas. Sprinkle with basil. Yield: 4 servings (serving size: 1 topped pita).

CALORIES 283 (27% from fat); FAT 8.5g (sat 4.7g, mono 2.4g, poly 0.7g); PROTEIN 11.9g; CARB 39.8g; FIBER 2.9g; CHOL 17mg; IRON 2.7mg; SODIUM 731mg; CALC 133mg

Curried Tofu

Serve with white rice or rice noodles and fresh orange slices.

2 teaspoons vegetable oil
1 (15-ounce) package reduced-fat firm tofu, drained and cut into ½-inch cubes
½ teaspoon salt
½ cup light coconut milk
1 teaspoon curry powder
1 cup matchstick-cut carrots
¼ teaspoon crushed red pepper
1 (15¼-ounce) can pineapple chunks in juice, drained
1 red bell pepper, thinly sliced
½ cup chopped fresh basil

1. Heat oil in a large nonstick skillet over medium-high heat. Add tofu, and sprinkle with salt. Cook 8 minutes or until golden brown, stirring frequently. Remove from pan; keep warm.
2. Add coconut milk and curry powder to pan, and cook 1 minute, stirring constantly. Add carrots, crushed red pepper, pineapple, and bell pepper; cook 5 minutes, stirring occasionally. Stir in tofu. Sprinkle with basil. Yield: 3 servings (serving size: about 1⅓ cups).

CALORIES 171 (34% from fat); FAT 6.4g (sat 2g, mono 0.9g, poly 2.4g); PROTEIN 8.9g; CARB 21.7g; FIBER 3.6g; CHOL 0mg; IRON 2.7mg; SODIUM 508mg; CALC 99mg

Food & Friendship

Cooking is a pleasure in itself, but sharing the results with friends and family is even better. That's why we've devoted 14 pages to entertaining. We offer a number of ways to make dining—and cooking—a communal event. You'll get tips from Chef Billy Strynkowski on how supper club members can team up in the kitchen (page 296), strategies from John and Caprial Pence on cooking together as a couple (page 298), planning ideas for a progressive dinner party (page 300), and authentic recipes and inspiration for hosting a Puerto Rican block party (page 309).

Live From New York

With a little help from Chef Billy Strynkowski, a Long Island supper club prepares a stellar dinner—together.

Supper Club Menu
serves 8

Grilled Eggplant with Caramelized Onion and Fennel

Crab-Stuffed Lobster with Citrus Vinaigrette

Corn Fritter Casserole

Summer Tomato Chopped Salad

Lemon-Buttermilk Panna Cotta with Blueberry Sauce

WINE NOTE: This menu is chock-full of flavor. As a result, the accompanying wine needs to be fresh, clean, lively, and flexible with a wide range of tastes. California Sauvignon Blanc, most of which have good, light herbal flavors with notes of green fig and melon, is a good choice. A fine example: Husch 2002 Sauvignon Blanc from Mendocino, California, $12.50.

Grilled Eggplant with Caramelized Onion and Fennel

To prepare this appetizer indoors, broil the eggplant rounds until browned, and continue the recipe as instructed. White balsamic vinegar offers the sweetness of regular balsamic but won't discolor the salad. You can use regular balsamic vinegar if white isn't available.

1 (1¼-pound) eggplant (about 4-inch diameter), peeled
Cooking spray
¼ teaspoon salt, divided
¼ teaspoon freshly ground black pepper, divided
2¾ cups chopped fennel bulb (about 1 large bulb)
2 cups finely chopped yellow onion
2 cups trimmed arugula
1 teaspoon white balsamic vinegar
1 teaspoon extravirgin olive oil
1 cup quartered cherry tomatoes
½ cup (2 ounces) crumbled goat cheese
2 tablespoons chopped fresh basil
1 tablespoon chopped fresh thyme

1. Prepare grill to medium heat.
2. Cut peeled eggplant crosswise into 8 (½-inch-thick) slices. Lightly coat both sides of slices with cooking spray; sprinkle with ⅛ teaspoon salt and ⅛ teaspoon pepper. Place on a grill rack coated with cooking spray; grill 7 minutes on each side or until browned. Set aside.
3. Heat a large nonstick skillet over medium-high heat. Coat with cooking spray. Add fennel and onion; sauté 8 minutes or until vegetables are tender and lightly browned.
4. Combine ⅛ teaspoon salt, ⅛ teaspoon pepper, arugula, vinegar, and oil in a medium bowl; toss gently to coat. Divide arugula mixture evenly among 8 appetizer plates; top each serving with 1 eggplant slice. Arrange about ⅓ cup fennel mixture on each eggplant slice; top with 2 tablespoons tomatoes and 1 tablespoon cheese. Sprinkle basil and thyme evenly over cheese. Yield: 8 servings.

CALORIES 73 (30% from fat); FAT 2.4g (sat 1.2g, mono 0.8g, poly 0.2g); PROTEIN 3.2g; CARB 11.3g; FIBER 3.8g; CHOL 3mg; IRON 0.9mg; SODIUM 122mg; CALC 49mg

Crab-Stuffed Lobster with Citrus Vinaigrette

Ask your fishmonger to briefly steam, split, and clean the lobsters; then skip Step 3.

STUFFING:
1 cup finely chopped leek
¼ cup finely chopped red bell pepper
¼ cup fresh corn kernels
1 pound lump crabmeat, shell pieces removed
1 tablespoon low-fat mayonnaise
1 tablespoon whole-grain Dijon mustard
1½ teaspoons Old Bay seasoning
1 teaspoon fresh lemon juice
1 large egg white, lightly beaten
3 tablespoons finely chopped fresh parsley
2 teaspoons minced fresh tarragon

LOBSTER:
5 quarts water
4 (1½-pound) whole Maine lobsters
Cooking spray
½ cup coarsely crushed cornflakes

VINAIGRETTE:
½ cup fresh orange juice
2 tablespoons chopped fresh chives
2 tablespoons fresh lemon juice
2 tablespoons fresh lime juice
2 tablespoons olive oil
1½ teaspoons sugar
1½ teaspoons whole-grain Dijon mustard
⅛ teaspoon salt
⅛ teaspoon freshly ground black pepper

1. To prepare stuffing, cook leek in boiling water 2 minutes. Drain and plunge leek into ice water; drain. Pat dry with a
Continued

paper towel. Place leek, bell pepper, corn, and crab in a large bowl; toss gently to combine. Combine mayonnaise and next 4 ingredients in a small bowl, stirring with a whisk. Add mayonnaise mixture to crab mixture; toss gently to coat. Gently fold in parsley and tarragon; set aside.

2. Preheat oven to 375°.

3. To prepare lobster, bring 5 quarts water to a boil in an 8-quart stockpot; plunge 2 lobsters headfirst, 1 at a time, into water. Return to a boil. Cover, reduce heat, and simmer 2 minutes. Remove lobsters from pan using tongs; drain well. Repeat procedure with remaining lobsters. Cool lobsters slightly. Remove claws; place claws on a baking sheet. Cut lobsters in half lengthwise; clean upper cavity of lobsters, leaving white meat intact.

4. Arrange lobster halves, cut sides up, on a jelly-roll pan coated with cooking spray; spoon ½ cup stuffing into cleaned cavity of each lobster half. Top stuffing in each lobster half with 1 tablespoon cornflakes, and lightly coat with cooking spray.

5. Place baking sheet with claws on bottom rack in oven; place jelly-roll pan with stuffed lobster halves on upper rack in oven. Bake at 375° for 20 minutes or until lobster halves are done and stuffing is lightly browned. Remove lobster halves from oven; cover and keep warm. Bake claws an additional 10 minutes or until done. Cool claws slightly; remove meat from cooked claws.

6. To prepare vinaigrette, combine orange juice and remaining 8 ingredients, stirring with a whisk. Serve vinaigrette with lobster. Yield: 8 servings (serving size: 1 stuffed lobster half, 1 claw, and 2 tablespoons vinaigrette).

CALORIES 228 (21% from fat); FAT 5.4g (sat 0.7g, mono 2.9g, poly 0.9g); PROTEIN 31.1g; CARB 12.7g; FIBER 0.7g; CHOL 120mg; IRON 2.3mg; SODIUM 774mg; CALC 128mg

---

STAFF FAVORITE
Corn Fritter Casserole

This dish is a cross between corn bread and corn pudding. Bake it before the lobsters go in the oven; if you cover it loosely with foil, it should still be warm enough when the lobsters are finished. Use 1½ cups fresh corn kernels in place of the canned corn, if you prefer.

3 tablespoons butter, softened
3 large egg whites, lightly beaten
1 (8-ounce) block fat-free cream cheese, softened
½ cup finely chopped onion
½ cup finely chopped red bell pepper
1 (15¼-ounce) can whole-kernel corn, drained
1 (14¾-ounce) can cream-style corn
1 (8½-ounce) package corn muffin mix (such as Jiffy)
¼ teaspoon black pepper
Cooking spray

1. Preheat oven to 375°.

2. Combine first 3 ingredients in a large bowl, stirring with a whisk until smooth. Stir in onion and next 3 ingredients; mix well. Add muffin mix and black pepper, stirring until well combined. Pour into an 11 x 7-inch baking dish coated with cooking spray. Bake at 375° for 50 minutes or until a wooden pick inserted in center comes out clean. Yield: 9 servings (serving size: about ⅔ cup).

CALORIES 247 (31% from fat); FAT 8.4g (sat 3.7g, mono 2.7g, poly 0.7g); PROTEIN 8.6g; CARB 36.7g; FIBER 1.9g; CHOL 31mg; IRON 1.3mg; SODIUM 629mg; CALC 72mg

---

QUICK & EASY
Summer Tomato Chopped Salad

Use heirloom-variety tomatoes from your local farmers' market to make this salad look and taste its best. Coarse sea salt offers visual appeal and crunch; you can also substitute ¼ teaspoon table salt.

7 cups (¾-inch) diced tomato (about 2¾ pounds)
¼ cup thinly sliced fresh basil
1 tablespoon extravirgin olive oil
½ teaspoon sea salt
¼ teaspoon freshly ground black pepper
1 tablespoon pine nuts, toasted

1. Place first 5 ingredients in a large bowl; toss gently to combine. Sprinkle with nuts. Serve immediately. Yield: 8 servings (serving size: about ¾ cup).

CALORIES 55 (46% from fat); FAT 2.8g (sat 0.4g, mono 1.5g, poly 0.6g); PROTEIN 1.6g; CARB 7.6g; FIBER 1.9g; CHOL 0mg; IRON 0.9mg; SODIUM 161mg; CALC 11mg

---

Chef Billy's Tips

At all *Cooking Light* Supper Club Events, Chef Billy Strynkowski distributes handouts with cooking tips, including:

• Garlic is great, but its smell lingers on your hands. To remove the scent, rub your hands against stainless steel, such as a kitchen faucet.

• Coat a knife with cooking spray before slicing a pie so sticky fillings won't cling to the blade.

• When roasting meats, poultry, and fish, rest the meat on rings (or "doughnuts") of crimped aluminum foil. This elevates the meat from the bottom of the pan so it roasts evenly and keeps it from sticking to the bottom of the pan.

• When preparing a marinade, use as little oil as possible. Oil seals the outer layer of proteins in the meat and prevents the flavor of the marinade from penetrating.

• To preserve fresh herbs, gently wrap them in a damp paper towel, place them in a zip-top plastic bag, and refrigerate up to 10 days.

• To dry your own herbs, arrange fresh herbs on a baking sheet lined with parchment paper, and dry for 5 to 7 hours in an oven set as low as possible. Store in the freezer in tightly capped jars.

• Be choosy when purchasing sea scallops. Make sure they're on a dry surface, as scallops shouldn't be sitting in water or any liquid. They should also be sticky to the touch.

• Use a rind of Parmesan cheese to impart a nice nutty flavor to homemade tomato sauce. Simply slip the rind into the sauce, and remove it when cooking is complete.

• Rice cookers make great rice, are foolproof, and are almost effortless to operate. They shut off automatically when the rice is cooked to keep it from burning.

• To get more juice from lemons or limes, poke a small hole into the fruit, microwave for 10 to 15 seconds, cut, and squeeze.

Lemon-Buttermilk Panna Cotta with Blueberry Sauce

The creamy texture of the panna cotta is a nice match for summer fruit. Running a knife around the edge of each prepared custard makes it easier to remove to a plate.

PANNA COTTA:
Cooking spray
1½ tablespoons unflavored gelatin
  1 cup whole milk
  ½ cup plus 2 tablespoons sugar
  3 cups low-fat buttermilk
  1 teaspoon grated lemon rind

SAUCE:
  ½ cup apple juice
  ¼ cup sugar
  1 tablespoon fresh lemon juice
  2 cups blueberries
Mint sprigs (optional)

1. To prepare panna cotta, coat 8 (6-ounce) custard cups with cooking spray. Sprinkle gelatin over whole milk in a small saucepan; let stand 10 minutes. Cook milk mixture over medium-low heat 10 minutes or until gelatin dissolves, stirring constantly with a whisk. Increase heat to medium; add ½ cup plus 2 tablespoons sugar, stirring with a whisk until sugar dissolves. Remove from heat. Add buttermilk and rind, stirring well. Divide mixture evenly among prepared custard cups. Cover and chill at least 5 hours or overnight.
2. To prepare sauce, combine apple juice, ¼ cup sugar, and lemon juice in a small saucepan. Bring to a boil over medium-high heat; stir until sugar dissolves. Reduce heat to medium; stir in blueberries. Cook mixture 8 minutes or until blueberries are warm and begin to pop. Cool sauce to room temperature.
3. Place a dessert plate, upside down, on top of each custard cup; invert panna cotta onto plates. Serve with sauce. Garnish with mint sprigs, if desired. Yield: 8 servings (serving size: 1 panna cotta and about ¼ cup sauce).

CALORIES 173 (10% from fat); FAT 2g (sat 1.2g, mono 0.6g, poly 0.1g); PROTEIN 5.4g; CARB 34.8g; FIBER 1g; CHOL 8mg; IRON 0.2mg; SODIUM 117mg; CALC 148mg

cooking class

In the Kitchen with Caprial and John

Caprial and John Pence, who work and cook together, share their tips for couples who want to team up at the stove.

Caprial and John have owned and operated Caprial's Bistro in Portland, Oregon, for 11 years. Last September, the couple coproduced a TV show: *Caprial & John's Kitchen: Cooking for Friends and Family.* Here they relate how to make the most of time together in the kitchen—and how to cook more happily with family and friends.

Flank Steak with Five-Spice Rub and Chile Relish

Caprial and John grill frequently. They make this dish on really busy nights.

RELISH:
  2 poblano chiles
  1 orange bell pepper
1½ tablespoons chopped dry-roasted peanuts
  1 tablespoon chopped fresh cilantro
  1 tablespoon seasoned rice vinegar
  ¼ teaspoon kosher salt
  ¼ teaspoon freshly ground black pepper
  1 garlic clove, minced

STEAK:
  1 tablespoon brown sugar
  2 teaspoons kosher salt
  1 teaspoon ground cumin
  ½ teaspoon five-spice powder
  ¼ teaspoon ground ginger
  1 (2-pound) flank steak, trimmed
Cooking spray

1. Preheat broiler.
2. To prepare relish, cut chiles and bell pepper in half lengthwise; discard seeds and membranes. Place halves, skin sides up, on a foil-lined baking sheet; flatten with hand. Broil 15 minutes or until blackened. Place in a zip-top plastic bag; seal. Let stand 15 minutes. Peel and chop. Combine chiles, bell pepper, peanuts, and next 5 ingredients in a small bowl; toss well. Set aside.
3. Prepare grill.
4. To prepare steak, combine sugar and next 4 ingredients in a small bowl. Sprinkle steak with sugar mixture. Place steak on a grill rack coated with cooking spray; grill 6 minutes on each side or until desired degree of doneness. Cut steak across grain into thin slices. Serve with relish. Yield: 8 servings (serving size: about 3 tablespoons relish and 3 ounces steak).

CALORIES 198 (42% from fat); FAT 9.2g (sat 3.7g, mono 3.7g, poly 0.6g); PROTEIN 22.8g; CARB 5.2g; FIBER 0.8g; CHOL 54mg; IRON 2.6mg; SODIUM 681mg; CALC 17mg

Spicy Fish Cakes
(pictured on page 306)

Serve as an appetizer, or atop greens.

  ⅓ cup chopped green onions
  ¼ cup panko (Japanese breadcrumbs)
  2 tablespoons chile paste with garlic
  1 tablespoon chopped fresh basil
  1 teaspoon grated peeled fresh ginger
  2 garlic cloves, chopped
  1 large egg white
  ¾ pound skinless halibut fillets, cut into ½-inch pieces
  ½ pound sea scallops
  2 teaspoons vegetable oil
Sliced green onions (optional)

1. Preheat oven to 350°.
2. Place first 9 ingredients in a food processor; pulse until coarsely ground. Divide fish mixture into 6 equal portions, shaping each into a ½-inch-thick patty.
3. Heat oil in a large nonstick skillet over medium-high heat. Add patties; cook 2 minutes on each side. Turn patties over; wrap handle of pan with foil. Bake at 350° for 5 minutes or until patties are golden brown and thoroughly heated. Garnish with chopped green onions, if desired. Yield: 6 servings (serving size: 1 patty).

CALORIES 134 (23% from fat); FAT 3.4g (sat 0.5g, mono 0.9g, poly 1.4g); PROTEIN 19.4g; CARB 6.1g; FIBER 0.4g; CHOL 31mg; IRON 0.9mg; SODIUM 211mg; CALC 49mg

Caprial and John's Cooking Tips

Tip 1: Team Up

Don't put one person in charge; this could lead to a conflict, especially if one of you always makes the sauces and sears the meat while the other is relegated to the grunt work, like chopping and peeling the garlic. To form a true partnership, write a simple prep list that splits the duties equally so that each person will play an essential role in preparing the meal.

Tip 2: Move in Sync

If your kitchen is small, divide the preparation chores so, for example, one person uses the cutting board while the other cooks at the stove or works at the sink. You may bump elbows a few times as you start to establish a routine, but before long, working together in the kitchen will become like a well-choreographed ballet.

Tip 3: Plan Ahead

Mapping out meals for the week will alleviate a great deal of stress—and eliminate those last-minute stops at the grocery store where you frantically browse the aisles trying to come up with dinner. Try to make one big shopping trip for the week, augmenting with fresh vegetables you pick up as needed. Another strategy is to plan for leftovers. If you make soup for dinner, make a double batch for those nights when you come home and really don't want to cook. Also, be sure to maintain a well-stocked pantry, which makes it easier to cook after a long day.

Tip 4: Keep It Simple

These recipes are simple enough to prepare for a weeknight supper and yet impressive enough for casual entertaining. You can combine one or more of these dishes with your own family favorites to create a stunning menu for a special occasion.

Curry Ginger Butternut Squash Soup

Straining this spicy-sweet soup gives the final product a velvety appearance and texture.

2 teaspoons vegetable oil
3 tablespoons finely chopped peeled fresh ginger
3 garlic cloves, minced
2 teaspoons curry powder
1 cup mirin (sweet rice wine)
6 cups (½-inch) cubed peeled butternut squash (about 2½ pounds)
6 cups fat-free, less-sodium chicken broth
2½ cups (½-inch) cubed peeled celeriac (celery root; 1 to 1½ pounds)
2 teaspoons thawed orange juice concentrate
1 teaspoon Sriracha (hot chile sauce, such as Huy Fong)
½ teaspoon salt
½ cup plain low-fat yogurt
2 teaspoons chopped fresh flat-leaf parsley

1. Heat oil in a Dutch oven over medium-high heat. Add ginger and garlic; sauté 1½ minutes. Add curry; cook 15 seconds, stirring constantly. Add mirin; cook until liquid is reduced to ½ cup (about 4 minutes). Add squash, broth, and celeriac; bring to a boil. Reduce heat; simmer 15 minutes or until tender.
2. Place one-fourth of squash mixture in a blender; process until smooth. Strain puréed squash mixture through a sieve into a large bowl; discard solids. Repeat procedure in 3 more batches with remaining squash mixture. Stir in orange juice concentrate, Sriracha, and salt. Dollop 1 tablespoon yogurt over each serving, and sprinkle with parsley. Yield: 8 servings (serving size: about 1 cup).

CALORIES 176 (9% from fat); FAT 1.7g (sat 0.4g, mono 0.4g, poly 0.8g); PROTEIN 5.2g; CARB 29.3g; FIBER 4.7g; CHOL 1mg; IRON 1.3mg; SODIUM 567mg; CALC 107mg

Spinach Salad with Grilled Shrimp

Add crusty bread to make this salad complete.

DRESSING:
2 tablespoons rice vinegar
2 tablespoons fresh orange juice
1½ tablespoons extravirgin olive oil
1 tablespoon honey
1 tablespoon low-sodium soy sauce
½ teaspoon grated peeled fresh ginger
½ teaspoon salt
⅛ teaspoon crushed red pepper

SHRIMP:
2 teaspoons extravirgin olive oil
1 teaspoon grated peeled fresh ginger
½ teaspoon ground cumin
¼ teaspoon salt
¼ teaspoon black pepper
2 garlic cloves, minced
2 pounds large shrimp, peeled and deveined
Cooking spray

SALAD:
8 cups baby spinach (about 8 ounces)
2 cups thinly sliced shiitake mushroom caps (about 4 ounces)
¾ cup thinly vertically sliced red onion

1. Prepare grill.
2. To prepare dressing, combine first 8 ingredients in a large bowl; stir well with a whisk. Set aside.
3. To prepare shrimp, combine 2 teaspoons oil and next 6 ingredients in a large bowl; toss well. Thread about 5 shrimp onto each of 6 (8-inch) skewers. Place skewers on a grill rack coated with cooking spray; grill 3 minutes or until done.
4. To prepare salad, add spinach, mushrooms, and onion to vinegar mixture; toss gently to coat. Serve with shrimp skewers. Yield: 6 servings (serving size: 1⅓ cups salad and 1 shrimp skewer).

CALORIES 181 (29% from fat); FAT 5.9g (sat 0.9g, mono 3g, poly 1.2g); PROTEIN 24.8g; CARB 6.9g; FIBER 1.3g; CHOL 172mg; IRON 3.9mg; SODIUM 478mg; CALC 96mg

Basmati Rice with Basil and Mint

1 cup basmati rice
2 teaspoons vegetable oil
2 teaspoons minced peeled fresh ginger
2 garlic cloves, minced
2¼ cups fat-free, less-sodium chicken broth
1 tablespoon chopped fresh basil
2 teaspoons chopped fresh mint
¼ teaspoon freshly ground black pepper

1. Preheat oven to 350°.
2. Place rice in a fine-mesh strainer. Rinse with cold water; drain.
3. Heat oil in a large saucepan over medium-high heat. Add ginger and garlic; cook 30 seconds, stirring constantly. Stir in rice; cook 1 minute, stirring constantly. Stir in broth and remaining ingredients; bring to a boil. Cover; wrap handle of pan with foil. Bake at 350° for 25 minutes, stirring once. Remove rice from oven; fluff rice with a fork. Yield: 4 servings (serving size: about ¾ cup).

CALORIES 215 (10% from fat); FAT 2.3g (sat 0.3g, mono 0.5g, poly 1.3g); PROTEIN 4.5g; CARB 46.7g; FIBER 1.5g; CHOL 0mg; IRON 1.5mg; SODIUM 254mg; CALC 5mg

Almond-Stuffed Baked Apples with Caramel-Apple Sauce
(pictured on page 306)

These stuffed apples bake while you enjoy dinner. When you caramelize the sugar, don't stir or move the pan until the sugar begins to color. Cook until the mixture becomes a deep amber color. The caramel mixture will splatter when you add the cider so use a long-handled wooden spoon for stirring.

FILLING:
½ cup sliced almonds, toasted
¼ cup sugar
2 teaspoons butter, melted
¼ teaspoon vanilla extract
⅛ teaspoon salt
Dash of ground nutmeg
1 large egg white, lightly beaten

APPLES:
4 Braeburn apples, halved
Cooking spray
1 tablespoon sugar
¼ teaspoon ground cinnamon

SAUCE:
½ cup sugar
3 tablespoons water
½ cup apple cider
1 tablespoon brandy
1 tablespoon Grand Marnier (orange-flavored liqueur)
1 teaspoon butter
Dash of salt

1. Preheat oven to 350°.
2. To prepare filling, place almonds in a food processor; process until finely ground. Combine ground almonds, ¼ cup sugar, and next 5 ingredients, stirring until well combined.
3. To prepare apples, core, remove seeds, and carefully scoop out 1 tablespoon from each apple half to form a cup. Cut a thin slice off the rounded side of each apple half to make a flat surface. Place apples, cup-sides up, on a jelly-roll pan coated with cooking spray. Combine 1 tablespoon sugar and cinnamon; sprinkle generously over apples. Spoon about 1 tablespoon filling in cup of each apple half. Bake at 350° for 40 minutes or until apples are golden and tender.
4. To prepare sauce, combine ½ cup sugar and 3 tablespoons water in a small saucepan. Cook over medium-high heat (do not stir) until mixture begins to brown; gently tilt pan, and swirl to evenly brown mixture. Reduce heat to low; slowly add cider, stirring constantly. Remove from heat; stir in brandy and remaining 3 ingredients. Serve over apples. Yield: 8 servings (serving size: 1 stuffed apple half and 1½ tablespoons sauce).

WINE NOTE: Since this dessert isn't supersweet, it's perfect for wine pairing. Very sweet desserts are harder to pair because they can make wine taste dull or neutral. A terrific choice is Muscat Beaumes-de-Venise from Jaboulet, France. The 2001 is about $16 for a 375-milliliter half-bottle. Just a small glass of this wonderful wine will make the baked apples taste like a three-star dessert course.

CALORIES 185 (22% from fat); FAT 4.5g (sat 1.1g, mono 2.3g, poly 0.8g); PROTEIN 1.7g; CARB 34.4g; FIBER 3.1g; CHOL 4mg; IRON 0.2mg; SODIUM 78mg; CALC 18mg

How to Prepare Apples

1. *Use a tablespoon measure to scoop out the flesh.*

2. *Cut off a sliver so the apple half balances.*

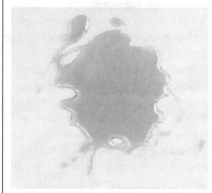

3. *Check the color of the caramel on white paper.*

Progressive Dinner

Hit the road for an evening of creative eating and fun.

If your supper club or group of friends is looking for a different way to entertain, try planning a progressive dinner. At this type of get-together, each course is served at a different home.

Here's how it works: The group splits into three teams—one for appetizers, one for the main course, and one for dessert. One person from each team hosts that group's course at his or her house. The evening begins with the entire group meeting at the first location for appetizers, then walking or driving to the other homes for subsequent courses. To get you moving, we've provided the menu, the recipes, and, all the tips.

Progressive Dinner Menu
serves 9

Our fusion menu features four appetizer options. Choose a couple to serve, or prepare them all. There are also two main-dish selections to choose from to suit your group.

Appetizer Stop

Baked Hoisin Chicken Buns

Tofu Larb

Galloping Horses

Crab and Scallop Sui Mei

Riesling or other sweet white wine

Main-Course Stop

Bitter Greens Salad with Sourdough Croutons and Warm Tomato Vinaigrette

Lamb Osso Buco over Parmesan Polenta or
Beef Bourguignonne with Egg Noodles

Cabernet Sauvignon

Dessert Stop

Individual Tiramisu Trifles

Coffee

How to Plan a Progressive Dinner Party

Teams

• Divide your friends into three teams—one for each course. Limit yourselves to three changes of locale.
• Draw names out of a hat to determine teams. Or have three people volunteer to be hosts, and let them choose teams.
• Split couples into separate teams to keep things interesting.
• Keep teams to a manageable size (about three to six so you don't end up with 30 guests to feed).
• Choose individual themes for each team or a single theme for the night. Entertain according to cuisine (Indian, French, etc.), culture (retro, book, or movie themes), or whatever members come up with. Or allow each team to choose a separate theme—like Mardi Gras appetizers (serve shrimp rémoulade and Hurricane cocktails), mystery theater main dish (stage a murder mystery), and *Love Boat* desserts (mimic the midnight buffet on a cruise ship).

Locations

• Pick homes that are close together and involve the least amount of travel time. Walking distance is ideal.
• Though a progressive dinner works best for people who live near each other, you can also stage this type of party in one house. Visit a different room or location within the home for each course (for example, appetizers on the patio, main course in the dining room, and dessert on the upstairs deck).

Timing and Travel

• A weekend night works best for this type of party. People will have all day to prepare and won't be rushing home from work.
• Set specific times for each course, and try to stick to them. Once you get off schedule, it's hard to get back on track.
• Allow extra time for appetizers at the first stop (people will want to talk more when they first come together) and dessert (folks will linger at the finale).

• Allow for travel time between houses.
• If you need to drive between locations, assign driving duty a day or two ahead so you don't waste time making that decision the night of the party.
• Provide a map, if needed.
• The main-dish and dessert teams need to leave a little early to get to their stations for last-minute touches before the rest of the group arrives.

Housekeeping

• Divide the recipes among team members so each person handles everything for one or two recipes.
• Ideally, each team should get together the night before, or at least earlier in the day, to set the table.
• Save receipts, and split costs among team members.
• Figure out clean-up duties ahead. Either plan to get back together at the end of the night to help your team's host clean up, or do it first thing the next morning.

Location 1: Appetizer

• Because the appetizer locale is the first stop, this team has the luxury of preparing dishes at the last minute.

• These starters have some make-ahead components, but a good bit of the work needs to be done just before serving: steaming the dumplings, baking the stuffed chicken buns, and cooking the *larb*. Designate one member to handle each chore shortly before guests are due to arrive.

• Divide the recipes so that each team member is responsible for purchasing the ingredients and preparing any make-ahead components.

Game Plan

Up to 1 day ahead:

• Prepare and refrigerate filling for dumplings.

• Combine juice mixture for larb; refrigerate in an airtight container.

• Separate cabbage leaves for larb; store leaves wrapped in damp paper towels in a zip-top plastic bag in refrigerator.

• Prepare and refrigerate filling for buns.

• Thaw dough for buns.

A few hours ahead:

• Prepare pork mixture and pineapple for Galloping Horses (recipe on page 302); cover and store separately in refrigerator.

Last-minute:

• Fill dumplings.

• Steam dumplings.

• Cook filling for larb; fill cabbage leaves.

• Bake chicken buns.

Baked Hoisin Chicken Buns

(pictured on page 305)

Most often, you'll see this type of stuffed bun steamed, but many Chinese dim sum restaurants also serve baked versions. Frozen roll dough is convenient and saves the trouble of making homemade dough; just be sure to thaw it in the refrigerator overnight. You can prepare the filling the day before the party, then fill and bake the buns so they'll be warm for arriving guests.

Cooking spray
12 ounces skinless, boneless chicken thighs
¼ cup finely chopped green onions
1½ tablespoons hoisin sauce
1 tablespoon oyster sauce
2 teaspoons rice vinegar
9 frozen white roll dough pieces, thawed (such as Rich's)
1 large egg, lightly beaten
1 teaspoon sesame seeds, toasted

1. Heat a nonstick skillet over medium-high heat. Coat pan with cooking spray. Add chicken; cook 4 minutes on each side or until done. Cool slightly, and shred meat with 2 forks. Place in a medium bowl. Add onions, hoisin sauce, oyster sauce, and vinegar; toss well to combine.

2. Roll each dough piece into a 4-inch circle on a lightly floured surface. Spoon about 2 tablespoons chicken mixture into center of each dough circle. Gather edges of dough over filling; pinch to seal. Place filled dough, seam sides down, on a baking sheet coated with cooking spray. Lightly coat with cooking spray. Cover and let rise 20 minutes.

3. Preheat oven to 375°.

4. Uncover filled dough. Gently brush with egg. Sprinkle evenly with sesame seeds. Bake at 375° for 15 minutes or until golden brown. Serve warm. Yield: 9 servings (serving size: 1 filled bun).

CALORIES 143 (26% from fat); FAT 4.1g (sat 1g, mono 1.3g, poly 1g); PROTEIN 10.4g; CARB 16.6g; FIBER 1.2g; CHOL 43mg; IRON 1.4mg; SODIUM 220mg; CALC 29mg

Tofu Larb

Traditionally made with ground chicken, larb is a spicy Thai appetizer. This rendition works well because the tofu readily absorbs the seasonings. Serve with lime wedges for extra zip.

⅓ cup fresh lime juice (about 3 limes)
1½ tablespoons fish sauce
1 tablespoon sugar
½ teaspoon salt
¼ teaspoon crushed red pepper
2 (14-ounce) packages water-packed firm reduced-fat tofu, drained and crumbled
2 teaspoons vegetable oil
½ teaspoon dark sesame oil
2 cups thinly vertically sliced red onion
3 garlic cloves, minced
2 serrano chiles, thinly sliced
½ cup chopped fresh basil
¼ cup chopped fresh mint
9 large green or red cabbage leaves

1. Combine first 5 ingredients, stirring until sugar dissolves; set aside.

2. Spread tofu in a single layer onto several layers of paper towels; cover with additional paper towels. Let stand 15 minutes, pressing down occasionally.

3. Heat oils in a large nonstick skillet over medium-high heat. Add onion, garlic, and chiles; sauté 3 minutes. Add tofu; cook 8 minutes or until lightly browned, stirring occasionally. Stir in juice mixture; cook 1 minute or until heated. Remove from heat; stir in basil and mint. Spoon about ½ cup tofu mixture into each cabbage leaf. Yield: 9 servings (serving size: 1 filled cabbage leaf).

CALORIES 80 (28% from fat); FAT 2.5g (sat 0.2g, mono 0.6g, poly 1.4g); PROTEIN 6.3g; CARB 7.5g; FIBER 1.2g; CHOL 0mg; IRON 1.1mg; SODIUM 426mg; CALC 66mg

Galloping Horses

This traditional Thai appetizer tops fresh pineapple slices with a sweet-savory-nutty mixture of ground pork mixed with green onions, cilantro, and peanuts. Its name, *ma hor* or *mah haw* in Thai, literally translates as "horses of the Haw people," a tribe that immigrated to Thailand from China. You can serve this dish at room temperature; for best results, don't prepare the pork mixture more than a few hours in advance.

- ¼ cup dry-roasted peanuts
- ⅓ cup chopped green onions
- ¼ cup fresh cilantro leaves
- 1 tablespoon sugar
- 1 tablespoon fish sauce
- 3 garlic cloves, chopped
- 1 serrano chile, halved
- 12 ounces pork tenderloin, trimmed and coarsely chopped
- Cooking spray
- ¼ teaspoon salt
- 9 (½-inch-thick) slices pineapple, each cut into quarters

1. Place peanuts in a food processor; process until finely ground. Spoon into a bowl; set aside.
2. Place onions and next 5 ingredients in food processor, and process until finely chopped. Spoon into a bowl; set aside.
3. Place pork in food processor; process until coarsely ground.
4. Heat a nonstick skillet over medium-high heat. Coat pan with cooking spray. Add ground pork; cook 4 minutes or until done, stirring to crumble. Stir in onion mixture; cook 2 minutes, stirring frequently. Stir in ground peanuts and salt. Serve pork mixture over pineapple pieces. Yield: 9 servings (serving size: about ¼ cup pork mixture and 4 pineapple pieces).

CALORIES 105 (30% from fat); FAT 3.5g (sat 0.7g, mono 1.6g, poly 0.9g); PROTEIN 8.7g; CARB 10g; FIBER 1.2g; CHOL 23mg; IRON 0.8mg; SODIUM 229mg; CALC 10mg

Crab and Scallop Sui Mei

(pictured on page 305)

These open-faced dumplings (pronounced "shoe-MY") are made with round gyoza skins. If you can't find gyoza skins, purchase wonton wrappers instead, and cut them into circles with a three-inch round biscuit cutter. You can make and refrigerate the seafood-and-vegetable filling up to 1 day in advance; fill and steam the dumplings shortly before serving them. If you don't have a bamboo steamer, prepare these in 2 or 3 batches in a collapsible metal steamer basket (be sure to line it with lettuce leaves so that the dumplings don't stick).

DUMPLINGS:
- ⅓ cup chopped shiitake mushroom caps
- ⅓ cup chopped water chestnuts
- 3 tablespoons chopped green onions
- 2 garlic cloves, chopped
- 1 teaspoon grated peeled fresh ginger
- ½ teaspoon dark sesame oil
- ¼ teaspoon salt
- 5 ounces sea scallops, chopped
- 1 (6-ounce) can lump crabmeat, drained (such as Chicken of the Sea)
- 1 large egg, lightly beaten
- 18 gyoza skins
- 1 teaspoon cornstarch
- 8 lettuce leaves

DIPPING SAUCE:
- 2 tablespoons low-sodium soy sauce
- 2 tablespoons rice vinegar
- 1 tablespoon water
- 1 tablespoon sugar
- 1 teaspoon sambal oelek (ground fresh chile paste) or Thai chile paste

1. To prepare dumplings, place first 4 ingredients in a food processor; pulse 8 times or until finely chopped. Add ginger, oil, salt, and scallops; pulse 4 times or until scallops are finely chopped. Spoon mixture into a medium bowl; add crabmeat and egg, tossing to combine.
2. Working with 1 gyoza skin at a time (cover remaining skins to prevent drying), spoon about 1 tablespoon filling into center of skin. Gather up edges of skin around filling; lightly squeeze skin to adhere to filling, leaving top of dumpling open. Smooth surface of filling

with back of a spoon dipped in water. Place dumplings on a baking sheet sprinkled with cornstarch; cover loosely with a damp towel to prevent drying.
3. Line each tier of a 2-tiered (10-inch) bamboo steamer with 4 lettuce leaves. Arrange 9 dumplings, 1 inch apart, over lettuce in each steamer basket. Stack tiers, and cover with steamer lid. Add water to a large skillet to a depth of 1 inch; bring to a boil. Place steamer in pan; steam dumplings 10 minutes. Remove dumplings from steamer.
4. To prepare sauce, combine soy sauce and remaining 4 ingredients; stir with a whisk until sugar dissolves. Serve with dumplings. Yield: 9 servings (serving size: 2 dumplings and about 1 teaspoon sauce).

CALORIES 100 (13% from fat); FAT 1.4g (sat 0.3g, mono 0.4g, poly 0.4g); PROTEIN 8.1g; CARB 13.3g; FIBER 0.6g; CHOL 43mg; IRON 0.9mg; SODIUM 370mg; CALC 31mg

How to Make Dumplings

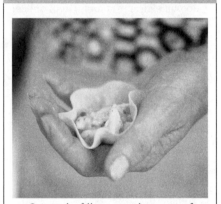

1. *Spoon the filling into the center of a gyoza skin.*

2. *Cup your hand around the gyoza skin while smoothing the filling with a spoon.*

Location 2: Main Course

- Serve food that can be heated early in the evening (before departing for appetizers) and stay warm in a slow cooker on low heat. Both our main-dish options can be made 1 day ahead, reheated, and held in a slow cooker until guests arrive at the main-course location.
- Leave the appetizer stop 10 or 15 minutes early to take care of last-minute preparations: cooking the egg noodles (for Beef Bourguignonne, recipe on page 304) or polenta (for Osso Buco, recipe at right), warming the salad dressing, and tossing the salad ingredients together.

Game Plan

Up to 2 days ahead:
- Bake croutons for salad; store at room temperature in an airtight container or zip-top plastic bag.

Up to 1 day ahead:
- Prepare beef or lamb mixture. Cover; chill.
- Make and refrigerate vinaigrette.

A few hours ahead:
- Combine greens for salad in the bowl you plan to serve from; cover and chill.
- Combine gremolata ingredients for Osso Buco; cover and refrigerate.
- Grate cheese for polenta; store in refrigerator in a zip-top plastic bag.
- Reheat beef or lamb mixture; keep warm in slow cooker set to low heat.

Last-minute:
- Boil egg noodles and chop parsley for Beef Bourguignonne, or prepare polenta for Osso Buco.
- Reheat vinaigrette and toss with salad; top salad with croutons.

Bitter Greens Salad with Sourdough Croutons and Warm Tomato Vinaigrette

Bake the croutons 1 or 2 days in advance; store at room temperature in a zip-top plastic bag. Make and refrigerate the vinaigrette 1 day ahead; reheat gently over low heat before tossing with the greens.

CROUTONS:
- 8 ounces sourdough bread, cut into ¾-inch cubes (about 6 cups)
- Cooking spray
- ½ teaspoon lemon pepper
- ¼ teaspoon garlic powder

SALAD:
- 6 cups trimmed arugula
- 3 cups thinly sliced radicchio
- 3 cups thinly sliced escarole

VINAIGRETTE:
- 1½ tablespoons extravirgin olive oil
- ¼ cup finely chopped shallots
- 4 garlic cloves, thinly sliced
- 1½ cups diced seeded plum tomato
- ¼ cup balsamic vinegar
- 1½ tablespoons brown sugar
- 2 teaspoons Dijon mustard
- ¼ teaspoon salt
- ¼ teaspoon black pepper

REMAINING INGREDIENT:
- ½ cup (2 ounces) grated fresh Parmesan cheese

1. Preheat oven to 350°.
2. To prepare croutons, arrange bread cubes on a baking sheet. Lightly coat with cooking spray. Sprinkle evenly with lemon pepper and garlic powder; toss to coat. Bake at 350° for 10 minutes or until crisp, stirring once.
3. To prepare salad, combine arugula, radicchio, and escarole in a large bowl.
4. To prepare vinaigrette, heat oil in a nonstick skillet over medium heat. Add shallots and garlic; cook 5 minutes, stirring occasionally. Add tomato; cook 2 minutes, stirring frequently. Stir in vinegar and next 4 ingredients. Reduce heat to low; cook 2 minutes or until warm. Drizzle over salad; toss gently to coat. Place 1 cup salad on each of 9 salad plates; top each serving with about 2½ teaspoons cheese. Divide croutons evenly among salads. Yield: 9 servings.

CALORIES 149 (30% from fat); FAT 5g (sat 1.6g, mono 2.5g, poly 0.6g); PROTEIN 5.8g; CARB 21g; FIBER 2g; CHOL 4mg; IRON 1.5mg; SODIUM 382mg; CALC 138mg

Lamb Osso Buco over Parmesan Polenta

Osso buco is an Italian dish that's traditionally made with veal shanks. This version uses lamb. We chose shoulder chops (sometimes labeled "arm chops"). Prepare the lamb and vegetable mixture 1 day in advance; combine the ingredients for the gremolata earlier in the day, and refrigerate until dinnertime. Make the polenta just before serving.

OSSO BUCO:
- Cooking spray
- 2 cups chopped onion
- 1 cup chopped carrot
- 6 garlic cloves, minced
- ⅓ cup all-purpose flour
- 9 (6-ounce) lamb shoulder chops (about 1 inch thick), trimmed
- 1¼ teaspoons salt, divided
- ½ teaspoon freshly ground black pepper, divided
- 1 tablespoon butter, divided
- 1 cup dry white wine
- 3 thyme sprigs
- 1 (14½-ounce) can diced tomatoes, drained
- 1 (14-ounce) can less-sodium beef broth

POLENTA:
- 3 cups water
- 3 cups fat-free milk
- 1½ cups yellow cornmeal
- ¾ cup (3 ounces) grated fresh Parmesan cheese
- 1 teaspoon salt

GREMOLATA:
- ½ cup chopped fresh flat-leaf parsley
- 1 tablespoon grated lemon rind
- ¼ teaspoon kosher salt
- 3 garlic cloves, minced

1. To prepare osso buco, heat a large Dutch oven over medium-high heat. Coat pan with cooking spray. Add onion, carrot, and 6 garlic cloves; sauté 7 minutes or until tender. Remove onion mixture from pan.
2. Place flour in a shallow dish. Sprinkle lamb with ½ teaspoon salt and ¼ teaspoon *Continued*

pepper; dredge lamb in flour. Melt 1 teaspoon butter in pan over medium-high heat. Add 3 lamb chops; cook 3 minutes on each side or until browned. Remove lamb from pan. Repeat procedure twice with 2 teaspoons butter and lamb.

3. Return onion mixture to pan. Add wine; cook 4 minutes or until most of liquid evaporates. Add ¾ teaspoon salt, ¼ teaspoon pepper, thyme, tomatoes, and broth. Return lamb to pan; bring to a boil. Cover, reduce heat, and simmer 1 hour. Uncover and simmer 45 minutes or until lamb is tender. Remove lamb from pan; cover and keep warm. Discard thyme sprigs.

4. Strain cooking liquid through a sieve into a large bowl; reserve vegetable mixture. Place a heavy-duty zip-top plastic bag inside a 2-cup glass measure. Pour cooking liquid into bag; let stand 10 minutes (fat will rise to top of bag). Seal bag; carefully snip off 1 bottom corner of bag. Drain liquid into bowl, stopping before fat layer reaches opening; discard fat. Add reserved vegetable mixture to liquid.

5. To prepare polenta, combine water and milk in a large saucepan; bring to a boil, stirring occasionally. Gradually add cornmeal, stirring constantly with a whisk. Cover and cook over medium heat 10 minutes or until thick, stirring frequently. Add cheese and 1 teaspoon salt, stirring until cheese melts.

6. To prepare gremolata, combine parsley, rind, kosher salt, and 3 garlic cloves. Serve gremolata over polenta, lamb, and vegetable mixture. Yield: 9 servings (serving size: about ⅔ cup polenta, 1 chop, about ½ cup vegetable mixture, and about 1 tablespoon gremolata).

CALORIES 420 (28% from fat); FAT 13.2g (sat 5.7g, mono 5.2g, poly 0.8g); PROTEIN 34g; CARB 40.4g; FIBER 4.9g; CHOL 88mg; IRON 3.3mg; SODIUM 975mg; CALC 264mg

---

STAFF FAVORITE • MAKE AHEAD
Beef Bourguignonne with Egg Noodles
(pictured on page 305)

This entrée tastes better when made 1 day in advance. Warm it in a Dutch oven over medium heat until thoroughly heated, and keep warm in a slow cooker set to low.

⅓ cup all-purpose flour
2 teaspoons salt, divided
¾ teaspoon freshly ground black pepper, divided
2¼ pounds beef stew meat
3 bacon slices, chopped and divided
1 cup chopped onion
1 cup sliced carrot
4 garlic cloves, minced
1½ cups dry red wine
1 (14-ounce) can less-sodium beef broth
8 cups halved mushrooms (about 1½ pounds)
2 tablespoons tomato paste
2 teaspoons chopped fresh thyme
2 bay leaves
1 (16-ounce) package frozen pearl onions
7 cups hot cooked medium egg noodles (about 6 cups uncooked noodles)
3 tablespoons chopped fresh flat-leaf parsley

1. Combine flour, 1 teaspoon salt, and ¼ teaspoon pepper in a large zip-top plastic bag. Add beef; seal and shake to coat.

2. Cook half of bacon in a large Dutch oven over medium-high heat until crisp. Remove bacon from pan with a slotted spoon; set aside. Add half of beef mixture to drippings in pan; cook 5 minutes, browning on all sides. Remove beef from pan; cover and keep warm. Repeat procedure with remaining bacon and beef mixture.

3. Add chopped onion, carrot, and garlic to pan; sauté 5 minutes. Stir in wine and broth, scraping pan to loosen browned bits. Add bacon, beef, 1 teaspoon salt, ½ teaspoon pepper, mushrooms, and next 4 ingredients; bring to a boil. Cover, reduce heat, and simmer 45 minutes. Uncover and cook 1 hour or until beef is tender. Discard bay leaves. Serve beef mixture over noodles; sprinkle with parsley. Yield: 9 servings (serving size: about 1 cup beef mixture, ¾ cup noodles, and 1 teaspoon parsley).

CALORIES 447 (29% from fat); FAT 14.6g (sat 5.1g, mono 6.1g, poly 1.5g); PROTEIN 32.7g; CARB 45.7g; FIBER 3.9g; CHOL 117mg; IRON 6mg; SODIUM 677mg; CALC 47mg

---

Location 3: Dessert

• This will be the last location of the night, so plan to have guests linger after dessert.
• Be sure to have coffee, dessert wines, and after-dinner drinks like port or brandy.
• Choose a dessert that can be completely prepared in advance, will hold up well in the refrigerator or at room temperature, and needs little or no last-minute fussing. Apart from our Individual Tiramisu Trifles (recipe below), good choices include crème brûlée, flan, cheesecake, and cakes.

Game Plan

Up to 1 day ahead:
• Assemble and refrigerate the trifles.
Last-minute:
• Brew coffee for guests.

MAKE AHEAD
Individual Tiramisu Trifles

1 cup cold strong brewed coffee
3 tablespoons Marsala wine
1 (8-ounce) block ⅓-less-fat cream cheese, softened
½ cup (4 ounces) block-style fat-free cream cheese, softened
¾ cup sugar
30 cakelike ladyfingers (2½ [3-ounce] packages)
1 teaspoon unsweetened cocoa

1. Combine coffee and wine; set aside.

2. Place cheeses in a medium bowl; beat with a mixer at medium speed until smooth. Gradually add sugar, beating until well blended.

3. Cut each ladyfinger crosswise into 3 pieces. Arrange 5 ladyfinger pieces in each of 9 wineglasses or small bowls; drizzle each serving with about 1 tablespoon coffee mixture. Spoon about 1½ tablespoons cheese mixture into each glass. Repeat layers once; sprinkle evenly with cocoa. Cover and chill at least 1 hour. Yield: 9 servings (serving size: 1 trifle).

CALORIES 228 (28% from fat); FAT 7.2g (sat 4.3g, mono 1.9g, poly 0.6g); PROTEIN 6.4g; CARB 34.2g; FIBER 0.3g; CHOL 62mg; IRON 0.7mg; SODIUM 340mg; CALC 71mg

---

Crab and Scallop Sui Mei, page 302, and Baked Hoisin Chicken Buns, page 301

Beef Bourguignonne with Egg Noodles, page 304

Spicy Fish Cakes, page 297

Almond-Stuffed Baked Apples with Caramel-Apple Sauce,
page 299

Pork and Grilled Vegetable Salad, page 314

Coconut Custard
Tembleque, **page 312**

Curb Appeal

A Puerto Rican-style block party is all about friends, family, and good food.

Puerto Rican ingredients and cooking techniques reflect the country's rich, multicultural history, with influences from the native Taíno Indians, Spanish colonists, African slaves who worked the fields, and, most recently, the United States. This block party menu highlights some typical Puerto Rican flavors—roast pork, rice and beans, and coconut. But even if you don't plan to go to Puerto Rico anytime soon, the flavors and aromas of these dishes will transport you and your guests to the island in spirit.

Puerto Rican Block Party Menu
serves 8

Appetizers

Crab-and-Mango Empanadas
Empanadas de Cangrejo y Mango

Ripe Plantain "Canoes" Stuffed with Ground Meat
Canoas

Citrus-Herb Shrimp
Camarones con Hierbas y Cítricos

Salad

Green Salad with Culantro and Cilantro Dressing
Ensalada Verde con Aderezo de Cilantro y Recao

Entrées

Roasted Pork
Pernil Asado

Pork Skewers with Guava Sauce
Pinchos de Cerdo con Salsa de Guayaba

Plantains and Pork Cracklings with Stewed Chicken
Mofongo Relleno de Pollo Guisado

Sides

Rice with Pigeon Peas
Arroz con Gandules

Rice with Stewed Pink Beans
Arroz con Habichuelas Rosadas Guisadas

Dessert

Coconut Custard
Tembleque

MAKE AHEAD
Empanada Dough
Masa de Empanadas

- 2 cups all-purpose flour, divided
- 6 tablespoons ice water
- 1 teaspoon cider vinegar
- 2 tablespoons powdered sugar
- ½ teaspoon salt
- ½ cup vegetable shortening

1. Lightly spoon flour into dry measuring cups, and level with a knife. Combine ½ cup flour, water, and vinegar, stirring with a whisk until well blended to form a slurry.
2. Combine 1½ cups flour, sugar, and salt in a bowl, stirring with a whisk; cut in shortening with a pastry blender or 2 knives until mixture resembles coarse meal. Add slurry; toss with a fork until flour mixture is moist.
3. Gently press mixture into a 4-inch circle on heavy-duty plastic wrap, and cover with additional plastic wrap. Roll dough, still covered, into an 18 x 12-inch rectangle; freeze 10 minutes or until plastic wrap can be easily removed. Remove plastic wrap, and place dough on a lightly floured surface; let stand 1 minute. Cut dough as directed according to specific recipe. Chill dough until ready to use. Yield: 1 Empanada Dough recipe.

CALORIES 1,690 (46% from fat); FAT 87.3g (sat 17.4g, mono 31.6g, poly 33.3g); PROTEIN 25.8g; CARB 198.5g; FIBER 6.8g; CHOL 0mg; IRON 11.6mg; SODIUM 1,177mg; CALC 39mg

Crab-and-Mango Empanadas
Empanadas de Cangrejo y Mango

- ½ cup chopped peeled mango
- ¼ cup frozen whole-kernel corn, thawed
- ¼ cup chopped green onions
- 2 tablespoons fat-free mayonnaise
- 1 tablespoon chopped fresh cilantro
- 4 ounces lump crabmeat, drained and shell pieces removed
- 1 jalapeño pepper, seeded and minced
- Empanada Dough (*Masa de Empanadas*) (recipe above)
- 1 tablespoon water
- 1 large egg, lightly beaten
- Cooking spray

1. Preheat oven to 425°.
2. Combine first 7 ingredients. Cut Empanada Dough into 12 circles using a 4-inch biscuit cutter. Spoon 1 tablespoon filling onto half of each circle, leaving a ½-inch border. Combine water and egg; brush egg mixture around edge of each circle. Fold dough over filling; press edges together with a fork or fingers to seal.
3. Place empanadas on a baking sheet coated with cooking spray; brush with remaining egg mixture. Bake at 425° for 25 minutes or until golden. Yield: 12 servings (serving size: 1 empanada).

(Totals include Empanada Dough) CALORIES 169 (43% from fat); FAT 8.1g (sat 1.6g, mono 2.9g, poly 3g); PROTEIN 4.8g; CARB 19.2g; FIBER 0.8g; CHOL 28mg; IRON 1.2mg; SODIUM 163mg; CALC 18mg

Ripe Plantain "Canoes" Stuffed with Ground Meat
Canoas

Use a spatula or dough scraper to hold open the hot plantain while you fill it.

STUFFING:
- ⅔ pound ground round
- Dash of salt
- 3 tablespoons tomato sauce
- 2 tablespoons chopped green bell pepper
- 2 tablespoons finely chopped lean smoked ham
- 2 teaspoons finely chopped garlic
- 1 teaspoon chopped fresh culantro
- 1 teaspoon chopped fresh cilantro
- ½ teaspoon dried oregano
- 1 bay leaf

PLANTAINS:
- 8 yellow plantains, peeled
- Cooking spray
- 1 teaspoon olive oil
- ¼ teaspoon salt
- ⅛ teaspoon ground red pepper
- ½ cup (2 ounces) shredded Cheddar cheese

1. Preheat oven to 350°.
2. To prepare stuffing, heat a large nonstick skillet over medium-high heat.
Continued

Add beef and salt; cook 2 minutes, stirring to crumble. Stir in tomato sauce and next 7 ingredients; cook 5 minutes or until bell pepper is tender. Discard bay leaf.

3. To prepare plantains, working with one plantain at a time, cut a small portion from outer curve to make a flat surface. Make a lengthwise cut on inside curve, being careful not to cut all the way through (plantain will now resemble a canoe). Carefully scoop out about 1 tablespoon of plantain from center cut to allow room for filling. Repeat with remaining plantains. Place plantains on a baking sheet coated with cooking spray. Brush oil evenly over plantains. Sprinkle with ¼ teaspoon salt and red pepper.

4. Bake at 350° for 25 minutes or until plantains are tender; let cool slightly. Fill each plantain with ¼ cup stuffing; top each with 1 tablespoon cheese. Bake an additional 10 minutes or until plantains are tender and cheese melts. Yield: 16 servings (serving size: ½ stuffed plantain).

CALORIES 170 (25% from fat); FAT 4.7g (sat 2.1g, mono 1.8g, poly 0.2g); PROTEIN 5.9g; CARB 29g; FIBER 2.2g; CHOL 18mg; IRON 1mg; SODIUM 116mg; CALC 33mg

---

Citrus-Herb Shrimp
*Camarones con Hierbas y
Cítricos*

This refreshing appetizer is a great snack when it's hot outside.

2   pounds unpeeled large shrimp
6   tablespoons chopped fresh mint
¼   cup chopped fresh cilantro
¼   cup fresh lime juice
2   tablespoons grated peeled fresh
    ginger
1   tablespoon vegetable oil
1   teaspoon salt
1   teaspoon crushed red pepper
½   teaspoon sugar
2   garlic cloves, minced

1. Peel and devein shrimp, leaving tails intact. Bring a large pot of water to a boil. Add shrimp; cook 5 minutes or just until shrimp are done. Drain; rinse with cold running water. Place shrimp in a large bowl; chill. Combine mint and remaining

---

8 ingredients. Add to shrimp; toss well to combine. Chill 1 hour. Yield: 10 servings (serving size: about 2½ ounces).

CALORIES 114 (24% from fat); FAT 3g (sat 0.5g, mono 0.6g, poly 1.4g); PROTEIN 18.7g; CARB 2.4g; FIBER 0.4g; CHOL 138mg; IRON 2.6mg; SODIUM 371mg; CALC 57mg

---

Green Salad with Culantro and Cilantro Dressing
*Ensalada Verde con Aderezo de
Cilantro y Recao*

DRESSING:
2   tablespoons extravirgin olive oil
2   tablespoons minced fresh
    cilantro
1   tablespoon finely chopped culantro
1½ teaspoons salt
2   garlic cloves, minced

SALAD:
5   cups torn iceberg lettuce
5   cups torn romaine lettuce
4   cups chopped tomato
1   cup (¼-inch-thick) slices cucumber
1   cup matchstick-cut carrots

1. To prepare dressing, combine first 5 ingredients, stirring with a whisk.
2. To prepare salad, combine lettuces and remaining 3 ingredients in a large bowl. Add dressing; toss gently to coat. Yield: 10 servings (serving size: about 1½ cups).

CALORIES 54 (52% from fat); FAT 3.1g (sat 0.4g, mono 2g, poly 0.4g); PROTEIN 1.7g; CARB 6.4g; FIBER 2g; CHOL 0mg; IRON 0.8mg; SODIUM 367mg; CALC 29mg

---

Roasted Pork
Pernil Asado

Double this recipe for a larger party.

1   teaspoon olive oil
½   teaspoon salt
½   teaspoon ground oregano
½   teaspoon freshly ground black
    pepper
4   garlic cloves, minced
2   (1¼-pound) pork tenderloins,
    trimmed
Cooking spray

---

1. Preheat oven to 350°.
2. Combine first 5 ingredients; rub evenly over pork. Place pork on a broiler pan coated with cooking spray. Bake at 350° for 50 minutes or until a thermometer registers 160°. Let stand 5 minutes before slicing. Yield: 8 servings (serving size: about 3 ounces).

CALORIES 181 (37% from fat); FAT 7.5g (sat 2.5g, mono 3.5g, poly 0.8g); PROTEIN 26.3g; CARB 0.6g; FIBER 0.1g; CHOL 84mg; IRON 1.6mg; SODIUM 208mg; CALC 11mg

---

Caribbean Pantry

Annatto seeds (also known as *achiote*) are used to infuse oil and give it a bright orange color. To prepare, combine ½ cup olive oil and 2 tablespoons annatto seeds in a small saucepan. Bring to a simmer over medium heat; cook 5 minutes. Let cool; strain over a bowl. Discard seeds.

Culantro is a green herb with long leaves, much like sorrel. It can be found in some supermarkets but will be more readily available in local Latino markets. Part of the parsley family, culantro has a bright, fresh taste, reminiscent of cilantro. If substituting cilantro for culantro, use about half as much cilantro as it has a stronger flavor.

Guava paste is firm, dark red, and sold in round, shallow tins or in bars. It isn't as delicate in flavor as the fruit, but it can be stored, unopened, indefinitely. It's a convenience product that's sliced and served with cheese as an appetizer or melted and used in glazes and sauces.

Pigeon peas (*gandules*) are the favorite bean of Puerto Rico. The beans are sold fresh, canned, or frozen, and they're often cooked with rice.

Plantains are relatives of bananas that are always eaten cooked—either green (unripe) or black (ripe). Store at room temperature until they reach the desired stage of ripeness.

Pork Skewers with Guava Sauce
Pinchos de Cerdo con Salsa de Guayaba

The oregano colors this pork slightly green—and gives it great flavor. If you grind dried oregano leaves in a spice grinder, the color is less green. Slice the remaining guava paste, and serve it as an appetizer with queso fresco cheese and crackers.

PORK:

1 tablespoon ground oregano
1½ teaspoons olive oil
¾ teaspoon salt
½ teaspoon freshly ground black pepper
2½ pounds boneless pork loin, cut into 1½-inch cubes
2 large onions, each cut into 16 wedges
Cooking spray

SAUCE:

1 cup chopped commercial guava paste (about 12 ounces)
½ cup less-sodium beef broth
2 tablespoons fresh lime juice
2 tablespoons dark rum
¼ teaspoon salt

1. To prepare pork, combine first 4 ingredients in a large bowl. Add pork; stir to coat. Cover and refrigerate 2 hours. Thread pork and onion alternately onto 16 (8-inch) skewers.
2. Prepare grill.
3. Place skewers on a grill rack coated with cooking spray, and grill 14 minutes or until done, turning occasionally. Arrange skewers on a serving platter, and keep warm.
4. To prepare sauce, combine guava paste and remaining 4 ingredients in a small saucepan. Bring to a simmer over medium heat; cook 8 minutes or until smooth, stirring constantly. Serve sauce with pork. Yield: 8 servings (serving size: 2 skewers and about 2½ tablespoons sauce).

CALORIES 357 (22% from fat); FAT 8.6g (sat 2.8g, mono 4.1g, poly 1g); PROTEIN 31.7g; CARB 34.2g; FIBER 1.3g; CHOL 78mg; IRON 1.5mg; SODIUM 361mg; CALC 47mg

Plantains and Pork Cracklings with Stewed Chicken
Mofongo Relleno de Pollo Guisado

Mofongo is mashed plantains with garlic, olive oil, and pork cracklings that are shaped into individual patties or molded with a mortar and pestle into a bowl to hold meat or fish.

CHICKEN:

1 tablespoon olive oil, divided
5 pounds skinless, boneless chicken breast, cut into bite-sized pieces
1 cup chopped onion
¼ cup minced fresh cilantro
¼ cup minced fresh culantro
1 teaspoon salt
3 garlic cloves, minced
1 (15-ounce) can tomato sauce

MOFONGO:

6 green plantains, peeled and cut into 1-inch pieces (about 3 pounds)
2 teaspoons salt, divided
6 bacon slices, cooked and crumbled (drained)
3 garlic cloves, minced
¾ cup fat-free, less-sodium chicken broth
6 tablespoons olive oil, divided

1. To prepare chicken, heat 1½ teaspoons oil in a large Dutch oven over medium-high heat. Add half of chicken; sauté 8 minutes or until browned. Remove chicken from pan. Repeat procedure with 1½ teaspoons oil and remaining chicken. Return chicken to pan; stir in onion and next 5 ingredients. Bring to a boil; cover, reduce heat, and simmer 20 minutes or until chicken is done. Keep warm.
2. To prepare mofongo, place plantains and ½ teaspoon salt in a large Dutch oven. Cover with water to 1 inch above plantains; stir to dissolve salt. Let stand 20 minutes. Drain plantains, and return to pan. Cover plantains with water to 1 inch above plantains. Bring to a boil over high heat. Reduce heat, and simmer 20 minutes or until tender. Drain plantains; return to pan. Mash plantains with a potato masher. Stir in 1½ teaspoons salt, bacon, garlic, and broth. Shape plantain mixture into 24 (½-inch-thick) patties.
3. Heat 2 tablespoons oil in a large non-stick skillet over medium-high heat. Add 8 patties; cook 3 minutes on each side or until browned. Repeat procedure twice with 4 tablespoons oil and remaining patties. Serve chicken mixture over patties. Yield: 12 servings (serving size: ⅔ cup chicken mixture and 2 patties).

CALORIES 426 (26% from fat); FAT 12.2g (sat 2.4g, mono 7.2g, poly 1.5g); PROTEIN 46.9g; CARB 32.9g; FIBER 2.8g; CHOL 112mg; IRON 2.3mg; SODIUM 864mg; CALC 35mg

Rice with Pigeon Peas
Arroz con Gandules

Look for canned pigeon peas in the Latino foods aisle at the supermarket. Serve with Roasted Pork (recipe on page 310).

1 teaspoon annatto oil (see "Caribbean Pantry" on page 310) or olive oil
½ cup chopped onion
2 garlic cloves, minced
1 (4-ounce) boneless center-cut loin pork chop, cubed
2 cups uncooked medium-grain rice
1 cup water
¼ cup lean smoked ham, cubed
½ teaspoon salt
½ teaspoon dried oregano
2 (14-ounce) cans less-sodium beef broth
½ cup Spanish stuffed olives, chopped
2 tablespoons chopped fresh cilantro
1 (15.5-ounce) can pigeon peas

1. Heat oil in a large Dutch oven over medium-high heat. Add onion, garlic, and pork; sauté 5 minutes. Stir in rice. Add water and next 4 ingredients; bring to a boil. Cover, reduce heat, and simmer 20 minutes or until liquid is absorbed and rice is tender. Stir in olives, cilantro, and peas. Yield: 10 servings (serving size: about ¾ cup).

CALORIES 241 (13% from fat); FAT 3.4g (sat 0.8g, mono 1.5g, poly 0.7g); PROTEIN 10.5g; CARB 41.3g; FIBER 3.7g; CHOL 10mg; IRON 2.9mg; SODIUM 282mg; CALC 38mg

Rice with Stewed Pink Beans

Arroz con Habichuelas Rosadas Guisadas

These beans turn pink when cooked; you can also use pinto beans, red kidney beans, or navy beans in this dish.

BEANS:

1½ cups dried small red beans (about ⅔ pound)
8 cups water
½ cup (½-inch) cubed salt pork (about 3 ounces)
½ cup (½-inch) cubed smoked ham (about 3 ounces)
⅓ cup (1-inch) cubed peeled baking potato
1 bay leaf
¼ cup chopped green bell pepper
1 tablespoon minced garlic
¼ cup tomato sauce
1 tablespoon chopped fresh culantro
1½ teaspoons chopped fresh cilantro
1 teaspoon olive oil
½ teaspoon salt

RICE:

1 tablespoon olive oil
1½ cups uncooked medium-grain rice
1¼ cups water
1 tablespoon chopped fresh culantro
½ teaspoon salt
1 (14-ounce) can fat-free, less-sodium chicken broth

1. To prepare beans, sort and wash beans; place in a large Dutch oven. Cover with water to 2 inches above beans; cover and let stand 8 hours. Drain beans.
2. Combine beans, 8 cups water, and next 4 ingredients in pan. Bring to a boil; cover, reduce heat, and simmer 30 minutes or until beans are almost tender. Stir in bell pepper and garlic; simmer, uncovered, 20 minutes or until beans are done. Drain in sieve over a bowl, reserving ⅓ cup cooking liquid. Discard bay leaf. Return bean mixture to pan. Add reserved ⅓ cup cooking liquid, tomato sauce, and next 4 ingredients; stir to combine.
3. To prepare rice, heat 1 tablespoon oil in a medium saucepan over medium-high heat. Add rice; sauté 2 minutes. Add 1¼ cups water, 1 tablespoon culantro, ½ teaspoon salt, and broth; bring to a boil. Cover, reduce heat, and simmer 13 minutes or until liquid is absorbed and rice is tender. Serve beans over rice. Yield: 12 servings (serving size: about ⅓ cup rice and about ⅓ cup beans).

CALORIES 265 (28% from fat); FAT 8.1g (sat 2.5g, mono 3.9g, poly 1g); PROTEIN 9.6g; CARB 38g; FIBER 3.9g; CHOL 12mg; IRON 3mg; SODIUM 517mg; CALC 43mg

---

MAKE AHEAD
Coconut Custard

Tembleque

(pictured on page 308)

This creamy coconut custard should be made the night before. Sprinkle with cinnamon before serving. We strained the custard before chilling to ensure it would be smooth.

¾ cup sugar
½ cup cornstarch
⅛ teaspoon salt
3 (13.5-ounce) cans light coconut milk
½ teaspoon vanilla extract
⅛ teaspoon coconut extract
⅛ teaspoon ground cinnamon

1. Combine first 4 ingredients in a heavy medium saucepan. Bring mixture to a boil over medium heat; cook 1 minute, stirring constantly. Remove from heat; stir in extracts. Strain through a sieve into a shallow 2-quart dish; cover surface of custard with plastic wrap. Chill overnight. Sprinkle with cinnamon before serving. Yield: 10 servings (serving size: about ⅔ cup).

CALORIES 157 (36% from fat); FAT 6.2g (sat 4.2g, mono 0g, poly 0g); PROTEIN 0g; CARB 25g; FIBER 0.1g; CHOL 0mg; IRON 0mg; SODIUM 75mg; CALC 1mg

---

What to Pour in Puerto Rico

Puerto Rico is famous for its rum, which is an ingredient in these refreshing choices. Make Classic Mojito, Mango Martini, and Puerto Rican Sangría individually, or prepare pitchers full.

QUICK & EASY
Classic Mojito

This Cuban drink is fast becoming a favorite in Puerto Rico; the mint and sugar go well with our traditional dishes. If you have access to Key limes, use those for the most authentic flavor.

2 tablespoons sugar
15 fresh mint leaves
¼ cup white rum
1½ tablespoons fresh lime juice
¼ cup club soda, chilled
½ cup ice

1. Place sugar and mint in a 2-cup glass measure; crush with a wooden spoon. Add rum and juice; stir until sugar dissolves. Just before serving, stir in club soda. Place ice in an 8-ounce glass; pour mint mixture over ice. Yield: 1 serving (serving size: about 1 cup).

CALORIES 234 (0% from fat); FAT 0g; PROTEIN 0.1g; CARB 27.2g; FIBER 0.2g; CHOL 0mg; IRON 0.1mg; SODIUM 14mg; CALC 7mg

QUICK & EASY
Mango Martini

Here's a fun twist on the classic martini that uses rum and tropical fruit for flavor.

Crushed ice
¼ cup white rum
2 tablespoons Triple Sec (orange-flavored liqueur)
2 tablespoons mango juice
2 teaspoons fresh lime juice
Mango slices (optional)

1. Place crushed ice in a martini shaker. Add rum, liqueur, and juices; shake to combine. Strain rum mixture into a martini glass; garnish with mango slices, if desired. Serve immediately. Yield: 1 serving (serving size: about ½ cup).

CALORIES 247 (1% from fat); FAT 0.2g (sat 0g, mono 0g, poly 0.1g); PROTEIN 0.3g; CARB 16.4g; FIBER 0.1g; CHOL 0mg; IRON 0.2mg; SODIUM 3mg; CALC 2mg

QUICK & EASY
Puerto Rican Sangría

Unlike many versions of sangría, which need to sit overnight to release the flavors of the fruit, this invigorating beverage is ready to serve immediately.

- 3 cups lemon-lime soda (such as Sprite), chilled
- 2 cups chopped fresh pineapple
- 2 cups chopped Granny Smith apple
- 1 cup chopped peeled ripe mango
- ½ cup fresh orange sections
- ½ cup dark rum
- ¼ cup sugar
- 1 (750-milliliter) bottle dry white wine

1. Combine all ingredients in a large pitcher. Serve immediately over ice. Yield: 12 servings (serving size: about 1 cup).

CALORIES 140 (1% from fat); FAT 0.2g (sat 0g, mono 0g, poly 0.1g); PROTEIN 0.3g; CARB 20.4g; FIBER 1.2g; CHOL 0mg; IRON 0.4mg; SODIUM 10mg; CALC 14mg

lunch box chronicles

Cook Now, Eat Later

The answer to your weekday lunchtime doldrums could be in Sunday night's dinner.

Here's the idea: On Sunday, when you have a little time on your hands, roast a three-pound pork loin. Season it lightly so you can adapt the leftovers to other flavors. Enjoy the warm pork for dinner, then transform the remaining meat into any of the nine exciting lunches featured here. (The leftover pork will keep for two days in the refrigerator.).

Simply Roasted Pork

Use apple jelly in place of the apricot preserves for a slightly sweeter flavor. Serve with roasted red skin potatoes or mashed potatoes, broccoli spears or collard greens, and rolls.

- ½ cup apricot preserves
- 1 teaspoon salt
- 1 teaspoon dried oregano
- ¾ teaspoon garlic powder
- ½ teaspoon freshly ground black pepper
- 1 (3-pound) boneless pork loin, trimmed
- Cooking spray

1. Preheat oven to 425°.
2. Place preserves in a small saucepan over medium-low heat, and cook 10 minutes or until melted. Keep warm over low heat.
3. Combine salt, oregano, garlic powder, and pepper; rub evenly over pork. Place pork on a rack coated with cooking spray; place rack in a shallow roasting pan. Bake at 425° for 30 minutes. Brush ¼ cup preserves evenly over pork. Bake an additional 10 minutes. Brush remaining preserves evenly over pork. Bake an additional 10 minutes or until thermometer registers 155° (slightly pink). Let stand 10 minutes before slicing. Yield: 14 servings (serving size: about 3 ounces).

CALORIES 159 (27% from fat); FAT 4.7g (sat 1.6g, mono 2.1g, poly 0.5g); PROTEIN 20.6g; CARB 7.6g; FIBER 0.2g; CHOL 59mg; IRON 0.9mg; SODIUM 232mg; CALC 24mg

MAKE AHEAD
Spicy Pork, Turkey, and Swiss Cubano Roll

- 4 teaspoons prepared yellow mustard
- 4 (8-inch) flour tortillas
- 4 (¾-ounce) slices reduced-fat Swiss cheese
- 1 cup thinly sliced Simply Roasted Pork (recipe above) (about 6 ounces)
- 4 (½-ounce) slices deli turkey breast
- ½ cup cilantro leaves
- 16 pickled jalapeño pepper slices, patted dry

1. Spread 1 teaspoon mustard evenly over each tortilla. Top each tortilla with 1 cheese slice, ¼ cup Simply Roasted Pork, and 1 turkey slice. Arrange 2 tablespoons cilantro and 4 jalapeño slices evenly over each tortilla; roll up.
2. Heat a large skillet over medium heat. Add rolls to pan. Place a cast-iron or heavy skillet on top of rolls; press gently to flatten. Cook 3 minutes on each side or until cheese melts and rolls are crisp (leave cast-iron skillet on rolls while they cook). Yield: 4 servings (serving size: 1 roll).

CALORIES 272 (22% from fat); FAT 6.6g (sat 2g, mono 2.7g, poly 0.7g); PROTEIN 18.6g; CARB 33.2g; FIBER 2g; CHOL 31mg; IRON 2.1mg; SODIUM 772mg; CALC 227mg

MAKE AHEAD
Thai Pork Salad with Chili Dressing

Thai roasted red chili paste combines the kick of chili paste with a smoky flavor. It can be found in most Asian markets. If it's unavailable, chili paste with garlic or Sriracha is a good substitute.

- 2 ounces uncooked bean threads (cellophane noodles)
- 2 cups shredded napa (Chinese) cabbage
- 1½ cups thinly sliced seeded cucumber
- 1½ cups (¼-inch-thick) slices Simply Roasted Pork (recipe at left) (about 9 ounces)
- 1 cup thinly sliced red bell pepper strips
- ¾ cup finely shredded carrot
- ½ cup thinly sliced red onion
- ¼ cup thinly sliced fresh basil
- ¼ cup finely chopped fresh mint
- 1 serrano chile, seeded and finely chopped
- ¼ cup finely chopped green onions
- 3 tablespoons fresh lime juice
- 3 tablespoons seasoned rice vinegar
- 2 tablespoons sugar
- 1 tablespoon fish sauce
- 1 tablespoon roasted peanut oil
- 1½ teaspoons roasted red chili paste (such as Thai Kitchen)
- ¼ teaspoon salt

Continued

1. Pour boiling water over noodles; let stand 8 minutes or until tender. Drain and rinse with cold water. Drain. Snip noodles with kitchen shears. Combine noodles, cabbage, and next 8 ingredients in a large bowl; toss gently. Combine green onions and remaining 7 ingredients; stir with a whisk. Pour green onion mixture over cabbage mixture; toss gently to coat. Yield: 6 servings (serving size: 1⅔ cups).

CALORIES 231 (22% from fat); FAT 5.7g (sat 1.3g, mono 2.5g, poly 1.4g); PROTEIN 11g; CARB 34.3g; FIBER 3.2g; CHOL 26mg; IRON 1mg; SODIUM 861mg; CALC 61mg

Pork and Grilled Vegetable Salad

(pictured on page 307)

⅔ pound red potatoes, cut into (⅛-inch-thick) slices
1½ tablespoons extravirgin olive oil, divided
Cooking spray
1 small zucchini, cut lengthwise into (¼-inch-thick) slices
1 yellow squash, cut lengthwise into (¼-inch-thick) slices
1 large red bell pepper, quartered
1 large orange bell pepper, quartered
1 red onion, cut into (¼-inch-thick) slices
4 (1-ounce) slices sourdough bread
1 garlic clove, peeled and halved
1½ cups thinly sliced Simply Roasted Pork (recipe on page 313) (about 8 ounces)
1½ tablespoons white wine vinegar
1 tablespoon honey
1 teaspoon chopped fresh oregano
1 teaspoon Dijon mustard
¾ teaspoon salt
½ teaspoon chopped fresh thyme
¼ teaspoon black pepper

1. Prepare grill.
2. Toss potatoes with 1 teaspoon oil. Place potatoes on grill rack coated with cooking spray; grill 4 minutes on each side or until tender. Place zucchini, squash, bell peppers, and onion on grill rack; cook 3 minutes on each side. Place bread slices on grill rack; grill 1 minute on each side or until well marked. Rub

both sides of each bread slice with cut sides of garlic. Coarsely chop zucchini, squash, and bell peppers. Combine potatoes, chopped vegetables and Simply Roasted Pork in a large bowl, tossing gently.
3. Combine vinegar and remaining 6 ingredients, stirring with a whisk. Gradually add 3½ teaspoons oil, stirring with a whisk. Drizzle vinegar mixture over vegetable mixture, tossing to coat. Serve bread with salad. Yield: 4 servings (serving size: 1¾ cups salad and 1 bread slice).

CALORIES 310 (25% from fat); FAT 8.5g (sat 1.7g, mono 5.1g, poly 1.1g); PROTEIN 15g; CARB 45.1g; FIBER 5.6g; CHOL 26mg; IRON 2.6mg; SODIUM 755mg; CALC 73mg

Pork Tabbouleh

Mint, lemon juice, and parsley brighten this refreshing salad.

1½ cups boiling water
1 cup uncooked bulgur
1½ cups (¼-inch) cubed Simply Roasted Pork (recipe on page 313) (about 8 ounces)
1½ cups chopped seeded plum tomato
1 cup chopped seeded cucumber
1 cup finely chopped fresh parsley
½ cup chopped green onions
½ cup chopped fresh mint
1 (15½-ounce) can chickpeas (garbanzo beans), drained
⅓ cup lemon juice (about 2 lemons)
1 tablespoon extravirgin olive oil
¾ teaspoon salt
¼ teaspoon freshly ground black pepper
1 garlic clove, minced

1. Combine water and bulgur in a large bowl; cover and let stand 15 minutes or until water is absorbed and bulgur is tender. Add Simply Roasted Pork and next 6 ingredients; toss gently to combine.
2. Combine lemon juice and remaining 4 ingredients, stirring with a whisk. Drizzle juice mixture over pork mixture; toss to combine. Chill at least 2 hours. Yield: 6 servings (serving size: 1⅔ cups).

CALORIES 382 (18% from fat); FAT 7.5g (sat 1.4g, mono 3.8g, poly 1.4g); PROTEIN 20g; CARB 62.3g; FIBER 13.5g; CHOL 26mg; IRON 4.2mg; SODIUM 887mg; CALC 98mg

Pork and Grilled Stone Fruit Couscous Salad

When nectarines and peaches go out of season, substitute plums.

¾ cup fresh orange juice
½ cup water
½ teaspoon ground cumin
⅛ teaspoon ground cinnamon
¾ teaspoon salt, divided
¼ teaspoon freshly ground black pepper, divided
1 cup uncooked couscous
2 teaspoons chopped peeled fresh ginger
2 teaspoons raspberry vinegar
2 teaspoons balsamic vinegar
1 teaspoon Dijon mustard
2 tablespoons extravirgin olive oil, divided
2 ripe nectarines, halved and pitted
2 ripe peaches, halved and pitted
1½ cups (¼-inch) cubed Simply Roasted Pork (recipe on page 313) (about 8 ounces)
⅓ cup chopped red onion
¼ cup chopped fresh cilantro

1. Combine first 4 ingredients in a small saucepan; stir in ½ teaspoon salt and ⅛ teaspoon pepper. Bring to a boil; stir in couscous. Cover, remove from heat, and let stand 5 minutes. Fluff with a fork.
2. Combine ¼ teaspoon salt, ⅛ teaspoon pepper, ginger, vinegars, and mustard, stirring with a whisk. Gradually add 1½ tablespoons oil, stirring with a whisk.
3. Heat a grill pan over medium-high heat. Brush 1½ teaspoons oil evenly over fruit. Cook 3 minutes on each side or until well marked; cool. Cut fruit into ¼-inch cubes.
4. Combine fruit, Simply Roasted Pork, onion, and cilantro in a large bowl, tossing gently. Stir in couscous. Drizzle vinegar mixture over couscous mixture, tossing gently to coat. Chill 1 hour. Yield: 4 servings (serving size: 1½ cups).

CALORIES 377 (23% from fat); FAT 9.7g (sat 1.7g, mono 6g, poly 1g); PROTEIN 16g; CARB 56.6g; FIBER 4.8g; CHOL 26mg; IRON 1.5mg; SODIUM 581mg; CALC 40mg

Horseradish and Caramelized Onion Pork Sandwiches

Sweet onions are paired with a spicy-hot, creamy sauce in this fancy sandwich.

1 tablespoon olive oil
4 cups vertically sliced onion (about 1¼ pounds)
1½ tablespoons sugar
1 tablespoon red wine vinegar
1 tablespoon low-sodium soy sauce
1 teaspoon chopped fresh thyme
⅛ teaspoon ground red pepper
2 garlic cloves, minced
2 tablespoons reduced-fat sour cream
2 tablespoons low-fat mayonnaise
1 tablespoon prepared horseradish
1 (8-ounce) loaf French bread, halved lengthwise
1 cup torn red leaf lettuce leaves
1½ cups thinly sliced Simply Roasted Pork (recipe on page 313) (about 8 ounces)

1. Heat oil in a large nonstick skillet over medium heat. Add onion and next 6 ingredients to pan; cook 30 minutes or until onion is golden, stirring occasionally. Remove from heat; cool.
2. Combine sour cream, mayonnaise, and horseradish; spread evenly over cut side of top half of bread. Arrange lettuce over bottom half of bread. Arrange onion and Simply Roasted Pork over lettuce. Top with top half of bread. Cut stuffed loaf into 4 pieces. Yield: 4 servings (serving size: 1 sandwich quarter).

CALORIES 369 (22% from fat); FAT 9.2g (sat 2.4g, mono 4.3g, poly 1.1g); PROTEIN 16.7g; CARB 55.8g; FIBER 5.1g; CHOL 30mg; IRON 2.6mg; SODIUM 666mg; CALC 113mg

Pork and Peanut Noodle Salad

The sweetness of the pork's apricot glaze is a great accompaniment to the spicy peanut sauce.

4 ounces uncooked soba (buckwheat) noodles
¼ cup creamy peanut butter
¼ cup hoisin sauce
2 tablespoons rice vinegar
2 tablespoons fresh lime juice
1 tablespoon low-sodium soy sauce
2 teaspoons Sriracha (hot chile sauce, such as Huy Fong)
¼ teaspoon crushed red pepper
1 cup (½-inch) cubed Simply Roasted Pork (recipe on page 313) (about 6 ounces)
½ cup finely chopped carrots
½ cup chopped green onions
⅓ cup finely chopped celery

1. Cook noodles according to package directions, omitting salt and fat.
2. Combine peanut butter and next 6 ingredients in a large bowl, stirring with a whisk. Add noodles, Simply Roasted Pork, and remaining ingredients, tossing gently to coat. Chill. Yield: 4 servings (serving size: 1¼ cups).

CALORIES 301 (31% from fat); FAT 10.5g (sat 2.3g, mono 4.8g, poly 2.7g); PROTEIN 15.9g; CARB 39.3g; FIBER 2.7g; CHOL 20mg; IRON 1.8mg; SODIUM 814mg; CALC 39mg

Sourdough Pork Sandwiches with Parsley-Pesto Mayonnaise

1 cup packed parsley leaves
1 tablespoon capers, drained
1 tablespoon water
1 tablespoon fresh lemon juice
2 teaspoons extravirgin olive oil
½ teaspoon anchovy paste
⅛ teaspoon freshly ground black pepper
1 garlic clove, minced
½ cup (2 ounces) crumbled feta cheese
¼ cup fat-free mayonnaise
8 (1-ounce) slices sourdough bread
2 cups trimmed arugula
2 cups thinly sliced Simply Roasted Pork (recipe on page 313) (about 12 ounces)
2 (7-ounce) bottles roasted red bell peppers, drained

1. Combine first 8 ingredients in a blender; process until smooth. Combine parsley mixture, cheese, and mayonnaise, stirring well.
2. Spread 1 tablespoon mayonnaise mixture over each bread slice; top each of 4 slices with ½ cup arugula and ½ cup Simply Roasted Pork. Arrange red bell peppers evenly over pork. Top each serving with a bread slice. Cut sandwiches in half diagonally. Yield: 4 servings (serving size: 1 sandwich).

CALORIES 371 (28% from fat); FAT 11.6g (sat 4.2g, mono 4.5g, poly 1.4g); PROTEIN 22.8g; CARB 43.5g; FIBER 3.5g; CHOL 55mg; IRON 3.8mg; SODIUM 1,170mg; CALC 178mg

Chipotle Pork and Avocado Wrap

For a bit more spice in your wrap, add another teaspoon of chipotle chiles to the avocado spread.

½ cup mashed peeled avocado
1½ tablespoons low-fat mayonnaise
2 teaspoons chopped canned chipotle chiles in adobo sauce
1 teaspoon fresh lime juice
¼ teaspoon salt
¼ teaspoon ground cumin
¼ teaspoon dried oregano
4 (8-inch) fat-free flour tortillas
1½ cups (¼-inch-thick) slices Simply Roasted Pork (recipe on page 313) (about 8 ounces)
1 cup shredded iceberg lettuce
¼ cup bottled salsa

1. Combine first 7 ingredients; stir well.
2. Warm tortillas according to package directions. Spread about 2 tablespoons avocado mixture over each tortilla, leaving a 1-inch border. Arrange Simply Roasted Pork slices down center of tortillas. Top each tortilla with ¼ cup shredded lettuce and 1 tablespoon salsa, and roll up. Yield: 4 servings (serving size: 1 wrap).

CALORIES 239 (22% from fat); FAT 5.8g (sat 1.3g, mono 2.8g, poly 0.7g); PROTEIN 13.9g; CARB 32.8g; FIBER 2.6g; CHOL 29mg; IRON 1mg; SODIUM 683mg; CALC 27mg

Mother Knows Best

A California woman seeks to improve her daughter's favorite soup.

Pat Philipps, of Davis, California, hints that her daughter, Lesley, isn't much of a cook: "A successful English teacher, yes. A master of the culinary arts, not exactly." So when Lesley proudly made her mom Chicken and Wild Rice Soup for dinner, Pat didn't want to be negative. "It was delicious and filling, but my heart sank as I watched her make it," Pat says. She sent the recipe to *Cooking Light* for "constructive criticism."

Using cooking spray instead of butter was a simple substitution that cut the recipe by more than 200 calories and 23 grams of fat. A cheese switch eliminated another 220 calories and 32 grams of fat. A small amount of all-purpose flour stirred into reduced-fat milk took the place of whole milk. We cooked peeled baking potato cubes in less-sodium chicken broth to create a thick, potato-infused broth that, combined with the slurry, gave us the cream-of-potato characteristics. These changes reduced the calories by 206 and the fat by 29.8 grams. Eliminating canned soup saved a whopping 3,610 milligrams of sodium.

BEFORE	AFTER
SERVING SIZE	
1 ¼ cups	
CALORIES PER SERVING	
337	280
FAT	
15.9g	7g
PERCENT OF TOTAL CALORIES	
42%	23%
SODIUM	
1,172mg	879mg

Chicken and Wild Rice Soup

  1 cup uncooked quick-cooking wild rice
    Cooking spray
  1 cup chopped onion
  2 garlic cloves, minced
  3 cups fat-free, less-sodium chicken broth
  1½ cups cubed peeled baking potato
  ⅓ cup all-purpose flour
  3 cups 2% reduced-fat milk
  10 ounces light processed cheese, cubed (such as Velveeta Light)
  2 cups chopped roasted skinless, boneless chicken breast (about 2 breasts)
  ½ teaspoon freshly ground black pepper
  ¼ teaspoon salt
  ¼ cup chopped fresh parsley (optional)

1. Cook rice according to package directions, omitting salt and fat.
2. Heat a large Dutch oven over medium-high heat. Coat pan with cooking spray. Add onion and garlic, and sauté 3 minutes. Add broth and potato; bring to a boil over medium-high heat. Cover, reduce heat, and simmer 5 minutes or until potato is tender.
3. Lightly spoon flour into a dry measuring cup; level with a knife. Combine flour and milk, stirring well with a whisk. Add milk mixture to potato mixture; cook 5 minutes or until slightly thick, stirring constantly. Remove from heat; add cheese, stirring until cheese melts. Stir in rice, chicken, pepper, and salt. Garnish with parsley, if desired. Yield: 8 servings (serving size: 1¼ cups).

CALORIES 280 (23% from fat); FAT 7g (sat 4g, mono 1g, poly 0.5g); PROTEIN 24.9g; CARB 28.7g; FIBER 1.6g; CHOL 52mg; IRON 1.1mg; SODIUM 879mg; CALC 329mg

Hip in the Heartland

Minneapolis/St. Paul is cool—and we don't just mean the weather.

Here's a "cool" appetizer from Bobino Café—a café and wine bar where Chef Jason Schellin comes up with a fresh menu every month.

Steamed Mussels with Cardamom, Orange, and Mint

This appetizer from Bobino Café contains cardamom—an important spice in Scandinavian cuisine and, hence, Minnesota cooking. Serve with toasted French bread.

  1 tablespoon olive oil
  ¼ cup finely chopped shallots
  1 teaspoon chopped peeled fresh ginger
  ½ teaspoon cardamom seeds
  2 teaspoons grated orange rind
  ¾ cup fresh orange juice (about 3 oranges)
  ½ cup sauvignon blanc or other dry white wine
  3 pounds small mussels, scrubbed and debearded
  ¼ cup chopped fresh mint
  ½ teaspoon sea salt
  ¼ teaspoon freshly ground black pepper

1. Heat oil in a large Dutch oven over medium heat. Add shallots, ginger, and cardamom; cook 2 minutes or until shallots are tender. Stir frequently. Add rind, juice, and wine; bring to a simmer. Add mussels; cover and cook 5 minutes or until shells open. Discard any unopened shells.
2. Sprinkle mussels with mint, salt, and pepper; stir gently to combine. Divide mussels and juice mixture among 8 shallow bowls. Yield: 8 servings (serving size: about 9 mussels and ¼ cup juice mixture).

CALORIES 119 (29% from fat); FAT 3.8g (sat 0.6g, mono 1.7g, poly 0.7g); PROTEIN 11.1g; CARB 7.2g; FIBER 0.3g; CHOL 25mg; IRON 3.8mg; SODIUM 404mg; CALC 32mg

Seafood Suppers

All aboard for a fabulous seafood supper.

Seafood Supper Menu 1

serves 6

Shrimp with Lemon, Mint, and Goat Cheese

Marinated mushrooms*

Garlic bread

*Combine 1 teaspoon grated orange rind, ½ cup fresh orange juice, 2 tablespoons white wine vinegar, 2 tablespoons honey, 1 tablespoon olive oil, 1 tablespoon chopped fresh tarragon, and 2 (8-ounce) packages quartered button mushrooms. Add ½ teaspoon salt and ¼ teaspoon pepper. Let stand 20 minutes before serving, stirring occasionally.

Game Plan

1. While mushrooms marinate:
- Prepare vegetables for shrimp dish
- Grate lemon rind and squeeze juice

2. While shrimp mixture cooks:
- Chop mint

QUICK & EASY
Shrimp with Lemon, Mint, and Goat Cheese

Serve over thin pasta, such as linguine.

TOTAL TIME: 30 MINUTES

- 1 tablespoon olive oil
- 6 small garlic cloves, minced
- 2¼ pounds peeled and deveined large shrimp
- 1 cup frozen green peas, thawed
- ¾ cup thinly sliced green onions
- ¼ cup mirin (sweet rice wine)
- 1 teaspoon grated lemon rind
- 2 tablespoons fresh lemon juice
- ½ teaspoon salt
- 4 plum tomatoes, diced (about 1 pound)
- ½ cup chopped fresh mint
- ½ cup (2 ounces) crumbled goat cheese

1. Heat oil in a large nonstick skillet over medium-high heat. Add garlic; sauté 1 minute or until browned. Add shrimp; cook 1 to 2 minutes, stirring constantly. Add peas and next 6 ingredients; cook 8 minutes or until shrimp are done. Top each serving with 4 teaspoons mint and 4 teaspoons goat cheese. Yield: 6 servings (serving size: 1 cup).

CALORIES 286 (22% from fat); FAT 7.1g (sat 2.7g, mono 2.6g, poly 1.2g); PROTEIN 40.3g; CARB 11.8g; FIBER 2.6g; CHOL 337mg; IRON 7.3mg; SODIUM 660mg; CALC 125mg

QUICK & EASY
Shrimp and Crab Gumbo

Traditionally, gumbo begins with a roux of butter and flour. Toasting the flour in a dry pan on the stove provides a flavorful, low-fat substitute for a roux in this Creole specialty.

TOTAL TIME: 45 MINUTES

QUICK TIP: To save time in the kitchen, buy peeled and deveined shrimp.

- ⅓ cup all-purpose flour
- 3 bacon slices, diced
- 2 cups finely chopped onion
- 1½ cups finely chopped green bell pepper (about 1 large)
- 4 celery stalks, thinly sliced
- 4 garlic cloves, minced
- 1 cup water
- 2 (14-ounce) cans fat-free, less-sodium chicken broth, divided
- 2 teaspoons salt-free Cajun seasoning
- ½ teaspoon salt
- ¼ teaspoon crushed red pepper
- 1 (16-ounce) bag frozen cut okra, thawed
- 1 pound peeled and deveined medium shrimp
- 2 (6-ounce) cans lump crabmeat (such as Chicken of the Sea), drained
- 3 cups hot cooked long-grain white rice
- Hot pepper sauce (optional)

1. Place flour in a small skillet; cook 5 minutes over medium heat or until flour is brown, stirring constantly. Place in a small bowl; cool.

2. Cook bacon in a Dutch oven over medium-high heat 3 minutes. Add onion, bell pepper, celery, and garlic; sauté 10 minutes or until vegetables are tender and lightly browned. Add water, and cook 1 minute, stirring constantly.

3. Combine toasted flour and 1 can chicken broth in a medium bowl, stirring well with a whisk. Gradually pour broth mixture into pan. Stir in 1 can chicken broth, Cajun seasoning, salt, crushed red pepper, and okra; bring to a boil. Cover, reduce heat, and simmer 15 minutes.

4. Add shrimp; cook 3 minutes or until shrimp are done. Gently stir in crabmeat. Remove from heat; serve gumbo over rice. Serve with hot pepper sauce, if desired. Yield: 6 servings (serving size: ½ cup rice and 1¼ cups gumbo).

CALORIES 464 (28% from fat); FAT 9g (sat 2.9g, mono 3.4g, poly 1.7g); PROTEIN 33.8g; CARB 60.2g; FIBER 5.4g; CHOL 160mg; IRON 5.5mg; SODIUM 955mg; CALC 192mg

Seafood Supper Menu 2

serves 6

Shrimp and Crab Gumbo

Green salad

Cherries in Zinfandel syrup*

*Combine 2 cups Zinfandel or other fruity dry red wine and ¼ cup sugar in a small saucepan. Boil 10 to 12 minutes or until reduced to ½ cup. Remove from heat; stir in 2 cups frozen dark pitted cherries. Serve over vanilla frozen yogurt.

Game Plan

1. While water for rice comes to a boil:
- Chop onion and bell pepper
- Slice celery

2. While rice cooks:
- Brown flour in skillet

3. While bacon mixture cooks:
- Bring Zinfandel syrup for cherries to a boil

Linguine with Clam Sauce

Cold cucumber soup*

Sautéed asparagus spears

*Combine 1 large coarsely chopped seeded peeled cucumber, 5 coarsely chopped green onions, 2 garlic cloves, and ¼ cup coarsely chopped fresh dill in a food processor; process until finely chopped. Add 2 (6-ounce) cartons plain low-fat yogurt, 1 (14-ounce) can fat-free, less-sodium chicken broth, and ½ teaspoon salt; process until combined.

Game Plan

1. While water for linguine comes to a boil:
- Mince garlic for linguine
- Chop parsley

2. While linguine cooks:
- Peel, seed, and chop cucumber
- Chop dill, onions, and garlic for soup
- Sauté asparagus

QUICK & EASY
Linguine with Clam Sauce

Store live clams in your refrigerator up to 2 days. Clams are a good source of iron; this dish provides almost half of the recommended daily allowance (18 milligrams) for women ages 25 to 50.

TOTAL TIME: 35 MINUTES

- 1   (12-ounce) package linguine
- 3   tablespoons butter
- 5   garlic cloves, minced
- ½   cup dry white wine
- ½   teaspoon salt
- 1   (8-ounce) bottle clam juice
- 2   (6½-ounce) cans minced clams, undrained
- 24 littleneck clams, scrubbed
- 1   cup finely chopped parsley
- 2   tablespoons fresh lemon juice
- ⅛   teaspoon freshly ground black pepper
- Lemon wedges (optional)

1. Cook linguine according to package directions, omitting salt and fat. Set aside.
2. Melt butter in a large skillet over medium heat. Add garlic to pan; cook 3 minutes or until golden.
3. Stir in wine, salt, and clam juice. Drain minced clams; add juice to pan (reserve minced clams). Simmer 5 minutes. Add littleneck clams; cover and cook 3 to 4 minutes or until shells open. Remove from heat, and discard any unopened shells. Add reserved minced clams, parsley, lemon juice, and pepper.
4. Place pasta in a large bowl. Add clam mixture to pasta, and toss well. Serve with lemon wedges, if desired. Yield: 6 servings (serving size: about 1 cup pasta mixture).

CALORIES 332 (19% from fat); FAT 7g (sat 3.8g, mono 1.7g, poly 0.3g); PROTEIN 17.1g; CARB 47.5g; FIBER 2.2g; CHOL 39mg; IRON 8.5mg; SODIUM 627mg; CALC 54mg

sound bites

Dry Goods

Sun-dried tomatoes add a burst of flavor and nutrition to many dishes.

Meat and Potatoes Menu
serves 8

The slowly simmered beef and creamy mashed potatoes make a welcome, hearty meal on a fall night.

Braised Beef with Sun-Dried Tomatoes

Mashed Yukon gold potatoes*

Green salad

*Place 4 pounds cubed Yukon gold potatoes in a large saucepan; cover with water. Bring to a boil. Reduce heat, and simmer 10 minutes or until tender; drain. Return potatoes to pan; add ½ cup low-fat buttermilk, 1 teaspoon salt, and ¼ teaspoon black pepper. Mash with a potato masher until desired consistency.

STAFF FAVORITE
Braised Beef with Sun-Dried Tomatoes

The tomatoes cook so long in the liquid that they soften to the point of falling apart, adding flavor and body to the braise. The long cooking time also makes the beef very tender.

- 2   teaspoons olive oil
- 2   pounds beef stew meat, cut into 1-inch cubes
- 2   onions, vertically sliced
- 2   garlic cloves, minced
- 1   tablespoon all-purpose flour
- 1¾   cups water
- 1   cup dry red wine
- 1   cup less-sodium beef broth
- 1   cup sun-dried tomato halves, packed without oil, cut into strips (about 2½ ounces)
- 1   tablespoon brown sugar
- 1   tablespoon Worcestershire sauce
- 1½   teaspoons chopped fresh rosemary
- ¾   teaspoon salt
- ¼   teaspoon freshly ground black pepper
- 1   bay leaf
- ¼   cup chopped fresh parsley

1. Heat oil in a large Dutch oven over medium-high heat. Add beef; cook 4 minutes, browning on all sides. Add onion; cook 7 minutes or until onion is softened, stirring occasionally. Add garlic; cook 1 minute, stirring frequently. Stir in flour; cook 2 minutes, stirring frequently.
2. Stir in water and next 9 ingredients. Reduce heat to medium-low; cover and simmer 1 hour. Uncover and simmer 30 minutes or until beef is tender. Discard bay leaf. Sprinkle each serving with parsley. Yield: 8 servings (serving size: ¾ cup beef stew and 1½ teaspoons parsley).

CALORIES 241 (35% from fat); FAT 9.4g (sat 3.2g, mono 4.4g, poly 0.5g); PROTEIN 23.8g; CARB 10g; FIBER 1.5g; CHOL 71mg; IRON 3.7mg; SODIUM 443mg; CALC 33mg

All About Sun-Dried Tomatoes

The Italians may have been the first to sun-dry tomatoes as a way of preserving their summery flavor, but American cooks use them with gusto. Drying Roma, or plum, tomatoes intensifies their naturally sweet taste and gives them a slightly chewy texture that adds richness to the consistency of a dish. While some gourmet producers still dry tomatoes in the sun, others use dehydrators or ovens.

Besides their vivid flavor, sun-dried tomatoes also have a health benefit. Drying concentrates the amount of lycopene, an antioxidant that may help reduce the risk of cardiovascular disease and certain cancers, including those that affect the prostate, colon, and breast. There's up to 12 times more lycopene in sun-dried tomatoes than in the same amount of fresh tomatoes.

Sun-dried tomatoes are available dry or packed in olive oil, sometimes with additional seasonings. Those packed in oil have about twice the calories of those that aren't. But if you need oil for a recipe anyway (as we do here in several recipes), use both the oil and the tomatoes for more flavor. Dry-packed tomatoes are best when you want to limit the fat in a recipe. Rehydrate dry-packed tomatoes in hot water to soften their texture in the final product, or add them to the cooking liquid in a saucy dish. They should be pliable; don't purchase any that are blackened, shriveled, or dusty looking. To make working with sun-dried tomatoes easier:

• Use sharp kitchen scissors to cut oil-packed tomatoes into smaller pieces; chopping them with a chef's knife can make a pulpy mess.

• To keep dry-packed tomatoes from sticking to the blade of a chef's knife, coat the blade with cooking spray before chopping.

QUICK & EASY
Sun-Dried Tomato Pesto and Chicken-Pasta Toss

Make the pesto ahead, and refrigerate or freeze until ready to use.

PESTO:
- 1 (7-ounce) jar oil-packed sun-dried tomato halves
- 1½ cups loosely packed fresh basil leaves
- 1 tablespoon water
- ¼ teaspoon salt
- 2 garlic cloves

PASTA:
- 2 teaspoons olive oil
- 1 pound skinless, boneless chicken breast, cut into 1-inch pieces
- ¼ teaspoon salt
- ¼ teaspoon freshly ground black pepper
- 2 garlic cloves, minced
- 2 tablespoons balsamic vinegar
- 1 (6-ounce) bag prewashed baby spinach
- 1 (12-ounce) can evaporated fat-free milk
- 1 (3-ounce) package goat cheese, crumbled
- 6 cups hot cooked cavatappi (about 4 cups uncooked pasta)

1. To prepare pesto, drain sun-dried tomatoes in a sieve over a bowl, reserving oil. Place 2 tablespoons reserved oil in a food processor. Place remaining oil in sun-dried tomato jar; refrigerate and reserve for another use. Coarsely chop ¼ cup drained tomatoes; set aside. Place remaining drained tomatoes in food processor. Add basil, water, ¼ teaspoon salt, and 2 garlic cloves to food processor; process until finely minced.

2. To prepare pasta, heat olive oil in a large nonstick skillet over medium-high heat. Sprinkle chicken with ¼ teaspoon salt and pepper. Add chicken to pan; sauté 5 minutes or until chicken is done. Remove chicken from pan. Add minced garlic; sauté 30 seconds. Add vinegar and spinach; cook 2 minutes or until spinach wilts. Stir in pesto and milk. Bring to a boil, and cook 2 minutes. Add cheese; cook until cheese melts, stirring constantly. Return chicken to pan; cook 1 minute or until thoroughly heated. Combine chicken mixture and pasta, tossing well to coat. Sprinkle with reserved chopped tomatoes. Yield: 6 servings (serving size: 2 cups).

CALORIES 423 (26% from fat); FAT 12g (sat 3g, mono 6.3g, poly 1.5g); PROTEIN 27.2g; CARB 52.1g; FIBER 3.6g; CHOL 39mg; IRON 3mg; SODIUM 300mg; CALC 203mg

Rosemary-Tomato Pinwheels

Serve with soup or as a quick snack.

- ¼ cup extravirgin olive oil
- 1 teaspoon minced fresh rosemary
- ¼ teaspoon salt
- 1 garlic clove, minced
- 1 cup sun-dried tomato halves, packed without oil (about 2½ ounces)
- 2 (13.8-ounce) cans refrigerated pizza crust dough
- 1 cup thinly sliced fresh basil leaves
- ½ cup (2 ounces) grated fresh Romano cheese
- 2 tablespoons chopped fresh rosemary

1. Combine first 4 ingredients; let stand 1 hour.

2. Cover sun-dried tomatoes with boiling water in a bowl; let stand 30 minutes or until soft. Drain and chop.

3. Preheat oven to 425°.

4. Working with one can of dough at a time, unroll dough onto a lightly floured surface; pat into a 15 x 10-inch rectangle. Brush about 1 tablespoon oil mixture over dough. Sprinkle half of sun-dried tomatoes, ½ cup basil, ¼ cup cheese, and 1 tablespoon chopped rosemary evenly over dough. Starting at long edge, roll up jelly-roll fashion. Cut into 12 (1-inch) slices; place 2 inches apart on a baking sheet lined with parchment paper. Flatten each pinwheel with hand. Brush tops with about 1 tablespoon oil mixture. Repeat procedure with remaining
Continued

can of dough, oil mixture, sun-dried tomatoes, basil, cheese, and rosemary.

5. Bake at 425° for 12 minutes or until golden. Yield: 24 pinwheels (serving size: 1 pinwheel).

CALORIES 122 (30% from fat); FAT 4.1g (sat 0.7g, mono 1.8g, poly 0.2g); PROTEIN 3.9g; CARB 17.2g; FIBER 0.8g; CHOL 2mg; IRON 1.1mg; SODIUM 317mg; CALC 28mg

MAKE AHEAD
Mixed Bean Salad with Sun-Dried Tomatoes

Here's a great choice for your next potluck party. You can make it ahead; it tastes even better after the flavors have had time to meld.

  1 (8-ounce) jar oil-packed sun-dried
    tomato halves
  ½ cup chopped fresh parsley
  ½ cup chopped fresh basil
  1 (15-ounce) can red kidney beans,
    rinsed and drained
  1 (15-ounce) can white kidney
    beans, rinsed and drained
  1 (15-ounce) can black beans, rinsed
    and drained
  1 (15.8-ounce) can black-eyed peas,
    rinsed and drained
  ½ red onion, thinly sliced
  ⅓ cup red wine vinegar
  ¼ cup sugar
  1 teaspoon salt
  ½ teaspoon dry mustard
  ¼ teaspoon freshly ground black
    pepper

1. Drain sun-dried tomatoes in a sieve over a bowl, reserving oil. Place ¼ cup oil in a medium bowl. Return remaining oil to sun-dried tomato jar; refrigerate and reserve for another use. Chop drained tomatoes; place in a large bowl. Add parsley and next 6 ingredients, and stir gently to combine.

2. Add vinegar and remaining 4 ingredients to ¼ cup reserved oil, stirring with a whisk. Drizzle over bean mixture; toss gently to coat. Cover and chill. Yield: 14 servings (serving size: ½ cup).

CALORIES 181 (28% from fat); FAT 5.7g (sat 0.7g, mono 3.6g, poly 0.9g); PROTEIN 7.2g; CARB 26.2g; FIBER 4.4g; CHOL 0mg; IRON 2.5mg; SODIUM 500mg; CALC 100mg

Weeknight Shrimp Dinner Menu
serves 4

Start marinating the shrimp as soon as you get home from work. The rest of the meal comes together in no time at all.

Sun-Dried Tomato Spiced Shrimp

Coconut-almond couscous*

Steamed broccoli spears with lemon rind

*Bring 1½ cups light coconut milk to a boil in a medium saucepan. Gradually stir in 1 cup uncooked couscous, ¼ cup chopped green onions, ¾ teaspoon salt, and ¼ teaspoon ground red pepper. Remove from heat; cover and let stand 5 minutes. Fluff with a fork. Sprinkle with ¼ cup toasted slivered almonds.

Sun-Dried Tomato Spiced Shrimp

To get the most flavor from the marinade, press the sides of the bag when you turn it during the marinating process.

  1 (8-ounce) jar oil-packed sun-dried
    tomato halves
  1 cup chopped fresh
    cilantro
  ½ teaspoon lemon rind
  2 tablespoons fresh lemon
    juice
  1¼ teaspoons curry paste
  1½ pounds large shrimp, peeled and
    deveined
  Cooking spray

1. Drain sun-dried tomatoes in a sieve over a bowl, reserving oil. Place 1 tablespoon oil in a food processor. Coarsely chop 1 cup tomatoes; add to food processor. Place remaining oil and sun-dried tomatoes in sun-dried tomato jar; refrigerate and reserve for another use. Add cilantro, rind, juice, and curry to food processor; process until smooth. Combine tomato mixture and shrimp in a large zip-top plastic bag. Seal and marinate in refrigerator 1 hour, turning bag occasionally. Remove shrimp from bag; discard marinade.

2. Prepare grill to medium-high heat.

3. Place shrimp on grill rack coated with cooking spray; grill 3 minutes on each side or until done. Yield: 4 servings (serving size: about 6 ounces).

CALORIES 224 (25% from fat); FAT 6.1g (sat 1g, mono 2.5g, poly 1.5g); PROTEIN 35.5g; CARB 5.7g; FIBER 1.2g; CHOL 259mg; IRON 4.8mg; SODIUM 292mg; CALC 102mg

QUICK & EASY
Olive and Sun-Dried Tomato Sauce over Chicken

This sauce is similar to a tapenade but has a thinner consistency.

  1 (8-ounce) jar oil-packed sun-dried
    tomato halves
  1¼ cups fat-free, less-sodium chicken
    broth
  ⅔ cup kalamata olives, pitted
  2 tablespoons chopped fresh
    parsley
  1 tablespoon capers
  1 teaspoon chopped fresh thyme
  1 teaspoon chopped fresh rosemary
  1 teaspoon balsamic vinegar
  1 garlic clove, minced
  4 (6-ounce) skinless, boneless
    chicken breast halves
  Cooking spray
  2 cups cooked couscous

1. Prepare grill to medium-high heat.

2. Drain sun-dried tomatoes in a sieve over a bowl, reserving oil. Place 1½ tablespoons oil in a blender or food processor. Coarsely chop ⅔ cup drained tomatoes; place in blender or food processor. Place remaining oil and tomatoes in sun-dried tomato jar; refrigerate and reserve for another use. Add broth and next 7 ingredients to blender; process until smooth.

3. Place chicken on grill rack coated with cooking spray; grill 5 minutes on each side or until done. Serve chicken over couscous; top with sauce. Yield: 4 servings (serving size: 1 chicken breast half, ½ cup couscous, and ½ cup sauce).

CALORIES 394 (28% from fat); FAT 12.3g (sat 2g, mono 7.6g, poly 1.6g); PROTEIN 44.5g; CARB 25g; FIBER 3.1g; CHOL 99mg; IRON 3mg; SODIUM 565mg; CALC 60mg

Savory Herb Sun-Dried Tomato Scones

You can freeze any extra scones. Cool completely; place in a heavy-duty zip-top plastic bag, and freeze up to 2 months. Let thaw at room temperature.

½ cup sun-dried tomato halves, packed without oil (about 1¼ ounces)
2 cups all-purpose flour
¼ cup (1 ounce) grated fresh Romano cheese
1 tablespoon chopped fresh thyme
2 teaspoons baking powder
2 teaspoons chopped fresh rosemary
2 teaspoons dried oregano
½ teaspoon salt
½ teaspoon baking soda
Dash of ground red pepper
¼ cup chilled butter, cut into small pieces
1 cup fat-free buttermilk

1. Cover sun-dried tomatoes with boiling water in a bowl; let stand 30 minutes or until soft. Drain well, and finely chop.
2. Preheat oven to 425°.
3. Cover a baking sheet with parchment paper.
4. Lightly spoon flour into a dry measuring cup; level with a knife. Combine flour, cheese, and next 7 ingredients in a bowl; cut in butter with a pastry blender or 2 knives until mixture resembles coarse meal. Stir in chopped tomatoes. Add buttermilk, stirring just until moist (dough will be sticky).
5. Turn dough out onto a lightly floured surface; knead lightly 4 times with floured hands. Divide dough in half. Pat each dough portion into a 6-inch circle on prepared baking sheet. Cut each circle into six wedges, cutting into but not through dough. Bake at 425° for 12 minutes or until golden. Yield: 12 servings (serving size: 1 wedge).

CALORIES 132 (32% from fat); FAT 4.7g (sat 2.8g, mono 1.3g, poly 0.3g); PROTEIN 4g; CARB 18.8g; FIBER 1g; CHOL 13mg; IRON 1.4mg; SODIUM 361mg; CALC 104mg

Sun-Dried Tomato Cheesecake

CRUST:

5 (1-ounce) slices whole wheat bread
½ cup chopped fresh parsley
½ teaspoon salt
½ teaspoon grated lemon rind
½ teaspoon freshly ground black pepper
1 tablespoon butter
1 teaspoon extravirgin olive oil
1 garlic clove, minced

FILLING:

1¼ cups sun-dried tomato halves, packed without oil (about 3 ounces)
1¼ cups 1% low-fat cottage cheese
1 tablespoon fresh lemon juice
1 tablespoon all-purpose flour
¼ teaspoon salt
2 (8-ounce) blocks ⅓-less-fat cream cheese
2 (8-ounce) blocks fat-free cream cheese
2 large egg whites
¼ cup coarsely chopped fresh basil
½ cup drained canned artichoke hearts, chopped
72 Melba toast rounds (about 12.5 ounces)

1. Preheat oven to 350°.
2. Line bottom of a 9-inch springform pan with parchment.
3. To prepare crust, place bread in a food processor; pulse 10 times or until coarse breadcrumbs measure 2 cups. Combine breadcrumbs, parsley, ½ teaspoon salt, rind, and pepper in a medium bowl. Melt butter in a small skillet over medium heat. Add oil and garlic; cook 1 minute, stirring constantly. Add butter mixture to breadcrumb mixture; stir with a fork. Press breadcrumb mixture evenly into bottom of prepared pan. Set aside.
4. To prepare filling, cover sun-dried tomatoes with boiling water in a bowl; let stand 30 minutes or until soft. Drain and finely chop.
5. Place cottage cheese in a food processor; process until smooth. Add lemon juice and next 5 ingredients; process until smooth. Add tomatoes, basil, and artichoke; process until well blended. Pour cream cheese mixture into prepared pan. Bake at 350° for 30 minutes or until almost set; cool to room temperature. Cover and chill for 2 hours; cut into 24 wedges. Serve at room temperature with Melba toast rounds. Yield: 24 servings (serving size: 1 wedge and 3 Melba toast rounds).

CALORIES 164 (34% from fat); FAT 6.2g (sat 3.5g, mono 1.9g, poly 0.5g); PROTEIN 9.3g; CARB 18.1g; FIBER 1.9g; CHOL 18mg; IRON 1.3mg; SODIUM 410mg; CALC 82mg

Sun-Dried Tomato Ketchup

This ketchup gets its richness from the sun-dried tomatoes and soaking liquid. Use it to perk up hamburgers or to baste grilled chicken or pork.

3 cups sun-dried tomato halves, packed without oil (about 7½ ounces)
4 cups boiling water
2 tablespoons olive oil
1½ cups chopped onion
1 garlic clove, minced
¼ cup balsamic vinegar
3 tablespoons dark brown sugar
1 tablespoon tomato paste
1 teaspoon salt

1. Cover sun-dried tomatoes with boiling water in a bowl; let stand 30 minutes or until soft.
2. Heat oil in a large saucepan over medium-high heat. Add onion and garlic; sauté 4 minutes or until onion is tender. Place tomato mixture, onion mixture, vinegar, sugar, paste, and salt in a blender; process until smooth. Place puréed tomato mixture in pan. Bring to a simmer over medium heat; partially cover, reduce heat, and simmer 30 minutes, stirring occasionally. Chill thoroughly. Yield: 3 cups (serving size: 1 tablespoon).
NOTE: Store in refrigerator up to 1 week.

CALORIES 20 (32% from fat); FAT 0.7g (sat 0.1g, mono 0.4g, poly 0.1g); PROTEIN 0.6g; CARB 3.4g; FIBER 0.5g; CHOL 0mg; IRON 0.4mg; SODIUM 121mg; CALC 6mg

QUICK & EASY
Sun-Dried Tomato-Tortellini Soup

The dry-packed tomatoes rehydrate in this quickly made soup, eliminating the need to steep them.

1½ teaspoons olive oil
1 cup chopped onion
1 cup (¼-inch-thick) slices carrot
⅔ cup chopped celery
2 garlic cloves, minced
5 cups fat-free, less-sodium chicken broth
2 cups water
1¼ cups sun-dried tomato halves, packed without oil, chopped (about 3 ounces)
½ teaspoon dried basil
¼ teaspoon freshly ground black pepper
1 bay leaf
3 cups fresh cheese tortellini (about 12 ounces)
1 cup chopped bok choy

1. Heat oil in a large Dutch oven over medium-high heat. Add onion, carrot, celery, and garlic; sauté 5 minutes. Add broth and next 5 ingredients; bring to a boil. Reduce heat; simmer 2 minutes. Add pasta and bok choy; simmer 7 minutes or until pasta is done. Discard bay leaf. Yield: 6 servings (serving size: about 1½ cups).

CALORIES 256 (28% from fat); FAT 8g (sat 2.6g, mono 3.9g, poly 0.7g); PROTEIN 12.1g; CARB 33.9g; FIBER 3.9g; CHOL 25mg; IRON 1.1mg; SODIUM 681mg; CALC 47mg

superfast
. . . And Ready in Just About 20 Minutes

Have the ingredients for these Asian-inspired recipes on hand, and you'll find little reason for ordering take-out.

STAFF FAVORITE • QUICK & EASY
Tofu Fried Rice

Using frozen peas and carrots plus bottled minced garlic and ginger speeds up preparation of this simple Chinese standby. Keep any leftover sake tightly capped in the refrigerator up to 3 weeks. You can substitute a tablespoon of rice wine vinegar for the sake.

2 cups uncooked instant rice
2 tablespoons vegetable oil, divided
1 (14-ounce) package reduced-fat firm tofu, drained and cut into (½-inch) cubes
2 large eggs, lightly beaten
1 cup (½-inch-thick) slices green onions
1 cup frozen peas and carrots, thawed
2 teaspoons bottled minced garlic
1 teaspoon bottled minced fresh ginger
3 tablespoons low-sodium soy sauce
2 tablespoons sake (rice wine)
1 tablespoon hoisin sauce
½ teaspoon dark sesame oil
Thinly sliced green onions (optional)

1. Cook rice according to package directions, omitting salt and fat.
2. While rice cooks, heat 1 tablespoon vegetable oil in a large nonstick skillet over medium-high heat. Add tofu; cook 4 minutes or until lightly browned, stirring occasionally. Remove from pan. Add eggs to pan; cook 1 minute or until done, breaking egg into small pieces. Remove from pan. Add 1 tablespoon vegetable oil to pan. Add 1 cup onions and next 3 ingredients; sauté 2 minutes.

3. While vegetable mixture cooks, combine soy sauce, sake, hoisin sauce, and sesame oil. Add cooked rice to pan; cook 2 minutes, stirring constantly. Add tofu, egg, and soy sauce mixture; cook 30 seconds, stirring constantly. Garnish with sliced green onions, if desired. Yield: 4 servings (serving size: 1½ cups).

CALORIES 376 (26% from fat); FAT 11g (sat 2g, mono 3g, poly 5.1g); PROTEIN 15.8g; CARB 50.6g; FIBER 3.2g; CHOL 106mg; IRON 3.8mg; SODIUM 629mg; CALC 79mg

QUICK & EASY
Coconut Curried Chicken

Enjoy authentic Thai flavor in this quick entrée. You can use cooked, peeled, and deveined shrimp instead of chicken. Just add the shrimp at the end to heat it up.

1½ cups water, divided
⅔ cup uncooked couscous
1 cup light coconut milk
1 tablespoon cornstarch
1 tablespoon fish sauce
2 teaspoons sugar
2 teaspoons bottled minced garlic
2 teaspoons bottled minced ginger
1 teaspoon green curry paste
2 teaspoons vegetable oil, divided
1 pound chicken breast tenders
½ teaspoon salt, divided
1 cup frozen green peas
½ cup prechopped onion
1 (8-ounce) package presliced mushrooms
1 teaspoon lime juice
Lime wedges (optional)

1. Bring 1 cup water to a boil in a medium saucepan. Stir in couscous; cover and remove from heat. Let stand 5 minutes. Fluff with a fork.
2. While couscous cooks, combine ½ cup water, coconut milk, and next 6 ingredients, stirring well with a whisk.
3. Heat 1 teaspoon oil in a large nonstick skillet over medium-high heat. Sprinkle chicken with ¼ teaspoon salt. Add chicken to pan; cook 6 minutes or until done, turning once. Remove from pan; keep warm.
4. Add 1 teaspoon oil to pan. Add peas, onion, and mushrooms; cook 3 minutes

or until mushrooms are tender. Add coconut milk mixture and ¼ teaspoon salt to pan; bring to a boil. Reduce heat, and simmer 1 minute. Add chicken and lime juice to pan; cook 1 minute or until thoroughly heated. Serve over couscous; garnish with lime wedges, if desired. Yield: 4 servings (serving size: 1½ cups chicken mixture and ½ cup couscous).

CALORIES 361 (18% from fat); FAT 7.2g (sat 2.6g, mono 1.8g, poly 1.2g); PROTEIN 34.4g; CARB 38.1g; FIBER 4.4g; CHOL 66mg; IRON 2.2mg; SODIUM 778mg; CALC 39mg

QUICK & EASY
20-Minute Peking Duck

Here's a simplified—and delicious—Peking duck with flour tortillas standing in for traditional thin pancakes.

- 2 teaspoons dark sesame oil
- 2 (8-ounce) packages boneless duck breast halves, thawed and skinned
- ⅓ cup hoisin sauce
- ½ teaspoon grated orange rind
- 2 tablespoons orange juice
- 2 teaspoons Sriracha (hot chile sauce, such as Huy Fong)
- 4 (6-inch) flour tortillas
- ½ cucumber, peeled, halved lengthwise, seeded, and cut lengthwise into 8 strips
- 2 green onion tops, cut into thin strips
- 2 teaspoons sesame seeds

1. Heat oil in a large nonstick skillet over medium-high heat. Add duck to pan; cook 2 minutes on each side. Reduce heat to medium; cover and cook 3 minutes on each side or until done. Cut duck diagonally across grain into thin slices.
2. Combine hoisin, orange rind, orange juice, and Sriracha. Heat tortillas according to package directions. Spread about 2 tablespoons hoisin mixture down center of each tortilla. Top each tortilla with ¼ of duck, 2 cucumber strips, ¼ of onions, and ½ teaspoon sesame seeds; roll up. Yield: 4 servings (serving size: 1 filled tortilla).

CALORIES 331 (29% from fat); FAT 10.8g (sat 2.6g, mono 3.9g, poly 2.6g); PROTEIN 26.6g; CARB 30.3g; FIBER 2.4g; CHOL 88mg; IRON 6.7mg; SODIUM 595mg; CALC 36mg

---

Speedy Southern Supper Menu
serves 4

This meal is ready in less than 20 minutes, thanks to convenience products like Cajun spice blend, packaged coleslaw mix, and bottled caramel sauce. Pick up corn bread or corn muffins from the deli to keep things extraeasy.

Pan-Fried Catfish with Cajun Tartar Sauce

Cider-mustard slaw*

Corn bread

Vanilla ice cream with caramel sauce

*Combine half of 1 (16-ounce) package cabbage-and-carrot coleslaw, 1 tablespoon brown sugar, 2 tablespoons cider vinegar, 1 tablespoon coarse ground mustard, and ⅛ teaspoon salt.

QUICK & EASY
Pan-Fried Catfish with Cajun Tartar Sauce

This fish is "fried" without the calories or trouble of deep-fat frying. For a spicier sauce, add more hot pepper sauce.

- 4 (6-ounce) farm-raised catfish fillets
- 2 teaspoons Cajun seasoning
- ¼ teaspoon salt
- Cooking spray
- ½ cup fat-free mayonnaise
- 1 tablespoon sweet pickle relish
- 1 tablespoon minced fresh onion
- 1 tablespoon capers, drained
- 1 teaspoon hot pepper sauce (such as Tabasco)
- ¼ teaspoon dried oregano

1. Heat a large nonstick skillet over medium-high heat. Sprinkle fish evenly with Cajun seasoning and salt. Coat pan with cooking spray. Add 2 fillets to pan; cook 4 minutes on each side or until fish flakes easily when tested with a fork. Remove fish from pan; keep warm. Wipe pan clean with paper towels; recoat with cooking spray. Repeat procedure with remaining 2 fillets.

2. While fish cooks, combine mayonnaise and remaining 5 ingredients. Serve mayonnaise mixture with fish. Yield: 4 servings (serving size: 1 fillet and about 3 tablespoons mayonnaise mixture).

CALORIES 262 (48% from fat); FAT 13.9g (sat 3.2g, mono 6.1g, poly 2.7g); PROTEIN 26.7g; CARB 6.3g; FIBER 1g; CHOL 83mg; IRON 1mg; SODIUM 815mg; CALC 20mg

---

QUICK & EASY
Pork Fattoush

This traditional Mediterranean bread salad uses pita; experiment with leftover whole wheat, French, or sourdough bread cut into cubes and toasted before tossing with the other ingredients.

- 1½ teaspoons bottled minced garlic
- ¾ teaspoon salt, divided
- 1 pound pork tenderloin, trimmed and cut into ¾-inch cubes
- 1 tablespoon olive oil
- 2 (7-inch) pitas
- 3 cups chopped tomato
- ½ cup chopped green onions
- ⅓ cup chopped fresh mint
- 1 tablespoon balsamic vinegar
- 1 teaspoon lemon juice
- 1 cucumber, peeled, quartered lengthwise, and sliced into ¼-inch pieces
- 1 (7-ounce) bottle roasted red bell peppers, drained and chopped

1. Preheat oven to 400°.
2. Combine garlic, ½ teaspoon salt, and pork, tossing well to coat. Let stand 5 minutes. Heat oil in a large nonstick skillet over medium-high heat.
3. Arrange pitas in a single layer directly on oven rack. Bake at 400° for 5 minutes or until crisp; transfer to a wire rack.
4. While pitas bake, add pork mixture to pan; cook 5 minutes or until done, stirring frequently. Place pork mixture in a large bowl. Stir in ¼ teaspoon salt, tomato, and remaining 6 ingredients. Break toasted pitas into bite-sized pieces. Add to pork mixture; toss to combine. Yield: 4 servings (serving size: 2 cups).

CALORIES 314 (25% from fat); FAT 8.6g (sat 2.1g, mono 4.6g, poly 1.3g); PROTEIN 28.9g; CARB 30g; FIBER 3.7g; CHOL 74mg; IRON 3.4mg; SODIUM 852mg; CALC 62mg

Corn and Two-Bean Burgers with Chipotle Ketchup

Chipotle chile powder adds a smoky Southwestern note.

BURGERS:
- 2 tablespoons olive oil
- 1 (15-ounce) can kidney beans, rinsed and drained
- 1 (15-ounce) can black beans, rinsed and drained
- ⅓ cup dry breadcrumbs
- ¼ cup canned whole-kernel yellow corn, drained
- ¼ cup prechopped onion
- 1 large egg, lightly beaten

KETCHUP:
- ⅓ cup ketchup
- 1 teaspoon honey
- 1 teaspoon lime juice
- ½ teaspoon chipotle chile powder
- ½ teaspoon ground cumin

REMAINING INGREDIENTS:
- 4 (2-ounce) Kaiser rolls or hamburger buns
- 4 lettuce leaves (optional)
- 4 (¼-inch-thick) slices tomato (optional)

1. To prepare burgers, heat oil in a large nonstick skillet over medium-high heat.
2. Combine kidney beans and black beans in a large bowl; partially mash with a fork. Add breadcrumbs, corn, onion, and egg; stir until well blended. Divide bean mixture into 4 equal portions, shaping each into a ½-inch-thick patty. Add patties to pan; cook 4 minutes on each side or until crisp and lightly browned.
3. To prepare ketchup, combine ketchup and next 4 ingredients, stirring with a whisk.
4. Spread 1 tablespoon ketchup on bottom half of each bun; top each serving with 1 patty, 1 lettuce leaf, 1 tomato slice if desired, and top half of bun. Yield: 4 servings (serving size: 1 burger).

CALORIES 447 (25% from fat); FAT 12.6g (sat 2.8g, mono 7g, poly 1.6g); PROTEIN 17.9g; CARB 68.8g; FIBER 11.2g; CHOL 53mg; IRON 5mg; SODIUM 979mg; CALC 130mg

Shrimp and Crab Rolls

To speed up prep time, purchase cooked, peeled, and deveined shrimp.

- ¼ cup light mayonnaise
- 2 teaspoons Dijon mustard
- ½ teaspoon hot pepper sauce (such as Tabasco)
- ¼ cup finely chopped celery
- 2 tablespoons finely chopped red onion
- 8 ounces chopped cooked medium shrimp
- 8 ounces lump crabmeat, shell pieces removed
- 4 hot dog buns, toasted
- 4 curly leaf lettuce leaves

1. Combine first 3 ingredients in a medium bowl. Add celery, onion, shrimp, and crab; stir well to combine. Line each bun with 1 lettuce leaf; top each serving with ½ cup shrimp mixture. Yield: 4 servings (serving size: 1 roll.)

CALORIES 290 (30% from fat); FAT 9.7g (sat 1.9g, mono 3.5g, poly 3.2g); PROTEIN 26.4g; CARB 24g; FIBER 1.7g; CHOL 161mg; IRON 3.8mg; SODIUM 713mg; CALC 130mg

season's best

Oven-Braised Pork Roast with Apples

When summer fades and the first brisk days of fall approach, you may crave the warmth of a dish roasting in the kitchen.

This pork roast recipe is a delightful reason to turn up the oven. Searing the pork jump-starts the process. Roasting takes less than an hour, tenderizing the meat and deepening its flavor. And the roast's savory juices are the start of a tangy-sweet sauce featuring Rome apples, a perennial accompaniment to pork. Whether you serve this at a dinner party or a family sit-down, it's a comforting entrée that will welcome the season.

Oven-Braised Pork Roast with Apples

- 2 tablespoons brown sugar
- 2 teaspoons ground cumin
- 1 teaspoon ground cinnamon
- 1 teaspoon garlic powder
- ½ teaspoon coarsely ground black pepper
- ¼ teaspoon ground ginger
- ¼ teaspoon ground red pepper
- ¼ teaspoon ground cloves
- 1 teaspoon salt, divided
- 1 (3½-pound) boneless pork loin roast, trimmed
- Cooking spray
- ½ cup chopped onion
- ½ cup chopped dried apricots
- ½ cup thawed orange juice concentrate
- ⅓ cup golden raisins
- 1 (14-ounce) can fat-free, less-sodium chicken broth
- 2 tablespoons butter
- 4 Rome apples, each cut into 8 wedges
- 1 tablespoon balsamic vinegar

1. Combine first 8 ingredients; stir in ¾ teaspoon salt. Rub evenly over pork. Cover and refrigerate 2 hours.
2. Preheat oven to 425°.
3. Heat a large Dutch oven over medium-high heat. Coat pan with cooking spray. Add pork to pan, and cook 4 minutes, browning on all sides. Remove pork from pan. Add onion to pan; sauté 1 minute. Return pork to pan. Add apricots, orange juice concentrate, raisins, and broth; bring to a boil. Cover and bake at 425° for 30 minutes. Reduce oven temperature to 325° (do not remove pork from oven); bake 20 minutes or until meat thermometer inserted into thickest portion of pork registers 160° (slightly pink). Remove pork from pan, reserving cooking liquid. Place pork on a platter; cover with foil.
4. Remove apricots and raisins from pan with a slotted spoon; set aside. Bring reserved cooking liquid to a boil over high heat; cook until reduced to ½ cup (about 5 minutes). Remove from heat.
5. Melt butter in a large nonstick skillet over medium-high heat. Add apples; cook 2 minutes on each side or until lightly browned. Stir in reserved apricots

and raisins, reduced broth mixture, ¼ teaspoon salt, and vinegar; cook 3 minutes. Slice pork into thick slices. Yield: 12 servings (serving size: 3 ounces pork and ½ cup apple mixture).

CALORIES 297 (31% from fat); FAT 10.1g (sat 3.8g, mono 4.1g, poly 1.1g); PROTEIN 29.7g; CARB 21.7g; FIBER 2.6g; CHOL 83mg; IRON 1.9mg; SODIUM 355mg; CALC 43mg

enlightened cook

Food for Thought

For Chef Cary Neff, mindful cooking is healthful and delicious.

"There are no bad foods," Chef Cary Neff says. "But there are bad portion sizes and bad decisions." Here are some examples of good choices.

White Bean, Tuna, and Onion Salad with Sprouts

VINAIGRETTE:

  2 tablespoons minced shallots
  1 tablespoon white balsamic vinegar
  1 tablespoon Dijon mustard
  1 teaspoon extravirgin olive oil
  1 teaspoon honey
  ¼ teaspoon sea salt
  ⅛ teaspoon freshly ground black pepper
  1 garlic clove, minced
  ¼ cup vegetable broth
  ½ teaspoon cornstarch
  1 tablespoon minced fresh parsley

SALAD:

  ⅓ cup chopped red onion
  1 (16-ounce) can cannellini beans or other white beans, rinsed and drained
  1 (6-ounce) can albacore tuna in water, drained and flaked
  4 cups fresh baby spinach (about 4 ounces)
  2 yellow tomatoes, halved and sliced
  2½ cups thinly sliced Belgian endive (about ½ pound)
  ¼ cup spicy radish sprouts

1. To prepare vinaigrette, combine first 8 ingredients in a small saucepan. Combine broth and cornstarch in a small bowl; stir with a whisk. Add cornstarch mixture to pan. Bring to a boil over medium-high heat, and cook 1 minute; stir constantly. Remove from heat, and stir in parsley. Cool to room temperature.
2. To prepare salad, combine vinaigrette, onion, beans, and tuna in a large bowl; toss gently to combine. Cover; chill 1 hour.
3. Arrange 1 cup spinach and ¼ of tomatoes on each of 4 plates, and top with about ⅔ cup endive. Arrange about ½ cup tuna mixture and 1 tablespoon sprouts on each serving. Yield: 4 servings.

CALORIES 179 (18% from fat); FAT 3.5g (sat 0.5g, mono 1.3g, poly 1.1g); PROTEIN 16.5g; CARB 21.4g; FIBER 5.5g; CHOL 18mg; IRON 4.5mg; SODIUM 694mg; CALC 122mg

Beef Tenderloin with Porcini Mushroom Sauce

Steamed baby carrots make a pretty side dish.

SAUCE:

  1 cup boiling water
  ½ cup dried porcini mushrooms (about ½ ounce)
  1 teaspoon extravirgin olive oil
  1½ cups chopped red onion
  ¼ cup finely chopped shallots
  1½ cups less-sodium beef broth
  ½ cup dry white wine
  ½ teaspoon chopped fresh thyme
  1 bay leaf
  2 tablespoons water
  2 teaspoons cornstarch
  ¼ teaspoon sea salt
  ⅛ teaspoon freshly ground black pepper

BEEF:

  4 (4-ounce) beef tenderloin steaks, trimmed (1½ inches thick)
  ½ teaspoon sea salt
  ⅛ teaspoon freshly ground black pepper
  Cooking spray

1. To prepare sauce, combine boiling water and mushrooms in a bowl; cover and let stand 10 minutes or until tender. Drain; rinse and drain mushrooms. Chop mushrooms.

2. Heat oil in a medium saucepan over medium-high heat. Add mushrooms, onion, and shallots; sauté 3 minutes or until onions are tender. Reduce heat to medium. Add broth, wine, thyme, and bay leaf. Bring to a simmer; cook 6 minutes. Discard bay leaf. Combine 2 tablespoons water and cornstarch in a small bowl; stir with a whisk. Add cornstarch mixture to pan; bring to a boil. Cook 1 minute; stir constantly. Remove from heat; stir in ¼ teaspoon salt and ⅛ teaspoon pepper. Keep warm.
3. Preheat oven to 400°.
4. To prepare beef, heat a large nonstick skillet over medium-high heat. Sprinkle beef with ½ teaspoon salt and ⅛ teaspoon pepper. Coat pan with cooking spray. Add beef to pan; cook 1 minute on each side or until browned. Wrap handle of pan with foil; place pan in oven. Bake at 400° for 5 minutes or until desired degree of doneness. Place beef on a platter; let stand 5 minutes before serving. Yield: 4 servings (serving size: 1 steak and ¼ cup sauce).

CALORIES 318 (30% from fat); FAT 10.5g (sat 3.4g, mono 4.5g, poly 0.8g); PROTEIN 32.2g; CARB 17.7g; FIBER 4.1g; CHOL 71mg; IRON 7.4mg; SODIUM 523mg; CALC 35mg

Minestrone with Chickpeas

Cooking spray
  1 cup chopped eggplant
  1 cup chopped zucchini
  1 cup chopped yellow squash
  ½ cup chopped red bell pepper
  ½ cup chopped onion
  1 garlic clove, minced
  2 (14-ounce) cans vegetable broth
  1 (28-ounce) can diced tomatoes, undrained
  1 bay leaf
  1 tablespoon chopped fresh parsley
  1 tablespoon commercial pesto
  1 teaspoon chopped fresh oregano
  ½ teaspoon sea salt
  ¼ teaspoon freshly ground black pepper
  2 (15½-ounce) cans chickpeas (garbanzo beans), rinsed and drained
  2 cups chopped spinach (about 1 ounce)

Continued

1. Heat a large saucepan over medium-high heat. Coat pan with cooking spray. Add eggplant and next 5 ingredients; sauté 4 minutes or until onion is tender. Stir in broth, tomatoes, and bay leaf, and bring to a boil. Reduce heat, and simmer 15 minutes. Discard bay leaf. Add parsley and next 5 ingredients; cook 5 minutes or until thoroughly heated. Stir in spinach; serve immediately. Yield: 8 servings (serving size: about 1 cup).

CALORIES 133 (21% from fat); FAT 3.1g (sat 0.3g, mono 1.2g, poly 1.1g); PROTEIN 6.2g; CARB 22.9g; FIBER 6.2g; CHOL 1mg; IRON 2mg; SODIUM 838mg; CALC 84mg

reader recipes

A New Classic

A time-tested recipe for banana loaf is tweaked for today's tastes.

When Kay Rothschild, of Dayton, Ohio, lightens a recipe, it's a minor change, not a major overhaul. Her Banana-Oatmeal Loaf, for example, started with an old-fashioned quick bread, with a little buttermilk for moisture and just the right amount of banana for sweetness. She added fiber-rich oats, which give the loaf a hearty crust and substantial texture. With all these delicious additions to an old standby, her new classic is something we can all enjoy.

MAKE AHEAD • FREEZABLE
Banana-Oatmeal Loaf

1½ cups all-purpose flour
⅔ cup sugar
1½ teaspoons baking powder
¼ teaspoon baking soda
¼ teaspoon salt
¾ cup regular oats
1 cup mashed ripe banana (about 2 large)
⅓ cup low-fat buttermilk
¼ cup vegetable oil
1 teaspoon vanilla extract
2 large eggs, lightly beaten
Cooking spray

1. Preheat oven to 350°.
2. Lightly spoon flour into dry measuring cups; level with a knife. Combine flour and next 4 ingredients in a large bowl, stirring well with a whisk. Stir in oats.
3. Combine mashed banana and next 4 ingredients; add to flour mixture. Stir just until moist.
4. Spoon batter into an 8 x 4-inch loaf pan coated with cooking spray. Bake at 350° for 55 minutes or until a wooden pick inserted in center comes out clean. Cool 15 minutes in pan on a wire rack; remove from pan. Cool completely on wire rack. Yield: 12 servings (serving size: 1 slice).

CALORIES 192 (28% from fat); FAT 6g (sat 1.1g, mono 1.5g, poly 2.9g); PROTEIN 3.8g; CARB 31.4g; FIBER 1.3g; CHOL 36mg; IRON 1.2mg; SODIUM 154mg; CALC 52mg

QUICK & EASY • MAKE AHEAD
Roasted Red Pepper on Mini-Bagel Sandwiches

"I came up with the idea for this after having a similar sandwich with roasted red pepper and fresh mozzarella. It's light, filling, and great for boxed lunches or on-the-go meals."
—Kerri Kwist, Carrollton, Texas

¾ cup (6 ounces) ⅓-less-fat cream cheese, softened
¼ cup (2 ounces) fat-free cream cheese, softened
¼ cup minced green onions
¼ teaspoon salt
⅛ teaspoon black pepper
2 garlic cloves, minced
12 mini bagels, halved and toasted
1 (12-ounce) bottle roasted red bell peppers, rinsed, drained, and chopped

1. Combine first 6 ingredients.
2. Spread cream cheese mixture evenly over cut sides of bagels. Arrange bell peppers evenly over bottom halves of bagels; top with top halves of bagels. Cut each sandwich in half. Yield: 24 servings (serving size: half a sandwich).

CALORIES 62 (29% from fat); FAT 2g (sat 1.1g, mono 0.5g, poly 0.2g); PROTEIN 2.6g; CARB 8.1g; FIBER 0.4g; CHOL 9mg; IRON 0.6mg; SODIUM 173mg; CALC 15mg

MAKE AHEAD
Apple-Orange Pie

"My mother, who was a very good cook, gave me the idea for this pie. I love to make it in the fall and for the holidays."
—Pat Habiger, Spearville, Kansas

2 thin-skinned oranges
1 cup water
¼ cup honey
1 tablespoon fresh lemon juice
½ cup packed brown sugar
3 tablespoons all-purpose flour
¼ teaspoon ground cinnamon
⅛ teaspoon ground ginger
Dash of salt
6 Golden Delicious apples, peeled, cored, and sliced
1 (15-ounce) package refrigerated pie dough (such as Pillsbury)
Cooking spray
1 large egg, lightly beaten

1. Carefully remove rind from oranges using a vegetable peeler, making sure to avoid white pithy part of rind (reserve oranges for another use). Cut rinds into 1 x ⅛-inch strips. Combine water, honey, and lemon juice in a small saucepan; bring to a boil over medium-high heat. Add orange rind; cover, reduce heat, and simmer 30 minutes or until rind is very soft. Remove rind from pan with a slotted spoon; discard cooking liquid.
2. Preheat oven to 350°.
3. Combine brown sugar and next 4 ingredients in a large bowl. Add apples; toss well to coat. Fit 1 portion of dough into a 9-inch deep-dish pie plate coated with cooking spray, allowing dough to extend over edge of plate. Spoon half of apple mixture into crust; arrange orange rind over top. Spoon remaining apple mixture over rind. Place remaining dough on apple mixture. Press edges of dough together. Fold edges under; flute. Cut 3 (1-inch) slits in top of pastry using a sharp knife. Brush top and edges with beaten egg.
4. Place pie on a baking sheet; bake at 350° for 1 hour or until golden. Cool on a wire rack. Yield: 10 servings.

CALORIES 333 (31% from fat); FAT 11.6g (sat 4.9g, mono 0.2g, poly 0.1g); PROTEIN 3g; CARB 56g; FIBER 4g; CHOL 29mg; IRON 1mg; SODIUM 185mg; CALC 24mg

Pork Medallions with Garlic-Ginger-Pomegranate Sauce

"I'm always creating recipes using the latest cooking trends. This simple, healthy pork recipe involves pomegranate juice, ginger, and cilantro."

—Tracey Medeiros, Atlanta, Georgia

½   cup water
¼   cup pomegranate juice
1½ tablespoons fresh lemon juice
1½ tablespoons low-sodium soy sauce
1   teaspoon minced peeled fresh ginger
2   garlic cloves, minced
½   teaspoon salt, divided
¼   teaspoon black pepper, divided
1   (1-pound) pork tenderloin, trimmed
2   tablespoons all-purpose flour
1½ teaspoons olive oil
1   tablespoon water
1   teaspoon cornstarch
2   tablespoons chopped fresh cilantro

1. Combine first 6 ingredients in a large zip-top plastic bag; add ¼ teaspoon salt and ⅛ teaspoon pepper. Add pork; seal and marinate in refrigerator 2 hours, turning bag occasionally. Remove pork from bag, reserving marinade. Sprinkle pork with ¼ teaspoon salt, ⅛ teaspoon pepper, and flour.
2. Preheat oven to 350°.
3. Heat oil in a large ovenproof skillet over medium-high heat. Add pork; cook 5 minutes, browning on all sides. Pour reserved marinade over pork. Bake at 350° for 10 minutes or until a thermometer registers 160° (slightly pink). Remove pork from pan; let stand 10 minutes. Cut crosswise into 8 pieces.
4. Combine 1 tablespoon water and cornstarch, stirring well with a whisk. Bring marinade to a boil over medium-high heat. Add cornstarch mixture to marinade; cook 1 minute or until sauce thickens, stirring constantly. Serve over pork; sprinkle with cilantro. Yield: 4 servings (serving size: 2 pieces pork and 1 tablespoon sauce).

CALORIES 170 (30% from fat); FAT 5.6g (sat 1.6g, mono 3g, poly 0.6g); PROTEIN 24.3g; CARB 4.6g; FIBER 0.2g; CHOL 74mg; IRON 1.6mg; SODIUM 551mg; CALC 12mg

---

QUICK & EASY • MAKE AHEAD
Beef and Green Chile Soup

"This soup is best served the same day you prepare it and doubles easily if you're feeding a crowd."

—Sally Cerny, Great Falls, Montana

½   pound ground round
1¼ cups chopped onion
⅔   cup chopped celery
½   cup chopped carrot
¼   teaspoon dried oregano
¼   teaspoon ground cumin
Dash of ground red pepper
1   garlic clove, minced
¼   teaspoon salt
2   (14-ounce) cans less-sodium beef broth
1   (4.5-ounce) can chopped green chiles, undrained
1¼ cups uncooked large elbow macaroni (about 4 ounces)

1. Heat a large Dutch oven over medium-high heat. Add beef; cook 3 minutes or until browned, stirring to crumble. Remove beef from pan. Add onion, celery, and carrot to pan; cook 6 minutes or until tender, stirring occasionally. Stir in oregano, cumin, pepper, and garlic; cook 1 minute. Return beef to pan. Stir in salt, broth, and chiles; bring to a boil. Add macaroni; reduce heat, and simmer 8 minutes or until macaroni is tender. Yield: 6 servings (serving size: about 1 cup).

CALORIES 202 (31% from fat); FAT 6.9g (sat 2.5g, mono 2.9g, poly 0.5g); PROTEIN 13.6g; CARB 21g; FIBER 2.5g; CHOL 26mg; IRON 2.1mg; SODIUM 197mg; CALC 32mg

---

QUICK & EASY • MAKE AHEAD
Tortilla Soup

"I had this soup at a restaurant. I played around with the ingredients and came up with a pretty close duplication."

—Jenny Thompson, Newton, Iowa

2   cups no-salt-added tomato sauce
1½ cups water
1   cup bottled salsa
1   cup frozen whole-kernel corn
1   teaspoon dried oregano
1   teaspoon dried basil
1   (14-ounce) can fat-free, less-sodium chicken broth
1   (16-ounce) can kidney beans, rinsed and drained
1   garlic clove, minced
1½ cups (6 ounces) shredded, reduced-fat Cheddar cheese
30 fat-free baked tortilla chips

1. Combine first 9 ingredients in a large saucepan; bring to a boil. Cover, reduce heat, and simmer 12 minutes. Ladle into bowls; sprinkle with cheese. Serve with chips. Yield: 6 servings (serving size: 1⅓ cups soup, ¼ cup cheese, and 5 chips).

CALORIES 226 (12% from fat); FAT 3g (sat 1.3g, mono 0.8g, poly 0.5g); PROTEIN 14g; CARB 36g; FIBER 7.9g; CHOL 6mg; IRON 2.5mg; SODIUM 766mg; CALC 178mg

---

Thai-Style Chicken Stir-Fry

"I love Thai chicken-coconut soup and wanted similar flavors in an entrée. We like it spicy, but you can reduce the jalapeño. Serve over jasmine rice or cellophane noodles."

—Elena Andrews Gaillard, New York, New York

1½ tablespoons fish sauce
1   tablespoon low-sodium soy sauce
1   tablespoon bottled minced fresh ginger
3   tablespoons fresh lime juice, divided
1   pound skinless, boneless chicken breast, cut into bite-sized pieces
1   tablespoon canola oil
2   cups (¼-inch-thick) slices zucchini
1   cup (½-inch-thick) slices onion
1   cup (¼-inch-thick) slices red bell pepper
4   garlic cloves, minced
2   jalapeño peppers, seeded and minced
¼   cup thinly sliced fresh basil
¼   cup minced fresh cilantro
¼   cup chopped green onions

Continued

1. Combine first 3 ingredients in a large zip-top plastic bag; add 1½ tablespoons lime juice. Add chicken; seal and marinate in refrigerator 25 minutes. Remove chicken from bag, reserving marinade.

2. Heat oil in a large nonstick skillet over medium-high heat. Add chicken; stir-fry 2 minutes or until chicken begins to brown. Add zucchini and next 4 ingredients; stir-fry 5 minutes or until chicken is done. Add reserved marinade, and cook 1 minute. Remove from heat; stir in 1½ tablespoons lime juice, basil, cilantro, and green onions. Yield: 4 servings (serving size: 1½ cups).

CALORIES 200 (23% from fat); FAT 5.2g (sat 0.7g, mono 2.4g, poly 1.5g); PROTEIN 28.3g; CARB 9.4g; FIBER 2.3g; CHOL 66mg; IRON 1.5mg; SODIUM 700mg; CALC 40mg

inspired vegetarian

Soy on the Sly

Sneak in a meatless version of a family standby.

MAKE AHEAD
Chicken-Green Chile Enchilada Casserole

Serve with sour cream, salsa, and fruit salad.

 1 teaspoon vegetable oil
 1 cup chopped onion
 3 garlic cloves, minced
 1 (4.5-ounce) can chopped green chiles, undrained
 2 (6-ounce) packages meatless fat-free chicken strips (such as Lightlife Smart Menu), chopped
 ½ teaspoon ground cumin
 ½ teaspoon chili powder
 2 (10-ounce) cans green chile enchilada sauce
    Cooking spray
 14 (6-inch) corn tortillas, cut into quarters
 1½ cups (6 ounces) preshredded reduced-fat Mexican blend cheese, divided
    Chopped fresh cilantro (optional)

1. Preheat oven to 375°.

2. Heat oil in a large nonstick skillet over medium-high heat. Add onion and garlic; sauté 5 minutes or until onion is tender. Add chiles; cook 3 minutes. Stir constantly. Remove from heat; stir in chicken strips.

3. Combine cumin, chili powder, and enchilada sauce. Pour ⅓ of sauce mixture into an 11 x 7-inch baking dish coated with cooking spray. Arrange ½ of tortilla quarters over sauce mixture; top with chicken mixture. Sprinkle with ¾ cup Mexican blend cheese; top with ⅓ of sauce mixture. Top with remaining tortillas and sauce mixture. Bake at 375° for 15 minutes. Sprinkle with ¾ cup cheese; bake an additional 10 minutes. Sprinkle with cilantro, if desired. Yield: 8 servings.

CALORIES 218 (29% from fat); FAT 7.3g (sat 2.3g, mono 1.4g, poly 1g); PROTEIN 17.8g; CARB 22.9g; FIBER 5.5g; CHOL 15mg; IRON 0.1mg; SODIUM 889mg; CALC 145mg

Biscuits and Vegetarian Sausage Gravy

Vegetarian sausage has a firmer texture than pork sausage. Crumbling it helps distribute it evenly throughout the gravy.

 1 (16.3-ounce) can reduced-fat refrigerated biscuit dough
 1 tablespoon vegetable oil
 ½ (14-ounce) package meatless fat-free sausage (such as Lightlife Gimme Lean)
 ¼ cup all-purpose flour
 3 cups 1% low-fat milk
 ½ teaspoon salt
 ¼ teaspoon freshly ground black pepper

1. Prepare biscuits according to package directions.

2. Heat oil in a large nonstick skillet over medium-high heat. Add sausage; cook 3 minutes or until browned, stirring to crumble. Remove from heat; cool slightly. Crumble sausage into ½-inch pieces; return to pan.

3. Lightly spoon flour into a dry measuring cup; level with a knife. Combine flour and milk, stirring with a whisk until smooth. Add milk mixture, salt, and pepper to pan; bring to a boil over medium-high heat.

Cover, reduce heat, and simmer 3 minutes or until thick. Split biscuits in half. Place 2 biscuit halves on each of 8 plates; top each serving with about ⅓ cup gravy. Serve immediately. Yield: 8 servings.

CALORIES 268 (29% from fat); FAT 8.7g (sat 2.4g, mono 4g, poly 1g); PROTEIN 11.4g; CARB 36.9g; FIBER 0.6g; CHOL 4mg; IRON 1mg; SODIUM 910mg; CALC 131mg

STAFF FAVORITE
Pepperoni, Provolone, and Pesto Stromboli

 1 cup warm water (100° to 110°)
 1 package dry yeast (about 2¼ teaspoons)
 3 cups plus 2 tablespoons all-purpose flour, divided
 1 tablespoon sugar
 ¼ teaspoon salt
    Cooking spray
 ⅓ cup commercial pesto (such as DiGiorno)
 1½ cups (6 ounces) shredded provolone cheese
 ¼ cup chopped pitted kalamata olives
 1 (7-ounce) bottle roasted red bell peppers, drained and chopped
 1 (4-ounce) package meatless fat-free pepperoni (such as Lightlife Smart Deli)

1. Combine warm water and yeast in a large bowl; let stand 5 minutes. Lightly spoon flour into dry measuring cups; level with a knife. Add 3 cups flour, sugar, and salt to yeast mixture; stir to form a dough. Turn dough out onto a floured surface. Knead until smooth and elastic (about 5 minutes); add enough of remaining flour, 1 tablespoon at a time, to prevent dough from sticking to hands (dough will feel sticky). Place dough in a large bowl coated with cooking spray, turning to coat top. Cover and let rise in a warm place (85°), free from drafts, 1 hour or until doubled in size. (Gently press two fingers into dough. If indentation remains, dough has risen enough.) Punch dough down; cover and let rest 5 minutes.

2. Preheat oven to 350°.

3. Press dough into a 15 x 10-inch jelly-roll pan coated with cooking spray.

Spread pesto over dough, leaving a 1-inch border; top evenly with cheese, olives, peppers, and pepperoni, pressing gently into dough. Beginning with a long side, roll up jelly-roll fashion. Press seam to seal. Place roll, seam side down, on pan. Cut 4 slits across top of dough using a sharp knife; let rise 30 minutes. Lightly coat dough with cooking spray. Bake at 350° for 40 minutes. Let stand 10 minutes before slicing. Cut crosswise into 8 slices. Yield: 8 servings (serving size: 1 slice).

CALORIES 361 (32% from fat); FAT 13g (sat 4.4g, mono 3.6g, poly 2.4g); PROTEIN 16.8g; CARB 44.7g; FIBER 2.4g; CHOL 18mg; IRON 3.2mg; SODIUM 708mg; CALC 167mg

Veggie Sausage and Egg Strata

2 (8-ounce) packages frozen meatless breakfast sausage patties (such as Boca)
Cooking spray
12 (1-ounce) slices white bread, crust removed
¾ cup (3 ounces) shredded reduced-fat sharp Cheddar cheese, divided
2½ cups fat-free milk
½ teaspoon salt
¼ teaspoon freshly ground black pepper
2 (8-ounce) cartons egg substitute

1. Heat a large nonstick skillet over medium-high heat. Lightly coat sausages with cooking spray. Add sausages to pan; cook 5 minutes or until browned, turning once. Chop sausages.
2. Arrange 6 bread slices in bottom of a 13 x 9-inch baking dish coated with cooking spray. Arrange sausage and ½ cup cheese over bread. Top with remaining bread slices. Combine milk, salt, pepper, and egg substitute, stirring with a whisk. Pour over bread mixture. Let stand 30 minutes.
3. Preheat oven to 400°.
4. Sprinkle ¼ cup cheese over bread mixture. Bake at 400° for 30 minutes or until puffed and browned. Let stand 5 minutes before serving. Yield: 8 servings.

CALORIES 284 (33% from fat); FAT 10.5g (sat 4.2g, mono 1.5g, poly 2.3g); PROTEIN 22.3g; CARB 25.1g; FIBER 3.7g; CHOL 10mg; IRON 3.3mg; SODIUM 952mg; CALC 234mg

Meet the Meatless

Bulk Sausage

What to expect: The texture is soft when cooked, and the flavor is similar to pork sausage because it contains many of the same seasonings. Found in refrigerated grocery section
Best uses: This is an excellent substitute for pork sausage. Cut to form patties, and brown in a skillet. Like some other bulk sausages (such as turkey Italian sausage), you'll need to break it up into smaller pieces as it cooks—it doesn't crumble on its own.
Our favorite: Lightlife Gimme Lean Sausage Style

Chicken

What to expect: It's a little chewier than chicken, more akin to light meat than dark. Found in refrigerated grocery section
Best uses: Chopped and stirred into saucy dishes, such as soup or creamy casseroles. This helps keep the texture from mimicking overcooked chicken.
Our favorite: Lightlife Smart Menu Chick'n Strips

Ground Beef

What to expect: The texture of meatless ground burger is soft and moist like raw ground beef, while soy crumbles are more like cooked and crumbled ground beef. Found in both refrigerated and freezer case grocery sections
Best uses: The combination of meatless ground burger and soy crumbles produces the best results when making something you need to shape and hold together, such as meat loaf, burgers, and meatballs. Either is fine in tacos, chili, or sloppy joes.

Our favorites: Boca Ground Burger, Yves Veggie Ground Round, and Lightlife Smart Ground

Italian Sausage

What to expect: These are similar in texture to cooked turkey Italian sausage, but they're closer in flavor to pork Italian sausage. Found in freezer case grocery section
Best uses: Whole, you can use it in any dish in which you would use link Italian sausage. Chopped, it substitutes well for cooked and crumbled Italian sausage.
Our favorite: Boca Italian Sausages

Pepperoni

What to expect: The slices are thicker and less chewy than real pepperoni, but the flavor is similar. Found in refrigerated grocery section
Best uses: Anywhere you'd use pepperoni
Our favorites: Lightlife Smart Deli Pepperoni Slices and Yves Veggie Pizza Pepperoni

Sausage Patties

What to expect: These have a firm, slightly crisp texture and a flavor similar to pork breakfast sausage. Be careful not to overcook them—they can become very dry and firm. Found in freezer case grocery section
Best uses: Anywhere you'd use breakfast sausage patties. You can also chop to use in casseroles where you'd use bulk breakfast sausage.
Our favorites: Boca Breakfast Patties and Morningstar Farms Veggie Breakfast Sausage Patties

Italian Sausage and Fennel Lasagna

A piece of this saucy lasagna provides 428 milligrams of calcium—almost half the recommended daily amount.

 2 teaspoons olive oil
 2 cups chopped fennel
    bulb
1½ cups chopped onion
4½ cups fat-free spaghetti
    sauce
 ½ cup water
 1 (10-ounce) package frozen
    meatless Italian sausages (such as
    Boca), thawed and chopped
 1 (8-ounce) can no-salt-added
    tomato sauce
 1 (12-ounce) carton 2% low-fat
    cottage cheese
 2 large egg whites
 1 cup fat-free ricotta cheese
 ½ teaspoon dried Italian
    seasoning
 2 garlic cloves, minced
 1 (8-ounce) package precooked
    lasagna noodles
1½ cups (6 ounces) shredded
    part-skim mozzarella cheese,
    divided
    Cooking spray

1. Preheat oven to 375°.
2. Heat oil in a Dutch oven over medium-high heat. Add fennel and onion; sauté 5 minutes or until tender. Add spaghetti sauce, water, sausage, and tomato sauce; cover, reduce heat, and simmer 5 minutes.
3. Combine cottage cheese and egg whites in a food processor; process until smooth. Place cottage cheese mixture in a medium bowl. Stir in ricotta, Italian seasoning, and garlic.
4. Spread about 1½ cups sausage mixture in bottom of a 13 x 9-inch baking dish. Arrange 3 noodles over sausage mixture, and top with about ¾ cup ricotta mixture, about 1¾ cups sausage mixture, and ⅓ cup mozzarella. Repeat layers, ending with noodles. Spread remaining sausage mixture over noodles. Cover with foil coated with cooking spray. Bake at 375° for 40 minutes.

Sprinkle with remaining mozzarella. Bake, uncovered, an additional 20 minutes or until lightly browned. Let stand 10 minutes before serving. Yield: 8 servings.

CALORIES 388 (21% from fat); FAT 9.2g (sat 2.8g, mono 2.8g, poly 1.8g); PROTEIN 25.5g; CARB 46.7g; FIBER 5.3g; CHOL 16mg; IRON 3.4mg; SODIUM 1,078mg; CALC 428mg

Vegetarian Meat Loaf

Using heart-healthy meatless crumbles instead of ground round saves about 10 grams of fat per serving and adds almost 5 grams of fiber.

 1 cup chopped celery
 1 cup sliced carrots
 1 onion, peeled and quartered
 3 garlic cloves, minced
 1 tablespoon vegetable oil
 ¾ cup ketchup, divided
 ⅓ cup dry breadcrumbs
 2 large eggs, lightly beaten
 1 (12-ounce) package meatless
    ground burger (such as Boca)
 1 (12-ounce) package meatless
    fat-free crumbles (such as Lightlife
    Smart Ground)
    Cooking spray

1. Preheat oven to 350°.
2. Combine first 4 ingredients in a food processor, and process until finely chopped.
3. Heat oil in a large nonstick skillet over medium-high heat. Add onion mixture; sauté 5 minutes or until tender. Place onion mixture, ½ cup ketchup, breadcrumbs, eggs, ground burger, and crumbles in a large bowl; mix well.
4. Place mixture in a 9 x 5-inch loaf pan coated with cooking spray. Spread ¼ cup ketchup over top. Bake at 350° for 35 minutes. Let stand 10 minutes before serving. Yield: 8 servings.

CALORIES 197 (16% from fat); FAT 3.7g (sat 0.7g, mono 1g, poly 1.3g); PROTEIN 20.5g; CARB 22.3g; FIBER 5.9g; CHOL 53mg; IRON 3mg; SODIUM 667mg; CALC 41mg

Shepherd's Pie

Soy crumbles provide 10 grams of soy protein and 3 grams of fiber per serving. They don't require browning in the skillet, which reduces your time in the kitchen.

 1 tablespoon vegetable oil
1½ cups diced onion
 3 garlic cloves, minced
14 large mushrooms (about
    12 ounces)
 1 (12-ounce) package meatless
    fat-free crumbles (such as Lightlife
    Smart Ground)
 ¼ cup all-purpose flour
1½ cups 1% low-fat milk
 ½ teaspoon salt
 ¼ teaspoon freshly ground black
    pepper
 1 (11-ounce) can no-salt-added
    whole-kernel corn, drained
 1 (20-ounce) package refrigerated
    mashed potatoes (such as Simply
    Potatoes)
 ½ cup reduced-fat sour cream
 2 tablespoons butter, melted

1. Preheat oven to 375°.
2. Heat oil in a large nonstick skillet over medium heat. Add onion, and cook 5 minutes or until tender, stirring frequently. Add garlic and mushrooms; cook 8 minutes or until liquid evaporates, stirring frequently. Stir in meatless crumbles. Lightly spoon flour into a dry measuring cup; level with a knife. Combine flour, milk, salt, and pepper, stirring with a whisk. Add to pan. Bring to a simmer; cook 2 minutes. Place mixture in an 11 x 7-inch baking dish. Top with corn.
3. Prepare potatoes according to package directions. Stir in sour cream and butter. Spread potatoes evenly over corn. Bake at 375° for 30 minutes or until browned. Yield: 6 servings.

CALORIES 340 (28% from fat); FAT 11g (sat 4.7g, mono 2.7g, poly 2g); PROTEIN 21g; CARB 42.5g; FIBER 7.4g; CHOL 20mg; IRON 2.3mg; SODIUM 749mg; CALC 114mg

Apple Appellations

While there are hundreds of apple varieties from which to choose, the best can be found close to home.

All it takes is a trip to a local farmers' market or a country orchard in the fall to remind us that the best apples are those that are selected, and eaten, not far from the tree. Apples are superior when picked fresh from an orchard.

Roast Pork with Apples, Cabbage, and Turnips

Showcasing the best of fall's flavors, this hearty dish combines tart apples with smoky bacon, pungent cabbage, and sweet maple syrup. The apples and vegetables cook along with the pork so the flavors are harmonious. Full-flavored, tart apples, such as Granny Smith, Jonagold, Albemarle (Newtown) Pippin, Roxbury Russet, or Winesap, provide the best flavor.

Cooking spray
1   (3-pound) boneless pork loin roast, trimmed
2   cups finely chopped onion
1   slice applewood-smoked bacon, chopped
5   cups thinly sliced peeled tart apple (about 1½ pounds)
3   cups thinly sliced green cabbage
3   cups (1-inch) cubed peeled turnips
¾   cup dry white wine
2   tablespoons maple syrup
2   tablespoons cider vinegar
1   teaspoon salt
¼   teaspoon freshly ground black pepper

1. Preheat oven to 375°.
2. Heat a large Dutch oven over medium-high heat. Coat pan with cooking spray. Add pork; cook 15 minutes, browning on all sides. Remove pork from pan. Add onion and bacon to pan; sauté 5 minutes or until onion is tender. Return pork to pan. Add apple and remaining ingredients, and bring to a simmer. Place pan in oven. Bake, uncovered, at 375° for 1 hour and 15 minutes or until a thermometer registers 155°, turning pork after 45 minutes. Yield: 10 servings (serving size: 3 ounces pork and about ½ cup apple mixture).

CALORIES 262 (34% from fat); FAT 9.8g (sat 3.5g, mono 4.3g, poly 0.9g); PROTEIN 25.7g; CARB 17.6g; FIBER 2.8g; CHOL 70mg; IRON 1.4mg; SODIUM 333mg; CALC 50mg

MAKE AHEAD
Overnight Apple Butter

A mixture of apple varieties, rather than just one type, will produce apple butter with rich, complex flavor. Good choices include Esopus Spitzenburg, Granny Smith, Jonathan, Northern Spy, Rome, Stayman, Winesap, and York. Enjoy the apple butter over toast or English muffins, or serve it with pork chops or chicken.

1   cup packed brown sugar
½   cup honey
¼   cup apple cider
1   tablespoon ground cinnamon
¼   teaspoon ground cloves
⅛   teaspoon ground mace
10 apples, peeled, cored, and cut into large chunks (about 2½ pounds)

1. Combine all ingredients in a 5-quart electric slow cooker. Cover and cook on low-heat setting 10 hours or until apples are very tender.
2. Place a large fine-mesh sieve over a bowl; spoon one-third of apple mixture into sieve. Press mixture through sieve using back of a spoon or ladle. Discard pulp. Repeat procedure with remaining apple mixture. Return apple mixture to slow cooker. Cook, uncovered, on high-heat setting 1½ hours or until mixture is thick, stirring occasionally. Spoon into a bowl; cover and chill up to 1 week. Yield: 4 cups (serving size: ¼ cup).

STOVETOP VARIATION: Combine all ingredients in a Dutch oven. Cover and cook over medium-low heat 1 hour or until apples are very tender, stirring occasionally. Strain through a sieve as recipe instructs in Step 2. Return mixture to pan. Cook, uncovered, over medium-low heat 15 minutes or until thick, stirring frequently.

CALORIES 132 (0% from fat); FAT 0g; PROTEIN 0.1g; CARB 35.3g; FIBER 3.1g; CHOL 0mg; IRON 0.7mg; SODIUM 6mg; CALC 18mg

QUICK & EASY
Autumn Apple and Spinach Salad
(pictured on page 342)

Goldrush, a recent apple cultivar, has a nice balance of sweetness and acidity that's ideal for this salad. Other suitable varieties include Albemarle (Newtown) Pippin, Honeycrisp, Pink Lady, Golden Russet, and Roxbury Russet.

2   tablespoons fresh orange juice
2   tablespoons fresh lime juice
2   teaspoons Dijon mustard
2   teaspoons honey
¼   teaspoon salt
⅛   teaspoon freshly ground black pepper
½   cup thinly vertically sliced red onion
8   cups bagged prewashed baby spinach (about 8 ounces)
1   large, firm, sweet-tart apple, cored and thinly sliced
¼   cup (1 ounce) crumbled blue cheese

Continued

1. Combine first 6 ingredients, stirring well with a whisk.

2. Combine onion, spinach, and apple in a large bowl. Drizzle with dressing; toss gently to coat. Sprinkle with cheese. Yield: 6 servings (serving size: about 1⅓ cups).

CALORIES 60 (29% from fat); FAT 1.9g (sat 1g, mono 0.5g, poly 0.1g); PROTEIN 2.7g; CARB 9.4g; FIBER 2.2g; CHOL 4mg; IRON 1.3mg; SODIUM 251mg; CALC 76mg

Apple-Cranberry Cobbler

Toss at least two kinds of apples into this juicy cobbler for heightened flavor. Recommended choices include Cortland, Crispin, Golden Delicious, Goldrush, Gravenstein, Ida Red, Jonagold, Northern Spy, Rhode Island Greening, Stayman, and Winesap.

CRUST:

1½ cups all-purpose flour
2 tablespoons cornmeal
¼ teaspoon salt
6 tablespoons chilled butter, cut into small pieces
¼ cup ice water
1 teaspoon cider vinegar

FILLING:

⅓ cup sugar
1 tablespoon all-purpose flour
1 teaspoon ground cinnamon
10 cups thinly sliced peeled sweet-tart apple (about 6 large)
1 cup dried cranberries
Cooking spray

1. Preheat oven to 425°.

2. To prepare crust, lightly spoon 1½ cups flour into dry measuring cups; level with a knife. Place 1½ cups flour, cornmeal, and salt in a food processor; pulse 2 or 3 times or until combined. Add butter, and pulse 10 times or until mixture resembles coarse meal. With processor on, slowly add ice water and vinegar through food chute, processing just until mixture is combined (do not form a ball). Press gently into a 4-inch circle on plastic wrap; cover and chill 15 minutes or until plastic wrap can be easily removed.

3. To prepare filling, combine sugar, 1 tablespoon flour, and cinnamon in a large bowl. Add apple and cranberries; toss well to coat. Spoon apple mixture into an 11 x 7-inch baking dish coated with cooking spray.

4. Unwrap dough; place on a lightly floured surface. Roll dough into a 12 x 8-inch rectangle. Fit dough over filling. Fold edges under; flute. Cut several slits in top of dough to allow steam to escape. Bake at 425° for 30 minutes or until crust is golden brown. Cool on a wire rack 10 minutes. Yield: 9 servings.

CALORIES 294 (25% from fat); FAT 8.2g (sat 4.8g, mono 2.2g, poly 0.5g); PROTEIN 2.7g; CARB 53.6g; FIBER 4.2g; CHOL 20mg; IRON 1.3mg; SODIUM 143mg; CALC 14mg

Apple Bisque with Chestnuts

This unique recipe pairs the homey sweetness of apples with the creamy texture and rich flavor of chestnuts. Choose at least two varieties of all-purpose cooking apples for the best flavor—try a combination of Cortland, Gravenstein, Stayman, Winesap, Granny Smith, McIntosh, Grimes Golden, or York.

1 tablespoon butter
2 teaspoons extravirgin olive oil
3 cups chopped onion
1 teaspoon finely chopped fresh thyme
1 (14-ounce) can fat-free, less-sodium chicken broth
2 cooking apples, peeled, cored, and chopped (about 3 cups)
2 cups water
1 cup coarsely chopped bottled chestnuts
¼ cup cream sherry
¾ teaspoon salt
¼ teaspoon freshly ground black pepper
Thyme leaves (optional)

1. Heat butter and oil in a large Dutch oven over medium heat. Add onion and chopped thyme; cook 10 minutes or until onion is tender, stirring frequently.

Stir in broth and apple; cover and cook 30 minutes, stirring occasionally.

2. Add water and next 4 ingredients. Reduce heat to medium-low; simmer, uncovered, 10 minutes, stirring occasionally. Remove from heat; cool 5 minutes.

3. Place half of apple mixture in a blender; process until smooth. Pour puréed bisque into a large bowl. Repeat procedure with remaining apple mixture. Return bisque to pan; cook over low heat 5 minutes or just until heated. Garnish with thyme leaves, if desired. Yield: 6 servings (serving size: about ¾ cup).

CALORIES 131 (25% from fat); FAT 3.7g (sat 1.4g, mono 1.7g, poly 0.3g); PROTEIN 2.5g; CARB 21.7g; FIBER 3.6g; CHOL 5mg; IRON 0.3mg; SODIUM 437mg; CALC 21mg

Apple and Chicken Hash

Here's an excellent use for leftover baked potatoes. This classic autumn skillet supper is elevated with the addition of apples. Use firm-fleshed varieties, such as Goldrush, Granny Smith, or Winesap; they will soften as they cook without breaking up entirely.

1 tablespoon olive oil, divided
1 cup chopped onion
2 tart cooking apples, peeled, cored, and finely chopped (about 3 cups)
2 cups cubed peeled baked potato (about 1 large)
1½ cups chopped skinless, boneless rotisserie chicken breast
1 teaspoon chopped fresh sage
¾ teaspoon salt
¼ teaspoon freshly ground black pepper
¼ teaspoon paprika

1. Heat 1½ teaspoons oil in a large non-stick skillet over medium-high heat. Add onion and apple; sauté 7 minutes or until mixture begins to brown. Spoon into a large bowl. Add potato and remaining 5 ingredients; toss well to combine.

2. Heat 1½ teaspoons oil in pan over medium heat. Add apple mixture, and

pat into an even layer in pan. Cook, without stirring, 2 minutes. Stir gently; cook 2 minutes or until potato begins to brown. Serve immediately. Yield: 4 servings (serving size: 1 cup).

CALORIES 226 (22% from fat); FAT 5.6g (sat 1.1g, mono 3.2g, poly 0.8g); PROTEIN 18.1g; CARB 26.3g; FIBER 2.9g; CHOL 45mg; IRON 1mg; SODIUM 483mg; CALC 24mg

Charleston Pudding

Also called Ozark Pudding, this classic Southern dessert has a texture between a sticky cake and a bread pudding. We used a combination of Fuji and McIntosh apples; you can also try Arkansas Black, Golden Russet, Jonagold, or Suncrisp apples.

    2 cups peeled, cored, coarsely
       chopped sweet-tart apple (about
       2 medium)
    1 tablespoon apple brandy
    ¼ cup all-purpose flour
    2 teaspoons baking powder
    ⅛ teaspoon salt
    1 cup packed brown sugar
    1 teaspoon vanilla extract
    2 large eggs
    ⅓ cup chopped pecans, toasted
       Cooking spray

1. Preheat oven to 350°.
2. Combine apple and brandy, tossing well to coat.
3. Lightly spoon flour into a dry measuring cup; level with a knife. Combine flour, baking powder, and salt in a medium bowl, stirring with a whisk.
4. Place sugar, vanilla, and eggs in a large bowl; beat with a mixer at medium speed 3 minutes or until thick. With mixer on low speed, gradually add flour mixture. Gently fold in apple mixture and pecans. Spoon batter into an 8-inch square baking pan coated with cooking spray. Bake at 350° for 25 minutes or until top is puffed and deep golden brown. Serve warm. Yield: 6 servings (serving size: about ½ cup).

CALORIES 263 (22% from fat); FAT 6.5g (sat 0.9g, mono 3.3g, poly 1.7g); PROTEIN 3.2g; CARB 48.6g; FIBER 2.5g; CHOL 71mg; IRON 1.6mg; SODIUM 246mg; CALC 135mg

Matchmaking

The essential guide to food and wine pairing, with six perfect matches to show how it's done.

Here's your complete guide to food and wine pairing by Karen MacNeil, the author of *The Wine Bible*, and host of the PBS series *Wine, Food, and Friends with Karen MacNeil*. Karen has created six delicious recipes and paired them with what she thinks are sensational wines. For Karen, such pairings must result in *both* the wine and the food tasting better. Karen is also the chairperson of the Professional Wine Studies Program at the Culinary Institute of America in Napa Valley, California and also won the 2004 James Beard Foundation Outstanding Wine and Spirits Professional Award.

QUICK & EASY
Duck Breast with Cherry-Pepper Sauce

Duck and Cabernet Sauvignon is an elegant combination—and a favorite for a dinner party. This easy cherry and black pepper sauce picks up on the black cherry and peppery flavors of many Cabernet Sauvignons. Red Bordeaux wines (which are usually a blend of Cabernet Sauvignon and Merlot) are also sensational with this dish, as are many Merlots. Serve with steamed green beans tossed in olive oil, salt, and black pepper.

    1 (14.5-ounce) can pitted
       tart red cherries in water,
       undrained
    1 tablespoon olive oil
    2 (12-ounce) packages frozen
       boneless whole duck breast,
       thawed, skinned, and cut in half
    1 teaspoon freshly ground black
       pepper, divided
    ½ teaspoon salt
    1 tablespoon minced shallots
    ½ cup dried tart cherries
    ½ cup ruby port or other sweet red
       wine
    ½ cup less-sodium beef broth
    2 tablespoons honey
    1 teaspoon chopped fresh
       thyme
    ½ teaspoon balsamic vinegar
    2 teaspoons butter

1. Drain canned cherries in a sieve over a bowl. Place ½ cup canned cherries and ¼ cup cherry liquid in a blender; reserve remaining canned cherries and liquid for another use. Process cherry mixture until smooth.
2. Heat oil in a large nonstick skillet over medium-high heat. Sprinkle duck with ¼ teaspoon pepper and salt. Add duck to pan; cook 5 minutes on each side or until desired degree of doneness. Remove from pan; keep warm. Add shallots to pan; sauté 1 minute. Stir in ¾ teaspoon pepper, dried cherries, and next 5 ingredients; cook 2 minutes. Remove from heat; add puréed cherry mixture and butter, stirring until butter melts. Slice duck; serve with sauce. Yield: 5 servings (serving size: about 3½ ounces duck and about ¼ cup sauce).

PERFECT WINE: Sebastiani Cabernet Sauvignon 2000 (Sonoma County), $17. Tasted alone, the Sebastiani Cabernet Sauvignon is a sleek wine with powerful black cherry and cassis flavors plus a lot of tannic grip. Once the Cabernet is paired with the duck, however, real magic happens. The richness of the duck softens the tannins, while the cherries and pepper in the sauce enliven those flavors in the wine to make it taste even more dramatic. It's an example of a truly great match.

CALORIES 323 (29% from fat); FAT 10.3g (sat 3.2g, mono 4.2g, poly 1.1g); PROTEIN 28.2g; CARB 22.6g; FIBER 0.7g; CHOL 109mg; IRON 7mg; SODIUM 340mg; CALC 20mg

Top Principles for Perfect Matches

Be aware of acidity.
Acidity plays a powerful role in successful matching. The key concepts are:
• Acidity makes wine versatile. High-acid wines (including Riesling, Sauvignon Blanc, Champagne and sparkling wines, Pinot Noir, and Sangiovese) are generally easy to pair with a wide variety of foods.
• High-acid wines and high-acid foods go well together (goat cheese and Sauvignon Blanc are a great example).
• High acidity in a wine will often balance and temper a food's saltiness (that's why Champagne is so good with caviar).
• High acidity in a wine is a terrific counterpoint to smoked foods (that's why Champagne is nice with smoked salmon).
• High acidity in food can make a wine seem dull. For example, acidic tomatoes make Chardonnay taste flat and lifeless.
• High acidity in food can make a tannic wine seem hard and tinny (tomatoes will be awful with Cabernet Sauvignon).

Pair salty and sweet.
A dish seasoned with a significant amount of soy sauce has a salty flavor that will dull the flavor of many wines, making them taste neutral. To counterbalance a food's saltiness, serve wine that has a touch of sweetness. An Asian stir-fry seasoned with soy sauce is often terrific with an American Gewürztraminer that's slightly sweet (not all are, so you'll have to ask the wineshop to recommend one).

Pair great with great, humble with humble.
This basic principle goes a long way toward success. Pot roast doesn't need a costly Pinot Noir to accompany it. But an expensive standing rib roast may be the perfect opportunity to spring for a pricey Merlot.

Match delicate to delicate, robust to robust.
Delicate wine tastes like water when served with a dramatically spiced dish. Bold, spicy, and hot flavors are ideal for bold, spicy, wines. Here are common wine varietals from most delicate to most bold:
Whites: Pinot Gris/Pinot Grigio, Riesling, Sauvignon Blanc, Viognier, Chardonnay
Reds: Pinot Noir, Merlot, Cabernet Sauvignon, Syrah/Shiraz, Zinfandel

Decide if you want to mirror flavors or create a contrast.
Chardonnay with chowder is an example of mirroring; both are thick, rich, buttery, and creamy. But some matches are based on the opposite strategy: contrast. Roast pork and Riesling are fabulous together because pork is meaty and rich, while Riesling is crisp and lean. As counterpoints, they create a delicious seesaw together. A bite of the rich pork makes you want a sip of the refreshing wine, and vice versa.

Incorporate fruit.
Not surprisingly, dishes with a significant fruit component—pork with sautéed apples, barbecued chicken with apricot glaze, and beef stew with dried plums—often pair beautifully with fruity wines that have superfruity aromas. Gewürztraminer, Muscat, Viognier, and Riesling are the fruitiest whites. Gamay (the grape that makes Beaujolais) and Australian Shiraz (Syrah) are examples of fruity reds.

Reconsider oak.
Wines with a lot of oak flavor often end up tasting hard, flat, and crude when you have them with food. California Chardonnays, which usually spend quite some time in oak barrels, are often overtly oaky and toasty. That makes them difficult as good food partners. By contrast, Sauvignon Blanc and Riesling, neither of which are made with oak, are more food friendly.

Consider complexity.
To showcase a wine that is complex and expensive, pair it with food that is simply prepared. For example, with a truly extraordinary Cabernet Sauvignon or top-notch Bordeaux, serve a high-quality, but simple, dish such as a fine steak and low-key roasted potatoes.

Consider the overall weight and intensity of the dish.
When it comes to choosing a good wine partner, a hot, spicy lamb curry, for example, is extremely different from lightly spiced lamb kebabs. You could pair Syrah with either of these dishes, but in the first case, you'd want a Syrah known to be powerful, bold, superfruity, and spicy to stand up to the intensity of the curry.

Incorporate "bridge" ingredients.
A bridge ingredient is a food that ties a dish and wine together. Adding crumbled goat cheese to a salad makes it a better match for Sauvignon Blanc because the cheese and wine share similar tangy flavors. Adding peppercorns to a sauce would help that sauce pair more perfectly with a peppery wine, such as Cabernet Sauvignon. A sprinkling of toasted nuts on top of a dish helps bridge it to toasty, buttery, and nutty Chardonnays.

Don't forget dessert.
Be sure the wine is sweeter than the dessert. A good example of this is Sauternes (a honied sweet wine) and a simple pear tart. The match works because the wine is sweeter than the dessert itself.

Spicy Lamb Stew with Parsnips and Figs

Syrah and lamb are often served together in the south of France, and tasting this dish, you'll see why. Syrah often has a meatiness of its own, plus a hint of spice and a rich fruitiness. Each of these characters is mirrored in the dish. Serve this over couscous, which adds a nutty flavor. Any ruby port will do fine such as Cockburn's Special Reserve Porto, $16, which belongs to a category of port known as Vintage Character Port. (Avoid using tawny port, which has a deep toffee character that will conflict with the fruitiness of the wine and the food.)

3 tablespoons olive oil, divided
1½ pounds boneless leg of lamb, trimmed and cut into 1-inch pieces
1 teaspoon salt, divided
½ teaspoon freshly ground black pepper, divided
1½ cups chopped onion
2 cups (1-inch-thick) slices parsnip
2 teaspoons ground cumin
½ teaspoon garam masala
1 cup ruby port or other sweet red wine
1 teaspoon chile paste with garlic
12 small dried figs, halved (about 5 ounces)
1 (14-ounce) can less-sodium beef broth
1¾ cups water, divided
2 teaspoons cornstarch
1 cup uncooked couscous
Chopped fresh parsley (optional)

1. Preheat oven to 325°.
2. Heat 2 teaspoons oil in a Dutch oven over medium-high heat. Sprinkle lamb with ¾ teaspoon salt and ¼ teaspoon pepper. Add half of lamb to pan; cook 5 minutes, browning on all sides. Remove from pan. Repeat procedure with 2 teaspoons oil and remaining lamb.
3. Heat 1 tablespoon oil in pan over medium-high heat. Add onion; sauté 4 minutes or until tender. Add ¼ teaspoon pepper, parsnip, cumin, and garam masala; cook 3 minutes, stirring frequently. Return lamb and accumulated juices to pan. Add port, chile paste, figs, and broth; bring to a boil. Cover and bake at 325° for 1 hour or until lamb is tender, stirring occasionally.
4. Combine ¼ cup water and cornstarch, stirring with a whisk. Add cornstarch mixture to pan; stir well to combine. Bring to a boil over medium-high heat. Cook 1 minute or until sauce is thick and bubbly, stirring constantly.
5. Bring 1½ cups water to a boil in a medium saucepan; gradually stir in 2 teaspoons oil, ¼ teaspoon salt, and couscous. Remove from heat; cover and let stand 5 minutes. Fluff with a fork. Serve lamb mixture over couscous. Garnish with parsley, if desired. Yield: 6 servings (serving size: about ¾ cup lamb mixture and ½ cup couscous).

PERFECT WINE: Grant Burge Barossa Vines Shiraz 2001 (Barossa Valley, Australia), $11. This Australian Shiraz (Syrah is known as Shiraz Down Under), has exotic, spicy flavors, which mirror the spices in the dish. And finally, this wine's thick, blackberry fruitiness and almost syrupy softness cushion the bold spices in the wine and the dish.

CALORIES 523 (24% from fat); FAT 14.1g (sat 3.3g, mono 7.8g, poly 1.5g); PROTEIN 29.6g; CARB 60.9g; FIBER 9g; CHOL 74mg; IRON 4.1mg; SODIUM 515mg; CALC 109mg

Braised Pork Shoulder in Hoisin-Wine Sauce with Dried Plums

The long, slow braising technique results in a pork roast that's ultraflavorful and moist. Though braising isn't quick, the oven does most of the work. As for wine, try the combination of pork and Riesling. It may seem surprising to pair a "big" meat like pork with a white wine, but in fact the two have been deliciously served together for centuries—especially in Germany, Austria, and Switzerland. Serve with a simple accompaniment of baby carrots and mashed potatoes.

MARINADE:
1 tablespoon sake (rice wine)
1 tablespoon hoisin sauce
2 teaspoons brown sugar
2 garlic cloves, minced

ROAST:
3½ pounds Boston Butt pork roast, trimmed
1½ teaspoons salt
2 cups chopped onion
3 garlic cloves, minced
1 cup fat-free, less-sodium chicken broth
¾ cup sake (rice wine)
¼ cup hoisin sauce
1 tablespoon chile paste with garlic
10 pitted dried plums, halved

1. To prepare marinade, combine first 4 ingredients; rub evenly over pork. Cover and marinate pork in refrigerator 24 hours.
2. Preheat oven to 300°.
3. To prepare roast, heat a Dutch oven over medium-high heat. Sprinkle pork with salt. Add pork to pan; cook 8 minutes, browning on all sides. Remove from pan. Add onion and 3 garlic cloves to pan; sauté 2 minutes. Stir in broth and next 3 ingredients. Return pork to pan; cover and bake at 300° for 3 hours. Reduce oven temperature to 250° (do not remove pork from oven); cook 30 minutes. Remove pork from pan; let stand 15 minutes. Use two forks to pull apart pork into bite-sized pieces. Remove and discard any visible fat.
4. Strain wine mixture through a sieve into a bowl; discard solids. Place a large zip-top plastic bag inside a 4-cup glass measure. Pour wine mixture into bag; let stand 10 minutes (fat will rise to the top). Seal bag; carefully snip off 1 bottom corner of bag. Drain wine mixture back into pan, stopping before fat layer reaches opening; discard fat. Add dried plums to pan; bring to a boil. Cook until sauce is reduced to 2 cups (about 10 minutes). Yield: 10 servings (serving size: about 4 ounces pork and about 3 tablespoons sauce).

PERFECT WINE: Dr. Weims-Prum Wehlener Sonnenuhr Riesling Spatlese 2002 (Mosel-Saar-Ruwer, Germany), $17. The clean crispness and high acidity of German Rieslings are great with rich pork roasts. This Riesling also has hints of apricot that work beautifully against the sweetness of the plums and hoisin sauce.

CALORIES 339 (42% from fat); FAT 15.7g (sat 5.5g, mono 7.1g, poly 1.6g); PROTEIN 30g; CARB 13.2g; FIBER 1.4g; CHOL 102mg; IRON 2.1mg; SODIUM 621mg; CALC 36mg

All About Wine

Wine Varietal	Herbs and Spices	Vegetables	Fish and Shellfish	Meats	Cheeses	Good Bridges
SAUVIGNON BLANC	Basil, bay leaf, cilantro, dill, fennel, lemongrass, marjoram, mint, parsley, savory, thyme	Carrots, eggplant, most green vegetables (lettuces, snow peas, zucchini), tomatoes	Sea bass, snapper, sole, swordfish, trout, tuna, clams, mussels, oysters, shrimp, scallops	Chicken, game birds, turkey	Buffalo mozzarella, feta, fontina, goat, Parmigiano-Reggiano, ricotta, Swiss	Bell peppers (fresh, roasted), capers, citrus (lemon, lime, orange), fennel, garlic, green figs, leeks, olives, sour cream, tomatoes (fresh, sun-dried)
CHARDONNAY	Basil, clove, tarragon, thyme	Corn, mushrooms, potatoes, pumpkin, squash	Grouper, halibut, monkfish, salmon, swordfish, tuna, crab, lobster, scallops, shrimp	Chicken, pork, turkey, veal	Brie, camembert, Monterey Jack, Swiss	Apples, avocado, bacon, butter, citrus (lemon juice, lemon zest), coconut milk, cream, Dijon mustard, milk, nuts (toasted hazelnuts, cashews, pine nuts, almonds), pancetta, pears, polenta, tropical fruits (mango, papaya, pineapple), vanilla
RIESLING	Chile pepper, cilantro, dill, five-spice, ginger, lemongrass, nutmeg, parsley	Carrots, corn, onions (roasted, sautéed), parsnips	Sole, smoked fish (salmon, trout), snapper, trout, crab, scallops	Chicken, game birds, pork	Emmenthal, Gouda	Apricots (fresh, dried), citrus (lime, orange, citrus zest), dried fruits (plums, figs, raisins), peaches, tropical fruits (mango, papaya)
PINOT NOIR	Basil, black pepper, cinnamon, clove, fennel, five-spice, oregano, rosemary, star anise, thyme	Beets, eggplant, mushrooms	Salmon (baked, grilled, sautéed), tuna	Beef, chicken, game birds, lamb, liver, rabbit, squab, turkey, veal	Aged Cheddar, Brie	Beets, butter, Dijon mustard, dried fruits (plums, cherries, raisins, cranberries), mushrooms, onions (roasted, sautéed), pomegranates, pomegranate molasses, shallots, tea, cooked tomatoes, truffles
SYRAH | SHIRAZ	Allspice, chile pepper, coriander, cumin, five-spice, pepper, rosemary, sage	Eggplant, onions (roasted, sautéed), root vegetables	Blackened "meaty" fish (salmon, tuna)	Bacon, duck, lamb, pancetta, pheasant, quail, sausage, short ribs, squab, venison	Cheddar, goat, Gouda, Gruyère	Black figs, black licorice, black olives, black pepper, cherries (fresh, dried), chocolate/cocoa
CABERNET SAUVIGNON	Juniper, oregano, rosemary, sage, savory, thyme	Mushrooms, potatoes, root vegetables	None	Beef (roasts, grilled steak), duck, lamb, venison	Camembert, cantal, carmody, aged Jack, aged Gouda	Balsamic vinegar, blackberries, black olives, black pepper, butter, cassis, cherries (fresh, dried), cream, currants, roasted red pepper, toasted nuts (walnuts, pecans)

Risotto with Butternut Squash, Pancetta, and Jack Cheese

Chardonnay is a varietal that's difficult to pair with foods. But the creamy, buttery sweetness of butternut squash makes a good complement to wine. The same is true of tarragon, which in small amounts is a delicious backdrop for most Chardonnays. Utterly satisfying, this pairing is comfort food and comfort wine at its best.

1½ pounds butternut squash, peeled, seeded, and cut into ½-inch cubes (about 3½ cups)
Cooking spray
2 cups fat-free, less-sodium chicken broth
1⅓ cups water
2 tablespoons Madeira wine or sweet Marsala
1 tablespoon minced fresh tarragon
4 ounces chopped pancetta
1 cup finely chopped onion
1 teaspoon olive oil
2 garlic cloves, minced
¾ cup uncooked Arborio rice or other short-grain rice
⅔ cup (about 2½ ounces) ½-inch cubed Monterey Jack cheese
½ teaspoon salt
¼ teaspoon freshly ground black pepper
2 tablespoons pine nuts, toasted
Tarragon sprigs (optional)

1. Preheat oven to 475°.
2. Place squash on a nonstick jelly-roll pan coated with cooking spray. Bake at 475° for 20 minutes or until tender, turning after 10 minutes.
3. Reduce oven temperature to 325°.
4. Combine broth, water, wine, and tarragon in a saucepan; bring to a simmer. Keep warm over low heat.
5. Cook pancetta in a large ovenproof Dutch oven over medium-high heat until crisp. Remove pancetta from pan; drain on a paper towel. Discard pan drippings. Add onion and oil to pan; sauté 10 minutes or until onion is tender. Add garlic; sauté 1 minute. Add rice to pan; sauté 1 minute. Stir in broth mixture; bring to a

boil over medium heat. Reduce heat, and simmer over low heat, uncovered, 10 minutes. (Do not stir; rice will have a liquid consistency similar to stew.)
6. Place pan in oven; bake at 325° for 15 minutes. Remove from oven. Stir in squash, pancetta, cheese, salt, and pepper. Cover with a clean cloth; let stand 10 minutes (rice will continue to cook). Sprinkle with pine nuts. Garnish with tarragon sprigs, if desired. Yield: 4 servings (serving size: ¾ cup).
PERFECT WINE: Clos du Val Chardonnay 2001 (Carneros, CA), $21. This Chardonnay has refined flavors reminiscent of custard, caramel, apple tarts, and honey. There's a hint of oak, but the wine isn't superbuttery, oaky, or toasty. This wine is complemented by the savoriness of the rice and the sweetness of the squash.

CALORIES 423 (30% from fat); FAT 14.2g (sat 5.5g, mono 5.6g, poly 1.9g); PROTEIN 14.5g; CARB 57.3g; FIBER 6.6g; CHOL 28mg; IRON 2mg; SODIUM 783mg; CALC 235mg

Pan-Grilled Pork Tenderloin with Pomegranate Molasses

One of the flavors often found in Pinot Noir is pomegranate, which is the inspiration for this easy dish. The sauce is based on pomegranate molasses, a thick, savory syrup used in Middle Eastern cooking that acts as a fascinating bridge to the Pinot Noir. Look for pomegranate molasses in Middle Eastern markets. Serve with a simple side dish of steamed asparagus and roasted onion wedges. To prepare the onions with the pork tenderloin, remove pork from pan after browning on all sides. Cook the onion wedges in the pan for one minute, then return the pork to the pan and bake as directed.

SAUCE:
1 cup less-sodium beef broth
½ cup Pinot Noir or other spicy dry red wine
2 tablespoons pomegranate molasses
1 tablespoon finely chopped shallots
1 tablespoon honey
1 tablespoon butter

PORK:
½ teaspoon salt
¼ teaspoon five-spice powder
¼ teaspoon freshly ground black pepper
1 (1-pound) pork tenderloin, trimmed
Cooking spray

1. To prepare sauce, combine first 5 ingredients in a small saucepan; cook over medium heat 30 minutes or until reduced to ⅓ cup. Remove from heat; strain through a sieve into a bowl. Discard solids. Add butter to molasses mixture, stirring with a whisk until butter melts.
2. To prepare pork tenderloin, preheat oven to 500°.
3. Heat a cast-iron skillet over medium-high heat. Combine salt, five-spice powder, and pepper; rub evenly over pork. Coat pan with cooking spray. Add pork to pan, and cook 1 minute, browning on all sides. Place pan in oven; bake at 500° for 12 minutes or until a thermometer registers 155° (slightly pink). Let stand 10 minutes. Cut pork into thin slices, and serve with sauce. Yield: 4 servings (serving size: about 3 ounces pork and about 1 tablespoon sauce).
PERFECT WINES: Sanford Pinot Noir 2001 "Santa Rita Hills" (Santa Barbara County, CA), $26. This wine's beautiful flavors of earth, pomegranate, grenadine, mocha, and cherry preserves come into focus when you serve it with the pork tenderloin and pomegranate sauce. The sauce also mirrors the wine's wonderful silky, plush texture. As a less expensive alternative, consider the Echelon 2002 Pinot Noir from the Central Coast of California, about $12.

CALORIES 220 (29% from fat); FAT 7.1g (sat 3.2g, mono 2.7g, poly 0.6g); PROTEIN 25.2g; CARB 13.1g; FIBER 0.1g; CHOL 81mg; IRON 2.3mg; SODIUM 404mg; CALC 37mg

Shrimp and Fennel in Hot Garlic Sauce

When friends come over, make this quick, easy appetizer and serve it family-style on a big white platter while everyone enjoys Sauvignon Blanc as the accompanying aperitif. The shrimp and fennel's fresh, lively flavors pair perfectly with Sauvignon Blancs that are medium-bodied, sassy, herbal, and citrusy. In particular, California Sauvignon Blancs are best here. Don't forget to add the lime at the end of the recipe. It's the flavorful ribbon that ties the food and wine together.

    1   tablespoon olive oil
    3½ cups thinly sliced fennel bulb
        (about ¾ pound)
    ¼   teaspoon salt
    ⅛   teaspoon freshly ground black
        pepper
    4   garlic cloves, thinly sliced
    1   bay leaf
    ½   teaspoon crushed red pepper
    ¾   pound large shrimp, peeled and
        deveined
    2   tablespoons fresh lime juice
Lime wedges (optional)

1. Heat oil in a large nonstick skillet over medium-high heat. Add fennel and next 4 ingredients; cook 5 minutes or until fennel is crisp-tender, stirring occasionally. Add red pepper and shrimp to pan; cook 3 minutes or until shrimp are done, stirring occasionally. Stir in lime juice. Serve with lime wedges, if desired. Yield: 4 servings (serving size: about 1 cup).

PERFECT WINE: Try St. Supery Sauvignon Blanc 2002 (Napa Valley, CA), $16. This very crisp wine has snappy, fresh flavors reminiscent of green figs, melon, herbs, lime, and fennel—a perfect fit with this recipe.

CALORIES 154 (30% from fat); FAT 5.1g (sat 0.8g, mono 2.7g, poly 0.9g); PROTEIN 18.6g; CARB 8.8g; FIBER 2.8g; CHOL 129mg; IRON 2.8mg; SODIUM 317mg; CALC 93mg

Chicken Thighs with Olives and Red Peppers

This Mediterranean-inspired chicken dish was created with Sauvignon Blanc in mind. The olives, roasted red peppers, leeks, and herbs act as a bridge of flavor between the chicken and the crisp white wine.

    1   (7-ounce) bottle roasted red bell
        peppers
    1   tablespoon olive oil
    2½ cups coarsely chopped leeks
        (about 3 large)
    8   (4-ounce) bone-in chicken thighs,
        skinned
    1   tablespoon chopped fresh thyme
    1   teaspoon dried rubbed sage
    ¾   teaspoon salt, divided
    ½   teaspoon Hungarian sweet paprika
    1   cup fat-free, less-sodium chicken
        broth
    ¾   cup kalamata olives, pitted and
        chopped
    2   tablespoons fresh lemon juice
    2   cups hot cooked orzo (about
        6½ ounces uncooked pasta)
    1   tablespoon butter

1. Remove 1 roasted pepper from bottle; cut into thin strips. Reserve remaining roasted peppers for another use.
2. Heat oil in a large nonstick skillet over medium-high heat. Add leeks to pan; sauté 5 minutes or until tender. Arrange roasted red pepper strips over leeks. Arrange chicken over pepper strips. Sprinkle chicken with thyme, sage, ¼ teaspoon salt, and paprika. Gently pour broth around chicken; bring to a boil. Reduce heat, and simmer, covered, 15 minutes. Turn chicken over; cover and simmer 10 minutes. Stir in olives and lemon juice. Cook, uncovered, 8 minutes or until chicken is done.
3. Toss orzo with ½ teaspoon salt and 1 tablespoon butter. Serve chicken and leek mixture over orzo. Yield: 4 servings (serving size: 2 chicken thighs, 1 cup leek mixture, and ½ cup orzo).

PERFECT WINE: Chateau St. Jean Fumé Blanc 2002 (Sonoma County, CA), $13. This medium-bodied Sauvignon Blanc (Fumé Blanc is another name for Sauvignon Blanc) has wonderful herbal flavors, plus a hint of vanilla and a long, vibrant finish. These provide an extravagant backdrop for the meaty, herbal flavors of the chicken. Though the dish is rather bold, the wine has enough weight, character, flavor, and crispness to stand up to it.

CALORIES 428 (30% from fat); FAT 14.2g (sat 3.9g, mono 6.7g, poly 1.8g); PROTEIN 30.4g; CARB 44.8g; FIBER 3.3g; CHOL 102mg; IRON 4.7mg; SODIUM 919mg; CALC 86mg

White Wine with . . .

We've all heard the advice: white wine with fish, red wine with meat. No one knows exactly when that rule was invented, but most food and wine historians think it was probably an aesthetic notion. In other words, some host or hostess thought white foods like fish *looked* better with white wines, as did red meats with red wine. It had little to do with flavor. Today, we know that many white wines do indeed taste great with fish. This is true of shellfish and crustaceans, which pair well with high-acid whites like sparkling wines, Riesling, and Sauvignon Blanc. But there are also some red wine and fish combinations that are knockouts. For example, try grilled salmon with Pinot Noir—it's a stellar combination.

A successful food-and-wine pairing must result in both the wine and the food tasting better.

Savory Bread Puddings

These toss-together entrées are welcome on any chilly autumn night.

Mention bread pudding, and most people think of dessert. But this classic dish can be made savory, too, with the same luscious, creamy texture that makes the sweet version so appealing. A frugal way to use stale bread, bread pudding combines convenience with the appeal of comfort food—a solution to the problem of dinner on a cool fall evening.

Use these recipes as guidelines, then experiment with your own favorite ingredients; add diced ham or chicken, use focaccia in place of the bread called for, or vary the cheese according to your taste preference.

Perfect Pudding

Bread puddings are among the most flexible of recipes. Assemble and bake them immediately, or cover and refrigerate them overnight before baking. Follow these tips for consistent success:

• Use day-old (very dry) bread for the best texture. Very fresh bread will yield a slightly spongy texture.

• Use the bread's ounce/weight measurement as a more accurate guide than the cup measurement.

• If you don't have a kitchen scale and are measuring the bread by cup amounts, be sure not to tightly pack the bread cubes into the measuring cup, or you'll end up with too much bread.

• Leave the crusts on for more texture.

• Whole-grain breads give these puddings a nutty taste and a slightly drier texture. But, they can be strong in flavor, which might overpower delicate ingredients. Be sure to taste the bread before using it for a bread pudding.

MAKE AHEAD

Mushroom, Roasted Red Pepper, and Goat Cheese Bread Pudding

Use any combination, or just one type, of your favorite mushrooms for this earthy vegetarian entrée. Crumbled feta cheese makes a fine substitute for goat cheese.

¼ cup chopped fresh parsley
1 teaspoon chopped fresh thyme
1 teaspoon chopped fresh rosemary
2 garlic cloves, minced
2 teaspoons olive oil
3 cups sliced cremini mushrooms (about 6 ounces)
3 cups sliced button mushrooms (about 6 ounces)
2 cups sliced shiitake mushroom caps (about 4 ounces)
1 cup thinly sliced leek
½ teaspoon salt, divided
¼ teaspoon black pepper, divided
1 (12-ounce) bottle roasted red bell peppers, drained and chopped
1½ cups 1% low-fat milk
1 cup egg substitute
1¼ cups (5 ounces) crumbled goat cheese, divided
8 ounces (1-inch) cubed day-old sourdough bread (about 9 cups)
Cooking spray

1. Preheat oven to 350°.
2. Combine first 4 ingredients. Set aside.
3. Heat oil in a large nonstick skillet over medium-high heat. Add mushrooms, leek, ¼ teaspoon salt, and ⅛ teaspoon black pepper; sauté 10 minutes or until liquid evaporates and mushrooms are lightly browned. Add half of parsley mixture; cook 1 minute, stirring constantly. Stir in bell peppers. Remove from heat; cool slightly.
4. Combine ¼ teaspoon salt, ⅛ teaspoon black pepper, remaining parsley mixture, milk, egg substitute, and ¾ cup cheese in a large bowl, stirring with a whisk. Stir in mushroom mixture. Add bread; stir gently to combine. Let stand

10 minutes. Spoon into a 2-quart baking dish coated with cooking spray. Sprinkle with ½ cup cheese. Bake at 350° for 45 minutes or until pudding is set and lightly browned. Yield: 6 servings.

CALORIES 273 (29% from fat); FAT 8.9g (sat 4.4g, mono 2.9g, poly 0.8g); PROTEIN 17.3g; CARB 31.9g; FIBER 2.9g; CHOL 13mg; IRON 3.9mg; SODIUM 766mg; CALC 174mg

---

MAKE AHEAD

Sausage, Apple, and Cheddar Bread Pudding

This dish is reminiscent of holiday stuffing. Leave the peel on the apple for color and texture.

8 ounces turkey Italian sausage
2 cups chopped Granny Smith apple
1 cup chopped onion
2 cups 1% low-fat milk
1 cup egg substitute
¾ cup (3 ounces) shredded sharp Cheddar cheese, divided
¼ cup chopped fresh parsley
¼ teaspoon salt
⅛ teaspoon black pepper
8 ounces (1-inch) cubed day-old sourdough bread (about 9 cups)
Cooking spray

1. Preheat oven to 350°.
2. Heat a large nonstick skillet over medium-high heat. Remove casings from sausage. Add sausage to pan; cook 4 minutes or until browned, stirring to crumble. Stir in apple and onion. Cover and cook over low heat 5 minutes or until apple is crisp-tender. Remove from heat; cool slightly.
3. Combine milk, egg substitute, ¼ cup cheese, parsley, salt, and pepper in a large bowl, stirring with a whisk. Stir in sausage mixture. Add bread, and stir gently to combine. Let stand 10 minutes. Spoon into a 2-quart baking dish coated with cooking spray. Sprinkle with ½ cup cheese. Bake at 350° for 45 minutes or until pudding is set and lightly browned. Yield: 6 servings.

CALORIES 308 (30% from fat); FAT 10.4g (sat 4.9g, mono 3.4g, poly 1.6g); PROTEIN 20.7g; CARB 32.4g; FIBER 2.7g; CHOL 50mg; IRON 2.5mg; SODIUM 762mg; CALC 256mg

Greek-Style Bread Pudding

Don't be surprised if this bread pudding puffs up as it bakes and rises above the edges of the baking dish.

        1   teaspoon olive oil
        6   cups sliced cremini mushrooms
             (about 12 ounces)
       ½   cup chopped onion
        1   garlic clove, minced
       ½   cup golden raisins
       ¼   teaspoon black pepper
       ⅛   teaspoon salt
        1   (14½-ounce) can Italian-style
             diced tomatoes, drained
        1   (10-ounce) package frozen
             chopped spinach, thawed,
             drained, and squeezed dry
        2   cups 1% low-fat milk
        1   cup (4 ounces) crumbled feta
             cheese, divided
        4   large eggs, lightly beaten
        8   ounces (1-inch) cubed day-old
             Italian bread (about 9 cups)
             Cooking spray

1. Preheat oven to 350°.
2. Heat oil in a large nonstick skillet over medium heat. Add mushrooms, onion, and garlic; cook 12 minutes or until mushrooms are tender, stirring occasionally. Stir in raisins, pepper, salt, tomatoes, and spinach. Remove from heat; cool slightly.
3. Combine milk, ½ cup cheese, and eggs in a large bowl, stirring with a whisk. Stir in mushroom mixture. Add bread; stir gently to combine. Let stand 10 minutes. Spoon into a 2-quart baking dish coated with cooking spray. Sprinkle with ½ cup cheese. Bake at 350° for 45 minutes or until pudding is set and lightly browned. Yield: 6 servings.

CALORIES 341 (28% from fat); FAT 10.5g (sat 4.9g, mono 3.3g, poly 1.3g); PROTEIN 17.9g; CARB 44.3g; FIBER 4.9g; CHOL 162mg; IRON 3.9mg; SODIUM 886mg; CALC 336mg

Corn and Chipotle Bread Pudding

A generous amount of chipotle chiles adds smoky heat to balance the sweetness of the corn. A whole jalapeño pepper adds more fire, but you can seed it if you prefer a milder pudding.

        2   teaspoons olive oil
       ½   cup finely chopped red bell pepper
       ½   cup finely chopped onion
        2   cups fresh corn kernels (about
             2 ears)
       ½   cup thinly sliced green onions
        1   jalapeño pepper, minced
        1   garlic clove, minced
        1   teaspoon salt, divided
        1   teaspoon ground cumin, divided
    1½   cups 1% low-fat milk
        1   cup egg substitute
        1   cup (4 ounces) shredded
             Monterey Jack cheese, divided
        1   tablespoon finely chopped canned
             chipotle chiles in adobo sauce
        9   ounces (1-inch) cubed day-old
             firm white bread (about 10 cups)
             Cooking spray

1. Preheat oven to 350°.
2. Heat oil in a large nonstick skillet over medium-high heat. Add bell pepper and chopped onion, and sauté 5 minutes or until tender. Add corn, green onions, jalapeño, and garlic; sauté 3 minutes. Stir in ½ teaspoon salt and ½ teaspoon cumin. Remove from heat; cool slightly.
3. Combine ½ teaspoon salt, ½ teaspoon cumin, milk, egg substitute, ½ cup cheese, and chipotle chiles in a large bowl, stirring with a whisk. Stir in corn mixture. Add bread; stir gently to combine. Let stand 10 minutes. Spoon into a 2-quart baking dish coated with cooking spray. Sprinkle with ½ cup cheese. Bake at 350° for 45 minutes or until pudding is set and lightly browned. Yield: 6 servings.

CALORIES 313 (30% from fat); FAT 10.6g (sat 4.8g, mono 3.6g, poly 0.7g); PROTEIN 16.5g; CARB 38.7g; FIBER 2.9g; CHOL 19mg; IRON 2.8mg; SODIUM 878mg; CALC 278mg

Butternut Squash and Parmesan Bread Pudding

(pictured on page 341)

A side of sautéed kale or mustard greens would provide a nice counterpoint to the sweet butternut squash.

        3   cups (½-inch) cubed peeled
             butternut squash
             Cooking spray
       ½   teaspoon salt, divided
        1   teaspoon olive oil
        1   cup chopped onion
        1   garlic clove, minced
        2   cups 1% low-fat milk
        1   cup (4 ounces) grated fresh
             Parmigiano-Reggiano cheese,
             divided
       ¼   teaspoon black pepper
       ⅛   teaspoon ground nutmeg
        3   large eggs, lightly beaten
        2   large egg whites, lightly beaten
        8   ounces (1-inch) cubed day-old
             French bread (about 9 cups)

1. Preheat oven to 400°.
2. Arrange squash in a single layer on a jelly-roll pan coated with cooking spray. Sprinkle with ¼ teaspoon salt. Bake at 400° for 12 minutes or until tender. Remove from oven; reduce oven temperature to 350°.
3. Heat oil in a medium nonstick skillet over medium-high heat. Add onion; sauté 5 minutes or until tender. Add garlic, and sauté 1 minute. Remove from heat; cool slightly.
4. Combine ¼ teaspoon salt, milk, ½ cup cheese, pepper, nutmeg, eggs, and egg whites in a large bowl, stirring with a whisk. Stir in squash and onion mixture. Add bread, and stir gently to combine. Let stand 10 minutes. Spoon into a 2-quart baking dish coated with cooking spray. Sprinkle with ½ cup cheese. Bake at 350° for 45 minutes or until pudding is set and lightly browned. Yield: 6 servings.

CALORIES 304 (30% from fat); FAT 10.3g (sat 4.8g, mono 3.7g, poly 0.9g); PROTEIN 18.1g; CARB 35.3g; FIBER 4g; CHOL 122mg; IRON 2.1mg; SODIUM 823mg; CALC 406mg

Butternut Squash and Parmesan Bread Pudding, page 340

Breaded Pork Chops, page 369

Autumn Apple and Spinach Salad, page 331

Marble Cheesecake Squares, page 370

Meatball Soup
Sopa de Albóndigas, page 355

Cider-Roasted Chicken, page 347,
Fall Green Salad, page 345, and
Spicy Sweet Potato Wedges, page 347

Cozy Cabin Retreat

Relax and celebrate the season with this make-ahead menu, ideal for casual get-togethers.

Fall Cabin Menu
serves 8

Red Pepper-Cheese Dip

Fall Green Salad

Rich Mushroom Soup or **Savory Beet Soup**

Cider-Roasted Pork Loin or **Cider-Roasted Chicken**

Spicy Sweet Potato Wedges

Country Rye Loaves

Pumpkin-Orange Cake

Fall Ahead of Schedule

• **Country Rye Loaves**: Make sponge 2 days ahead. Bake bread 1 day ahead. Cool completely on a wire rack; store in an airtight container.

• Make **Red Pepper-Cheese Dip** 1 day ahead; cover and chill. Let stand at room temperature 30 minutes before serving.

• Prepare soup according to recipe (except for sour cream swirl in **Savory Beet Soup** or parsley in **Rich Mushroom Soup**). Cover and chill up to 1 day. Reheat, covered, in a saucepan over low heat until thoroughly heated. Add garnishes to each serving.

• Prepare brine for **Cider-Roasted Chicken** or **Cider-Roasted Pork Loin** up to 5 days ahead; refrigerate until ready to use. Brine chicken or pork overnight.

• **Spicy Sweet Potato Wedges**: Peel and cut potatoes into wedges while meat cooks.

• Prepare vinaigrette for **Fall Green Salad** 1 day ahead; cover and chill.

• Prepare **Pumpkin-Orange Cake** 1 day ahead; cover loosely and refrigerate until ready to serve.

MAKE AHEAD
Red Pepper-Cheese Dip

Make this the day before for entertaining ease. It's great with crisp breadsticks and does double duty as a sandwich spread.

 1 large red bell pepper
 1 small onion, peeled and halved
Cooking spray
 1 whole garlic head
 1 cup plain fat-free yogurt
 ½ cup (4 ounces) block-style fat-free cream cheese
 ¼ teaspoon ground cumin
 ⅛ teaspoon ground red pepper
 ¼ cup chopped fresh flat-leaf parsley

1. Preheat broiler.
2. Cut bell pepper in half lengthwise, and discard seeds and membranes. Place pepper halves, skin sides up, on a foil-lined baking sheet; flatten with hand. Broil 15 minutes or until blackened. Place in a zip-top plastic bag; seal. Let stand 10 minutes. Remove and discard peel. Set roasted pepper aside.
3. Reduce oven temperature to 400°.
4. Place onion halves, cut sides down, on a baking sheet coated with cooking spray. Remove white papery skin from garlic head (do not peel or separate cloves). Wrap in foil. Place garlic on baking sheet with onion. Bake at 400° for 15 minutes; turn over onion halves. Bake an additional 15 minutes or until onions are soft and begin to brown. Place onion halves on a plate. Return garlic to oven, and bake an additional 15 minutes. Cool 10 minutes. Separate cloves; squeeze to extract garlic pulp. Discard skins.
5. Place roasted pepper, onion, and garlic pulp in a food processor; process until fairly smooth. Add yogurt, cheese, cumin seed, and ground red pepper; process until smooth. Spoon dip into a bowl, and stir in parsley. Cover and chill. Yield: 16 servings (servings size: 2 tablespoons).

CALORIES 20 (9% from fat); FAT 0.2g (sat 0.1g, mono 0g, poly 0g); PROTEIN 1.9g; CARB 3.1g; FIBER 0.3g; CHOL 1mg; IRON 0.2mg; SODIUM 85mg; CALC 37mg

QUICK & EASY
Fall Green Salad
(pictured on page 344)

Using three types of greens lends a variety of textures and flavors to this simple salad.

VINAIGRETTE:
 ¼ cup water
 3 tablespoons fresh lemon juice
 ½ teaspoon cornstarch
 1 tablespoon honey
 ½ teaspoon white wine vinegar
 ¼ teaspoon salt
 ¼ teaspoon freshly ground black pepper
 ¼ cup (1 ounce) grated fresh Parmesan cheese

SALAD:
 4 cups torn curly leaf lettuce
 4 cups torn romaine lettuce
 3 cups trimmed arugula
 ½ cup thinly sliced red onion

1. To prepare vinaigrette, combine water, juice, and cornstarch in a small saucepan, stirring with a whisk. Bring to a boil over medium-high heat; cook 1 minute, stirring frequently. Remove from heat. Stir in honey, vinegar, salt, and pepper. Place in a blender or food processor. Add cheese, and process until well blended. Cool to room temperature.
2. To prepare salad, combine greens and onion in a large bowl. Drizzle with vinaigrette, tossing gently to combine. Serve immediately. Yield: 8 servings (serving size: 1 cup).

CALORIES 38 (24% from fat); FAT 1g (sat 0.6g, mono 0.3g, poly 0.1g); PROTEIN 2.4g; CARB 5.9g; FIBER 1.4g; CHOL 2mg; IRON 0.5mg; SODIUM 145mg; CALC 80mg

Rich Mushroom Soup

This smooth and satisfying soup can also be made with 2% milk rather than 1% and half-and-half. Any combination of fresh mushrooms works just fine.

    2 tablespoons all-purpose flour
    1 cup boiling water
    1 cup dried porcini mushrooms
       (about 1 ounce)
    2 teaspoons butter
 1½   cups chopped onion
    2 teaspoons chopped garlic
    2 teaspoons finely chopped fresh
       thyme
   ¼ teaspoon salt
   ¼ teaspoon freshly ground black
       pepper
 6½   cups thinly sliced shiitake
       mushroom caps (about 1 pound
       mushrooms)
    2 (8-ounce) packages presliced
       button mushrooms
    4 cups fat-free, less-sodium chicken
       broth
    1 cup 1% low-fat milk
   ½ cup half-and-half
   ¼ cup dry sherry
       Chopped fresh flat-leaf parsley
       (optional)

1. Place flour in a small skillet over medium-high heat; cook 2 minutes or until flour turns light brown, stirring constantly. Transfer flour to a small plate; cool.
2. Combine boiling water and porcini mushrooms in a bowl; cover and let steep 20 minutes. Drain porcini mushrooms in a sieve over a bowl, reserving liquid. Chop mushrooms.
3. Melt butter in a Dutch oven over medium-high heat. Add onion; sauté 5 minutes or until tender. Add garlic, thyme, salt, and pepper; sauté 30 seconds. Add shiitake mushrooms; cook 3 minutes, stirring constantly. Add button mushrooms; cook 3 minutes, stirring constantly. Add chopped porcini mushrooms and broth to pan.
4. Combine reserved porcini soaking liquid with toasted flour; stir with a whisk, and add to pan. Bring to a boil; reduce

heat, and simmer, uncovered, 15 minutes. Add milk; simmer 10 minutes, stirring frequently. Remove from heat; stir in half-and-half and sherry. Place 2 cups soup in a blender; process until smooth. Return puréed soup to pan. Warm soup over low heat 5 minutes or until thoroughly heated. Divide soup among 8 bowls, and sprinkle with parsley, if desired. Yield: 8 servings (serving size: 1 cup).

CALORIES 114 (24% from fat); FAT 3.1g (sat 1.8g, mono 0.9g, poly 0.1g); PROTEIN 7.1g; CARB 13.3g; FIBER 1.9g; CHOL 11mg; IRON 1.9mg; SODIUM 341mg; CALC 72mg

Savory Beet Soup

For added creaminess and a lovely presentation, we swirled this vibrantly colored soup with sour cream.

    1 teaspoon olive oil
    1 cup chopped onion
    4 cups fat-free, less-sodium chicken
       broth
    2 cups water
   ½ teaspoon salt
   ¼ teaspoon freshly ground black
       pepper
    3 beets, peeled and halved
    1 medium baking potato, peeled and
       halved crosswise
    1 bay leaf
    1 teaspoon lemon juice
    8 teaspoons reduced-fat sour cream

1. Heat oil in a Dutch oven over medium-high heat. Add onion; sauté 3 minutes or until tender. Add broth and next 6 ingredients. Bring to a boil; reduce heat, and simmer, uncovered, 20 minutes or until beets and potato are tender. Discard bay leaf.
2. Place one-third of broth mixture in a blender or food processor; process until smooth. Place puréed mixture in a large bowl. Repeat procedure twice with remaining broth mixture. Return puréed mixture to pan. Warm soup over low heat 5 minutes or until thoroughly heated. Remove from heat, and stir in lemon juice.
3. Combine ½ cup soup and sour cream, stirring with a whisk. Divide soup evenly

among 8 bowls. Top each serving with 1 tablespoon sour cream mixture; swirl sour cream mixture using tip of a knife. Yield: 8 servings (serving size: about ¾ cup soup).

CALORIES 74 (16% from fat); FAT 1.3g (sat 0.5g, mono 0.4g, poly 0.1g); PROTEIN 3.3g; CARB 12.3g; FIBER 2.2g; CHOL 3mg; IRON 0.7mg; SODIUM 343mg; CALC 23mg

Cider-Roasted Pork Loin

Fresh herbs and sweet cider syrup combine in this savory main dish. Overnight brining tenderizes the roast. If the cider reduction becomes too thick to brush on the pork, warm it in a saucepan over low heat.

    3 cups water
    3 cups apple cider
   ¼ cup kosher salt
    1 tablespoon black peppercorns
    1 tablespoon coriander seeds
    1 bay leaf
    1 (2-pound) boneless pork loin,
       trimmed
    2 cups apple cider
       Cooking spray
 1½   teaspoons chopped fresh
       rosemary
 1½   teaspoons chopped fresh sage
   ⅛ teaspoon freshly ground black
       pepper

1. Combine first 6 ingredients in a saucepan; bring to a boil, stirring until salt dissolves. Remove from heat; cool. Pour brine into a 2-gallon zip-top plastic bag. Add pork; seal. Refrigerate 8 hours or overnight, turning bag occasionally.
2. Preheat oven to 350°.
3. Bring 2 cups cider to a boil in a small saucepan over medium-high heat. Cook until cider is thickened and reduced to ¼ cup (about 15 minutes). Set aside.
4. Remove pork from bag; discard brine. Place pork on rack of a broiler pan coated with cooking spray. Lightly coat pork with cooking spray. Combine rosemary, sage, and ground black pepper; sprinkle evenly over pork. Bake at 350° for 1 hour or until thermometer registers 155°, basting twice with cider reduction during final 20 minutes of cooking. Remove

from oven; baste with remaining cider reduction. Let stand 10 minutes before slicing. Yield: 8 servings (serving size: about 3 ounces pork).

CALORIES 200 (30% from fat); FAT 6.6g (sat 2.2g, mono 3g, poly 0.7g); PROTEIN 24.4g; CARB 9.2g; FIBER 0.3g; CHOL 67mg; IRON 1.1mg; SODIUM 419mg; CALC 25mg

MAKE AHEAD
Cider-Roasted Chicken
(pictured on page 344)

Brining overnight in a salt-and-cider mixture makes this chicken incredibly flavorful and moist; basting with reduced apple cider adds a hint of sweetness to the finished chicken. Use tongs to carefully remove the skin from the hot chicken.

    3   quarts water
    1   quart apple cider
    ¼   cup kosher salt
    1   tablespoon black peppercorns
    1   bay leaf
    1   (6-pound) roasting chicken
    2   cups apple cider
    1   large onion, peeled and
        halved
    4   flat-leaf parsley sprigs
    4   garlic cloves, peeled

1. Combine first 5 ingredients in a saucepan; bring to a boil, stirring until salt dissolves. Remove from heat; cool completely. Remove and discard giblets and neck from chicken. Rinse chicken with cold water; pat dry. Trim excess fat. Pour brine into a 2-gallon zip-top plastic bag. Add chicken; seal. Refrigerate 8 hours or overnight, turning bag occasionally.
2. Preheat oven to 400°.
3. Bring 2 cups cider to a boil in a small saucepan over medium-high heat. Cook until cider is thickened and reduced to ¼ cup (about 15 minutes). Set aside.
4. Remove chicken from bag; discard brine. Pat chicken dry with paper towels. Place onion halves, parsley, and garlic in cavity. Lift wing tips up and over back; tuck under chicken. Tie legs. Place chicken on rack of a broiler pan. Bake at 400° for 1½ hours or until thermometer registers 175°. Remove from oven (do not turn oven off). Carefully remove and

discard skin. Baste chicken with half of reduced cider; return to 400° oven for 10 minutes. Remove from oven; baste with remaining cider reduction. Transfer chicken to a platter.
5. Place a zip-top plastic bag inside a 2-cup glass measure. Pour drippings into bag; let stand 10 minutes (fat will rise to top). Seal bag; carefully snip off 1 bottom corner of bag. Drain drippings into a small bowl, stopping before fat layer reaches opening; discard fat. Serve jus over chicken. Yield: 8 servings (serving size: about 4 ounces chicken and about 1 tablespoon jus).

CALORIES 224 (29% from fat); FAT 7.1g (sat 2g, mono 2.7g, poly 1.7g); PROTEIN 26.9g; CARB 11.3g; FIBER 0.4g; CHOL 80mg; IRON 1.4mg; SODIUM 452mg; CALC 26mg

QUICK & EASY
Spicy Sweet Potato Wedges
(pictured on page 344)

These peppery-sweet potatoes are delicious with roasted meats. Cooking them at high heat makes their interior tender just as the sugar-and-spice coating begins to caramelize and brown the outside.

    6   sweet potatoes (about 2¼
        pounds)
    Cooking spray
    2   teaspoons sugar
    ½   teaspoon salt
    ¼   teaspoon ground red
        pepper
    ⅛   teaspoon black pepper

1. Preheat oven to 500°.
2. Peel potatoes; cut each lengthwise into quarters. Place potatoes in a large bowl; coat with cooking spray. Combine sugar, salt, and peppers, and sprinkle over potatoes, tossing well to coat. Arrange potatoes, cut sides down, in a single layer on a baking sheet. Bake at 500° for 10 minutes; turn wedges over. Bake an additional 10 minutes or until tender and beginning to brown. Yield: 8 servings (serving size: 3 wedges).

CALORIES 153 (2% from fat); FAT 0.4g (sat 0.1g, mono 0g, poly 0.2g); PROTEIN 2.4g; CARB 35.5g; FIBER 2.3g; CHOL 0mg; IRON 0.9mg; SODIUM 166mg; CALC 31mg

MAKE AHEAD • FREEZABLE
Country Rye Loaves

This bread has hearty flavor with a thick crust and soft interior. Combine the yeast, water, rye flour, and molasses the night before so it has time to ferment and create a sponge; this makes for tangy, dense loaves. The dough is soft, so be patient when kneading, and add only as much flour as is necessary to keep the dough from sticking to your hands.

    2   packages dry yeast (about
        2¼ teaspoons)
    3   cups warm water (100° to 110°)
    3   cups rye flour
    6   tablespoons molasses
    1   tablespoon olive oil
 2½   teaspoons salt
    2   cups whole wheat flour
    2   cups bread flour, divided
    Cooking spray
    2   teaspoons cornmeal
    2   tablespoons bread flour

1. Dissolve yeast in warm water in a large bowl; let stand 5 minutes. Lightly spoon rye flour into dry measuring cups; level with a knife. Add rye flour and molasses to yeast mixture, and stir until combined. Cover and let stand at room temperature 8 hours or overnight to make a sponge.
2. Stir oil and salt into sponge. Lightly spoon whole wheat flour and bread flour into dry measuring cups; level with a knife. Add whole wheat flour and 1½ cups bread flour to sponge; stir until a soft dough forms. Turn dough out onto a lightly floured surface. Knead until smooth and elastic (about 8 minutes); add enough of remaining ½ cup bread flour, 1 tablespoon at a time, to prevent dough from sticking to hands (dough will feel tacky).
3. Place dough in a large bowl coated with cooking spray, turning to coat top. Cover and let rise in a warm place (85°), free from drafts, 1 hour or until doubled in size. (Press two fingers into dough. If indentation remains, dough has risen enough.) Punch dough down; cover and let rest 5 minutes. Divide dough into
Continued

2 equal portions. Shape each portion into a 6-inch round. Place dough rounds on a baking sheet sprinkled with 2 teaspoons cornmeal. Lightly coat surface of dough with cooking spray. Cover and let rise in a warm place (85°), free from drafts, 20 minutes or until doubled in size.

4. Preheat oven to 350°.

5. Uncover loaves. Place 2 tablespoons bread flour in a small sifter, and sift flour evenly over loaves. Cut a shallow (¼-inch) X in center of each loaf. Bake at 350° for 1 hour or until bread is browned on bottom and sounds hollow when tapped. Cool on a wire rack. Yield: 2 loaves, 10 servings per loaf (serving size: 1 slice).

CALORIES 170 (7% from fat); FAT 1.4g (sat 0.1g, mono 0.6g, poly 0.2g); PROTEIN 5.6g; CARB 34.5g; FIBER 4.6g; CHOL 0mg; IRON 1.9mg; SODIUM 301mg; CALC 17mg

---

STAFF FAVORITE • MAKE AHEAD
Pumpkin-Orange Cake

You can also prepare this in a 13 x 9-inch pan (bake for 40 minutes, and cool in pan for 10 minutes) or a tube pan (bake for 55 minutes, and cool in pan for 20 minutes). For the pan variations, you'll need an extra pomegranate and can of oranges for the topping.

  ½ cup granulated sugar
  ½ cup butter, softened
  1 (15-ounce) can pumpkin
  ¼ cup egg substitute
  ½ teaspoon vanilla extract
  2¾ cups sifted cake flour
  1 teaspoon baking soda
  ½ teaspoon salt
  ½ teaspoon baking powder
  ½ teaspoon ground cinnamon
  ¼ teaspoon ground ginger
  ¼ teaspoon ground nutmeg
  1 (12-ounce) can evaporated fat-free milk
  Cooking spray
  3 cups sifted powdered sugar, divided
  ¾ cup (6 ounces) ⅓-less-fat cream cheese, softened
  1 teaspoon grated orange rind
  2 (11-ounce) cans mandarin oranges in light syrup, drained (2 cups)
  1 cup pomegranate seeds (about 2)

1. Preheat oven to 350°.

2. Place granulated sugar and butter in a large bowl, and beat with a mixer at medium speed until well blended. Add pumpkin; beat well. Add egg substitute and vanilla; beat until well blended.

3. Combine flour and next 6 ingredients, stirring with a whisk. Add flour mixture and milk alternately to butter mixture, beginning and ending with flour mixture. Pour batter into 2 (9-inch) round cake pans coated with cooking spray; sharply tap pans once on counter to remove air bubbles. Bake at 350° for 30 minutes or until a wooden pick inserted in center comes out clean. Cool in pans 10 minutes on a wire rack; remove from pans. Cool completely on wire rack.

4. Place 1 cup powdered sugar and cream cheese in a large bowl; beat with a mixer at medium speed until well blended. Add 2 cups powdered sugar and rind; beat until fluffy.

5. Place 1 cake layer on a plate. Spread ⅔ cup cream cheese frosting evenly over top of cake. Top with remaining cake layer; spread remaining cream cheese frosting over top, but not sides, of cake. Arrange orange slices in a ring around outer edge of top cake layer. Sprinkle pomegranate seeds over center of top cake layer. Store cake loosely covered in refrigerator. Yield: 14 servings (serving size: 1 slice).

CALORIES 338 (26% from fat); FAT 9.6g (sat 5.9g, mono 2g, poly 0.4g); PROTEIN 5.9g; CARB 58.5g; FIBER 1.2g; CHOL 28mg; IRON 2.3mg; SODIUM 354mg; CALC 102mg

---

Sandwiching Leftovers

Save the second Country Rye Loaf (recipe on page 347) to make sandwiches with any leftovers. Use Red Pepper-Cheese Dip (recipe on page 345) as a sandwich spread, add a layer of remaining lettuce purchased for the salad, and top with Cider-Roasted Pork Loin (recipe on page 346) or Cider-Roasted Chicken (recipe on page 347) for the filling.

. . . And Ready in Just About 20 Minutes

These recipes span the globe—and the supermarket—with Greek, Asian, Italian, and Caribbean choices.

Speedy Supper Menu
serves 4

The ricelike pasta side dish is simply seasoned, making it a good match for the intensely flavored entrée. Look for packaged, peeled, trimmed baby carrots in the produce section.

Chicken Piccata

Orzo with peas*

Roasted baby carrots

*Combine 2 cups hot cooked orzo; ½ cup frozen, thawed green peas; ⅓ cup crumbled feta cheese; 1 tablespoon extravirgin olive oil; ¼ teaspoon salt; and ¼ teaspoon cracked black pepper.

QUICK & EASY
Chicken Piccata

Substitute chicken breast tenders or veal cutlets, if you like. Serve over orzo, angel hair pasta, or rice.

  1 tablespoon olive oil
  4 (6-ounce) skinless, boneless chicken breast halves
  ½ teaspoon salt
  ¼ teaspoon black pepper
  ⅓ cup fat-free, less-sodium chicken broth
  2 tablespoons dry white wine
  1½ tablespoons fresh lemon juice
  ¼ cup chopped fresh parsley
  1 tablespoon capers, drained

1. Heat oil in a large nonstick skillet over medium-high heat.

2. Place each chicken breast half between 2 sheets of heavy-duty plastic wrap; pound to ½-inch thickness using a meat mallet or rolling pin. Sprinkle chicken evenly with salt and pepper. Add chicken to pan; cook 4 minutes on each side or until done. Remove from pan. Add broth, wine, and lemon juice to pan; reduce heat, and simmer 1 minute. Stir in parsley and capers. Spoon sauce over chicken. Yield: 4 servings (serving size: 1 breast half and 1 tablespoon sauce).

CALORIES 227 (22% from fat); FAT 5.5g (sat 1g, mono 3g, poly 0.8g); PROTEIN 39.7g; CARB 1.1g; FIBER 0.3g; CHOL 99mg; IRON 1.6mg; SODIUM 505mg; CALC 27mg

QUICK & EASY

Pasta with Sun-Dried Tomato Pesto and Feta Cheese

The oil in the sun-dried tomatoes gives the almond-spiced pesto a rich consistency.

- 1 (9-ounce) package refrigerated fresh linguine
- ¾ cup oil-packed sun-dried tomato halves, drained
- ¼ cup loosely packed basil leaves
- 2 tablespoons slivered almonds
- 2 tablespoons preshredded fresh Parmesan cheese
- 1 tablespoon bottled minced garlic
- ½ teaspoon salt
- ¼ teaspoon black pepper
- ½ cup (2 ounces) crumbled feta cheese

1. Cook pasta according to package directions, omitting salt and fat. Drain in a sieve over a bowl, reserving 1 cup cooking liquid. Return pasta to pan.
2. While pasta cooks, place tomatoes and next 6 ingredients in a food processor; process until finely chopped.
3. Combine tomato mixture and reserved 1 cup cooking liquid, stirring with a whisk. Add to pasta; toss well to coat. Sprinkle with feta. Yield: 4 servings (serving size: 1 cup).

CALORIES 300 (30% from fat); FAT 9.9g (sat 3.3g, mono 3.9g, poly 1.6g); PROTEIN 12.3g; CARB 42g; FIBER 4.3g; CHOL 61mg; IRON 3.1mg; SODIUM 570mg; CALC 141mg

QUICK & EASY

Chili-Glazed Tofu over Asparagus and Rice

Cooking the rice and asparagus in the same pot of boiling water saves a little time.

- 4 cups water
- 1 (3½-ounce) bag boil-in-bag long-grain rice
- 2¼ cups chopped asparagus (about 1 pound)
- 1 tablespoon peanut oil
- 2 tablespoons rice vinegar
- 2 tablespoons low-sodium soy sauce
- 1 tablespoon sugar
- 1 teaspoon bottled minced ginger
- 1 teaspoon hot chili sauce with garlic (such as KA·ME)
- 1 pound extrafirm tofu, drained and cut lengthwise into 9 pieces
- 1 teaspoon salt, divided
- ¼ teaspoon black pepper
- ¾ cup preshredded carrot
- 1 teaspoon dark sesame oil

1. Bring 4 cups water to a boil in a 2-quart saucepan. Add bag of rice, submerging bag completely in water. Boil 10 minutes. Carefully remove bag from pan, leaving boiling water in pan. Add asparagus to pan; cook 1 minute. Drain.
2. While rice cooks, heat peanut oil in a large nonstick skillet over medium-high heat. Combine vinegar and next 4 ingredients in a small bowl. Sprinkle tofu with ½ teaspoon salt and pepper. Add tofu to pan; cook 3 minutes on each side or until browned. Add soy sauce mixture; cook 20 seconds, stirring constantly. Remove from heat. Combine rice, asparagus, ½ teaspoon salt, carrot, and sesame oil. Serve tofu over rice mixture. Yield: 3 servings (serving size: 3 tofu pieces and 1⅓ cups rice mixture).

CALORIES 296 (26% from fat); FAT 8.4g (sat 1.1g, mono 2.8g, poly 2.3g); PROTEIN 15.7g; CARB 41g; FIBER 4.9g; CHOL 0mg; IRON 3.7mg; SODIUM 913mg; CALC 126mg

QUICK & EASY

Cannellini Stew with Sausage and Kale and Cheese Toasts

Try this dish with various flavored chicken sausages and other mild cheeses, such as fontina or mozzarella.

- 2 teaspoons vegetable oil
- 1 teaspoon bottled minced garlic
- 4 (2-ounce) smoked turkey and duck sausages with fennel, cut into ¼-inch-thick slices (such as Gerhard's)
- 1 cup water
- 1 cup fat-free, less-sodium chicken broth
- 2 (19-ounce) cans cannellini beans or other white beans, rinsed and drained
- 4 cups bagged chopped kale
- ½ teaspoon black pepper
- ¼ teaspoon crushed red pepper
- ⅛ teaspoon salt
- 2 tablespoons fresh lemon juice
- 6 tablespoons (1½ ounces) shredded provolone cheese
- 6 (1-ounce) slices French bread baguette

1. Preheat broiler.
2. Heat oil in a large saucepan over medium-high heat. Add garlic and sausage; sauté 1 minute. Add water, broth, and beans; bring to a boil. Stir in kale, black pepper, red pepper, and salt; bring to a boil. Cover, reduce heat, and simmer 5 minutes or until kale is tender. Remove from heat; stir in lemon juice.
3. While stew simmers, sprinkle 1 tablespoon cheese over each bread slice; broil 1 minute or until cheese melts. Serve toasts with soup. Yield: 6 servings (serving size: 1 cup stew and 1 toast).

CALORIES 349 (26% from fat); FAT 10.2g (sat 3.6g, mono 1.7g, poly 2.7g); PROTEIN 19.3g; CARB 45.3g; FIBER 8.5g; CHOL 39mg; IRON 4.9mg; SODIUM 981mg; CALC 214mg

Sirloin Steak with Dijon-Port Sauce

The port and mustard create a rich, sweet, spicy sauce.

- 3 cups uncooked medium egg noodles
- 1 pound trimmed sirloin (about 1 inch thick)
- ½ teaspoon salt
- ½ teaspoon black pepper
- Cooking spray
- ½ cup port or other sweet red wine
- ¼ cup minced shallots
- 1 teaspoon bottled minced garlic
- ½ cup less-sodium beef broth
- 1 tablespoon Dijon mustard
- ½ teaspoon fresh thyme leaves

1. Cook noodles according to package directions, omitting salt and fat. Drain; keep warm.
2. While noodles cook, heat a nonstick skillet over medium-high heat. Sprinkle both sides of steak with salt and pepper. Lightly coat steak with cooking spray. Add steak to pan; cook 4 minutes on each side or until desired degree of doneness. Transfer meat to a platter; keep warm.
3. Add port to pan, scraping to loosen browned bits. Stir in shallots and garlic; cook 45 seconds, stirring frequently. Add beef broth; bring to a boil. Cook 20 seconds; remove from heat. Add mustard and thyme, stirring with a whisk.
4. Cut steak diagonally across grain into thin slices. Serve steak and sauce with noodles. Yield: 4 servings (serving size: about 3 ounces steak, 2 tablespoons sauce, and 1 cup noodles).

CALORIES 344 (29% from fat); FAT 11g (sat 4.1g, mono 4.6g, poly 0.8g); PROTEIN 28.5g; CARB 23.6g; FIBER 1g; CHOL 97mg; IRON 4.3mg; SODIUM 501mg; CALC 36mg

Tropical Chopped Salad with Shrimp

We use English cucumbers so you can skip the step of seeding regular cucumbers.

- 2 cups packaged Italian-blend salad greens
- 2 cups chopped bottled mango
- 1¼ cups chopped peeled English cucumber
- 1 cup cherry tomatoes, halved
- 1 tablespoon rice vinegar
- 1 teaspoon kosher salt
- ½ teaspoon crushed red pepper
- 1½ pounds medium shrimp, cooked and peeled
- 1 cup diced peeled avocado
- 1 tablespoon chopped cashews

1. Combine first 8 ingredients, tossing well. Place 2 cups salad on each of 4 plates; top each serving with ¼ cup avocado and ¾ teaspoon chopped cashews. Yield: 4 servings.

CALORIES 317 (29% from fat); FAT 10.2g (sat 1.7g, mono 4.6g, poly 2.2g); PROTEIN 36.7g; CARB 21.1g; FIBER 3.3g; CHOL 259mg; IRON 6.8mg; SODIUM 747mg; CALC 119mg

Lamb Chops with Herbed Yogurt over Couscous

- 1 cup water
- ¾ cup uncooked couscous
- 8 (4-ounce) lamb loin chops, trimmed
- ½ teaspoon salt
- ¼ teaspoon black pepper, divided
- Cooking spray
- ⅓ cup plain fat-free yogurt
- 1 tablespoon chopped fresh parsley
- 1 tablespoon chopped fresh mint
- 1 tablespoon chopped fresh basil
- 1 teaspoon honey

1. Preheat broiler.
2. Bring water to a boil in a medium saucepan; gradually stir in couscous. Remove from heat; cover and let stand 5 minutes. Fluff with a fork.
3. While couscous stands, sprinkle lamb with salt and ⅛ teaspoon pepper. Place lamb on a broiler pan coated with cooking spray; broil 5 minutes on each side or until desired degree of doneness.
4. While lamb cooks, combine ⅛ teaspoon pepper, yogurt, and remaining 4 ingredients. Serve lamb over couscous with yogurt sauce. Yield: 4 servings (serving size: 2 lamb chops, ½ cup couscous, and 2 tablespoons sauce).

CALORIES 282 (27% from fat); FAT 8.4g (sat 3g, mono 3.6g, poly 0.6g); PROTEIN 21.5g; CARB 28.4g; FIBER 1.8g; CHOL 54mg; IRON 1.8mg; SODIUM 363mg; CALC 68mg

reader recipes

One Fine Chili

A Pennsylvania cook fine-tunes her favorite chicken chili recipe.

Mercy Ingraham, a retired psychiatric nurse who now works part-time as a health educator, has been making White Chicken Chili for years. The recipe starts out as a simple one-pot chicken dish with common chili spices. She then adjusts the ingredient list depending on whom she's serving and what's in season.

White Chicken Chili

- Cooking spray
- 2 pounds skinless, boneless chicken breast, cut into bite-sized pieces
- 2 cups finely chopped onion
- 2 garlic cloves, minced
- 2 teaspoons ground cumin
- ½ teaspoon dried oregano
- 1 teaspoon ground coriander
- 2 (4.5-ounce) cans chopped green chiles, undrained
- 1 cup water
- 2 (15.5-ounce) cans cannellini beans, rinsed and drained (such as Goya)
- 1 (14-ounce) can fat-free, less-sodium chicken broth
- ½ teaspoon hot pepper sauce
- 1 cup (4 ounces) shredded Monterey Jack cheese
- ½ cup chopped fresh cilantro
- ½ cup chopped green onions

1. Heat a large nonstick skillet over medium-high heat. Coat pan with cooking spray. Add chicken to pan; cook 10 minutes or until browned, stirring frequently.

2. Heat a large Dutch oven over medium-high heat. Coat pan with cooking spray. Add onion to pan; sauté 6 minutes or until tender, stirring frequently. Add garlic; sauté 2 minutes, stirring frequently. Stir in cumin, oregano, and coriander; sauté 1 minute. Stir in chiles; reduce heat to low, and cook 10 minutes, partially covered. Add chicken, water, cannellini beans, and broth; bring to a simmer. Cover and simmer 10 minutes. Stir in hot sauce. Ladle 1 cup chili into each of 8 bowls; sprinkle each serving with 2 tablespoons cheese, 1 tablespoon cilantro, and 1 tablespoon green onions. Yield: 8 servings.

CALORIES 233 (23% from fat); FAT 5.9g (sat 3.1g, mono 1.6g, poly 0.5g); PROTEIN 32.7g; CARB 11.7g; FIBER 3.4g; CHOL 78mg; IRON 3.2mg; SODIUM 694mg; CALC 180mg

Eggplant Parmesan Pizza

"I came up with this recipe when trying to expand my usual pizza repertoire. Eggplant soaks up the flavors so well that it has become one of my favorite pizza toppings."

—Kristen Laise, Martinsburg, West Virginia

    1   cup (½-inch-thick) slices
        zucchini
    1   (1-pound) eggplant, cut into
        ¼-inch-thick slices
    Cooking spray
    1   (14-ounce) Italian cheese-
        flavored pizza crust (such as
        Boboli)
    1½ cups fat-free marinara sauce (such
        as Muir Glen Organic)
    ½   cup (2 ounces) shredded
        part-skim mozzarella cheese
    ½   cup turkey pepperoni (about
        2 ounces, such as Hormel)
    ¼   cup (1 ounce) grated fresh
        Parmesan cheese
    ¼   teaspoon crushed red
        pepper
    ¼   teaspoon dried oregano

1. Preheat oven to 400°.

2. Place zucchini and eggplant in a single layer on 2 baking sheets coated with cooking spray; lightly coat eggplant and zucchini with cooking spray. Bake at 400° for 15 minutes on each side or until tender and lightly browned.

3. Increase oven temperature to 425°.

4. Place crust on a baking sheet. Spread marinara over crust, leaving a 1-inch border. Layer zucchini and eggplant evenly over sauce; top with mozzarella, pepperoni, Parmesan, pepper, and oregano. Bake at 425° for 10 minutes or until cheese melts. Let stand 5 minutes. Yield: 6 servings.

CALORIES 290 (23% from fat); FAT 7.3g (sat 2.6g, mono 1.9g, poly 2.3g); PROTEIN 15.6g; CARB 40.6g; FIBER 3.3g; CHOL 20mg; IRON 2.3mg; SODIUM 782mg; CALC 293mg

Salmon with Orange Marmalade

"When I ran out of orange juice, I substituted marmalade in a broiled salmon recipe I've been making for years. It turned out to be the best salmon I ever had."

—Gail Sheriff, Fairfield, Connecticut

    ¼   cup orange marmalade
    2   tablespoons low-sodium soy
        sauce
    2   garlic cloves, minced
    1   (1½-pound) salmon fillet
    ¼   teaspoon salt

1. Preheat oven to 400°.

2. Combine first 3 ingredients, stirring with a whisk. Place salmon on rack of a broiler pan lined with foil; sprinkle fillet evenly with salt. Spread half of marmalade mixture over fillet. Bake at 400° for 18 minutes or until fish flakes easily when tested with a fork. Remove from oven. Spread remaining marmalade mixture evenly over fish.

3. Preheat broiler.

4. Broil fish 3 minutes or until topping browns. Yield: 4 servings (serving size: about 4½ ounces).

CALORIES 328 (36% from fat); FAT 13.1g (sat 3.1g, mono 5.7g, poly 3.2g); PROTEIN 36.8g; CARB 14.4g; FIBER 0.1g; CHOL 87mg; IRON 0.8mg; SODIUM 505mg; CALC 32mg

Butternut Squash and Red Pepper

"This recipe is reason enough to keep a rosemary plant in a sunny window in your house, because it provides the freshest rosemary possible."

—Robin Inman, Malden, Massachusetts

    7   cups (1-inch) cubed peeled
        butternut squash (about 3½ pounds)
    1½ cups (1-inch) pieces red bell pepper
    3   tablespoons minced fresh parsley
    1   tablespoon minced fresh rosemary
    2   teaspoons olive oil
    ¾   teaspoon salt
    2   garlic cloves, minced
    Cooking spray
    2   tablespoons grated fresh Parmesan
        cheese

1. Preheat oven to 450°.

2. Combine first 7 ingredients, tossing well. Place in a 13 x 9-inch baking dish coated with cooking spray. Bake at 450° for 30 minutes or until tender. Sprinkle with cheese. Yield: 5 servings (serving size: 1 cup).

CALORIES 160 (19% from fat); FAT 3.4g (sat 0.9g, mono 1.6g, poly 0.5g); PROTEIN 6.2g; CARB 31.5g; FIBER 5.8g; CHOL 2mg; IRON 2.3mg; SODIUM 412mg; CALC 143mg

Lentil Spread

"My husband and I frequent a great little fusion restaurant in town. They serve bread with a lentil spread instead of butter. This is my version. It's best with crusty Italian bread."

—Rebekka Clavin, Libertyville, Illinois

    2   cups water
    ¾   cup dried lentils
    1   tablespoon olive oil
    2   tablespoons finely chopped shallots
    1   tablespoon minced garlic
    ½   cup chopped peeled tomato
    2   tablespoons thinly sliced green
        onions
    1½ tablespoons chopped fresh basil
    1   teaspoon salt

Continued

1. Combine water and lentils in a medium saucepan, and bring to a boil. Cover, reduce heat, and simmer 40 minutes or until tender.
2. Heat oil in a small skillet over medium heat. Add shallots and garlic; cook 2 minutes or until shallots are tender, stirring occasionally. Place lentils in a large bowl; mash to desired consistency. Stir in shallot mixture, tomato, and remaining ingredients. Cool to room temperature. Yield: 2¾ cups (serving size: ¼ cup).

CALORIES 60 (21% from fat); FAT 1.4g (sat 0.2g, mono 0.9g, poly 0.2g); PROTEIN 3.9g; CARB 8.5g; FIBER 4.2g; CHOL 0mg; IRON 1.3mg; SODIUM 213mg; CALC 11mg

Green Rice

"This is one of my favorite recipes to make because it's always well received. It has a wonderful aroma that envelops the house."
—Arundathi Krishna, San Mateo, California

    4 cups water, divided
    1 cup basmati rice
    1 cup chopped fresh cilantro
    2 tablespoons water
    2 poblano chiles, seeded and
       coarsely chopped
 1½ teaspoons olive oil
    1 cup finely chopped onion
   ½ cup chopped green bell
       pepper
   ¼ cup chopped green onions
    1 garlic clove, minced
   ½ teaspoon salt

1. Combine 2 cups water and rice; let stand 30 minutes. Drain well.
2. Place cilantro, 2 tablespoons water, and poblanos in a blender or food processor; process until smooth.
3. Heat oil in Dutch oven over medium-high heat. Add onion, bell pepper, green onions, and garlic; sauté 3 minutes. Add poblano mixture; sauté 2 minutes. Stir in rice, 2 cups water, and salt; bring to a boil. Cover, reduce heat, and simmer 15 minutes or until liquid is absorbed. Yield: 4 servings (serving size: 1 cup).

CALORIES 243 (9% from fat); FAT 2.5g (sat 0.3g, mono 1.3g, poly 0.6g); PROTEIN 4.5g; CARB 55.1g; FIBER 4.7g; CHOL 0mg; IRON 2.8mg; SODIUM 311mg; CALC 28mg

Southwest Meat Loaf

"Since I was looking for a way to jazz up the traditional American meat loaf, I added Tex-Mex ingredients, and the result was fantastic. You can even use hot banana pepper rings, if you like."
—Patricia Moed, Manchester, Connecticut

   ½ cup seasoned breadcrumbs
   ½ cup finely chopped onion
   ¼ cup chopped fresh cilantro
   ¼ cup pickled banana pepper rings,
       finely chopped
    2 tablespoons Dijon mustard
    2 tablespoons Worcestershire sauce
    1 tablespoon onion powder
   ½ teaspoon dried oregano
Dash of crushed red pepper
    2 pounds ground turkey
    2 large egg whites, lightly beaten
Cooking spray
    1 cup bottled salsa

1. Preheat oven to 350°.
2. Combine first 11 ingredients. Divide meat mixture into 2 portions, and shape each portion into a 6 x 3-inch loaf. Place loaves in a 13 x 9-inch baking dish coated with cooking spray; pour ½ cup salsa over each loaf. Bake at 350° for 1 hour or until a thermometer registers 165°. Let stand 10 minutes. Cut each loaf into 8 slices. Yield: 8 servings (serving size: 2 slices).

CALORIES 239 (41% from fat); FAT 10.8g (sat 3.6g, mono 3.6g, poly 3.2g); PROTEIN 23.1g; CARB 10.6g; FIBER 1.3g; CHOL 96mg; IRON 2.1mg; SODIUM 582mg; CALC 37mg

Enjoy the Soup, Salad, and Bread Menu and the changing color of the leaves from the comfort of your porch.

Under the Maple Tree

October is a fantastic month to enjoy a comforting meal outside under the golden-hued branches of color-changing trees.

Make this soup, salad, and bread, and be prepared not only to savor a delicious meal, but the dazzling view of Mother Nature's work as well.

Soup, Salad, and Bread Menu
serves 6

Chardonnay or Pinot Noir pair nicely with this fall menu.

Green Salad with Roasted Poblanos and Cumin-Lime Dressing

Butternut Squash-White Bean Soup

Cornmeal Scones

Vanilla Bean Sorbet with Pineapple Topping

QUICK & EASY
Green Salad with Roasted Poblanos and Cumin-Lime Dressing

A little heat, a little honey, and a pungent spice enliven this simple salad and dressing.

    2 poblano chiles, seeded and
       halved
    2 tablespoons fresh lime juice
    1 tablespoon extravirgin olive
       oil
    1 tablespoon honey
   ¼ teaspoon salt
   ¼ teaspoon freshly ground black
       pepper
   ⅛ teaspoon ground cumin
  10 cups gourmet salad greens

1. Preheat broiler.
2. Place chiles, cut sides down, on a foil-lined baking sheet; broil 6 minutes or

until blackened. Place in a zip-top plastic bag; seal. Let stand 15 minutes. Peel and discard skins, stems, and seeds. Cut chiles into thin strips.

3. Combine lime juice and next 5 ingredients in a large bowl, stirring with a whisk. Add chile strips and salad greens; toss gently to coat. Yield: 6 servings (serving size: 1½ cups).

CALORIES 52 (43% from fat); FAT 2.5g (sat 0.3g, mono 1.7g, poly 0.3g); PROTEIN 1.8g; CARB 7.2g; FIBER 2.2g; CHOL 0mg; IRON 1.4mg; SODIUM 122mg; CALC 54mg

Butternut Squash-White Bean Soup

Cream adds a smooth finish to the soup, while crumbled bacon and toasted pumpkinseeds lend crunch.

3 bacon slices
1 cup chopped onion
⅔ cup chopped celery
3 garlic cloves, minced
4 cups (¾-inch) cubed peeled butternut squash (about 1½ pounds)
¼ cup dry white wine
4 cups fat-free, less-sodium chicken broth
1 teaspoon ground cumin
¼ teaspoon ground red pepper
⅛ teaspoon ground cinnamon
⅛ teaspoon ground cloves
¼ cup whipping cream
1 tablespoon chopped fresh oregano
1 teaspoon salt
¼ teaspoon freshly ground black pepper
2 (15-ounce) cans Great Northern beans, rinsed and drained
3 tablespoons unsalted pumpkinseed kernels, toasted

1. Cook bacon in a Dutch oven over medium heat until crisp. Remove bacon from pan, reserving 2 teaspoons drippings in pan; crumble bacon, and set aside.
2. Add onion, celery, and garlic to pan; cook 3 minutes or until tender, stirring occasionally. Add squash; cook 3 minutes, stirring occasionally. Add wine;

cook until liquid almost evaporates. Stir in broth, cumin, red pepper, cinnamon, and cloves; bring to a boil. Reduce heat; simmer 5 minutes or until squash is tender. Stir in cream, oregano, salt, black pepper, and beans; bring to a boil. Remove from heat. Sprinkle each serving with bacon and pumpkinseeds. Yield: 6 servings (serving size: 1½ cups).

CALORIES 324 (30% from fat); FAT 10.7g (sat 4.3g, mono 3.4g, poly 2.1g); PROTEIN 17.7g; CARB 42.2g; FIBER 9.2g; CHOL 18mg; IRON 4.1mg; SODIUM 774mg; CALC 129mg

Cornmeal Scones

These scones are a good match for thick and hearty Butternut Squash-White Bean Soup (recipe at left).

1⅔ cups all-purpose flour
⅓ cup yellow cornmeal
3 tablespoons sugar
2½ teaspoons baking powder
¼ teaspoon salt
3½ tablespoons chilled butter, cut into small pieces
½ cup 1% low-fat milk
1 large egg, lightly beaten
Cooking spray

1. Preheat oven to 375°.
2. Lightly spoon flour into dry measuring cups; level with a knife. Combine flour, cornmeal, sugar, baking powder, and salt in a large bowl; cut in butter with a pastry blender or 2 knives until mixture resembles coarse meal. Add milk and egg to cornmeal mixture; stir just until moist.
3. Turn dough out onto a lightly floured surface, and knead lightly 4 times with floured hands. Cover a baking sheet with parchment paper; coat with cooking spray. Pat dough into a 7-inch circle on prepared baking sheet. Cut dough into 8 wedges, cutting into but not through dough.
4. Bake at 375° for 22 minutes or until golden brown and a wooden pick inserted in center comes out clean. Serve warm. Yield: 8 servings (serving size: 1 scone).

CALORIES 187 (28% from fat); FAT 5.8g (sat 3.4g, mono 1.8g, poly 0.3g); PROTEIN 4.3g; CARB 30.1g; FIBER 0.8g; CHOL 41mg; IRON 1.5mg; SODIUM 265mg; CALC 72mg

Vanilla Bean Sorbet with Pineapple Topping

On its own, this sorbet is sweet, but the spicy tartness of the pineapple topping is the perfect foil. A touch of corn syrup in the sorbet keeps it from freezing solid and allows for easy scooping.

SORBET:

4 cups water
1 cup sugar
¼ cup light corn syrup
1 (3-inch) piece vanilla bean, split lengthwise
1 tablespoon fresh lemon juice

TOPPING:

½ cup dark rum
¼ cup water
2 tablespoons sugar
1 (1-inch) slice peeled fresh ginger, halved
1½ cups diced pineapple

1. To prepare sorbet, combine first 3 ingredients in a medium saucepan; bring to a boil over high heat. Cook 2 minutes or until sugar dissolves, stirring frequently. Scrape seeds from vanilla bean into a medium bowl. Add vanilla bean and lemon juice. Pour hot sugar mixture over vanilla mixture; stir well with a whisk. Cover and chill completely. Remove and discard vanilla bean. Pour mixture into freezer can of an ice-cream freezer; freeze according to manufacturer's instructions. Spoon sorbet into a freezer-safe container; cover and freeze 4 hours or until firm.
2. To prepare topping, combine rum and next 3 ingredients in a small saucepan. Bring to a boil; cook 2 minutes. Remove from heat; cool to room temperature. Remove and discard ginger. Pour rum mixture over pineapple; chill 1 hour. Yield: 8 servings (serving size: about ⅔ cup sorbet and about 3 tablespoons topping).

CALORIES 185 (0% from fat); FAT 0.1g (sat 0g, mono 0g, poly 0.1g); PROTEIN 0.1g; CARB 39.7g; FIBER 0.4g; CHOL 0mg; IRON 0.2mg; SODIUM 13mg; CALC 3mg

Mexican Soups & Stews

Warm and pleasantly spicy, this authentic fare is a delicious way to enjoy a real taste of the cuisine.

Mexican Kitchen

Most of these ingredients can be found in your local supermarket, but a few might require a trip to a Latino market.

Crema Mexicana: looks like and has a tanginess similar to sour cream, but it's thinner and richer, like heavy cream

Queso fresco: grainy, crumbly cheese with a mild, slightly acidic flavor

Achiote paste: often used in Yucatan and Oaxacan cuisine; made from grinding earthy-flavored, red-colored annatto seeds into a paste; found in Latino markets

Hominy: corn kernels that have been soaked in a slaked lime or lye solution to remove the hulls; sold dried or rehydrated and canned

Tomatillos: not actually tomatoes, even though they look like small green tomatoes with a papery husk; have hints of lemon and herbs, and a sharp tartness when eaten raw; cooking slightly mellows the tartness

Chayote: gourdlike squash that looks like a large green pear; also known as a mirliton in Louisiana

---

MAKE AHEAD
Calabaza and Poblano Stew

Redolent with honey, cinnamon, and aniseed, this stew highlights mild but exotic flavors typically associated with European cuisine, but which are also commonly used in Mexico. Calabaza is a pumpkinlike winter squash. Butternut squash is a good substitute. If you prefer a smoother consistency, use a potato masher to break up the squash.

5   poblano chiles (about 1 pound)
1   teaspoon aniseed
1   (3-inch) cinnamon stick, broken
1   tablespoon peanut oil
3½ cups chopped onion
4   garlic cloves, minced
10 cups (2-inch) pieces peeled calabaza squash (about 3 pounds)
4   cups vegetable broth
2   cups water
3   tablespoons honey
½   teaspoon salt
6   tablespoons Crema Mexicana
½   cup roasted pumpkinseed kernels

1. Preheat broiler.

2. Cut chiles in half; discard seeds and membranes. Place chile halves, skin sides up, on a foil-lined baking sheet; flatten with hand. Broil 5 minutes or until blackened. Place in a heavy-duty zip-top plastic bag; seal. Let stand 15 minutes. Peel chiles; discard skins. Chop chiles.

3. Place aniseed and cinnamon in a spice or coffee grinder; process until finely ground.

4. Heat oil in a large Dutch oven over medium-high heat. Add onion; sauté 5 minutes or until browned. Add garlic; sauté 1 minute. Add cinnamon mixture to pan; sauté 1 minute. Add chopped chiles, squash, broth, water, honey, and salt; bring to a boil. Reduce heat, and simmer 30 minutes or until squash is tender.

5. Drizzle each serving with Crema Mexicana; sprinkle with pumpkinseeds. Yield: 8 servings (serving size: 1½ cups stew, about 2 teaspoons Crema Mexicana, and 1 tablespoon pumpkinseeds).

CALORIES 266 (35% from fat); FAT 10.4g (sat 2.6g, mono 2.7g, poly 3.4g); PROTEIN 9g; CARB 40.7g; FIBER 8.4g; CHOL 8mg; IRON 4mg; SODIUM 669mg; CALC 118mg

---

STAFF FAVORITE • MAKE AHEAD
Pork Posole

There are three main versions of this hominy stew, each representing a color of the Mexican flag. Red posole, like this version, is made from dried chiles; our stew features ancho chiles. The green version is made from fresh chiles; white posole has no chiles.

4   ancho chiles, stemmed and seeded
2   cups boiling water
1   tablespoon cumin seeds
1   tablespoon peanut oil
1½ pounds boneless pork loin, trimmed and cut into ½-inch pieces
1½ cups chopped onion
4   garlic cloves, minced
4   cups fat-free, less-sodium chicken broth
2   tablespoons sugar
¾   teaspoon salt
2   (15.5-ounce) cans white hominy, undrained
6   tablespoons sliced radishes
6   tablespoons chopped green onions
6   tablespoons minced fresh cilantro
6   lime slices

1. Heat a cast-iron skillet over high heat. Place chiles in pan; flatten with a spatula. Cook 10 seconds on each side or until blackened. Combine toasted chiles and boiling water in a bowl; let stand 10 minutes or until soft. Place chile mixture in a blender or food processor; process until smooth.

2. Cook cumin seeds in a large Dutch oven over medium heat 1 minute or until toasted and fragrant. Place in a spice or coffee grinder; process until finely ground.

3. Heat oil in Dutch oven over medium-high heat. Add pork; cook 5 minutes, browning on all sides. Remove pork from pan. Reduce heat to medium. Add onion and garlic to pan; cook 8 minutes or until onion is browned, stirring frequently. Stir in pork, puréed chiles, toasted ground cumin, broth, sugar, salt, and hominy; bring to a simmer. Cook 30 minutes or until pork is tender. Spoon 1⅔ cups posole into each of 6 bowls; top each serving with 1 tablespoon radishes, 1 tablespoon green onions, and 1 tablespoon cilantro. Serve with lime slices. Yield: 6 servings.

CALORIES 376 (27% from fat); FAT 11.2g (sat 2.9g, mono 4.5g, poly 2.6g); PROTEIN 30.7g; CARB 37.4g; FIBER 7.4g; CHOL 67mg; IRON 4mg; SODIUM 971mg; CALC 67mg

MAKE AHEAD
Meatball Soup
Sopa de Albóndigas
(pictured on page 343)

In Mexico, *albóndigas* (meatballs) are sometimes made with rice used as the binding agent. Other times, rice is in the soup.

    2   teaspoons coriander seeds
  1½   teaspoons cumin seeds
    4   whole cloves
    1   (3-inch) cinnamon stick, broken
    ½   cup uncooked long-grain white rice
    2   tablespoons grated fresh onion
    ½   teaspoon salt
    1   pound ground round
    1   large egg white, lightly beaten
    1   garlic clove, minced
  Cooking spray
    3   cups chopped green cabbage
    2   cups chopped onion
    1   cup sliced carrot
    ½   cup chopped celery
    1   tablespoon chili powder
  1½   tablespoons drained chopped
        chipotle chile in adobo sauce
    ¼   teaspoon salt
    2   (14-ounce) cans fat-free,
        less-sodium chicken broth
    1   (14.5-ounce) can fire-roasted
        whole tomatoes, undrained and
        chopped (such as Muir Glen)
  1½   cups cubed peeled baking potato

1. Cook coriander seeds and cumin seeds in a large Dutch oven over medium heat 1 minute or until toasted and fragrant. Place toasted spices, cloves, and cinnamon in a spice or coffee grinder; process until finely ground.
2. Combine 2 teaspoons cinnamon mixture, rice and next 5 ingredients in a large bowl; set remaining cinnamon mixture aside. Shape beef mixture into 24 (1-inch) meatballs.

3. Heat pan over medium heat. Coat pan with cooking spray. Add cabbage, chopped onion, carrot, and celery to pan; cook 8 minutes, stirring frequently. Add remaining cinnamon mixture, chili powder, and chipotle; cook 1 minute, stirring constantly. Stir in ¼ teaspoon salt, broth, and tomatoes; bring to a boil. Reduce heat to simmer. Add meatballs; cover and cook 15 minutes. Add potato; cook, uncovered, over medium heat 20 minutes or until potato is tender. Yield: 6 servings (serving size: 1⅔ cups).

CALORIES 330 (34% from fat); FAT 12.4g (sat 4.6g, mono 5.2g, poly 0.6g); PROTEIN 20.6g; CARB 34.5g; FIBER 4.9g; CHOL 51mg; IRON 4mg; SODIUM 780mg; CALC 97mg

STAFF FAVORITE • MAKE AHEAD
Chicken Green Chili with White Beans

Our kitchen has found that Anaheim chiles run the gamut from mild to fairly hot.

    6   Anaheim chiles
    1   tablespoon peanut oil
    3   chicken leg quarters, skinned
        (about 1¾ pounds)
  1¾   cups chopped onion
    4   garlic cloves, minced
    4   cups fat-free, less-sodium chicken
        broth
    2   cups water, divided
  1½   teaspoons ground cumin
    1   (15.5-ounce) can cannellini beans
        (such as Goya) or other white
        beans, rinsed and drained
    3   tablespoons all-purpose flour
    1   teaspoon salt
    3   tablespoons reduced-fat sour cream
    6   lime slices

1. Preheat broiler.
2. Cut chiles in half; discard seeds and membranes. Place halves, skin sides up, on a foil-lined baking sheet; flatten with hand. Broil 5 minutes or until blackened. Place in a heavy-duty zip-top plastic bag; seal. Let stand 15 minutes. Peel chiles; discard skins. Chop chiles.
3. Heat oil in a large Dutch oven over medium-high heat. Add chicken; cook 4 minutes on each side or until browned. Remove chicken from pan. Add onion

and garlic to pan, and sauté 6 minutes or until browned, stirring frequently. Return chicken to pan. Add broth, 1½ cups water, and cumin; bring to a simmer. Cook 20 minutes or until chicken is done. Remove chicken; cool slightly. Remove chicken from bones; cut meat into bite-sized pieces. Discard bones. Add chicken to pan; stir in chopped chiles and beans.
4. Combine ½ cup water and flour, stirring with a whisk. Stir into chicken mixture. Bring to a simmer; cook 15 minutes. Stir in salt. Spoon about 1½ cups soup into each of 6 bowls; top each serving with 1½ teaspoons sour cream. Serve with lime slices. Yield: 6 servings.

CALORIES 248 (20% from fat); FAT 5.6g (sat 1.5g, mono 1.9g, poly 1.4g); PROTEIN 19.1g; CARB 25.1g; FIBER 4.8g; CHOL 45mg; IRON 3.2mg; SODIUM 903mg; CALC 87mg

---

Chile Course

These soups and stews rely on chiles for heat and much of their flavor. Here are the fresh and dried chiles used in these recipes in order of their heat index (mildest to hottest).

Fresh Chiles
Anaheim: generally mild chiles that can occasionally be hot; often chopped, canned, and labeled "green chiles"
Poblano: dark-colored with meaty flesh; mild to medium in heat; often used to make chiles rellenos
Jalapeño: small chiles that range in heat from hot to fiery; perhaps the most popular and widely available hot chile

Dried Chiles
Guajillo: sweet, medium heat with berry undertones
Ancho: dried poblano chiles that possess a medium heat level; the sweetest of the dried chiles, with a fruity, raisin-like aroma
Chipotle: dried jalapeño peppers that have been smoked; most often found canned in adobo sauce (oniony tomato sauce); have a subtle, deep heat with slight chocolate undertones

MAKE AHEAD

Garbanzo and Greens Stew

There are two types of chorizo sausage in American markets. Mexican chorizo is raw, spiced pork that resembles breakfast sausage, and Spanish chorizo is cured, spiced pork, similar to smoked sausage or salami. Though Mexican chorizo would be more traditional in this soup, it's often much fattier than the Spanish version. If you can't find Spanish chorizo, substitute smoked sausage or kielbasa.

    4 dried guajillo chiles, stemmed and
       seeded
    2 cups boiling water
 2½ cups chopped onion
    8 ounces chopped Spanish chorizo
       sausage
    3 garlic cloves, minced
    9 cups coarsely chopped Swiss
       chard (about ¾ pound)
  ¾ teaspoon ground cumin
  ¼ to ½ teaspoon ground cinnamon
    2 (14-ounce) cans fat-free,
       less-sodium chicken broth
    2 (15½-ounce) cans chickpeas
       (garbanzo beans), rinsed and
       drained
    1 (14.5-ounce) can fire-roasted
       crushed tomatoes, undrained
       (such as Muir Glen)
    8 (6-inch) corn tortillas
    1 cup (4 ounces) crumbled queso fresco

1. Heat a cast-iron skillet over high heat. Place chiles in pan; flatten with a spatula. Cook 5 seconds on each side or until blackened. Combine toasted chiles and boiling water in a bowl; let stand 20 minutes or until soft. Place chile mixture in a blender or food processor; process until smooth.
2. Heat a Dutch oven over medium-high heat. Add onion, chorizo, and garlic; cook 5 minutes or until browned, stirring frequently. Add puréed chile mixture, Swiss chard, and next 5 ingredients; bring to a boil. Reduce heat; simmer 30 minutes. Warm tortillas according to package directions. Sprinkle soup with queso fresco; serve with tortillas. Yield: 8 servings (serving size: about 1½ cups soup, 1 tortilla, and 2 tablespoons cheese).

CALORIES 401 (32% from fat); FAT 14.3g (sat 5.1g, mono 6.1g, poly 2g); PROTEIN 19.4g; CARB 50.9g; FIBER 9.2g; CHOL 30mg; IRON 4.3mg; SODIUM 972mg; CALC 182mg

MAKE AHEAD

Beef and Vegetable Soup
Cocido

When handling achiote paste, wear gloves to avoid staining your hands. If you can't find chayote, use summer squash instead.

    2 tablespoons achiote paste
    2 teaspoons chili powder
 1½ teaspoons salt
    1 teaspoon ground cumin
    1 teaspoon olive oil
  ¼ teaspoon ground red pepper
    4 garlic cloves, minced
    2 pounds boneless sirloin steak,
       trimmed and cut into 1-inch pieces
    1 tablespoon olive oil
    4 cups chopped onion
    2 (14-ounce) cans fat-free,
       less-sodium chicken broth
    1 (14.5-ounce) can fire-roasted
       diced tomatoes with green chiles,
       undrained (such as Muir Glen)
    4 cups cubed peeled baking potato
    3 cups cubed peeled chayote squash
    2 cups (½-inch-thick) slices carrot
    1 tablespoon white wine vinegar

1. Combine first 7 ingredients, stirring with a fork until mixture resembles coarse meal; sprinkle 1½ tablespoons achiote mixture evenly over beef, tossing to coat. Set remaining achiote mixture aside.
2. Heat oil in a Dutch oven over medium-high heat. Add beef mixture; cook 2 minutes, browning on all sides. Remove beef from pan. Add onion to pan; sauté 3 minutes. Add remaining achiote mixture; cook 2 minutes, stirring frequently. Return beef mixture to pan. Stir in broth and tomatoes; bring to a boil. Cover, reduce heat, and simmer 35 minutes. Add potato, chayote, and carrot; cover and simmer 35 minutes or until potato is tender. Remove from heat. Stir in vinegar. Yield: 10 servings (serving size: 1½ cups).

CALORIES 243 (25% from fat); FAT 6.8g (sat 2.1g, mono 3.3g, poly 0.5g); PROTEIN 21.1g; CARB 24.9g; FIBER 4.1g; CHOL 50mg; IRON 2.9mg; SODIUM 607mg; CALC 51mg

Seafood Soup
Caldo de Mariscos

A specialty of the Veracruz coast, this soup is similar to bouillabaisse. Seafood soup—depending on the catch of the day—is found across Mexico, where it's commonly sold in markets as a hangover remedy. We used green-lipped mussels, but blue mussels will give you the same result.

    3 poblano chiles
 1½ teaspoons aniseed
 1½ teaspoons cumin seeds
    2 tablespoons vegetable oil
 1½ cups finely chopped onion
    4 garlic cloves, minced
    2 tablespoons sugar
  ½ teaspoon salt
    4 (8-ounce) bottles clam juice
    2 jalapeño peppers, seeded and
       finely chopped
    1 (28-ounce) can fire-roasted
       crushed tomatoes, undrained
       (such as Muir Glen)
  ¼ cup fresh lime juice
    2 (6-ounce) tilapia fillets, cut into
       2-inch pieces
    1 pound medium shrimp, peeled
       and deveined
    1 pound mussels, scrubbed and
       debearded
  ¾ cup minced fresh cilantro
    8 lime slices

1. Preheat broiler.

2. Cut chiles in half; discard seeds and membranes. Place halves, skin sides up, on a foil-lined baking sheet; flatten with hand. Broil 5 minutes or until blackened. Place in a heavy-duty zip-top plastic bag, and seal. Let stand 15 minutes. Peel chiles; discard skins. Finely chop chiles.

3. Cook aniseed and cumin seeds in a saucepan over medium heat 1 minute or until toasted and fragrant. Place in a spice or coffee grinder, and process until finely ground.

4. Heat oil in a large Dutch oven over medium heat. Add onion and garlic; cook 15 minutes or until onion is browned, stirring occasionally. Add toasted ground spices; cook 1 minute. Add sugar and next 4 ingredients; bring to a simmer. Cook 10 minutes, stirring occasionally. Add chopped poblano chiles, lime juice, tilapia, shrimp, and mussels; bring to a simmer. Cook 5 minutes or until shrimp are done and mussels open; discard any unopened shells. Stir in cilantro, and serve with lime slices. Yield: 8 servings (serving size: 1¾ cups).

CALORIES 253 (24% from fat); FAT 6.8g (sat 1.1g, mono 1.4g, poly 3g); PROTEIN 29.5g; CARB 19.8g; FIBER 3.4g; CHOL 126mg; IRON 6.1mg; SODIUM 806mg; CALC 124mg

Thanks to wider availability of ingredients used in Mexican cooking, you can enjoy the deep, complex flavors of this food at home.

After-School Special

A Chicago teacher uses cooking to teach kids about reading, writing, math—and nutrition.

Seven years ago, Chicago's Douglas Taylor Elementary School principal, Sally Culhane, was searching for ways to keep her students involved in school—always a challenge in Chicago's rough southeast side. Knowing of Gloria Hafer's passion for cooking and excellent rapport with the kids, Culhane asked the physical education teacher to expand her teaching beyond the gymnasium and into the kitchen to form the after-school cooking class and safe haven. Hafer readily agreed to the double duty, and the kids have been just as excited.

While most students can't wait for the bell to ring and rush home, Gloria Hafer's students can't wait to get into the kitchen and start cooking. Here are some of the recipes that Hafer and her students enjoy preparing.

Chicken Vegetable Stew

- 1 tablespoon olive oil
- 4 chicken thighs (about 1 pound), skinned
- 2 chicken breast halves (1 pound), skinned
- 4 cups (1-inch) cubed red potato (about 1¼ pounds)
- 3 cups (1-inch-thick) slices carrot (about 1 pound)
- 1½ cups (1-inch) pieces onion
- 1½ teaspoons garlic powder
- 1 teaspoon onion powder
- ¾ teaspoon black pepper
- ¾ teaspoon salt
- 4 (14-ounce) cans fat-free, less-sodium chicken broth
- ¼ cup all-purpose flour
- ¾ cup water
- 1 (16-ounce) package frozen green peas

1. Heat oil in a large Dutch oven over medium-high heat. Add chicken to pan; cook 5 minutes. Brown on all sides. Add potato and next 6 ingredients; stir well. Add broth; bring to a boil. Cover, reduce heat, and simmer 45 minutes or until chicken is done.

2. Lightly spoon flour into a dry measuring cup; level with a knife. Combine flour and water; stir with a whisk until smooth. Add flour mixture and peas to pan. Bring to a boil; cook 5 minutes. Remove chicken from pan; cool slightly. Remove chicken from bones, and discard bones. Return chicken to pan; stir to combine. Yield: 7 servings (serving size: 2 cups).

CALORIES 332 (23% from fat); FAT 8.4g (sat 2g, mono 3.7g, poly 1.7g); PROTEIN 27.8g; CARB 35.2g; FIBER 6.9g; CHOL 56mg; IRON 3mg; SODIUM 813mg; CALC 56mg

Chicken Cacciatore

Gloria Hafer uses this recipe to teach students how to avoid cross contamination by using separate cutting boards and utensils. Depending on the size of your Dutch oven, you may need to brown the chicken in batches.

- 1 teaspoon onion powder
- 1 teaspoon garlic powder
- 1 teaspoon dried oregano
- 1 teaspoon dried basil
- ¾ teaspoon salt
- ¾ teaspoon freshly ground black pepper
- 6 bone-in chicken breast halves (about 3 pounds), skinned
- 1 tablespoon olive oil
- 2 cups sliced mushrooms
- 1½ cups red bell pepper strips
- 1½ cups green bell pepper strips
- 1 cup thinly vertically sliced onion
- 1 tablespoon balsamic vinegar
- 2 bay leaves
- 1 (28-ounce) can whole tomatoes, undrained and chopped
- 1 (6-ounce) can tomato paste
- 6 cups hot cooked penne (about ¾ pound uncooked tube-shaped pasta)
- ½ cup (2 ounces) grated fresh Parmesan cheese

Continued

1. Combine first 6 ingredients, and sprinkle 4 teaspoons oregano mixture evenly over chicken. Set remaining oregano mixture aside.

2. Heat oil in a large Dutch oven over medium-high heat. Add chicken to pan; cook 2 minutes on each side or until browned. Remove chicken from pan. Add mushrooms, bell peppers, and onion to pan; sprinkle with remaining oregano mixture. Cover and cook 5 minutes or until tender, stirring occasionally. Stir in vinegar, bay leaves, tomatoes, and tomato paste. Arrange chicken over tomato mixture, and bring to a boil. Cover, reduce heat, and simmer 50 minutes or until chicken is done.

3. Place 1 cup pasta in each of 6 shallow bowls; top each serving with 1 chicken breast half. Ladle 1 cup sauce over each serving, and sprinkle each with 4 teaspoons Parmesan cheese. Yield: 6 servings.

CALORIES 533 (13% from fat); FAT 7.8g (sat 2.7g, mono 2.9g, poly 0.8g); PROTEIN 53.9g; CARB 60.6g; FIBER 5.5g; CHOL 105mg; IRON 4.3mg; SODIUM 813mg; CALC 207mg

Chicken Meatball Soup with Pasta

Using ground chicken breast makes the meatballs lower in fat than when using ground beef. If you can't find it, substitute ground turkey breast. This recipe teaches uniformity of size to ensure that all of the meatballs finish cooking at the same time.

MEATBALLS:
- ¾ cup seasoned breadcrumbs
- ½ cup chopped onion
- ¼ cup (1 ounce) grated fresh Parmesan cheese
- 1 tablespoon garlic powder
- 1 tablespoon chopped fresh parsley
- 1 teaspoon onion powder
- 1 teaspoon black pepper
- ½ teaspoon salt
- 2 pounds ground chicken breast
- 2 large eggs, lightly beaten
- Cooking spray

SOUP:
- 3 cups water
- 3 (14-ounce) cans fat-free, less-sodium chicken broth
- 2 cups chopped celery
- ½ cup chopped green onions
- 1 (16-ounce) package frozen mixed vegetables
- 1 cup uncooked small pasta shells
- ¼ cup chopped fresh parsley

1. Preheat oven to 400°.

2. To prepare meatballs, combine first 10 ingredients in a bowl; shape mixture into 48 (1-inch) meatballs. Place meatballs on a jelly-roll pan coated with cooking spray. Bake at 400° for 20 minutes or until done.

3. To prepare soup, bring water and broth to a boil in a Dutch oven. Add celery, onions, and frozen vegetables; cook 10 minutes or until vegetables are tender. Add pasta; cook 8 minutes or until done. Add meatballs, and cook 2 minutes or until thoroughly heated. Place 6 meatballs in each of 8 bowls; divide soup among bowls. Sprinkle evenly with parsley. Yield: 8 servings (serving size: about 1⅓ cups).

CALORIES 302 (13% from fat); FAT 4.4g (sat 1.5g, mono 1.3g, poly 0.8g); PROTEIN 36.3g; CARB 27.8g; FIBER 4.2g; CHOL 121mg; IRON 2.8mg; SODIUM 920mg; CALC 109mg

Chicken Breasts Stuffed with Spinach and Ricotta

"When kids make this recipe, they substitute apple juice or apple cider for the wine," Hafer says. "It makes it sweeter, and the kids enjoy it. This is a great way to get them to eat their spinach because it's rolled with cheese."

FILLING:
- 1 cup part-skim ricotta cheese
- ⅓ cup (about 1½ ounces) grated fresh Parmesan cheese
- ¼ teaspoon salt
- ¼ teaspoon garlic powder
- ¼ teaspoon black pepper
- 1 (10-ounce) package frozen chopped spinach, thawed, drained, and squeezed dry
- 1 large egg, lightly beaten

CHICKEN:
- 6 (6-ounce) skinless, boneless chicken breast halves
- ½ cup dry white wine

1. To prepare filling, combine first 7 ingredients.

2. Preheat oven to 350°.

3. To prepare chicken, place each chicken breast half between 2 sheets of heavy-duty plastic wrap; pound to ¼-inch thickness using a meat mallet or rolling pin. Divide filling into 6 equal portions, and spread evenly over chicken breast halves. Roll up jelly-roll fashion. Tuck in sides; place chicken, seam sides down, in a 13 x 9-inch baking dish. Pour wine over chicken. Cover dish with foil.

4. Bake at 350° for 30 minutes, basting chicken with wine every 10 minutes. Uncover and bake an additional 15 minutes or until chicken is done. Remove chicken from baking dish; keep warm. Strain wine mixture through a sieve into a bowl; discard solids. Serve wine mixture over chicken. Yield: 6 servings (serving size: 1 stuffed breast and 3 tablespoons wine mixture).

CALORIES 265 (25% from fat); FAT 7.3g (sat 3.6g, mono 2.1g, poly 0.7g); PROTEIN 40.5g; CARB 4.7g; FIBER 1.5g; CHOL 131mg; IRON 2.4mg; SODIUM 367mg; CALC 247mg

in season

Sensational Sunchokes

Try these delightful dishes from the kitchen.

In season from October to March, knobby, thin-skinned vegetables called Jerusalem artichokes or "sunchokes" sometimes resemble fresh gingerroot. They possess the crunch of water chestnuts and the sweet, nutty taste of artichoke hearts. It's easy to remove their skin with a vegetable peeler, but because the skin is so thin, sunchokes can also be left unpeeled. Raw, their crunch and delicate flavor are right at home in salads. They also work well roasted, steamed, or boiled and mashed with or in place of potatoes.

Roasted Sunchokes and Fennel

Roasting minimally seasoned sunchokes allows their true flavor to shine through. With crisp, browned skin and tender flesh, they taste like a cross between a baked potato and an artichoke heart.

1 tablespoon olive oil
1 teaspoon finely chopped fresh rosemary
½ teaspoon salt
¼ teaspoon black pepper
1½ pounds Jerusalem artichokes (sunchokes), quartered
1 fennel bulb, cut into 8 wedges
Cooking spray

1. Preheat oven to 475°.
2. Combine first 6 ingredients in a large bowl, tossing well to coat. Arrange artichoke mixture in a single layer on a baking sheet coated with cooking spray. Bake at 475° for 35 minutes or until golden brown and tender. Yield: 4 servings (serving size: 1¼ cups).

CALORIES 138 (23% from fat); FAT 3.5g (sat 0.5g, mono 2.5g, poly 0.3g); PROTEIN 3.1g; CARB 24.9g; FIBER 3.7g; CHOL 0mg; IRON 4.5mg; SODIUM 329mg; CALC 48mg

A Sunchoke by Any Other Name

Jerusalem artichokes don't come from Jerusalem, nor are they artichokes. So why the confusing moniker? There are several explanations. One has to do with the fact that this native North American tuber, which tastes something like globe artichokes, became a staple in the New World, which was often referred to as "new Jerusalem." Another is that the "Jerusalem" name is a corruption of Ter Neusen, the place in Holland that exported the tubers to England. But perhaps the most widespread explanation is that "Jerusalem" sounds very much like the Italian word for sunflower, *girasol*.

Spicy Chicken and Sunchoke Stir-Fry

Sunchokes take the place of water chestnuts in this tasty stir-fry. Look for Thai peanut sauce in your supermarket's ethnic foods aisle.

8 ounces wide rice stick noodles (*banh pho*)
2 tablespoons vegetable oil
4 cups vertically sliced onion
3 garlic cloves, minced
1½ pounds Jerusalem artichokes (sunchokes), peeled and cut into ½-inch pieces (about 3 cups)
1 pound skinless, boneless chicken breast, cut into 1-inch strips
3 tablespoons Thai peanut sauce
2 tablespoons low-sodium soy sauce
2 tablespoons natural-style peanut butter (such as Smucker's)
6 cups broccoli florets
2 cups (¼-inch) red bell pepper strips
1 cup water
½ teaspoon crushed red pepper

1. Cook noodles in boiling water 5 minutes or until done. Drain noodles; keep warm.
2. Heat oil in a wok or large nonstick skillet over medium-high heat. Add onion and garlic; stir-fry 2 minutes. Add artichokes and chicken; stir-fry 4 minutes. Remove from heat; stir in peanut sauce, soy sauce, and peanut butter. Place pan over medium-high heat; cook 4 minutes, stirring frequently. Add broccoli, bell pepper, water, and crushed red pepper; cook 5 minutes or until broccoli is tender, stirring frequently. Serve immediately over noodles. Yield: 6 servings (serving size: 1 cup noodles and 1⅓ cups stir-fry).

CALORIES 432 (21% from fat); FAT 10.2g (sat 1.6g, mono 2.7g, poly 3.9g); PROTEIN 26g; CARB 60.5g; FIBER 6.6g; CHOL 44mg; IRON 4.8mg; SODIUM 469mg; CALC 87mg

---

Sunchoke Latkes

Use the shredder blade of a food processor to quickly shred the artichokes, potato, and carrot. Cook the latkes soon after combining the ingredients so the mixture doesn't become watery; if it does, though, remove the mixture from the liquid using a slotted spoon.

1½ pounds Jerusalem artichokes (sunchokes), peeled and shredded
1 pound baking potatoes, peeled and shredded
1 large carrot, peeled and shredded
⅓ cup all-purpose flour
1 teaspoon salt
¼ teaspoon black pepper
1 large egg, lightly beaten
1 large egg white, lightly beaten
2½ tablespoons olive oil, divided
6 tablespoons fat-free sour cream

1. Place first 3 ingredients in a large bowl, and toss gently to combine. Lightly spoon flour into a dry measuring cup; level with a knife. Add flour, salt, and pepper to artichoke mixture; toss gently to combine. Add egg and egg white; stir just until combined.
2. Heat half of oil in a large nonstick skillet over medium-high heat. Spoon about ¼ cup artichoke mixture for each of 9 latkes into pan. Cook 3 minutes on each side or until browned. Remove from pan. Repeat procedure with remaining oil and artichoke mixture. Serve with sour cream. Yield: 6 servings (serving size: 3 latkes and 1 tablespoon sour cream).

CALORIES 216 (28% from fat); FAT 6.6g (sat 1g, mono 4.5g, poly 0.6g); PROTEIN 6.8g; CARB 32.1g; FIBER 3.1g; CHOL 38mg; IRON 3.7mg; SODIUM 445mg; CALC 54mg

Sunchoke and Tomato Gratin

Tomatoes, basil, olives, and Parmesan cheese add a taste of the Mediterranean to nutty-flavored sunchokes. Parboiling the sunchokes is necessary to ensure that they're tender.

 1 pound Jerusalem artichokes (sunchokes), cut into ¼-inch-thick slices (about 4 cups)
 2 teaspoons olive oil
 4 cups thinly vertically sliced onion
 2 garlic cloves, minced
 ½ cup thinly sliced celery
 2 tablespoons tomato paste
 ½ teaspoon fennel seeds, crushed
 ⅛ teaspoon salt
 1 (28-ounce) can whole tomatoes, undrained and coarsely chopped
 1 bay leaf
 Cooking spray
 ½ cup (2 ounces) grated fresh Parmesan cheese
 ¼ cup sliced ripe olives
 2 tablespoons thinly sliced fresh basil

1. Preheat oven to 375°.
2. Cook artichokes in boiling water 5 minutes. Drain; set aside.
3. Heat oil in a large nonstick skillet over medium-high heat. Add onion and garlic; sauté 5 minutes or until tender. Add artichokes, celery, and next 5 ingredients; cook 5 minutes or until thoroughly heated. Discard bay leaf. Spoon onion mixture into a 13 x 9-inch baking dish coated with cooking spray. Sprinkle with cheese and olives. Cover and bake at 375° for 20 minutes. Uncover and bake an additional 35 minutes or until artichokes are tender and cheese is golden brown. Sprinkle with basil. Yield: 6 servings (serving size: about ¾ cup).

CALORIES 160 (28% from fat); FAT 4.9g (sat 1.9g, mono 2.3g, poly 0.4g); PROTEIN 7.1g; CARB 24g; FIBER 4.2g; CHOL 6mg; IRON 3.2mg; SODIUM 462mg; CALC 188mg

How to Purchase and Store Sunchokes

Green grocers, health-food stores, and some large supermarkets stock Jerusalem artichokes from fall to spring, available either in bulk or in packages labeled "sunchokes." You can also find them on farm stands throughout the United States and Canada. Select unblemished large, firm tubers. Keep them wrapped in plastic (to help prevent moisture loss) in the refrigerator up to 1 week. To prevent peeled tubers from discoloring, keep them submerged in water.

QUICK & EASY
Sunchoke-Chicken Salad Wraps

This recipe highlights the crunchy texture of raw sunchokes, which add a nutty flavor that heightens the taste of the pecans.

 ¼ cup chopped pecans, toasted
 5 ounces Jerusalem artichokes (sunchokes), peeled and chopped (about 1 cup)
 ½ cup (4 ounces) block-style fat-free cream cheese, softened
 3 tablespoons light mayonnaise
 1 tablespoon fresh lemon juice
 ¼ teaspoon salt
 ⅛ teaspoon ground red pepper
 2 cups shredded skinless, boneless rotisserie chicken breast
 6 (8-inch) fat-free flour tortillas
 12 (⅛-inch-thick) slices tomato
 3 cups shredded leaf lettuce

1. Combine pecans and artichokes in a food processor; pulse 5 times or until finely chopped.
2. Combine cream cheese and next 4 ingredients in a large bowl; stir until smooth. Stir in artichoke mixture and chicken. Spread ⅓ cup artichoke mixture over each tortilla; top each with 2 tomato slices and ½ cup lettuce. Roll up. Yield: 6 servings (serving size: 1 wrap).

CALORIES 298 (24% from fat); FAT 8g (sat 1.3g, mono 4.1g, poly 1.5g); PROTEIN 20.6g; CARB 25.4g; FIBER 3.7g; CHOL 46mg; IRON 1.7mg; SODIUM 512mg; CALC 87mg

season's best
Candy Corn Popcorn Balls

Sweet, crunchy, buttery, and studded with a quintessential Halloween treat, our Candy Corn Popcorn Balls go hand in hand with trick-or-treating and fall festivals.

They're a sure hit with kids, who will delight in shaping the gooey marshmallows and popcorn into their own masterpieces. (Who says popcorn balls have to be round?) Since this is the season of mystery, it's a good time to ponder how popcorn pops. Each kernel contains a small amount of water that expands as the kernel heats up. When the pressure becomes too great, it bursts. Happy Halloween!

QUICK & EASY • MAKE AHEAD
Candy Corn Popcorn Balls

If kids are helping shape these treats, make sure the marshmallow mixture is cool enough for them to handle. Store the confections in an airtight container up to 3 days.

 8 cups popped light butter microwave popcorn (about 1 [3-ounce] bag)
 1 cup candy corn
 ¼ cup butter
 ¼ teaspoon salt
 1 (10-ounce) bag marshmallows
 Cooking spray

1. Combine popcorn and candy corn in a large bowl.
2. Melt butter in a large saucepan over medium heat; stir in salt and marshmallows. Reduce heat to low; cook 7 minutes or until marshmallows melt and mixture is smooth, stirring frequently.
3. Pour marshmallow mixture over popcorn mixture; stir to coat well. Lightly coat hands with cooking spray; shape popcorn mixture into 20 (2-inch) balls. Yield: 20 servings (serving size: 1 popcorn ball).

CALORIES 212 (12% from fat); FAT 2.9g (sat 1.6g, mono 0.1g, poly 0.1g); PROTEIN 0.5g; CARB 47.6g; FIBER 0.4g; CHOL 6mg; IRON 0.1mg; SODIUM 73mg; CALC 1mg

Stress-Free Entertaining with Donata Maggipinto

Successful dinner parties don't have to be complicated or fussy. Keep it simple, yet stylish, to make a big impression.

Donata Maggipinto is the entertaining and home style contributor for NBC's *Today* show. Donata advocates a relaxed, real-life approach to entertaining. "I'm a hybrid cook, stylist, and nester," she says. "I'm often referred to as a 'lifestyle expert' but consider myself a creative spark for those who want to punctuate their cooking with simple, yet stylish, recipes, their tables with graceful settings, and their homes with beauty and comfort.

"When it comes to entertaining, great food and easy style are symbiotic. My entertaining philosophy can be summed up in five words: the simplest route to 'wow.' The recipes here all have casual, stylish flair. Use them together as a complete menu, or integrate them with your own favorite dishes. Remember, all you need to entertain are an enthusiastic attitude and a desire to share your home and hospitality with others."

Mix-and-Match Dinner Party Menu
serves 6

Warm Olives with Fennel and Orange

Peppered Garlic Confit with Prosciutto

Persimmon-Walnut Oil Salad or **Red Lettuce Salad with Citrus Vinaigrette**

Mustard-Crusted Lamb Chops served with **Bay Leaf and Thyme-Scented Roasted Winter Squash and Garlic**
or
Triple-Pepper Steamed Halibut served with **Saffron Couscous**

Sautéed Cherry Tomatoes with Shallots

Bittersweet Chocolate Sorbet

MAKE AHEAD
Warm Olives with Fennel and Orange

It's amazing what changing the expected temperature of a dish can do to incite cocktail conversation. Gentle heat from the oven awakens the briny richness of olives, while fennel, orange, rosemary, and balsamic vinegar assert their own personalities to brighten the overall flavor of this appetizer. Purchase pitted kalamata olives to speed up preparation.

  1 tablespoon extravirgin olive oil
1½ teaspoons grated orange rind
  1 teaspoon chopped fresh rosemary
 ½ teaspoon fennel seeds
  1 small fennel bulb, cut into ¼-inch-thick wedges
12 kalamata olives, pitted
12 pimiento-stuffed olives
  1 tablespoon balsamic vinegar

1. Heat oil in a large nonstick skillet over medium heat. Add rind, rosemary, fennel seeds, and fennel wedges; cook 5 minutes, stirring frequently. Add olives; cook 1 minute. Remove from heat; stir in vinegar. Place fennel mixture in an 8-inch square baking dish. Cover and let stand at least 2 hours.
2. Preheat oven to 250°.
3. Uncover olive mixture. Bake at 250° for 10 minutes or until heated; stir once. Yield: 6 servings (serving size: about ⅓ cup).

CALORIES 72 (71% from fat); FAT 5.7g (sat 0.3g, mono 4.7g, poly 0.7g); PROTEIN 0.5g; CARB 5.2g; FIBER 1.3g; CHOL 0mg; IRON 0.4mg; SODIUM 331mg; CALC 24mg

---

STAFF FAVORITE • MAKE AHEAD
Peppered Garlic Confit with Prosciutto

Though it's best eaten straightaway, you can also make the confit up to 1 day in advance, and warm before serving. The flavors are concentrated, so a little goes a long way.

  2 whole garlic heads
  3 tablespoons olive oil
 ¼ cup chopped prosciutto (about 1 ounce)
  1 teaspoon coarsely ground black pepper
24 (½-inch-thick) slices diagonally cut French bread baguette
Chopped fresh parsley (optional)

1. Preheat oven to 350°.
2. Remove white papery skin from garlic heads (do not peel or separate cloves). Wrap each head separately in foil. Bake at 350° for 1 hour; cool 10 minutes. Separate cloves; squeeze to extract garlic pulp. Discard skins.
3. Heat oil in a small saucepan over medium heat. Add prosciutto and pepper; cook 5 minutes, stirring occasionally. Combine garlic pulp and prosciutto mixture in a small bowl, stirring with a fork until well blended. Serve with bread slices. Garnish with parsley, if desired. Yield: 12 servings (serving size: 2 bread slices and 1½ teaspoons garlic mixture).

CALORIES 120 (34% from fat); FAT 4.5g (sat 0.7g, mono 2.9g, poly 0.5g); PROTEIN 3.4g; CARB 16.5g; FIBER 1g; CHOL 1mg; IRON 0.9mg; SODIUM 209mg; CALC 31mg

All you need to entertain is an enthusiastic attitude and a desire to share your home and hospitality with others.

Entertaining Ideas and Know-How

Creating a Beautiful Presentation

We feast with our eyes as well as our palates. For memorable dishes, do the following:

• Consider the **colors and shapes** that will be on the plate, and strive for variation. A rectangular-shaped grilled salmon fillet looks wonderful beside small, round roasted red potatoes and long, slender green beans.

• The more **natural** you are with the food, the better. Don't worry about fancy presentations. Instead, garnish plates simply with fresh herbs or slices of lemon and lime.

• **Present** in a way that makes you—and your guests—comfortable. Plate each dish individually, serve food family-style on large platters, or assemble a buffet and let guests help themselves.

How to Compose a Menu

It's a snap to compose a visually appealing, palate-pleasing menu when you keep these tips in mind.

• **Color.** Strive for a variety of hues on the plate. An all-white menu of poached halibut, cauliflower, and mashed potatoes is as boring to look at as it is to eat. On the other hand, multicolored Triple-Pepper Steamed Halibut (recipe on page 363), golden Saffron Couscous (recipe on page 363), and bright-red Sautéed Cherry Tomatoes with Shallots (recipe on page 364) are fresh and vibrant.

• **Texture.** Again, variety is key. Opt for a combination of chewy, creamy, and crunchy foods, such as Mustard-Crusted Lamb Chops (recipe on page 363), Bay Leaf and Thyme-Scented Roasted Winter Squash and Garlic (recipe on page 363), and Red Lettuce Salad with Citrus Vinaigrette (recipe on page 363).

• **Flavor.** Don't go overboard on any one flavor. For example, a chicken breast marinated in soy sauce shouldn't be served with asparagus with black olives and roasted potatoes with sea salt—too salty. A good rule of thumb: Stick with seasonal ingredients, vary them, and minimally season them so their true flavors shine, and you'll be fine.

Five Must-Have Ingredients for Autumn Entertaining

Not counting Champagne and macadamia nuts, which transform any occasion into a party, here are five foods that will ensure you can handle a last-minute get-together with finesse:

1. Arborio rice
2. Dried porcini mushrooms
3. Marinated artichoke hearts
4. Frozen organic spinach
5. A selection of sorbets

   Use the rice to make a risotto flavored with the mushrooms and artichoke hearts; serve alongside the spinach (sautéed with a little olive oil, lemon zest, and red pepper). Finish the meal with sorbet. And don't forget the Champagne and macadamias.

Persimmon-Walnut Oil Salad

This simple salad is made special with the use of high-quality ingredients. Choose crisp, globe-shaped Fuyu persimmons, which remain firm even when ripe—making them an ideal ingredient for fall salads. The heart-shaped Hachiya persimmon, which doesn't become sweet until its flesh is quite soft, is better suited for baking.

3 tablespoons Champagne vinegar
1 tablespoon walnut oil
¼ teaspoon salt
¼ teaspoon freshly ground black pepper
8 cups torn romaine lettuce
3 Fuyu persimmons, peeled, cored, and thinly sliced (about 2 cups)

1. Combine first 4 ingredients in a large bowl, stirring with a whisk. Add lettuce and persimmons; toss gently to coat. Yield: 6 servings (serving size: about 1¼ cups).

CALORIES 47 (48% from fat); FAT 2.5g (sat 0.2g, mono 0.5g, poly 1.5g); PROTEIN 1.3g; CARB 6g; FIBER 1.5g; CHOL 0mg; IRON 1.2mg; SODIUM 105mg; CALC 31mg

Easy Uptown Dinner Menu
serves 6

Supersimple doesn't have to mean predictable. This meal has an upscale feel while still being appropriate for a weeknight dinner. Prepare the salad while the beef cooks.

Red Lettuce Salad with Citrus Vinaigrette

Peppercorn and mustard-crusted beef tenderloin*

French bread

*Rub 1½ tablespoons whole-grain Dijon mustard, ¾ teaspoon chopped fresh thyme, ½ teaspoon salt, and ½ teaspoon cracked black pepper over a 1½-pound beef tenderloin. Secure beef at 1-inch intervals with twine. Place on a broiler pan coated with cooking spray. Bake at 475° for 30 minutes or until desired degree of doneness. Let stand 10 minutes before slicing.

Red Lettuce Salad with Citrus Vinaigrette

Make the vinaigrette up to 1 day ahead; toss with the salad just before serving.

1½ tablespoons fresh orange juice
1½ tablespoons fresh grapefruit juice
2 teaspoons extravirgin olive oil
1 teaspoon grated lemon rind
1 teaspoon fresh lemon juice
1 teaspoon honey
¼ teaspoon salt
¼ teaspoon freshly ground black pepper
8 cups torn red leaf lettuce
2 cups torn radicchio
⅓ cup dried cranberries
1 tablespoon roasted sunflower seed kernels

1. Combine first 8 ingredients in a large bowl, stirring with a whisk. Add lettuce and remaining ingredients; toss gently to coat. Yield: 6 servings (serving size: about 1⅓ cups).

CALORIES 68 (33% from fat); FAT 2.5g (sat 0.3g, mono 1.3g, poly 0.8g); PROTEIN 1.6g; CARB 11g; FIBER 2.1g; CHOL 0mg; IRON 1.3mg; SODIUM 108mg; CALC 57mg

Mustard-Crusted Lamb Chops

Marinate the lamb earlier in the day.

¼ cup stone-ground mustard
3 tablespoons chopped fresh rosemary
3 tablespoons red wine vinegar
¾ teaspoon Worcestershire sauce
½ teaspoon salt
½ teaspoon freshly ground black pepper
5 garlic cloves, minced
12 (4-ounce) lamb loin chops, trimmed
Cooking spray

1. Combine first 7 ingredients in a large zip-top plastic bag. Add lamb; seal and marinate in refrigerator 1 hour or up to 8 hours, turning bag occasionally.
2. Prepare grill or grill pan to medium-high heat.

3. Remove lamb from bag; discard marinade. Place lamb on grill rack or grill pan coated with cooking spray; cook 6 minutes on each side or until medium-rare or desired degree of doneness. Yield: 6 servings (serving size: 2 chops).

CALORIES 230 (37% from fat); FAT 9.5g (sat 3.4g, mono 4.1g, poly 0.6g); PROTEIN 29.4g; CARB 3.6g; FIBER 1.5g; CHOL 90mg; IRON 2.4mg; SODIUM 443mg; CALC 41mg

Bay Leaf and Thyme-Scented Roasted Winter Squash and Garlic

Whole, unpeeled garlic cloves roast along with butternut squash in this aromatic side dish. Give each guest a couple of garlic cloves, and invite them to extract the mellow roasted pulp over the squash.

10 cups (2-inch) cubed peeled butternut squash (about 3 pounds)
1 tablespoon olive oil
¾ teaspoon salt
¼ teaspoon freshly ground black pepper
12 garlic cloves, unpeeled
8 thyme sprigs
6 bay leaves
Cooking spray

1. Preheat oven to 450°.
2. Combine first 7 ingredients in a large bowl; toss to coat. Arrange in a single layer on a jelly-roll pan coated with cooking spray. Bake at 450° for 45 minutes or until tender, stirring after 20 minutes. Discard thyme and bay leaves before serving. Yield: 6 servings (serving size: 1 cup).

CALORIES 131 (17% from fat); FAT 2.5g (sat 0.4g, mono 1.7g, poly 0.3g); PROTEIN 2.7g; CARB 28.6g; FIBER 7.9g; CHOL 0mg; IRON 1.7mg; SODIUM 303mg; CALC 120mg

Triple-Pepper Steamed Halibut

This colorful entrée is inspired by the Italian vegetable dish *peperonata*, which includes sweet bell peppers, garlic, and onions. Use a large, 2-inch-deep skillet to make sure everything fits.

1½ tablespoons olive oil
4 cups vertically sliced yellow onion
2½ cups (½-inch) strips red bell pepper (about 2 large)
2½ cups (½-inch) strips yellow bell pepper (about 2 large)
2½ cups (½-inch) strips orange bell pepper (about 2 large)
¾ teaspoon salt, divided
½ teaspoon freshly ground black pepper, divided
4 garlic cloves, minced
1 cup dry white wine
¼ cup chopped fresh basil
2 tablespoons chopped fresh oregano
6 (6-ounce) halibut fillets

1. Heat oil in a large nonstick skillet over medium-high heat. Add onion, bell peppers, ¼ teaspoon salt, ¼ teaspoon black pepper, and garlic; sauté 20 minutes or until tender. Stir in wine, basil, and oregano; cook 1 minute. Sprinkle fillets with ½ teaspoon salt and ¼ teaspoon black pepper; arrange fillets over bell pepper mixture. Cover, reduce heat, and simmer 10 minutes or until fish flakes easily when tested with a fork. Yield: 6 servings (serving size: 1 fillet and ¾ cup bell pepper mixture).

CALORIES 298 (24% from fat); FAT 7.8g (sat 1.1g, mono 3.8g, poly 1.8g); PROTEIN 38.1g; CARB 18.8g; FIBER 4.8g; CHOL 54mg; IRON 2.7mg; SODIUM 394mg; CALC 127mg

Saffron Couscous

Earthy saffron is lifted by peppery green onions in this quick side dish. Serve with Triple-Pepper Steamed Halibut (recipe at left) to soak up the tasty juices.

2¼ cups fat-free, less-sodium chicken broth
¼ teaspoon saffron threads, crushed
2 tablespoons olive oil
1½ cups uncooked couscous
½ teaspoon hot pepper sauce
¼ teaspoon salt
¼ teaspoon freshly ground black pepper
⅓ cup chopped green onion tops

Continued

1. Bring broth to a simmer in a small saucepan. Add saffron, stirring to dissolve. Cover and keep warm.

2. Heat oil in a medium saucepan over medium-high heat. Add couscous; cook 1 minute, stirring constantly. Add broth mixture, hot sauce, salt, and pepper; bring to a boil. Cover, remove from heat, and let stand 5 minutes. Fluff with a fork; stir in onions. Yield: 6 servings (serving size: ⅔ cup).

CALORIES 212 (20% from fat); FAT 4.8g (sat 0.7g, mono 3.4g, poly 0.5g); PROTEIN 6.7g; CARB 34.4g; FIBER 2.4g; CHOL 0mg; IRON 0.5mg; SODIUM 275mg; CALC 11mg

---

QUICK & EASY
Sautéed Cherry Tomatoes with Shallots

Heat brings out the inherent sweetness of the tomatoes, while shallots give them a soft garlic-onion bite. Once the tomatoes pop, they're ready to serve. The ripeness of the tomatoes will determine how long they need to cook; the riper the tomatoes, the less time they'll need to pop. Grape tomatoes also work well in this recipe.

  2 teaspoons olive oil
  3 tablespoons finely chopped
     shallots (about 1 large)
  4 cups cherry tomatoes
  ¼ cup chopped fresh parsley
  ½ teaspoon salt
  ¼ teaspoon freshly ground black
     pepper

1. Heat oil in a large nonstick skillet over medium heat. Add shallots; cook 2½ minutes or until tender, stirring occasionally. Add tomatoes; cook 5 minutes or until slightly soft and thoroughly heated. Remove from heat. Stir in parsley, salt, and pepper. Serve immediately. Yield: 6 servings (serving size: about ½ cup).

CALORIES 39 (44% from fat); FAT 1.9g (sat 0.3g, mono 1.2g, poly 0.3g); PROTEIN 1.1g; CARB 5.7g; FIBER 1.2g; CHOL 0mg; IRON 0.7mg; SODIUM 206mg; CALC 11mg

---

MAKE AHEAD • FREEZABLE
Bittersweet Chocolate Sorbet

The deep chocolate flavor and rich consistency belie this dessert's low-fat status. Freeze the sorbet up to 2 days in advance; let stand at room temperature 15 minutes to soften before scooping.

  2½ cups water
  1¼ cups sugar
   ½ cup unsweetened cocoa
    3 ounces bittersweet chocolate,
       finely chopped
    2 teaspoons vanilla extract

1. Bring water to a boil in a medium saucepan. Stir in sugar and cocoa; reduce heat, and simmer 5 minutes, stirring frequently. Remove from heat; add chocolate and vanilla, stirring until chocolate melts. Cover and chill completely.

2. Pour chocolate mixture into freezer can of an ice-cream freezer; freeze according to manufacturer's instructions. Spoon sorbet into a freezer-safe container; cover and freeze 1 hour or until firm. Yield: 6 servings (serving size: about ⅔ cup).

CALORIES 253 (25% from fat); FAT 7.1g (sat 4.3g, mono 1.2g, poly 0.1g); PROTEIN 2.4g; CARB 52.8g; FIBER 3.4g; CHOL 0mg; IRON 1.4mg; SODIUM 2mg; CALC 10mg

---

inspired vegetarian

Fall's Convenient Comforts

Turn to the slow cooker for easy meatless meals.

The first chill of autumn stirs our cravings for rich bean soups, warming stews, and other hearty fare. But many folks put off such long-cooking dishes until the weekend, when they have more time to devote to the task. With an electric slow cooker, though, you can enjoy these dishes any night of the week, even after a long day at work. Here are just a few vegetarian slow-cooker greats.

MAKE AHEAD
White Bean, Artichoke, and Chard Ragoût with Fennel Relish

A crunchy topping of raw fennel and bell peppers makes an ideal accompaniment to the mellow flavors of this slow-simmered stew of beans and vegetables. You can make and refrigerate the relish up to 1 day ahead to save time.

RAGOÛT:

  1 tablespoon olive oil
  3 cups thinly sliced leek (about
     2 large)
  1 cup (½-inch-thick) slices carrot
  3 garlic cloves, minced
  3 cups cooked cannellini or Great
     Northern beans
  2½ cups chopped fennel bulb (about
     1 large)
  2 cups (½-inch) cubed red potatoes
  1 cup chopped red bell pepper
  ¾ cup water
  1 teaspoon dried basil
  ¾ teaspoon salt
  ¼ teaspoon dried oregano
  ¼ teaspoon black pepper
  1 (14.5-ounce) can diced tomatoes with
     basil, garlic, and oregano, drained
  1 (14-ounce) can vegetable broth
  1 (9-ounce) package frozen
     artichoke hearts, thawed
  2 cups chopped Swiss chard

RELISH:

  1 cup boiling water
  6 sun-dried tomatoes, packed
     without oil
  3 cups shredded fennel bulb (about
     1 large)
  1 cup coarsely chopped yellow bell
     pepper
  ¼ cup chopped fresh parsley
  1 tablespoon fresh lemon juice
  2 teaspoons olive oil
  ½ teaspoon sugar
  ¼ teaspoon salt
  ⅛ teaspoon black pepper

1. To prepare ragoût, heat 1 tablespoon oil in a large nonstick skillet over medium heat. Add leek, carrot, and garlic; cover and cook 5 minutes or until tender.

2. Place leek mixture in a 5-quart electric slow cooker. Add beans and next 11 ingredients. Cover and cook on high-heat setting 8 hours or until vegetables are tender. Add chard; stir until chard wilts.

3. To prepare relish, combine boiling water and sun-dried tomatoes; let stand 15 minutes or until soft. Drain; chop. Combine sun-dried tomatoes and remaining 8 ingredients; let stand 30 minutes. Yield: 6 servings (serving size: 2 cups ragoût and about ½ cup relish).

CALORIES 290 (16% from fat); FAT 5.3g (sat 0.8g, mono 2.8g, poly 0.7g); PROTEIN 13.6g; CARB 52.4g; FIBER 15.6g; CHOL 0mg; IRON 5.5mg; SODIUM 885mg; CALC 191mg

MAKE AHEAD

Vegetable and Chickpea Curry

Aromatic Indian spices mingle with chickpeas, green beans, and potatoes. Coconut milk is stirred into the cooked curry for a creamy finish. Serve over quick-cooking couscous.

- 1 tablespoon olive oil
- 1½ cups chopped onion
- 1 cup (¼-inch-thick) slices carrot
- 1 tablespoon curry powder
- 1 teaspoon brown sugar
- 1 teaspoon grated peeled fresh ginger
- 2 garlic cloves, minced
- 1 serrano chile, seeded and minced
- 3 cups cooked chickpeas (garbanzo beans)
- 1½ cups cubed peeled baking potato
- 1 cup coarsely chopped green bell pepper
- 1 cup (1-inch) cut green beans
- ½ teaspoon salt
- ¼ teaspoon black pepper
- ⅛ teaspoon ground red pepper
- 1 (14.5-ounce) can diced tomatoes, undrained
- 1 (14-ounce) can vegetable broth
- 3 cups fresh baby spinach
- 1 cup light coconut milk
- 6 lemon wedges

1. Heat oil in a large nonstick skillet over medium heat. Add onion and carrot;

cover and cook 5 minutes or until tender. Add curry powder and next 4 ingredients; cook 1 minute, stirring constantly.

2. Place onion mixture in a 5-quart electric slow cooker. Stir in chickpeas and next 8 ingredients. Cover and cook on high-heat setting 6 hours or until vegetables are tender. Add spinach and coconut milk; stir until spinach wilts. Serve with lemon wedges. Yield: 6 servings (serving size: 1⅓ cups vegetable mixture and 1 lemon wedge).

CALORIES 276 (23% from fat); FAT 7.2g (sat 1.9g, mono 2.3g, poly 1.3g); PROTEIN 10.9g; CARB 44.7g; FIBER 10.6g; CHOL 0mg; IRON 4.3mg; SODIUM 623mg; CALC 107mg

MAKE AHEAD

Barley-Stuffed Cabbage Rolls with Pine Nuts and Currants

This dish works well assembled the night before, so a little planning gives you a great head start on the next day's dinner. Trimming away part of the thick center vein from the cabbage leaves makes them more pliable and easier to roll up. Try stirring in one cup thawed frozen meatless crumbles in place of or in addition to the feta cheese. You can also cook the rolls on low-heat setting for 6 to 8 hours.

- 1 large head green cabbage, cored
- 1 tablespoon olive oil
- 1½ cups finely chopped onion
- 3 cups cooked pearl barley
- ¾ cup (3 ounces) crumbled feta cheese
- ½ cup dried currants
- 2 tablespoons pine nuts, toasted
- 2 tablespoons chopped fresh parsley
- ½ teaspoon salt, divided
- ¼ teaspoon black pepper, divided
- ½ cup apple juice
- 1 tablespoon cider vinegar
- 1 (14.5-ounce) can crushed tomatoes, undrained

1. Steam cabbage head 8 minutes; cool slightly. Remove 16 leaves from cabbage head; reserve remaining leaves for another use. Cut off raised portion of

center vein of each cabbage leaf (do not cut out vein); set trimmed cabbage leaves aside.

2. Heat oil in a large nonstick skillet over medium heat. Add onion; cover and cook 6 minutes or until tender. Remove from heat; stir in barley and next 4 ingredients. Stir in ¼ teaspoon salt and ⅛ teaspoon pepper.

3. Place cabbage leaves on a flat surface; spoon about ⅓ cup barley mixture into center of each cabbage leaf. Fold in edges of leaves over barley mixture; roll up. Arrange cabbage rolls in bottom of a 5-quart electric slow cooker.

4. Combine ¼ teaspoon salt, ⅛ teaspoon pepper, apple juice, vinegar, and tomatoes; pour evenly over cabbage rolls. Cover and cook on high-heat setting 2 hours or until thoroughly heated. Yield: 4 servings (serving size: 4 cabbage rolls and 2 tablespoons sauce).

CALORIES 402 (25% from fat); FAT 11.3g (sat 4.2g, mono 4.4g, poly 1.9g); PROTEIN 11.3g; CARB 70.1g; FIBER 11.3g; CHOL 19mg; IRON 5mg; SODIUM 693mg; CALC 234mg

---

Tips for Slow-Cooking Success

- For the best results, be sure your cooker is between half and three-quarters full when beginning a recipe. Slow cookers come in a variety of sizes, from one to seven quarts. These recipes were tested in a five-quart model.
- Many recipes benefit when you sauté some of the ingredients (such as onions) for a few minutes before adding them to the slow cooker. Doing so enhances the flavors and ensures that all the components of the dish will be done at the same time.
- Add delicate ingredients, such as fresh herbs, at the end of cooking time for the brightest, freshest flavor.
- Prepare starchy ingredients like pasta and rice separately, since they can become gummy when prepared in the slow cooker.

How to Slow-Cook Beans

For any of the recipes that call for cooked beans, try these basic instructions for slow-cooked beans. Or you can use canned beans that have been rinsed and drained.

1. Sort 1 pound dried beans, discarding misshapen or broken ones and pebbles.

2. Place beans in a colander; rinse under cold running water. Drain.

3. Place beans in a large bowl or Dutch oven. (Allow enough room for beans to expand as they absorb water.) Cover with cold water to 2 inches above beans; cover and let stand 8 hours or overnight.

4. Drain beans. Combine beans; 6 cups water; 1 small onion, cut in half; 1 crushed garlic clove; and 1 bay leaf in a 5-quart electric slow cooker.

5. Cover and cook on high-heat setting until tender. Times differ according to many variables: the type of bean, age of bean, and slow cooker used.

Here's a general guideline of cooking times.

• Black beans, small red beans, and Great Northern beans: 4 to 5 hours

• Pinto beans and navy beans: 5 to 7 hours

• Chickpeas (garbanzo beans): 9 to 12 hours

6. Drain cooked beans in a colander; discard onion and bay leaf.

7. Separate beans into 1-cup portions; freeze for later use. Rinse in a colander under cold running water to thaw.

African Sweet Potato Stew with Red Beans

Vivid colors and fragrant spices are the hallmarks of this thick stew, which is garnished with crunchy peanuts. A squeeze of lime juice at the table brightens the rich, earthy flavors.

    2   teaspoons olive oil
 1½   cups chopped onion
    1   garlic clove, minced
    4   cups (½-inch) cubed peeled sweet
        potato (about 1½ pounds)
 1½   cups cooked small red beans
 1½   cups vegetable broth
    1   cup chopped red bell pepper
  ½   cup water
    1   teaspoon grated peeled fresh
        ginger
  ½   teaspoon salt
  ½   teaspoon ground cumin
  ¼   teaspoon black pepper
    1   (14.5-ounce) can diced tomatoes,
        drained
    1   (4.5-ounce) can chopped green
        chiles, drained
    3   tablespoons creamy peanut butter
    3   tablespoons chopped dry-roasted
        peanuts
    6   lime wedges

1. Heat oil in a nonstick skillet over medium heat. Add onion and garlic; cover and cook 5 minutes or until tender.

2. Place onion mixture in a 5-quart electric slow cooker. Add sweet potato and next 10 ingredients. Cover and cook on low-heat setting 8 hours or until vegetables are tender.

3. Spoon 1 cup cooking liquid into a small bowl. Add peanut butter; stir well with a whisk. Stir peanut butter mixture into stew. Top with peanuts; serve with lime wedges. Yield: 6 servings (serving size: 1⅓ cups stew, 1½ teaspoons peanuts, and 1 lime wedge).

CALORIES 308 (26% from fat); FAT 8.8g (sat 1.5g, mono 4.2g, poly 2.3g); PROTEIN 11.1g; CARB 49.9g; FIBER 10.2g; CHOL 0mg; IRON 2.7mg; SODIUM 574mg; CALC 64mg

Pinto Bean Chili with Corn and Winter Squash

The spiciness of this light yet satisfying chili is complemented by the subtle sweetness of corn and winter squash. Queso fresco is a crumbly, slightly salty Mexican cheese that's available in many large supermarkets. If you can't find it, substitute crumbled feta or farmer cheese. For a heartier chili, add 1 cup thawed frozen meatless crumbles. For a vegan version, use shredded soy Cheddar or mozzarella cheese.

    1   tablespoon olive oil
 1½   cups chopped onion
 1½   cups chopped red bell pepper
    1   garlic clove, minced
    2   tablespoons chili powder
  ½   teaspoon ground cumin
    4   cups (½-inch) cubed peeled
        butternut squash (about 1 pound)
    3   cups cooked pinto beans
 1½   cups water
    1   cup frozen whole-kernel corn
    1   teaspoon salt
    1   (14.5-ounce) can crushed
        tomatoes, undrained
    1   (4.5-ounce) can chopped green
        chiles, undrained
  ¾   cup (3 ounces) crumbled queso
        fresco
    6   lime wedges

1. Heat oil in a large nonstick skillet over medium heat. Add onion, bell pepper, and garlic; cover and cook 5 minutes or until tender. Add chili powder and cumin; cook 1 minute, stirring constantly.

2. Place onion mixture in a 5-quart electric slow cooker. Add squash and next 6 ingredients. Cover and cook on low-heat setting 8 hours or until vegetables are tender and chili is thick. Sprinkle with cheese; serve with lime wedges. Yield: 6 servings (serving size: 1½ cups chili, 2 tablespoons cheese, and 1 lime wedge).

CALORIES 296 (20% from fat); FAT 6.5g (sat 2.2g, mono 2.7g, poly 1g); PROTEIN 15.1g; CARB 49.6g; FIBER 13.3g; CHOL 10mg; IRON 4.8mg; SODIUM 640mg; CALC 206mg

Thyme-Scented White Bean Cassoulet

Butter-tossed breadcrumbs stirred in at the end give this dish a robust stewlike consistency. Meatless Italian sausage stands in for the traditional pork sausage. With this recipe, you can also sauté the sausage slices in a nonstick skillet over medium-high heat until browned, then stir them into the dish.

  1   tablespoon olive oil
1½ cups chopped onion
1½ cups (½-inch-thick) slices
     diagonally cut carrot
  1   cup (½-inch-thick) slices
     diagonally cut parsnip
  2   garlic cloves, minced
  3   cups cooked Great Northern beans
 ¾ cup vegetable broth
 ½ teaspoon dried thyme
 ¼ teaspoon salt
 ¼ teaspoon black pepper
  1   (28-ounce) can diced tomatoes, undrained
  1   bay leaf
 ¼ cup dry breadcrumbs
 ¼ cup (1 ounce) grated fresh Parmesan cheese
  2   tablespoons butter, melted
  2   links frozen meatless Italian sausage (such as Boca), thawed and chopped
  2   tablespoons chopped fresh parsley

1. Heat oil in a large nonstick skillet over medium heat. Add onion, carrot, parsnip, and garlic; cover and cook 5 minutes or until tender.
2. Place parsnip mixture in a 5-quart electric slow cooker. Add beans and next 6 ingredients. Cover and cook on low-heat setting 8 hours or until vegetables are tender. Discard bay leaf.
3. Combine breadcrumbs, cheese, and butter in a small bowl; toss with a fork until moist. Stir breadcrumb mixture and sausage into bean mixture; sprinkle with parsley. Yield: 6 servings (serving size: 1⅓ cups).

CALORIES 314 (29% from fat); FAT 10.2g (sat 3.7g, mono 3.7g, poly 1.7g); PROTEIN 16.4g; CARB 41.9g; FIBER 11.6g; CHOL 13mg; IRON 3.6mg; SODIUM 777mg; CALC 177mg

Slow and Steady

Slow cookers, as their name implies, are designed to cook food slowly over a long period of time. They come equipped with a tight-fitting lid, which traps steam so food stays moist. Another advantage of the tight cover is that it traps heat so, even though food might cook all day, your kitchen never heats up.

When testing these recipes in our Test Kitchens, we found that cooking times can vary significantly between one slow cooker and another—even ones of the same size. Different brands and models cook differently—some faster than others. These recipes provide the most consistent cooking times that we got in our Test Kitchens with the various cookers we used. Understand that you might need to cook a little longer, or a little less, depending on the slow cooker you use.

enlightened traveler

Undiscovered Wine Countries

Off-the-beaten-track wineries are producing the next wave of America's best vintages.

In wine country, the pace is relaxed, the scenery beguiling, the wines sensational, and fitness is a way of life. Plus, where there's good wine, there's often fresh, delicious food.

The wine country most people know is the area north of San Francisco, particularly Napa Valley and Sonoma County. But America boasts dozens of wine regions that are less known but worth visiting—beautiful places for lazy-day exploring—such as the "Sonoma Valley of the Eastern seaboard" (Northern Virginia and the Shenandoah Valley). Here's a harvest recipe that pairs well with that region.

Brunswick Stew with Smoked Paprika

This recipe is said to have originated in Brunswick County, Virginia, in the 1800s. We spiced it up with a little smoked Spanish paprika (available at gourmet specialty stores and some supermarkets). Use rotisserie chicken to speed up preparation. The strong, smoky flavors in this dish pair well with Champagne or sparkling wine. It's a delicious combination that could become a regular autumn weeknight treat.

  2   cups (¾-inch) cubed Yukon gold potato
  2   cups thinly sliced yellow onion
  2   cups frozen corn kernels, thawed
  1   cup frozen baby lima beans, thawed
 ½ cup tomato sauce
  2   (14-ounce) cans fat-free, less-sodium chicken broth
  2   bacon slices, cut crosswise into ½-inch strips
  3   cups shredded cooked chicken breast
 ½ teaspoon sweet Spanish smoked paprika
 ½ teaspoon kosher salt
 ¼ teaspoon ground red pepper

1. Combine first 7 ingredients in a Dutch oven over medium-high heat; bring to a boil. Reduce heat to low; simmer 30 minutes or until potatoes are tender, stirring occasionally. Stir in chicken, paprika, salt, and pepper; simmer 15 minutes. Yield: 6 servings (serving size: about 1½ cups).

CALORIES 308 (22% from fat); FAT 7.5g (sat 2.4g, mono 3g, poly 1.4g); PROTEIN 29.4g; CARB 31.6g; FIBER 4.9g; CHOL 65mg; IRON 2.2mg; SODIUM 645mg; CALC 36mg

Quick Chops

Prepare pork chops for quick meals.

Quick Chops Menu 1
serves 4

Buttermilk-Brined Pork Chops

Roasted butternut squash*

Steamed green beans

*Preheat oven to 400°. Coat a nonstick baking sheet with cooking spray. Arrange 4 cups (½-inch) diced butternut squash in a single layer on pan; sprinkle with ½ teaspoon salt, ¼ teaspoon ground cinnamon, and ¼ teaspoon ground nutmeg. Coat squash with cooking spray. Bake at 400° for 10 minutes; turn with a spatula. Bake an additional 10 minutes or until squash is soft and begins to brown.

Game Plan

1. Brine pork chops overnight.
2. While oven preheats:
   • Dice squash
3. While squash roasts:
   • Cook pork chops
   • Steam green beans

Buttermilk-Brined Pork Chops

Brine these chops up to 2 days ahead. After an overnight soak, cover in plastic wrap, and refrigerate until ready to cook.

TOTAL TIME: 10 MINUTES (doesn't include brining time)

- 2 cups fat-free buttermilk
- 2 tablespoons kosher salt
- 2 tablespoons sugar
- 1 tablespoon grated lemon rind
- 1 teaspoon chopped fresh rosemary
- 1 teaspoon chopped fresh sage
- 4 (6-ounce) bone-in center-cut pork chops (about ½ inch thick)
- 2 teaspoons freshly ground black pepper

Cooking spray

1. Combine first 6 ingredients in a large zip-top plastic bag; shake well to dissolve salt and sugar. Add pork; seal and refrigerate overnight, turning bag occasionally. Remove pork from bag; discard brine. Pat pork dry with a paper towel. Sprinkle pork with pepper.
2. Heat a large nonstick grill pan over medium-high heat. Coat pan with cooking spray. Add pork; cook 3½ minutes on each side or until desired degree of doneness. Yield: 4 servings (serving size: 1 chop).

CALORIES 183 (35% from fat); FAT 7.2g (sat 2.5g, mono 3.2g, poly 0.6g); PROTEIN 26g; CARB 2g; FIBER 0.3g; CHOL 69mg; IRON 0.8mg; SODIUM 345mg; CALC 43mg

Quick Chops Menu 2
serves 4

Grilled Plum and Prosciutto-Stuffed Pork Chops

Hominy sauté*

Strawberry sorbet

*Melt 2 teaspoons butter in a large nonstick skillet. Add ½ cup chopped onion and 2 minced garlic cloves; sauté 2 minutes or until tender. Add 1 (15.5-ounce) can drained white hominy, ¼ cup chopped green onions, ¼ teaspoon salt, and ¼ teaspoon freshly ground black pepper. Cook 2 minutes or until thoroughly heated.

Game Plan

1. While grill heats:
   • Chop sage and rosemary
   • Soak dried plums in boiling water
2. While pork grills:
   • Sauté hominy

Grilled Plum and Prosciutto-Stuffed Pork Chops

Balsamic vinegar and sweet molasses balance the spicy rub.

TOTAL TIME: 35 MINUTES

QUICK TIP: Get a head start by assembling the stuffed pork chops the night before. Sprinkle them with the fennel mixture just prior to grilling.

- 4 pitted dried plums, halved
- 2 very thin slices prosciutto (about ¾ ounce), halved
- ½ teaspoon crushed fennel seeds
- ½ teaspoon paprika
- ½ teaspoon chopped fresh sage
- ½ teaspoon chopped fresh rosemary
- ¼ teaspoon kosher salt
- ¼ teaspoon crushed red pepper
- ¼ teaspoon freshly ground black pepper
- 4 (4-ounce) boneless center-cut loin pork chops (about ¾ inch thick)

Cooking spray

- 2 teaspoons balsamic vinegar
- 2 teaspoons molasses

1. Prepare grill.
2. Soak plum halves in boiling water 5 minutes. Drain.
3. Wrap 2 plum halves in each prosciutto piece.
4. Combine fennel seeds and next 6 ingredients in a small bowl.
5. Cut a horizontal slit through thickest portion of each pork chop to form a pocket. Stuff 1 prosciutto wrap into each pocket. Sprinkle pork chops with fennel mixture. Place pork chops on grill rack coated with cooking spray; grill 5 minutes on each side or until desired degree of doneness. Combine vinegar and molasses; brush over pork chops. Yield: 4 servings (serving size: 1 chop).

CALORIES 205 (32% from fat); FAT 7.2g (sat 2.6g, mono 2.9g, poly 0.5g); PROTEIN 25.7g; CARB 8.5g; FIBER 0.9g; CHOL 70mg; IRON 1.3mg; SODIUM 270mg; CALC 42mg

Quick Chops Menu 3

serves 4

Sautéed Boneless Pork Chops with Tomato-Sage Pan Sauce

Penne pasta with butter and Parmesan cheese*

Lettuce salad with marinated artichoke hearts and tomatoes

*Cook 8 ounces penne pasta according to package directions, omitting salt and fat. Drain well; toss with 1 tablespoon butter and ¼ cup grated fresh Parmesan cheese. Sprinkle with chopped fresh parsley.

Game Plan

1. While water for pasta comes to a boil:
- Grate Parmesan cheese
- Chop sage
- Chop and seed tomatoes
- Season chops

2. While pasta cooks:
- Make salad
- Cook chops and sauce

QUICK & EASY

Sautéed Boneless Pork Chops with Tomato-Sage Pan Sauce

Serve pork chops whole or sliced and spooned over pasta.

TOTAL TIME: 24 MINUTES

QUICK TIP: Use drained canned Italian-style diced tomatoes as a substitute for chopped and seeded fresh tomatoes.

- 2 teaspoons chopped fresh sage, divided
- ½ teaspoon kosher salt
- ½ teaspoon freshly ground black pepper
- 4 (4-ounce) boneless center-cut loin pork chops (about ¾ inch thick)
- Cooking spray
- ½ cup dry white wine
- 2 garlic cloves, minced
- 1 cup chopped seeded tomato
- ¼ cup fat-free, less-sodium chicken broth
- ¼ teaspoon kosher salt
- ⅛ teaspoon freshly ground black pepper

1. Combine 1 teaspoon sage, ½ teaspoon salt, and ½ teaspoon pepper in a small bowl. Sprinkle both sides of pork with sage mixture.

2. Heat a large nonstick skillet over medium-high heat. Coat pan with cooking spray. Add pork; cook 3 minutes on each side or until browned. Remove from pan; set aside.

3. Add 1 teaspoon sage, wine, and garlic to pan, scraping to loosen browned bits. Cook 1½ minutes or until reduced to about ¼ cup. Stir in tomato and broth, and cook 4 minutes or until slightly thick. Return pork and accumulated juices to pan. Cover and cook 1 minute or until heated. Sprinkle with ¼ teaspoon salt and ⅛ teaspoon pepper. Yield: 4 servings (serving size: 1 chop and about 1 tablespoon sauce).

CALORIES 175 (34% from fat); FAT 6.6g (sat 2.4g, mono 2.9g, poly 0.5g); PROTEIN 24.6g; CARB 3.3g; FIBER 0.6g; CHOL 65mg; IRON 1.1mg; SODIUM 435mg; CALC 35mg

Quick Chops Menu 4

serves 4

Breaded Pork Chops

Garlic-scented turnip greens*

Garlic bread

*Cook 1 (1-pound) bag prewashed turnip greens in boiling water 5 minutes or until tender; drain and set aside. Add 2 teaspoons minced garlic and 2 teaspoons olive oil to pan; cook over medium-high heat 1 minute. Add greens and ½ teaspoon hot pepper sauce. Cook 2 minutes, stirring frequently. Add 2 teaspoons red wine vinegar, ½ teaspoon kosher salt, and ¼ teaspoon freshly ground black pepper.

Game Plan

1. While water for turnip greens comes to a boil:
- Set up 3 shallow dishes for coating chops
- Make breadcrumbs

2. While turnip greens cook:
- Cook chops
- Prepare garlic bread
- Cut lemon wedges

QUICK & EASY

Breaded Pork Chops

(pictured on page 341)

Once you have coated the pork chops, place them on a wire rack that's resting over a baking sheet. This prevents the chops from getting soggy while the pan heats.

TOTAL TIME: 25 MINUTES

- 2 (1-ounce) slices white bread
- ¾ teaspoon kosher salt
- ½ teaspoon freshly ground black pepper
- ½ teaspoon dried rubbed sage
- ½ teaspoon dried thyme
- 8 (2-ounce) boneless center-cut loin pork chops (¼ inch thick)
- ¼ cup all-purpose flour
- 3 large egg whites, lightly beaten
- 2 teaspoons vegetable oil
- Cooking spray
- 4 lemon wedges

1. Place bread slices in a food processor; pulse 10 times or until coarse crumbs measure 1 cup. Place breadcrumbs in a shallow dish.

2. Combine salt, pepper, sage, and thyme; sprinkle over both sides of pork. Place flour in a shallow dish; place egg whites in another shallow dish. Dredge pork in flour, dip in egg whites, and dredge in breadcrumbs. Heat oil in a large nonstick skillet over medium-high heat. Add pork to pan. Cook 2½ minutes or until lightly browned. Lightly coat surface of chops with cooking spray; turn chops over. Cook 2½ minutes or until done. Serve with lemon wedges. Yield: 4 servings (serving size: 2 pork chops and 1 lemon wedge).

CALORIES 245 (29% from fat); FAT 8g (sat 2.2g, mono 2.9g, poly 1.8g); PROTEIN 28.4g; CARB 13g; FIBER 0.8g; CHOL 70mg; IRON 1.9mg; SODIUM 502mg; CALC 33mg

Dressed-Up Desserts

These make-ahead treats will end your dinner parties with ease and elegance.

Have you ever listened to your guests laugh festively in the next room while you mop your brow, try to remedy the mess of your thrown-together dessert catastrophe, and pray that the dish ends up tasting better than it actually looks? Well if you can answer "yes" to this question, then these desserts are for you.

Now you can make desserts before the party. Some can even be dressed up at the last minute such as Pineapple-Rum Granita, served elegantly in martini glasses, or Rice Pudding with Port and Dried Plum Sauce, whose rich layers can reside in the refrigerator until the dinner plates are cleared.

With these desserts at the ready, you're in business—the business of basking in well-earned praise.

MAKE AHEAD • FREEZABLE

Pineapple-Rum Granita

Mix the ingredients the night before, and freeze. Scrape the mixture just before serving so it will be light and fluffy.

    1   cup water
    ¾   cup pineapple juice
    ⅓   cup sugar
    2   tablespoons dark rum

1. Combine first 3 ingredients in a medium saucepan; bring to a boil. Cook 1 minute or until sugar dissolves, stirring frequently. Remove from heat; stir in rum. Cool completely. Pour into an 8-inch square baking dish. Cover and freeze 8 hours or until firm.
2. Remove mixture from freezer; scrape entire mixture with a fork until fluffy. Yield: 8 servings (serving size: ½ cup).

CALORIES 55 (0% from fat); FAT 0g; PROTEIN 0.1g; CARB 11.6g; FIBER 0.1g; CHOL 0mg; IRON 0.1mg; SODIUM 1mg; CALC 5mg

---

MAKE AHEAD

Marble Cheesecake Squares

(pictured on page 342)

If you've forgotten to set out the cream cheese to soften, arrange the unwrapped blocks in a single layer in a large bowl, and microwave at HIGH 1 minute or until slightly soft.

    1   cup chocolate graham cracker
         crumbs (about 9 cookie
         sheets)
    Cooking spray
    1   tablespoon butter, melted
    2   (8-ounce) blocks fat-free cream
         cheese, softened
    1   (8-ounce) block ⅓-less-fat cream
         cheese, softened
    1   cup sugar
    3   tablespoons all-purpose flour
    1   tablespoon vanilla extract
    3   large egg whites
    1   large egg
    1   ounce semisweet chocolate

1. Preheat oven to 325°.
2. Place crumbs in a 9-inch square baking pan coated with cooking spray; drizzle with butter. Toss with a fork until moist. Press into bottom of pan. Bake at 325° for 8 minutes; cool on a wire rack.
3. Place cheeses in a large bowl; beat with a mixer at high speed until smooth. Add sugar and flour; beat well. Add vanilla, egg whites, and egg; beat until well blended. Pour cheese mixture into prepared pan.
4. Place chocolate in a small microwave-safe bowl; microwave at HIGH 1½ minutes or until soft, stirring after 45 seconds (chocolate should not completely melt). Stir until smooth. Drop melted chocolate onto cheese mixture to form 9 mounds. Swirl chocolate into batter using tip of a knife. Bake at 325° for 35 minutes or until almost set. Cool on a wire rack. Cover and chill at least 4 hours. Yield: 12 servings.

CALORIES 239 (29% from fat); FAT 7.6g (sat 4.1g, mono 2.1g, poly 0.2g); PROTEIN 9.7g; CARB 31.4g; FIBER 0.6g; CHOL 41mg; IRON 0.6mg; SODIUM 355mg; CALC 124mg

---

MAKE AHEAD

Vanilla-Almond Panna Cotta with Mango Sauce

Make and refrigerate the sauce up to 2 days ahead and the panna cotta up to 1 day ahead. Look for almond milk in aseptic containers on the organic food aisle of your supermarket. If you can't find it, substitute whole milk.

    1   envelope unflavored gelatin
    1⅔   cups almond milk (such as
         Almond Breeze), divided
    ⅔   cup half-and-half
    ⅓   cup sugar
    1   (6-inch) piece vanilla bean, split
         lengthwise and divided
    Cooking spray
    1½   cups mango nectar
    1   tablespoon fresh lime
         juice
    Fresh raspberries (optional)

1. Sprinkle gelatin over ⅓ cup almond milk in a small bowl; let stand 4 minutes.
2. Combine 1⅓ cups almond milk, half-and-half, sugar, and half vanilla bean in a medium saucepan; bring to a simmer over medium heat (do not boil). Remove from heat. Add gelatin mixture, stirring until gelatin dissolves. Remove vanilla bean. Pour mixture evenly into 6 (6-ounce) custard cups coated with cooking spray. Cover and chill 8 hours or overnight.
3. Combine remaining half of vanilla bean and nectar in a small saucepan; bring to a boil. Reduce heat to medium, and cook until reduced to 1 cup (about 15 minutes). Remove from heat; stir in lime juice. Cover and chill. Remove vanilla bean.
4. Loosen edges of custards with a knife or rubber spatula. Place a dessert plate, upside down, on top of each cup; invert onto plates. Spoon sauce around custards. Garnish with fresh raspberries, if desired. Yield: 6 servings (serving size: 1 custard and 2½ tablespoons sauce).

CALORIES 137 (24% from fat); FAT 3.6g (sat 1.9g, mono 1.4g, poly 0g); PROTEIN 2.3g; CARB 24g; FIBER 0.7g; CHOL 13mg; IRON 0.2mg; SODIUM 60mg; CALC 96mg

---

European dishes such as panna cotta and flan can be made the day before the party and unmolded just before serving.

MAKE AHEAD
Individual Anise-Orange Flans

Refrigerate these flans 1 day ahead; invert onto dessert plates just before serving.

- ½ cup sugar
- 1 tablespoon water
- Cooking spray
- ½ teaspoon aniseed
- 1 cup 1% low-fat milk
- 1 teaspoon grated orange rind
- 1 teaspoon vanilla extract
- Dash of salt
- 3 large eggs, lightly beaten
- 1 (14-ounce) can fat-free sweetened condensed milk

1. Preheat oven to 350°.
2. Combine sugar and water in a small, heavy saucepan over medium-high heat; cook until sugar dissolves, stirring frequently. Continue cooking until golden (about 3 minutes), stirring occasionally. Immediately pour into 6 (6-ounce) ramekins or custard cups coated with cooking spray, tipping quickly until caramelized sugar coats bottom of cups.
3. Place aniseed in a spice or coffee grinder; process until finely ground. Combine aniseed and remaining 6 ingredients, stirring well with a whisk. Pour into prepared ramekins. Place ramekins in a 13 x 9-inch baking pan; add hot water to pan to a depth of 1 inch. Bake at 350° for 30 minutes or until a knife inserted in center comes out clean. Remove cups from pan; cool completely on a wire rack. Cover and chill at least 4 hours or overnight.
4. Loosen edges of custards with a knife or rubber spatula. Place a dessert plate, upside down, on top of each cup; invert onto plates. Drizzle any remaining caramelized syrup over custards. Yield: 6 servings (serving size: 1 flan).

CALORIES 306 (9% from fat); FAT 3.1g (sat 1g, mono 1.1g, poly 0.4g); PROTEIN 10.4g; CARB 59.1g; FIBER 0.1g; CHOL 112mg; IRON 0.5mg; SODIUM 146mg; CALC 250mg

MAKE AHEAD
Rice Pudding with Port and Dried Plum Sauce

Layers of creamy rice pudding alternate with a sauce of dried plums enhanced with sweet port wine.

- 1 cup pitted dried plums
- ¾ cup port or other sweet red wine
- 2 tablespoons water
- 2 cups fat-free milk, divided
- 1½ cups water
- ½ cup uncooked long-grain rice
- ½ teaspoon salt
- ⅓ cup granulated sugar
- 1 teaspoon vanilla extract
- ⅓ cup whipping cream
- 2 tablespoons port or other sweet red wine
- 2 teaspoons powdered sugar
- 2 tablespoons slivered almonds, toasted

1. Combine plums and ¾ cup port in a small saucepan; bring to a boil. Reduce heat; simmer 15 minutes or until plums are tender. Let stand 5 minutes. Place plum mixture and 2 tablespoons water in a blender. Process until smooth.
2. Combine 1 cup milk, 1½ cups water, rice, and salt in a medium saucepan; bring to a boil. Cover, reduce heat, and simmer 25 minutes. Stir in 1 cup milk, granulated sugar, and vanilla. Cover and simmer 30 minutes. Remove from heat; let stand 10 minutes.
3. Spoon about 4 teaspoons plum sauce into each of 6 (6-ounce) martini or parfait glasses; top each serving with ⅓ cup rice pudding. Repeat layers once. Cover and chill at least 4 hours.
4. Combine whipping cream, 2 tablespoons port, and powdered sugar in a medium bowl; beat with a mixer at high speed until light and fluffy. Top each serving with 2 tablespoons cream mixture and 1 teaspoon slivered almonds. Yield: 6 servings.

CALORIES 293 (21% from fat); FAT 6.7g (sat 3.3g, mono 2.5g, poly 0.6g); PROTEIN 5.5g; CARB 49.2g; FIBER 2.5g; CHOL 20mg; IRON 1.6mg; SODIUM 247mg; CALC 137mg

MAKE AHEAD • FREEZABLE
Chocolate-Mint Sorbet

Look for peppermint oil at health-food stores, large supermarkets, and specialty stores that sell candy-making ingredients; don't substitute peppermint extract. For a simple chocolate sorbet, omit the oil.

- 4 cups water
- 1 cup sugar
- ¼ cup light-colored corn syrup
- ¼ cup unsweetened cocoa
- 4 ounces semisweet chocolate, chopped
- 4 drops peppermint oil

1. Combine first 3 ingredients in a medium saucepan; bring to a boil. Cook 2 minutes or until sugar dissolves, stirring frequently.
2. Place cocoa and chocolate in a medium bowl. Pour hot sugar mixture over chocolate mixture; let stand 2 minutes. Stir with a whisk until smooth. Stir in peppermint oil. Cover and chill for about 2 hours.
3. Pour mixture into freezer can of an ice-cream freezer; freeze according to manufacturer's instructions. Spoon sorbet into a freezer-safe container; cover and freeze 4 hours or until firm. Yield: 11 servings (serving size: ½ cup).

CALORIES 147 (20% from fat); FAT 3.3g (sat 2g, mono 1g, poly 0.1g); PROTEIN 1g; CARB 31.6g; FIBER 2.1g; CHOL 0mg; IRON 0.6mg; SODIUM 10mg; CALC 3mg

Temptation Rolls

A slimmed-down version of a young couple's family recipe earns our Test Kitchens' highest rating.

Ever since they began dating, Desiree Schneider of Pittsburgh, Pennsylvania, had listened to her husband, Paul, reminisce about the gooey orange rolls of his childhood. So as a part of his 25th birthday celebration, she secretly obtained a copy of the recipe from her mother-in-law and surprised him by baking a batch of his favorite treat.

Desiree felt there was a good chance that Paul would overindulge in the rolls anytime she made them. We took her concerns to heart.

Switching from regular to reduced-fat sour cream saved about 120 calories and 19 grams of fat in the recipe. Another 72 calories and almost 5 grams of fat were trimmed by using one egg instead of two. The biggest change occurred when we slashed the butter content to ¼ cup, but we kept enough in the dough to maintain the original's tender, almost pillowlike texture. We kept most of the butter originally in the glaze because it imparts rich flavor at first bite. Still, the rolls contain only half the butter of the original recipe, which knocks out a whopping 792 calories and 91 grams of fat. All the modifications make for a rich-tasting baked delight with only 178 calories per serving and about half the fat of the original.

Orange Rolls

Keep any remaining rolls in the baking pan. Cover pan with foil, and store it in the refrigerator. To reheat, place foil-covered pan in a 300° oven for 15 minutes or until rolls are warm.

DOUGH:

- 1 package dry yeast (about 2¼ teaspoons)
- ½ cup warm water (100° to 110°)
- 1 cup sugar, divided
- ½ cup reduced-fat sour cream
- 2 tablespoons butter, softened
- 1 teaspoon salt
- 1 large egg, lightly beaten
- 3½ cups all-purpose flour, divided
- Cooking spray
- 2 tablespoons butter, melted
- 2 tablespoons grated orange rind

GLAZE:

- ¾ cup sugar
- ¼ cup butter
- 2 tablespoons fresh orange juice
- ½ cup reduced-fat sour cream

1. To prepare dough, dissolve yeast in warm water in a large bowl; let stand 5 minutes. Add ¼ cup sugar, ½ cup sour cream, softened butter, salt, and egg, and beat with a mixer at medium speed until smooth. Lightly spoon flour into dry measuring cups; level with a knife. Add 2 cups flour to yeast mixture; beat until smooth. Add 1 cup flour to yeast mixture, stirring until a soft dough forms. Turn dough out onto a floured surface. Knead until smooth and elastic (about 10 minutes); add enough remaining flour, 1 tablespoon at a time, to prevent dough from sticking to hands (dough will feel sticky).

2. Place dough in a large bowl coated with cooking spray, turning to coat top. Cover and let rise in a warm place (85°), free from drafts, 1 hour and 15 minutes or until doubled in size. (Gently press two fingers into dough. If indentation remains, dough has risen enough.)

3. Punch dough down; cover and let rest 5 minutes. Divide dough in half. Working with 1 portion at a time (cover remaining dough to prevent drying), roll dough into a 12-inch circle on a floured surface. Brush surface of circle with 1 tablespoon melted butter. Combine ¾ cup sugar and rind. Sprinkle half of sugar mixture over each circle. Cut each circle into 12 wedges. Roll up wedge tightly, beginning at wide end. Place rolls, point sides down, in a 13 x 9-inch baking pan coated with cooking spray. Cover and let rise 25 minutes or until doubled in size.

4. Preheat oven to 350°.

5. Uncover dough. Bake at 350° for 25 minutes or until golden brown.

6. While rolls bake, prepare glaze. Combine ¾ cup sugar, ¼ cup butter, and orange juice in a small saucepan; bring to a boil over medium-high heat. Cook 3 minutes or until sugar dissolves, stirring occasionally. Remove from heat; cool slightly. Stir in ½ cup sour cream. Drizzle glaze over warm rolls; let stand 20 minutes before serving. Yield: 2 dozen (serving size: 1 roll).

CALORIES 178 (28% from fat); FAT 5.6g (sat 3.2g, mono 1.3g, poly 0.3g); PROTEIN 2.8g; CARB 30g; FIBER 0.6g; CHOL 24mg; IRON 1mg; SODIUM 146mg; CALC 23mg

BEFORE	AFTER
SERVING SIZE	
1 roll	
CALORIES PER SERVING	
218	178
FAT	
10.2g	5.6g
PERCENT OF TOTAL CALORIES	
41%	28%

Thanksgiving

Consult our five-day planner for recipes that ensure
lots of Thanksgiving-week food and fun.

Thanksgiving has evolved into more than a day of gratitude and favorite holiday dishes. Now many families spend part or all of the long weekend together. That adds up to a lot of meals to prepare. We've designed this five-day planner to make it easier. Start with a casual stew to greet guests as they arrive on Wednesday night, followed by a traditional turkey-and-all-the-trimmings meal on Thursday. For Friday, we show you how to put leftovers to delicious use, while Saturday's supper features Asian flavors for those weary of turkey. On Sunday morning, send everyone off with a hearty breakfast. They'll be glad you planned ahead.

Wednesday Night Welcome

Have a comforting, slow-cooked stew ready and waiting when company arrives.

STAFF FAVORITE
Beef Daube Provençal

Serve with a whole-grain baguette, bagged salad greens, and bottled vinaigrette.

     2   teaspoons olive oil
    12   garlic cloves, crushed
     1   (2-pound) boneless chuck roast, trimmed and cut into 2-inch cubes
    1½   teaspoons salt, divided
     ½   teaspoon freshly ground black pepper, divided
     1   cup red wine
     2   cups chopped carrot
    1½   cups chopped onion
     ½   cup less-sodium beef broth
     1   tablespoon tomato paste
     1   teaspoon chopped fresh rosemary
     1   teaspoon chopped fresh thyme
    Dash of ground cloves
     1   (14½-ounce) can diced tomatoes
     1   bay leaf
     3   cups hot cooked medium egg noodles (about 4 cups uncooked noodles)

1. Preheat oven to 300°.

2. Heat oil in a small Dutch oven over low heat. Add garlic; cook 5 minutes or until garlic is fragrant, stirring occasionally. Remove garlic with a slotted spoon, and set aside. Increase heat to medium-high. Add beef to pan; sprinkle with ½ teaspoon salt and ¼ teaspoon pepper. Cook 5 minutes, browning on all sides. Remove beef from pan. Add wine to pan; bring to a boil, scraping pan to loosen browned bits. Add garlic, beef, 1 teaspoon salt, ¼ teaspoon pepper, carrot, and next 8 ingredients, and bring to a boil.

3. Cover and bake at 300° for 2½ hours or until beef is tender. Discard bay leaf. Serve over noodles. Yield: 6 servings (serving size: about ¾ cup stew and ½ cup noodles).

NOTE: To make in a slow cooker, prepare through Step 2. Place beef mixture in an electric slow cooker. Cover and cook on high-heat setting 5 hours.

CALORIES 367 (31% from fat); FAT 12.8g (sat 4.3g, mono 5.8g, poly 0.9g); PROTEIN 29.1g; CARB 33.4g; FIBER 3.9g; CHOL 105mg; IRON 4.3mg; SODIUM 776mg; CALC 76mg

Thursday The Big Event

Offer this tantalizing Thanksgiving feast of beloved favorites and new twists.

Now is the time to bring out your good china and create a special mood for your friends and family.

Classic Thanksgiving Menu
serves 12

Roasted Butternut Squash Dip
served with toasted baguette slices or pita chips

Spinach-Pear Salad with Mustard Vinaigrette

Apple Cider-Brined Turkey with Savory Herb Gravy

Herbed Bread Stuffing with Mushrooms and Sausage

Brown Sugar-Glazed Sweet Potato Wedges

Shredded Brussels Sprouts with Bacon and Hazelnuts

Cranberry-Pear Chutney

Dinner rolls

Pumpkin Pie with Pecan Pastry Crust or **Pecan Pie with Spiked Cream**

WINE NOTE: With our Thanksgiving dinner, one wine needs to match a variety of dishes. Luckily, there is a wine that can do it all: Pinot Noir. Because it's a red wine, Pinot Noir has a savory, earthy character that complements many fall dishes. Yet it also has good underlying acidity—the secret ingredient when you need a single wine to work with a big range of flavors. Buy a current vintage Pinot from any of these producers: Sanford, Pisoni, Robert Mondavi Winery, Robert Sinskey, or Sebastiani.

Continued

(pictured on page 377)

Holiday Countdown

Up to three weeks ahead:
• Make chutney; refrigerate in glass jars.

Up to one week ahead:
• Make and freeze piecrust dough in pie plate(s) for either or both pies.

Up to four days ahead:
• Place frozen turkey in refrigerator to thaw. (Allow 1 full day for every 4 pounds to thaw, plus an extra day to brine.)

Up to three days ahead:
• Prepare and chill the dip.
• Toast bread cubes for stuffing; store at room temperature in a zip-top plastic bag.

Up to two days ahead:
• Toast baguette slices (if using) to accompany the dip; store at room temperature in a zip-top plastic bag.
• Prepare and refrigerate salad vinaigrette.
• Prepare and refrigerate brining liquid (minus ice).
• Make and refrigerate sweet potatoes.
• Toast hazelnuts for Brussels sprouts; store at room temperature in a zip-top plastic bag.

Up to one day ahead:
• Shave cheese for salad; store in refrigerator in a zip-top plastic bag.
• Place turkey in brining liquid with ice; refrigerate in plastic oven bags.
• Prepare gravy through Step 1. Cover; chill.
• Bake and chill pecan pie.

Thanksgiving morning:
• Bake stuffing.
• Slice Brussels sprouts and chop bacon; store separately in the refrigerator.
• Bake pumpkin pie.

A few hours before dinner:
• Place turkey in oven (tent cooked turkey with foil to keep it warm).

At the last minute:
• Reheat squash dip in microwave.
• Toss salad.
• Bake or reheat stuffing and sweet potatoes together in oven.
• Finish preparing gravy while turkey rests.
• Warm purchased dinner rolls in oven.
• Cook Brussels sprouts.
• Stir bourbon into topping for pecan pie.

MAKE AHEAD • FREEZABLE
Roasted Butternut Squash Dip

Terrific with toasted baguette slices or pita chips, this creamy, sweet-savory dip can be prepared up to 3 days in advance. Refrigerate in a microwave-safe container, then reheat in a microwave on HIGH 1 to 2 minutes or just until warmed.

  1 (2-pound) butternut squash
  1 small Walla Walla or other sweet onion, trimmed and quartered
  4 garlic cloves, unpeeled
1½ teaspoons olive oil
  2 tablespoons crème fraîche or whole sour cream
¾ teaspoon salt
⅛ teaspoon ground red pepper
⅛ teaspoon ground nutmeg
⅛ teaspoon freshly ground black pepper

1. Preheat oven to 350°.
2. Cut squash in half lengthwise; discard seeds and membrane. Brush cut sides of squash halves, cut sides of onion quarters, and garlic cloves with oil. Arrange squash halves, cut sides down, on a jelly-roll pan; arrange onion quarters and garlic cloves on pan. Bake at 350° for 45 minutes or until tender. Cool slightly. Peel squash. Squeeze garlic cloves to extract pulp.
3. Place squash, onion, and garlic pulp in a food processor; process until smooth. Add crème fraîche and remaining ingredients; process to combine. Serve warm. Yield: 4 cups (serving size: ¼ cup).

CALORIES 35 (28% from fat); FAT 1.1g (sat 0.5g, mono 0.5g, poly 0.1g); PROTEIN 0.6g; CARB 6.3g; FIBER 1.7g; CHOL 1mg; IRON 0.4mg; SODIUM 113mg; CALC 29mg

---

QUICK & EASY • MAKE AHEAD
Spinach-Pear Salad with Mustard Vinaigrette

A fresh salad featuring ripe fall pears is a welcome addition to the Thanksgiving table. Save time by using packaged, pre-washed spinach. Prepare and refrigerate the vinaigrette up to 2 days ahead, and shave and refrigerate the cheese up to 1 day ahead.

  2 Bosc pears, cored and thinly sliced
  1 (6-ounce) package fresh baby spinach
  3 tablespoons water
  2 tablespoons balsamic vinegar
  5 teaspoons extravirgin olive oil
1½ teaspoons stone-ground mustard
  1 teaspoon sugar
¾ teaspoon salt
½ teaspoon coarsely ground black pepper
¼ cup (1 ounce) shaved Parmigiano-Reggiano cheese

1. Combine pear slices and spinach in a large bowl. Combine water and next 6 ingredients, stirring with a whisk. Drizzle vinaigrette over salad, and toss gently to coat. Sprinkle with cheese. Yield: 12 servings (serving size: ⅔ cup salad and about 1 teaspoon cheese).

CALORIES 52 (47% from fat); FAT 2.7g (sat 0.7g, mono 1.6g, poly 0.2g); PROTEIN 1.7g; CARB 6.1g; FIBER 1.4g; CHOL 2mg; IRON 0.8mg; SODIUM 215mg; CALC 58mg

---

STAFF FAVORITE
Apple Cider-Brined Turkey with Savory Herb Gravy
(pictured on page 377)

This turkey received our highest Test Kitchens rating. Brining is an overnight process, so if you're using a frozen turkey, be sure to thaw it well in advance (see Holiday Countdown at left). Choose turkey-sized plastic oven bags for brining the turkey. Use 2 bags to prevent brine from leaking, and place the turkey in a large stockpot as another precaution.

BRINE:

  8 cups apple cider
⅔ cup kosher salt
⅔ cup sugar
  1 tablespoon black peppercorns, coarsely crushed
  1 tablespoon whole allspice, coarsely crushed
  8 (⅛-inch-thick) slices peeled fresh ginger
  6 whole cloves
  2 bay leaves
  1 (12-pound) fresh or frozen turkey, thawed
  2 oranges, quartered
  6 cups ice

REMAINING INGREDIENTS:

- 4 garlic cloves
- 4 sage leaves
- 4 thyme sprigs
- 4 parsley sprigs
- 1 onion, quartered
- 1 (14-ounce) can fat-free, less-sodium chicken broth
- 2 tablespoons unsalted butter, melted and divided
- 1 teaspoon freshly ground black pepper, divided
- ½ teaspoon salt, divided
- Savory Herb Gravy

1. To prepare brine, combine first 8 ingredients in a large saucepan; bring to a boil. Cook 5 minutes or until sugar and salt dissolve. Cool completely.

2. Remove giblets and neck from turkey; reserve for Savory Herb Gravy. Rinse turkey with cold water; pat dry. Trim excess fat. Stuff body cavity with orange quarters. Place a turkey-sized oven bag inside a second bag to form a double thickness. Place bags in a large stockpot. Place turkey inside inner bag. Add cider mixture and ice. Secure bags with several twist ties. Refrigerate 12 to 24 hours, turning occasionally.

3. Preheat oven to 500°.

4. Remove turkey from bags, and discard brine, orange quarters, and bags. Rinse turkey with cold water; pat dry. Lift wing tips up and over back; tuck under turkey. Tie legs together with kitchen string. Place garlic, sage, thyme, parsley, onion, and broth in bottom of a roasting pan. Place roasting rack in pan. Arrange turkey, breast side down, on roasting rack. Brush turkey back with 1 tablespoon butter; sprinkle with ½ teaspoon pepper and ¼ teaspoon salt. Bake at 500° for 30 minutes.

5. Reduce oven temperature to 350°.

6. Remove turkey from oven. Carefully turn turkey over (breast side up) using tongs. Brush turkey breast with 1 tablespoon butter; sprinkle with ½ teaspoon pepper and ¼ teaspoon salt. Bake at 350° for 1 hour and 15 minutes or until a thermometer inserted into meaty part of thigh registers 170° (make sure not to touch bone). (Shield turkey with foil if it browns too quickly.) Remove turkey from

oven; let stand 20 minutes. Reserve pan drippings for Savory Herb Gravy. Discard skin before serving; serve with gravy. Yield: 12 servings (serving size: 6 ounces turkey and about 3 tablespoons gravy).

(Totals include Savory Herb Gravy) CALORIES 338 (30% from fat); FAT 11.3g (sat 4.2g, mono 2.5g, poly 3g); PROTEIN 51.3g; CARB 4.5g; FIBER 0.1g; CHOL 138mg; IRON 3.3mg; SODIUM 770mg; CALC 45mg

MAKE AHEAD

SAVORY HERB GRAVY:

The gravy, through Step 1, can be made 1 day in advance; just cover and refrigerate. Finish the gravy while the turkey rests before being carved.

- 2 teaspoons vegetable oil
- Reserved turkey neck and giblets
- 4 cups water
- 6 black peppercorns
- 4 parsley sprigs
- 2 thyme sprigs
- 1 yellow onion, unpeeled and quartered
- 1 carrot, cut into 2-inch pieces
- 1 celery stalk, cut into 2-inch pieces
- 1 bay leaf
- Reserved turkey drippings
- 3 tablespoons all-purpose flour
- ½ teaspoon salt
- ¼ teaspoon freshly ground black pepper

1. Heat oil in a large saucepan over medium-high heat. Add turkey neck and giblets; cook 5 minutes, browning on all sides. Add water and next 7 ingredients; bring to a boil. Reduce heat, and simmer until liquid is reduced to about 2½ cups (about 1 hour). Strain through a colander into a bowl, reserving cooking liquid and turkey neck. Discard remaining solids. Chill cooking liquid completely. Skim fat from surface, and discard. Remove meat from neck; finely chop meat. Discard neck bone. Add neck meat to cooking liquid.

2. Strain reserved turkey drippings through a colander into a shallow bowl; discard solids. Place strained drippings in freezer 20 minutes. Skim fat from surface; discard.

3. Place flour in a medium saucepan; add ¼ cup cooking liquid, stirring with a whisk until smooth. Add remaining cooking liquid, turkey drippings, salt, and pepper; bring to a boil, stirring frequently. Reduce heat; simmer 5 minutes or until slightly thickened. Yield: 2½ cups (serving size: about 3 tablespoons).

CALORIES 21 (43% from fat); FAT 1g (sat 0.2g, mono 0.2g, poly 0.5g); PROTEIN 1.3g; CARB 1.7g; FIBER 0.1g; CHOL 4mg; IRON 0.2mg; SODIUM 160mg; CALC 2mg

MAKE AHEAD

Herbed Bread Stuffing with Mushrooms and Sausage

Making your own bread cubes is easy and yields delicious results. You can prepare the toasted bread cubes 2 to 3 days before Thanksgiving; store at room temperature in a zip-top plastic bag. If there's space in the oven, bake the stuffing while the turkey roasts at 350°. Otherwise, bake it in the morning, cover with foil, and reheat at 350° for 20 minutes.

- 1½ pounds peasant-style white bread
- 4 (4-ounce) links sweet turkey Italian sausage
- 2 teaspoons butter
- 1 pound cremini mushrooms, quartered
- Cooking spray
- 2 cups chopped onion
- 1¼ cups chopped carrot
- 1¼ cups chopped celery
- ½ cup minced fresh parsley
- 1 tablespoon fresh thyme leaves
- 1 tablespoon minced fresh sage
- ½ teaspoon salt
- ¼ teaspoon freshly ground black pepper
- 2 large eggs, lightly beaten
- 1 (14-ounce) can fat-free, less-sodium chicken broth

1. Preheat oven to 400°.

2. Trim crust from bread. Cut bread into 1½-inch cubes. Arrange bread cubes in a single layer on 2 jelly-roll pans. Bake at 400° for 10 minutes or until toasted.

3. Reduce oven temperature to 350°.

Continued

4. Cook sausage in a large nonstick skillet over medium-high heat 10 minutes, browning on all sides. Remove from pan; cut crosswise into ¼-inch-thick slices.

5. Melt butter in skillet over medium-high heat. Add mushrooms; sauté 4 minutes. Combine bread cubes, sausage, and mushrooms in a large bowl.

6. Heat skillet over medium-high heat. Coat pan with cooking spray. Add onion, carrot, and celery; sauté 5 minutes or until lightly browned. Add parsley, thyme, sage, salt, and pepper; sauté 1 minute. Add to bread mixture. Combine eggs and broth, stirring with a whisk. Add to bread mixture; toss to coat. Spoon into a 13 x 9-inch baking dish coated with cooking spray. Bake at 350° for 45 minutes or until browned. Yield: 12 servings (serving size: about 1 cup).

CALORIES 208 (27% from fat); FAT 6.2g (sat 1.7g, mono 1.9g, poly 1.2g); PROTEIN 13.6g; CARB 25.9g; FIBER 4.1g; CHOL 68mg; IRON 2mg; SODIUM 635mg; CALC 46mg

MAKE AHEAD
Brown Sugar-Glazed Sweet Potato Wedges

Make this tasty side dish up to 2 days ahead, and store, covered, in the refrigerator. Reheat at 350°, covered, 20 minutes or until heated through; if desired, finish the dish under the broiler to recrisp the edges of the potato.

¼ cup unsalted butter
¾ cup packed dark brown sugar
¼ cup water
1 teaspoon salt
½ teaspoon ground nutmeg
¼ teaspoon ground ginger
1 (3-inch) cinnamon stick
4 pounds sweet potatoes, peeled, cut in half crosswise, and cut into ½-inch wedges
Cooking spray

1. Preheat oven to 400°.
2. Melt butter in a medium saucepan over medium heat. Add sugar and next 5 ingredients; bring to a simmer. Cook 5 minutes, stirring frequently. Discard cinnamon stick. Combine sugar mixture

and potato wedges in a large bowl; toss well to coat. Arrange potato mixture on a large jelly-roll pan coated with cooking spray. Bake at 400° for 40 minutes or until tender, stirring after 20 minutes. Yield: 12 servings (serving size: ⅔ cup).

CALORIES 182 (19% from fat); FAT 3.9g (sat 2.4g, mono 1.1g, poly 0.2g); PROTEIN 1.7g; CARB 36.1g; FIBER 3g; CHOL 10mg; IRON 0.8mg; SODIUM 211mg; CALC 44mg

QUICK & EASY
Shredded Brussels Sprouts with Bacon and Hazelnuts

To get a head start before the Thanksgiving meal, chop the bacon and slice the Brussels sprouts in the morning, and toast the hazelnuts up to 2 days ahead.

QUICK TIP: Use a food processor's thin slicing blade attachment to prepare the Brussels sprouts.

½ cup chopped bacon (about 3 slices)
½ cup fat-free, less-sodium chicken broth
13 cups thinly sliced Brussels sprouts (about 2 pounds)
1 teaspoon salt
½ teaspoon freshly ground black pepper
3 tablespoons chopped hazelnuts, toasted

1. Cook bacon in a large Dutch oven over medium-high heat 4 minutes or until crisp. Remove bacon from pan, reserving 1½ teaspoons drippings in pan; set bacon aside. Add broth to pan; bring to a simmer. Add Brussels sprouts; cook 4 minutes or until crisp-tender, stirring frequently. Sprinkle with salt and pepper, tossing gently to combine. Sprinkle evenly with bacon and hazelnuts. Serve immediately. Yield: 12 servings (serving size: ¾ cup).

CALORIES 59 (41% from fat); FAT 2.7g (sat 0.7g, mono 1.5g, poly 0.4g); PROTEIN 3.4g; CARB 7.2g; FIBER 3.1g; CHOL 2mg; IRON 1.2mg; SODIUM 262mg; CALC 35mg

MAKE AHEAD
Cranberry-Pear Chutney

This ruby-colored chutney can be made up to 3 weeks ahead and stored in airtight jars in the refrigerator until you're ready to serve. It also makes a great hostess gift when packed in small, decorative glass jars.

1½ cups sugar
1 cup water
1 teaspoon salt
⅛ teaspoon ground cloves
2 (3-inch) cinnamon sticks
1 (12-ounce) package fresh cranberries
2 cups chopped peeled Bosc pear (about 3 medium)
1 cup chopped peeled Granny Smith apple (about 1 small)
¾ cup golden raisins
⅓ cup chopped onion
¼ cup chopped crystallized ginger
2 tablespoons fresh lemon juice

1. Combine first 6 ingredients in a large saucepan; bring to a boil, stirring until sugar dissolves. Reduce heat, and simmer 10 minutes or until cranberries begin to pop. Stir in pear, apple, raisins, onion, and ginger; cook 20 minutes or until fruit is tender. Remove from heat; stir in juice. Cool to room temperature, and discard cinnamon. Cover and chill. Yield: 4¾ cups (serving size: ¼ cup).

CALORIES 107 (2% from fat); FAT 0.2g (sat 0g, mono 0g, poly 0.1g); PROTEIN 0.4g; CARB 27.8g; FIBER 1.6g; CHOL 0mg; IRON 0.3mg; SODIUM 125mg; CALC 9mg

Continued on page 381

Apple Cider-Brined Turkey with Savory Herb Gravy, page 374

Spinach-Parmesan Dip, page 409

Red Wine-Marinated Steak Sandwiches, page 400

Sour Cream-Hazelnut Bundt Cake, page 389,
Pistachio Granola, page 388, and Fruit Salad
with Honey-Yogurt Sauce, page 388

Pecan Pie with Spiked Cream, page 381

Pumpkin Pie with Pecan Pastry Crust

Many supermarkets stock ground pecans with the other nuts; if you can't find pre-ground nuts, grind the pecans in a food processor or spice grinder. Make the crust up to 1 week ahead; arrange pastry dough in the pie plate, and freeze. Cover tightly with plastic wrap once it's frozen so the wrap won't stick to the dough. On Thanksgiving morning, quickly mix the filling, add it to the frozen crust, and bake.

CRUST:

    1   cup all-purpose flour, divided
    3½   tablespoons ice water
    1   teaspoon fresh lemon juice
    3   tablespoons ground pecans, toasted
    2   tablespoons powdered sugar
    ¼   teaspoon salt
    3   tablespoons vegetable shortening
    Cooking spray

FILLING:

    1   cup fat-free sour cream
    ⅓   cup granulated sugar
    2   tablespoons molasses
    1½   teaspoons pumpkin-pie spice
    1   teaspoon vanilla extract
    ¼   teaspoon salt
    2   large egg whites, lightly beaten
    1   large egg, lightly beaten
    1   (15-ounce) can pumpkin

1. Preheat oven to 350°.
2. To prepare crust, lightly spoon flour into a dry measuring cup, and level with a knife. Combine ¼ cup flour, ice water, and lemon juice, stirring with a whisk until well blended to form a slurry. Combine ¾ cup flour, pecans, powdered sugar, and ¼ teaspoon salt in a large bowl; cut in shortening with a pastry blender or 2 knives until mixture resembles coarse meal. Add slurry; toss with a fork until flour mixture is moist.
3. Gently press mixture into a 4-inch circle on 2 sheets of overlapping heavy-duty plastic wrap; cover with 2 additional sheets of overlapping plastic wrap. Roll dough, still covered, into a 12-inch circle. Freeze dough 10 minutes or until plastic wrap can be easily removed.

4. Remove dough from freezer. Remove top 2 sheets of plastic wrap; let dough stand 1 minute or until pliable. Fit dough, plastic wrap side up, into a 9-inch pie plate coated with cooking spray, allowing dough to extend over edge. Remove remaining plastic wrap. Press dough into bottom and up sides of pie plate. Fold edges under, and flute. Place in freezer until ready to fill.
5. To prepare filling, combine sour cream and remaining 8 ingredients, stirring with a whisk until well blended. Pour filling into prepared crust. Bake at 350° for 45 minutes or until a knife inserted in center comes out clean; cool on a wire rack. Yield: 8 servings (serving size: 1 wedge).

CALORIES 234 (30% from fat); FAT 7.9g (sat 1.9g, mono 2.9g, poly 1.9g); PROTEIN 5.6g; CARB 35.8g; FIBER 2.5g; CHOL 29mg; IRON 2.1mg; SODIUM 322mg; CALC 83mg

Pecan Pie with Spiked Cream

(pictured on page 380)

Brown rice syrup is a sweetener with soft, delicate flavor. It's sold in jars in the baking section of supermarkets or health-food stores. You can substitute dark corn syrup. You can make and freeze the unbaked crust up to 1 week ahead; bake the pie up to 1 day in advance, and refrigerate. Remove from the refrigerator about 1 hour before serving.

CRUST:

    1   cup all-purpose flour, divided
    3   tablespoons ice water
    1   teaspoon fresh lemon juice
    2   tablespoons powdered sugar
    ¼   teaspoon salt
    3   tablespoons vegetable shortening

FILLING:

    1   cup brown rice syrup or dark corn
         syrup
    ¼   cup maple syrup
    2   tablespoons all-purpose flour
    ¼   teaspoon salt
    2   large eggs
    1   large egg white
    ½   cup pecan halves
    1   teaspoon vanilla extract

TOPPING:

    ⅔   cup frozen fat-free whipped
         topping, thawed
    1   tablespoon bourbon

1. Preheat oven to 350°.
2. To prepare crust, lightly spoon 1 cup flour into a dry measuring cup, and level with a knife. Combine ¼ cup flour, ice water, and lemon juice, stirring with a whisk until well blended to form a slurry. Combine ¾ cup flour, powdered sugar, and ¼ teaspoon salt in a large bowl; cut in shortening with a pastry blender or 2 knives until mixture resembles coarse meal. Add slurry; toss with a fork until flour mixture is moist.
3. Gently press mixture into a 4-inch circle on 2 sheets of overlapping heavy-duty plastic wrap; cover with 2 additional sheets of overlapping plastic wrap. Roll dough, still covered, into a 12-inch circle. Freeze dough 10 minutes or until plastic wrap can be easily removed.
4. Remove dough from freezer. Remove top 2 sheets of plastic wrap; let dough stand 1 minute or until pliable. Fit dough, plastic wrap side up, into a 9-inch pie plate, allowing dough to extend over edge. Remove remaining plastic wrap. Press dough into bottom and up sides of pie plate. Fold edges under; flute. Bake at 350° for 8 minutes. Cool on wire rack.
5. To prepare filling, place rice syrup and next 5 ingredients in a large bowl; beat with a mixer at medium speed until well blended. Stir in pecans and vanilla. Pour filling into prepared crust. Bake at 350° for 50 minutes or until edges puff and center is set (shield edges of piecrust with foil if crust gets too brown). Cool on wire rack.
6. To prepare topping, combine whipped topping and bourbon until blended. Serve with pie. Yield: 10 servings (serving size: 1 wedge and about 1 tablespoon topping).

CALORIES 295 (27% from fat); FAT 8.8g (sat 1.6g, mono 3.9g, poly 2.3g); PROTEIN 3.9g; CARB 48.8g; FIBER 0.8g; CHOL 43mg; IRON 1.1mg; SODIUM 194mg; CALC 21mg

Friday
For the Day After

Holiday leftovers star in these quick and simple recipes that are excellent for casual meals.

We designed these recipes so you can use leftover turkey, turkey gravy, and cranberry sauce. If you didn't end up with many leftovers from Thanksgiving dinner, rotisserie chicken and canned whole-berry cranberry sauce work fine. We weren't pleased with the results when we used canned or jarred turkey gravy, so we developed a quick version called Quick Gravy (recipe on page 383) to make when you need it.

QUICK & EASY
Jack Quesadillas with Cranberry Salsa

The salsa is also great on turkey sandwiches. To make meatless quesadillas, use sautéed vegetables in place of the turkey.

SALSA:
- 1 cup whole-berry cranberry sauce
- ¼ cup chopped fresh cilantro
- 2 tablespoons chopped green onions
- 1 tablespoon fresh lime juice
- ½ teaspoon ground cumin
- 1 Anjou pear, cored and finely diced
- 1 jalapeño pepper, seeded and minced

QUESADILLAS:
- Cooking spray
- ¼ cup (2-inch) slices green onions
- 1 cup (4 ounces) shredded Monterey Jack cheese with jalapeño peppers
- 8 (8-inch) flour tortillas
- 2 cups chopped cooked turkey
- ½ cup fat-free sour cream

1. To prepare salsa, combine first 7 ingredients. Cover and chill.
2. To prepare quesadillas, heat a large nonstick skillet over medium-high heat. Coat pan with cooking spray. Add sliced onions to pan; sauté 3 minutes or until tender. Remove onions from pan; reduce heat to medium. Sprinkle 2 tablespoons cheese over each of 4 tortillas. Top each cheese-covered tortilla with one-fourth of onions, ½ cup turkey, 2 tablespoons cheese, and 1 tortilla.
3. Recoat pan with cooking spray. Place over medium heat. Add 1 quesadilla to pan; cook 2 minutes on each side or until lightly browned and cheese is melted. Repeat with remaining quesadillas. Cut each quesadilla into 6 wedges. Serve with cranberry salsa and sour cream. Yield: 8 servings (serving size: 3 wedges, about ¼ cup salsa, and 1 tablespoon sour cream).

CALORIES 356 (25% from fat); FAT 9.7g (sat 4.2g, mono 3.5g, poly 1.2g); PROTEIN 19.4g; CARB 47.8g; FIBER 3g; CHOL 42mg; IRON 2.7mg; SODIUM 372mg; CALC 218mg

QUICK & EASY • MAKE AHEAD
Curry Turkey Salad

This flavorful salad is chock-full of grapes, cashews, and turkey, and it's dressed with a creamy honey-lime sauce.

- 2 tablespoons reduced-fat sour cream
- 2 tablespoons plain yogurt
- 1 tablespoon fresh lime juice
- 1 tablespoon honey
- 1 teaspoon curry powder
- ¼ teaspoon salt
- ¼ teaspoon freshly ground black pepper
- 2 cups chopped cooked turkey
- 1 cup seedless red grapes, halved
- ½ cup chopped celery
- ¼ cup chopped red onion
- 2 tablespoons cashew pieces
- 20 mini pita rounds (about 5 ounces, such as Toufayan Pitettes)

1. Combine first 7 ingredients in a large bowl. Add turkey, grapes, celery, onion, and cashews; stir gently to combine. Serve with pitas. Yield: 4 servings (serving size: about 1 cup salad and 5 pitas).

CALORIES 309 (21% from fat); FAT 7.3g (sat 2.4g, mono 2.2g, poly 1.7g); PROTEIN 25.5g; CARB 35.3g; FIBER 2g; CHOL 57mg; IRON 2.8mg; SODIUM 419mg; CALC 83mg

QUICK & EASY
Mushroom and Turkey Casserole

This one-dish meal needs only a green salad to make it complete. Day-old bread is best for breadcrumbs, but you can bake fresh bread cubes in a 350° oven until toasted.

- 1 (6-ounce) package long-grain and wild rice (such as Uncle Ben's)
- 1 ounce French bread or other firm white bread, cubed
- 1 tablespoon butter, melted and divided
- ¾ cup (3 ounces) grated fresh Parmesan cheese
- ½ cup chopped onion
- 2 garlic cloves, minced
- 1 (8-ounce) package presliced mushrooms
- 1½ cups chopped cooked turkey
- 1 cup turkey gravy
- ½ cup 2% reduced-fat milk
- ½ cup reduced-fat sour cream
- ¼ cup chopped fresh parsley
- ¾ teaspoon minced fresh or ¼ teaspoon dried sage
- ½ teaspoon salt
- ¼ teaspoon freshly ground black pepper
- Cooking spray
- ¾ cup whole-berry cranberry sauce

1. Preheat oven to 325°.
2. Prepare rice according to package directions, omitting fat and seasoning packet. Set aside.
3. While rice cooks, place bread in a food processor; pulse 15 times or until fine crumbs measure ½ cup. Add 1 teaspoon butter to processor; pulse until combined. Add cheese to processor, and pulse until combined.
4. Heat a large skillet over medium-high heat. Add 2 teaspoons butter, onion, garlic, and mushrooms; sauté 7 minutes or until onion is tender. Stir in turkey and next 7 ingredients. Add cooked rice; stir.
5. Spoon rice mixture into a 1½-quart casserole coated with cooking spray. Sprinkle with breadcrumb mixture. Bake at 325° for 30 minutes or until golden brown. Serve with cranberry sauce.

Yield: 6 servings (serving size: about 1 cup casserole and 2 tablespoons sauce).

CALORIES 363 (27% from fat); FAT 10.8g (sat 6g, mono 2.3g, poly 0.8g); PROTEIN 23g; CARB 44.3g; FIBER 1.9g; CHOL 62mg; IRON 2.6mg; SODIUM 766mg; CALC 268mg

QUICK & EASY
Quick Gravy

If you're out of turkey gravy, try this recipe.

    1   tablespoon butter
    2   tablespoons all-purpose flour
    ¼   teaspoon poultry seasoning
    ⅛   teaspoon salt
    ⅛   teaspoon black pepper
    1   cup fat-free, less-sodium chicken
        broth

1. Melt butter in a small saucepan over medium heat; add flour, poultry seasoning, salt, and black pepper, stirring with a whisk. Gradually add broth, stirring until blended. Cook 2 minutes or until thick, stirring constantly. Yield: about 1 cup (serving size: 2 tablespoons).

CALORIES 22 (57% from fat); FAT 1.4g (sat 0.9g, mono 0.4g, poly 0.1g); PROTEIN 0.6g; CARB 1.7g; FIBER 0.1g; CHOL 4mg; IRON 0.1mg; SODIUM 107mg; CALC 1mg

QUICK & EASY
Bacon and Hash Brown Casserole

This quick side dish is well-suited for a casual brunch.

    1   cup turkey gravy or Quick Gravy
        (recipe above)
    ¾   cup (3 ounces) shredded extra-
        sharp Cheddar cheese, divided
    ½   cup thinly sliced green onions
    ¼   teaspoon freshly ground black
        pepper
    ½   (32-ounce) package frozen shredded
        hash brown potatoes, thawed
    1   (8-ounce) carton fat-free sour cream
    Cooking spray
    2   slices bacon, cooked and crumbled

1. Preheat oven to 350°.
2. Combine turkey gravy, ½ cup cheese, onions, pepper, potatoes, and sour cream.

Spoon into a shallow 1-quart casserole coated with cooking spray. Bake at 350° for 35 minutes. Sprinkle with ¼ cup cheese and bacon. Bake an additional 5 minutes or until cheese melts. Yield: 6 servings (serving size: about ⅔ cup).

CALORIES 184 (32% from fat); FAT 6.5g (sat 3.5g, mono 2g, poly 0.6g); PROTEIN 7.6g; CARB 22.2g; FIBER 1.6g; CHOL 22mg; IRON 1.2mg; SODIUM 400mg; CALC 159mg

QUICK & EASY
English Muffin Hot Browns

Hot Browns, sandwiches that are a cross between grilled cheese and BLT, were created at the Brown Hotel in Louisville, Kentucky, in the 1930s. This version uses English muffins instead of regular bread.

    4   English muffins, split and toasted
    Cooking spray
    1   teaspoon butter
    1½ tablespoons all-purpose flour
    1   cup 2% low-fat milk
    1   cup turkey gravy or Quick Gravy
        (recipe at left)
    Dash of ground red pepper
    1   cup chopped cooked turkey
    2   slices Canadian bacon, cut into
        thin strips
    8   (¼-inch-thick) slices tomato
    ¼   cup (1 ounce) grated fresh
        Parmesan cheese
    ¼   teaspoon freshly ground black
        pepper

1. Preheat broiler.
2. Arrange English muffin halves in a single layer in a 13 x 9-inch baking dish coated with cooking spray.
3. Melt butter in a small saucepan over medium heat. Add flour; stir with a whisk until combined. Gradually add milk; stir with a whisk until blended. Cook 2 minutes or until bubbly and slightly thick; stir constantly with a whisk. Add gravy and red pepper; cook 1 minute or until thoroughly heated, stirring constantly. Add turkey; stir gently to combine.
4. Spoon turkey mixture evenly over muffin halves; sprinkle evenly with bacon. Broil 5 minutes or until top is lightly browned. Remove from oven. Place 1 tomato slice over each muffin half; sprinkle

evenly with Parmesan cheese. Broil 1 minute or until cheese is lightly browned. Sprinkle with black pepper. Yield: 4 servings (serving size: 2 muffin halves).

CALORIES 326 (24% from fat); FAT 8.8g (sat 3.7g, mono 2.6g, poly 1.6g); PROTEIN 23.9g; CARB 36.6g; FIBER 2.3g; CHOL 46mg; IRON 3mg; SODIUM 967mg; CALC 257mg

QUICK & EASY
Chicken with Cranberry Barbecue Sauce

Like all barbecue sauces, this one contains flavors ranging from sweet to spicy. The chicken is pounded thin so it cooks evenly, but you'll need to cook it in 2 batches because all 6 breast halves won't fit in the pan at one time.

    1   cup whole-berry cranberry sauce
    ⅓   cup apricot preserves
    2   tablespoons tomato paste
    2   tablespoons balsamic vinegar
    2   teaspoons prepared mustard
    1   teaspoon chili powder
    ¼   teaspoon ground cumin
    6   (6-ounce) skinless, boneless
        chicken breast halves
    ¾   teaspoon ground coriander
    ½   teaspoon salt
    ¼   teaspoon freshly ground black
        pepper
    1   tablespoon olive oil, divided

1. Combine first 7 ingredients in a small saucepan; bring to a boil. Reduce heat, and simmer 10 minutes.
2. Place each chicken breast half between 2 sheets of plastic wrap; pound to a ¼-inch thickness using a meat mallet or rolling pin. Combine coriander, salt, and pepper in a small bowl; sprinkle evenly over chicken.
3. Heat 1½ teaspoons oil in a large nonstick skillet over medium-high heat. Add half of chicken; cook 2 minutes on each side or until done. Repeat with 1½ teaspoons oil and remaining chicken. Serve with sauce. Yield: 6 servings (serving size: 1 chicken breast half and about 3 tablespoons sauce).

CALORIES 332 (13% from fat); FAT 4.7g (sat 0.9g, mono 2.3g, poly 0.8g); PROTEIN 39.9g; CARB 31.8g; FIBER 1.3g; CHOL 99mg; IRON 1.7mg; SODIUM 394mg; CALC 33mg

QUICK & EASY
Cranberry Jezebel Sauce with Sautéed Ham

This classic Southern sauce combines the fruitiness of cranberry sauce and pineapple preserves with the tanginess of horseradish and mustard. It's a piquant partner for ham. Don't lean over the pan when you add the water and onion; they can splatter.

    ½ cup sugar
    ¼ cup hot water
    ½ red onion, thinly sliced
    1 cup whole-berry cranberry sauce
    ⅓ cup pineapple preserves
    1 tablespoon prepared
       horseradish
    1 teaspoon Dijon mustard
    8 (3-ounce) slices reduced-fat ham

1. Place sugar in a heavy skillet over medium-high heat; cook 2 minutes, stirring until sugar dissolves. Cook 1 minute or until golden brown (do not stir). Remove from heat; gently stir in water and onion. Place in a medium bowl; cool completely. Stir in cranberry sauce, preserves, horseradish, and mustard. Cover and chill.

2. Heat a grill pan over medium-high heat. Add 4 ham slices; cook 3 minutes on each side or until grill marks form. Remove ham from pan. Repeat procedure with remaining ham slices. Serve with cranberry Jezebel sauce. Yield: 8 servings (serving size: 1 ham slice and ¼ cup sauce).

CALORIES 229 (15% from fat); FAT 3.7g (sat 1g, mono 1.7g, poly 0.5g); PROTEIN 15.4g; CARB 35.5g; FIBER 0.5g; CHOL 41mg; IRON 1.2mg; SODIUM 883mg; CALC 5mg

QUICK & EASY
Turkey-Pasta Soup
(pictured on page 379)

To ensure that the pasta cooks properly, make sure the soup is boiling when you add the ditali and that it comes back to a boil for the remaining cook time.

    1   tablespoon olive oil
    ½   cup chopped carrot
    ¼   cup chopped celery
    ¼   cup minced onion
    1   garlic clove, minced
    2   cups water
    ⅓   cup chopped 33%-less-sodium
         ham (about 2 ounces)
    ¼   teaspoon freshly ground black
         pepper
    4   (14-ounce) cans fat-free,
         less-sodium chicken broth
    1   cup uncooked ditali (about
         4 ounces short tube-shaped
         macaroni)
    3   cups chopped cooked turkey
    3   cups thinly sliced napa (Chinese)
         cabbage

1. Heat oil in a large Dutch oven over medium-high heat. Add carrot, celery, onion, and garlic; sauté 3 minutes or until tender. Add water, ham, pepper, and broth; bring to a boil. Add pasta; cook 8 minutes or until pasta is done. Stir in turkey and cabbage; cook 2 minutes or until cabbage wilts. Yield: 8 servings (serving size: 1½ cups).

CALORIES 194 (23% from fat); FAT 4.9g (sat 1.3g, mono 2g, poly 1g); PROTEIN 21.8g; CARB 14.2g; FIBER 1.2g; CHOL 44mg; IRON 1.6mg; SODIUM 483mg; CALC 45mg

QUICK & EASY
Asiago-Artichoke-Turkey Spread

Blending the mixture in the food processor is the secret to a smooth texture in this appetizer spread. Adding the garlic to the running food processor finely minces the cloves, and it ensures that they're completely chopped before the other ingredients are added.

    2   garlic cloves, peeled
    2   cups chopped cooked turkey
    1   cup sliced green onions
    1   (14-ounce) can artichoke hearts,
         drained and coarsely chopped
    1   cup (4 ounces) shredded part-skim
         mozzarella cheese
    ½   cup (2 ounces) grated fresh
         Parmesan cheese
    ½   cup (2 ounces) shredded Asiago
         cheese
    ½   cup (4 ounces) ⅓-less-fat cream
         cheese, softened
    ⅓   cup fat-free mayonnaise
    ¼   teaspoon freshly ground black
         pepper
    Cooking spray
    80   Melba toast rounds (about 14
         ounces)

1. Preheat oven to 350°.

2. With food processor running, drop garlic through food chute, and process until minced. Add turkey, green onions, and artichoke hearts to processor; process until combined.

3. Combine mozzarella and next 5 ingredients in a large bowl. Stir in turkey mixture. Spoon mixture into a shallow 1-quart casserole dish coated with cooking spray. Bake at 350° for 30 minutes or until bubbly and top is golden. Serve hot with Melba toast rounds. Yield: 20 servings (serving size: 4 Melba toast rounds and about 3 tablespoons spread).

CALORIES 146 (31% from fat); FAT 5g (sat 2.7g, mono 1.3g, poly 0.5g); PROTEIN 10.2g; CARB 14.5g; FIBER 1.5g; CHOL 23mg; IRON 1.1mg; SODIUM 308mg; CALC 120mg

The texture of these turkey cakes is similar to crab cakes, but a bit denser. They offer a great way to use leftover turkey, though you can also use rotisserie chicken.

Sesame Turkey Cakes with Sweet Chili Sauce

Asian slaw*

Steamed sugar snap peas

*Combine 8 cups shredded napa cabbage, 1 cup red bell pepper strips, ¼ cup chopped green onions, and ¼ cup shredded carrot. Combine 3 tablespoons rice vinegar, 1 tablespoon roasted peanut oil, 1 teaspoon chile paste with garlic, and ¼ teaspoon salt, stirring with a whisk. Drizzle vinaigrette over slaw; toss to combine.

QUICK & EASY

Sesame Turkey Cakes with Sweet Chili Sauce

These savory cakes with a slightly Asian flair are best served just out of the skillet with a side of stir-fried vegetables. You can use leftover Chinese takeout rice or prepared boil-in-bag rice instead of basmati. Look for sweetened chili sauce in Asian markets, and offer the remaining sauce with spring rolls.

2 cups chopped cooked turkey
1 cup cooked basmati rice
½ cup finely chopped green onions
½ cup chopped water chestnuts
¼ cup finely chopped celery
¼ cup light mayonnaise
1 teaspoon ground cumin
⅛ teaspoon ground red pepper
⅛ teaspoon freshly ground black pepper
2 large egg whites, lightly beaten
1 garlic clove, minced
½ cup dry breadcrumbs
2 teaspoons sesame seeds, toasted
1 tablespoon vegetable oil, divided
½ cup sweetened chili sauce

1. Combine first 11 ingredients in a large bowl. Add dry breadcrumbs and sesame seeds; stir until well blended. Divide turkey mixture into 6 equal portions; shape each portion into a ¾-inch-thick patty.

2. Heat 1½ teaspoons oil in a large non-stick skillet over medium heat. Add 3 patties; cook 3 minutes. Carefully turn patties; cook 3 minutes or until golden. Remove patties from pan. Repeat procedure with 1½ teaspoons oil and remaining patties. Serve patties immediately with chili sauce. Yield: 6 servings (serving size: 1 patty and about 1½ tablespoons sauce).

CALORIES 295 (28% from fat); FAT 9.1g (sat 1.8g, mono 2.4g, poly 4g); PROTEIN 17.3g; CARB 36.6g; FIBER 1.2g; CHOL 39mg; IRON 2.1mg; SODIUM 419mg; CALC 45mg

---

Saturday Casual Dinner

For a change of pace, enjoy the bright, intense flavors of this easy Asian-inspired meal.

QUICK & EASY

Hot-and-Sour Coconut Soup

Infuse a simple base of canned chicken broth with authentic Thai flavors of ginger, cilantro, garlic, and lemongrass. Thai fish sauce and *sambal oelek* are available in the ethnic food aisle at most large supermarkets; both are versatile condiments to keep on hand.

½ cup (1-inch) slices peeled fresh ginger
¼ cup chopped fresh cilantro
3 garlic cloves, halved
2 (14-ounce) cans fat-free, less-sodium chicken broth
2 (10-inch) stalks fresh lemongrass, each cut into 2-inch pieces
1 cup light coconut milk
1 tablespoon Thai fish sauce
2 teaspoons sambal oelek (ground fresh chile paste)
8 ounces skinless, boneless chicken breast, cut into bite-sized pieces
1 (15-ounce) can whole straw mushrooms, rinsed and drained
1 cup snow peas, halved crosswise
¼ cup chopped fresh basil
2 tablespoons fresh lime juice

1. Place first 5 ingredients in a large saucepan; bring to a boil. Cover, reduce heat, and simmer 20 minutes. Strain mixture through a sieve into a bowl; discard solids. Return infused broth to pan. Add coconut milk and next 4 ingredients; bring to a boil. Reduce heat, and simmer 10 minutes. Add peas; cook 3 minutes. Remove from heat; stir in basil and lime juice. Yield: 6 servings (serving size: about 1 cup).

CALORIES 101 (26% from fat); FAT 2.9g (sat 1.5g, mono 0.2g, poly 0.3g); PROTEIN 12.9g; CARB 5.9g; FIBER 1.7g; CHOL 22mg; IRON 1.5mg; SODIUM 742mg; CALC 17mg

---

QUICK & EASY • MAKE AHEAD

Shrimp and Spinach Soup

You can prepare the seasoned broth up to one day in advance, omitting the shrimp and spinach. Shortly before serving, reheat the broth, and stir them in.

½ cup water
½ cup matchstick-cut peeled fresh ginger
¼ cup mirin (sweet rice wine)
2 tablespoons low-sodium soy sauce
2 (14-ounce) cans vegetable broth
1 pound medium shrimp, peeled and deveined
2 cups bagged prewashed spinach (about 2 ounces)

Continued

1. Combine first 5 ingredients in a large saucepan; bring to a boil. Cover, reduce heat, and simmer 10 minutes. Stir in shrimp; cook over medium heat 2 minutes or until shrimp are almost done. Stir in spinach; cook 1 minute, stirring occasionally. Yield: 6 servings (serving size: about ¾ cup).

CALORIES 120 (14% from fat); FAT 1.9g (sat 0.3g, mono 0.2g, poly 0.5g); PROTEIN 17.1g; CARB 6.5g; FIBER 0.3g; CHOL 115mg; IRON 2.2mg; SODIUM 861mg; CALC 52mg

QUICK & EASY • MAKE AHEAD
Singapore Mai Fun

Long popular in take-out menus, this curried noodle dish is a sure hit and ready in a snap—provided you have the ingredients prepped before you start. The leftovers are good cold, as well. You'll find skinny rice noodles in the supermarket's ethnic food section.

    1   (6-ounce) package skinny rice
        noodles (*py mai fun*)
    ½   cup fat-free, less-sodium chicken
        broth
    3   tablespoons low-sodium soy
        sauce
    1   teaspoon sugar
    ½   teaspoon salt
    Cooking spray
    1   tablespoon peanut oil,
        divided
    1   large egg, lightly beaten
    ½   cup red bell pepper strips
    1   tablespoon grated peeled fresh
        ginger
    ¼   teaspoon crushed red
        pepper
    3   garlic cloves, minced
    8   ounces skinless, boneless chicken
        breast, thinly sliced
    1   tablespoon curry powder
    8   ounces medium shrimp, peeled
        and deveined
    1   cup (1-inch) slices green
        onions

1. Cook rice noodles according to package directions, omitting salt and fat. Drain.
2. Combine broth, soy sauce, sugar, and salt; stir until sugar dissolves.

3. Heat a large nonstick skillet over medium-high heat; coat pan with cooking spray. Add 1 teaspoon oil. Add egg; stir-fry 30 seconds or until soft-scrambled, stirring constantly. Remove from pan. Wipe pan clean with a paper towel. Heat 2 teaspoons oil in pan over medium-high heat. Add bell pepper strips, ginger, crushed red pepper, and garlic; stir-fry 15 seconds. Add chicken, and stir-fry 2 minutes. Add curry and shrimp; stir-fry 2 minutes. Stir in noodles, broth mixture, and egg; cook 1 minute or until thoroughly heated. Sprinkle with green onions. Yield: 6 servings (serving size: 1 cup).

CALORIES 237 (17% from fat); FAT 4.6g (sat 1g, mono 1.7g, poly 1.3g); PROTEIN 19.7g; CARB 27.8g; FIBER 1.3g; CHOL 115mg; IRON 2.2mg; SODIUM 646mg; CALC 53mg

QUICK & EASY
Pan-Fried Noodles
with Scallops

Pat noodles and scallops dry with paper towels to remove excess moisture before pan-frying. They'll be nicely crisp.

    8   ounces uncooked Chinese egg
        noodles
    1   pound large sea scallops, cut in
        half horizontally
    ¼   cup yellow cornmeal
    3   tablespoons peanut oil,
        divided
    2   teaspoons dark sesame oil
    1   cup chopped green onions
    1   teaspoon minced peeled fresh
        ginger
    3   garlic cloves, minced
    3   tablespoons low-sodium soy
        sauce
    3   tablespoons rice wine
        vinegar
    3   tablespoons oyster sauce
    1   teaspoon toasted sesame seeds

1. Cook noodles according to package directions, omitting salt and fat. Drain well. Pat noodles dry with paper towels; set aside.
2. Pat scallops dry with paper towels. Place cornmeal in a shallow dish; dredge scallops in cornmeal. Heat 1 tablespoon peanut oil in a large nonstick skillet over

medium-high heat. Add scallops; cook 3 minutes on each side or until browned. Remove from pan; cover and keep warm.
3. Heat 2 tablespoons peanut oil in pan over medium-high heat. Add noodles; pat into an even layer in pan. Cook 3 minutes or until browned, shaking pan occasionally. Carefully turn noodles over in sections; cook 3 minutes or until browned, shaking pan occasionally. Place browned noodles on a platter.
4. Heat sesame oil in pan over medium-high heat. Add green onions, ginger, and garlic; stir-fry 2 minutes. Stir in soy sauce, vinegar, and oyster sauce; cook 1 minute or until thoroughly heated. Drizzle sauce over noodles; top with scallops. Sprinkle with sesame seeds. Yield: 6 servings (serving size: about 1¼ cups).

CALORIES 308 (29% from fat); FAT 10g (sat 1.4g, mono 3.8g, poly 3g); PROTEIN 18g; CARB 38.6g; FIBER 6g; CHOL 25mg; IRON 2.8mg; SODIUM 447mg; CALC 40mg

Pork and Squash Stir-Fry

Chinese black vinegar, available in Asian markets, has a deep, smoky flavor that's slightly sweet; substitute balsamic vinegar or Worcestershire sauce, if desired.

    1   (2-pound) butternut squash,
        peeled and cut into ½-inch
        cubes
    2   tablespoons peanut oil
    2   tablespoons coarsely grated
        orange rind
    1   tablespoon minced peeled fresh
        ginger
    ½   teaspoon crushed red pepper
    1   (3-inch) cinnamon stick,
        broken
    1¼ pounds pork tenderloin, trimmed
        and cut into 2-inch strips
    2   tablespoons sugar
    3   tablespoons low-sodium soy
        sauce
    2   tablespoons Chinese black
        vinegar
    2   tablespoons red wine vinegar
    1   teaspoon cornstarch
    ¼   teaspoon salt
    1   cup chopped green onions

1. Place squash in a large microwave-safe bowl. Add water to a depth of 1 inch. Cover with plastic wrap; vent. Microwave at HIGH 8 minutes or until tender. Drain and set aside.

2. Heat oil in a large nonstick skillet over medium heat. Add rind, ginger, red pepper, and cinnamon stick pieces; cook 1 minute, stirring constantly. Remove and discard cinnamon stick pieces.

3. Increase heat to medium-high. Add pork to pan, and sauté 4 minutes or until browned. Combine sugar and next 5 ingredients, stirring with a whisk. Add sugar mixture to pan; cook 2 minutes or until sauce is slightly thickened, stirring constantly. Add squash; toss to coat. Stir in green onions. Yield: 6 servings (serving size: 1 cup).

CALORIES 257 (28% from fat); FAT 7.9g (sat 1.9g, mono 3.6g, poly 1.9g); PROTEIN 21.9g; CARB 25.9g; FIBER 6.2g; CHOL 61mg; IRON 2.5mg; SODIUM 423mg; CALC 84mg

MAKE AHEAD • FREEZABLE
Green Tea Granita

Any flavor of tea will work in this recipe. Brew it stronger or weaker according to your preference. Garnish this delicate dessert with wafer-thin slices of lemon.

    3   cups boiling water
    4   regular-sized green tea bags
    1   (2-inch) piece peeled fresh ginger, quartered
    ½   cup honey
    3   tablespoons fresh lemon juice

1. Pour boiling water over tea bags and ginger in a medium bowl. Cover and let stand 5 minutes. Add honey and lemon juice; stir to combine. Strain tea mixture through a sieve into a bowl; discard solids. Cool completely. Pour mixture into an 8-inch square baking dish. Cover and freeze 8 hours or until firm.

2. Remove tea mixture from freezer; scrape entire mixture with a fork until fluffy. Yield: 6 servings (serving size: about ½ cup).

CALORIES 88 (0% from fat); FAT 0g; PROTEIN 0.1g; CARB 23.9g; FIBER 0.1g; CHOL 0mg; IRON 0.1mg; SODIUM 1mg; CALC 2.2mg

Sunday
Brunch Buffet

End the weekend on a graceful note with this relaxing spread.

Brunch Buffet Menu
serves 6

Holiday Brunch Tonic

Whole Wheat Apricot Muffins

Grits Casserole with Mushrooms, Prosciutto, and Provolone

Pistachio Granola served with milk or vanilla low-fat yogurt

Fruit Salad with Honey-Yogurt Sauce

Sour Cream-Hazelnut Bundt Cake

Holiday Brunch Tonic

This fizzy beverage takes on a festive feel with the scent of rosemary-infused sugar syrup. Garnish with extra rosemary sprigs, if desired. Serve shortly after mixing everything together so the tonic will sparkle.

    1   cup sugar
    1   cup water
    4   rosemary sprigs
    4   cups cranberry juice cocktail, chilled
    3   cups club soda, chilled
    2   cups fresh orange juice (about 6 oranges), chilled

1. Combine sugar and water in a small saucepan; bring to a boil. Reduce heat, and simmer 4 minutes or until sugar dissolves. Add rosemary; simmer 5 minutes. Remove from heat. Pour sugar syrup into a bowl; cover and refrigerate overnight.

2. Uncover sugar syrup; remove and discard rosemary sprigs. Combine sugar syrup, cranberry juice, soda, and orange juice in a large pitcher. Serve immediately over ice. Yield: 12 servings (serving size: about ¾ cup).

CALORIES 131 (1% from fat); FAT 0.2g (sat 0g, mono 0g, poly 0.1g); PROTEIN 0.3g; CARB 33.1g; FIBER 0.2g; CHOL 0mg; IRON 0.2mg; SODIUM 15mg; CALC 10mg

MAKE AHEAD
Whole Wheat Apricot Muffins

These muffins are best served warm, so reheat before serving if you've made them 1 or 2 days ahead. Wrap the muffins in aluminum foil, and heat at 350° for 10 to 15 minutes. Try varying the recipe by using dried fruit in place of the apricots—dried cherries or dates, for instance.

    1   cup all-purpose flour
    ⅔   cup whole wheat flour
    ½   cup sugar
    1¼   teaspoons grated orange rind
    1   teaspoon baking soda
    ¼   teaspoon salt
    1   cup low-fat buttermilk
    ¼   cup butter, melted
    ½   teaspoon vanilla extract
    1   large egg, lightly beaten
    1   cup finely chopped dried apricots
    Cooking spray

1. Preheat oven to 375°.

2. Lightly spoon flours into dry measuring cups; level with a knife. Combine flours, sugar, orange rind, baking soda, and salt in a large bowl, stirring with a whisk; make a well in center of mixture. Combine buttermilk, butter, vanilla, and egg; add to flour mixture, stirring just until moist. Fold in apricots.

3. Spoon batter into 12 muffin cups coated with cooking spray. Bake at 375° for 15 minutes or until muffins spring back when touched lightly in center. Remove muffins from pan, and place on a wire rack. Yield: 1 dozen (serving size: 1 muffin).

CALORIES 167 (25% from fat); FAT 4.7g (sat 2.6g, mono 1.3g, poly 0.3g); PROTEIN 3.6g; CARB 29g; FIBER 1.9g; CHOL 29mg; IRON 1.1mg; SODIUM 221mg; CALC 37mg

Grits Casserole with Mushrooms, Prosciutto, and Provolone

Use yellow grits for the best presentation; white grits may look gray under the mushroom topping.

MAKE-AHEAD TIP: Cook the grits, spoon into the baking dish, and refrigerate overnight. Let the baking dish stand at room temperature while you prepare the mushroom topping; top the grits, and bake as directed.

- 5 cups water
- 1¼ cups stone-ground yellow grits
- ¾ cup (3 ounces) shredded sharp provolone cheese, divided
- 1 teaspoon salt, divided
- Cooking spray
- 1½ teaspoons butter
- ¾ cup chopped onion
- 2 garlic cloves, minced
- 4 cups thinly sliced portobello mushrooms (about 6 ounces)
- 3 cups thinly sliced shiitake mushroom caps (about 4½ ounces)
- 1 teaspoon dried herbes de Provence
- ¼ teaspoon freshly ground black pepper
- 1 cup chopped prosciutto (about 3 ounces)
- ⅓ cup dry white wine
- 3 large eggs, lightly beaten
- 2 large egg whites, lightly beaten
- 1 tablespoon minced fresh parsley

1. Bring water to a boil in a large saucepan; gradually stir in grits. Reduce heat, and simmer 30 minutes or until thick, stirring frequently. Remove from heat. Stir in ¼ cup cheese and ½ teaspoon salt. Spoon grits mixture into an 11 x 7-inch baking dish coated with cooking spray.

2. Preheat oven to 350°.

3. Melt butter in a large nonstick skillet over medium-high heat. Add onion and garlic; sauté 3 minutes or until tender. Add ½ teaspoon salt, mushrooms, herbes de Provence, and pepper; cook 6 minutes or until mushrooms are tender, stirring frequently. Stir in prosciutto and wine; cook 5 minutes or until liquid almost evaporates. Remove from heat; cool slightly. Stir in eggs and egg whites. Spread mushroom mixture over grits mixture; sprinkle with ½ cup cheese. Bake at 350° for 30 minutes or until cheese melts and grits are thoroughly heated. Let stand 5 minutes before serving. Sprinkle with parsley. Yield: 6 servings.

CALORIES 287 (30% from fat); FAT 9.6g (sat 4.4g, mono 3.1g, poly 0.9g); PROTEIN 16.3g; CARB 35.7g; FIBER 2.3g; CHOL 131mg; IRON 2.9mg; SODIUM 832mg; CALC 136mg

Pistachio Granola
(pictured on page 379)

This easy stovetop method makes preparing granola a breeze. Handle the cooled granola according to your preference—leave it in larger chunks, or break it into smaller pieces. Serve with vanilla low-fat yogurt, over ice cream, in a bowl with milk, or as a snack.

- ⅔ cup packed brown sugar
- ¼ cup apple cider
- 2 cups regular oats
- ⅔ cup chopped pistachios
- ⅔ cup nutlike cereal nuggets (such as Grape-Nuts)
- ⅔ cup dried sweet cherries
- ½ cup sunflower seed kernels
- ½ teaspoon ground cinnamon
- ¼ teaspoon salt

1. Combine sugar and cider in a large nonstick skillet; cook over medium-high heat 3 minutes or until sugar dissolves, stirring frequently. Stir in oats and remaining ingredients; cook 5 minutes or until granola is lightly browned, stirring frequently. Cool completely. Store in an airtight container up to 1 week. Yield: 5 cups (serving size: ½ cup).

CALORIES 263 (29% from fat); FAT 8.4g (sat 1g, mono 3.1g, poly 3.7g); PROTEIN 6.9g; CARB 42.9g; FIBER 4.6g; CHOL 0mg; IRON 3.9mg; SODIUM 149mg; CALC 45mg

Fruit Salad with Honey-Yogurt Sauce
(pictured on page 379)

You can prepare and refrigerate the yogurt sauce up to 1 day in advance. You can also combine and refrigerate the fruit mixture (except the banana) up to 3 hours ahead; stir in the banana just before serving to prevent discoloring.

- 1 cup vanilla low-fat yogurt
- 1 tablespoon honey
- 1½ teaspoons grated lime rind
- 3 cups cubed pineapple (about 1 medium)
- 1½ cups chopped Braeburn apple (about 1 large)
- 1 cup orange sections (about 2 oranges)
- 1 cup chopped peeled kiwi (about 2 large)
- ⅓ cup flaked sweetened coconut
- 1 banana, sliced
- ¼ cup slivered almonds, toasted

1. Combine yogurt, honey, and lime rind in a small bowl.

2. Combine pineapple and next 4 ingredients in a large bowl; toss gently. Just before serving, stir in banana. Top fruit mixture with yogurt sauce; sprinkle with almonds. Yield: 6 servings (serving size: 1¼ cups fruit mixture, 2 tablespoons sauce, and 2 teaspoons almonds).

CALORIES 196 (22% from fat); FAT 4.8g (sat 1.8g, mono 1.7g, poly 0.8g); PROTEIN 4.3g; CARB 37.9g; FIBER 4.7g; CHOL 2mg; IRON 0.9mg; SODIUM 40mg; CALC 111mg

Set out this breakfast buffet so that your guests can eat whenever they want and at their own pace.

Sour Cream-Hazelnut Bundt Cake

(pictured on page 379)

Bake the cake up to 2 days ahead; store at room temperature. Or bake it up to 1 month ahead. Freeze; thaw at room temperature.

Cooking spray
1 tablespoon dry breadcrumbs
1½ cups granulated sugar
½ cup butter, softened
2 large eggs
1 teaspoon vanilla extract
1 (16-ounce) carton fat-free sour cream
2½ cups all-purpose flour
1 teaspoon baking powder
½ teaspoon baking soda
¼ teaspoon salt
¼ cup chopped hazelnuts, toasted
2 tablespoons chocolate-hazelnut spread (such as Nutella)
1 teaspoon powdered sugar

1. Preheat oven to 350°.
2. Coat a 12-cup Bundt pan with cooking spray; dust with breadcrumbs.
3. Place granulated sugar and butter in a large bowl; beat with a mixer at medium speed until well blended (about 2 minutes). Add eggs, 1 at a time, beating well after each addition. Add vanilla and sour cream; beat until well blended.
4. Lightly spoon flour into dry measuring cups; level with a knife. Combine flour, baking powder, baking soda, and salt in a medium bowl; stir with a whisk until well combined. Add flour mixture to sugar mixture; stir just until combined.
5. Spoon half of batter into prepared Bundt pan; sprinkle evenly with hazelnuts. Drop small spoonfuls of chocolate spread over nuts. Spoon remaining batter over chocolate spread; swirl batter using tip of a knife. Bake at 350° for 55 minutes or until a wooden pick inserted in center comes out clean. Cool in pan on a wire rack 15 minutes; remove cake from pan. Cool completely on wire rack. Sprinkle cake with powdered sugar. Yield: 14 servings (serving size: 1 slice).

CALORIES 293 (30% from fat); FAT 9.8g (sat 4.8g, mono 3.6g, poly 0.7g); PROTEIN 5.4g; CARB 46.1g; FIBER 1g; CHOL 51mg; IRON 1.4mg; SODIUM 226mg; CALC 82mg

Rick Rodgers Talks Turkey

The author of Thanksgiving 101 teaches how to make delicious dishes with the season's most popular bird.

As a chef, cooking teacher, and former spokesperson for a major poultry producer, Rick Rodgers knows all about turkey. And as the author of *Thanksgiving 101: Celebrate America's Favorite Holiday with America's Thanksgiving Expert*, Rodgers takes the most pride in applying this knowledge to everyday cooking for "real people."

Turkey is a great medium for all kinds of cooking. "Versatile" doesn't begin to describe this bird. Of course, a roast turkey remains the star of the winter holiday dinner table, but turkey can be turned into hearty stews, satisfying braises, simple sautés, and more, all year long. And turkey can do it with less fat and more flavor than its cousin, the chicken.

Beyond a whole bird, the supermarket offers a variety of turkey options: boneless and skinless cuts; turkey parts in their natural, skin-on, bone-in state (such as drumsticks and wings); ground turkey; and processed turkey products like fresh Italian and breakfast sausages and cooked sausages. These recipes will show you how to cook with different turkey parts to create more than the centerpiece at your Thanksgiving table.

Italian Turkey Sausage with Three Peppers

Use a variety of bell peppers for visual appeal. Crushed red and ground black round out the peppers of the recipe's title.

3 pounds red potatoes, quartered
Cooking spray
4 teaspoons olive oil, divided
¾ teaspoon salt, divided
¼ teaspoon freshly ground black pepper
6 hot Italian turkey sausages (about 1 [19½-ounce] package)
3 bell peppers, cut into ½-inch strips
2 garlic cloves, minced
2 tablespoons balsamic vinegar
1 teaspoon dried rosemary
¼ teaspoon crushed red pepper

1. Preheat oven to 375°.
2. Arrange potatoes in a single layer in a roasting pan coated with cooking spray. Drizzle with 1 teaspoon oil, and sprinkle with ½ teaspoon salt and black pepper. Toss to coat. Bake at 375° for 40 minutes or until tender, turning occasionally.
3. While potatoes cook, heat 1 teaspoon oil in a large nonstick skillet over medium-high heat. Pierce sausage casings several times with a fork. Add sausages to pan; cook 5 minutes or until lightly browned. Remove sausages from pan.
4. Heat 2 teaspoons oil in pan. Add bell pepper; sauté 5 minutes or until tender. Add garlic; sauté 1 minute. Stir in ¼ teaspoon salt, vinegar, rosemary, and red pepper. Return sausages to pan; cover and cook over medium-low heat 15 minutes or until sausages are done. Yield: 6 servings (serving size: 1 sausage link, ⅓ cup bell pepper mixture, and about 1 cup potatoes).

CALORIES 358 (30% from fat); FAT 12.1g (sat 3.1g, mono 5.6g, poly 3g); PROTEIN 21.3g; CARB 41.2g; FIBER 5.2g; CHOL 78mg; IRON 2.1mg; SODIUM 861mg; CALC 35mg

Turkey Cooking Tips

The main thing to consider with turkey is the white meat versus dark meat issue. White meat is very lean. Its lack of intra-muscular fat (which melts during cooking and contributes to moistness) can make the cooked meat dry, but only if cooked improperly. Here are a few tricks to remember:

• When appropriate, choose a method that creates a moist cooking environment, such as braising.
• Use medium heat when cooking boneless white-meat cuts on the stove-top. High heat forces moisture out of the meat.
• Don't cook thick white-meat cuts, such as breasts or tenderloins, above 170°.
• Dark meat is fattier, which translates into moister end results. Dark meat comes from areas that get lots of exercise, so it's tougher and needs a longer cooking time. Dark meat isn't tender until it reaches 180°.

White Meat

White-meat turkey cuts come from the breast. You can find whole turkey breasts with skin that come boneless or bone-in. Tell your butcher the weight of skinless, boneless turkey breast you need, and have him remove skin and bone while you shop. A boneless turkey breast half, with skin, is sometimes labeled "bone-less turkey breast roast." These cuts are wrapped in netting and aren't always one whole breast half; you may find small portions of meat in addition to the breast half. To remove the skin, you need to remove the netting, cut off the skin, and replace the netting to hold the roast together. Skinless, boneless turkey cutlets, also known as turkey scaloppine, are a good substitute for veal cutlets in sautéed dishes. Turkey tenderloins can be roasted or cut into thick medallions or "boneless chops" for sautéing; they don't brown well when baked as a whole tenderloin.

Dark Meat

Economical and tasty dark meat parts include drumsticks, wings, and thighs. It's no secret that poultry skin contains plenty of fat, and removing it reduces the fat by about one-third, but these cuts aren't always skinless. It's easy to remove the skin from drumsticks and thighs. Skinless drumsticks are best cooked in a moist medium to braise the tough meat and tenderize it, rather than with the familiar roasting method. Cut-up skinless, boneless turkey thighs, which must also be simmered to juicy tender-ness, are a good replacement for red meat in stews. Taking the skin off raw turkey wings is virtually impossible. Instead, simmer them in broth to flavor soups, then remove the skin from the wings, and chop the meat to add to the soup. Chill the chopped wing meat and broth separately, and skim the fat before finishing the soup.

Ground Turkey

Not all ground turkey is created equal. Regular ground turkey (labeled 93 per-cent lean) is a combination of white and dark meat and is fairly high in calories and fat, but it's still leaner than ground round (usually 85 percent lean). Frozen ground turkey, which is all dark meat and can contain skin, can be just as high in fat as ground beef. Ground turkey breast is the lowest in fat, but it can dry out.

When cooking turkey burgers and meatballs, use regular ground turkey, and add something to moisten it and a little binder (like breadcrumbs) to retain moisture. Use ground turkey breast in saucy and soupy applications to keep it from becoming dry.

Turkey Sausage

Fresh turkey sausages are pork-free, as the casings are made from vegetable cellulose. They're made from ground turkey seasoned in various ways. Remove the casings, and cook in a pan, stirring to crumble. Or broil, grill, or pan sauté whole sausages with the casings. To help avoid curling at the edges, pierce whole sausages several times before cooking.

Cooked turkey sausages can be lower in fat than traditional sausages, but they may be smoked and relatively high in sodium, so reserve them for an occasional treat.

Timing Whole Turkeys

Be sure to take into account all the steps needed to get your bird ready to roast.

Thawing: The best way to thaw a frozen turkey is in the refrigerator. A 12-pound turkey takes 2½ to 3 days to thaw. If you run out of time, thaw the bird, wrapped in its original packaging, in cold water, changing the water every 30 minutes. Figure 30 minutes per pound, or 6 hours for a 12-pound bird.

Salting or brining: The basic roast turkey recipe offered within this Cooking Class calls for salting the bird and storing it uncovered in the refrigerator for 24 hours. Other recipes (for example, Apple Cider-Brined Turkey with Savory Herb Gravy, recipe on page 374) may call for brining (soaking it in a saltwater solution). Both procedures provide juicy, flavorful results.

Get ready to roast: Preparation can take up to 1 hour. Allow 30 minutes if you're brining or salting the turkey; you'll need to rinse, pat dry, and remove the lumps of fat from the tail area of the bird before seasoning and refrigerating, then rinse and pat it dry again. Chopping aromatic vegetables to stuff into the body cavity and tying the legs can take another 30 minutes. If your turkey came with a metal clip attached to the legs, use that instead of kitchen string to hold the legs together.

Carving: Place the roasted turkey on a platter, tent it loosely with foil, and let it stand for 30 minutes. This lets juices redistribute in the meat so it's moister and firmer when carved.

Amish Potpie with Turkey Wings

In Amish cookery, potpie is a poultry soup with noodles. Turkey wings add lots of flavor to the broth. Make the broth ahead, and skim the fat from the surface. Cutting the turkey wings at the joints makes it easier to lay them flat in the pan for even browning. The turkey meat and broth are stored separately because the broth needs to cool to room temperature before being placed in the refrigerator to keep the steam from warming up the fridge. The turkey needs to be chilled as soon as possible, though. To cook the noodles properly, make sure the broth mixture is boiling before adding them.

  3 pounds turkey wings
  2 teaspoons vegetable oil, divided
  2 cups chopped onion
  1 cup chopped carrot
  1 cup chopped celery
 12 cups water
1½ teaspoons salt
  1 teaspoon dried thyme
 ½ teaspoon freshly ground black pepper
  2 bay leaves
2½ cups uncooked medium egg noodles
  3 tablespoons chopped fresh parsley
 ½ teaspoon saffron threads, crushed

1. Cut turkey wings apart at the joints. Heat 1 teaspoon oil in a large Dutch oven over medium-high heat. Add half of turkey; cook 7 minutes, browning on all sides. Remove from pan. Repeat procedure with 1 teaspoon oil and remaining turkey.
2. Add onion, carrot, and celery to pan; sauté 5 minutes or until lightly browned. Return turkey to pan; add 12 cups water. Bring to a boil; skim any foam from surface of broth. Stir in salt, thyme, pepper, and bay leaves. Reduce heat; simmer 1½ hours.
3. Remove turkey; cool slightly. Discard skin and bones; coarsely chop turkey meat. Place turkey meat in a medium bowl; cover and chill. Place broth mixture in a large bowl; cool 1 hour at room temperature. Cover and chill 8 hours. Skim solidified fat from surface.
4. Place broth mixture in a large Dutch oven. Bring to a boil over medium-high heat. Add turkey meat, noodles, parsley, and saffron; cook 6 minutes or until noodles are tender. Discard bay leaves. Yield: 8 servings (serving size: 1½ cups).

CALORIES 188 (25% from fat); FAT 5.3g (sat 1.4g, mono 1.5g, poly 1.7g); PROTEIN 20g; CARB 14.4g; FIBER 1.9g; CHOL 70mg; IRON 2.2mg; SODIUM 518mg; CALC 50mg

Turkey Kielbasa Choucroute

Draining and rinsing sauerkraut gives it a cleaner taste and reduces the sodium content. Broiling browns the sausage and intensifies the spices. Nestling it in the sauerkraut mixture helps the flavors permeate the entire dish.

  2 pounds refrigerated sauerkraut, drained
     Cooking spray
1½ cups chopped onion
  3 cups sliced peeled Golden Delicious apple
  1 cup Riesling or other dry white wine
  1 cup fat-free, less-sodium chicken broth
  1 teaspoon caraway seeds
 ½ teaspoon dried thyme
 ¼ teaspoon freshly ground black pepper
  1 bay leaf
  2 (14-ounce) packages turkey kielbasa, cut into 18 pieces

1. Soak sauerkraut in cold water 10 minutes. Drain in a colander; press to remove excess moisture.
2. Heat a Dutch oven over medium heat. Coat pan with cooking spray. Add onion; sauté 5 minutes or until tender. Stir in sauerkraut, apple, and next 6 ingredients; bring to a boil. Cover, reduce heat, and simmer 30 minutes or until apple is just tender, stirring occasionally.
3. Preheat broiler.
4. Place kielbasa on a baking sheet; cut several ¼-inch-deep slits in each piece. Broil 8 minutes or until lightly browned, turning occasionally. Nestle kielbasa pieces into sauerkraut mixture; cover and simmer 15 minutes. Uncover; cook 5 minutes or until liquid almost evaporates. Discard bay leaf. Yield: 9 servings (serving size: about 1 cup).

CALORIES 195 (33% from fat); FAT 7.2g (sat 2.2g, mono 2.7g, poly 2.2g); PROTEIN 15g; CARB 13.8g; FIBER 2.9g; CHOL 58mg; IRON 2.4mg; SODIUM 1,063mg; CALC 45mg

Belgian Turkey Ragoût

This recipe is based on the Belgian beef dish *carbonnade à la flamande*, a thick stew with bacon, beer, onions, and sugar. With turkey instead of beef, it's also like the rich French stew called ragoût. Purchase 3½ pounds of turkey thighs with skin and bone, or 2¼ pounds of skinless, boneless turkey thighs.

3½ pounds turkey thighs
  1 teaspoon salt, divided
 ½ teaspoon black pepper, divided
  2 teaspoons vegetable oil
  1 tablespoon butter
  4 cups thinly sliced leek (about 5 large)
  2 cups (½-inch) pieces carrot
  3 tablespoons all-purpose flour
  1 cup fat-free, less-sodium chicken broth
  1 tablespoon brown sugar
  1 (12-ounce) bottle amber lager
  1 tablespoon Dijon mustard
  1 tablespoon white wine vinegar
  2 tablespoons chopped fresh parsley

1. Preheat oven to 300°.
2. Remove skin from turkey; cut meat from bones. Discard skin and bones; cut meat into 1½-inch pieces. Sprinkle with ½ teaspoon salt and ¼ teaspoon pepper.
3. Heat oil in a small Dutch oven over medium-high heat. Add turkey; cook 6 minutes or until browned, stirring
Continued

occasionally. Remove turkey and juices from pan. Reduce heat to medium; melt butter in pan. Add leek and carrot; cover and cook 12 minutes or until leek begins to brown, stirring occasionally.

4. Return turkey and juices to pan. Sprinkle flour over turkey mixture; stir well to coat. Add ½ teaspoon salt, ¼ teaspoon pepper, broth, sugar, and beer. Bring to a boil; cover. Place in oven. Bake at 300° for 50 minutes or until turkey is tender. Stir in mustard and vinegar; sprinkle with parsley. Yield: 8 servings (serving size: 1 cup).

CALORIES 253 (30% from fat); FAT 8.4g (sat 2.9g, mono 1.9g, poly 2.5g); PROTEIN 26.8g; CARB 14.7g; FIBER 2g; CHOL 89mg; IRON 3.5mg; SODIUM 538mg; CALC 67mg

Turkey Breast with Spinach-Feta Stuffing

Don't pound the turkey breast meat too hard; it's delicate and can tear. After spreading the spinach mixture and rolling the turkey, secure it with twine.

    4   tablespoons water, divided
    1   (6-ounce) package prewashed
        baby spinach
    1   tablespoon olive oil, divided
    ¼   cup finely chopped shallots,
        divided
    1   garlic clove, minced
    ½   cup (2 ounces) crumbled feta
        cheese
    1   tablespoon dry breadcrumbs
    ½   teaspoon dried oregano
    ¾   teaspoon salt, divided
    ⅛   teaspoon freshly ground black
        pepper
    1   large egg white, lightly beaten
    1   (1¾-pound) boneless turkey
        breast half
    ¼   teaspoon freshly ground black
        pepper
    ½   cup dry white wine
    ¾   cup fat-free, less-sodium chicken
        broth
    1½ teaspoons cornstarch
    1   tablespoon butter

1. Heat a large saucepan over medium-high heat. Add 1 tablespoon water and spinach; cover and cook 5 minutes or until spinach wilts, stirring occasionally. Place spinach mixture in a colander, pressing until barely moist.

2. Heat 1 teaspoon oil in a small saucepan over medium-high heat. Add 2 tablespoons chopped shallots, 2 tablespoons water, and garlic; cover and cook 3 minutes or until moisture evaporates. Spoon shallot mixture into a medium bowl. Add spinach, feta, breadcrumbs, oregano, ¼ teaspoon salt, ⅛ teaspoon pepper, and egg white.

3. Cut horizontally through center of breast, cutting to, but not through, other side using a sharp knife; open flat as you would a book. Place breast between 2 sheets of plastic wrap; pound to an even ½-inch thickness using a meat mallet or rolling pin. Discard plastic wrap. Spread spinach mixture over turkey, leaving a 1-inch border. Roll up breast, jelly-roll fashion, starting with one short side. Secure at 2-inch intervals with twine. Rub ½ teaspoon salt and ¼ teaspoon pepper evenly over turkey.

4. Preheat oven to 325°.

5. Heat 2 teaspoons oil in a large Dutch oven over medium-high heat. Add turkey; cook 5 minutes, browning on all sides. Remove turkey from pan. Add 2 tablespoons shallots to pan; sauté 30 seconds. Stir in wine, scraping pan to loosen browned bits. Add turkey and broth to pan; bring to a boil. Cover and bake at 325° for 40 minutes or until a thermometer inserted in thickest portion of turkey registers 170°. Remove turkey from pan; keep warm.

6. Place pan on stovetop over high heat. Combine cornstarch and 1 tablespoon water, stirring with a whisk. Add cornstarch mixture to pan; bring to a boil. Cook 1 minute or until slightly thick, stirring constantly. Remove from heat. Add butter, stirring with a whisk. Remove and discard twine from turkey. Cut turkey into 8 slices. Serve sauce with turkey. Yield: 8 servings (serving size: 1 turkey slice and 1½ tablespoons sauce).

CALORIES 191 (28% from fat); FAT 5.9g (sat 2.8g, mono 2.2g, poly 0.5g); PROTEIN 27.4g; CARB 3.6g; FIBER 0.7g; CHOL 74mg; IRON 2.1mg; SODIUM 449mg; CALC 86mg

How to Stuff a Turkey Breast

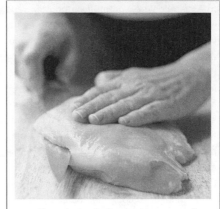

1. *Slice through the thickest part of the breast, leaving it attached at one side.*

2. *When spreading the filling over the flattened breast, leave a 1-inch border so it doesn't fall out.*

3. *Secure with twine to hold the breast together.*

Turkey-Jasmine Rice Meatballs with Baby Bok Choy

Use a box grater to shred the ginger after you've peeled away the outer layer. Jasmine rice underscores the other Asian ingredients, but any long-grain white rice will work. Chopped bok choy can substitute for whole baby bok choy.

MEATBALLS:

    1   cup water
    ⅓   cup uncooked jasmine rice
    ¼   cup dry breadcrumbs
    ¼   cup chopped green onions
    ¾   teaspoon salt
    ¼   teaspoon freshly ground black pepper
    1¼ pounds ground turkey
    2   large egg whites, lightly beaten
    1   garlic clove, minced
    Cooking spray

BOK CHOY:

    6   baby bok choy (about 1⅓ pounds)
    2   teaspoons vegetable oil
    ¼   cup chopped green onions
    1   tablespoon shredded peeled fresh ginger
    1   garlic clove, minced
    1   cup water
    ¾   cup fat-free, less-sodium chicken broth
    3   tablespoons low-sodium soy sauce
    1½ teaspoons sugar
    ½   teaspoon crushed red pepper
    1½ tablespoons dry sherry
    2   teaspoons cornstarch

1. To prepare meatballs, bring 1 cup water to a boil in a small saucepan. Stir in rice; reduce heat, and simmer 15 minutes or until rice is almost tender. Drain; cool. Combine rice, breadcrumbs, and next 6 ingredients. Shape mixture into 18 meatballs.

2. Heat a large nonstick skillet over medium-high heat; coat pan with cooking spray. Add meatballs; cook 5 minutes, browning on all sides. Cover and reduce heat to medium; cook 10 minutes or until done, turning frequently. Remove from heat; keep warm.

3. While meatballs cook, prepare bok choy. Cut each bok choy in half lengthwise. Rinse with cold running water; drain well. Arrange bok choy in a steamer basket, overlapping pieces.

4. Heat oil in a Dutch oven over medium-high heat. Add ¼ cup onions, ginger, and 1 garlic clove; sauté 30 seconds. Place steamer basket in pan. Combine 1 cup water, broth, and next 3 ingredients; pour over bok choy. Bring to a boil; cover, reduce heat, and steam over medium-low heat 20 minutes or until bok choy is tender, rearranging bok choy after 10 minutes. Remove bok choy and steamer basket from pan; cover and keep warm.

5. Combine sherry and cornstarch; add to pan. Bring to a boil; cook 1 minute or until slightly thick. Yield: 6 servings (serving size: 3 meatballs, 2 bok choy halves, and 3 tablespoons sauce).

CALORIES 251 (35% from fat); FAT 9.8g (sat 2.4g, mono 3.4g, poly 2.9g); PROTEIN 21.3g; CARB 18g; FIBER 1.9g; CHOL 75mg; IRON 2.6mg; SODIUM 832mg; CALC 135mg

Turkey Scaloppine with Porcini and Marsala

Scaloppine is a very lean, thin cut and will dry out if cooked over high heat. Serve with mashed potatoes, rice, or pasta.

    1   cup fat-free, less-sodium chicken broth
    ⅓   cup dry Marsala
    1   ounce dried porcini mushrooms
    1   tablespoon olive oil, divided
    4   (½-inch-thick) turkey breast cutlets (about 1 pound)
    ½   teaspoon salt
    ¼   teaspoon freshly ground black pepper
    3   cups sliced cremini mushrooms (about 8 ounces)
    2   tablespoons finely chopped shallots
    1   tablespoon all-purpose flour

1. Bring first 3 ingredients to a boil in a small saucepan. Cover; remove from heat. Let stand 20 minutes or until mushrooms are tender. Drain mushrooms in a fine sieve over a bowl, reserving soaking liquid. Coarsely chop porcini mushrooms.

2. Heat 1 teaspoon oil in a nonstick skillet over medium heat. Sprinkle turkey with salt and pepper. Add turkey to pan; cook 2 minutes on each side or just until browned. Remove turkey from pan.

3. Heat 2 teaspoons oil in pan over medium-high heat. Add cremini mushrooms; sauté 5 minutes. Add porcini mushrooms and shallots, and sauté 2 minutes. Sprinkle with flour, stirring to coat. Stir in reserved soaking liquid; bring to a boil. Return turkey to pan. Reduce heat to medium-low. Cover and cook 5 minutes or until turkey is done and sauce is slightly thick. Yield: 4 servings (serving size: 1 turkey cutlet and about ¼ cup sauce).

CALORIES 246 (16% from fat); FAT 4.4g (sat 0.7g, mono 2.8g, poly 0.6g); PROTEIN 33.7g; CARB 10.3g; FIBER 2.5g; CHOL 70mg; IRON 3.5mg; SODIUM 488mg; CALC 18mg

MAKE AHEAD • FREEZABLE
Homemade Turkey Stock

Refrigerate this speedy stock in an airtight container for 1 week, or freeze up to 3 months.

    2   teaspoons vegetable oil
    Turkey heart, neck, and gizzard from 1 (12-pound) turkey
    ½   cup chopped onion
    ½   cup chopped carrot
    ½   cup chopped celery
    8   cups cold water
    2   (14-ounce) cans fat-free, less-sodium chicken broth
    ½   teaspoon dried thyme
    ¼   teaspoon black peppercorns
    3   parsley sprigs
    1   bay leaf

1. Heat oil in a large stockpot over medium-high heat. Add heart, neck, and gizzard; sauté 5 minutes. Add onion, carrot, and celery; sauté 4 minutes. Add water and broth; bring to a boil. Add thyme, peppercorns, parsley, and bay leaf. Reduce heat; simmer 2 hours. Strain through a sieve into a bowl; discard solids. Cool to room temperature. Cover and chill overnight. Skim solidified fat from surface. Yield: 7 cups (serving size: 1 cup).

CALORIES 31 (55% from fat); FAT 1.9g (sat 0.3g, mono 0.5g, poly 0.9g); PROTEIN 2.4g; CARB 0.9g; FIBER 0.2g; CHOL 3mg; IRON 0.3mg; SODIUM 228mg; CALC 10mg

Roast Turkey with Sausage Gravy

Salting the turkey and refrigerating it 24 hours lets the seasoning spread throughout the meat and keeps moisture in. You get the benefits of brining, but it takes up less space in the refrigerator. To keep the breast area of the turkey moist, cover tightly with aluminum foil to deflect heat and slow the cooking.

   1   (12-pound) fresh or frozen turkey, thawed
 4½   teaspoons salt, divided
   2   cups chopped onion
   1   cup chopped celery
   8   rosemary sprigs
  12   thyme sprigs
  12   sage sprigs
  ¾   teaspoon black pepper, divided
   5   cups fat-free, less-sodium chicken broth, divided
   2   (3.5-ounce) links sweet Italian turkey sausage, casings removed
  ⅓   cup all-purpose flour
   2   tablespoons cornstarch
   1   tablespoon water

1. Remove giblets, neck, and heart from turkey, and reserve for Homemade Turkey Stock (recipe on page 393). Rinse turkey with cold water; pat dry. Trim excess fat. Sprinkle 4 teaspoons salt over turkey and in body cavity; refrigerate, uncovered, 24 hours.
2. Preheat oven to 325°.
3. Rinse turkey with cold water; pat dry. Stuff body cavity with onion, celery, herbs, and ¼ teaspoon pepper. Lift wing tips up and over back; tuck under turkey. Tie legs together with kitchen string. Place turkey, breast side up, on a rack in a roasting pan. Insert a meat thermometer into meaty part of thigh, making sure not to touch bone. Sprinkle turkey with ½ teaspoon salt and ½ teaspoon pepper. Cover breast with foil. Bake at 325° for 2 hours, basting turkey with ⅓ cup broth every 30 minutes. Remove foil; bake an additional 1 hour and 45 minutes or until thermometer registers 180°, basting turkey with broth every 30 minutes. Remove turkey from oven. Place on a platter, reserving pan drippings. Cover turkey loosely with foil, and let stand 30 minutes before carving. Discard skin.
4. Cook sausage in a large nonstick skillet over medium-high heat until browned, stirring to crumble. Drain and set aside.
5. Place a zip-top plastic bag in a 2-cup measure. Pour reserved drippings into bag; let stand 10 minutes (fat will rise to the top). Seal bag, and snip off 1 bottom corner. Drain into a medium saucepan; stop before fat reaches opening. Reserve 1 tablespoon fat; discard remaining fat. Cook reserved fat and flour in roasting pan over medium heat 1 minute; stir constantly with a whisk. Add drippings, 3 cups broth, and sausage. Combine cornstarch and water; add to pan. Bring to a boil. Cook 2 minutes or until thick; stir constantly. Yield: 12 servings (serving size: 6 ounces turkey and ⅓ cup gravy).

CALORIES 353 (28% from fat); FAT 11.1g (sat 3.6g, mono 2.8g, poly 3.1g); PROTEIN 54.5g; CARB 4.8g; FIBER 0.2g; CHOL 144mg; IRON 3.2mg; SODIUM 603mg; CALC 45mg

from the pantry

Delectable Dates

This rich fruit is a delicious match with sweet and savory dishes.

Although dates are commonly used in North African and Middle Eastern kitchens, Americans most often use them for holiday baking. But dates can add variety to meals all year round. Their versatility has made them a staple food for at least 5,000 years.

Many different types of dates are available in grocery stores, including soft, semidry, and dried dates (see "Know Your Date," on page 396). When shopping, choose plump, soft fruit with smooth, shiny, dark-amber skin. Avoid those that are badly cracked, smell sour, or have formed sugar crystals (a sure sign that they're past their prime). When at home, store dried dates in a cool, dark place up to one year. Tightly wrap soft and semidry dates in plastic wrap, and store them in the refrigerator up to one month.

Cardamom-Date Snack Cake

This spicy little cake welcomes a glass of milk or cup of hot tea. The dates make this treat extremely moist and tender, so use a serrated knife to cut it.

CAKE:
      Cooking spray
   2   cups all-purpose flour
   1   teaspoon baking powder
   1   teaspoon baking soda
  ½   teaspoon salt
  ½   teaspoon ground cardamom
  ½   teaspoon ground cinnamon
   1   cup packed brown sugar
   1   cup applesauce
   5   tablespoons butter, softened
   1   teaspoon vanilla extract
   3   large eggs
  ¾   cup chopped pitted dates

TOPPING:
  ⅓   cup sliced almonds
   3   tablespoons all-purpose flour
   3   tablespoons brown sugar
   2   tablespoons butter, melted

1. Preheat oven to 350°.
2. To prepare cake, coat a 9-inch square baking pan with cooking spray; set aside.
3. Lightly spoon 2 cups flour into dry measuring cups; level with a knife. Combine 2 cups flour and next 5 ingredients in a large bowl; make a well in center of mixture. Combine 1 cup brown sugar and next 4 ingredients in a medium bowl; beat with a mixer at medium speed until blended. Add to flour mixture; stir just until moist. Stir in dates. Spoon batter into prepared pan.
4. To prepare topping, combine sliced almonds and remaining 3 ingredients, stirring with a fork until blended. Sprinkle evenly over batter. Bake at 350° for 35 minutes or until a wooden pick inserted in center comes out clean. Cool completely in pan. Yield: 16 servings.

CALORIES 230 (30% from fat); FAT 7.6g (sat 3.6g, mono 2.6g, poly 0.8g); PROTEIN 3.9g; CARB 37.8g; FIBER 1.7g; CHOL 53mg; IRON 1.6mg; SODIUM 248mg; CALC 52mg

Date-Orange Breakfast Spread

Enjoy this spread over bagels, waffles, English muffins, toast, or apples for a healthful, great-tasting breakfast in an instant.

1 cup finely chopped pitted dates
   (about ½ pound)
1 tablespoon finely grated orange rind
2 tablespoons fresh orange juice
½ teaspoon ground cinnamon
⅛ teaspoon salt
4 ounces ⅓-less-fat cream cheese,
   softened

1. Combine all ingredients, stirring until blended. Chill 30 minutes. Yield: 1¾ cups (serving size: 1 tablespoon).
NOTE: Store, covered, in refrigerator up to 2 weeks.

CALORIES 29 (31% from fat); FAT 1g (sat 0.6g, mono 0.3g, poly 0g); PROTEIN 0.6g; CARB 5.1g; FIBER 0.6g; CHOL 3mg; IRON 0.1mg; SODIUM 27mg; CALC 6mg

Saffron Chicken and Rice with Dates

North African staples transform this simple supper.

1 tablespoon vegetable oil
1 pound skinless, boneless chicken
   breast, cut into bite-sized pieces
½ teaspoon salt, divided
¼ teaspoon freshly ground black
   pepper
1½ cups chopped onion
¼ teaspoon saffron threads, crushed
   and divided
2 garlic cloves, minced
2 cups tomato juice
6 whole pitted dates, quartered
2 cups water
1 cup uncooked long-grain rice
3 green onions, thinly sliced
Lemon wedges (optional)

1. Heat oil in a large saucepan over medium-high heat. Sprinkle chicken with ¼ teaspoon salt and pepper. Add chicken to pan, and sauté 5 minutes,

browning on all sides. Remove chicken from pan; keep warm.
2. Add onion, ⅛ teaspoon saffron, and garlic to pan; sauté 5 minutes or until onion is tender. Stir in chicken, tomato juice, and dates; cover. Reduce heat to low, and cook 15 minutes. Uncover; cook 10 minutes. Remove from heat; keep warm.
3. Combine ¼ teaspoon salt, ⅛ teaspoon saffron, 2 cups water, and rice in a saucepan; bring to a boil. Cover, reduce heat, and simmer 20 minutes or until rice is tender and water is absorbed. Fluff with a fork. Serve chicken mixture over rice mixture. Garnish with green onions and lemon wedges, if desired. Yield: 6 servings (serving size: ½ cup rice and ⅔ cup chicken mixture).

CALORIES 273 (12% from fat); FAT 3.5g (sat 0.7g, mono 0.8g, poly 1.6g); PROTEIN 20.8g; CARB 38.6g; FIBER 2.5g; CHOL 44mg; IRON 2.8mg; SODIUM 500mg; CALC 43mg

Individual Goat Cheese and Date Tortas

Prepare the components of this appetizer ahead, and assemble it at the last minute.

½ cup chopped pitted dates
2 (3-ounce) packages goat cheese
1 tablespoon balsamic vinegar
2 teaspoons extravirgin olive oil
½ teaspoon Dijon mustard
¼ teaspoon salt
¼ teaspoon sugar
¼ teaspoon Spanish smoked paprika
1 garlic clove, minced
1 cup arugula or baby spinach
24 (¼-inch-thick) slices French
   bread baguette, toasted (about
   12 ounces)
12 pecan halves, each cut in half
3 tablespoons diced red bell pepper

1. Combine dates and cheese; set aside. Combine vinegar and next 6 ingredients, stirring with a whisk. Add arugula to vinaigrette; toss gently to coat. Divide arugula mixture evenly over bread slices. Top each bread slice with 1 rounded tablespoon date mixture and 1 pecan half. Sprinkle red pepper evenly over

bread slices. Serve immediately. Yield: 12 servings (serving size: 2 tortas).

CALORIES 166 (34% from fat); FAT 6.2g (sat 2.5g, mono 2.4g, poly 0.8g); PROTEIN 5.8g; CARB 22.5g; FIBER 1.6g; CHOL 7mg; IRON 1.2mg; SODIUM 302mg; CALC 51mg

Date and Apricot Chutney

Serve this savory-sweet condiment with curry dishes or roasted meats, or as a spread on ham sandwiches. Also try it on wheat toast in the morning or as an appetizer spread spooned over cream cheese.

½ cup dried apricots, halved
1 cup chopped pitted dates (about 1
   pound)
¾ cup packed brown sugar
½ cup cider vinegar
1 teaspoon minced peeled fresh ginger
1 teaspoon tomato paste
½ teaspoon ground coriander
¼ teaspoon salt
⅛ teaspoon crushed red pepper
½ onion, thinly sliced
2 tablespoons chopped fresh cilantro

1. Place apricots in a medium bowl. Cover with boiling water, and let stand 1 hour. Drain.
2. Combine apricots, dates, and next 8 ingredients in a medium heavy saucepan. Bring to a boil; reduce heat, and simmer 25 minutes or until thickened. Remove from heat; stir in cilantro.
3. Pack chutney in clean jars. Cover and cool chutney completely; chill. Yield: 2¼ cups (serving size: ¼ cup).
NOTE: Store chutney in refrigerator up to 6 weeks.

CALORIES 153 (1% from fat); FAT 0.2g (sat 0.1g, mono 0g, poly 0g); PROTEIN 0.9g; CARB 39.5g; FIBER 2.2g; CHOL 0mg; IRON 1.1mg; SODIUM 74mg; CALC 30mg

Nutritional Powerhouse

Dates are high in complex carbohydrates, so they're a good energy source. They also provide a healthy dose of potassium and iron, as well as plenty of fiber—1.6 grams in one Medjool date.

Know Your Date

In these recipes, we used soft and semidry dates, which are less sweet and more aromatic than fully dried fruit. Unless a recipe specifies a variety, any of the following will work.

SOFT DATES have the highest moisture content and should be stored in the refrigerator.

Medjool dates are dark-brown, sweet, rich in flavor, meaty, moist, and sticky. They vary greatly in size, but are generally the largest type of date.

Amer Hajj dates have coloring similar to Medjools but are spicier with a caramel flavor and have a soft, sticky texture. They're called "the visitor's date" in the Middle East, where they're a delicacy served to guests. Their shape is similar to plum tomatoes but smaller in size.

Halaway dates have a sweet, buttery flavor with thick flesh and a light-brown, blond color.

Barhi dates have amber skin with a deep brownish-maroon color. They're soft, not too sweet, and have a light, buttery, caramel flavor.

SEMIDRY DATES are firmer and should be stored in a dark, cool place.

Deglet Noor are amber-colored, elongated dates that have a delicate honey flavor. They're firmer than Amer Hajj, and aren't as sweet or moist as Medjool. They're the most popular date sold in the United States; in grocery stores they're often in round packages labeled "fresh pitted dates."

Empress dates have a yellow crown at the top. They're soft, not too sweet, and a bit chewy with a deep caramel flavor.

Zahidi dates have large seeds and fibrous flesh. This variety is often used for diced dates. The flavor is similar to brown sugar.

Onion, Date, and Brie Crostini

These simple hors d'oeuvres combine the Mediterranean flavors of dates, rosemary, and balsamic vinegar with buttery Brie.

24 (½-inch-thick) slices diagonally cut French bread baguette (about 12 ounces)
1 teaspoon butter
3 cups thinly sliced onion
2 teaspoons finely chopped fresh rosemary
½ teaspoon salt
½ teaspoon freshly ground black pepper
1 garlic clove, minced
2 teaspoons sugar
2 teaspoons balsamic vinegar
1 teaspoon Worcestershire sauce
¼ cup chopped pitted dates
4 ounces chopped Brie or Camembert cheese

1. Preheat broiler.
2. Arrange bread in a single layer on a baking sheet. Broil 2 minutes on each side or until toasted.
3. Reduce oven temperature to 300°.
4. Melt butter in a large nonstick skillet over medium heat. Add onion and next 4 ingredients; cook 10 minutes or until onion is translucent, stirring frequently. Increase heat to medium-high; sauté 4 minutes or until onion begins to brown. Add sugar; sauté 2 minutes. Stir in vinegar and Worcestershire; remove from heat. Add dates and cheese; stir until combined.
5. Top each toast with about 2 teaspoons onion mixture. Bake at 300° for 4 minutes or until cheese melts. Yield: 24 crostini (serving size: 1 crostini).

CALORIES 68 (25% from fat); FAT 1.9g (sat 1g, mono 0.6g, poly 0.2g); PROTEIN 2.4g; CARB 10.5g; FIBER 0.8g; CHOL 5mg; IRON 0.5mg; SODIUM 169mg; CALC 24mg

Sephardic Beef Stew

The classic Sephardic Jewish New Year's meal called *tzimmes*—a stew of meat, potatoes, carrots, and dried fruit—inspired this comforting dish.

½ teaspoon olive oil
1½ cups chopped onion
½ cup chopped celery
½ teaspoon salt
½ teaspoon freshly ground black pepper
½ teaspoon ground red pepper
1 tablespoon cornstarch
1 pound sirloin, trimmed and cut into 1½-inch cubes
½ cup dry white wine
2½ cups fat-free, less-sodium chicken broth
½ cup water
1 teaspoon minced peeled fresh ginger
2 garlic cloves, minced
2 cups chopped carrot
1 cup whole pitted dates, halved
¼ cup whole dried apricots, halved
1 large (8-ounce) baking potato, peeled and chopped

1. Preheat oven to 350°.
2. Heat oil in a large Dutch oven over medium-high heat. Add onion, celery, salt, and peppers to pan; sauté 6 minutes or until onion is tender.
3. Combine cornstarch and beef, tossing well to coat. Add beef mixture to pan; cook 5 minutes, browning on all sides. Stir in wine, scraping pan to loosen browned bits. Stir in broth, water, ginger, and garlic; bring to a boil. Cover and place in oven. Bake at 350° for 1 hour.
4. Stir in carrot, dates, apricots, and potato. Return to oven. Cover and bake at 350° for 1 hour. Stir well; cover and bake an additional 30 minutes or until beef is tender. Yield: 6 servings (serving size: about 1 cup).

CALORIES 350 (23% from fat); FAT 8.9g (sat 3.4g, mono 4g, poly 0.4g); PROTEIN 20.2g; CARB 45.9g; FIBER 5.4g; CHOL 45mg; IRON 2.4mg; SODIUM 472mg; CALC 52mg

Spiced Orzo Pilaf

This pasta is cooked in a manner similar to traditional rice pilaf.

  1   tablespoon olive oil
  ¼   teaspoon ground cinnamon
  ¼   teaspoon ground cumin
  ¼   teaspoon paprika
  1½ cups vegetable broth
  1   cup uncooked orzo (rice-shaped pasta)
  ½   cup fresh orange juice
  2   garlic cloves, minced
  ½   cup chopped pitted dates
  ¼   cup finely chopped green onions
  1   teaspoon grated lemon rind
  ¼   teaspoon salt
  ¼   teaspoon freshly ground black pepper
  ¼   cup finely chopped carrot
  2   tablespoons chopped fresh cilantro
  1   tablespoon fresh lemon juice

1. Heat oil in a medium saucepan over low heat. Add cinnamon, cumin, and paprika; cook 1 minute or until fragrant. Increase heat to medium-high. Stir in broth, orzo, orange juice, and garlic; bring to a boil. Cover, reduce heat, and simmer 10 minutes or until liquid is almost absorbed. Stir in dates and next 4 ingredients; cook, uncovered, 2 minutes. Remove from heat; cover and let stand 5 minutes or until liquid is absorbed. Fluff with a fork. Stir in carrot, cilantro, and lemon juice. Yield: 4 servings (serving size: ¾ cup).

CALORIES 280 (15% from fat); FAT 4.6g (sat 0.7g, mono 2.5g, poly 0.4g); PROTEIN 7.6g; CARB 55g; FIBER 4g; CHOL 0mg; IRON 1.9mg; SODIUM 534mg; CALC 30mg

---

Internet Dating

If you can't find the varieties of dates that you need in the supermarket, go to www.sphinxdateranch.com to order online or www.browndategarden.com to print a price list and mail-order form.

Spiced Date-Walnut Snacks

Extramoist Medjool dates act as the binding agent in these snacks. A can of beans makes a handy weight.

  2   tablespoons fresh orange juice
  ½   teaspoon ground cinnamon
  ½   teaspoon ground ginger
  ¾   cup walnut halves
  2   cups Medjool dates, pitted and chopped
  1   teaspoon grated orange rind

1. Preheat oven to 350°.
2. Combine first 3 ingredients in a medium bowl, stirring with a whisk. Add walnuts; toss to coat. Arrange walnuts in a single layer on a baking sheet. Bake at 350° for 8 minutes or until toasted.
3. Combine dates and orange rind. Line a 9 x 5-inch loaf pan with plastic wrap, allowing plastic wrap to extend 2 inches over edge of pan. Firmly press one-third of date mixture into bottom of pan; top with half of walnuts. Repeat layers, ending with dates. Fold overhanging plastic wrap over the top. Place a heavy weight on plastic wrap, and let stand overnight. Remove weight; invert loaf onto a serving plate. Discard plastic wrap. Cut into squares. Yield: 20 servings (serving size: 1 square).

CALORIES 81 (33% from fat); FAT 3g (sat 0.3g, mono 0.4g, poly 2.1g); PROTEIN 1.1g; CARB 14.2g; FIBER 1.8g; CHOL 0mg; IRON 0.4mg; SODIUM 1mg; CALC 12mg

---

enlightened cook

Election-Night Surprise

A volunteer cooks for poll workers, and her dishes win their palates by a landslide.

Barbara Lauterbach of Center Harbor, New Hampshire, enjoys providing meals for fellow poll workers on election night. Here are a few samples of what she serves.

Hot Chicken and Chips Retro

This recipe has a nostalgic appeal that harks back to the 1950s and '60s. If you make it ahead, don't add the baked potato chips until it's time to bake the casserole, or they'll become soggy.

  4   cups chopped roasted skinless, boneless chicken breast (about 4 breasts)
  ¼   cup chopped green onions
  ¼   cup chopped red bell pepper
  2   tablespoons finely chopped fresh flat-leaf parsley
  1   (8-ounce) can sliced water chestnuts, drained and chopped
  ½   cup low-fat mayonnaise
  ¼   cup reduced-fat sour cream
  2   tablespoons fresh lemon juice
  2   teaspoons Dijon mustard
  ½   teaspoon salt
  ½   teaspoon freshly ground black pepper
Cooking spray
  ¾   cup (3 ounces) shredded Swiss cheese
  ¾   cup crushed baked potato chips (about 2 ounces)

1. Preheat oven to 400°.
2. Combine first 5 ingredients in a large bowl; stir well. Combine mayonnaise and next 5 ingredients in a small bowl, stirring with a whisk. Add mayonnaise mixture to chicken mixture; stir well to combine. Spoon chicken mixture into an 11 x 7-inch baking dish coated with cooking spray, and sprinkle with cheese. Top evenly with chips. Bake at 400° for 13 minutes or until filling is bubbly and chips are golden. Yield: 6 servings.

CALORIES 321 (31% from fat); FAT 10.9g (sat 4.1g, mono 2.6g, poly 1g); PROTEIN 34.3g; CARB 20.4g; FIBER 2.6g; CHOL 96mg; IRON 11.4mg; SODIUM 606mg; CALC 175mg

Venison Chili

Many New Englanders have freezers stocked with venison from autumn hunting expeditions. If venison isn't available, substitute ground sirloin. Garnish with reduced-fat sour cream and/or reduced-fat shredded Cheddar, if desired. You can make the chili 1 day ahead and refrigerate; reheat in the microwave or on the stovetop.

Cooking spray
1 pound ground venison
1 cup chopped sweet onion
1 cup chopped green bell pepper
4 garlic cloves, minced
1 jalapeño pepper, seeded and chopped
2 tablespoons chili powder
½ teaspoon salt
½ teaspoon ground cumin
½ teaspoon ground red pepper
½ teaspoon freshly ground black pepper
1 (14.5-ounce) can diced tomatoes, undrained
1 (14-ounce) can fat-free, less-sodium chicken broth
1 tablespoon tomato paste
1 (15-ounce) can red kidney beans, rinsed and drained

1. Heat a small Dutch oven over medium-high heat. Coat pan with cooking spray. Add venison; cook 3 minutes or until browned, stirring to crumble. Remove from pan with a slotted spoon. Cover and keep warm.
2. Reduce heat to medium. Add onion, bell pepper, garlic, and jalapeño to pan; cook 10 minutes or until tender, stirring frequently. Stir in chili powder and next 4 ingredients. Stir in venison, tomatoes, broth, and tomato paste; bring to a boil. Cover, reduce heat, and simmer 30 minutes. Add beans; cook, uncovered, 15 minutes. Yield: 4 servings (serving size: 1½ cups).

CALORIES 319 (12% from fat); FAT 4.1g (sat 1.2g, mono 0.9g, poly 1g); PROTEIN 35.8g; CARB 35.8g; FIBER 12.5g; CHOL 96mg; IRON 6.6mg; SODIUM 941mg; CALC 87mg

Potato, Leek, and Ham Gratin

This dish can be assembled 1 day ahead and refrigerated. Remove from the refrigerator, and let stand at room temperature 30 minutes before baking. Look for cooked, diced ham at the grocery store.

8 large peeled Yukon gold potatoes, cut into ¼-inch-thick slices (about 2¾ pounds)
Cooking spray
4 cups thinly sliced leek (about 4 large)
1 teaspoon vegetable oil
2 cups fat-free, less-sodium chicken broth
2 tablespoons Dijon mustard
¼ teaspoon freshly ground black pepper
Dash of ground nutmeg
½ cup all-purpose flour
2 cups 1% low-fat milk
3 cups diced 33%-less-sodium ham (about ¾ pound)
1½ cups (6 ounces) shredded Gruyère cheese

1. Preheat oven to 375°.
2. Place potato in a Dutch oven, and cover with water. Bring to a boil; remove from heat. Drain; set aside.
3. Heat pan over medium heat. Coat with cooking spray. Add leek and oil, stirring to coat leek. Cover and cook 10 minutes or until leek is tender. Remove from pan; set aside.
4. Add broth, mustard, pepper, and nutmeg to pan, stirring with a whisk until well blended. Lightly spoon flour into a dry measuring cup; level with a knife. Place flour in a medium bowl; gradually add milk, stirring with a whisk to form a slurry. Add slurry to broth mixture, stirring to combine; bring to a boil. Reduce heat, and simmer 3 minutes or until mixture thickens, stirring constantly.
5. Pour 1 cup milk mixture into bottom of a 13 x 9-inch baking dish coated with cooking spray; arrange 2⅓ cups potato over milk mixture. Top with 1½ cups ham and 1 cup leek; sprinkle with ½ cup cheese. Repeat layers once, and top with remaining potatoes. Pour remaining milk mixture over potatoes; sprinkle with ½ cup cheese. Bake at 375° for 45 minutes or until bubbly and golden brown. Let stand 15 minutes before serving. Yield: 10 servings.

CALORIES 320 (31% from fat); FAT 11.5g (sat 5.1g, mono 2g, poly 0.7g); PROTEIN 22.8g; CARB 35.2g; FIBER 3.3g; CHOL 60mg; IRON 2.1mg; SODIUM 940mg; CALC 266mg

New Hampshire Maple-Mustard Salad Dressing

"New Hampshire folk feel almost as strongly about their maple syrup as they do about their presidential primary. They like this dressing, which I toss with bagged, washed salad greens just before serving."
—Barbara Lauterbach, Center Harbor, New Hampshire

⅓ cup maple syrup
3 tablespoons whole-grain Dijon mustard
2 tablespoons red wine vinegar
2 tablespoons finely chopped shallots
1 tablespoon canola oil
¼ teaspoon freshly ground black pepper
⅛ teaspoon salt

1. Combine all ingredients in a medium bowl, stirring with a whisk. Yield: about ¾ cup (serving size: 1 tablespoon).

CALORIES 40 (34% from fat); FAT 1.5g (sat 0.1g, mono 0.8g, poly 0.5g); PROTEIN 0.3g; CARB 6.7g; FIBER 0.1g; CHOL 0mg; IRON 0.3mg; SODIUM 120mg; CALC 12mg

These election-day dishes can be made ahead, are easily portable, and are guaranteed winners.

Pork Stroganoff

For the smoothest results, turn the heat down well before adding the sour cream to the sauce.

- 1 tablespoon vegetable oil
- ½ teaspoon salt, divided
- ¼ teaspoon freshly ground black pepper, divided
- 1 (1-pound) pork tenderloin, trimmed and cut into 3 x ¼-inch-thick strips
- 1½ cups thinly vertically sliced onion
- 1 (8-ounce) package presliced mushrooms
- 1½ cups dry white wine
- ¾ cup reduced-fat sour cream
- 1 tablespoon Dijon mustard
- 1 teaspoon fresh lemon juice
- 1 tablespoon chopped fresh parsley
- 2 cups hot cooked medium egg noodles (about 4 ounces uncooked pasta)

1. Heat oil in a large heavy skillet over high heat. Sprinkle ¼ teaspoon salt and ⅛ teaspoon pepper over pork, tossing to coat. Add pork to pan; cook 4 minutes or until browned, stirring occasionally. Remove pork from pan. Reduce heat to medium-high. Add onion to pan; cook 2 minutes, stirring frequently. Add mushrooms, and cook 6 minutes or until mushrooms release moisture, stirring occasionally. Add wine; simmer until wine is reduced by half (about 7 minutes). Reduce heat to medium-low.
2. Combine sour cream and mustard in a small bowl, stirring with a whisk. Stir sour cream mixture into wine mixture; add pork, ¼ teaspoon salt, and ⅛ teaspoon pepper. Cook 3 minutes or until heated; stir in juice. Sprinkle with parsley. Serve over noodles. Yield: 4 servings (serving size: about 1 cup pork mixture and ½ cup noodles).

CALORIES 438 (30% from fat); FAT 14.5g (sat 5.5g, mono 4.6g, poly 3.1g); PROTEIN 31.7g; CARB 31.2g; FIBER 2.8g; CHOL 118mg; IRON 4mg; SODIUM 480mg; CALC 92mg

dinner tonight

Warm Sandwiches

Warm sandwiches heat up chilly autumn evenings.

Balsamic-Glazed Chicken Sandwiches with Red Onions and Goat Cheese

This tangy chicken sandwich takes less than a half-hour to prepare from pan to plate. The addition of antipasto salad and pears rounds it out into a full meal.

TOTAL TIME: 26 MINUTES

- ¾ cup balsamic vinegar
- ½ cup dry red wine
- 2 teaspoons brown sugar
- 1 teaspoon low-sodium soy sauce
- 2 (6-ounce) skinless, boneless chicken breast halves
- ½ teaspoon salt
- ¼ teaspoon freshly ground black pepper
- Cooking spray
- 1 tablespoon olive oil
- 1½ cups thinly vertically sliced red onion
- 1 (3-ounce) package goat cheese
- 4 (2-ounce) hoagie or Kaiser rolls
- 1 cup trimmed arugula

1. Combine first 4 ingredients in a small saucepan over medium heat. Bring mixture to a boil, stirring until sugar dissolves. Cook until reduced to ⅓ cup (about 12 minutes). Remove from heat; cool slightly.
2. While vinegar mixture cooks, heat a large nonstick skillet over medium-high heat. Sprinkle chicken with salt and pepper. Coat pan with cooking spray. Add chicken to pan; cook 4 minutes on each side or until done. Remove chicken from pan, and cut into thin slices. Cover and keep warm.
3. Add oil to pan; reduce temperature to medium-low. Add onion; cook 5 minutes or until onion is soft and beginning to brown, stirring frequently. Remove onion from heat.
4. Spread about 1½ tablespoons goat cheese evenly over bottom half of each roll; arrange chicken and onion evenly over cheese. Drizzle each serving with about 1 tablespoon balsamic mixture, and top with ¼ cup arugula and top half of a roll. Serve immediately. Yield: 4 servings (serving size: 1 sandwich).

CALORIES 424 (25% from fat); FAT 11.6g (sat 4.2g, mono 4.4g, poly 1.7g); PROTEIN 30.1g; CARB 43.9g; FIBER 2.2g; CHOL 59mg; IRON 3.7mg; SODIUM 796mg; CALC 129mg

Warm Sandwich Menu 1
serves 4

Balsamic-Glazed Chicken Sandwiches with Red Onions and Goat Cheese

Antipasto salad*

Cubed winter pears

*Combine 1 cup quartered mushrooms, ½ cup sliced bottled roasted red bell peppers, ¼ cup low-fat balsamic vinaigrette, 1 (15-ounce) can drained chickpeas, and 1 (14-ounce) can drained and halved artichoke hearts in a medium bowl; toss well to coat.

Game Plan

1. While vinegar mixture cooks:
- Slice onion
- Begin cooking chicken
2. While onion cooks:
- Prepare salad
- Continue cooking vinegar mixture
- Cube pears

Red Wine-Marinated Steak Sandwiches

(pictured on page 378)

TOTAL TIME: 35 MINUTES (doesn't include marinating time)

QUICK TIP: Prepare the marinade the night before and refrigerate, then add the steak in the morning to marinate until you're ready to make dinner.

BEEF:

- ½ cup dry red wine
- 3 tablespoons low-sodium soy sauce
- 2 tablespoons Worcestershire sauce
- 2 tablespoons fresh lemon juice
- 2 tablespoons Dijon mustard
- 1½ teaspoons coarsely ground black pepper
- 1 teaspoon dried thyme
- 1 pound flank steak, trimmed

HORSERADISH CREAM:

- ¼ cup fat-free sour cream
- 1 tablespoon prepared horseradish
- 1 tablespoon Dijon mustard

GREENS:

- 1 tablespoon minced shallots
- ¼ teaspoon grated lemon rind
- 1 tablespoon fresh lemon juice
- 1 teaspoon Dijon mustard
- ½ teaspoon extravirgin olive oil
- ⅛ teaspoon black pepper
- 3 cups mixed salad greens

REMAINING INGREDIENTS:

- 8 (1-ounce) slices diagonally cut French bread, toasted
- ½ cup (2 ounces) shaved fresh Parmesan cheese

1. To prepare beef, combine first 7 ingredients in a large zip-top plastic bag. Add steak; seal. Marinate in refrigerator 8 hours or overnight.

2. Heat a grill pan over medium-high heat. Remove steak from marinade; discard marinade. Add steak to pan; cook 4 minutes on each side or until desired degree of doneness. Let stand 5 minutes; cut into thin slices.

3. To prepare horseradish cream, combine sour cream, horseradish, and 1 tablespoon mustard.

4. To prepare greens, combine shallots and next 5 ingredients in a large bowl. Add salad greens; toss to coat.

5. Spread about 1 tablespoon horseradish cream evenly over each of 4 bread slices; arrange steak and greens evenly over bread slices. Top each serving with 2 tablespoons cheese and 1 bread slice. Yield: 4 servings (serving size: 1 sandwich).

CALORIES 432 (32% from fat); FAT 15.2g (sat 6.6g, mono 5.9g, poly 1.1g); PROTEIN 35.6g; CARB 36.6g; FIBER 3.3g; CHOL 69mg; IRON 4.9mg; SODIUM 889mg; CALC 292mg

Pacific Rim Pork Sandwiches with Hoisin Slaw

Since the pork marinates for 1 to 2 hours, add it to the marinade as soon as you arrive home from work. The pork is also delicious stir-fried with Asian vegetables and served over rice.

TOTAL TIME: 15 MINUTES (doesn't include marinating time)

QUICK TIP: Pork tenderloin cooks quickly, especially when cut into thin slices and pan-fried.

PORK:

- 3 tablespoons low-sodium soy sauce
- 3 tablespoons dry sherry
- 3 tablespoons hoisin sauce
- 2 tablespoons minced peeled fresh ginger
- 1 tablespoon dark sesame oil
- 1½ teaspoons hot Chinese mustard
- ¼ teaspoon five-spice powder
- 1 garlic clove, minced
- 1 pound pork tenderloin, trimmed and cut into ¼-inch slices

2 tablespoons seasoned rice wine vinegar
1 tablespoon hoisin sauce
2 teaspoons dark sesame oil
1 teaspoon low-sodium soy sauce
1 teaspoon minced peeled fresh ginger
¼ teaspoon hot Chinese mustard
1 garlic clove, minced
2½ cups packaged cabbage-and-carrot coleslaw
¼ cup sliced green onions

REMAINING INGREDIENTS:

Cooking spray
4 (2-ounce) sesame seed buns, toasted

1. To prepare pork, combine first 8 ingredients in a large zip-top plastic bag. Add pork, and seal. Marinate in refrigerator 1 to 2 hours, turning occasionally.
2. To prepare slaw, combine vinegar and next 6 ingredients in a large bowl. Add coleslaw and green onions; toss well.
3. Heat a large nonstick skillet over medium-high heat. Remove pork from bag, and discard marinade. Coat pan with cooking spray. Add pork to pan; cook 2 minutes on each side or until done.
4. Divide pork evenly among bottom halves of buns. Top each serving with about ½ cup slaw mixture and top half of bun. Yield: 4 servings (serving size: 1 sandwich).

CALORIES 360 (23% from fat); FAT 9.2g (sat 2.1g, mono 3.5g, poly 2.6g); PROTEIN 30.4g; CARB 37.1g; FIBER 2.8g; CHOL 74mg; IRON 3.6mg; SODIUM 697mg; CALC 84mg

This flavorful pork sandwich is a delicious tribute to the Pacific Rim nations.

Warm Sandwich Menu 4

serves 4

Wasabi Salmon Sandwiches

Miso soup*

Sliced cucumbers and red onions tossed with seasoned rice vinegar and black pepper

*Bring 3 cups water to a boil. Combine 3 tablespoons boiling water and 2 tablespoons white miso in a medium bowl, stirring to form a paste. Add remaining boiling water, 1 tablespoon slivered green onions, 1 teaspoon low-sodium soy sauce, and ½ teaspoon fish sauce.

Game Plan

1. While salmon marinates:
 • Prepare ginger-garlic mayonnaise
 • Whisk sesame oil into dressing
 • Prepare cucumbers; chill until ready to serve
2. While salmon cooks:
 • Toss greens and dressing
 • Prepare miso soup

Wasabi Salmon Sandwiches

TOTAL TIME: 45 MINUTES

QUICK TIP: The shallot mixture does double duty as a marinade for the fish and dressing for the greens.

FISH:

⅓ cup rice vinegar
¼ cup minced shallots
2 tablespoons brown sugar
2 tablespoons minced peeled fresh ginger
1 tablespoon minced garlic (about 3 cloves)
3 tablespoons low-sodium soy sauce
1½ teaspoons wasabi paste
4 (6-ounce) salmon fillets (about 1 inch thick), skinned

GINGER-GARLIC MAYONNAISE:

2 tablespoons low-fat mayonnaise
2 tablespoons plain fat-free yogurt
1 teaspoon wasabi paste
¾ teaspoon grated peeled fresh ginger
½ teaspoon rice vinegar
1 garlic clove, minced

REMAINING INGREDIENTS:

1 tablespoon dark sesame oil
4 cups baby spinach leaves
8 (1-ounce) slices ciabatta bread, toasted

1. To prepare fish, combine first 7 ingredients. Place ¾ cup shallot mixture in a large zip-top plastic bag. Set remaining shallot mixture aside. Add fish to bag; seal and marinate in refrigerator 30 minutes, turning once.
2. To prepare ginger-garlic mayonnaise, combine mayonnaise and next 5 ingredients.
3. Preheat broiler.
4. Remove fish from bag; discard marinade. Place fish on a broiler pan; broil 10 minutes or until fish flakes easily when tested with a fork.
5. Combine reserved shallot mixture and sesame oil in a large bowl. Add spinach; toss well.
6. Spread about 1 tablespoon ginger-garlic mayonnaise evenly over each of 4 bread slices; top each with 1 fillet and about 1 cup spinach mixture. Top with remaining bread slices. Yield: 4 servings (serving size: 1 sandwich).

CALORIES 434 (33% from fat); FAT 15.7g (sat 3.3g, mono 6.5g, poly 4.5g); PROTEIN 33.8g; CARB 37.6g; FIBER 2.6g; CHOL 65mg; IRON 2.8mg; SODIUM 682mg; CALC 103mg

Seaside in San Diego

Spend a weekend in America's fittest city.

Autumn is a subtle season in the border city of San Diego. The temperature hovers in the 60s, and skies are quintessentially blue, making it a great time to kayak the bays, bike through historic neighborhoods, claim fire rings at the beach, or eat delicious foods at fine restaurants such as Arterra at the San Diego Marriott.

Kabocha Squash Soup

Chef Carl Schroeder of Arterra uses fresh, locally grown produce. Kabocha squash, known as sweet Japanese squash, have a flavor between sweet potatoes and pumpkin. If you can't find kabocha squash, try either pumpkin or acorn squash.

    1   (2½-pound) kabocha squash
        Cooking spray
    1   tablespoon butter
    1   cup chopped leek
    ¾   cup chopped onion
    ¾   teaspoon grated peeled fresh
        ginger
    ⅛   teaspoon black pepper
    3   garlic cloves, chopped
    1   (1-inch) piece crushed fresh
        lemongrass
    2½ cups vegetable broth
    1½ cups water
    ¼   cup packed brown sugar
    ½   cup light coconut milk
    1½ teaspoons grated lime rind
    2   tablespoons diagonally cut green
        onions
    1   tablespoon chopped fresh cilantro

1. Preheat oven to 350°.
2. Cut squash in half lengthwise; discard seeds. Place squash, cut sides down, on a baking sheet coated with cooking spray. Bake at 350° for 45 minutes or until tender; cool. Scoop out pulp; discard skins.

3. Melt butter in a large Dutch oven over medium-high heat. Stir in leek and next 5 ingredients. Reduce heat to medium; cover and cook 5 minutes or until tender, stirring occasionally. Stir in squash pulp, broth, water, and sugar, and bring to a boil. Reduce heat to medium-low; simmer 45 minutes. Place half of squash mixture in a blender or food processor; process until smooth. Strain puréed mixture through a sieve into a bowl; discard solids. Repeat procedure with remaining squash mixture. Return puréed mixture to pan; stir in coconut milk and rind. Cook over medium-high heat until thoroughly heated. Sprinkle with green onions and cilantro. Yield: 8 servings (serving size: about ¾ cup).

CALORIES 153 (19% from fat); FAT 3.3g (sat 1.5g, mono 0.6g, poly 0.4g); PROTEIN 2.7g; CARB 32.5g; FIBER 6.8g; CHOL 4mg; IRON 1.9mg; SODIUM 341mg; CALC 83mg

Harvest Celebration

Fall colors, fragrant spices, and hearty flavors showcase seasonal produce in this memorable menu.

Meatless Thanksgiving Menu
serves 8

Roasted Tomato-Harissa Soup with Olive Toasts

Phyllo Purses with Roasted Squash, Peppers, and Artichokes

Glazed Carrots and Cipollini Onions with Coriander and Orange

Spinach with Chickpeas and Spices or
Fruited Couscous Pilaf

Fall Salad with Buttermilk Dressing

Chile-Lime Pineapple with Cardamom-Lime Ice Cream

Roasted Tomato-Harissa Soup with Olive Toasts

Harissa is a Moroccan spice paste found at Middle-Eastern markets or specialty food shops. You can make the soup a couple of days ahead, refrigerate, and reheat over medium heat; or freeze it up to 4 weeks, thaw in the refrigerator, and reheat. The olive spread can be prepared up to 3 days in advance. The tomatoes release flavorful juices when roasted; just add the juices to the soup.

SOUP:

    2¼ pounds plum tomatoes, cut in half
        lengthwise
    2   garlic cloves, unpeeled
    2   Walla Walla or other sweet
        onions, cut into ½-inch-thick
        slices (about 1½ pounds)
    ½   red bell pepper, seeded
        Cooking spray
    1½ teaspoons olive oil
    ½   teaspoon ground cumin
    ½   teaspoon ground coriander
    1   teaspoon commercial harissa
    ¼   teaspoon Spanish smoked paprika
        or chipotle chile powder
    2½ cups vegetable broth
    ½   cup water
    ½   teaspoon chopped fresh
        thyme
    1½ teaspoons fresh lemon juice
    ⅛   teaspoon salt
    ⅛   teaspoon freshly ground black
        pepper

TOASTS:

    1   garlic clove, halved
    8   (¼-inch-thick) slices diagonally
        cut French bread baguette, toasted
        (about 2 ounces)
    ¼   cup chopped pitted kalamata
        olives
    1½ teaspoons chopped fresh
        parsley
    ¼   teaspoon balsamic vinegar
    ⅛   teaspoon chopped fresh
        thyme

REMAINING INGREDIENT:

    8   teaspoons plain low-fat
        yogurt

1. Preheat oven to 425°.

2. To prepare soup, arrange tomatoes, cut sides up, 2 garlic cloves, onion slices, and bell pepper half on a jelly-roll pan coated with cooking spray. Bake at 425° for 1 hour and 10 minutes or until golden. Cool. Chop tomatoes, onion, and bell pepper. Set aside ⅓ cup chopped onion for toasts. Squeeze garlic cloves to extract pulp; discard skins.

3. Heat oil in a Dutch oven over medium heat. Add remaining chopped onion, bell pepper, cumin, and coriander; cook 5 minutes, stirring frequently. Add harissa and paprika; cook 2 minutes. Stir in tomatoes, garlic pulp, broth, water, and ½ teaspoon thyme; bring to a boil. Cover, reduce heat, and simmer 15 minutes. Remove from heat, and let stand 5 minutes. Stir in lemon juice, salt, and black pepper. Place half of tomato mixture in a blender, and process until smooth. Pour into a bowl. Repeat procedure with remaining tomato mixture.

4. To prepare toasts, rub cut sides of halved garlic clove over one side of each bread slice. Combine reserved ⅓ cup chopped onion, olives, parsley, vinegar, and ⅛ teaspoon thyme. Top each bread slice with about 1 tablespoon olive mixture. Ladle about ½ cup soup into each of 8 bowls. Top each serving with 1 teaspoon yogurt; serve with 1 olive toast. Yield: 8 servings.

CALORIES 108 (20% from fat); FAT 2.4g (sat 0.4g, mono 1.1g, poly 0.4g); PROTEIN 3.6g; CARB 20.9g; FIBER 3.3g; CHOL 0mg; IRON 1.2mg; SODIUM 425mg; CALC 49mg

Phyllo Purses with Roasted Squash, Peppers, and Artichokes

A vegetarian Thanksgiving menu demands a centerpiece as dramatic and satisfying as a turkey. This recipe is it: crusty phyllo pouches full of lightly spiced fall vegetables. The cool, creamy yogurt sauce balances the heat from the green poblano chiles in the filling. You can prepare the filling and sauce earlier in the day, and refrigerate until ready to assemble and bake the purses.

SAUCE:

1½ cups plain low-fat yogurt
2 tablespoons chopped fresh cilantro
2 tablespoons chopped fresh mint
½ teaspoon paprika
¼ teaspoon salt
¼ teaspoon freshly ground black pepper

PURSES:

2 cups (1-inch) cubed peeled butternut or kabocha squash
2 large green bell peppers, halved lengthwise and seeded
Cooking spray
½ teaspoon salt, divided
½ teaspoon freshly ground black pepper, divided
1 teaspoon cumin seeds
2 teaspoons olive oil
3 cups thinly sliced leek (about 3 large)
3 large poblano chiles, seeded and chopped
2 tablespoons chopped fresh cilantro
1 (14-ounce) can artichoke hearts, drained and coarsely chopped
16 (18 x 14-inch) sheets frozen phyllo dough, thawed
1½ cups (6 ounces) crumbled feta cheese

1. To prepare sauce, combine first 6 ingredients; cover and chill.

2. Preheat oven to 375°.

3. To prepare purses, arrange squash and bell pepper halves in a single layer on a baking sheet coated with cooking spray; coat vegetables with cooking spray. Sprinkle evenly with ¼ teaspoon salt and ¼ teaspoon black pepper. Bake at 375° for 40 minutes or until squash is tender, stirring after 20 minutes. Cool slightly. Cut bell pepper halves into thin slices, and set aside.

4. Reduce oven temperature to 350°.

5. Cook cumin seeds in a large nonstick skillet over medium heat 1 minute or until toasted and fragrant. Add oil to pan; increase heat to medium-high heat. Add leek and poblanos; sauté 8 minutes or until leek is tender. Cool slightly.

6. Combine squash, bell peppers, leek mixture, ¼ teaspoon salt, ¼ teaspoon black pepper, 2 tablespoons cilantro, and artichokes, tossing gently.

7. Place 1 phyllo sheet on a large cutting board or work surface (cover remaining dough to prevent drying); lightly coat with cooking spray. Top with another phyllo sheet; lightly coat with cooking spray. Gently press coated phyllo sheets together. Spoon about 1¼ cups squash mixture into center of phyllo stack; top with 3 tablespoons cheese. Gather 4 corners of phyllo, and crimp and twist to seal, forming a purse. Lightly coat purse with cooking spray; place on a baking sheet. Repeat procedure with remaining phyllo, squash mixture, and cheese to form 8 purses. Bake at 350° for 30 minutes or until phyllo is browned and crisp. Serve with sauce. Yield: 8 servings (serving size: 1 purse and 3 tablespoons sauce).

CALORIES 304 (29% from fat); FAT 9.7g (sat 4.6g, mono 3.6g, poly 0.9g); PROTEIN 11.5g; CARB 44.2g; FIBER 4.3g; CHOL 22mg; IRON 3.9mg; SODIUM 836mg; CALC 239mg

Glazed Carrots and Cipollini Onions with Coriander and Orange

If you can't find cipollini onions, substitute pearl onions. To make peeling the onions easier, drop them into boiling water and cook for 1 minute. Drain, rinse with cold water, and trim the ends; the peels will slip off easily. Prepare this dish up to 1 day in advance; reheat in a skillet over medium heat, adding 1 to 2 tablespoons water, if necessary.

1 tablespoon butter
1¼ pounds cipollini onions, peeled
1 cup water
1 teaspoon grated orange rind
⅓ cup fresh orange juice
2 tablespoons brown sugar
2 tablespoons sherry vinegar or cider vinegar
1 teaspoon crushed coriander seeds
1½ pounds carrots, peeled and cut into ½-inch diagonal slices
2 tablespoons coarsely chopped fresh cilantro
½ teaspoon salt
¼ teaspoon freshly ground black pepper

Continued

1. Melt butter in a large nonstick skillet over medium-high heat. Add onions, and sauté 3 minutes or until golden. Add water and next 6 ingredients; bring to a boil. Reduce heat; simmer 18 minutes or until vegetables are tender and liquid almost evaporates, stirring occasionally. Remove from heat; stir in cilantro, salt, and pepper. Yield: 8 servings (serving size: about ⅔ cup).

CALORIES 100 (16% from fat); FAT 1.8g (sat 0.9g, mono 0.5g, poly 0.2g); PROTEIN 2g; CARB 20.7g; FIBER 3.7g; CHOL 4mg; IRON 0.8mg; SODIUM 195mg; CALC 46mg

---

QUICK & EASY
Spinach with Chickpeas and Spices

Espinacas con garbanzos (spinach with garbanzo beans) is a popular dish in southern Spain's Andalusia region. There, it's often served as a *tapa*, or appetizer, piled on pieces of toast and presented with a glass of sherry. In this menu, it accompanies the phyllo purses. The breadcrumbs help thicken the liquid to coat the spinach and chickpeas.

 1 tablespoon olive oil
1½ cups chopped onion
 ¼ teaspoon crushed red pepper
 4 garlic cloves, minced
 ¾ teaspoon ground cumin
1½ cups water
 ¼ cup dry breadcrumbs
 2 tablespoons dry sherry
 ¼ teaspoon saffron threads, crushed
 2 (15½-ounce) cans chickpeas (garbanzo beans), rinsed and drained
 2 (10-ounce) packages fresh spinach
 1 tablespoon chopped fresh parsley
 1 tablespoon fresh lemon juice
 ¾ teaspoon salt
 ½ teaspoon freshly ground black pepper

1. Heat oil in a Dutch oven over medium-high heat. Add onion; sauté 2 minutes. Add red pepper and garlic, and sauté 1 minute. Add cumin; cook 30 seconds, stirring constantly. Add water and next 4 ingredients; cook 2 minutes or until slightly thick, stirring frequently. Add half of spinach; cook 2 minutes or until

spinach wilts. Repeat procedure with remaining spinach. Remove from heat. Stir in parsley and remaining ingredients. Yield: 8 servings (serving size: about ⅔ cup).

CALORIES 141 (25% from fat); FAT 3.9g (sat 0.3g, mono 2g, poly 1.3g); PROTEIN 6.3g; CARB 21.6g; FIBER 6g; CHOL 0mg; IRON 3.6mg; SODIUM 490mg; CALC 116mg

---

Fruited Couscous Pilaf

This side dish studded with autumn-hued dried fruits would enliven any holiday meal. Stir cubes of fresh mozzarella cheese into leftovers for a satisfying pasta salad lunch.

 ½ cup dried currants or raisins
 ½ cup chopped dried tart cherries
 ½ cup chopped dried apricots
 ½ cup fresh orange juice (about 1 orange)
 ¾ cup warm water, divided
 2 (14-ounce) cans vegetable broth
2½ cups uncooked couscous
 1 tablespoon extravirgin olive oil
 1 cup chopped green onions
 ¼ cup chopped fresh parsley
 ¼ cup chopped fresh cilantro
 2 tablespoons chopped fresh mint
 2 tablespoons fresh lemon juice
 ½ teaspoon salt
 ¼ teaspoon freshly ground black pepper
 2 tablespoons pine nuts, toasted

1. Place first 4 ingredients in a medium bowl; add ¼ cup water. Let stand 45 minutes, stirring twice. Drain well; discard orange juice mixture.
2. Bring ½ cup water and broth to a boil in a large saucepan; gradually stir in fruit mixture and couscous. Remove from heat; cover and let stand 8 minutes. Fluff with a fork; place in a large bowl.
3. Heat oil in a nonstick skillet over medium heat. Add onions; sauté 2 minutes. Add onions, parsley, and next 5 ingredients to couscous mixture; stir until well blended. Sprinkle with nuts. Yield: 12 servings (serving size: about 1 cup).

CALORIES 217 (11% from fat); FAT 2.7g (sat 0.3g, mono 1.1g, poly 0.7g); PROTEIN 6.1g; CARB 42.5g; FIBER 3.4g; CHOL 0mg; IRON 1mg; SODIUM 387mg; CALC 21mg

---

MAKE AHEAD
Fall Salad with Buttermilk Dressing

Crisp lettuces and fresh oranges are tossed with a creamy homemade dressing similar to ranch. Feathery fennel fronds make a pretty garnish. Prepare the croutons and dressing the day before; store the croutons at room temperature in a zip-top plastic bag, and put the dressing in the refrigerator. Dress the salad just before serving.

CROUTONS:
 4 ounces Hawaiian sweet bread, cut into ½-inch cubes
Cooking spray

DRESSING:
 1 tablespoon finely chopped shallots
 ¼ teaspoon ground cumin
 ¼ teaspoon ground coriander
 ¼ cup fresh orange juice, divided
 1 teaspoon white wine vinegar
 ⅓ cup low-fat buttermilk
 1 tablespoon finely chopped fresh chives
 1 tablespoon chopped fresh cilantro
 1 teaspoon Dijon mustard
 ¼ teaspoon salt
 ⅛ teaspoon freshly ground black pepper

SALAD:
 4 cups torn Boston lettuce
 3 cups thinly sliced fennel bulb (about 1 large bulb)
 2 cups torn radicchio
1½ cups orange sections (about 3 oranges)
 ½ cup thinly sliced red onion
 ¼ cup chopped fennel fronds (optional)

1. Preheat oven to 350°.
2. To prepare croutons, place bread cubes on a baking sheet; coat with cooking spray. Bake at 350° for 12 minutes or until lightly browned and crisp, stirring once. Cool completely.
3. To prepare dressing, heat a large nonstick skillet over medium-high heat. Coat pan with cooking spray. Add shallots, cumin, and coriander; sauté 3 minutes or until shallots are tender. Stir in

2 tablespoons orange juice and vinegar; cook 2 minutes or until liquid evaporates, stirring constantly. Remove from heat; cool slightly.

4. Combine 2 tablespoons orange juice, buttermilk, and next 5 ingredients, stirring with a whisk. Stir in shallot mixture.

5. To prepare salad, combine lettuce, fennel bulb, and radicchio in a large bowl. Drizzle with dressing; toss gently to combine. Arrange about 1¼ cups salad on each of 8 salad plates; top evenly with orange sections and onion. Sprinkle evenly with croutons and fennel fronds, if desired. Yield: 8 servings.

CALORIES 90 (15% from fat); FAT 1.5g (sat 0.5g, mono 0.5g, poly 0.2g); PROTEIN 3.1g; CARB 17g; FIBER 2.5g; CHOL 5mg; IRON 1mg; SODIUM 160mg; CALC 64mg

How to Peel Pineapple and Lime

Use a heavy chef's knife to peel the pineapple.

Use a vegetable peeler to remove lime rind without any bitter white pith.

MAKE AHEAD • FREEZABLE

Chile-Lime Pineapple with Cardamom-Lime Ice Cream

ICE CREAM:

    1   cup sugar
    ½   cup water
    ¼   teaspoon ground cardamom
    2   large pasteurized egg whites
    ¼   teaspoon cream of tartar
    1   cup low-fat buttermilk
    ½   cup heavy cream
    1   teaspoon grated lime rind
    ⅓   cup fresh lime juice (about 3 limes)

PINEAPPLE:

    2   cups boiling water, divided
    2   tablespoons (1-inch) julienne-cut lime rind
    ½   cup sugar
    ½   cup water
    ¼   cup fresh lime juice (about 2 limes)
    1   hot red or green chile, seeded and minced
    1   large pineapple, peeled, cored, and cut into 8 (½-inch) slices

1. To prepare ice cream, combine first 3 ingredients in a saucepan; bring to a boil. Stir to dissolve sugar; cook 3 minutes.

2. While sugar syrup cooks, place egg whites in a large bowl; beat with a mixer at high speed until foamy. Add cream of tartar; beat at high speed until stiff peaks form. Gradually pour hot sugar syrup in a thin stream over egg whites, beating at high speed until mixture is glossy and stiff (about 5 minutes).

3. Combine buttermilk, cream, grated rind, and ⅓ cup juice, stirring with a whisk; gently fold into egg white mixture. Spoon into a freezer-safe bowl; cover and freeze 8 hours or overnight.

4. To prepare pineapple, pour 1 cup boiling water over julienne-cut rind in a small bowl; let stand 5 minutes. Drain. Repeat procedure with 1 cup boiling water and rind (soak rind 2 times).

5. Combine ½ cup sugar and ½ cup water in a small saucepan. Bring to a boil over medium-high heat, stirring constantly. Cook 3 minutes or until slightly thick (do not stir). Remove from heat; stir in julienne-cut rind, ¼ cup juice, and chile. Cool completely.

6. Place pineapple slices on a platter. Pour chile-lime syrup over pineapple; cover and chill at least 30 minutes. Serve pineapple and syrup with ice cream. Yield: 8 servings (serving size: 1 pineapple slice, ¾ cup ice cream, and 4 teaspoons syrup).

CALORIES 248 (21% from fat); FAT 5.9g (sat 3.6g, mono 1.7g, poly 0.3g); PROTEIN 2.7g; CARB 49g; FIBER 1.2g; CHOL 22mg; IRON 0.2mg; SODIUM 53mg; CALC 58mg

season's best

Spiced Cranberry and Zinfandel Sauce

This version of the traditional Thanksgiving relish is updated with the addition of spices and wine.

MAKE AHEAD

Spiced Cranberry and Zinfandel Sauce

    2   cups Zinfandel or other fruity dry red wine
    ¾   cup sugar
    5   (2-inch) orange rind strips
    ½   cup fresh orange juice
    6   whole cloves
    4   slices peeled fresh ginger
    2   (3-inch) cinnamon sticks
    1   (12-ounce) package fresh cranberries

1. Combine first 7 ingredients in a medium saucepan; bring to a boil over high heat. Reduce heat to medium, and cook 15 minutes or until mixture begins to thicken and sugar dissolves, stirring occasionally. Strain mixture through a sieve into a bowl, and discard solids. Return mixture to pan.

2. Add cranberries to pan; cook over high heat 10 minutes or until berries pop. Reduce heat to low; simmer 30 minutes or until mixture is slightly thick. Pour into a bowl; cool. Yield: 10 servings (serving size: ¼ cup).

CALORIES 119 (0% from fat); FAT 0g; PROTEIN 0.2g; CARB 22.1g; FIBER 1.3g; CHOL 0mg; IRON 0.2mg; SODIUM 3mg; CALC 5mg

Hot Off the Griddle

A Massachusetts reader transforms traditional pancakes using a breakfast staple.

Inspiration for Michelle Collins's Hearty Pancakes struck at a local pancake house where Michelle and her husband, Matt, ate breakfast. There was something in the pancakes that made them "crunchy and different," she says. Matt asked the waitress what was in the batter, and she whispered, "The secret is Cream of Wheat!"

Back in their kitchen in Amesbury, Massachusetts, the Collinses both went to work. Once the recipe, complete with Cream of Wheat, was nailed down, it became a regular on the family's breakfast menu. The Collinses complete their pancake breakfast with a fruit and soy milk smoothie. "It's a favorite duo for a power breakfast," Michelle says.

QUICK & EASY • FREEZABLE
Hearty Pancakes

- 1 cup whole wheat flour
- ¼ cup all-purpose flour
- ⅓ cup uncooked farina (such as Cream of Wheat)
- ⅓ cup sugar
- 1 teaspoon baking soda
- 1 teaspoon baking powder
- ½ teaspoon salt
- 1½ cups vanilla soy milk
- ¼ cup applesauce
- 1 large egg, lightly beaten
- Cooking spray
- ½ cup golden raisins, divided
- ½ cup coarsely chopped walnuts, divided
- ¼ cup maple syrup

1. Lightly spoon flours into dry measuring cups; level with a knife. Combine flours, farina, and next 4 ingredients in a large bowl, stirring with a whisk. Combine milk, applesauce, and egg in a medium bowl, stirring until well blended. Add milk mixture to flour mixture, stirring until well combined. Let batter stand 5 minutes.

2. Heat a nonstick griddle or skillet over medium heat; coat pan with cooking spray. Pour about ¼ cup batter per pancake onto pan; sprinkle each with 2 teaspoons raisins and 2 teaspoons walnuts. Cook 1 minute or until tops are covered with bubbles and edges look cooked. Carefully turn pancakes over, and cook 1 minute or until bottoms are lightly browned. Repeat procedure with remaining batter, raisins, and walnuts. Serve with syrup. Yield: 6 servings (serving size: 2 pancakes and 2 teaspoons maple syrup).

CALORIES 347 (23% from fat); FAT 9g (sat 1g, mono 1.3g, poly 5.1g); PROTEIN 8.8g; CARB 61.1g; FIBER 4.3g; CHOL 35mg; IRON 4.8mg; SODIUM 537mg; CALC 142mg

QUICK & EASY • MAKE AHEAD
Seco de Quinoa

"I grew up in Ecuador, where my mom often made soup with quinoa, potatoes, and peanuts. Quinoa is believed to have been the Incan kings' grain of choice, and this is a basic recipe for preparing it."

—Ximena Cardoso-Sloane,
Seattle, Washington

- 1¾ cups uncooked quinoa (about 12 ounces)
- 1 tablespoon olive oil
- 3 garlic cloves, minced
- 1 cup finely chopped onion
- 3½ cups water
- ¾ teaspoon salt

1. Place quinoa in a fine sieve; rinse with cold water, and drain.

2. Heat oil in a large saucepan over medium-high heat. Add garlic; sauté 30 seconds. Add onion; sauté 4 minutes or until tender. Stir in quinoa, water, and salt; bring to a boil. Cover, reduce heat, and simmer 15 minutes or until liquid is absorbed and quinoa is tender. Remove from heat; fluff with a fork. Yield: 8 servings (serving size: ½ cup).

CALORIES 163 (21% from fat); FAT 3.9g (sat 0.5g, mono 1.8g, poly 1g); PROTEIN 5.2g; CARB 27.7g; FIBER 2.6g; CHOL 0mg; IRON 3.5mg; SODIUM 233mg; CALC 30mg

MAKE AHEAD
Stuffed Green Pepper Soup

"This recipe is a good way to get my husband to eat vegetables. It's a comforting soup for a cold day with corn bread or another hearty bread; it's better the day after."

—Chris Sunderman,
Morgantown, West Virginia

- ½ pound ground round
- 2 cups chopped green bell pepper
- 1 cup chopped onion
- ¼ teaspoon black pepper
- 1 (14-ounce) can less-sodium beef broth
- 1 (14.5-ounce) can diced tomatoes, undrained
- 1 (10¾-ounce) can tomato soup, undiluted
- 1½ cups hot cooked white rice

1. Heat a small Dutch oven over medium-high heat. Add beef; cook 3 minutes or until browned, stirring to crumble. Add bell pepper and onion; cook 8 minutes or until vegetables are tender. Stir in black pepper, broth, tomatoes, and tomato soup; bring to a boil. Reduce heat, and simmer 45 minutes.

2. Spoon ¼ cup rice into each of 6 bowls; top with 1 cup soup. Yield: 6 servings.

CALORIES 219 (30% from fat); FAT 7.2g (sat 2.6g, mono 2.9g, poly 0.8g); PROTEIN 11.7g; CARB 27.5g; FIBER 3.2g; CHOL 26mg; IRON 2.7mg; SODIUM 444mg; CALC 39mg

---

Great Grains

In the recipe for Hearty Pancakes (recipe at left), we call for farina—a.k.a. Cream of Wheat. Farina is a fine meal, or flour, that is usually combined with hot water and eaten as a breakfast cereal.

Quinoa, featured in Seco de Quinoa (recipe at left) is deeply rooted in ancient South American cuisine. It has more protein than other grains and contains all eight essential amino acids, so it's a complete protein. Use quinoa as a side dish in place of rice or as the basis of a satisfying meatless entrée.

Portobello Mushrooms with Mediterranean Stuffing

"This is great to serve as a first course at Thanksgiving or Christmas. I came up with the idea when I was looking for a vegetarian dish with a traditional feel. It's easy, tasty, and always a hit."

—Angela McKinlay, Everett, Washington

- 4 (4-inch) portobello caps (about ¾ pound)
- ¼ cup finely chopped onion
- ¼ cup finely chopped celery
- ¼ cup finely chopped carrot
- ¼ cup finely chopped red bell pepper
- ¼ cup finely chopped green bell pepper
- ¼ teaspoon dried Italian seasoning
- 2 garlic cloves, minced
- Cooking spray
- 3 cups (¼-inch) cubed French bread, toasted
- ½ cup vegetable broth
- ½ cup (2 ounces) crumbled feta cheese
- 3 tablespoons low-fat balsamic vinaigrette, divided
- 4 teaspoons grated fresh Parmesan cheese
- ¼ teaspoon black pepper
- 4 cups mixed salad greens

1. Preheat oven to 350°.
2. Remove stems from mushrooms, and finely chop stems to measure ¼ cup. Discard remaining stems. Combine ¼ cup chopped stems, onion, and next 6 ingredients.
3. Heat a large nonstick skillet over medium heat; coat pan with cooking spray. Add onion mixture to pan; cook 10 minutes or until vegetables are tender. Combine onion mixture and bread in a large bowl, tossing to combine. Slowly add broth to bread mixture, tossing to coat. Add feta; toss gently.
4. Remove brown gills from undersides of mushroom caps using a spoon; discard gills. Place mushrooms, stem side up, on a baking sheet coated with cooking spray. Brush mushrooms evenly with 1 tablespoon vinaigrette. Sprinkle Parmesan and black pepper evenly over mushrooms; top each with ½ cup bread mixture. Bake at 350° for 25 minutes or until mushrooms are tender.
5. Combine 2 tablespoons vinaigrette and greens, tossing gently. Place 1 cup greens on each of 4 plates; top each serving with 1 mushroom. Yield: 4 servings.

CALORIES 182 (32% from fat); FAT 6.4g (sat 3.5g, mono 1.3g, poly 0.5g); PROTEIN 9.3g; CARB 22.7g; FIBER 4.1g; CHOL 20mg; IRON 2.2mg; SODIUM 691mg; CALC 189mg

Super Sloppy Joe Sandwiches

"My family loves Sloppy Joes, so I came up with this recipe. It works well with just about any combination of vegetables. When I want a change from bell pepper and celery, I substitute a package of broccoli slaw, chopped eggplant, and shredded carrots."

—Rebecca Fulcher, Monument, Colorado

- 1 pound ground round
- 1¼ cups chopped green bell pepper
- 1¼ cups chopped celery
- 1 cup chopped onion
- 3 garlic cloves, minced
- 1 cup water
- 1 cup ketchup
- 1 tablespoon brown sugar
- 1 tablespoon fresh lemon juice
- 1 tablespoon red wine vinegar
- 2 teaspoons Worcestershire sauce
- 1 teaspoon paprika
- 1 teaspoon Dijon mustard
- ¼ teaspoon fennel seeds
- ¼ teaspoon hot pepper sauce
- 1 (8-ounce) package presliced mushrooms, chopped
- 6 (2-ounce) Kaiser rolls or hamburger buns, toasted

1. Heat a large nonstick skillet over medium-high heat. Add beef; cook 3 minutes or until browned, stirring to crumble. Add bell pepper, celery, onion, and garlic; cook 7 minutes or until vegetables are tender, stirring occasionally. Stir in water and next 10 ingredients; bring to a boil. Reduce heat, and simmer 25 minutes or until mixture begins to thicken, stirring occasionally. Spoon ⅔ cup meat mixture onto bottom half of each roll; cover with top half of roll. Yield: 6 servings (serving size: 1 sandwich).

CALORIES 404 (31% from fat); FAT 14.2g (sat 5.1g, mono 5.5g, poly 1.8g); PROTEIN 21.3g; CARB 49.4g; FIBER 4.1g; CHOL 51mg; IRON 4.1mg; SODIUM 929mg; CALC 97mg

Creamy Squash and Apple Soup

"This is a way to get my daughter, Clara, to eat squash, and we all love it. It's so adaptable; I just sprinkle the squash with cheese or croutons or maybe even a drizzle of puréed cranberries."

—Molly Swetnam-Burland, Brunswick, Maine

- 5¾ cups fat-free, less-sodium chicken broth
- 1 (1½-pound) butternut squash, peeled and cut into 1-inch cubes
- 1 large peeled sweet potato, cut into 1-inch pieces
- 4 teaspoons butter, divided
- 2 cups vertically sliced onion
- 1½ cups sliced peeled Granny Smith apple
- 1 tablespoon all-purpose flour
- ½ teaspoon salt
- ¼ teaspoon black pepper

1. Combine first 3 ingredients in a Dutch oven; bring to a boil. Cover, reduce heat, and simmer 15 minutes or until squash and potato are tender. Remove squash and potato from pan with a slotted spoon, reserving broth. Mash squash mixture to desired consistency.
2. While squash and potato cook, melt 1 teaspoon butter in a medium nonstick skillet over medium-low heat. Add onion and apple; cook 20 minutes or until lightly browned, stirring occasionally. Remove onion mixture from pan; set aside. Increase heat to medium-high. Melt 3 teaspoons butter in pan. Add flour; cook 5 minutes or until golden brown, stirring constantly with a whisk. Gradually add 1 cup reserved broth, and cook 3 minutes
Continued

or until slightly thickened.

3. Add thickened broth mixture, mashed squash mixture, onion mixture, salt, and pepper to remaining broth in Dutch oven. Cook over medium heat 5 minutes, stirring occasionally. Yield: 8 servings (serving size: about 1 cup).

CALORIES 115 (16% from fat); FAT 2.1g (sat 1.2g, mono 0.5g, poly 0.1g); PROTEIN 3.8g; CARB 22.8g; FIBER 2.9g; CHOL 5mg; IRON 0.9mg; SODIUM 546mg; CALC 59mg

entertaining

Make-ahead Snacks

Offer these no-fuss dips and spreads to hungry guests to nibble while you finish making dinner.

When you're busy putting the final touches on a holiday feast, you don't need the distraction of well-intentioned people hovering in the kitchen. A 15-minute investment the night before will pay big dividends. That's all the time it takes to prepare one or two of these make-ahead dips and spreads. Then, when a would-be helper ambles into the kitchen on the big day, simply hand him or her a platter of dip and crackers, pre-cut vegetables, or bread to share with the other guests. It's the ideal diversion to keep hungry company satisfied.

Crunching Calories

The percent of calories from fat may appear high in some of these recipes, but when you pair them with dippers, the numbers add up nicely. If you eat one serving of Tapenade (recipe at right) with two toasted baguette slices, the proportion of calories from fat drops to 39 percent. Enjoy four carrot sticks, four broccoli florets, and four crackers with one serving of Spinach-Parmesan Dip (recipe on page 409), and it's 33 percent of calories from fat.

Sandwich Night Menu
serves 4

Creamy Mushroom Spread (recipe below box) is versatile enough to elevate a simple chicken sandwich to a memorable meal.

Chicken, provolone, and mushroom sandwiches*

Red seedless grapes

*Heat 2 teaspoons olive oil in a large nonstick skillet over medium-high heat. Rub ½ teaspoon salt, ¼ teaspoon black pepper, and ¼ teaspoon ground red pepper evenly over 4 (6-ounce) skinless, boneless chicken breast halves. Place chicken in pan; cook 4 minutes on each side or until done. Spread 2 tablespoons Creamy Mushroom Spread (recipe below) over each of 4 (1-ounce) slices toasted sourdough bread; top each with 1 chicken breast half, 1 (1-ounce) slice provolone cheese, ¼ cup trimmed arugula, and 1 (1-ounce) slice toasted sourdough bread.

QUICK & EASY • MAKE AHEAD
Creamy Mushroom Spread

This spread is delicious either warm or cold.

    2 (8-ounce) packages presliced
       mushrooms
    1 tablespoon olive oil
    ¼ cup finely chopped shallots
    1½ teaspoons chopped fresh thyme
    2 garlic cloves, minced
    ½ teaspoon salt
    ¼ teaspoon freshly ground black
       pepper
    ½ cup light sour cream

1. Place mushrooms in a food processor; process until finely chopped. Heat oil in a large nonstick skillet over medium-high heat. Add mushrooms, shallots, thyme, and garlic; cook 10 minutes or until liquid evaporates, stirring occasionally. Stir in salt and pepper.
2. Place mushroom mixture in a bowl; stir in sour cream. Serve spread at room temperature or chilled. Yield: 1¼ cups (serving size: 2 tablespoons).

CALORIES 42 (54% from fat); FAT 2.5g (sat 1g, mono 1g, poly 0.2g); PROTEIN 2.4g; CARB 3.2g; FIBER 0.6g; CHOL 4mg; IRON 0.3mg; SODIUM 130mg; CALC 21mg

---

QUICK & EASY • MAKE AHEAD
Black Bean Spread with Lime and Cilantro

Fresh lime juice and cilantro dress up canned black beans for a simple, delicious appetizer. Serve with baked tortilla chips, and use any remaining spread in quesadillas or burritos.

    3 garlic cloves, peeled
    ½ cup chopped fresh cilantro
    2 tablespoons fresh lime juice
    1½ tablespoons extravirgin olive oil
    ½ teaspoon salt
    1 (15-ounce) can black beans,
       rinsed and drained
    1 (15-ounce) can black beans,
       undrained
    Cilantro sprig (optional)

1. With food processor running, drop garlic through food chute; process until minced. Add chopped cilantro and next 5 ingredients, and process until smooth. Garnish with cilantro sprig, if desired. Yield: 2½ cups (serving size: ¼ cup).

CALORIES 64 (28% from fat); FAT 2g (sat 0.3g, mono 1.5g, poly 0.2g); PROTEIN 3.2g; CARB 11.2g; FIBER 3.8g; CHOL 0mg; IRON 1.2mg; SODIUM 325mg; CALC 28mg

---

QUICK & EASY • MAKE AHEAD
Tapenade

Serve this thick olive paste from Provençe with toasted baguette slices. It's also great stirred into pasta, used as a sandwich spread, or as a pizza topping.

    2 garlic cloves, peeled
    2 cups pitted kalamata olives
    ¼ cup capers
    2 canned anchovy fillets
    ¼ cup finely chopped fresh parsley

1. With food processor running, drop garlic through food chute, and process until minced. Add olives, capers, and anchovies; process until finely chopped. Add parsley; pulse to combine. Yield: 1¼ cups (serving size: 2 tablespoons).

CALORIES 56 (80% from fat); FAT 5g (sat 0.6g, mono 3.8g, poly 0.6g); PROTEIN 0.7g; CARB 2.2g; FIBER 0.3g; CHOL 1mg; IRON 0.3mg; SODIUM 433mg; CALC 13mg

Spinach-Parmesan Dip
(pictured on page 378)

At first, the spinach will seem to overflow in the skillet, but keep stirring—as it begins to wilt, it reduces in volume. Serve with crudités or hearty wheat crackers.

    1   teaspoon olive oil
    3   garlic cloves, chopped
    ¼   teaspoon salt
    1   (10-ounce) package fresh spinach
    ½   cup basil leaves, loosely packed
    ⅓   cup (about 3 ounces) ⅓-less-fat
        cream cheese, softened
    ⅛   teaspoon black pepper
    ⅓   cup plain fat-free yogurt
    ¼   cup (1 ounce) grated fresh
        Parmesan cheese

1. Heat oil in a large skillet over medium-high heat. Add garlic; sauté 1 minute. Add salt and spinach; sauté 3 minutes or until spinach wilts. Place spinach mixture in a colander, pressing until mixture is barely moist.
2. Place spinach mixture, basil, cream cheese, and pepper in a food processor; process until smooth. Spoon spinach mixture into a medium bowl. Stir in yogurt and Parmesan. Cover and chill. Yield: 2 cups (serving size: ¼ cup).

CALORIES 63 (60% from fat); FAT 4.2g (sat 2.3g, mono 1.4g, poly 0.2g); PROTEIN 4.1g; CARB 3g; FIBER 0.9g; CHOL 11mg; IRON 1.1mg; SODIUM 209mg; CALC 112mg

Cumin Curried Hummus

The flavor of the hummus is similar to that of Indian *lentil dal* but is much easier to prepare. Serve with warm pita wedges.

    1   tablespoon olive oil
    3   garlic cloves, chopped
    1   tablespoon curry powder
    ½   teaspoon cumin seeds
    ½   cup water
    3   tablespoons fresh lemon juice
    ¾   teaspoon salt
    2   (15½-ounce) cans chickpeas
        (garbanzo beans), rinsed and drained

1. Heat oil in a small skillet over medium heat. Add garlic; cook 30 seconds, stirring constantly. Add curry and cumin; cook 30 seconds or until fragrant, stirring constantly. Place garlic mixture, water, and remaining ingredients in a food processor; process until smooth. Yield: 3 cups (serving size: ¼ cup).

CALORIES 82 (29% from fat); FAT 2.6g (sat 0.2g, mono 1.4g, poly 1g); PROTEIN 3g; CARB 12.2g; FIBER 3g; CHOL 0mg; IRON 1.2mg; SODIUM 254mg; CALC 27mg

Red Pepper-Walnut Dip

Serve with toasted pita wedges or sourdough baguette slices.

    ¾   cup walnuts, toasted
    ½   cup raisins
    ½   cup plain low-fat yogurt
    ¼   teaspoon salt
    ⅛   teaspoon ground red pepper
    1   (12-ounce) bottle roasted red bell
        peppers, drained

1. Place all ingredients in a food processor, and process until smooth. Yield: 12 servings (serving size: about 2½ tablespoons).

CALORIES 75 (53% from fat); FAT 4.4g (sat 0.5g, mono 0.6g, poly 3.1g); PROTEIN 2.1g; CARB 7.9g; FIBER 0.9g; CHOL 1mg; IRON 0.5mg; SODIUM 160mg; CALC 31mg

Smoked Trout Spread

Thanks to the rich flavor of the smoked trout, there's no need to season this spread with extra salt or pepper. Look for smoked trout in the same section of the grocery store that has fresh fish. Bagel chips or Melba toasts provide crunchy contrast to the creamy dip, but toasted baguette slices are good, too.

    1   (8-ounce) package smoked trout
    ½   cup fat-free sour cream
    ⅓   cup low-fat mayonnaise
    ⅓   cup finely chopped red
        onion
    ⅓   cup shredded carrot
    ⅓   cup finely chopped green bell
        pepper

1. Remove and discard skin from fish; finely chop fish. Place fish, sour cream, and mayonnaise in a medium bowl, and mash with a fork. Stir in onion, carrot, and bell pepper. Yield: 2 cups (serving size: ¼ cup).

CALORIES 77 (29% from fat); FAT 2.5g (sat 0.7g, mono 0.6g, poly 0.9g); PROTEIN 6.9g; CARB 6.5g; FIBER 0.3g; CHOL 18mg; IRON 0.1mg; SODIUM 534mg; CALC 26mg

Cool and Crunchy Crab Dip

While fresh crabmeat makes this dip extraspecial, canned lump crabmeat is a great substitute and can be kept in the pantry to use at a moment's notice. Serve with your favorite crackers and crisp raw vegetables.

    ¾   cup fat-free sour cream
    4   ounces block-style ⅓-less-fat
        cream cheese, softened
    1   cup finely chopped celery
    ¼   cup minced fresh chives
    ¼   cup fat-free Thousand Island
        dressing
    ¾   teaspoon salt
    1   (8-ounce) container lump crabmeat,
        drained and shell pieces removed
    Chopped chives (optional)

1. Combine sour cream and cream cheese in a large bowl; stir with a whisk until smooth. Stir in celery, minced chives, dressing, and salt. Gently fold in crabmeat. Garnish with chopped chives, if desired. Yield: 12 servings (serving size: ¼ cup).

CALORIES 67 (38% from fat); FAT 2.8g (sat 1.6g, mono 0.7g, poly 0.2g); PROTEIN 5.6g; CARB 4.5g; FIBER 0.4g; CHOL 28mg; IRON 0.2mg; SODIUM 304mg; CALC 54mg

happy endings

Crisps and Crumbles

These simple desserts have the luscious appeal of baked fruit pies—without the work of making a pastry crust.

The difference between a crisp and a crumble is subtle in these recipes. Our crisps have a buttery, streusel-like topping sprinkled over the fruit. The butter is cut into a flour-sugar mixture that's dry and separates easily. For our crumbles, a wet mixture of oil and egg is stirred into the flour mixture until moist. This topping is more moist and dense than a crisp, so use your hands to form little pieces of dough to drop onto the filling.

Most of these desserts use apples and pears because firm fruits hold their shape and don't release much liquid when they cook. But several of the recipes incorporate berries and dried fruits for added interest. Once you've tried these techniques, use our basic crisp and crumble recipes for your own creations.

Vanilla-Scented Harvest Crisp with Pistachios

The dried fruits and apples under a crusty oatmeal-pistachio topping make a great ending to a fall evening.

FILLING:
- 1 tablespoon butter
- 1 cup dried apricots, chopped
- 1 cup apricot nectar
- ½ cup dried figs, chopped
- ¼ cup dried currants or dried cranberries
- 2 tablespoons honey
- 1 tablespoon brown sugar
- 1 tablespoon vanilla extract
- 1½ pounds Granny Smith apples, peeled and chopped (about 4 apples)
- 1 (2-inch) cinnamon stick
- Cooking spray

TOPPING:
- ½ cup regular oats
- ½ cup all-purpose flour
- ¼ cup packed brown sugar
- ¼ teaspoon salt
- ¼ teaspoon ground cinnamon
- 3 tablespoons chilled butter, cut into small pieces
- 1 cup chopped pistachios

1. Preheat oven to 375°.
2. To prepare filling, melt 1 tablespoon butter in a large saucepan over medium-high heat. Add apricots and next 8 ingredients; bring to a boil. Reduce heat; simmer 10 minutes or until fruit is tender, stirring occasionally. Discard cinnamon stick.
3. Place filling in an 8-inch square baking dish coated with cooking spray.
4. To prepare topping, place oats in a food processor; pulse until coarsely chopped. Place oats in a large bowl. Lightly spoon flour into a dry measuring cup; level with a knife. Add flour, ¼ cup brown sugar, salt, and ground cinnamon to oats; stir to combine. Cut in chilled butter with a pastry blender or 2 knives until mixture resembles coarse meal. Add pistachios; toss well. Sprinkle topping over filling. Bake at 375° for 25 minutes or until golden. Yield: 12 servings.

CALORIES 272 (30% from fat); FAT 9g (sat 3g, mono 3.6g, poly 1.6g); PROTEIN 4.4g; CARB 45.5g; FIBER 5.6g; CHOL 10mg; IRON 2.1mg; SODIUM 92mg; CALC 40mg

Pear-Berry Crisp with Lavender Topping

Lavender lends a subtle floral note to this crisp and complements the berries and pears. Use either fresh or frozen berries. Lavender buds can be found in gourmet specialty stores.

FILLING:
- 1 cup blackberries
- 1 cup fresh raspberries
- 3 tablespoons sugar
- 1 tablespoon fresh lemon juice
- 1½ teaspoons cornstarch
- 2 pounds pears, peeled and cut into 1-inch pieces (about 6 pears)
- Cooking spray

TOPPING:
- ½ cup regular oats
- 1 teaspoon lavender buds
- ¾ cup all-purpose flour
- ½ cup sugar
- ½ teaspoon salt
- ¼ cup chilled butter, cut into small pieces
- 3 tablespoons honey

1. Preheat oven to 375°.
2. To prepare filling, combine first 6 ingredients, tossing well. Spoon mixture into an 8-inch square baking dish coated with cooking spray.
3. To prepare topping, place oats in a food processor; pulse until coarsely ground. Add lavender buds; pulse 8 times or until combined. Place oat mixture in a large bowl. Lightly spoon flour into dry measuring cups; level with a knife. Add flour, ½ cup sugar, and salt to oat mixture; stir to combine. Cut in butter with a pastry blender or 2 knives until mixture resembles coarse meal. Add 3 tablespoons honey to oat mixture; stir just until moistened. Sprinkle topping over filling. Bake at 375° for 30 minutes or until golden and bubbly. Yield: 10 servings.

CALORIES 235 (21% from fat); FAT 5.5g (sat 2.9g, mono 1.4g, poly 0.4g); PROTEIN 2.4g; CARB 47.1g; FIBER 4.7g; CHOL 12mg; IRON 1.1mg; SODIUM 164mg; CALC 21mg

Gingered Pear Crisp

FILLING:
- 2 tablespoons sugar
- 1 teaspoon vanilla extract
- 3 pounds ripe pears, peeled and chopped (about 8 pears)
- 2 tablespoons all-purpose flour
- Cooking spray

TOPPING:
- ¾ cup plus 2 tablespoons all-purpose flour
- ½ cup sugar
- ½ teaspoon salt
- ¼ cup chilled butter, cut into small pieces
- ½ cup crystallized ginger, minced (about 4 ounces)
- 3 tablespoons honey

1. Preheat oven to 375°.
2. To prepare filling, combine first 3 ingredients in a large bowl. Sprinkle with 2 tablespoons flour; toss gently to coat. Spoon filling into an 8-inch square baking dish coated with cooking spray.
3. To prepare topping, lightly spoon ¾ cup flour into dry measuring cups; level with a knife. Combine ¾ cup flour, 2 tablespoons flour, ½ cup sugar, and salt in a large bowl, stirring with a whisk. Cut in butter with a pastry blender or 2 knives until mixture resembles coarse meal. Add ginger and honey; stir just until moistened. Sprinkle over filling. Bake at 375° for 40 minutes or until golden and bubbly. Yield: 10 servings.

CALORIES 274 (18% from fat); FAT 5.5g (sat 2.9g, mono 1.3g, poly 0.2g); PROTEIN 2.2g; CARB 57.6g; FIBER 3.6g; CHOL 12mg; IRON 1mg; SODIUM 168mg; CALC 35mg

STAFF FAVORITE
Orange Crisp with Coconut Topping

To distribute the topping better, use a shallow baking dish.

FILLING:
6 large navel oranges
1½ tablespoons uncooked quick-cooking tapioca
1 tablespoon Grand Marnier (orange-flavored liqueur)
Cooking spray

TOPPING:
⅔ cup all-purpose flour
⅔ cup sugar
½ teaspoon salt
¼ cup chilled butter, cut into small pieces
⅔ cup flaked sweetened coconut

1. Preheat oven to 375°.
2. To prepare filling, peel and section oranges over a large bowl, reserving ¼ cup juice. Add tapioca and liqueur to reserved ¼ cup juice; stir until well blended. Add orange sections; stir gently. Let stand 20 minutes, stirring occasionally.
3. Place filling in an 11 x 7-inch baking dish or shallow 2-quart baking dish coated with cooking spray.

4. To prepare topping, lightly spoon flour into dry measuring cups; level with a knife. Combine flour, sugar, and salt in a large bowl, stirring with a whisk. Cut in butter with a pastry blender or 2 knives until mixture resembles coarse meal. Add coconut; toss well. Sprinkle topping evenly over filling. Bake at 375° for 35 minutes or until crisp is golden and bubbly. Yield: 8 servings.

CALORIES 231 (31% from fat); FAT 7.9g (sat 5.3g, mono 1.8g, poly 0.3g); PROTEIN 2.2g; CARB 40g; FIBER 2.5g; CHOL 15mg; IRON 0.7mg; SODIUM 221mg; CALC 38mg

Crisp and Crumble Basics

How to Make Your Own Filling:

- If you're using only firm fruit (apple, pear, plum, or peach), use 7 cups peeled and sliced or chopped fruit.
- To add berries, replace 1 or 2 cups of firm fruit with your choice of berries. Any more berries, and your filling will have too much liquid.
- To use dried fruit, replace ¾ cup to 1¾ cups of the firm fruit with the dried fruit of your choice. In order to rehydrate and soften the dried fruit as it cooks, you'll need to add about ½ cup fruit juice for every ¾ cup dried fruit.
- Use a light hand when sweetening the filling. Since the sweetness of fresh fruits can vary significantly, use your own judgment and flavor preference when adding sweeteners, such as sugar, brown sugar, or honey.

How to Make Your Own Topping:

Basic Crisp Topping: Place ½ cup regular oats in a food processor; pulse until coarsely ground. Place ¾ cup all-purpose flour, ½ cup sugar, and ½ teaspoon salt in a large bowl; stir to combine. Cut ¼ cup chilled butter into small pieces. Add butter to flour mixture; cut in with a pastry blender or two knives until mixture resembles coarse meal. Stir in ground oats. Add 3 tablespoons honey; toss well.

Basic Crumble Topping: Place ½ cup regular oats in a food processor; pulse until coarsely ground. Place oats in a large bowl; add ¾ cup all-purpose flour, ½ cup whole wheat pastry flour, ¼ cup chopped walnuts (or any nut of your choice), ¼ cup packed brown sugar, ½ teaspoon salt, ½ teaspoon ground cinnamon, and ¼ teaspoon ground nutmeg; stir to combine. Combine 3 tablespoons honey, 2 tablespoons walnut oil (or canola oil), and 1 egg yolk, stirring with a whisk. Add to flour mixture; stir just until moist.

How to Prepare Your Dessert:

- Preheat oven to 375°.
- Lightly coat a baking dish with cooking spray. For crisps you can use an 8-inch square baking pan. For crumbles, we recommend a shallow dish with a large surface area (such as an 11 x 7-inch baking dish) so the denser topping is better distributed and cooks evenly.
- Add filling to prepared dish.
- For a crisp, sprinkle topping evenly over fruit.
- For a crumble, squeeze handfuls of dough to form clumps; crumble dough pieces evenly over fruit.
- Bake at 375° for 35 minutes or until golden and bubbly.

If you're looking for a yummy no-pastry-crust dessert, try one of our humble crisps or crumbles.

Pear Crumble with Dried Tart Cherries and Almond Streusel

The traditional pairing of almonds with cherries gets a triple dose with almond oil, almond paste, and chopped almonds.

FILLING:

¾ cup dried cherries
½ cup apple cider
2½ pounds ripe pears, peeled and chopped (about 7 pears)
2 tablespoons sugar
2 tablespoons all-purpose flour
Cooking spray

TOPPING:

¾ cup all-purpose flour
½ cup whole wheat pastry flour
¼ cup sugar
¼ cup toasted almonds, finely chopped
½ teaspoon salt
2 tablespoons almond paste
3 tablespoons honey
2 tablespoons almond oil
1 large egg yolk, lightly beaten

1. Preheat oven to 375°.
2. To prepare filling, combine cherries and cider in a small saucepan; bring to a boil. Remove from heat. Cover; let stand 10 minutes or until cherries are soft. Drain. Combine cherries and pears in a bowl. Sprinkle with 2 tablespoons sugar and 2 tablespoons flour; toss gently to coat. Spoon filling into an 11 x 7-inch baking dish coated with cooking spray.
3. To prepare topping, lightly spoon ¾ cup all-purpose flour and pastry flour into dry measuring cups; level with a knife. Combine flours, ¼ cup sugar, almonds, and salt in a large bowl, stirring with a whisk. Cut in almond paste with a pastry blender or 2 knives until mixture resembles coarse meal. Combine honey, oil, and egg yolk, stirring with a whisk. Add to flour mixture; stir just until moistened. Squeeze handfuls of topping to form large pieces. Crumble over filling. Bake at 375° for 35 minutes or until golden and bubbly. Yield: 10 servings.

CALORIES 270 (21% from fat); FAT 6.2g (sat 0.6g, mono 3.4g, poly 1.1g); PROTEIN 4g; CARB 53.3g; FIBER 2.6g; CHOL 21mg; IRON 1.1mg; SODIUM 121mg; CALC 35mg

Brandied Caramel-Apple Crumble

Apple brandy gives the filling a sweet, intense flavor as a contrast to the spices.

FILLING:

1½ tablespoons butter, divided
3 pounds Granny Smith apples, peeled and cut into ½-inch slices (about 8 apples)
1 teaspoon ground cinnamon
2 teaspoons vanilla extract
½ teaspoon ground allspice
½ cup Calvados (apple brandy)
¼ cup packed dark brown sugar
2 tablespoons half-and-half
3 tablespoons Calvados (apple brandy)
2 teaspoons cornstarch
Cooking spray

TOPPING:

¾ cup all-purpose flour
½ cup whole wheat pastry flour
½ cup finely chopped walnuts, toasted
¼ cup finely chopped pecans, toasted
¼ cup packed dark brown sugar
1 teaspoon ground cinnamon
½ teaspoon salt
3 tablespoons honey
2 tablespoons walnut or canola oil
1 large egg yolk, lightly beaten

1. Preheat oven to 375°.
2. To prepare filling, melt 1 tablespoon butter in a large nonstick skillet over medium-high heat. Add apples; sauté 8 minutes or until crisp-tender. Stir in 1 teaspoon cinnamon, vanilla, and allspice; cook 1 minute. Add ½ cup brandy; cook 1 minute or until liquid is absorbed. Remove from heat.
3. Combine 1½ teaspoons butter, ¼ cup sugar, and half-and-half in a small saucepan. Cook over medium heat just until sugar dissolves and mixture is slightly thick (about 5 minutes). Remove from heat.
4. Combine 3 tablespoons brandy and cornstarch, stirring with a whisk. Add half-and-half mixture and cornstarch mixture to apple mixture; spoon into a 2-quart baking dish coated with cooking spray.
5. To prepare topping, lightly spoon flours into dry measuring cups; level with a knife. Combine flours, walnuts, and next 4 ingredients in a large bowl. Combine honey, oil, and egg yolk; add to flour mixture. Stir just until moistened. Squeeze handfuls of topping to form large pieces. Crumble over filling. Bake at 375° for 30 minutes or until golden and bubbly. Yield: 12 servings.

CALORIES 287 (30% from fat); FAT 9.7g (sat 1.9g, mono 2.6g, poly 4.6g); PROTEIN 3g; CARB 41.6g; FIBER 3.7g; CHOL 22mg; IRON 1.2mg; SODIUM 118mg; CALC 30mg

Cranberry-Apple Crumble

Apples, cranberries, and an oat topping are an ideal combination of flavors for the holidays. Vary this dessert by using different nuts and nut oils in the topping.

FILLING:

1¾ cups granulated sugar, divided
½ cup cranberry juice
1 (12-ounce) package fresh cranberries
2 pounds Gala apples, peeled, cored, and thinly sliced (about 6 apples)
1 tablespoon all-purpose flour
¼ teaspoon ground cinnamon
Cooking spray

TOPPING:

½ cup regular oats
¾ cup all-purpose flour
½ cup whole wheat pastry flour
½ cup chopped walnuts
¼ cup packed dark brown sugar
½ teaspoon salt
¼ teaspoon ground cinnamon
⅛ teaspoon ground cardamom
¼ cup walnut or canola oil
3 tablespoons honey
2 large egg yolks, lightly beaten

1. Preheat oven to 375°.
2. To prepare filling, combine 1½ cups granulated sugar, cranberry juice, and fresh cranberries in a medium saucepan

over medium-high heat; bring to a boil. Reduce heat, and simmer until cranberries pop, stirring occasionally (about 10 minutes). Set aside.

3. Combine apples, ¼ cup granulated sugar, 1 tablespoon all-purpose flour, and ¼ teaspoon cinnamon in a large zip-top plastic bag. Seal; shake to coat.

4. Place cranberry mixture in an 11 x 7-inch baking dish coated with cooking spray; top evenly with apple mixture.

5. To prepare topping, place oats in a food processor, and pulse until coarsely chopped. Place oats in a large bowl. Lightly spoon ¾ cup all-purpose flour and pastry flour into dry measuring cups; level with a knife. Add flours and next 5 ingredients to oats; stir to combine. Combine oil, honey, and egg yolks, stirring with a whisk. Add to flour mixture; stir just until moistened. Squeeze handfuls of topping to form large pieces. Crumble over filling. Bake at 375° for 40 minutes or until topping is golden and bubbly. Yield: 14 servings.

CALORIES 302 (24% from fat); FAT 7.9g (sat 0.9g, mono 1.6g, poly 4.7g); PROTEIN 3g; CARB 58g; FIBER 4.6g; CHOL 30mg; IRON 1.2mg; SODIUM 88mg; CALC 17mg

superfast

...And Ready in Just About 20 Minutes

This superfast column provides valuable lessons in cooking with a skillet.

Many of these recipes instruct you to begin heating the skillet before other preparations to give it time to reach the right temperature. A hot skillet (or grill pan) sears the outside of fish or meat while leaving a rare middle in Tuna with White Bean-Cucumber Salad or Filet Mignon with Mushroom-Wine Sauce. It allows you to stir-fry for quick cooking that retains the crisp texture of fresh vegetables, and it helps to create a satisfying crust on the Peanut-Crusted Snapper and Chicken with Black Bean Sauce.

These two recipes instruct you to heat the skillet before all other preparations so it reaches the right temperature.

Peanut-Crusted Snapper

Coat the flesh side of the fillets, but not the skin side, with the peanut mixture. Serve with rice tossed with green onions.

¼   cup fat-free milk
2   large egg whites, lightly beaten
⅓   cup panko (Japanese) breadcrumbs
¼   cup finely chopped roasted peanuts
2   teaspoons ground coriander
1   teaspoon sugar
1   teaspoon ground cumin
¾   teaspoon salt
¾   teaspoon curry powder
¼   teaspoon ground cinnamon
4   (6-ounce) red snapper fillets
Cooking spray
4   lime wedges

1. Preheat oven to 475°.
2. Heat a large ovenproof skillet over medium-high heat.
3. Combine milk and egg whites in a shallow dish, stirring with a whisk. Combine breadcrumbs and next 7 ingredients in another shallow dish. Working with 1 fillet at a time, dip fillet, skin side up, in egg mixture; dredge fillet, skin side up, in breadcrumb mixture. Repeat procedure with remaining fillets, egg mixture, and breadcrumb mixture.
4. Coat pan with cooking spray. Add snapper fillets, skin sides up, to pan, and cook 1½ minutes. Turn fillets over; place pan in oven. Bake at 475° for 10 minutes or until fish flakes easily when tested with a fork. Serve with lime wedges. Yield: 4 servings (serving size: 1 fillet and 1 lime wedge).

CALORIES 266 (30% from fat); FAT 9g (sat 1.5g, mono 3.4g, poly 2.8g); PROTEIN 35.5g; CARB 9.4g; FIBER 1.8g; CHOL 136mg; IRON 2.1mg; SODIUM 600mg; CALC 67mg

Filet Mignon with Mushroom-Wine Sauce

This quick but posh dinner for two goes nicely with packaged refrigerated mashed potatoes and bagged salad greens with bottled dressing.

½   cup less-sodium beef broth
¼   cup water
2   teaspoons all-purpose flour
¾   teaspoon Dijon mustard
½   teaspoon bottled minced garlic
¼   teaspoon salt
⅛   teaspoon black pepper
Cooking spray
2   (4-ounce) beef tenderloin steaks
1   cup presliced mushrooms
½   cup sweet Marsala

1. Heat a large cast-iron skillet over high heat.
2. Combine first 7 ingredients in a bowl.
3. Coat pan with cooking spray. Add steaks to pan; cook 5 minutes on each side or until desired degree of doneness. Remove steaks from pan. Add mushrooms to pan, and cook 3 minutes or until lightly browned. Remove mushrooms from pan. Remove pan from heat; add Marsala, scraping pan to loosen browned bits. Reduce heat to medium. Return pan to heat. Add broth mixture to pan; bring to a boil. Cook 1 minute, stirring frequently. Stir in mushrooms. Yield: 2 servings (serving size: 1 steak and ¼ cup sauce).

CALORIES 318 (31% from fat); FAT 11.1g (sat 4.2g, mono 4.5g, poly 0.6g); PROTEIN 26.3g; CARB 11.9g; FIBER 0.6g; CHOL 78mg; IRON 2.3mg; SODIUM 410mg; CALC 32mg

Shrimp and Snow Pea Stir-Fry

Serve with rice and jasmine tea.

    1   teaspoon dark sesame oil
    3   tablespoons low-sodium soy
        sauce
    2   tablespoons seasoned rice
        vinegar
    2   tablespoons bottled minced fresh
        ginger
    2   teaspoons sugar
    1   teaspoon bottled minced
        garlic
    1   small red bell pepper, cut into
        1½-inch pieces
    1   small red onion, cut into 8
        wedges
    1   cup snow peas, trimmed
  1½   pounds peeled and deveined large
        shrimp
    3   tablespoons sesame seeds,
        toasted

1. Heat oil in a large nonstick skillet over medium-high heat.
2. Combine soy sauce, vinegar, ginger, sugar, and garlic, stirring with a whisk.
3. Add bell pepper and onion to pan; stir-fry 2 minutes or until crisp-tender. Add snow peas and shrimp; stir-fry 3 minutes or until shrimp are done. Add soy sauce mixture, and cook 1 minute. Sprinkle with sesame seeds. Yield: 7 servings (serving size: 1⅔ cups).

CALORIES 274 (23% from fat); FAT 7.1g (sat 1.2g, mono 2g, poly 3g); PROTEIN 37.4g; CARB 14.1g; FIBER 2.7g; CHOL 259mg; IRON 5.4mg; SODIUM 838mg; CALC 117mg

Chicken with Black Bean Sauce

Look for black bean sauce in the Asian section of the supermarket. Serve with rice stick noodles.

  1½   tablespoons vegetable oil,
        divided
    1   cup fresh orange juice
    ¼   cup black bean sauce
    1   tablespoon low-sodium soy
        sauce
    2   teaspoons sugar
    1   teaspoon cornstarch
    1   teaspoon bottled minced
        garlic
    ¼   teaspoon black pepper
    1   pound skinless, boneless chicken
        breast cutlets
    ¼   teaspoon salt
    ½   cup panko (Japanese)
        breadcrumbs

1. Heat 1 tablespoon oil in a large non-stick skillet over medium-high heat.
2. Combine orange juice and next 6 ingredients, stirring with a whisk.
3. Sprinkle chicken with salt. Dredge chicken in breadcrumbs. Add half of chicken to pan; cook 2 minutes on each side or until done. Repeat procedure with 1½ teaspoons oil and remaining chicken. Remove from pan. Add orange juice mixture to pan, and bring to a boil. Cook 1 minute, stirring constantly. Serve sauce over chicken. Yield: 4 servings (serving size: about 3 ounces chicken and ¼ cup sauce).

CALORIES 256 (27% from fat); FAT 7.6g (sat 1.3g, mono 1.9g, poly 3.6g); PROTEIN 28.1g; CARB 17.1g; FIBER 0.7g; CHOL 66mg; IRON 1.2mg; SODIUM 476mg; CALC 28mg

Pork Marsala

Smoky Marsala wine brings out the woodsy note of the mushrooms.

    1   (9-ounce) package refrigerated
        angel hair pasta
    1   tablespoon butter
    ¾   teaspoon salt, divided
    1   tablespoon olive oil, divided
    ¼   cup all-purpose flour
    8   (2-ounce) boneless center-cut loin
        pork chops (¼ inch thick),
        trimmed
    ¼   teaspoon black pepper
    ½   cup chopped shallots
    1   (8-ounce) package presliced
        mushrooms
    ¾   cup fat-free, less-sodium chicken
        broth
    ¾   cup Marsala wine
    ¼   cup chopped green onions

1. Cook pasta according to package directions, omitting salt and fat. Drain; toss with butter and ¼ teaspoon salt.
2. While pasta cooks, heat 1½ teaspoons oil in a large nonstick skillet over medium-high heat.
3. Place flour in a shallow dish. Sprinkle pork with ½ teaspoon salt and pepper; dredge pork in flour. Add half of pork to pan; cook 2 minutes on each side or until browned. Remove pork from pan. Repeat procedure with 1½ teaspoons oil and remaining pork.
4. Add shallots and mushrooms to pan; sauté 2 minutes. Add broth and wine; bring to a boil. Reduce heat, and simmer 2 minutes, stirring occasionally. Return pork to pan; cover and simmer 3 minutes or until pork is done. Serve pork mixture over pasta. Sprinkle with onions. Yield: 4 servings (serving size: 2 chops, about 1 cup pasta, and 1 tablespoon onions).

CALORIES 495 (25% from fat); FAT 13.7g (sat 4.5g, mono 6.1g, poly 1.7g); PROTEIN 35.9g; CARB 49.9g; FIBER 3.8g; CHOL 126mg; IRON 4.4mg; SODIUM 651mg; CALC 50mg

Pasta with Beet Greens and Raisins

8 ounces uncooked pennette (mini penne)
¼ cup raisins
1½ tablespoons olive oil
2 cups coarsely chopped trimmed beet greens
2 teaspoons bottled minced garlic
⅓ cup slivered almonds, toasted
½ teaspoon salt
⅛ teaspoon black pepper
Cracked black pepper (optional)

1. Cook pasta according to package directions, omitting salt and fat. Drain.
2. While pasta cooks, place raisins in a small bowl; cover with hot water. Let stand 10 minutes. Drain.
3. While pasta cooks and raisins soak, heat oil in a large nonstick skillet over medium-high heat. Add greens and garlic; sauté 3 minutes or until greens are tender. Stir in pasta, raisins, almonds, salt, and ⅛ teaspoon black pepper; toss to combine. Sprinkle with cracked black pepper, if desired. Yield 4 servings (serving size: about 1 cup).

CALORIES 345 (26% from fat); FAT 10g (sat 1.3g, mono 6.3g, poly 1.4g); PROTEIN 10.9g; CARB 55.2g; FIBER 5.2g; CHOL 0mg; IRON 4mg; SODIUM 409mg; CALC 110mg

Pan-Seared Scallops with Tomatoes and Pesto

For a golden-brown crust on the scallops, don't disturb them while they cook except to turn them over once.

1½ pounds sea scallops
¼ teaspoon salt
¼ teaspoon black pepper
Cooking spray
¼ teaspoon grated lemon rind
2 tablespoons fresh lemon juice
2 tablespoons balsamic vinegar
2 teaspoons olive oil
½ teaspoon bottled minced garlic
2 cups grape tomatoes
3 tablespoons commercial pesto
1 tablespoon chopped fresh basil

1. Heat a large cast-iron skillet over high heat. Pat scallops dry with paper towels; sprinkle with salt and pepper. Lightly coat pan with cooking spray. Add scallops to pan; cook 2 minutes on each side or until golden brown. Remove scallops from pan; keep warm. Reduce heat to medium. Add rind and next 4 ingredients to pan; bring to a simmer. Add tomatoes; cook 45 seconds, tossing to coat.
2. Spoon about 2 teaspoons pesto on each of 4 plates. Arrange one-fourth of scallops and about ½ cup tomato mixture on each plate. Sprinkle with basil. Yield: 4 servings.

CALORIES 252 (33% from fat); FAT 9.1g (sat 1.9g, mono 5g, poly 1.1g); PROTEIN 31.4g; CARB 10.4g; FIBER 1.3g; CHOL 60mg; IRON 1.4mg; SODIUM 517mg; CALC 133mg

Pennette with Asparagus and Pine Nuts

Serve this colorful pasta dish with a salad tossed in sherry vinaigrette.

8 ounces uncooked pennette (mini penne)
2 teaspoons olive oil
2 teaspoons bottled minced garlic
⅛ teaspoon crushed red pepper
3 cups (1-inch) slices asparagus (about 1 pound)
½ cup fat-free, less-sodium chicken broth
¼ cup fresh lemon juice
½ cup chopped drained oil-packed sun-dried tomato halves
½ teaspoon salt
½ cup (2 ounces) shredded Asiago cheese
2 tablespoons pine nuts, toasted

1. Cook pasta according to package directions, omitting salt and fat. Drain; place in a large bowl.
2. While pasta cooks, heat oil in a large nonstick skillet over medium heat. Add garlic and pepper; cook 2 minutes, stirring constantly. Add asparagus, broth, and lemon juice; reduce heat to medium. Cook 5 minutes or until asparagus is tender. Stir in tomato and salt; cook 1 minute. Add asparagus mixture to pasta, and toss to coat. Sprinkle with cheese and nuts. Yield: 4 servings (serving size: about 1½ cups).

CALORIES 369 (27% from fat); FAT 10.9g (sat 3.5g, mono 4.6g, poly 1.5g); PROTEIN 16.2g; CARB 53.4g; FIBER 5.3g; CHOL 12mg; IRON 3.1mg; SODIUM 422mg; CALC 176mg

Tuna with White Bean-Cucumber Salad

The creamy cannellini beans, the crunchy cucumber, and the tangy dressing make for a refreshing meal.

⅔ cup chopped cucumber
¼ cup minced red onion
¼ cup fat-free Italian dressing
2 tablespoons chopped fresh parsley
2 tablespoons fat-free buttermilk
1 (15.5-ounce) can cannellini beans or other white beans (such as Goya), rinsed and drained
½ teaspoon salt, divided
¼ teaspoon black pepper, divided
4 (6-ounce) Bluefin tuna steaks (about ¾ inch thick)
Cooking spray
Lemon wedges

1. Heat a large nonstick grill pan over medium-high heat.
2. Combine first 6 ingredients, ¼ teaspoon salt, and ⅛ teaspoon pepper. Sprinkle tuna with ¼ teaspoon salt and ⅛ teaspoon pepper. Coat pan with cooking spray. Add tuna to pan; cook 3 minutes on each side or until desired degree of doneness. Slice tuna; serve over bean salad. Serve with lemon wedges. Yield: 4 servings (serving size: 1 tuna steak and about ½ cup bean salad).

CALORIES 353 (23% from fat); FAT 9.1g (sat 2.3g, mono 2.7g, poly 2.9g); PROTEIN 44.9g; CARB 19.5g; FIBER 4.9g; CHOL 66mg; IRON 3.6mg; SODIUM 684mg; CALC 72mg

A Whodunit Dinner Dilemma

Lightening this vegetarian lasagna was no mystery.

Among the many dinner parties Lisa Fazio of Asheville, North Carolina, has hosted, the "murder mystery" party in which she and her friends played assigned characters trying to solve a game of whodunit was among the most memorable. "The mystery theme I chose was set in the 1960s," she says. "The scenario had a groovy, sort of hippie feel, so naturally I picked an earthy vegetarian entrée— Roasted Butternut Squash, Rosemary, and Garlic Lasagna." But Fazio said she'd prepared it for the last time until *Cooking Light* could lighten it.

The lasagna's savoriness comes from the butternut squash, Parmigiano-Reggiano cheese, and a top layer of whipped cream. To keep these ingredients close to the original dish, we looked for creative ways to lower the calories and fat. Using an ample amount of cooking spray on the squash provided the coating needed for roasting. This simple technique eliminated 3 tablespoons of oil, and thus 36 grams of fat and 331 calories from the entire recipe.

Before, the lasagna's sauce was a traditional roux made of butter and flour blended with whole milk. For the lightened version, we made a white sauce. This slashed 75 grams of fat and 656 calories. Reducing the cheese to ¾ cup still allowed for generous layering among all the other ingredients and shaved more than 2½ grams of fat per serving. Cutting the whipped cream topping in half retained its luxurious texture while reducing the fat grams even further. And lastly, the new-and-improved lasagna has less sodium than its predecessor.

Roasted Butternut Squash, Rosemary, and Garlic Lasagna

This dish is easy to divide into make-ahead steps. Roast the squash and prepare the white sauce the night before, then layer the lasagna up to 6 hours before the party. Just before guests arrive, top with cream and the last layering of Parmesan cheese, then bake.

8¼ cups (½-inch) cubed peeled butternut squash (about 3 pounds)
Cooking spray
4 cups fat-free milk, divided
2 tablespoons dried rosemary
¼ cup all-purpose flour
1 tablespoon butter
1 tablespoon minced garlic
1½ teaspoons salt, divided
½ teaspoon freshly ground black pepper
1 (8-ounce) package precooked lasagna noodles
¾ cup (3 ounces) grated fresh Parmigiano-Reggiano, divided
½ cup whipping cream

1. Preheat oven to 450°.
2. Arrange squash in a single layer in a large roasting pan coated with cooking spray. Coat squash with cooking spray. Bake at 450° for 25 minutes or until squash is just tender, stirring once. Set aside.
3. Reduce oven temperature to 350°.
4. Combine 3½ cups milk and rosemary in a 1-quart glass measuring cup, and microwave at HIGH 5 minutes or until mixture begins to boil. Let stand 10 minutes. Strain milk through a fine sieve into a bowl; discard rosemary.
5. Lightly spoon flour into a dry measuring cup; level with a knife. Combine flour and ½ cup milk, stirring with a whisk until well blended to form a slurry.
6. Melt butter in a large saucepan over medium heat. Add garlic; cook 1 minute or until tender, stirring constantly. Stir in steeped milk, and increase heat to medium-high. Gradually add slurry to pan, stirring constantly with a whisk. Cook 15 minutes or until thick, stirring frequently. Remove from heat; stir in ¾ teaspoon salt and pepper. Combine milk mixture and squash, tossing gently.
7. Spread about 1½ cups squash mixture into the bottom of an 11 x 7-inch baking dish coated with cooking spray. Arrange 3 noodles over squash mixture; top with 2 cups squash mixture and ¼ cup cheese. Repeat layers once with 3 noodles, 2 cups of squash, and ¼ cup of cheese. Top with 3 noodles.
8. Beat whipping cream and ¾ teaspoon salt with mixer at high speed until soft peaks form. Spread whipping cream mixture over noodles; sprinkle with ¼ cup cheese. Cover with foil coated with cooking spray. Bake at 350° for 30 minutes. Uncover and bake an additional 15 minutes or until golden. Let lasagna stand 10 minutes. Yield: 8 servings.

CALORIES 376 (29% from fat); FAT 12.3g (sat 6.9g, mono 2.4g, poly 0.8g); PROTEIN 12.2g; CARB 54.3g; FIBER 6.3g; CHOL 38mg; IRON 3mg; SODIUM 712mg; CALC 430mg

BEFORE	AFTER
SERVING SIZE	
1 piece	
CALORIES PER SERVING	
589	376
FAT	
33.7g	12.3g
PERCENT OF TOTAL CALORIES	
51%	29%

cooking class

Pasta Perfected by Lidia Bastianich

America's foremost authority on Italian cooking shows how to make great dishes using a pantry staple.

Lidia Bastianich has popularized traditional Italian cooking in America. She is the owner of five Italian restaurants: Felidia, Becco, and Esca in New York City; Lidia's Kansas City; and Lidia's Pittsburgh. She also hosts two Italian cooking shows on public television and has written three Italian cookbooks, *La Cucina di Lidia (Lidia's Italian Kitchen)*, *Lidia's Italian-American Kitchen*, and the newly released *Lidia's Family Table*. Here are some of her pasta basics ("Pasta by Lidia" on page 418) along with some of her favorite pasta recipes.

STAFF FAVORITE • QUICK & EASY
Whole Wheat Pasta with Sausage, Leeks, and Fontina

Whole wheat pasta makes this dish hearty. The flavors meld and provide just enough of each element to keep you wanting more.

  6   quarts water
2½   teaspoons salt, divided
  1   pound uncooked whole wheat penne or rigatoni
  1   tablespoon olive oil
  1   (4-ounce) link sweet Italian sausage
  2   cups chopped leek
  4   cups shredded Savoy cabbage (about 10 ounces)
  1   cup fat-free, less-sodium chicken broth
  ¼   teaspoon freshly ground black pepper
  ½   cup (2 ounces) shredded fontina cheese

1. Bring 6 quarts water and 2 teaspoons salt to a boil in a large stockpot. Stir in pasta; partially cover, and return to a boil, stirring frequently. Cook 8 minutes or until pasta is almost al dente, stirring occasionally. Drain.
2. While pasta cooks, heat olive oil in a Dutch oven over medium-high heat. Remove casing from sausage. Add sausage to Dutch oven; cook 2 minutes or until lightly browned, stirring to crumble. Add leek; cook 2 minutes or until leek is soft, stirring frequently. Add cabbage; cook 2 minutes or until cabbage wilts, stirring frequently. Add remaining ½ teaspoon salt, broth, and pepper; bring to a boil. Reduce heat, and simmer 15 minutes or until vegetables are very tender.
3. Add pasta to Dutch oven, tossing well to coat; bring to a boil. Reduce heat, and cook 1 minute or until pasta is al dente, stirring constantly. Remove from heat; stir in cheese. Serve immediately. Yield: 6 servings (serving size: 1⅔ cups).

CALORIES 385 (21% from fat); FAT 8.9g (sat 3.2g, mono 3.8g, poly 1.2g); PROTEIN 17.3g; CARB 64.3g; FIBER 8.3g; CHOL 18mg; IRON 3.8mg; SODIUM 658mg; CALC 119mg

QUICK & EASY
Spaghettini with Oil and Garlic

In Italian, simple garlic and olive oil sauce is known as *aglio e olio*. This classic pasta dish comes together quickly, so it's a good weeknight dinner. Just pair it with a green salad and a bottle of wine. Spaghettini is in between the sizes of vermicelli and spaghetti, so either of those is a good substitute. Be careful not to overcook the garlic, as browned garlic tastes bitter. Push the garlic to one side of the pan so it will cook evenly.

  6   quarts water
2¾   teaspoons salt, divided
  1   pound uncooked spaghettini
  2   tablespoons extravirgin olive oil
 10   garlic cloves, sliced
  ½   cup chopped fresh flat-leaf parsley
  ½   teaspoon crushed red pepper
  1   cup (4 ounces) grated Parmigiano-Reggiano cheese

1. Bring 6 quarts water and 2 teaspoons salt to a boil in a large stockpot. Stir in pasta; partially cover, and return to a boil, stirring frequently. Cook 6 minutes or until pasta is almost al dente, stirring occasionally. Drain pasta in a colander over a bowl, reserving 1 cup cooking liquid.
2. While pasta cooks, heat oil in a large nonstick skillet over medium heat. Add garlic; cook 2 minutes or until fragrant and beginning to turn golden, stirring constantly. Remove from heat; stir in remaining ¾ teaspoon salt, reserved 1 cup cooking liquid, parsley, and pepper.
3. Add pasta to pan, stirring well to coat. Return pan to medium heat; cook 1 minute or until pasta is al dente, tossing to coat. Place 1 cup pasta mixture in each of 8 bowls; sprinkle each serving with 2 tablespoons cheese. Serve immediately. Yield: 8 servings.

CALORIES 303 (24% from fat); FAT 8g (sat 2.9g, mono 3.7g, poly 0.8g); PROTEIN 12.7g; CARB 44.4g; FIBER 1.6g; CHOL 10mg; IRON 2.6mg; SODIUM 603mg; CALC 190mg

Fresh or Dry?

I'm often asked which is better, fresh or dry pasta. Actually, they're two different things, though both end up in a pot of boiling water. Fresh pasta is made with regular soft wheat flour or a mixture of other flours, such as whole wheat, barley, and semolina, with the addition of eggs and sometimes olive oil. The rich flavor and silky texture of fresh pasta work best with delicate oil sauces or smooth cream sauces.

Dry pasta is made from durum wheat (the hardest wheat grain), salt, and water. Sauces cling better to dry pasta, and that's what these recipes use. Dry pasta also retains some firmness when cooked, and it comes in a myriad of shapes, so it's the ideal palette for all of the wonderful Italian sauces. When buying pasta, look for "100% durum semolina wheat" on the label, which indicates that only hard durum wheat was used. This pasta will have a pleasantly chewy bite and a nutty wheat flavor.

Although dry pasta has a long shelf life, it's best cooked and eaten sooner rather than later. White spots on dry pasta are an indication that it's old. Blotchy, unevenly colored pasta may have been dried or stored improperly. Also look for a slightly rough texture on the outside of the pasta. This is an indication that it was shaped in bronze dies instead of Teflon-coated ones. Sauces cling better to rough-textured pasta than to pasta with a smooth surface.

Many Sizes, Fun Shapes

There are three main types of dried pasta—short, long, and various pastinas (or little pastas). Short pasta has the widest selection, with more than 100 different shapes. They can be smooth or have a ridged finish, in which case they'll have the addition of "rigati" or "rigate" in their name. These shapes vary from tubular (rigatoni, ziti, penne, and mezzani) to tubular with a twist (gomiti [elbow], lumache [snails], and creste di galli [cock's comb]). Other distinctive shapes include rotelle (wheels), dischi volanti (flying saucers), radiatore (radiators), and tofe (a shell-like shape).

Among the long pastas, the main difference is the diameter. Some are long and round, like spaghetti, vermicelli, and capellini, while others are long and flat, like linguine and fresine. Some, like perciatelli, bucatini, and mezzanelli, are hollow and round. Pastinas, such as rice-shaped orzo, are best used in soups.

Tossing with Sauce

Add sauce to pasta immediately after cooking, while it's still hot. And use a judicious hand so the sauce doesn't overwhelm the pasta. In most pasta dishes, the idea is to make just enough sauce to lightly coat the noodles. Especially for tubular or creviced pasta, you want to be sure to drain it well, or the excess water will keep the sauce from adhering to the pasta and may also dilute the flavor of the sauce. I usually drain the pasta over a bowl to reserve some cooking water, which can be used to loosen up a too-thick sauce. Warmed bowls will keep the pasta hot when ready to serve.

Perfect pasta pairings—linguine and clam sauce, cavatelli and broccoli, ziti and meat sauce—have been a part of the Italian culinary repertoire for centuries. The possible combinations of pasta and sauce are limitless and may even seem a little intimidating. But follow a good Italian pasta recipe, and your dish should be on track.

In Italy, cheese is used with pasta very selectively (it's not offered with seafood pastas, for example) and with careful attention to timing. Toss cheese with the pasta at the last minute, after removing it from the heat. Otherwise the heat will cause the proteins of the cheese to separate from the fat, and you might end up with a serving spoon filled with stringy cheese and oily pasta. To add the final touch, grate or shave a little extra cheese over the plated pasta. The steam from the pasta will lift and intensify the aroma of the cheese.

Finding Fancy Pasta

If you can't find certain shapes, sizes, and well-made pasta at local gourmet food stores, you can order specialty pasta via the Internet. Try www.bellaitaliaonline.com; www.farawayfoods.com; www.flyingnoodle.com; and www.amazon.com for specialty Italian pasta.

Al Dente

To make great pasta, cook it al dente, or "to the tooth." Pasta cooked al dente results in a sensation of slight resistance when chewed, and it's an important part of the overall enjoyment of pasta (and rice, too).

Al dente is easy to recognize. Properly cooked, pasta will be tender and not raw tasting, but it will have a firm texture and even a little "snap" at the center. It's easy to tell pasta that has been cooked al dente by looking at it. With long pasta shapes, like spaghetti and linguine, there will be a dot of white at the center; in round pasta shapes, like ziti or penne, there will be a faint but clear ring of white that runs around the center of the pasta.

If you're going to simmer cooked pasta together with a sauce, as I do most of the time, then the pasta should be slightly less cooked than al dente. It will finish cooking in the sauce.

QUICK & EASY
Gomiti with Broccoli Rabe, Chickpeas, and Prosciutto

Ask your butcher or deli manager to give you the end of the prosciutto for this dish. It's much easier to cut into strips and tends to be meatier. Gomiti is similar in shape to elbow macaroni. Grana Padano is a hard cheese that is usually found with Parmesan cheese near the deli section in the grocery store.

- 6 quarts water
- 2 teaspoons salt
- 1 pound uncooked gomiti (short, curled, tube-shaped pasta)
- 3 tablespoons olive oil
- ½ cup sliced garlic (about 10 to 12 garlic cloves)
- 1 (3-ounce) prosciutto end piece, cut into ¼-inch-wide julienne strips
- ½ teaspoon crushed red pepper
- 1 (16-ounce) can chickpeas (garbanzo beans), rinsed and drained
- 10 cups coarsely chopped broccoli rabe (about 1 [1-pound] bunch)
- ½ cup (2 ounces) grated Grana Padano cheese

1. Bring 6 quarts water and 2 teaspoons salt to a boil in a large stockpot. Stir in pasta; partially cover, and return to a boil, stirring frequently. Cook 8 minutes or until pasta is almost al dente, stirring occasionally. Drain pasta in a colander over a bowl, reserving 2 cups cooking liquid.

2. While pasta cooks, heat oil in a Dutch oven over medium-high heat. Add garlic and prosciutto; cook 1 minute, stirring constantly. Add pepper; cook 2½ minutes or until prosciutto is crisp, stirring frequently. Add reserved 2 cups cooking liquid and chickpeas; bring to a boil. Add broccoli rabe (do not stir); cover, reduce heat, and simmer 7 minutes or until broccoli rabe is tender. Uncover; simmer 15 minutes or until liquid almost evaporates. Add pasta, and cook 1 minute or until pasta is al dente, tossing to combine. Remove from heat; stir in cheese. Serve immediately. Yield: 8 servings (serving size: about 1⅔ cups).

CALORIES 374 (23% from fat); FAT 9.6g (sat 2.3g, mono 4.2g, poly 0.7g); PROTEIN 17.4g; CARB 56.4g; FIBER 5.9g; CHOL 14mg; IRON 3.2mg; SODIUM 767mg; CALC 126mg

QUICK & EASY
Campanelle with Salsa Arrabbiata

A tomato-based pasta sauce, *salsa arrabbiata*—literally "angry sauce"—is made in countless versions in Italy, sometimes with meat, sometimes without, but always with some kind of hot pepper. The heat comes from small, whole, pickled peppers that are labeled pepperoncini or pepperoncino. Although these are milder than pickled cherry peppers, they provide plenty of spice. The sauce should have a pleasing play of textures, as well as tastes, and should provide distinctive bites of all the ingredients. Place the tomatoes and juices in a large bowl, and use your hands to squeeze the tomatoes into chunks. Cut the onions, pepperoncini, and prosciutto thick enough so that they don't get lost in the tomato sauce. Campanelle (sometimes called gigli) is trumpet-shaped pasta; torch-shaped torchio is a good substitute.

- 6 quarts water
- 2 teaspoons salt
- 1 pound uncooked campanelle pasta
- 1½ tablespoons olive oil
- 1½ cups (¼-inch-thick) onion wedges
- 3 bay leaves
- 1 (3-ounce) prosciutto end piece, cut into ½-inch pieces
- ½ cup pepperoncini peppers, drained, seeded, and sliced
- 1 (28-ounce) can plum tomatoes, undrained and chopped
- 1 cup (4 ounces) grated Parmigiano-Reggiano cheese

1. Bring 6 quarts water and 2 teaspoons salt to a boil in a large stockpot. Stir in campanelle pasta; partially cover, and return to a boil, stirring frequently. Cook 6 minutes or until pasta is almost al dente, stirring occasionally. Drain pasta in a colander over a bowl, reserving 1 cup cooking liquid.

2. While pasta cooks, heat oil in a Dutch oven over medium-high heat. Add onion, bay leaves, and prosciutto; sauté 5 minutes or until onion softens. Add peppers, and sauté 1 minute. Stir in reserved 1 cup cooking liquid and tomatoes; bring to a boil. Reduce heat, and simmer 10 minutes or until sauce thickens. Discard bay leaves.

3. Add pasta to Dutch oven; cook 1 minute or until pasta is al dente, stirring well to coat. Remove from heat; stir in cheese. Yield: 6 servings (serving size: 1⅓ cups).

CALORIES 331 (21% from fat); FAT 7.7g (sat 2.7g, mono 2.8g, poly 0.8g); PROTEIN 15.1g; CARB 50.6g; FIBER 2g; CHOL 18mg; IRON 2.6mg; SODIUM 965mg; CALC 182mg

Linguine with White Clam and Broccoli Sauce

"This is a popular dish at my restaurant Felidia. Sometimes we substitute broccoli rabe for the regular broccoli, which is also delicious. You can chop the garlic if you like, but I prefer slices. They are mellower in flavor and become part of the texture of the dish. Unlike the light amount of sauce served with most pastas, when combining clam sauce and linguine, there should be a little extra broth. I love littleneck clams for this sauce, but other types of hard-shelled clams, such as Manila or butter clams, make a good substitute."

—Lidia Bastianich

- ¾ cup water
- 36 littleneck clams in shells, scrubbed (about 2½ pounds)
- 6 quarts water
- 2½ teaspoons salt, divided
- 3 cups broccoli florets
- 1 pound uncooked linguine
- 3 tablespoons extravirgin olive oil, divided
- 6 garlic cloves, sliced
- ½ teaspoon crushed red pepper
- ¼ cup chopped fresh flat-leaf parsley

Continued

1. Bring ¾ cup water to a boil in a large stockpot. Add clams; cover and cook 4 minutes or until shells open. Remove clams from pan, and reserve cooking liquid. Discard any unopened shells. Cool clams. Remove meat from shells; chop. Discard shells.

2. Bring 6 quarts water and 2 teaspoons salt to a boil in stockpot. Add broccoli, and cook 2 minutes or until broccoli is bright green. Remove broccoli with a slotted spoon (do not drain water from stockpot). Place broccoli in a colander, and rinse with cold water. Drain broccoli; coarsely chop.

3. Return water to a boil in stockpot. Stir in pasta; partially cover, and return to a boil, stirring frequently. Cook 6 minutes or until pasta is al dente, stirring occasionally. Drain.

4. While pasta cooks, heat 2 tablespoons oil in a large nonstick skillet over medium heat. Add garlic; cook 1 minute or until fragrant and beginning to turn golden, stirring constantly. Add broccoli and pepper; cook 2 minutes or until broccoli sizzles. Stir in clams and reserved 1 cup cooking liquid; bring to a boil. Reduce heat, and simmer 2 minutes or until broccoli is tender.

5. Add pasta to pan, stirring well to coat. Bring mixture to a boil. Stir in remaining ½ teaspoon salt and chopped parsley; cook 1 minute, stirring constantly. Place about 1 cup pasta mixture in each of 6 bowls; drizzle each serving with ½ teaspoon oil. Serve immediately. Yield: 6 servings.

CALORIES 420 (19% from fat); FAT 9g (sat 1.2g, mono 5.2g, poly 1.5g); PROTEIN 22.1g; CARB 61.8g; FIBER 3g; CHOL 30mg; IRON 15.7mg; SODIUM 484mg; CALC 80mg

Ziti with Sausage, Onions, and Fennel

By moving ingredients to one side and adding a new ingredient in the open space, each can be sautéed in direct contact with the pan to achieve the right browning, instead of steaming in the mass of ingredients. Keep more than 2 cups of the pasta cooking water to adjust the sauce. If the pasta appears dry, ladle in more cooking water; if it's soupy, increase the heat to cook it rapidly and thicken the sauce.

    1   (1¼-pound) fennel bulb with
        stalks
    6   quarts water
    2¼ teaspoons salt, divided
    1   pound uncooked ziti (short,
        tube-shaped pasta)
    1   tablespoon olive oil
    1   pound sweet Italian sausage
    2   cups (¼-inch-thick) onion
        wedges (about 2 medium)
    ½   teaspoon crushed red pepper
    ¼   cup tomato paste
    ¼   cup (1 ounce) grated fresh
        pecorino Romano cheese

1. Trim fennel, reserving fronds and bulb. Cut fennel bulb in half lengthwise; cut each bulb half lengthwise into (¼-inch-thick) slices. Cut bulb slices into 2-inch-long pieces. Chop fennel fronds to measure ⅓ cup.

2. Bring 6 quarts water and 2 teaspoons salt to a boil in a large stockpot. Stir in pasta; partially cover, and return to a boil, stirring frequently. Cook 8 minutes or until pasta is almost al dente, stirring occasionally. Drain pasta in a colander over a bowl, reserving 3 cups cooking liquid.

3. While pasta cooks, heat oil in a large Dutch oven over medium-high heat. Remove sausage from casings. Add sausage to Dutch oven; cook 2 minutes or until lightly browned, stirring to crumble. Push sausage to one side of pan. Add onion to open space in pan; cook 1 minute or until onion begins to soften. Stir onion into sausage. Push onion mixture to one side of pan. Add fennel bulb to open space in pan; cook

1 minute or until fennel begins to soften. Stir fennel into onion mixture. Stir in pepper and ¼ teaspoon salt; cook 1 minute. Move sausage and fennel mixture to outside edges of pan, leaving an open space in center. Add ¼ cup tomato paste to open space in pan; cook 1 minute, stirring constantly. Stir tomato paste into fennel mixture.

4. Add 3 cups reserved cooking liquid to pan; bring to a boil. Reduce heat, and simmer 6 minutes or until fennel is tender. Add fennel fronds and pasta; cook 2 minutes or until pasta is al dente, tossing to combine. Remove from heat; stir in cheese. Serve immediately. Yield: 8 servings (serving size: about 1¾ cups).

CALORIES 352 (21% from fat); FAT 8.3g (sat 2.9g, mono 3.6g, poly 0.5g); PROTEIN 19g; CARB 51.7g; FIBER 3.8g; CHOL 20mg; IRON 3.2mg; SODIUM 669mg; CALC 88mg

---

Preparing Pasta

Cook pasta in an abundant amount of water: One pound of pasta to 6 quarts of water in an 8-quart stockpot is a good rule. Salt is a matter of taste, but Lidia likes to use it in her cooking water to enhance the flavor of the pasta (much of the salt drains out with the water). Make sure the water is at a full rolling boil before you stir in the pasta, and return it to a boil as soon as possible. Try this trick: After adding the pasta to the water, put the lid on the pot, but prop it open slightly with a wooden spoon so the water doesn't boil over.

"I'm not sure how the practice of adding oil to the pasta cooking water came about," Lidia says. "But I discourage it. Oil reduces the starchiness of the pasta's surface, so sauce won't adhere as well. The exception to this rule is the large shapes of pasta, such as lasagna noodles, because they tend to stick together and tear."

Riviera Maya

Mexico's newest hot spot is the destination for active travelers who adore the outdoors.

With a holiday season that extends to early January and a favorable exchange rate, Riviera Maya is a great place to go. If you can't make it to the Yucatán, try this recipe that's a Riviera Maya specialty.

QUICK & EASY
Grilled Grouper with Lime and Mexican Confetti Rice

Fresh grouper is a favorite at the Zamas resort in Tulum, Mexico. If you can't find chayote, use zucchini.

    4 (6-ounce) grouper fillets
    2 teaspoons olive oil
    ½ teaspoon salt
    ¼ teaspoon pepper
    Cooking spray
    4 lime wedges
    Mexican Confetti Rice

1. Rub fish with oil. Sprinkle with salt and pepper.
2. Heat a large nonstick grill pan over medium-high heat; coat pan with cooking spray. Add fish; cook 5 minutes on each side or until fish flakes easily when tested with a fork. Serve with lime wedges and Mexican Confetti Rice. Yield: 4 servings (serving size: 1 fillet and 1¼ cups rice).

(Totals include Mexican Confetti Rice) CALORIES 409 (15% from fat); FAT 7g (sat 1.2g, mono 3.9g, poly 1.3g); PROTEIN 37.7g; CARB 47.1g; FIBER 2.6g; CHOL 63mg; IRON 3.9mg; SODIUM 848mg; CALC 78mg

QUICK & EASY
MEXICAN CONFETTI RICE:
    2 teaspoons olive oil
    ½ cup chopped onion
    1 garlic clove minced
    1 cup long-grain rice
    ¾ cup finely chopped peeled chayote
    ⅔ cup fresh corn kernels
    ½ finely chopped carrot
    2 cups water
    ¾ teaspoon salt

1. Heat oil in a large saucepan over medium-high heat. Add onion; sauté 2 minutes. Add garlic; sauté 1 minute. Stir in rice, chayote, corn, and carrot; sauté 3 minutes. Stir in water and salt; bring to a boil. Cover, reduce heat, and simmer 20 minutes or until rice is tender. Yield: 4 servings (serving size: 1¼ cups).

CALORIES 231 (12% from fat); FAT 3g (sat 0.5g, mono 1.9g, poly 0.5g); PROTEIN 4.7g; CARB 46.6g; FIBER 2.5g; CHOL 0mg; IRON 2.3mg; SODIUM 463mg; CALC 31mg

New Chicken Dinners

New ways with a supper standby: chicken.

Cuban Chicken Pizza Menu
serves 4

Cuban Chicken Pizza

Celery and bell pepper sticks

Tequila-cardamom syrup and vanilla ice cream*

*Combine ½ cup water, ¼ cup sugar, and 2 whole crushed cardamom pods in a medium saucepan. Boil 5 minutes, stirring to dissolve sugar. Strain into a bowl; discard cardamom pods. Stir in 2 tablespoons tequila and 2 tablespoons lime juice, and chill in freezer 20 minutes. Serve over low-fat vanilla ice cream.

Game Plan

1. While syrup for ice cream comes to a boil:
  • Mince garlic
  • Shred cheese
2. While syrup freezes:
  • Toast tortillas
  • Cook corn
  • Combine topping ingredients

QUICK & EASY
Cuban Chicken Pizza

Toasting the corn in a skillet brings out its natural sweetness and adds a smoky note.

TOTAL TIME: 36 MINUTES

QUICK TIP: Use rotisserie chicken from the deli counter, or thaw frozen, cooked, and diced chicken breast (such as Tyson).

    4 (8-inch) fat-free flour tortillas
    Cooking spray
    1 (11-ounce) can no-salt-added whole-kernel corn, drained
    ½ teaspoon cumin seeds
    2 cups diced roasted chicken breast
    1 (15-ounce) can black beans, rinsed and drained
    1 garlic clove, minced
    2 tablespoons fresh lime juice
    ¾ cup shredded Monterey Jack cheese with jalapeño peppers
    4 teaspoons chopped fresh cilantro

1. Preheat oven to 350°.
2. Place flour tortillas on a baking sheet coated with cooking spray. Bake at 350° for 10 minutes or until edges are light brown. Remove from oven; stack and press down to flatten. Set aside.
3. Heat a large nonstick skillet over medium-high heat; coat pan with cooking spray. Add corn to pan, and cook 1 minute or until lightly charred. Add cumin seeds; cook 5 seconds, stirring constantly. Add chicken, black beans, and garlic; cook 2 minutes or until thoroughly heated. Remove from heat; stir in lime juice.
4. Place tortillas on baking sheet. Spoon ¾ cup bean mixture onto each tortilla; top each with 3 tablespoons cheese. Bake at 350° for 2 minutes or until cheese melts. Sprinkle each pizza with 1 teaspoon cilantro. Yield: 4 servings (serving size: 1 pizza).

CALORIES 460 (20% from fat); FAT 10.2g (sat 4.8g, mono 2.9g, poly 1.7g); PROTEIN 37.7g; CARB 54.3g; FIBER 8.4g; CHOL 78mg; IRON 3.6mg; SODIUM 760mg; CALC 210mg

Thai-Style Chicken Menu

serves 4

Thai-Style Stir-Fried Chicken

Rice noodles*

Green tea

*Place 6 ounces thin rice vermicelli (thin rice noodles) in a large bowl; cover with boiling water. Let stand 20 minutes. Drain; serve chicken over noodles.

Game Plan

1. While noodles soak:
   - Prepare marinade for chicken
2. While chicken marinates:
   - Chop onion, carrot, and cilantro

Thai-Style Stir-Fried Chicken

Once the chicken and vegetables are prepped, the cooking goes quickly. Have all the ingredients close at hand to whip up this sweet-hot dinner on a busy evening.

TOTAL TIME: 40 MINUTES (includes marinating time)

QUICK TIP: Look for prechopped onion in the supermarket produce aisle.

- ¼ cup rice vinegar
- 2 tablespoons brown sugar
- 2 tablespoons fresh lime juice
- 2 teaspoons red curry paste
- ⅛ teaspoon crushed red pepper
- 1 pound skinless, boneless chicken breast, cut into bite-sized pieces
- 1½ tablespoons vegetable oil, divided
- 1 cup chopped onion
- 1 cup chopped carrot
- 1 (8-ounce) package presliced mushrooms
- ½ cup light coconut milk
- 1 tablespoon fish sauce
- ½ teaspoon salt
- 1 cup fresh bean sprouts
- ¼ cup chopped fresh cilantro

1. Combine first 5 ingredients in a large zip-top plastic bag. Add chicken; seal and marinate in refrigerator 15 minutes, turning once.

2. Remove chicken from bag, reserving marinade. Heat 1 tablespoon oil in a large nonstick skillet or wok over medium-high heat. Add chicken; stir-fry 4 minutes. Remove chicken from pan; keep warm. Add remaining 1½ teaspoons oil to pan. Add onion and carrot; stir-fry 2 minutes. Add mushrooms; stir-fry 3 minutes. Add reserved marinade, scraping pan to loosen browned bits. Add coconut milk and fish sauce; bring to a boil. Reduce heat, and simmer 1 minute. Stir in chicken and salt; cook 1 minute. Top with sprouts and cilantro. Yield: 4 servings (serving size: 1 cup chicken mixture, ¼ cup sprouts, and 1 tablespoon cilantro).

CALORIES 271 (28% from fat); FAT 8.4g (sat 2.2g, mono 1.6g, poly 3.4g); PROTEIN 29.7g; CARB 19.6g; FIBER 2.9g; CHOL 66mg; IRON 2.2mg; SODIUM 767mg; CALC 43mg

Chicken with Sherry Vinegar Sauce Menu

serves 4

Pan-sautéed chicken, mashed potatoes, and green beans make a classic combination.

Chicken with Sherry Vinegar Sauce

Rustic mashed potatoes*

Steamed green beans

*Place 3 cups refrigerated new potato wedges (such as Simply Potatoes) in a medium saucepan. Cover with water; bring to a boil over high heat. Reduce heat to medium; cook 5 minutes or until tender. Drain potatoes. Mash with 1 tablespoon butter, ½ teaspoon salt, and ¼ teaspoon pepper.

Game Plan

1. While chicken cooks:
   - Mince shallots
   - Chop parsley
2. While potatoes boil:
   - Make sauce

Chicken with Sherry Vinegar Sauce

Simple and luscious, this dish comes together in a hurry and requires only one pan.

TOTAL TIME: 35 MINUTES

- 4 (6-ounce) skinless, boneless chicken breast halves
- ½ teaspoon salt
- ¼ teaspoon black pepper
- 1 teaspoon butter
- 1 teaspoon olive oil
- ½ cup minced shallots
- ¾ cup fat-free, less-sodium chicken broth
- 3 tablespoons sherry vinegar
- 2 tablespoons whipping cream
- 1 tablespoon chopped fresh parsley

1. Sprinkle chicken with salt and pepper. Heat butter and oil in a large nonstick skillet over medium-high heat. Add chicken; cook 4 minutes on each side. Remove from pan; keep warm. Add shallots to pan; sauté 1 minute. Stir in chicken broth and vinegar, and cook 2 minutes. Add whipping cream; cook 1 minute. Serve sauce with chicken. Sprinkle with parsley. Yield: 4 servings (serving size: 1 chicken breast half and 1 tablespoon sauce).

CALORIES 194 (29% from fat); FAT 6.3g (sat 2.9g, mono 2.2g, poly 0.6g); PROTEIN 27.4g; CARB 5.6g; FIBER 0.4g; CHOL 78mg; IRON 1.3mg; SODIUM 457mg; CALC 33mg

Instead of starting from scratch, look for prepared mashed potatoes in the refrigerator section of the supermarket.

Pass the Pancakes

Potato latkes take center stage at one couple's annual Hanukkah party.

When Marge Perry and her husband, David Bonom, host their annual Hanukkah party, they make a few nontraditional latkes in addition to the traditional pancakes—along with other holiday buffet recipes.

Orange Cardamom Cake

CAKE:
Cooking spray
1 tablespoon all-purpose flour
3 cups all-purpose flour
2 cups granulated sugar
1 tablespoon baking powder
1¾ teaspoons ground cardamom
½ teaspoon ground cinnamon
½ teaspoon salt
¾ cup fresh orange juice
⅔ cup canola oil
1 tablespoon grated orange rind
2 teaspoons grated lemon rind
1 teaspoon vanilla extract
3 large eggs

GLAZE:
1 cup powdered sugar
4½ teaspoons fresh orange juice
½ teaspoon fresh lemon juice

1. Preheat oven to 350°.
2. To prepare cake, coat a 10-inch tube pan or Bundt pan with cooking spray; dust with 1 tablespoon flour. Set aside.
3. Lightly spoon 3 cups flour into dry measuring cups; level with a knife. Combine flour, sugar, and next 4 ingredients in a large bowl. Make a well in center of mixture. Add ¾ cup orange juice and next 5 ingredients to flour mixture; beat with a mixer at low speed until well combined, scraping sides of bowl occasionally.
4. Spoon batter into prepared cake pan, spreading evenly. Bake at 350° for 55 minutes or until a wooden pick inserted in center comes out clean. Cool in pan 5 minutes on a wire rack; remove from pan.
5. To prepare glaze, combine 1 cup powdered sugar, 4½ teaspoons orange juice, and lemon juice in a small bowl, stirring well with a whisk. Drizzle glaze over warm cake; cool cake completely on wire rack. Yield: 16 servings (serving size: 1 slice).

CALORIES 318 (29% from fat); FAT 10.6g (sat 1g, mono 5.9g, poly 3g); PROTEIN 3.8g; CARB 52.8g; FIBER 0.9g; CHOL 40mg; IRON 1.5mg; SODIUM 179mg; CALC 63mg

Middle Eastern Slow-Cooked Stew with Lamb, Chickpeas, and Figs

Make this dish, aromatic with spices, up to 2 days ahead; store it in the refrigerator. Reheat before serving in a slow cooker.

1 teaspoon olive oil
Cooking spray
1½ pounds boneless leg of lamb, trimmed and cubed
4 cups onion, sliced and separated into rings
1¾ cups water, divided
5 garlic cloves, minced
½ teaspoon ground cumin
½ teaspoon ground coriander
½ teaspoon ground ginger
¼ teaspoon saffron threads, crushed
¼ teaspoon ground allspice
⅛ teaspoon ground red pepper
1 (3-inch) cinnamon stick
1 (14-ounce) can less-sodium beef broth
1 (15½-ounce) can chickpeas (garbanzo beans), drained
2 cups baby carrots
1 cup golden raisins
½ cup dried figs, halved
2 tablespoons chopped fresh mint
1 teaspoon salt

1. Heat oil in a large Dutch oven over medium-high heat; coat pan with cooking spray. Add half of lamb; sauté 8 minutes or until browned. Remove from pan. Repeat procedure with remaining lamb. Return first batch of lamb to pan. Add onion, ¼ cup water, and garlic to pan; cook 4½ minutes or until lightly browned, scraping pan to loosen browned bits. Add cumin and next 6 ingredients; cook 30 seconds, stirring constantly. Stir in broth and 1½ cups water; bring to a boil. Cover, reduce heat, and simmer 1 hour. Stir in chickpeas and next 3 ingredients; cover and simmer 20 minutes or until carrots are tender. Stir in mint and salt. Yield: 8 servings (serving size: about ¾ cup).

CALORIES 310 (18% from fat); FAT 6.2g (sat 1.8g, mono 2.5g, poly 0.6g); PROTEIN 21.4g; CARB 44.5g; FIBER 6.6g; CHOL 49mg; IRON 2.7mg; SODIUM 542mg; CALC 90mg

Work Ahead, and Have Fun at the Party

If you don't plan to position yourself at the stove and flip latkes on demand, here are tips for a make-ahead latke party. First, create the menu.
• Choose dishes you can prepare in advance that taste good served warm or at room temperature, such as Honey-Pomegranate Roasted Chicken Thighs (recipe on page 424) or Middle Eastern Slow-Cooked Stew with Lamb, Chickpeas, and Figs (recipe at left).
• Offer something that appeals to meat-eaters and vegetarians alike.

Aside from selecting the menu, there are other strategies to help a holiday buffet go smoothly.
• At least 1 day ahead, take out serving platters and utensils, and label them with the name of the dish for which they'll be used (sticky notes work well for this).
• When guests offer to bring food, accept. Be sure you know whether their contributions will require oven or refrigerator space. Ask them to bring appropriate serving dishes and utensils. Orange Cardamom Cake (recipe at left) and Sweet Onion, White Bean, and Artichoke Dip (recipe on page 424) are easy for helpful guests to prepare and transport.
• Tuck a small basket of cleaning supplies out of sight but within easy reach so it's easy to clean up spills.

Honey-Pomegranate Roasted Chicken Thighs

You can find pomegranate molasses in Middle Eastern and specialty stores. Serve chicken warm or at room temperature.

¾ cup honey
⅓ cup finely chopped shallots
1 tablespoon grated lemon rind
¼ cup fresh lemon juice (about 3 small lemons)
2 tablespoons pomegranate molasses
1 teaspoon Worcestershire sauce
1 teaspoon hot sauce
6 garlic cloves, minced
16 chicken thighs (about 4 pounds), skinned
1 tablespoon cornstarch
1 tablespoon water
Cooking spray
1 teaspoon salt
¼ teaspoon freshly ground black pepper

1. Combine first 9 ingredients in a large bowl; marinate in refrigerator 2 hours, stirring occasionally.
2. Preheat oven to 425°.
3. Remove chicken from bowl, reserving marinade. Combine cornstarch and water in a small bowl. Place reserved marinade in a small saucepan; bring to a boil. Stir in cornstarch mixture, and cook 3 minutes or until thickened, stirring frequently. Remove from heat. Place chicken on a broiler pan coated with cooking spray; sprinkle with salt and pepper. Bake at 425° for 30 minutes or until chicken is done, basting with marinade mixture every 10 minutes. Yield: 8 servings (serving size: 2 thighs).

CALORIES 378 (31% from fat); FAT 13.1g (sat 3.7g, mono 5g, poly 3g); PROTEIN 31.7g; CARB 33.8g; FIBER 0.3g; CHOL 114mg; IRON 2.6mg; SODIUM 416mg; CALC 36mg

QUICK & EASY
Potato Latkes

Place cooked patties on paper towels to lightly drain some of the oil. The potato mixture releases moisture as it sits, so squeeze the latkes before cooking them. Serve with light sour cream and applesauce.

4 cups shredded peeled baking potato (about 1½ pounds)
1 cup grated fresh onion (about 2 medium)
¼ cup all-purpose flour
1 teaspoon chopped fresh thyme
1 teaspoon salt
¼ teaspoon freshly ground black pepper
1 large egg, lightly beaten
1 large egg white, lightly beaten
3 tablespoons olive oil, divided

1. Combine potato and onion in a sieve; squeeze moisture from potato mixture, discarding liquid. Lightly spoon flour into a dry measuring cup; level with a knife. Combine potato mixture, flour, and next 5 ingredients in a large bowl. Divide mixture into 12 equal portions; squeeze out any remaining liquid. Shape each portion into a ¼-inch-thick patty.
2. Heat 1½ tablespoons oil in a large nonstick skillet over medium heat. Add 6 patties; cook 5 minutes on each side or until golden. Repeat procedure with 1½ tablespoons oil and patties. Yield: 12 servings (serving size: 1 patty).

CALORIES 81 (31% from fat); FAT 2.8g (sat 0.4g, mono 1.8g, poly 0.3g); PROTEIN 2.6g; CARB 11.2g; FIBER 1.3g; CHOL 18mg; IRON 0.6mg; SODIUM 210mg; CALC 10mg

QUICK & EASY • MAKE AHEAD
Vegetable Party Latke

Use the shredding blade attachment on a food processor to shred the vegetables.

1 pound shredded peeled baking potato
4 ounces shredded peeled sweet potato
4 ounces shredded zucchini
1 carrot, peeled and shredded
½ medium onion, shredded
½ cup all-purpose flour
¾ teaspoon salt
¼ teaspoon freshly ground black pepper
1 large egg, lightly beaten
1 large egg white, lightly beaten
2 tablespoons olive oil, divided

1. Preheat oven to 350°.

2. Combine first 10 ingredients in a large bowl.
3. Heat 1 tablespoon oil in a large non-stick skillet over medium-high heat. Add potato mixture. Press mixture into an even layer in pan; cook 10 minutes or until golden brown. Place a large plate upside down on top of pan; invert latke onto plate. Add remaining 1 tablespoon oil to pan. Slide latke, uncooked-side down, into pan; wrap skillet handle with foil. Bake at 350° for 20 minutes or until golden brown. Cut latke into 8 wedges. Yield: 8 servings (serving size: 1 wedge).

CALORIES 146 (25% from fat); FAT 4.2g (sat 0.7g, mono 2.7g, poly 0.5g); PROTEIN 3.7g; CARB 24.1g; FIBER 2g; CHOL 26mg; IRON 0.8mg; SODIUM 252mg; CALC 16mg

QUICK & EASY • MAKE AHEAD
Sweet Onion, White Bean, and Artichoke Dip

This dip comes together in about 15 minutes; prepare and store it in the refrigerator up to 2 days in advance.

2 tablespoons olive oil
1 cup chopped onion
2 teaspoons sugar
4 garlic cloves, sliced
1 tablespoon fresh lemon juice
1 teaspoon chopped fresh oregano
⅛ teaspoon ground red pepper
¼ teaspoon salt
¼ teaspoon freshly ground black pepper
1 (15.5-ounce) can Great Northern beans, rinsed and drained
1 (14-ounce) can artichoke hearts, drained
4 (6-inch) pitas, each cut into 8 wedges

1. Heat oil in a nonstick skillet over medium-high heat. Add onion, sugar, and garlic; cook 5 minutes or until golden brown. Combine onion mixture, lemon juice, and next 6 ingredients in a food processor; process until smooth. Serve with pita wedges. Yield: 8 servings (serving size: about ⅓ cup dip and 4 pita wedges).

CALORIES 185 (18% from fat); FAT 4g (sat 0.5g, mono 2.5g, poly 0.5g); PROTEIN 7.8g; CARB 33.3g; FIBER 5.4g; CHOL 0mg; IRON 1.5mg; SODIUM 725mg; CALC 60mg

Eggnog Cheese Pie with Bourbon Cream

Our Eggnog Cheese Pie with Bourbon Cream is a make-ahead dessert that chills overnight prior to serving, so it fits nicely into a busy holiday schedule.

The pie is reminiscent of cheesecake and made with fresh eggnog, available in the dairy section through New Year's Day. A nip of bourbon in the creamy topping adds the finishing touch.

MAKE AHEAD
Eggnog Cheese Pie with Bourbon Cream

CRUST:

32 low-fat graham crackers (8 cookie sheets)
2 tablespoons granulated sugar
1½ tablespoons butter, melted
1 large egg white
Cooking spray

FILLING:

½ cup plain fat-free yogurt
½ cup (4 ounces) block-style ⅓-less-fat cream cheese, softened
½ cup (4 ounces) block-style fat-free cream cheese, softened
1 teaspoon vanilla extract
2 large eggs
⅓ cup granulated sugar
2 tablespoons all-purpose flour
⅛ teaspoon salt
⅔ cup eggnog
2 large egg whites
2 tablespoons granulated sugar

BOURBON CREAM:

¾ cup frozen fat-free whipped topping, thawed
2 tablespoons eggnog
1 teaspoon bourbon
⅛ teaspoon grated nutmeg

1. Preheat oven to 350°.

2. To prepare crust, place crackers in a food processor; process until crumbly. Add 2 tablespoons sugar, butter, and 1 egg white; pulse 5 times or just until moist. Press crumb mixture evenly into a 9-inch pie plate coated with cooking spray. Bake at 350° for 8 minutes; cool on a wire rack 15 minutes.

3. Reduce oven temperature to 325°.

4. To prepare filling, spoon yogurt onto several layers of heavy-duty paper towels; spread yogurt to ½-inch thickness. Cover with additional paper towels, and let stand 5 minutes. Scrape into a bowl using a rubber spatula. Place cream cheeses and vanilla in a bowl, and beat with a mixer at medium speed until smooth. Add eggs, one at a time, beating well after each addition. Combine ⅓ cup sugar, flour, and salt, stirring with a whisk. Add mixture to cheese mixture, and beat until combined. Add yogurt and ⅔ cup eggnog to cheese mixture. Beat at low speed just until combined.

5. Beat 2 egg whites with a mixer at medium speed until soft peaks form, using clean, dry beaters. Add 2 tablespoons sugar, 1 tablespoon at a time, beating until stiff peaks form. Gently fold egg whites into cheese mixture. Pour filling into prepared crust. Bake at 325° for 40 minutes or until center is almost set. Cool completely on wire rack. Chill overnight.

6. To prepare bourbon cream, place whipped topping in a bowl. Gently fold in 2 tablespoons eggnog and bourbon; chill. Top each pie slice with bourbon cream; sprinkle with nutmeg before serving. Yield: 10 servings (serving size: 1 pie slice and about 2 teaspoons bourbon cream).

CALORIES 263 (29% from fat); FAT 8.6g (sat 4.3g, mono 1.5g, poly 0.4g); PROTEIN 8.4g; CARB 37.8g; FIBER 0.9g; CHOL 68mg; IRON 1.2mg; SODIUM 293mg; CALC 87mg

---

About Eggnog

Eggnog is a rich, chilled Christmas beverage made of eggs, cream or milk, sugar, nutmeg, flavoring, and sometimes liquor. The name comes from the word "noggin," a small mug or cup in which eggnog was served in earlier days.

Pudding Bread

A Wisconsin mom adds a creative ingredient to update a hand-me-down recipe.

Sarah Brinkley of Endeavor, Wisconsin, inherited the recipe for Chocolate Chip Pumpkin Bread from a friend but knew she wanted to give it her own twist when she saw the ingredients.

Her first step was to reduce the amount of oil and substitute egg whites for whole eggs. Then she turned to a trick she learned from a banana bread recipe in *Cooking Light* that used sour cream to make a light, moist loaf. "I was out of sour cream, so on a whim I used vanilla pudding. Pudding cups like Hunt's Snack Pack work well, or you can use instant pudding mix," she says.

The pudding made the bread tender, and "it's a phenomenal treat," says Sarah. "I eat it for breakfast, and it's my husband's favorite dessert." Sometimes she bakes the batter in muffin cups to make kid-sized snacks for her daughter. She continues to experiment with the recipe and makes another version with whole wheat flour and less sugar.

MAKE AHEAD • FREEZABLE
Chocolate Chip Pumpkin Bread

2 cups sugar
2 cups canned pumpkin
½ cup canola oil
½ cup fat-free vanilla pudding
4 large egg whites, lightly beaten
3 cups all-purpose flour
2 teaspoons ground cinnamon
1¼ teaspoons salt
1 teaspoon baking soda
1 cup semisweet chocolate chips
Cooking spray

1. Preheat oven to 350°.

2. Combine first 5 ingredients in a large bowl, stirring well with a whisk. Lightly spoon flour into dry measuring cups;

Continued

level with a knife. Combine flour and next 3 ingredients in a medium bowl, stirring well with a whisk. Add flour mixture to pumpkin mixture, stirring just until moist. Stir in chocolate chips.

3. Spoon batter into 2 (8 x 4-inch) loaf pans coated with cooking spray. Bake at 350° for 1 hour and 15 minutes or until a wooden pick inserted in center comes out clean. Cool 10 minutes in pans on a wire rack, and remove from pans. Cool completely on wire rack. Yield: 32 servings (serving size: 1 slice).

CALORIES 152 (30% from fat); FAT 5g (sat 1.2g, mono 2.5g, poly 1.1g); PROTEIN 2g; CARB 26.5g; FIBER 1.1g; CHOL 0mg; IRON 1mg; SODIUM 137mg; CALC 10mg

Swiss Chard with Almonds and Shallots

"I had some greens left over from another recipe. I thought the almonds might complement them, and happily, it turned out well. This makes a great side dish for two people."

—Alisa Davis, Washington, DC

1 teaspoon olive oil
2 tablespoons thinly sliced shallots
3 cups sliced Swiss chard (about 3 ounces)
⅛ teaspoon salt
⅛ teaspoon black pepper
1 teaspoon slivered almonds, toasted

1. Heat oil in a large skillet over medium heat. Add shallots; cook 2 minutes or until shallots begin to brown, stirring frequently. Stir in chard. Cover and cook 2 minutes or until chard wilts. Remove from heat; stir in salt and pepper. Sprinkle with almonds. Yield: 2 servings (serving size: ½ cup).

CALORIES 44 (59% from fat); FAT 2.9g (sat 0.4g, mono 2.1g, poly 0.4g); PROTEIN 1.5g; CARB 4g; FIBER 1.2g; CHOL 0mg; IRON 1.2mg; SODIUM 264mg; CALC 35mg

Seared Beef Tenderloin Mini Sandwiches with Mustard-Horseradish Sauce

"While I was visiting a friend, she prepared these mini open-faced sandwiches. They make delightful appetizers for holiday guests, and the Mustard-Horseradish Sauce can be made ahead of time."

—Susan Wambui Thiong'o, Nairobi, Kenya

⅔ cup fat-free sour cream
¼ cup Dijon mustard
2 tablespoons minced fresh tarragon
2 tablespoons prepared horseradish
1 (1½-pound) beef tenderloin, trimmed
½ teaspoon freshly ground black pepper
Cooking spray
2 tablespoons fresh lemon juice
3 cups trimmed watercress (about 1 bunch)
1 (8-ounce) French bread baguette, cut diagonally into 16 slices
2 tablespoons capers
½ cup (2 ounces) shaved fresh Parmesan cheese

1. Combine first 4 ingredients, stirring well with a whisk. Cover and chill.

2. Secure beef at 2-inch intervals with twine. Sprinkle beef with pepper. Heat a large nonstick skillet over medium-high heat; coat pan with cooking spray. Add beef to pan; cook 15 minutes or until desired degree of doneness, turning frequently. Let stand 15 minutes. Cut into 16 slices. Sprinkle with lemon juice.

3. Arrange watercress evenly on bread slices. Place 1 beef slice and about 1 tablespoon chilled sauce over each bread slice. Arrange capers and cheese evenly over sauce. Yield: 16 servings (serving size: 1 sandwich).

CALORIES 136 (33% from fat); FAT 5g (sat 1.8g, mono 1.5g, poly 0.3g); PROTEIN 12.6g; CARB 10g; FIBER 0.6g; CHOL 25mg; IRON 1.7mg; SODIUM 314mg; CALC 94mg

...And Ready in Just About 20 Minutes

Quick-cooking meat, poultry, and fish make these dishes easy weeknight meals.

It takes less than 10 minutes to broil bass and snapper—leaving you plenty of time for sides, such as tomato-cucumber salad or steamed sugar snap peas. Pork chops take even less time when cooked on a hot grill pan. Or you can purchase a rotisserie chicken for the Roasted Chicken and Goat Cheese Roll-Ups.

Mojo Bass

Mojo sauce is a staple of the Canary Islands, where it's often served on fish. For even cooking, choose fillets of a uniform thickness. Serve with a tomato and cucumber salad.

1 tablespoon fresh orange juice
1 tablespoon fresh lime juice
1 teaspoon ground coriander
1 teaspoon bottled minced garlic
1 teaspoon olive oil
½ teaspoon ground cumin
4 (6-ounce) striped bass fillets (about 1 inch thick)
Cooking spray
2 tablespoons chopped fresh mint

1. Preheat broiler.

2. Combine first 6 ingredients, stirring with a whisk.

3. Arrange fish, skin side down, on a foil-lined baking sheet coated with cooking spray. Brush half of orange juice mixture over fish; broil 4 minutes. Brush with remaining orange juice mixture; broil 4 minutes or until fish flakes easily when tested with a fork. Sprinkle with mint. Yield: 4 servings (serving size: 1 fillet).

CALORIES 183 (26% from fat); FAT 5.3g (sat 1g, mono 2g, poly 1.5g); PROTEIN 30.4g; CARB 1.5g; FIBER 0.5g; CHOL 136mg; IRON 1.6mg; SODIUM 409mg; CALC 35mg

Hoisin Grilled Sirloin

A grill pan makes quick work on the steak. Serve with snow peas and rice.

2 tablespoons hoisin sauce
1 tablespoon apricot preserves
1½ teaspoons fresh lime juice
⅛ teaspoon crushed red pepper
½ teaspoon salt
1 pound top sirloin

1. Heat a grill pan over medium-high heat.
2. Combine first 4 ingredients, stirring with a whisk. Sprinkle salt over beef. Add beef to pan; cook 3 minutes on each side or until desired degree of doneness. Let stand 5 minutes before slicing. Brush both sides of beef with hoisin mixture. Cut beef across grain into thin slices. Yield: 4 servings (serving size: about 3 ounces).

CALORIES 213 (37% from fat); FAT 8.8g (sat 3.4g, mono 3.7g, poly 0.5g); PROTEIN 25.3g; CARB 7g; FIBER 0.3g; CHOL 76mg; IRON 2.9mg; SODIUM 477mg; CALC 13mg

Roasted Chicken and Goat Cheese Roll-Ups

If you'd prefer, use queso fresco or Monterey Jack in place of the goat cheese.

1½ teaspoons olive oil
1½ cups vertically sliced red onion
2 cups shredded roasted skinless, boneless chicken breasts
¾ cup (3 ounces) crumbled goat cheese
½ cup canned salsa verde
6 (8-inch) fat-free flour tortillas
Cooking spray

1. Heat oil in a large nonstick skillet over medium-high heat. Add onion; sauté 3 minutes or until tender. Add chicken; sauté 30 seconds or until thoroughly heated. Remove from heat; stir in cheese and salsa.
2. Warm tortillas according to package directions. Spoon about ½ cup chicken mixture down center of each tortilla; roll up. Wipe pan clean with a paper towel. Heat pan over medium-high heat; coat pan with cooking spray. Place filled tortillas in pan, seam sides down; cook 4 minutes, turning to brown on all sides. Yield: 6 roll-ups (serving size: 1 roll-up).

CALORIES 267 (24% from fat); FAT 7g (sat 3.6g, mono 2.4g, poly 0.6g); PROTEIN 20.8g; CARB 28.6g; FIBER 1.4g; CHOL 51mg; IRON 0.8mg; SODIUM 512mg; CALC 56mg

Red Snapper over Sautéed Spinach and Tomatoes

Serve this simple dish with boil-in-bag brown rice or crusty dinner rolls.

3 tablespoons country-style Dijon mustard
3 tablespoons reduced-fat Italian dressing
4 (6-ounce) red snapper fillets
Cooking spray
½ cup chopped onion
1 (10-ounce) package fresh spinach (about 10 cups)
1 cup chopped red or yellow tomato
4 lemon wedges

1. Preheat broiler.
2. Combine mustard and dressing, stirring with a whisk.
3. Arrange fish, skin side down, on a foil-lined baking sheet coated with cooking spray. Brush half of mustard mixture over fish. Broil 8 minutes or until fish flakes easily when tested with a fork.
4. While fish cooks, combine onion and remaining mustard mixture in a large nonstick skillet over medium heat. Cover and cook 2 minutes. Add half of spinach; cover and cook 1 minute or until spinach wilts. Add remaining spinach and tomato; cover and cook 1 minute or until spinach wilts. Stir well to combine. Serve fish over spinach mixture; serve with lemon wedges. Yield: 4 servings (serving size: 1 fillet, about ¾ cup spinach mixture, and 1 lemon wedge).

CALORIES 227 (26% from fat); FAT 6.5g (sat 1g, mono 1.5g, poly 1.8g); PROTEIN 33.5g; CARB 8.4g; FIBER 2.5g; CHOL 136mg; IRON 3.9mg; SODIUM 588mg; CALC 120mg

Mole-Style Pork Chops

1 tablespoon brown sugar
1 teaspoon smoked paprika
1 teaspoon ground cumin
1 teaspoon unsweetened cocoa powder
1 teaspoon ground chipotle chile peppers
½ teaspoon salt
4 (6-ounce) bone-in center-cut pork chops (about ½ inch thick)
Cooking spray

1. Heat a grill pan over medium heat.
2. Combine first 6 ingredients; rub evenly over both sides of pork. Lightly coat pork with cooking spray. Place pork on grill pan; cover and grill 3 minutes on each side or until done. Let stand 3 minutes. Yield: 4 servings (serving size: 1 pork chop).

CALORIES 180 (32% from fat); FAT 6.4g (sat 2.1g, mono 3g, poly 1.2g); PROTEIN 25.4g; CARB 4.4g; FIBER 0.8g; CHOL 70mg; IRON 0.5mg; SODIUM 376mg; CALC 11mg

Rosemary Fried Scallops with Tomato-Caper Salad

Cornmeal gives the scallops a crunchy crust. Serve with orzo tossed with olive oil and salt.

1 tablespoon olive oil
2 cups chopped tomato
1 tablespoon chopped fresh parsley
1 tablespoon capers
2 teaspoons rice vinegar
¼ teaspoon sugar
¼ teaspoon salt
¼ teaspoon freshly ground black pepper
2 tablespoons cornmeal
1 teaspoon chopped fresh rosemary
1½ pounds sea scallops

1. Heat oil in a large nonstick skillet over medium-high heat.
2. Combine tomato and next 6 ingredients. Combine cornmeal, rosemary, and scallops in a zip-top plastic bag; seal and shake well to coat.

Continued

3. Add scallops to pan; cook 3 minutes on each side or until done. Serve with tomato salad. Yield: 4 servings (serving size: about 4 ounces scallops and about ½ cup salad).

CALORIES 217 (21% from fat); FAT 5.1g (sat 0.7g, mono 2.6g, poly 0.9g); PROTEIN 30g; CARB 12.1g; FIBER 1.5g; CHOL 56mg; IRON 1.2mg; SODIUM 464mg; CALC 49mg

---

QUICK & EASY
Turkey Cutlets with Smoky Black Bean Sauce

You can also use chicken tenders instead of turkey breast cutlets. Serve with black beans and tortilla chips.

- ¼ cup fat-free, less-sodium chicken broth
- 2 teaspoons onion powder
- 1 teaspoon bottled minced garlic
- ½ teaspoon chili powder
- ½ teaspoon white wine vinegar
- ⅛ teaspoon salt
- Dash of ground red pepper
- 1 (15-ounce) can black beans, rinsed and drained
- 1 (14.5-ounce) can diced tomatoes, drained
- ½ teaspoon barbecue smoked seasoning (such as Hickory Liquid Smoke)
- 2 tablespoons butter
- 8 (2-ounce) turkey breast cutlets
- ⅛ teaspoon salt
- Cooking spray

1. Combine first 9 ingredients in a small saucepan; bring to a boil. Reduce heat, and simmer 8 minutes. Stir in smoked seasoning; cook 2 minutes. Remove from heat; stir in butter.
2. While sauce cooks, heat a large nonstick skillet over medium-high heat. Sprinkle turkey with ⅛ teaspoon salt. Coat pan with cooking spray. Add turkey to pan; cook 2 minutes on each side or until done. Serve with sauce. Yield: 4 servings (serving size: 2 cutlets and ½ cup sauce).

CALORIES 291 (23% from fat); FAT 7.3g (sat 3.9g, mono 1.6g, poly 1.2g); PROTEIN 34.7g; CARB 19.7g; FIBER 7.4g; CHOL 85mg; IRON 3.9mg; SODIUM 617mg; CALC 67mg

---

lighten up

Scallop Success

An Alabama reader dusts off a recipe and calls on Cooking Light *for help.*

As a newlywed in the early 1980s, Debra Palmer of Huntsville, Alabama, looked forward to preparing meals for her husband. One of her earliest successes was Scallops au Gratin. With a cup of whipping cream and a half-cup of butter, the recipe is no longer in line with Debra's commitment to healthy cooking. So she called on *Cooking Light* for help.

We created a lightened cream sauce that showcases the scallops, the tangy flavor of the sherry, and the sharpness of the Parmesan cheese. We replaced the cup of whipping cream in the original recipe with ½ cup reduced-fat sour cream and ½ cup half-and-half. This dropped 118 calories and 15 grams of fat per serving. Omitting the excessive butter used to broil the English muffins and sauté the vegetables saved another 108 calories and 12 grams of fat per serving. In total, each serving is 261 calories and about 30 grams of fat lighter.

QUICK & EASY
Scallops au Gratin

- 1 tablespoon butter
- 1 pound sea scallops
- ½ cup chopped onion
- ½ cup chopped green bell pepper
- 1 cup fat-free, less-sodium chicken broth
- ½ cup half-and-half
- ½ cup reduced-fat sour cream
- 3 tablespoons all-purpose flour
- ¼ teaspoon salt
- ¼ teaspoon paprika
- ⅛ teaspoon freshly ground black pepper
- ⅛ teaspoon ground nutmeg
- 2 tablespoons sherry
- 1 (2-ounce) jar diced pimiento, drained
- 4 English muffins, split and toasted
- ¼ cup dry breadcrumbs
- 2 tablespoons grated Parmesan cheese

1. Preheat broiler.
2. Melt butter in a large nonstick skillet over medium-high heat. Add scallops; cook 3 minutes on each side or until done. Remove from pan, and keep warm. Add onion and bell pepper to pan; sauté 5 minutes or until tender.
3. Combine chicken broth and next 7 ingredients in a medium bowl; stir well with a whisk. Add broth mixture to pan; bring to a boil. Reduce heat to medium-low; simmer 5 minutes or until thick, stirring constantly. Remove from heat; stir in scallops, sherry, and diced pimiento.
4. Place English muffins on a foil-lined jelly-roll pan. Spoon about ½ cup scallop mixture over each muffin half. Sprinkle each muffin half with 1½ teaspoons breadcrumbs and about ¾ teaspoon Parmesan cheese. Broil 5 minutes or until browned and bubbly. Serve immediately. Yield: 4 servings (serving size: 2 topped muffin halves).

CALORIES 420 (26% from fat); FAT 12.1g (sat 7g, mono 1.5g, poly 0.9g); PROTEIN 29.5g; CARB 45g; FIBER 1.3g; CHOL 77mg; IRON 3.1mg; SODIUM 809mg; CALC 232mg

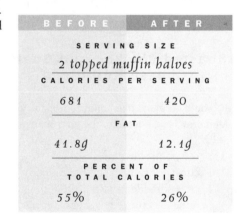

BEFORE	AFTER
SERVING SIZE	
2 topped muffin halves	
CALORIES PER SERVING	
681	420
FAT	
41.8g	12.1g
PERCENT OF TOTAL CALORIES	
55%	26%

Fruited Basmati Pilaf with Pistachios,
page 444, with roasted pork and Brussels sprouts

Yeasted Corn Bread, page 438

Chicken Chowder with Chipotle
Chupe de Pollo con Chipotle, **page 437**

Peppermint Brownie à la Mode, page 448

Roasted Chicken with Asiago Polenta and Truffled Mushrooms, page 440

Smoked Salmon Crostini, page 434

Christmas Sugar Wafers with Vanilla Icing, page 453,
White Chocolate-Cashew Coffee Biscotti, page 453,
Ginger Shortbread, page 454, and Toasted Pecan
Divinity, page 453

The *Cooking Light*® Holiday Cookbook

Here's our gift to you: All the recipes you need for holiday entertaining and dining, from delicious entrées to surprising gifts from the kitchen. We've also included technique photos along with a generous helping of make-ahead tips and menu suggestions.

Table of Contents

Appetizers & Beverages, page 433

Soups, Salads, & Breads, page 436

Main Dishes, page 440

On the Side, page 444

Desserts, page 447

Gifts from the Kitchen, page 451

Holiday Menus, page 455

Appetizers & Beverages

Whether you're entertaining a crowd or feeding the family, we have snacks and beverages to jump-start the festivities.

Spinach, Sun-Dried Tomato, and Parmesan Rolls

Use a serrated knife to cut the delicate layers of cooked phyllo dough. Be sure to use the small phyllo sheets for this recipe. If all you can find are the large (18 x 14-inch) sheets, cut them in half crosswise to form (14 x 9-inch) sheets.

1 cup boiling water
½ cup sun-dried tomatoes, packed without oil
2 teaspoons olive oil
1 cup chopped onion
1 teaspoon dried oregano
1 teaspoon dried basil
4 garlic cloves, minced
2 (10-ounce) packages frozen chopped spinach, thawed, drained, and squeezed dry
¾ cup fat-free ricotta cheese
½ cup part-skim ricotta cheese
½ cup (2 ounces) grated fresh Parmesan cheese
½ teaspoon salt
¼ teaspoon freshly ground black pepper
1 large egg white, lightly beaten
10 (14 x 9-inch) sheets frozen phyllo dough, thawed
Cooking spray
¼ cup dry breadcrumbs

1. Combine boiling water and tomatoes in a bowl; let stand 30 minutes or until soft. Drain and chop tomatoes.
2. Preheat oven to 350°.
3. Heat oil in a large nonstick skillet over medium-high heat. Add onion, oregano, basil, and garlic; sauté 4 minutes or until onion begins to brown. Stir in tomatoes and spinach; cook 1 minute. Remove from heat; cool 10 minutes. Stir in cheeses, salt, pepper, and egg white; mix well.
4. Place 1 phyllo sheet on a large cutting board or work surface (cover remaining dough to prevent drying); lightly coat with cooking spray. Sprinkle with 1½ teaspoons breadcrumbs. Repeat layers 3 times; top with 1 phyllo sheet. Gently press phyllo layers together. Lightly coat top phyllo sheet with cooking spray. Spoon half of spinach mixture along 1 long edge of phyllo, leaving a 2-inch border. Fold over short edges of phyllo to cover 2 inches of spinach mixture on each end. Starting at long edge, roll up jelly-roll fashion. Place roll, seam side down, on a baking sheet coated with cooking spray. Cut diagonal slits into top of roll using a sharp knife. Lightly coat with cooking spray. Repeat procedure with remaining phyllo, cooking spray, breadcrumbs, and spinach mixture. Bake at 350° for 22 minutes or until golden. Let stand 5 minutes. Cut each roll into 5 equal slices. Yield: 10 servings (serving size: 1 slice).

CALORIES 135 (29% from fat); FAT 4.4g (sat 1.9g, mono 1.8g, poly 0.4g); PROTEIN 8.7g; CARB 15.5g; FIBER 2.7g; CHOL 11mg; IRON 2.2mg; SODIUM 363mg; CALC 214mg

---

QUICK & EASY
Cheddar with Sautéed Apples and Brown Bread

The combination of Cheddar and apples is timeless, but this dish gives that classic pair a slightly different twist.

2 tart-sweet apples (such as Gala, Braeburn, or Fuji), each cored and cut into 16 wedges
⅓ cup sugar
¼ teaspoon ground cinnamon
Cooking spray
4 (1-ounce) slices pumpernickel bread
4 ounces extrasharp Cheddar cheese, cut into 16 slices

Continued

1. Preheat oven to 400°.

2. Heat a large nonstick skillet over medium-high heat. Place apples in a medium bowl; sprinkle with sugar and cinnamon. Toss well to coat. Coat pan with cooking spray. Add apple mixture; cook 4 minutes or until thoroughly heated, turning frequently. Remove from heat; cool slightly.

3. Cut each bread slice crosswise into 4 strips. Arrange in a single layer on a baking sheet. Bake at 400° for 5 minutes or until tops are toasted. Turn strips over; bake 3 minutes or until tops are toasted. Cool completely. Serve with apples and cheese. Yield: 8 servings (serving size: 2 bread strips, 4 apple wedges, and 2 cheese slices).

CALORIES 150 (30% from fat); FAT 5g (sat 2.6g, mono 1.4g, poly 0.4g); PROTEIN 4.9g; CARB 22.9g; FIBER 2.2g; CHOL 15mg; IRON 0.5mg; SODIUM 186mg; CALC 114mg

Smoked Salmon Crostini
(pictured on page 431)

You can prepare the salmon topping earlier in the day and keep it refrigerated until ready to assemble. These appetizers look great assembled like canapés; however, for a more informal get-together, you can set the toasts, cheese, and salmon mixture out and invite guests to build their own crostini.

½ cup chopped fennel bulb
¼ cup chopped green onions
1 tablespoon extravirgin olive oil
2 teaspoons chopped fresh dill
1 teaspoon grated lemon rind
1½ tablespoons fresh lemon juice
1 teaspoon freshly ground black pepper
¾ pound cold-smoked salmon, cut into thin strips
48 (½-inch-thick) slices French bread baguette, toasted (about 1½ pounds)
½ cup light garlic-and-herbs spreadable cheese (such as Alouette Light)
Dill sprigs (optional)

1. Combine first 8 ingredients; cover and chill at least 1 hour. Spread each toast slice with ½ teaspoon cheese; top each with 1 tablespoon salmon mixture. Garnish with fresh dill sprigs, if desired. Yield: 24 servings (serving size: 2 crostini).

CALORIES 112 (24% from fat); FAT 3g (sat 0.9g, mono 1.4g, poly 0.4g); PROTEIN 5.7g; CARB 15.5g; FIBER 1g; CHOL 6mg; IRON 0.9mg; SODIUM 482mg; CALC 28mg

Blood Orange Sangría

Any good-quality, fruity red wine works well in this cold sipper; a combination of Pinot Noir and Beaujolais is particularly good. The vermilion flesh of blood oranges (which come into season in December) is lovely. But if they're not available, substitute navel oranges.

2 cups sliced strawberries
2 cups apple juice
⅔ cup Triple Sec (orange-flavored liqueur)
½ cup sugar
4 whole cloves
3 seedless blood oranges, each cut into 16 wedges
2 (750-milliliter) bottles fruity red wine
2 (3-inch) cinnamon sticks
1 lemon, cut into 8 wedges
1 lime, cut into 8 wedges

1. Combine all ingredients in a large pitcher; stir until sugar dissolves. Cover and chill 8 hours or overnight. Discard cloves and cinnamon sticks. Pour sangría into individual glasses, including fruit. Yield: 16 servings (serving size: about 1 cup).

CALORIES 157 (1% from fat); FAT 0.1g (sat 0g, mono 0g, poly 0.1g); PROTEIN 0.6g; CARB 20.5g; FIBER 1.2g; CHOL 0mg; IRON 0.6mg; SODIUM 7mg; CALC 23mg

Mulled Cranberry-Guava Toddies

This warm beverage is just as good without the rum. Guava nectar has a sweet, strawberry-banana-pineapple flavor and is available in the ethnic section of most supermarkets (and sometimes with the fruit juices, as well). Float an orange slice in each toddy mug for a pretty presentation.

3 quarts cranberry juice cocktail
¼ cup sliced peeled fresh ginger
2 teaspoons whole cloves
16 (¼-inch-thick) slices orange (about 4 oranges)
1 (12-ounce) can guava nectar
2 cups dark rum

1. Combine first 5 ingredients in a large saucepan; bring to a boil. Cover, reduce heat, and simmer 10 minutes. Discard ginger and cloves. Stir in rum. Yield: 16 servings (serving size: about ¾ cup).

CALORIES 185 (1% from fat); FAT 0.2g (sat 0g, mono 0g, poly 0.1g); PROTEIN 0g; CARB 30.4g; FIBER 0.2g; CHOL 0mg; IRON 0.3mg; SODIUM 5mg; CALC 15mg

Caramelized Onion, Red Pepper, and Mushroom Pizzetti

Guests will adore these mini pizzas topped with sweet caramelized onions, earthy mushrooms, and sharp cheeses.

¾ cup warm water (100° to 110°)
2½ tablespoons extravirgin olive oil, divided
4 teaspoons sugar, divided
1 package dry yeast (about 2¼ teaspoons)
2¼ cups all-purpose flour, divided
1½ teaspoons salt, divided
Cooking spray
8 cups vertically sliced onion
3 cups sliced mushrooms
3 tablespoons Madeira wine
½ cup bottled roasted red bell peppers, cut into strips
½ cup (2 ounces) shredded sharp provolone cheese
¼ cup (1 ounce) grated fresh Parmesan cheese
2 tablespoons cornmeal

1. Combine water, 1 tablespoon oil, 1 teaspoon sugar, and yeast in a large bowl; let stand 5 minutes or until foamy. Lightly spoon flour into dry measuring cups; level with a knife. Combine 2 cups flour and 1 teaspoon salt, stirring with a

whisk. Add to yeast mixture; stir until a rough dough forms. Turn dough out onto a lightly floured surface. Knead until smooth and elastic (about 10 minutes); add enough of remaining flour, 1 tablespoon at a time, to prevent dough from sticking to hands (dough will feel tacky). Place dough in a large bowl coated with cooking spray, turning to coat top. Cover and let rise in a warm place (85°), free from drafts, 45 minutes or until doubled in size. (Press two fingers into dough. If indentation remains, dough has risen enough.)

2. Preheat oven to 450°.

3. Heat 2½ teaspoons oil in a large non-stick skillet over medium-high heat. Add onion, remaining 1 tablespoon sugar, and remaining ½ teaspoon salt; cover and cook 15 minutes or until golden brown, stirring frequently. Spoon into a medium bowl. Add remaining 2 teaspoons oil and mushrooms to pan; sauté 5 minutes. Add Madeira; cook 30 seconds or until liquid evaporates. Add mushroom mixture and bell peppers to onion mixture; stir well.

4. Combine cheeses in a small bowl, and set aside.

5. Punch dough down; cover and let rest 5 minutes. Divide into 12 equal portions; roll each dough portion into a 5-inch circle on a floured surface. Coat 2 baking sheets with cooking spray; sprinkle each with 1 tablespoon cornmeal. Place 6 dough circles on each baking sheet. Top each dough circle with about ¼ cup onion mixture and 1 tablespoon cheese mixture, leaving a ¼-inch border. Bake at 450° for 12 minutes. Yield: 12 servings (serving size: 1 pizzetta).

CALORIES 190 (26% from fat); FAT 5.4g (sat 1.7g, mono 2.3g, poly 0.5g); PROTEIN 6.1g; CARB 29.9g; FIBER 2.2g; CHOL 6mg; IRON 1.6mg; SODIUM 417mg; CALC 86mg

QUICK & EASY
Cheese Dip with Crawfish

Here's an intriguing version of the standard two-ingredient party dip. Be sure to rinse the crawfish after they thaw to remove any fishy taste. Substitute cooked shrimp for the crawfish, if you prefer; if they're large, roughly chop them so they're easier to scoop with the dip.

- 2 teaspoons butter
- ½ cup chopped onion
- 3 garlic cloves, minced
- 1 pound frozen cooked peeled and deveined crawfish tail meat, thawed, rinsed, and drained
- 1 pound light processed cheese, cubed (such as Velveeta Light)
- 1 (10-ounce) can diced tomatoes and green chiles, undrained
- 1 (10-ounce) can diced tomatoes and green chiles, drained
- ½ cup chopped green onions
- 5½ ounces baked tortilla chips
  Green onion strips (optional)

1. Melt butter in a large saucepan over medium heat. Add ½ cup onion and garlic; cook 5 minutes or until tender, stirring frequently. Add crawfish; cook 2 minutes, stirring frequently. Remove mixture from pan; cover and keep warm.

2. Add cheese and tomatoes to pan; cook over medium-low heat 5 minutes or until cheese melts. Stir in crawfish mixture and chopped green onions. Serve with tortilla chips. Garnish with green onion strips, if desired. Yield: about 6 cups dip (serving size: ⅓ cup dip and about 6 chips).

CALORIES 115 (29% from fat); FAT 3.7g (sat 2.1g, mono 0.9g, poly 0.4g); PROTEIN 13.7g; CARB 12g; FIBER 1g; CHOL 39mg; IRON 0.7mg; SODIUM 559mg; CALC 166mg

---

Pomegranates

The red juice from pomegranate seeds can stain your clothes, countertops, and hands, so use caution when handling the fruit. Wear an apron and latex gloves. Cut and seed the fruit under water (in a bowl or sink) to prevent unwanted splashes of juice.

Blackened Shrimp with Pomegranate-Orange Salsa

The jewel-toned salsa features fresh seasonal fruit and serves as a fitting complement to the heavily seasoned shrimp. It also makes a nice accompaniment to grilled chicken breasts.

SALSA:

- 2 cups pomegranate seeds (about 4 pomegranates)
- 1 cup finely chopped orange sections (about 2 oranges)
- ⅓ cup chopped green onions
- 2 tablespoons minced seeded jalapeño pepper
- 2 tablespoons chopped fresh cilantro
- ¼ teaspoon salt

SHRIMP:

- 1 tablespoon paprika
- 2 teaspoons ground cumin
- 1 teaspoon garlic powder
- 1 teaspoon dried oregano
- ¾ teaspoon dried thyme
- ¾ teaspoon ground red pepper
- ½ teaspoon salt
- ½ teaspoon ground allspice
- 36 large shrimp, peeled and deveined (about 1½ pounds)
- 5 teaspoons olive oil, divided

1. To prepare salsa, combine first 6 ingredients.

2. To prepare shrimp, combine paprika and next 7 ingredients in a large zip-top plastic bag. Add shrimp to bag; seal and shake well to coat. Remove shrimp from bag.

3. Heat 2½ teaspoons oil in a large non-stick skillet over medium-high heat. Add half of shrimp mixture; cook 2 minutes on
Continued

Choose appetizers that can be served at room temperature so you don't have to fuss with last-minute cooking.

each side or until done. Remove from pan. Repeat procedure with remaining 2½ teaspoons oil and remaining shrimp mixture. Serve warm with salsa. Yield: 12 servings (serving size: 3 shrimp and ¼ cup salsa).

CALORIES 127 (23% from fat); FAT 3.2g (sat 0.5g, mono 1.6g, poly 0.7g); PROTEIN 12.4g; CARB 12.6g; FIBER 1.3g; CHOL 86mg; IRON 1.9mg; SODIUM 235mg; CALC 45mg

QUICK & EASY
Mocha Mudslides

Using a whisk to stir this milk-shake cocktail keeps it thick. For the grated chocolate, you can use a couple of mini-sized dark-chocolate candy bars. To soften the ice cream, microwave at MEDIUM 10 to 20 seconds.

2 cups chocolate low-fat ice cream, softened
½ cup 1% chocolate low-fat milk
¼ cup Kahlúa (coffee-flavored liqueur)
1 tablespoon grated semisweet or bittersweet chocolate (about ½ ounce)
½ teaspoon instant coffee granules
½ teaspoon vanilla extract

1. Combine all ingredients in a medium bowl; stir with a whisk until blended. Serve immediately. Yield: 4 servings (serving size: ½ cup).

CALORIES 181 (15% from fat); FAT 3.1g (sat 1.9g, mono 0.2g, poly 0g); PROTEIN 3.3g; CARB 27.7g; FIBER 0.9g; CHOL 6mg; IRON 0.5mg; SODIUM 70mg; CALC 96mg

Soups, Salads, & Breads

These recipes are light enough to round out a holiday spread—and hearty enough to make a terrific dinner on their own.

Onion Soup Gratinée

Canned beef broth and aromatic celery, carrots, and mushrooms create the stock for this classic French soup. Yellow onions work best in this application.

Cooking spray
2 cups coarsely chopped celery
½ cup chopped carrot
1 (8-ounce) package presliced mushrooms
1 cup dry red wine
4 cups less-sodium beef broth
4 cups water
3 parsley sprigs
2 thyme sprigs
7 cups thinly sliced yellow onion (about 3 large)
½ teaspoon salt
3 tablespoons dry red wine
¼ teaspoon freshly ground black pepper
8 (½-ounce) slices French bread baguette
¾ cup (3 ounces) shredded Gruyère cheese
Thyme sprigs (optional)

1. Heat a large Dutch oven over medium-high heat; coat pan with cooking spray. Add celery, carrot, and mushrooms; sauté 5 minutes or until lightly browned. Remove from heat; slowly stir in 1 cup wine, scraping pan to loosen browned bits. Add broth, water, parsley, and 2 thyme sprigs. Bring to a simmer over medium heat; cook 30 minutes. Strain broth mixture through a sieve into a bowl; discard solids.
2. Heat pan over medium heat; coat pan with cooking spray. Add onion and salt; cook 20 minutes or until golden brown, stirring frequently. Stir in strained broth; bring to a boil. Reduce heat, and simmer 20 minutes or until onions are very tender. Remove from heat; stir in 3 tablespoons wine and pepper.
3. Preheat broiler.
4. Ladle about ¾ cup soup into each of 8 ovenproof bowls. Place bowls on a jelly-roll pan. Top each serving with 1 bread slice and 1½ tablespoons cheese. Broil 1 minute or until cheese begins to brown. Garnish with thyme sprigs, if desired. Serve immediately. Yield: 8 servings.

CALORIES 146 (29% from fat); FAT 4.7g (sat 2.3g, mono 1.6g, poly 0.5g); PROTEIN 7.8g; CARB 18.6g; FIBER 1.9g; CHOL 12mg; IRON 1mg; SODIUM 311mg; CALC 148mg

Carrot-Parsnip Soup with Parsnip Chips

Winter root vegetables lend their complementary, slightly sweet flavors to this hearty soup. Stir in more water or broth if you prefer a thinner consistency.

2 tablespoons olive oil, divided
2½ cups chopped yellow onion
3 cups coarsely chopped parsnip (about 1 pound)
3 cups water
2½ cups coarsely chopped carrot (about 1 pound)
2 (14-ounce) cans fat-free, less-sodium chicken broth
¼ teaspoon salt
¼ teaspoon freshly ground black pepper
½ cup (⅛-inch-thick) slices parsnip
1 tablespoon chopped fresh chives

1. Heat 1 teaspoon oil in a Dutch oven over medium heat. Add onion; cook 10 minutes or until tender, stirring occasionally. Add chopped parsnip, water, carrot, and broth; bring to a boil. Reduce heat, and simmer 50 minutes or until vegetables are tender. Remove from heat; let stand 5 minutes.
2. Place half of carrot mixture in a blender; process until smooth. Pour puréed carrot mixture into a large bowl. Repeat procedure with remaining carrot mixture. Stir in salt and pepper.
3. Heat remaining 5 teaspoons oil in a small saucepan over medium-high heat. Add parsnip slices; cook 5 minutes or until lightly browned, turning occasionally. Drain on paper towels. Ladle 1⅓ cups soup into each of 6 bowls. Sprinkle parsnip chips and chives over soup. Serve immediately. Yield: 6 servings (serving size: 1⅓ cups soup, about 2 teaspoons parsnip chips, and ½ teaspoon chives).

CALORIES 159 (28% from fat); FAT 4.9g (sat 0.7g, mono 3.4g, poly 0.6g); PROTEIN 3.7g; CARB 26.4g; FIBER 6.4g; CHOL 0mg; IRON 0.8mg; SODIUM 388mg; CALC 61mg

Celery-Celeriac Soup with Roquefort Croutons

Even folks in our Test Kitchens who say they don't like celery loved this soup.

SOUP:
- 1 tablespoon butter
- 1 cup thinly sliced leek (about 1 large)
- ½ cup chopped shallots
- 4 cups chopped peeled celeriac (celery root; about 2 medium)
- 1½ cups cubed peeled Yukon gold potato
- 1 cup water
- 2 (14-ounce) cans fat-free, less-sodium chicken broth
- 2 thyme sprigs
- 2 bay leaves
- 2 cups thinly sliced celery
- 1 cup 2% reduced-fat milk
- ½ teaspoon salt
- ½ teaspoon coarsely ground black pepper
- ¼ cup half-and-half

CROUTONS:
- 8 (½-inch-thick) slices French bread baguette
- Cooking spray
- ½ cup (2 ounces) crumbled Roquefort cheese

1. To prepare soup, melt butter in a large Dutch oven over medium heat. Add leek and shallots; cook 5 minutes or until tender, stirring frequently. Stir in celeriac and next 5 ingredients; bring to a boil. Cover, reduce heat, and simmer 15 minutes or until vegetables are tender. Stir in celery, milk, salt, and pepper; simmer 10 minutes (do not boil). Remove from heat; let stand 5 minutes. Discard bay leaves and thyme.
2. Place half of celery mixture in a blender; process until smooth. Pour puréed celery mixture into a large bowl. Repeat procedure with remaining celery mixture. Stir in half-and-half.
3. Preheat broiler.
4. To prepare croutons, arrange bread in a single layer on a baking sheet; coat with cooking spray. Broil 1 minute or until golden. Turn bread over; sprinkle each bread slice with 1 tablespoon cheese. Broil 1 minute or until cheese melts; cool 1 minute on baking sheet. Place bread on a cutting board; cut each bread slice into 6 wedges to form croutons. Ladle about 1 cup soup into each of 8 bowls; top each with 6 croutons. Serve immediately. Yield: 8 servings.

CALORIES 178 (28% from fat); FAT 5.6g (sat 3.3g, mono 1.6g, poly 0.4g); PROTEIN 7.3g; CARB 25g; FIBER 3g; CHOL 16mg; IRON 1.4mg; SODIUM 585mg; CALC 161mg

Chicken Chowder with Chipotle
Chupe de Pollo con Chipotle
(pictured on page 429)

This hearty soup makes enough to feed a crowd.

- 1 (7-ounce) can chipotle chiles in adobo sauce
- 1 tablespoon extravirgin olive oil
- 2 cups chopped onion
- 1 cup chopped carrot
- ½ cup chopped celery
- 1 teaspoon ground cumin
- ½ teaspoon dried oregano
- ½ teaspoon dried thyme
- 6 garlic cloves, crushed
- 6 cups fat-free, less-sodium chicken broth
- 1½ pounds skinless, boneless chicken breast
- 2 medium red potatoes (about 12 ounces), cut into ½-inch pieces
- 1 (15.5-ounce) can white or golden hominy, drained and rinsed
- ¼ cup whipping cream
- 1 cup chopped seeded plum tomato
- ¼ cup chopped fresh cilantro
- ½ teaspoon salt
- 8 lime wedges

1. Remove 1 chile and 1 teaspoon adobo sauce from can; reserve remaining chiles and sauce for another use. Finely chop chile; set chile and sauce aside separately.
2. Heat oil in a large Dutch oven over medium heat. Add chopped chile, onion, and next 6 ingredients; cook 7 minutes or until onion is tender, stirring frequently. Stir in broth; bring to a boil. Add chicken; cover, reduce heat to medium-low, and simmer 30 minutes or until chicken is tender. Remove chicken with a slotted spoon; cool slightly. Shred chicken with 2 forks; cover and keep warm.
3. Remove pan from heat; let stand 5 minutes. Place one-third broth mixture in a blender; process until smooth. Pour puréed broth mixture into a large bowl. Repeat procedure in two more batches with remaining broth mixture. Return puréed broth mixture to pan. Stir in potatoes and hominy; bring to a simmer over medium heat. Cook, uncovered, 20 minutes or until potatoes are tender. Stir in chicken and cream; simmer 5 minutes. Remove from heat; stir in reserved 1 teaspoon adobo sauce, tomato, cilantro, and salt. Serve with lime wedges. Yield: 8 servings (serving size: about 1⅓ cups soup and 1 lime wedge).

CALORIES 246 (23% from fat); FAT 6.2g (sat 2.3g, mono 2.4g, poly 0.8g); PROTEIN 24.5g; CARB 21.8g; FIBER 3.5g; CHOL 60mg; IRON 1.7mg; SODIUM 672mg; CALC 52mg

Escarole and Fennel Salad with Pears and Gruyère

Escarole has a pleasant bitterness and sturdy leaves that can withstand being tossed in dressing and still look appealing when it's passed around the table. If you can't find almond oil, try hazelnut or walnut oil. Sprinkle with cracked black pepper, if desired.

- 3 tablespoons sherry vinegar or cider vinegar
- 1 tablespoon almond oil
- ½ teaspoon salt
- ⅛ teaspoon freshly ground black pepper
- 6 cups torn escarole (about 1 head)
- 4 cups thinly sliced fennel bulb (about 1 medium bulb)
- 3 Bartlett or Anjou pears, cored and thinly sliced
- ¼ cup (1 ounce) finely shredded Gruyère cheese

Continued

1. Combine first 4 ingredients, stirring with a whisk.

2. Combine escarole and fennel in a large bowl. Add pears; toss gently to combine. Drizzle dressing over salad; toss gently to coat. Sprinkle with cheese. Yield: 6 servings (serving size: about 1⅔ cups).

CALORIES 113 (33% from fat); FAT 4.1g (sat 1.1g, mono 2.1g, poly 0.5g); PROTEIN 2.9g; CARB 18.6g; FIBER 5.3g; CHOL 5mg; IRON 0.9mg; SODIUM 247mg; CALC 103mg

---

Blood Oranges

This variety has a striking red flesh and juice, and tastes like regular oranges with a hint of berry undertones. Use as you would regular oranges; the color will add a festive touch.

Citrus Salad with Shrimp and Watercress

This salad takes advantage of the citrus fruits in season.

VINAIGRETTE:

- 1 teaspoon grated grapefruit rind
- 3 tablespoons fresh grapefruit juice
- 2 tablespoons extravirgin olive oil
- 1 tablespoon white wine vinegar
- ½ teaspoon salt
- ¼ teaspoon freshly ground black pepper

SALAD:

- 1¼ pounds jumbo shrimp, peeled and deveined
- 2 navel oranges
- 2 blood oranges
- 1 pink grapefruit
- ½ cup thinly sliced red onion
- 1 tablespoon chopped fresh mint
- 2 cups trimmed watercress (about 1 bunch)
- 10 kumquats, seeded and thinly sliced

1. To prepare vinaigrette, combine first 6 ingredients, stirring with a whisk.

2. To prepare salad, add shrimp to a large saucepan of boiling water. Remove from heat; let stand 5 minutes or until shrimp are done. Drain and rinse with cold water; drain.

3. Cut a ¼-inch slice off top and bottom of oranges and grapefruit. Cut away peel so no white pith remains. Cut fruit crosswise into ¼-inch-thick slices; discard any seeds. Cut grapefruit slices into quarters. Arrange fruit on a serving platter. Drizzle with 2 tablespoons vinaigrette.

4. Combine shrimp, onion, mint, and 1 tablespoon vinaigrette, tossing gently to coat. Arrange shrimp mixture over fruit.

5. Combine remaining vinaigrette, watercress, and kumquats; toss gently to coat. Arrange watercress mixture over shrimp mixture. Serve immediately. Yield: 6 servings (serving size: about ⅓ cup watercress mixture, ½ cup shrimp mixture, and ½ cup fruit).

CALORIES 226 (26% from fat); FAT 6.5g (sat 1g, mono 3.6g, poly 1.1g); PROTEIN 20g; CARB 22.5g; FIBER 4.1g; CHOL 144mg; IRON 1.5mg; SODIUM 345mg; CALC 114mg

---

MAKE AHEAD • FREEZABLE
Yeasted Corn Bread

(pictured on page 429)

Although this bread contains yeast, it's more of a batter bread. *Masa harina*, sometimes labeled corn flour, is the fine yellow cornmeal used to make corn tortillas.

- 2 cups all-purpose flour
- 2 cups masa harina
- 2 tablespoons sugar
- 1½ teaspoons salt
- 1 package quick-rise yeast (about 2¼ teaspoons)
- 2 cups warm 1% low-fat milk (100° to 110°)
- 6 tablespoons butter, melted
- 2 large eggs, lightly beaten
- Cooking spray

1. Lightly spoon flour and masa into dry measuring cups; level with a knife. Combine flour, masa, and next 3 ingredients in a large bowl, stirring with a whisk. Add milk, butter, and eggs; stir with a wooden spoon 1 minute or until smooth.

2. Spread dough into a 13 x 9-inch baking pan coated with cooking spray. Cover

with plastic wrap; let rise in a warm place (85°), free from drafts, 1 hour or until doubled in size.

3. Preheat oven to 375°.

4. Bake at 375° for 25 minutes or until bread is golden brown and springs back when touched lightly in center. Cool in pan 5 minutes before serving. Serve warm. Yield: 12 servings (serving size: 1 piece).

CALORIES 159 (31% from fat); FAT 5.4g (sat 2.9g, mono 1.4g, poly 0.7g); PROTEIN 4.5g; CARB 24g; FIBER 1.6g; CHOL 35mg; IRON 1.2mg; SODIUM 246mg; CALC 65mg

---

MAKE AHEAD • FREEZABLE
Peppernut Tea Bread

Dark and delicious, this quick bread features all the spices of Russian-Mennonite peppernuts, or spice cookies: star anise, cinnamon, nutmeg, and black pepper. Grind the star anise in a coffee or spice grinder.

- 1½ cups all-purpose flour
- 1 teaspoon baking soda
- ¾ teaspoon salt
- ½ teaspoon grated whole nutmeg
- ½ teaspoon ground cinnamon
- ¼ teaspoon ground star anise
- ¼ teaspoon freshly ground black pepper
- 1 cup apple butter
- ¼ cup sugar
- ¼ cup honey
- 2 large eggs, lightly beaten
- ½ cup golden raisins
- 2 tablespoons sliced almonds, divided
- Cooking spray

1. Preheat oven to 325°.

2. Lightly spoon flour into dry measuring cups; level with a knife. Combine flour, baking soda, and next 5 ingredients in a large bowl, stirring with a whisk. Add apple butter, sugar, honey, and eggs; stir with a whisk until well combined. Fold in raisins and 1 tablespoon almonds.

3. Spoon batter into a 9 x 5-inch loaf pan coated with cooking spray. Sprinkle with 1 tablespoon almonds. Bake at 325° for 35 minutes or until a wooden pick inserted in center comes out clean. Loosen bread from sides of pan using a narrow metal spatula; turn out onto a wire rack; cool. Yield: 1 loaf, 16 servings (serving size: 1 slice).

CALORIES 130 (8% from fat); FAT 1.2g (sat 0.3g, mono 0.5g, poly 0.2g); PROTEIN 2.4g; CARB 28.1g; FIBER 0.9g; CHOL 27mg; IRON 0.8mg; SODIUM 198mg; CALC 13mg

MAKE AHEAD • FREEZABLE
Dinner Rolls, Five Ways

One dough yields five dinner roll variations. To freeze rolls, bake, cool completely, wrap in heavy-duty foil, and freeze. Thaw, and reheat (still wrapped) at 350° for 12 minutes or until warm. Heat the milk in the microwave or on the stovetop; if it's too hot, be sure to let it cool to no warmer than 110° so your dough will rise nicely.

  2 teaspoons sugar
  1 package dry yeast (about 2¼ teaspoons)
  1 (12-ounce) can evaporated fat-free milk, warmed (100° to 110°)
  4 cups all-purpose flour, divided
  1 large egg, lightly beaten
  1 teaspoon salt
Cooking spray
  1 teaspoon cornmeal
  2 tablespoons butter, melted and cooled
Poppy seeds (optional)

1. Dissolve sugar and yeast in warm milk in a large bowl; let stand 5 minutes.
2. Lightly spoon flour into dry measuring cups; level with a knife. Add 3 cups flour and egg to milk mixture, stirring until smooth; cover and let stand 15 minutes.
3. Add ¾ cup flour and salt; stir until a soft dough forms. Turn dough out onto a floured surface. Knead until smooth and elastic (about 8 minutes); add enough of remaining flour, 1 tablespoon at a time, to prevent dough from sticking to hands (dough will feel tacky).
4. Place dough in a large bowl coated with cooking spray, turning to coat top. Cover and let rise in a warm place (85°), free from drafts, 40 minutes or until doubled in size. (Press two fingers into dough. If indentation remains, dough

Five Ways to Shape Dinner Rolls

Shaping Directions

Roll: Divide dough into 16 equal portions; shape each portion into a ball.

Knot: Divide dough into 16 equal portions; shape each portion into an 8-inch rope. Tie each rope into a single knot; tuck top end of rope under bottom edge of roll.

Snail: Divide dough into 16 equal portions; shape each portion into a 20-inch rope. Working on a flat surface, coil each rope around itself in a spiral; pinch tail of coil to seal.

Twist: Divide dough into 16 equal portions; shape each portion into an 18-inch rope. Fold each rope in half so that both ends meet. Working with one folded rope at a time, hold ends of rope in one hand and folded end in the other hand; gently twist.

Cloverleaf: Divide dough into 16 equal portions; divide each portion into 3 balls. Working with 3 balls at a time, press balls together to form a cloverleaf roll on baking sheet (be sure balls are touching each other).

has risen enough.) Punch dough down; cover and let rest 5 minutes.
5. Divide dough into 16 equal portions. Working with one portion at a time (cover remaining dough to prevent drying), shape portion into desired form (see "Five Ways to Shape Dinner Rolls" above). Place shaped dough portions on 2 baking sheets, each lightly sprinkled with ½ teaspoon cornmeal. Lightly coat shaped dough portions with cooking spray; cover with plastic wrap. Let rise in a warm place (85°), free from drafts, 20 minutes or until doubled in size.
6. Preheat oven to 400°.

7. Gently brush shaped dough portions with butter; sprinkle with poppy seeds, if desired. Place 1 baking sheet on bottom oven rack and 1 baking sheet on middle oven rack. Bake at 400° for 10 minutes; rotate baking sheets. Bake an additional 10 minutes or until lightly browned on top and hollow-sounding when tapped on bottom. Place on wire racks. Serve warm, or cool completely on wire racks. Yield: 16 servings (serving size: 1 roll).

CALORIES 151 (13% from fat); FAT 2.1g (sat 1.1g, mono 0.5g, poly 0.2g); PROTEIN 5.4g; CARB 27g; FIBER 0.9g; CHOL 18mg; IRON 1.7mg; SODIUM 187mg; CALC 69mg

Main Dishes

From turkey to pork, these satisfying entrées render any meal memorable.

Roasted Chicken with Asiago Polenta and Truffled Mushrooms

(pictured on page 430)

Look for packages of mixed wild mushrooms in the produce section, or use any combination of oyster, shiitake, chanterelle, and cremini mushrooms.

CHICKEN:

1 (5-pound) roasting chicken
2 teaspoons fresh orange juice
1½ teaspoons finely chopped fresh thyme
¼ teaspoon salt
¼ teaspoon freshly ground black pepper
2 garlic cloves, minced
1 orange, halved
6 garlic cloves, peeled
2 thyme sprigs
1 (14-ounce) can fat-free, less-sodium chicken broth, divided
Cooking spray
½ cup white wine
2 teaspoons all-purpose flour

MUSHROOMS:

2 teaspoons butter
½ teaspoon salt
¼ teaspoon freshly ground black pepper
12 ounces mixed wild mushrooms, sliced (about 8 cups)
1 (8-ounce) package presliced mushrooms
2 teaspoons truffle oil

POLENTA:

2 cups fat-free milk
¾ cup water
½ teaspoon salt
¼ teaspoon freshly ground black pepper
¾ cup instant dry polenta
½ cup (2 ounces) grated Asiago cheese

1. Preheat oven to 325°.

2. To prepare chicken, remove and discard giblets and neck from chicken. Rinse chicken with cold water; pat dry. Trim excess fat. Starting at neck cavity, loosen skin from breast and drumsticks by inserting fingers, gently pushing between skin and meat. Combine juice and next 4 ingredients; rub over breast and drumsticks under loosened skin. Place orange halves in body cavity. Lift wing tips up and over back; tuck under chicken.

3. Combine 6 garlic cloves, thyme sprigs, and 1 cup broth in a shallow roasting pan. Place chicken on a rack coated with cooking spray; place rack in pan. Insert meat thermometer into meaty part of thigh, making sure not to touch bone.

4. Bake at 325° for 2 hours or until thermometer registers 180°. Let stand 10 minutes. Discard skin. Place chicken on a platter, reserving drippings in pan; cover chicken, and keep warm. Add wine to drippings in pan, scraping pan to loosen browned bits; discard thyme and garlic.

5. Place flour in a small saucepan; gradually add remaining ¾ cup broth, stirring with a whisk until blended. Set aside. Place a zip-top plastic bag inside a 2-cup glass measure. Pour pan drippings into bag; let stand 10 minutes (fat will rise to top). Seal bag; carefully snip off 1 bottom corner of bag. Drain drippings into flour mixture in saucepan, stopping before fat layer reaches opening; discard fat. Bring mixture to a boil; cook 1 minute or until thick, stirring constantly with a whisk. Keep warm.

6. To prepare mushrooms, melt butter in a large nonstick skillet over medium-high heat. Add ½ teaspoon salt, ¼ teaspoon pepper, and mushrooms; cook 5 minutes or until mushrooms release moisture and darken, stirring frequently. Remove from heat; stir in truffle oil.

7. To prepare polenta, combine milk, water, ½ teaspoon salt, and ¼ teaspoon pepper in a medium saucepan over medium-high heat; bring to a boil. Gradually add polenta, stirring constantly with a whisk; reduce heat, and cook 2 minutes or until thick, stirring constantly. Remove from heat; stir in cheese. Serve with chicken, gravy, and mushrooms. Yield: 6 servings (serving size: about 6 ounces chicken, 2½ tablespoons gravy, ½ cup polenta, and ½ cup mushrooms).

CALORIES 467 (30% from fat); FAT 15.8g (sat 5.6g, mono 5.9g, poly 2.7g); PROTEIN 52.4g; CARB 27.5g; FIBER 3.4g; CHOL 135mg; IRON 2.9mg; SODIUM 814mg; CALC 221mg

How to Wrap a Turkey Breast

1. *Press half of fig mixture onto each turkey breast half, leaving a 1-inch border. Roll up, starting at short end. Sprinkle each roll with thyme, salt, and pepper. Wrap each in heavy-duty plastic wrap.*

2. *Wrap each roll in aluminum foil; twist ends to seal.*

Fig and Stilton-Stuffed Turkey Breast with Port Sauce

Ask the butcher to remove the bone and skin from the turkey breast halves, and specify the weight of skinless, boneless breast meat you'll need. Also, tell the butcher that you intend to flatten the meat so you can roll it up. Wrapping the turkey in plastic wrap and then foil keeps the meat moist. The plastic wrap won't melt in the oven because it's protected by the foil.

1½ cups ruby port or other sweet red
wine
1 cup chopped onion
1 tablespoon fresh lemon juice
⅛ teaspoon salt
10 dried Calimyrna figs, stemmed and
coarsely chopped (about ¾ cup)
6 whole black peppercorns,
crushed
3 thyme sprigs
2 bay leaves
1 rosemary sprig
2 cups (½-inch) cubed French
bread baguette
1 cup (4 ounces) crumbled Stilton
or other blue cheese
1 cup fat-free, less-sodium chicken
broth, divided
2 tablespoons coarsely chopped
fresh thyme, divided
1 teaspoon salt, divided
1 teaspoon freshly ground black
pepper, divided
2 (1½-pound) skinless, boneless
turkey breast halves
Cooking spray
3 tablespoons finely chopped
shallots
2 tablespoons butter
2 tablespoons all-purpose flour
Rosemary and thyme sprigs (optional)

1. Combine first 9 ingredients in a medium
saucepan. Bring to a boil; cover, reduce
heat, and simmer 20 minutes or until figs
are tender. Drain fig mixture in a colander over a bowl, reserving cooking liquid. Discard thyme sprigs, bay leaves,
and rosemary sprig. Combine fig
mixture, bread, cheese, ¼ cup broth, 2
teaspoons chopped thyme, ¼ teaspoon
salt, and ½ teaspoon pepper, tossing
until well blended.
2. Preheat oven to 350°.
3. Place each turkey breast half between
2 sheets of heavy-duty plastic wrap; carefully pound to about ½-inch thickness.
Remove plastic wrap. Press half of fig
mixture onto each turkey breast half,
leaving a 1-inch border. Roll up, starting
at short end. Sprinkle each roll with 2
teaspoons chopped thyme, ¼ teaspoon
salt, and ¼ teaspoon pepper. Wrap each
roll in heavy-duty plastic wrap, then
wrap each roll in aluminum foil; twist

ends to seal. Place on a jelly-roll pan.
Bake at 350° for 1 hour and 20 minutes.
Remove from oven; let stand 20 minutes.
4. Heat a small saucepan over medium
heat. Coat pan with cooking spray. Add
shallots to saucepan; cook 3 minutes or
until tender, stirring frequently. Add
reserved cooking liquid, remaining ¾
cup broth, and remaining ¼ teaspoon
salt; bring to a boil. Combine butter and
flour in a small bowl; mash with fingertips to form a paste. Drop butter mixture
into pan by small spoonfuls, stirring with
a whisk. Cook 2 minutes or until thick,
stirring constantly with a whisk.
5. Remove foil and plastic wrap from
turkey. Cut each roll into 8 slices. Serve
with sauce. Garnish with rosemary and
thyme, if desired. Yield: 8 servings (serving size: 2 turkey slices and about 3
tablespoons sauce).

CALORIES 371 (21% from fat); FAT 8.6g (sat 4.6g, mono 2.6g,
poly 0.7g); PROTEIN 47.3g; CARB 25.3g; FIBER 3.2g; CHOL 124mg;
IRON 3.5mg; SODIUM 748mg; CALC 159mg

QUICK & EASY
Sesame Halibut
en Papillote

En papillote refers to a method of baking
food in parchment paper. Steam is trapped
inside, and this keeps the food moist and
flavorful. The impressive presentation
belies this dish's simple preparation.

1 tablespoon dark sesame oil, divided
2 garlic cloves, minced
4 cups shredded bok choy
½ teaspoon salt, divided
½ teaspoon chile paste with garlic
4 (6-ounce) halibut or flounder
fillets (about 1 inch thick)
¼ teaspoon freshly ground black
pepper
1 teaspoon sesame seeds, toasted

1. Preheat oven to 400°.
2. Heat 1 teaspoon oil in a large nonstick skillet over medium-high heat. Add
garlic; sauté 30 seconds. Add bok choy
and ¼ teaspoon salt; sauté 5 minutes or
until crisp-tender. Remove from heat;
stir in chile paste. Sprinkle fillets evenly
with ¼ teaspoon salt and pepper.

3. Cut 4 (15-inch) squares of parchment
paper. Fold each square in half; open
each. Place ½ cup bok choy near fold;
top with 1 fillet. Drizzle each serving
with ½ teaspoon oil; sprinkle with ¼
teaspoon sesame seeds. Fold papers; seal
edges with narrow folds. Place packets
on a baking sheet. Bake at 400° for 18
minutes or until paper is puffy and lightly
browned. Place 1 packet on each of 4
plates; cut open. Serve immediately.
Yield: 4 servings.

CALORIES 233 (30% from fat); FAT 7.8g (sat 1.1g, mono 2.8g,
poly 2.9g); PROTEIN 36.7g; CARB 2.3g; FIBER 0.9g; CHOL 54mg;
IRON 2.1mg; SODIUM 459mg; CALC 158mg

Pappardelle with
Roasted Winter Squash,
Arugula, and Pine Nuts

Easy and filling, this handsome entrée is a
good choice for a weeknight vegetarian
dinner.

4 cups (1-inch) cubed peeled
butternut squash
2 tablespoons balsamic vinegar
2 teaspoons olive oil
½ teaspoon salt, divided
Cooking spray
8 ounces uncooked pappardelle
(wide ribbon pasta) or fettuccine
1 tablespoon butter
2 tablespoons pine nuts
1 tablespoon chopped fresh sage
2 garlic cloves, minced
2 cups trimmed arugula
½ cup (2 ounces) grated Asiago
cheese
½ teaspoon coarsely ground black
pepper

1. Preheat oven to 475°.
2. Combine squash, vinegar, oil, and ¼
teaspoon salt in a large bowl; toss well to
coat. Arrange squash mixture in a single
layer on a jelly-roll pan coated with
cooking spray. Bake at 475° for 25
minutes or until tender and lightly
browned, stirring occasionally.
3. While squash bakes, cook pasta
according to package directions, omitting
Continued

salt and fat. Drain pasta in a colander over a bowl, reserving 1 tablespoon cooking liquid.

4. Melt butter in a large nonstick skillet over medium heat. Add pine nuts, sage, and garlic; cook 3 minutes or just until pine nuts begin to brown, stirring occasionally. Place pasta, reserved cooking liquid, pine nut mixture, and squash mixture in a large bowl; toss gently to combine. Add remaining ¼ teaspoon salt, arugula, cheese, and pepper; toss gently to combine. Serve immediately. Yield: 6 servings (serving size: about 2 cups).

CALORIES 270 (27% from fat); FAT 8.2g (sat 3.5g, mono 2.9g, poly 1g); PROTEIN 9.8g; CARB 41.6g; FIBER 4.8g; CHOL 14mg; IRON 2.4mg; SODIUM 249mg; CALC 162mg

---

Tangerines

Tangerines have thinner, looser skins than oranges, and their sections separate easily. The juice is sweeter than orange juice, and some find it less acidic. Petite clementines are another loose-skinned orange that have virtually no seeds.

Seared Sea Scallops with Spicy Citrus Sauce

A cast-iron skillet is ideal for searing the scallops, but you can also use a nonstick pan. Serve with steamed basmati rice tossed with chopped cilantro.

- 1 cup fresh tangerine juice (about 5 tangerines)
- ½ cup seeded, thinly sliced kumquat
- ¼ cup minced shallots
- 2 tablespoons fresh lime juice
- ½ teaspoon coarsely ground black pepper
- 2 tablespoons fresh tangerine juice
- ½ teaspoon ancho chile powder
- ¼ teaspoon ground red pepper
- ¼ teaspoon salt
- 40 sea scallops (about 3 pounds)
- ¼ cup dry white wine
- 1 tablespoon butter
- 8 teaspoons chopped pistachios

1. Combine first 5 ingredients in a small saucepan. Bring to a boil; reduce heat, and simmer 3 minutes or until mixture is slightly thick.

2. Heat a large cast-iron skillet over medium-high heat. Combine 2 tablespoons tangerine juice, chile powder, red pepper, and salt in a large bowl; add scallops, tossing gently to coat. Add scallops to pan; cook 2 minutes on each side or until browned. Remove from pan; keep warm. Add wine to pan, scraping pan to loosen browned bits; bring to a boil. Add kumquat mixture and butter. Reduce heat to low; stir until butter melts. Arrange 5 scallops on each of 8 plates; top each serving with 3 tablespoons sauce, and sprinkle with 1 teaspoon nuts. Yield: 8 servings.

CALORIES 209 (18% from fat); FAT 4.2g (sat 1.2g, mono 1.1g, poly 0.9g); PROTEIN 29.8g; CARB 12.1g; FIBER 1.4g; CHOL 60mg; IRON 1mg; SODIUM 363mg; CALC 61mg

---

Horseradish and Mustard-Crusted Beef Tenderloin

Prep this entrée up to 1 day ahead, then just pop it in the oven. It'll be ready in only 35 minutes. Be sure to ask for a center-cut beef tenderloin; it's a consistent width and cooks more evenly than a piece with a tapered end.

- 2 tablespoons Dijon mustard
- 1 tablespoon prepared horseradish
- 1 (2-pound) center-cut beef tenderloin, trimmed
- ½ cup dry breadcrumbs
- Cooking spray

1. Combine mustard and horseradish; spread evenly over tenderloin. Pat breadcrumbs into mustard mixture. Wrap tenderloin in plastic wrap; refrigerate 1 to 24 hours.

2. Preheat oven to 400°.

3. Remove and discard plastic wrap from tenderloin. Place tenderloin on a broiler pan coated with cooking spray. Bake at 400° for 25 minutes or until a thermometer registers 145° (medium-rare) or desired degree of doneness.

Place tenderloin on a cutting board; cover and let stand 10 minutes before slicing. Yield: 8 servings (serving size: 3 ounces).

CALORIES 205 (40% from fat); FAT 9g (sat 3.3g, mono 3.6g, poly 0.6g); PROTEIN 24.1g; CARB 5.5g; FIBER 0.4g; CHOL 63mg; IRON 1.8mg; SODIUM 199mg; CALC 37mg

---

Jambalaya

This Creole dish works well for busy nights after holiday shopping. It's great when you need a meal that can stand for a while once it's ready, and it reheats well. Serve with hot sauce.

- 2 teaspoons vegetable oil
- ¼ pound skinless, boneless chicken breast, cut into bite-sized pieces
- ¼ pound skinless, boneless chicken thighs, cut into bite-sized pieces
- ¼ teaspoon salt
- ¼ teaspoon freshly ground black pepper
- 1 cup chopped smoked turkey sausage (about 4 ounces)
- 1 cup chopped onion
- ½ cup chopped green bell pepper
- ½ cup chopped celery
- 1 garlic clove, minced
- 1½ cups uncooked long-grain white rice
- 2¾ cups fat-free, less-sodium chicken broth
- 2 teaspoons paprika
- ½ teaspoon dried thyme
- ¼ teaspoon ground red pepper
- 1 (14.5-ounce) can diced tomatoes, undrained
- ¼ pound large shrimp, peeled, deveined, and chopped
- ¼ cup thinly sliced green onions

1. Heat oil in a large skillet over medium-high heat. Sprinkle chicken with salt and black pepper. Add chicken to pan; cook 5 minutes or until lightly browned, stirring occasionally. Remove chicken from pan; cover and keep warm. Add sausage to pan; cook 5 minutes or until lightly browned, stirring occasionally. Add 1 cup onion, bell pepper, celery, and garlic; cover, reduce heat to low, and cook 12 minutes or until vegetables are tender, stirring occasionally.

2. Stir in rice; cook 2 minutes, stirring constantly. Add broth, paprika, thyme, and red pepper. Bring to a boil; cover, reduce heat, and simmer 15 minutes. Add chicken and tomatoes; cook, uncovered, 10 minutes or until liquid is absorbed. Stir in shrimp; cover and cook 5 minutes or until shrimp are done. Remove from heat; let stand 5 minutes. Fluff with a fork. Sprinkle with green onions. Yield: 6 servings (serving size: 1⅓ cups).

CALORIES 322 (14% from fat); FAT 5.1g (sat 1.1g, mono 1.5g, poly 1.9g); PROTEIN 20.4g; CARB 46.8g; FIBER 3.2g; CHOL 68mg; IRON 3.3mg; SODIUM 640mg; CALC 72mg

---

Kumquats

This tiny, oval citrus fruit contains little flesh and is mostly skin. You can eat the entire fruit; the skin is subtly sweet and tart but without the bitter pith that oranges have.

Duck Breasts with Kumquat Chutney

If you or someone on your gift list loves kumquats, stock up on them and make a double batch of chutney. The chutney makes a great gift; attach a recipe card with instructions for cooking the duck, or suggest serving with chicken or pork tenderloin.

DUCK:

- ¼ cup fresh lime juice (about 2 limes)
- 1 tablespoon grated peeled fresh ginger
- 1 tablespoon olive oil
- 3 garlic cloves, crushed
- 6 (6-ounce) boneless duck breast halves, skinned
- ¼ teaspoon salt
- Cooking spray

CHUTNEY:

- 1 cup kumquats, halved and seeded (about 15)
- ⅔ cup sugar
- ½ cup white wine vinegar
- ¼ cup finely chopped red onion
- 1 teaspoon minced peeled fresh ginger
- ½ jalapeño pepper, finely chopped
- ½ cup dried cherries
- ¼ cup finely chopped fresh basil
- 2 tablespoons finely chopped fresh parsley
- 2 tablespoons fresh lime juice

1. To prepare duck, combine first 4 ingredients in a large zip-top plastic bag. Add duck; seal and marinate in refrigerator 2 hours, turning bag occasionally. Remove duck from marinade; discard marinade. Sprinkle salt evenly over duck. Heat a large nonstick skillet over medium-high heat. Coat pan with cooking spray. Add duck; cook 2 minutes on each side or until desired degree of doneness.

2. To prepare chutney, while duck marinates, combine kumquats and next 5 ingredients in a saucepan. Bring to a boil; cover, reduce heat, and simmer 40 minutes. Add cherries; cover and simmer 15 minutes. Remove from heat; stir in basil, parsley, and 2 tablespoons lime juice. Serve warm or at room temperature over duck. Yield: 6 servings (serving size: 1 duck breast half and ¼ cup chutney).

CALORIES 379 (20% from fat); FAT 8.3g (sat 2.4g, mono 2.6g, poly 1.1g); PROTEIN 35.4g; CARB 39.9g; FIBER 3.9g; CHOL 131mg; IRON 8.6mg; SODIUM 203mg; CALC 43mg

---

STAFF FAVORITE

Maple and Calvados-Glazed Pork Crown Roast with Apple-Chestnut Purée

This simple yet spectacular-looking crown roast earned our Test Kitchens' highest rating. If you can't find Calvados, use a combination of 3 parts brandy to 1 part apple cider.

ROAST:

- ½ cup Calvados (apple brandy)
- ¼ cup maple syrup
- 1 sage sprig
- 1 (16-rib) crown roast of pork (about 10¼ pounds), trimmed
- Cooking spray
- 1½ teaspoons salt
- 1 teaspoon freshly ground black pepper

PURÉE:

- 4 cups chopped peeled Granny Smith apple (about 1½ pounds)
- 1 cup bottled chestnuts
- ½ cup Calvados (apple brandy)
- ⅓ cup packed brown sugar
- 2 tablespoons maple syrup
- 2 tablespoons half-and-half
- 2 tablespoons Calvados (apple brandy)
- ½ teaspoon salt
- 1 teaspoon finely chopped fresh sage

1. Preheat oven to 450°.

2. To prepare roast, combine ½ cup Calvados, ¼ cup syrup, and sage sprig in a small saucepan. Bring to a boil over medium-high heat. Reduce heat; simmer 5 minutes or until slightly thick. Remove glaze from heat; discard sage sprig.

3. Lightly coat roast with cooking spray; rub 1½ teaspoons salt and pepper over roast. Place roast on a broiler pan coated with cooking spray. Brush one-fourth of glaze over roast. Bake at 450° for 25 minutes or until browned.

4. Reduce oven temperature to 300° (do not remove roast from oven); bake at 300° for 1 hour and 45 minutes, brushing with glaze every 30 minutes. (Cover bones with foil if they start to become too brown.)

5. Increase oven temperature to 400° (do not remove roast from oven); bake an additional 25 minutes or until a thermometer inserted in meaty part of roast registers 150°. Remove roast from oven; let stand 20 minutes before carving.

6. To prepare purée, while roast bakes, combine apple, chestnuts, ½ cup Calvados, sugar, and 2 tablespoons syrup

Continued

in a medium saucepan. Bring to a boil; reduce heat, and simmer 15 minutes or until apple is tender. Place mixture in a food processor; add half-and-half, 2 tablespoons Calvados, ½ teaspoon salt, and chopped sage. Process 1 minute or until smooth.

7. Slice vertically between rib bones. Serve pork with purée. Yield: 16 servings (serving size: 1 pork rib chop and about 2½ tablespoons purée).

WINE NOTE: A dish with flavors as complex as our Maple and Calvados-Glazed Pork Crown Roast deserves an equally complex wine. And one varietal in particular fills the bill: Pinot Noir. It has an earthy character that's a great foil to maple and chestnut flavors. Plus, compared to other reds, Pinot Noir has good underlying acidity to balance the richness of roast pork. Alas, great Pinot Noir is usually expensive, but one moderately priced example is the 2001 Thomas Fogarty Pinot Noir ($25) from the Santa Cruz Mountains of California.

CALORIES 374 (29% from fat); FAT 11.9g (sat 4.4g, mono 5.3g, poly 0.9g); PROTEIN 43.8g; CARB 16.2g; FIBER 0.9g; CHOL 119mg; IRON 1.5mg; SODIUM 385mg; CALC 58mg

On the Side

Supporting dishes for simple weeknight suppers and celebratory feasts.

Carrot Coins with Maple-Balsamic Browned Butter

This recipe tastes best when you start with whole carrots. The peeling and slicing take less than 5 minutes.

3¼ cups (¼-inch-thick) slices peeled carrots (about 1 pound)
1 tablespoon butter
1 tablespoon maple syrup
1 teaspoon balsamic vinegar
⅛ teaspoon salt
⅛ teaspoon freshly ground black pepper
1 teaspoon chopped fresh parsley

1. Steam carrots, covered, 15 minutes or until tender.

2. Melt butter in a medium nonstick skillet over medium heat. Cook butter 3 minutes or until lightly browned, stirring occasionally. Stir in syrup, vinegar, salt, and black pepper. Add carrots; cook 1 minute or until thoroughly heated, stirring to coat. Stir in parsley. Yield: 4 servings (serving size: about ⅔ cup).

CALORIES 86 (32% from fat); FAT 3.1g (sat 1.8g, mono 0.8g, poly 0.2g); PROTEIN 1.1g; CARB 14.5g; FIBER 3.4g; CHOL 8mg; IRON 0.5mg; SODIUM 173mg; CALC 43mg

Meringue and Streusel-Topped Sweet Potatoes

If you don't have a pastry bag, simply fill a zip-top plastic bag with the meringue, and snip a corner with kitchen shears. Personalize the meringue design any way you desire.

SWEET POTATO PURÉE:
8 cups cubed peeled sweet potatoes (about 3¼ pounds)
1 cup sweetened dried cranberries, coarsely chopped
½ cup half-and-half
⅓ cup maple syrup
1 teaspoon salt
1 teaspoon vanilla extract
½ teaspoon ground cinnamon
½ teaspoon maple flavoring
2 large eggs
Cooking spray

STREUSEL:
⅔ cup chopped pecans
½ cup packed light brown sugar
2 tablespoons all-purpose flour
2 tablespoons butter, melted
¼ teaspoon ground cinnamon

MERINGUE:
4 large egg whites
2⅓ cups granulated sugar

1. Preheat oven to 350°.

2. To prepare sweet potato purée, place sweet potatoes in a stockpot, and cover with water; bring to a boil. Reduce heat,

and simmer 20 minutes or until tender. Drain potatoes; place in a large bowl. Add cranberries and next 7 ingredients; beat with a mixer at high speed 2 minutes or until smooth. Spoon sweet potato purée into a 13 x 9-inch baking dish coated with cooking spray.

3. To prepare streusel, combine pecans, brown sugar, flour, butter, and ¼ teaspoon cinnamon. Sprinkle streusel evenly over sweet potato purée. Bake at 350° for 30 minutes; remove from oven (do not turn oven off).

4. To prepare meringue, place egg whites in a large bowl; beat with mixer at high speed until soft peaks form using clean, dry beaters. Gradually add granulated sugar, 1 tablespoon at a time, beating until stiff peaks form (about 4 minutes). Spoon meringue into a pastry bag fitted with a star tip. Pipe meringue in a lattice design over streusel. Bake at 350° for 15 minutes or until lightly browned. Yield: 16 servings (serving size: ½ cup).

CALORIES 267 (26% from fat); FAT 7.6g (sat 2.3g, mono 3.1g, poly 1.4g); PROTEIN 4.3g; CARB 46g; FIBER 3.6g; CHOL 73mg; IRON 1.1mg; SODIUM 201mg; CALC 53mg

Fruited Basmati Pilaf with Pistachios
(pictured on page 429)

Serve with roasted pork and Brussels sprouts. If your cinnamon stick is larger than 1 inch, just break it to get a 1-inch piece.

2 tablespoons butter
1 cup thinly sliced shallots
2½ cups water
1½ cups uncooked basmati rice
¾ cup frozen green peas
¾ cup golden raisins
1½ teaspoons salt
¾ teaspoon fennel seeds, lightly crushed
¼ teaspoon freshly ground black pepper
⅛ teaspoon ground cardamom
⅛ teaspoon saffron threads, crushed
1 (1-inch) cinnamon stick
1 bay leaf
½ cup chopped pistachios, toasted

1. Melt butter in a large nonstick skillet over medium-high heat. Add shallots; sauté 8 minutes or until golden brown. Remove from heat.

2. Combine water and rice in a medium saucepan over medium-high heat; bring to a boil. Stir in green peas and next 8 ingredients; cover, reduce heat, and simmer 20 minutes or until liquid is absorbed and rice is tender. Discard cinnamon stick and bay leaf. Stir in shallots and pistachios. Yield: 10 servings (serving size: ¾ cup).

CALORIES 196 (30% from fat); FAT 6.6g (sat 2.3g, mono 2.6g, poly 1.2g); PROTEIN 4.5g; CARB 31.9g; FIBER 2.4g; CHOL 8mg; IRON 1.2mg; SODIUM 482mg; CALC 30mg

Herbed Parmesan Soufflé

Potato starch (sometimes called potato flour) gives this soufflé light, airy texture. Look for it on the baking aisle. Coating the dish with breadcrumbs gives the soufflé traction to climb.

Cooking spray
⅓ cup dry breadcrumbs
2 tablespoons potato starch
½ teaspoon salt
⅛ teaspoon ground red pepper
⅛ teaspoon ground nutmeg
1 cup fat-free milk
¾ cup (3 ounces) grated fresh Parmesan cheese
1 tablespoon chopped fresh or 1 teaspoon dried thyme
1 tablespoon chopped fresh parsley
1 large egg yolk, lightly beaten
6 large egg whites
⅛ teaspoon cream of tartar

1. Preheat oven to 350°.

2. Coat a 1½-quart soufflé dish with cooking spray; sprinkle with ⅓ cup dry breadcrumbs.

3. Combine potato starch, salt, pepper, and nutmeg in a medium saucepan; gradually add 1 cup milk, stirring with a whisk. Bring to a boil over medium heat, stirring constantly with a whisk. Cook 1 minute or until thick, stirring constantly (mixture will be thick). Remove from heat; stir in cheese, thyme, and parsley.

Spoon mixture into a large bowl; let stand 1 minute. Whisk in egg yolk.

4. Place egg whites and cream of tartar in a large bowl; beat with a mixer at high speed until stiff peaks form, using clean, dry beaters. Gently stir one-fourth of egg whites into cheese mixture; gently fold in remaining egg whites. Gently spoon mixture into prepared dish. Bake at 350° for 35 minutes or until puffed and golden. Serve immediately. Yield: 6 servings.

CALORIES 120 (32% from fat); FAT 4.3g (sat 2.3g, mono 1.4g, poly 0.3g); PROTEIN 10.3g; CARB 9.5g; FIBER 0.2g; CHOL 44mg; IRON 0.7mg; SODIUM 509mg; CALC 210mg

QUICK & EASY
Golden Rutabagas and Shallots

A rutabaga's skin is thick, waxy, and tough, so a paring knife works best for peeling. After peeling, chop the rutabaga in half with a heavy knife or cleaver, and then cube, slice, or dice as needed.

5 cups (1-inch) cubed peeled rutabaga (about 1½ pounds)
1 tablespoon butter
12 shallots, peeled and halved
1 cup fat-free, less-sodium chicken broth
½ cup Madeira wine or dry sherry
2 tablespoons honey
¼ teaspoon salt
½ teaspoon minced fresh thyme
⅛ teaspoon freshly ground black pepper

1. Place rutabaga in a large saucepan, and cover with water; bring to a boil. Reduce heat, and simmer 25 minutes or until tender. Drain.

2. While rutabaga cooks, melt butter in a large nonstick skillet over medium-high heat. Add shallots; sauté 2 minutes. Add broth, wine, honey, and salt; bring to a boil. Reduce heat, and simmer until reduced to ½ cup (about 20 minutes). Add rutabaga, thyme, and pepper to pan; toss gently to coat. Yield: 6 servings (serving size: about ¾ cup).

CALORIES 130 (16% from fat); FAT 2.3g (sat 1.2g, mono 0.5g, poly 0.2g); PROTEIN 2.6g; CARB 21.2g; FIBER 3.5g; CHOL 5mg; IRON 1mg; SODIUM 204mg; CALC 69mg

Peppery Baked Onions with Sage and Gruyère

These onions have all the rich flavor of French onion soup and are a good accompaniment to roast beef, baked ham, or lamb.

4 medium yellow onions, peeled and halved
Cooking spray
1½ teaspoons olive oil
¾ teaspoon freshly ground black pepper
¼ teaspoon salt
⅔ cup less-sodium beef broth
2 teaspoons low-sodium soy sauce
¼ teaspoon dried rubbed sage
¼ cup (1 ounce) finely shredded Gruyère cheese

1. Preheat oven to 400°.

2. Arrange onions, cut sides up, in a single layer in a shallow 2-quart baking dish coated with cooking spray. Brush tops of onions with oil; sprinkle with pepper and salt. Bake at 400° for 40 minutes. Add broth and soy sauce; bake 1 hour, basting every 15 minutes. Sprinkle sage and cheese evenly over onions. Bake an additional 5 minutes or until cheese melts. Yield: 4 servings (serving size: 2 onion halves).

CALORIES 110 (34% from fat); FAT 4.1g (sat 1.6g, mono 2g, poly 0.3g); PROTEIN 4.7g; CARB 14.6g; FIBER 3.2g; CHOL 8mg; IRON 0.6mg; SODIUM 271mg; CALC 116mg

Sugar Snap Peas with Lemon and Toasted Almonds

Sugar snap peas make this a crisper, sweeter version of green beans amandine.

1 cup water
2½ cups sugar snap peas, trimmed (about 8 ounces)
1½ teaspoons butter, melted
½ teaspoon grated lemon rind
2 tablespoons sliced almonds, toasted
¼ teaspoon salt
⅛ teaspoon freshly ground black pepper

Continued

1. Bring water to a boil in a medium saucepan. Add peas; cook 2 minutes or until crisp-tender. Drain peas in a colander over a bowl; reserve 1 teaspoon cooking liquid.
2. Combine peas, reserved cooking liquid, butter, and lemon rind, tossing gently to combine. Sprinkle with almonds, salt, and pepper; toss gently to combine. Yield: 4 servings (serving size: ½ cup).

CALORIES 80 (36% from fat); FAT 3.2g (sat 1.1g, mono 1.4g, poly 0.4g); PROTEIN 3.5g; CARB 9.9g; FIBER 3.4g; CHOL 4mg; IRON 1.5mg; SODIUM 173mg; CALC 77mg

Butternut Squash and Leek Gratins

Individual gratins bake more quickly than a large casserole would.

    1   (2-pound) butternut squash,
        halved lengthwise and seeded
    Cooking spray
    1   teaspoon butter
    4   cups finely chopped leek (about
        6 large)
    1   tablespoon sugar
    ¾   teaspoon salt
    ¼   teaspoon freshly ground black
        pepper
    Dash of ground nutmeg
    4   large eggs, lightly beaten
    1   large egg yolk, lightly beaten
    ¼   cup (1 ounce) grated fresh
        Parmesan cheese

1. Preheat oven to 375°.
2. Place squash halves, cut sides down, on a baking sheet coated with cooking spray. Bake at 375° for 45 minutes or until tender. Cool 30 minutes. Scoop out pulp; mash with a potato masher or fork until smooth.
3. Reduce oven temperature to 325°.
4. Heat a large nonstick skillet over medium heat; coat pan with cooking spray. Melt butter in pan. Add leek; cover and cook 20 minutes or until tender, stirring once. Reduce heat to medium-low; uncover and cook 10 minutes or until lightly browned, stirring occasionally. Cool slightly.
5. Combine sugar and next 5 ingredients in a large bowl, stirring with a whisk. Add

squash and leek; stir until well combined. Divide squash mixture evenly among 6 (6-ounce) ramekins or custard cups coated with cooking spray. Place ramekins in a 13 x 9-inch baking pan; add hot water to pan to a depth of 1 inch. Cover pan with foil; bake at 325° for 25 minutes. Uncover, and bake an additional 15 minutes or until a knife inserted in center comes out clean. Remove from oven; place ramekins on a baking sheet.
6. Sprinkle 2 teaspoons cheese over each ramekin.
7. Preheat broiler.
8. Broil gratins 2 minutes or until cheese melts and begins to brown. Yield: 6 servings (serving size: 1 gratin).

CALORIES 186 (31% from fat); FAT 6.4g (sat 2.6g, mono 2.2g, poly 0.8g); PROTEIN 8.6g; CARB 25.9g; FIBER 3.6g; CHOL 181mg; IRON 2.9mg; SODIUM 437mg; CALC 170mg

Chianti-Stained Risotto with Pears and Blue Cheese

This winter risotto would enhance a beef tenderloin seasoned with pepper and sea salt. Serve remaining Chianti with your meal.

    1   cup pear nectar
    ¼   teaspoon ground cinnamon
    3   (14-ounce) cans fat-free,
         less-sodium chicken broth
    1½   tablespoons olive oil, divided
    ¼   cup chopped shallots
    1½   teaspoons chopped fresh thyme
    3   garlic cloves, minced
    1½   cups Arborio rice
    ½   cup Chianti or other dry red wine
    ¼   teaspoon salt
    ¼   teaspoon freshly ground black
         pepper
    1   teaspoon butter
    2   firm Bosc pears, peeled, cored, and
         cut lengthwise into ¼-inch-thick
         slices
    ½   cup (2 ounces) crumbled blue cheese
    ⅓   cup chopped walnuts, toasted
    2   tablespoons chopped fresh parsley

1. Bring first 3 ingredients to a simmer in a medium saucepan (do not boil). Keep warm over low heat.

2. Heat 1 tablespoon oil in a large saucepan over medium-high heat. Add shallots, thyme, and garlic; sauté 2 minutes. Add rice; cook 3 minutes, stirring constantly. Stir in wine; cook 2 minutes or until liquid is nearly absorbed, stirring constantly. Add broth mixture, ¾ cup at a time, stirring constantly until each portion of broth is absorbed before adding next (about 30 minutes total). Stir in salt and pepper.
3. Heat remaining 1½ teaspoons oil and butter in a large nonstick skillet over medium-high heat. Add pear slices; sauté 4 minutes. Serve pears over risotto; sprinkle with cheese, nuts, and parsley. Yield: 10 servings (serving size: about ½ cup risotto, about ¼ cup pears, about 1 tablespoon cheese, 1½ teaspoons nuts, and about ½ teaspoon parsley).

CALORIES 247 (27% from fat); FAT 7.5g (sat 2.2g, mono 2.9g, poly 2.1g); PROTEIN 7.6g; CARB 36.6g; FIBER 1.8g; CHOL 6mg; IRON 0.6mg; SODIUM 379mg; CALC 51mg

---

Nuts

This is the time of year to dig out your nutcracker and buy unshelled nuts. They keep longer than shelled nuts—up to 8 months in a cool, dark place. One pound of unshelled nuts usually yields about ½ pound, or 2 cups, of nuts.

Barley with Shiitakes and Spinach

Serve this side dish with beef or chicken.

    2   teaspoons olive oil
    1   cup chopped onion
    ½   teaspoon dried crushed rosemary
    3   garlic cloves, minced
    8   cups sliced shiitake mushroom
         caps (about 1¼ pounds)
    ¾   cup uncooked quick-cooking barley
    ⅓   cup water
    1   (10½-ounce) can beef consommé
    8   cups torn spinach
    3   tablespoons grated fresh Parmesan
         cheese
    ¼   teaspoon freshly ground black
         pepper

1. Heat oil in a large nonstick skillet over medium-high heat. Add onion, rosemary, and garlic; sauté 3 minutes or until onion is tender. Add mushrooms; sauté 6 minutes or until tender. Stir in barley, water, and consommé; bring to a boil. Cover, reduce heat, and simmer 10 minutes or until barley is tender. Add spinach, cheese, and pepper; cook 3 minutes or until spinach wilts, stirring frequently. Yield: 6 servings (serving size: 1 cup).

CALORIES 172 (17% from fat); FAT 3.3g (sat 0.9g, mono 1.5g, poly 0.5g); PROTEIN 8.6g; CARB 26.7g; FIBER 6.7g; CHOL 2mg; IRON 3.7mg; SODIUM 362mg; CALC 94mg

Creamed Cauliflower with Herbed Crumb Topping

Making fresh breadcrumbs from sourdough bread and tossing them with garlic butter gives the topping the flavor of garlic bread and a crispy texture that contrasts with the creamy filling.

    6 (1-ounce) slices sourdough bread
   10 cups coarsely chopped cauliflower
       florets (about 2 heads)
    4 teaspoons butter, divided
    3 cups chopped leek (about 4 large)
    6 garlic cloves, minced and divided
   ½ cup all-purpose flour
   3½ cups 2% reduced-fat milk
    1 teaspoon salt, divided
    1 cup (4 ounces) grated Parmigiano-
       Reggiano cheese
   ¼ teaspoon freshly ground black
       pepper
       Cooking spray
    2 tablespoons finely chopped fresh
       parsley
    2 teaspoons chopped fresh thyme

1. Preheat oven to 400°.
2. Place bread slices in a food processor; process until fine crumbs measure 3 cups. Set aside.
3. Cook cauliflower in boiling water 15 minutes or until tender; drain.
4. Melt 1 tablespoon butter in a large nonstick skillet over medium heat. Add leek and 3 garlic cloves; cook 7 minutes or until tender, stirring frequently.

Lightly spoon flour into a dry measuring cup; level with a knife. Combine flour and milk, stirring with a whisk; add to pan. Bring to a simmer; cook 2 minutes or until thick, stirring constantly. Stir in ¾ teaspoon salt, cheese, and pepper. Remove from heat; stir in cauliflower. Spoon cauliflower mixture into a 13 x 9-inch baking dish coated with cooking spray.
5. Melt remaining 1 teaspoon butter in a small skillet over medium heat. Add remaining 3 garlic cloves; cook 30 seconds or until lightly browned, stirring constantly. Remove from heat. Combine breadcrumbs, remaining ¼ teaspoon salt, parsley, and thyme. Drizzle with garlic-butter mixture; toss to combine. Sprinkle breadcrumb mixture evenly over cauliflower mixture. Bake at 400° for 30 minutes or until bubbly and browned. Yield: 10 servings (serving size: about 1¼ cups).

CALORIES 214 (29% from fat); FAT 6.9g (sat 4g, mono 1.9g, poly 0.4g); PROTEIN 11.6g; CARB 27.9g; FIBER 3.8g; CHOL 18mg; IRON 2mg; SODIUM 612mg; CALC 295mg

Desserts

Cakes, tarts, pudding, and other delectable treats to delight a yuletide sweet tooth.

STAFF FAVORITE • MAKE AHEAD
Red Raspberry Velvet Cake

Culinary historians believe this cake originated in New York City in the 1950s at Oscar's at the Waldorf-Astoria Hotel.

CAKE:
       Cooking spray
    3 cups sifted cake flour
    2 tablespoons unsweetened cocoa
    1 teaspoon baking soda
    1 teaspoon baking powder
   ½ teaspoon salt
   1⅔ cups granulated sugar
   ½ cup butter, softened
    4 large egg whites
    2 cups fat-free buttermilk
    1 (1-ounce) bottle red food coloring
    1 teaspoon vanilla extract

FROSTING:
    7 ounces ⅓-less-fat cream cheese
    1 teaspoon vanilla extract
   2¾ cups powdered sugar

REMAINING INGREDIENT:
   ½ cup seedless raspberry jam

1. Preheat oven to 350°.
2. Coat 2 (9-inch) round cake pans with cooking spray, and line bottoms of pans with wax paper.
3. Combine flour and next 4 ingredients. Set aside.
4. Beat granulated sugar and butter with a mixer at medium speed 4 minutes or until well blended. Add egg whites to sugar mixture; beat at medium speed 5 minutes or until fluffy. Combine buttermilk, food coloring, and 1 teaspoon vanilla in a small bowl; stir well with a whisk. Add flour mixture and buttermilk mixture alternately to sugar mixture, beginning and ending with flour mixture; mix just until moistened.
5. Pour batter into prepared cake pans. Sharply tap pans once on counter to remove air bubbles. Bake at 350° for 28 minutes or until a wooden pick inserted in center comes out clean (do not overbake). Cool in pans 10 minutes; remove from pans. Cool cake layers completely on wire racks.
6. To prepare frosting, combine cream cheese and 1 teaspoon vanilla in a medium bowl; beat with mixer at high speed 3 minutes or until fluffy. Add powdered sugar; beat at low speed just until blended (do not overbeat).
7. To assemble cake, place 1 cake layer on a plate. Spread with jam; top with second cake layer. Spread frosting over top and sides of cake. Store cake loosely covered in refrigerator. Yield 18 servings (serving size: 1 cake slice).

CALORIES 308 (23% from fat); FAT 7.9g (sat 4.9g, mono 2.1g, poly 0.3g); PROTEIN 3.9g; CARB 56.7g; FIBER 0.5g; CHOL 22mg; IRON 1.3mg; SODIUM 269mg; CALC 29mg

Upside-Down Cranberry-Ginger Cake

A seasonal version of the classic upside-down cake, this is easy to make and yields impressive-looking results.

Cooking spray
¾ cup packed light brown sugar
2 tablespoons butter
1½ tablespoons grated peeled fresh ginger
3 cups fresh cranberries
1½ cups all-purpose flour
2 teaspoons baking powder
¼ teaspoon salt
¼ cup butter, softened
1 cup granulated sugar
2 large egg yolks
½ cup fat-free milk
1 teaspoon vanilla extract
2 large egg whites
¼ teaspoon cream of tartar
⅔ cup frozen fat-free whipped topping, thawed

1. Preheat oven to 350°.
2. Heat a 9-inch round cake pan over medium heat; coat pan with cooking spray. Add brown sugar and 2 tablespoons butter to pan, stirring until melted. Stir in ginger; cook 1 minute, stirring constantly. Remove from heat; arrange cranberries on brown sugar mixture.
3. Lightly spoon flour into dry measuring cups; level with a knife. Combine flour, baking powder, and salt. Combine ¼ cup butter and granulated sugar in a large bowl; beat with a mixer at high speed until fluffy. Add egg yolks, 1 at a time, beating well after each addition. Add flour mixture and milk alternately to butter mixture, beginning and ending with flour mixture; mix after each addition. Beat in vanilla.
4. Beat egg whites and cream of tartar with a mixer at medium speed until stiff peaks form, using clean, dry beaters. Fold egg whites into batter; pour batter over cranberries in prepared pan. Bake at 350° for 55 minutes or until a wooden pick inserted in center comes out clean. Cool in pan 15 minutes; run a knife around outside edge. Place a plate upside down on top of cake pan; invert cake onto plate. Top each serving with whipped topping. Yield: 10 servings (serving size: 1 wedge and about 1 tablespoon whipped topping).

CALORIES 312 (23% from fat); FAT 8g (sat 4.7g, mono 2.2g, poly 0.5g); PROTEIN 3.8g; CARB 57.3g; FIBER 2g; CHOL 59mg; IRON 1.5mg; SODIUM 185mg; CALC 96mg

Ginger-Hazelnut Pumpkin Tart

Prebaking the empty crust ensures a crisp pastry.

Cooking spray
½ (15-ounce) package refrigerated pie dough (such as Pillsbury)
⅔ cup granulated sugar
½ cup part-skim ricotta cheese
½ cup fat-free milk
1 teaspoon vanilla extract
½ teaspoon pumpkin-pie spice
¼ teaspoon salt
1 (15-ounce) can pumpkin
1 large egg, lightly beaten
3 tablespoons chopped hazelnuts, toasted
2 tablespoons chopped crystallized ginger
2 tablespoons brown sugar
3⅓ cups vanilla low-fat ice cream

1. Preheat oven to 375°.
2. Coat bottom only of a 9-inch round removable-bottom tart pan with cooking spray. Press dough into bottom and up sides of pan. Pierce dough on bottom and sides with a fork. Bake at 375° for 10 minutes. Cool on a wire rack.
3. Combine granulated sugar and next 7 ingredients in a food processor; process until well blended. Spoon pumpkin mixture into prepared crust. Combine hazelnuts, ginger, and brown sugar; sprinkle evenly over pumpkin mixture. Bake at 375° for 45 minutes or until set. Cool 20 minutes on a wire rack. Serve with ice cream. Yield: 10 servings (serving size: 1 tart slice and ⅓ cup ice cream).

CALORIES 294 (30% from fat); FAT 9.8g (sat 4g, mono 4g, poly 0.9g); PROTEIN 6g; CARB 45.6g; FIBER 2.1g; CHOL 33mg; IRON 1mg; SODIUM 200mg; CALC 138mg

Peppermint Brownie à la Mode
(pictured on page 430)

This is a fun way to use all the candy canes that come your way this time of year. If you really like mint, substitute mint chocolate chip ice cream.

1 cup all-purpose flour
½ cup unsweetened cocoa powder
¼ teaspoon baking soda
¼ teaspoon salt
¼ cup warm fat-free milk
2 teaspoons instant coffee
1 teaspoon vanilla extract
1 cup granulated sugar
2 large eggs, lightly beaten
5 tablespoons butter
¼ cup semisweet chocolate chips
Cooking spray
4 cups reduced-fat chocolate chip ice cream (such as Healthy Choice), softened
4 candy canes (2 ounces), coarsely chopped
2 teaspoons powdered sugar
¼ cup coarsely chopped candy canes (optional)

1. Preheat oven to 350°.
2. Lightly spoon flour into a dry measuring cup; level with a knife. Combine flour, cocoa, baking soda, and salt in a large bowl, stirring with a whisk. Set aside.
3. Combine milk, coffee, and vanilla in a medium bowl. Add granulated sugar and eggs, stirring with a whisk until well combined. In a small microwave-safe bowl, melt butter and chocolate chips at HIGH in 20-second intervals until completely melted, stirring after each interval. Add chocolate mixture to egg mixture, stirring with a whisk until well combined.
4. Fold egg mixture into flour mixture, stirring just until moist. Spread batter into an 8-inch square baking pan coated with cooking spray. Bake at 350° for 20 minutes or until a wooden pick inserted in center comes out clean. Cool in pan on a wire rack. Cut into 12 pieces.
5. Place ice cream in a large bowl. Add 4 coarsely chopped candy canes to ice cream, stirring with a wooden spoon

until well combined. Return to freezer until ready to serve.

6. Place each brownie on a plate; sprinkle with about ⅛ teaspoon powdered sugar. Top with ⅓ cup ice cream. Garnish with additional candy cane pieces, if desired. Yield: 12 servings.

CALORIES 294 (30% from fat); FAT 10.2g (sat 6.2g, mono 2.1g, poly 0.4g); PROTEIN 5.2g; CARB 47.9g; FIBER 1.7g; CHOL 61mg; IRON 1.3mg; SODIUM 160mg; CALC 20mg

Lemon-Scented Coconut Macaroon Bars

Butter and lemon juice help make a flaky crust. To slice the bars cleanly, use a thin, sharp knife, and wipe it off with a moist towel between cuts.

CRUST:

    6 tablespoons sugar
    5 tablespoons butter, softened
    1 tablespoon fresh lemon juice
    ⅛ teaspoon almond extract
 1½ cups all-purpose flour
    Cooking spray

TOPPING:

    4 large egg whites
    ½ teaspoon cream of tartar
    ¼ teaspoon salt
    1 cup sugar
    1 cup flaked sweetened coconut
 2½ teaspoons grated lemon rind

1. Preheat oven to 350°.
2. To prepare crust, place first 4 ingredients in a large bowl; beat with a mixer at medium speed until well blended. Lightly spoon flour into dry measuring cups; level with a knife. Add flour to sugar mixture, beating until mixture resembles coarse meal. Press into bottom of a 13 x 9-inch baking dish coated with cooking spray. Bake at 350° for 12 minutes or until lightly browned; cool on a wire rack. Set aside.
3. Lower oven temperature to 325°.
4. To prepare topping, combine 4 egg whites, cream of tartar, and salt in a large bowl; beat with a mixer at high speed until soft peaks form. Gradually add 1 cup sugar, 1 tablespoon at a time, beating until stiff

peaks form, using clean, dry beaters. Fold in coconut and lemon rind; spread evenly over prepared crust. Bake at 325° for 40 minutes or until top is dry and lightly browned. Cool completely in pan on wire rack. Cut into 32 pieces. Store in an airtight container. Yield: 32 servings (serving size: 1 bar).

CALORIES 83 (28% from fat); FAT 2.6g (sat 1.8g, mono 0.5g, poly 0.1g); PROTEIN 1.1g; CARB 14.1g; FIBER 0.3g; CHOL 5mg; IRON 0.3mg; SODIUM 49mg; CALC 1mg

Black Forest Icebox Cookies

Keep these on hand for company; they can be made ahead and stored in the freezer up to 2 weeks. Work quickly when assembling them because the ice cream becomes difficult to handle as it melts. If this happens, return the ice cream to the freezer 10 minutes before continuing. We preferred chocolate ice cream, but vanilla is good, too. Make some of each. You also could use multicolored sprinkles instead of chocolate.

 1¼ cups low-fat chocolate ice cream, slightly softened
  ⅔ cup frozen pitted dark sweet cherries
    1 tablespoon brandy
  20 chocolate wafers (such as Nabisco's Famous Chocolate Wafers)
  ¼ cup chocolate sprinkles

1. Combine ice cream, cherries, and brandy in a small bowl. Cover and freeze 20 minutes, stirring after 10 minutes.
2. Working quickly, spoon about 1½ tablespoons ice cream mixture onto each of 10 wafers; top with remaining wafers, pressing firmly. Freeze 10 minutes. Place sprinkles on a small plate. Roll edges of cookies in sprinkles. Store in an airtight container in freezer until ready to serve. Yield: 10 servings (serving size: 1 cookie).

CALORIES 117 (26% from fat); FAT 3.4g (sat 1.6g, mono 0.6g, poly 0.2g); PROTEIN 1.6g; CARB 19.2g; FIBER 0.7g; CHOL 5mg; IRON 0.4mg; SODIUM 103mg; CALC 0mg

Vanilla-Bourbon Bread Pudding

The liquor flavor in the sauce is robust; reduce the amount if you prefer a subtler effect. For best results, use day-old bread.

PUDDING:

 1½ cups 1% low-fat milk
  ¾ cup packed dark brown sugar
  ½ cup golden raisins
  ¼ cup bourbon
    1 tablespoon vanilla extract
  ¼ teaspoon ground nutmeg
    2 large eggs, lightly beaten
    1 large egg white, lightly beaten
    1 (12-ounce) can evaporated fat-free milk
    8 cups (1-inch) cubed white bread (about 12 [1-ounce] slices)
    Cooking spray

SAUCE:

  ⅓ cup granulated sugar
    2 tablespoons butter
    1 cup 1% low-fat milk
    1 tablespoon cornstarch
    2 tablespoons bourbon

1. To prepare pudding, combine first 9 ingredients in a large bowl, stirring with a whisk. Add bread; toss gently to combine. Cover and chill 1 hour.
2. Preheat oven to 350°.
3. Spoon bread mixture into an 11 x 7-inch baking dish coated with cooking spray. Bake bread mixture at 350° for 50 minutes or until set.
4. To prepare sauce, combine ⅓ cup granulated sugar and butter in a medium saucepan over medium heat. Combine 1 cup milk and cornstarch in a small bowl, stirring with a whisk. Add milk mixture to pan; bring to a boil. Cook 4 minutes or until thick, stirring constantly. Reduce heat to medium-low; stir in 2 tablespoons bourbon. Cook 2 minutes; serve over pudding. Yield: 10 servings (serving size: 1 bread pudding scoop and about 2½ teaspoons sauce).

CALORIES 329 (16% from fat); FAT 5.6g (sat 2.6g, mono 1.6g, poly 0.3g); PROTEIN 9.5g; CARB 54.5g; FIBER 0.7g; CHOL 52mg; IRON 1.8mg; SODIUM 315mg; CALC 228mg

Apple Crumb Tart with Maple Ice Milk

We like to use whole wheat pastry flour because it adds color and texture, but all-purpose flour also works.

CRUST:

½ cup whole wheat pastry flour
½ cup all-purpose flour
2 teaspoons brown sugar
½ teaspoon baking powder
⅛ teaspoon sea salt
¼ cup chilled butter, cut into small pieces
5 tablespoons ice water
Cooking spray

FILLING:

6 cups sliced peeled Granny Smith apple (about 1½ pounds)
1 tablespoon cornstarch
2 tablespoons brown sugar
2 tablespoons maple syrup
1 teaspoon lemon juice
½ teaspoon ground cinnamon

TOPPING:

¼ cup whole wheat pastry flour
⅓ cup all-purpose flour
3 tablespoons brown sugar
¼ teaspoon baking powder
Dash of sea salt
2 tablespoons butter, melted
Maple Ice Milk

1. Preheat oven to 375°.
2. To prepare crust, lightly spoon ½ cup whole wheat pastry flour and ½ cup all-purpose flour into dry measuring cups; level with a knife. Combine flours and next 3 ingredients in a bowl; cut in chilled butter with a pastry blender or 2 knives until mixture resembles coarse meal. Sprinkle surface with ice water, 1 tablespoon at a time, tossing with a fork until moist and crumbly (do not form a ball). Press mixture gently into a 4-inch circle on plastic wrap. Cover and chill 5 minutes in freezer. Slightly overlap 2 sheets plastic wrap on a slightly damp surface. Unwrap and place chilled dough on plastic wrap. Cover dough with 2 additional sheets of overlapping plastic wrap. Roll dough, still covered, into a 10-inch circle. Place dough in freezer 5 minutes or until plastic wrap can be easily removed. Remove top sheets of plastic wrap; fit dough, plastic wrap side up, into a 9-inch round removable-bottom tart pan coated with cooking spray. Remove remaining plastic wrap. Fold edges under; flute. Cover and refrigerate.
3. To prepare filling, place apple in a large bowl. Sprinkle with cornstarch; toss well to coat. Stir in 2 tablespoons brown sugar and next 3 ingredients.
4. To prepare topping, lightly spoon ¼ cup whole wheat pastry flour and ⅓ cup all-purpose flour into dry measuring cups; level with a knife. Combine flours, 3 tablespoons sugar, ¼ teaspoon baking powder, and dash of salt; drizzle with melted butter. Toss with a fork just until combined (mixture will be lumpy).
5. Spread apple mixture in crust; sprinkle evenly with topping. Bake at 375° for 50 minutes or until fruit bubbles and topping is golden brown. Cool in pan to room temperature on a wire rack. Yield 10 servings (serving size: 1 tart slice and ⅔ cup ice cream).

(Totals include Maple Ice Milk) CALORIES 326 (31% from fat); FAT 11.1g (sat 6.9g, mono 3.1g, poly 0.5g); PROTEIN 4.7g; CARB 53.1g; FIBER 2.3g; CHOL 36mg; IRON 1.5mg; SODIUM 181mg; CALC 139mg

MAPLE ICE MILK:

1⅓ cups half-and-half
1⅓ cups 2% reduced-fat milk
¾ cup maple syrup
Dash of salt

1. Combine all ingredients. Pour mixture into freezer can of an ice-cream freezer; freeze according to manufacturer's instructions. Spoon ice cream into a freezer-safe container; cover and freeze 1 hour or until firm. Yield: 10 servings (serving size: about ⅔ cup).

CALORIES 121 (29% from fat); FAT 3.9g (sat 2.5g, mono 1.3g, poly 0.1g); PROTEIN 2.2g; CARB 18.7g; FIBER 0g; CHOL 18mg; IRON 0.3mg; SODIUM 49mg; CALC 98mg

How to Prepare Apple Crumb Tart Crust

1. *Roll dough, still covered, into a 10-inch circle.*

2. *After freeze time, remove top sheets of plastic wrap; fit dough, plastic wrap side up, into a 9-inch round removable-bottom tart pan coated with cooking spray. Remove remaining plastic wrap.*

Coffee-Chocolate Torte

Chill 2 mixing bowls in the freezer to give yourself time to work the cocoa and chocolate into the ice cream.

CRUST:

14 chocolate wafer cookies
1 tablespoon butter, melted
1 tablespoon sugar
1 large egg white
Cooking spray

WALNUTS:

3 tablespoons sugar
1 tablespoon water
⅛ teaspoon ground cinnamon
¼ cup chopped walnuts

FILLING:

- 4 cups low-fat coffee ice cream, softened and divided
- 3 tablespoons unsweetened cocoa, divided
- 1 (½-ounce) piece bittersweet or semisweet baking chocolate, grated

1. Preheat oven to 350°.

2. To prepare crust, place cookies in a food processor or blender; pulse until crumbs form. Add butter, 1 tablespoon sugar, and egg white; pulse 5 times or until combined. Press into bottom of an 8-inch springform pan coated with cooking spray. Bake at 350° for 8 minutes. Cool in pan on a wire rack.

3. To prepare walnuts, combine 3 tablespoons sugar, water, and cinnamon in a small saucepan over medium heat. Cook 1 minute, stirring constantly until sugar nearly dissolves. Stir in walnuts; cook 2 minutes. Remove from heat; spoon mixture onto wax or parchment paper. Cool until brittle. Break into small pieces. Set aside.

4. To prepare filling, spoon 1 cup ice cream into a chilled bowl. Stir in 2 tablespoons cocoa. Cover and freeze.

5. Place 3 cups ice cream in a chilled bowl; stir in chocolate. Cover and freeze 30 minutes. Spoon half of chocolate mixture into crust, spreading with a rubber spatula or wooden spoon. Freeze 1 hour. Spread cocoa mixture over chocolate mixture; freeze 30 minutes. Spread remaining half of chocolate mixture over cocoa mixture. Cover, and freeze overnight.

6. Place torte in refrigerator 30 minutes before serving. Uncover and dust with 1 tablespoon cocoa; sprinkle with candied walnuts. Yield: 9 servings (serving size: 1 tart slice).

CALORIES 231 (30% from fat); FAT 7.8g (sat 2.9g, mono 1.4g, poly 2.1g); PROTEIN 4.1g; CARB 37g; FIBER 2.1g; CHOL 31mg; IRON 0.8mg; SODIUM 138mg; CALC 12mg

Chocolate and cranberries spark sweet holiday treats.

Cranberry-Pear Crumb Pie

Frozen vanilla yogurt is an icy contrast to the tart cranberries and crumb topping.

CRUST:

- 1 cup all-purpose flour
- ⅛ teaspoon salt
- 3 tablespoons chilled butter, cut into small pieces
- 3 tablespoons vegetable shortening
- 3 to 3½ tablespoons ice water
- Cooking spray

FILLING:

- 5 cups thinly sliced peeled pear (about 2½ pounds)
- 1½ cups fresh cranberries
- ⅔ cup packed brown sugar
- 3 tablespoons uncooked quick-cooking tapioca
- 1 tablespoon fresh lemon juice
- 1 teaspoon grated lemon rind
- 1 teaspoon vanilla extract
- ¼ teaspoon ground nutmeg

TOPPING:

- ¼ cup all-purpose flour
- ¼ cup packed brown sugar
- ¼ cup regular oats
- ¼ teaspoon ground cinnamon
- 2 tablespoons chilled butter, cut into small pieces

1. To prepare crust, lightly spoon 1 cup flour into a dry measuring cup; level with a knife. Combine flour and salt in a bowl; cut in 3 tablespoons butter and shortening with a pastry blender or 2 knives until mixture resembles coarse meal. Sprinkle surface with ice water, 1 tablespoon at a time, tossing with a fork until dough is moist. Gently press dough into a 4-inch circle on heavy-duty plastic wrap; cover with additional plastic wrap. Chill 30 minutes.

2. Preheat oven to 400°.

3. Roll dough, still covered, into a 12-inch circle. Remove 1 sheet plastic wrap; fit dough into a 9-inch pie plate coated with cooking spray. Remove top sheet of plastic wrap. Fold edges of dough under; flute.

4. To prepare filling, combine pear and cranberries in a large bowl. Add ⅔ cup

sugar and next 5 ingredients, tossing well to combine. Spoon pear mixture into crust.

5. To prepare topping, lightly spoon ¼ cup flour into a dry measuring cup; level with a knife. Combine flour, ¼ cup sugar, oats, and cinnamon in a bowl; cut in 2 tablespoons butter with a pastry blender or 2 knives until mixture resembles coarse meal. Sprinkle topping over pear filling.

6. Cover loosely with foil; bake at 400° for 30 minutes. Uncover and bake an additional 30 minutes or until browned and bubbly. Let stand 20 minutes before serving. Yield: 10 servings.

CALORIES 310 (27% from fat); FAT 9.8g (sat 4.6g, mono 2.8g, poly 1.3g); PROTEIN 2.5g; CARB 55.5g; FIBER 4.9g; CHOL 15mg; IRON 1.5mg; SODIUM 80mg; CALC 35mg

Gifts from the Kitchen

From bread and biscotti to delicious divinity, these are sure to spread seasonal cheer.

Sugar-Frosted Cardamom Braid

Use a thermometer to be sure the liquid reaches the correct temperature before adding it to the yeast.

- 1⅓ cups 2% reduced-fat milk
- ½ cup granulated sugar
- 2 tablespoons butter
- 2 tablespoons grated lemon rind
- ½ to 1 teaspoon ground cardamom
- ½ teaspoon salt
- 4½ to 4¾ cups all-purpose flour, divided
- 1 package dry yeast (about 2¼ teaspoons)
- 1 large egg
- Cooking spray
- 1 large egg white, lightly beaten
- 1 tablespoon water
- 1 tablespoon coarse-grain sugar

Continued

1. Combine first 6 ingredients in a heavy saucepan over low heat. Cook 5 minutes or until sugar dissolves and a thermometer registers 115°, stirring frequently. Remove saucepan from heat.

2. Lightly spoon flour into dry measuring cups; level with a knife. Combine 2½ cups flour and yeast in a large bowl, stirring well with a whisk. Add milk mixture and egg; beat with a heavy-duty stand mixer at low speed 30 seconds or just until blended. Increase speed to medium; beat 2 to 3 minutes. Gradually add 2 cups flour; beat at low speed until mixture forms a ball.

3. Turn dough out onto a floured surface. Knead until smooth and elastic (about 8 minutes); add enough of remaining flour, 1 tablespoon at a time, to prevent dough from sticking to hands (dough will feel sticky). Place dough in a large bowl coated with cooking spray, turning to coat top. Cover and let rise in a warm place (85°), free from drafts, 1 hour or until doubled in size. (Press two fingers into dough. If indentation remains, dough has risen enough.) Punch dough down; cover and let rest 5 minutes.

4. Divide dough into 3 equal portions, shaping each portion into a 20-inch rope. Pinch ends together at one end to seal. Braid ropes on a lightly floured surface; pinch loose ends to seal. Place braid on a baking sheet coated with cooking spray. (The braid should be about 15 inches long.) Cover and let rise 30 minutes or until doubled in size.

5. Preheat oven to 375°.

6. Combine egg white and water; brush over top of loaf. Sprinkle 1 tablespoon coarse-grain sugar over loaf. Bake at 375° for 25 minutes or until golden and loaf sounds hollow when tapped. Remove from oven; cool on a wire rack. Yield: 24 servings (serving size: 1 slice).

CALORIES 130 (13% from fat); FAT 1.9g (sat 0.9g, mono 0.5g, poly 0.3g); PROTEIN 3.6g; CARB 24.5g; FIBER 0.8g; CHOL 13mg; IRON 1.3mg; SODIUM 71mg; CALC 23mg

Mini Cranberry Panettones

This classic Italian holiday sweet bread is a cross between a coffee cake and dessert that's now served year-round the world over. Lining the muffin cups with strips of parchment makes it easy to remove the panettones after baking. You can also prepare this recipe in traditional muffin tins for a yield of 18; trim the parchment paper for the muffin cups to 6 x 2½ inches, and shorten the baking time to 20 minutes.

 2 packages dry yeast (about 4½ teaspoons)
 1¼ cups warm water (100° to 110°)
 5¾ cups all-purpose flour, divided
 ¾ cup sugar
 7 tablespoons butter
 1 tablespoon finely chopped fresh orange rind
 ½ teaspoon salt
 2 large eggs
 2½ cups sweetened dried cranberries
 ¼ cup finely chopped crystallized ginger
 Cooking spray
 2 tablespoons sliced almonds

1. Dissolve yeast in water in a large bowl; let stand 5 minutes. Lightly spoon 1¼ cups flour into dry measuring cups; level with a knife. Add to yeast mixture, stirring with a whisk to combine. Cover; let rise in a warm place (85°), free from drafts, 1 hour.

2. Combine sugar and next 3 ingredients in a large bowl; beat with a heavy-duty stand mixer at medium speed until light and fluffy (about 3 minutes). Add eggs, beating until combined; beat in yeast mixture. Lightly spoon 4½ cups flour into dry measuring cups; level with a knife. Add 4 cups flour to egg mixture, beating at medium speed until smooth. Turn dough out onto a floured surface. Knead until smooth and elastic (about 3 minutes); add enough of remaining flour, 1 tablespoon at a time, to prevent dough from sticking to hands (dough will feel sticky). Knead in cranberries and ginger until well incorporated.

3. Place dough in a large bowl coated with cooking spray, turning to coat top. Cover and let rise in a warm place (85°), free from drafts, 1 hour or until doubled in size. (Gently press two fingers into dough. If indentation remains, dough has risen enough.)

4. Coat 6 (1 cup) muffin cups with cooking spray. Cut 6 (5 x 12-inch) strips of parchment paper; place paper in muffin cups to extend 3 inches from top of muffin cups. Divide dough evenly among muffin cups. Lightly spray each muffin with cooking spray; sprinkle with nuts. Let rise in a warm place (85°), free from drafts, 1 hour or until doubled in size.

5. While muffins rise, preheat oven to 375°.

6. After muffins have doubled in size, bake at 375° for 25 minutes or until muffins are lightly browned. Yield: 24 servings (serving size: ¼ muffin).

CALORIES 219 (18% from fat); FAT 4.5g (sat 2.3g, mono 1.2g, poly 0.5g); PROTEIN 4g; CARB 42.6g; FIBER 1.7g; CHOL 26mg; IRON 1.7 mg; SODIUM 81mg; CALC 14mg

Candied Hazelnut Brittle

Store the brittle in an airtight container.

 Cooking spray
 ½ cup sugar
 3 tablespoons water
 ⅛ teaspoon cream of tartar
 ⅓ cup chopped roasted hazelnuts
 1 teaspoon vanilla extract

1. Line a baking sheet with foil; coat foil with cooking spray.

2. Combine sugar, water, and cream of tartar in a medium saucepan; stir to dissolve sugar. Bring to a boil over medium-high heat. Cook until mixture is golden brown (about 6 minutes), stirring occasionally. Remove from heat, and stir in hazelnuts and vanilla. Spread mixture onto prepared baking sheet. Cool completely. Break into pieces. Yield: 11 servings (serving size: 1 tablespoon).

CALORIES 58 (31% from fat); FAT 2.1g (sat 0.2g, mono 1.6g, poly 0.3g); PROTEIN 0.5g; CARB 9.7g; FIBER 0.3g; CHOL 0mg; IRON 0.2mg; SODIUM 1mg; CALC 4mg

White Chocolate-Cashew Coffee Biscotti
(pictured on page 432)

A drizzle of white chocolate adds holiday flair to these biscotti. For contrast, melt semi-sweet chocolate to drizzle over half the batch.

½ cup granulated sugar
½ cup packed brown sugar
2 tablespoons butter, softened
1 teaspoon vanilla extract
2 large eggs
1 large egg white
2½ cups all-purpose flour
¼ cup instant coffee granules
3 tablespoons unsweetened cocoa
1 teaspoon baking soda
½ teaspoon ground cinnamon
¼ teaspoon salt
⅛ teaspoon ground nutmeg
¾ cup dry-roasted cashews, coarsely chopped
Cooking spray
1 tablespoon granulated sugar
3 ounces premium white chocolate, chopped

1. Preheat oven to 350°.
2. Place first 6 ingredients in a large bowl, and beat with a mixer at medium speed until well blended.
3. Lightly spoon flour into dry measuring cups; level with a knife. Combine flour and next 6 ingredients; gradually add to sugar mixture, beating until well blended. Stir in cashews. Turn dough out onto a lightly floured surface; knead lightly 7 times. Divide dough in half. Shape each portion into a 12-inch-long roll. Place rolls on a baking sheet coated with cooking spray; pat to ¾-inch thickness. Sprinkle rolls evenly with 1 tablespoon granulated sugar.
4. Bake at 350° for 22 minutes. Remove rolls from baking sheet; cool 10 minutes on a wire rack. Cut each roll diagonally into 21 (½-inch) slices. Carefully stand slices upright on baking sheet. Reduce oven temperature to 325°; bake 20 minutes (cookies will be slightly soft in center but will harden as they cool). Remove from baking sheet, and cool completely on wire rack.

5. Place chocolate in a small heavy-duty zip-top plastic bag; microwave at HIGH 1 minute or until chocolate is soft. Knead bag until smooth. Snip a tiny hole in 1 corner of bag; drizzle chocolate over biscotti. Yield: 3½ dozen (serving size: 1 biscotto).

CALORIES 83 (30% from fat); FAT 2.8g (sat 1.1g, mono 0.9g, poly 0.3g); PROTEIN 1.8g; CARB 13g; FIBER 0.4g; CHOL 12mg; IRON 0.7mg; SODIUM 56mg; CALC 13mg

Christmas Sugar Wafers with Vanilla Icing
(pictured on page 432)

Freezing the dough before cutting makes these low-fat cookies crunchy.

COOKIES:
6 tablespoons sugar
¼ cup butter
2 tablespoons dark brown sugar
1½ teaspoons vanilla extract
2 large egg whites
1½ cups all-purpose flour
3 tablespoons cornstarch
½ teaspoon baking powder
¼ teaspoon baking soda
¼ teaspoon salt
Cooking spray

VANILLA ICING:
1 cup powdered sugar
2 teaspoons warm water
1 teaspoon light-colored corn syrup
¼ teaspoon vanilla extract
Dash of salt

1. Preheat oven to 375°.
2. To prepare cookies, place first 3 ingredients in a large bowl; beat with a mixer at medium speed until well blended (about 5 minutes). Beat in 1½ teaspoons vanilla. Add egg whites, 1 at a time, beating well after each addition.
3. Lightly spoon flour into dry measuring cups; level with a knife. Combine flour and next 4 ingredients, stirring well with a whisk. Add to butter mixture; beat well. Turn dough out onto a lightly floured surface (dough will be soft). Divide dough into 4 equal portions. Roll

each portion into an 8-inch circle between 2 sheets of plastic wrap. Freeze dough 20 minutes or until plastic wrap can be easily removed.
4. Working with 1 portion of dough at a time (keep remaining dough in freezer), remove top sheet of plastic wrap. Cut dough with a 3-inch cookie cutter, dipping cutter in flour before each use; place cookies on baking sheets coated with cooking spray. Discard bottom sheet of plastic wrap; reserve remaining dough scraps. Repeat procedure with remaining frozen dough.
5. Gently gather reserved dough into a ball; repeat rolling, freezing, and cutting procedure.
6. Bake at 375° for 8 minutes or until cookies are lightly browned. Remove from baking sheet; cool on a wire rack.
7. To prepare vanilla icing, combine powdered sugar and remaining 4 ingredients in a small bowl; stir with a fork until combined. Drizzle icing over cookies, or spoon icing into a small heavy-duty zip-top plastic bag; cut a tiny hole in 1 corner of bag, and pipe designs onto cookies. Yield: 24 servings (serving size: 1 cookie).

CALORIES 94 (22% from fat); FAT 2.3g (sat 1.4g, mono 0.6g, poly 0.3g); PROTEIN 0.1g; CARB 17.9g; FIBER 0.3g; CHOL 5mg; IRON 0.4mg; SODIUM 75mg; CALC 5mg

Toasted Pecan Divinity
(pictured on page 432)

Here's a traditional holiday candy that contrasts the sweetness of a confection with the flavor of buttery toasted pecans. Use a candy thermometer to ensure you get perfect results.

4 dozen pecan halves (about 4 ounces)
1 tablespoon butter, melted
¼ teaspoon salt
2½ cups sugar
⅔ cup water
½ cup light-colored corn syrup
2 large egg whites
1 teaspoon vanilla extract

Continued

1. Preheat oven to 350°.
2. Combine pecans and butter, and toss well. Spread mixture evenly onto a jelly-roll pan. Bake at 350° for 12 minutes, stirring once. Remove from oven; sprinkle with salt.
3. Combine sugar, water, and corn syrup in a medium saucepan. Bring to a boil over medium heat; cover and cook 3 minutes. Uncover and cook without stirring, until a candy thermometer registers 250° (about 8 minutes). Remove from heat.
4. Beat egg whites in a large bowl with a heavy-duty stand mixer at high speed until stiff peaks form; beat in vanilla. Pour hot syrup in a thin stream over beaten egg whites while continuing to beat at high speed. Beat until mixture is stiff (about 3 minutes). Working quickly, drop by rounded teaspoonfuls onto wax paper. Gently press a pecan half on top of each piece of candy. Store divinity in an airtight container. Yield: 4 dozen (serving size: 1 piece).

CALORIES 70 (24% from fat); FAT 1.9g (sat 0.3g, mono 1g, poly 0.5g); PROTEIN 0.4g; CARB 13.5g; FIBER 0.2g; CHOL 1mg; IRON 0.1mg; SODIUM 20mg; CALC 2mg

---

MAKE AHEAD
Ginger Shortbread
(pictured on page 432)

Though it's lightened, this traditional-style shortbread has all of the buttery flavor and tender flaky texture of the original. For more pronounced ginger flavor, increase the ground ginger by ½ teaspoon. (Leave out the ginger for a plain version.) Wedges are a classic shortbread shape. To keep the texture of the bread pleasantly light, handle the dough as little as possible.

¾ cup plus 3 tablespoons cake flour
¼ cup granulated sugar
1 teaspoon ground ginger
Dash of salt
5 tablespoons unsalted butter, softened
1 tablespoon ice water
Cooking spray
1 tablespoon turbinado or other coarse sugar
¼ ounce crystallized ginger, cut into 16 thin slices

1. Lightly spoon flour into dry measuring cups; level with a knife. Combine flour, ¼ cup sugar, ground ginger, and salt, stirring with a whisk.
2. Place butter in a medium bowl; beat with a mixer at medium speed until smooth (about 1 minute). Add flour mixture; beat at low speed just until combined. Add ice water, and stir just until combined. Press mixture gently into a 4-inch circle on plastic wrap; cover with additional plastic wrap. Chill 20 minutes.
3. Preheat oven to 350°.
4. Slightly overlap 2 sheets of plastic wrap on a slightly damp surface. Unwrap and place chilled dough on plastic wrap. Cover dough with 2 additional sheets of overlapping plastic wrap. Roll dough, still covered, into an 8-inch circle (edges of circle will crack slightly). Remove top sheets of plastic wrap, and fit dough, plastic wrap side up, onto a baking sheet coated with cooking spray. Remove remaining plastic wrap.
5. Sprinkle dough with 1 tablespoon coarse sugar; press gently to help sugar adhere to dough. Lightly score dough into 16 wedges, cutting into, but not through, dough. Place 1 piece of crystallized ginger in each wedge; press gently to adhere.
6. Bake at 350° for 25 minutes or until light gold in color. Remove from oven; cool 5 minutes. Cut through score lines to make 16 wedges. Place on a wire rack; cool completely. Yield: 16 cookies (serving size: 1 cookie).

CALORIES 77 (42% from fat); FAT 3.6g (sat 2.3g, mono 0.9g, poly 0.2g); PROTEIN 0.7g; CARB 10.7g; FIBER 0.2g; CHOL 9mg; IRON 0.6mg; SODIUM 10mg; CALC 3mg

---

MAKE AHEAD
Kumquats in Spiced Syrup with Cloves, Cinnamon, and Star Anise

This spiced fruit can be chopped and stirred into couscous or served with ham. For optimum texture and flavor, refrigerate the kumquats for 2 weeks before they're used.

2 pounds kumquats (about 8 cups)
4 cups water
2 cups sugar
9 whole cloves, divided
3 (3-inch) cinnamon sticks, divided
3 star anise, divided
1 vanilla bean, halved lengthwise and divided
1 cup brandy, divided

1. Pierce each kumquat several times with a wooden skewer.
2. Combine water and sugar in a large saucepan; bring to a boil, stirring until sugar dissolves. Add 3 cloves, 1 cinnamon stick, and 1 star anise. Reduce heat, and simmer 5 minutes. Add kumquats, and simmer 20 minutes or until tender.
3. Using a slotted spoon, remove kumquats from pan, and divide evenly between 2 (1-quart) jars. Tuck 3 whole cloves, 1 cinnamon stick, 1 star anise, and half of vanilla bean into each jar.
4. Bring cooking liquid to a boil; cook 4 minutes. Remove from heat. Strain mixture through a sieve into a bowl, discarding solids. Pour 2 cups cooking liquid and ½ cup brandy into each jar. Seal jars; shake well. Store in refrigerator 2 weeks before using. Yield: 8 cups kumquats (serving size: ¼ cup).

CALORIES 87 (2% from fat); FAT 0.2g (sat 0g, mono 0g, poly 0.1g); PROTEIN 0.5g; CARB 17g; FIBER 1.8g; CHOL 0mg; IRON 0.3mg; SODIUM 3mg; CALC 18mg

Spoil loved ones with warm holiday flavors of ginger and spice with the recipe for kumquats in spiced syrup.

Six Holiday Menus

To make planning meals easier, we composed six all-occasion menus with recipes from our holiday cookbook.

Holiday Dinner Menu
serves 8

Celery-Celeriac Soup with Roquefort Croutons (recipe on page 437)

Horseradish and Mustard-Crusted Beef Tenderloin (recipe on page 442)

Steamed haricot verts tossed with butter

Dinner Rolls, Five Ways (recipe on page 439)

Mashed potatoes

Upside-Down Cranberry-Ginger Cake (recipe on page 448)

Red wine

Cocktail Party Menu
serves 12

Blood Orange Sangría (recipe on page 434)

Blackened Shrimp with Pomegranate-Orange Salsa (recipe on page 435)

Caramelized Onion, Red Pepper, and Mushroom Pizzetti (recipe on page 434)

Cheese and crackers

Fresh fruit tray

White Chocolate-Cashew Coffee Biscotti (recipe on page 453)

Movie Night Menu
serves 6

Tossed salad

Jambalaya (recipe on page 442)

Yeasted Corn Bread (recipe on page 438)

Lemon-Scented Coconut Macaroon Bars (recipe on page 449)

Beer and root beer

Popcorn

Brunch Menu
serves 6

Sugar-Frosted Cardamom Braid (recipe on page 451)

Herbed Parmesan Soufflé (recipe on page 445)

Escarole and Fennel Salad with Pears and Gruyère (recipe on page 437)

Pan-sautéed ham slices

Fresh orange juice

Open House Menu
serves 8

Mulled Cranberry-Guava Toddies (recipe on page 434)

Cheddar with Sautéed Apples and Brown Bread (recipe on page 433)

Cheese Dip with Crawfish (recipe on page 435)

Chicken Chowder with Chipotle
Chupe de Pollo con Chipotle
(recipe on page 437)

Garlic bread

Red Raspberry Velvet Cake (recipe on page 447)

Sunday Supper Menu
serves 4

Roasted pork tenderloin

Garden salad

Carrot Coins with Maple-Balsamic Browned Butter (recipe on page 444)

Peppery Baked Onions with Sage and Gruyère (recipe on page 445)

Vanilla ice cream with gingersnaps

Dry white wine

Menu Index

A topical guide to all the menus that appear in Cooking Light *Annual Recipes 2004*.
See page 478 for the General Recipe Index.

Dinner Tonight

Bell Pepper Frittata Menu (page 11)
serves 4
Red Bell Pepper Frittata
Toasted English muffins with jam
Roasted vanilla-scented apples

Huevos Rancheros Menu (page 11)
serves 4
Huevos Rancheros with Queso Fresco
Orange, pineapple, and coconut ambrosia
Margaritas

Shrimp and Grits Menu (page 12)
serves 6
Southern Shrimp and Grits
Green salad with avocado and tomatoes
Orange sorbet

Joe's Special Menu (page 12)
serves 4
Joe's Special
Crisp oven potatoes
Beer

Halibut Menu (page 72)
serves 4
Cornflake-Crusted Halibut with
Chile-Cilantro Aïoli
Oven fries
Cabbage salad

Pan-Seared Cod Menu (page 73)
serves 4
Pan-Seared Cod with Basil Sauce
Garlic smashed potatoes
Sautéed spinach

Striped Bass Menu (page 73)
serves 4
Asian Marinated Striped Bass
Rice noodles
Steamed baby bok choy

Trout with Lentils Menu (page 74)
serves 4
Trout with Lentils
Mixed greens salad with goat
cheese croutons
Angel food cake with lemon curd

Fettuccine Menu (page 103)
serves 4
Fettuccine with Shrimp and Portobellos
Arugula salad
Garlic bread

Garlicky Pasta Menu (page 104)
serves 6
Garlicky Pasta with Fresh
Tomatoes and Basil
Sautéed broccoli rabe
Fresh berries

Lasagna Rolls Menu (page 104)
serves 4
Lasagna Rolls with Roasted Red
Pepper Sauce
Sugar snap peas
Amaretto pears

Greek Pasta Salad Menu (page 105)
serves 4
Greek Pasta Salad
Pita crisps
Orange sorbet

**Chicken and Couscous
Salad Menu** (page 151)
serves 4
Chicken and Couscous Salad
Pita crisps
Lemon sorbet

Chicken Salad Pita Menu (page 151)
serves 4
Smoky Bacon and Blue Cheese Chicken
Salad Pitas
Herbed carrots
Fresh berries

**Chicken, Potato, and Green Bean
Salad Menu** (page 152)
serves 4
Chicken, Red Potato, and
Green Bean Salad
Garlic-Parmesan toasts
Sliced fresh plum tomatoes with salt and
pepper

**Chicken Salad with Nectarines
Menu** (page 152)
serves 5
Chicken Salad with Nectarines in
Mint Vinaigrette
Peppery cheese breadsticks
Lemonade

Pork Tacos Menu (page 197)
serves 4
Lime-Cilantro Pork Tacos
Black bean salad with
bell peppers and onions
Lemon sorbet

Chicken and Rice Menu (page 198)
serves 4
Parmesan Chicken and Rice
Green beans amandine
Dinner rolls

Flank Steak Menu (page 198)
serves 6
Rice Noodles with Sesame-Ginger
Flank Steak
Orange sections tossed with
chopped fresh mint
Herbed green tea

**Mushroom-Prosciutto
Pizza Menu** (page 199)
serves 4
Mushroom-Prosciutto Pizza
Arugula salad with garlic-sherry vinaigrette
Angel food cake topped with fresh berries

Rub Menu 1 (page 240)
serves 4
Herbes de Provence-Crusted Lamb Chops
Grilled red potatoes with mint
Steamed green beans

Rub Menu 2 (page 240)
serves 4
Lemon and Oregano-Rubbed
Chicken Paillards
Greek farmers' salad
Basmati rice

Rub Menu 3 (page 241)
serves 4
Classic Steak House Rubbed Filet Mignon
Grilled asparagus with lemon
Baked potatoes with chives and
reduced-fat sour cream

Rub Menu 4 (page 241)
serves 4
Grilled Pastrami-Style Salmon
Red cabbage and apple slaw
Rye bread

Wrap Menu (page 288)
serves 6
Thai Beef Salad Wraps
Grilled soy-glazed eggplant
Iced green tea

Stromboli Menu (page 288)
serves 4
Prosciutto and Gruyère Strombolis
Tomato-basil soup
Cantaloupe cubes tossed with mint

Crêpe Menu (page 289)
serves 6
Creamy Chicken and Mushroom Crêpes
Broccoli with balsamic-butter sauce
White and wild rice blend

Focaccia Menu (page 289)
serves 6
Spinach and Feta-Stuffed
Focaccia
Romaine, strawberry, and orange salad
Vanilla low-fat ice cream with caramel sauce

Seafood Supper Menu 1 (page 317)
serves 6
Shrimp with Lemon, Mint, and
Goat Cheese
Marinated mushrooms
Garlic bread

Seafood Supper Menu 2 (page 317)
serves 6
Shrimp and Crab Gumbo
Green salad
Cherries in Zinfandel syrup

Seafood Supper Menu 3 (page 318)
serves 6
Linguine with Clam Sauce
Cold cucumber soup
Sautéed asparagus spears

Quick Chops Menu 1 (page 368)
serves 4
Buttermilk-Brined Pork Chops
Roasted butternut squash
Steamed green beans

Quick Chops Menu 2 (page 368)
serves 4
Grilled Plum and Prosciutto-Stuffed
Pork Chops
Hominy sauté
Strawberry sorbet

Quick Chops Menu 3 (page 369)
serves 4
Sautéed Boneless Pork Chops with
Tomato-Sage Pan Sauce
Penne pasta with butter and Parmesan cheese
Lettuce salad with marinated artichoke
hearts and tomatoes

Quick Chops Menu 4 (page 369)
serves 4
Breaded Pork Chops
Garlic-scented turnip greens
Garlic bread

Warm Sandwich Menu 1 (page 399)
serves 4
Balsamic-Glazed Chicken Sandwiches with
Red Onions and Goat Cheese
Antipasto salad
Cubed winter pears

Warm Sandwich Menu 2 (page 400)
serves 4
Red Wine-Marinated Steak
Sandwiches
Roasted herbed potatoes
Steamed baby carrots

Warm Sandwich Menu 3 (page 400)
serves 4
Pacific Rim Pork Sandwiches
with Hoisin Slaw
Sesame noodle salad
Orange and grapefruit slices

Warm Sandwich Menu 4 (page 401)
serves 4
Wasabi Salmon Sandwiches
Miso soup
Sliced cucumbers and red onions tossed
with seasoned rice vinegar and black pepper

**Cuban Chicken
Pizza Menu** (page 421)
serves 4
Cuban Chicken Pizza
Celery and bell pepper sticks
Tequila-cardamom syrup and
vanilla ice cream

Thai-Style Chicken Menu (page 422)
serves 4
Thai-Style Stir-Fried Chicken
Rice noodles
Green tea

**Chicken with Sherry Vinegar Sauce
Menu** (page 422)
serves 4
Chicken with Sherry Vinegar Sauce
Rustic mashed potatoes
Steamed green beans

Simple Suppers

Sandwich Night Menu (page 79)
serves 4
Chicken Sandwich with Arugula and
Sun-Dried Tomato Vinaigrette
Sour cream and bacon potato salad
Bread-and-butter pickles

Sandwich Night Menu (page 134)
serves 8
Ham and brie sandwich
Sweet potato chips
Honeydew melon wedge

**Quick Dinner for
One Menu** (page 252)
serves 1
Bell Pepper and Fresh
Mozzarella Couscous
Green salad
Balsamic-brown sugar strawberries

**Breakfast for Dinner
Menu** (page 256)
serves 4
Wild Rice, Asparagus, and Goat
Cheese Frittata
Potato and bell pepper hash
English muffins with jam

Meat and Potatoes Menu (page 318)
serves 8
Braised Beef with Sun-Dried Tomatoes
Mashed Yukon gold potatoes
Green salad

**Weeknight Shrimp
Dinner Menu** (page 320)
serves 4
Sun-Dried Tomato Spiced Shrimp
Coconut-almond couscous
Steamed broccoli spears with lemon rind

**Speedy Southern
Supper Menu** (page 323)
serves 4
Pan-Fried Catfish with Cajun Tartar Sauce
Cider-mustard slaw
Corn bread
Vanilla ice cream with caramel sauce

Brunch & Lunch

Speedy Supper Menu (page 348)
serves 4
Chicken Piccata
Orzo with peas
Roasted baby carrots

Soup and Salad Night Menu
(page 356)
serves 8
Garbanzo and Greens Stew
Tomato salad
Mexican beer

Brown-Bag Lunch Menu (page 20)
serves 1
Pasta salad with chicken
Carrot and cucumber sticks
Pecan Bar Cookies

Family Picnic Menu (page 213)
serves 4
Couscous Salad with Chicken and
Chopped Vegetables
Cream cheese roll-ups
Gingersnaps

Brown-Bag Lunch Menu
(page 253)
serves 2
Soba Noodles with Shrimp
Sesame green beans
Orange wedges

Brunch Buffet Menu (page 387)
serves 6
Holiday Brunch Tonic
Whole Wheat Apricot Muffins
Grits Casserole with Mushrooms,
Prosciutto, and Provolone
Pistachio Granola served with milk or
vanilla low-fat yogurt
Fruit Salad with Honey-Yogurt Sauce
Sour Cream-Hazelnut Bundt Cake

Brunch Menu (page 455)
serves 6
Sugar-Frosted Cardamom Braid
Herbed Parmesan Soufflé
Escarole and Fennel Salad with
Pears and Gruyère
Pan-sautéed ham slices
Fresh orange juice

Casual Entertaining

Warming Winter Menu (page 7)
serves 6
Crisp and Spicy Snack Mix
Broccoli, Orange, and Watercress Salad
Beef Stew
Creamy Mashed Potatoes
Sloppy Joes
Hearty Wheat Bread
Mulled Cranberry-Apple Cider
Oatmeal-Walnut Cookies
Cranberry and Apple Crumble

Easy Entertaining Menu (page 77)
serves 4
Caramelized Onion Dip
Pork chops with tomato chutney
Mashed potatoes
Collard greens

Backyard Entertaining Menu (page 134)
serves 8
Romaine Salad with Avocado-Lime
Vinaigrette
Mahimahi fish tacos
Chips and salsa
Margaritas

Quick Tex-Mex Dinner Menu (page 215)
serves 6
Taco Rice Salad
Easy guacamole with chips
Lemonade
Angel food cake with fat-free caramel sauce

Seaside Supper Menu (page 242)
serves 6
Spicy Shrimp and Scallop Seviche
Baked flour tortilla chips
Citrus-Spiked Jícama and Carrot Slaw
Grilled Pork Chops with Tomatillo,
Corn, and Avocado Salsa
Basmati rice
Key Lime Pie Ice Cream

Waterside Menu (page 263)
serves 4
Herbed Cracker Bread
Roasted Fig and Arugula Salad
Grilled Lemon-Bay Shrimp
Barley Risotto with Fennel and Olives
Cherries in Spiced Wine Syrup with
Pound Cake Croutons
Pimm's Cup, Slushy Watermelon Mojitos,
or Sparkling Peach Splash

Santa Fe Menu (page 273)
serves 8
Farmers' Market Quesadillas
Red Cabbage and Spinach Salad with
Balsamic Vinaigrette
Fiery Turkey Fillets with Mango Salsa
Mexican Chocolate Cake
Lemon Southwest Rice

Supper Club Menu (page 295)
serves 8
Grilled Eggplant with Caramelized Onion
and Fennel
Crab-Stuffed Lobster with Citrus Vinaigrette
Corn Fritter Casserole
Summer Tomato Chopped Salad
Lemon-Buttermilk Panna Cotta with
Blueberry Sauce

Fall Cabin Menu (page 345)
serves 8
Red Pepper-Cheese Dip
Fall Green Salad
Rich Mushroom Soup or
Savory Beet Soup
Cider-Roasted Pork Loin or
Cider-Roasted Chicken
Spicy Sweet Potato Wedges
Country Rye Loaves
Pumpkin-Orange Cake

**Soup, Salad, and Bread
Menu** (page 352)
serves 6
Green Salad with Roasted Poblanos and
Cumin-Lime Dressing
Butternut Squash-White Bean Soup
Cornmeal Scones
Vanilla Bean Sorbet with
Pineapple Topping

Easy Uptown Dinner Menu (page 362)
serves 6
Red Lettuce Salad with Citrus Vinaigrette
Peppercorn and mustard-crusted
beef tenderloin
French bread

Sweet Heat Menu (page 384)
serves 8
Cranberry Jezebel Sauce with Sautéed Ham
Almond rice pilaf
Steamed broccoli spears

Try Something New Menu (page 385)
serves 6
Sesame Turkey Cakes with Sweet Chili
Sauce
Asian slaw
Steamed sugar snap peas

Sandwich Night Menu (page 408)
serves 4
Chicken, provolone, and mushroom sandwiches
Red seedless grapes

Movie Night Menu (page 455)
serves 6
Tossed salad
Jambalaya
Yeasted Corn Bread
Lemon-Scented Coconut Macaroon Bars
Beer and root beer
Popcorn

Sunday Supper Menu (page 455)
serves 4
Roasted pork tenderloin
Garden salad
Carrot Coins with Maple-Balsamic
Browned Butter
Peppery Baked Onions with Sage and Gruyère
Vanilla ice cream with gingersnaps
Dry white wine

Special Occasions

Social Saturday Menu (page 47)
Breakfast
Bran flakes
1% milk
Banana
Lunch
Subway (6-inch) turkey breast
Baked Lays potato chips
Diet soda
Dinner
Olive assortment
Peppercorn-Crusted Filet Mignon with
Port Jus
Creamy Parmesan Orzo
Chive Green Beans
Merlot
Chocolate Soufflés with Pistachios

Relaxing Sunday Menu (page 49)
Brunch
Mushroom and Bell Pepper Omelet
with Fontina
Sweet Potato Hash
Sesame-seed bagel
Cubed melon
Bloody Mary
Dinner
Moroccan Chicken with Almond Couscous
Lemony Asparagus-Mushroom Stir-Fry
Light vanilla ice cream

Busy Weekday Menu (page 51)

<u>Breakfast</u>
Egg McMuffin
Hash browns
Orange juice
Black coffee
<u>Snack</u>
Oats and Honey Granola Bar
<u>Lunch</u>
Roasted Chicken and Bow Tie
Pasta Salad
Rye dinner roll
Apple
Iced tea
<u>Dinner</u>
Sesame Tofu Stir-Fry over Rice
Fresh pineapple
Fortune cookie
Lite Beer

**Mix-and-Match
Shower Menu** (page 96)
serves 12
Grilled Chicken Salad with
Feta and Cucumbers
Shrimp and White Bean Salad
over Watercress
Spanish Tortilla with Almond Romesco
Salad of Papaya, Mango, and Grapefruit
Fennel, Orange, and Parmigiano Salad
Millet Muffins with Honey-Pecan Butter
Raspberry-Almond Muffins
Strawberries and Oranges with
Vanilla-Scented Wine

**Easter Dinner Alfresco
Menu** (page 106)
serves 4
Mushroom and Parmigiano Bruschetta
Rosemary and Pepper-Crusted
Pork Tenderloin
Three-Grain Risotto with
Asparagus Spears
Green salad
Strawberry Granita

Progressive Dinner Menu
(page 300)
serves 9
<u>Appetizer Stop</u>
Baked Hoisin Chicken Buns
Tofu Larb
Galloping Horses
Crab and Scallop Sui Mei
Riesling or other sweet white wine
<u>Main-Course Stop</u>
Bitter Greens Salad with Sourdough
Croutons and Warm Tomato Vinaigrette
Lamb Osso Buco over Parmesan Polenta
or Beef Bourguignonne with
Egg Noodles
Cabernet Sauvignon
<u>Dessert Stop</u>
Individual Tiramisu Trifles
Coffee

**Elegant Weeknight
Dinner Menu** (page 160)
serves 4
Seared Duck Breast with
Ginger-Rhubarb Sauce
Garlic-fontina polenta
Steamed baby bok choy

**Mix-and-Match Dinner
Party Menu** (page 361)
serves 6
Warm Olives with Fennel and Orange
Peppered Garlic Confit with Prosciutto
Persimmon-Walnut Oil Salad or Red
Lettuce Salad with Citrus Vinaigrette
Mustard-Crusted Lamb Chops
served with Bay Leaf and Thyme-Scented
Roasted Winter Squash and Garlic or
Triple-Pepper Steamed Halibut served
with Saffron Couscous
Sautéed Cherry Tomatoes with Shallots
Bittersweet Chocolate Sorbet

Classic Thanksgiving Menu (page 373)
serves 12
Roasted Butternut Squash Dip served with
toasted baguette slices or pita chips
Spinach-Pear Salad with
Mustard Vinaigrette
Apple Cider-Brined Turkey with
Savory Herb Gravy
Herbed Bread Stuffing with
Mushrooms and Sausage
Brown Sugar-Glazed Sweet
Potato Wedges
Shredded Brussels Sprouts with
Bacon and Hazelnuts
Cranberry-Pear Chutney
Dinner rolls
Pumpkin Pie with Pecan Pastry Crust
or
Pecan Pie with Spiked Cream

Holiday Dinner Menu (page 455)
serves 8
Celery-Celeriac Soup with
Roquefort Croutons
Horseradish and Mustard-Crusted
Beef Tenderloin
Steamed haricot verts tossed with butter
Dinner Rolls, Five Ways
Mashed potatoes
Upside-Down Cranberry-Ginger Cake
Red wine

Cocktail Party Menu (page 455)
serves 12
Blood Orange Sangría
Blackened Shrimp with
Pomegranate-Orange Salsa
Caramelized Onion, Red Pepper,
and Mushroom Pizzetti
Cheese and crackers
Fresh fruit tray
White Chocolate-Cashew Coffee Biscotti

Open House Menu (page 455)
serves 8
Mulled Cranberry-Guava Toddies
Cheddar with Sautéed Apples
and Brown Bread
Cheese Dip with Crawfish
Chicken Chowder with Chipotle
Chupe de Pollo con Chipotle
Garlic bread
Red Raspberry Velvet Cake

Hot off the Grill

Steak and Potatoes Menu (page 118)
serves 6
Asiago, Potato, and Bacon Gratin
Grilled marinated flank steak
Steamed green beans

Farmers' Market Menu (page 178)
serves 8
Italian Stuffed Summer Vegetables
Field peas with green beans
Grilled flank steak

**Summertime Grilling
Menu** (page 196)
serves 4
Grilled Vegetable Salad with Creamy
Blue Cheese Dressing
Jamaican Jerk Turkey Burgers with
Papaya-Mango Salsa
Baked potato chips
Apricot-Cherry Upside-Down Mini Cakes

Moroccan Grilling Menu (page 217)
serves 8
Tomato Salad with Avocado and
Preserved Lemons
Brochettes of Lamb
Carrots with Paprika and Capers
Couscous with Apple-Ginger Topping
and Orange Sauce
Iced Mint Tea

Vegetarian

Appalachian Menu (page 14)
serves 8
Simple Slaw
Quick Buttermilk Corn Bread
Winter Greens and Potato Casserole
Corn Chow-Chow
Savory Soup Beans
Unfried Apple Pies

Beans and Greens Menu (page 55)
serves 8
Baked Gigantes in Tomato Sauce
Artichoke-kalamata olive salad
Vanilla low-fat ice cream topped with
toasted slivered almonds

Southwestern Veggie Plate Menu
(page 93)
serves 9
Southwestern Succotash Pot Pie
Creamy coleslaw
Vanilla ice cream with fat-free caramel sauce

Sicilian Menu (page 135)
serves 6
Shaved Fennel Salad with
Almonds and Mint
Baked Frittata Ribbons in Tomato Sauce
Bucatini with Eggplant and Roasted Peppers
Ricotta-Honey Mousse with Summer Berries

Tuscan Menu (page 137)
serves 6
Wild Mushroom Bruschetta
Stuffed Onions with Chianti Sauce
Penne in Creamy Basil-Walnut Sauce
Sweet Chocolate Log

Star-Spangled Menu (page 229)
serves 6
Watermelon Agua Fresca
Summer Baked Beans
Green Bean, Chickpea, and
Tomato Salad
Red, White, and Blue Potato Salad
Grilled Summer Squash
Grilled Corn with Creamy
Chipotle Sauce
Santa Rosa Plum Crumble

Meatless Thanksgiving Menu (page 402)
serves 8
Roasted Tomato-Harissa Soup with
Olive Toasts
Phyllo Purses with Roasted Squash,
Peppers, and Artichokes
Glazed Carrots and Cipollini Onions with
Coriander and Orange
Spinach with Chickpeas and Spices or
Fruited Couscous Pilaf
Fall Salad with Buttermilk Dressing
Chile-Lime Pineapple with Cardamom-
Lime Ice Cream

Global Kitchen

Quick Asian Menu (page 27)
serves 4
Sweet Black Pepper Fish
Snow pea and red pepper stir-fry
Steamed white rice

**A Taste of the
Caribbean Menu** (page 39)
serves 6
Pork and Plantains
Cuban bread with tomatoes
Tossed salad
Pineapple sherbet

Irish-Inspired Menu (page 61)
Cabbage and Mixed Greens Salad with
Tangy Herb Vinaigrette
Vegetable-Beef Stew
Brown Soda Bread
Gingered Pear Crisp

Asian Flavors Menu (page 86)
serves 4
Vegetarian Gyoza with Spicy Dipping Sauce
Tofu stir-fry
Hot cooked short-grain rice

Greek/Asian Dinner Menu (page 251)
serves 4
Yogurt-Marinated Beef Kebabs with
Wasabi Aïoli
Greek chickpea salad
Pita bread

Italian Pasta Supper Menu (page 279)
serves 4
Penne Pasta with Roasted Fennel, Cherry
Tomatoes, and Black Olives
Garlic-Parmesan rolls
Garden salad

Asian Menu (page 287)
serves 8
Garlic and Ginger Rice
Five-spice shrimp
Snow peas

**Puerto Rican Block Party
Menu** (page 309)
serves 8
Appetizers
Crab-and-Mango Empanadas
Empanadas de Cangrejo y Mango
Ripe Plantain "Canoes" Stuffed
with Ground Meat
Canoas
Citrus-Herb Shrimp
Camarones con Hierbas y Cítricos
Salad
Green Salad with Culantro
and Cilantro Dressing
*Ensalada Verde con Aderezo
de Cilantro y Recao*
Entrées
Roasted Pork
Pernil Asado
Pork Skewers with Guava Sauce
Pinchos de Cerdo con Salsa de Guayaba
Plantains and Pork Cracklings
with Stewed Chicken
Mofongo Relleno de Pollo Guisado
Sides
Rice with Pigeon Peas
Arroz con Gandules
Rice with Stewed Pink Beans
Arroz con Habichuelas Rosadas Guisadas
Dessert
Coconut Custard
Tembleque

Mix-and-Match Asian Menu (page 385)
serves 6
Hot and Sour Coconut Soup or
Shrimp and Spinach Soup
Singapore Mai Fun or
Pan-Fried Noodles with Scallops or
Pork and Squash Stir-Fry with steamed
white rice
Green Tea Granita
Jasmine tea
Beer

Recipe Title Index

*An alphabetical listing of every recipe title that appeared
in the magazine in 2004. See page 478 for the General Recipe Index.*

African Sweet Potato Stew with Red Beans, 366
All-Purpose Southwestern Corn and Black Bean Salad, 166
Almond Rice Pilaf, 384
Almond-Stuffed Baked Apples with Caramel-Apple Sauce, 299
Amaretto Pears, 104
Amaretto-Scented Pear Parfaits with Gingersnaps, 267
Amish Potpie with Turkey Wings, 391
Antipasto Salad, 399
Apple and Chicken Hash, 332
Apple and Horseradish-Glazed Salmon, 159
Apple Bisque with Chestnuts, 332
Apple Cider-Brined Turkey with Savory Herb Gravy, 374
Apple-Cranberry Cobbler, 332
Apple-Cream Cheese Strudel, 138
Apple Crumb Tart with Maple Ice Milk, 450
Apple-Orange Pie, 326
Apple Pie à la Mode Parfaits, 267
Apple, Rhubarb, and Sour Cherry Passover Cobbler, 91
Apple Spice Cake, 44
Apricot-Cherry Upside-Down Mini Cakes, 197
Apricot-Glazed Roasted Asparagus, 87
Apricot-Lavender Sauce, 275
Arctic Lime Freeze, 128
Arroz con Pollo, 70
Artichoke-Kalamata Olive Salad, 55
Arugula Salad, 103
Arugula Salad with Garlic-Sherry Vinaigrette, 199
Asiago-Artichoke-Turkey Spread, 384
Asiago, Potato, and Bacon Gratin, 118
Asian Chicken Noodle Soup, 294
Asian Chicken over Noodles, 37
Asian Chicken Stock, 287
Asian Marinated Striped Bass, 73
Asian Noodles with Asparagus and Shrimp, 32
Asian Slaw, 385
Asopao, 72
Asparagus and Chicken Carbonara, 212
Asparagus-Fontina Tart, 140
Asparagus-Potato Soup, 244
Asparagus Salad with Mustard-Soy Dressing, 26
Autumn Apple and Spinach Salad, 331

Baby Spinach Salad with Candied Hazelnuts, 133
Bacon and Hash Brown Casserole, 383

Baked Chiles Rellenos, 223
Baked Eggplant with Savory Cheese Stuffing, 54
Baked Figs and Nectarines over Ice Cream, 291
Baked Frittata Ribbons in Tomato Sauce, 136
Baked Gigantes in Tomato Sauce, 55
Baked Hoisin Chicken Buns, 301
Baked Sesame Chicken Noodles, 41
Baked Ziti with Shrimp and Scallops, 43
Balsamic-Brown Sugar Strawberries, 252
Balsamic-Glazed Chicken Sandwiches with Red Onions and Goat Cheese, 399
Balsamic Rosemary Pork, 124
Balsamic Strawberry Topping, 191
Banana-Oatmeal Loaf, 326
Banana-Walnut Napoleons, 133
Barbecue Beans, 166
Barbecue Beef Sandwiches, 38
Barley-Chicken Salad with Fresh Corn and Sweet Onions, 283
Barley Risotto with Fennel and Olives, 264
Barley-Stuffed Cabbage Rolls with Pine Nuts and Currants, 365
Barley with Shiitakes and Spinach, 446
Basmati Chicken Salad, 214
Basmati Rice with Basil and Mint, 299
Bay Leaf and Thyme-Scented Roasted Winter Squash and Garlic, 363
Bayou Catfish Fillets, 126
Beef and Barley-Stuffed Peppers, 208
Beef and Green Chile Soup, 327
Beef and Vegetable Soup (Cocido), 356
Beef Bourguignonne with Egg Noodles, 304
Beef Cooked with Carrots, Onions, and Dried Plums, 115
Beef Daube Provençal, 373
Beef Stew, 7
Beef Tenderloin with Porcini Mushroom Sauce, 325
Beet and Red Onion Salad with Ricotta-Provolone Topping, 179
Belgian Turkey Ragoût, 391
Bell Pepper and Fresh Mozzarella Couscous, 252
Bell Pepper and Tomato Penne with Meatballs, 118
Bell Pepper Chicken with Feta Orzo, 149
Berries and Almond Milk, 161
Berry French Toast, 102
Bierocks, 33
Biscuits and Vegetarian Sausage Gravy, 328
Bistro Chicken and Peppers, 207

Bitter Greens Salad with Sourdough Croutons and Warm Tomato Vinaigrette, 303
Bittersweet Chocolate Sorbet, 364
Black Bean Chicken, 38
Black Bean Quesadillas with Corn Salsa, 78
Black Bean Salad with Bell Peppers and Onions, 197
Black Bean Soup, 188
Black Bean Spread with Lime and Cilantro, 408
Blackberry-Peach Smoothie with Walnuts, 246
Blackberry-Zinfandel Quail, 161
Blackened Shrimp with Pomegranate-Orange Salsa, 435
Black Forest Cheesecake Parfaits, 268
Black Forest Icebox Cookies, 449
Blood Orange Sangría, 434
Bloody Mary, 53
BLT Bread Salad, 243
Blueberry-Blackberry Shortcakes, 237
Blueberry Blender, 196
Blueberry Cheesecake, 239
Blueberry Cinnamon-Burst Muffins, 239
Blueberry Gingerbread Cake, 238
Blueberry-Pumpkin Pound Cake, 238
Braised Baby Artichokes and New Potatoes, 56
Braised Beef with Sun-Dried Tomatoes, 318
Braised Kale with Bacon and Cider, 19
Braised Pork Shoulder in Hoisin-Wine Sauce with Dried Plums, 335
Braised Seafood and Vegetable Noodles, 220
Brandied Caramel-Apple Crumble, 412
Breaded Pork Chops, 369
Breakfast Polenta with Warm Berry Compote, 19
Broccoli, Orange, and Watercress Salad, 7
Broccoli with Balsamic-Butter Sauce, 289
Brochettes of Lamb, 217
Brown Soda Bread, 61
Brown Sugar-Glazed Sweet Potato Wedges, 376
Brunch Parfaits, 190
Brunswick Stew with Smoked Paprika, 367
Bruschetta with Warm Tomatoes, 276
Bucatini with Eggplant and Roasted Peppers, 136
Buttered Spaetzle, 82
Butterflied Shrimp and Vegetable Stir-Fry, 68
Buttermilk-Brined Pork Chops, 368
Butternut Squash and Leek Gratins, 446

Butternut Squash and Parmesan Bread Pudding, 340
Butternut Squash and Red Pepper, 351
Butternut Squash-White Bean Soup, 353

Cabbage and Mixed Greens Salad with Tangy Herb Vinaigrette, 61
Cactus Salad, 129
Café Brûlot, 52
Café con Leche Cream Pie, 158
Cajun Garlic Pork Roast, 127
Cajun Sausage and Rice Skillet, 32
Cajun Shrimp and Catfish, 40
Cajun-Spiced Chicken Fettuccine, 216
Calabaza and Poblano Stew, 354
Caldo de Bolas, 86
Camarones Fritoes with Mexican Cocktail Sauce, 156
Campanelle with Salsa Arrabbiata, 419
Candied Hazelnut Brittle, 452
Candy Corn Popcorn Balls, 360
Cannellini Stew with Sausage and Kale and Cheese Toasts, 349
Caramelized Condensed Milk, 169
Caramelized Onion Dip, 77
Caramelized Onion, Red Pepper, and Mushroom Pizzetti, 434
Cardamom-Date Snack Cake, 394
Carrot Coins with Maple-Balsamic Browned Butter, 444
Carrot-Parsnip Soup with Parsnip Chips, 436
Carrots with Paprika and Capers, 218
Cashew Chicken Salad Sandwiches, 122
Cashew Chicken Salad with Mandarin Oranges, 284
Celery-Celeriac Soup with Roquefort Croutons, 437
Chamomile-Fruit Smoothie, 195
Chardonnay-Braised Radishes, 108
Charleston Pudding, 333
Cheddar with Sautéed Apples and Brown Bread, 433
Cheese Dip with Crawfish, 435
Cherries in Spiced Wine Syrup with Pound Cake Croutons, 264
Cherries in Zinfandel Syrup, 317
Cherry-Apricot Turnovers, 142
Cherry-Hazelnut Oatmeal, 132
Chianti-Stained Risotto with Pears and Blue Cheese, 446
Chicken and Barley Stew, 30
Chicken and Blue Cheese Slaw, 212
Chicken and Couscous Salad, 151
Chicken and Rosemary Dumplings, 82
Chicken and Shrimp Paella, 71
Chicken and Soba Noodle Soup, 120
Chicken and Wild Rice Soup, 316
Chicken Biriyani, 72
Chicken Braised in Walnut Sauce, 16
Chicken Braised with Leeks and Figs, 291
Chicken Breasts Stuffed with Goat Cheese and Sun-Dried Tomatoes, 67
Chicken Breasts Stuffed with Spinach and Ricotta, 358

Chicken Breasts with Tarragon-Caper Sauce, 247
Chicken Cacciatore, 357
Chicken Chowder with Chipotle (Chupe de Pollo con Chipotle), 437
Chicken, Date, and Apricot Tagine, 65
Chicken Fried Rice with Bok Choy, 71
Chicken-Green Chile Enchilada Casserole, 328
Chicken Green Chili with White Beans, 355
Chicken Meatball Soup with Pasta, 358
Chicken, Mushroom, and Cheese Quesadillas, 247
Chicken Philly Sandwiches, 187
Chicken Piccata, 348
Chicken, Provolone, and Mushroom Sandwiches, 408
Chicken, Red Potato, and Green Bean Salad, 152
Chicken Salad with Nectarines in Mint Vinaigrette, 152
Chicken Sandwich with Arugula and Sun-Dried Tomato Vinaigrette, 79
Chicken Saté Wraps, 283
Chicken Scaloppine over Broccoli Rabe, 293
Chicken Tenders with Apricots and Sautéed Spinach, 80
Chicken Thighs with Olives and Red Peppers, 338
Chicken Vegetable Stew, 357
Chicken with Black Bean Sauce, 414
Chicken with Cherry Tomato and Olive Topping, 163
Chicken with Chunky Pepper Sauce, 163
Chicken with Citrus, 113
Chicken with Cranberry Barbecue Sauce, 383
Chicken with Cremini Mushrooms and Asparagus, 203
Chicken with Ginger and Green Onion-Salt Dip, 287
Chicken with Green Olives, 25
Chicken with Morels (Pollo con Jugo de Morillas), 74
Chicken with Port Wine Sauce, 205
Chicken with Sherry Vinegar Sauce, 422
Chickpeas with Spinach, 130
Chile-Glazed Risotto, 201
Chile-Lime Pineapple with Cardamom-Lime Ice Cream, 405
Chili-Glazed Tofu over Asparagus and Rice, 349
Chilled Corn Bisque with Basil, Avocado, and Crab, 156
Chipotle-Bacon Corn Bread, 251
Chipotle Macaroni and Cheese, 248
Chipotle Pork and Avocado Wrap, 315
Chipotle Pork Tenderloin with Corn Salsa, 205
Chipotle Pulled-Pork Barbecue Sandwiches, 186
Chipotle Shrimp Cups, 215
Chive Green Beans, 48
Chochoyones in Black Bean Soup, 85

Chocolate and Peanut Butter Cookies, 88
Chocolate-Cherry Chunk Meringues, 170
Chocolate Chip Dutch Baby, 19
Chocolate Chip Pumpkin Bread, 425
Chocolate Chip Zucchini Bread, 224
Chocolate-Mint Sorbet, 371
Chocolate Pudding Cake, 19
Chocolate Soufflés with Pistachios, 48
Chopstick Noodle Salad, 262
Christmas Sugar Wafers with Vanilla Icing, 453
Chunky Vegetable Soup with Toasted Cheese Croutons, 202
Cider-Glazed Chicken with Dried Cranberries, 203
Cider-Mustard Slaw, 323
Cider-Roasted Chicken, 347
Cider-Roasted Pork Loin, 346
Citrus-Herb Shrimp (Camarones con Hierbas y Cítricos), 310
Citrus Salad with Shrimp and Watercress, 438
Citrus Salmon with Garlicky Greens, 167
Citrus-Spiked Jícama and Carrot Slaw, 242
Clams with Cherry Tomatoes (Almejas con Tomates), 75
Classic Mojito, 312
Classic Steak House Rubbed Filet Mignon, 241
Coconut-Almond Couscous, 320
Coconut Cream Pie Parfaits, 268
Coconut Curried Chicken, 322
Coconut Curry Shrimp Cakes with Papaya-Lime Sauce, 158
Coconut Custard (Tembleque), 312
Coconut French Toast with Grilled Pineapple and Tropical Salsa, 195
Coconut Frushi, 195
Coconut Meringues, 171
Coffee and Molasses-Brined Pork Chops, 176
Coffee-Chocolate Torte, 450
Cold Cucumber Soup, 318
Cool and Crunchy Crab Dip, 409
Cool Melon Sipper, 246
Corn and Chipotle Bread Pudding, 340
Corn and Sun-Dried Tomato Quesadilla with Smoked Mozzarella, 254
Corn and Two-Bean Burgers with Chipotle Ketchup, 324
Corn Bread with Fresh Corn, 222
Corn Chow-Chow, 15
Cornflake-Crusted Halibut with Chile-Cilantro Aïoli, 72
Corn Fritter Casserole, 296
Cornmeal Scones, 353
Cornmeal Shortcakes with Tomato-Ginger Jam, 258
Corn Tortillas, 155
Country Rye Loaves, 347
Couscous-Chickpea Salad with Ginger-Lime Dressing, 194
Couscous Salad with Chicken and Chopped Vegetables, 213
Couscous with Apple-Ginger Topping and Orange Sauce, 218

Crab-and-Mango Empanadas (Empanadas de Cangrejo y Mango), 309
Crab and Scallop Sui Mei, 302
Crab Cakes with Rémoulade, 29
Crab Quesadillas, 121
Crab-Stuffed Lobster with Citrus Vinaigrette, 295
Cranberry and Apple Crumble, 9
Cranberry-Apple Crumble, 412
Cranberry Jezebel Sauce with Sautéed Ham, 384
Cranberry-Pear Chutney, 376
Cranberry-Pear Crumb Pie, 451
Cranberry Walnut Tabbouleh, 132
Cran-Grape Syrup, 16
Crawfish and Rice Casserole, 215
Cream Cheese Roll-ups, 213
Creamed Cauliflower with Herbed Crumb Topping, 447
Creamy Chicken and Mushroom Crêpes, 289
Creamy Coleslaw, 93
Creamy Dill Variation, 107
Creamy Gruyère and Shrimp Pasta, 42
Creamy Mashed Potatoes, 8
Creamy Mushroom Spread, 408
Creamy Parmesan Orzo, 48
Creamy Pasta with Chicken and Mushrooms, 206
Creamy Shrimp and Corn Bowl, 163
Creamy Squash and Apple Soup, 407
Crisp and Spicy Snack Mix, 7
Crisp Oven Potatoes, 12
Cuban Bread with Tomatoes, 39
Cuban Chicken Pizza, 421
Cumin Curried Hummus, 409
Cumin-Lime Vinaigrette, 143
Curried Chicken Penne with Fresh Mango Chutney, 188
Curried Chicken Salad, 253
Curried Couscous with Broccoli and Feta, 30
Curried Couscous with Pine Nuts and Currants, 193
Curried Lamb Chops with Minted Chutney, 206
Curried Noodles, 279
Curried Tofu, 294
Curry Ginger Butternut Squash Soup, 298
Curry Turkey Salad, 382

Date and Apricot Chutney, 395
Date-Orange Breakfast Spread, 395
Deconstructed Flan, 74
Dijon Vinaigrette, 142
Dilled Goat Cheese Sandwiches with Roasted Plum Tomatoes, 209
Dinner Rolls, Five Ways, 439
Double Vanilla Meringues, 172
Dry-Rub Chicken with Honey Barbecue Sauce, 126
Duck Breasts with Kumquat Chutney, 443
Duck Breast with Cherry-Pepper Sauce, 333
Dulce de Leche-Filled Cookies, 169

Easy Gnocchi with Thick Marinara Sauce, 244
Easy Guacamole with Chips, 215
Easy Ravioli Bake, 43
Ecuadoran Shrimp Seviche, 200
Edamame and Bean Salad with Shrimp and Fresh Salsa, 254
Edamame, Quinoa, and Shiitake Mushroom Salad, 283
Eggnog Cheese Pie with Bourbon Cream, 425
Eggplant and Tomato Gratin, 275
Eggplant Parmesan Pizza, 351
Eggplant Stew over Couscous, 210
Eggplant, Tomato, and Smoked Mozzarella Tart, 116
Eggs Hussarde, 53
Empanada Dough (Masa de Empanadas), 309
English Muffin Hot Browns, 383
Ensalada de Repollo (Cabbage Salad), 162
Escarole and Fennel Salad with Pears and Gruyère, 437
Escarole Soup with Ginger and Cilantro, 205

Fall Green Salad, 345
Fall Salad with Buttermilk Dressing, 404
Farmers' Market Quesadillas, 273
Farm Hand Potatoes (Papas de Caserio), 76
Fennel-Brined Pork Chops, 174
Fennel, Orange, and Parmigiano Salad, 97
Feta and Lemon-Stuffed Lamb with Potato-Parsnip Mash, 257
Feta-Chicken Pasta, 262
Feta-Chile Spread, 55
Feta-Spinach Tarts, 141
Fettuccine with Shrimp and Portobellos, 103
Field Greens with Eggs and Enoki Mushrooms, 102
Field Greens with Mississippi Caviar, 127
Field Peas with Green Beans, 178
Fiery Turkey Fillets with Mango Salsa, 274
Fig and Chile-Glazed Pork Tenderloin, 159
Fig and Mascarpone Focaccia, 120
Fig and Stilton-Stuffed Turkey Breast with Port Sauce, 440
Filet Mignon with Mushroom-Wine Sauce, 413
Filet Mignon with Red Currant-Green Peppercorn Sauce, 160
Fire-Grilled Pork Chops, 114
Fish Chowder, 260
Five-Spice Chicken Breasts with Hoisin Glaze, 175
Five-Spice Shrimp, 287
Flank Steak with Five-Spice Rub and Chile Relish, 297
Flatbread with Oven-Dried Figs, Caramelized Onions, and Blue Cheese, 291
Fresh Cherry Cobbler, 180

Fresh Corn Frittata with Smoked Mozzarella, 275
Fresh Corn Risotto with Seared Shrimp and Salsa Verde, 227
Fresh Fig Salad with Crème Fraîche, Mint, and Prosciutto, 290
Fresh Spring Rolls with Dipping Sauce, 87
Fresh Strawberry Jam, 191
Fresh Tomato Lasagna, 105
Fresh Tuna Stew (Marmitako), 76
Frittata with Mushrooms, Linguine, and Basil, 209
Frozen Banana Latte, 245
Frozen Strawberry Daiquiris, 190
Fruited Basmati Pilaf with Pistachios, 444
Fruited Couscous Pilaf, 404
Fruit Salad with Honey-Yogurt Sauce, 388
Funky Monkey Parfaits, 267

Galloping Horses, 302
Garbanzo and Greens Stew, 356
Garden Salad with Citrus Vinaigrette, 144
Garlic and Bell Pepper Farfalle, 189
Garlic and Ginger Rice (Com Gung Tuong), 287
Garlic and Sun-Dried Tomato Hummus, 13
Garlic-Fontina Polenta, 160
Garlicky Pasta with Fresh Tomatoes and Basil, 104
Garlic-Parmesan Rolls, 279
Garlic-Parmesan Toasts, 152
Garlic-Rosemary Lamb Pita, 29
Garlic-Scented Turnip Greens, 369
Garlic Smashed Potatoes, 73
Gazpacho Panzanella, 211
Gazpacho Salad with Tomato Vinaigrette, 143
Gemelli Pasta with Clams, Scallops, and Shrimp, 281
Ginger Beef, 31
Ginger-Curry Pork and Rice, 207
Gingered Pear Crisp, 62, 410
Ginger-Hazelnut Pumpkin Tart, 448
Ginger-Lemon Tonic, 245
Ginger Shortbread, 454
Glazed Carrots and Cipollini Onions with Coriander and Orange, 403
Glazed Peaches in Phyllo Baskets with Ricotta Cream, 256
Goat Cheese, Artichoke, and Smoked Ham Strata, 177
Golden Gazpacho, 14
Golden Rutabagas and Shallots, 445
Golden Summer Soup, 227
Gomiti with Broccoli Rabe, Chickpeas, and Prosciutto, 419
Greek Black-Eyed Peas and Greens, 56
Greek Chickpea Salad, 251
Greek Farmers' Salad, 240
Greek Greens and Sweet Onion Pie, 95
Greek Pasta Salad, 105
Greek Pasta with Seared Tuna, 282
Greek-Style Bread Pudding, 340
Green and White Salad with Blue Cheese Dressing, 143

Green Bean, Chickpea, and Tomato Salad, 229

Green Bean, Corn, and Roasted Poblano Chile Salad, 144

Green Beans Amandine, 198

Green Chile Sopes with Chipotle Mayonnaise, Shrimp, and Pineapple Slaw, 157

Green Eggs and Ham, 194

Green Enchiladas with Crab, 157

Green Papaya Salad (Goi Du Du), 287

Green Rice, 352

Green Rice with Roasted Chiles and Leeks, 276

Green Salad with Avocado and Tomatoes, 12

Green Salad with Culantro and Cilantro Dressing (Ensalada Verde con Aderezo de Cilantro y Recao), 310

Green Salad with Roasted Poblanos and Cumin-Lime Dressing, 352

Green Tea Granita, 387

Grillades and Gravy over Grits, 52

Grilled Asparagus with Lemon, 241

Grilled Beef Salad with Lemongrass Dressing, 221

Grilled Chicken and Roasted Red Pepper Sandwiches with Fontina Cheese, 185

Grilled Chicken Breasts with Yellow Tomato Curry Sauce and Thai Ratatouille, 228

Grilled Chicken Salad with Feta and Cucumbers, 96

Grilled Chicken with Pinot-Plum Sauce, 258

Grilled Cornish Hens with Apricot-Mustard Glaze, 160

Grilled Corn with Creamy Chipotle Sauce, 230

Grilled Eggplant with Caramelized Onion and Fennel, 295

Grilled Goat Cheese Sandwiches with Fig and Honey, 186

Grilled Grouper with Lime and Mexican Confetti Rice, 421

Grilled Ham and Cheese with Tomato, 187

Grilled Lamb Chops, 170

Grilled Lemon-Bay Shrimp, 263

Grilled Marinated Flank Steak, 118

Grilled Pastrami-Style Salmon, 242

Grilled Plum and Prosciutto-Stuffed Pork Chops, 368

Grilled Pork Chops with Fiery Salsa, 248

Grilled Pork Chops with Rhubarb Chutney, 154

Grilled Pork Chops with Tomatillo, Corn, and Avocado Salsa, 243

Grilled Portobello-Goat Cheese Pitas, 294

Grilled Red Potatoes with Mint, 240

Grilled Soy-Glazed Eggplant, 288

Grilled-Steak Soft Tacos, 149

Grilled Summer Squash, 230

Grilled Tuna with Avocado Salsa, 232

Grilled Vegetable and Mozzarella Sandwiches, 187

Grilled Vegetable Salad with Creamy Blue Cheese Dressing, 196

Grits Casserole with Mushrooms, Prosciutto, and Provolone, 388

Grouper with Puttanesca Sauce, 231

Guacamole and Turkey Sandwiches, 123

Ham and Asparagus Frittata, 124

Ham and Brie Sandwich, 134

Ham and Cheese Hash Browns, 122

Ham and Potato Omelet, 101

Hamburger, Cheddar, and Macaroni Toss, 279

Hanoi Beef and Rice Noodle Soup (Pho Bo), 286

Hearty Fresh Tomato Salsa, 261

Hearty Pancakes, 406

Hearty Sour Rye Bread, 36

Hearty Wheat Bread, 8

Herbed Bread Stuffing with Mushrooms and Sausage, 375

Herbed Carrots, 151

Herbed Cracker Bread, 263

Herbed Green Tea, 198

Herbed Parmesan Soufflé, 445

Herbes de Provence-Crusted Lamb Chops, 240

Hoisin Chicken and Broccoli Stir-Fry, 32

Hoisin Grilled Sirloin, 427

Holiday Brunch Tonic, 387

Homemade Beet Horseradish, 89

Homemade Turkey Stock, 393

Hominy Sauté, 368

Honey and Thyme-Brined Turkey Breast, 173

Honey-Pomegranate Roasted Chicken Thighs, 424

Hoppin' John, 32

Horseradish and Caramelized Onion Pork Sandwiches, 315

Horseradish and Mustard-Crusted Beef Tenderloin, 442

Hot-and-Sour Coconut Soup, 385

Hot Chicken and Chips Retro, 397

Huevos Rancheros Tostados, 204

Huevos Rancheros with Queso Fresco, 11

Hummus-Stuffed Pitas with Vegetables, 150

Iced Mint Tea, 218

Indian Chickpeas over Garlic Spinach, 210

Indian-Spiced Roast Salmon, 203

Individual Anise-Orange Flans, 371

Individual Goat Cheese and Date Tortas, 395

Individual Pizzas with Broccoli, Cheese, and Meat Sauce, 150

Individual Tiramisu Trifles, 304

Insalata Pizzas, 163

Irish Oatmeal Bread, 16

Island Rice, 125

Italian Garbanzo Salad, 129

Italian Sausage and Fennel Lasagna, 330

Italian Sausage Puttanesca, 44

Italian Sausage Soup, 232

Italian Stuffed Summer Vegetables, 178

Italian Turkey Sausage with Three Peppers, 389

Jack Quesadillas with Cranberry Salsa, 382

Jamaican Jerk Turkey Burgers with Papaya-Mango Salsa, 196

Jambalaya, 442

Jerk-Style Chicken, 125

Joe's Special, 12

Jook (Rice Porridge), 27

Kabocha Squash Soup, 402

Kale with Garlic and Hot Red Pepper, 178

Key Lime Cheesecake, 101

Key Lime Curd, 101

Key Lime Pie Ice Cream, 243

Key Lime Pie Parfaits, 268

Korean Beef Strip Steak, 201

Kumquats in Spiced Syrup with Cloves, Cinnamon, and Star Anise, 454

Kung Pao Tofu Rice Salad, 254

Lamb Chops with Herbed Yogurt over Couscous, 350

Lamb Osso Buco over Parmesan Polenta, 303

Lamb Stew (Txilindron de Cordero), 75

Lasagna Rolls with Roasted Red Pepper Sauce, 104

Lattice-Topped Rhubarb Pie, 153

Leg of Lamb with Herbs and Mustard, 115

Lemon and Oregano-Rubbed Chicken Paillards, 241

Lemon-Basil Risotto with Tomato Topping, 164

Lemon-Buttermilk Panna Cotta with Blueberry Sauce, 297

Lemon Chicken and Rice with Artichokes, 13

Lemon Garbanzo Salad with Feta, 253

Lemongrass Shrimp over Rice Vermicelli and Vegetables (Bun Tom Nuong Xa), 285

Lemon Noodles with Curry Leaves and Cashews, 282

Lemon Pound Cake with Mixed Berries, 125

Lemon-Scented Coconut Macaroon Bars, 449

Lemon Southwest Rice, 274

Lemon Tarragon-Brined Whole Chicken, 173

Lemony Asparagus-Mushroom Stir-Fry, 50

Lemony Fruit Dip, 45

Lemony Lentils with Black Olives, 53

Lentil and Fennel Salad, 191

Lentil Couscous with Spinach, 244

Lentil Dal Wraps, 284

Lentil Spread, 351

Lime-Cilantro Pork Tacos, 197

Linguine Carbonara, 203

Linguine with Clam Sauce, 318

Linguine with White Clam and Broccoli Sauce, 419

Lobster Newburg, 260

Louisiana Crab Cakes with Creole Tartar
Sauce, 248
Louisiana Goulash, 46
Low-Fat Strawberry-Cinnamon
Muffins, 45

Macadamia and Ginger Cookies, 256
Macadamia Nut-Pesto Fettuccine, 123
Mac and Cheese Florentine, 208
Mahimahi Fish Tacos, 134
Maine Lobster and Pepper Salad with
Asian Herbs, 225
Mango-Cucumber Salad, 261
Mango Mahi Seviche, 51
Mango Martini, 312
Maple and Calvados-Glazed Pork Crown
Roast with Apple-Chestnut
Purée, 443
Maple Ice Milk, 450
Maple-Orange Chicken, 205
Marble Cheesecake Squares, 370
Marinara Magnifica, 261
Marinated Mushrooms, 317
Marinated Salmon with Mango-Kiwi
Relish, 79
Mashed Yukon Gold Potatoes, 318
Matzo Ball Soup, 85
Matzo Buttercrunch, 89
Matzo, Mushroom, and Onion Kugel, 89
Meatball Soup (Sopa de Albóndigas), 355
Mediterranean Shrimp and Pasta, 88
Mediterranean-Style Poached Eggs, 103
Mediterranean Vegetable Soup, 123
Mediterranean Vegetable Stew over Soft
Polenta, 79
Melon Balls with Port, 265
Melon Chicken Salad, 219
Meringue and Streusel-Topped Sweet
Potatoes, 444
Mexican Chocolate Cake, 274
Mexican Confetti Rice, 421
Mexican Corn and Bean Soup, 31
Mexican Pizza, 10
Middle Eastern Slow-Cooked Stew with
Lamb, Chickpeas, and Figs, 423
Miller's Cinnamon-Raisin Bread, 35
Millet Muffins with Honey-Pecan
Butter, 99
Minestrone with Chickpeas, 325
Mini Cranberry Panettones, 452
Miso Soup, 401
Mixed Bean Salad with Sun-Dried
Tomatoes, 320
Mixed Greens Salad with Goat Cheese
Croutons, 74
Mixed Pepper Pizza with Basil and Pine
Nuts, 10
Mocha Mudslides, 436
Moist 'n' Dark Nut Bread, 47
Mojo Bass, 426
Mole-Style Pork Chops, 427
Moroccan Chicken and Lentils, 208
Moroccan Chicken with Almond
Couscous, 50
Moroccan-Spiced Bulgur and Chickpea
Salad, 283

Moroccan Summer Vegetable and Sausage
Stew, 167
Muffuletta, 159
Mulled Cranberry-Apple Cider, 8
Mulled Cranberry-Guava Toddies, 434
Mushroom and Bell Pepper Omelet with
Fontina, 49
Mushroom and Parmigiano
Bruschetta, 106
Mushroom and Turkey Casserole, 382
Mushroom and Yellow Pepper
Lasagna, 280
Mushroom Lasagna with Creamy
Béchamel, 93
Mushroom Pasta Bake, 42
Mushroom-Prosciutto Pizza, 199
Mushroom, Roasted Red Pepper, and Goat
Cheese Bread Pudding, 339
Mussel Salad, 170
Mussels with Tomato-Wine Broth, 168
Mustard-Crusted Lamb Chops, 363

Napa Cabbage and Snow Pea Slaw, 143
New England-Style Pickled Beef, 174
New Hampshire Maple-Mustard Salad
Dressing, 398
Normandy Seafood Stew, 114
Nutty Pasta Toss with Shrimp, 207

Oatmeal-Walnut Cookies, 9
Old-Fashioned Oatmeal, 161
Olive and Sun-Dried Tomato Sauce over
Chicken, 320
Olive-Tomato Grilled Cheese
Sandwiches, 204
Omelet with Summer Vegetables, 231
Onion, Date, and Brie Crostini, 396
Onion Soup Gratinée, 436
Orange-Brined Pork Loin, 175
Orange Cardamom Cake, 423
Orange Crisp with Coconut Topping, 411
Orange-Pecan French Toast
Casserole, 216
Orange-Pecan Tea Bread, 119
Orange, Pineapple, and Coconut
Ambrosia, 11
Orange Rolls, 372
Orecchiette with Tomatoes, Fresh
Mozzarella, and Basil, 192
Orzo-Bell Pepper Salad, 192
Orzo with Peas, 348
Oven-Braised Cornish Hens with Cider
Vinegar and Warm Vegetable
Sauce, 100
Oven-Braised Pork Roast with Apples, 324
Oven-Dried Figs, 290
Oven Fries, 72
Oven Fries with Crisp Sage Leaves, 180
Overnight Apple Butter, 331

Pacific Rim Pork Sandwiches with Hoisin
Slaw, 400
Pain Perdu, 52
Pan-Fried Bass, 201
Pan-Fried Catfish with Cajun Tartar
Sauce, 323

Pan-Fried Noodles with Scallops, 386
Pan-Fried Tofu with Spicy Lemongrass
Sauce (Tofu Nuong Xa), 286
Pan-Grilled Pork Tenderloin with
Pomegranate Molasses, 337
Pan-Seared Cod with Basil Sauce, 73
Pan-Seared Oatmeal with Warm Fruit
Compote and Cider Syrup, 194
Pan-Seared Pork Chops with Molasses-
Plum Sauce, 119
Pan-Seared Scallops with Tomatoes and
Pesto, 415
Papaya Lime Soup, 162
Pappardelle with Roasted Winter Squash,
Arugula, and Pine Nuts, 441
Parmesan Chicken and Rice, 198
Parmesan-Corn Bread Muffins, 189
Parmesan-Herb Baked Flounder, 31
Passover Baklava Cake, 90
Passover Chopped Layered Salad, 90
Passover Pecan Bars, 91
Pasta Primavera, 91
Pasta Salad with Chicken, 20
Pasta with Anchovies and Walnuts, 27
Pasta with Asparagus, Lemon, and
Prosciutto, 122
Pasta with Beet Greens and Raisins, 415
Pasta with Mushrooms and Radicchio, 210
Pasta with Roasted Shiitakes and Tomato
Purée, 280
Pasta with Sun-Dried Tomato Pesto and
Feta Cheese, 349
Pastel de Choclo, 168
Peach and Raspberry Pavlova Parfaits, 267
Peaches Chilled in Red Wine, 180
Peanut Butter-Chocolate Meringue
Sandwiches, 172
Peanut Chicken Soba Salad, 132
Peanut-Crusted Snapper, 413
Pear-Berry Crisp with Lavender
Topping, 410
Pear Crumble with Dried Tart Cherries and
Almond Streusel, 412
Pear, Pecorino, and Prosciutto Panini, 186
Pebre, 169
Pecan Bar Cookies, 20
Pecan Pie with Spiked Cream, 381
Penne in Creamy Basil-Walnut Sauce, 138
Penne Pasta with Butter and Parmesan
Cheese, 369
Penne Pasta with Roasted Fennel, Cherry
Tomatoes, and Olives, 279
Pennette with Asparagus and Pine
Nuts, 415
Penne with Mushroom Sauce, 277
Peppercorn and Mustard-Crusted Beef
Tenderloin, 362
Peppercorn-Crusted Filet Mignon with
Port Jus, 48
Peppered Garlic Confit with
Prosciutto, 361
Pepper-Garlic Spice Rub, 176
Peppermint Brownie à la Mode, 448
Peppernut Tea Bread, 438
Pepperoni, Provolone, and Pesto
Stromboli, 328

Peppery Baked Onions with Sage and Gruyère, 445
Peppery Cheese Breadsticks, 152
Peppery Chicken Pasta Salad, 214
Persimmon-Walnut Oil Salad, 362
Phyllo Éclairs, 141
Phyllo Purses with Roasted Squash, Peppers, and Artichokes, 403
Picadillo Soft Tacos, 202
Pickled Hot Peppers, 179
Pierogi Dough, 83
Pilaf with Chicken, Spinach, and Walnuts, 70
Pimm's Cup, 264
Pineapple-Coconut-Banana Upside-Down Cake, 20
Pineapple-Rum Granita, 370
Pineapple Seviche Mixto, 199
Pinto Bean Chili with Corn and Winter Squash, 366
Pistachio Granola, 388
Pistachio Rice, 132
Pita Crisps, 105, 151
Pizza Dough, 10
Pizza Frittata, 150
Pizza with Escarole, Roasted Peppers, and Olives, 9
Pizzeria Bianco Watermelon, Fennel, and Parsley Salad, 228
Plantains and Pork Cracklings with Stewed Chicken (Mofongo Relleno de Pollo Guisado), 311
Polenta with Smoky Mushroom Ragoût, 92
Popovers, 92
Pork and Chestnuts, 40
Pork and Grilled Stone Fruit Couscous Salad, 314
Pork and Grilled Vegetable Salad, 314
Pork and Peanut Noodle Salad, 315
Pork and Plantains, 39
Pork and Squash Stir-Fry, 386
Pork Chops with Country Gravy and Mashed Potatoes, 31
Pork Chops with Tomato Chutney, 77
Pork Fattoush, 323
Pork Loin with Dried-Plum Stuffing, 17
Pork Marsala, 414
Pork Medallions with Garlic-Ginger-Pomegranate Sauce, 327
Pork Medallions with Port Wine-Dried Cherry Pan Sauce, 64
Pork Posole, 354
Pork Skewers with Guava Sauce (Pinchos de Cerdo con Salsa de Guayaba), 311
Pork Stew with Pearl Onions, Green Olives, and Figs, 292
Pork Stroganoff, 399
Pork Tabbouleh, 314
Pork Tenderloin in Phyllo, 139
Pork Tenderloin with Olive-Mustard Tapenade, 204
Pork Tenderloin with Plum Sauce, 222
Pork Tenderloin with Xec, 28
Pork with Cranberry-Apple Salsa, 206

Portobello Mushrooms with Mediterranean Stuffing, 407
Posole, 76
Potato and Bell Pepper Hash, 256
Potato and Cabbage Mash (Patatas y Berzas), 76
Potato and Summer Vegetable Stovetop Casserole, 277
Potatoes with Spicy Cheese Sauce, 169
Potato Gnocchi with Bolognese, 84
Potato Latkes, 424
Potato, Leek, and Ham Gratin, 398
Potato Pierogi, 83
Prairie Fields Wheat and Soy Bread, 35
Pressed Cubano with Bacon, 185
Prosciutto and Gruyère Strombolis, 288
Prosciutto and Picholine Pasta Salad, 282
Prussian Leaf-Wrapped Breadsticks, 34
Puerto Rican Sangría, 313
Pumpkin-Orange Cake, 348
Pumpkin Pie with Pecan Pastry Crust, 381

Quick Buttermilk Corn Bread, 14
Quick Gravy, 383
Quick Preserved Lemons, 217

Rachel's Tropical Fruit Salsa, 129
Radish Raita, 107
Radish Slaw with New York Deli Dressing, 107
Radish Vichyssoise, 108
Rainbow Seviche, 200
Raspberry-Almond Muffins, 99
Ratatouille Pizza with Chicken, 211
Red Bell Pepper Frittata, 11
Red Cabbage and Apple Slaw, 241
Red Cabbage and Spinach Salad with Balsamic Vinaigrette, 273
Red Lettuce Salad with Citrus Vinaigrette, 363
Red Pepper-Cheese Dip, 345
Red Pepper-Walnut Dip, 409
Red Raspberry Velvet Cake, 447
Red Snapper over Sautéed Spinach and Tomatoes, 427
Red, White, and Blue Potato Salad, 230
Red Wine-Marinated Steak Sandwiches, 400
Refrigerator Fig Preserves, 290
Rhubarb, Pear, and Apple Compote, 154
Rhubarb Pudding Cake, 154
Rhubarb Sorbet, 154
Rhubarb-Strawberry Crumble, 155
Rice Noodles, 73, 422
Rice Noodles with Sesame-Ginger Flank Steak, 198
Rice Pudding with Port and Dried Plum Sauce, 371
Rice with Pigeon Peas (Arroz con Gandules), 311
Rice with Stewed Pink Beans (Arroz con Habichuelas Rosadas Guisadas), 312
Rich Mushroom Soup, 346
Ricotta-Honey Mousse with Summer Berries, 136
Ripe Plantain "Canoes" Stuffed with Ground Meat (Canoas), 309

Risotto with Butternut Squash, Pancetta, and Jack Cheese, 337
Roast Chicken Chimichangas, 122
Roasted Beet Salad with Raspberry Vinaigrette, 144
Roasted Butternut Squash, 368
Roasted Butternut Squash and Bacon Pasta, 41
Roasted Butternut Squash Dip, 374
Roasted Butternut Squash, Rosemary, and Garlic Lasagna, 416
Roasted Chicken and Bow Tie Pasta Salad, 51
Roasted Chicken and Goat Cheese Roll-Ups, 427
Roasted Chicken-Artichoke Calzones, 252
Roasted Chicken with Asiago Polenta and Truffled Mushrooms, 440
Roasted Fig and Arugula Salad, 263
Roasted Garlic and Corn Soufflé, 102
Roasted Garlic Vinaigrette, 142
Roasted Herbed Potatoes, 400
Roasted Loin of Pork with Apricot-Rum Glaze, 100
Roasted Pork (Pernil Asado), 310
Roasted Red Pepper on Mini-Bagel Sandwiches, 326
Roasted Red Pepper Spread Sandwiches, 193
Roasted Salmon and Leeks in Phyllo Packets, 140
Roasted Sunchokes and Fennel, 359
Roasted Tomato-Harissa Soup with Olive Toasts, 402
Roasted Vanilla-Scented Apples, 11
Roast Pork Porchetta-Style, 179
Roast Pork Sandwiches au Jus with Rosemary, 261
Roast Pork with Apples, Cabbage, and Turnips, 331
Roast Turkey with Sausage Gravy, 394
Romaine Lettuce with Red Pepper and Olives, 144
Romaine Salad with Avocado-Lime Vinaigrette, 134
Romaine, Strawberry, and Orange Salad, 289
Rosemary and Pepper-Crusted Pork Tenderloin, 106
Rosemary Fried Scallops with Tomato-Caper Salad, 427
Rosemary-Tomato Pinwheels, 319
Rustic Mashed Potatoes, 422

Saffron Chicken and Rice with Dates, 395
Saffron Couscous, 363
Salad of Papaya, Mango, and Grapefruit, 97
Salmon with Orange Marmalade, 351
Salmon with Roasted Cherry Tomatoes, 88
Salmon with Sweet-and-Sour Pan Sauce, 64
Salmon with Wilted Watercress and Balsamic Drizzle, 293
Salsa Chicken, 123

Santa Rosa Plum Crumble, 230
Sausage and Egg Burrito, 123
Sausage, Apple, and Cheddar Bread
    Pudding, 339
Sautéed Boneless Pork Chops with
    Tomato-Sage Pan Sauce, 369
Sautéed Broccoli Rabe, 104
Sautéed Cherry Tomatoes with
    Shallots, 364
Sautéed Chicken Breasts with Balsamic
    Vinegar Pan Sauce, 62
Sautéed Chicken Breasts with Latin Citrus
    Sauce, 204
Sautéed Pork Chops Niçoise, 29
Sautéed Tilapia with Lemon-Peppercorn
    Pan Sauce, 62
Sautéed Turkey Cutlets with Orange-
    Cranberry Pan Sauce, 64
Savory Beet Soup, 346
Savory Dill-Salmon Strudel, 69
Savory Herb Gravy, 375
Savory Herb Sun-Dried Tomato
    Scones, 321
Savory Soup Beans, 15
Savory Yogurt Cheesecake with
    Caramelized Onions, 18
Scallops au Gratin, 428
Scallops Gremolata, 29
Scallops with Cucumber-Horseradish
    Sauce, 124
Seafood Salad with Lime Vinaigrette, 265
Seafood Soup (Caldo de Mariscos), 356
Seared Beef Tenderloin Mini Sandwiches
    with Mustard-Horseradish Sauce, 426
Seared Chicken with Sriracha Barbecue
    Dipping Sauce, 249
Seared Duck Breast with Ginger-Rhubarb
    Sauce, 160
Seared Scallops on Braised Wild
    Mushrooms, 255
Seared Scallops, Sweet Potato, and Pecan
    Salad, 77
Seared Scallops with Port-Poached Figs
    and Apple Salad, 100
Seared Sea Scallops with Spicy Citrus
    Sauce, 442
Seared Shrimp with Thai Cocktail
    Sauce, 249
Seco de Quinoa, 406
Sephardic Beef Stew, 396
Sesame Chicken Salad, 294
Sesame-Crusted Tuna with Ginger-Peanut
    Rice, 78
Sesame-Crusted Tuna with Wasabi-Ponzu
    Sauce, 251
Sesame Farfalle with Roasted Tofu, 192
Sesame Green Beans, 253
Sesame Halibut en Papillote, 441
Sesame Noodle Salad, 400
Sesame Pork Lo Mein, 278
Sesame Tofu Stir-Fry over Rice, 50
Sesame Turkey Cakes with Sweet Chili
    Sauce, 385
Shaved Fennel Salad with Almonds and
    Mint, 135
Shepherd's Pie, 330

Shireen Palow (Afghan Orange Rice with
    Chicken), 70
Shredded Brussels Sprouts with Bacon and
    Hazelnuts, 376
Shrimp and Crab Gumbo, 317
Shrimp and Crab Rolls, 324
Shrimp and Fennel in Hot Garlic
    Sauce, 338
Shrimp and Snow Pea Stir-Fry, 414
Shrimp and Spinach Soup, 385
Shrimp and White Bean Salad over
    Watercress, 96
Shrimp, Corn, and Potato Soup, 216
Shrimp Creole, 121
Shrimp in Green Sauce, 26
Shrimp Lo Mein, 25
Shrimp-Poblano Rice, 164
Shrimp Salad with White Beans, Broccoli,
    and Toasted Garlic, 80
Shrimp Sautéed with Fresh Tomatoes,
    Wine, and Basil, 176
Shrimp Tacos with Spiked Sour
    Cream, 252
Shrimp with Lemon, Mint, and Goat
    Cheese, 317
Simple Peach Ice Cream, 284
Simple Slaw, 14
Simply Roasted Pork, 313
Singapore Mai Fun, 386
Sirloin Steak with Dijon-Port Sauce, 350
Skillet Stuffed Peppers, 162
Skinny Turkey-Spinach Meat Loaf, 78
Sloppy Joes, 8
Slow Cooker Beef Stew, 88
Slushy Watermelon Mojitos, 264
Smoked Paprika-Spiced Chicken over
    Lentils with Yogurt-Cumin
    Sauce, 128
Smoked Salmon, 175
Smoked Salmon Crostini, 434
Smoked Trout Spread, 409
Smoky Bacon and Blue Cheese Chicken
    Salad Pitas, 151
Smoky Eggplant Purée with Crostini, 56
Snow Pea and Red Pepper Stir-Fry, 27
Soba Noodles with Broccoli and
    Chicken, 150
Soba Noodles with Shrimp, 253
Soba with Garlic Chives, Mushrooms, and
    Bok Choy, 281
Sour Cream and Bacon Potato Salad, 79
Sour Cream Babka, 33
Sour Cream Coffee Cake, 127
Sour Cream-Hazelnut Bundt Cake, 389
Sour Cream Pound Cake with Rum
    Glaze, 259
Sourdough Panzanella with Grilled Flank
    Steak, 67
Sourdough Pork Sandwiches with Parsley-
    Pesto Mayonnaise, 315
Southeast Asian Grilled Beef Salad, 46
Southern Shrimp and Grits, 12
Southwestern Chicken Roll-Ups, 189
Southwestern Pasta with Beans, 280
Southwestern Salad Bar, 213
Southwestern Steak and Pinto Beans, 202

Southwestern Succotash Pot Pie, 93
Southwest Meat Loaf, 352
Spaetzle Baked with Ham and Gruyère, 82
Spaghettini with Oil and Garlic, 417
Spanish-Style Brined Pork Tenderloin, 177
Spanish Tortilla with Almond Romesco, 97
Sparkling Peach Splash, 265
Spiced Beef with Wine Sauce and Roasted
    Potatoes, 266
Spiced Blueberry Muffins, 240
Spiced Chicken with Black-Eyed Peas and
    Rice, 246
Spiced Cranberry and Zinfandel
    Sauce, 405
Spiced Date-Walnut Snacks, 397
Spiced Fig Upside-Down Cake, 292
Spiced Orzo Pilaf, 397
Spiced Shrimp with Avocado Oil, 135
Spiced Turkey Cutlets, 28
Spicy Chicken and Arugula Sandwich, 30
Spicy Chicken and Sunchoke Stir-Fry, 359
Spicy Chicken Pasta, 121
Spicy Corn Relish, 262
Spicy Fish Cakes, 297
Spicy Lamb Stew with Parsnips and
    Figs, 335
Spicy Lentils with Chorizo, 168
Spicy Mango-Orange Slush, 245
Spicy Noodle Salad with Tofu and Peanut
    Dressing, 278
Spicy Orange Beef, 38
Spicy Pork, Turkey, and Swiss Cubano
    Roll, 313
Spicy Sausage Pizza, 202
Spicy Shrimp and Scallop Seviche, 242
Spicy Sriracha Bread, 250
Spicy Sweet Potato Wedges, 347
Spicy Yellow Soybean, Lentil, and Carrot
    Curry, 18
Spinach and Feta-Stuffed Focaccia, 289
Spinach-Parmesan Dip, 409
Spinach-Pear Salad with Mustard
    Vinaigrette, 374
Spinach Salad with Grilled Shrimp, 298
Spinach, Sun-Dried Tomato, and Parmesan
    Rolls, 433
Spinach with Chickpeas and Spices, 404
Springtime Pea Soup, 129
Spring Vegetables, 114
Steak with Mustard-Caper Sauce, 262
Steamed Mussels with Cardamom, Orange,
    and Mint, 316
Steamed Pork Buns, 81
Steamed Salmon with Savory Black Bean
    Sauce, 221
Strawberries and Oranges with Vanilla-
    Scented Wine, 99
Strawberry-Basil Sorbet, 161
Strawberry Granita, 107
Strawberry Parfait with Fresh Normandy
    Cream, 116
Strawberry Pie, 190
Strawberry-Rhubarb Tart, 190
Striped Bass with Heirloom Tomatoes and
    Herbs, 225
Stuffed Green Pepper Soup, 406

Stuffed Onions with Chianti Sauce, 137
Stuffed Portobellos, 224
Sugar-Frosted Cardamom Braid, 451
Sugar Snap Peas with Lemon and Toasted
    Almonds, 445
Summer Baked Beans, 229
Summer Pappardelle with Tomatoes,
    Arugula, and Parmesan, 278
Summer Squash Soup with Pasta and
    Parmesan, 282
Summer Succotash with Chicken, 212
Summer Tomato Chopped Salad, 296
Sunchoke and Tomato Gratin, 360
Sunchoke-Chicken Salad Wraps, 360
Sunchoke Latkes, 359
Sun-Dried Tomato Cheesecake, 321
Sun-Dried Tomato Ketchup, 321
Sun-Dried Tomato Pesto and Chicken-
    Pasta Toss, 319
Sun-Dried Tomato Spiced Shrimp, 320
Sun-Dried Tomato-Tortellini Soup, 322
Super Sloppy Joe Sandwiches, 407
Sweet Black Pepper Fish, 27
Sweet Chocolate Log, 138
Sweet Coconut Tapioca Soup with Bananas
    (Che Chuoi), 285
Sweet Onion, White Bean, and Artichoke
    Dip, 424
Sweet Pepper and Green Bean Risotto, 94
Sweet Potato and Carrot Tzimmes, 90
Sweet Potato Hash, 49
Sweet Potato Trifle, 214
Sweet Vanilla Cheese Pierogi, 84
Swiss Chard with Almonds and Shallots, 426
Swiss Chard with Pine Nuts and Raisins, 162

Taco Rice Salad, 215
Tamale Pie, 30
Tapenade, 408
Tarte Tatin, 20
Tequila-Cardamom Syrup and Vanilla Ice
    Cream, 421
Tex-Mex Beef Tacos, 129
Tex-Mex Lasagna, 209
Thai Beef and Radish Salad, 108
Thai Beef Salad Wraps, 288
Thai Pork Salad with Chili Dressing, 313
Thai Roast Duck Salad, 249
Thai Shrimp Rolls with Julienne of
    Vegetables, 68
Thai-Style Chicken, 232
Thai-Style Chicken Stir-Fry, 327
Thai-Style Stir-Fried Chicken, 422
Thin French Apple Tart, 65
Three-Grain Risotto with Asparagus
    Spears, 106
Three-Pepper Beef, 219
Thumbprint Meringues, 172
Thyme-Scented White Bean
    Cassoulet, 367
Toasted Bagels with Avocado-Cilantro
    Spread, 284
Toasted Hazelnut Focaccia, 134
Toasted Pecan Divinity, 453
Tofu and Mushrooms, 39
Tofu Fried Rice, 322

Tofu Larb, 301
Tofu Stir-Fry, 86
Tofu Teriyaki Noodle Salad, 193
Tomatillo Shrimp Fajitas, 231
Tomato and Cucumber Salad, 192
Tomato and Cucumber Salad with Feta, 143
Tomato and Lentil Soup, 54
Tomato-Basil Soup, 288
Tomatoes Roasted with Rosemary and
    Lemon, 178
Tomato Salad, 356
Tomato Salad with Avocado and Preserved
    Lemons, 217
Tortilla Soup, 165, 327
Tricolor Bitter Greens Salad, 69
Triple Berry Freeze, 245
Triple-Pepper Steamed Halibut, 363
Triple Sesame Asparagus, 46
Tropical Breeze, 245
Tropical Chopped Salad with Shrimp, 350
Trout Topped with Cucumber Salsa, 167
Trout with Lentils, 74
Truffled Shrimp and Crab Risotto, 135
Tuna and Red Pepper Pasta Salad, 281
Tuna Tartare in Endive with Horseradish
    Sauce, 258
Tuna with Miso-Chile Sauce, 28
Tuna with White Bean-Cucumber Salad, 415
Turkey Bolognese, 188
Turkey Breast with Spinach-Feta
    Stuffing, 392
Turkey Cutlets with Coleslaw, 206
Turkey Cutlets with Smoky Black Bean
    Sauce, 428
Turkey-Jasmine Rice Meatballs with Baby
    Bok Choy, 393
Turkey Kielbasa Choucroute, 391
Turkey-Pasta Soup, 384
Turkey Scaloppine with Porcini and
    Marsala, 393
Tuscan Bean and Wilted Arugula
    Salad, 119
Tweed Meringues, 171
Twenty-Minute Chili, 80
20-Minute Peking Duck, 323
Tzatziki, 54

Unfried Apple Pies, 15
Upside-Down Cranberry-Ginger
    Cake, 448

Vanilla-Almond Panna Cotta with Mango
    Sauce, 370
Vanilla Bean Sorbet with Pineapple
    Topping, 353
Vanilla-Bourbon Bread Pudding, 449
Vanilla-Honey-Nut Smoothie, 246
Vanilla-Nut Pudding, 117
Vanilla-Scented Harvest Crisp with
    Pistachios, 410
Veal Piccata, 232
Vegetable and Chickpea Curry, 365
Vegetable-Beef Stew, 61
Vegetable Party Latke, 424
Vegetable Salad with Roasted Garlic
    Vinaigrette, 144

Vegetables à la Grecque, 266
Vegetarian Gyoza with Spicy Dipping
    Sauce, 86
Vegetarian Meat Loaf, 330
Veggie Sausage and Egg Strata, 329
Venison Chili, 398
Versatile Vinaigrette, 142
Vichyssoise, 165

Walnut-Chicken Linguine, 133
Warm Eggplant and Goat Cheese
    Sandwiches, 45
Warm Olives with Fennel and
    Orange, 361
Warm Salad of Grilled Figs, Grapes, and
    Bitter Greens, 293
Wasabi Salmon Sandwiches, 401
Watermelon Agua Fresca, 229
White Bean and Roasted Chicken
    Salad, 211
White Bean, Artichoke, and Chard Ragoût
    with Fennel Relish, 364
White Bean Dip, 223
White Beans with Roasted Red Pepper and
    Pesto, 165
White Bean, Tomato, and Green Bean
    Salad, 191
White Bean, Tuna, and Onion Salad with
    Sprouts, 325
White Chicken Chili, 350
White Chocolate-Cashew Coffee
    Biscotti, 453
White Pizza, 46
Wholesome Morning Granola, 13
Whole Wheat Apricot Muffins, 387
Whole Wheat Pasta with Sausage, Leeks,
    and Fontina, 417
Whole Wheat Penne with Broccoli, Green
    Olives, and Pine Nuts, 276
Wildflower Inn Blueberry Jam, 237
Wild Mushroom Bruschetta, 137
Wild Mushroom Pizza with Truffle
    Oil, 130
Wild Rice, Asparagus, and Goat Cheese
    Frittata, 256
Wilted Greens with Rice, 55
Winter Fruit Compote (Compota de
    Frutas), 75
Winter Greens and Potato Casserole, 14
Winter Vegetable Stew over Couscous, 94

Yakitori, 247
Yeasted Corn Bread, 438
Yellow Squash Gratin, 95
Yogurt-Marinated Beef Kebabs with
    Wasabi Aïoli, 251

Zesty Garden Sauce, 224
Ziti Baked with Spinach, Tomatoes, and
    Smoked Gouda, 43
Ziti with Sausage, Onions, and
    Fennel, 420
Zucchini-Buttermilk Soup with Watercress
    Pesto, 255
Zucchini-Spinach Bisque, 223
Zwieback, 36

Month-by-Month Index

A month-by-month listing of every food story with recipe titles that appeared in the magazine in 2004. See page 478 for the General Recipe Index.

January-February

... And Ready in Just About 20 Minutes, 28
- Asian Noodles with Asparagus and Shrimp, 32
- Cajun Sausage and Rice Skillet, 32
- Chicken and Barley Stew, 30
- Crab Cakes with Rémoulade, 29
- Curried Couscous with Broccoli and Feta, 30
- Garlic-Rosemary Lamb Pita, 29
- Ginger Beef, 31
- Hoisin Chicken and Broccoli Stir-Fry, 32
- Mexican Corn and Bean Soup, 31
- Parmesan-Herb Baked Flounder, 31
- Pork Chops with Country Gravy and Mashed Potatoes, 31
- Sautéed Pork Chops Niçoise, 29
- Scallops Gremolata, 29
- Spiced Turkey Cutlets, 28
- Spicy Chicken and Arugula Sandwich, 30
- Tamale Pie, 30

A Perfect Winter's Day, 7
- Beef Stew, 7
- Broccoli, Orange, and Watercress Salad, 7
- Cranberry and Apple Crumble, 9
- Creamy Mashed Potatoes, 8
- Crisp and Spicy Snack Mix, 7
- Hearty Wheat Bread, 8
- Mulled Cranberry-Apple Cider, 8
- Oatmeal-Walnut Cookies, 9
- Sloppy Joes, 8

Appalachian Menu, 14
- Corn Chow-Chow, 15
- Quick Buttermilk Corn Bread, 14
- Savory Soup Beans, 15
- Simple Slaw, 14
- Unfried Apple Pies, 15
- Winter Greens and Potato Casserole, 14

Breakfast Tonight, 11
- Huevos Rancheros with Queso Fresco, 11
- Joe's Special, 12
- Red Bell Pepper Frittata, 11
- Southern Shrimp and Grits, 12

Feeding the Mind, 13
- Garlic and Sun-Dried Tomato Hummus, 13
- Golden Gazpacho, 14
- Lemon Chicken and Rice with Artichokes, 13
- Wholesome Morning Granola, 13

Hoppin' John, 32
- Hoppin' John, 32

In the Red, 37
- Asian Chicken over Noodles, 37
- Barbecue Beef Sandwiches, 38
- Black Bean Chicken, 38
- Pork and Chestnuts, 40
- Pork and Plantains, 39
- Spicy Orange Beef, 38
- Tofu and Mushrooms, 39

On the Greens Path, 9
- Mexican Pizza, 10
- Mixed Pepper Pizza with Basil and Pine Nuts, 10
- Pizza Dough, 10
- Pizza with Escarole, Roasted Peppers, and Olives, 9

Power Up Your Plate, 16
- Braised Kale with Bacon and Cider, 19
- Breakfast Polenta with Warm Berry Compote, 19
- Chicken Braised in Walnut Sauce, 16
- Cran-Grape Syrup, 16
- Irish Oatmeal Bread, 16
- Pork Loin with Dried-Plum Stuffing, 17
- Savory Yogurt Cheesecake with Caramelized Onions, 18
- Spicy Yellow Soybean, Lentil, and Carrot Curry, 18

Prairie Home Baking, 33
- Bierocks, 33
- Hearty Sour Rye Bread, 36
- Miller's Cinnamon-Raisin Bread, 35
- Prairie Fields Wheat and Soy Bread, 35
- Prussian Leaf-Wrapped Breadsticks, 34
- Sour Cream Babka, 33
- Zwieback, 36

Surfing for Succulence, 40
- Cajun Shrimp and Catfish, 40

The Minimalist Mark Bittman, 25
- Asparagus Salad with Mustard-Soy Dressing, 26
- Chicken with Green Olives, 25
- Jook (Rice Porridge), 27
- Pasta with Anchovies and Walnuts, 27
- Pork Tenderloin with Xec, 28
- Shrimp in Green Sauce, 26
- Shrimp Lo Mein, 25
- Sweet Black Pepper Fish, 27
- Tuna with Miso-Chile Sauce, 28

While the Iron Is Hot, 19
- Chocolate Chip Dutch Baby, 19
- Chocolate Pudding Cake, 19
- Pecan Bar Cookies, 20
- Pineapple-Coconut-Banana Upside-Down Cake, 20
- Tarte Tatin, 20

March

... And Ready in Just About 20 Minutes, 78
- Black Bean Quesadillas with Corn Salsa, 78
- Chicken Sandwich with Arugula and Sun-Dried Tomato Vinaigrette, 79
- Chicken Tenders with Apricots and Sautéed Spinach, 80
- Marinated Salmon with Mango-Kiwi Relish, 79
- Mediterranean Vegetable Stew over Soft Polenta, 79
- Sesame-Crusted Tuna with Ginger-Peanut Rice, 78
- Shrimp Salad with White Beans, Broccoli, and Toasted Garlic, 80
- Twenty-Minute Chili, 80

Chicken with Rice Is Nice, 70
- Arroz con Pollo, 70
- Asopao, 72
- Chicken and Shrimp Paella, 71
- Chicken Biriyani, 72
- Chicken Fried Rice with Bok Choy, 71
- Pilaf with Chicken, Spinach, and Walnuts, 70
- Shireen Palow (Afghan Orange Rice with Chicken), 70

Fish Fillets, 72
- Asian Marinated Striped Bass, 73
- Cornflake-Crusted Halibut with Chile-Cilantro Aïoli, 72
- Pan-Seared Cod with Basil Sauce, 73
- Trout with Lentils, 74

Foolproof Dinners with Pam Anderson, 62
- Pork Medallions with Port Wine-Dried Cherry Pan Sauce, 64
- Salmon with Sweet-and-Sour Pan Sauce, 64
- Sautéed Chicken Breasts with Balsamic Vinegar Pan Sauce, 62
- Sautéed Tilapia with Lemon-Peppercorn Pan Sauce, 62
- Sautéed Turkey Cutlets with Orange-Cranberry Pan Sauce, 64

Getting an Edge, 65
- Butterflied Shrimp and Vegetable Stir-Fry, 68
- Chicken Breasts Stuffed with Goat Cheese and Sun-Dried Tomatoes, 67
- Chicken, Date, and Apricot Tagine, 65
- Savory Dill-Salmon Strudel, 69
- Sourdough Panzanella with Grilled Flank Steak, 67
- Thai Shrimp Rolls with Julienne of Vegetables, 68

March (continued)

Thin French Apple Tart, 65
Tricolor Bitter Greens Salad, 69

Gimme the Skinny, 77
Caramelized Onion Dip, 77
Seared Scallops, Sweet Potato, and Pecan Salad, 77
Skinny Turkey-Spinach Meat Loaf, 78

Irish Inspired, 61
Brown Soda Bread, 61
Cabbage and Mixed Greens Salad with Tangy Herb Vinaigrette, 61
Gingered Pear Crisp, 62
Vegetable-Beef Stew, 61

Meals That Add Up, 47
Chive Green Beans, 48
Chocolate Soufflés with Pistachios, 48
Creamy Parmesan Orzo, 48
Lemony Asparagus-Mushroom Stir-Fry, 50
Moroccan Chicken with Almond Couscous, 50
Mushroom and Bell Pepper Omelet with Fontina, 49
Peppercorn-Crusted Filet Mignon with Port Jus, 48
Roasted Chicken and Bow Tie Pasta Salad, 51
Sesame Tofu Stir-Fry over Rice, 50
Sweet Potato Hash, 49

Muffin Magic, 45
Lemony Fruit Dip, 45
Louisiana Goulash, 46
Low-Fat Strawberry-Cinnamon Muffins, 45
Moist 'n' Dark Nut Bread, 47
Southeast Asian Grilled Beef Salad, 46
Triple Sesame Asparagus, 46
Warm Eggplant and Goat Cheese Sandwiches, 45
White Pizza, 46

New Orleans Brunch, 52
Bloody Mary, 53
Café Brûlot, 52
Eggs Hussarde, 53
Grillades and Gravy over Grits, 52
Pain Perdu, 52

Posole, 76
Posole, 76

Puerto Rico, 51
Mango Mahi Seviche, 51

Snack Time, 44
Apple Spice Cake, 44

The Basque Way, 74
Chicken with Morels (Pollo con Jugo de Morillas), 74
Clams with Cherry Tomatoes (Almejas con Tomates), 75
Deconstructed Flan, 74
Farm Hand Potatoes (Papas de Caserio), 76
Fresh Tuna Stew (Marmitako), 76
Lamb Stew (Txilindron de Cordero), 75

Potato and Cabbage Mash (Patatas y Berzas), 76
Winter Fruit Compote (Compota de Frutas), 75

The Lenten Tastes of Greece, 53
Baked Eggplant with Savory Cheese Stuffing, 54
Baked Gigantes in Tomato Sauce, 55
Braised Baby Artichokes and New Potatoes, 56
Feta-Chile Spread, 55
Greek Black-Eyed Peas and Greens, 56
Lemony Lentils with Black Olives, 53
Smoky Eggplant Purée with Crostini, 56
Tomato and Lentil Soup, 54
Tzatziki, 54
Wilted Greens with Rice, 55

Warming Trend, 41
Baked Sesame Chicken Noodles, 41
Baked Ziti with Shrimp and Scallops, 43
Creamy Gruyère and Shrimp Pasta, 42
Easy Ravioli Bake, 43
Italian Sausage Puttanesca, 44
Mushroom Pasta Bake, 42
Roasted Butternut Squash and Bacon Pasta, 41
Ziti Baked with Spinach, Tomatoes, and Smoked Gouda, 43

April

. . . And Ready in Just About 20 Minutes, 121
Balsamic Rosemary Pork, 124
Cashew Chicken Salad Sandwiches, 122
Crab Quesadillas, 121
Guacamole and Turkey Sandwiches, 123
Ham and Asparagus Frittata, 124
Ham and Cheese Hash Browns, 122
Macadamia Nut-Pesto Fettuccine, 123
Mediterranean Vegetable Soup, 123
Pasta with Asparagus, Lemon, and Prosciutto, 122
Roast Chicken Chimichangas, 122
Salsa Chicken, 123
Sausage and Egg Burrito, 123
Scallops with Cucumber-Horseradish Sauce, 124
Shrimp Creole, 121
Spicy Chicken Pasta, 121

Delightful Dumplings, 81
Buttered Spaetzle, 82
Caldo de Bolas, 86
Chicken and Rosemary Dumplings, 82
Chochoyones in Black Bean Soup, 85
Matzo Ball Soup, 85
Pierogi Dough, 83
Potato Gnocchi with Bolognese, 84
Potato Pierogi, 83
Spaetzle Baked with Ham and Gruyère, 82
Steamed Pork Buns, 81
Sweet Vanilla Cheese Pierogi, 84

Vegetarian Gyoza with Spicy Dipping Sauce, 86

Easter Dinner Alfresco, 106
Mushroom and Parmigiano Bruschetta, 106
Rosemary and Pepper-Crusted Pork Tenderloin, 106
Strawberry Granita, 107
Three-Grain Risotto with Asparagus Spears, 106

Gourmet Getaways, 105
Fresh Tomato Lasagna, 105

In a Pinch, 116
Asiago, Potato, and Bacon Gratin, 118
Bell Pepper and Tomato Penne with Meatballs, 118
Chicken and Soba Noodle Soup, 120
Eggplant, Tomato, and Smoked Mozzarella Tart, 116
Fig and Mascarpone Focaccia, 120
Orange-Pecan Tea Bread, 119
Pan-Seared Pork Chops with Molasses-Plum Sauce, 119
Tuscan Bean and Wilted Arugula Salad, 119
Vanilla-Nut Pudding, 117

Little Red Radishes, 107
Chardonnay-Braised Radishes, 108
Radish Raita, 107
Radish Slaw with New York Deli Dressing, 107
Radish Vichyssoise, 108
Thai Beef and Radish Salad, 108

Passover Suite, 89
Apple, Rhubarb, and Sour Cherry Passover Cobbler, 91
Homemade Beet Horseradish, 89
Matzo Buttercrunch, 89
Matzo, Mushroom, and Onion Kugel, 89
Passover Baklava Cake, 90
Passover Chopped Layered Salad, 90
Passover Pecan Bars, 91
Sweet Potato and Carrot Tzimmes, 90

Pasta Primavera, 91
Pasta Primavera, 91

Pasta Tonight, 103
Fettuccine with Shrimp and Portobellos, 103
Garlicky Pasta with Fresh Tomatoes and Basil, 104
Greek Pasta Salad, 105
Lasagna Rolls with Roasted Red Pepper Sauce, 104

Popovers Anytime, 92
Popovers, 92

Putting a Wrap on Spring, 87
Apricot-Glazed Roasted Asparagus, 87
Chocolate and Peanut Butter Cookies, 88
Fresh Spring Rolls with Dipping Sauce, 87
Mediterranean Shrimp and Pasta, 88
Salmon with Roasted Cherry Tomatoes, 88
Slow Cooker Beef Stew, 88

Something for Everyone, 92
    Greek Greens and Sweet Onion Pie, 95
    Mushroom Lasagna with Creamy
      Béchamel, 93
    Polenta with Smoky Mushroom
      Ragoût, 92
    Southwestern Succotash Pot Pie, 93
    Sweet Pepper and Green Bean
      Risotto, 94
    Winter Vegetable Stew over
      Couscous, 94
    Yellow Squash Gratin, 95
Spring Showers, 96
    Fennel, Orange, and Parmigiano
      Salad, 97
    Grilled Chicken Salad with Feta and
      Cucumbers, 96
    Millet Muffins with Honey-Pecan
      Butter, 99
    Raspberry-Almond Muffins, 99
    Salad of Papaya, Mango, and
      Grapefruit, 97
    Shrimp and White Bean Salad over
      Watercress, 96
    Spanish Tortilla with Almond
      Romesco, 97
    Strawberries and Oranges with Vanilla-
      Scented Wine, 99
Susan Loomis: An American Near
Paris, 113
    Beef Cooked with Carrots, Onions, and
      Dried Plums, 115
    Chicken with Citrus, 113
    Fire-Grilled Pork Chops, 114
    Leg of Lamb with Herbs and
      Mustard, 115
    Normandy Seafood Stew, 114
    Spring Vegetables, 114
    Strawberry Parfait with Fresh
      Normandy Cream, 116
The Chef Shapes Up, 100
    Oven-Braised Cornish Hens with Cider
      Vinegar and Warm Vegetable
      Sauce, 100
    Roasted Loin of Pork with Apricot-Rum
      Glaze, 100
    Seared Scallops with Port-Poached Figs
      and Apple Salad, 100
The Essential Egg, 101
    Berry French Toast, 102
    Field Greens with Eggs and Enoki
      Mushrooms, 102
    Ham and Potato Omelet, 101
    Key Lime Cheesecake, 101
    Mediterranean-Style Poached
      Eggs, 103
    Roasted Garlic and Corn Soufflé, 102

May

A Legacy of Soulful Food, 125
    Bayou Catfish Fillets, 126
    Cajun Garlic Pork Roast, 127
    Dry-Rub Chicken with Honey
      Barbecue Sauce, 126
    Field Greens with Mississippi
      Caviar, 127

Island Rice, 125
Jerk-Style Chicken, 125
Lemon Pound Cake with Mixed
    Berries, 125
. . . And Ready in Just About 20
Minutes, 162
    Chicken with Cherry Tomato and
      Olive Topping, 163
    Chicken with Chunky Pepper
      Sauce, 163
    Creamy Shrimp and Corn
      Bowl, 163
    Insalata Pizzas, 163
    Shrimp-Poblano Rice, 164
    Skillet Stuffed Peppers, 162
Applying Pressure, 164
    All-Purpose Southwestern Corn and
      Black Bean Salad, 166
    Barbecue Beans, 166
    Lemon-Basil Risotto with Tomato
      Topping, 164
    Moroccan Summer Vegetable and
      Sausage Stew, 167
    Tortilla Soup, 165
    Vichyssoise, 165
    White Beans with Roasted Red Pepper
      and Pesto, 165
A Tart Tale of Rhubarb, 153
    Grilled Pork Chops with Rhubarb
      Chutney, 154
    Lattice-Topped Rhubarb Pie, 153
    Rhubarb, Pear, and Apple
      Compote, 154
    Rhubarb Pudding Cake, 154
    Rhubarb Sorbet, 154
    Rhubarb-Strawberry Crumble, 155
Beyond Olive Oil, 130
    Baby Spinach Salad with Candied
      Hazelnuts, 133
    Banana-Walnut Napoleons, 133
    Cherry-Hazelnut Oatmeal, 132
    Cranberry Walnut Tabbouleh, 132
    Peanut Chicken Soba Salad, 132
    Pistachio Rice, 132
    Romaine Salad with Avocado-Lime
      Vinaigrette, 134
    Spiced Shrimp with Avocado
      Oil, 135
    Toasted Hazelnut Focaccia, 134
    Truffled Shrimp and Crab Risotto, 135
    Walnut-Chicken Linguine, 133
    Wild Mushroom Pizza with Truffle
      Oil, 130
Chopped Salads, 142
    Garden Salad with Citrus
      Vinaigrette, 144
    Gazpacho Salad with Tomato
      Vinaigrette, 143
    Green and White Salad with Blue
      Cheese Dressing, 143
    Green Bean, Corn, and Roasted
      Poblano Chile Salad, 144
    Napa Cabbage and Snow Pea
      Slaw, 143
    Roasted Beet Salad with Raspberry
      Vinaigrette, 144

Romaine Lettuce with Red Pepper and
    Olives, 144
Tomato and Cucumber Salad with
    Feta, 143
Vegetable Salad with Roasted Garlic
    Vinaigrette, 144
Versatile Vinaigrette, 142
Farmer Bob's Veggie Vision, 149
    Bell Pepper Chicken with Feta
      Orzo, 149
    Grilled-Steak Soft Tacos, 149
    Hummus-Stuffed Pitas with
      Vegetables, 150
    Individual Pizzas with Broccoli, Cheese,
      and Meat Sauce, 150
    Pizza Frittata, 150
    Soba Noodles with Broccoli and
      Chicken, 150
Fast From the Sea, 167
    Citrus Salmon with Garlicky Greens, 167
    Mussels with Tomato-Wine Broth, 168
    Trout Topped with Cucumber Salsa, 167
In Chile, 168
    Dulce de Leche-Filled Cookies, 169
    Grilled Lamb Chops, 170
    Mussel Salad, 170
    Pastel de Choclo, 168
    Pebre, 169
    Potatoes with Spicy Cheese Sauce, 169
    Spicy Lentils with Chorizo, 168
Jam-Packed with Flavor, 159
    Apple and Horseradish-Glazed
      Salmon, 159
    Blackberry-Zinfandel Quail, 161
    Fig and Chile-Glazed Pork
      Tenderloin, 159
    Filet Mignon with Red Currant-Green
      Peppercorn Sauce, 160
    Grilled Cornish Hens with Apricot-
      Mustard Glaze, 160
    Seared Duck Breast with Ginger-
      Rhubarb Sauce, 160
    Strawberry-Basil Sorbet, 161
London's Calling, 128
    Smoked Paprika-Spiced Chicken over
      Lentils with Yogurt-Cumin
      Sauce, 128
Meringue Cookies, 170
    Chocolate-Cherry Chunk
      Meringues, 170
    Coconut Meringues, 171
    Double Vanilla Meringues, 172
    Peanut Butter-Chocolate Meringue
      Sandwiches, 172
    Thumbprint Meringues, 172
    Tweed Meringues, 171
Muffuletta, 158
    Muffuletta, 159
New Classic Salads, 151
    Chicken and Couscous Salad, 151
    Chicken, Red Potato, and Green Bean
      Salad, 152
    Chicken Salad with Nectarines in Mint
      Vinaigrette, 152
    Smoky Bacon and Blue Cheese Chicken
      Salad Pitas, 151

May (continued)

Out in the Open, 135
Baked Frittata Ribbons in Tomato Sauce, 136
Bucatini with Eggplant and Roasted Peppers, 136
Penne in Creamy Basil-Walnut Sauce, 138
Ricotta-Honey Mousse with Summer Berries, 136
Shaved Fennel Salad with Almonds and Mint, 135
Stuffed Onions with Chianti Sauce, 137
Sweet Chocolate Log, 138
Wild Mushroom Bruschetta, 137

Scoop of the Day, 128
Arctic Lime Freeze, 128
Cactus Salad, 129
Chickpeas with Spinach, 130
Italian Garbanzo Salad, 129
Rachel's Tropical Fruit Salsa, 129
Springtime Pea Soup, 129
Tex-Mex Beef Tacos, 129

She Takes the Cake, 127
Sour Cream Coffee Cake, 127

Terry Conlan: Redefining Spa Cuisine, 155
Café con Leche Cream Pie, 158
Camarones Fritoes with Mexican Cocktail Sauce, 156
Chilled Corn Bisque with Basil, Avocado, and Crab, 156
Coconut Curry Shrimp Cakes with Papaya-Lime Sauce, 158
Corn Tortillas, 155
Green Chile Sopes with Chipotle Mayonnaise, Shrimp, and Pineapple Slaw, 157
Green Enchiladas with Crab, 157

The Raw Edge, 161
Berries and Almond Milk, 161
Ensalada de Repollo (Cabbage Salad), 162
Old-Fashioned Oatmeal, 161
Papaya Lime Soup, 162
Swiss Chard with Pine Nuts and Raisins, 162

Wrap and Roll, 138
Apple-Cream Cheese Strudel, 138
Asparagus-Fontina Tart, 140
Cherry-Apricot Turnovers, 142
Feta-Spinach Tarts, 141
Phyllo Éclairs, 141
Pork Tenderloin in Phyllo, 139
Roasted Salmon and Leeks in Phyllo Packets, 140

June

. . . And Ready in Just About 20 Minutes, 201
Chicken with Cremini Mushrooms and Asparagus, 203
Chicken with Port Wine Sauce, 205
Chile-Glazed Shrimp, 201
Chipotle Pork Tenderloin with Corn Salsa, 205
Chunky Vegetable Soup with Toasted Cheese Croutons, 202
Cider-Glazed Chicken with Dried Cranberries, 203
Creamy Pasta with Chicken and Mushrooms, 206
Curried Lamb Chops with Minted Chutney, 206
Escarole Soup with Ginger and Cilantro, 205
Huevos Rancheros Tostados, 204
Indian-Spiced Roast Salmon, 203
Linguine Carbonara, 203
Maple-Orange Chicken, 205
Olive-Tomato Grilled Cheese Sandwiches, 204
Pan-Fried Bass, 201
Picadillo Soft Tacos, 202
Pork Tenderloin with Olive-Mustard Tapenade, 204
Pork with Cranberry-Apple Salsa, 206
Sautéed Chicken Breasts with Latin Citrus Sauce, 204
Southwestern Steak and Pinto Beans, 202
Spicy Sausage Pizza, 202
Turkey Cutlets with Coleslaw, 206

Brining with Bruce Aidells, 173
Coffee and Molasses-Brined Pork Chops, 176
Fennel-Brined Pork Chops, 174
Five-Spice Chicken Breasts with Hoisin Glaze, 175
Honey and Thyme-Brined Turkey Breast, 173
Lemon Tarragon-Brined Whole Chicken, 173
New England-Style Pickled Beef, 174
Orange-Brined Pork Loin, 175
Shrimp Sautéed with Fresh Tomatoes, Wine, and Basil, 176
Smoked Salmon, 175
Spanish-Style Brined Pork Tenderloin, 177

Burger Cookout, 196
Apricot-Cherry Upside-Down Mini Cakes, 197
Grilled Vegetable Salad with Creamy Blue Cheese Dressing, 196
Jamaican Jerk Turkey Burgers with Papaya-Mango Salsa, 196

Celebration of Heritage, 178
Beet and Red Onion Salad with Ricotta-Provolone Topping, 179
Italian Stuffed Summer Vegetables, 178
Kale with Garlic and Hot Red Pepper, 178
Oven Fries with Crisp Sage Leaves, 180
Peaches Chilled in Red Wine, 180
Pickled Hot Peppers, 179
Roast Pork Porchetta-Style, 179
Tomatoes Roasted with Rosemary and Lemon, 178

Currying Flavor, 188
Black Bean Soup, 188
Curried Chicken Penne with Fresh Mango Chutney, 188
Garlic and Bell Pepper Farfalle, 189
Parmesan-Corn Bread Muffins, 189
Southwestern Chicken Roll-Ups, 189
Turkey Bolognese, 188

Feeding a Crowd, 214
Cajun-Spiced Chicken Fettuccine, 216
Chipotle Shrimp Cups, 215
Crawfish and Rice Casserole, 215
Orange-Pecan French Toast Casserole, 216
Shrimp, Corn, and Potato Soup, 216
Sweet Potato Trifle, 214
Taco Rice Salad, 215

Fresh Cherry Cobbler, 180
Fresh Cherry Cobbler, 180

Great Grilled Sandwiches, 185
Chicken Philly Sandwiches, 187
Chipotle Pulled-Pork Barbecue Sandwiches, 186
Grilled Chicken and Roasted Red Pepper Sandwiches with Fontina Cheese, 185
Grilled Goat Cheese Sandwiches with Fig and Honey, 186
Grilled Ham and Cheese with Tomato, 187
Grilled Vegetable and Mozzarella Sandwiches, 187
Pear, Pecorino, and Prosciutto Panini, 186
Pressed Cubano with Bacon, 185

Meals to Go, 191
Couscous-Chickpea Salad with Ginger-Lime Dressing, 194
Curried Couscous with Pine Nuts and Currants, 193
Lentil and Fennel Salad, 191
Orecchiette with Tomatoes, Fresh Mozzarella, and Basil, 192
Orzo-Bell Pepper Salad, 192
Roasted Red Pepper Spread Sandwiches, 193
Sesame Farfalle with Roasted Tofu, 192
Tofu Teriyaki Noodle Salad, 193
Tomato and Cucumber Salad, 192
White Bean, Tomato, and Green Bean Salad, 191

Meatless Main, 209
Dilled Goat Cheese Sandwiches with Roasted Plum Tomatoes, 209
Eggplant Stew over Couscous, 210
Frittata with Mushrooms, Linguine, and Basil, 209
Indian Chickpeas over Garlic Spinach, 210
Pasta with Mushrooms and Radicchio, 210
Tex-Mex Lasagna, 209

Moroccan Barbecue, 217
Brochettes of Lamb, 217
Carrots with Paprika and Capers, 218
Couscous with Apple-Ginger Topping and Orange Sauce, 218
Iced Mint Tea, 218

Quick Preserved Lemons, 217
Tomato Salad with Avocado and
Preserved Lemons, 217
Northwest Exposure, 201
Korean Beef Strip Steak, 201
Pop Goes the Breakfast, 194
Blueberry Blender, 196
Chamomile-Fruit Smoothie, 195
Coconut French Toast with Grilled
Pineapple and Tropical Salsa, 195
Coconut Frushi, 195
Green Eggs and Ham, 194
Pan-Seared Oatmeal with Warm Fruit
Compote and Cider Syrup, 194
Quick One-Dish Wonders, 207
Beef and Barley-Stuffed Peppers, 208
Bistro Chicken and Peppers, 207
Ginger-Curry Pork and Rice, 207
Mac and Cheese Florentine, 208
Moroccan Chicken and Lentils, 208
Nutty Pasta Toss with Shrimp, 207
Rotisserie Chicken, 211
Asparagus and Chicken
Carbonara, 212
Basmati Chicken Salad, 214
Chicken and Blue Cheese Slaw, 212
Couscous Salad with Chicken and
Chopped Vegetables, 213
Gazpacho Panzanella, 211
Peppery Chicken Pasta Salad, 214
Ratatouille Pizza with Chicken, 211
Southwestern Salad Bar, 213
Summer Succotash with Chicken, 212
White Bean and Roasted Chicken
Salad, 211
Sauté in No Time, 197
Lime-Cilantro Pork Tacos, 197
Mushroom-Prosciutto Pizza, 199
Parmesan Chicken and Rice, 198
Rice Noodles with Sesame-Ginger
Flank Steak, 198
Serving Mom's Seviche, 199
Ecuadoran Shrimp Seviche, 200
Pineapple Seviche Mixto, 199
Rainbow Seviche, 200
Strata Makeover, 177
Goat Cheese, Artichoke, and Smoked
Ham Strata, 177
Summer Sweethearts, 190
Balsamic Strawberry Topping, 191
Brunch Parfaits, 190
Fresh Strawberry Jam, 191
Frozen Strawberry Daiquiris, 190
Strawberry Pie, 190
Strawberry-Rhubarb Tart, 190

July

**. . . And Ready in Just About 20
Minutes, 231**
Grilled Tuna with Avocado Salsa, 232
Grouper with Puttanesca Sauce, 231
Italian Sausage Soup, 232
Omelet with Summer Vegetables, 231
Thai-Style Chicken, 232
Tomatillo Shrimp Fajitas, 231
Veal Piccata, 232

A Plum Recipe for Pork, 222
Baked Chiles Rellenos, 223
Chocolate Chip Zucchini Bread, 224
Pork Tenderloin with Plum Sauce, 222
Stuffed Portobellos, 224
White Bean Dip, 223
Zesty Garden Sauce, 224
Zucchini-Spinach Bisque, 223
BLT Bread Salad, 243
BLT Bread Salad, 243
Creative Chicken, 246
Chicken Breasts with Tarragon-Caper
Sauce, 247
Chicken, Mushroom, and Cheese
Quesadillas, 247
Spiced Chicken with Black-Eyed Peas
and Rice, 246
Yakitori, 247
Fresh Take on the Fourth, 229
Green Bean, Chickpea, and Tomato
Salad, 229
Grilled Corn with Creamy Chipotle
Sauce, 230
Grilled Summer Squash, 230
Red, White, and Blue Potato Salad, 230
Santa Rosa Plum Crumble, 230
Summer Baked Beans, 229
Watermelon Agua Fresca, 229
Great Places for Active Getaways, 228
Grilled Chicken Breasts with Yellow
Tomato Curry Sauce and Thai
Ratatouille, 228
Inspiration From the Garden, 225
Fresh Corn Risotto with Seared Shrimp
and Salsa Verde, 227
Golden Summer Soup, 227
Maine Lobster and Pepper Salad with
Asian Herbs, 225
Pizzeria Bianco Watermelon, Fennel,
and Parsley Salad, 228
Striped Bass with Heirloom Tomatoes
and Herbs, 225
Maine's Got the Blues, 237
Blueberry-Blackberry Shortcakes, 237
Blueberry Cheesecake, 239
Blueberry Cinnamon-Burst
Muffins, 239
Blueberry Gingerbread Cake, 238
Blueberry-Pumpkin Pound Cake, 238
Spiced Blueberry Muffins, 240
Wildflower Inn Blueberry Jam, 237
Martin Yan Can Teach, 219
Braised Seafood and Vegetable
Noodles, 220
Grilled Beef Salad with Lemongrass
Dressing, 221
Melon Chicken Salad, 219
Steamed Salmon with Savory Black
Bean Sauce, 221
Three-Pepper Beef, 219
More of a Good Thing, 222
Corn Bread with Fresh Corn, 222
Refresher Course, 245
Blackberry-Peach Smoothie with
Walnuts, 246
Cool Melon Sipper, 246

Frozen Banana Latte, 245
Ginger-Lemon Tonic, 245
Spicy Mango-Orange Slush, 245
Triple Berry Freeze, 245
Tropical Breeze, 245
Vanilla-Honey-Nut Smoothie, 246
Seaside Supper, 242
Citrus-Spiked Jícama and Carrot
Slaw, 242
Grilled Pork Chops with Tomatillo,
Corn, and Avocado Salsa, 243
Key Lime Pie Ice Cream, 243
Spicy Shrimp and Scallop Seviche, 242
Tasty Rubs, 240
Classic Steak House Rubbed Filet
Mignon, 241
Grilled Pastrami-Style Salmon, 242
Herbes de Provence-Crusted Lamb
Chops, 240
Lemon and Oregano-Rubbed Chicken
Paillards, 241
The Gourmet Athlete, 244
Asparagus-Potato Soup, 244
Easy Gnocchi with Thick Marinara
Sauce, 244
Lentil Couscous with Spinach, 244
Turn Up the Heat, 248
Chipotle-Bacon Corn Bread, 251
Chipotle Macaroni and Cheese, 248
Grilled Pork Chops with Fiery
Salsa, 248
Louisiana Crab Cakes with Creole
Tartar Sauce, 248
Seared Chicken with Sriracha Barbecue
Dipping Sauce, 249
Seared Shrimp with Thai Cocktail
Sauce, 249
Sesame-Crusted Tuna with Wasabi-
Ponzu Sauce, 251
Shrimp Tacos with Spiked Sour
Cream, 252
Spicy Sriracha Bread, 250
Thai Roast Duck Salad, 249
Yogurt-Marinated Beef Kebabs with
Wasabi Aïoli, 251
What to Eat After a Workout, 252
Bell Pepper and Fresh Mozzarella
Couscous, 252
Corn and Sun-Dried Tomato
Quesadilla with Smoked
Mozzarella, 254
Curried Chicken Salad, 253
Edamame and Bean Salad with Shrimp
and Fresh Salsa, 254
Kung Pao Tofu Rice Salad, 254
Lemon Garbanzo Salad with Feta, 253
Roasted Chicken-Artichoke
Calzones, 252
Soba Noodles with Shrimp, 253

August

Air Fare, 282
Barley-Chicken Salad with Fresh Corn
and Sweet Onions, 283
Cashew Chicken Salad with Mandarin
Oranges, 284

August (*continued*)

Chicken Saté Wraps, 283
Edamame, Quinoa, and Shiitake
Mushroom Salad, 283
Lentil Dal Wraps, 284
Moroccan-Spiced Bulgur and Chickpea
Salad, 283
Prosciutto and Picholine Pasta
Salad, 282
Toasted Bagels with Avocado-Cilantro
Spread, 284

**. . . And Ready in Just About 20
Minutes, 293**
Asian Chicken Noodle Soup, 294
Chicken Scaloppine over Broccoli
Rabe, 293
Curried Tofu, 294
Grilled Portobello-Goat Cheese Pitas, 294
Salmon with Wilted Watercress and
Balsamic Drizzle, 293
Sesame Chicken Salad, 294

Charting a Healthy Course, 259
Fish Chowder, 260
Lobster Newburg, 260
Sour Cream Pound Cake with Rum
Glaze, 259

Cooking for the Company, 273
Farmers' Market Quesadillas, 273
Fiery Turkey Fillets with Mango
Salsa, 274
Lemon Southwest Rice, 274
Mexican Chocolate Cake, 274
Red Cabbage and Spinach Salad with
Balsamic Vinaigrette, 273

Culinary Crossroads, 285
Asian Chicken Stock, 287
Chicken with Ginger and Green
Onion-Salt Dip, 287
Garlic and Ginger Rice (Com Gung
Tuong), 287
Green Papaya Salad (Goi Du Du), 287
Hanoi Beef and Rice Noodle Soup (Pho
Bo), 286
Lemongrass Shrimp over Rice
Vermicelli and Vegetables (Bun Tom
Nuong Xa), 285
Pan-Fried Tofu with Spicy Lemongrass
Sauce (Tofu Nuong Xa), 286
Sweet Coconut Tapioca Soup with
Bananas (Che Chuoi), 285

Farmers' Market Treasures, 275
Apricot-Lavender Sauce, 276
Bruschetta with Warm Tomatoes, 276
Eggplant and Tomato Gratin, 275
Fresh Corn Frittata with Smoked
Mozzarella, 275
Green Rice with Roasted Chiles and
Leeks, 276
Potato and Summer Vegetable Stovetop
Casserole, 277
Whole Wheat Penne with Broccoli,
Green Olives, and Pine Nuts, 276

Fresh Figs, 290
Baked Figs and Nectarines over Ice
Cream, 291

Chicken Braised with Leeks and
Figs, 291
Flatbread with Oven-Dried Figs,
Caramelized Onions, and Blue
Cheese, 291
Fresh Fig Salad with Crème Fraîche,
Mint, and Prosciutto, 290
Oven-Dried Figs, 290
Pork Stew with Pearl Onions, Green
Olives, and Figs, 292
Refrigerator Fig Preserves, 290
Spiced Fig Upside-Down Cake, 292
Warm Salad of Grilled Figs, Grapes,
and Bitter Greens, 293

**In Virginia, Romancing French
Cuisine, 265**
Melon Balls with Port, 265
Seafood Salad with Lime
Vinaigrette, 265
Spiced Beef with Wine Sauce and
Roasted Potatoes, 266
Vegetables à la Grecque, 266

Keeping It Simple with Sally James, 255
Cornmeal Shortcakes with Tomato-
Ginger Jam, 258
Feta and Lemon-Stuffed Lamb with
Potato-Parsnip Mash, 257
Glazed Peaches in Phyllo Baskets with
Ricotta Cream, 256
Grilled Chicken with Pinot-Plum
Sauce, 258
Macadamia and Ginger Cookies, 256
Seared Scallops on Braised Wild
Mushrooms, 255
Tuna Tartare in Endive with
Horseradish Sauce, 258
Wild Rice, Asparagus, and Goat Cheese
Frittata, 256
Zucchini-Buttermilk Soup with
Watercress Pesto, 255

Marinara *Magnifica*, 260
Chopstick Noodle Salad, 262
Feta-Chicken Pasta, 262
Hearty Fresh Tomato Salsa, 261
Mango-Cucumber Salad, 261
Marinara Magnifica, 261
Roast Pork Sandwiches au Jus with
Rosemary, 261
Spicy Corn Relish, 262
Steak with Mustard-Caper Sauce, 262

Perfectly Parfait, 267
Amaretto-Scented Pear Parfaits with
Gingersnaps, 267
Apple Pie à la Mode Parfaits, 267
Black Forest Cheesecake Parfaits, 268
Coconut Cream Pie Parfaits, 268
Funky Monkey Parfaits, 267
Key Lime Pie Parfaits, 268
Peach and Raspberry Pavlova
Parfaits, 267

Simple Peach Ice Cream, 284
Simple Peach Ice Cream, 284

The Long and Short of It, 277
Curried Noodles, 279
Gemelli Pasta with Clams, Scallops,
and Shrimp, 281

Greek Pasta with Seared Tuna, 282
Hamburger, Cheddar, and Macaroni
Toss, 279
Lemon Noodles with Curry Leaves and
Cashews, 282
Mushroom and Yellow Pepper
Lasagna, 280
Pasta with Roasted Shiitakes and
Tomato Purée, 280
Penne Pasta with Roasted Fennel,
Cherry Tomatoes, and
Olives, 279
Penne with Mushroom Sauce, 277
Sesame Pork Lo Mein, 278
Soba with Garlic Chives, Mushrooms,
and Bok Choy, 281
Southwestern Pasta with Beans, 280
Spicy Noodle Salad with Tofu and
Peanut Dressing, 278
Summer Pappardelle with Tomatoes,
Arugula, and Parmesan, 278
Summer Squash Soup with Pasta and
Parmesan, 282
Tuna and Red Pepper Pasta
Salad, 281

Waterside Menu, 263
Barley Risotto with Fennel and
Olives, 264
Cherries in Spiced Wine Syrup with
Pound Cake Croutons, 264
Grilled Lemon-Bay Shrimp, 263
Herbed Cracker Bread, 263
Pimm's Cup, 264
Roasted Fig and Arugula Salad, 263
Slushy Watermelon Mojitos, 264
Sparkling Peach Splash, 265

Wrap It Up, 288
Creamy Chicken and Mushroom
Crêpes, 289
Prosciutto and Gruyère
Strombolis, 288
Spinach and Feta-Stuffed Focaccia, 289
Thai Beef Salad Wraps, 288

September

**. . . And Ready in Just About 20
Minutes, 322**
Coconut Curried Chicken, 322
Corn and Two-Bean Burgers with
Chipotle Ketchup, 324
Pan-Fried Catfish with Cajun Tartar
Sauce, 323
Pork Fattoush, 323
Shrimp and Crab Rolls, 324
Tofu Fried Rice, 322
20-Minute Peking Duck, 323

A New Classic, 326
Apple-Orange Pie, 326
Banana-Oatmeal Loaf, 326
Beef and Green Chile Soup, 327
Pork Medallions with Garlic-Ginger-
Pomegranate Sauce, 327
Roasted Red Pepper on Mini-Bagel
Sandwiches, 326
Thai-Style Chicken Stir-Fry, 327
Tortilla Soup, 327

Cook Now, Eat Later, 313
Chipotle Pork and Avocado Wrap, 315
Horseradish and Caramelized Onion Pork Sandwiches, 315
Pork and Grilled Stone Fruit Couscous Salad, 314
Pork and Grilled Vegetable Salad, 314
Pork and Peanut Noodle Salad, 315
Pork Tabbouleh, 314
Simply Roasted Pork, 313
Sourdough Pork Sandwiches with Parsley-Pesto Mayonnaise, 315
Spicy Pork, Turkey, and Swiss Cubano Roll, 313
Thai Pork Salad with Chili Dressing, 313
Curb Appeal, 309
Citrus-Herb Shrimp (Camarones con Hierbas y Cítricos), 310
Classic Mojito, 312
Coconut Custard (Tembleque), 312
Crab-and-Mango Empanadas (Empanadas de Cangrejo y Mango), 309
Empanada Dough (Masa de Empanadas), 309
Green Salad with Culantro and Cilantro Dressing (Ensalada Verde con Aderezo de Cilantro y Recao), 310
Mango Martini, 312
Plantains and Pork Cracklings with Stewed Chicken (Mofongo Relleno de Pollo Guisado), 311
Pork Skewers with Guava Sauce (Pinchos de Cerdo con Salsa de Guayaba), 311
Puerto Rican Sangría, 313
Rice with Pigeon Peas (Arroz con Gandules), 311
Rice with Stewed Pink Beans (Arroz con Habichuelas Rosadas Guisadas), 312
Ripe Plantain "Canoes" Stuffed with Ground Meat (Canoas), 309
Roasted Pork (Pernil Asado), 310
Dry Goods, 318
Braised Beef with Sun-Dried Tomatoes, 318
Mixed Bean Salad with Sun-Dried Tomatoes, 320
Olive and Sun-Dried Tomato Sauce over Chicken, 320
Rosemary-Tomato Pinwheels, 319
Savory Herb Sun-Dried Tomato Scones, 321
Sun-Dried Tomato Cheesecake, 321
Sun-Dried Tomato Ketchup, 321
Sun-Dried Tomato Pesto and Chicken-Pasta Toss, 319
Sun-Dried Tomato Spiced Shrimp, 320
Sun-Dried Tomato-Tortellini Soup, 322
Food for Thought, 325
Beef Tenderloin with Porcini Mushroom Sauce, 325
Minestrone with Chickpeas, 325

White Bean, Tuna, and Onion Salad with Sprouts, 325
Food & Friendship, 295
Hip in the Heartland, 316
Steamed Mussels with Cardamom, Orange, and Mint, 316
In the Kitchen with Caprial and John, 297
Almond-Stuffed Baked Apples with Caramel-Apple Sauce, 299
Basmati Rice with Basil and Mint, 299
Curry Ginger Butternut Squash Soup, 298
Flank Steak with Five-Spice Rub and Chile Relish, 297
Spicy Fish Cakes, 297
Spinach Salad with Grilled Shrimp, 298
Live From New York, 295
Corn Fritter Casserole, 296
Crab-Stuffed Lobster with Citrus Vinaigrette, 295
Grilled Eggplant with Caramelized Onion and Fennel, 295
Lemon-Buttermilk Panna Cotta with Blueberry Sauce, 297
Summer Tomato Chopped Salad, 296
Mother Knows Best, 316
Chicken and Wild Rice Soup, 316
Oven-Braised Pork Roast with Apples, 324
Oven-Braised Pork Roast with Apples, 324
Progressive Dinner, 300
Baked Hoisin Chicken Buns, 301
Beef Bourguignonne with Egg Noodles, 304
Bitter Greens Salad with Sourdough Croutons and Warm Tomato Vinaigrette, 303
Crab and Scallop Sui Mei, 302
Galloping Horses, 302
Individual Tiramisu Trifles, 304
Lamb Osso Buco over Parmesan Polenta, 303
Tofu Larb, 301
Seafood Suppers, 317
Linguine with Clam Sauce, 318
Shrimp and Crab Gumbo, 317
Shrimp with Lemon, Mint, and Goat Cheese, 317
Soy on the Sly, 328
Biscuits and Vegetarian Sausage Gravy, 328
Chicken-Green Chile Enchilada Casserole, 328
Italian Sausage and Fennel Lasagna, 330
Pepperoni, Provolone, and Pesto Stromboli, 328
Shepherd's Pie, 330
Vegetarian Meat Loaf, 330
Veggie Sausage and Egg Strata, 329

October
After-School Special, 357
Chicken Breasts Stuffed with Spinach and Ricotta, 358
Chicken Cacciatore, 357
Chicken Meatball Soup with Pasta, 358
Chicken Vegetable Stew, 357
. . . And Ready in Just About 20 Minutes, 348
Cannellini Stew with Sausage and Kale and Cheese Toasts, 349
Chicken Piccata, 348
Chili-Glazed Tofu over Asparagus and Rice, 349
Lamb Chops with Herbed Yogurt over Couscous, 350
Pasta with Sun-Dried Tomato Pesto and Feta Cheese, 349
Sirloin Steak with Dijon-Port Sauce, 350
Tropical Chopped Salad with Shrimp, 350
Apple Appellations, 331
Apple and Chicken Hash, 332
Apple Bisque with Chestnuts, 332
Apple-Cranberry Cobbler, 332
Autumn Apple and Spinach Salad, 331
Charleston Pudding, 333
Overnight Apple Butter, 331
Roast Pork with Apples, Cabbage, and Turnips, 331
Candy Corn Popcorn Balls, 360
Candy Corn Popcorn Balls, 360
Cozy Cabin Retreat, 345
Cider-Roasted Chicken, 347
Cider-Roasted Pork Loin, 346
Country Rye Loaves, 347
Fall Green Salad, 345
Pumpkin-Orange Cake, 348
Red Pepper-Cheese Dip, 345
Rich Mushroom Soup, 346
Savory Beet Soup, 346
Spicy Sweet Potato Wedges, 347
Dressed-Up Desserts, 370
Chocolate-Mint Sorbet, 371
Individual Anise-Orange Flans, 371
Marble Cheesecake Squares, 370
Pineapple-Rum Granita, 370
Rice Pudding with Port and Dried Plum Sauce, 371
Vanilla-Almond Panna Cotta with Mango Sauce, 370
Fall's Convenient Comforts, 364
African Sweet Potato Stew with Red Beans, 366
Barley-Stuffed Cabbage Rolls with Pine Nuts and Currants, 365
Pinto Bean Chili with Corn and Winter Squash, 366
Thyme-Scented White Bean Cassoulet, 367
Vegetable and Chickpea Curry, 365
White Bean, Artichoke, and Chard Ragoût with Fennel Relish, 364

Matchmaking, 333
Braised Pork Shoulder in Hoisin-Wine
Sauce with Dried Plums, 335
Chicken Thighs with Olives and Red
Peppers, 338
Duck Breast with Cherry-Pepper
Sauce, 333
Pan-Grilled Pork Tenderloin with
Pomegranate Molasses, 337
Risotto with Butternut Squash,
Pancetta, and Jack Cheese, 337
Shrimp and Fennel in Hot Garlic
Sauce, 338
Spicy Lamb Stew with Parsnips and
Figs, 335

Mexican Soups & Stews, 354
Beef and Vegetable Soup (Cocido), 356
Calabaza and Poblano Stew, 354
Chicken Green Chili with White
Beans, 355
Garbanzo and Greens Stew, 356
Meatball Soup (Sopa de Albóndigas), 355
Pork Posole, 354
Seafood Soup (Caldo de Mariscos), 356

One Fine Chili, 350
Butternut Squash and Red Pepper, 351
Eggplant Parmesan Pizza, 351
Green Rice, 352
Lentil Spread, 351
Salmon with Orange Marmalade, 351
Southwest Meat Loaf, 352
White Chicken Chili, 350

Quick Chops, 368
Breaded Pork Chops, 369
Buttermilk-Brined Pork Chops, 368
Grilled Plum and Prosciutto-Stuffed
Pork Chops, 368
Sautéed Boneless Pork Chops with
Tomato-Sage Pan Sauce, 369

Savory Bread Puddings, 339
Butternut Squash and Parmesan Bread
Pudding, 340
Corn and Chipotle Bread Pudding, 340
Greek-Style Bread Pudding, 340
Mushroom, Roasted Red Pepper, and
Goat Cheese Bread Pudding, 339
Sausage, Apple, and Cheddar Bread
Pudding, 339

Sensational Sunchokes, 358
Roasted Sunchokes and Fennel, 359
Spicy Chicken and Sunchoke Stir-
Fry, 359
Sunchoke and Tomato Gratin, 360
Sunchoke-Chicken Salad Wraps, 360
Sunchoke Latkes, 359

**Stress-Free Entertaining with Donata
Maggipinto, 361**
Bay Leaf and Thyme-Scented Roasted
Winter Squash and Garlic, 363
Bittersweet Chocolate Sorbet, 364
Mustard-Crusted Lamb Chops, 363
Peppered Garlic Confit with
Prosciutto, 361
Persimmon-Walnut Oil Salad, 362

Red Lettuce Salad with Citrus
Vinaigrette, 363
Saffron Couscous, 363
Sautéed Cherry Tomatoes with
Shallots, 364
Triple-Pepper Steamed Halibut, 363
Warm Olives with Fennel and
Orange, 361

Temptation Rolls, 372
Orange Rolls, 372

Under the Maple Tree, 352
Butternut Squash-White Bean Soup, 353
Cornmeal Scones, 353
Green Salad with Roasted Poblanos and
Cumin-Lime Dressing, 352
Vanilla Bean Sorbet with Pineapple
Topping, 353

Undiscovered Wine Countries, 367
Brunswick Stew with Smoked
Paprika, 367

November

**. . . And Ready in Just About 20
Minutes, 413**
Chicken with Black Bean Sauce, 414
Filet Mignon with Mushroom-Wine
Sauce, 413
Pan-Seared Scallops with Tomatoes and
Pesto, 415
Pasta with Beet Greens and Raisins, 415
Peanut-Crusted Snapper, 413
Pennette with Asparagus and Pine
Nuts, 415
Pork Marsala, 414
Shrimp and Snow Pea Stir-Fry, 414
Tuna with White Bean-Cucumber
Salad, 415

A Whodunit Dinner Dilemma, 416
Roasted Butternut Squash, Rosemary,
and Garlic Lasagna, 416

Crisps and Crumbles, 410
Brandied Caramel-Apple Crumble, 412
Cranberry-Apple Crumble, 412
Gingered Pear Crisp, 410
Orange Crisp with Coconut Topping, 411
Pear-Berry Crisp with Lavender
Topping, 410
Pear Crumble with Dried Tart Cherries
and Almond Streusel, 412
Vanilla-Scented Harvest Crisp with
Pistachios, 410

Delectable Dates, 394
Cardamom-Date Snack Cake, 394
Date and Apricot Chutney, 395
Date-Orange Breakfast Spread, 395
Individual Goat Cheese and Date
Tortas, 396
Onion, Date, and Brie Crostini, 396
Saffron Chicken and Rice with Dates, 395
Sephardic Beef Stew, 396
Spiced Date-Walnut Snacks, 397
Spiced Orzo Pilaf, 397

Election-Night Surprise, 397
Hot Chicken and Chips Retro, 397
New Hampshire Maple-Mustard Salad
Dressing, 398

Pork Stroganoff, 399
Potato, Leek, and Ham Gratin, 398
Venison Chili, 398

Friday **For the Day After, 382**
Asiago-Artichoke-Turkey Spread, 384
Bacon and Hash Brown Casserole, 383
Chicken with Cranberry Barbecue
Sauce, 383
Cranberry Jezebel Sauce with Sautéed
Ham, 384
Curry Turkey Salad, 382
English Muffin Hot Browns, 383
Jack Quesadillas with Cranberry
Salsa, 382
Mushroom and Turkey Casserole, 382
Quick Gravy, 383
Sesame Turkey Cakes with Sweet Chili
Sauce, 385
Turkey-Pasta Soup, 384

Harvest Celebration, 402
Chile-Lime Pineapple with Cardamom-
Lime Ice Cream, 405
Fall Salad with Buttermilk
Dressing, 404
Fruited Couscous Pilaf, 404
Glazed Carrots and Cipollini Onions
with Coriander and Orange, 403
Phyllo Purses with Roasted Squash,
Peppers, and Artichokes, 403
Roasted Tomato-Harissa Soup with
Olive Toasts, 402
Spinach with Chickpeas and Spices, 404

Hot Off the Griddle, 406
Creamy Squash and Apple Soup, 407
Hearty Pancakes, 406
Portobello Mushrooms with
Mediterranean Stuffing, 407
Seco de Quinoa, 406
Stuffed Green Pepper Soup, 406
Super Sloppy Joe Sandwiches, 407

Make-ahead Snacks, 408
Black Bean Spread with Lime and
Cilantro, 408
Cool and Crunchy Crab Dip, 409
Creamy Mushroom Spread, 408
Cumin Curried Hummus, 409
Red Pepper-Walnut Dip, 409
Smoked Trout Spread, 409
Spinach-Parmesan Dip, 409
Tapenade, 408

Rick Rodgers Talks Turkey, 389
Amish Potpie with Turkey Wings, 391
Belgian Turkey Ragoût, 391
Homemade Turkey Stock, 393
Italian Turkey Sausage with Three
Peppers, 389
Roast Turkey with Sausage Gravy, 394
Turkey Breast with Spinach-Feta
Stuffing, 392
Turkey-Jasmine Rice Meatballs with
Baby Bok Choy, 393
Turkey Kielbasa Choucroute, 391
Turkey Scaloppine with Porcini and
Marsala, 393

Saturday **Casual Dinner, 385**
Green Tea Granita, 387

Hot-and-Sour Coconut Soup, 385
Pan-Fried Noodles with Scallops, 386
Pork and Squash Stir-Fry, 386
Shrimp and Spinach Soup, 385
Singapore Mai Fun, 386
Seaside in San Diego, 402
Kabocha Squash Soup, 402
**Spiced Cranberry and Zinfandel
Sauce, 405**
Spiced Cranberry and Zinfandel
Sauce, 405
Sunday **Brunch Buffet, 387**
Fruit Salad with Honey-Yogurt
Sauce, 388
Grits Casserole with Mushrooms,
Prosciutto, and Provolone, 388
Holiday Brunch Tonic, 387
Pistachio Granola, 388
Sour Cream-Hazelnut Bundt Cake, 389
Whole Wheat Apricot Muffins, 387
Thursday **The Big Event, 373**
Apple Cider-Brined Turkey with Savory
Herb Gravy, 374
Brown Sugar-Glazed Sweet Potato
Wedges, 376
Cranberry-Pear Chutney, 376
Herbed Bread Stuffing with Mushrooms
and Sausage, 375
Pecan Pie with Spiked Cream, 381
Pumpkin Pie with Pecan Pastry
Crust, 381
Roasted Butternut Squash Dip, 374
Shredded Brussels Sprouts with Bacon
and Hazelnuts, 376
Spinach-Pear Salad with Mustard
Vinaigrette, 374
Warm Sandwiches, 399
Balsamic-Glazed Chicken Sandwiches
with Red Onions and Goat
Cheese, 399
Pacific Rim Pork Sandwiches with
Hoisin Slaw, 400
Red Wine-Marinated Steak
Sandwiches, 400
Wasabi Salmon Sandwiches, 401
Wednesday **Night Welcome, 373**
Beef Daube Provençal, 373

December

**. . . And Ready in Just About 20
Minutes, 426**
Hoisin Grilled Sirloin, 427
Mojo Bass, 426
Mole-Style Pork Chops, 427
Red Snapper over Sautéed Spinach and
Tomatoes, 427
Roasted Chicken and Goat Cheese
Roll-Ups, 427
Rosemary Fried Scallops with Tomato-
Caper Salad, 427
Turkey Cutlets with Smoky Black Bean
Sauce, 428
**Eggnog Cheese Pie with Bourbon
Cream, 425**
Eggnog Cheese Pie with Bourbon
Cream, 425

New Chicken Dinners, 421
Chicken with Sherry Vinegar
Sauce, 422
Cuban Chicken Pizza, 421
Thai-Style Stir-Fried Chicken, 422
Pass the Pancakes, 423
Honey-Pomegranate Roasted Chicken
Thighs, 424
Middle Eastern Slow-Cooked Stew
with Lamb, Chickpeas, and Figs, 423
Orange Cardamom Cake, 423
Potato Latkes, 424
Sweet Onion, White Bean, and
Artichoke Dip, 424
Vegetable Party Latke, 424
Pasta Perfected by Lidia Bastianich, 417
Campanelle with Salsa Arrabbiata, 419
Gomiti with Broccoli Rabe, Chickpeas,
and Prosciutto, 419
Linguine with White Clam and
Broccoli Sauce, 419
Spaghettini with Oil and Garlic, 417
Whole Wheat Pasta with Sausage,
Leeks, and Fontina, 417
Ziti with Sausage, Onions, and
Fennel, 420
Pudding Bread, 425
Chocolate Chip Pumpkin Bread, 425
Seared Beef Tenderloin Mini
Sandwiches with Mustard-
Horseradish Sauce, 426
Swiss Chard with Almonds and
Shallots, 426
Riviera Maya, 421
Grilled Grouper with Lime and
Mexican Confetti Rice, 421
Scallop Success, 428
Scallops au Gratin, 428

The *Cooking Light* Holiday Cookbook

Appetizers & Beverages, 433
Blackened Shrimp with Pomegranate-
Orange Salsa, 435
Blood Orange Sangría, 434
Caramelized Onion, Red Pepper, and
Mushroom Pizzetti, 434
Cheddar with Sautéed Apples and
Brown Bread, 433
Cheese Dip with Crawfish, 435
Mocha Mudslides, 436
Mulled Cranberry-Guava Toddies, 434
Smoked Salmon Crostini, 434
Spinach, Sun-Dried Tomato, and
Parmesan Rolls, 433
Desserts, 447
Apple Crumb Tart with Maple Ice
Milk, 450
Black Forest Icebox Cookies, 449
Coffee-Chocolate Torte, 450
Cranberry-Pear Crumb Pie, 451
Ginger-Hazelnut Pumpkin Tart, 448
Lemon-Scented Coconut Macaroon
Bars, 449
Peppermint Brownie à la Mode, 448
Red Raspberry Velvet Cake, 447

Upside-Down Cranberry-Ginger
Cake, 448
Vanilla-Bourbon Bread Pudding, 449
Gifts from the Kitchen, 451
Candied Hazelnut Brittle, 452
Christmas Sugar Wafers with Vanilla
Icing, 453
Ginger Shortbread, 454
Kumquats in Spiced Syrup with Cloves,
Cinnamon, and Star Anise, 454
Mini Cranberry Panettones, 452
Sugar-Frosted Cardamom Braid, 451
Toasted Pecan Divinity, 453
White Chocolate-Cashew Coffee
Biscotti, 453
Main Dishes, 440
Duck Breasts with Kumquat Chutney, 443
Fig and Stilton-Stuffed Turkey Breast
with Port Sauce, 440
Horseradish and Mustard-Crusted Beef
Tenderloin, 442
Jambalaya, 442
Maple and Calvados-Glazed Pork
Crown Roast with Apple-Chestnut
Purée, 443
Pappardelle with Roasted Winter
Squash, Arugula, and Pine Nuts, 441
Roasted Chicken with Asiago Polenta
and Truffled Mushrooms, 440
Seared Sea Scallops with Spicy Citrus
Sauce, 442
Sesame Halibut en Papillote, 441
On the Side, 444
Barley with Shiitakes and Spinach, 446
Butternut Squash and Leek Gratins, 446
Carrot Coins with Maple-Balsamic
Browned Butter, 444
Chianti-Stained Risotto with Pears and
Blue Cheese, 446
Creamed Cauliflower with Herbed
Crumb Topping, 447
Fruited Basmati Pilaf with
Pistachios, 444
Golden Rutabagas and Shallots, 445
Herbed Parmesan Soufflé, 445
Meringue and Streusel-Topped Sweet
Potatoes, 444
Peppery Baked Onions with Sage and
Gruyère, 445
Sugar Snap Peas with Lemon and
Toasted Almonds, 445
Soups, Salads, & Breads, 436
Carrot-Parsnip Soup with Parsnip
Chips, 436
Celery-Celeriac Soup with Roquefort
Croutons, 437
Chicken Chowder with Chipotle
(Chupe de Pollo con Chipotle), 437
Citrus Salad with Shrimp and
Watercress, 438
Dinner Rolls, Five Ways, 439
Escarole and Fennel Salad with Pears
and Gruyère, 437
Onion Soup Gratinée, 436
Peppernut Tea Bread, 438
Yeasted Corn Bread, 438

General Recipe Index

*A listing by major ingredient and food category
for every recipe that appeared in the magazine in 2004.*

Almonds
Apples with Caramel-Apple Sauce, Almond-Stuffed Baked, 299
Rice Pilaf, Almond, 384
Romesco, Spanish Tortilla with Almond, 97
Streusel, Pear Crumble with Dried Tart Cherries and Almond, 412
Ambrosia, Orange, Pineapple, and Coconut, 11
Anchovies and Walnuts, Pasta with, 27
Appetizers. *See also* Snacks.
Beef Tenderloin Mini Sandwiches with Mustard-Horseradish Sauce, Seared, 426
Bruschetta, Mushroom and Parmigiano, 106
Bruschetta with Warm Tomatoes, 276
Cheddar with Sautéed Apples and Brown Bread, 433
Cheesecake, Sun-Dried Tomato, 321
Chicken Buns, Baked Hoisin, 301
Confit with Prosciutto, Peppered Garlic, 361
Crostini, Onion, Date, and Brie, 396
Crostini, Smoked Salmon, 434
Dips
Caramelized Onion Dip, 77
Cheese Dip with Crawfish, 435
Crab Dip, Cool and Crunchy, 409
Fruit Dip, Lemony, 45
Guacamole with Chips, Easy, 215
Onion, White Bean, and Artichoke Dip, Sweet, 424
Red Pepper-Cheese Dip, 345
Red Pepper-Walnut Dip, 409
Roasted Butternut Squash Dip, 374
Spinach-Parmesan Dip, 409
White Bean Dip, 223
Galloping Horses, 302
Larb, Tofu, 301
Lobster and Pepper Salad with Asian Herbs, Maine, 225
Mussels with Cardamom, Orange, and Mint, Steamed, 316
Olives with Fennel and Orange, Warm, 361
Pizzetti, Caramelized Onion, Red Pepper, and Mushroom, 434
Scallops, Sweet Potato, and Pecan Salad, Seared, 77
Seviche, Mango Mahi, 51
Shrimp with Pomegranate-Orange Salsa, Blackened, 435
Spinach, Sun-Dried Tomato, and Parmesan Rolls, 433
Spreads
Black Bean Spread with Lime and Cilantro, 408
Hummus, Cumin Curried, 409
Mushroom Spread, Creamy, 408
Smoked Trout Spread, 409
Spring Rolls with Dipping Sauce, Fresh, 87

Sui Mei, Crab and Scallop, 302
Tapenade, 408
Tortas, Individual Goat Cheese and Date, 395
Tuna Tartare in Endive with Horseradish Sauce, 258
Apples
Baked Apples with Caramel-Apple Sauce, Almond-Stuffed, 299
Bisque with Chestnuts, Apple, 332
Butter, Overnight Apple, 331
Cake, Apple Spice, 44
Cider-Brined Turkey with Savory Herb Gravy, Apple, 374
Cobbler, Apple-Cranberry, 332
Cobbler, Apple, Rhubarb, and Sour Cherry Passover, 91
Crumble, Brandied Caramel-Apple, 412
Hash, Apple and Chicken, 332
Parfaits, Apple Pie à la Mode, 267
Pie, Apple-Orange, 326
Pies, Unfried Apple, 15
Pork Roast with Apples, Oven-Braised, 324
Pork with Apples, Cabbage, and Turnips, Roast, 331
Pudding, Charleston, 333
Purée, Maple and Calvados-Glazed Pork Crown Roast with Apple-Chestnut, 443
Roasted Vanilla-Scented Apples, 11
Salad, Autumn Apple and Spinach, 331
Salmon, Apple and Horseradish-Glazed, 159
Sautéed Apples and Brown Bread, Cheddar with, 433
Strudel, Apple-Cream Cheese, 138
Tarte Tatin, 20
Tart, Thin French Apple, 65
Tart with Maple Ice Milk, Apple Crumb, 450
Topping and Orange Sauce, Couscous with Apple-Ginger, 218
Apricots
Asparagus, Apricot-Glazed Roasted, 87
Cakes, Apricot-Cherry Upside-Down Mini, 197
Chicken Tenders with Apricots and Sautéed Spinach, 80
Glaze, Grilled Cornish Hens with Apricot-Mustard, 160
Glaze, Roasted Loin of Pork with Apricot-Rum, 100
Muffins, Whole Wheat Apricot, 387
Sauce, Apricot-Lavender, 275
Artichokes
Braised Baby Artichokes and New Potatoes, 56
Calzones, Roasted Chicken-Artichoke, 252
Chicken and Rice with Artichokes, Lemon, 13
Salad, Artichoke-Kalamata Olive, 55
Sunchoke and Tomato Gratin, 360
Sunchoke-Chicken Salad Wraps, 360

Sunchoke Latkes, 359
Sunchokes and Fennel, Roasted, 359
Sunchoke Stir-Fry, Spicy Chicken and, 359
Asparagus
Carbonara, Asparagus and Chicken, 212
Glazed Roasted Asparagus, Apricot-, 87
Grilled Asparagus with Lemon, 241
Noodles with Asparagus and Shrimp, Asian, 32
Pasta with Asparagus, Lemon, and Prosciutto, 122
Pennette with Asparagus and Pine Nuts, 415
Risotto with Asparagus Spears, Three-Grain, 106
Salad with Mustard-Soy Dressing, Asparagus, 26
Sesame Asparagus, Triple, 46
Soup, Asparagus-Potato, 244
Stir-Fry, Lemony Asparagus-Mushroom, 50
Tart, Asparagus-Fontina, 140
Avocados
Guacamole with Chips, Easy, 215
Oil, Spiced Shrimp with Avocado, 135
Salad with Avocado and Tomatoes, Green, 12
Salsa, Grilled Tuna with Avocado, 232
Spread, Toasted Bagels with Avocado-Cilantro, 284

Bacon. *See also* **Ham.**
Brussels Sprouts with Bacon and Hazelnuts, Shredded, 376
Carbonara, Linguine, 203
Casserole, Bacon and Hash Brown, 383
Cubano with Bacon, Pressed, 185
Eggs Hussarde, 53
Kale with Bacon and Cider, Braised, 19
Pitas, Smoky Bacon and Blue Cheese Chicken Salad, 151
Salad, BLT Bread, 243
Bananas
Latte, Frozen Banana, 245
Loaf, Banana-Oatmeal, 326
Napoleons, Banana-Walnut, 133
Parfaits, Funky Monkey, 267
Soup with Bananas (Che Chuoi), Sweet Coconut Tapioca, 285
Barbecue. *See also* **Grilled.**
Beans, Barbecue, 166
Beef Sandwiches, Barbecue, 38
Pulled-Pork Barbecue Sandwiches, Chipotle, 186
Sauces
Cranberry Barbecue Sauce, Chicken with, 383
Honey Barbecue Sauce, Dry-Rub Chicken with, 126
Sriracha Barbecue Dipping Sauce, Seared Chicken with, 249

Barley
Cabbage Rolls with Pine Nuts and Currants, Barley-Stuffed, 365
Risotto with Fennel and Olives, Barley, 264
Salad with Fresh Corn and Sweet Onions, Barley-Chicken, 283
Shiitakes and Spinach, Barley with, 446
Beans. *See also* **Lentils, Salads.**
Baked Beans, Summer, 229
Barbecue Beans, 166
Black
Chicken, Black Bean, 38
Quesadillas with Corn Salsa, Black Bean, 78
Sauce, Chicken with Black Bean, 414
Sauce, Steamed Salmon with Savory Black Bean, 221
Sauce, Turkey Cutlets with Smoky Black Bean, 428
Soup, Black Bean, 188
Soup, Chochoyones in Black Bean, 85
Spread with Lime and Cilantro, Black Bean, 408
Burgers with Chipotle Ketchup, Corn and Two-Bean, 324
Chickpeas and Spices, Spinach with, 404
Chickpeas, Minestrone with, 325
Chickpeas over Garlic Spinach, Indian, 210
Chickpeas with Spinach, 130
Garbanzo and Greens Stew, 356
Gigantes in Tomato Sauce, Baked, 55
Green
Amandine, Green Beans, 198
Chive Green Beans, 48
Field Peas with Green Beans, 178
Sesame Green Beans, 253
Hummus, Cumin Curried, 409
Hummus, Garlic and Sun-Dried Tomato, 13
Hummus-Stuffed Pitas with Vegetables, 150
Pasta with Beans, Southwestern, 280
Pink Beans (Arroz con Habichuelas Rosadas Guisadas), Rice with Stewed, 312
Pinto Bean Chili with Corn and Winter Squash, 366
Pinto Beans, Southwestern Steak and, 202
Red Beans, African Sweet Potato Stew with, 366
Soup Beans, Savory, 15
Tabbouleh, Pork, 314
White
Cannellini Stew with Sausage and Kale and Cheese Toasts, 349
Cassoulet, Thyme-Scented White Bean, 367
Chili with White Beans, Chicken Green, 355
Dip, White Bean, 223
Ragoût with Fennel Relish, White Bean, Artichoke, and Chard, 364
Roasted Red Pepper and Pesto, White Beans with, 165
Beef. *See also* **Beef, Ground; Grilled.**
Bolognese, Potato Gnocchi with, 84
Bourguignonne with Egg Noodles, Beef, 304
Braised Beef with Sun-Dried Tomatoes, 318
Orange Beef, Spicy, 38
Pickled Beef, New England-Style, 174

Roasts
Carrots, Onions, and Dried Plums, Beef Cooked with, 115
Daube Provençal, Beef, 373
Soup (Pho Bo), Hanoi Beef and Rice Noodle, 286
Sandwiches with Mustard-Horseradish Sauce, Seared Beef Tenderloin Mini, 426
Sirloin, Hoisin Grilled, 427
Steaks
Filet Mignon with Mushroom-Wine Sauce, 413
Filet Mignon with Port Jus, Peppercorn-Crusted, 48
Flank Steak, Rice Noodles with Sesame-Ginger, 198
Ginger Beef, 31
Grillades and Gravy over Grits, 52
Mustard-Caper Sauce, Steak with, 262
Pepper Beef, Three-, 219
Salad, Thai Beef and Radish, 108
Sandwiches, Barbecue Beef, 38
Sandwiches, Red Wine-Marinated Steak, 400
Sirloin Steak with Dijon-Port Sauce, 350
Soup (Cocido), Beef and Vegetable, 356
Southwestern Steak and Pinto Beans, 202
Spiced Beef with Wine Sauce and Roasted Potatoes, 266
Tenderloin with Porcini Mushroom Sauce, Beef, 325
Stew, Beef, 7
Stew, Sephardic Beef, 396
Stew, Slow Cooker Beef, 88
Stew, Vegetable-Beef, 61
Tenderloin, Horseradish and Mustard-Crusted Beef, 442
Tenderloin, Peppercorn and Mustard-Crusted Beef, 362
Beef, Ground
Caldo de Bolas, 86
Hamburger, Cheddar, and Macaroni Toss, 279
Meatball Soup (Sopa de Albóndigas), 355
Peppers, Skillet Stuffed, 162
Plantain "Canoes" Stuffed with Ground Meat (Canoas), Ripe, 309
Sloppy Joes, 8
Soup, Beef and Green Chile, 327
Stuffed Peppers, Beef and Barley-, 208
Tacos, Tex-Mex Beef, 129
Beets
Breadsticks, Prussian Leaf-Wrapped, 34
Horseradish, Homemade Beet, 89
Salad with Raspberry Vinaigrette, Roasted Beet, 144
Salad with Ricotta-Provolone Topping, Beet and Red Onion, 179
Soup, Savory Beet, 346
Beverages
Agua Fresca, Watermelon, 229
Alcoholic
Bloody Mary, 53
Café Brûlot, 52
Daiquiris, Frozen Strawberry, 190
Martini, Mango, 312

Mocha Mudslides, 436
Mojito, Classic, 312
Mojitos, Slushy Watermelon, 264
Pimm's Cup, 264
Sangría, Blood Orange, 434
Sangría, Puerto Rican, 313
Splash, Sparkling Peach, 265
Toddies, Mulled Cranberry-Guava, 434
Blueberry Blender, 196
Breeze, Tropical, 245
Cider, Mulled Cranberry-Apple, 8
Freeze, Triple Berry, 245
Latte, Frozen Banana, 245
Sipper, Cool Melon, 246
Slush, Spicy Mango-Orange, 245
Smoothies
Blackberry-Peach Smoothie with Walnuts, 246
Chamomile-Fruit Smoothie, 195
Vanilla-Honey-Nut Smoothie, 246
Tea, Herbed Green, 198
Tea, Iced Mint, 218
Tonic, Ginger-Lemon, 245
Tonic, Holiday Brunch, 387
Biscuits and Vegetarian Sausage Gravy, 328
Blackberry-Peach Smoothie with Walnuts, 246
Blackberry Shortcakes, Blueberry-, 237
Blackberry-Zinfandel Quail, 161
Blueberries
Blender, Blueberry, 196
Cake, Blueberry Gingerbread, 238
Cake, Blueberry-Pumpkin Pound, 238
Cheesecake, Blueberry, 239
French Toast, Berry, 102
Jam, Wildflower Inn Blueberry, 237
Muffins, Blueberry Cinnamon-Burst, 239
Muffins, Spiced Blueberry, 240
Sauce, Lemon-Buttermilk Panna Cotta with Blueberry, 297
Shortcakes, Blueberry-Blackberry, 237
Bok Choy, Chicken Fried Rice with, 71
Bok Choy, Turkey-Jasmine Rice Meatballs with Baby, 393
Breads. *See also* specific types.
Banana-Oatmeal Loaf, 326
Breadsticks, Peppery Cheese, 152
Brown Soda Bread, 61
Bruschetta, Wild Mushroom, 137
Cracker Bread, Herbed, 263
Cuban Bread with Tomatoes, 39
Fattoush, Pork, 323
Focaccia, Spinach and Feta-Stuffed, 289
Nut Bread, Moist 'n' Dark, 47
Pain Perdu, 52
Popovers, 92
Puddings
Butternut Squash and Parmesan Bread Pudding, 340
Corn and Chipotle Bread Pudding, 340
Greek-Style Bread Pudding, 340
Mushroom, Roasted Red Pepper, and Goat Cheese Bread Pudding, 339
Sausage, Apple, and Cheddar Bread Pudding, 339
Vanilla-Bourbon Bread Pudding, 449
Pumpkin Bread, Chocolate Chip, 425

Breads (*continued*)

Rolls, Garlic-Parmesan, 279
Salad, BLT Bread, 243
Scones, Cornmeal, 353
Scones, Savory Herb Sun-Dried Tomato, 321
Shortcakes with Tomato-Ginger Jam,
    Cornmeal, 258
Sopes with Chipotle Mayonnaise, Shrimp, and
    Pineapple Slaw, Green Chile, 157
Tea Bread, Orange-Pecan, 119
Tea Bread, Peppernut, 438
Toasts, Garlic-Parmesan, 152
Yeast
    Babka, Sour Cream, 33
    Braid, Sugar-Frosted Cardamom, 451
    Breadsticks, Prussian Leaf-Wrapped, 34
    Cinnamon-Raisin Bread, Miller's, 35
    Flatbread with Oven-Dried Figs,
        Caramelized Onions, and Blue
        Cheese, 291
    Focaccia, Fig and Mascarpone, 120
    Focaccia, Toasted Hazelnut, 134
    Oatmeal Bread, Irish, 16
    Panettones, Mini Cranberry, 452
    Pizza Dough, 10
    Rolls, Five Ways, Dinner, 439
    Rolls, Orange, 372
    Rye Loaves, Country, 347
    Sour Rye Bread, Hearty, 36
    Sriracha Bread, Spicy, 250
    Wheat and Soy Bread, Prairie Fields, 35
    Wheat Bread, Hearty, 8
    Zwieback, 36
Zucchini Bread, Chocolate Chip, 224
Broccoli
Balsamic-Butter Sauce, Broccoli with, 289
Couscous with Broccoli and Feta, Curried, 30
Penne with Broccoli, Green Olives, and Pine
    Nuts, Whole Wheat, 276
Pizzas with Broccoli, Cheese, and Meat Sauce,
    Individual, 150
Rabe, Chicken Scaloppine over Broccoli, 293
Rabe, Chickpeas, and Prosciutto, Gomiti with
    Broccoli, 419
Rabe, Sautéed Broccoli, 104
Salad, Broccoli, Orange, and Watercress, 7
Soba Noodles with Broccoli and Chicken, 150
Brussels Sprouts with Bacon and Hazelnuts,
    Shredded, 376
Bulgur and Chickpea Salad, Moroccan-Spiced, 283
Burrito, Sausage and Egg, 123
Butter
Apple Butter, Overnight, 331
Honey-Pecan Butter, Millet Muffins with, 99
Maple-Balsamic Browned Butter, Carrot Coins
    with, 444
Sauce, Broccoli with Balsamic-Butter, 289

Cabbage. *See also* **Salads.**
Bierocks, 33
Mash (Patatas y Berzas), Potato and
    Cabbage, 76
Stuffed Cabbage Rolls with Pine Nuts and
    Currants, Barley-, 365
Cactus Salad, 129

Cakes
Apple Spice Cake, 44
Baklava Cake, Passover, 90
Blueberry Gingerbread Cake, 238
Cheesecakes
    Blueberry Cheesecake, 239
    Key Lime Cheesecake, 101
    Yogurt Cheesecake with Caramelized
        Onions, Savory, 18
Chocolate Cake, Mexican, 274
Chocolate Pudding Cake, 19
Coffee Cake, Sour Cream, 127
Pound
    Blueberry-Pumpkin Pound Cake, 238
    Croutons, Cherries in Spiced Wine Syrup
        with Pound Cake, 264
    Lemon Pound Cake with Mixed
        Berries, 125
    Sour Cream Pound Cake with Rum
        Glaze, 259
Pumpkin-Orange Cake, 348
Red Raspberry Velvet Cake, 447
Rhubarb Pudding Cake, 154
Shortcakes, Blueberry-Blackberry, 237
Snack Cake, Cardamom-Date, 394
Sour Cream-Hazelnut Bundt Cake, 389
Upside-Down Cake, Pineapple-Coconut-
    Banana, 20
Upside-Down Cake, Spiced Fig, 292
Upside-Down Cranberry-Ginger Cake, 448
Upside-Down Mini Cakes, Apricot-
    Cherry, 197
Candies
Brittle, Candied Hazelnut, 452
Divinity, Toasted Pecan, 453
Caramel
Condensed Milk, Caramelized, 169
Cookies, Dulce de Leche-Filled, 169
Crumble, Brandied Caramel-Apple, 412
Pie, Café con Leche Cream, 158
Sauce, Almond-Stuffed Baked Apples with
    Caramel-Apple, 299
Carrots
Beef Cooked with Carrots, Onions, and Dried
    Plums, 115
Coins with Maple-Balsamic Browned Butter,
    Carrot, 444
Glazed Carrots and Cipollini Onions with
    Coriander and Orange, 403
Herbed Carrots, 151
Paprika and Capers, Carrots with, 218
Soup with Parsnip Chips, Carrot-Parsnip, 436
Casseroles. *See also* **Lasagna.**
Asiago, Potato, and Bacon Gratin, 118
Bacon and Hash Brown Casserole, 383
Chicken and Chips Retro, Hot, 397
Chicken Fettuccine, Cajun-Spiced, 216
Chicken-Green Chile Enchilada Casserole, 328
Chicken Noodles, Baked Sesame, 41
Crawfish and Rice Casserole, 215
French Toast Casserole, Orange-Pecan, 216
Gigantes in Tomato Sauce, Baked, 55
Grits Casserole with Mushrooms, Prosciutto,
    and Provolone, 388
Italian Sausage Puttanesca, 44
Mac and Cheese Florentine, 208

Macaroni and Cheese, Chipotle, 248
Mushroom and Turkey Casserole, 382
Pasta, Creamy Gruyère and Shrimp, 42
Pastel de Choclo, 168
Potato, Leek, and Ham Gratin, 398
Ravioli Bake, Easy, 43
Roasted Butternut Squash and Bacon
    Pasta, 41
Strata, Goat Cheese, Artichoke, and Smoked
    Ham, 177
Strata, Veggie Sausage and Egg, 329
Vegetable
    Corn Fritter Casserole, 296
    Greens and Potato Casserole, Winter, 14
    Mushroom Pasta Bake, 42
    Potato and Summer Vegetable Stovetop
        Casserole, 277
    Spinach, Tomatoes, and Smoked Gouda,
        Ziti Baked with, 43
    Sweet Potato and Carrot Tzimmes, 90
    Yellow Squash Gratin, 95
Ziti with Shrimp and Scallops, Baked, 43
Cauliflower with Herbed Crumb Topping,
    Creamed, 447
Cheese. *See also* **Breads, Salads, Sandwiches.**
Bruschetta, Mushroom and Parmigiano, 106
Casseroles
    Asiago, Potato, and Bacon Gratin, 118
    Goat Cheese, Artichoke, and Smoked
        Ham Strata, 177
    Pasta, Creamy Gruyère and Shrimp, 42
Cheddar with Sautéed Apples and Brown
    Bread, 433
Cheesecake, Sun-Dried Tomato, 321
Chicken Breasts Stuffed with Goat Cheese and
    Sun-Dried Tomatoes, 67
Chiles Rellenos, Baked, 223
Couscous, Bell Pepper and Fresh
    Mozzarella, 252
Desserts
    Cheesecake Parfaits, Black
        Forest, 268
    Cheesecake Squares, Marble, 370
    Pierogi, Sweet Vanilla Cheese, 84
    Strudel, Apple-Cream Cheese, 138
    Tiramisu Trifles, Individual, 304
Dip, Red Pepper-Cheese, 345
Dip with Crawfish, Cheese, 435
Huevos Rancheros with Queso Fresco, 11
Lamb with Potato-Parsnip Mash, Feta and
    Lemon-Stuffed, 257
Mac and Cheese Florentine, 208
Macaroni and Cheese, Chipotle, 248
Mousse with Summer Berries, Ricotta-
    Honey, 136
Orzo, Bell Pepper Chicken with Feta, 149
Orzo, Creamy Parmesan, 48
Pasta, Feta-Chicken, 262
Pasta with Butter and Parmesan Cheese,
    Penne, 369
Pie with Bourbon Cream, Eggnog
    Cheese, 425
Pizza, Eggplant Parmesan, 351
Pizza, White, 46
Polenta, Garlic-Fontina, 160
Polenta, Lamb Osso Buco over Parmesan, 303

Quesadillas with Cranberry Salsa, Jack, 382
Roll-Ups, Cream Cheese, 213
Roll-Ups, Roasted Chicken and Goat
    Cheese, 427
Sauce, Potatoes with Spicy Cheese, 169
Soufflé, Herbed Parmesan, 445
Spread, Asiago-Artichoke-Turkey, 384
Spread, Feta-Chile, 55
Stuffing, Baked Eggplant with Savory
    Cheese, 54
Tarts, Feta-Spinach, 141
Tortas, Individual Goat Cheese and Date, 395
Cherries
Cobbler, Fresh Cherry, 180
Cookies, Black Forest Icebox, 449
Dried Cherry Pan Sauce, Pork Medallions with
    Port Wine-, 64
Dried Tart Cherries and Almond Streusel, Pear
    Crumble with, 412
Meringues, Chocolate-Cherry Chunk, 170
Oatmeal, Cherry-Hazelnut, 132
Parfaits, Black Forest Cheesecake, 268
Sauce, Duck Breast with Cherry-Pepper, 333
Spiced Wine Syrup with Pound Cake Croutons,
    Cherries in, 264
Turnovers, Cherry-Apricot, 142
Zinfandel Syrup, Cherries in, 317
Chicken. *See also* **Grilled/Poultry; Salads/Chicken;**
    Sandwiches/Chicken; Soups/Chicken.
Arroz con Pollo, 70
Asian Chicken over Noodles, 37
Asopao, 72
Baked Sesame Chicken Noodles, 41
Bell Pepper Chicken with Feta Orzo, 149
Biriyani, Chicken, 72
Bistro Chicken and Peppers, 207
Black Bean Chicken, 38
Black Bean Sauce, Chicken with, 414
Braised in Walnut Sauce, Chicken, 16
Braised with Leeks and Figs, Chicken, 291
Breasts Stuffed with Goat Cheese and Sun-
    Dried Tomatoes, Chicken, 67
Breasts Stuffed with Spinach and Ricotta,
    Chicken, 358
Breasts with Tarragon-Caper Sauce,
    Chicken, 247
Brunswick Stew with Smoked Paprika, 367
Cacciatore, Chicken, 357
Carbonara, Asparagus and Chicken, 212
Casserole, Chicken-Green Chile
    Enchilada, 328
Cherry Tomato and Olive Topping, Chicken
    with, 163
Chiles Rellenos, Baked, 223
Chili, White Chicken, 350
Chili with White Beans, Chicken Green, 355
Chimichangas, Roast Chicken, 122
Chowder with Chipotle (Chupe de Pollo con
    Chipotle), Chicken, 437
Citrus, Chicken with, 113
Cranberry Barbecue Sauce, Chicken
    with, 383
Cremini Mushrooms and Asparagus, Chicken
    with, 203
Crêpes, Creamy Chicken and Mushroom, 289
Curried Chicken, Coconut, 322

Curried Chicken Penne with Fresh Mango
    Chutney, 188
Dry-Rub Chicken with Honey Barbecue
    Sauce, 126
Dumplings, Chicken and Rosemary, 82
Fettuccine, Cajun-Spiced Chicken, 216
Fried Rice with Bok Choy, Chicken, 71
Ginger and Green Onion-Salt Dip, Chicken
    with, 287
Glazed Chicken with Dried Cranberries,
    Cider-, 203
Green Olives, Chicken with, 25
Hash, Apple and Chicken, 332
Hot Chicken and Chips Retro, 397
Jambalaya, 442
Jerk-Style Chicken, 125
Lemon Chicken and Rice with Artichokes, 13
Linguine, Walnut-Chicken, 133
Maple-Orange Chicken, 205
Morels (Pollo con Jugo de Morillas), Chicken
    with, 74
Moroccan Chicken and Lentils, 208
Moroccan Chicken with Almond Couscous, 50
Paella, Chicken and Shrimp, 71
Parmesan Chicken and Rice, 198
Pasta, Feta-Chicken, 262
Pasta, Spicy Chicken, 121
Pasta Toss, Sun-Dried Tomato Pesto and
    Chicken-, 319
Pasta with Chicken and Mushrooms,
    Creamy, 206
Pastel de Choclo, 168
Pepper Sauce, Chicken with Chunky, 163
Piccata, Chicken, 348
Pilaf with Chicken, Spinach, and Walnuts, 70
Pizza, Cuban Chicken, 421
Pizza with Chicken, Ratatouille, 211
Port Wine Sauce, Chicken with, 205
Quesadillas, Chicken, Mushroom, and
    Cheese, 247
Roasted Chicken and Goat Cheese Roll-
    Ups, 427
Roasted Chicken, Cider-, 347
Roasted Chicken Thighs, Honey-
    Pomegranate, 424
Roasted Chicken with Asiago Polenta and
    Truffled Mushrooms, 440
Saffron Chicken and Rice with Dates, 395
Salsa Chicken, 123
Sautéed Chicken Breasts with Balsamic Vinegar
    Pan Sauce, 62
Sautéed Chicken Breasts with Latin Citrus
    Sauce, 204
Scaloppine over Broccoli Rabe, Chicken, 293
Seared Chicken with Sriracha Barbecue
    Dipping Sauce, 249
Sherry Vinegar Sauce, Chicken with, 422
Shireen Palow (Afghan Orange Rice with
    Chicken), 70
Singapore Mai Fun, 386
Smoked Paprika-Spiced Chicken over Lentils
    with Yogurt-Cumin Sauce, 128
Soba Noodles with Broccoli and Chicken, 150
Southwestern Chicken Roll-Ups, 189
Spiced Chicken with Black-Eyed Peas and
    Rice, 246

Stew, Chicken and Barley, 30
Stew, Chicken Vegetable, 357
Stewed Chicken (Mofongo Relleno de Pollo
    Guisado), Plantains and Pork Cracklings
    with, 311
Stir-Fried Chicken, Thai-Style, 422
Stir-Fry, Hoisin Chicken and Broccoli, 32
Stir-Fry, Spicy Chicken and Sunchoke, 359
Stir-Fry, Thai-Style Chicken, 327
Succotash with Chicken, Summer, 212
Tagine, Chicken, Date, and Apricot, 65
Tenders with Apricots and Sautéed Spinach,
    Chicken, 80
Thai-Style Chicken, 232
Thighs with Olives and Red Peppers,
    Chicken, 338
Yakitori, 247
Chili
Chicken Chili, White, 350
Chicken Green Chili with White Beans, 355
Pinto Bean Chili with Corn and Winter
    Squash, 366
Twenty-Minute Chili, 80
Venison Chili, 398
Chocolate
Bars and Cookies
Biscotti, White Chocolate-Cashew
    Coffee, 453
Brownie à la Mode, Peppermint, 448
Icebox Cookies, Black Forest, 449
Meringue Sandwiches, Peanut Butter-
    Chocolate, 172
Meringues, Chocolate-Cherry
    Chunk, 170
Meringues, Tweed, 171
Peanut Butter Cookies, Chocolate and, 88
Bread, Chocolate Chip Pumpkin, 425
Bread, Chocolate Chip Zucchini, 224
Buttercrunch, Matzo, 89
Cakes and Torte
Coffee-Chocolate Torte, 450
Mexican Chocolate Cake, 274
Pudding Cake, Chocolate, 19
Dutch Baby, Chocolate Chip, 19
Éclairs, Phyllo, 141
Log, Sweet Chocolate, 138
Mocha Mudslides, 436
Parfaits, Black Forest Cheesecake, 268
Parfaits, Funky Monkey, 267
Sorbet, Bittersweet Chocolate, 364
Sorbet, Chocolate-Mint, 371
Soufflés with Pistachios, Chocolate, 48
Chowder, Fish, 260
Chowder with Chipotle (Chupe de Pollo con
    Chipotle), Chicken, 437
Chutneys. *See also* **Pesto, Relishes, Salsas, Sauces.**
Cranberry-Pear Chutney, 376
Date and Apricot Chutney, 395
Kumquat Chutney, Duck Breasts with, 443
Mango Chutney, Curried Chicken Penne with
    Fresh, 188
Minted Chutney, Curried Lamb Chops
    with, 206
Rhubarb Chutney, Grilled Pork Chops
    with, 154
Tomato Chutney, Pork Chops with, 77

Clams

Cherry Tomatoes (Almejas con Tomates), Clams with, 75

Pasta with Clams, Scallops, and Shrimp, Gemelli, 281

Sauce, Linguine with Clam, 318

Sauce, Linguine with White Clam and Broccoli, 419

Coconut

Chicken, Coconut Curried, 322

Couscous, Coconut-Almond, 320

Custard (Tembleque), Coconut, 312

French Toast with Grilled Pineapple and Tropical Salsa, Coconut, 195

Frushi, Coconut, 195

Macaroon Bars, Lemon-Scented Coconut, 449

Meringues, Coconut, 171

Parfaits, Coconut Cream Pie, 268

Shrimp Cakes with Papaya-Lime Sauce, Coconut Curry, 158

Soup, Hot-and-Sour Coconut, 385

Soup with Bananas (Che Chuoi), Sweet Coconut Tapioca, 285

Topping, Orange Crisp with Coconut, 411

Cookies

Bars and Squares

Brownie à la Mode, Peppermint, 448

Coconut Macaroon Bars, Lemon-Scented, 449

Pecan Bar Cookies, 20

Pecan Bars, Passover, 91

Biscotti, White Chocolate-Cashew Coffee, 453

Chocolate and Peanut Butter Cookies, 88

Dulce de Leche-Filled Cookies, 169

Icebox Cookies, Black Forest, 449

Macadamia and Ginger Cookies, 256

Oatmeal-Walnut Cookies, 9

Shortbread, Ginger, 454

Sugar Wafers with Vanilla Icing, Christmas, 453

Corn. *See also* **Salads, Salsas.**

Bisque with Basil, Avocado, and Crab, Chilled Corn, 156

Burgers with Chipotle Ketchup, Corn and Two-Bean, 324

Casserole, Corn Fritter, 296

Chipotle Bread Pudding, Corn and, 340

Chow-Chow, Corn, 15

Corn Bread with Fresh Corn, 222

Frittata with Smoked Mozzarella, Fresh Corn, 275

Grilled Corn with Creamy Chipotle Sauce, 230

Pastel de Choclo, 168

Quesadilla with Smoked Mozzarella, Corn and Sun-Dried Tomato, 254

Relish, Spicy Corn, 262

Risotto with Seared Shrimp and Salsa Verde, Fresh Corn, 227

Soufflé, Roasted Garlic and Corn, 102

Soup, Mexican Corn and Bean, 31

Tortillas, Corn, 155

Corn Breads

Buttermilk Corn Bread, Quick, 14

Chipotle-Bacon Corn Bread, 251

Corn, Corn Bread with Fresh, 222

Yeasted Corn Bread, 438

Cornish Hens

Grilled Cornish Hens with Apricot-Mustard Glaze, 160

Oven-Braised Cornish Hens with Cider Vinegar and Warm Vegetable Sauce, 100

Couscous. *See also* **Salads.**

Almond Couscous, Moroccan Chicken with, 50

Apple-Ginger Topping and Orange Sauce, Couscous with, 218

Bell Pepper and Fresh Mozzarella Couscous, 252

Coconut-Almond Couscous, 320

Curried Couscous with Broccoli and Feta, 30

Curried Couscous with Pine Nuts and Currants, 193

Lentil Couscous with Spinach, 244

Pilaf, Fruited Couscous, 404

Saffron Couscous, 363

Crab

Bisque with Basil, Avocado, and Crab, Chilled Corn, 156

Cakes with Creole Tartar Sauce, Louisiana Crab, 248

Cakes with Rémoulade, Crab, 29

Dip, Cool and Crunchy Crab, 409

Empanadas (Empanadas de Cangrejo y Mango), Crab-and-Mango, 309

Enchiladas with Crab, Green, 157

Lobster with Citrus Vinaigrette, Crab-Stuffed, 295

Quesadillas, Crab, 121

Sui Mei, Crab and Scallop, 302

Cranberries. *See also* **Salsas, Sauces.**

Cake, Upside-Down Cranberry-Ginger, 448

Chutney, Cranberry-Pear, 376

Cider, Mulled Cranberry-Apple, 8

Crumble, Cranberry and Apple, 9

Crumble, Cranberry-Apple, 412

Dried Cranberries, Cider-Glazed Chicken with, 203

Panettones, Mini Cranberry, 452

Pie, Cranberry-Pear Crumb, 451

Syrup, Cran-Grape, 16

Tabbouleh, Cranberry Walnut, 132

Toddies, Mulled Cranberry-Guava, 434

Crawfish and Rice Casserole, 215

Crawfish, Cheese Dip with, 435

Crêpes, Creamy Chicken and Mushroom, 289

Croutons

Cheese Croutons, Chunky Vegetable Soup with Toasted, 202

Goat Cheese Croutons, Mixed Greens Salad with, 74

Pound Cake Croutons, Cherries in Spiced Wine Syrup with, 264

Roquefort Croutons, Celery-Celeriac Soup with, 437

Sourdough Croutons and Warm Tomato Vinaigrette, Bitter Greens Salad with, 303

Cucumbers

Pita, Garlic-Rosemary Lamb, 29

Raita, Radish, 107

Salsa, Trout Topped with Cucumber, 167

Sauce, Scallops with Cucumber-Horseradish, 124

Soup, Cold Cucumber, 318

Tzatziki, 54

Curry, Spicy Yellow Soybean, Lentil, and Carrot, 18

Curry, Vegetable and Chickpea, 365

Custards

Coconut Custard (Tembleque), 312

Flan, Deconstructed, 74

Flans, Individual Anise-Orange, 371

Panna Cotta with Blueberry Sauce, Lemon-Buttermilk, 297

Panna Cotta with Mango Sauce, Vanilla-Almond, 370

Desserts. *See also* specific types.

Apples with Caramel-Apple Sauce, Almond-Stuffed Baked, 299

Berries and Almond Milk, 161

Buttercrunch, Matzo, 89

Caramelized Condensed Milk, 169

Cheesecake Squares, Marble, 370

Cherries in Spiced Wine Syrup with Pound Cake Croutons, 264

Cherries in Zinfandel Syrup, 317

Chocolate Log, Sweet, 138

Compote (Compota de Frutas), Winter Fruit, 75

Compote, Rhubarb, Pear, and Apple, 154

Curd, Key Lime, 101

Dutch Baby, Chocolate Chip, 19

Figs and Nectarines over Ice Cream, Baked, 291

Frozen

Cookies, Black Forest Icebox, 449

Granita, Green Tea, 387

Granita, Pineapple-Rum, 370

Granita, Strawberry, 107

Ice Milk, Maple, 450

Lime Freeze, Arctic, 128

Pineapple with Cardamom-Lime Ice Cream, Chile-Lime, 405

Sorbet, Bittersweet Chocolate, 364

Sorbet, Chocolate-Mint, 371

Sorbet, Rhubarb, 154

Sorbet, Strawberry-Basil, 161

Sorbet with Pineapple Topping, Vanilla Bean, 353

Torte, Coffee-Chocolate, 450

Melon Balls with Port, 265

Parfaits

Apple Pie à la Mode Parfaits, 267

Black Forest Cheesecake Parfaits, 268

Coconut Cream Pie Parfaits, 268

Funky Monkey Parfaits, 267

Key Lime Pie Parfaits, 268

Peach and Raspberry Pavlova Parfaits, 267

Pear Parfaits with Gingersnaps, Amaretto-Scented, 267

Strawberry Parfait with Fresh Normandy Cream, 116

Peaches Chilled in Red Wine, 180

Sauce, Apricot-Lavender, 275

Soufflés with Pistachios, Chocolate, 48
Soup with Bananas (Che Chuoi), Sweet
  Coconut Tapioca, 285
Strawberries and Oranges with Vanilla-Scented
  Wine, 99
Strawberries, Balsamic-Brown Sugar, 252
Tequila-Cardamom Syrup and Vanilla Ice
  Cream, 421
Topping, Balsamic Strawberry, 191
Trifles, Individual Tiramisu, 304
Trifle, Sweet Potato, 214

Duck
Breasts with Kumquat Chutney, Duck, 443
Breast with Cherry-Pepper Sauce, Duck, 333
Breast with Ginger-Rhubarb Sauce, Seared
  Duck, 160
Peking Duck, 20-Minute, 323
Salad, Thai Roast Duck, 249

Dumplings
Caldo de Bolas, 86
Chicken and Rosemary Dumplings, 82
Chochoyones in Black Bean Soup, 85
Gnocchi with Bolognese, Potato, 84
Gnocchi with Thick Marinara Sauce, Easy, 244
Gyoza with Spicy Dipping Sauce,
  Vegetarian, 86
Matzo Ball Soup, 85
Pierogi Dough, 83
Pierogi, Potato, 83
Pierogi, Sweet Vanilla Cheese, 84
Pork Buns, Steamed, 81
Spaetzle Baked with Ham and Gruyère, 82
Spaetzle, Buttered, 82
Sui Mei, Crab and Scallop, 302

Edamame and Bean Salad with Shrimp and Fresh
  Salsa, 254
Edamame, Quinoa, and Shiitake Mushroom
  Salad, 283
Eggnog Cheese Pie with Bourbon Cream, 425

Eggplant
Baked Eggplant with Savory Cheese
  Stuffing, 54
Bucatini with Eggplant and Roasted
  Peppers, 136
Gratin, Eggplant and Tomato, 275
Grilled Eggplant with Caramelized Onion and
  Fennel, 295
Grilled Soy-Glazed Eggplant, 288
Pizza, Eggplant Parmesan, 351
Purée with Crostini, Smoky Eggplant, 56
Sandwiches, Warm Eggplant and Goat
  Cheese, 45
Stew over Couscous, Eggplant, 210
Tart, Eggplant, Tomato, and Smoked
  Mozzarella, 116

Eggs. *See also* **Omelets.**
Burrito, Sausage and Egg, 123
Frittata, Ham and Asparagus, 124
Frittata Ribbons in Tomato Sauce, Baked, 136
Frittata, Wild Rice, Asparagus, and Goat
  Cheese, 256
Frittata with Mushrooms, Linguine, and
  Basil, 209
Frittata with Smoked Mozzarella, Fresh
  Corn, 275

Green Eggs and Ham, 194
Greens with Eggs and Enoki Mushrooms,
  Field, 102
Huevos Rancheros Tostados, 204
Huevos Rancheros with Queso Fresco, 11
Hussarde, Eggs, 53
Poached Eggs, Mediterranean-Style, 103
Special, Joe's, 12
Empanada Dough (Masa de Empanadas), 309
Empanadas (Empanadas de Cangrejo y Mango),
  Crab-and-Mango, 309
Enchilada Casserole, Chicken-Green Chile, 328
Enchiladas with Crab, Green, 157

Fajitas, Tomatillo Shrimp, 231
Fennel. *See also* **Salads.**
Olives with Fennel and Orange, Warm, 361
Pasta with Roasted Fennel, Cherry Tomatoes,
  and Olives, Penne, 279
Pork Chops, Fennel-Brined, 174
Relish, White Bean, Artichoke, and Chard
  Ragoût with Fennel, 364
Risotto with Fennel and Olives, Barley, 264

Fettuccine
Asparagus, Lemon, and Prosciutto, Pasta
  with, 122
Chicken Fettuccine, Cajun-Spiced, 216
Macadamia Nut-Pesto Fettuccine, 123
Shrimp and Portobellos, Fettuccine with, 103

Figs
Baked Figs and Nectarines over Ice
  Cream, 291
Cake, Spiced Fig Upside-Down, 292
Chicken Braised with Leeks and Figs, 291
Focaccia, Fig and Mascarpone, 120
Grilled Figs, Grapes, and Bitter Greens, Warm
  Salad of, 293
Oven-Dried Figs, 290
Oven-Dried Figs, Caramelized Onions, and
  Blue Cheese, Flatbread with, 291
Poached Figs and Apple Salad, Seared Scallops
  with Port-, 100
Pork Stew with Pearl Onions, Green Olives,
  and Figs, 292
Pork Tenderloin, Fig and Chile-Glazed, 159
Preserves, Refrigerator Fig, 290
Roasted Fig and Arugula Salad, 263
Salad with Crème Fraîche, Mint, and Prosciutto,
  Fresh Fig, 290
Turkey Breast with Port Sauce, Fig and Stilton-
  Stuffed, 440

Fish. *See also* specific types and **Seafood.**
Bass, Mojo, 426
Bass, Pan-Fried, 201
Cakes, Spicy Fish, 297
Catfish, Cajun Shrimp and, 40
Catfish Fillets, Bayou, 126
Catfish with Cajun Tartar Sauce, Pan-
  Fried, 323
Chowder, Fish, 260
Cod with Basil Sauce, Pan-Seared, 73
Flounder, Parmesan-Herb Baked, 31
Grouper with Lime and Mexican Confetti Rice,
  Grilled, 421
Grouper with Puttanesca Sauce, 231
Halibut en Papillote, Sesame, 441

Halibut, Triple-Pepper Steamed, 363
Halibut with Chile-Cilantro Aïoli, Cornflake
  Crusted, 72
Mahimahi Fish Tacos, 134
Mahi Seviche, Mango, 51
Red Snapper over Sautéed Spinach and
  Tomatoes, 427
Seviche, Rainbow, 200
Snapper, Peanut-Crusted, 413
Striped Bass, Asian Marinated, 73
Striped Bass with Heirloom Tomatoes and
  Herbs, 225
Sweet Black Pepper Fish, 27
Tilapia with Lemon-Peppercorn Pan Sauce,
  Sautéed, 62
Trout Spread, Smoked, 409
Trout Topped with Cucumber Salsa, 167
Trout with Lentils, 74

French Toast
Berry French Toast, 102
Casserole, Orange-Pecan French Toast, 216
Coconut French Toast with Grilled Pineapple
  and Tropical Salsa, 195

Fruit. *See also* specific types and **Salads.**
Berries and Almond Milk, 161
Chicken with Citrus, 113
Compote and Cider Syrup, Pan-Seared
  Oatmeal with Warm Fruit, 194
Compote, Breakfast Polenta with Warm
  Berry, 19
Compote (Compota de Frutas), Winter
  Fruit, 75
Couscous Pilaf, Fruited, 404
Dip, Lemony Fruit, 45
Frushi, Coconut, 195
Gazpacho, Golden, 14
Grilled Stone Fruit Couscous Salad, Pork
  and, 314
Pain Perdu, 52
Pilaf with Pistachios, Fruited Basmati, 444
Pork Tenderloin with Xec, 28
Salsa, Rachel's Tropical Fruit, 129

Garlic
Beef Daube Provençal, 373
Carrots with Paprika and Capers, 218
Cauliflower with Herbed Crumb Topping,
  Creamed, 447
Chicken Breasts with Yellow Tomato Curry
  Sauce and Thai Ratatouille, Grilled, 228
Chicken over Noodles, Asian, 37
Chicken Thighs, Honey-Pomegranate
  Roasted, 424
Chowder with Chipotle (Chupe de Pollo con
  Chipotle), Chicken, 437
Confit with Prosciutto, Peppered Garlic, 361
Grillades and Gravy over Grits, 52
Lamb Chops, Mustard-Crusted, 363
Lamb Osso Buco over Parmesan Polenta, 303
Lasagna Rolls with Roasted Red Pepper
  Sauce, 104
Marinara Magnifica, 261
Plantains and Pork Cracklings with Stewed
  Chicken (Mofongo Relleno de Pollo
  Guisado), 311
Pork Porchetta-Style, Roast, 179

Garlic (continued)

Pork Roast, Cajun Garlic, 127
Roasted Garlic and Corn
Soufflé, 102
Roasted Garlic Vinaigrette, 142
Rub, Pepper-Garlic Spice, 176
Salad with Sourdough Croutons and Warm
Tomato Vinaigrette, Bitter Greens, 303
Sandwiches with Fontina Cheese, Grilled
Chicken and Roasted Red Pepper, 185
Shrimp in Green Sauce, 26
Shrimp with Lemon, Mint, and Goat
Cheese, 317
Soft Tacos, Grilled-Steak, 149
Spaghettini with Oil and Garlic, 417
Stew (Txilindron de Cordero), Lamb, 75
Stew with Lamb, Chickpeas, and Figs, Middle
Eastern Slow-Cooked, 423
Toasted Garlic, Shrimp Salad with White Beans,
Broccoli, and, 80
Winter Squash and Garlic, Bay Leaf and
Thyme-Scented Roasted, 363
Gifts
Biscotti, White Chocolate-Cashew
Coffee, 453
Braid, Sugar-Frosted Cardamom, 451
Brittle, Candied Hazelnut, 452
Divinity, Toasted Pecan, 453
Kumquats in Spiced Syrup with Cloves,
Cinnamon, and Star Anise, 454
Panettones, Mini Cranberry, 452
Shortbread, Ginger, 454
Wafers with Vanilla Icing, Christmas
Sugar, 453
Granola, Pistachio, 388
Granola, Wholesome Morning, 13
Grapefruit, Salad of Papaya, Mango, and, 97
Gravies
Country Gravy and Mashed Potatoes, Pork
Chops with, 31
Grillades and Gravy over Grits, 52
Herb Gravy, Savory, 375
Quick Gravy, 383
Sausage Gravy, Roast Turkey with, 394
Vegetarian Sausage Gravy, Biscuits and, 328
Greens
Beet Greens and Raisins, Pasta with, 415
Black-Eyed Peas and Greens, Greek, 56
Greek Greens and Sweet Onion Pie, 95
Kale with Bacon and Cider, Braised, 19
Kale with Garlic and Hot Red Pepper, 178
Salad of Grilled Figs, Grapes, and Bitter Greens,
Warm, 293
Turnip Greens, Garlic-Scented, 369
Wilted Greens with Rice, 55
Winter Greens and Potato Casserole, 14
Grilled
Beef
Filet Mignon, Classic Steak House
Rubbed, 241
Filet Mignon with Red Currant-Green
Peppercorn Sauce, 160
Flank Steak, Grilled Marinated, 118
Flank Steak, Sourdough Panzanella with
Grilled, 67

Flank Steak with Five-Spice Rub and Chile
Relish, 297
Kebabs with Wasabi Aïoli, Yogurt-
Marinated Beef, 251
Salad, Southeast Asian Grilled Beef, 46
Salad with Lemongrass Dressing, Grilled
Beef, 221
Steak Soft Tacos, Grilled-, 149
Strip Steak, Korean Beef, 201
Thai Beef Salad Wraps, 288
Fish and Shellfish
Grouper with Lime and Mexican Confetti
Rice, Grilled, 421
Mahimahi Fish Tacos, 134
Mussel Salad, 170
Salmon, Grilled Pastrami-Style, 242
Salmon, Smoked, 175
Shrimp and White Bean Salad over
Watercress, 96
Shrimp, Five-Spice, 287
Shrimp, Grilled Lemon-Bay, 263
Shrimp over Rice Vermicelli and
Vegetables (Bun Tom Nuong Xa),
Lemongrass, 285
Shrimp Seviche, Ecuadoran, 200
Shrimp, Spinach Salad with Grilled, 298
Shrimp, Sun-Dried Tomato Spiced, 320
Tuna with Avocado Salsa, Grilled, 232
Lamb, Brochettes of, 217
Lamb Chops, Grilled, 170
Lamb Chops, Herbes de Provence-
Crusted, 240
Lamb Chops, Mustard-Crusted, 363
Pineapple and Tropical Salsa, Coconut French
Toast with Grilled, 195
Pork
Chops, Coffee and Molasses-Brined
Pork, 176
Chops, Fennel-Brined Pork, 174
Chops, Fire-Grilled Pork, 114
Chops, Grilled Plum and Prosciutto-
Stuffed Pork, 368
Chops with Fiery Salsa, Grilled
Pork, 248
Chops with Rhubarb Chutney, Grilled
Pork, 154
Chops with Tomatillo, Corn, and Avocado
Salsa, Grilled Pork, 243
Skewers with Guava Sauce (Pinchos de
Cerdo con Salsa de Guayaba),
Pork, 311
Tenderloin, Fig and Chile-Glazed
Pork, 159
Tenderloin, Spanish-Style Brined
Pork, 177
Poultry
Chicken and Roasted Red Pepper
Sandwiches with Fontina Cheese,
Grilled, 185
Chicken Breasts with Hoisin Glaze, Five-
Spice, 175
Chicken Breasts with Yellow Tomato
Curry Sauce and Thai Ratatouille,
Grilled, 228
Chicken, Lemon Tarragon-Brined
Whole, 173

Chicken, Olive and Sun-Dried Tomato
Sauce over, 320
Chicken Paillards, Lemon and Oregano-
Rubbed, 241
Chicken Salad with Feta and Cucumbers,
Grilled, 96
Chicken with Pinot-Plum Sauce,
Grilled, 258
Cornish Hens with Apricot-Mustard
Glaze, Grilled, 160
Quail, Blackberry-Zinfandel, 161
Turkey Burgers with Papaya-Mango Salsa,
Jamaican Jerk, 196
Stone Fruit Couscous Salad, Pork and
Grilled, 314
Vegetables
Asparagus with Lemon, Grilled, 241
Corn with Creamy Chipotle Sauce,
Grilled, 230
Eggplant, Grilled Soy-Glazed, 288
Eggplant with Caramelized Onion and
Fennel, Grilled, 295
Muffuletta, 159
Red Potatoes with Mint, Grilled, 240
Salad, Pork and Grilled Vegetable, 314
Salad with Creamy Blue Cheese Dressing,
Grilled Vegetable, 196
Sandwiches, Grilled Vegetable and
Mozzarella, 187
Squash, Grilled Summer, 230
Grits
Casserole with Mushrooms, Prosciutto, and
Provolone, Grits, 388
Grillades and Gravy over Grits, 52
Shrimp and Grits, Southern, 12
Gumbo, Shrimp and Crab, 317

Ham. See also **Bacon, Pork.**
Cubano with Bacon, Pressed, 185
Eggs and Ham, Green, 194
Frittata, Ham and Asparagus, 124
Gratin, Potato, Leek, and Ham, 398
Grilled Ham and Cheese with
Tomato, 187
Hash Browns, Ham and Cheese, 122
Omelet, Ham and Potato, 101
Prosciutto and Gruyère Strombolis, 288
Prosciutto and Picholine Pasta Salad, 282
Prosciutto, and Provolone, Grits Casserole with
Mushrooms, 388
Prosciutto, Fresh Fig Salad with Crème Fraîche,
Mint, and, 290
Prosciutto, Gomiti with Broccoli Rabe,
Chickpeas, and, 419
Prosciutto Panini, Pear, Pecorino, and, 186
Prosciutto, Pasta with Asparagus, Lemon,
and, 122
Prosciutto, Peppered Garlic Confit with, 361
Prosciutto Pizza, Mushroom-, 199
Prosciutto-Stuffed Pork Chops, Grilled Plum
and, 368
Sandwich, Ham and Brie, 134
Sautéed Ham, Cranberry Jezebel Sauce
with, 384
Smoked Ham Strata, Goat Cheese, Artichoke,
and, 177

Spaetzle Baked with Ham and
    Gruyère, 82
Hominy
    Posole, 76
    Posole, Pork, 354
    Sauté, Hominy, 368

Ice Creams
    Key Lime Pie Ice Cream, 243
    Peach Ice Cream, Simple, 284

Jambalaya
    Jambalaya, 442
    Louisiana Goulash, 46
Jams
    Blueberry Jam, Wildflower Inn, 237
    Strawberry Jam, Fresh, 191
    Tomato-Ginger Jam, Cornmeal Shortcakes
        with, 258

Kebabs
    Beef Kebabs with Wasabi Aïoli, Yogurt-
        Marinated, 251
    Lamb, Brochettes of, 217
    Pork Skewers with Guava Sauce (Pinchos de
        Cerdo con Salsa de Guayaba), 311
    Shrimp, Five-Spice, 287
    Yakitori, 247
Kugel, Matzo, Mushroom, and Onion, 89
Kumquat Chutney, Duck Breasts with, 443
Kumquats in Spiced Syrup with Cloves,
    Cinnamon, and Star Anise, 454

Lamb
    Brochettes of Lamb, 217
    Chops
        Curried Lamb Chops with Minted
            Chutney, 206
        Grilled Lamb Chops, 170
        Herbed Yogurt over Couscous, Lamb
            Chops with, 350
        Herbes de Provence-Crusted Lamb
            Chops, 240
        Mustard-Crusted Lamb Chops, 363
    Leg of Lamb with Herbs and Mustard, 115
    Osso Buco over Parmesan Polenta, Lamb, 303
    Pita, Garlic-Rosemary Lamb, 29
    Stew (Txilindron de Cordero), Lamb, 75
    Stew with Lamb, Chickpeas, and Figs, Middle
        Eastern Slow-Cooked, 423
    Stew with Parsnips and Figs, Spicy Lamb, 335
    Stuffed Lamb with Potato-Parsnip Mash, Feta
        and Lemon-, 257
Lasagna
    Italian Sausage and Fennel Lasagna, 330
    Mushroom and Yellow Pepper Lasagna, 280
    Mushroom Lasagna with Creamy Béchamel, 93
    Roasted Butternut Squash, Rosemary, and Garlic
        Lasagna, 416
    Rolls with Roasted Red Pepper Sauce, Lasagna, 104
    Tex-Mex Lasagna, 209
    Tomato Lasagna, Fresh, 105
Latkes
    Orange Cardamom Cake, 423
    Potato Latkes, 424
    Sunchoke Latkes, 359

Vegetable Party Latke, 424
Leeks and Figs, Chicken Braised with, 291
Lemon
    Asparagus with Lemon, Grilled, 241
    Chicken and Rice with Artichokes, Lemon, 13
    Chicken, Lemon Tarragon-Brined Whole, 173
    Chicken Paillards, Lemon and Oregano-
        Rubbed, 241
    Chicken Piccata, 348
    Lamb with Potato-Parsnip Mash, Feta and
        Lemon-Stuffed, 257
    Noodles with Curry Leaves and Cashews,
        Lemon, 282
    Panna Cotta with Blueberry Sauce, Lemon-
        Buttermilk, 297
    Pound Cake with Mixed Berries, Lemon, 125
    Preserved Lemons, Quick, 217
    Rice, Lemon Southwest, 274
    Risotto with Tomato Topping, Lemon-Basil, 164
    Salad with Feta, Lemon Garbanzo, 253
    Sauce, Sautéed Tilapia with Lemon-Peppercorn
        Pan, 62
    Shrimp, Grilled Lemon-Bay, 263
    Shrimp with Lemon, Mint, and Goat
        Cheese, 317
    Sugar Snap Peas with Lemon and Toasted
        Almonds, 445
    Tomatoes Roasted with Rosemary and Lemon, 178
    Tonic, Ginger-Lemon, 245
    Veal Piccata, 232
Lentils
    Chicken and Lentils, Moroccan, 208
    Chorizo, Spicy Lentils with, 168
    Couscous with Spinach, Lentil, 244
    Curry, Spicy Yellow Soybean, Lentil, and
        Carrot, 18
    Dal Wraps, Lentil, 284
    Lemony Lentils with Black Olives, 53
    Salad, Lentil and Fennel, 191
    Soup, Tomato and Lentil, 54
    Spread, Lentil, 351
    Trout with Lentils, 74
Lime
    Dressing, Couscous-Chickpea Salad with
        Ginger-Lime, 194
    Dressing, Green Salad with Roasted Poblanos
        and Cumin-Lime, 352
    Freeze, Arctic Lime, 128
    Grouper with Lime and Mexican Confetti Rice,
        Grilled, 421
    Key Lime Cheesecake, 101
    Key Lime Curd, 101
    Key Lime Pie Ice Cream, 243
    Key Lime Pie Parfaits, 268
    Mojito, Classic, 312
    Pineapple with Cardamom-Lime Ice Cream,
        Chile-Lime, 405
    Pork Tacos, Lime-Cilantro, 197
    Soup, Papaya Lime, 162
    Spread with Lime and Cilantro, Black Bean, 408
    Vinaigrette, Cumin-Lime, 143
    Vinaigrette, Seafood Salad with
        Lime, 265
Linguine
    Carbonara, Linguine, 203
    Clam Sauce, Linguine with, 318

Frittata with Mushrooms, Linguine, and
    Basil, 209
    Greek Pasta with Seared Tuna, 282
    Sun-Dried Tomato Pesto and Feta Cheese, Pasta
        with, 349
    Walnut-Chicken Linguine, 133
    White Clam and Broccoli Sauce, Linguine with, 419
Lobster
    Newburg, Lobster, 260
    Salad with Asian Herbs, Maine Lobster and
        Pepper, 225
    Stuffed Lobster with Citrus Vinaigrette, Crab-, 295

Macaroni
    Cheese, Chipotle Macaroni and, 248
    Cheese Florentine, Mac and, 208
    Toss, Hamburger, Cheddar, and
        Macaroni, 279
Mangoes
    Chutney, Curried Chicken Penne with Fresh
        Mango, 188
    Martini, Mango, 312
    Relish, Marinated Salmon with Mango-Kiwi, 79
    Salad, Mango-Cucumber, 261
    Salsa, Fiery Turkey Fillets with Mango, 274
    Sauce, Vanilla-Almond Panna Cotta with
        Mango, 370
    Seviche, Mango Mahi, 51
    Slush, Spicy Mango-Orange, 245
Meatballs
    Chicken Meatball Soup with Pasta, 358
    Penne with Meatballs, Bell Pepper and
        Tomato, 118
    Soup (Sopa de Albóndigas), Meatball, 355
    Turkey-Jasmine Rice Meatballs with Baby Bok
        Choy, 393
Meat Loaf
    Southwest Meat Loaf, 352
    Turkey-Spinach Meat Loaf, Skinny, 78
    Vegetarian Meat Loaf, 330
Melons
    Port, Melon Balls with, 265
    Salad, Melon Chicken, 219
    Sipper, Cool Melon, 246
    Watermelon Agua Fresca, 229
    Watermelon, Fennel, and Parsley Salad, Pizzeria
        Bianco, 228
    Watermelon Mojitos, Slushy, 264
Meringues
    Chocolate-Cherry Chunk Meringues, 170
    Coconut Meringues, 171
    Sandwiches, Peanut Butter-Chocolate
        Meringue, 172
    Thumbprint Meringues, 172
    Tweed Meringues, 171
    Vanilla Meringues, Double, 172
Microwave
    Desserts
        Biscotti, White Chocolate-Cashew
            Coffee, 453
        Brownie à la Mode, Peppermint, 448
        Cake, Mexican Chocolate, 274
        Cheesecake Squares, Marble, 370
        Compote (Compota de Frutas), Winter
            Fruit, 75
        Éclairs, Phyllo, 141

Microwave (continued)

Parfaits, Funky Monkey, 267
Pie, Café con Leche Cream, 158
Tart, Thin French Apple, 65
Main Dishes
Eggs Hussarde, 53
Ham and Cheese Hash Browns, 122
Huevos Rancheros with Queso Fresco, 11
Lasagna, Roasted Butternut Squash,
Rosemary, and Garlic, 416
Lasagna Rolls with Roasted Red Pepper
Sauce, 104
Lasagna with Creamy Béchamel,
Mushroom, 93
Peppers, Beef and Barley-Stuffed, 208
Peppers, Skillet Stuffed, 162
Pork and Squash Stir-Fry, 386
Pork Tenderloin in Phyllo, 139
Pork with Apricot-Rum Glaze, Roasted
Loin of, 100
Stew over Couscous, Eggplant, 210
Parfaits, Brunch, 190
Salad, Kung Pao Tofu Rice, 254
Salad with Ricotta-Provolone Topping, Beet and
Red Onion, 179
Vegetables
Broccoli with Balsamic-Butter
Sauce, 289
Green Beans Amandine, 198
Sweet Potato Hash, 49
Mousse with Summer Berries, Ricotta-
Honey, 136
Muffins
Apricot Muffins, Whole Wheat, 387
Blueberry Cinnamon-Burst Muffins, 239
Blueberry Muffins, Spiced, 240
Millet Muffins with Honey-Pecan
Butter, 99
Parmesan-Corn Bread Muffins, 189
Raspberry-Almond Muffins, 99
Strawberry-Cinnamon Muffins, Low-Fat, 45
Mushrooms
Bread Pudding, Mushroom, Roasted Red
Pepper, and Goat Cheese, 339
Bruschetta, Mushroom and Parmigiano, 106
Casserole, Mushroom and Turkey, 382
Casserole with Mushrooms, Prosciutto, and
Provolone, Grits, 388
Cremini Mushrooms and Asparagus, Chicken
with, 203
Kugel, Matzo, Mushroom, and Onion, 89
Lasagna, Mushroom and Yellow
Pepper, 280
Lasagna with Creamy Béchamel,
Mushroom, 93
Marinated Mushrooms, 317
Morels (Pollo con Jugo de Morillas), Chicken
with, 74
Omelet with Fontina, Mushroom and Bell
Pepper, 49
Pasta Bake, Mushroom, 42
Pasta with Mushrooms and Radicchio, 210
Pizza, Mushroom-Prosciutto, 199
Porcini and Marsala, Turkey Scaloppine
with, 393

Porcini Mushroom Sauce, Beef Tenderloin
with, 325
Pork Marsala, 414
Portobello-Goat Cheese Pitas, Grilled, 294
Portobello Mushrooms with Mediterranean
Stuffing, 407
Portobellos, Stuffed, 224
Ragoût, Polenta with Smoky Mushroom, 92
Sauce, Filet Mignon with Mushroom-
Wine, 413
Shiitakes and Spinach, Barley with, 446
Shiitakes and Tomato Purée, Pasta with
Roasted, 280
Soba with Garlic Chives, Mushrooms, and Bok
Choy, 281
Soup, Rich Mushroom, 346
Spread, Creamy Mushroom, 408
Stuffing with Mushrooms and Sausage, Herbed
Bread, 375
Tofu and Mushrooms, 39
Wild Mushroom Bruschetta, 137
Wild Mushroom Pizza with Truffle
Oil, 130
Wild Mushrooms, Seared Scallops on
Braised, 255
Mussels
Salad, Mussel, 170
Steamed Mussels with Cardamom, Orange, and
Mint, 316
Tomato-Wine Broth, Mussels with, 168

Nectarines in Mint Vinaigrette, Chicken Salad
with, 152
Nectarines over Ice Cream, Baked Figs and, 291
Noodles
Asian Noodles with Asparagus and
Shrimp, 32
Baked Sesame Chicken Noodles, 41
Chicken over Noodles, Asian, 37
Curried Noodles, 279
Lemon Noodles with Curry Leaves and
Cashews, 282
Lo Mein, Sesame Pork, 278
Noodles, Beef Bourguignonne with Egg, 304
Pan-Fried Noodles with Scallops, 386
Rice Noodles, 73, 422
Rice Noodle Soup (Pho Bo), Hanoi Beef
and, 286
Rice Noodles with Sesame-Ginger Flank
Steak, 198
Salad, Chopstick Noodle, 262
Salad, Pork and Peanut Noodle, 315
Salad, Sesame Noodle, 400
Salad, Tofu Teriyaki Noodle, 193
Salad with Tofu and Peanut Dressing, Spicy
Noodle, 278
Seafood and Vegetable Noodles,
Braised, 220
Singapore Mai Fun, 386
Soba Noodle Soup, Chicken and, 120
Soba Noodles with Broccoli and Chicken, 150
Soba Noodles with Shrimp, 253
Soba Salad, Peanut Chicken, 132
Soba with Garlic Chives, Mushrooms, and Bok
Choy, 281
Soup, Asian Chicken Noodle, 294

Oatmeal
Bread, Irish Oatmeal, 16
Cherry-Hazelnut Oatmeal, 132
Cookies, Oatmeal-Walnut, 9
Granola, Wholesome Morning, 13
Loaf, Banana-Oatmeal, 326
Old-Fashioned Oatmeal, 161
Pan-Seared Oatmeal with Warm Fruit Compote
and Cider Syrup, 194
Olives
Black Olives, Lemony Lentils with, 53
Chicken Thighs with Olives and Red Peppers, 338
Fennel and Orange, Warm Olives with, 361
Green Olives, Chicken with, 25
Pork Chops Niçoise, Sautéed, 29
Sandwiches, Olive-Tomato Grilled
Cheese, 204
Sauce over Chicken, Olive and Sun-Dried
Tomato, 320
Tapenade, 408
Tapenade, Pork Tenderloin with Olive-
Mustard, 204
Toasts, Roasted Tomato-Harissa Soup with
Olive, 402
Omelets
Ham and Potato Omelet, 101
Mushroom and Bell Pepper Omelet with
Fontina, 49
Tortilla with Almond Romesco, Spanish, 97
Vegetables, Omelet with Summer, 231
Onions
Baked Onions with Sage and Gruyère,
Peppery, 445
Caramelized Onion and Fennel, Grilled
Eggplant with, 295
Caramelized Onion Dip, 77
Caramelized Onion Pork Sandwiches,
Horseradish and, 315
Caramelized Onion, Red Pepper, and
Mushroom Pizzetti, 434
Caramelized Onions, Savory Yogurt
Cheesecake with, 18
Cipollini Onions with Coriander and Orange,
Glazed Carrots and, 403
Crostini, Onion, Date, and Brie, 396
Green Onion-Salt Dip, Chicken with Ginger
and, 287
Kugel, Matzo, Mushroom, and Onion, 89
Larb, Tofu, 301
Pearl Onions, Green Olives, and Figs, Pork
Stew with, 292
Pebre, 169
Pie, Greek Greens and Sweet Onion, 95
Pizza, Mexican, 10
Quinoa, Seco de, 406
Red Onion Salad with Ricotta-Provolone
Topping, Beet and, 179
Soup Gratinée, Onion, 436
Special, Joe's, 12
Stuffed Onions with Chianti Sauce, 137
Sweet Onion, White Bean, and Artichoke
Dip, 424
Vichyssoise, 165
Oranges
Ambrosia, Orange, Pineapple, and Coconut, 11
Beef, Spicy Orange, 38

Blood Orange Sangría, 434
Bread, Orange-Pecan Tea, 119
Casserole, Orange-Pecan French Toast, 216
Chicken, Maple-Orange, 205
Desserts
    Cake, Orange Cardamom, 423
    Cake, Pumpkin-Orange, 348
    Crisp with Coconut Topping,
        Orange, 411
    Flans, Individual Anise-Orange, 371
    Pie, Apple-Orange, 326
    Vanilla-Scented Wine, Strawberries and
        Oranges with, 99
Mandarin Oranges, Cashew Chicken Salad
    with, 284
Pork Loin, Orange-Brined, 175
Rice with Chicken), Shireen Palow (Afghan
    Orange, 70
Rolls, Orange, 372
Salmon with Orange Marmalade, 351
Sauce, Couscous with Apple-Ginger Topping
    and Orange, 218
Sauce, Sautéed Turkey Cutlets with Orange-
    Cranberry Pan, 64
Slush, Spicy Mango-Orange, 245
Spread, Date-Orange Breakfast, 395
Orzo
    Feta Orzo, Bell Pepper Chicken with, 149
    Parmesan Orzo, Creamy, 48
    Peas, Orzo with, 348
    Pilaf, Spiced Orzo, 397

Paella, Chicken and Shrimp, 71
Pancakes, Hearty, 406
Papaya
    Salad (Goi Du Du), Green Papaya, 287
    Salad of Papaya, Mango, and
        Grapefruit, 97
    Salsa, Jamaican Jerk Turkey Burgers with
        Papaya-Mango, 196
    Sauce, Coconut Curry Shrimp Cakes with
        Papaya-Lime, 158
    Soup, Papaya Lime, 162
Parsnip Chips, Carrot-Parsnip Soup with, 436
Parsnips and Figs, Spicy Lamb Stew with, 335
Pasta. See also specific types.
    Anchovies and Walnuts, Pasta with, 27
    Bake, Mushroom Pasta, 42
    Beans, Southwestern Pasta with, 280
    Beet Greens and Raisins, Pasta with, 415
    Bow Tie Pasta Salad, Roasted Chicken
        and, 51
    Bucatini with Eggplant and Roasted
        Peppers, 136
    Cacciatore, Chicken, 357
    Campanelle with Salsa Arrabbiata, 419
    Chicken Pasta, Spicy, 121
    Chicken-Pasta Toss, Sun-Dried Tomato Pesto
        and, 319
    Creamy Pasta with Chicken and
        Mushrooms, 206
    Farfalle, Garlic and Bell Pepper, 189
    Farfalle with Roasted Tofu, Sesame, 192
    Feta-Chicken Pasta, 262
    Garlicky Pasta with Fresh Tomatoes and
        Basil, 104

Gemelli Pasta with Clams, Scallops, and
    Shrimp, 281
Gomiti with Broccoli Rabe, Chickpeas, and
    Prosciutto, 419
Gruyère and Shrimp Pasta, Creamy, 42
Mushrooms and Radicchio, Pasta with, 210
Orecchiette with Tomatoes, Fresh Mozzarella,
    and Basil, 192
Orzo-Bell Pepper Salad, 192
Pappardelle with Roasted Winter Squash,
    Arugula, and Pine Nuts, 441
Pappardelle with Tomatoes, Arugula, and
    Parmesan, Summer, 278
Penne in Creamy Basil-Walnut Sauce, 138
Penne Pasta with Butter and Parmesan
    Cheese, 369
Penne Pasta with Roasted Fennel, Cherry
    Tomatoes, and Olives, 279
Pennette with Asparagus and Pine Nuts, 415
Penne with Broccoli, Green Olives, and Pine
    Nuts, Whole Wheat, 276
Penne with Fresh Mango Chutney, Curried
    Chicken, 188
Penne with Meatballs, Bell Pepper and
    Tomato, 118
Penne with Mushroom Sauce, 277
Picholine Pasta Salad, Prosciutto and, 282
Primavera, Pasta, 91
Roasted Butternut Squash and Bacon
    Pasta, 41
Roasted Shiitakes and Tomato Purée, Pasta
    with, 280
Salad, Greek Pasta, 105
Salad, Peppery Chicken Pasta, 214
Salad, Tuna and Red Pepper Pasta, 281
Salad with Chicken, Pasta, 20
Shrimp and Pasta, Mediterranean, 88
Shrimp, Nutty Pasta Toss with, 207
Soup, Turkey-Pasta, 384
Soup with Pasta and Parmesan, Summer
    Squash, 282
Soup with Pasta, Chicken Meatball, 358
Spaghettini with Oil and Garlic, 417
Tortellini Soup, Sun-Dried Tomato-, 322
Whole Wheat Pasta with Sausage, Leeks, and
    Fontina, 417
Ziti Baked with Spinach, Tomatoes, and
    Smoked Gouda, 43
Ziti with Sausage, Onions, and Fennel, 420
Ziti with Shrimp and Scallops, Baked, 43
Peaches
    Chilled in Red Wine, Peaches, 180
    Glazed Peaches in Phyllo Baskets with Ricotta
        Cream, 256
    Ice Cream, Simple Peach, 284
    Parfaits, Peach and Raspberry Pavlova, 267
    Smoothie with Walnuts, Blackberry-Peach, 246
    Splash, Sparkling Peach, 265
Peanut Butter
    Cookies, Chocolate and Peanut Butter, 88
    Meringue Sandwiches, Peanut Butter-
        Chocolate, 172
    Parfaits, Funky Monkey, 267
Pears. See also Pies and Pastries.
    Amaretto Pears, 104
    Chutney, Cranberry-Pear, 376

Compote, Rhubarb, Pear, and Apple, 154
Panini, Pear, Pecorino, and Prosciutto, 186
Parfaits with Gingersnaps, Amaretto-Scented
    Pear, 267
Risotto with Pears and Blue Cheese, Chianti-
    Stained, 446
Salad with Mustard Vinaigrette, Spinach-Pear, 374
Salad with Pears and Gruyère, Escarole and
    Fennel, 437
Peas
    Black-Eyed
        Caviar, Field Greens with Mississippi, 127
        Chicken with Black-Eyed Peas and Rice,
            Spiced, 246
        Greek Black-Eyed Peas and Greens, 56
        Hoppin' John, 32
    Field Peas with Green Beans, 178
    Orzo with Peas, 348
    Pigeon Peas (Arroz con Gandules), Rice with, 311
    Snow Peas
        Slaw, Napa Cabbage and Snow Pea, 143
        Stir-Fry, Shrimp and Snow Pea, 414
        Stir-Fry, Snow Pea and Red Pepper, 27
    Soup, Springtime Pea, 129
    Sugar Snap Peas with Lemon and Toasted
        Almonds, 445
Pecans
    Bars, Passover Pecan, 91
    Bread, Moist 'n' Dark Nut, 47
    Cookies, Pecan Bar, 20
    Divinity, Toasted Pecan, 453
    Pastry Crust, Pumpkin Pie with Pecan, 381
    Pie with Spiked Cream, Pecan, 381
Peppers
    Beef, Three-Pepper, 219
    Bell Pepper and Fresh Mozzarella Couscous, 252
    Bell Pepper and Tomato Penne with
        Meatballs, 118
    Bell Pepper Chicken with Feta Orzo, 149
    Bell Pepper Farfalle, Garlic and, 189
    Chicken and Peppers, Bistro, 207
    Chile
        Aïoli, Cornflake-Crusted Halibut with
            Chile-Cilantro, 72
        Chipotle-Bacon Corn Bread, 251
        Chipotle Macaroni and Cheese, 248
        Chipotle Pork and Avocado Wrap, 315
        Chipotle Pork Tenderloin with Corn
            Salsa, 205
        Chipotle Pulled-Pork Barbecue
            Sandwiches, 186
        Chipotle Sauce, Grilled Corn with
            Creamy, 230
        Chipotle Shrimp Cups, 215
        Green Chile Sopes with Chipotle
            Mayonnaise, Shrimp, and Pineapple
            Slaw, 157
        Pickled Hot Peppers, 179
        Poblanos and Cumin-Lime Dressing,
            Green Salad with Roasted, 352
        Rellenos, Baked Chiles, 223
        Roasted Chiles and Leeks, Green Rice
            with, 276
        Sriracha Bread, Spicy, 250
    Chile Relish, Flank Steak with Five-Spice Rub
        and, 297

Peppers (continued)

Green Pepper Soup, Stuffed, 406
Halibut, Triple-Pepper Steamed, 363
Pizza with Basil and Pine Nuts, Mixed Pepper, 10
Red
Butternut Squash and Red Pepper, 351
Dip, Red Pepper-Cheese, 345
Dip, Red Pepper-Walnut, 409
Frittata, Red Bell Pepper, 11
Pepper Stir-Fry, Snow Pea and Red, 27
Risotto, Sweet Pepper and Green Bean, 94
Roasted Red Pepper and Pesto, White Beans with, 165
Roasted Red Pepper on Mini-Bagel Sandwiches, 326
Roasted Red Pepper Sauce, Lasagna Rolls with, 104
Roasted Red Pepper Spread Sandwiches, 193
Romaine Lettuce with Red Pepper and Olives, 144
Rice, Green, 352
Roasted Peppers, and Olives, Pizza with Escarole, 9
Salad with Asian Herbs, Maine Lobster and Pepper, 225
Salad with Bell Peppers and Onions, Black Bean, 197
Salsa Arrabbiata, Campanelle with, 419
Sauce, Chicken with Chunky Pepper, 163
Sausage with Three Peppers, Italian Turkey, 389
Stuffed Peppers, Beef and Barley-, 208
Stuffed Peppers, Skillet, 162
Yellow Pepper Lasagna, Mushroom and, 280
Pesto
Sun-Dried Tomato Pesto and Chicken-Pasta Toss, 319
Sun-Dried Tomato Pesto and Feta Cheese, Pasta with, 349
Watercress Pesto, Zucchini-Buttermilk Soup with, 255
Pies and Pastries
Apple-Orange Pie, 326
Apple Pies, Unfried, 15
Café con Leche Cream Pie, 158
Cobblers, Crisps, and Crumbles
Apple-Cranberry Cobbler, 332
Apple Crumble, Brandied Caramel-, 412
Apple, Rhubarb, and Sour Cherry Passover Cobbler, 91
Cherry Cobbler, Fresh, 180
Cranberry and Apple Crumble, 9
Cranberry-Apple Crumble, 412
Harvest Crisp with Pistachios, Vanilla-Scented, 410
Orange Crisp with Coconut Topping, 411
Pear-Berry Crisp with Lavender Topping, 410
Pear Crisp, Gingered, 62, 410
Pear Crumble with Dried Tart Cherries and Almond Streusel, 412
Plum Crumble, Santa Rosa, 230
Rhubarb-Strawberry Crumble, 155

Cranberry-Pear Crumb Pie, 451
Eggnog Cheese Pie with Bourbon Cream, 425
Greens and Sweet Onion Pie, Greek, 95
Main Dish
Bierocks, 33
Phyllo Purses with Roasted Squash, Peppers, and Artichokes, 403
Pork Tenderloin in Phyllo, 139
Roasted Chicken-Artichoke Calzones, 252
Salmon and Leeks in Phyllo Packets, Roasted, 140
Salmon Strudel, Savory Dill-, 69
Shepherd's Pie, 330
Succotash Pot Pie, Southwestern, 93
Tamale Pie, 30
Pastries
Éclairs, Phyllo, 141
Empanada Dough (Masa de Empanadas), 309
Empanadas (Empanadas de Cangrejo y Mango), Crab-and-Mango, 309
Napoleons, Banana-Walnut, 133
Phyllo Baskets with Ricotta Cream, Glazed Peaches in, 256
Pierogi Dough, 83
Pierogi, Potato, 83
Pierogi, Sweet Vanilla Cheese, 84
Rolls, Spinach, Sun-Dried Tomato, and Parmesan, 433
Strudel, Apple-Cream Cheese, 138
Turnovers, Cherry-Apricot, 142
Pecan Pie with Spiked Cream, 381
Pumpkin Pie with Pecan Pastry Crust, 381
Rhubarb Pie, Lattice-Topped, 153
Strawberry Pie, 190
Tarts
Apple Crumb Tart with Maple Ice Milk, 450
Apple Tart, Thin French, 65
Asparagus-Fontina Tart, 140
Eggplant, Tomato, and Smoked Mozzarella Tart, 116
Feta-Spinach Tarts, 141
Pumpkin Tart, Ginger-Hazelnut, 448
Strawberry-Rhubarb Tart, 190
Tatin, Tarte, 20
Pineapple
Cake, Pineapple-Coconut-Banana Upside-Down, 20
Chile-Lime Pineapple with Cardamom-Lime Ice Cream, 405
Galloping Horses, 302
Granita, Pineapple-Rum, 370
Grilled Pineapple and Tropical Salsa, Coconut French Toast with, 195
Mixto, Pineapple Seviche, 199
Slaw, Green Chile Sopes with Chipotle Mayonnaise, Shrimp, and Pineapple, 157
Topping, Vanilla Bean Sorbet with Pineapple, 353
Pizza
Chicken Pizza, Cuban, 421
Dough, Pizza, 10
Eggplant Parmesan Pizza, 351

Escarole, Roasted Peppers, and Olives, Pizza with, 9
Frittata, Pizza, 150
Individual Pizzas with Broccoli, Cheese, and Meat Sauce, 150
Insalata Pizzas, 163
Mexican Pizza, 10
Mushroom-Prosciutto Pizza, 199
Pepper Pizza with Basil and Pine Nuts, Mixed, 10
Pizzetti, Caramelized Onion, Red Pepper, and Mushroom, 434
Ratatouille Pizza with Chicken, 211
Sausage Pizza, Spicy, 202
White Pizza, 46
Wild Mushroom Pizza with Truffle Oil, 130
Plantains
Caldo de Bolas, 86
"Canoes" Stuffed with Ground Meat (Canoas), Ripe Plantain, 309
Pork and Plantains, 39
Pork Cracklings with Stewed Chicken (Mofongo Relleno de Pollo Guisado), Plantains and, 311
Plums
Crumble, Santa Rosa Plum, 230
Dried Plum Sauce, Rice Pudding with Port and, 371
Dried Plums, Braised Pork Shoulder in Hoisin-Wine Sauce with, 335
Dried-Plum Stuffing, Pork Loin with, 17
Grilled Plum and Prosciutto-Stuffed Pork Chops, 368
Sauce, Grilled Chicken with Pinot-Plum, 258
Sauce, Pan-Seared Pork Chops with Molasses-Plum, 119
Sauce, Pork Tenderloin with Plum, 222
Polenta
Asiago Polenta and Truffled Mushrooms, Roasted Chicken with, 440
Breakfast Polenta with Warm Berry Compote, 19
Garlic-Fontina Polenta, 160
Parmesan Polenta, Lamb Osso Buco over, 303
Ragoût, Polenta with Smoky Mushroom, 92
Soft Polenta, Mediterranean Vegetable Stew over, 79
Pomegranate-Orange Salsa, Blackened Shrimp with, 435
Pomegranate Roasted Chicken Thighs, Honey, 424
Pork. *See also* **Bacon; Grilled/Pork; Ham; Sausage.**
Bolognese, Potato Gnocchi with, 84
Chestnuts, Pork and, 40
Chops
Boneless Pork Chops with Tomato-Sage Pan Sauce, Sautéed, 369
Breaded Pork Chops, 369
Buttermilk-Brined Pork Chops, 368
Country Gravy and Mashed Potatoes, Pork Chops with, 31
Cranberry-Apple Salsa, Pork with, 206
Ginger-Curry Pork and Rice, 207
Marsala, Pork, 414
Mole-Style Pork Chops, 427
Pan-Seared Pork Chops with Molasses-Plum Sauce, 119

Sautéed Pork Chops Niçoise, 29
Tomato Chutney, Pork Chops with, 77
Cracklings with Stewed Chicken (Mofongo
Relleno de Pollo Guisado), Plantains and
Pork, 311
Loin, Orange-Brined Pork, 175
Loin with Dried-Plum Stuffing, Pork, 17
Posole, Pork, 354
Roasted Pork Loin, Cider-, 346
Roasted Pork, Simply, 313
Roasts
Apples, Cabbage, and Turnips, Roast Pork
with, 331
Braised Pork Shoulder in Hoisin-Wine
Sauce with Dried Plums, 335
Buns, Steamed Pork, 81
Cajun Garlic Pork Roast, 127
Crown Roast with Apple-Chestnut Purée,
Maple and Calvados-Glazed Pork, 443
Loin of Pork with Apricot-Rum Glaze,
Roasted, 100
Oven-Braised Pork Roast with
Apples, 324
Porchetta-Style, Roast Pork, 179
Posole, 76
Stew with Pearl Onions, Green Olives,
and Figs, Pork, 292
Roll, Spicy Pork, Turkey, and Swiss
Cubano, 313
Salad, Pork and Grilled Stone Fruit
Couscous, 314
Salad, Pork and Grilled Vegetable, 314
Salad, Pork and Peanut Noodle, 315
Salad with Chili Dressing, Thai Pork, 313
Sandwiches, Horseradish and Caramelized
Onion Pork, 315
Sandwiches with Parsley-Pesto Mayonnaise,
Sourdough Pork, 315
Tabbouleh, Pork, 314
Tenderloin
Balsamic Rosemary Pork, 124
Chipotle Pork Tenderloin with Corn
Salsa, 205
Fattoush, Pork, 323
Galloping Horses, 302
Medallions with Garlic-Ginger-
Pomegranate Sauce, Pork, 327
Medallions with Port Wine-Dried Cherry
Pan Sauce, Pork, 64
Olive-Mustard Tapenade, Pork Tenderloin
with, 204
Pan-Grilled Pork Tenderloin with
Pomegranate Molasses, 337
Phyllo, Pork Tenderloin in, 139
Plantains, Pork and, 39
Plum Sauce, Pork Tenderloin with, 222
Roasted Pork (Pernil Asado), 310
Rosemary and Pepper-Crusted Pork
Tenderloin, 106
Sandwiches au Jus with Rosemary, Roast
Pork, 261
Sandwiches, Chipotle Pulled-Pork
Barbecue, 186
Sandwiches with Hoisin Slaw, Pacific Rim
Pork, 400
Sesame Pork Lo Mein, 278

Stir-Fry, Pork and Squash, 386
Stroganoff, Pork, 399
Tacos, Lime-Cilantro Pork, 197
Xec, Pork Tenderloin with, 28
Wrap, Chipotle Pork and Avocado, 315
Potatoes. *See also* **Salads, Sweet Potatoes.**
Casserole, Potato and Summer Vegetable
Stovetop, 277
Cheese Sauce, Potatoes with Spicy, 169
Farm Hand Potatoes (Papas de Caserio), 76
Fries, Oven, 72
Gnocchi with Bolognese, Potato, 84
Gratin, Asiago, Potato, and Bacon, 118
Gratin, Potato, Leek, and Ham, 398
Hash Brown Casserole, Bacon and, 383
Hash Browns, Ham and Cheese, 122
Hash, Potato and Bell Pepper, 256
Latkes, Potato, 424
Mashed
Cabbage Mash (Patatas y Berzas), Potato
and, 76
Creamy Mashed Potatoes, 8
Garlic Smashed Potatoes, 73
Parsnip Mash, Feta and Lemon-Stuffed
Lamb with Potato-, 257
Pork Chops with Country Gravy and
Mashed Potatoes, 31
Rustic Mashed Potatoes, 422
Shepherd's Pie, 330
Yukon Gold Potatoes, Mashed, 318
New Potatoes, Braised Baby Artichokes and, 56
Omelet, Ham and Potato, 101
Oven Fries with Crisp Sage Leaves, 180
Oven Potatoes, Crisp, 12
Pierogi, Potato, 83
Red Potatoes with Mint, Grilled, 240
Roasted Herbed Potatoes, 400
Roasted Potatoes, Spiced Beef with Wine Sauce
and, 266
Tortilla with Almond Romesco, Spanish, 97
Vichyssoise, Radish, 108
Preserves, Refrigerator Fig, 290
Pressure Cooker
Beans, Barbecue, 166
Risotto with Tomato Topping, Lemon-Basil, 164
Salad, All-Purpose Southwestern Corn and
Black Bean, 166
Soup, Tortilla, 165
Stew, Moroccan Summer Vegetable and
Sausage, 167
Vichyssoise, 165
White Beans with Roasted Red Pepper and
Pesto, 165
Puddings. *See also* **Breads/Puddings; Custards;
Mousse.**
Cake, Chocolate Pudding, 19
Cake, Rhubarb Pudding, 154
Charleston Pudding, 333
Rice Pudding with Port and Dried Plum Sauce, 371
Vanilla-Nut Pudding, 117
Pumpkin
Bread, Chocolate Chip Pumpkin, 425
Cake, Blueberry-Pumpkin Pound, 238
Cake, Pumpkin-Orange, 348
Pie with Pecan Pastry Crust, Pumpkin, 381
Tart, Ginger-Hazelnut Pumpkin, 448

Quail, Blackberry-Zinfandel, 161
Quesadillas
Black Bean Quesadillas with Corn Salsa, 78
Chicken, Mushroom, and Cheese
Quesadillas, 247
Corn and Sun-Dried Tomato Quesadilla with
Smoked Mozzarella, 254
Crab Quesadillas, 121
Farmers' Market Quesadillas, 273
Jack Quesadillas with Cranberry Salsa, 382
Quinoa
Risotto with Asparagus Spears, Three-
Grain, 106
Salad, Edamame, Quinoa, and Shiitake
Mushroom, 283
Seco de Quinoa, 406

Radishes
Braised Radishes, Chardonnay-, 108
Raita, Radish, 107
Salad, Thai Beef and Radish, 108
Slaw with New York Deli Dressing,
Radish, 107
Vichyssoise, Radish, 108
Ragoûts. *See also* **Stews.**
Mushroom Ragoût, Polenta with Smoky, 92
Turkey Ragoût, Belgian, 391
White Bean, Artichoke, and Chard Ragoût with
Fennel Relish, 364
Raspberries
Cake, Red Raspberry Velvet, 447
French Toast, Berry, 102
Meringues, Thumbprint, 172
Muffins, Raspberry-Almond, 99
Vinaigrette, Roasted Beet Salad with
Raspberry, 144
Ravioli Bake, Easy, 43
Relishes. *See also* **Chutneys, Pesto, Salsas, Sauces,
Toppings.**
Chile Relish, Flank Steak with Five-Spice Rub
and, 297
Corn Chow-Chow, 15
Corn Relish, Spicy, 262
Mango-Kiwi Relish, Marinated Salmon
with, 79
Rhubarb
Cake, Rhubarb Pudding, 154
Chutney, Grilled Pork Chops with
Rhubarb, 154
Compote, Rhubarb, Pear, and Apple, 154
Crumble, Rhubarb-Strawberry, 155
Pie, Lattice-Topped Rhubarb, 153
Sauce, Seared Duck Breast with Ginger-
Rhubarb, 160
Sorbet, Rhubarb, 154
Rice
Asopao, 72
Basmati Rice with Basil and Mint, 299
Beans (Arroz con Habichuelas Rosadas
Guisadas), Rice with Stewed Pink, 312
Biriyani, Chicken, 72
Chicken and Rice, Parmesan, 198
Chicken and Rice with Artichokes,
Lemon, 13
Chicken and Rice with Dates, Saffron, 395
Fried Rice, Tofu, 322

Rice *(continued)*

Fried Rice with Bok Choy, Chicken, 71
Frushi, Coconut, 195
Garlic and Ginger Rice (Com Gung Tuong), 287
Ginger-Peanut Rice, Sesame-Crusted Tuna with, 78
Goulash, Louisiana, 46
Green Rice, 352
Green Rice with Roasted Chiles and Leeks, 276
Greens with Rice, Wilted, 55
Island Rice, 125
Jook (Rice Porridge), 27
Lemon Southwest Rice, 274
Mexican Confetti Rice, 421
Orange Rice with Chicken), Shireen Palow (Afghan, 70
Pigeon Peas (Arroz con Gandules), Rice with, 311
Pilaf, Almond Rice, 384
Pilaf with Chicken, Spinach, and Walnuts, 70
Pilaf with Pistachios, Fruited Basmati, 444
Pistachio Rice, 132
Pollo, Arroz con, 70
Pork and Rice, Ginger-Curry, 207
Pudding with Port and Dried Plum Sauce, Rice, 371
Risotto
    Barley Risotto with Fennel and Olives, 264
    Butternut Squash, Pancetta, and Jack Cheese, Risotto with, 337
    Chianti-Stained Risotto with Pears and Blue Cheese, 446
    Corn Risotto with Seared Shrimp and Salsa Verde, Fresh, 227
    Lemon-Basil Risotto with Tomato Topping, 164
    Shrimp and Crab Risotto, Truffled, 135
    Sweet Pepper and Green Bean Risotto, 94
    Three-Grain Risotto with Asparagus Spears, 106
Salad, Kung Pao Tofu Rice, 254
Salad, Taco Rice, 215
Sausage and Rice Skillet, Cajun, 32
Shrimp-Poblano Rice, 164
Wild Rice, Asparagus, and Goat Cheese Frittata, 256
Wild Rice Soup, Chicken and, 316
Rutabagas and Shallots, Golden, 445

Salads and Salad Dressings
Antipasto Salad, 399
Apple Salad, Seared Scallops with Port-Poached Figs and, 100
Artichoke-Kalamata Olive Salad, 55
Arugula Salad, 103
Arugula Salad with Garlic-Sherry Vinaigrette, 199
Asparagus Salad with Mustard-Soy Dressing, 26
Bean
    Black Bean Salad, All-Purpose Southwestern Corn and, 166
    Black Bean Salad with Bell Peppers and Onions, 197
    Chickpea Salad, Greek, 251
    Chickpea Salad, Moroccan-Spiced Bulgur and, 283
    Chickpea Salad with Ginger-Lime Dressing, Couscous-, 194
    Garbanzo Salad, Italian, 129
    Garbanzo Salad with Feta, Lemon, 253
    Green Bean, Chickpea, and Tomato Salad, 229
    Green Bean, Corn, and Roasted Poblano Chile Salad, 144
    Green Bean Salad, Chicken, Red Potato, and, 152
    Mixed Bean Salad with Sun-Dried Tomatoes, 320
    Tuscan Bean and Wilted Arugula Salad, 119
    White Bean and Roasted Chicken Salad, 211
    White Bean Salad over Watercress, Shrimp and, 96
    White Bean, Tomato, and Green Bean Salad, 191
    White Bean, Tuna, and Onion Salad with Sprouts, 325
Beef and Radish Salad, Thai, 108
Beef Salad, Southeast Asian Grilled, 46
Beef Salad with Lemongrass Dressing, Grilled, 221
Beef Salad Wraps, Thai, 288
Beet and Red Onion Salad with Ricotta-Provolone Topping, 179
Bitter Greens Salad with Sourdough Croutons and Warm Tomato Vinaigrette, 303
Bread Salad, BLT, 243
Broccoli, Orange, and Watercress Salad, 7
Cabbage and Mixed Greens Salad with Tangy Herb Vinaigrette, 61
Cactus Salad, 129
Chicken
    Bacon and Blue Cheese Chicken Salad Pitas, Smoky, 151
    Barley-Chicken Salad with Fresh Corn and Sweet Onions, 283
    Basmati Chicken Salad, 214
    Cashew Chicken Salad Sandwiches, 122
    Cashew Chicken Salad with Mandarin Oranges, 284
    Couscous Salad, Chicken and, 151
    Curried Chicken Salad, 253
    Grilled Chicken Salad with Feta and Cucumbers, 96
    Melon Chicken Salad, 219
    Nectarines in Mint Vinaigrette, Chicken Salad with, 152
    Pasta Salad, Peppery Chicken, 214
    Pasta Salad with Chicken, 20
    Peanut Chicken Soba Salad, 132
    Red Potato, and Green Bean Salad, Chicken, 152
    Roasted Chicken and Bow Tie Pasta Salad, 51
    Sesame Chicken Salad, 294
    Southwestern Salad Bar, 213
White Bean and Roasted Chicken Salad, 211
    Wraps, Sunchoke-Chicken Salad, 360
Chopped Layered Salad, Passover, 90
Chopped Salad with Shrimp, Tropical, 350
Citrus Salad with Shrimp and Watercress, 438
Couscous Salad with Chicken and Chopped Vegetables, 213
Couscous with Pine Nuts and Currants, Curried, 193
Duck Salad, Thai Roast, 249
Edamame and Bean Salad with Shrimp and Fresh Salsa, 254
Edamame, Quinoa, and Shiitake Mushroom Salad, 283
Ensalada de Repollo (Cabbage Salad), 162
Escarole and Fennel Salad with Pears and Gruyère, 437
Fall Salad with Buttermilk Dressing, 404
Farfalle with Roasted Tofu, Sesame, 192
Fennel, Orange, and Parmigiano Salad, 97
Fennel Salad with Almonds and Mint, Shaved, 135
Field Greens with Eggs and Enoki Mushrooms, 102
Fig Salad with Crème Fraîche, Mint, and Prosciutto, Fresh, 290
Figs, Grapes, and Bitter Greens, Warm Salad of Grilled, 293
Fruit Salad with Honey-Yogurt Sauce, 388
Garden Salad with Citrus Vinaigrette, 144
Gazpacho Salad with Tomato Vinaigrette, 143
Greek Farmers' Salad, 240
Green
    Avocado and Tomatoes, Green Salad with, 12
    Bitter Greens Salad, Tricolor, 69
    Culantro and Cilantro Dressing (Ensalada Verde con Aderezo de Cilantro y Recao), Green Salad with, 310
    Fall Green Salad, 345
    Field Greens with Mississippi Caviar, 127
    Mixed Greens Salad with Goat Cheese Croutons, 74
    Roasted Poblanos and Cumin-Lime Dressing, Green Salad with, 352
    Romaine Lettuce with Red Pepper and Olives, 144
    White Salad with Blue Cheese Dressing, Green and, 143
Lentil and Fennel Salad, 191
Lobster and Pepper Salad with Asian Herbs, Maine, 225
Mango-Cucumber Salad, 261
Maple-Mustard Salad Dressing, New Hampshire, 398
Mussel Salad, 170
Noodle Salad, Chopstick, 262
Noodle Salad with Tofu and Peanut Dressing, Spicy, 278
Orecchiette with Tomatoes, Fresh Mozzarella, and Basil, 192
Orzo-Bell Pepper Salad, 192
Panzanella, Gazpacho, 211
Panzanella with Grilled Flank Steak, Sourdough, 67

Papaya, Mango, and Grapefruit, Salad of, 97
Papaya Salad (Goi Du Du), Green, 287
Pasta Salad, Greek, 105
Pasta Salad, Prosciutto and Picholine, 282
Persimmon-Walnut Oil Salad, 362
Pizzas, Insalata, 163
Pork and Grilled Stone Fruit Couscous
    Salad, 314
Pork and Grilled Vegetable Salad, 314
Pork and Peanut Noodle Salad, 315
Pork Fattoush, 323
Pork Salad with Chili Dressing, Thai, 313
Potato
        Red Potato, and Green Bean Salad,
            Chicken, 152
        Red, White, and Blue Potato Salad, 230
        Sour Cream and Bacon Potato Salad, 79
Red Lettuce Salad with Citrus Vinaigrette, 363
Rice Salad, Kung Pao Tofu, 254
Rice Salad, Taco, 215
Roasted Beet Salad with Raspberry
    Vinaigrette, 144
Roasted Fig and Arugula Salad, 263
Romaine Salad with Avocado-Lime
    Vinaigrette, 134
Romaine, Strawberry, and Orange Salad, 289
Seafood Salad with Lime Vinaigrette, 265
Seared Scallops, Sweet Potato, and Pecan
    Salad, 77
Sesame Noodle Salad, 400
Shrimp and White Bean Salad over
    Watercress, 96
Shrimp Salad with White Beans, Broccoli, and
    Toasted Garlic, 80
Slaws
        Asian Slaw, 385
        Chicken and Blue Cheese Slaw, 212
        Cider-Mustard Slaw, 323
        Creamy Coleslaw, 93
        Dill Variation, Creamy, 107
        Jícama and Carrot Slaw, Citrus-
            Spiked, 242
        Napa Cabbage and Snow Pea Slaw, 143
        Pineapple Slaw, Green Chile Sopes with
            Chipotle Mayonnaise, Shrimp,
            and, 157
        Radish Slaw with New York Deli
            Dressing, 107
        Red Cabbage and Apple Slaw, 241
        Simple Slaw, 14
Spinach
        Apple and Spinach Salad, Autumn, 331
        Baby Spinach Salad with Candied
            Hazelnuts, 133
        Grilled Shrimp, Spinach Salad with, 298
        Pear Salad with Mustard Vinaigrette,
            Spinach-, 374
        Red Cabbage and Spinach Salad with
            Balsamic Vinaigrette, 273
Tabbouleh, Pork, 314
Tofu Teriyaki Noodle Salad, 193
Tomato and Cucumber Salad, 192
Tomato and Cucumber Salad with Feta, 143
Tomato-Caper Salad, Rosemary Fried Scallops
    with, 427
Tomato Chopped Salad, Summer, 296

Tomato Salad, 356
Tomato Salad with Avocado and Preserved
    Lemons, 217
Tuna and Red Pepper Pasta Salad, 281
Tuna with White Bean-Cucumber Salad, 415
Turkey Salad, Curry, 382
Vegetable Salad with Creamy Blue Cheese
    Dressing, Grilled, 196
Vegetable Salad with Roasted Garlic
    Vinaigrette, 144
Vinaigrette
        Cumin-Lime Vinaigrette, 143
        Dijon Vinaigrette, 142
        Roasted Garlic Vinaigrette, 142
        Versatile Vinaigrette, 142
Watermelon, Fennel, and Parsley Salad, Pizzeria
    Bianco, 228
Salmon
    Cherry Tomatoes, Salmon with Roasted, 88
    Citrus Salmon with Garlicky Greens, 167
    Glazed Salmon, Apple and Horseradish-, 159
    Grilled Pastrami-Style Salmon, 242
    Marinated Salmon with Mango-Kiwi Relish, 79
    Orange Marmalade, Salmon with, 351
    Roasted Salmon and Leeks in Phyllo
        Packets, 140
    Roast Salmon, Indian-Spiced, 203
    Smoked Salmon, 175
    Smoked Salmon Crostini, 434
    Steamed Salmon with Savory Black Bean
        Sauce, 221
    Strudel, Savory Dill-Salmon, 69
    Sweet-and-Sour Pan Sauce, Salmon with, 64
    Wasabi Salmon Sandwiches, 401
    Watercress and Balsamic Drizzle, Salmon with
        Wilted, 293
Salsas. *See also* **Pesto, Relishes, Sauces.**
    Avocado Salsa, Grilled Tuna with, 232
    Corn Salsa, Black Bean Quesadillas with, 78
    Corn Salsa, Chipotle Pork Tenderloin with, 205
    Cranberry-Apple Salsa, Pork with, 206
    Cranberry Salsa, Jack Quesadillas with, 382
    Cucumber Salsa, Trout Topped with, 167
    Fiery Salsa, Grilled Pork Chops with, 248
    Fruit Salsa, Rachel's Tropical, 129
    Mango Salsa, Fiery Turkey Fillets with, 274
    Papaya-Mango Salsa, Jamaican Jerk Turkey
        Burgers with, 196
    Pomegranate-Orange Salsa, Blackened Shrimp
        with, 435
    Tomatillo, Corn, and Avocado Salsa, Grilled
        Pork Chops with, 243
    Tomato Salsa, Hearty Fresh, 261
    Tropical Salsa, Coconut French Toast with
        Grilled Pineapple and, 195
    Verde, Fresh Corn Risotto with Seared Shrimp
        and Salsa, 227
Sandwiches
    Bagels with Avocado-Cilantro Spread,
        Toasted, 284
    Beef
        Barbecue Beef Sandwiches, 38
        Sloppy Joes, 8
        Sloppy Joe Sandwiches, Super, 407
        Steak Sandwiches, Red Wine-
            Marinated, 400

        Tenderloin Mini Sandwiches with
            Mustard-Horseradish Sauce, Seared
            Beef, 426
    Burgers with Chipotle Ketchup, Corn and Two-
        Bean, 324
    Burgers with Papaya-Mango Salsa, Jamaican
        Jerk Turkey, 196
    Chicken
        Arugula and Sun-Dried Tomato
            Vinaigrette, Chicken Sandwich with, 79
        Balsamic-Glazed Chicken Sandwiches
            with Red Onions and Goat
            Cheese, 399
        Buns, Baked Hoisin Chicken, 301
        Calzones, Roasted Chicken-
            Artichoke, 252
        Cashew Chicken Salad Sandwiches, 122
        Grilled Chicken and Roasted Red Pepper
            Sandwiches with Fontina Cheese, 185
        Philly Sandwiches, Chicken, 187
        Pitas, Smoky Bacon and Blue Cheese
            Chicken Salad, 151
        Provolone, and Mushroom Sandwiches,
            Chicken, 408
        Spicy Chicken and Arugula Sandwich, 30
    Cubano with Bacon, Pressed, 185
    Eggplant and Goat Cheese Sandwiches,
        Warm, 45
    Goat Cheese Sandwiches with Roasted Plum
        Tomatoes, Dilled, 209
    Grilled Cheese Sandwiches, Olive-
        Tomato, 204
    Grilled Goat Cheese Sandwiches with Fig and
        Honey, 186
    Grilled Ham and Cheese with Tomato, 187
    Grilled Portobello-Goat Cheese Pitas, 294
    Grilled Vegetable and Mozzarella
        Sandwiches, 187
    Guacamole and Turkey Sandwiches, 123
    Ham and Brie Sandwich, 134
    Hot Browns, English Muffin, 383
    Mini-Bagel Sandwiches, Roasted Red Pepper
        on, 326
    Muffuletta, 159
    Panini, Pear, Pecorino, and Prosciutto, 186
    Pita, Garlic-Rosemary Lamb, 29
    Pitas with Vegetables, Hummus-Stuffed, 150
    Pork
        Barbecue Sandwiches, Chipotle Pulled-
            Pork, 186
        Horseradish and Caramelized Onion Pork
            Sandwiches, 315
        Pacific Rim Pork Sandwiches with Hoisin
            Slaw, 400
        Roast Pork Sandwiches au Jus with
            Rosemary, 261
        Roll, Spicy Pork, Turkey, and Swiss
            Cubano, 313
        Sourdough Pork Sandwiches with Parsley-
            Pesto Mayonnaise, 315
    Roasted Red Pepper Spread Sandwiches, 193
    Salmon Sandwiches, Wasabi, 401
    Shrimp and Crab Rolls, 324
    Stromboli, Pepperoni, Provolone, and
        Pesto, 328
    Strombolis, Prosciutto and Gruyère, 288

Sandwiches *(continued)*

Wraps

Beef Salad Wraps, Thai, 288

Chicken Saté Wraps, 283

Lentil Dal Wraps, 284

Pork and Avocado Wrap, Chipotle, 315

Sunchoke-Chicken Salad Wraps, 360

Sauces. *See also* **Chutneys, Pesto, Relishes, Salsas, Toppings.**

Almond Romesco, Spanish Tortilla with, 97

Arrabbiata, Campanelle with Salsa, 419

Balsamic-Butter Sauce, Broccoli with, 289

Balsamic Vinegar Pan Sauce, Sautéed Chicken Breasts with, 62

Basil Sauce, Pan-Seared Cod with, 73

Basil-Walnut Sauce, Penne in Creamy, 138

Béchamel, Mushroom Lasagna with Creamy, 93

Black Bean Sauce, Chicken with, 414

Black Bean Sauce, Steamed Salmon with Savory, 221

Black Bean Sauce, Turkey Cutlets with Smoky, 428

Cheese Sauce, Potatoes with Spicy, 169

Cherry-Pepper Sauce, Duck Breast with, 333

Chianti Sauce, Stuffed Onions with, 137

Chili Sauce, Sesame Turkey Cakes with Sweet, 385

Chipotle Sauce, Grilled Corn with Creamy, 230

Citrus Sauce, Sautéed Chicken Breasts with Latin, 204

Citrus Sauce, Seared Sea Scallops with Spicy, 442

Clam Sauce, Linguine with, 318

Cocktail Sauce, Camarones Fritoes with Mexican, 156

Cocktail Sauce, Seared Shrimp with Thai, 249

Cranberry and Zinfandel Sauce, Spiced, 405

Cranberry Barbecue Sauce, Chicken with, 383

Cranberry Jezebel Sauce with Sautéed Ham, 384

Dijon-Port Sauce, Sirloin Steak with, 350

Dipping Sauce, Fresh Spring Rolls with, 87

Dipping Sauce, Vegetarian Gyoza with Spicy, 86

Garden Sauce, Zesty, 224

Garlic-Ginger-Pomegranate Sauce, Pork Medallions with, 327

Ginger and Green Onion-Salt Dip, Chicken with, 287

Ginger-Rhubarb Sauce, Seared Duck Breast with, 160

Green Sauce, Shrimp in, 26

Guava Sauce (Pinchos de Cerdo con Salsa de Guayaba), Pork Skewers with, 311

Hoisin-Wine Sauce with Dried Plums, Braised Pork Shoulder in, 335

Horseradish Sauce, Tuna Tartare in Endive with, 258

Hot Garlic Sauce, Shrimp and Fennel in, 338

Lemongrass Sauce (Tofu Nuong Xa), Pan-Fried Tofu with Spicy, 286

Lemon-Peppercorn Pan Sauce, Sautéed Tilapia with, 62

Marinara Magnifica, 261

Marinara Sauce, Easy Gnocchi with Thick, 244

Meat Sauce, Individual Pizzas with Broccoli, Cheese, and, 150

Miso-Chile Sauce, Tuna with, 28

Molasses-Plum Sauce, Pan-Seared Pork Chops with, 119

Mushroom-Wine Sauce, Filet Mignon with, 413

Mustard-Caper Sauce, Steak with, 262

Mustard-Horseradish Sauce, Seared Beef Tenderloin Mini Sandwiches with, 426

Olive and Sun-Dried Tomato Sauce over Chicken, 320

Orange-Cranberry Pan Sauce, Sautéed Turkey Cutlets with, 64

Papaya-Lime Sauce, Coconut Curry Shrimp Cakes with, 158

Pebre, 169

Pepper Sauce, Chicken with Chunky, 163

Pinot-Plum Sauce, Grilled Chicken with, 258

Plum Sauce, Pork Tenderloin with, 222

Pomegranate Molasses, Pan-Grilled Pork Tenderloin with, 337

Porcini Mushroom Sauce, Beef Tenderloin with, 325

Port Sauce, Fig and Stilton-Stuffed Turkey Breast with, 440

Port Wine-Dried Cherry Pan Sauce, Pork Medallions with, 64

Port Wine Sauce, Chicken with, 205

Puttanesca Sauce, Grouper with, 231

Raita, Radish, 107

Red Currant-Green Peppercorn Sauce, Filet Mignon with, 160

Rémoulade, Crab Cakes with, 29

Roasted Red Pepper Sauce, Lasagna Rolls with, 104

Scallops with Cucumber-Horseradish Sauce, 124

Sherry Vinegar Sauce, Chicken with, 422

Sriracha Barbecue Dipping Sauce, Seared Chicken with, 249

Sweet-and-Sour Pan Sauce, Salmon with, 64

Tarragon-Caper Sauce, Chicken Breasts with, 247

Tartar Sauce, Louisiana Crab Cakes with Creole, 248

Tartar Sauce, Pan-Fried Catfish with Cajun, 323

Tomato-Sage Pan Sauce, Sautéed Boneless Pork Chops with, 369

Tomato Sauce, Baked Frittata Ribbons in, 136

Tomato Sauce, Baked Gigantes in, 55

Vegetable Sauce, Oven-Braised Cornish Hens with Cider Vinegar and Warm, 100

Walnut Sauce, Chicken Braised in, 16

Wasabi-Ponzu Sauce, Sesame-Crusted Tuna with, 251

White Clam and Broccoli Sauce, Linguine with, 419

Wine Sauce and Roasted Potatoes, Spiced Beef with, 266

Yellow Tomato Curry Sauce and Thai Ratatouille, Grilled Chicken Breasts with, 228

Yogurt-Cumin Sauce, Smoked Paprika-Spiced Chicken over Lentils with, 128

Sausage

Bread Pudding, Sausage, Apple, and Cheddar, 339

Burrito, Sausage and Egg, 123

Cajun Sausage and Rice Skillet, 32

Chorizo, Spicy Lentils with, 168

Frittata, Pizza, 150

Goulash, Louisiana, 46

Gravy, Roast Turkey with Sausage, 394

Italian Sausage and Fennel Lasagna, 330

Italian Sausage Puttanesca, 44

Italian Sausage Soup, 232

Italian Turkey Sausage with Three Peppers, 389

Kielbasa Choucroute, Turkey, 391

Pasta with Sausage, Leeks, and Fontina, Whole Wheat, 417

Pepperoni, Provolone, and Pesto Stromboli, 328

Pizza, Spicy Sausage, 202

Special, Joe's, 12

Stew, Moroccan Summer Vegetable and Sausage, 167

Stew with Sausage and Kale and Cheese Toasts, Cannellini, 349

Vegetarian Sausage Gravy, Biscuits and, 328

Veggie Sausage and Egg Strata, 329

Ziti with Sausage, Onions, and Fennel, 420

Scallops

au Gratin, Scallops, 428

Cucumber-Horseradish Sauce, Scallops with, 124

Fried Scallops with Tomato-Caper Salad, Rosemary, 427

Gremolata, Scallops, 29

Noodles with Scallops, Pan-Fried, 386

Pan-Seared Scallops with Tomatoes and Pesto, 415

Seared Scallops on Braised Wild Mushrooms, 255

Seared Scallops, Sweet Potato, and Pecan Salad, 77

Seared Scallops with Port-Poached Figs and Apple Salad, 100

Sea Scallops with Spicy Citrus Sauce, Seared, 442

Seafood. *See also* specific types and **Fish.**

Braised Seafood and Vegetable Noodles, 220

Salad with Lime Vinaigrette, Seafood, 265

Seviche Mixto, Pineapple, 199

Soup (Caldo de Mariscos), Seafood, 356

Stew, Normandy Seafood, 114

Seasonings

Pepper-Garlic Spice Rub, 176

Preserved Lemons, Quick, 217

Seviche

Pineapple Seviche Mixto, 199

Rainbow Seviche, 200

Shrimp and Scallop Seviche, Spicy, 242

Shrimp Seviche, Ecuadoran, 200

Shrimp. *See also* **Grilled/Fish and Shellfish;**
   Salads.
   Blackened Shrimp with Pomegranate-Orange
      Salsa, 435
   Bowl, Creamy Shrimp and Corn, 163
   Cajun Shrimp and Catfish, 40
   Cakes with Papaya-Lime Sauce, Coconut Curry
      Shrimp, 158
   Camarones Fritoes with Mexican Cocktail
      Sauce, 156
   Chile-Glazed Shrimp, 201
   Chipotle Shrimp Cups, 215
   Citrus-Herb Shrimp (Camarones con Hierbas y
      Cítricos), 310
   Creole, Shrimp, 121
   Fajitas, Tomatillo Shrimp, 231
   Fettuccine with Shrimp and Portobellos, 103
   Garlic Sauce, Shrimp and Fennel in Hot, 338
   Goulash, Louisiana, 46
   Green Sauce, Shrimp in, 26
   Grits, Southern Shrimp and, 12
   Gumbo, Shrimp and Crab, 317
   Jambalaya, 442
   Lemon, Mint, and Goat Cheese, Shrimp with, 317
   Lo Mein, Shrimp, 25
   Noodles with Asparagus and Shrimp, Asian, 32
   Paella, Chicken and Shrimp, 71
   Pasta, Creamy Gruyère and Shrimp, 42
   Pasta, Mediterranean Shrimp and, 88
   Pasta Toss with Shrimp, Nutty, 207
   Pasta with Clams, Scallops, and Shrimp,
      Gemelli, 281
   Rice, Shrimp-Poblano, 164
   Rolls, Shrimp and Crab, 324
   Rolls with Julienne of Vegetables, Thai
      Shrimp, 68
   Salad with Shrimp and Watercress, Citrus, 438
   Sautéed with Fresh Tomatoes, Wine, and Basil,
      Shrimp, 176
   Seared Shrimp and Salsa Verde, Fresh Corn
      Risotto with, 227
   Seared Shrimp with Thai Cocktail Sauce, 249
   Seviche, Spicy Shrimp and Scallop, 242
   Singapore Mai Fun, 386
   Soba Noodles with Shrimp, 253
   Sopes with Chipotle Mayonnaise, Shrimp, and
      Pineapple Slaw, Green Chile, 157
   Soup, Shrimp and Spinach, 385
   Soup, Shrimp, Corn, and Potato, 216
   Spiced Shrimp with Avocado Oil, 135
   Spring Rolls with Dipping Sauce, Fresh, 87
   Stir-Fry, Butterflied Shrimp and Vegetable, 68
   Stir-Fry, Shrimp and Snow Pea, 414
   Tacos with Spiked Sour Cream, Shrimp, 252
   Truffled Shrimp and Crab Risotto, 135
   Ziti with Shrimp and Scallops, Baked, 43
Slaws. *See also* **Salads/Slaws.**
Slow Cooker
   Butter, Overnight Apple, 331
   Main Dishes
      Beef Daube Provençal, 373
      Cabbage Rolls with Pine Nuts and
         Currants, Barley-Stuffed, 365
      Vegetable and Chickpea Curry, 365
   Soups and Stews
      Beef Stew, Slow Cooker, 88

Cassoulet, Thyme-Scented White
   Bean, 367
Chili with Corn and Winter Squash, Pinto
   Bean, 366
Ragoût with Fennel Relish, White Bean,
   Artichoke, and Chard, 364
Sweet Potato Stew with Red Beans,
   African, 366
Snacks
   Cake, Cardamom-Date Snack, 394
   Cracker Bread, Herbed, 263
   Crisps, Pita, 105, 151
   Date-Walnut Snacks, Spiced, 397
   Figs, Oven-Dried, 290
   Mix, Crisp and Spicy Snack, 7
   Pinwheels, Rosemary-Tomato, 319
   Popcorn Balls, Candy Corn, 360
Soufflés
   Chocolate Soufflés with Pistachios, 48
   Parmesan Soufflé, Herbed, 445
   Roasted Garlic and Corn Soufflé, 102
Soups. *See also* **Chowder, Gumbo, Jambalayas,**
   Ragoûts, Stews.
   Amish Potpie with Turkey Wings, 391
   Apple Bisque with Chestnuts, 332
   Asparagus-Potato Soup, 244
   Bean
      Black Bean Soup, 188
      Black Bean Soup, Chochoyones in, 85
      Chickpeas, Minestrone with, 325
      Corn and Bean Soup, Mexican, 31
      White Bean Soup, Butternut Squash-, 353
   Beef and Green Chile Soup, 327
   Beef and Rice Noodle Soup (Pho Bo),
      Hanoi, 286
   Beef and Vegetable Soup (Cocido), 356
   Beet Soup, Savory, 346
   Bisque with Basil, Avocado, and Crab, Chilled
      Corn, 156
   Bisque, Zucchini-Spinach, 223
   Butternut Squash Soup, Curry Ginger, 298
   Butternut Squash-White Bean Soup, 353
   Caldo de Bolas, 86
   Carrot-Parsnip Soup with Parsnip Chips, 436
   Celery-Celeriac Soup with Roquefort
      Croutons, 437
   Chicken
      Meatball Soup with Pasta, Chicken, 358
      Noodle Soup, Asian Chicken, 294
      Soba Noodle Soup, Chicken and, 120
      Stock, Asian Chicken, 287
      Wild Rice Soup, Chicken and, 316
   Coconut Soup, Hot-and-Sour, 385
   Coconut Tapioca Soup with Bananas (Che
      Chuoi), Sweet, 285
   Cucumber Soup, Cold, 318
   Escarole Soup with Ginger and Cilantro, 205
   Gazpacho, Golden, 14
   Green Pepper Soup, Stuffed, 406
   Italian Sausage Soup, 232
   Kabocha Squash Soup, 402
   Matzo Ball Soup, 85
   Meatball Soup (Sopa de Albóndigas), 355
   Miso Soup, 401
   Mushroom Soup, Rich, 346
   Onion Soup Gratinée, 436

Papaya Lime Soup, 162
Pea Soup, Springtime, 129
Roasted Tomato-Harissa Soup with Olive
   Toasts, 402
Seafood Soup (Caldo de Mariscos), 356
Shrimp and Spinach Soup, 385
Shrimp, Corn, and Potato Soup, 216
Squash and Apple Soup, Creamy, 407
Summer Soup, Golden, 227
Summer Squash Soup with Pasta and
   Parmesan, 282
Tomato and Lentil Soup, 54
Tomato-Basil Soup, 288
Tortellini Soup, Sun-Dried Tomato-, 322
Tortilla Soup, 165, 327
Turkey-Pasta Soup, 384
Turkey Stock, Homemade, 393
Vegetable Soup, Mediterranean, 123
Vegetable Soup with Toasted Cheese Croutons,
   Chunky, 202
Vichyssoise, 165
Vichyssoise, Radish, 108
Zucchini-Buttermilk Soup with Watercress
   Pesto, 255
Spaetzle Baked with Ham and Gruyère, 82
Spaetzle, Buttered, 82
Spinach. *See also* **Salads/Spinach.**
   Chicken Breasts Stuffed with Spinach and
      Ricotta, 358
   Chickpeas and Spices, Spinach with, 404
   Chickpeas with Spinach, 130
   Dip, Spinach-Parmesan, 409
   Florentine, Mac and Cheese, 208
   Focaccia, Spinach and Feta-Stuffed, 289
   Garlicky Greens, Citrus Salmon with, 167
   Pilaf with Chicken, Spinach, and Walnuts, 70
   Pizza, White, 46
   Rolls, Spinach, Sun-Dried Tomato, and
      Parmesan, 433
   Sautéed Spinach and Tomatoes, Red Snapper
      over, 427
   Stuffing, Turkey Breast with Spinach-Feta, 392
   Tarts, Feta-Spinach, 141
   Ziti Baked with Spinach, Tomatoes, and
      Smoked Gouda, 43
Spreads
   Asiago-Artichoke-Turkey Spread, 384
   Avocado-Cilantro Spread, Toasted Bagels
      with, 284
   Black Bean Spread with Lime and Cilantro, 408
   Date-Orange Breakfast Spread, 395
   Feta-Chile Spread, 55
   Hummus, Garlic and Sun-Dried Tomato, 13
   Lentil Spread, 351
   Mayonnaise, Sourdough Pork Sandwiches with
      Parsley-Pesto, 315
   Mushroom Spread, Creamy, 408
   Red Pepper-Cheese Dip, 345
   Roasted Red Pepper Spread Sandwiches, 193
   Smoked Trout Spread, 409
Squash. *See also* **Zucchini.**
   Butternut
      Bread Pudding, Butternut Squash and
         Parmesan, 340
      Dip, Roasted Butternut Squash, 374
      Gratins, Butternut Squash and Leek, 446

Squash *(continued)*

    Lasagna, Roasted Butternut Squash,
        Rosemary, and Garlic, 416
    Red Pepper, Butternut Squash and, 351
    Risotto with Butternut Squash, Pancetta,
        and Jack Cheese, 337
    Roasted Butternut Squash, 368
    Roasted Butternut Squash and Bacon
        Pasta, 41
    Soup, Butternut Squash-White Bean, 353
    Soup, Creamy Squash and Apple, 407
    Soup, Curry Ginger Butternut
        Squash, 298
    Stir-Fry, Pork and Squash, 386
Calabaza and Poblano Stew, 354
Kabocha Squash Soup, 402
Roasted Squash, Peppers, and Artichokes,
    Phyllo Purses with, 403
Summer Squash, Grilled, 230
Summer Squash Soup with Pasta and
    Parmesan, 282
Winter Squash and Garlic, Bay Leaf and
    Thyme-Scented Roasted, 363
Winter Squash, Arugula, and Pine Nuts,
    Pappardelle with Roasted, 441
Winter Squash, Pinto Bean Chili with Corn
    and, 366
Yellow Squash Gratin, 95

Stews. *See also* **Chili, Chowder, Gumbo,**
    Jambalayas, Ragoûts, Soups.
Beef Stew, 7
Beef Stew, Sephardic, 396
Beef Stew, Slow Cooker, 88
Brunswick Stew with Smoked Paprika, 367
Calabaza and Poblano Stew, 354
Cannellini Stew with Sausage and Kale and
    Cheese Toasts, 349
Chicken and Barley Stew, 30
Chicken, Date, and Apricot Tagine, 65
Chicken Vegetable Stew, 357
Eggplant Stew over Couscous, 210
Garbanzo and Greens Stew, 356
Lamb Stew (Txilindron de Cordero), 75
Lamb Stew with Parsnips and Figs, Spicy, 335
Middle Eastern Slow-Cooked Stew with Lamb,
    Chickpeas, and Figs, 423
Pork Posole, 354
Pork Stew with Pearl Onions, Green Olives,
    and Figs, 292
Posole, 76
Seafood Stew, Normandy, 114
Sweet Potato Stew with Red Beans,
    African, 366
Tuna Stew (Marmitako), Fresh, 76
Vegetable and Sausage Stew, Moroccan
    Summer, 167
Vegetable-Beef Stew, 61
Vegetable Stew over Couscous, Winter, 94
Vegetable Stew over Soft Polenta,
    Mediterranean, 79
White Bean Cassoulet, Thyme-Scented, 367

Strawberries
Balsamic-Brown Sugar Strawberries, 252
Daiquiris, Frozen Strawberry, 190
Granita, Strawberry, 107

Jam, Fresh Strawberry, 191
Muffins, Low-Fat Strawberry-Cinnamon, 45
Parfaits, Brunch, 190
Parfait with Fresh Normandy Cream,
    Strawberry, 116
Pie, Strawberry, 190
Salad, Romaine, Strawberry, and
    Orange, 289
Sorbet, Strawberry-Basil, 161
Tart, Strawberry-Rhubarb, 190
Topping, Balsamic Strawberry, 191
Vanilla-Scented Wine, Strawberries and
    Oranges with, 99
Stroganoff, Pork, 399

Stuffings
Cheese Stuffing, Baked Eggplant with
    Savory, 54
Dried-Plum Stuffing, Pork Loin with, 17
Herbed Bread Stuffing with Mushrooms and
    Sausage, 375
Mediterranean Stuffing, Portobello Mushrooms
    with, 407
Spinach-Feta Stuffing, Turkey Breast with, 392
Succotash Pot Pie, Southwestern, 93
Succotash with Chicken, Summer, 212

Sweet Potatoes
Glazed Sweet Potato Wedges, Brown
    Sugar-, 376
Hash, Sweet Potato, 49
Meringue and Streusel-Topped Sweet
    Potatoes, 444
Salad, Seared Scallops, Sweet Potato, and
    Pecan, 77
Spicy Sweet Potato Wedges, 347
Stew with Red Beans, African Sweet
    Potato, 366
Trifle, Sweet Potato, 214
Tzimmes, Sweet Potato and Carrot, 90
Swiss Chard with Almonds and Shallots, 426
Swiss Chard with Pine Nuts and Raisins, 162

Syrups
Cider Syrup, Pan-Seared Oatmeal with Warm
    Fruit Compote and, 194
Cran-Grape Syrup, 16
Spiced Syrup with Cloves, Cinnamon, and Star
    Anise, Kumquats in, 454
Spiced Wine Syrup with Pound Cake Croutons,
    Cherries in, 264
Tequila-Cardamom Syrup and Vanilla Ice
    Cream, 421
Zinfandel Syrup, Cherries in, 317

Tabbouleh, Cranberry Walnut, 132
Tabbouleh, Pork, 314

Tacos
Beef Tacos, Tex-Mex, 129
Mahimahi Fish Tacos, 134
Pork Tacos, Lime-Cilantro, 197
Salad, Taco Rice, 215
Shrimp Tacos with Spiked Sour Cream, 252
Soft Tacos, Grilled-Steak, 149
Soft Tacos, Picadillo, 202
Tamale Pie, 30

Tofu
Curried Tofu, 294
Freeze, Arctic Lime, 128

Fried Rice, Tofu, 322
Glazed Tofu over Asparagus and Rice,
    Chili-, 349
Larb, Tofu, 301
Mushrooms, Tofu and, 39
Pan-Fried Tofu with Spicy Lemongrass Sauce
    (Tofu Nuong Xa), 286
Rice Salad, Kung Pao Tofu, 254
Roasted Tofu, Sesame Farfalle with, 192
Salad, Tofu Teriyaki Noodle, 193
Salad with Tofu and Peanut Dressing, Spicy
    Noodle, 278
Stir-Fry over Rice, Sesame Tofu, 50
Stir-Fry, Tofu, 86
Tomatillo, Corn, and Avocado Salsa, Grilled Pork
    Chops with, 243
Tomatillo Shrimp Fajitas, 231

Tomatoes. *See also* **Salads.**
Bread with Tomatoes, Cuban, 39
Broth, Mussels with Tomato-Wine, 168
Bruschetta with Warm Tomatoes, 276
Campanelle with Salsa Arrabbiata, 419
Cherry Tomato and Olive Topping, Chicken
    with, 163
Cherry Tomatoes (Almejas con Tomates),
    Clams with, 75
Cherry Tomatoes, and Olives, Penne Pasta with
    Roasted Fennel, 279
Cherry Tomatoes, Salmon with Roasted, 88
Cherry Tomatoes with Shallots, Sautéed, 364
Chutney, Pork Chops with Tomato, 77
Gratin, Eggplant and Tomato, 275
Gratin, Sunchoke and Tomato, 360
Heirloom Tomatoes and Herbs, Striped Bass
    with, 225
Jam, Cornmeal Shortcakes with Tomato-
    Ginger, 258
Lasagna, Fresh Tomato, 105
Orecchiette with Tomatoes, Fresh Mozzarella,
    and Basil, 192
Pappardelle with Tomatoes, Arugula, and
    Parmesan, Summer, 278
Pasta with Fresh Tomatoes and Basil,
    Garlicky, 104
Pinwheels, Rosemary-Tomato, 319
Plum Tomatoes, Dilled Goat Cheese
    Sandwiches with Roasted, 209
Purée, Pasta with Roasted Shiitakes and
    Tomato, 280
Ravioli Bake, Easy, 43
Salsa, Hearty Fresh Tomato, 261

Sauces
    Gigantes in Tomato Sauce, Baked, 55
    Marinara Magnifica, 261
    Marinara Sauce, Easy Gnocchi with
        Thick, 244
    Olive and Sun-Dried Tomato Sauce over
        Chicken, 320
    Puttanesca Sauce, Grouper with, 231
    Tomato Sauce, Baked Frittata Ribbons
        in, 136
Scallops with Tomatoes and Pesto, Pan-
    Seared, 415
Shrimp Sautéed with Fresh Tomatoes, Wine,
    and Basil, 176
Soup, Tomato and Lentil, 54

Soup, Tomato-Basil, 288
Soup with Olive Toasts, Roasted Tomato-
    Harissa, 402
Sun-Dried Tomato, and Parmesan Rolls,
    Spinach, 433
Sun-Dried Tomato Cheesecake, 321
Sun-Dried Tomatoes, Braised Beef with, 318
Sun-Dried Tomatoes, Mixed Bean Salad
    with, 320
Sun-Dried Tomato Hummus, Garlic and, 13
Sun-Dried Tomato Ketchup, 321
Sun-Dried Tomato Pesto and Chicken-Pasta
    Toss, 319
Sun-Dried Tomato Pesto and Feta Cheese, Pasta
    with, 349
Sun-Dried Tomato Scones, Savory Herb, 321
Sun-Dried Tomato Spiced Shrimp, 320
Sun-Dried Tomato-Tortellini Soup, 322
Sun-Dried Tomato Vinaigrette, Chicken
    Sandwich with Arugula and, 79
Tomatoes Roasted with Rosemary and
    Lemon, 178
Topping, Lemon-Basil Risotto with
    Tomato, 164
Vinaigrette, Bitter Greens Salad with
    Sourdough Croutons and Warm
    Tomato, 303
Vinaigrette, Gazpacho Salad with Tomato, 143
Yellow Tomato Curry Sauce and Thai
    Ratatouille, Grilled Chicken Breasts
    with, 228
Toppings
Aïoli, Cornflake-Crusted Halibut with Chile-
    Cilantro, 72
Apple-Ginger Topping and Orange Sauce,
    Couscous with, 218
Apricot-Rum Glaze, Roasted Loin of Pork
    with, 100
Balsamic Drizzle, Salmon with Wilted
    Watercress and, 293
Berry Compote, Breakfast Polenta with Warm, 19
Bourbon Cream, Eggnog Cheese Pie with, 425
Cherries in Zinfandel Syrup, 317
Cherry Tomato and Olive Topping, Chicken
    with, 163
Citrus Vinaigrette, Crab-Stuffed Lobster
    with, 295
Crumb Topping, Creamed Cauliflower with
    Herbed, 447
Eggplant Purée with Crostini, Smoky, 56
Figs, Oven-Dried, 290
Ketchup, Corn and Two-Bean Burgers with
    Chipotle, 324
Ketchup, Sun-Dried Tomato, 321
Ricotta-Provolone Topping, Beet and Red
    Onion Salad with, 179
Strawberry Topping, Balsamic, 191
Tomato Topping, Lemon-Basil Risotto
    with, 164
Tortillas. *See also* **Burrito, Enchiladas, Fajitas,**
    Quesadillas, Tacos.
Chimichangas, Roast Chicken, 122
Corn Tortillas, 155
Pizza, Cuban Chicken, 421
Roll, Spicy Pork, Turkey, and Swiss
    Cubano, 313

Roll-Ups, Cream Cheese, 213
Roll-Ups, Roasted Chicken and Goat
    Cheese, 427
Soup, Tortilla, 165, 327
Spanish Tortilla with Almond Romesco, 97
Wraps
    Chicken Saté Wraps, 283
    Pork and Avocado Wrap, Chipotle, 315
    Sunchoke-Chicken Salad Wraps, 360
    Thai Beef Salad Wraps, 288
Tuna. *See also* **Salads.**
Grilled Tuna with Avocado Salsa, 232
Miso-Chile Sauce, Tuna with, 28
Seared Tuna, Greek Pasta with, 282
Sesame-Crusted Tuna with Ginger-Peanut
    Rice, 78
Sesame-Crusted Tuna with Wasabi-Ponzu
    Sauce, 251
Stew (Marmitako), Fresh Tuna, 76
Tartare in Endive with Horseradish Sauce,
    Tuna, 258
Turkey
Apple Cider-Brined Turkey with Savory Herb
    Gravy, 374
Bierocks, 33
Bolognese, Turkey, 188
Breast, Honey and Thyme-Brined Turkey, 173
Breast with Port Sauce, Fig and Stilton-Stuffed
    Turkey, 440
Breast with Spinach-Feta Stuffing, Turkey, 392
Burgers with Papaya-Mango Salsa, Jamaican
    Jerk Turkey, 196
Cakes with Sweet Chili Sauce, Sesame
    Turkey, 385
Chili, Twenty-Minute, 80
Cutlets, Spiced Turkey, 28
Cutlets with Coleslaw, Turkey, 206
Cutlets with Orange-Cranberry Pan Sauce,
    Sautéed Turkey, 64
Cutlets with Smoky Black Bean Sauce,
    Turkey, 428
Fillets with Mango Salsa, Fiery Turkey, 274
Hot Browns, English Muffin, 383
Kielbasa Choucroute, Turkey, 391
Meatballs, Bell Pepper and Tomato Penne
    with, 118
Meatballs with Baby Bok Choy, Turkey-Jasmine
    Rice, 393
Meat Loaf, Skinny Turkey-Spinach, 78
Meat Loaf, Southwest, 352
Ragoût, Belgian Turkey, 391
Roast Turkey with Sausage Gravy, 394
Roll, Spicy Pork, Turkey, and Swiss
    Cubano, 313
Salad, Curry Turkey, 382
Sandwiches, Guacamole and Turkey, 123
Sausage with Three Peppers, Italian
    Turkey, 389
Scaloppine with Porcini and Marsala,
    Turkey, 393
Soup, Turkey-Pasta, 384
Spread, Asiago-Artichoke-Turkey, 384
Stock, Homemade Turkey, 393
Tacos, Picadillo Soft, 202
Wings, Amish Potpie with Turkey, 391
Tzimmes, Sweet Potato and Carrot, 90

Vanilla
Apples, Roasted Vanilla-Scented, 11
Bread Pudding, Vanilla-Bourbon, 449
Crisp with Pistachios, Vanilla-Scented
    Harvest, 410
Flan, Deconstructed, 74
Icing, Christmas Sugar Wafers with Vanilla, 453
Meringues, Double Vanilla, 172
Panna Cotta with Mango Sauce, Vanilla-
    Almond, 370
Pierogi, Sweet Vanilla Cheese, 84
Pudding, Vanilla-Nut, 117
Smoothie, Vanilla-Honey-Nut, 246
Sorbet with Pineapple Topping, Vanilla Bean, 353
Wine, Strawberries and Oranges with Vanilla-
    Scented, 99
Veal Piccata, 232
Vegetables. *See also* specific types and **Salads,**
    Soups, Stews.
à la Grecque, Vegetables, 266
Asopao, 72
Casserole, Potato and Summer Vegetable
    Stovetop, 277
Curry, Vegetable and Chickpea, 365
Gyoza with Spicy Dipping Sauce,
    Vegetarian, 86
Julienne of Vegetables, Thai Shrimp Rolls
    with, 68
Latke, Vegetable Party, 424
Muffuletta, 159
Noodles, Braised Seafood and Vegetable, 220
Pitas with Vegetables, Hummus-Stuffed, 150
Primavera, Pasta, 91
Quesadillas, Farmers' Market, 273
Ratatouille, Grilled Chicken Breasts with Yellow
    Tomato Curry Sauce and Thai, 228
Ratatouille Pizza with Chicken, 211
Rice, Mexican Confetti, 421
Sandwiches, Grilled Vegetable and
    Mozzarella, 187
Sauce, Oven-Braised Cornish Hens with Cider
    Vinegar and Warm Vegetable, 100
Sauce, Zesty Garden, 224
Shrimp Lo Mein, 25
Shrimp over Rice Vermicelli and Vegetables
    (Bun Tom Nuong Xa), Lemongrass, 285
Spring Rolls with Dipping Sauce, Fresh, 87
Spring Vegetables, 114
Stir-Fry, Butterflied Shrimp and Vegetable, 68
Stuffed Summer Vegetables, Italian, 178
Summer Vegetables, Omelet with, 231
Venison Chili, 398

Yogurt
Cheesecake with Caramelized Onions, Savory
    Yogurt, 18
Herbed Yogurt over Couscous, Lamb Chops
    with, 350
Raita, Radish, 107
Tzatziki, 54

Zucchini
Bisque, Zucchini-Spinach, 223
Bread, Chocolate Chip Zucchini, 224
Soup with Watercress Pesto, Zucchini-
    Buttermilk, 255

HOW TO USE IT AND WHY Glance at the end of any *Cooking Light* recipe, and you'll see how committed we are to helping you make the best of today's light cooking. With six chefs, three registered dietitians, three home economists, and a computer system that analyzes every ingredient we use, *Cooking Light* gives you authoritative dietary detail like no other magazine. We go to such lengths so you can see how our recipes fit into your healthful eating plan. If you're trying to lose weight, the calorie and fat figures will probably help most. But if you're keeping a close eye on the sodium, cholesterol, and saturated fat in your diet, we provide those numbers, too. And because many women don't get enough iron or calcium, we can also help there, as well. Finally, there's a fiber analysis for those of us who don't get enough roughage.

Here's a helpful guide to put our nutrition analysis numbers into perspective. Remember, one size doesn't fit all, so take your lifestyle, age, and circumstances into consideration when determining your nutrition needs. For example, women who are pregnant or breast-feeding need more protein, calories, and calcium. And men over 50 need 1,200mg of calcium daily, 200mg more than the amount recommended for younger men.

IN OUR NUTRITIONAL ANALYSIS, WE USE THESE ABBREVIATIONS:

sat	saturated fat	**CHOL**	cholesterol
mono	monounsaturated fat	**CALC**	calcium
poly	polyunsaturated fat	**g**	gram
CARB	carbohydrates	**mg**	milligram

Daily Nutrition Guide

	WOMEN AGES 25 TO 50	WOMEN OVER 50	MEN OVER 24
Calories	2,000	2,000 or less	2,700
Protein	50g	50g or less	63g
Fat	65g or less	65g or less	88g or less
Saturated Fat	20g or less	20g or less	27g or less
Carbohydrates	304g	304g	410g
Fiber	25g to 35g	25g to 35g	25g to 35g
Cholesterol	300mg or less	300mg or less	300mg or less
Iron	18mg	8mg	8mg
Sodium	2,400mg or less	1,300mg or less	1,500mg or less
Calcium	1,000mg	1,200mg	1,000mg

The nutritional values used in our calculations either come from The Food Processor, Version 7.5 (ESHA Research), or are provided by food manufacturers.

Contributing Recipe Developers

Bruce Aidells
Pam Anderson
Patricia Baird
Kathy Baruffi
Lidia Bastianich
Peter Berley
Chris Bianco
Mark Bittman
David Bonom
Julie Grimes Bottcher
James Boyce
Barbara Seelig Brown
Greg Brown
Jennifer Brulé
Nancy Byal
Maureen Callahan
Viviana Carballo
Claudia M. Caruana
Rebecca Charles
Cindy Chavich
Barbara Chernetz

Holly Clegg
Katherine Cobbs
Martha Condra
Terry Conlan
Jenny Cornbleet
Lorrie Hulston Corvin
Culinary Institute of America
Janice Daciuk
Cynthia DePersio
Abby Dinces
Dave DiResta
Charla Draper
Melissa Dupree
Kathy Farrell-Kingsley
Judith Fertig
Allison Fishman
John Folse
Jose Garces
Brian Glover
Marcy Goldman

Sandra Granseth
Ken Haedrich
Jacques Haeringer
Gloria Hafer
Ryan Hardy
Tamar Haspel
Jan Turner Hazard
Lia Mack Huber
Nancy Hughes
Dana Jacobi
Sally James
Patsy Jamieson
Bill Jamison
Cheryl Alters Jamison
Wendy Kalen
Elizabeth Karmel
Robin Kline
Jean Kressy
Barbara Lauterbach
Jeanne Lemlin
Karen Levin

Alison Lewis
John Littlewood
Judy Lockhart
Susan Loomis
Ronni Lundy
Karen MacNeil
Deborah Madison
Elaine Magee
Donata Maggipinto
Domenica Marchetti
Jennifer Martinkus
Dana McCauley
Maggie Melanson
Jill Melton
Matt Miller
Janet Mitchell
Paulette Mitchell
Maira Isabel Morales
Diane Morgan
Kitty Morse
Joan Nathan

Cary Neff
Micol Negrin
Kate Nelson
Cynthia Nicholson
Daniel Orr
Greg Patent
Caprial Pence
John Pence
Marge Perry
Steven Raichlen
Victoria Riccardi
Robin Robertson
Rick Rodgers
Sharon Sanders
Santa Fe School of Cooking
Mark Scarbrough
Jason Schellin
Chris Schlesinger
Johnny Schmitt
Carl Schroeder

Martha Rose Shulman
Marie Simmons
Annie Somerville
Lisë Stern
Billy Strynkowski
Elizabeth Taliaferro
Corinne Trang
Robert Trevino
Robin Vitetta-Miller
Robyn Webb
Bruce Weinstein
Joanne Weir
Laura Werlin
Chris Whittaker
Carla Fitzgerald Williams
Martin Yan
Lisa Zwirn